THE ROAD TO
Armageddon

D1521787

Latin American and Caribbean Series

Hendrik Kraay, General Editor

ISSN 1498-2366 (PRINT), ISSN 1925-9638 (ONLINE)

This series sheds light on historical and cultural topics in Latin America and the Caribbean by publishing works that challenge the canon in history, literature, and postcolonial studies. It seeks to print cutting-edge studies and research that redefine our understanding of historical and current issues in Latin America and the Caribbean.

No. 1 · **Waking the Dictator: Veracruz, the Struggle for Federalism and the Mexican Revolution** Karl B. Koth

No. 2 · **The Spirit of Hidalgo: The Mexican Revolution in Coahuila** Suzanne B. Pasztor · Copublished with Michigan State University Press

No. 3 · **Clerical Ideology in a Revolutionary Age: The Guadalajara Church and the Idea of the Mexican Nation, 1788–1853** Brian F. Connaughton, translated by Mark Allan Healey · Copublished with University Press of Colorado

No. 4 · **Monuments of Progress: Modernization and Public Health in Mexico City, 1876–1910** Claudia Agostoni · Copublished with University Press of Colorado

No. 5 · **Madness in Buenos Aires: Patients, Psychiatrists and the Argentine State, 1880–1983** Jonathan Ablard · Copublished with Ohio University Press

No. 6 · **Patrons, Partisans, and Palace Intrigues: The Court Society of Colonial Mexico, 1702–1710** Christoph Rosenmüller

No. 7 · **From Many, One: Indians, Peasants, Borders, and Education in Callista Mexico, 1924–1935** Andrae Marak

No. 8 · **Violence in Argentine Literature and Film (1989–2005)** Edited by Carolina Rocha and Elizabeth Montes Garcés

No. 9 · **Latin American Cinemas: Local Views and Transnational Connections** Edited by Nayibe Bermúdez Barrios

No. 10 · **Creativity and Science in Contemporary Argentine Literature: Between Romanticism and Formalism** Joanna Page

No. 11 · **Textual Exposures: Photography in Twentieth Century Spanish American Narrative Fiction** Dan Russek

No. 12 · **Whose Man in Havana? Adventures from the Far Side of Diplomacy** John W. Graham

No. 13 · **Journalism in a Small Place: Making Caribbean News Relevant, Comprehensive, and Independent** Juliette Storr

No. 14 · **The Road to Armageddon: Paraguay versus the Triple Alliance, 1866–70** Thomas L. Whigham

UNIVERSITY OF CALGARY
Press

THE ROAD TO
Armageddon

PARAGUAY VERSUS THE TRIPLE ALLIANCE, 1866–70

Thomas L. Whigham

Latin American and
Caribbean Series
ISSN 1498-2366 (Print)
ISSN 1925-9638 (Online)

UNIVERSITY OF CALGARY
FACULTY OF ARTS
Latin American Research Centre

University of Calgary Press
2500 University Drive NW
Calgary, Alberta
Canada T2N 1N4
press.ucalgary.ca

LIBRARY AND ARCHIVES CANADA CATALOGUING IN PUBLICATION

Whigham, Thomas, 1955-, author
          The road to Armageddon : Paraguay versus the Triple Alliance, 1866-70 / Thomas L. Whigham.

(Latin American and Caribbean series ; no. 14)
Includes bibliographical references and index.
Issued in print and electronic formats.
ISBN 978-1-55238-809-9 (softcover).—ISBN 978-1-55238-810-5 (open access PDF).—
ISBN 978-1-55238-811-2 (PDF).—ISBN 978-1-55238-812-9 (EPUB).—
ISBN 978-1-55238-813-6 (Kindle)

     1. Paraguayan War, 1865-1870. 2. Paraguay—History—1811-1870. 3. Brazil—
History—Empire, 1822-1889. 4. Uruguay—History—1830-1875. 5. Argentina—History—
1860-1910. I. Title. II. Series: Latin American and Caribbean series ; no. 14

F2687.W45 2017   989.2'05   C2017-906271-9
                                                             C2017-906272-7

The University of Calgary Press acknowledges the support of the Government of Alberta through the Alberta Media Fund for our publications. We acknowledge the financial support of the Government of Canada. We acknowledge the financial support of the Canada Council for the Arts for our publishing program.

Cover image: *Episodio de la 2da División Buenos Aires en la batalla de Tuyutí, Mayo 24 de 1866.* The Paraguayan cavalry attacks during the first phase of the Battle of Tuyutí, 24 May 1866. Painting by Cándido López, 1866. From the collection of Museo Historico Nacional, Buenos Aires. Image courtesy of Marco Fano.

Copyediting by Ryan Perks
Cover design, page design, and typesetting by Melina Cusano

For my sons Alex and Nicholas

Maps

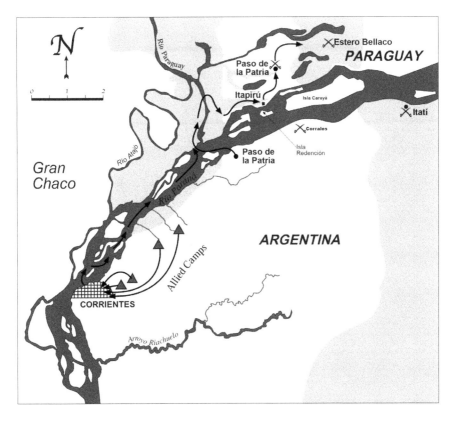

MAP 1. THE CROSSING OF THE RIVERS (APRIL 1866)

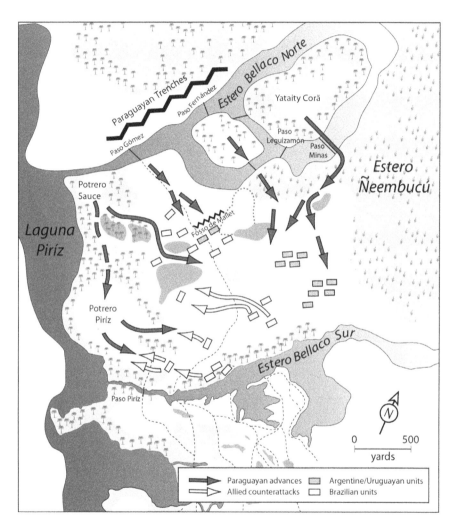

Paraguayan Trenches

Estero Bellaco Norte

Paso Fernández

Yataity Corã

Paso Gómez

Paso Leguizamón

Paso Minas

Estero Ñeembucú

Potrero Sauce

Laguna Piríz

Fosso de Mallet

Potrero Piríz

Estero Bellaco Sur

Paso Piríz

N

0   500

yards

➡ Paraguayan advances	▨ Argentine/Uruguayan units
⇨ Allied counterattacks	☐ Brazilian units

MAP 2. THE BATTLE OF TUYUTÍ (24 MAY 1866)

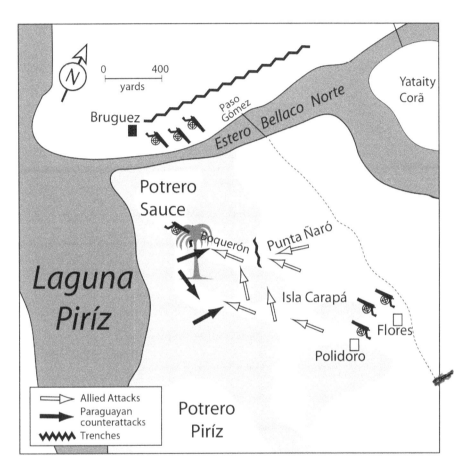

Bruguez

Paso Gómez

Estero Bellaco Norte

Yataity Corã

Potrero Sauce

Boquerón

Punta Ñaró

Laguna Piríz

Isla Carapá

Flores

Polidoro

Allied Attacks
Paraguayan counterattacks
Trenches

Potrero Piríz

0   400
yards

MAP 3. THE BATTLE OF BOQUERÓN (16-18 JULY 1866)

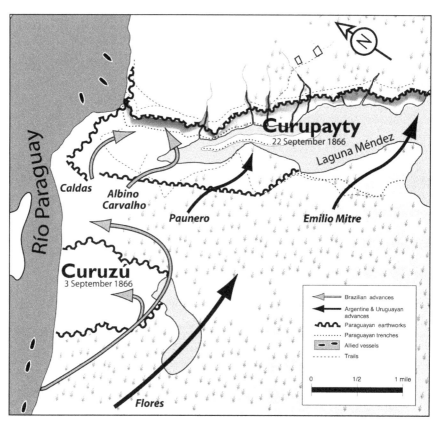

Map 4. The Battles of Curuzú and Curupayty (September 1866)

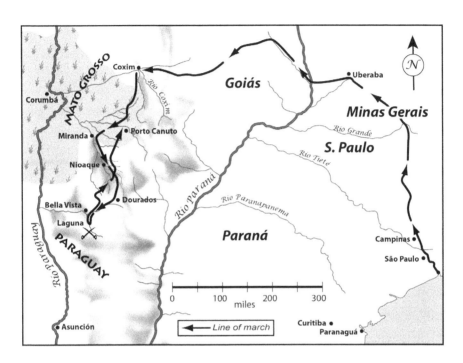

MAP 5. THE MATO GROSSO CAMPAIGN (1865-1867)

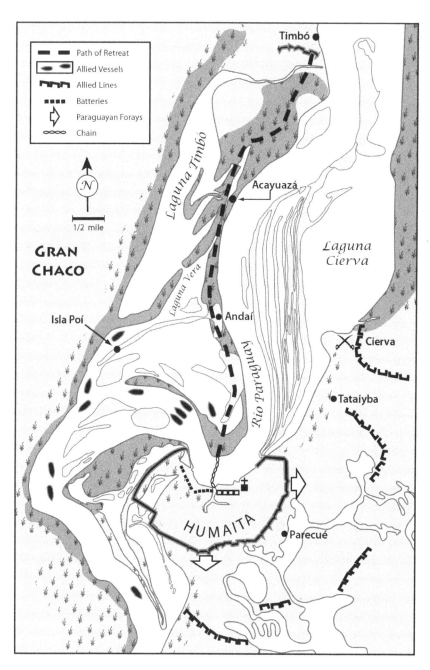

MAP 6. THE RETREAT FROM HUMAITÁ (MARCH–AUGUST 1868)

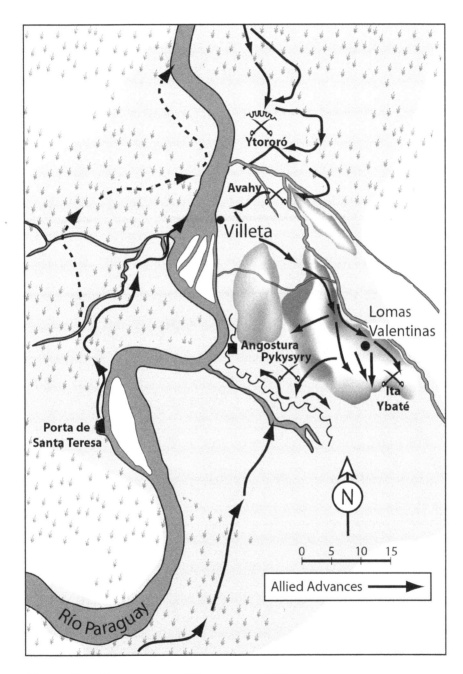

Río Paraguay

Ytororó

Avahy

Villeta

Lomas
Valentinas

Angostura
Pykysyry

Ita
Ybaté

Porta de
Santa Teresa

N

0   5   10   15

Allied Advances

MAP 7. THE DEZEMBRADA (DECEMBER 1868)

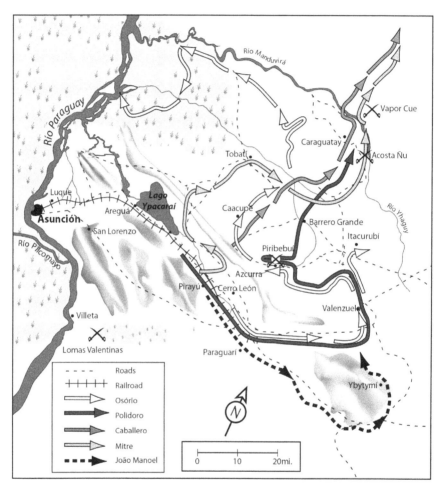

Rio Manduvirá

Vapor Cue

Rio Paraguay

Caraguatay

Acosta Ñu

Tobatí

Luque

Lago Ypacaraí

Caacupé

Rio Yhaguy

Aregúa

Asunción

Barrero Grande

San Lorenzo

Itacurubí

Río Pilcomayo

Piribebuy

Azcurra

Pirayú

Cerro León

Valenzuela

Villeta

Lomas Valentinas

Paraguarí

Ybytymí

	Roads
	Railroad
	Osório
	Polidoro
	Caballero
	Mitre
	João Manoel

N

0   10   20mi.

MAP 8. THE CORDILLERA CAMPAIGN (MAY-AUGUST 1869)

TABLE OF CONTENTS

Acknowledgments

Every serious scholar is an apprentice who depends on the wisdom of others. I am no different. In researching and writing for twenty years on the Paraguayan War of 1864–1870, I have necessarily accumulated many debts, both to scholars and, not infrequently, to thoughtful and friendly acquaintances who have appeared serendipitously on the scene with new information and points of view that I had never considered. That which is well written and solid in the present volume owes everything to the efforts of those people. They shared their ideas, their documents, and their reactions freely with me and I can never properly repay them for all their attention to our common *inquietud*.

I am grateful to the directors and staffs of various archives and libraries, including Asunción's Archivo Nacional, Biblioteca Nacional, Centro Paraguayo de Estudios Sociológicos, and Museo Historico Militar; the Archivo General de la Nación (Buenos Aires), Archivo del Banco de la Provincia de Buenos Aires, Museo Mitre, Archivo General de la Provincia de Corrientes, Instituto de Investigaciones Geo-Históricas (Resistencia); Rio de Janeiro's Instituto Histórico e Geografico Brasileiro, Biblioteca Nacional, Biblioteca e Arquivo do Exercito, and Serviço Documental Geral da Marinha, and Porto Alegre's Arquivo Historico do Rio Grande do Sul; the Biblioteca Nacional, Archivo General de la Nación, and Museo Histórico Nacional in Montevideo; the Oliveira Lima Library (Catholic University, Washington), Nettie Lee Benson Library (University of Texas at Austin), Spencer Library (University of Kansas), Tomás Rivera Library (University of California at Riverside), Washburn-Norlands Library (Livermore Falls, Maine), and the Hispanic Division of the Library of Congress (Washington).

Research was made possible by grants from the Fulbright-Hays Program, the American Philosophical Society, and the University of Georgia Faculty Research program.

Scholars in many countries lent me critical counsel. Canadians Roderick J. Barman, Stephen Bell, and Hendrik Kraay were particularly helpful, as were Brazilians Francisco Doratioto, Reginaldo da Silva Bacchi, Adler Homero Fonseca de Castro, Heraldo Makrakis, Max Justo Guedes, and Eduardo Italo

Pesce. Uruguayans Alicia Barán, Fernando Aguerre, Alberto del Pino Menck, Ana Ribeiro, Andrea Gayoso, and especially Juan Manuel Casal alerted me to some unusual sources and corrected errors and weaknesses in the manuscript. I received other useful suggestions and advice from Argentines Dardo Ramirez Braschi, Liliana Brezzo, Ignacio Telesca, María Lucrecia Johansson, Miguel Angel de Marco, and *mi querido profe*, the late Tulio Halperín Donghi; from Paraguayans Milda Rivarola, Adelina Pusineri, Alfredo Boccia Romanach, Herib Caballero Campos, Armando Rivarola, Ricardo Scavone Yegros, Guido Rodriguez Alcalá, and *los siempre recordados* "Tito" Duarte and Aníbal Solis; from Britons Denis Wright, Chris Leuchars, Andrew Nickson, and Leslie Bethell; from Germans Wolf Lustig and Barbara Potthast; Spaniards Eva Morales Raya and Mar Langa Pizarro; Frenchman Luc Capdevila; Italian Marco Fano (who generously shared some wonderful nineteenth-century images of the war); and Costa Rican Roberto Arguedas.

In the United States, I benefited from the valuable suggestions of Peter Hoffer, John T. LaSaine, Jr., Richard Graham, Steve Huggins, Erick Langer, Karl Friday, John Chasteen, Bridget Chesterton, Jennifer French, and especially Jeffrey Needell. Theodore Webb, Kerck Kelsey, Joseph Howell, and the late Billie Gammon shared some fascinating documents from the Washburn-Norlands Library with me. Wendy Giminski helped with the maps.

I also wish to acknowledge the support and hard work of Peter Enman, Karen Buttner, Brian Scrivener, Helen Hajnoczky, Alison Cobra, and Melina Cusano at the University of Calgary Press, and Ryan Perks, whose quick eye saved my manuscript again and again. I also want to thank the staff of Jittery Joe's Coffee of Watkinsville, Georgia, whose premises afforded me the equivalent of a second office, and in which I composed a surprisingly large portion of this text. Thanks for the caffeine and the good cheer.

My greatest appreciation of all goes to Lieutenant Colonel Loren "Pat" Patterson and my dear friend, the late Jerry W. Cooney, who read pretty much everything I wrote. These two gentlemen-scholars contributed immeasurably to the realization of this project. I simply could not have done it without them.

Finally, I wish to thank my dear wife Pamela Towle, who showed me that the historical muse can come in many forms and can provide happy support, good humor, and a laugh or two to put it all in perspective.

Thomas L. Whigham
July 2017
Watkinsville, Georgia, USA

Abbreviations

AGNBA	Archivo General de la Nación, Buenos Aires
AGNM	Archivo General de la Nación, Montevideo
ANA	Archivo Nacional de Asunción
ANA-CRB	Archivo Nacional de Asunción, Colección Rio Branco
ANA-SH	Archivo Nacional de Asunción, Sección Histórica
ANA-SJC	Archivo Nacional de Asunción, Sección Judicial Criminal
ANA-SNE	Archivo Nacional de Asunción, Sección Nueva Encuadernación
APEMT	Arquivo Publico do Estado do Mato Grosso do Sul, Campo Grande
BNA	Biblioteca Nacional de Asunción
BNA-CJO	Biblioteca Nacional de Asunción, Colección Juan O'Leary
BNRJ	Biblioteca Nacional, Rio de Janeiro
IHGB	Instituto Histórico e Geográfico Brasileiro, Rio de Janeiro
MG	University of Texas, Austin, Manuel Gondra Collection
MHMA	Museo Histórico Militar, Asunción
MHMA-CGA	Museo Histórico Militar, Asunción, Colección Gill Aguinaga
MHMA-CZ	Museo Histórico Militar, Asunción, Colección Zeballos
MHNM	Museo Histórico Nacional, Montevideo
NARA	National Archives and Records Administration, Washington, DC
PRO-FO	Public Records Office, London, Foreign Office Documents
UCR-JSG	University of California, Riverside, Juan Silvano Godoi Collection
WNL	Washburn-Norlands Library, Livermore Falls, Maine

Illustrations

Portrait of Francisco Solano López, photographed by Doménico Parodi in the Azcurra camp. See Alfred Marbais du Graty, *La République du Paraguay* (Bruxelles: C. Muquardt, 1862).

Marshal Francisco Solano López (1825–70), whose ragged troops resisted the combined armies of Brazil, Argentina, and Uruguay for over five years.

Portrait of Bartolomé Mitre, drawn by T. Hutchison, 1865. See Thomas L. Whigham, *The Paraguayan War. Causes and Early Conduct* (Lincoln: University of Nebraska Press, 2002), image 5.

Bartolomé Mitre (1821–1906), poet, historian, and president of Argentina during the early stages of the Paraguayan War. His alliance with Brazil was unpopular in his country.

Portrait of Dom Pedro II, 1870, dressed as Admiral. Photograph by Joaquim Insley Pacheco.

Pedro II (1825–91), emperor of Brazil for over forty years. He regarded the Paraguayan occupation of Mato Grosso as a personal affront.

Itapiru, 19 de Abril de 1866, República del Paraguay. Painting by Cándido López, 1866. Collection of Museo Historico Nacional, Buenos Aires. Image courtesy of Marco Fano.

Itapirú and Paso de la Patria fell into Allied hands, with little resistance, in April 1866.

Manuel Luís Osório, c. 1868.
Photographer unknown. See Silva
Costa, *A Vida dos Grandes Brasileiros
- Duque de Caxias* (Rio de Janeiro:
Editora Três, 2003).

Manuel Osório (1808–79), Marquis of
Herval. A Riograndense cavalryman
with long experience of command,
Osório was Brazil's most capable
field commander.

"Cadaveres paraguayos de la batalla de Tuyutí." Lithograph by Francisco Fortuny. See *Album de la
Guerra del Paraguay* (Buenos Aires: Asociación Guerreros del Paraguay, 1893).

Mounds of Paraguayan cadavers after Tuyutí. The bodies were said to be so lean that they did
not catch fire when Allied burial teams initially tried to cremate them.

Portrait of Joaquim Marques Lisboa, the Baron of Tamandaré, 1873. Photographer unknown. See Thomas L. Whigham, *The Paraguayan War. Causes and Early Conduct* (Lincoln: University of Nebraska Press, 2002), image 9.

Admiral Tamandaré (1807–97), whose fleet of iron-clads bombarded Paraguayan river defenses for many months but generally failed to silence them.

"Spanish-born León de Palleja's death during the Battle of Potrero Sauce, 18 July 1866." Photographer unknown. See Ricardo Salles, *Guerra do Paraguai. Memórias e Imagens* (Rio de Janeiro: Edições Biblioteca Nacional, 2003), 71.

Colonel León de Palleja (1816–66) was as well-known for his war diaries as for his skill at command. His death at Boquerón was universally mourned and even his Paraguayan adversaries praised his kindness and humanity.

Bateria Londres, 1868.
Postcard, painting by
E.C. Jourdan.

The fortress of Humaitá,
with its many casemented
batteries, was considered
by many to be the
"Sebastopol of South
America."

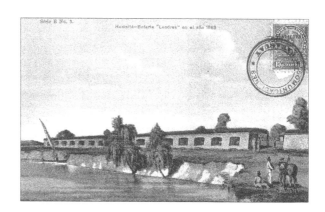

"Dernière entrevue des généraux Florès, Mitre et du maréchal Lopez. – D'apres un dessin de
M. Meyer." Drawing from *L'illustration: journal universel* (v. 48 Jul-Dec 1866): 316.

The conference at Yataity-Corã in September 1866 failed to inspire a negotiated settlement
to the war.

Marcha del Ejército Argentino a tomar posiciones para el ataque a Curupaytí el 22/09/1866. Painting by Cándido López, 1902. Collection of Museo Historico Nacional, Buenos Aires. Image courtesy of Marco Fano.

Allied troops advance on well-defended positions at Curupayty, 22 September 1866.

Después de la Batalla de Curupaytí. Painting by Cándido López, 1893. Collection of Museo Historico Nacional, Buenos Aires. Image courtesy of Marco Fano.

The bloody defeat at Curupayty set back Allied hopes for victory for nearly a year.

Portrait of Venancio Flores,
President of Uruguay, c.1865.
Photographer unknown.

Though a brave commander and
strong supporter of the Triple
Alliance, Uruguayan president
Venancio Flores (1808–68)
found himself increasingly out
of step with his countrymen as
the war progressed.

Portrait of Luís Alves de Lima e Silva.
Engraving by Goupil, 1878. See cover of
Padre Joaquim Pinto de Campos, *Vida do
grande cidadão brasileiro Luís Alves
de Lima e Silva* (Lisbon: Imprensa
Nacional, 1878).

As Allied commander, the Marquis de
Caxias (1803–80) won fame as much for
his political acumen as for his intelligent
handling of the military challenges in the
campaign against Paraguay.

Hon. C. A. Washburn
1885

131 POST ST.
SAN FRANCISCO.

Photograph of Charles Ames Washburn, 1885. Photograph by I. W. Taber, San Francisco. Image courtesy of Marco Fano.

Charles Ames Washburn lived from 1822 to 1889. As U.S. Minister to Asunción, Washburn tried to initiate peace negotiations and was later accused of conspiracy against the López government.

Portrait of Joaquim José Inácio, Viscount of Inhaúma, c.1861. Drawing by Sébastien Auguste Sisson. See Sébastien Auguste Sisson, *Galeria dos brasileiros ilustres* (Brasília: Federal Senate, Special Secretariat for Publishing and Publication, 1999).

Whereas his predecessor, Admiral Tamandaré, had been flamboyant, Admiral Joaquim José Ignácio, Viscount of Inhaúma (1808–69) was steady and thoughtful, a stance that helped assure Allied supremacy on the rivers. He was also deeply religious.

Portrait of General José Eduvigis Díaz, c. 1867. Photographer unknown.

The always audacious General José Eduvigis Díaz (1833–67) was the most significant Paraguayan commander of the war save for Marshal López himself.

"Vista de la Asuncion tomada del Arsenal." Illustration, date unknown. See Juan F. Pérez Acosta, *Carlos Antonio López. Obrero Máximo* (Asunción: Guarania, 1948), photo section, II.

Organized in part by the Marshal's British engineers, the Asunción arsenal continued to supply the Paraguayan army with arms and munitions up to the end of 1868.

Illustration from the third page of the newspaper *El Centinela*, 13 June 1867.

The evident willingness of Paraguayan women to take up arms against their country's enemies gave rise to rumors that the Marshal had formed women's battalions. Here he responds by mocking a non-existent unit of Brazilian female troopers.

La actualidad de la alianza.

Illustration from the second page of the newspaper *El Centinela*, 24 October 1867.

The Allied commanders seem to have spent every lull in the fighting arguing among themselves, as this satirical woodcut indicates with great clarity.

Eliza Alicia Lynch, c. 1864. Photographer unknown. See *Revista de História da Biblioteca Nacional* (Issue 54), March 2010.

Eliza Alicia Lynch (1835–86), the Marshal's lover and confidante and mother of many of his children, she was a power in her own right in Paraguay.

Photograph of Juana Pabla Carrillo. Photographer and date unknown. Image courtesy of Marco Fano.

The widow of President Carlos Antonio López, dona Juana Pabla accompanied her son the Marshal into the eastern districts of Paraguay, and actually survived him as the war came to an end.

"Prisioneros de guerra y familias paraguayas tortuados por Lopéz en el campamento de San Fernando." Drawing by Francisco Fortuny. See *Album de la Guerra del Paraguay* (Buenos Aires: Asociación Guerreros del Paraguay, 1893).

The "Tribunals of Blood" at San Fernando, where so many Paraguayans were condemned, was perhaps the worst, though by no means the only example of López turning on his own people.

The Battle of Avaí. Painting by Pedro Americo, 1872–79. Collection of Museu Nacional de Belas Artes.

The battle of Avay, as presented by painter Pedro Americo (1843–1905), was a glorious achievement for the Marquis de Caxias. In truth, it was a bloody scrimmage entirely destitute of glory.

"Guerre du Paraguay: La ville de l'Assumption occupée par l'armée alliée." Artist unknown. From *Le Monde illustré: journal hebdomadaire*, (no. 625) 3 April 1869.

The Brazilian fleet arrives at the port of Asunción.

Portrait of Count d'Eu. "Gaston d´Orléans, conde d´Eu, esposo de Isabel, Princesa Imperial do Brasil no Rio de Janeiro, c.1870." Photography by Christiano Júnior. See *De Volta a Luz: Fotografias Nunca Vistas do Imperador* (São Paulo: Instituto Cultural Banco Santos, 2003).

The Count d'Eu (1842–1922) had to be pressured to assume Allied command in 1869, but nonetheless took very seriously his mission to hunt down Marshal López.

Portrait of José Maria da Silva Paranhos, viscount of Rio Branco, c.1875. Photograph by Alberto Henschel.

José Maria da Silva Paranhos (1819–80), later Baron of Rio Branco, was tasked with reconstructing the Paraguayan government in 1869–70.

Photography of
a starving boy.
Photographer unknown,
no date. See *I Die with
My Country. Perspectives
on the Paraguayan War,
1864–1870*, edited by
Hendrik Kraay and
Thomas L. Whigham
(Lincoln and London:
University of Nebraska
Press, 2004), 78–79.

Starving refugees and
boy-soldiers from
the Marshal's army
continued to arrive in the
city, some of them barely
recognizable as
human beings.

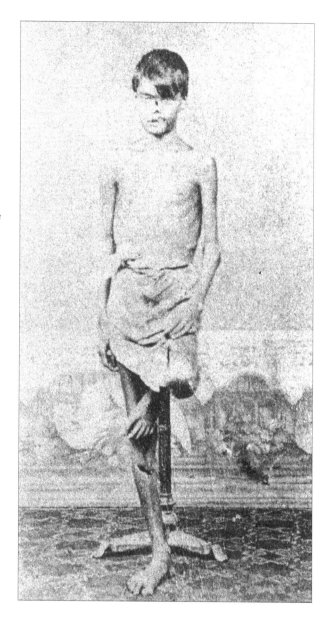

Mother with dead child. Drawing from *Harper's New Monthly Magazine* (no. CCXXXIX April 1870 vol. XL): 646.

The grieving *destinadas* became the iconic symbol for Paraguay not just in 1870 but for a hundred years or more.

INTRODUCTION

The hot breath of war blew furiously across South America during the summer of 1865, and, like the sand-laden *viento norte* that regularly sweeps the south-central parts of the continent, it was a merciless wind. It spared neither man nor animal; alike it blasted churches, ranch houses, and the whitewashed huts of the poor; and it caused otherwise level-headed people to contemplate killing on a vast scale. Worst of all, the violence had only just begun, for nearly five more years would pass before side arms were holstered, and swords returned to their scabbards.

As the Paraguayan War (1864–1870)—also known as the War of the Triple Alliance—unfolded, it brought the usual litany of human disasters, and perhaps a bit more. The Paraguayan War enjoys the dubious distinction of being the bloodiest inter-state war ever fought in South America—and yet it is easily the least understood. Like many serious conflicts, it offers a chance to reflect on the folly of human interactions, the bravery of individual fighters, the stupidity, the confusion, the terror, the camaraderie, and the willingness of people to sacrifice themselves for a cause. But the Paraguayan campaign was unusual in that it went on and on beyond all reason, so much so that contemporary observers—and modern historians—have had a difficult time trying to understand it.

The war began, like a great many wars of the nineteenth century, as an outgrowth of differing views on borders, national identities, and power relations in a continent little accustomed to self-rule. Control over the Platine waterways—the Paraná, Paraguay, and Uruguay Rivers—remained a strategic goal for most of the governments involved, just as it had for the previous colonial regimes. But honor was also at stake, as was personal interest. In these ways the war was straightforward enough at the beginning. But it soon evolved into a struggle for survival, not just for individual soldiers, but for the Paraguayan people as a whole.

While the inhabitants of South America had inherited a vast geographical space from Spain and Portugal, the former colonial empires gave them only the barest notion of how to govern their new nations after independence in the 1810s and '20s.[1] Political systems and visions of the future were bitterly contested. Social elites and political factions in the two largest countries, Brazil and Argentina, had to concern themselves with administering thousands of miles of coastlines, grasslands, mountains, and forested hills. The very size of these territories frustrated attempts at governance on all sides, and those who aspired to the status of statesmen worried about how much they ought to draw from colonial precedents or break with the past. Brazilian and Argentine elites offered their peoples distinct models of nationhood—the former monarchical and slavocrat, the latter oligarchical. Both options had advantages and disadvantages, yet it was never clear which model could better meet the political aspirations of the greatest number of people. Besides, in both countries there were provincial chieftains, or caudillos, who for opportunistic reasons wished to frustrate the consolidation of any political order they could not control.

And then there was the exceptional case of Paraguay. Located far up the rivers in the South American interior, the Republic of Paraguay offered to a largely heterogeneous, Guaraní-speaking people a frankly dictatorial model that promised order amid every uncertainty. Authoritarianism had a long pedigree in the country, with some scholars tracing its roots to eighteenth-century Jesuit influences.[2] While the missionary priests may or may not have convinced their Indigenous charges that salvation was ultimately contingent on unquestioning obedience, the governments that came to power after independence clearly convinced the majority of Paraguayans of the need to obey their dictates as the price of national survival. The fact that most people in the country already harbored a xenophobic mistrust of outsiders made it easier to accept the leaders' decisions for the community as a whole. So it had been during the Supreme Dictatorship of José Gaspar Rodríguez de Francia (1814–1840) and the only slightly more liberal presidency of Carlos Antonio López (1844–1862).[3] And when the latter's eldest son, Francisco Solano López (1826–1870), inherited the mantle of power from his father, he hoped to use his considerable legitimacy to keep Paraguay free from trouble with its neighbors. In fact, López steered the country directly into a hornet's nest.

Many writers have portrayed the younger López as either a hero or a despot.[4] He was clearly a bit of both. But he was also the leader of a nation at war, who was challenged mercilessly by the enemy and by his own preconceptions about statecraft and duty; as will become clear, he had a great many human weaknesses, too. And yet he often showed military skill, especially while on the defensive. His selfishness and physical cowardice have been condemned, but in trying to understand his behavior we might keep in mind that we do not know how his opponents would have acted in his place. They, too, had to act under pressure and sometimes cracked. All of them were affected by the fighting.

The Paraguayan War stemmed from ongoing debates over the status of the Banda Oriental, the Spanish-speaking territory along the northern bank of the Río de la Plata that had been fashioned into the independent Oriental

Republic of Uruguay in 1828. The establishment of this new nation—which was separated from Paraguay by three hundred miles—was the result of a political compromise that satisfied neither the Brazilians nor their Argentine rivals, nor their respective surrogates in the region. Two political factions, the Colorado and Blanco Parties, had jostled for power ever since, appealing for support to whatever friends they could find beyond Uruguay's borders, without ever managing to dominate the government in Montevideo, the Oriental capital, for any length of time. A series of civil wars was the inevitable result.

By the early 1860s, these tensions had come to threaten the broader peace in the Platine region. Across the river in Buenos Aires, President Bartolomé Mitre (1821–1906) had recently triumphed over provincial caudillos at the battle of Pavón, and now sought the restoration of Argentina's traditional hegemony over Uruguay. Next door in Brazil, however, various members of the emperor's government were thinking along similar lines. Pedro II (1825–1891) had seen his country torn by civil conflicts only a few years earlier and now felt anxious to see his rule properly consolidated. His ministers argued that this meant developing a sphere of influence in the Río de la Plata, especially in Uruguay, where the Portuguese had exercised considerable influence in colonial times.

In taking this stand, the politicians were egged on by Brazilian ranchers who owned land in the Oriental Republic and who felt vexed that the Blanco government had required them to pay taxes like other landowners. The emperor himself attempted to stay aloof from these questions of diplomacy, but certain influential members of Parliament were not so squeamish. Some even felt receptive to the suggestion that Brazil should intervene militarily in the Banda Oriental. Thus the empire could uphold the immediate interests of the Brazilian ranchers while simultaneously assuring long-term imperial advantages in the region by sponsoring the caudillo Venancio Flores (1808–1868), a man of decidedly traditional sensibilities, more at home in the saddle than in the halls of government. Flores had been a perennial contender for power in Uruguay, and would see to it that the Colorados would replace the Blancos in Montevideo and presumably follow a pro-Brazilian line from that point forward. The fact that Flores also enjoyed the tacit support of Mitre meant that the Blancos lacked any obvious foreign support and would necessarily have to find new friends or else yield to Flores.

It was in these circumstances that the Blancos turned to López and Paraguay. Had their appeal for support been made to Dr. Francia or the elder López it would certainly have been spurned as impractical and politically unwise. But the younger López lived in a different era of Paraguayan national development, and thus had different ambitions. The country's isolation over the previous decades had been the stuff of legend in South America, and many statesmen still could not fathom how to best cultivate good relations with its government.[5] In fact, during the 1850s, the prickly Carlos Antonio López waded into minor confrontations with Brazil, Britain, France, Argentina, and even the United States, which sent a flotilla up the Paraná River to force the resolution of an incident in which an American sailor was killed.[6]

Paraguay had backed down in all these confrontations, a humiliation of sorts that the younger López had never forgotten. It convinced him that the country's security could not be secured through negotiations with foreign powers—it would take a strong army. With this in mind, he used his position as his father's war minister to build a substantial military. The armed forces he created may not have been as awe-inspiring as later commentators claimed, but it featured some modern aspects, and it employed near-universal conscription, something that was absent in Brazil and Argentina.[7]

As Paraguay developed a respectable military force, Solano López began to conceive of a greater role for his country in broader Platine affairs. This was not an entirely inappropriate desire. During the struggle that the Argentine Confederation had experienced with the breakaway province of Buenos Aires between 1858 and 1859, the contending parties had actually called upon López to act as mediator, a role carried out with dignity and evenhandedness, and for which he was widely praised by the Porteños (inhabitants of the city of Buenos Aires).[8] Given his ambition and point of view, it was natural that when the Banda Oriental was convulsed by the Flores revolt from 1863 to 1864, he would presume that the belligerents would turn to him for help.

Only the Blancos did so. They were desperate for support, having been rejected by traditional friends in the Argentine provinces and elsewhere, and now faced with the possibility of an imminent Brazilian invasion. Blanco diplomats in Asunción, the Paraguayan capital, approached López with a new and curious argument about power relations that had been inspired by events in Europe, but which they now hoped to apply to the crisis in the Plata. They maintained that the empire, in contemplating an aggrandized role in the Banda Oriental, was threatening a balance of power that had assured the general peace in the region, and that if the Brazilians were successful in this endeavor, Uruguay would soon fall, but then so would Paraguay.

It is not clear that López bought every aspect of this argument, though it later appeared as a sort of gospel truth in his government's proclamations and decrees. What does seem likely is that he felt that the events in Uruguay required some demonstration of seriousness on his part.[9] And once he had decided on the necessity of action, events started to take their own baleful course.

Flores received some not-so-clandestine supplies of arms from Buenos Aires throughout 1864.[10] While this was happening, Brazilian politicians issued a series of threats to the Blancos, who instructed their representatives in Asunción to pressure López for some kind of commitment. Instead, he issued letters of concern, which the politicians in Rio and Buenos Aires dismissed. Then, after the Brazilians formally threatened military intervention against the government in Montevideo, López issued an ultimatum on 30 August, announcing that the "Republic of Paraguay would consider any occupation of Uruguayan territory by imperial forces … as an attack upon the balance of power of the Platine states," and an action requiring an immediate response. As López also warned, the Paraguayan government disclaimed "any responsibility for the ultimate consequences."[11]

Though a casus belli could not have been more clearly defined, the Brazilians chose to ignore the note. Imperial troops crossed the Uruguayan frontier on 16 October 1864 and swiftly drove the Blanco troops into strongholds at Salto and Paysandú. Flores soon coordinated his efforts with those of the intervening forces, breaking all resistance at Salto within a matter of weeks and laying siege to Paysandú. The Blanco minister to Asunción urged López to move expeditiously in accordance with his previous ultimatum, but for a time he vacillated, evidently hoping that the Brazilians would come to their senses. Then, on 12 November he sent his naval units to seize the Brazilian steamer *Marqués de Olinda*, which had passed upriver from Asunción the previous day on its way to Corumbá in Mato Grosso. The Brazilian officers and crew, who had not expected a confrontation, now found themselves prisoners, unsure of what would happen next. López had no such doubts. His country now had a sizable army and navy, though not nearly as large as that of the empire, and it seemed as if time were running against him. "If we don't have a war now with Brazil," he remarked, "we shall have one at a less convenient time for ourselves."[12] Thus he decided to sow the wind. His country would reap the whirlwind.

In my earlier study, *The Paraguayan War, Causes and Early Conduct*, I offered a detailed analysis of the offensive that Marshal López launched, first against Brazil, and then against Argentina, between 1864 and 1865. The campaign took a simple, if not quite predictable, course. As a landlocked country, Paraguay had always suffered from a strategic disadvantage vis-à-vis its neighbors; it thus needed to act with care and hopefully with the aid of allies like the Uruguayan Blancos. In a surprise move, however, the army of Marshal López surged not to the south, to aid the Blancos in Uruguay, but to the north, where it seized some waterlogged districts (and stockpiled armaments) in Mato Grosso. Thereafter the Paraguayans faced a dilemma. To link up with their Uruguayan allies—or what was left of them—they needed to move southward as quickly as possible, probably by way of the rivers. But this led in short order to a seemingly insurmountable barrier—Argentine neutrality—which the government in Buenos Aires strongly defended, and which it was unlikely to waive in order to permit the Paraguayan army to strike across its national territory.

López's answer to the problem of transit was typically unambiguous—he attacked, occupying the port of Corrientes in April 1865, and ordered his army into northeastern Argentina and Rio Grande do Sul in two widely dispersed columns. From the outset, this invasion seemed risky. Neither the Argentines nor their new allies in Brazil and Uruguay could hope to counter its effects in the short term, but since the Marshal had little hope of defeating these countries, all his opponents needed was a series of delaying actions to slow his progress. Eventually, a war of attrition would evolve, one that would distinctly favor Paraguay's enemies. López, they presumed, would sue for peace.

The Paraguayans, however, enjoyed a few advantages. There was no reason, for instance, to suppose that the Argentines and Brazilians would cooperate effectively, since they had never done so previously. The Marshal's action had tethered the two powers in an unnatural alliance with Flores, who had just succeeded in obliterating the Blanco stronghold at Paysandú. This apparent victory might now work against the Argentines and Brazilians, who were sure to squabble over the spoils. Besides, the Paraguayans expected to receive concrete aid from anti-Brazilian and anti-Porteño factions in the Argentine Litoral and Uruguay. Seven months later each of these assumptions was laid bare by the facts. The Marshal's exhausted troops stumbled back into Paraguay from Corrientes to reconsider their position. They were badly chastened, to be sure, but they were not defeated.

López's offensive in Corrientes and Rio Grande do Sul in 1865 revealed strengths and weaknesses on both sides. The Allies—Argentina, Brazil, and Uruguay—had made no initial preparations to counter any Paraguayan attack; they conducted raids and minor guerrilla actions, but they developed no general plan for resistance. As López had predicted, they bickered among themselves over strategy, tactics, and command. Like the proverbial scorpion and turtle, they mistrusted each other's motives, and saw only minimal need to share supplies and transport. Morale was low.

Even so, the alliance between Argentina, Brazil, and Uruguay held, and López provided the reason. In order to preserve itself, a small country surrounded by unfriendly neighbors either must exploit the jealousies that exist outside its borders, or else find some way to stay aloof. For many years, Paraguay had pursued the latter course, but the Marshal's rapid expansion of his military forces, his unpredictability, and his arrogance convinced many in Buenos Aires and Rio de Janeiro to doubt him more than they doubted each other. Besides, they reasoned, he had drawn the first blood and now had to pay the price for his conceit.

Ultimately, when forces friendly to López failed to materialize in Corrientes, his men had to face an increasingly well-armed and better-organized enemy without any benefit of succor. The Paraguayan offensive soon began to sputter out. First came a disastrous river engagement at the Riachuelo in June 1865, during which Paraguay lost the use of the Paraná River as its main supply route for troops and supplies. This was followed by a land battle at Yataí in August—another defeat—that set the stage for a protracted siege at Uruguaiana in Rio Grande do Sul, and ultimately for the surrender of its starving and demoralized garrison one month later. Put together, these encounters cost López more than a third of his army. He had no choice but to pull his remaining forces back to Paraguay and into the labyrinthine swamps that guarded his great fortress of Humaitá.

Few on the Allied side had doubted that victory would eventually be theirs. The Marshal had exhausted his diplomatic options, and the Brazilians and Argentines had isolated his country with an impenetrable blockade. López had lost the better part of his river fleet and some thirty to forty thousand dead, wounded, and missing by the beginning of 1866.[13] Dysentery hit many of the survivors, and cases of measles and smallpox had cropped up in the ranks. It could only be a matter of time before the Paraguayans yielded.

And yet, the Marshal succeeded in rallying his troops, who had no intention of admitting defeat. He argued—unconvincingly—that the Allies had purposely sent infected troops through the lines to introduce smallpox into Paraguay, and that his brave stalwarts would survive even this example of perfidy.[14] Foreign observers tended to treat such hyperbole as the product of panic. In their eyes, logic demanded a prompt end to hostilities, either through direct negotiation or some frank admission of the military facts at the beginning of 1866.

Instead, as this study will show, the fighting went on. My earlier account addressed the causes and earliest stages of the war, when the Paraguayans still believed that their offensive was unstoppable. The present one traces what happened afterwards, how the Marshal's men endured everything that the Allies could throw at them in a defense that lasted four years. The Paraguayans gave up only bit by bit, losing an enormous number of men until the final resisters died in combat alongside Marshal López in March 1870. How they kept up the fight while their country was tumbling down around them is at the center of this story, which even the most implacable enemies of the Marshal see as an epic as well as a tragedy.

During the war, diplomats and foreign observers consistently expressed a desire for peace. But the rationalizations that they voiced in favor of a negotiated settlement left the common Paraguayan soldier unconvinced and ambitious generals on all sides thirsting for further measures of glory. As I will show, aspiration outweighed prudence until very late in the day—a sad truth for which López and the Allied leaders must share the blame.[15]

Brazil's Pedro II regarded the struggle against Paraguay as a kind of personal crusade. He was a thoughtful yet rather peevish individual, and, as a sovereign, was keenly aware of his duties and prerogatives. He considered Brazil a civilized, if flawed, realm whose dignity the Marshal had offended with his invasion of Mato Grosso. While the physical immensity of the empire might have mitigated the need to respond to such pinpricks, in fact the government in Rio had a surprisingly fragile structure—more like a piece of fine china than an iron chisel. Slavery had already blotted Brazil's reputation in the eyes of the world, and there was no need to likewise admit to weakness vis-à-vis an ambitious tyrant like López. To move beyond Brazil's obvious defects, to allow the noble spirit of his empire to shine through, and to spread civilization to a benighted people, Pedro needed an absolute victory over Paraguay; for him, the road to Brazil's future had to pass through Asunción. This was not so much a matter of seeking vengeance against López as it was a way of setting the universe right. Along the way, Pedro and his ministers—who should have known better—became prisoners of an unbending policy.

Bartolomé Mitre, the Argentine president and overall Allied commander at the beginning of the conflict, was cut of a less refined but worldlier cloth: his was a bourgeois background, not a regal one. He had weaned himself on the grittiest political infighting while in exile in Montevideo in the 1840s and '50s, and afterwards traded his bloody shirt for the frock coat of the cultured statesman. Nonetheless he was most comfortable writing diatribes in the editorial offices of his newspaper, *La Nación Argentina*, or in drawing-room debate; an austere and distant palace held no charms for him. Unlike Pedro, Mitre saw the struggle against Paraguay in political terms, and like a chess player, he treated armies as pawns that might be sacrificed so long as it brought the requisite gain. So it had been during the 1850s, when Mitre's partisans ousted one set of rural caudillos and stalemated another. Driving López out of Corrientes gave Mitre still greater leverage over his domestic opponents in Argentina, and he could ill afford to squander this advantage. Nor did he intend to concede to the Brazilians a larger sphere of influence on the continent than they already enjoyed. Taking Asunción could undercut his enemies on all sides, and might even herald the unification of the Plata under an unquestioned Porteño hegemony.

Such thoughts might have animated Mitre, but they were repellant, of course, to López. The Paraguayan leader had launched the war in an illusory quest to impose—or restore—a balance of power in the region. In the Marshal's view, the liberal and supposedly progressive forces in the Plata (as represented by the oligarchs of Buenos Aires) had united with Brazilian monarchists to stifle "true American republicanism." The troubles in Uruguay were thus an augury of what would happen if López could not guarantee for Paraguay its rightful share of power and prestige. Now, come what may, the enemy had to be combated by deed as well as by word.

As the Allies pressed hard upon the Paraguayan frontier the nature of the war changed, but the Marshal stayed the same. His family had ruled Paraguay since 1841, ushering the country away from the traditional social patterns of the eighteenth century toward those of a modern capitalist state. There were many benefits to this modernization, but also many costs, of which López himself surely was one. Paraguay now had a constitution comparable to that of many new nations in Latin America; it had a cash economy and a growing export trade in cattle, tobacco, hides, and yerba mate; it had a responsible state apparatus, with a sizeable bureaucracy and a rational tax system; it even had primary education and a weekly newspaper. At the same time, however, far too much power was concentrated in the hands of the López family. Francisco Solano López never hesitated to use—and abuse—this power. His brash and sensual impulses, so noticeable in his youth, still dominated his heart. He was attracted to low women and fine uniforms like a child to a pretty toy, and like a child, he could never admit a mistake; it followed, then, that his army's reverses in Corrientes and Rio Grande would be blamed on his subordinates, against whom he always directed a cascade of invective. After Uruguaiana fell, he singled out Antonio de la Cruz Estigarribia, the colonel who had surrendered the garrison, threatening him with heavy consequences should he ever fall into Paraguayan hands, and consigning his wife and family to the streets. Then, to the officers assembled at Humaitá, he issued a stern warning:

> I am working for my country, for the good and honor of you all, and none help me. I stand alone—I have confidence in none of you—I cannot trust one amongst you. ... *Cuidado*! But take care! Hitherto I have pardoned offenses, taken pleasure in pardoning, but now, from this day, I pardon no one.[16]

There was calculation as well as bad temper in this attitude. López's attitudes suggested that the rabble—of which he considered his men members—had to be led by terror as much as by example.[17]

On their side, the Allies liked to think that a broad patriotism inspired their soldiers. Presuming that this was the case, they thought it a simple matter to turn the Marshal's violent predilection towards his own people to their advantage. In a letter to Washington, the US minister to Asunción noted the common presumption among Allied officers that Paraguayan obstinacy amounted to "a superstitious fear and belief that if they fail[ed] to obey orders to the fullest extent they [would] sooner or later fall into the hands of López and then be put to inconceivable torture."[18] Surely this situation favored the Allied cause—or so the men in Rio de Janeiro and Buenos Aires wanted to believe.

In truth, as I hope to show, the Paraguayans were motivated by something more powerful than fear. López could command obedience from his soldiers and suppress every inkling of dissent, but he could not command courage: the Paraguayans gave this of their own volition, for although they knew that López and the nation were not one and the same, they nonetheless accepted the basic need to defend home and family.[19] Certainly the Marshal could arouse great trepidation, just as the Allies had claimed. But then, what else could they say? To admit that the Paraguayans acted from a love of country that went beyond submission to the López family might legitimize their struggle, which was the last thing that Mitre and the others wished to do. Allied leaders could speak contemptuously of the Paraguayans' "blind" or slavish loyalty, but still they envied it.

Constancy is but one element in war, and the operation of armies and logistical networks will also receive attention in the following pages. British military engineer George Thompson, who would one day rise to the rank of colonel on López's staff, noted how grateful the Marshal's men felt in late 1865 to be back in Paraguay. Regrouping near the perimeter of Humaitá, they slept, sent messages to their families, and received medical attention.[20] Those who were badly wounded were evacuated to Asunción or to the army's hospitals at Cerro León.

The men who stayed behind at Humaitá initially had plenty of food. The officers ordered the men to reinforce the defenses at the main camp, and dispatched new units to the auxiliary works at Itapirú and Santa Teresa, both on the Paraná River. Another three thousand men under Major Manuel Núñez rode east to Encarnación to guard against any Allied attacks that might come through Misiones. A spate of rest revived the Paraguayan troops, who now could prepare for a long siege. The Marshal's men moved quickly to refit the eight batteries at Humaitá with gabions of packed earth. They built a new series of huts and powder magazines and dug some rudimentary trenches. What was left of the Paraguayan navy busied itself in logistical support, ferrying munitions and foodstuffs from Asunción.[21] Cattle and horses were likewise driven southward along a meandering route through the Ñe'embucú swamplands to Humaitá.

In order to repulse any Allied invasion, López also needed to strengthen his defenses along the Paraná. His father had long before established a military post at Itapirú, located along the shortest invasion route from the Allied camps in Corrientes. This same "fort" had witnessed an armed confrontation with the US warship *Water Witch* in the late 1850s, and the younger López had never forgotten its strategic significance. Now he dispatched his engineers to build hidden batteries at nearby Paso de la Patria. They erected "a fine work, with redans and curtains, resting on two lagoons and impassible *carrizal* [sloughs], and mounting thirty field guns" and other smaller pieces.[22] It was no Sebastopol, nor even an Humaitá, but before the Allies could even think of raiding Paraguayan territory they would have to get past it.

López showed great enthusiasm in directing the work at Paso de la Patria. Thanks to a new recruitment campaign he had already assembled another thirty thousand troops to add to those he already had at Humaitá, giving him a total of eighteen battalions of infantry, eighteen regiments of cavalry, and two of artillery.[23] Though his army now included many old men and teenaged boys, in numbers alone it represented a formidable challenge to the Allies. The new troops clearly intended a long stay. They reached Paso by December 1865, and immediately began to sow the adjacent fields with Indian corn, peanuts, sweet potatoes, manioc, garbanzos, and other crops. They also constructed hundreds of thatched huts, built an extensive line of trenches, and moved sixty pieces of artillery into strategic spots.[24]

Across the Paraná, Allied preparations were more spasmodic. Horses, munitions, and foodstuffs remained in short supply. In their retreat from Corrientes, López's men had stripped the province's farms and ranch lands of everything, including some one hundred thousand head of cattle that they drove across the river to Paraguay.[25] The Brazilian, Argentine, and Uruguayan commissariats needed provisions and could not make good these losses right away. Heavy rains interrupted the northward flow of supplies by land. This left the Allied troops to subsist on what could be transported upriver on merchant or naval vessels—support that always seemed slipshod, inadequate, or reluctantly given.[26] In the end, it took five months to properly establish forward bases in Corrientes. Entrerriano Governor Justo José de Urquiza, once the most powerful figure in all of Argentina, provided the greatest number of cattle and horses for the camps, and also sent some of the toughest and most practiced fighters in the region. It was a mixed blessing, however: units from Entrerriano had already disbanded at Toledo and Basualdo some months earlier, and some of the disaffected men had been pressed back into the Allied forces. Many of the Argentine provincials—not just the Entrerrianos—detested the Brazilians, whom they suspected of expansionist designs in the Litoral.[27] To these men, López posed the lesser danger, and, indeed, his political ideas had more in common with their own than either's did with the Argentine national government. Now that the Paraguayans had abandoned Corrientes, they felt that Mitre ought to negotiate an early end to the conflict rather than sheepishly follow the Brazilian lead.

For their part, Pedro's troops chafed under Argentine command. Most officers—and certainly most state ministers—regretted the emperor's earlier concession in Rio Grande, by which Mitre retained command over Allied forces even while on Brazilian soil. They reciprocated the bad feelings directed at them and bristled at every show of Argentine highhandedness. The internal problems of the Litoral provinces were of no concern to them—pursuing the war against Paraguay was.

The longer the Allied troops went without fighting their common enemy, the better the Paraguayans' chances of watching these units dissolve as a coherent force. The Triple Alliance of Brazil, Argentina, and the newly conquered Uruguay linked three governments to the common end of destroying López. But smooth cooperation among them proved elusive. Mitre had to keep this fact constantly in mind as he pondered his next move. Several options suggested themselves. As early as September 1865, the Brazilian military engineer André Rebouças composed a "Project for the Prompt Conclusion of the Campaign against Paraguay". It presented a dispassionate recounting of Allied strengths and weaknesses, as well as those of the Marshal. Rebouças claimed that battlefield reverses had brought Paraguayan morale to its lowest point since the war began. The arms captured from the enemy, he noted, included the most antiquated flintlocks, unrifled cannons, locally made sabers, and bamboo lances.

All this contrasted with the strength of the Allied armies, which boasted a well-equipped and vigorous force ready to slash its way northward at any time. Rebouças recognized that certain deficiencies, especially the lack of adequate mounts, might delay the Allied advance for a time. Yet, this was a minor matter. While the army waited, Brazilian ironclads could pulverize the earthworks below Humaitá just as the Yankees had done at Fort Henry during the US Civil War. A short but unremitting siege of the fortress would commence once the Allies crossed into Paraguay, and Marshal López would strike his colors shortly thereafter.[28]

Rebouças's plan reflected accepted military thinking among the Brazilians, but the Argentines were less sanguine about the war ending quickly. The Paraguayans had fought the Argentines in 1849, and on that occasion, the barefooted soldiers of López's father had not acted like the sort of men who would easily crumble before superior force.[29] The Argentines also understood better than the policymakers in Rio the difficulty of the terrain they needed to traverse should the Allied navies fail to force the rivers. Perhaps most critically, the Argentines recognized their own domestic weaknesses better than the Brazilians did. Despite Mitre's rash prediction of "to the barracks in twenty-four hours, to the field in fifteen days, and to Asunción in three months,"[30] the Argentine national army needed more time to become fully operational. It had only been established in 1864 and still seemed woefully unprepared. Worst of all, it lacked the unqualified support of the Argentine public.

Furthermore, Argentine leaders quietly perceived what should have been obvious: the war had failed to stir popular support in either their country or Brazil. Such a reaction, smacking in some quarters of indifference, might eventually undermine the whole campaign. The Brazilian public initially responded to the war with a strong show of volunteerism, offering the government everything from good wishes to money to shirts for the troops.[31] The ranks of the Voluntários da Pátria, or volunteer units, swelled into the thousands. Few noticed at that moment that sympathy for the fight seemed strongest in the provinces that abutted the Plata. Men whose families owned property in the Banda Oriental saw the struggle against Paraguay as a reasonable business, even congenial up to a point. In Pernambuco and other areas of the north and northeast, on the other hand, draft evasions and a general contempt for the fighting were already in evidence. The northeasterners tended to be individualists, like the gauchos of the Pampas, and their unit of community never extended beyond the clan.[32] At a local level this may have been a source of strength, but it contributed to Brazil's weakness as a nation. Even now, forty years after independence, many northeasterners still found it painful to subordinate their interests to those of Rio de Janeiro. And unlike the southerners—who had seen their own lands invaded by López—these men regarded Paraguay as impossibly far away. They might periodically join in verbally abusing the Marshal, but they showed little enthusiasm for the cause, and sent few troops as a result.

In Argentina and Uruguay, the situation was worse, with large portions of the population either disaffected from their governments' military campaign in Paraguay (and from the cost in lives and resources it occasioned) or secretly supporting López. So-called Americanist factions commanded considerable respect in the Litoral provinces and to a lesser extent in Buenos Aires. Neither the famous jurist Juan Bautista Alberdi, nor the willful son of Urquiza, nor José Hernández, future author of *Martín Fierro*, made any effort to conceal their dislike of the national government's pro-Brazilian stance. And they were not the only dissenters. In the western provinces, Mitre's governors had to use iron shackles to smooth their recruitment efforts.[33] As for the Banda Oriental, public opinion there held that Uruguay's participation in the Paraguayan War was nothing more than Flores's way of paying a political debt to Mitre and the Brazilians.[34]

The sense of uncertainty so common in the Allied countries found no parallel on the Paraguayan side. From the distance of one hundred forty years, it is easy to stress the authoritarian aspect of the López regime in explaining the coherence of the Paraguayan response to the war. And yet the Paraguayan people were not simply browbeaten into putting up a good fight—they accepted the burden of defending their country because it came naturally to them. They saw their homes and way of life threatened; any struggle to repel foreign invaders thus seemed to them legitimate and honorable. Perhaps this did signal López's manipulation of his people—he was a skilled propagandist who knew how to appeal to the Paraguayan masses in the Guaraní language they understood and cherished. But to relegate popular support for the war to a nebulous realm of false consciousness misses the fact that the Paraguayans had already reflected soberly on their situation. They knew what the stakes were and if they could not win the war, perhaps they could at least make it unwinnable for the enemy. Negotiation was not an option; neither was surrender. If the Allies chose to continue the fight, then they would reap only the blackest of tragedies together with their Paraguayan opponents. On the long road to Armageddon, all would suffer.

1

THE ARMIES INVADE

The confluence of the Paraná and Paraguay Rivers offers a spectacular panorama, with the blue-green Paraguay mixing unevenly with the muddy Paraná amidst a landscape of forests and cream-colored sandbanks. Everywhere one looks the waters predominate; they blend and flow onward to Buenos Aires, breaking into seven great currents before coming together again and overtaking the low-lying territory on either side. In such an environment, the works of man can seem puny. Yet in January 1866, human activity was very much in evidence. More than a mile separated the Argentine and Paraguayan banks of the Paraná, but to the armed men on either side the distance must have appeared far smaller.

Imagination can exert a powerful hold over soldiers who have too little to eat and too much time to complain. The Allied camps, spread in an arc from Corrientes to the little river port of Itatí, had lately been rife with worries. Months before, when the men had enlisted in a rush of enthusiasm, they had assumed that they would soon face the enemy, but all they had done was drill, and then drill some more. Very few had seen more than an occasional Paraguayan picket, and almost no one had fired a weapon in anger.[1] When would they receive proper rations and decent uniforms? When would the summer heat let up? And, most of all, when would they be ordered north into Paraguay?

The Brazilians, who had established camps near Corrientes at Laguna Brava and Tala Corã, were better placed to answer these questions. Their navy dominated river traffic, and the high command enjoyed good communications with Buenos Aires and Rio. Despite an imperfect supply line, General Manoel Osório's troops still managed better than their Argentine and Uruguayan allies in gathering provisions. Indeed, they had assembled such extensive stores of hardtack, flour, salt, and dried beef (*charqui*) that their quartermasters could trade rations for the steers offered by Correntino ranchers. No one in the Argentine camp could as yet afford such an arrangement. Though their food-stuffs were "the object of some envy," the Brazilians still had much to complain about. Their bland fare depended too heavily on meat for a people whose diet featured many fruits and grains. The omnipresent flies and stinging gnats (*mbarigui*), moreover, made eating a test of will with the insects, which had to be scooped away by the spoonful at every meal.[2]

In other respects, life for the Brazilian soldiers was not so bad. They built straw huts with palm-frond roofs, which made for cool and comfortable billets. The number of Brazilians stationed in the sector had grown by the end of January to around forty thousand, including both regular units and Voluntários da Pátria.[3] With such numbers on hand, the troops could count on the presence of furniture makers, carpenters, leatherworkers, and tailors, all of whom found extra employment catering to their comrades' needs. Less reputably, there were liquor runners, cardsharps, and purveyors of pornographic booklets.[4] And there were hunters and would-be hunters. The Brazilian soldiers enjoyed hunting caimans, which were plentiful in the Correntino lagoons. But the animals could prove a dangerous prey; on one occasion, a large caiman burst into a soldier's hut at night, seized the man by the legs, and would have dragged him back to the water had his comrades not beaten the creature back.[5]

The Brazilian camps' proximity to the town of Corrientes offered many temptations. Tricksters ran their variant of three-card Monte on every corner of this normally sleepy community, which now boasted makeshift grogshops, brothels, and dance halls for the men, and passable restaurants for the officers (many of whom were "Rio lawyers" who demanded—and got—a better class of eating).[6] Not all was pleasurable, however; harsh words and knife fights between the Brazilians and their allies—and even a few murders—sometimes disturbed the town, though never so often as to interfere with making money.[7] Having expressed ambiguous feelings toward the Paraguayan occupation at the beginning of the conflict, the locals now threw themselves into the Allied war effort. Like the other Argentines, the Correntinos still suspected Brazilian intentions. Yet, given the potential profits to be made as sutlers, the merchants of the town put aside their doubts and triple-charged their new clients, Brazilians and Argentines alike.[8] As the correspondent for *The Standard* observed:

> Words cannot give you an idea of Corrientes at the present moment—every house or room that is inhabitable is filled with Brazilian officers. Two and a half ounces [of gold] are paid for the rental of a place hardly large enough to contain a bed and two chairs. ... There are no such persons as cooks or washerwomen

to be had; poor women and girls who never possessed an ounce have now bags of gold; ... Sharpers who are conversant with the localities of Baden-Baden, Germany, or Poles who have held rank in the rebel States of the North [America], congregate at hotels, where they live in great style. Where they come from, or how they get money to pay their way, no one can tell.[9]

This pattern lasted to the end of the war and included hundreds of foreign merchants who came to Corrientes to add to the general atmosphere of speculation.[10]

Unlike the Brazilian forces, the Argentine troops still suffered from the same confusion that dogged their efforts at Yataí and Uruguaiana. This was not just a matter of poor logistics. Though 24,522 soldiers from various provinces had come together at Ensenaditas, they had yet to develop any obvious military cohesion, except in the most formal sense.[11] Despite the constant exercises, the near-endless marching, and the encouragement of President Mitre, much bitterness divided the men of the interior from the Porteños of Buenos Aires.[12]

Mitre had appointed Vice President Marcos Paz to take charge of supply, and both men were shrewd enough to recognize that good morale counted for as much as good provisioning. Paz therefore hastened to ship new tents and summer uniforms from the capital as a way to build *esprit de corps*. When he toured the camp, "don Bartolo," as Mitre was known by his men, noted the positive effect of these uniforms, but condemned the accompanying kepis as an inadequate means of providing shade from the blistering sun. He himself made a point of using the regulation headgear until broad-brimmed replacements arrived, but he suffered along with his soldiers.[13]

The Argentines and Uruguayans spent many hours at drill. This accustomed them to the stern barks of sergeants, but they still found it difficult to get beyond the irregular, indecisive skirmishes so typical of warfare in the Pampas. Although they were heroic to a fault, they found it difficult to focus on a single objective, and, in general, never thought of themselves as soldiers, much less as Argentines or Uruguayans.[14] Officers had to tread lightly on what the men considered God-given prerogatives, and they often looked the other way when it came to unauthorized absences. As one correspondent observed, the temptation to stray was particularly acute among men conscripted from nearby districts: "The Correntino soldiers take French leave ... complaining of having more than their share of fighting to do, of bad pay, no clothes, and very little tobacco, yerba, soap ... [and] of the injuries done them by purveyors, paymasters, and sutlers, of the cruel and wicked *món dá* [theft] that is being done with impunity."[15]

Allied commanders could dismiss some soldiers going AWOL as a minor nuisance; desertion, on the other hand, presented a serious threat. The mutinies of Entrerriano troops at Basualdo and Toledo still elicited comment in camp. With so many troops simply leaving the field, how much easier was it for individual malcontents and small groups to follow their lead? No matter that reinforcements had already set sail for Corrientes—they, too, might become disaffected and abandon their posts.[16] If this happened, Mitre would have to concede a greater and more dangerous measure of authority to his Brazilian partners. It could even excite open rebellions in other areas of Argentina. It was thus imperative to keep such talk contained.

The most striking example of this problem was found among the Uruguayan units encamped near Itatí. These forces were commanded by Venancio Flores, head of the Colorado Party, victor at Yataí, and now his country's head of state. The war never enjoyed much support back in Uruguay, and the general found it difficult to obtain fresh troops from Montevideo. He had had to rely on the weary, threadbare men he had brought with him at the beginning of the campaign, and to bring the total number of soldiers under his command up to around seven thousand, Flores filled his army with Paraguayan prisoners. Though they ate their rations and took their pay, these "recruits" had never learned to appreciate their new masters. And now that they found themselves close to López's army, many broke away and made the risky swim to Paraguay.

It might seem odd that Flores expected his Paraguayan levies to stay faithful to him. As a traditional chieftain accustomed to the civil wars in the grasslands, however, he expected nothing less, for in similar conflicts the gaucho troops sided with whatever faction was the strongest. Paraguayans, however, were not gauchos, and they were not so readily swayed by the force of any caudillo's personality, not even that of López. To them, the considerations of patriotism cancelled out any doubts voiced against the Marshal, and whenever they could, they fled the Allied camp and rejoined their countrymen.

Flustered at this "ingratitude," General Flores had one recaptured deserter shot before his assembled battalion.[17] When this action failed to stem the problem, he heeded the counsel of one of his senior commanders, the Spanish-born Colonel León de Palleja, who recommended that the Paraguayan recruits be disarmed and sent downriver to Montevideo to serve in the public works.[18] A sizable number nonetheless stayed behind, biding their time until they too could slip away.[19]

The Paraguayan "deserters" who managed the short but arduous dash to Itapirú took a considerable gamble. Not only were the river currents strong, and the various pickets trigger-happy, but on the other side López's troops had orders to arrest anyone who crossed; the Marshal considered the escapees spies. The less fortunate among them—those found in new Allied uniforms, especially—were executed as traitors. Even so, their numbers grew until López changed his ruthless policy, giving orders to welcome them.[20] He remained suspicious, however, of those Paraguayans who had spent much time beyond his grasp. Emotionally, the Marshal reflected the harsh and insecure history of his country, whose inhabitants generally reacted with passivity to the trials of life, though they became volatile when agitated by unexpected threats. López understood this inclination because he shared it, and at this critical stage of the war, he had no wish to see his army infiltrated by rumormongers or potential assassins.[21]

The Paraguayans on the "far shore" wasted no time with these matters. The majority were smallholders or peasants who, in their daily lives, rarely concerned themselves with distant events. Now that the greater part of the troops had moved south to Paso de la Patria, they needed to arrange its defenses as quickly as possible. This left Humaitá with a skeletal garrison of just a few artillery units to guard the main positions. Soldiers dragged a few cannons to new sites at Curuzú and Curupayty, where they stretched three thick iron chains across the Río Paraguay to the Gran Chaco to prevent Allied vessels from ascending the river.

At Paso, the sixty cannons that guarded the edge of the river were manned by the experienced gunners of Colonel José María Bruguez, a man who had distinguished himself seven months earlier at the battle of the Riachuelo. To strengthen their defensive positions still further, the colonel dispatched artillery units to occupy the small island of Redención, adjacent to Itapirú, eventually placing eight guns there to provide cover for raiding parties. Meanwhile, the Marshal transformed several thousand of his cavalrymen into infantry, and set them to work building wooden huts for billets. The soldiers constructed a fine headquarters, a large building of whitewashed adobe braced with hardwood lapacho logs for López and his staff. The building was high enough to permit a good view of the Paraná, but far enough back to avoid salvoes from Allied warships.

From the safety of this position, López could observe the far bank of the river, and the many flickering cook fires that illuminated the Allied camps at night. The nearness of the enemy both vexed and tempted him; already, in the first days of December, he determined to do something about it. After inspecting the work at Itapirú, he returned to Paso to attend mass together with his Irish lover, Eliza Lynch. On leaving the chapel, the couple happened to spot a party of Allied pickets on the opposite bank of the Paraná, and the Marshal had his men fire a 12-pounder at them. The shot missed, but it scattered the enemy troopers. López then dispatched four canoes with twelve men each to gain the opposite bank and pursue the startled Correntinos. The Marshal took pleasure at the havoc this had caused. Thereafter he sent raiders across the river at every opportunity, urging his soldiers to kill as many of the enemy as possible.[22]

These raids, which usually involved less than a hundred men, proved popular with the Paraguayans, especially with Lieutenant Colonel José Eduvigis Díaz, whom López charged with their organization. Díaz had an intuitive understanding of his men, and sensed that the majority thirsted for battle. He had about him what the Paraguayans call *mbareté*, an air of self-assurance and resolution that instilled a sense of loyalty in those around him. The trick was to focus these sentiments. Also, with so many inexperienced men coming from Humaitá and points north, the colonel made sure to include new recruits in these hit-and-run operations, testing their mettle and giving them some experience of combat.[23] These short engagements illustrated the merciless zeal of the Paraguayans. On one occasion in mid-January, Díaz's soldiers killed twelve unarmed men who had come to the riverbank to wash their clothes. Two of the dead were decapitated, and their heads brought back as trophies for the Marshal, who upbraided this act as "barbarous, worthy only of savages."[24] And yet he punished no one.

The senior Allied leaders understood the limited nature of the raids, and presented them in their official accounts as inconsequential. Try as they might, however, they could not shake the suspicion that their own efforts against the Paraguayans were half-hearted. The journalists who had come from the south were flustered by this same image, though they had a hand in propagating it. The average citizen in Brazil and Argentina probably felt more irritated still, for the longer the Allies failed to stem the incursions, the more it seemed as if the Paraguayans were winning significant victories.

Part of the trouble involved the Allied fleet. The imperial navy had sixteen war steamers at Corrientes, three of them ironclads. This was more than enough to counter any raids, and yet the ships refused to engage the Paraguayans. This seeming timidity earned the navy a bad name from Mitre, Flores, and even Osório and the other Brazilian officers, who wondered why the fleet commander, Admiral Francisco Manoel Barroso, had failed to direct a single warship upriver.[25] Such a deployment would end Díaz's daytime raiding—and yet the Brazilian fleet had failed to budge an inch for four months. As "Sindbad," the pseudonymous correspondent for the English-language *Standard* observed, "no launch, no boat [had] ever been sent to make a reconnaissance, or to watch the enemy's movement; no effort made … to curb the barefaced insolence of the Paraguayans, no … target firing, boat racing, or the exercising of the great guns."[26]

There were several possible explanations for this inaction. For one thing, many of the ships had been designed for ocean transport and drew upwards of twelve feet of water. With such shallow drafts, any maneuvering on the Paraná was dangerous, a fact that had been obvious since the loss of the steamer *Jequitinhonha* during the battle of the Riachuelo. That ship had run aground on an unseen sandbar and Bruguez's gunners had raked her to pieces. No naval commander wanted to face a similar situation in this riverine environment.[27] At the Riachuelo, Admiral Barroso had depended on local Correntino pilots, and though they had done right by him, even they could not predict the river currents or know where the Marshal's men might have scattered mines.

A weakness in the command structure also helped explain the Brazilian inaction. Article 3 of the Treaty of Triple Alliance had assigned the navy an authority independent from that of the land forces. The Allied naval commander, Admiral João Marques de Lisboa, Baron of Tamandaré, took this as a license to set his own terms for the fleet's engagement. An arrogant officer with a reputation for testiness, he had yet to join the fleet, preferring to stay in Buenos Aires to engage in the intricate politics of alliance building, take in the city's night life, and loudly portray himself as the right-hand man of the emperor. This left his friend Admiral Barroso in acting command of naval forces at Corrientes.

Tamandaré had contributed to the public adulation that attended Barroso's victory at the Riachuelo, but he had no wish to see the navy deviate from its greater mission. He wanted to fight the war on his terms, never admitting to any Brazilian subservience. In the alliance between his country and Argentina, he insisted that politicians and military men on all sides see Brazil as the coachman and Argentina as the horse—the better to drive toward a proper hegemony in the region. As a result, the admiral ordered Barroso to do nothing, and though he obeyed, it made him look as if he were shirking his duties. Barroso's reputation thus suffered because of Tamandaré. This opened the door for the Paraguayans, and López stepped through it in grand fashion.

Corrales

The most serious of the Marshal's raids began on 30 January 1866, when two hundred fifty men under the command of Lieutenant Celestino Prieto made the passage across the river to Corrientes. The initial plan called for a three-staged attack that would culminate in over a thousand men hitting the Allied positions opposite Itapirú. The guns at Redención Island concentrated covering fire on Corrales, an exposed spot on the Correntino bank that the Paraguayans had used in colonial times as a holding area for smuggled cattle. It was a good day for the attack: the skies had cleared after a week of torrential rains, and the men were evidently in good spirits. Their departure at mid-morning was heralded by cheering, the distribution of cigars and sweets, and the playing of martial tunes. The men had grown so contemptuous of Allied prowess on the rivers that they stood up in their canoes and jeered at the enemy as if the war had been arranged for their amusement.

The Allies knew that the Marshal intended a major incursion. The Argentines had been humiliated by the earlier raids on their national soil and wanted to lay a trap. On this occasion, Correntino General Manuel Hornos readied several crack cavalry regiments about a league behind the Paraná. Colonel Emilio Conesa, a Porteño, simultaneously elected a wooded site at the far edge of the Peguajó Creek, a mile closer to the river, and moved nineteen hundred Bonaerense (inhabitants of Buenos Aires province) national guardsmen into position for an ambush.

Just before noon, scouts brought word that Prieto's men were advancing toward a little bridge that spanned the Peguajó. The Argentines should have enjoyed near-total surprise. At the last moment, however, the forty-two-year-old Conesa gathered his officers together, removed his white gloves, and instead of offering quiet encouragement, gave a rousing, impromptu speech to the assembled four battalions of infantry. The men responded with *vivas* to don Bartolo, Buenos Aires, and the Alliance—cheers that grew louder and louder.

Prieto, who was only three hundred yards away, immediately realized the danger and pulled back at once, firing his sixteen Congreve rockets into the Argentine lines as he withdrew. Though they survived, the sharpshooters that Conesa had stationed in the treetops were knocked over by the concussions. The remaining Bonaerenses fell back in momentary disarray, leaving the barefooted Paraguayans to strike at the Argentine center. Prieto's men went through the water and kept up close pursuit as they advanced to the Peguajó. A veil of gray smoke soon covered the space between the two forces; though visibility fell accordingly, lead continued to fly. Columns of troops lunged forwards and backwards, over and over, leaving many men to fall along the way. Slowly, after a spate of heavy fighting, Colonel Conesa pushed the Paraguayans back, first across the Peguajó, then northward across another creek, the San Juan.[28]

At Mitre's behest, General Hornos's cavalry then charged forward to link up with Conesa. General Osório offered to send his infantry to help, but Mitre demurred, wanting to keep the engagement an all-Argentine effort.[29] In any case, the Allied advantage in numbers soon began to have an effect, for Prieto fell back slowly through the marshes to his original landing place. The Argentines had hoped to encircle him, but, as they came over the rise from the south, they fell under sustained fire from Bruguez's artillery on Redención Island.[30] Several of the Argentines continued to fight like duelists, standing erect and making targets of their bodies, while others fell to their feet, hoping to shield themselves but finding it impossible to properly charge their weapons. Flustered, Conesa and Hornos abruptly halted, and their troops scurried for cover among the brambles and quagmires.

The plucky Argentines nonetheless kept firing, and this forced Prieto's raiders to flee into dense foliage just east of Corrales.[31] There they received some welcome support from a two-hundred-man force under Lieutenant Saturnino Viveros of the 3rd Battalion, who had crossed at two in the afternoon, bringing substantial quantities of ammunition.[32] He was accompanied by Julián N. Godoy, aide-de-camp to López, who left a rousing account of the horrible five-hour engagement that followed.[33]

Throughout this battle, the Argentines outnumbered the Paraguayans by over eight to one, and yet they could not gain control in the wet, wooded, and irregular terrain.[34] The austral sun beat down heavily on them and no wind or rain lessened the heat or dissipated the stench of the spent powder. Prieto, Viveros, and Godoy fought doggedly. The men got their feet caught in the thorny vines and could not wheel about and fire through the foliage, yet they made the enemy suffer for every foot gained. Though Conesa later tried to justify his minimal progress by inflating the number of obstacles in his path, in fact it was Paraguayan discipline that prevented his outright victory.[35] What could have been an easy win proved costly for the Allies, and only the quick and efficient work of the Argentine medical corps kept the battle from becoming costlier still.[36]

By late afternoon, Prieto and Viveros realized with some shock that the enemy had nearly surrounded their position, and ordered a retreat from the forested areas toward the safety of the Paraná. Conesa then saw his last chance. His troops closed with the Paraguayans, and wave after wave of Argentine infantry fell on the now exposed enemy. Low on ammunition, the Paraguayans fixed bayonets and charged into the Argentine left flank, and from that point both sides smelled victory and refused to yield. Bodies littered the field and every tree and bush seemed twisted and torn with violence.[37] On several occasions, the Paraguayans were seen throwing stones at the enemy.[38] Though Conesa himself received a serious chest contusion, he kept fighting sword in hand.

But it was too late. As had already happened to the Paraguayans, the Argentines ran low on ammunition, and as Conesa's exhausted men neared the river, they glimpsed in the distance the landing of a third Paraguayan force, this one composed of seven hundred men from Colonel Díaz's 12th Battalion. Not wishing to challenge these fresh troops after such a trying day, and having no reserves, Conesa broke off his pursuit. The Paraguayans maintained their tenuous control over the Correntino riverbank that evening and returned home the next morning without further incident. They carried back one hundred seventy of their men *hors de combat* (killed and wounded).[39]

The Paraguayans can perhaps be forgiven for believing that Corrales offered convincing proof of the superiority of their arms. They had, after all, killed or maimed several hundred enemy combatants, including some fifty officers; they had momentarily driven Conesa from the field; and their opponents had even failed to seize the Paraguayans' canoes, which they could have easily done at the outset.[40] In the end, there was no way that the colonel, or any other Argentine military man who had seen action at Corrales, could call it a victory.

The Buenos Aires newspapers initially cast the action at Corrales in a positive light.[41] Yet a feeling of dread nonetheless permeated the Argentine capital. The British minister reported to the Earl of Clarendon that "upon intelligence of the engagement reaching Buenos Ayres the greatest consternation prevailed; a victory was proclaimed [but] anxiety was universally felt, festivities announced for the approaching carnival were cancelled, and the public journals teemed with articles of censure on the inactivity of the Brazilian squadron and on President Mitre."[42]

For his part, Marshal López smirked at the ineptitude of his enemy. Natalicio Talavera, the war correspondent of Asunción's *El Semanario*, underlined the general sentiment: "Doesn't this [defeat] serve as a lesson to the Argentines, who make themselves the vile instruments of the empire, and are then pushed into battle [by the Brazilians, whose own] army takes pleasure at seeing its ally destroyed? When will these victims of such a fatal deception awake from their slumber?"[43]

In fact, the fight at Corrales yielded nothing of consequence. The Allies smarted from embarrassment, but it was the sort of humiliation from which they could recover. The medical corps had responded well and so had individual commanders, some acting with conspicuous gallantry. The weakness in Conesa's leadership, the poor communication with Hornos and the other units, the insufficiency of ammunition, the want of a reserve force—all these could be overcome. The Paraguayans, in future engagements, would no longer seem so awe-inspiring, and if they stuck with the same tactics, they could be defeated. A raid must have a specific objective, such as the destruction of a gun position or displacement of a command center. Or, as with General Wenceslao Paunero's raid on Paraguayan-controlled Corrientes in May 1865, it must frustrate enemy timetables. Nothing about Corrales, however, suggested even a temporary setback to the Allies' main objective of crossing the Paraná and taking the war to Paraguayan soil. More Allied ships and troops arrived every day, and it was only a matter of time before Mitre made his move.

Itatí

Having whetted his appetite for raiding, Marshal López planned another major incursion for mid-February. His new objective was the port town of Itatí, which today boasts the largest cathedral in the Argentine northeast. The building's main edifice houses a jewel-encrusted statue of the Virgin, which, by 1866, had already become the focus of public veneration. Catholics from all over the region made pilgrimages to Itatí to beg her intercession.

Much as he needed a miracle, López seems to have had little interest in the religious character of the community; rather, he knew that Itatí lay close to the headquarters of the old Army of the Van—commanded by Flores—which he rightly judged as the most disaffected force on the Allied side. A strike on these units, even a glancing blow, might cause the less resolute among the Uruguayans to lose their nerve. If the Army of the Van disintegrated, Mitre and the emperor might have to reconsider their invasion plans, and bring the war to an honorable, if not wholly satisfactory, end. Of course, the odds of gaining a success were long, but in López's active imagination, such an assault had much to recommend it. He frequently expressed contempt for the fighting qualities of his adversaries, and thought Mitre and Osório fools. He believed that reckless decisions by his subordinates and a simple spate of bad luck had cost him the campaign in Corrientes.[44] In a war of attrition, the Allies held the stronger hand, so his only hope lay in maneuver—the more audacious, the better. Allied incompetence would do the rest.[45]

The Marshal perceived one advantage in the problematic Uruguayan command. Flores had traveled south to Montevideo to recruit more troops and left his units to the care of General Gregorio "Goyo" Suárez, the Colorado stalwart and supposed "butcher" of Paysandú. Suárez had had a checkered career in the civil wars against the Blancos and was widely disparaged for being too close to the Brazilians. In Uruguay, this made him suspect enough, but in Corrientes, as commander of the weakest link in the Allied line, the perception that he acted as a lackey of the empire was a clear liability in the eyes of his own men. The Argentines trusted him far less than they trusted Flores, and no one could guess how well they might work with him. It was true that Suárez had considerable experience: he had defeated the Blancos along the Uruguay River in mid-1865, and his cavalry units had likewise beaten the Paraguayans at Yataí. General "Goyo" certainly understood the enemy, and he expected ferocious resistance.

What the Paraguayans encountered with Suárez, therefore, was a naturally pugnacious commander of uncertain troops, a man trusted by one ally but probably not the other, who faced a determined enemy willing to take on superior numbers. It was a circumstance that should have inspired caution. And yet, perhaps because he had to be careful, Suárez yearned to do something risky or capricious. At the end of January, just as the battle of Corrales ended, the general decamped from San Cosme and ordered the Army of the Van to advance to Itatí. In fact, he had had strict instructions from Flores to do nothing of the kind, for such a move put thirty miles between him and the rest of the Allied army.

Itatí, a relatively wooded spot, was more accessible from the river than by the twisting paths that connected it to Corrientes. In the event of a Paraguayan incursion, other Allied land forces could never get to Suárez in time. López knew this, for spies on the Correntino side of the river had given him regular reports on enemy positions. At this stage of the war, he had far better military intelligence than his opponents, and he used it more effectively. With Suárez now in an exposed position, the Marshal decided to attack him.

This latest raid started in atypical fashion. Having learned that the Brazilian squadron in Corrientes would do nothing to stop his canoes, the Marshal decided to bring up what was left of his fleet. On the 16 February, three vessels, the *Ygurey*, the *Gualeguay*, and the *25 de Mayo*, departed Humaitá and followed the meandering Paraguay into the Paraná. Their course took them past an Allied picket ship that had earlier reported all quiet. As López had guessed, not a single Brazilian ship responded.

Of the three ships that steamed toward Paso de la Patria, only the 548-ton *Ygurey* had flown the Paraguayan ensign before the war. The Marshal's navy had taken the other two vessels from the Argentines at Corrientes the previous April. Each now boasted a crew of Paraguayan officers and men with a few British machinists contracted by the Marshal's government to act as advisors. This day their mission took them first to the camp at Paso, where they attached towlines to flatboats, onto which boarded one thousand soldiers chosen from a variety of units. As before, the mood in camp was triumphant, with bands playing, and crowds shouting for the heads of Mitre and the emperor.

The little flotilla steamed toward Itatí. General Suárez had no inkling that a major raid had begun and assumed the worst. Given all that had occurred in recent weeks, it was not too much to suppose that the entire Paraguayan army would soon fall upon him. Unlike Marshal López, who already understood something of his opponent's movements at Corrientes, neither Suárez nor any other Allied commander had any idea of what they faced.

At the head of the Paraguayan raiding force was the same Colonel Díaz whose plan of attack had supposedly reaped so many rewards at Corrales. Díaz, whose ascent as one of López's favorites was now assured, was a natural disciplinarian with a Van Dyke beard and piercing blue eyes that suggested a strict attention to the smallest detail. His military background was limited, and it was assumed that this would put him at a disadvantage. Yet, for a man who had served as police chief in the somnolent neighborhoods of Asunción, he had a keen sense of military judgment. On this occasion, he believed that Suárez would run.

He was right. The Uruguayan general enjoyed a superiority of numbers, with 2,846 of his own men (and six pieces of artillery), as well as 1,500 Brazilians and 971 Argentines under his direct command, for a total of 5,317 men.[46] Yet the events at Corrales played on Suárez's mind; at that battle, Conesa had depended on Hornos's cavalry to get him through, and he had placed himself, in the event of a failure by the cavalry, so that he could at least fall back to dry ground. At Itatí, Suárez enjoyed neither advantage. Given the looming presence of the Paraguayan steamers on 17 February, it seemed probable that Marshal López intended to strike a heavy blow. Rather than risk its destruction, Suárez ordered the Army of the Van to strike the tents and abandon Itatí to the invaders, who landed unopposed in the late afternoon.[47]

A great many of the tents, in fact, were left intact for the enemy, who picked up some curious loot, including "Goyo's" private possessions, including his papers, his spare uniform, his gold watch and chain. As they sacked first the camp, then the town, the Paraguayans fired after the retreating Uruguayan soldiers, shouting, "Where are the heroes of Yataí?"[48] The gibe was mean-spirited but fair, for Suárez could have made the enemy pay dearly for the incursion. Instead, he left the village to the mercy of Díaz.

The treatment the Paraguayans had meted out to captured towns in Mato Grosso and Rio Grande had had something wild and uncontrolled about it. Not here. Itatí was sparsely populated and heavily wooded along its eastern approaches. Díaz ordered his men to go from *rancho* to *rancho*, house to house, and take everything of value. This amounted to eight rifles, three sabers, a few head of emaciated cattle, some sheep, and a few tiny stores of rice, flour, and hardtack (*galleta*). The men proceeded to set fire to the town's residences, emptying the court building of its archives and writing materials; they then reboarded the flatboats, and departed for Paso de la Patria just before midnight. Though they detained the town priest for a number of hours, they left the church and its miraculous virgin untouched.[49] They also left behind one man, a common soldier of the 8th Regiment, who, when ordered to search a *rancho*, happened upon a demijohn of raw rum (*caña*) and drank himself into a stupor. When he awoke the next day, he found himself a prisoner.[50]

General Suárez and his men spent an uncomfortable day two leagues to the south. They had passed through some of the swampiest terrain in Corrientes to reach an outcropping of dry land. The troops had had to drag themselves through waist-deep water, and quite a few became lost along the way. No one had eaten anything save for a little salted beef, and they had had little or no communication with the main Allied forces further west. Eventually, a rider got through from General Osório. He carried a message that expressed both frustration and anxiety. Osório begged the Uruguayan general to release the Brazilian infantrymen under his command to prevent their slaughter by the Paraguayans.[51] Since Díaz had already departed by this time, we are left to wonder, along with Suárez: who was going to rescue whom?

The "serenade" that the Paraguayans had thus given Itatí had even less strategic significance than the earlier engagement at Corrales. The quantity of booty seized was laughable. And because no one had died on either side, no one could speak of dealing a decisive blow one way or the other. Yet the raid did have one important effect: it concentrated the animus of the Allies not against the Paraguayans—whose audacity everyone recognized—but against the imperial navy. There were now forty warships and transports moored at the port of Corrientes, and though they mounted 112 guns, they failed to stop the "ragamuffin savages" on the Alto Paraná. A few weeks before, Allied officers had asked when they could move forward into Paraguay. Now they were asking when they would cease being made fools of. Only one man, Admiral Tamandaré, could answer that question.

Cat and Mouse with the Chatas

Though they hardly realized it, the Allies held all the best cards during the last weeks of February 1866. Their forces in Corrientes had grown appreciably, and they benefited from a parallel deployment of twelve thousand Brazilian troops under Tamandaré's cousin, the Baron of Porto Alegre, who had crossed into the province near Santo Tomé and was advancing northward along the old Jesuit trails into Misiones. Aside from a nominal force left behind for scouting purposes, the Paraguayans had long since fled this area, leaving Porto Alegre with little to do. Eventually his army emerged on the Alto Paraná some seventy miles east of Corrientes.

The river was wide at this point with treacherous currents separating the two banks. On the opposite side, Major Manuel Núñez stood ready with three thousand troops and twelve pieces of artillery to defend the little town of Encarnación. Like the other Paraguayan commanders, Núñez understood that this eastern route—not Paso de la Patria—provided the traditional entry point for those invading his country. It had happened during the Comuneros Rebellion of the early 1700s and again in 1811 during the independence wars. It might happen again.[52]

Back in Corrientes, the long-awaited Tamandaré arrived in port. He had departed Buenos Aires, on board the steamer *Onze de Junho*, on 8 February, but because he refused to pay full price for coal while en route, he was forced to use his sails to tack upriver; it thus took him nearly three weeks to make the voyage. The admiral felt stung by the many accusatory stories he had read in the Porteño newspapers, and he carried this resentment to his northern station.[53]

Tamandaré blamed Bartolomé Mitre for the critical stance that Argentines had taken toward him. This accusation had some basis in fact, but it put the president in a difficult position; Mitre the politician could afford, secretly, to take pleasure in the public censure of Tamandaré, but Mitre the general had to uphold the dignity of his prickly ally. The admiral had clearly acted unreasonably, never acknowledging, for instance, that many in the Brazilian land forces also blamed him for the poor showing in the war thus far.[54] Besides, he clearly had delayed too long. This gave the Paraguayans renewed hope and frustrated the entire array of Allied commanders. Worst of all, Tamandaré's procrastination had called into question the basic cohesion of the Triple Alliance, upon which all future progress depended.

Within hours of his arrival on 21 February, Tamandaré received Mitre's invitation to attend a council of war. Flores, who had returned one day earlier, also begged the Brazilian naval commander to hurry to the meeting. But the admiral quite publicly insisted that don Bartolo first offer an apology for the impudent behavior of the press. The Argentine president, already angry at such a demand, had also just received news that his vice president, Marcos Paz, wished to resign because of conflicts with the war minister, General Juan A. Gelly y Obes; Paz threatened to make his dissatisfaction public if the general was not sacked. Mitre, however, needed both of these men as much as he needed Tamandaré, Osório, and Flores; despite all his frustrations and headaches, then, he had to employ his best diplomacy once more.

On 25 February, the council of war met at Ensenaditas. Mitre started by offering Tamandaré full authority to organize the invasion of Paraguay. In doing so, the Argentine president assigned a crucial role to the navy in future operations, declaring that its commander deserved the honor of setting the agenda for the upcoming fight. Though usually sensitive to false praise, Tamandaré nonetheless reached for the sop. He had already received satisfaction on the insulting newspaper articles, and now seemed mollified. He outlined in detail the strengths of his squadron and the outstanding qualities of his officers, especially Barroso. Now he promised Mitre to smash the enemy defenses from Paso de la Patria to Humaitá. With a wave of his arm, the admiral assured all present that by 25 May—the Argentine national holiday—they would all dine in Asunción.

It was a grandiloquent boast, yet believable enough, as long as the navy fulfilled its assigned role. Tamandaré suggested an amphibious assault on Paso, after which the navy would transport the entire Allied army across the river. This notion coincided with general strategic understandings agreed to when the Treaty of Triple Alliance was signed nine months earlier. Mitre hastened to endorse the plan, though, like Osório, he raised an eyebrow when the admiral assured him that the passage could be completed in a single day.

Perhaps Mitre felt that discussing the operation at this time would risk conceding to Tamandaré a portion of power greater than that he already enjoyed. This was a real danger, for the admiral tended to see his allies as footstools. Or perhaps don Bartolo had simply grown tired of the ongoing friction. For now, he had the admiral's word on supplying the necessary naval force to sweep the enemy from the Paraná and make the passage feasible. Once on Paraguayan soil, it hardly mattered that Mitre had promised too much to the Brazilians: the battlefield victories would be his to savor, along with the political gain.

It had proven impossible for the Allies to coordinate tactics except in the most general sense. With the Paraguayans, the opposite was true; for all the Marshal's evident pride in making every military decision himself, he could delegate authority when it came to logistical matters, and he was well served by staff officers in preparing national defenses. He needed all the help he could muster since his recruitment efforts had slowed to a trickle. Moreover, many of his men had come down with dysentery and fever. One deserter claimed to Allied interrogators that sixteen to twenty men died of measles and cholera every day at Humaitá, and the situation was worsening.[55]

On 23 February, the Marshal responded to these problems by issuing a decree that called every able-bodied citizen into military service. Though this decree made no mention of women, they, too, were enlisted under rules that obligated them to weave cloth for uniforms and blankets, sow their local fields with food crops for the army, and donate what was left of their valuables to the cause. All these activities were supervised by local functionaries (*jefes políticos*) in the different villages, men who reported directly to Vice President Francisco Sánchez and the war minister.[56]

At Paso de la Patria, preparations to repel an Allied invasion had already begun. Despite the supposedly positive results of the attack on Itatí, López decided to scale back on raiding, save for an occasional reconnaissance along the left bank of the river. Tamandaré's arrival at Corrientes meant that the Paraguayans could no longer count on a quiescent imperial navy. Once Mitre and Tamandaré patched up their differences, moreover, their coordinated forces could assault Paso de la Patria and the war would move on to a more furious stage.

The Paraguayans may have had sufficient time but they never repaired the holes in their southern defense. With the eight guns that Bruguez had stationed on Redención Island now removed to Paso de la Patria, only two 12-pounders guarded Itapirú proper. Earthworks at the latter site should by now have rivaled those at Humaitá, but in fact work had hardly begun. The principal structure had as its base a volcanic knoll reinforced with brickwork (though one of its sides had fallen down). Its greatest interior diameter was a mere thirty yards, and it stood out plainly against the horizon, thus making it an easy target. It was hardly a major obstacle, for in mounting the elaborate raids on Corrales and Itatí, the Marshal had failed to build strong defenses at Itapirú, evidently convincing himself that he already possessed the necessary bulwark. His officers did not disabuse him of this conviction.

The lack of preparation was already evident on 21 March, when Tamandaré ordered three warships to reconnoiter directly in front of the fort. The Paraguayans received these vessels with an indifferent cannonade. One of the Allied ships went aground upriver but managed to pull itself off the sandbar before the Paraguayans could pour fire onto it. The Brazilians continued to take soundings near Itapirú, thus signaling their intention to cause still greater mischief.[57] The admiral's assumption of active command caused the Paraguayans to act with greater caution once the regular shelling of Itapirú began.

But López was still capable of a trick or two. On 22 March, he sent the *Gualeguay* into the open channel of the Alto Paraná just in front of Paso. The steamer towed a *chata*, a small, undecked, double-prowed punt that carried a crew of three or four and a single, 8-inch gun. The chata, which had seen action at the Riachuelo, rode low in the water, and easily blended with the vegetation along the riverbank. One British observer made a careful inspection of these unusual craft and left the following description:

> In construction, the shape resembled an English canal barge, Except that it is more gracefully tapering at the ends and not so long, whilst at each extremity is a rudder. ... The top of the bulwark is only 18 inches over the water. Being flat-bottomed, it must have a very shallow draught of water. In its centre, the deck has a depression of a foot in depth, within a circle, that permits a brass swivel, whereon a ... gun is turned to any point of the compass which the commander may desire. The whole length of the craft is but 18 feet, and there is no protection for the crew.[58]

Though the *Gualeguay* offered a tempting target for the Brazilian gunners on the warships off Corrales, its accompanying craft was practically invisible. But because the chata had no motive power of its own, it had to be towed close enough to fire at the enemy ships.

The Paraguayans scored several hits before the Brazilians even realized where the shells were coming from. In the distance, the Gualeguay twisted and looped, and the little vessel followed. Soon the Allied ships were firing and missing their mark. Amid the shelling, two ironclads surged forward to cut the chata's towline, and, as the vessels approached, the Paraguayan crew leapt into the water and swam away toward the northern bank. The Brazilians lowered three skiffs that gave chase until a unit of Paraguayan infantry, lying hidden among the nearby reeds, rose and fired their muskets. The Brazilian ensign in charge of the skiffs tried to urge his men onward, but a second discharge of six hundred muskets drove them back.[59] The Paraguayans later recovered their chata, though its gun had been damaged beyond repair.

Over the next week, the Marshal repeated these daring provocations on six different occasions, much to the delight of his men and the consternation of the imperial navy.[60] On 26 March, the Brazilians scored a direct hit on a chata. This set off its powder supply and handed its crew a "rapid and instantaneous passport to the hereafter."[61] The next afternoon, with the thermometer hovering around one hundred degrees Fahrenheit, the Paraguayans evened the score when another chata's lucky shot ripped through a gunport and onto the bridge of the ironclad *Tamandaré*. The vessel's portholes were guarded from musket fire by chain curtains, but this heavy shot struck and shattered the chain, sending shards of hot metal and wooden splinters flying in every direction. The captain was mortally wounded, and four officers and eighteen crewmen were killed as well. This new vessel, named for the admiral, was his particular pride, and the horrible death of her officers sickened him.[62] The next day his gunners struck back at the chata, leaving it "a heap of shattered wood."[63] When López ordered another sent down from Humaitá a few days later, the Brazilians captured it intact, and its crew escaped into the nearby forests.[64]

Save for some periodic and inconsequential forays by the *Gualeguay*, this ended the duel. In general, though the "battle" of the chatas annoyed the Allies, it failed to slow their preparations for the greater offensive. It forced the Allied fleet to take greater care in its movements, but the damage done to the Brazilian ships was light and easily repaired. For his part, Tamandaré had spent several days on the bridge of the warship *Apa*, gaining some firsthand understanding of his Paraguayan foes (though he learned no lessons that could help his land-based allies). The only thing that the chata episode did was to lift the already high morale of the Marshal's men, who never failed to volunteer for the perilous duty aboard the craft. Their courage added to the reputation of the Paraguayan soldiers as fighters—but it could not stop the Allies.

Redención Island

Everything came alive in the weeks after Tamandaré's meeting with Mitre, Osório, and Flores. The Brazilian army had operated two factories in Corrientes since the beginning of the year, one for the production of munitions and the other for the repair of weapons. These establishments now added their efforts to those of the main arms factory at Campinho, in Rio de Janeiro. They provided cartridges for every soldier, all of whom seemed eager for the fray. The same was true for the Argentines, who had finally received both ample rations and reinforcements.[65] Even Flores's Uruguayans appeared ready. The Allied army received orders to break camp, march to the river, and prepare for war. The men did as they were told, despite the fact that their commanders had yet to name a date or place for the invasion.

Most Allied warships had by now deployed to the Alto Paraná, and, when not occupied chasing the chatas or the *Gualeguay*, were busily pounding Itapirú. They shot the main structure of the fort to pieces, sending bricks flying, and on several occasions knocking down the flagstaff, which was always immediately replaced. The bombardment littered the field for a mile around with cannonballs, but, strictly speaking, it did little harm, for the Marshal had pulled his men back beyond the range of Allied guns. At night, small parties of Paraguayans crept back to Itapirú to collect the spent shot, which they hoped to return to the Brazilians at the first opportunity.

With less success, Tamandaré also attempted to shell the main Paraguayan camp at Paso de la Patria. The Marshal's troops had sunk two stone-filled canoes into the shallows of the northern channel above Carayá Island. This limited the fleet's passage to the broader southern channel, which was too distant for accurate firing on the Paraguayan position.[66] Furthermore, while the Paraguayans had failed to entrench Itapirú, preparations continued at Paso de la Patria under the direction of George Thompson, a British engineer under contract to the López government. Thompson prepared a trench eleven feet wide and six feet deep that followed the crest of high ground overlooking the camp, dipping low at only one point to circle around the Marshal's headquarters. This trench had various small redoubts for flanking and for obtaining fire over the front; thousands of troops could fit comfortably into its recesses, and thirty field guns provided good enfilade. The Allies were not going to maul this position as easily as Itapirú.

In front of the fort, within rifle range, was the small, sandy Redención Island, sometimes called the Banco de Purutué, half a mile across and covered with tall grass (*sarandí*).[67] Bruguez's gunners, who had assiduously defended this speck of land during the attack at Corrales, had now redeployed to the mainland near Paso. The Allies decided to take advantage of the Paraguayans' departure. On the night of 5 April, Brazilian troops under Lieutenant Colonel João Carlos de Vilagran Cabrita landed, making the island the first piece of Paraguayan territory to fall into Allied hands. Cabrita set to work immediately. In spite of a humidity that did not abate, during even the darkest hours, his men labored to dig trenches and pits for batteries. The Brazilians soon had two thousand men on Redención, guarded by four LaHitte 12-pounders and four heavy mortars. At daybreak, as sunlight replaced the haze, the Brazilians rose up from their trenches and rained cannon and rifle fire all over Itapirú.[68] Their shocked Paraguayan opponents responded at once, giving shot for shot, and keeping up a regular fusillade for several days.[69]

Perhaps Mitre and Osório thought to gain a foothold at this islet to ease the passage of the Allied armies. Or perhaps it was a diversion, with the Argentines, Brazilians, and Uruguayans not yet sure of a precise route or timetable for invasion. In either case, with the island in Cabrita's hands, the Paraguayans could no longer count on uncontested control of the waters above Carayá Island. For his part, the Brazilian colonel was an austere officer of engineers who understood the advantages and the perils of his position. He knew his opponents well, having served as artillery instructor in Asunción in the mid-1850s. Now, assisted by the fleet's steady bombardment of Itapirú, his men dug two extra lines of trenches, filling sandbags and gabions and leaving a disguised track on an oblique angle to the rear to aid, if need be, in a hasty retreat.[70]

The night of 10 April 1866 was barely lit by a quarter moon when eight hundred Paraguayan troopers crossed the river in fifty canoes. Colonel Díaz, who directed the attack from Itapirú, had hoped that darkness would favor their effort, but doubted that his men could get ashore without major losses. Madame Lynch and the Marshal's eldest son had seen the soldiers off with promises of promotion and reward. In the event, though the Brazilian sentries had warnings of an impending attack, they nonetheless were shocked when the enemy stormed ashore. One sleepy trooper lifted his rifle to challenge the first of the intruders, and received a taunt in return: "We are Paraguayans come to kill you blacks [*kambáes*]!"[71]

The Marshal's men crashed into the Brazilian front line and struck down a score of defenders before they knew what had happened. Cabrita recovered quickly, however. His troops fired many rounds of canister at the advancing Paraguayans, cutting up a great number, including some two hundred dismounted cavalrymen from a four-hundred-man reserve sent by Díaz to join the attack. If the Paraguayans had pressed hard on the enemy center, and used their few guns more effectively, they might have overwhelmed the first line of trenches at Redención.

As it was, confusion reigned among the Paraguayan attackers. This was hardly surprising, with more than three thousand men contesting a tiny island in near-complete darkness. Thompson (and the Marshal's state gazette *El Semanario*) claimed that Díaz's men, "many of whom were armed only with sabers," had stormed a portion of the trenches repeatedly but were always driven back.[72] The Brazilians denied that this had happened, just as they denied that the Paraguayans captured several of their guns.[73] Either way, Cabrita successfully kept his fire directed at the approaching enemy, and this proved the key factor in stalling the assault.

By daybreak, the Brazilians had run critically short of ammunition, and, though the Paraguayan attack was losing its impetus, the Marshal's men kept coming. As three of Tamandaré's warships moved in to provide supporting fire, Cabrita ordered his fatigued troops to fix bayonets and charge. López's so-called Indian mercenaries had not foreseen this, and as the Brazilians drove into them, the Marshal's soldiers fell over each other to get away.

Díaz's beaten men fought their way to the water's edge and what they prayed was the safety of their canoes. Once there, however, they came under a rain of fire from the Brazilian warships, which had steamed forward to attempt the coup de grâce. The Paraguayans paddled desperately, or swam beside the canoes towards Itapirú. Many were blown from the water. The few that made it ashore could hear the trumpet blasts of Cabrita's military band in the distance; they were playing the Brazilian anthem on Redención. It was the final insult.

The Allies traded barrages with the Paraguayans at Itapirú for the rest of the day, but there was no doubt they had won a stupendous victory. The Paraguayans lost over nine hundred killed and wounded, and hundreds of pistols, sabers, and muskets littered the island.[74] Cabrita's men even managed to capture thirty canoes.[75] López thus gained no advantage whatsoever for this foray. He could not make up for such losses, and with Redención in Brazilian hands, Itapirú had no future as a bulwark. The Marshal now had to reconsider his entire defensive strategy.

On the Brazilian side, Lieutenant Colonel Cabrita had won the engagement, and he deserved the credit for it all. His victory highlighted the value of empirical data and precise planning, something that military engineers at the War College of Praia Vermelha had stressed ever since the establishment of the academy; in war, there is no substitute for good training and preparation. This principle served as an exalted mantra for the Brazilian engineers. Cabrita's skilled construction of deep, well-buttressed trenches, the accuracy of his artillery, and his coolness under fire made it possible for his men to react well even though they were dog-tired before the battle began. He lost around two hundred troops, and perhaps even more—but they were easily replaced.[76]

The Allied capitals celebrated long into the night once word of Cabrita's victory on Redención arrived.[77] In Rio, the news brought a double satisfaction, for it was the work of one of Brazil's own. An elated Pedro II started to draft a jubilant proclamation that included citations for the colonel and his men. Then came a second signal from Corrientes that cast a pall over the festive mood: Cabrita was dead. Six hours after the last Paraguayan had left the island, the colonel had boarded a raft towed by the gunship *Fidelis*. As he journeyed back across the river, he began to write a summary report of the action just concluded. Before he could sign the document, however, a 68-pound projectile fired from Itapirú ripped through him and two other officers before crashing into the *Fidelis*, which later sank. The commander of the Paraguayan battery that had done the deed was none other than José María Bruguez, one of Cabrita's best pupils in the gunnery course he had conducted at Asunción twelve years before.[78]

The Crossing of the Paraná

The colonel's ironic death gave small comfort to Marshal López. The Brazilians controlled Redención and could now almost certainly strike Itapirú, where the Marshal had his trenches and cannons at the ready, along with four thousand of his best troops. In previous weeks, his soldiers had constructed a series of low wooden bridges that connected the fort with the Marshal's headquarters at Paso de la Patria, but nothing was assured. The Paraguayans had prided themselves on the supposed impregnability of their defenses, but now they were beginning to have second thoughts—and the invasion was nearly upon them.

But where? Itapirú was the most likely target, but the Allied commanders had yet to decide on a landing site for the invading army. In an extensive letter to Marcos Paz on 30 March, Mitre had already outlined the perils facing an invasion force. He rejected a passage by way of Itatí, the Paso Lenguas, or above Carayá Island, all three options involving terrain too swampy for the safe movement of large units. This left Itapirú, which, though it allowed for quick passage, also promised a bloody landing. Mitre was willing to bear the responsibility for any lives and equipment lost, the alternative being to hand the Marshal a victory by default. Even so, because of previous tensions, don Bartolo had to wonder whether he could trust Tamandaré in any joint venture against Itapirú or at any other point on the Paraguayan riverbank.[79]

Mitre reiterated the need to attack Itapirú in a letter to Paz two weeks later. He observed that, with Redención in Brazilian hands, it was more important than ever for the Allies to move against the fort. He announced his intention to land fifteen thousand Argentines on the morning of 16 April; if all went well, thirty-two thousand troopers would advance from Itapirú to Paso de la Patria before nightfall.[80] At the same time that Mitre was penning this letter to Paz, however, Tamandaré suggested an alternative: instead of a head-on assault against Itapirú, he asked, why not land the army on the banks of the Paraguay River, a mile or two from its confluence with the Paraná? Though this involved a longer passage, the spot for disembarkation was undefended and could accommodate the landing of thousands of troops before the Marshal could react. Surprised at the obvious good sense of the admiral's proposition, Mitre assented, and Osório sent a small force to reconnoiter the area.[81] Two days later the Allied army followed.

Given the friction that for months had clouded relations among the Allies, and the many disputes about the conduct of the fighting, the decision to invade was made swiftly, its execution largely left to field commanders. Mitre noted that the landing could constitute a primary or secondary objective, all depending on the conditions Osório encountered.

At eleven at night on 15 April some ten thousand Brazilian troops crowded onto transport ships, canoes, and every other sort of river craft at Corrientes. The engineers there had been busy building temporary quays right up to the last moment. Mess orderlies distributed extra rations of charqui and hardtack to the men. Behind the Brazilian units, five thousand Uruguayans made ready to board the ships as they returned. Flores's men constituted the second wave, with ten thousand Argentines under General Paunero making up the third. The Marshal, still encamped at Paso de la Patria, had no idea that a landing would take place on the Paraguay. He seems to have thought the main fighting would occur at Itapirú; he thus positioned four thousand men, with most of his biggest guns, along the mile-long stretch between the fort and Paso.

Osório made his move on the morning of 16 April. The Brazilian squadron made a feint toward Itapirú, and Tamandaré's gunners fired heavily onto that position. As López's men ducked into their trenches, the Allied transports changed course, steamed back to the confluence of the rivers, then directly up the Paraguay. In what must have been the most anticlimactic moment of the whole campaign, Osório and his men landed on Paraguayan territory without firing a shot.[82]

Since his childhood in Rio Grande do Sul, the Brazilian general had shown a certain enigmatic quality. On some occasions, he was pensive, almost indifferent to the world. At other times, his impulsiveness seemed so dramatic as to infect everyone around him, pushing his officers in directions that no one wished to go, and in the most reckless fashion.[83] Now, having ordered the landing force to dig in, he himself galloped full-speed into the swamps at the head of a scouting party of twelve men.

Given that the Allies lacked even the barest information about the topography that lay ahead, some intelligence gathering made sense. But why should the commanding general undertake such a task, and at such a moment? He later explained that his was an army of untrained men who needed to be led by example—an excuse that rings as hollow today as it did to the war minister, Mitre, and Pedro.[84] The peril facing Osório was more than symbolic. After a mile, twenty Paraguayan pickets caught sight of the general's party and started firing. The Brazilians fled behind a stand of trees and returned fire. Osório, revolver in hand, coolly directed their efforts. For a time, the twelve were completely isolated, but eventually several units of Voluntários da Pátria made their way forward and into the fray.[85] By now, however, the Paraguayans had been reinforced with over two thousand men and two cannons. It no longer seemed a simple skirmish.

Osório ordered a bayonet charge that drove the Paraguayans further into the forest, yet they continued to fire in his direction. By late afternoon, more Brazilian units worked their way up from the river, and under a heavy downpour, the Paraguayans broke off the engagement.[86] They had lost 400 killed and another 100 wounded, while the Brazilians lost 62 killed and 290 wounded. [87] As for the unscathed general, he returned to the main force to supervise the landing of Argentine troops and the unloading of cannon and equipment. All the men who had heard of his bravery under fire wanted to step up and congratulate him, but he waved them off, seemingly surprised that his behavior elicited any comment.

When word of Osório's landing reached Rio de Janeiro, the city went wild with excitement. After the unexpectedly long wait, here, finally, was proof that the Allies could move expeditiously. They had gained a foothold in the Marshal's country, and amazingly enough, as Tamandaré had boasted, the navy succeeded in transporting almost fifteen thousand troops across the river in a single day. General Osório became a hero, the subject of ornate poetry published in the Rio and São Paulo press, and soon thereafter, the emperor named him the Baron of Herval.

Osório, however, could not yet afford to enjoy his triumph. A heavy downpour had prevented a concentrated Paraguayan counterattack, but the last enemy units he observed on 16 April doubtlessly came from Itapirú. With a poor knowledge of the numbers against him, and no knowledge at all of the terrain, Osório needed to get his men on dry ground as soon as possible.

Sheer confusion reigned in the Paraguayan camps. The men had expected an attack and had spent several sleepless nights waiting for it, and the Marshal was forced to defend an extremely long front. The Allied invasion might have come by way of Itatí, the Paso Lenguas, the island of Apipé, even (utilizing the troops of Porto Alegre) by way of Encarnación. There had been bombardments at Encarnación, and more particularly, at Itapirú, which for López remained the logical route for the Allies. Yet because he had insufficient manpower to defend the entire length of the Paraná, he chose to defend the line between Itapirú and Paso de la Patria. This was the reasonable decision, but it turned out to be wrong.

There was only one solution for the Paraguayans: in spite of the rain, they had to rush and immediately attack Osório with all available force, hoping that the advantage provided by Tamandaré's warships would be cancelled out by poor visibility. López had men at the ready, but any delay, even just a few hours, might prove disastrous. As Colonel León de Palleja remarked, this "night would test López's luck; if he did not attack and repel the disembarked troops, by noon the next day he would be facing twenty thousand men and it would be too late."[88]

On the Brazilian side, Osório stood to gain a far more significant victory. If he attacked the Marshal's troops while they were still disoriented he could take both Itapirú and Paso de la Patria and, more importantly, cut off their escape to Humaitá; for once, the swampy terrain might work for him. For López, everything depended on timing, and on the morning of 17 April, he and his staff travelled halfway from Paso to Itapirú—a scant two thousand yards. This proved enough, however, for the Marshal to judge as untenable the Paraguayan position at the fort. He ordered his artillery withdrawn from Itapirú, save for the two 8-inch guns that were too heavy to pull without oxen. (The Paraguayans buried these cannons in the hope of recovering them later.[89]) He then instructed his remaining soldiers to fly straightaway to Paso and the safety of the trenches there. The army made no attempt to pivot and attack Osório, who was moving in from the west.

In choosing not to counterattack, to abandon Itapirú and to concentrate on defending Paso, the Marshal lost his last chance to expel the Allies from Paraguayan soil. Having wasted his manpower in the assault on Redención, he now avoided contact with the enemy when a prompt, aggressive move might have made the difference. Meanwhile, don Bartolo, who never stayed away from the scene of action for very long, landed at Itapirú with a force of Argentine infantry.[90] The president's officers had wanted to dress in gala uniforms, but he forbade this, reminding them of the Russian sharpshooters who had cut down the bemedaled British guards officers in the Crimea.[91] For now, he had to rush to meet his Brazilian allies, who had already arrived to inspect the fort that had once seemed so imposing, so untouchable, but which now had the appearance of a rocky outcropping studded with broken brick and rubble—a place to erect a flagstaff and little else.

Mitre joined Generals Flores and Osório to make a reconnaissance on 18 April. Several small Paraguayan units fired upon the three commanders, but they managed to return unscathed to their respective camps. Having previously lacked even basic details of the terrain in this part of the Marshal's territory, they now began to grasp its daunting nature. From the point of confluence of the two great rivers to Curupayty on the north and Paso de la Patria on the northeast, the riverbanks were crisscrossed by lagoons and deep mud that extended far inland. On either side grew prickly bushes, jungle vine, and grass so tall that no amount of hacking would clear it. When the main river channels were low, they might cut paths along the dried mud from lagoon to lagoon, but when they were high, everything fell under water too shallow for the passage of canoes yet too high for cannon. Only men on horseback could pass through the quagmire-like *carrizal*, and then only with difficulty.

The one permanent road through this morass linked Itapirú to Paso de la Patria, but even there two lagoons prevented a dry passage. López had constructed wooden bridges to get over the deepest stretch, which were destroyed as his men retreated. This made it necessary for Tamandaré to approach Paso by the river. The Allies had sixty-eight steamers at Itapirú, together with forty-eight sailing vessels. Never before had the Paraná witnessed such a naval gathering, and the admiral supposed that his firepower alone could dislodge the Paraguayans from Paso.[92]

It was not easily accomplished. The trench works at the main camp were well established and deep, so without the aid of Allied cavalry and foot soldiers the Paraguayans could probably outlast any barrage by simply staying deep behind the parapets. Neither Osório, nor Mitre, nor Flores coordinated the land forces so as to benefit from a naval bombardment. Besides, though the landings at Itapirú and on the Paraguay had proven successful, the men had few provisions. As it was, the transport of their horses, artillery, and foodstuffs took upwards of a fortnight to complete.[93] By that time, the momentum was gone.

Tamandaré kept up his fight nonetheless. On the evening of 19 April, he brought his squadron in front of Paso and made ready to bombard the position. Had the admiral fired right away, the Paraguayans probably would have taken heavy casualties because Marshal López had disappeared from camp without issuing orders and no one could find him.[94] And no one knew what to do. There were nearly one thousand women camp followers at Paso de la Patria, and these now bolted en masse, adding to the confusion and to the impression that López had abandoned them to their fate. General Francisco Resquín had done good work retreating from Corrientes a year before, but he now lacked instructions. With the situation worsening by the moment, he ordered the garrison out of the trenches to follow the women. He left Bruguez behind to cover their withdrawal.

All this movement occurred at night, and when the first rays of the sun broke across the carrizal the next day, Tamandaré opened fire. It was the biggest bombardment thus far and lasted all day long. In the absence of an effective command, the remaining troops at Paso de la Patria elected to slip away in small groups. Before they left, however, they and the remaining civilians helped themselves to the Marshal's wine and provisions and emptied the government's money chest of its paper money. Amazingly enough, only five or six men were killed or wounded, though there were many close calls. The telegraph operator saw his station pierced through by a 68-pounder and his uniform splashed with ink from an open pot, yet neither he nor his instruments were damaged, and both were soon relocated to the north side of the Estero Bellaco, where the Paraguayans hoped to regroup.

During these hours, Marshal López reappeared. He had fled to a high point some three miles distant to observe the Allied bombardment and perhaps to prepare a new defensive line. He had left his staff officers, the bishop, and even Madame Lynch and his children to fend for themselves. Unlike Osório, López never had any use for personal heroics. Sadly, as Thompson sarcastically noted, the Marshal "possessed a peculiar kind of courage: when out of range of fire, even though completely surrounded by the enemy, he was always in high spirits, but he could not endure the whistle of a ball."[95] The appearance of cowardice in a common soldier can have serious consequences for his unit; when displayed by a commanding general, however, even a whiff of trepidation can provoke total collapse. Yet nothing of the kind happened here. Whether through fear, patriotism, or a deep sense of loyalty to the regime, the Paraguayans had tied themselves to López, and they refused to forsake him.

Paso de la Patria, however, was doomed. Osório's men had constructed land batteries to pound the site to pieces, while Tamandaré and Mitre kept up an active fire of canister. On 21 and 22 April, the Marshal met some of the last troops out of Paso. His scouts and staff officers had determined that the northern Estero Bellaco, "an enormous marsh split by a grassy island into two halves," provided the best chance for a new defensive line. It enjoyed direct communication with Humaitá, and the Allies could not hope to cross its watery expanse. Satisfied, López reassembled his forces at a dry spot, called Rojas, and dug in. He sent word to evacuate the remaining handful of men from Paso de la Patria, and simultaneously ordered the sinking of the *Gualeguay*, which the enemy squadron had hounded for some days. The ship, which had served the Paraguayans well, had her pump valves removed. She sank fast.[96] The last of López's soldiers at Paso left the fort on 23 April. They fired whatever remained of the buildings and made their way north through the marshes. Only the little chapel and López's bungalow escaped unscathed. Before leaving, the men scattered about the charred ruins scores of copies of the Marshal's order of the day in which he instructed his men to respect the rights of prisoners. Even at this late hour, it seems, López thought he could encourage the enemy to desert.

The Allies had expected a long siege. Osório and Mitre had moved their armies into a broad pincer-like posture, cutting off Paso de la Patria on three sides. The engineers constructed pontoon bridges and batteries into which they situated forty guns so as to pound the Paraguayans by land as well as by water. Now the Allied soldiers entered Paso without resistance. They rang the bells of the chapel all day long in celebration.

The Paraguayans made two fundamental mistakes in the last days of the campaign. Having been surprised at Osório's landing on the Paraguay (which came without benefit of gunboat protection), they squandered the chance to repel this force before it became fully established. They compounded this error by a precipitous and uncontrolled flight from Paso. The trenches there were among the best in the entire theater, and Thompson, who had built them, was not alone in thinking them impregnable. "If instead of sending his men to fight on the banks of the river," he wrote, "López had defended the trenches of Paso de la Patria, he would have cut up perhaps eight or ten-thousand of the Allies, with hardly any loss on his own side."[97]

Perhaps Thompson, Palleja, and others were right to criticize the Marshal's withdrawal. Even so, the extensive trench works at Paso seemed to invite flanking at various points, and they were always falling under the guns of the enemy fleet. They might not have been as secure as many believed. In the end, the Marshal deserved censure not so much for abandoning an established position in favor of a new defensive line, as for retreating in a manner so sloppy and undisciplined that it almost brought disaster.

As it was, the fall of Paso de la Patria provided the Allies with an open door. The twelve thousand men of Porto Alegre's column soon arrived at the site, having decided against a passage at Encarnación, Apipé, or Santa Teresa. By concentrating these forces together with the Allied units already present at Paso, Mitre and his commanders could now challenge the remnants of the Marshal's army with an unstoppable force.

VAST FIELDS OF DEATH

Having gained a foothold in Paraguay with relative ease and minimal loss of life, the Allied commanders evidently felt reassured in their strategy. The Marshal had given up his powerful defenses at Paso de la Patria after a scant resistance. With men and supplies pouring across the river, his adversaries felt confident; they flattered themselves by assuming that López's ineptitude would continue to bring happy results. The editors of the Buenos Aires *Standard* were hardly alone in crowing at the expectation of a speedy triumph. "Half the campaign is now over," they wrote. "The grand feat of crossing the Paraná is accomplished, and the Allies flushed with victory will quickly advance their resistless [*sic*] legions to the last bulwark of López's power, the fort of Humayta."[1]

Allied optimism rested on the belief that the Marshal could ill afford a pitched battle. Raids and night skirmishes were his proven forte, Mitre and Osório reasoned, and the Paraguayan leader would never risk facing their superior artillery. The benefits of fighting on home ground near his base of supply might provide him a short respite, but each day the Allies grew stronger, and Mitre, it seems, felt particularly buoyant. In his various dispatches from Itapirú, he maintained full confidence in the Allied armies. The details of command had been left undecided in the Triple Alliance Treaty, which stipulated that Mitre should direct operations on Argentine soil; General Osório, or some other imperial commander, in Brazil; and General Flores in Uruguay, should the fortunes of war carry the Allied armies that far south. Thus far, Mitre's successes provided justification for his continued command, and no one—not even Admiral Tamandaré—questioned his right to carry on in that capacity.

For the moment, however, the Argentine president needed to address his army's logistical needs. His soldiers were still hungry and ill-clad. They had received few provisions, and the navy had had no opportunity to land supplies by way of the Paraguay River, which was still contested. So don Bartolo arranged for some fifty-four ocean-going steamers, together with another forty-eight sailing vessels, to transport arms and powder, cattle, cavalry horses, blankets, and other matériel. Ships large and small, flying all flags, now plied the river for the short distance between Corrientes and Paso de la Patria. At Paso, hundreds of soldiers briskly, even jauntily, unloaded the supplies, conveying everything forward through the marshes in oxcart caravans.[2]

The Allied troops had to carry their rations on the march northward to Humaitá, at least until they reached the pastures where the cattle the Paraguayans had seized in Corrientes might be located. No one was accustomed to moving over such sodden ground, and foraging presented a serious challenge. At least the Brazilian military engineers managed to assemble a series of temporary bridges, which helped somewhat.[3]

The men found few occasions to rest. On 22 April 1866, Mitre issued each Argentine soldier a ration of fourteen biscuits of galleta—the first time many had tasted bread in over a month—and it went down well with the usual portion of charqui and yerba mate.[4] The Brazilians seem to have eaten a bit better, and the Uruguayans a bit worse—but even then, few could boast of a full stomach. The soldiers faced many other inconveniences. For one thing, a minor but noticeable outbreak of what the doctors called "tetanus" had hit the Allied ranks, a situation aggravated by the rainy weather. Only a few units had received tents. At night, Allied soldiers huddled onto whatever high ground they could find, their woolen ponchos held up to their faces and their headgear pulled down as far as possible. Combat may have failed to break them, but the mud, rain, sickness, and mosquitoes exacted a heavy toll for every mile the Allies advanced. And in the distance, the Paraguayans were waiting.

After the retreat from Paso de la Patria, López assumed a new position, one conveniently out of range of Tamandaré's guns. Though not as well situated for the defensive as Paso, the new Paraguayan line was still secure at the edge of a low plateau extending a league northward towards Humaitá. The Marshal ordered his men to bivouac just behind a narrow ford that linked the Estero Bellaco swamp with its shallower counterpart, the Laguna Pirís. The trails that linked the old camps on the Paraná with the fortress passed along this thin spit of land, and if the Allies hoped to approach Humaitá over any kind of firm ground, they would have to break through at this chokepoint.

For all the confusion of the moment, the Paraguayans maintained good discipline, their conduct belying the Allied claim that they were a defeated rabble. As a rule, the Paraguayans were unassuming as soldiers; they were wiry, and though often malnourished, could go for days with only a small portion of manioc or charqui and still fight with exceptional ruthlessness. They could withstand privation that the Argentines or Brazilians could not. Just the same, the Paraguayans usually lacked the "can-do" spirit their enemies frequently displayed, for to act independently or to call attention to any need for improvement was to question their subordination to the Marshal. They had to meticulously obey orders, even complex directives issued by distant commanders who were in no position to understand the circumstances at hand. To do so without question had become second nature among the Paraguayans. Their unbending resistance to the enemy thus drew its strength not so much from individual displays of bravery as from a collective obedience.[5] This was an asset as well as a liability.

One other factor came into relief at this time. The "secret" text of the Triple Alliance Treaty of 1 May 1865, which anticipated Allied appropriation of several portions of Paraguayan territory, had become known to the world. Some months earlier, the British minister in Montevideo, W. G. Lettsom, had wondered aloud to General Flores's foreign minister, Carlos de Castro, whether the Allies planned a general appropriation of Paraguayan territory so as to leave the country partitioned, like some South American Poland. Hoping to assuage the Briton, Castro begged his confidence and passed him an uncensored copy of the treaty that included the two sensitive articles. But Lettsom, worried that this proposed seizure of land was no better than a general annexation, decided to forward his copy of the treaty to the prime minister, Lord John Russell, whose government had long opposed territorial cessions of any kind in Uruguay, and, by extension, anywhere in the Plata.

The text of the treaty seemed to violate long-established diplomacy in the region. The British government decided to ignore Lettsom's promises of discretion, and hastened to publish the entire treaty as part of a "Blue Book" report that was read before Parliament in March 1866.[6] The London newspapers picked up the story, and denounced the Allies, who had hitherto portrayed themselves as aggrieved parties whose common security had come under the threat from a madman.[7] The desire to liberate Paraguay by expelling the country's "tyrant" was untainted, the Allies had always argued, by base motives or special interests.

This hypocrisy now received a just scrutiny in Europe. In Paris and London, many people who had previously displayed a certain romantic or patrician attachment to Pedro II now realized that the Paraguayan conflict was a real war, with real interests and real costs. And this was still only a prelude, for, when news of the "secret clauses" reached South America a few weeks later, it brought strong public condemnation. Many who had supported the Allied war effort felt dismayed by the none-too-subtle imperialism expressed in the treaty. The Marshal's soldiers learned of the "Blue Paper" at the end of April, but they had to wait until the first week of May to see a non-truncated text published in *La*

América, an anti-war newspaper in Buenos Aires.[8] By that time, however, its key points were well understood by the Paraguayans, who were now apt to think of their country being turned, figuratively speaking, into an artichoke, to be eaten leaf by leaf.

The revelation of the full text of the treaty brought an important shift in the struggle. Questions about the politics of the war had never risen above a whisper in the Paraguayan camp, where opinions were fashioned from two parts patriotism and three parts fear, but in this case open expression favored the Marshal. Paraguayan soldiers responded with a fortitude born not of some traditional deference to the will of a father figure (*karaí*), nor of a simple xenophobia, but rather of an increasingly offended nationalism.

For the Allied commanders in the field, the war remained an extension of regional conflicts that could be pressed or ignored according to circumstances. Given the loss of life and property that had already occurred, why did López refuse to purchase peace by relinquishing a part of his dominion? Was it just that the Allies insisted on his departure, while he refused to meet that condition? Or was it a question of honor? For the Paraguayans, it seems, the war had become an issue of national survival.[9]

Estero Bellaco

The Estero Bellaco consisted of two parallel streams some three miles apart, separated by a dense stand of yataí palms, which grew thickly at thirty to a hundred feet above the lagoon and obscured everything in the near distance. The main current of the Bellaco flows westward into the Paraguay by way of the Laguna Pirís, while its seasonal overflow falls into the Paraná some one hundred miles to the east through the Ñe'embucú marshes. The water of these *esteros*, or sloughs, was crystalline, good to drink, and attracted all manner of birds and wildlife. The streams were broken at many places by half-drowned trees, which in turn abounded with green vines that spread riotously as much as nine feet above the water line. These made a home for tadpoles and frogs, who every evening proclaimed their sovereignty in an incessant croaking over these watery expanses. The bottom of the lagoon was shaped by a deep mud of caramel color, over which flowed some three feet of water, which made them impassable, save at the fords, where the Paraguayans had previously torn out rushes and shoveled sand over the mud. Even at these passes transit was impractical for all but oxcarts and horses. The Marshal could count on the estero to offer a natural defense for his army.

By the end of April, López had between thirty and thirty-five thousand men in the immediate vicinity. He had situated a hundred guns of varied calibers on the north side of the northern Bellaco together with the majority of his troops. A Paraguayan vanguard positioned itself with six field pieces on the north side of the southern Bellaco. The Allies, for their part, had fifty thousand men encamped on the heights running east and west a mile above Paso de la Patria, which left a phalanx of Uruguayan units separated from the Paraguayans by a narrow marsh. Not surprisingly, troops often spotted each other and exchanged fire.

General Flores launched skirmishes near the fords on 26 and 29 April, but López's men drove off the attackers. This should have signaled that the Marshal could still count on his troops, but the Allies continued to treat the enemy with careless indifference. At that time, Flores had no more reason to expect trouble, but he later blamed Mitre for making light of the threat, quoting his commander's soothing but erroneous evaluation of the facts: "Don't alarm yourself, general. The aggression of the barbarians is nil, for the hour of their extermination has sounded."[10]

The Marshal had four possible courses of action other than surrender or withdrawal. He could take advantage of the terrain and remain in place at the Estero Bellaco, though a purely defensive deployment could do nothing to prevent an Allied buildup along the Paraná. He could continue the spoiling actions that had brought success at Corrales and Itatí, but this course would never force Mitre's withdrawal from Paraguay. He could launch an all-out attack, committing every reserve in a last-ditch effort to drive the enemy back across the river, but it was too late to believe that such an assault stood any chance of success; besides, except at the Riachuelo, the Marshal had never appeared as an "all-or-nothing" commander. This left the possibility of a limited offensive action, in which López could risk a portion of his troops in a swift movement to try to cause a major Allied misstep. Though neither a decisive victory nor an outright defeat was likely, the Marshal found himself most attracted to this latter approach.

On 2 May, under the rays of a bright noonday sun, the Paraguayans attacked. They caught the Allies napping: Colonel Léon de Palleja had just set up his table at the opening of his tent and had started to pen his weekly report to the Montevideo newspapers, in which he noted the cool of the morning hours and the tedium of camp life.[11] Suddenly, the roar of cannon fire rent the air and thousands of enemy infantrymen came streaming up along the Sidra Pass. They soon overwhelmed the first Brazilian units they encountered, the 7th Infantry Battalion of Pecegueiro's 12th Brigade.

In a flash, the Allied front was teeming with Paraguayans, coming ever stronger, cutting into Palleja's own Florida Battalion. Jumping up, the colonel managed to rouse his troops, who rushed forward to support the Brazilians, but it was too late. The loss of control associated with combat—the sensation of helplessness—fell on the bewildered Allies like a torrent of mud, and they panicked. The 21st and 38th Voluntários da Pátria broke and fled under tremendous pressure, leaving scores of dead behind them.[12] Then came the turn of the other

Uruguayan battalions—the Libertad and 24th Abril—which were torn by a murderous Paraguayan fusillade. General Flores himself narrowly escaped capture. In the melee, the Uruguayans failed to guard the four LaHitte field guns given them by the Brazilians; these the Paraguayans dragged back to their line.[13]

The Marshal had ordered three thousand infantry and one thousand cavalry to advance along the passes at the southern end of the estero and make contact with the enemy. Major Bruguez brought up his guns and Congreve rockets and pounded the Allied positions while Colonel José Eduvigis Díaz pushed through to the enemy center with his foot soldiers. As smoke covered the scene, Paraguayan cavalry units came across the Paso Carreta, pivoted, and tore into the Argentine 1st Regiment, which faced the Paraguayans on their extreme left. Like the Uruguayans, the Argentines recoiled at the audacity of the enemy, whose horsemen came directly at them, their lances extended, the drops of water glistening in the manes and fetlocks of their animals. They seemed to be galloping impossibly fast.

The Argentines had no time to prepare before the Paraguayans reached them, whereupon it became a matter of saber, bayonet, and bludgeon. Both sides recorded striking acts of heroism during this interchange: one Paraguayan corporal, the standard bearer for the 13th Regiment, had his stallion shot out from under him, and when three enemy soldiers closed in, he ran one through with the finial of his flagstaff and drove the other two off.[14] Colonel Silvestre Aveiro recorded another tale of courage in which two infantrymen, one Paraguayan and one Uruguayan, both with broken legs, berated each other with insults amidst the noise of battle. The two soldiers, thinking alike, crawled forward to within musket range and fired simultaneously. Both died on the spot.[15]

All this fighting took just a few minutes, and it brought good results for López. The Argentines retreated half a mile while the Uruguayans and Brazilians were mauled. Had López's men withdrawn straightaway, they likely would have gained a convincing success. Díaz, however, felt tempted by the prospect of a broader victory. Allied reports had claimed that he had been killed or wounded at Redención Island when he had in fact escaped unscathed.[16] He had just been promoted to full colonel the day before and sought laurels befitting his new rank. His orders encompassed only a spoiling attack, but watching the Allies take to their heels, he followed them in hopes of inflicting still more damage. Díaz reasoned that the Allied units opposite his center would scatter and leave him still more trophies. Fresh Allied units started to move up, however, and the pandemonium that had stymied their deployment started to subside. Allied ranks regrouped within easy striking distance of the Paraguayans, yet the colonel did nothing but survey the scene before him.[17]

Mitre had been lunching with Osório and other officers aboard a Brazilian warship when the battle began. He now rushed to a forward position and ordered his troops to envelop those of Díaz, whose flanks were exposed. The colonel's dithering cost the Paraguayans all the advantages they had just won, and the narrow passes over which they had launched their sorties now became death traps.

A poor cowboy from the grasslands of Argentina, Brazil, or Uruguay might bite every coin to test its metal, but, once converted into a soldier, the same man had no surefire way of testing his commanders before coming under fire. Even so, at the battle of the Estero Bellaco, everything fell into place: officers led from the front, the men followed from behind. Once again, General Osório displayed great personal valor, receiving one slight wound, and, like Flores, he had a horse shot out from under him. Despite the momentary confusion this caused, he managed to get his men to press ahead.[18] They seemed to lose their fear and any remaining inhibitions against taking human life. As comrades fell, their natural restraint vanished, and the rage of battle took hold. The Allied soldiers fired wildly and the contending forces seesawed back and forth over the field for the next four hours.

In the end, however, there was little that the outmatched Díaz could do but retreat with as much good order as his men could muster. He had to slug it out the entire way. The Argentines attempted to cut off the Pirís and Sidra Passes and met determined resistance everywhere. Two Allied battalions managed to get across to the north side of the latter ford, but could not hold. Major Bruguez again provided covering fire for the Paraguayans, whereupon Mitre's troops brought up their own guns, and the engagement tuned into a classic artillery duel.

Díaz's infantry counterattacked, suffering heavy casualties from canister. This gave Mitre his opportunity. Seizing the moment, he ordered his battalions to storm the enemy positions along the Carreta Pass. Díaz countered with a bloody bayonet charge that drove the Argentines back and gained him sufficient time to reach the Paraguayan lines at the other side of the Bellaco, but it took the lives of many men in his favorite unit, the 40th Battalion.

Finally, at the hour of vespers, the armies broke contact and began to take stock of the day's bloody work. The battle of the Estero Bellaco had started with the Paraguayans exploiting one of the great military principles—surprise. It ended with them disregarding another great principle—the objective. The Allies had left themselves opened by placing their pickets in wooded areas too distant from the main body of their own army to sound the alarm. As a result, when Díaz attacked, he achieved complete surprise. Yet the Marshal had never defined the objective he wished to attain, so when the colonel failed to follow through and request reinforcements, the Paraguayans lost momentum and never recovered it. Only in exceptional circumstances should a smaller force challenge a larger one when ample room exists for maneuver. On his own, Díaz lacked the manpower to wreck the enemy forces in detail, but he could have disrupted any movement of Allied units coming from the south. This, however, was not his decision to make.

If López had always intended a major spoiling action, his colonel should have ordered a quick retreat after the damage was done. Díaz had all the virtues of courage and a dog's loyalty to the Marshal, but he lacked the shrewdness, the breadth of vision, and the tactical flexibility that winning this battle required.[19] López had always discouraged any independent decision making among his officers, and Díaz, refusing to deviate from this standing policy, failed to capitalize on the enemy's confusion. He hesitated while the Allies reformed their lines. From that point onward, he could only mount a fighting retreat back to where he had started.

It is tempting in this context to blame López. The army he created relied too heavily on central command and control; the Marshal demanded unconditional obedience from his officers, and this often frustrated his objectives. Those who showed any initiative might win but more often would suffer for their impudence. (General Wenceslao Robles, the former Paraguayan commander in Corrientes, had been executed in January 1866 for just such a show of temerity.[20]) Knowing this, Paraguayan field commanders would always signal for López to confirm their decisions, even amid the smoke of battle.[21] In this case, the Marshal had given orders to attack a superior force without explaining what he wished to accomplish afterwards. Díaz's attack thus created a tactical opening that the rest of the army could not exploit.

Mitre, by contrast, always gave his officers considerable freedom of action, and both Flores and his subordinate Palleja used that freedom to good effect whenever the opportunity presented itself. At the Estero Bellaco, the Allies quickly recovered from their surprise, and though they failed to surround the entire Paraguayan force, as Mitre had wished, still they pressed the enemy mercilessly.

Losses on both sides were staggering. The Marshal's army counted twenty-three hundred *hors de combat*, including his principal colonel of cavalry, who died in the initial assault. The Allies suffered fifteen hundred killed, wounded, and missing.[22] The Paraguayans had throttled the Uruguayan battalions so badly that they lost combat effectiveness, with the Florida Battalion, for instance, mustering only eight officers out of twenty-seven by the end of the day.[23] The Brazilians likewise suffered, so much so that Colonel Manoel Lopes Pecegueiro, commander of the 12th Brigade, demanded a court-martial to clear himself.[24]

It now seems plain that if Pecegueiro had failed to prepare for the Paraguayan assault, so, too, had all the other Allied commanders. Few forgot this lesson. Henceforth, pickets were stationed closer to forward units, so that communications could never again be so easily disrupted. The Allies also learned that, in spite of the Marshal's poor leadership and want of supplies, his soldiers were still a match for their own troops, one-on-one. The Paraguayans could withstand both cavalry and artillery and maintain their line. Even when facing far superior numbers, they yielded only in the last extremity. Against such soldiers, any war of attrition was bound to last a long time.

In the aftermath of the battle of the Estero Bellaco, a dispassionate observer could see that the basic strategic situation still favored an Allied offensive, which sooner or later would sweep the Marshal's army before it. Mitre continued to receive reinforcements and supplies at Paso de la Patria, while the Paraguayans to the north could not replace their losses. The Marshal's obduracy might now be recognized and countered by the Allies building at least a threefold advantage in men and matériel.

For their part, the Paraguayans refused to recognize the scale of their losses at the Bellaco. Neither Díaz nor any other field commander admitted that the engagement occasioned greater casualties than expected. And when reports appeared in the state gazette, they were upbeat, claiming that "the enemy could not resist [Paraguayan] bravery … [such that] many begged for mercy at the end of a bayonet."[25] A timely show of ferocity and stubbornness might have fired López's imagination, but, like most of the readers of El Semanario, he had kept well back from the actual fighting.[26] In 1860s South America, journalists portrayed events in the rosiest possible light, and whether it was in liberal Buenos Aires, monarchist Rio de Janeiro, or authoritarian Asunción, they rarely failed to give bad news a positive slant. A Roman wag once observed that the throng likes to be deceived and gets what it wants, but even in classical times it was already an old story.

Medical Realities

The battle of the Estero Bellaco witnessed a horrifying tableaux of cruelty and carnage. Yet the most repugnant sights came after the shooting stopped, when orderlies and would-be rescuers stumbled through the gathering darkness in search of the wounded. One young Brazilian officer described "an extensive rack of corpses piled in irregular mounds [with] decapitated heads and eyes wide open; some heads were … split clean in half, the brain matter flowing out … such was the enemy's path to death and glory … a glory [drenched] with tears … the glory of Osório, of Napoleon, of Frederick the Great—the glory of death."[27]

Many times, the searchers found soldiers facedown at the edge of the marsh, seemingly unscathed but for a tiny nick in the cheek; when turned over, the other side of their faces were blasted away. This was the work of the Minié ball. By now, many soldiers on the Allied side used new percussion rifles to fire this heavy, half-inch tapered projectile. If a lead missile thus constructed chanced to clip a bone, it tore all the tissue behind it. This almost always necessitated amputation to stanch the bleeding. Thus, for every man the Minié ball killed, it left many others with shattered limbs requiring immediate attention. Those wounded in the gut could only moan intermittently for water.

Considering the terrain, the absence of medicines, and the general deficiency in qualified personnel, the Allied medical units did reasonably well in rescuing the wounded. They formed a flying ambulance of first aid and set up tents for field hospitals. They laid out instruments, linens, and compresses, and brought out the antiseptic. Estero Bellaco provided them with an opportunity to test their skills, for never before, not even at the Riachuelo and Yataí, had there been so many casualties in so small a place.

Oxcarts, horse-driven ambulances, dual-saddled *cacolets*, and simple stretchers brought the wounded back from the battlefield.[28] As they were received at the field hospitals, nurses performed standard triage to note which men needed immediate attention, which could wait, and which were beyond hope. The physicians and orderlies who attended to the first of these categories showed some courage, if the ability to withstand screams and bloody tribulations might be so described.[29] Though surgeons carried a variety of scalpels, bone saws, and probes, no one seemed to have sufficient ligatures, disinfectants, splints, bandages, and laudanum. Even soap was a minor luxury that often had to be procured from the sutlers who accompanied the army.

The surgeon's tent had the appearance of a nocturnal slaughterhouse. The oil lamps gave off an eerie, intermittent light, whose flickering made work difficult and uncertain. The balls and shrapnel had mangled many men beyond recognition, and limbs could not always be saved. Scores of wounded soldiers passed into the tents, and amid their cries for pity, the doctors sawed off arms and legs, throwing them into a grisly pile before sponging down the tables and starting over. Military chaplains offered spiritual relief to the dying and solace to the survivors, but most men could not hear their words.[30]

Those who lived through amputations often died later from shock and infection. Many soldiers had no understanding of sepsis, and despite the application of carbolic acid, they could not keep themselves clean. The wounded often had no way to resist the simple surface infections that abounded in this dirty environment. In general, if a wounded man could reach the larger field hospitals at Paso de la Patria, he stood a good chance of surviving; if he made it to Corrientes, the odds were better still. There, he would find some of the best-trained staff in the Brazilian and Argentine medical services, and many more supplies. The Allies constructed several impressive hospitals at Corrientes, all of which received shipments of modern equipment and medicines.[31] Later, they inaugurated a floating hospital aboard the Brazilian ship *Onze de Junho* that also saw much service.[32]

For every defect in the Allied medical services, the Paraguayans had three. While they had established adequate medical facilities at Humaitá, and still better ones at Asunción and Cerro León, little provision had been made for the immediate evacuation of the wounded.[33] Thus the proportion of dead to wounded near the battlefield tended to be far greater among the Paraguayans than among the Allies. Paraguayan field hospitals were rudimentary, and few—if any—possessed the instruments needed for surgery. Amputations were conducted with the sharpened edge of a machete or cane knife wielded by some unlettered sergeant who had little in common with the Allied surgeons. The Paraguayans always pretended that their men could bear the terrible pain of operations if the nurses, who were usually women, were looking into their eyes—as if vanity could do for the wounded what the absence of opiates could not.

Despite these drawbacks, the Marshal's men displayed a more flexible attitude toward the treatment of wounds and medical complaints than did the Allies. In the Argentine and Brazilian services, doctors stressed the efficacy of modern scientific methods; this left them few substitutes when medicines were unavailable. The Paraguayans, by contrast, showed an extraordinary inventiveness, using aloes to treat cuts and burns and a variety of herbs and tisanes as sedatives and tonics. The British pharmacist George Frederick Masterman often expressed contempt for the Paraguayan medics under his command, yet when it came to local medicines, he found much to praise.[34] There were ample astringents among the mimosas. Purgatives and calomel were easily manufactured along with absorbent mixtures (made out of "mountain limestone"). Masterman used arsenic in place of quinine, but opium, which he needed most of all, could not be produced no matter what.[35] The various drug substitutes found a successful place in the wartime pharmacopeia of the Paraguayans. But innovations were useless without trained medics, who could not even reach their wounded at the Estero Bellaco since the site of the battle had fallen to the Allies.

Masterman's highlighting of drugs suggests that only a small number of those on sick call in either army actually suffered from battle wounds. After the Allies had occupied the Misiones south of the Alto Paraná, the military hospital at Encarnación filled with Paraguayan patients. In a report of 11 November 1865, the officer in charge noted thirty men with combat wounds out of a total of 554 men interned. Of those remaining, 40 percent were down with diarrhea, caused by tainted meat and bad water. Fifty men had measles.[36] Save for this latter disease, whose rate of incidence would later be surpassed by cholera, smallpox, and yellow fever, the breakdown of medical complaints remained the same on both sides throughout the war.[37] This report also suggests something further about the physical state of many troops: at the Estero Bellaco, as at all the other major battles, a certain portion of the soldiers engaged—perhaps a significant portion—were stomach-sick at the outset. When combined with fever, fear, and a general dissipation, this ailment had a significant impact on how the fighting unfolded.

Tuyutí

As the orderlies scrubbed the blood and filth from the field hospitals, the Allied and Paraguayan commanders took stock of the situation facing them. In one respect, both sides benefited from a windfall of information. At the time of the battle of Estero Bellaco, several Paraguayans whose families were out of favor with López made use of the confusion and deserted to the other side. They reported a growing malaise among the Marshal's troops caused by the starvation diet. There was not enough food to keep them going much longer.

Mitre had woken to the danger of false optimism, and did not accept this news at face value. He now understood how fiercely the Paraguayans fought on their own soil; besides, the desertions at Estero Bellaco had not all been on one side. Masterman asserted that seven hundred Paraguayans who had joined the Allies after the capitulation at Uruguaiana "went over to a man [at the Bellaco], taking their arms with them" once they caught sight of their own flag. While this suggested a commitment to the national cause on the part of the Paraguayans, Masterman offered a tragic nuance when he observed that "López repaid their devotion by shooting all the more respectable among them for not returning sooner."[38]

The Marshal's suspicions of the Paraguayan elite are clear enough in this anecdote, and though the judicious reader may doubt the figure of seven hundred deserters, the general tone of the story is nonetheless believable. López came to look upon all his upper-class countrymen as potential traitors. This led him to whittle away at their presence in the senior ranks of his army. As the old elites receded into insignificance, both at the front and in Asunción, it was noteworthy that the European veneer of Paraguayan nationalism likewise receded, leaving in its place something earthier, more rural, more redolent of the Guaraní past. To judge from the shifting tenor of wartime newspapers in the country, this change in the national spirit was unmistakable.[39]

As for the newly arrived deserters, the Marshal tended to credit the information they brought him from behind enemy lines, for it confirmed what his spies had already told him. The Allies were growing stronger, and his men kept probing for fissures in the enemy morale. They had prisoners call out to their comrades at twilight from across the swamps, beckoning them to cross the lines for a good meal of galleta.[40] And they kept sniping at the Allied positions.

Over the next two weeks, regular small-scale encounters erupted between the frontline units. None of these amounted to much—just a few shots exchanged.[41] But the incidents kept everyone on edge. At nighttime, Allied sentries heard suspicious noises in the darkness ahead of them and grew jittery, firing often on the flickering glimmers of fireflies or swamp gas.[42] The nervousness on the Allied side was palpable. One twenty-two-year-old Brazilian officer, Joaquim Silverio de Azevedo Pimentel, recorded how this felt at one in the morning on 16 May:

> Suddenly we heard shouts of "long live the Paraguayan Republic and death to the Brazilian darkies!" mixed with a rising, dull, truly terrifying growl. Our advance pickets, who were not asleep, fired off a general volley and continued shooting as if they were being attacked. The night was extremely dark. Our [troops] stood firm by their posts, despite hearing the uproar, or something similar to thunder, which rolled along the surface of the ground [and] which could already be heard in the rear, although it first appeared at our front. … The Paraguayans had captured some wild horses, firmly tied ropes on their tails, at the ends of which they attached whole cowhides, and whipped them toward us. … Artillery, infantry, and cavalry, the latter reduced to walking [for their mounts had fled], took up arms and waited until daybreak … [while] the enemy remained peacefully in his camp [sleeping the night away].[43]

In fact, a good deal was happening behind the Paraguayan lines. López had moved northward and sought safety at Paso Pucú, where he had several battalions in reserve. This site, which would serve as López's operational headquarters for the next two years, boasted a reinforced blockhouse with rooms for Madame Lynch and their children, an array of telescopes, bookcases, and charts, and an auxiliary telegraph line that provided communication with Humaitá and Asunción. Paso Pucú was safe and provided an excellent view of the front, several miles away.

The civilian populations south of the Río Tebicuary had been evacuated on López's orders back in November 1865, and now most areas below Humaitá were vacant save for military personnel.[44] The main body of the Paraguayan army dug in some four miles above the southern arm of the Bellaco. The Marshal now instructed his commanders to avoid pitched battle at the fords, and instead retire whenever the Allies made their move. Mitre advanced along the expected line of march on 20 May, and the Paraguayans retreated in good order to the prepared positions at the northern Bellaco. The Allies moved up in three columns and stopped to bivouac near a dense palm forest. Flores, who again commanded Mitre's vanguard, established his camp on sandy ground just below the Bellaco. The main Paraguayan units were right in front of him.

The Uruguayan chieftain, who had fought in so many battles since the 1850s, now found himself commanding a force only nominally Uruguayan. He had two Brazilian divisions assigned to him as well as a regiment of Argentine cavalry. Most of his veteran troops from the Banda Oriental were dead or missing, replaced now by Paraguayan prisoners and a few European adventurers.[45]

Flores might take pride in the twenty-eight Brazilian guns that don Bartolo had transferred to him at the last moment, yet his command no longer exemplified the Uruguayan nation as such.

Flores's Blanco opponents had always condemned his support of the Triple Alliance as proof of a mercenary inclination, but up to this point he could reply that his Colorado stalwarts had mostly been born in the Banda Oriental and represented Uruguayan interests; now he could make no such claim. Galling though this might have been for his countrymen in general, members of the majority faction of the Colorados had by now accepted that their influence depended on Brazil even more than an earlier generation of Uruguayans had depended on Great Britain. This fact festered as a wound within the body politic, and Flores, now an absentee president, had to wonder about events in Montevideo.[46]

The details of political infighting in Uruguay mattered little to Mitre at this particular juncture; he needed to prepare for the next engagement. The perimeter of the new Allied line resembled a long horseshoe that enclosed a broad and relatively dry rise called Tuyutí ("white mud"). General Osório's Brazilian units, which held the left third of the semicircle, were encamped in an extended arc from the Potrero Pirís to a point near Flores's battalions, which once again occupied the center. The Argentines, under Generals Wenceslao Paunero, who was born in Uruguay, Juan Andrés Gelly y Obes, whose father was Paraguayan, and Emilio Mitre, who was the younger brother of the president, occupied the right on a line that extended to the Ñe'embucú. As a whole, the revamped Allied army amounted to some forty-five thousand men (not counting several thousand still at Paso de la Patria and Corrientes). They had one hundred fifty guns, almost all of them rifled, situated along the perimeter. To make this line stronger, they built two redoubts, one in the center and one on the left.

The artillery at the center was commanded by Brazilian Lieutenant Colonel Emílio Luiz Mallet, a dark-haired, owl-eyed engineer who had attended the French War Academy at Saint-Cyr and whose skills were now well demonstrated in his preparations along the Allied line. On Osório's orders, the colonel had constructed a deep ditch, later christened the Fôsso de Mallet, which provided protection for his LaHitte guns.

Irrespective of the Allied numerical superiority, all was not well in the Brazilian, Argentine, and Uruguayan camps. Supply problems still hampered operations, especially for the cavalry, which remained short of mounts. At the same time, the terrain presented little security with no more than three miles of front for the whole of an enormous army, with woods and marshes on both sides, extending well into the rear. As one Brazilian officer reported:

> Our camp is not all terra firma. It greatly resembles an archipelago. In order to visit my comrades … I am obliged to turn and wind for miles around the lakes and swamps. Amphibious

creatures abound. … Every morning I find myself accompanied by a bodyguard of fifteen or twenty monstrous toads which have quietly spent the night under the corners of the hides that serve as my bed. Enormous alligators [*sic*—caimans] promenade regularly from lake to lake every night. In a major's tent the other day, one was killed that measured about six feet in length.[47]

The soldiers also needed to fear the tiniest mosquitoes. The malaria from the sloughs had already brought down between three and four thousand men, and various fevers threatened to carry away many more. Given the pestilential character of the land and the general anxiety of the troops, all hoped for a prompt attack so as to leave the place behind.

For its part, the Marshal's army held a long line from Paso Gómez to Paso Rojas, with a few smaller units encamped further east. The Paraguayan right flank abutted the impenetrable carrizal around the Potrero Sauce, a natural clearing in the palm forest that the Allies could reach by way of a narrow mouth that faced east, near their main camps. Colonel Thompson and the other foreign engineers had sealed this opening with a small ditch from which enemy columns might be enfiladed at some distance.[48]

The Paraguayans had spent a fortnight cutting a trail through the dense forest from the Potrero Sauce to the Potrero Pirís, another clearing to the south. They felled hundreds of short yataí palms and scores of heavy hardwood trees and purple-flowered lapachos. It was back-breaking labor, and only partly successful in trimming out the green tangles of boughs and creepers. At the end, even the clearest spot along the trail provided visibility for less than twenty yards.

Where it flowed in front of the Paraguayan positions, the northern arm of the Bellaco was more than six feet deep to the west of Paso Gómez, and a bit over four feet deep to the east. If Mitre attacked the Paraguayans head-on, his armies would first have to traverse two deep passes while under fire; if they attempted to turn the Paraguayan left, they would see their communications cut. The Marshal thus enjoyed a strong position, and the Allies had no easy way around it. They would have to face a strongly entrenched enemy contingent that had now grown to twenty-five thousand able-bodied men.

On the day that the Allies drove in upon the Paraguayan vanguard, Thompson constructed a deep trench above the Potrero Sauce that linked the palm forest on the right with the marshes at the left of Paso Fernández. He laced the outer edges of these works with thorny brambles called "the crown of thorns" (*espina de corona*), which acted as barbed wire. The line of his trenches at Sauce was around fifteen hundred yards in length and fixed with twenty-six barbettes for artillery.[49] And this was not all: Thompson constructed trenches at the other passes, where the Paraguayans intended to await the attack, and when the Allies began, to throw ten thousand men on their rear from the Potrero

Sauce. These men would not be "perceived till they were cutting up the rear of the Allies."[50]

Had López followed this plan, he might have inflicted a serious defeat on the Allied army, which would have taken heavy losses through enfilade, blunting its teeth in a full-scale assault. To everyone's surprise, however, the Marshal changed his mind on 23 May, and called together his commanders to announce that he intended to attack the following morning. Juan Crisóstomo Centurión, who would one day gain the rank of colonel on López's staff, later derided this decision as the worst mistake the Paraguayans made during the entire war. The attack, he claimed, made no sense militarily, but instead issued from the whims of the Marshal's rash intuition.[51]

At Tuyutí, the Paraguayans enjoyed every advantage that the defense could hope for. They were well dug in, their artillery well mounted, their infantry ready; the terrain favored them far more than it had at Paso de la Patria. And yet the Marshal abandoned his excellent defenses in favor of a risky frontal assault. Why? Speaking of the engagement a year later, López remarked that he had anticipated an enemy attack sometime on 25 May, the Argentine independence day and one-year anniversary of Paunero's raid on Paraguayan-occupied Corrientes.[52] To frustrate this plan, which "frankly he did not like," the Marshal reasoned that a surprise attack of his own stood the best chance of success. He also knew that Porto Alegre's army in the Misiones might soon work its way downriver to link its twelve thousand men with Mitre's forty-five thousand. Such a force, combined with a naval attack on Curupayty, might prove overpowering. The Marshal thus had to move quickly.

On the afternoon of 23 May, the Paraguayan president rode out to address his reserve battalions at Paso Pucú. He reminded the men how the Brazilians had invaded the country to enslave its people; that they, his trusted soldiers, might find themselves in the place of those "unfortunate negroes of Africa"; that their wives and daughters, after being outraged by the "contemptible monkeys," would soon end up in the slave markets of Rio; and that their lands would be wrested from them in the interim and their villages burned. "Tomorrow," he intoned, "the whole army will throw itself … on these cowardly scoundrels … [and] exterminate them! No mercy, no pity upon them! I … know every one of you will do his duty! Let us defeat them tomorrow and, if needs be, let us die, shouting 'Long live the Republic of the Paraguay! Independence or Death!' "[53]

Whatever the real contours of his thinking, López had grown tired of halfway measures and yearned for a decisive battle. He spent the entire evening with his officers outlining their instructions for the upcoming engagement. He had studied the terrain and measured the enemy's strengths and weaknesses. Now, speaking as a father speaks to his children, he called in his field commanders one at a time and explained what he wanted each man to do.[54]

On the extreme left, at some distance from the main force, the Marshal's brother-in-law, General Vicente Barrios, would attack from within the Potrero Pirís with 8,700 men in ten battalions of infantry and two regiments of cavalry. At the same time, Colonel Díaz would assault from the right with 5,030 men in five battalions of infantry and two regiments of cavalry. On Díaz's immediate left, Lieutenant Colonel Hilario Marcó was to advance against the enemy center with 4,200 men in four battalions of infantry and two regiments of cavalry. General Resquín, for his part, would advance on the enemy right with 6,300 men in two battalions of infantry and eight regiments of cavalry.

On paper, the attacking forces totaled 24,230 men, though some witnesses thought the figure might have been several thousand less.[55] The attacks were to begin simultaneously at the firing of a Congreve rocket from the Paso Gómez. The resulting surprise, the Marshal predicted, would break the Allied front, bringing total confusion to the enemy, who would scatter like frightened deer into the swamps where the Paraguayans could pick them off. Neither Mitre nor the Brazilians could bear the political costs of such a defeat, and López could dictate the terms of peace.

Success depended on Barrios. His men had to creep through the heavy brambles and carrizal all the way into the Potrero Pirís and lie there in wait for the signal. This meant moving in single file along an undercut path with his cavalrymen dismounted and leading their horses forward. The Marshal ordered Díaz to advance to within earshot of the enemy, all the while keeping himself hidden from view. At the right moment, the colonel would rush the Allied vanguard. For his part, Resquín would quietly move across the Laguna Rojas during the nighttime to concentrate his forces behind the palms at Yataity Corã. These units would also remain concealed from the enemy's pickets until the signal came for the battle to commence. Resquín's cavalry would then sweep around the Allied rear to join with those of Barrios bearing down from the opposite direction. Thus would the Paraguayans envelop the Allied army.

When first he announced the battle plan, Colonel Franz Wisner von Morgenstern raised an objection. An advisor to the López family for twenty years, this Hungarian engineer understood his own political limitations in his adopted country as well as its problematic topography. He noted that abandoning the prepared entrenchments in order to take the offensive meant leaving behind the cover fire that Bruguez could provide. The Marshal admitted the problem, but tried to reassure his old counselor that surprise would carry the day.[56] Wisner remained skeptical but held his tongue.

The following morning, 24 May, as the moment of decision neared, the Paraguayan field officers smelled trouble. General Barrios was supposed to have eased past the defile by nine in the morning, but even men long accustomed to marching barefoot found it difficult to traverse a path strewn with the branches of thorn bushes. It was thus almost noon before his troops scrambled beyond that point. Díaz, Marcó, and Resquín had already reached their appointed spots and were waiting impatiently. Some men had drunk a concoction of caña and gunpowder to steel their mettle. Even so, their mouths stayed dry, their muscles tightened, and they could hear their own heartbeats.[57]

At that moment a party of skirmishers from the Brazilian 4th Infantry happened to be gathering firewood near the edge of the Potrero Pirís. They were led by Lieutenant Dionísio Cerqueira, the dapper "Beau Brummell of Bahia," who later wrote one of the most evocative memoirs to come from the Allied side. On this crisp and clear morning, his pistol was holstered and he had his eyes to the ground in search of dry kindling.

Just after ten o'clock, the men to his front glimpsed hundreds of Paraguayans in scarlet tunics moving through the brambles. Though Cerqueira's skirmishers were likewise visible, the Marshal's troops held their fire and began to arrange themselves by units. This signaled a major battle in the offing. Amazed at what he had seen, one of the Brazilian soldiers hurried back to the lieutenant, caught his breath, and in an excited voice blurted out that the forest had "gone red with Paraguayans."[58]

Cerqueira and his men slipped back to the Allied lines without incident, but just as he was making his report, the signal rocket blazed across the sky and fell harmlessly among the soldiers of the Florida Battalion. The Paraguayans immediately surged forward on all sides, bellowing their war cries. Some were singing the national anthem, while others cried, "Ya jha! Ya jha!" (Let's go! Let's go!).

Mitre, however, had previously ordered an extensive reconnaissance for the afternoon, and so all of his men were already under arms.[59] The surprise therefore had few of the effects that López predicted. As the rocket struck the ground, guns erupted on both sides and the fighting became general. The Allies might have been lax on 2 May, but now they stood ready for all that the Paraguayans could throw at them. Thompson, who witnessed it all, remarked that over the next four hours the "musketry was so well kept up, that only one continuous sound was heard, which was relieved by the cannonading of the Allies."[60]

On the Allied left flank, the Paraguayans pushed the Brazilians down to the waters of the Bellaco, where Osório's men rallied, and, with an impressive discipline turned the Paraguayans back to the Potrero. On reaching the line of palms, the Marshal's troops rallied themselves, and forced the Brazilians back three times.

Amid the fighting, the General Antônio Sampaio, commander of the Brazilian 3rd Division, sent six of his eight battalions forward to aid the stricken Uruguayans. Each man carried ten cartridge boxes and one hundred twenty-five firing caps, and each battalion was trailed by several ammunition carts, more than enough to make the difference.[61] The smoke and fire into which the Brazilians surged nonetheless shocked their senses; within minutes, their faces were sooty, their ears rang with sound, and their mouths bore the bitter taste of powder. Every finger trembled.

Nothing could disguise the unfolding carnage. One of those who fell wounded in this seesaw of battle was Sampaio.[62] According to one story, his troops began to falter when medical teams evacuated their wounded commander on a stretcher. At that moment, however, General Osório swept in on horseback, having ordered his 1st Division to the rescue. When the soldiers hesitated, he swung his mount toward them and gestured with his saber, urging the "Baianada" forward with supreme contempt for their race, promising each man three months' "soldo e cachaça" (pay and sugarcane liquor).[63] Whether or not he used these precise words (and a good officer realizes that he can sometimes get good results by shaming his men), the 1st Division moved into the fray as Osório commanded.

As the Brazilians advanced, they found Barrios's cavalry still cutting into the ranks of their retreating comrades, causing tremendous confusion among them. The Paraguayan horses were short-jointed and scrawny but gregarious. Individual animals would seek safety in flight whenever distressed. When in herds, however, instinct took over and wherever the first animal led, all would follow—even, as in this case, into the concentrated fire of the enemy's musketry. Whenever a horse took a hit, a thud would signal a ball entering some fleshy mass. He would jerk for a bare moment and then push on as if the wound were little more than a scratch. A horse hit in one leg usually went ahead on three, and even mortally wounded animals kept going until the loss of blood caused them to stumble, hesitate, and drop.

The horses' courage could do nothing, however, to reverse the horror of what every man beheld. Bunched up and frightened by the noise, the cavalry horses were torn to shreds by artillery and the lances of their own disoriented riders.[64] The Allied cannons kept up a sustained fire and the Paraguayans fell by the dozens before the canister. The German-educated Francisco Seeber, who started the war as a second lieutenant and had been promoted to captain in the Argentine National Guard, noted the glee of the Allied gunners and the tragedy of the men they killed: "men can become drunk on murder and killing is a pleasure that at certain moments [can be elevated] to the sublime, [but these wars are really nothing] … more than the products of human perversity, and of the ignoble ambition of despots."[65]

The Brazilians, flushed with the same rush of success, pushed back hard from the flanks of their own artillery. Then the Marshal's cavalry gave way.[66] At the center and center-left, Díaz and Marcó had to contend with General Flores, whose artillery pieces were twenty-eight to their four. When the Paraguayans attacked, the Allied troops wavered, leaving large sections of the field to Marcó. The Independencia and Libertad Battalions began to break up and some of the Brazilian and Uruguayan soldiers took to their heels, racing as far as Itapirú, where their appearance caused great alarm.[67] Some in Corrientes assumed that López was about to make good on his threats.

Mallet's gunners, however, soon recovered from the initial surprise. The instant the Paraguayans came into the open they encountered the full sweep of his artillery, which spewed shrapnel charges and 9- and 10-pound shot at such speed that the Brazilians later nicknamed it the "repeating cannon" (*artilharía revólver*).[68] Díaz's own guns proved useless against the well-defended Fôsso de Mallet.

Throughout the battle, the Allies enjoyed a distinct advantage, not just in numbers, but also in the preeminence of their artillery. The Paraguayans made no use of their own artillery reserve, for, as Wisner had noted, Bruguez was too far back to provide support. The Allies also counted on the efficiency of their small arms, which included Minié rifles that could be fired three times a minute with good accuracy. Their enemies had no such weapons. The few modern rifles the Paraguayans possessed they lost back at the Estero Bellaco, and the muskets that remained to them were mostly flintlocks.

With all of this, Colonel Díaz still had to face another obstacle. To get at the enemy, his men needed to cross over a deep ford, holding their muskets above their heads. They made easy targets. Soon the morass was choked with bodies, and to push ahead, the Paraguayans had to step upon the semi-sunken corpses of their comrades. The men of the 25th Battalion, all new recruits from the countryside, "heaped themselves up like a flock of sheep, [and] were easily shot down."[69]

On the Allied right, General Resquín's cavalry performed well in the first charge, tearing up the same Correntino cavalry units they had once fought on the other side of the Paraná. Generals Nicanor Cáceres and Manuel Hornos, who commanded these Allied units, could not get their men to rally against the "monkey-tailed" Acá-Carajá Regiment that swept in among them. Resquín's men cut through to the artillery, losing about half their number in the process. They seized twenty guns and started to drag them toward their own lines when, out of nowhere, an Argentine cavalry reserve swept in and retook the cannon. Allied artillery units also poured fire onto the field, killing almost as many Argentines as Paraguayans.[70] Resquín's cavalrymen were annihilated—not a single man survived. His infantrymen, with their machetes at the ready, charged up from the rear at this moment, determined to aid their comrades.[71] It did no good; they shared the same fate in the unequal contest with enemy artillery.

The reserve Paraguayan cavalry units rushed around the Allied right and into the palm forest. They had hoped to encircle the enemy as planned, but it was far too late: General Osório, who seemed to be everywhere at once, had already grasped the danger behind him and shunted twelve regiments of dismounted cavalry to the rear together with most of his unoccupied artillery, which fired into Barrios's cavalry as it emerged from the scrub. Almost no one got through. Inspecting their work a half-hour later, the Brazilians encountered—and killed—a horribly wounded Paraguayan sergeant who was eating his regimental colors rather than see them fall into enemy hands.[72]

Just a portion of Resquín's 17th Regiment, commanded by Major Antonio Olabarrieta, managed to break through the Argentine line and ride along the Allied rear. As he approached the spot designated for the linkup with Barrios, Olabarrieta found himself isolated, for the general had long since retreated before the Allied guns. In the absence of all support, the major turned and fought his way through the Brazilian infantry until he could reach the safety of the Potrero Sauce. He arrived badly wounded and almost alone.

The fighting subsided just before four in the afternoon, when the remnants of the Paraguayan army retired in confusion across the fords of the northern Bellaco and into their fortified lines. As the last vindictive cracks sputtered out, Díaz ordered the remnants of his military band (*Banda paí*) to play their cornets to convince the Allies that superior numbers still awaited them in the near distance.[73] In truth, however, the Paraguayans had been soundly defeated.

As the Smoke Cleared

Save for the Marshal, everyone agreed that it had been an appalling day for his army. He had lost four artillery pieces, five hundred muskets, seven hundred swords and sabers, two hundred machetes, four hundred lances, fifty thousand bullets, twelve drums, fifteen bugles, and eight battle flags and regimental colors.[74] Initial reports fixed the number of Paraguayan dead at forty-two hundred, though in the end, something closer to six thousand bodies were found among the brush and esteros.[75] The Allies took another three hundred fifty men prisoner, all of them wounded. The number of Paraguayan soldiers that reached the hospital at Humaitá and points further north approached seven thousand, and those with slight wounds received no leave to join them, but were instead ordered to resume their positions within the trenches along the northern arm of the Bellaco. The dearth of medicines and the filthy conditions the men found there meant that, inevitably, many of these walking wounded would later succumb.

Given the scale of the carnage, it was odd that the Marshal lost but one field officer, a major so fat and aged that he could barely make the roll call. All the junior officers, however, had been hit, often grievously.[76] Unit cohesion therefore vanished. Díaz's old 40th Battalion, for instance, suffered an 80 percent loss, and the much-admired Nambí-í Battalion, composed of Afro-Paraguayans, was annihilated.

The slaughter before the Allied cannons left a gruesome impression, and León de Palleja was not alone on the Allied side in feeling sympathy for the enemy's plight:

This virile and pure race, whom vices and comforts have [yet] to feminize, has been strengthened by its misery, nakedness, and privation; [these curses] have turned the Paraguayan soldier into ... a first-rate [fighting man]. I look with great pain at the extermination they have suffered in so many repeated and disgraceful battles over this last year, and I ask, why? Because of one man. ... The Paraguayan soldier deserves a better fate.[77]

Putting aside Allied displays of sympathy, there was much to pity in the Paraguayans' obstinacy. After all, casualties among López's men were high because they would neither surrender nor deviate from orders.[78] In the absence of flexible instructions (or field officers willing to act on their own initiative), Paraguayan bravery could not be properly focused on a tactical goal, for every time an officer went down, his men would push blindly ahead. The Paraguayans might win momentary victories, but defeating the Allies required much more than that.

The Paraguayans always remained implacable—and dangerous—in refusing defeat. This intransigence, while commendable in some ways, brought a terrible response from the Allies, especially the Brazilian enlisted men (*praças*), who wanted to take no chances. Minister Washburn, who was nearby at Corrientes, noted that the Brazilians were "disinclined to take prisoners but [rather] kill alike wounded and deserters to their side," since the Paraguayans had a habit of feigning surrender only to fire on their would-be captors at the last moment; "when any number of Paraguayans [are] found together though they make signs of surrendering, they [are therefore] shot down without trust or mercy."[79]

Losses on the Allied side amounted to less than a thousand dead and another three thousand wounded, the great majority Brazilian.[80] Captain Seeber speculated that the Paraguayans preferred to concentrate their attacks on Brazilians rather than Argentines or Uruguayans.[81] This may have reflected López's own hatreds, or perhaps a Paraguayan prejudice against those who for years had encouraged the raids of the Guaicurú from the Chaco. Whether it was sound for the Marshal to focus on the Brazilians was another matter. Certainly, the Paraguayans found in their preferred opponent some stolid fighters. It was not just Osório and Sampaio who displayed a stiff resistance at Tuyutí—it was the entire Brazilian contingent.

Paraguay's losses at this battle had a qualitative as well as a quantitative effect on the war effort—and not one that the Allies could have predicted. As we have seen, López despised many members of his own elite class and lost few opportunities to assign them frontline duties. On this occasion, their numbers fell so dramatically that Masterman could claim that Tuyutí had "annihilated the Spanish race in Paraguay; in the front ranks were the males of all the best families in the country, and they were killed almost to a man; hundreds of families, especially in the capital, had not a husband, father, son, or brother left."[82] The death of so many well-placed, literate citizens in one fell swoop was bound to leave an enormous wound. In other countries, such a loss would have ended the war; in authoritarian Paraguay, however, it assured that the bloodletting would go on, for those same men who might have abandoned the struggle as hopeless, and who would have resisted the Marshal's course as equivalent to national suicide, now lay dead with only the obedient peasant troopers left behind to keep up the fight.

The medical teams on both sides were busy over the next days, much more so than after Estero Bellaco. The sheer number of wounded soldiers overwhelmed even the most energetic medical practitioners. Dr. Manoel Feliciano Pereira de Carvalho, head of the Brazilian field hospital at Paso de la Patria, praised the efforts of the mobile ambulances, noting that the wounded in his tent "included one brigadier, one lieutenant colonel, four majors, seven captains, fourteen lieutenants, twenty-one sub-lieutenants, one cadet, and 215 soldiers, for a total of 261."[83] Dr. Carvalho's field hospital was one of several on the Allied side that operated into the late hours of the night and into the next day.[84] Some of the wounded were taken aboard Allied transports and fitfully tended to before evacuation to Corrientes. *The Standard* reported from aboard the Brazilian transport *Presidente* as it received the wounded on the night of 25 May:

> Three hundred of the maimed embarked, a large proportion of whom were officers. The cabins, state-rooms, tables, floors, and decks were covered with them, some remaining upon the litters in which they came. A night of suffering followed, not easily to be forgotten by those who witnessed it. "Groans, not loud but deep," reverberated on every side, as utterances to the pangs caused by every class of lance, bayonet, saber, or gunshot wounds. All were begrimed with blood, little pools of it were seen in many places oozing from the yet unstaunched gashes. ... The [ship's captain] ... did all that could be done to lessen the afflictions of the passengers. Himself an invalid (as were most of the crewmembers), still he was seen with his servants softening with tepid water and cutting the saturated garments that were made stiff ... by clotted blood, furnishing from his own wardrobe shirts to replace those that were thus reduced to shreds.[85]

Burying the dead presented a thankless task under normal conditions, but at Tuyutí, the sheer scale of the work made it thoroughly repugnant. The bloated bodies of men and horses bobbed up and down in the esteros, merging with the branches and tree trunks that had been torn apart by cannon fire. Buzzards flew in from the Chaco by the hundreds and pecked at the corpses with raucous delight, hopping amid the shredded uniforms, kepis, broken muskets, and lances.

Given the relentless process of putrefaction, and the diseases that accompanied it, the burial teams could not afford to waste time. Bodies rotted so swiftly that, when lifted, they often came apart or ruptured, letting out a nauseating stench that caused every man nearby to retch uncontrollably. The wetness of the ground made it impossible to bury the cadavers where they lay, so they had to be moved or cremated, a task that took days to complete. The Allied burial details piled the bodies into mounds of fifty or more, interspersed them with firewood, and set them aflame during the evening hours. One man noticed that the Allied dead burned with a steady glow, while the Paraguayans, who had no fat left on their bodies, refused to ignite unless drenched with oil.[86] Unspent cartridges exploded from the bottom of these heaps, sending shreds of flesh in every direction, and splattering everyone present with gore. Some of the corpses twitched as if still alive within the fire. And in the following days, the air stank with a putrescence that could not be kept out of the food that survivors tasted or the water that they drank.

Everyone could agree that Tuyutí was a momentous battle, and that soldiers from both sides had shown extraordinary courage. In terms of sheer numbers it was the greatest battle ever waged in South America. But should it have ever been fought? The Marshal's defenses north of the Bellaco were well established, and he expected an Allied attack in that quarter. Why did he not await Mitre's assault and trust in his prepared defenses, the steadfastness of his soldiers, and the advantages of the terrain?

In pushing ahead with his own attack, López responded to several incontestable facts. The Paraguayan army may have been inferior in numbers and armament, but the Marshal saw no reason to concede the initiative to the Allies if that meant having to wait while they built up still greater strength. If Porto Alegre's troops had had time to arrive from the Misiones, so much the worse, for the Paraguayans could not hope to counter the increased enemy force. Also, the one clear Allied weakness at Tuyutí was an inability to use the fleet, which was too far out of range to help. But if the river had been given time to rise, Tamandaré could blast away at Curuzú and Curupayty as a prelude to breaking through at Humaitá. The Paraguayans would have been outflanked and could not have recovered. López's attack might best be seen in that light.

Having decided to take the initiative, the Marshal needed a workable plan. He never intended a suicidal attack, but what he came up with was still flawed, since it featured simultaneous assaults on all Allied positions without covering fire from Bruguez. But precise timing could never transpire without Barrios, and the latter general stood little chance of gaining the Potrero Pirís in good time (in this sense, the Marshal had set him a near-impossible task). Besides, the idea of turning both flanks of the Allied army while breaking the center at the same time made no allowance for the enemy's artillery. Had López brought up his own guns and concentrated his forces against the poorly defended Allied right, it is doubtful that the Argentines (who had few cannons and no Fôsso de Mallet) could have prevented his destruction of most of their army.[87] The Paraguayans would then have the Brazilians outflanked, and they would have to withdraw to Paso de la Patria. This would delay, although not alter, the course of the campaign.

As matters unfolded, the Allies gained complete command of the field. The Paraguayan army was wrecked beyond easy recovery. As the cries from inside the brambles and yataí stands died down, and the last of López's wounded bled to death, the Allied soldiers permitted themselves an ounce of hard-earned optimism. Humaitá might soon fall, and they could move upriver to Asunción and final victory.

Within the Paraguayan trenches, many were thinking along similar lines, and even those who had escaped unscathed began to despair. Colonel Díaz, with tears in his eyes, bit his lip and reported to the Marshal that "I gave the darkies a good bruising, sir, but I couldn't strip them of their hide."[88] "But you did your duty," answered López, "and guaranteed the safe return of Barrios, who would have been cut off otherwise; you've shown energy never before seen, and reorganized your forces three times under a withering enemy fire."[89] The next day Díaz was promoted to general, along with Bruguez, whose artillery had played no role in the engagement.

The Marshal's liberality on this occasion contrasted with his usual impatience. He did not bother to reprimand those officers who had done less than sterling work; Barrios, for example, had failed to initiate his attack at the right time, and Resquín had returned to his point of departure before completing the assigned maneuver.[90] Marcó was alone in receiving a reproach from López, a smirk at the colonel's supposed lack of fortitude for having abandoned the field after receiving an inconsequential wound (the bones of his left hand, in fact, had been pulverized by a ball).[91] Perhaps the Marshal failed to grasp the magnitude of his defeat, despite the evidence before his eyes. Perhaps he could not accept its implications even if he understood them. Either way, he dictated a report for El Semanario that depicted Tuyutí as a tremendous victory.[92]

Why did López seem so complacent and calm in the face of a disaster that cost him thirteen thousand casualties? To understand his reaction, we need only recall a passing comment he made to Colonel Wisner as the battle raged: in mid-afternoon, as the two men inspected a battalion of soldiers returning wounded from the field, the Marshal turned to the Hungarian and asked, "Well, what do you think?" "Sir," Wisner responded, "it is the greatest battle ever fought in South America." Visibly pleased with this statement, López nodded in agreement, and before he rode off, he said, "I think the same as you."[93] He felt flattered, it seemed, to be the author of so much glory and bloodshed.

3

A MARCH THROUGH THE SWAMPS

The Allied victory at Tuyutí certainly provided the necessary impetus to eliminate López. While Mitre's troops had sustained serious losses in men and matériel, these could be replaced—something the Paraguayans found increasingly difficult to do. The Allies also enjoyed positive momentum. Their navy, still fresh and ready for the fight, could shell the half-constructed river defenses just south of Humaitá at Curuzú and Curupayty, before pushing on with relative ease against the fortress of Humaitá, outflanking the enemy in the process. Moreover, despite the Marshal's reassurances that his losses amounted to little, the true costs of Tuyutí were sure to dampen Paraguayan spirits in short order. From disappointment would come disenchantment, and from disenchantment would come victory—or so Mitre and the other Allied commanders hoped.

The Argentine president had a comprehensive win within his reach. But he squandered this opportunity, and this was neither the first nor the last time that this occurred during the war. Instead of following the triumph at Tuyutí with unremitting attacks, the Allies suspended operations and established defenses along the south side of the northern Bellaco. The Paraguayans did the same on the north side. A lull set in, and for no good reason.

The Marshal's men were physically exhausted. The recent defeat had challenged their resolve, but they showed no sign of panic, or even anxiety. Instead, they set themselves to the laborious task of entrenchment, extending and reinforcing a series of works already in place, something accomplished with little real effort. Their commander still seemed unflappable, despite the odds against him, and he ordered heavy artillery from Humaitá and Asunción placed along the line. As Thompson noted, the trenches

> were dug with activity, and artillery … was mounted at the parapets. Three 8-inch guns were placed in the center, between Paso Gómez and Paso Fernández. In this short line of trench … thirty-seven pieces of artillery were crowded, of every imaginable size and shape. All sorts of old honeycombed carronades, 18-pounders—everything which by a stretch of courtesy could be called a gun—were made to do service by the Paraguayans. Artillery was also placed at the trench of the Potrero Sauce.[1]

These preparations provided clear proof of the Marshal's determination to continue his resistance, even though the Allies had severely tested his army.

Mitre could be criticized for giving the Paraguayans a breathing space, but in truth he never showed a fondness for the attack; the battles of Estero Bellaco and Tuyutí had come about through the Marshal's initiative. Though in tactical terms the Allies fought well on both occasions, their final strategic goal—Asunción—remained distant and unlikely to fall without a major effort. Every day they dawdled kept them that much further from victory.

Mitre cited supply problems for the delay, and there was something to this. His field commanders had complained about the shortage of cavalry horses and draft animals, which predated Tuyutí, if we are to believe the correspondence that passed between Mitre, his vice president, and other functionaries.[2] A council of war that included Flores, Osório, and Mitre (but not Tamandaré) took place at Tuyutí on 30 May; the lack of horses and mules received a full hearing, as did the need for cohesion among the Allied land forces. The commanders certainly vented their frustration, but they failed to mount any significant naval action. The Allies made no advances along the Chaco bank of the river, not was any serious reconnaissance north or east of their line attempted.

The Argentine president may have wished to weigh practical considerations, but he also had to think about politics. Though official reports made no allusions to it, ongoing friction between Mitre and Tamandaré made inter-service cooperation difficult. A year earlier, when the Allies decided, as a matter of strategy, to keep naval advance even with the army's line of march, they failed to anticipate the soggy terrain. They repeatedly lost the chance to turn the enemy flank because Mitre and Tamandaré refused to deviate from the agreed strategy. The admiral worried about the loss of ships to mines or hidden sandbars; both men worried about politics.

How did Tamandaré perceive his role now that Mitre's armies had won so convincingly at Tuyutí without his aid? The admiral had always judged himself senior to his Argentine rival, who let him think that way in exchange for naval cooperation; now the Brazilian could no longer feel so secure. He had already lambasted Mitre as "everything save a general," but the Argentine had the command, and this vexed the admiral to no end.[3] Real cohesion between the two Allied forces remained elusive as a result. Tamandaré had made only one recent attempt to get into the fight, when, on 20 May, he sent sixteen gunboats up the Paraguay to survey the enemy works at Curupayty. The squadron took a brief look, then retired downriver. Thereafter the admiral refused to retake the offensive, and instead remained anchored far to the south of the enemy.

Mitre viewed the issue of offensive action differently. He may have lacked the killer instinct so useful in war, but in any case he had slipped into a bad habit of waiting for the Paraguayans to make the first move. They made no sign of renewing their attacks, however. Inertia on one side led to inertia on the other, to the point where outside observers could begin speaking of a stalemate.

The First of Many Lulls

Behind the lines, preparations for a more protracted struggle had already begun. For Paraguay, this meant yet another spate of recruitment in the most distant *pueblitos* of the country. On 1 June 1866, Vice President Sánchez issued a circular that required the immediate conscription of those still fit for service. Each village could exempt its resident *juez de paz* or *jefe de milícias* from the call-up, and each state ranch (*estancia de la república*) could retain two older men (with their families) to care for the cattle and ranch houses. All other *peones*, however, had to report for duty, bringing their remaining horses. Private ranchers also had to supply two horses each for the war effort. The Payaguáes, who lived in encampments (*tolderías*) on the outskirts of the capital, were likewise pressed into service. Even convicts and church wardens received orders to travel south at once. The general conscription omitted only slaves and the foreign-born.[4]

The new recruits gathered at Asunción and Villa Franca, where they were joined by groups of walking wounded released from hospital, and given the bare minimum of training. All boarded steamers bound for Humaitá.[5] The efficiency of the new recruitment was such that, within three weeks' time, the Marshal had increased his troop strength in the south to around twenty thousand men.[6]

Scouring the Paraguayan countryside may have solved the immediate need for manpower, but it dealt a blow to the production of foodstuffs. Though Paraguayan women had engaged extensively in agricultural labor even before the war, they could not have welcomed the added responsibility. As men were impressed, horses and oxen were seized, which made it impossible to maintain levels of productivity in maize and other crops that required plowing. Though malnutrition had yet to affect areas far removed from the fight, it soon would as a result.

The men journeying south had positions waiting for them at the Bellaco. While these trench works might once have stopped, or at least delayed, the Allied army, the Paraguayans could no longer count on this. The Marshal had acted rashly at Tuyutí, and now he had to stay within his lines. His artillery still presented the Allies with a major challenge, though they could not know how formidable these defenses were.

Before Mitre could advance, he had to understand his opponent's strengths—and yet he tended to discount the crumbs of intelligence that came his way. He had no maps of the area, just a general sense of lagoons behind other lagoons, but he failed to call for scouts to identify possible lines of attack, or even inspect the terrain. Instead, he ordered his men to hold their positions, before abruptly telling them, on 2 June, to pull back beyond the range of Paraguayan guns. He then constructed a long line of trenches, complete with parapets and wooden observation platforms (*mangrullos*), some sixty feet high, from which his frontline units attempted to learn what they could of enemy intentions.

Mitre refused to launch any new attacks. The reason is a little obscure, though much of the explanation—or blame—must rest on the inefficiency of a military command in which real power was shared by Mitre, Flores, Osório, Tamandaré, and, in part, Porto Alegre. But there were also the political challenges that Mitre faced as Argentine head of state. He could never afford to discount the long-term political costs of his unpopular alliance with Brazil; now that he had won an unmistakable victory, he could only hope that the Paraguayans would face facts and accede to Allied territorial demands. López could then depart for a comfortable European exile with Madame Lynch and their children—a resolution to the conflict that would satisfy honor and leave Mitre to consolidate the political gains he had won in Argentina. Even a miniscule show of common sense on all sides might well facilitate an end to hostilities: it had worked that way after the 1861 battle of Pavón, when Mitre arranged the honorable withdrawal of his chief provincial rival, Justo José de Urquiza. Why not now?

López took pleasure in claiming that Mitre had abandoned the offensive out of sheer fright. This was a comforting bit of self-delusion. Any realistic appraisal of the situation should have inclined the Marshal toward greater prudence, and caused him to ask why the Allies had slowed their advance when so little impeded them. In general, when forced onto the defensive, he calculated quite well. In this case, though he could no longer spare men for large-scale raiding, he still thought Mitre could be goaded into a costly assault. He thus ordered regular bombardments of the Allied lines, causing the enemy troopers to flatten themselves upon the sodden ground like field mice squeezing under a closed door. He also sent sharpshooters to harass the Allies on the other side of the Bellaco in an attempt to make his army irksome, if not quite lethal, to the enemy.

Mitre had been weaned on many hours of drawing-room debate with other Argentine exiles in Santiago and Montevideo. These experiences taught him that mutual concessions and deal-making could yield a thousand benefits, even for the backward caudillos of the interior—a rustic class of men into which he mistakenly placed Marshal López. Mitre felt certain that, given time for reflection, both his Paraguayan opponents and Brazilian allies would come around to his pragmatic way of thinking. Inaction might even open the door to peace.

Mitre had to act as Allied commander as well, and here his reticence to attack drew upon a different rationale. He owed his reputation as a general to his skill as an organizer rather than as a tactician. He had put the Allied army together during the winter and early spring of 1865, overseeing its outfitting and training. Now, this very unmilitary military man once again had to address practical concerns. While Osório, Flores, and all the others insisted that he attack without delay, he saw the need to rearm his troops, bring up horses, and restock his victuals.

There was much to do. At Cerrito Island, near the confluence of the Paraná and the Paraguay, the Brazilians constructed storehouses, clinics, and workshops to repair Tamandaré's steamers. At the Bellaco itself, Allied soldiers set up new camps. One of their most pressing tasks, even now, was to bury the dead from the earlier battle. The stench of unburied corpses among the brambles gave their position away, but on the front lines, where enemy snipers remained active, the Allied troops could ill afford to leave their trenches; they would have to tolerate the nauseating smell as best they could. Mitre's officers insisted on keeping the camps orderly. The men pitched their tents in regular rows, gathered firewood, cleaned their weapons, and scraped mud from their boots. They butchered cattle and doled out portions of meat to every squad. They dug latrines and set up laundries. It was nonetheless difficult to keep tidy, for filth always accumulated on the ground, and the freezing rain pelted the men incessantly.

The *viento sur* scattered dirt into every tent and cook pot. Even the thickest woolens refused to stay dry in such weather. Every man complained of a cough or a skin rash. And this was not all. Malaria (*chucho*), dysentery, measles, and smallpox worked their way into camp and carried away many unfortunates, including the Riograndense General Antonio de Souza Netto, a white-haired sexagenarian who took ill and died in hospital two weeks later.[7] The number of afflicted who reached the medical facilities at Corrientes amounted to over five thousand in June, and this figure excluded patients in intermediate *puestos*, or aid stations.[8] Since the total number of trained physicians for the entire theater rarely exceeded twenty men, the medical situation must have been desperate.

The sanitary conditions in the Allied camps at Tuyutí left much to be desired, and the medical situation was intolerable. But the supply line to the camp did start to improve in June 1866. Caravans of oxcarts ferried ammunition and powder, food, blankets, and clothing from Paso de la Patria; and, as the river rose, some supplies got through by way of the Río Paraguay. Every arrival of provisions inspired celebration, especially among the officers, who competed to see who could host the most resplendent "banquet" made from recently arrived victuals.[9] German and Italian sutlers also hawked a variety of general merchandise out of wagons and merchant ships, catering to soldiers with enough money to afford canned oysters, liquor, or a new pair of shoes. Even the shoddiest goods demanded a high price.[10]

It was not all profit for the sutlers, however. Every one of them was new to the area, and apt to feel disoriented and nervous. One observer reported that, like the soldiers, the operatives of the "floating bakeries" had all come down with fever. They nonetheless kept their ovens roaring into the night to supply fresh bread in exchange for a substantial return.[11] And there were other dangers. Lucio Mansilla tells the tale of a drunken corporal condemned to death for knifing a sutler, the murdered man having sold him the liquor.[12]

Observers writing in June 1866 cited the Paraguayan artillery, which suggests the general effectiveness of López's gunners. Most Allied positions lay beyond Paraguayan range, however, and few of the shells hit their targets. Even so, no one could get used to the shelling. General Flores, who the Marshal frequently targeted, had a few narrow escapes during these barrages. On 8 June, a shell exploded in front of his tent. Eleven days later the enemy gunners scored a direct hit on it (though the Uruguayan president was absent at the time).[13] The older veterans treated Paraguayan marksmanship with utter contempt, yet none could claim to be getting unbroken sleep. They all understood that enemy projectiles had been recast from spent Allied shells, and if López's men showed enough ingenuity, they might even be capable of another attack.

On 14 June López ordered an artillery barrage to coincide with a major feint at the Allied left and center. The black-bearded Bruguez, now a general, gave the signal for all batteries to commence firing at 11:30 a.m. The shots fell wide at the outset, but the Paraguayans adjusted their fire, and over the next six hours threw an uninterrupted shower of shot and canister. No fewer than 3,000 shells fell on Mitre's forces, leaving 103 men killed or wounded.[14] A wide-ranging assault was likely to start after dusk, and the Allied soldiers steeled themselves accordingly. The Paraguayans opened up at that time with several sharp volleys of musketry, somehow managing to set fire to several enemy tents, but their dreaded attack never came. For its part, the Allied artillery barely answered.[15]

As the weeks went by, Allied troopers began to understand that the victory at Tuyutí would not compel a Paraguayan collapse. Quite the contrary: the enemy had shown such resilience that few doubted the Marshal's intention to take the offensive again. Having fostered a buoyant, cheerful feeling among his men, Mitre watched it evaporate, and no amount of provisions could restore the optimism once it had fled. Every show of despondency on the Allied side fed the Marshal's belief that he could hold out. His strategy stressed an active defense, and if he could not attack, then he probed, harassed, and kept the enemy bewildered. All the while, his men dug more trenches, extending the line until it abutted the Allied left, and from that spot, they concentrated fire on selected points and shouted insults at the enemy in Guaraní. At night, López's military bands played *malambos* and *galopas* until a late hour in what seemed to the Allies a most improbable revelry.[16] The Paraguayan cause was still alive.

Protest, Dissillusionment, and Attempts at Peacemaking

It was natural that the soldiers' exasperation would soon be communicated to the home front. Though war-weariness on a large scale had yet to emerge in the Allied countries, various factions called for a negotiated settlement. In Argentina, some of these appeals reflected a pragmatic temperament, like that of Mitre's. More often, demands for peace overlapped with a broader disavowal of the national government's alliance with Brazil. In its editorial of 22 June 1866, the opposition newspaper *El Nacional* denounced the senseless turn of events:

> The campaign in Paraguay has entered its second year, and [led] the Argentine Republic [into the deepest] tragedy. … [We find ourselves] bloodied and exhausted of resources, of gold and credit. … Such is the campaign against the Russia of South America, defended by its marshes and sloughs, its diseases and thick forests, and by inhabitants who never surrender save at the tip of a sword. Thus far, the engagements have all been massacres without result save to pile up thousands of killed and wounded, without our advancing a step forward nor breaking the will of an enemy disposed to defend his soil, man by man, inch by inch. [It has become] a war of extermination, and if things continue, within five months the Argentine army will be decimated by disease and by the shot of the Paraguayans; [even if we win] we will see our flag shredded into a skeleton.[17]

These sentiments were hardly novel. Ever since the fall of Rosas fourteen years earlier, the Argentine political system had tolerated a degree of dissension. The Mitre government reflected a consensus between urban elites, certain caudillos from the Interior and Litoral provinces, and wealthy Bonaerense landowners. The system permitted public rebukes of specific policies, including Mitre's alliance with Brazil and his prosecution of the war. By mid-1866, most Argentine politicians realized that the Marshal had ceased to pose a credible threat.

Since national survival was no longer at stake, much of the political divisiveness that had vanished with the initial Paraguayan invasion started to reassert itself. Hence it followed for Mitre that the most desirable road to peace was also the shortest. If he delayed negotiations because of prior commitments to the empire, he needed to disavow those obligations. A number of well-placed Argentines had already issued calls for peace. These included future president Manuel Quintana; José Hernández, future author of the gaucho epic *Martín Fierro*; writer José Mármol, best known for his heartrending romantic novel *Amalia* (1851); and Juan Bautista Alberdi, the animating force behind the 1853 constitution.[18] For his part Mitre tolerated this hectoring as the price of conducting politics.

But he had his limits.[19] On 20 June 1866 his police arrested Agustín de Vedia, the editor of the opposition newspaper *La América*, and a supposed "agent of Paraguayan and Chilean interests." The editor, whose real offense had been to denounce the war, was sent into internal exile in Patagonia.[20] His arrest, however, proved an exceptional act, for neither the president's liberal instincts nor his own background as a journalist encouraged the suppression of antiwar newspapers. He might stigmatize dissent, but he could not criminalize it without risking opposition from within his own Liberal Party.

Some pro-war newspapers did revise their stance around this time. The once-bellicose *El Nacional* now alluded to an Argentina "drained of resources." The paper reported that law students at the local *facultad* had protested the presence in Buenos Aires of wounded veterans, who, filthy and unclothed, and at risk of infection from tetanus, could only survive through begging. The message could not be clearer: the war had to stop.[21]

The most stinging criticism of Mitre's leadership came in the form of an essay serialized in *La Tribuna* of Buenos Aires. Entitled "El gobierno y la alianza," it was written by Carlos Guido y Spano (1827–1916), a poet of no mean accomplishments and the scion of an old family whose senior members had served Rosas.[22] Guido y Spano's bona fides as an Argentine patriot were as good as Mitre's, a fact that gave his antiwar diatribe legitimacy in the eyes of many Porteños. Guido y Spano insisted that the president had subverted the national interest in favor of Brazil, first in the Banda Oriental and now in Paraguay. By playing stooge to the crafty diplomats of Rio de Janeiro, Mitre had jettisoned the dream of Argentine grandeur, and ceded to the empire his country's primacy on the continent.[23] Despite these doubts, the president could depend on political associates in Buenos Aires, quite a few of whom had made fortunes selling beef, galleta, and other supplies to the Brazilian army.[24] These men would willingly spend their own capital to counter any protests against such a profitable alliance.

It was a bit more complex in the Litoral provinces, where longstanding anti-Brazilian sympathies were difficult to stanch even with the promise of big earnings. One figure who enriched himself was General Urquiza, former head of the old confederal government, whose ranches supplied horses and cattle to the imperial army. These sales—and the pro-Brazilian political inclination they signaled—irritated many of Urquiza's fellow Entrerrianos, who had already made their dissension felt in a variety of ways (including mass desertions from the Mitre's army in July and November 1865).[25] Urquiza encountered more friction with his fellow provincials as the war dragged on—unavoidable, perhaps, for a caudillo whose idea of authority conflicted with a people known for their spirit of independence.

The latent opposition of the rural poor and the eloquent disdain of urban intellectuals gave the antiwar sentiment palpable energy. The Brazilians had everything to gain from the continued campaign against López, Guido y Spano had argued, for not only would the Plata remain divided (one of Rio's long-term foreign policy goals), but Paraguay would fall to the empire. This would leave "Mitre, like General Flores, a Brazilian commander with a handful of men."[26]

This was logical reasoning, but it disregarded one inconvenient fact: in Brazil, one could find almost as much nascent opposition to the war as in Argentina. And it took a similar form. For the Brazilians, antiwar opinion stemmed from both regional and class identities. In general, the further one went from the cities of Rio and São Paulo, the less one met with unbroken support for the war. The peasants had never shown much animus toward Paraguay. They had joined in the earlier war fever because the offended dignity of the emperor demanded a show of loyalty. Those who lived in the north and northeast were inclined to think the conflict irrelevant, an attitude shared by politicians in regional centers like Fortaleza, Natal, and Recife.

In the larger cities of the center and south, and in the countryside of Rio Grande do Sul, pro-war sentiment still retained its sway among most sectors of the population. The patriotic enthusiasm shown at the time of the Mato Grosso invasion had nevertheless worn thin. Middle-class citizens no longer displayed the earlier spirit of volunteerism, as in 1865. Like their Argentine counterparts, they asked when the campaign would end so that their sons could come home.

Though the Brazilian elite had yet to produce a Carlos Guido y Spano who could crystallize these feelings into a coherent political critique, an ample array of commentators did deride government war policies. The most eloquent was the novelist José de Alencar (1829–1877), the Balzac of Brazil, who, under the pseudonym Erasmus, published a series of letters, first to the general public and then to the emperor, calling for a prompt end to the war and for the emancipation of the slaves.[27] Dom Pedro, who was shackled to his own brand of liberal paternalism, never tried to suppress these jabs at his ministers. Instead, he condescended to treat his critics with an affected indifference. They may have emitted an irritating and monotonous trilling like the insects in the tropical night, he believed, but they were just as harmless.

In Uruguay, the partisan frictions that had given rise to the war in 1864 and 1865 had never abated. The Brazilian military presence kept Flores's Blanco opponents in check, but they were just biding their time, waiting to rebel once again. More importantly, a growing number of dissidents from within the president's own Colorado Party had started to raise their voices against *his* war. So strong was anti-war sentiment in Montevideo that Flores announced his intention in late June to return to the Uruguayan capital to arrange new recruitment, though in truth he hoped to shore up wavering Colorado support for the campaign. That he had to delay his departure proved galling, for he had a good sense of the trouble brewing back home and the need to address grievances.[28]

The lull in the fighting after Tuyutí thus brought uncertainty in the Allied countries. It also spurred talk among outsiders who hoped to see a negotiated and prompt end to the conflict; rumors of a French mediation had evidently made the rounds in both Buenos Aires and Rio. But with the Quai d'Orsay so notoriously committed to preserving the unpopular Maximilian regime in Mexico, this was hardly a propitious time for a new diplomatic campaign in South America.[29]

One of the Andean countries might have played the role of mediator. All had remained neutral, but none could afford to be indifferent to the conflict in Paraguay. The war had already cost thousands of lives and had not advanced the interests of the continent in any way. The recent Spanish intervention in Peru's Chincha Islands had inspired fears of renewed European imperialism in South America (which Pedro II, as a monarch with European antecedents, was thought to support). According to this notion, the "in-fighting" between Paraguay and Argentina constituted a significant diversion from a genuine need for continental defense. Thus, on 21 June 1866, the Peruvian representative in Montevideo directed a letter to the governments of the Triple Alliance offering to arrange a cease-fire. The Marshal and his ministers never received word of this offer, however, as it was impossible to get the message through the Allied blockade.

The Peruvian's gesture was taken independently of a similar initiative started weeks earlier by Andean ministers in Buenos Aires. But it, too, stood little chance of success.[30] Policymakers in Rio understood the mistrust with which the Peruvian, Chilean, and Bolivian governments regarded them; they were thus unwilling to accept the agents of these republics as honest brokers. Besides, no one had consulted López, and no one could predict his reaction. The Marshal's artillery barrages, his new recruitment, his execution by beheading of nine deserters (and one loose-lipped defeatist) suggested nothing if not continued truculence.[31] So did the words of *El Semanario*, which insisted that Paraguay neither "desired, nor needed, mediations" from anyone.[32]

The one person in a position to offer real help was Charles Ames Washburn, the US minister to Asunción. The United States was regarded as a powerful though distant country with limited commercial interests in the region, a fact that promised genuine and irreproachable neutrality. Washburn, moreover, had an ambitious streak. Having been relegated by fate to a secondary role in a family of over-achievers, he badly wanted to shine like his brothers; the Paraguayan War presented him with the right challenge, if only he could get the contending parties to the conference table.[33] For the time being, however, a meeting proved impossible. Washburn had earlier forged good relations with the Marshal and his officials in the Paraguayan Foreign Ministry, and had enjoyed correct—if lukewarm—relations with Brazilian and Argentine representatives. But after the war began he took home leave and ended up stranded for six months in Corrientes, where the Allied military commanders seemed little inclined to expedite his passage upriver; they would have preferred that López have no accredited foreign diplomats in the country at all. Washburn, not surprisingly, seethed at the delay (and the implied disrespect to his flag). He sent notes of protest to Mitre, to Tamandaré, and to his superiors in Washington, but this got him nowhere.

Yataity Corã

Washburn and the others might have failed no matter what; all we know for sure is that the Allies had to plan for the next engagement. One key element in their strategy was the disposition of Porto Alegre's army. The high command had hoped at one time to use this twelve-thousand-man force to open a front through Encarnación in an attempt to draw enemy troops away from Humaitá and guard the Allied right flank above Tuyutí. A perusal of the map made this mission look desirable, for an attacking force should strike against the enemy's most vulnerable point rather than against his strongest bulwark at Humaitá.

But Encarnación was never a reasonable objective. For one thing, Porto Alegre seemed a reluctant subordinate who bristled under superior orders, and from the beginning he expressed doubts about the wisdom of such a gambit. Though he was willing to accept Mitre's initial instructions, he nonetheless complained to the Brazilian war minister about their impracticality. Many Paraguayan launches blocked the river channel and were sure to challenge the passage of his army. Even if he managed to get all of his troops across the Paraná, they would need to pass through two hundred miles of "wasteland" where foraging would yield little, at least until the vanguard reached Villarrica.[34] The Brazilians would have to build supply depots in their rear as they advanced, and they lacked everything they needed to do so. The suggested line of march north of Encarnación precluded naval support, and almost nothing was understood of the terrain and whatever enemy forces might lie ahead.

In the end, Mitre and the Brazilian generals shelved the idea of a new front. Porto Alegre, whose troops had already met the Paraguayans in a few skirmishes in the Misiones, received orders to advance down the left bank of the Paraná to link up with the main Allied force. This was no easy going, either, and by late June he had gotten no closer than Itatí, still twenty leagues from the front.[35]

If the Allied command had as yet found no way to use Porto Alegre's troops, the Paraguayans could not afford to ignore them. If they joined with Mitre or launched an attack from an alternative direction, the Marshal might need to yield his strong position at the Bellaco. This possibility suggested to López that he attack with all available forces and disrupt the Allied buildup before the new troops arrived. This might delay the inevitable, or it might bring concessions at the negotiating table.

The Paraguayans had probed the enemy's forward lines and discovered a weak spot on the Allied right near a large grove of palm trees called Yataity Corã. At three in the afternoon on 10 July, López's men struck at this point with two infantry battalions. The assault succeeded for a time in cutting off several Allied units recently arrived from the western Argentine province of Catamarca. The Paraguayans had fired their Congreve rockets at close range, setting the grass aflame, blanketing the scene with so much smoke that it became impossible to observe Allied reserves moving up from the south.[36] The latter units, all of them Correntino infantry, set up a loud fusillade, which drove the Paraguayans back toward their own lines.[37]

The next day, they tried again. This time, their attack was preceded by a bombardment of rockets and 68-pounders against the entire Allied line. General Díaz, who had received two wounds at Tuyutí, led the charge down the Leguizamón Pass with twenty-five hundred men at his side. His troops punched their way into the foremost of the enemy units, but the five Argentine battalions they encountered at the opening of the Pass put up a stolid resistance. Then, to add to the confusion occasioned by the smoke and noise of battle, an ugly sandstorm blew in from the Chaco. These storms, which are a normal part of the irksome *viento norte*, are familiar occurrences in that part of Paraguay. On this occasion, they caused the Argentines to hesitate. They might have given way completely had it not been for Colonel Ignacio Rivas, who remained cool under fire and kept his men steady.

The white-whiskered General Wenceslao Paunero (who, like Rivas, was born in Uruguay) had moved up to reinforce the frontline units, and, seeing that the sun had already started to set, wanted to break off the engagement. The general evidently believed that the Paraguayans would make no further advances under the veil of darkness, and so held his troops back. Yet just as the firing started to die down, at seven in the evening, he received instructions from Mitre to launch a counterattack.

Paunero had little confidence in this order. His men had already grown fatigued and could see nothing through the smoke, sand, and gathering darkness. Yet they pushed ahead as he gave the command to attack. Within minutes, what had been an uncomfortable but limited clash erupted into complete chaos. Soldiers fired their weapons blindly toward the enemy, and the Paraguayan infantry barreled into the Argentine line, only to be pushed back. Mitre then moved up with two more battalions and managed to seize the contested ground, after which he was attacked even more fiercely by Díaz, who rained rockets down upon him. One exploded a few feet from the Argentine president, and another came close to killing General Flores, who had ridden over from the center to observe the action.

At this juncture, Colonel Rivas brought five fresh battalions from the rear. This gave the Allies an advantage of eleven battalions against the Paraguayans' four. This proved too much even for the hard-fighting Díaz, who gave the order to retreat at 9:00 p.m., leaving the greater part of the field smoldering. The battle of Yataity Corã cost the Paraguayans four hundred dead and wounded. The Argentines lost just under three hundred, including three field officers.[38]

Predictably, both sides claimed victory. Natalicio Talavera, correspondent for *El Semanario*, declared himself unable to describe the jubilation he witnessed in the Paraguayan camp.[39] In truth, the Paraguayans should not have celebrated. As Thompson observed, the battle was "just another instance in which López weakened himself in small combats, where there was no advantage to be gained."[40] Nevertheless, Mitre refused to throw the weight of his army against the strong Paraguayan lines at the north end of the Bellaco. If Yataity Corã is best understood as an effort to excite the Allies into a major attack, then it failed. On the other hand, the engagement demonstrated the efficacy of the Congreve rocket, which came close to killing both Mitre and Flores. The battle also underlined a certain hesitation on the part of the Argentine commanders, who might have destroyed the enemy force had they pursued it with greater determination.

Boquerón

Some two thousand of Porto Alegre's cavalrymen reached the Estero Bellaco on 12 July, followed by the bulk of the baron's forces, which included fourteen thousand horses. López continued to hope that he could inveigle the Allies into a frontal assault on the Paraguayan line, although Porto Alegre's reinforcements made that proposition more dangerous. The Marshal remained undeterred, however, for even now his strongest positions could withstand anything.

The Allied left had many weaknesses. Enclosed on three sides by palmettos, the adjacent Potreros Sauce and Pirís enjoyed protection from Allied fire, yet contained various little openings in the undergrowth through which the Paraguayans could pour troops at will. Tuyutí had demonstrated the imprudence of launching a general engagement using these openings, but the pastures still permitted less ambitious incursions. López now decided to move several of his heavier artillery pieces into the mouth of the Sauce so as to direct fire on the enemy headquarters. As Mitre, Flores, and Osório were breakfasting, they could expect a ration of round shot with their black beans (*feijão*) and coffee. Even if every senior officer survived the shelling, they would have to silence the guns. This, López hoped, would bring on the major assault.

On 13 July, the Marshal ordered General Díaz, Colonel José Elizardo Aquino, and Major George Thompson to reconnoiter the no-man's land as far as the Punta Ñaró. Thompson reported back that the woods were strewn with unburied corpses from the battle of 24 May, and that his party of fifty riflemen had spotted Allied pickets on several occasions. Yet the Brazilians, who had also caught sight of the Paraguayans, seemed less interested in fighting than in protecting their herds of cattle from what they presumed was a raiding party. There was also a frightening moment for the fifty intruders when an enormous river mine detonated several miles up the Paraguay, drawing the attention of every enemy soldier along the line. Luckily for Thompson and his men, the Allied troopers did nothing except wonder aloud if a Brazilian warship had gone down. None had, and the Paraguayan reconnaissance party slipped through unscathed.[41]

Thompson assured López that he could erect a line of deep trenches, one at the northern mouth of the Potrero Sauce near the Punta Ñaró, and another at the southern mouth below the thickly wooded Carapá Island. The latter afforded a full view of the Allied position some five hundred yards from Mitre's headquarters.[42]

The Marshal wasted no time upon hearing this news. That same night,

> all the spades, shovels, and picks in the army, amounting to about 700, were sent down to Sauce, and … the greatest silence was enjoined on the men, lest they should let their spades and arms clank, as the enemy would inevitably hear them. A hundred men were posted in skirmishing order, twenty yards from the line to be dug to cover the work; and in order better to see anyone approaching, they lay down on their stomachs. In some places they were so mixed up with the corpses that it was impossible to tell which was which in the dark. [They erected cowhides to conceal the light of their lanterns] … and began by digging a trench one yard wide and one deep, throwing the earth to the front, so as to get a cover for their bodies as quickly as possible. The enemy's lines were so near that we could distinctly hear … the laughing and coughing in their camp … but, wonderfully enough, the enemy perceived nothing till the sun rose, when the whole length of the trench, 900 yards, was [visible to all].[43]

The next morning the Brazilians stared at this work with a cold fury. Not only had López succeeded in erecting a major trench in front of the Allied line; he had done so in a most audacious and insulting manner after Mitre had claimed the Paraguayans were finished. The new trench ran obliquely to the front, so as to threaten the entire Allied left and menace their communications. Don Bartolo, who could never tolerate the enemy's establishing such a strong redoubt, now had to attack with his full force after all. And he needed to do it quickly, "since today it [would] cost 200 men, tomorrow 500, and afterwards who [knew] how many, for every advance in the enemy construction [would result in an Allied] loss."

In considerable pain from recurrent gout and fed up with Mitre's vacillations, General Osório was plainly frustrated.[44] He still felt uncertain of his place in the Allied hierarchy. His command was on the verge of passing to General Polidoro de Fonseca Quintinilha Jordão, though he had yet to assume his duties and Osório had no desire to push ahead without a clear sense of what his successor proposed to do. Polidoro was already overdue, and another two days went by before he reached the front. In the interim, the Paraguayans dug more trenches just below the Carapá and brought up four heavy guns to better enfilade the opposite units. The Marshal's men accomplished all this under a light Allied bombardment that did no better than pepper the ground.

Mitre doubted the capacity of the new Brazilian commander. Save for a short tour of duty during the Farrapo Rebellion of the 1840s, Polidoro had had no combat experience, and on that occasion—now twenty years past—he had worked exclusively on fortifications. Since then, he had held bureaucratic posts in the army, serving, for example, as head of the military academy in Rio de Janeiro since 1858. His fellow officers considered Polidoro a martinet: honest, proficient, even meticulous. But unlike Osório, he was no soldier's soldier, and he could not transform himself into one overnight.[45]

Mitre met with the other Allied commanders (save for Tamandaré) on the night of 15 July, and together they conceived a plan of attack. Just before dawn the next day, the hesitant Polidoro struck with all the force he could manage. The eastern sky had just started to redden when Flores's artillery boomed and eight battalions of Brazilian infantrymen lunged forward together with a unit of engineers operating four LaHitte field guns. Their objective was to seize the southernmost of the two trench works.

The Brazilians advanced in two columns, with General José Luis Mena Barreto's 5th Brigade hugging the palmettos on the left, and General Guilherme Xavier de Souza's main force attacking the center. The morning fog allowed Mena Barreto to wriggle his way unseen through the undergrowth above the Potrero Pirís; from there, his troops fell upon the Paraguayan flank, while the remaining units attacked the trenches head-on.[46] López's soldiers were surprised while still engaged in entrenching, and attempted to beat back the thirty-five hundred Brazilians with their shovels. The Marshal's guns opened fire, but defending against such numbers was asking too much. An hour later, General Guilherme, as he was universally called, carried the newly dug trench and drove the enemy northward to the woods, where they turned and resumed fire. The Brazilians now held the southern trenches, but this offered minimal protection from enemy musketry.

Paraguayan reserves poured in from the Sauce as the Allies pressed ahead from the shorter mouth of the Pirís. General Guilherme's men managed to get within thirty paces of the Paraguayans before they were thrown back in disarray. At 11:00 a.m., after six hours of hard fighting and a loss of over one-third of their strength, the Brazilians withdrew to the same line of trenches they had taken in the morning. Here they learned that Mena Barreto had also been driven back. The Brazilians now held their position and waited for the reinforcements they knew Polidoro would send. To resume the attack, they needed to silence the Paraguayan guns at Punta Ñaró, which had fired so many Congreve rockets that it resembled a public fireworks display.[47]

At noon, a fresh Brazilian division commanded by a forty-five-year-old brigadier from Bahia, Alexandre Gomes Argolo Ferrão, replaced Guilherme's and the fight started all over again.[48] Although the hawk-faced Argolo had hoped to get behind the Paraguayan guns, he had to satisfy himself with holding the trenches recently won. This proved costly. Every half hour the Marshal sent fresh battalions to attack in waves, hoping to achieve with bayonets, lances, and sabers what they had failed to achieve with artillery.

Colonel Aquino, who commanded these assaults, maintained the fiercest enthusiasm for the work at hand, calling out to all who could hear him how he wished to kill a *kambá* with his bare hands. Aquino was a complex man, sharp-eyed and attentive to the tiniest of details. Though modest and reserved in peacetime, in war he displayed the same rude courage of a Díaz or an Osório, the feeling Shakespeare's Henry V described as a "stiffening of the sinews, a summoning up of the blood, a hard-favour'd rage."

This was much in evidence during one of the last charges of the day. On horseback and far ahead of his men, Aquino swung his saber to either side as he plunged headlong into a troop of enemy infantry, killing one man before a Minié ball struck him in the gut. But he did not fall. Instead, he galloped back to the Paraguayan lines and, with his hand across his extruded viscera, relinquished command to his subordinate. The mortally wounded commander received a promotion to general, and died in agony two days later. As so often happened during the war, the zeal of an individual soldier brought no real benefit. Aquino's sacrifice might have yielded another dead hero for the soldiers to eulogize, but the Paraguayans continued to hold their position at Punta Ñaró. They failed to drive Argolo from the mouth of the Sauce.

Around ten in the evening, Brigadier Vitorino José Carneiro Monteiro's brigade of five Brazilian battalions moved up to relieve Argolo, with Colonel Emilio Conesa's four Argentine battalions as a reserve. The Allies had enough time to lick their wounds as the last rockets spread a fleeting light over a field of corpses. They had lost fifteen hundred men, the same number as the Paraguayans, and still the battle was only half concluded. The Brazilian engineers began digging the trenches deeper, keeping their labors hidden as best they could from the enemy, who could hear, but not see, what was happening.[49]

A sense of foreboding pervaded both armies as darkness fell. Brigadier Vitorino, who was wounded a few hours later, seems to have had misgivings about surviving the battle. He was not alone. The Uruguayan Colonel Palleja was also nervous. True to habit, he had sat down in front of his tent and composed another letter to the newspapers. To judge from the general tenor of those letters, he had become more pensive of late, more downhearted, more convinced of his own mortality. Less than a week earlier, he had lost his favorite dog "Compañero," who had been blown to bits by a Paraguayan shell while the colonel was inspecting another unit.[50] The little cur had offered good cheer in the long months since the war began, and now that the dog was gone, Palleja felt edgy. His mind turned to thoughts of faraway Spain, of his wife in Montevideo, and of his son, who was also a soldier. He reflected on the recent engagement, noting how keenly Osório's absence had been felt. He also begged his readers to remember to give proper credit to the men who had spilled their blood.[51]

17 July brought a de facto truce that permitted both sides to bury the dead and call for reinforcements. No one considered the issue settled, however. The next morning appeared crisp and clear, with nary a cloud in the sky. López had removed his artillery pieces from the Punta Ñaró, leaving a single rocket stand guarded by an infantry battalion. His men had spent the previous hours cutting a new path (*picada*) through the palmettos of the Carapá so they could again threaten the southern trenches. The Allies got wind of this activity and dispatched infantry to flush the Paraguayans into the open. This brought a heavy response in musketry, for the Marshal's men had hidden themselves well and opened up as soon as the enemy came into view. The Brazilians returned fire, giving lick for lick.

As the casualties mounted around the Carapá, frustration was brewing back at the Allied headquarters. General Flores, who could see the plumes of smoke rising from the nearby forests, apparently believed that the Paraguayans were about to attack. Rather than cede the field, he ordered his best units, including Palleja's Florida Battalion, to storm the Punta Ñaró—not necessarily a thoughtless action, for everyone expected Flores to attack in this quarter, but a risky one nonetheless. The men of the defending 9th Battalion were a seasoned lot, and their commander, the aptly named Major Marcelino Coronel, was as obstinate an officer as could be found in the Marshal's army. Every man in the battalion sought to avenge Aquino.

They did not have to wait long. The Uruguayans approached from two directions, and as they neared, Coronel fired his rockets into them. The barrage was seconded by Bruguez's cannons from the main Paraguayan line above the Paso Gómez. Shell after shell fell among the Uruguayans. The main force managed to get through, charging ahead at the last instant and spilling into the trench. The Paraguayans had time for a single volley and then fled into the bush. Coronel himself got away, only to be killed a few hours later.

With Punta Ñaró in Uruguayan hands, the battle should have ended, for the Allies had secured all the places in contention since 16 July. General Flores, however, wanted to secure the final redoubt guarding the entrance to the Potrero Sauce. Seizing that position would require a charge up the entire length of the Boquerón, a natural break in the underbrush some forty yards across and four hundred long. The Paraguayans had left sharpshooters hidden on either side of this meadow, and they could pour considerable fire onto any units moving in from the south. And in the rear three well-protected guns could wreak havoc from a still greater distance.

If the Allies seized this last entrenchment, they could compromise López's right, which just might force a general retreat from the Bellaco. Flores evidently thought the gamble worth taking and, as at Yataí the previous year, he decided to attack even though his artillery could not yet provide supporting fire.

The Boquerón had never much figured in the Marshal's defensive strategy, but when the Allies started to charge up the clearing, the men under his command realized its value. Flores had embarked on a foolhardy attack and the farther the Allied troops advanced, the more difficult it would be to withdraw. Just getting in position to attack was costly enough, for the Paraguayans laid down a continuous fire—first one shell, then another, and another. No one surprised the Marshal's army this time.

The Allied vanguard was composed of green units of Argentine national guardsmen, the majority from Buenos Aires. They enjoyed support from Palleja's Florida Battalion, which, if anything, had spent too much time in combat. The Argentine commander, a stocky, square-jawed officer of threescore years named Cesáreo Domínguez, ordered the troops to advance in two columns along the margins, with the San Juaninos and Cordobeses on the left, the Entrerrianos and Mendocinos on the right. Since he expected the Paraguayans to focus their fire on the center, he left that part of the field open. It made little difference. As one observer put it, "the Paraguayan demons fought with desperation; drunk with the frenzy of battle, they seemed like angry lions. ...They defended their trench with a blind courage, [and struck out] with bayonet thrusts, with stones and round-shot that they threw by hand, with shovels full of sand flung into the faces of the assaulting troops, with rifle butts, with blows from ramrods, with sabers, with lances."[52]

The Argentine attackers may have lacked experience, and there were moments when their resolve wavered, but they had some daring officers among them. One major, an immigrant called Teófilo Iwanovski, shouted at his Mendocino troopers in a blend of Spanish and German, and gesticulated with a bullet-shattered hand toward the enemy.[53] They may not have understood his language, but they understood what he meant to say. Another major, a displaced *Bersagliere* named Rómulo Giuffra, bled so much that his upper torso looked like a sieve, yet he still urged the San Juaninos forward.[54] The soldiers of the different Argentine provinces were now united in a single body, leaving their regional loyalties behind and acting as patriots rather than rivals.

Together with the Florida Battalion, the Argentines succeeded in scaling the trench and forcing the enemy out. It was a euphoric moment for the Allies to see López's battalions take to their heels. Some of the soldiers climbed the parapets and shouted themselves hoarse with *vivas* to the Alliance, to the national government, and to their home provinces. Others slumped to the ground exhausted, and began biting into rations of charqui and galleta.

Suddenly, even before the last man had drunk from his canteen, a blizzard of musketry erupted from either side of the underbrush, followed by the sound of Paraguayan reinforcements moving down from the Sauce. The happy feeling of victory, which had seemed so sweet a few minutes before, turned sour at once. Colonel Domínguez faced six battalions of fresh Paraguayan infantry and a regiment of dismounted cavalry, all under the command of an irate General Díaz, who led from the front as usual.

The Argentine commander had no time for hesitation. He called for reinforcements and ordered his soldiers to spike the cannons that had so recently fallen into his hands. The men might well have panicked, for everything was pandemonium, but, for want of simple energy, they could not run. Instead, they abandoned the trench and fought as best they could while pulling back toward their original lines. Many fell dead as López's men rushed down the Boquerón like a torrent.

Domínguez, who had had two horses shot from underneath him during the battle, tried to direct fire with the little ammunition he had at his disposal. Now on foot, he turned to address Palleja, who had come up to stand near him, but before the words could leave the Argentine colonel's lips, he realized that the Spaniard was dead, split open by a cannon ball, and lying crumpled upon the ground. Domínguez cursed, and ordered his men to carry away the body.[55]

Less than ten minutes later, the last of the Argentine soldiers hobbled back to their original lines. They looked dejected, with torn uniforms and faces splattered with mud. A few had lost their muskets and rucksacks and all seemed disoriented, perhaps even ashamed. The men in the Uruguayan units probably felt much worse. They had lost their commander, whom even the Paraguayan recruits among them had learned to admire. Without question, Palleja had proven a heroic leader, and he was also decent and humane. He had dedicated his life to the profession of arms, and whether he defended the Carlists in Spain, or the political interests of the Colorados in the Banda Oriental, he always showed solicitude for the men around him. His letters from the Paraguayan front, later assembled as *Diário de la campaña*, provided a model of reasoned analysis, untouched by any rancor toward the enemy. Even today, they carry the authority of a moral witness to the best and worst aspects of the conflict, and Palleja is justly praised for the cogency and evenhandedness of his testimony.

The colonel's men, however, loved him with an even more genuine affection: the type reserved for a comrade. The balls continued to whiz overhead at the instant of his death, and yet the soldiers stopped in their tracks and presented arms over Palleja's lifeless body. They then brought up a stretcher that bore him from the scene, pausing along the way so that photographers could record the sad event. These dapper professionals, so incongruous in the muck and devastation of Paraguay, had arrived from Montevideo at the beginning of June, and now produced an image recognizable to a generation of veterans in every country affected by the war.[56] Colonel Palleja's name was thus immortalized, even in Paraguay, where his nobility of spirit always received an elaborate eulogy.[57] As he himself would have insisted, however, he was but one of hundreds of men who died that day.[58]

And yet the battle was not over. Flores felt nonplussed to see the Allied soldiers stumbling back so bloodied and spent, and now he acted with petulance. As Domínguez arrived, so, too, did the brother of the president, General Emilio Mitre, who commanded the units sent to reinforce the now defeated colonel. Seeing that he was too late, the general approached Flores to ask for instructions. Visibly irritated, the Uruguayan caudillo ordered Mitre to retake the trench. At this, the Argentine general bit his lip. Of the two brothers, Emilio was the more impetuous—but not on this occasion; he knew that nothing but further butchery could come from another assault at the Boquerón. He responded to the order with hesitance, hoping to beg off, but Flores repeated the instruction. He had no intention of being held back this time.[59]

Emilio Mitre had to explain the situation to Colonel Luis N. Argüero, commander of the 6th Division, who was ordered to mount the new attack. He, too, had no illusions about the peril of the mission. He saluted the general, bid him "goodbye forever," and started to advance toward the clearing.[60] Even before his men reached the opening, the Paraguayan guns had blown apart several of their number.

In the many histories of the war written since the 1860s, Paraguay is often portrayed as a pigmy faced with the overwhelming might of an Allied giant. On this occasion, however, the Marshal's army held the cards. Díaz had brought several pieces of artillery down from the northern Bellaco only to discover that the Argentines had failed to spike their cannons after all. He turned all these guns on the advancing enemy. The 68-pounders at the Paso Gómez continued to rain shot on the same troops. Thus, as Centurión put it, the Boquerón became "a vortex that swallowed masses of human flesh like an insatiable monster."[61]

As before, the attackers arranged themselves in two columns, with the right led this time by Argüero and the left by Colonel Adolfo Orma, who received a bullet wound in the foot within a minute of signaling the charge against the Paraguayan position. Major Francisco Borges, grandfather of the famous author, moved to take his place, but as the smoke drifted over his position, a Minié ball struck him, and he, too, had to be evacuated. Amid the chaos, and with every man coughing from the stench of sulfur, the column stalled.

On the right, Argüero's men pressed forward along the margin of the Boquerón, stepping across the bodies of their fallen comrades. In short order, the new troops reached the outer line of the earthworks as their predecessors had done. A few got close enough to peer across the top to see masses of Paraguayan soldiers huddled behind their cannon, proof positive that an attack could never succeed. Argüero had already ascertained the same thing. Now, as if on cue, the Paraguayan guns cut him down like a machete slicing through a stalk of corn. The Brazilians failed to send help, for López set up a barrage on his flank to make them think another attack was imminent. With no reinforcements in sight by two in the afternoon, Argüero's second-in-command called for the retreat, keeping his voice low so that the Marshal's men, who were thirty feet ahead, would hear nothing.[62] He left his colonel's body for the Paraguayans to bury.

The Tally

One half hour later the last of the Allied troops crawled back to their original position, where a livid Emilio Mitre was waiting.[63] They had seen such total devastation that it shocked the sensibility of every other man on the field. The battle of the Riachuelo had occasioned more confusion, and Tuyutí a far greater loss of life, but Boquerón, because its worst effects were confined to a small space, seemed infinitely more terrible. The Allies had suffered around three thousand casualties at the mouth of the clearing, which brought their losses for the three days to just over five thousand.[64] As Centurión described it, "mountains of cadavers [appeared] in which the Argentines, Brazilians, Orientals and also Paraguayans were mixed into a common disgrace, and in which bodies could be found in every curious position. ... [They] covered that enclosed space of land right up to the foot of the trenches, [and those] who were still alive twitched uncontrollably in the final exertions of their pain."[65] These grotesque mounds caught the eye of photographers, who, in the manner of moths drawn to the light of an oil lamp, kept returning to record these terrible vistas. They set up their bulky cameras and took picture after picture, producing so many different photos of dead bodies that in the minds of many people downriver this specific image of slaughter became emblematic of the war.[66]

The Paraguayans lost around twenty-five hundred men between 16 and 18 July, together with many wounded. Since this amounted to half those lost by the Allies, Marshal López could claim a clear-cut victory, and so he did, ordering celebrations from Humaitá to Asunción. This was not simple gloating, for in contrast to Yataity Corã, the results at Boquerón demonstrated the skill of the Marshal's defensive planning. He had lured the Allies into making a frontal assault against a position where they could be enfiladed, and the trick had worked far better than anyone could have expected.

When assigning blame for the Allied reverse, the best candidate for criticism was Flores. The Uruguayan president had brought to the battle his usual fortitude and bravery, but he acted with limited knowledge of the challenges his men might face. His decision to attack the rearmost trenches proved reckless, and his sending Argüero on a final suicidal charge criminally so. Perhaps he should have satisfied himself with holding the Punta Ñaró, but anger seized hold of him and he could not shake it off.[67]

Rather than laying blame on a single officer, it might be better to fault the entire Allied command, which favored a makeshift arrangement over a centralized authority. This way of doing things might have held its political attractions in an alliance of near-equals, but it also fostered many unnecessary delays and obstructions. As a rule, whichever Allied unit the Marshal attacked, its commander would take charge while the others would follow along. This modus operandi, which provided for independence of action for each unit along the line, had worked well on 24 May, when López attacked along a broad front and every Allied commander faced a common threat. At Boquerón, by contrast, the Paraguayans had relinquished the first move to an untried Brazilian corps commander and the irate president of Uruguay. The result was a series of ill-considered charges against a strong redoubt, a misuse of reserve troops, and a near-total lack of coordination between units.

The Allied generals pointed at each other in the battle's aftermath, and they were less than generous in their appraisal of López, whose dispositions had won the day for Paraguay.[68] Almost to a man the Argentine and Brazilian commentators stressed that the Marshal was far removed from the action and had little meaningful control over events south of the Bellaco. They forgot that his engineers had constructed ancillary telegraph lines to keep him in regular contact with his field officers. He also had his telescope trained on the engagement for most of the day, and thus knew when to send in his own reserves.[69] And to reiterate a point that military writers have turned into a cliché, López made fewer mistakes that day, and he had his victory. It had cost him twenty-five hundred lives—men he could not replace. But for the moment, he had won.

4

RISKS AND SETBACKS

In hindsight, it is obvious that the strategic situation remained unchanged. The Allies controlled every approach to Paraguay, and despite the recent setbacks, their armies remained formidable. Tamandaré's naval units had yet to mount a serious attack, but no one doubted their ability to do so. The Marshal's military, by contrast, might bask in the glow of a meaningless tactical victory, yet it was unable to break the enemy stranglehold on the south. López could contemplate defensive tactics, nothing more.

Notwithstanding this major limitation, the Paraguayans did benefit from certain geopolitical realities. Their adversaries mistrusted each other's intentions more than ever, and could not count on political stability in their respective countries. Argentina and Brazil had complex societies with large economies that only intersected with the war effort parenthetically. Mitre may have been Allied commander but he was also the conscientious president of a country where many factions opposed his policies. Revolution was already brewing against a Mitrista governor in Corrientes, and the western provinces were similarly uneasy. Rumors suggested that General Urquiza of Entre Ríos would soon switch his allegiance to López. These stories may have lacked foundation, but Mitre could not afford to ignore them. As for Brazil, politicians there had less to fear from provincial dissidents per se, but the parliamentary system suffered under its own constraints and weaknesses, which made decision-making difficult.

Tuyutí had to some extent slaked the thirst for vengeance that many in the Allied capitals had felt in 1865, yet a comprehensive victory remained a distant objective. Boquerón had shown that the war would be protracted, and if the conflict dragged on for much longer, the signatories of the Triple Alliance would need to find new and more convincing justifications for the immense expenditure of lives and treasure. All this suggested the need for Mitre to renew the fight as soon as possible. Perhaps he could still find some way to direct Tamandaré's guns against the Paraguayan flank. The admiral always boasted that he could destroy Humaitá whenever he chose—perhaps that time had come. He could deploy his steamers and draw the enemy's attention while Mitre launched a new attack by land.

But Tamandaré had made almost no moves upriver since May. This inaction gave the Paraguayans time to prepare batteries at the water's edge, and more ominously, to experiment with both anchored and floating mines. Their earliest efforts in this respect dated from just after the battle of the Riachuelo.[1] These mines were simple—demijohns stuffed with powder launched from rafts at the anchored Brazilian ships. The makeshift fuses of these "torpedoes" (*máquinas infernales*) tended to get wet as the rafts floated with the uneven current, and hardly ever exploded.[2] When they did go off, they made a noise that could be heard miles away at Tuyutí, but did little damage to Allied vessels.

In June the Paraguayans improved this technology. López had assembled a team of chemists and naval technicians at Humaitá under the direction of William Kruger, an American who may have had some previous experience in fabricating explosive devices during the US Civil War. He took to his new job with gusto, regarding it as a personal challenge to whip the problem of delayed or ineffective detonation. The English pharmacist George Frederick Masterman took leave from his hospital duties to join him as chemist, together with Ludwik Mieszkowski, a Polish engineer who had married one of the Marshal's cousins. The team also had a Paraguayan member, Escolástico Ramos, who had studied engineering with the Blyth Brothers firm in London.[3]

The failure of the earlier trials caused Kruger and his men to experiment with alternative designs. One device was launched by swimmers toward the Brazilian ironclad *Bahia* on the night of 16 June. Despite its disguise, the mine failed to fool alert crewmembers, who gently eased it away with poles and nets. After removing the percussion caps, they discovered that Kruger had fitted the raft-like construction with bamboo poles that jutted from the outer surface of three concentric boxes.[4] When the poles struck the hull of an enemy ship, metallic hammers would shatter a capsule of sulfuric acid onto a mixture of potassium chlorate and sugar within the innermost box, releasing enough heat to ignite the powder with a thunderous result.[5]

These mines were cheap to produce so long as powder was available.[6] López, however, tended to treat the torpedoes as more dangerous to their handlers than to the enemy. Even so, Kruger zealously promoted the devices, and the Marshal eventually let him have the chemicals and gunpowder he needed. The mines might have done severe damage to the Allied fleet, had the individual rafts proved steadier; as it were, they had to be bolstered by multiple buoys.

The trigger mechanism, moreover, never worked right, so getting the powder to explode at the correct moment proved almost impossible.

While Marshal López had doubts about the efficacy of these and later explosive devices, Kruger retained his enthusiasm to the end. One night, while aboard a canoe with Ramos, one of the two mines he was carrying went off prematurely and killed both men. This left Mieszkowski in charge of the project. Over the next two months, he launched scores, perhaps hundreds, of mines downriver. In one sense, they met with little success, for the Brazilians soon learned to keep their own canoes and skiffs in the water to give warning of any oncoming danger. They had some close calls. On one occasion in July, a mine loaded with fifteen hundred pounds of powder burst a scant three hundred yards from the bow of an Allied warship. The resulting blast was heard as far away as Corrientes. It threw a fleeting light upon the entire line at the Estero Bellaco, almost revealing the nocturnal trench making of the Marshal's troops.

In another sense, though, Mieszkowski's mines more than repaid the effort the Paraguayans put into them. Each evening the Allies encountered mines on the river, a great many of them empty boxes disguised to resemble bombs. Whether real or fake, their presence always sent the lookouts into a panic, and as they cried out "Paraguá! Paraguá!," the men aboard the nearby ironclads scrambled about in bewilderment.[7] The reaction was no less frantic every time the Marshal's men launched a raft onto the river piled high with blazing brushwood and oakum soaked in oil. Though these fire ships never got close to any Allied shipping, they nevertheless inspired a frenzied reaction. They also confirmed Tamandaré in his decision to stay anchored far below the enemy position and wait until the land forces moved in from the east.[8]

Mitre and the generals wanted more support from Tamandaré but he refused to concede it as long as the threat on the river remained unchanged. In Buenos Aires, the admiral's inaction had already set off a series of rumors that the fleet was being restrained in preparation for a sneak attack against Argentina. There was nothing to this tale, but that it was being repeated at all demonstrated once again how fragile the alliance was.[9]

Tamandaré depicted his lack of forward momentum as good politics. The battles at Sauce and Boquerón had called into question the appropriate route of Allied advance, which was constantly shifting as coalition strategy evolved. So long as the land forces continued to press into areas beyond the reach of naval fire, Mitre expected to carry the day on any matter of strategy. Tamandaré, however, rejected this attitude as placing Argentine interests over those of the empire. For his part, he always favored a line of advance parallel to the Paraguay River, so that the Allied armies could overwhelm the Marshal's batteries south of Humaitá before moving on to Asunción. Until he got his way on this point, he saw little reason to play dice with either his ships or his reputation.[10]

Tamandaré's emphasis on a naval-based strategy involved practical concerns as well. During the Crimean conflict and the US Civil War, armies could move forward by using existing lines of communication or by requisitioning supplies from local populations. This was never possible in the isolated circumstances of Argentina and Paraguay, where supply caravans needed to travel long distances and carry fodder for their draft animals. A law of diminishing returns set in whenever the caravans failed to carry sufficient supplies for themselves, much less for the Allied forces at the end of the line. In the previous wars in the Pampas and the Banda Oriental, cavalrymen always had to keep moving in order to find pastures for their mounts, something that was impractical in the swampy environment of southern Paraguay. Until the Allied generals developed a more thoughtful system of foraging in 1867, moving forward along the river line made sense since it ensured that adequate supplies reached the army.

Tamandaré understood this fact very well and the arrival of Porto Alegre's 2nd Corps on 29 July refocused the admiral's determination to have it his way. Unlike Polidoro, whose orientation was careerist, or Osório, who was essentially a fighting man, the Baron of Porto Alegre looked at life through a lens of class entitlement, since he shared the admiral's aristocratic origins and sense of privilege. More to the point, he was Tamandaré's first cousin, and could prove a useful ally in tipping de facto command to the Brazilians. Both Porto Alegre and Tamandaré were members of the Liberal Party; both were more than ten years older than their Argentine commander; and both retained the best political connections back in Rio de Janeiro. These things counted for something in the ongoing test of wills with Mitre.

They also counted for something vis-à-vis Polidoro. He might have been a Brazilian, but he was a Conservative, a political outsider whom the admiral and the baron trusted only as a subordinate. He might retain command over his 1st Corps, but he should exercise no further authority in Paraguay. With his cousin's help, Porto Alegre's word could carry meaningful weight within the Brazilian land forces, and this, for the moment, was all he wanted. Tamandaré, who had been isolated since Mitre assumed command, now had much to gain, and in matters of personal ambition, where he could conflate the interests of the empire with his own, he never failed to press his case. In this sense, his previous lassitude was less truant than strategic.

Mitre could not have missed any of this. He had gained certain benefits as commander in chief, but now, as meaningful authority in the field was shifting to the empire, he could no longer claim his previous influence. He still hoped to advance Argentine interests on the cheapest basis possible and preserve a tolerable modus vivendi with the Brazilians. But don Bartolo felt tired. He had proven his personal courage, his political acumen, and his skill as a military organizer. That the Paraguayans had yet to surrender was an awkward fact, but an enormous quantity of Brazilian treasure had flowed into Argentine coffers as a result of the alliance, and Mitre could certainly take credit for that. If circumstances now compelled the president to concede some real power to the admiral, then that was something he was prepared to bear.

As it turned out, Porto Alegre proved less pliant than Tamandaré expected. The baron's campaign in the Misiones, during which he faced no serious Paraguayan resistance, had hardly prepared him for the heavy fighting expected along the Estero Bellaco. The twelve thousand troops who landed with him at Itapirú did help to lift spirits in the Allied camp and raise the odds against López. Questions about command, however, clouded the arrival of the force. Mitre wanted to break through to the east of Humaitá, and outflank the Paraguayans. Porto Alegre and Tamandaré considered López's position in that quarter unassailable; they suggested instead a more straightforward assault, which would direct the main Allied force through the trench works at Curuzú and Curupayty before moving against the fortress from the south.

For a time, the Allied commanders failed to act on either plan. After holding a council of war on 18 August, however, they agreed to a combination of the two. This decision—the product of an unwanted compromise—might have fanned the embers of an already obvious jealousy had not Mitre swallowed his pride. He worried about splitting his forces, but since Polidoro and the Argentines could not move against the Bellaco, Mitre warily approved Tamandaré's ambitious plan for an attack on Curuzú. The admiral needed to detach several thousand of Porto Alegre's soldiers from the main force to mount the assault. Mitre agreed to this condition, but insisted that the Brazilians guarantee positive results within fifteen days so that he could follow up with an attack on the Paraguayan left. Tamandaré, who had already made a great many promises, gave his word on this occasion as well.

Porto Alegre refused to let it go, however. Mitre could spare no more than six thousand men for the Curuzú operation, yet the baron announced on 26 August that he was taking eighty-five hundred. Don Bartolo again kept his temper, even though this show of insubordination irked him profoundly. Nor was Tamandaré happy, for by asserting a right to command these land forces, Porto Alegre appeared to usurp the authority of the admiral, whose commission was slightly more recent than his own. The resulting squabble brought about another colloquy two days later. It was the most uncomfortable meeting that the Argentine president attended during the entire war: he begged, he cajoled, he danced around the problem, and he threatened to resign overall command while retaining control of the Argentine host—then he let the baron have his way.[11]

By now, the mutual antagonisms among the Allied commanders had become common knowledge. López's spies, who on this relatively open front penetrated the Allied ranks with considerable ease, were well aware of them, and their reports gave the Marshal cause for comfort, and even delight. The more his enemies quarreled over trivial matters, the more time López had to prepare his defenses.

Curuzú

Southwestern Paraguay had by now become one of the most fortified spots on earth. Aside from the earthworks along the Estero Bellaco and at Humaitá proper, the Marshal's engineers started to build a jagged line of trenches at Curupayty. Located a mile and a half to the south of the fortress, these works ran perpendicular for three miles from the bank of the Paraguay to the swampy Laguna Méndez. Just below Curupayty, thirty feet from the river's edge, stood the subsidiary trench works at Curuzú, whose single battery constituted López's first line of defense along the river. It was this position that the Brazilians now proposed to attack.

Aware of the weakness on their right flank, the Paraguayans dug a new trench from Paso Gómez in an arc around the inside of the Potrero Sauce. (The opening at Sauce was later deepened and shaped into a channel to divert the course of the Bellaco.[12]) Construction had also continued at Curupayty, where the Paraguayans set up a chain boom that stretched across the river to the Chaco. But they had yet to complete the trench just to the south at Curuzú. Moreover, though López had reserves of veteran troops in the camps above Tuyutí, he failed to move these men to the banks of the Paraguay. As a result, Curuzú was left exposed.

On 29 August, Porto Alegre's 2nd Corps began embarkation near Itapirú. More than half the expeditionary force had boarded the twelve transport ships when word came that the baron had postponed departure, citing a drop in the barometric pressure and the consequent threat of rain; and indeed, it poured heavily over the next thirty-six hours. On 1 September, the troops again boarded vessels for the short but hazardous voyage up the Paraguay. The Brazilians had to worry not only about shore batteries and mines; López's men had also sunk several rock-filled barges that could tear the keel out of any Allied warship. The hulks had drifted with the heavy current, and no one knew where.

Tamandaré decided to take a chance. His engineers charted a way through the mines at dawn on 1 August. Around 7:30 a.m., the admiral steamed ahead aboard the *Magé*, followed by six ironclads, ten other gunboats, the dozen transports, two command vessels, and one hospital ship. This was an impressive flotilla, boasting over eighty guns, mostly 32- and 68-pounders (with 150-pound Whitworths for the ironclads). Yet, despite this firepower, the Brazilians had reason to feel apprehensive, for they had to fight in a riverine setting they had only just started to understand. At 11:00 a.m., the ironclads left the wooden vessels anchored off the island of Palmar, and proceeded upriver to blast away at the enemy batteries at Curuzú and Curupayty.

Meanwhile, Porto Alegre landed his units half a league to the south. He sent one small party to the Chaco side to find an advantageous angle from which to pour fire on the Paraguayans across the river. Meanwhile, the rest of Porto Alegre's units undertook a speedy advance northward against Curupayty to block any reinforcements that the Marshal might send from that direction. All told, the baron's command counted 4,141 infantry, 3,564 cavalry (most of whom fought dismounted that day), and 710 artillery.[13] In short order, this substantial force encountered a single platoon of enemy infantry. Surprised by the large number of Allied soldiers moving toward them, the Paraguayans got off a single volley of musketry and retired to the trench at Curuzú.

The Allied shelling of this same trench did not go well. The Paraguayan batteries were guarded by vine-covered traverses, and this elastic layer resisted the impact of every projectile. Over several hours, the fleet fired on the enemy trench works, but the naval gunners had had little experience under fire. The gray smoke careened through the gun casements and into their eyes, such that they could barely see the target. López's gunners, by contrast, did good work with their one 8-inch gun and two 32-pounders. At one point, the gunboat *Ivaí* steamed too close and the Paraguayans blasted a sizable hole through one of her boilers. Few of the other Allied vessels escaped a thrashing.

At sunset, the fleet retired, only to recommence bombardment at the same spot the next morning. The ironclads *Lima Barros, Brasil, Bahia*, and *Barroso* steamed up the main channel toward Curupayty, firing the entire way, though again with limited effect. The Paraguayans resisted for hours, and though they managed to hit the *Bahia* on thirty-eight different occasions, the ship defiantly steamed on.[14]

For the Paraguayans crouching inside the shallow earthwork, the most satisfying moment came around two in the afternoon. Up to that point, the din had been deafening, and the soldiers pushed hard against the damp sides of the trench, jamming their fingers into their ears. Through the smoke, they caught sight of the *Rio de Janeiro,* which had already had its four-inch plates shot through twice. The ship was easing her way back toward the Chaco bank when she ran over two of Mieszkowski's submerged torpedoes. The resulting explosion ripped the bottom out of the vessel, sinking the ship within minutes. Fifty-one crewmen and four officers drowned, including the ship's commander.[15]

This was the Polish engineer's one great triumph. No further Allied vessels were lost to Paraguayan mines during the war. As for the men at Curuzú, they could not pause to celebrate, for the shelling went on until dusk. The navy fired some four hundred projectiles on 2 September, but only one Paraguayan died, a scout who had climbed a tree to observe enemy movements and was blown to pieces.[16]

Thus far, the naval investment of Curuzú had not rewarded the Brazilian effort. Tamandaré, having struck at the Paraguayan works for two days, failed to damage it, and Porto Alegre felt tense about the upcoming land engagement. He begged Mitre to launch a diversionary attack against the Paraguayan left.[17] The baron had no reason for real concern, however; though the enemy had thus far put up a spirited fight, the positive results were illusory. The trench works at Curuzú were incomplete, amounting to a single trench that wound nine hundred yards from the river up to a broad and little-visited estero. Its adjoining trench was still so shallow that a concentrated cannonade could hit any part of it. The navy's failure to reduce the "fort" had more to do with the absence of room for maneuver on the river (and the skittishness of Tamandaré's gunners) than with the efficiency or sophistication of Paraguayan defenses.

On the morning of 3 September, the true weakness of the trench works at Curuzú came into full perspective. The Marshal's men spent the late hours of the previous evening burning the brushwood at the front of their trenches in an effort to ruin the enemy timetable. The wind refused to cooperate, however, and at a late hour the fire swept back toward the Paraguayans. It was still smoldering when Porto Alegre attacked, just before dawn.[18] His troops advanced in three columns from the south, taking advantage of the fact that the Paraguayan battery that had so pestered the fleet was fixed on a westward angle toward the river. The baron therefore had to concern himself only with enemy sharpshooters. The day before the battle, however, the Paraguayans brought up ten more artillery pieces from Curupayty, along with troop reinforcements that increased their contingent at Curuzú to twenty-five hundred men. Most of the soldiers (including the entire 10th Battalion) had recently been recruited for frontline service.[19]

This should have constituted a formidable force, but the commanding colonel, Manuel A. Giménez, did not know these new men very well. He had served with distinction at Tuyutí as a subordinate to Díaz, but had little of his commander's charisma. Now, as Porto Alegre's left and center columns approached, the colonel failed to direct proper fire upon them. As a result, the bulk of the Brazilian units got through to the trench in less than forty minutes.[20] But when they reached the near side of the Paraguayan position, they discovered that the ramparts were several feet higher than expected; since they brought no scaling ladders, they had to stay in the hollow of the parapet, where the Paraguayans could not draw a bead on them. This provided some momentary safety, but they could not win the battle from such a position.[21]

The Brazilian advance had not been effectively covered by artillery. The draft animals refused to pass near the burning foliage, so the Brazilian gunners had to drag the gun carriages forward. They could not join the action, which left the forward infantry units isolated.[22] The men who huddled against the Paraguayan line were badly frightened; at one point, a grenade rolled over the rampart and onto a troop of the 47th Voluntários of Paraíba, killing two corporals and wounding another two.[23] At about the same moment, further down the line, a Zouave who had enlisted under the name José Luiz de Souza Reis, fell into an epileptic fit and was carried, still shaking, to the rear. It later emerged that the man was an escaped slave from Bahia.[24]

Despite the difficult circumstances that they faced on the left, the Brazilians in fact took far more casualties on the right, where the column turned the Paraguayan flank. A reconnaissance mission had already established the shallowness of the lagoon (perhaps four feet at its deepest), so the Brazilians could wade across. This was slow going, and for a time they were enfiladed from the Curuzú trench, but they nonetheless pressed through to dry land, and fell upon Giménez from the rear.[25]

At this crucial moment, the Paraguayan 10th Battalion broke. Its soldiers, many of whom had failed to discharge their weapons, fled in confusion along a narrow footpath toward Curupayty. Only the battalion commander stayed and resisted. He cursed and called upon his men to turn and fight, but his voice was lost in the clamor, and when the Brazilians caught sight of him, they gunned him down.

The other units in the trench fought on. Balls zipped through the smoky air and into faces, throats, and ribcages. The soldiers closed, and with sabers and lances cut into each other's ranks with a terrible fury. No one asked for quarter; none was offered. The air came alive with explosions, with shouts of anger and invocations of the Blessed Virgin, with muffled pleas for mothers, and desperate cries of agony. A Paraguayan and a Brazilian soldier were seen to lunge at one other so forcefully that each was run through by the other's bayonet.[26]

Hundreds of soldiers were killed or wounded over the next thirty minutes while the Brazilians stormed through on every side. What remained of Curuzú's defenders escaped northward through the scrub brush, carrying their wounded men along the same thorny path the 10th Battalion had taken. A few of the Brazilians gave chase all the way to the Curupayty line. Flushed with excitement, they jeered and swore and fired their rifles wildly in the air. Then, realizing that they had advanced too far and that buglers were sounding recall, they turned back to Curuzú.

The Brazilians found good reason to celebrate. They had taken two battle standards and thirteen of the enemy's guns in seizing this strategic point, and they put at least seven hundred Paraguayan troopers out of action. Morale in the Marshal's army had taken a serious whipping thanks to Porto Alegre's daring assault, a fact that quickly became common knowledge throughout the Paraguayan forces. As the last volleys died down, the baron's men unfurled their standards and shouted themselves hoarse. Then, as their voices grew to a crescendo, an enormous blast blotted out the revelry. A Paraguayan powder magazine had exploded right next to the Brazilians, killing twelve and sending a broad, vivid sheet of flame and blood skyward, before spreading out in every direction.[27] It was a telling reminder that each Allied victory brought ironies as well as lives lost.

The Brazilian achievement at Curuzú was far more conspicuous and far more significant than anything the Marshal had accomplished at Boquerón. Porto Alegre had pierced López's line at his weakest point and upset his plans for building an impregnable defense from the river to the esteros. The tactical advantage the Allies won could not be undone, and in this sense justified the one thousand Brazilian lives lost on 3 September.[28] The victory belonged to Porto Alegre's troops, a fact that irked Tamandaré and the other Allied commanders almost as much as the overall result infuriated the Marshal.[29]

In spite of his victory, the baron failed to follow through. Curupayty lay before him unprotected, and with seventy-five hundred soldiers of his 2nd Corps still fit for duty, it was unforgivable that he attempted no reconnaissance. He would have discovered a series of incomplete earthworks manned by dispirited Paraguayan units. Had the Brazilians attacked these positions right away, they probably would have carried the other trenches as well, leaving the Marshal's position on the Estero Bellaco outflanked and the trail open to Humaitá.

Porto Alegre chose to mount no new attacks because, as he later asserted, his men were too tired to go on. Even though troops returning from the fray had reported that the trenches on the Paraguayan left were lightly defended, the baron still lacked a good understanding of the terrain ahead and the number of Paraguayans he might encounter.[30] Centurión, however, argues that Porto Alegre felt satisfied with his signal achievement, and that a decisive win was at that moment quite far from his mind. In fact, rather than push ahead to Curupayty, he sent word to Mitre to send more troops to help maintain control of Curuzú.[31] Perhaps he needed these reinforcements to launch a broader attack, but most indications suggest that he only wanted to hold what he had already taken. He had no idea of how weak the enemy was—yet another example of the failure of the Allies' intelligence, and their unwillingness to take risks.

The Marshal reacted to his defeat at Curuzú with seething rage. He had spent the battle at Paso Pucú, where his telescope clearly revealed the scale of the setback. Up to now, he had acted with surprising serenity, having only just learned of the diplomatic support that the Andean countries had extended to his government. He even imagined that US Minister Washburn would rush from Corrientes to effect a negotiated peace. But the shock of Porto Alegre's easy victory at Curuzú brought López back to the issue at hand. He felt incensed that the men of the 10th Battalion had failed him, a dereliction of duty that, to his mind, smacked of treason and deserved a harsh punishment. That dutiful men could get caught up in a panic-stricken flight never once occurred to him.

It took a brave man to be a coward in the Marshal's army. It was well understood that, at times of personal stress, López could lash out with violence even at those closest to him. On this occasion, he first threw blame on General

Díaz, who had commanded the troops in that sector. Díaz was by now a court favorite, and thus felt sufficiently secure in his position to hazard a protest. The unit commanders, he argued, should be held responsible for the behavior of the 10th Battalion, not he.

The Marshal considered this, then turned on the officers who had participated in the battle. He reduced Colonel Giménez to sergeant. He did the same with Giménez's deputy, Major Albertano Zayas. Then López gave the order to decimate the battalion, with every tenth man taken from the line and shot.[32] Officers had to choose lots, and those unlucky enough to pick the long straw suffered the same. All others were broken to the ranks. While such a draconian response might be cited as an example of the Marshal's brutality, the Paraguayans had long since grown accustomed to making unreasonable sacrifices, and if the 10th Battalion had not stood its ground, it was not merely unfortunate, it was scandalous. Centurión spoke for a good many in Paraguay when he argued that cowards should expect swift execution.

What was left unsaid in these evaluations is that, by blaming the 10th Battalion for the loss at Curuzú, the Marshal effectively absolved those who had prepared the Paraguayan defenses along the river. And yet, if the general plan for protecting the army's right flank had failed once, it might fail again. In this sense, Curupayty beckoned to the Brazilians from across an expanse no greater than a mile. Porto Alegre had only to reach out and take it.

López met with his senior officers on 8 September, and they informed him that while the construction of the defenses at Curupayty had progressed to some extent, they were still incomplete. Díaz agreed, and stressed his dissatisfaction with what had thus far been achieved: "Oí porã kuatiápe, pero peixa ña mopuáramo la trinchera, nda ja jocoí xene los kambápe" (it might look good on paper, but if we leave the trenches [thus unfinished], we won't be able to stop the darkies).[33]

A Chance for Peace?

On the day that Curuzú fell to the Brazilians, the main Allied army at Tuyutí limited its activities to a minor movement against the enemy center. Ten men died in demonstrating what Mitre already understood—that he could not take the Paraguayan trenches north of the line without incurring serious losses. One day later, General Flores followed up with a major reconnaissance at the Bellaco, using three thousand cavalrymen to probe the Paraguayan left flank. When he encountered a vigorous report from the 68-pounders and Congreve rockets, he pulled back, needing no further proof that the enemy had fortified the entire line.

Flores, Mitre, and Polidoro then met in council. The celerity of Porto Alegre's victory at Curuzú offered them some room for optimism, but also much apprehension. Was not the 2nd Corps overextended on the left flank? If López possessed troop reserves, he might counterattack and cut off Porto Alegre at Curuzú. In such a case, Admiral Tamandaré could only evacuate the Brazilian troops under heavy fire, and it was not farfetched to presume he would be unwilling to do so.

The Argentine president remained committed to a new attack against the Bellaco line, but the events along the Paraguay River imposed new priorities. The Brazilians wanted the 2nd Corps reinforced as soon as practicable, and on 6 September the assembled Allied commanders worked out a provisional plan to this effect. Mitre ordered the detachment of twelve thousand men at Tuyutí for immediate deployment to Curuzú, where they would join the seventy-five hundred men already there. Once in position, they would mount an overwhelming attack against Curupayty with covering fire provided by the fleet. Meanwhile, the cavalry under Flores would stay behind and deliver a series of diversions to keep the enemy's attention focused on Tuyutí; once the main assault started along the river, the Uruguayan general would then rush his units northward across the esteros with Polidoro's infantry covering his left. By the time Flores reached Curupayty, the principal Paraguayan earthworks there should already have fallen to Mitre and Porto Alegre. After a short rest, the reunited Allied army could move on unopposed to Humaitá.[34]

The plan had many drawbacks. It envisioned enveloping the Marshal's forces on both flanks, though neither the distance nor the swampy terrain suggested this as a practical possibility. The generals had already rejected a frontal attack against the Bellaco trenches as too hazardous, and a broad flanking maneuver through the same well-defended area had as little to recommend it. Moreover, Porto Alegre still lacked intelligence about Paraguayan dispositions at Curupayty. His men had erected no mangrullos at Curuzú, nor dispatched any scouts north of the forward lines. The baron could not know whether he was facing three thousand men or fifty thousand. Finally, as each of the army commanders had already learned, any plan of attack that depended on Tamandaré's support was bound to involve risks.

General Polidoro had to feel uneasy. A clean-shaven Carioca with a world-weary look in his eye, the general had already gained a reputation for taking the long view of things. On this occasion, he observed that the units under his command lacked the strength to attempt extended movements. He recommended dispatching spies into the Chaco, from where they might observe the Paraguayans arranging their gun positions at Curupayty. He also sent sappers to identify possible routes for Flores's cavalry (and his own infantry) to traverse the marshes at the edge of the Potrero Pirís.

Polidoro was wise to question the details of the plan. Its apparent simplicity hid myriad uncertainties that were too inconvenient to mention. The want of unity of command still dogged the Allied campaign. True enough, don Bartolo remained commander in chief, and thus demanded the honor of launching the main attack on Curupayty, now slated for 17 September. Yet he could not coordinate the efforts of subordinate commanders; they always seemed determined to question each other's motives and authority, even in minor matters. That it was difficult to discern where one officer's command ended and another's began is hardly surprising: they did not know themselves.

For several days, the Allied commanders prepared their attack. Troops were ferried to Curuzú from Itapirú on an almost hourly basis. Mitre inspected the recently captured trench works and gazed at Curupayty through his spyglass. Pickets reported from the Chaco that they could glimpse considerable activity behind the Paraguayan line, though they knew little beyond this. And news came from the Bellaco that several lines of approach over dry land were available to Flores and Polidoro, but again the details were sketchy. From his flagship, Admiral Tamandaré signaled his readiness.

Then, on 10 September, a surprise occurred. In the late afternoon, a picket of four Paraguayan soldiers and an officer appeared before the Argentine lines under a flag of truce. Shocked by this unexpected sight, the gaucho cavalrymen fired and the little group scrambled back into the marshes. When Mitre learned of the incident, he reprimanded his soldiers, telling their officer that if the Paraguayans wanted to parley, he wanted to listen.

Sure enough, at noon the next day, the picket appeared again, and this time the Argentines held their fire. The Paraguayan officer, a handsome, dark-whiskered captain named Francisco Martínez, stepped toward the assembled enemy troopers and announced that he bore a formal message from Marshal López to the Allied commander in chief. In short order, Martínez found himself in don Bartolo's presence. The Argentine president, visibly excited, broke the seal on the envelope and read the message. It was brief and to the point: "To His Excellency, Brigadier General don Bartolomé Mitre, I have the honor to invite your Excellency to a personal interview between our lines on the day and hour that Your Excellency might indicate. May God keep you many years. [Signed] Francisco Solano López."[35]

One can easily guess what coursed through Mitre's mind. The prospect of peace after such a campaign must have attracted him. Moreover, this offer of a conference shifted the scene of action to a venue that the Argentine president found more amenable than the battlefield; Flores and Polidoro might have greater military experience, but when it came to diplomacy, Mitre was their senior. The Marshal's message, vague though it was, implied many possibilities, all of which cast the Argentine president back into a position of real dominance over both his enemies and his colleagues.

Mitre excused himself and rode at once to Polidoro's headquarters, where both men were soon joined by Flores. For thirty minutes the three commanders discussed the situation. Polidoro expressed open cynicism, grumbling that he lacked orders to engage in any negotiations, and that his superiors had instructed him to forego any communication with the Paraguayans while López was still in charge.[36] This rigid stance mirrored the views of the emperor, who, who from his palace in Rio de Janeiro, had long since rejected any negotiation that was not preconditioned by López's departure from South America. And, in any case, by this time both Polidoro and dom Pedro had apparently concluded that Allied victory was imminent, and they had little tolerance for any discussion that might delay it.

Modern theorists of international relations often attempt to convert complex motivations into straightforward propositions. Yet personalities frequently shape broader interests, and, in this case, the vanity and whims of Marshal López were more than balanced by the obstinacy of dom Pedro. The emperor's appreciation of the Vienna treaties of 1814–1815 caused him to regard the waging of preemptive war as illegal. He reasoned that previous Paraguayan actions in Mato Grosso and Rio Grande do Sul could never be justified under international law, and that any moves toward a lasting peace would therefore have to be predicated on bringing the Marshal's criminal leadership to an end. This view was consistent, even if it also marked a less dignified penchant for vengefulness. Yet Polidoro and the other Brazilian generals knew the emperor's heart, understood his wishes, and refused to challenge them.

Not wanting to be left out, Flores endorsed Brazilian intransigence with an exclamation of rough-hewn contempt: it was hopeless to deal with the likes of López, he maintained. Mitre, however, seemed to think that any diplomatic progress could only occur if the Allies understood Paraguayan intentions. The Argentine president therefore drafted a response in which he agreed to meet with López between the lines at nine the next morning. Martínez carried this simple message back to Paso Pucú.

The Paraguayan captain had spent the half-hour chatting with the Argentines under the shade of a yataí palm. He gave them word of their comrades held as prisoners north of the line, but answered their more substantial questions with a determined "no sé." When several officers of the Paraguayan Legion approached and tried to sound him out for news of their relatives in Asunción, he emphatically turned his back. With traitors there could be no fraternization. Then, as Martínez rode past his enemies, a procession of Argentine well-wishers followed, acclaiming him as a veritable "Moses, [and regaling him with] vivas and shouts of peace."[37]

That night word spread among the Allied troops that happy news was in the offing. Mitre himself started this rumor by instructing his staff members to prepare to receive the much-maligned López as a high-ranking guest. His comment elicited murmurs of surprise that soon were repeated as proof of an impending end to the war. Under the starlit sky, the soldiers broke out in song, and even the most battle-hardened veterans unbridled their emotions and let their voices grow to a ringing crescendo. Peace! Peace! Peace was at hand! They would soon be going home.[38]

On the Paraguayan side of the line, the mood was also hopeful, though perhaps more reserved, and colored more by relief than by joy. All the senior officers got caught up in the mood of the moment, and the men, normally so sullen, allowed themselves a flicker of optimism. Even Madame Lynch expressed happy anticipation, and she encouraged her paramour to demand the best possible terms. But López had much to preoccupy him. The fall of Curuzú had upset his entire defense strategy, and even a trifling attack on Curupayty might now bring disaster. He had dispatched Wisner and Thompson after the 8 September meeting to oversee the construction of earthworks by five thousand new arrivals. These soldiers, brought from the north by Captain Bernardino Caballero, also cut down trees and scrub brush, and shaped the mass into sharp-ended abatis. Though they worked without rest for days, they were still far behind in their labors. The Marshal's plea for a meeting gave them what they badly needed—more time.

Scholars have long debated whether López had any genuine interest in opening serious negotiations at this juncture. Perhaps he just wished to buy time.[39] But now that Mitre had agreed to a meeting, he had to take his own initiative seriously and reflect on what he hoped to gain from the Allies, as well as what he might have to concede.

López also ruminated on his personal safety. So far, he had spent the war in secure surroundings at Paso Pucú, but a meeting with the Allied commanders meant moving into a glade at Yataity Corã where the enemy might murder him and end the war with the simple thrust of a dagger. López understood his priorities. He sent a squad of sharpshooters to cover the meeting from as close a distance as they dared. He may have lacked the personal bravery that was so typical of his countrymen, but his position in Paraguay was also unique; whatever the plans for Paraguay's survival as an independent state, López remained indispensable. And yet his removal was explicitly called for in the Treaty of Triple Alliance. Any chance for diplomatic success hinged on his willingness to make this fundamental concession. The Marshal knew it and so did Mitre, though it was uncertain whether either would offer any flexibility.

12 September 1866 was a radiant day and López awoke already convinced that he had to make a good show. He arranged his hair and dressed in his most immaculate uniform, replete with gold braid, a blue military frock and kepi—the whole assemblage suggestive not so much of Napoleon Bonaparte as of a contemporary Italian *Generale di Divisione*. He also wore white gloves and heavy grenadier boots emblazoned with the national symbols to highlight his status as Paraguayan president. Over all this he placed a scarlet poncho, lined with vicuña wool—a gift that the Marquis of São Vicente had brought López's father from Rio several years before. He chose this cloak, emblazoned with the

image of a Bragança imperial crown, to further indicate his authority and to symbolize, above all, that he was no supplicant.[40]

López was the first to arrive at the appointed spot, followed a few minutes later by Mitre, who rode in with a small staff and escort of twenty lancers. In contrast to the Marshal, he had given minimal attention to his appearance, wearing just a frock coat, white sword belt, and an "old breakdown wideawake hat which gave him a Quixotic appearance."[41] He looked unkempt, distracted, and emotionally unguarded. Yet this was also a show, for in affecting this image, Mitre hid the cold detachment of a skilled diplomatist. His indifference to dress had caused many a previous opponent to underestimate him, and this had often worked to his favor.

The escorts halted and don Bartolo came forward to greet the Marshal. The two men had traded diplomatic niceties once before, in 1859, when López had served as mediator in the struggle between Buenos Aires and Urquiza's confederal government. On that occasion, all the Argentines present had praised the stranger from Asunción as fair, intelligent, tactful, and anxious to help. Mitre had hoped to find some of that same spirit in the more mature man who now extended his hand.

The two presidents dismounted and began to chat within calling distance of their aides-de-camp. Their opening words seem to have been correct rather than gracious. After a few minutes, Mitre sent word to Flores and Polidoro to invite them to attend the proceedings, but the latter declined, noting that with the Allied commander in chief present, his own participation would be redundant.[42] As a matter of fact, he had in mind the standing order from Rio de Janeiro that forbade any contact with the Paraguayans.

As for Flores, the Uruguayan president came along more out of curiosity than a commitment to negotiation. For the first time in the campaign he put on his gala uniform and white gloves. López, however, proved less than polite, accusing Flores of having fomented the war by encouraging Brazilian intervention in the Banda Oriental in 1864. The Colorado chieftain retorted that no one wished to safeguard Uruguayan independence more than he; besides, he wondered, what did any of that have to do with Paraguay? To this, the Marshal could only respond with hackneyed but impassioned references to a balance of power in the Plata—an interpretation accepted by no one save López.

Flores soon wearied of the give and take. In his brief account of the meeting, the Uruguayan president's secretary later observed that the Marshal could not tolerate having his word contradicted.[43] The gruff Flores, who was just as touchy, and with little interest in hearing himself called a Brazilian puppet, stopped listening. López shrugged his shoulders, then introduced the Uruguayan to his brother Venancio and his brother-in-law General Barrios. The three spoke cordially for a few minutes and then Flores tipped his hat, mounted his horse and galloped away. No one protested. From the Marshal's perspective, it was better to converse with the master than with the servant.

López called for chairs, paper, pen and ink, and a carafe of water. He and the Argentine leader then commenced a five-hour dialogue. While the two presidents concerned themselves with weighty matters, the Allied troopers mixed with their Paraguayan counterparts, and chatted amicably. The Marshal's men offered beef, biscuits, and yerba, and received various small gifts in return. Two Brazilian majors distributed silver sovereigns among the Paraguayans, who declared their surprise at so strange a kind of money.[44]

Meanwhile, Mitre and López sat or paced or poured cups of caña or water. At certain moments, their conversation looked friendly, at others tense. The specifics of what was said remain sketchy, which is curious given Mitre's penchant for recording details. The letter he penned to Vice President Marcos Paz offered only generalities.[45] It is clear, however, that in the meeting they spoke of many things: of the siege at Uruguaiana, of Bismarck's campaign in Austria, of the deficiencies of their respective armies, and of the urgent need for peace. They even seem to have found time to discuss books written in Guaraní and the polemics of the Chilean historian Diego Barros Arana.[46] Neither man, it emerged, could afford to deviate from previously established positions. The Marshal hinted that border alterations favorable to the Argentine Republic might still be arranged. He had launched the war, he explained, to frustrate imperial ambitions in Uruguay, and the opportunistic alliance between Argentina and Brazil should not now prevent an honorable peace.

It should be emphasized here that, as a general rule, the Paraguayans admired the Argentines for their education and worldliness, though they also considered them corrupt, materialistic, and untrustworthy. By contrast, the Paraguayans viewed the Brazilians as degenerate and cowardly—an estimation that many Argentines in the Litoral provinces shared as well. On both banks of the Paraná, the Brazilians were vilified as people who might be tolerated but never embraced. This view, which was tinged with a long history of bad relations and more than a little racism, entailed a glaring hypocrisy. Even those who profited from collaboration with the empire never seemed to rise above a patronizing appraisal of their benefactors or avoid an opportunity for a racist jibe.

Paraguayan revulsion towards Brazil had grown more intense since Tuyutí, and no one, least of all López, wanted more than cursory contact with the kambáes. It was one thing to confer with Mitre, the leader of a disreputable regime: the corruption of his ministers need not sully the dignity of a potential peace treaty. But it would be quite another matter for the Marshal to turn the welfare of his children over to the Brazilian rabble. And by spurning the offer of negotiation, Polidoro was demanding just such a capitulation. The war was a matter of honor for López, and while he was willing to concede much to the Argentine president, he would not offer his own resignation.

Mitre had heard this all before. He explained that, as commander in chief of the Allied forces, he was bound by the 1865 treaty. The Marshal would have to leave the country or further progress was impossible. Surely the needs of the Paraguayan nation took precedence over the political future of a single individual? López blanched at these words, looked for an instant or two at his feet, and then nodded his understanding. It was altogether reasonable to privilege *raison d'état* over personal needs in a modern city like Buenos Aires, but in Paraguay, López was the state, and he could no more vote himself out of office than he could change the course of a great river. He pursed his lips in a grimace, and intoned his refusal: "Such conditions your excellency can only dictate over my dead body in the most distant trench works of Paraguay."[47]

There was nothing more to say. The two presidents exchanged riding crops as a memento of the occasion and Mitre accepted a good Paraguayan cigar from López.[48] (Flores, who had returned at the last minute, spurned the cigar offered him.) The men parted with an affable wave and the Marshal rode back to Paraguayan headquarters, taking the same roundabout path that had brought him to Yataity Corã in the first place. The conference required a final act, and this came in the form of a memorandum agreed to by both men. It stated for the record that the Marshal had "suggested conciliatory means equally honorable to both belligerents, so that the blood hitherto spilt [might] be considered sufficient expiation of mutual differences, and thus put an end to the bloodiest war on this continent … and guaranteeing permanent … amity." Mitre passed these words on to the Argentine national government and to Allied representatives "in accordance with the obligations [previously] agreed to."[49] He advised López on 14 September that he had just completed this task, which brought an acknowledgment from the Marshal the subsequent morning. In this final communication, López summed up the various proceedings at Yataity Corã, and hinted at the terrible consequences that divine judgement would now reserve for all concerned. "For my part," he wrote, "I am gratified to have given the highest testimony of patriotism to my country, of consideration for the enemy government [against] whom we fight, and of humanity in presence of an impartial universe whose eyes are turned to this war."[50]

Curupayty

López had never endorsed negotiations with Mitre in the first place, and even though he had relented in this, he now had to yield to disappointment. His spies and informants at Montevideo and Buenos Aires had asserted that public opinion there had already shifted against the war, and many politicians were clamoring for an end to hostilities. This made no difference, however, for on the very point upon which the Marshal would make no concessions—his own resignation and voluntary exile—the Allies were intractable. When the Marshal rejected Mitre's unalterable demand, he pronounced the death sentence for a generation of his countrymen. Perhaps the Argentine president, practiced as he was in the art of the political gambit, should have found some way to offer López a broader concession, but in this he failed.

Whatever his intentions in calling a meeting with the Allied leaders, the Marshal had used his time well. Behind the lines at Curupayty, the Paraguayans had mounted eight 68-pounders onto raised platforms, four commanding the river approaches, two directed upon the land, and the final two ready to sweep both river and land. They set up forty-one lesser guns (including two rocket stands and the four guns previously captured from Flores) at advantageous intervals along the perimeter. Directed by Wisner and Thompson, the Paraguayans had worked day and night digging several shallow ditches and one major trench six feet deep and eleven wide.[51] A thin fringe of abatis completed the formidable works by providing a shield for two thousand yards of front from the edge of the river to the Laguna Méndez. The placement of the guns and the depth of the lagoon made it impractical for the Allies to turn the Paraguayan left as they had done at Curuzú, so they would have to execute a frontal attack. And when they began this assault, they found heavy guns waiting for them together with five thousand troops in seven battalions of infantry, three regiments of cavalry, and five of artillery, all coordinated by the redoubtable Díaz.[52]

Rain had fallen heavily on several occasions since 12 September—first a few drops, large and heavy, and then a metallic tapping, as on a snare drum, followed precipitously by water falling in torrents. One Brazilian officer cursed the effects of so much rain; the camp, he observed, had taken on the aspect of a mud pit in which the soldiers, with trousers pulled to the knee, skated and slipped about in the mire, trying to find their tents in the blinding downpour.[53] Since everyone's powder had gotten wet and close to no work had been accomplished on the Allied side, the commanding generals evidently felt sure that the enemy had made no progress digging trenches at Curupayty. Moreover, with eighteen thousand troops at their disposal (eleven thousand Brazilians, and seven thousand Argentines and Uruguayans), the Allies had every reason to be confident.

The attack was originally scheduled for 17 September 1866. The navy was champing at the bit and reinforcements in the form of the 1st and 2nd Argentine Corps had just disembarked at Curuzú. The Allied staff had already prepared a detailed plan. It called for the fleet to force its way upriver to a point opposite Curupayty, then launch a general barrage as prelude to the ground assault. The land forces, organized into four immense columns of equal size, would press the attack simultaneously. A unit of sharpshooters would cross the river into the Chaco to aid the battalion of sappers already posted there in providing cover fire. Just to the south, Polidoro's artillery would add more fire to discourage the Marshal's sending reinforcements from the Bellaco. To his right, Flores would launch a flanking maneuver to draw Paraguayan attention away from the main effort out of Curuzú. As the Allies enjoyed a four-to-one advantage in numbers, they should be able to carry the enemy works with minimal losses.[54]

Tamandaré had initially announced his readiness to give cover fire but begged off on the morning of 17 September, citing the inclement weather. The correspondent of *The Standard* treated this decision as yet another example of ineptitude or pusillanimity.[55] One can understand the contempt of the Anglo-Argentine correspondent, but Tamandaré deserved criticism more for an excess of caution than for sloppiness in executing orders; he showed more attention to the needs of the sailors than to those of the Allied infantrymen on shore, and this cost him all their respect. Intimations of cowardice directed at him by the press, however, were unfair. Tamandaré unhesitatingly went under fire many times. Eighteen years earlier, while a young captain in command of the frigate *Dom Affonso*, he risked his own life while rescuing the 396 passengers and crewmembers of the American ship *Ocean Monarch*, which had caught fire just off the port of Liverpool. The admiral may have been a prickly fellow, but he was no coward.[56]

This, of course, meant little to the Argentines. Their 2nd Corps had already gotten within five hundred yards of the Paraguayan front lines and was poised to strike despite the driving rain. As he waited for the order to attack, General Emilio Mitre pushed his kepi far back on his head and took repeated sips of caña from his canteen.[57] And then, as the rain soaked his poncho, the attack was called off.

Unbeknownst to the Allies, the Paraguayans had in fact kept digging even in the worst downpour. During three straight days of bad weather, they prepared more elevated gun positions together with powder magazines fashioned from adobe bricks and hardwood braces, and they carted quantities of sand up from the riverbank to reinforce the edges of the southernmost trenches. The men did not sleep, or else napped while leaning against the muddy edges of the trench in an attempt to forget their labors; any soldier caught drifting off would get a swift blow. It was a superhuman effort. And when Thompson conducted a last-minute inspection of the Curupayty trenches on the evening of 21 September, he could report that the men had just completed the final section and now felt ready to repel any attack.[58] General Díaz, who had conducted an inspection of his own, rode to Paso Pucú the same evening, and emphatically endorsed Thompson's findings in a conversation with López. The Marshal, who had been in bed with stomach cramps, perked up at this news, and, seconded by Madame Lynch, expressed himself eager, even itching, for the fight ahead.

Quite another sentiment permeated the Allied camp at Curuzú, at least among the senior officers. None of the Argentines had forgiven Tamandaré's procrastination. President Mitre, pensive as usual, had not forgotten that he had given Porto Alegre a fortnight to make substantial progress. Though the baron had succeeded in taking Curuzú, his failure to advance any further should have called for a reversion to the original strategy of outflanking the Paraguayans at the Estero Bellaco, or so Mitre fancied. Tamandaré and Porto Alegre, however, evidently thought that previous approach obsolete and now persisted in painting Curupayty as the enemy's weakest point. The two Brazilian commanders had only to convince don Bartolo to go along with the scheme. He had dawdled over minor matters in the past, and, to their eyes, seemed resistant to good advice. This time, however, they thought that he would do the right thing.

Mitre read this as political game-playing, but as he had lost some ground with his Brazilian officers since the failed negotiations with López, it made no sense to argue now. He regarded Tamandaré and Porto Alegre as churlish or idiotic in their behavior, and said as much in a letter to his foreign minister on 13 September.[59] And yet the Brazilians might just be right. Working in tandem, they managed to wear down any lingering doubts that the commander in chief still entertained. Now he announced his unqualified support.

Mitre needed to voice commitment to the plan or else look foolish when it succeeded. He also had to consider politics back home. With the rise of the Autonomist faction in the most recent elections in Buenos Aires, support for the alliance had started to dwindle among many Porteños. A triumph over López might give a boost to his Liberal supporters and put his rivals in the capital on the defensive. He not only wanted a victory at Curupayty—he needed one.

His Argentine subordinates had much less affection for the battle plan. On the night of 21 September, Captain Francisco Seeber took yerba mate together with a group of his officers that included Captain José I. Garmendia, Major Ruperto Fuentes, and Colonel Manuel Roseti, who affected the manner of a no-nonsense aristocrat. He was in fact the scion of a wealthy family of Italian immigrants, and had entered the army in the 1850s against the wishes of his parents. He was straight-shouldered, modest, and reassuring, but this evening his face was clouded with somber thoughts. "Comrades," he murmured,

> tomorrow we are going to be defeated. The Paraguayans are strongly entrenched, with fifty cannons. [Their] front is defended by spiny tree trunks. The terrain is mostly swampy, the pits deep and the bluffs steep. Our artillery is weak and insignificant. The enemy positions have not been sufficiently reconnoitered, and above all, [no one] has bothered to construct a line of parallel trenches to allow us to approach the [Paraguayans with any hope of acceptable] casualties. The fleet cannot act with any efficacy because the river banks are too high. I have a premonition that I will be among the first to fall with a ball to the gut; and I've already told Major Fuentes to be ready to replace me.[60]

At 5:30 a.m. the attacking columns began to move north in a slow, orderly fashion. The troops advanced in grand lines, like waves along a beachfront. The soggy ground prevented the use of horses, and the lack of oxen prevented the Allies from bringing up their artillery. The soldiers proceeded in silence for an hour and a half and then halted and crouched down as salvos from the fleet sliced through the air just in front of them.

The Paraguayans replied with a score of simultaneous discharges that shook the adjoining woods with a thunder "most awful and unearthly."[61] Tamandaré kept firing. He assumed that his shells had cleared out many of the enemy defenders, but the eight-foot bluff alongside the river obscured his view, and he could not actually measure the destruction his guns had wrought. A brick fortification, moreover, can be blasted apart, but firing on an earthwork was akin to striking a pillow with a clenched fist. Given the probable trajectory of his shells, the admiral would have to keep the fleet crowded against the right bank of the Paraguay to do anything other than overshoot the enemy batteries. As it turned out, only one of his shells did any damage—a 150-pound ball that struck a Paraguayan battery, dismounting an 8-inch gun and killing an unfortunate major who just the previous day had been released from detention to take part in the action.[62]

Over the next four hours, the whole fleet attempted to engage the Paraguayans. Ignoring the danger of torpedoes, two of the eight ironclads ran past the main enemy position, cut the chain near one end of the boom, and anchored in the battery's rear. Still, they could see no better than the other ships. An enormous cloud of smoke swept over the scene, and the Brazilian gunners could do no more than imagine the devastation that lay behind it. But the Paraguayans kept giving shell for shell. Their heavy projectiles hit the *Brasil* fifty times, the *Tamandaré* eleven, the *Barroso* thirteen, the *Lima Barros* fifteen, the *Bahia* nineteen, and the *Parnahyba* three.[63] Twenty-three men aboard these ships died.[64]

Sometime around eleven that morning, Tamandaré called an end to the barrage. He had fired five thousand shells, many of which were recovered and later reused by the Paraguayans.[65] After consulting his pocket watch, he raised red, then white, then blue signal flags to register mission accomplished—an assertion more hopeful than accurate.[66] A few minutes later the Argentine artillery opened up from the southeast. Smoke covered the scene once more, obscuring the fact that half these shells had fallen short.

At noon, the four great Allied columns again pushed forward to the sound of bugles and drums.[67] It was a bright spring day and the troops had dressed in their parade uniforms. They looked splendid in a display of colors clearly discernible against the background of tropical green—white pantaloons, butternut and navy-blue tunics, all moving forward as if part of some improbable parade. The soldiers had less than a mile to go, and as they pushed ahead, each individual let off a battle whoop, a triumphant, almost celebratory noise that the Correntinos and Paraguayans alike called the *sapukaí*. It was loud, spirited, and unanimous.[68] Unlike Roseti, these men had few doubts about their mission, and no officer had warned them of any extraordinary danger.

On the left, the troops of the first Brazilian column marched through the high grass near the river. Porto Alegre, who possessed as much courage as the dearly missed Osório, had filled his men with enthusiasm for fighting, not for dragging themselves through wet foliage. The vegetation, which had seemed so irksome, now provided Porto Alegre's men with the only cover they could find that day.

The Argentines soon understood the folly of the assault. Just one artillery unit supported their advance on the extreme right, and its fire proved ineffective. Before the Argentines had come halfway from Curuzú the fire against them was continuous. Ten minutes before, the soldiers had confidently shouted raucous insults at López and cheers for the Allied cause; now, with the first peals of cannon fire, they stumbled. The men coughed, gulped for air, and jabbed into the smoke with their rifles. They were unable to form words, unable to stay in line. Their confidence vanished.

Some carried wooden ladders fifteen feet long to scale the earthworks. Others carried fascines—bundles of cane and branches to bridge the ditches along the line of march. The burdens were heavy, and since every man likewise carried a rifle, rations of galleta, a canteen, a saucepan, and cartridge box, some soldiers were almost doubled over under the weight.[69] As the Paraguayan fire reached them, many sunk or pitched forward and disappeared into the sarandí. Others waded on, forming and reforming a line.

As the Argentines reached the outermost line of abatis, they received orders to take the adjacent trenches at a trot. This broke up the columns, for as some units tried to cut through the spiny branches, others sought to scale the obstacle with ladders. General Díaz had already withdrawn his men and field pieces from the outer ditches, but this brought no benefit to his Argentine opponents, for

> when they came to close quarters, notwithstanding the gallant manner in which they advanced, the Allies were thrown into disorder by the terrible artillery fire ... which was crossed upon them from all sides—the enormous canisters of the 8-inch guns doing terrible execution at a distance of two or three-hundred yards. Some of the Argentine commanding officers, [the only ones] on horseback, got quite to the edge of the trench, where they animated their soldiers, but almost all of them were killed. The column which attacked the right had the best road, but it was subject the whole way to enfilade fire.[70]

Word soon reached Mitre that his men had captured the first line of trenches—a false impression, since the Argentines had gained only the initial ditch. Acting on this error, however, Mitre ordered his troops to charge the hostile batteries. His brother Emilio and his fellow general, Wenceslao Paunero, commanded the right and right-center columns, respectively, and relayed their commander's instructions to unbelieving soldiers, who shuddered in collective disbelief. Then, with bewildered looks, they staggered to their feet to face the fury of enemy fire, rushing forward and scrambling over the bodies of their comrades. When the Argentines came within twenty-five yards of the Paraguayan line an impassable barrier of felled trees waited for them. Stymied once again, they huddled together as the Marshal's men hurled grenades at them. In contrast to the projectiles fired by Tamandaré's gunners, these missiles found their mark.

As the minutes passed, the grape, canister, rockets, shell, and shrapnel tore through the Argentine ranks, and the Paraguayan infantry at the flanks of the batteries poured blizzards of musketry upon them. The Allies' own lack of light artillery was glaringly obvious at this juncture, as every foot gained was marked with lines of the dismembered, the insensible, the slain. It was here that the "flower" of the Argentine military—Roseti, Manuel Fraga, Gianbattista Charlone, and many others—met their end.[71] Roseti assumed a look of near-serenity as he sank wounded to the ground. As his men came to aid him, he waved them away with a smile and a gesture of impatience, then lapsed into unconsciousness.

The Italian-born Charlone, with his shiny pate and flowing beard, had become a legend in the army, and had lost none of his élan in the engagement. In a voice controlled and steady amid the din, he reported to Colonel Ignacio Rivas, commander of the 1st Division, and calmly asked for reinforcements. His own brigade, which had included around three hundred men an hour earlier, now counted a mere eighty. Before Rivas could answer, however, a fragment of hot metal blew through the Italian's arm and into his chest. Three more balls hit him in succession, and down he went. A Brazilian medic took one look at the man and pronounced his wounds mortal.[72] Four of Charlone's legionnaires rushed to evacuate their commander in spite of this verdict, but as they eased him onto a stretcher, a canister round exploded nearby and killed all five men. Rivas felt the wind of shot go past him, then he, too, fell back wounded.

Bravery and steadfastness under fire were qualities not limited to these particular officers; courage was ubiquitous among Allied soldiers. The painter Cándido López, of the San Nicolás Battalion, lost his right arm in the engagement (and lived to provide the most eloquent testimony of the war's brutality through his fifty-odd renderings in oil, all of which were painted years after he learned to work with his left hand).[73] Another man, one Corporal Gómez of the Santafecino Battalion, caught a ball in the calf as he neared the Paraguayan line. This caused him to drop to one knee, but when ordered to withdraw, he refused, and dug the projectile out with a pen knife before rejoining his unit in the attack. Another member of the same battalion, a seventeen-year-old color-bearer named Mariano Grandoli, inspired all his comrades by pushing ahead through a cloud of shrapnel, and when struck no less than fourteen times, wrapped himself in the national ensign, fell, and died.[74] Yet the simplest, most straightforward evocation of Argentine audacity came that day from yet another Santafecino, Captain Martín Viñales, who was encountered after the action with the entire trunk of his body covered in blood. "It is nothing," he observed, "just one arm less—my country deserves more."[75]

As scores and scores of men succumbed to enemy fire, the support that Charlone had requested started to arrive in the form of fresh units whose commanding officers all perished before they had come thirty paces. Four more Argentine battalions moved up in total, but these were all horribly ravaged in the advance. Colonel José Miguel Arredondo, commander of the 2nd Division and ranking officer on the scene, pulled a ladder out from underneath one of the dead men, and with consummate daring prepared to scale the nearest parapet. Suddenly, the Allied fleet, which had held its fire while the troops advanced on land, resumed its bombardment. This time the heavy rounds fell not among the Paraguayans, or into the swamps, but among the Argentines.

Arrendondo and all the others scattered pell-mell across the field. General Paunero, who had seen the Argentine vanguard collapse, rode up at this juncture and found a young lieutenant wearing the kepi of a lieutenant colonel and directing the men as best he could. "Where is the 1st Division?" the general demanded. "Here it is, sir," came the answer, "four flags escorted by sixty men."[76]

General Díaz had waited for this moment, and at his command the Paraguayans sallied out from the flanks of their battery and emptied their muskets at the retreating enemy. Díaz yearned to send his cavalry after them but was restrained, it seems, by Marshal López, who had no wish to lose any horsemen in a victory already guaranteed. Some of the Argentines ran straight across the Brazilian rear and into the Río Paraguay, where they drowned, though by far the greatest number was swallowed up in the marshes.

The wounded Colonel Rivas made a miraculous escape. Roseti's corps searched every spot of the field looking for him and came away thinking that he had died in the retreat. In reality, the colonel had made it to the Brazilian lines, where he vainly begged Porto Alegre for reinforcements. In tribute to Rivas's bravery, Mitre promoted him to general on the field of battle.[77] But no one could save his men.

All this time, on the left, the Brazilians were experiencing a similar slaughter.[78] The center-left column, under Colonel Albino Carvalho, managed to approach the first trench under a withering fire, but was thwarted by a watery morass that paralleled the line. Pivoting to the left in an effort to get around the enemy position, Carvalho's troops re-formed into a single column, which quickly came under enemy fire. The powder-blackened Paraguayan artillerymen could not see these Brazilian troopers, but kept firing mechanically through the smoke, displaying an improbable discipline. So strained were the Paraguayan cannons that at each discharge they leapt up from their carriages; the water-clogged sponges thrust down their bores crackled and sizzled at the touch of hot metal. Some of the gunners' ears bled from the relentless detonations, but they could still see Díaz, who rode the length of the line on horseback, shouting and waving his sword in the air. Carvalho's men could never have heard these cries either, but the horrible toll exacted by the Paraguayan grapeshot and rockets was unmistakable.

The Brazilian column nearest the river seems to have had the best luck in avoiding the enemy's gunfire. Colonel Augusto Caldas, who had earlier resented the tall grass along the line of advance, was now thankful for it. At spots, the Voluntários da Patria and Riograndense national guardsmen had to cut through the brush. One company of dismounted cavalry managed to reach the Paraguayan line, but, finding itself isolated, was soon discovered and torn to shreds.[79] A reserve brigade, sent to reinforce the forward units, mistook the survivors emerging from the smoke for the vanguard of an enemy counterattack. This caused everyone to break. Neither Caldas nor his officers could check the alarm as the men fled southward.[80]

Panic also erupted among Carvalho's units around two thirty in the afternoon, caused not so much by the precipitous flight on the far left, but rather by someone—probably Mitre—issuing the reasonable order to pull back.[81] Those troops that had gone furthest forward reacted to this order by dropping their rucksacks and running as fast as they could. When units at either side caught sight of their hasty withdrawal, everyone presumed that López was just behind. This caused the newcomers to panic and flee across the field—a scurrying mass of men, stampeding around each other to reach safety at Curuzú.[82]

At this late hour, when it looked as if common sense might finally prevail, an order came from the rear countermanding the recall. This was madness, as experienced officers like Arredondo and Rivas later declared.[83] Yet all along the front, the battle resumed on the premise that advances on the far left had taken place. None had. And as the dejected and incredulous men again approached the Paraguayan line, still adamantine in its resistance, they were cut down. Concentrated blasts of canister and grape ripped into the Allied units as they made a desperate charge, the last of the day.

Those men not wounded or killed played dead or managed to hide themselves under the heaps of the slain, hoping to crawl away at nighttime.[84] The mind of at least one man snapped under the stress as Díaz's infantrymen picked off the last of the fleeing Allied soldiers.[85] Up and down the trenches, the Paraguayans raged with a bloodlust. The ledger for the defeats at Tuyutí and Uruguaiana had been balanced. As the last cannonades died down, the soldiers could make out the shouts of their officers: "Oguerekó porã mako! Oguerekó porã mako!" (At last they get what they deserve! At last they get what they deserve!)[86] Just before 4:00 p.m., Mitre ordered a general retreat.

After the Battle

It took many hours for the Allies to calculate the extent of the disaster, but when the count was finally taken, they could not contain their shock. The Argentines had lost 2,082 men wounded or killed in action, including sixteen senior and 147 junior officers; this amounted to nearly half the Argentine soldiers who participated in the attack.[87] Roseti was gone, as were Charlone, Francisco Paz (son of the vice president), Lieutenant Colonel Alejandro Díaz, Colonel Manuel Fraga, and Captain Octavio Olascoaga, the latter three battalion commanders.

Another loss that registered heavily was that of Captain Domingo Fidel Sarmiento, the adopted (and possibly biological) son of the Argentine minister to the United States. The twenty-one-year old "Dominguito" had been everyone's favorite, an intelligent, sensitive, and kind young man who was idealized by his parents. He had a heartrending death at Curupayty: hit by grapeshot in the Achilles tendon, he could not stanch the bleeding and slipped away while his friends watched.[88]

The day was also costly for the Brazilians, with 2,011 men out of action, including 201 officers.[89] Six battalion commanders died, including Major Manoel Antunes de Abreu and Captain Joaquim Fabricio de Matos, both infantry officers of more than twenty-five years' standing, and both Knights of the Order of the Rose.[90] In an army badly in need of professional experience, these men could not easily be replaced.

Among the Brazilian wounded, hospital orderlies discovered one individual whose presence at the battle gave rise to considerable comment. Her name was María Francisca de Conceição, and she was a thirteen-year-old girl from Pernambuco who had followed her soldier-husband to the front. After his death at Curuzú, she disguised herself as an infantryman, participated in the 22 September assault, and was wounded in the head by a saber cut. When the other Brazilian troopers learned her gender, they hailed her as a great heroine, and rechristened her "María Curupaity."[91]

More than twenty-four hours passed before details of the defeat reached Allied soldiers on the peripheries. The two battalions of sharpshooters that Porto Alegre had sent into the Chaco to provide cover fire had the distinction of being the most successful Allied unit at the battle of Curupayty. Their musketry claimed the great majority of the Paraguayan casualties, which numbered only fifty-four killed and another one hundred fifty wounded.[92]

At the other end of the Allied line, closer to the Bellaco, Generals Polidoro and Flores had heard the unwelcome tidings somewhat earlier. Relegated to a subordinate role from the beginning, Polidoro had spent the day waiting for the final signal to launch his attack against the Paraguayan position above Tuyutí; but either the order never arrived or else he chose to ignore it. Considering his previous irritation with Porto Alegre and Tamandaré, and their predilection for sidelining him, it seems surprising that more lapses in communication had not occurred. Polidoro held his position the entire day and avoided any clash with the enemy. His superiors—and the armchair warriors in Rio de Janeiro—castigated him at length for this inactivity, yet in hindsight, his failure to close with the enemy probably saved the empire a good many men.

Flores proved far more aggressive and punctilious in his obedience to orders. Early in the day, he led his cavalry units on a sweep around the Paraguayan left. He crossed the Estero Bellaco at Paso Canoa, fought a couple of quick, bloody skirmishes, and captured twenty men. He had almost reached Tuyucué (future site of Allied headquarters) when runners arrived to report what had happened at Curupayty. He narrowly escaped capture when the Marshal sent two cavalry regiments to intercept him, and when Flores rode into Tuyutí toward the end of the day, he learned from Polidoro that the Allies had suffered an unmitigated disaster.

The implications of the defeat had yet to sink in with senior commanders, but there was much finger-pointing in the weeks and months ahead. The time had not yet come to assign blame or ask questions about what to do next. The field was still clogged with wounded men and corpses. Some of the survivors were evacuated to field hospitals and to the major medical facilities in Corrientes, all of which were soon overwhelmed with cases numbering in the thousands.[93] These men were the lucky ones, for far up toward the Paraguayan lines lay many Argentines and Brazilians whom the Allied medical teams could not reach without risking their own lives. In the absence of a truce, they were left to the clemency of an enemy who had precious little mercy to offer.[94]

Very few Allied prisoners were taken—Thompson claims half a dozen. Two Paraguayans who had joined the Allied host after Uruguaiana were captured and hanged on orders from Díaz. One of them took a long time in dying, and such were his torments that he begged the general to finish him; Díaz rejected the appeal out of hand, saying that the man had earned a painful death. As with his master, the general answered any whiff of treason with an unbounded cruelty.[95]

Only a week before, the interview at Yataity Corã had offered a chance for honorable peace and reconciliation. No longer. Bitterness and revenge had now seized hold of every combatant. The Paraguayans stripped the Allied dead of their uniforms and either dropped the corpses into adjacent lagoons, or, tying them together in chain-like formations, hurled them into the waters of the Paraguay. Early the next day, while Díaz and López slept off the effects of a celebratory champagne dinner, these monstrous garlands floated past Curuzú in full view of the Allied forces. Mitre, Porto Alegre, and Tamandaré looked on and said nothing.

5

THE ALLIES STUMBLE

Save for the ultra-chauvinistic writers working for *El Semanario*, no one, on either side, had predicted the scale of the Paraguayan victory at Curupayty. In its simplest form, the Allied failure reflected an underappreciation of Paraguayan strengths. Though the Marshal's soldiers had only just completed the trench works at Curupayty, they were good defenses, well-guarded by experienced gunners with ample shot and powder. The local terrain also favored the Paraguayans, who enjoyed clear fields of fire, except on the extreme flanks—and even here, brush or deep water hindered the Allied advance. The imperial navy could possibly have suppressed Paraguayan fire, had the preliminary bombardment hit any of the main batteries. But this did not happen: Tamandaré claimed to have pulverized the enemy works, when in fact he had hardly touched them. The smoke and thunder had obscured his failure, and the admiral flattered himself with an imaginary victory.

This fundamental mistake was not the only one that Allied commanders committed. Porto Alegre could have sent out scouts in advance of the attack. He could have built mangrullos at Curuzú to scan the nearest line of trenches in order to gauge the enemy's potential strength. He did neither. But Mitre must also share the blame. His Brazilian subordinates had bristled under his direction, doubted his strategy of continued confrontation at the Bellaco, and pointed to the earlier victory at Curuzú to illustrate what they could accomplish when final authority over military matters rested with them. Such attitudes may have smacked of insubordination, but the Argentine president refused to force the Brazilians to toe the line. He was worn down by the near-constant bickering with Tamandaré and Porto Alegre. Perhaps he reasoned that, having missed the chance for a settlement with López, the time had come for a decisive action along the lines suggested by the Brazilians. Curupayty provided a direct means to test this contention.

From late September 1866 to August 1867, when the Allies resumed their original tactic of outflanking the Paraguayans, the front remained static.[1] Whole weeks went by without any meaningful contact between enemies, apart from the occasional shouted insult or sniper's shot. The fleet regularly laid barrages in the direction of Curupayty, "thinking nothing of throwing 2,000 shells before breakfast," but little damage ensued.[2] This eleven-month period might be considered a breathing space or an unfortunate delay. But such interludes in war usually present opportunities for broad reflection and redefinition, and so it was after Curupayty.

Exit Flores

No sooner had the news of the setback reached the Allied camp at Tuyutí than General Flores packed his bags and set sail for Montevideo. He had intended to leave for the south two weeks earlier but had stayed on in order to participate in a battle in which his role was negligible and his performance lackluster.[3] His inability to rise to the occasion, though not his fault, was lost in the general gloom of defeat, and ultimately counted for little. He left behind General Enrique Castro, who now commanded a token force only nominally Uruguayan in composition. Though the División Oriental, as it was known, continued to maintain some semblance of the national standard in the fields of Paraguay, it remained for all intents and purposes irrelevant. Flores had been one of the war's outstanding personalities; tenacious, if not always thoughtful, he had favored a gaucho manner of fighting in which charisma and a lion-hearted audacity counted far more than strategy.[4] His departure from the front brought an end to that older, more personalized style of war making.

Just before leaving, Flores issued a proclamation calling upon all Allied soldiers to continue "along the honorable path ... so that each man would become a hero, destined to avenge the loss of illustrious [comrades such as] Sampaio, Rivero, Palleja, Argüero, and so many other noble victims immolated by the fanaticism of our enemies."[5] His defenders argued that "having finished the mission of a warrior, [Flores] now embarks on that of an administrator," but few apparently believed this.[6] In fact, the heroic caudillo now appeared as a defeated general slinking home in disgrace.

The Brazilians stayed loyal to Flores; they had little choice if they wanted to attain their policy goals in the Platine estuary: they still had troops stationed in Montevideo and along the frontier, and could guarantee internal peace in Uruguay after a fashion. But any dissension among the ruling Colorados cast

Brazil more obviously in the role of an occupying power and their leader—the president of the Oriental Republic of the Uruguay—as a lackey.

In light of the conflicts Flores faced on the domestic scene, he found it useful to treat his Brazilian sponsors with a newfound wariness. In a personal communication to Polidoro on 20 October, he affirmed his allegiance to the Allied cause and stated that he "would always side with the imperial government, without this [fact] signifying that [he] would ignore the advantages that might accrue from a dignified peace."[7] This was certainly indicative of an ambiguous posture, but then again, Flores had also lost confidence in his Argentine allies. Upon his return to Montevideo, he instructed his personal secretary, Dr. Julio Herrera y Obes, to prepare for a confidential mission to Rio de Janeiro to report to dom Pedro on the inept comportment of Brazilian generals in the field, and on the "incompetence of General Mitre as commander-in-chief of the Allied forces."[8] Flores considered the Argentine president his friend of many years standing and had fought by his side from the Bonaerense grasslands to the hill country of Santa Fe. Now his political survival at home depended on putting distance between himself and both his erstwhile Allies.

A day or two before Dr. Herrera left for his meeting with Pedro, Flores received a copy of a communication the Argentine cabinet had sent to Mitre on 26 September. Its contents confirmed Flores's worst suspicions. The Porteños appeared eager to quit the war and authorized Mitre to reopen negotiations with Marshal López, separating Argentina from the Triple Alliance "in all that is neither transcendental nor compromises the honor and permanent interests of the republic."[9] It appeared that the treaty of May 1865 now meant little to the Argentine national government. Flores instructed Herrera to ask the emperor point-blank how the Allies could continue to trust a man whose government had called for peace at any price.

Out With the Old, In With the New

The pessimism with which Flores had to contemplate his options paralleled that of certain ministers and members of Parliament in Brazil. The news of Mitre's meeting with López at Yataity Corã had been poorly received and had encouraged those who had always questioned the wisdom of an alliance with Argentina.[10] Furthermore, the nationalist fervor unleashed by the Paraguayan invasions of Mato Grosso and Rio Grande do Sul had evaporated. The various paeans to the victors of Curuzú now rang hollow, and a distinct feeling of weariness hung in the air.[11] Every man who could evade service in the National Guard now did so.[12] To make up the difference and to provide recruits for the regular army, officials resorted to forced conscription, a practice that one parliamentarian from Minas Gerais condemned as an excuse to dispose of personal enemies through outright kidnapping.[13] His attitude was not uncommon. There were no longer any "children ardent for desperate glory," and many Brazilians now considered the Paraguayan War the equivalent of a peptic ulcer—irritating, if not fatal.

Certain Brazilian statesmen wondered the same thing. Seven weeks before the Curupayty disaster, a new cabinet came into office. Headed by Zacharias de Góes e Vasconcelos, it was composed of Conservatives and moderate Liberals who had banded together in a "Progressive League." The cabinet faced many opponents. The radical Liberals—those who had pushed the empire into the Uruguayan imbroglio in 1864 and who still professed the most enthusiasm for the war—opposed the ministry almost as much as did the old-guard Conservatives. The latter showed more concern about their exclusion from power than about the prosecution of the war. Too many outstanding issues urgently required attention, and most Brazilian politicians preferred to concentrate on those questions rather continue the struggle with Paraguay.[14]

The one significant figure who remained focused on winning the final victory was Emperor Pedro II. Early in October he wrote: "They talk about peace in the Rio de la Plata but *I* won't make peace with López, and public opinion is on my side; therefore I don't doubt the honorable outcome of the campaign for Brazil." [15] Whether the *vox populi* in Rio de Janeiro supported Pedro on the war was irrelevant, however; he could nominate or remove ministers as he saw fit. Given that fact, no politician, least of all Zacharias, could afford to make himself "incompatible" with Pedro.

A clean-shaven Conservative law professor and landowner from Bahia, the prime minister was well fitted to head the cabinet. Until the 1860s, his career had taken an orthodox course. He had served as president of three provinces before assuming office as a deputy, and in 1852, at the time of the Urquiza uprising against Rosas in Argentina, he joined the cabinet as its youngest minister. At the end of the decade, Zacharias found his political advancement blocked by the sclerotic Conservative senators, which left his continued success as a statesman in the hands of the emperor. When his third cabinet was established in 1866, Zacharias reluctantly submitted to the monarch's demand to pursue the fight against Paraguay despite Curupayty. Pedro had insisted on victory as the only "honorable outcome of the campaign," and once again, Zacharias did as his imperial majesty directed.

Neither an outright triumph nor an improvised peace could be achieved with the same strategy or under the same military leadership. Porto Alegre, Argolo, and Tamandaré, moreover, were all Liberals and each in his own way had sought to enhance the party's standing in the imperial government, a goal that became unrealistic after 22 September. This left Polidoro, the Conservative commander of the 1st Corps, who had always seemed a better administrator than a field officer. Aged sixty-four, he suffered from neuralgia and recurrent fatigue and he told his officers that he would prefer to yield supreme command to someone else.[16] But which general in the Brazilian army could rise above the misfortune of Curupayty and face the present adversity?

Only the emperor could say. In making his nomination, Pedro recognized that Zacharias, who had once argued for legal limitations on the imperial prerogative, now needed the monarch to cut the Gordian knot. Quietly and without fanfare Pedro put forward the name of the one man with sufficient prestige and experience to lead the imperial forces in Paraguay: Luís Alves de Lima e Silva, the Marquis of Caxias.

Born near Rio de Janeiro in 1803, Caxias was the scion of a notable family. He entered the army as a teenager and participated with distinction in every campaign in which the empire was involved. But Caxias was more than a good officer; the tactful and intelligent diplomacy he used in quelling the Farrapo secession in 1845 demonstrated an ability beyond the military sphere, hastening his entry onto the political stage, where he could always speak authoritatively. By the 1850s, Caxias was incontestably the army's most famous general, the most resourceful, and thus the most likely to succeed in any political endeavor.[17]

Caxias's aristocratic bearing was apparent to all of his contemporaries, but his character was decidedly intricate. Apprehensive in personality, he compensated by cultivating a demanding, even severe, professional standard. Over the years, his perfectionism manifested itself in impressive administrative skills, an unshakable loyalty to the monarch, and a broad military acumen. In Caxias's brain, moreover, there was always a guiding spirit that whispered: "control, control, control."[18] It made him the best candidate to save the Allied war effort. Polidoro had to preach to incredulous listeners, but the marquis's arguments always carried conviction.

As the emperor had noted some years earlier, "I believe Caxias to be loyal and my friend especially because he is so little a politician."[19] In fact, the marquis's father, a regent, had been close to those who had founded the Party of Order; it was hardly surprising that this connection, as well as his general outlook and his defense of the status quo aligned him with the Conservatives. That party, however, remained in opposition as the Triple Alliance War began.

Though Caxias appreciated the need for a unified campaign against López, he refused to cooperate on Zacharias's terms. A year earlier, the Progressives had kept him from the presidency of the province of Rio Grande do Sul. In addition, he was piqued that Zacharias had given the portfolio of war to Àngelo Moniz da Silva Ferraz, a man whom the marquis detested. He therefore abstained from command in the earliest stages of the Paraguayan War. The defeat at Curupayty, however, placed the question of his participation in a different light. Even though Caxias was only one year younger than Polidoro, no one doubted his physical stamina or fitness for command.

The marquis's selection offered few immediate benefits for Zacharias and his colleagues. Given Caxias's party loyalties, the appointment meant admitting a dissident into the inner circle of power. Though Pedro had urged the nomination, it proved difficult for the Progressives nonetheless; Ferraz, after all, was not only Zacharias's political ally, but a kinsman and a friend. Now the war minister was called upon to act the patriot, something he did not hesitate to do: he resigned the ministry at the beginning of October 1866. His replacement, João Lustosa da Cunha Paranaguá, wasted no time in aligning his policies with those of Caxias.

Having made the painful concession, Zacharias directed an evocative appeal to the marquis that stressed the same call of patriotism that had excited Ferraz. Caxias could not resist. He met with the various cabinet ministers in order to guarantee their future support for any strategies he might contemplate at the front. Then, donning his uniform, he embarked for Paraguay. As if to foreshadow the challenges that awaited him, the steam engine of the French packet *Carmel*, upon which he departed, soon broke down and had to be towed back to port. Caxias left aboard another vessel.[20]

The Argentine Reaction

Mitre was waiting for Caxias. Of all the Allied leaders who faced the Paraguayans at Curupayty, the Argentine president received the most blame for the setback. His political opponents called him lazy and predictable, and hinted at his cowardice.[21] He had given the order for the ill-fated attack and now had to take responsibility for what had happened. Many families had lost sons, and there was no lack of people accusing Mitre for their misfortunes.[22]

Buenos Aires was a city that thrived on rumors, and the defeat in the north set off considerable speculation, subdued at first, then very vocal indeed. Certain members of the national government called for another round of negotiations with the Marshal. Others, still recalling the warnings of Alberdi and Guido y Spano, and moved by the desperate tales circulating in the streets, suggested withdrawal as soon as possible.[23] Only those closest to Mitre—Marcos Paz, Guillermo Rawson, and Rufino de Elizalde—continued to express full confidence in the president's military leadership. Elizalde, who was both foreign minister and Mitre's presumptive heir, ignored the political implications and persisted in treating the war as a narrowly military challenge.[24]

The optimism Elizalde expressed in this missive of 3 October was little better than flat champagne. Though still imbued with the "flavor" of a once serious and potent argument, it had lost its vitality as far as the Argentine public was concerned. Patriotism had been a powerful lever in the hands of the Porteño Liberals since before Mitre's victory over Urquiza at Pavón—but it was fast slipping away. Buenos Aires had arrayed itself in mourning, as required by tradition, but even the most lugubrious displays could not hide the fact that most people wanted the war pushed from the headlines.

In the minds of a great many Bonaerenses, Uruguay and Paraguay remained buffer states with little right to independent existence. Uruguay had fallen into its proper place in early 1865; that Paraguay had not followed suit could only be ascribed to incompetence—Mitre's, as military commander, or, more likely, his Brazilian allies', as fighters.[25] Few of the old Argentine fire-eaters would concede that the Paraguayans had won at Curupayty through skill and mettle, and yet the general opinion in Buenos Aires held otherwise. As *The Standard* observed:

> We [thought that] the military strength of Paraguay was far inferior to its natural resources. The inhabitants have always been quiet and inoffensive, and extremely obedient, but the present war has no doubt called forth a warlike disposition, and this is enhanced by the studied care of President López to inculcate amongst his people the fixed belief that the humblest Paraguayan is more than a match for any foreigner. ... The tedious march of this campaign is fast converting this country of peasants into a nation of warriors, and the longer it lasts the more durable the change.[26]

With so many people questioning the pace, and, indeed, the value of the war effort, it took don Bartolo's associates weeks of concentrated work to shore up political support. Though chastened by recent events, these Liberals could still boast certain organizational advantages over the other factions, most of which represented a variety of regional and personal interests and found it difficult to work together as a result. Thus, when closing the congressional session on 10 October, Vice President Paz still had to sound the appropriate patriotic note. He enjoined the deputies to return to their homes to tell their "fellow citizens that the consolidation of the Republic [was] being strengthened every day, that there [were] no fears for the future of the nation or the cause of unity ... and that the valor of the army in the field [promised] a speedy and happy conclusion of the campaign against despotism."[27]

But it did nothing of the kind. Try as they might, the Liberals failed to find a new well of nationalism among the people. Instead, they discovered a growing insistence that while the alliance with Brazil remained good business, it was not always good politics. For the Bonaerense Autonomists, the era of glum acquiescence in Mitre's war making had ended. Now they hoped to exact a toll for every concession they offered the national government.

The Autonomists had always gauged good politics by its impact on the market. As with other Argentines, they had been angered by Paraguay's attack on Corrientes, and had adopted a pro-Brazil policy as a necessary step to setting things in their proper place. But now that the Allies had driven López back, the Autonomists explicitly sought to mold the war into a commercial venture—not so crucial to the nation as the Atlantic wool trade, but a profitable enterprise nevertheless.[28] In this fashion, the Bonaerenses began to redefine their stake in the war. To be sure, they continued to evoke national dignity and pay lip service to the Triple Alliance, but in military matters they preferred that the republic recede from active leadership. Moreover, while the Bonaerenses continued to formally support President Mitre in international affairs, they had lost interest, for now, in his protracted struggle against the Paraguayans. Let the slavocrats in Brazil have their foolish campaign of vengeance—it counted for little so long as they paid for their war supplies in Buenos Aires.[29]

In the Argentine Litoral and Interior, many people were resentful of the course of events and some even called for rebellion. In Corrientes, Tucumán, and Santiago del Estero, local Liberals continued to support Mitre and the national government, but this was more opportunistic than ideological.[30] The arrangement contrasted with the skepticism of those *provincianos* who saw the Alliance as an unnatural marriage that should be annulled without further delay, and who rejected any concept of Argentine nationalism dictated by the narrow ambitions of Buenos Aires.

There were also international questions to consider. The Chileans had asserted a degree of influence in the western provinces (and Patagonia) that contradicted local Argentine interests and from which the Bonaerenses remained rather insulated. In Salta and Jujuy, moreover, a disturbing rumor held that Bolivia might soon launch an invasion in support of Paraguay.[31] The Bolivian president, Mariano Melgarejo, had previously shown himself partial to Paraguayan interests; at the same time, he wanted to take advantage of Argentine disunity in order to project his country's influence in the bordering provinces. At least one important newspaper in La Paz endorsed this position despite the fact that it drew undisguised scorn from the Allied countries.[32]

In Entre Ríos, Governor Justo José de Urquiza barely managed to restrain his associates from an open break with the national government, this in spite of the profits local *estancieros* had earned from the sale of horses and cattle to the Brazilian army. A year earlier, Bonaerense agents had tried to appease the Entrerriano draftees, and all they got for their trouble were mutinies at Basualdo and Toledo. Now, Urquiza's own wife pressed him to abandon the distasteful contacts with the empire and reclaim his rightful position of seniority vis-à-vis Mitre.[33]

Old "war horses" such as the Entrerriano Ricardo López Jordan and the Catamarqueño Felipe Varela urged him in the same direction. This set off scuttlebutt about the governor's intentions that reached Mitre's ears at Tuyutí. It proved most unwelcome news. The president was well aware that Urquiza could not bear to speak of the Brazilians without calling them "monkeys" (*macacos*). Mitre felt sufficiently worried about this to send his personal secretary, José M. Lafuente, to query the Entrerriano caudillo about recent events.[34] The resulting report of 10 October made fascinating reading and provided Mitre with a useful appraisal of conditions in the Litoral. Lafuente observed that

> the general is your loyal friend and, although the constant clamor of his entourage may gradually erode this feeling and encourage his baser passions, especially envy, when he is addressed in your name ... he forgets his worst fears, turns his back on his most odious advisors ... and returns to the straight and narrow path. ... [He longs for the] role of peace-maker; his ambition is to return to the presidency and he sees this as the ladder he must use to ascend to that position.[35]

Urquiza's province might remain a thorn in the side of the national government but, for the moment, he appeared dependable.

At any rate, the real obstacle to Argentine national cohesion at the end of 1866 was not in the Litoral provinces but in the far west. Curupayty had kindled a signal fire for a hodgepodge of rural interests in Cuyo and La Rioja, some of which had links with the old Federalists and the Uruguayan Blancos, and all of which resented the national government's tax regimen, its recruitment efforts, its demands for "national organization," and its alliance with Brazil. These westerners were Mitre's longtime opponents, the "barbarians" that his "civilized" Liberals had always sought to contain.

Mitre thought the westerners Luddites, a doomed breed of traditionalists insensibly rejecting the modern age and its new system of values. For their part, the Cuyanos and Riojanos detested the "odious Unitarians" of the capital city, whose masculinity they doubted and whose pretensions to national leadership they treated with derision. To these "Americanists" of the west, the principle of monarchy, whether in Brazil or elsewhere, suggested an Old World wickedness that stunk of false dignity, corruption, and more than a taint of madness.[36]

The rebellion that many westerners longed for finally came in November 1866, and it had the covert support of those politicians in Santiago de Chile who were still smarting from the indifference that Mitre had shown during the Chincha Islands conflict. The Spaniards, they recalled, had bombarded Valparaiso after taking on provisions at Buenos Aires, and now the Chileans took pleasure in returning the favor by arming Mitre's opponents. The Argentine Montoneros, for their part, well understood what happens when the lamb begs the fox for aid, but greedily accepted Chilean support all the same.

"Volunteers" from the other side of the border joined with various gaucho insurgents in San Juan, after which the rebels set out to conquer Cuyo. As success followed success, the Montonero caudillos hoped to turn a limited uprising into a national revolution and to this end dispatched messages to Urquiza.[37] The westerners had loudly proclaimed their adherence to the 1853 Constitution as well as their support for Marshal López. Urquiza, they knew, had an explosive personality, but now he was no longer a self-assured young rebel, but a nervous old man with dyed sideburns. He had exchanged the role of insurgent for that of livestock purveyor, and spurned the Montoneros' offer.

Even without his help, however, some three thousand rebel troops managed to seize a huge swath of western territory within just a few weeks. This encouraged the enemies of the national government in every province of the republic.[38] In short order, the numerous revolutionary chieftains issued a series of flowery manifestos announcing their intention to march eastward—possibly, even, to Buenos Aires. Would Urquiza stay loyal to the national government under the pressure of their victories? Only he could say.

At the Front

Since Curupayty, Mitre had lived two months of self-pity, confusion, and persistent ague. At various times during the campaign, when all was deceptively quiet, he retired to his tent or timber-lined quarters to immerse himself in the poetry of Dante. He found it impossible, however, to free himself from the monsters the war had created. He had once shown skill in juggling political interests and beating a vulnerable enemy in the field. Now, the fighting seemed endless; the Paraguayans would never surrender, he worried, and he could find no way around the military dilemma.[39]

Worse still, his political rivals, both among the Argentines and the Brazilians, were ready to pounce upon his indecision. Reassuring messages from Buenos Aires could no longer hide the hard fact that everything Mitre had constructed in his own country might well disintegrate. If he wanted the Argentine republic to survive, he had to decide which adversary to face first—López, the Montonero leaders, or the various dissenters in Buenos Aires. If he chose the first, then he had to worry what the Brazilians might do and whether the Marquis of Caxias might become less a friend than a competitor.

Though no one expected a Paraguayan attack in the wake of Curupayty, the Allied commander took no chances. He ordered his troops to fortify the line from Curuzú to Tuyutí. At the former site, the Argentines evacuated, leaving the labor to the Brazilians, who built strong trenches and an earthen citadel reinforced with brick and defended by cannon. For convenience' sake, Porto Alegre lived aboard a steamer just opposite this position which offered him a degree of comfort and an ample view of the front. His men, however, led a much more cramped existence and suffered through Paraguayan barrages, which, according to Thompson, were much more successful than their own.[40] Meanwhile, the bulk of the Argentine army was redeployed several miles to the southeast, where the men worked to fortify their Tuyutí position (at the Paso Gómez) with a double line of trenches and a great many Whitworth 32-pounders and mortars. As with the Brazilian naval and land forces, the Argentines continued to fire on the Paraguayan lines with an indifferent result.

The one hope that the Allies cherished, at least for the near future, lay with Caxias, who arrived in Buenos Aires on 6 November. While lunching with his presumed friends in the Mitre government, the marquis coolly announced that the empire would send twenty thousand reinforcements before the end of the year. He observed that General Osório stood ready in Rio Grande do Sul with an additional fifteen thousand men to push into Paraguay via Encarnación if such an attack proved necessary.[41] This determination sounded perfect to Elizalde, who right away reported to Mitre that Caxias "was free of any nuisances that might [disrupt] the prosecution of the war."[42] The Argentine president was duly impressed with this news, as he knew the men at the front would be: far better to have one meticulous and optimistic general than three bickering prima donnas.

One figure who was not so contented was Tamandaré. On the sixteenth of the month he met with Caxias in Corrientes. The marquis gave him official word that under the new arrangement, the fleet no longer operated independently under the admiral, but fell directly under Caxias's authority. Tamandaré, unfailingly grumpy, snorted at this. The marquis contrived to soften the blow by offering his old comrade-in-arms three months' leave in accordance with a directive from the minister of marine, after which Tamandaré might resume his important duties in Paraguay if he so chose. In making this offer, Caxias realized that the admiral could never accept it. The next day, Tamandaré dictated a letter to his superiors in Rio de Janeiro formally asking to be relieved.

On 18 November 1866, the Marquis of Caxias issued his first order of the day from Allied headquarters. He announced his assumption of command in simple terms and ordered his officers to forego wearing headgear or epaulettes that might distinguish them from their men, and thereby offer Paraguayan snipers a more tempting target.[43] It was a significant indication that things would be different from now on, and that all the old aristocratic twaddle could be jettisoned if it interfered with winning the war. Caxias had a facility for stripping down problems to their simplest components, and Mitre, reassured, prepared for some long and productive conversations with the new commander.

North of the line, the Paraguayans jeered: one kambá more or less made no difference to them.

A Quandary for the Paraguayans

One might think that the triumph at Curupayty would have filled the Paraguayan troops with new confidence—and indeed, for several days, every town in the republic celebrated with games, songs, foot races for children, speeches in praise of the Marshal and the glorious cause, skyrockets and firecrackers, and considerable drinking. Dances were held at Humaitá, where soldiers stepped lively in their newly captured Brazilian or Argentine uniforms, their pockets bulging with loot.[44] Surely this meant that greater successes might follow?

Yet the tremendous achievement of Paraguayan arms only counted if the political balance in the Plata now tipped fundamentally against the Allies, and no one could be sure that this had even happened. The number of sick and wounded continued to mount and the Marshal could not replace these men.[45] Thus, the happy mood at Humaitá slowly dissipated into the same somber resignation that characterized the Allied soldiers on the opposite side.

Most Paraguayans scrupulously avoided any loose talk or show of disaffection, for such behavior would bring a swift punishment from López's Acá Verá guardsmen or the many spies in camp.[46] After the war, veterans claimed that even before the end of 1866 they already knew that the Allied powers would prevail. But at the time they could do nothing to stave off the unfolding disaster, nor would their notion of duty permit them any path but obedience. Their prospects of success were limited. Manpower shortages could only be alleviated by dipping still further into the shrinking adolescent population, and the increased hardship could only alienate country people; they had always led difficult lives, but they were still unaccustomed to so much outside pressure. It might prove necessary to subject both civilians and soldiers to even more coercion.

In this important sense, the Paraguayan achievement at Curupayty had a perverse effect. It confirmed López's belief that the war was a contest of wills in which the enormous material advantage of the Allies counted for little; with determination and courage, he could still win. This supposition provided a glossy veneer to the war's tragedy—for the unspoken recognition among many Paraguayans that the struggle was hopeless did not lessen the vigor of their resistance. Exceptions to this attitude existed, but they were very few.

For now, such conjecture was beside the point. Closer to the action, the men could only see what was happening in their immediate vicinity, and when actually fighting, that perspective was all they could afford. Certainly the Paraguayan soldiers had much to do at this time. The trench at Curupayty, which they had completed just hours before the assault began, was now widened and extended and the banquette raised. The men fashioned rawhide huts at the parapet's edge to keep their lines of fire unimpeded in the event of a new Allied attack. They also cut new trenches and a supply road through the woods and around the carrizal from the main fort at Curupayty all the way to Sauce—a distance of almost eighteen miles. They erected various mangrullos and a telegraph line that linked López's headquarters at Paso Pucú with Asunción and the forward positions.[47] The British consul at Rosario, Thomas Hutchinson, observed that the Paraguayan telegraph system bore more than a passing resemblance to that operated by Napoleon III during his Italian campaigns. It was a *telégrafo ambulante* (mobile telegraph) made up of wires, batteries, and bamboo poles sufficient to cover a very wide circuit.[48]

Thompson and the other foreign engineers worked well into 1867 in designing and constructing a series of ever more elaborate defenses. Thompson himself was a phlegmatic Briton who disliked the histrionics of his Paraguayan associates—and was disliked in turn—but usually got his way since the Marshal so manifestly appreciated his efforts. In due course, the engineers finished some 12,300 yards of trenches, the majority nine feet deep, with parapets buttressed with fascines of brambles and logs of heavy lapacho. Since the batteries along the trench line were placed far apart, the soldiers packed the intervening spaces with tree trunks wrapped in ox hides to resemble cannons—a ruse that served its purpose well, for the Allied officers in charge of reconnoitering parties invariably took them for guns.[49]

The Paraguayans also experienced considerable problems with water seeping in from the swamp and wrecking their efforts at reinforcing the parapets. In the end, when Thompson completed the vast defensive work, he linked the two previously separated sets of trenches at Sauce and Curupayty, which now formed an immense protective rectangle over forty miles in length. The Allies dubbed this trench work the "Cuadrilátero," and they had many opportunities to get to know it over the next two years.[50]

Having demonstrated his mastery of moist earth, stone, and tree branches, Thompson turned to water. His men dammed the northern channel of the Bellaco. This flooded the adjacent area, making it impassable save for movement along several wooden plank bridges that could be destroyed at a moment's notice. They then dug a channel leading to the old trenches at Sauce, which could be flooded by means of a sluice gate.[51]

The Marshal understood that disguised tree trunks, torpedoes, and flooded channels could provide only minimal security for his army, so he augmented his active batteries with cannon transported from Humaitá. This brought the total number of Paraguayan guns facing the river at Curupayty to thirty-five. Two of the older 24-pounders were sent from Humaitá to the Asunción arsenal, where workers rebored and rifled them to permit the use of a 50-pound shot. These guns, too, found their way south to Curupayty.[52] The Ybycuí foundry produced one noteworthy artillery piece during this period. Weighing twelve tons and capable of throwing a spherical 10-inch shell some five thousand yards, it was hauled by oxen and mules to the Asunción arsenal for mounting before being added to the other guns along the river at Curupayty. Because they had cast the cannon from bells contributed from churches, the men christened it "El Cristiano."[53]

The Paraguayans used these cannons to teach the Allies many lessons over the next several months. Casual observers of the artillery duels asked how López's army remained so well stocked with powder and shot. In fact, saltpeter deposits at San Juan Nepomuceno and the headwaters of the Ypané River provided much of the raw material for the former, and the latter came mostly from the Allies themselves.[54] Tamandaré's fleet, as we have seen, thought nothing of firing more than a thousand shells a day at Curupayty, and much of this spent ordnance was gathered for later use by López's men. Every armload of shell fragments that could be collected and reused earned a cup of maize as a reward.[55]

Only rarely did the Allies get off a lucky shot, as occurred, for example, in December 1866, when a shell hit a Paraguayan powder magazine, setting off an explosion that killed forty-six. Since this event coincided with a brief Allied bombardment against Paso Gómez, the various Paraguayan field commanders evidently expected the enemy to launch a frontal assault. It never came to pass. With the barrages doing little damage, the Paraguayans responded by blowing on rustic "cornets" made of cow horn and styled *turútutú* in imitation of the wail that they made. Their cacophonous taunts, which conveyed an unmistakable sarcasm, could be heard aboard every ship in the enemy fleet and, so it was said, drove Caxias to distraction.[56]

Activities on the Paraguayan side of the line focused on making that line impregnable, the better to buy time. One could easily depict the Marshal's stance as rigid in its truculence. The Allied debacle at Curupayty filled him with reassurance that his estimation of the enemy had been right all along. At the same time, López had to consider his army's strategic disposition, which had remained the same since before 22 September.

Enter Washburn

The slow war of attrition that had now commenced was painful. The Paraguayans had to depend on shrinking material and human resources behind long extended trenches. Moreover, for all their divisions, the Allies still commanded enormous resources and with Caxias on the scene, they might also claim the political will to keep fighting. López could not cancel these facts, and he could not attack without risking another Tuyutí; indeed, he could do nothing except defend the previously established lines. It seemed, therefore, as if the Allies would strangle the country.

This assumption reinforced the need for an honorable way out. But it was doubtful that the Marshal had the imagination—or even the necessary humility—to find a diplomatic solution at this stage. López had entered the Yataity Corã negotiation somewhat warily, and had been snubbed through Argentine deceit and Brazilian hostility. He had no interest in diplomacy if it meant further dishonor.

Previously, any talk of outside mediation brought guffaws from the Allies, who had presumed that a determined assault would take them to Humaitá and then to Asunción. The Paraguayans, trusting in the justice of their cause, had speculated that outside powers—the United States, Great Britain, France, or some combination of the three—might somehow impose a peace that would leave the Allies well short of victory.[57] The officials of the López government were careful not to state this openly, for such a proposition might be read as defeatism. If the foreigners could see the broad disadvantages for all concerned, surely they would insist on a new round of diplomacy. Had not something similar happened when the British brokered a peace between Brazil and Argentina in 1828?

The chief figure to argue this viewpoint was Charles Ames Washburn. Of all the people to play a central role during the Triple Alliance War, he probably felt the most frustrated by this position. The fifth son of an influential Republican family from Maine, he had always seemed a latecomer, a man of talent and introspection who watched from the side as accolades rained down on his brothers. As a favor to the family, President Lincoln named Washburn commissioner to Asunción in 1861, and subsequently upgraded his position to minister. This gave Washburn diplomatic authority. The post was no plum, however, for Paraguay was the most obscure of the South American republics, and so isolated that many responsible people in American government doubted the need for any diplomatic presence there at all.

Washburn, whatever his true opinions, reacted with verve once he arrived in the Paraguayan capital, as if to show his brothers that he was up to their standards. He even offered, in November 1864, to assist the government in Asunción in mediating the dispute between Uruguay and the empire.[58] Regrettably, his forthright and unambiguous behavior, which might have been common enough among the New Englanders of his day, found little sympathy in the authoritarian environment of Paraguay.

During his first stay in the country, from November 1861 to January 1865, Washburn managed to irritate both Lópezes, father and son. State officials and important figures on the social scene tended to snub Washburn in consequence. When not calling him a fool outright, they intimated that he was a man destitute of finesse who never made concessions to local sensibilities. He neither hid his opinions nor apologized for them. And for someone who took pleasure in parroting the egalitarian slogans of his faraway nation, he had the graceless habit of treating most strangers, Paraguayans and Americans alike, as his social inferiors. In a country where only one man was supreme, his attitude amounted to wanton arrogance and was deeply out of place in a diplomat.[59]

Now, in late 1866, in what must have seemed an irony, Washburn found himself in a situation where he might bring peace to Paraguay. While on home leave a year earlier, he had married Sallie Cleaveland, a high-strung, rather flighty woman from New York who was twenty-one years his junior. The couple spent months in Buenos Aires and Corrientes, trying to obtain Allied permission to pass through the blockade in order to reach Washburn's post upriver. Mitre seemed agreeable but Admiral Tamandaré peevishly refused to cooperate, probably not wanting to add legitimacy to the Marshal's status as head of state any more than he had to.[60] Washburn fumed at all the delays, his wife droned on about the lack of proper lodgings in Corrientes, and neither made any headway with the Allied authorities.

In late October, the commander of the USS *Shamokin*, a warship on station in the Río de la Plata, received orders to provide the couple passage to Asunción, and to force the Allied blockade should the Brazilians continue to stonewall. Clearly, Washburn's family connections had finally worked their magic in Washington. US naval officers had avoided helping Washburn up to that point, seeing little advantage in offending the Argentines and Brazilians by pushing the issue of the minister's right of access to Paraguay. Now that they had received their instructions, however, the officers were determined to get the minister through to his post and out of their hands.

As it turned out, the Paraguayans already knew of Washburn's misadventures in Corrientes, and had hoped that Tamandaré would have blundered into a confrontation with the United States. When this did not occur, they met the American ship coming upriver under a flag of truce and warned that torpedoes prevented unimpeded passage above Curupayty. Washburn agreed to disembark there, and was provided conveyance to Humaitá. All along the route the minister was received with military bands and the jubilant acclamations of Paraguayan soldiers, who celebrated his "breaking" the blockade as much as the possibility of any negotiations.[61]

Washburn expressed surprise that no invitation was forthcoming from the Marshal at Paso Pucú, but López was sick in bed and could receive no one.[62] So the American proceeded to Asunción, set up his legation once again, and met with his French counterpart, Consul Emile Laurent-Cochelet. The French consul, conceivably the most polished and educated foreigner in Paraguay, reported that some districts in the country faced imminent starvation. The police had recently started arresting foreigners, and many of the British engineers who had aided the Paraguayan cause had fallen into their clutches.[63]

In subsequent years, Washburn would interpret this news in the worst possible way. A general decline had already begun in Paraguay, brought on by the exigencies of the war, and there was no relief in sight. As Washburn began to prepare his case for American mediation, he also tried to place a diplomatic shield in front of as many people as he could—a practice that caused him and his government considerable trouble.

An official welcome ceremony for Washburn took place in the early hours of 26 November that included speeches in favor of the United States and, with the help of various musical bands, several improvised dances.[64] A few days later, Foreign Minister José Berges wrote to the US minister to note his government's pleasure in welcoming Washburn's return: "I am pleased to rejoice with you that the flag of the great American republic has forced the outrageous blockade of the Triple Alliance, commanded the respect and justice it deserves, saluted the national banner of the republic, waving in triumph over Curupayty, [and] in support of the cause of liberty that has just finally triumphed in the United States of America." [65]

Berges was thinking about the long-term geopolitical implications of the Paraguayan War. In contrast to the Marshal's other ministers, who had never left the country and who were apt to say the most exaggerated things about foreign intentions, he had a good grasp of the larger picture and favored American offers of help even if they only bought a bit of time.[66] His career as a diplomatist may have crested, and the Marshal had less and less use for him, but this issue of US mediation gave him a new chance to shine.

The Americans, Berges reasoned, had just finished their own Civil War, and were, at that moment, aiding the Juárez government in ousting the French interventionists from Mexico. President Grant was known to entertain a strongly pro-Mexican, and presumably pro-republican, view of continental affairs.[67] In the South American context, such an inclination redounded in favor of Paraguay. As the US minister in Brazil put it as early as the previous August, "we should impress all the American governments with a conviction, that it is alike their interest and their duty, to look to the United States for protection and advice; protection from European interference, and friendly counsel and advice in regard to difficulties with their neighbors."[68]

As the Platine states settled down to one of the hottest summers in memory, Washburn prepared a written proposal for mediation. He probably knew that, while the State Department remained uninterested in the idea of American interference in the Paraguayan struggle, his brothers' friends in the US Congress could be persuaded otherwise. Indeed, in mid-December, the House of Representatives passed a resolution suggesting the possibility of US mediation in both the Paraguayan conflict and the war between Spain and the Pacific republics of South America.[69] A circular letter to that effect was dispatched to the warring nations, and it proposed that they send plenipotentiaries to attend a conference to be held in Washington. Paraguay was asked to name one delegate, while the Allies might select one from each of their governments or one for all three. The president of the United States would appoint a presiding officer to advise and inform but not vote. All resolutions adopted at the conference had to be unanimous and ratified by the respective governments. The US president could appoint an umpire in case of disagreement. Once general propositions were accepted by all representatives, talks leading to an armistice could begin in earnest.[70]

The American offer was well intentioned, and, in general, well designed. It was also certain to be ignored by politicians and military commanders who had no desire for outside mediation. Washburn, unperturbed, worked on tirelessly. He drank cold yerba mate (*tereré*) from a tall glass while organizing details for his own comprehensive offer of mediation, little supposing that the various governments involved would find polite ways to rebuff his offer.

End-of-Year Certainties

The last days of 1866 were insufferably hot. Most men at the front did what they could to escape the blistering sun, and in the various halls of government politicians schemed to take advantage of whatever opportunities arose. With so much doubt and ambiguity in the wind, anything appeared possible. The arrival of Caxias suggested that things might soon change for the Allies. Though Mitre retained overall command, he now spent nearly as much time pondering the ramifications of the distant Montonero uprisings as he did directing the fight in Paraguay. Almost by default, the marquis saw his star rising. He still needed the Argentine president, however, and Mitre still craved a proper deference, so there was bound to be much give-and-take in their relationship.

On 3 December, word came from Rio de Janeiro that the emperor had named Tamandaré's replacement, and three weeks later the new man arrived off Itapirú, ready to take command. A sense of happy anticipation seems to have pervaded the Allied camp, with everyone, save for the admiral, assuming that things would improve. On his last day in Paraguay, Tamandaré ordered four warships upriver to shell the enemy positions at Curupayty. It was not much of a swansong, however, and although the barrage succeeded in silencing the enemy's guns for a time, it did no damage.[71]

Tamandaré's ultimate failure in Paraguay resulted from several factors. He was a decade older than most of the men with whom he shared command and could not help but lecture them on occasions that called for tact. He was plagued with severe bouts of rheumatism, far worse than those of Polidoro, and in the admiral's case, the pain incapacitated him on key occasions. And even when he was healthy, he could not hide his hatred of the Argentines, against whom he had fought in the 1820s. He was also prone to making exaggerated claims regarding the success of his naval units, which had proven his undoing at Curupayty. Worst of all, he was utterly unwilling to convey bad news to the emperor, even when duty required that he do so.[72] Pedro was far away in Rio, and could never make informed decisions on a war he insisted on winning but refused to direct. He and his advisors needed clear-cut information and loyal underlings who could act independently as the occasion required. In this, Tamandaré simply could not deliver.

The admiral steamed back to Montevideo, then to Rio, ostensibly on a three-month leave for health reasons. He made no speeches en route, no grandiloquent claims in favor of Brazilian arms. He never returned to Paraguay. Instead, after the invariable show of public acclaim in the capital, he sank insensibly into the role that the imperial system had prepared for him—that of an aged roué who enjoyed all the pomp and dignity his rank and status merited, but who was kept isolated from real power.

The new Allied naval commander in Paraguay was Vice Admiral Joaquim José Ignácio, rumored to be everything his predecessor was not. Born in Lisbon in 1808, Ignácio came to Brazil at a tender age. Similar to Caxias, he showed a pronounced affinity for study and hard work: he learned Latin and French while a teenager and gained some knowledge of English during his various tours in Europe; he earned high marks in advanced mathematics and basic seamanship while a naval cadet, and took readily to affecting the dress and manner of a British officer.

Ignácio had a distinguished record in the Cisplatine conflict of 1825–1828. During the fight, he was captured on the high seas off Bahia Blanca. Taking an aggressive, "now-or-never" attitude, he helped raise a revolt among ninety Brazilian prisoners being ferried into Argentine confinement aboard the captured schooner *Constança*. He managed to retake the ship and escape to Brazilian-held Montevideo.[73]

When the war with Paraguay began in 1864, Ignácio found himself at the admiralty in Rio de Janeiro, far from the scene of bloodshed. But the conflict still touched him deeply. His son, a gifted officer, thirty-one years old, and commander of a Brazilian ironclad, was mortally wounded in the assault on Itapirú, and died aboard a hospital ship in Tamandaré's arms. Ignácio never recovered from this blow and he adopted thereafter a Catholicism that was at once more profound and more obscurantist than that usually found among the men of his generation. This conservative and emotive faith offered him both solace and direction, but it also set him apart from other officers.

Ignácio would need all the help he could get once he got to Paraguay. The men at the front had already compared his reputation with that of his predecessor and he always came off looking better than the impetuous Tamandaré. Those who were tired of inaction trusted that Ignácio would break the impasse with a bolder approach. It had already been proven that the ironclads could stand up against the fury of the Paraguayan gunners, though as yet no one felt reassured about the river mines. Ignácio had thirty-eight warships at his command with 186 guns and 4,037 men.[74] He had the power and a great deal of authority; he could have taken the vote of confidence that his officers and men had given him as an inducement to move upriver, or at least to discuss the matter with Mitre and Caxias. Instead, Ignácio "marked the beginning of his reign by doubling the intensity of the bombardment." Same tactics, same results.[75]

Charles Ames Washburn was not so complacent. On 20 December 1866, the secretary of state directed him and the US ministers to Buenos Aires, Montevideo, and Rio de Janeiro to announce to their respective host governments that the United States was ready to offer its good offices in pursuit of a general peace. The mediation offer took the form outlined by Congress some months earlier, its chief feature being a proposed meeting in Washington to which the belligerent powers would send plenipotentiaries. Washburn would have taken seriously his charge as prospective mediator had he known of his government's instructions, but he had in fact already left Asunción for Humaitá, having been summoned by López. The Marshal had recovered from his recent illness and was anxious to see if Washburn had any useful information.

When Washburn arrived at Paso Pucu on 22 December, he found the atmosphere tense.

> Before I had left Paraguay, though the [resident Englishmen] all knew López was a tyrant capable of any atrocity, they had never supposed that they were themselves in any personal danger. But it was all changed now. They had seen that López was resolved that, if he could not continue to rule over Paraguay, no one else should, and [he] was bent on the destruction of the entire people. They early warned me to be very careful in my intercourse with him; that, if I could keep in favor with him, my presence in the country might somewhat restrain his barbarities; but that, were he to quarrel with me, it would have been infinitely better for them all had I never returned.[76]

Things had gotten worse at the front, and with a seemingly endless struggle facing his country, Marshal López had grown more abrupt—more apt, evidently, to cast blame on those closest to him even in tiny matters.

In his interviews with the Marshal, Washburn found the man thoughtful rather than menacing. He was willing, for example, to concede far more bravery to the Brazilian soldiers than most Paraguayans would have done at that time. It was not courage that was wanting among the kambáes, he maintained, but leadership, and this would not change with the arrival of Caxias and Ignácio. The situation had improved for López since the fall of Itapirú, when Tamandaré's warships had shelled his army night and day. Now, he told Washburn, the Allies would quarrel among themselves and see their alliance disintegrate, and the resulting strains to the imperial exchequer would likely force the Brazilians to give up the effort.[77]

As Washburn had yet to receive instructions on mediation, he confined himself to asking after six Americans imprisoned in the country. To his surprise, López ordered their release.[78] The Marshal also agreed to pay reparations to an American merchant whose shop Paraguayan troopers had sacked during their 1865 invasion of Corrientes.[79] López proved so obliging on these issues, in fact, that Washburn began to think the warnings of his English friends had little foundation. He was wrong.

After Washburn returned to Asunción, he learned that the police had arrested his landlord, don Luis Jara, evidently because of the latter's friendliness toward him.[80] Though he had no official leave even to protest this move, it did cause him to question the extent of the Marshal's "great politeness and civility." The foreigners in the Paraguayan capital had gone through some unexpected stress, with the police reprimanding them for their supposed lack of public enthusiasm for the war. Paraguayan women had contributed their jewelry, their labor, and their loved ones, and the men their fortunes and lives—why had these outsiders given so little?

One can sense in this pressure the hands of Lopista sycophants, who, having failed to deliver military victory to the Marshal, now wished to protect themselves by turning on anyone who betrayed an independent stance. The foreign community responded by issuing a message more militantly patriotic than that of the Asunción government: "How could we remain indifferent to all the benefits, to all the solicitude for our welfare? … We wish to remain neutral—that is true enough. But if neutrality is meant to show a cold indifference to the benefits we have received, then we reject with indignation any [questioning of our] gratitude [to] the Paraguayan people with whom we share links of the most cordial brotherhood."[81] The Marshal apparently smirked at this tardy show of support, but let it go anyway. As for the foreigners, not one of them, not even Washburn or Laurent-Cochelet, could afford to take his or his family's continued safety for granted.

In spite of the growing anxiety throughout Paraguay, there was some potentially good news for Washburn. On 28 December, while still at Paso Pucú, the dispatches he had expected finally reached him under a flag of truce. They contained word of his government's offer of mediation.[82] This opened a new opportunity. Seeking to ascertain the opinions of the US ministers to Brazil and Argentina, Washburn proposed to go through the lines to Caxias's headquarters to learn what he could.

The New Year thus began with the barest hint of hope. In a letter to his wife, the Argentine general Juan Andrés Gelly y Obes noted that the entire army had attended mass at four thirty in the morning, followed by two long days of music, dances, and drunkenness.[83] The Paraguayans had just finished celebrating their own independence day less than a week earlier, singing lustily from their water-soaked trenches while the military bands played patriotic marches. Now they sang again, partly in hope, partly in frustration, partly in envy of the Allied soldiers with their full stomachs.

Eight days later Admiral Ignácio launched the most blistering attack against the Paraguayan batteries since 22 September 1866. The shells of the fleet "rained down without let-up, exploding in mid-air [above the earthworks], leaving the whole horizon of Curupayty covered with gunsmoke."[84] When the Allied army failed to lunge forward, General Díaz ordered his gunners to fire back, directing all their murderous energy toward the enemy vessels. The iron-clad *Brasil* was holed by six cannonballs and withdrew quickly to Corrientes to save itself from sinking. Other ships were also hit. The Allies fired three thousand shells at Curupayty and another fifteen hundred at Sauce. The Paraguayans responded in kind. Yet again no real damage was done. On 13 January, the fleet opened a barrage on the same positions, gaining the same results. The Allied land forces probed the line near Sauce over the next few days. Once again, nothing came of it.

The Death of General Díaz

As with many military heroes who find themselves converted into legends during their own lifetimes, it is difficult with José Eduvigis Díaz to separate the man from the legend. Born near the little village of Pirayú, he had an obscure background, and his short stint as police chief of Asunción before the war was hardly conspicuous.[85] His actions in combat, however, made him famous in the eyes of the common Paraguayan soldier. He was plainspoken, and he eschewed material comforts. He never slept in a bed while on campaign, preferring the simplest hammock.[86] He could stare the life out of a man for some infraction of the rules one moment and afterwards slap him on the back with honest friendliness and encouragement the next. In fighting he was skilled, ruthless, and unafraid of bullets, just like Osório.

Unique among the Paraguayan commanders, however, Díaz enjoyed López's absolute confidence. This might seem odd, for the Marshal's evident narcissism—the product, it seems, of an adolescence that went on too long—drove him to envy men of much lesser rank. There was something in him, however, that yearned for the heroic, and he found much in Díaz that he wanted to find in himself.

Even before the war, the Paraguayans had constructed a surprisingly modern "cult of personality" around López. Every correct decision was ascribed to his genius and every public pronouncement glorified his name; both his birthday and the day of his assumption of the presidency became public holidays, replete with fireworks and elaborate speeches. The god-like status that this cult conferred explained why the Marshal deserved a jewel-encrusted sword, a golden "wreath of victory," a magnificently designed book of valedictories, and suffocating praise in the official press.[87] Actual heroics, however, remained something too plebeian, too "physical" in its implications. López had crafted himself into a superhuman entity—a beau ideal that stood above the masses—but now he had to live within its limits.

Díaz, by contrast, was "more Paraguayan than the manioc root," and never took any interest in fancy uniforms or shows of superiority.[88] He always displayed unquestioning deference to the Marshal, and this was an indispensable virtue—something that other Paraguayan commanders sometimes lacked. Even the Marshal's own brothers could not be trusted on occasions when General Díaz would willingly step forward and obey.

The favor of an absolute ruler does not always imply a want of merit in the object of patronage; without intending it, the ruler can reward a man of ability, or he might find such a man useful. Díaz had neither the independence of a Wenceslao Robles, nor the ineptitude of an Ignacio Meza or Antonio Estigarribia, all of whom López had long since dismissed as traitors. What he did have was courage and undeniable loyalty, and his actions resulted not from some servile obedience, but from a patriotic belief that the Marshal and the nation were one and the same.

Indeed, on one occasion early in the war, the Marshal asked Díaz, who at the time was only a captain, how he should go about defeating the empire, to which the man answered, "I would only wish to know your Excellency's orders in order to carry them out." When López insisted on a frank response, the future general stood as tall as his frame would allow, pursed his lips, and declared:

> Well, sir, it would be the greatest honor of my life to receive your order to assemble an army of our best 7,000 men, and embarking them all upon the steamers of our fleet, make straight for the Atlantic Ocean, passing through the Río de la Plata, leaving the Brazilian ships along the coastline, where they would never sense [our presence], then enter in sight of Rio de Janeiro on the ninth day, penetrating the bay at midnight [unseen] by the enemy forts … disembarking in thirty minutes … crossing the city and falling [in silence] upon the palace of San Cristobal, wherein I would seize Dom Pedro and the imperial family, returning to embark my prisoners and in twenty days' time, I would present them to Your Excellency in the capital, where thereafter you would impose the peace.[89]

Díaz's answer, uttered quickly and with full conviction, spoke volumes about his hubris, his dedication, and his ignorance of the greater world. Marshal López could not help but love the man.

Over the next months, Díaz proved that his fierceness was more than a matter of words. Again and again, he displayed an appetite for violent scrapes with the enemy. He convinced his men that not only would they survive the combat of that particular day, but they would rid the fatherland of its enemies. This conviction had gotten him into danger more than once. In late January 1867, it would lead him to take a fatal risk.

Díaz chafed under the forced inactivity that developed along the line of military contact after Curupayty. Never one to be dilatory, he understood that an attack en masse had little to recommend it, but was nonetheless anxious to keep the Allies guessing. Aggressive reconnaissance, hit-and-run raids, sniping, and active provocations—these were the tactics he had perfected in fulfilling the Marshal's orders and those he was most comfortable with.

General Díaz had an understandable contempt for the Brazilian navy. On the morning of 26 January, he slipped aboard a canoe and rowed from Curupayty into the main channel of the Paraguay. He intended to spy on the enemy warships and show them how little heed he took of their much-vaunted firepower. One of his paddlers, a Payaguá sergeant whom he had adopted as his godson, advised the general that they were approaching too close, but Díaz, a look of total disdain in his eye, calmly baited a fishing hook and dropped it into the water. He counted the number of enemy warships, and had a lieutenant note their disposition. Just at that moment, a Brazilian warship fired a single 13-inch shell, which burst in a flash above the canoe. The lieutenant and one of the paddlers died instantly. Díaz's godson, not realizing the extent of his wounds, managed to pull him to shore, where he saw that the unconscious general's leg was horribly mangled.

The Marshal sent at once for Dr. Frederick Skinner, who amputated the leg and told the general's friends and family to prepare for bad news. Madame Lynch arrived in Curupayty to carry Díaz back to Paso Pucú in her buggy. There he was lodged next to López's own quarters. The Marshal visited him daily and even ordered that a casket be fashioned for the severed leg, which was embalmed and placed in the room next to the general's bed. As Díaz drifted in and out of consciousness, however, he complained that he had left the job unfinished, that his men needed his help now more than ever. López tried to calm him, but it did no good.

After the surgery, Díaz could not keep his food down, which weakened him still further. On the morning of 7 February, he awoke feeling better than ever, and spoke cheerfully to his nurses and associates from the old 40th Battalion. He made a few disparaging jokes at the expense of the kambáes. Then, at noon, he took a bad turn. He announced his willingness to die, but loudly regretted that he would not live to see the final victory. He slipped away at 4:45 p.m.[90] He was thirty-four years old.

The general's death cast a pall over the entire country. Díaz received an elaborate funeral and was interred in Asunción together with what was left of his severed leg.[91] In the years to come, López and the propagandists of *El Semanario* inflated Díaz's reputation out of all proportion to what he had achieved. Though he was hardly the only Paraguayan to have died for his country during the war, he became the iconic representation of selfless patriotism. Even the Allies paid tribute to him.

Exit Mitre

The Argentine president had seen his fortunes decline ever since Curupayty. His name, once associated with claims of prompt victory, was now mentioned only in the context of stalemate, lost lives, and squandered opportunities. Asunción would not fall "in three months"—indeed it was unlikely to fall in three years. At the front, as at Buenos Aires, Mitre was no longer appreciated as the farsighted statesman that in many ways he remained. His humanism was forgotten, his achievements decried. The Paraguayans laughed at him, the Brazilians could no longer contain their resentment, and his own people argued that his sun had set.

In these circumstances, Mitre kept a low profile. The arrival of Caxias had seen de facto command pass to the Brazilians, which was in any case reasonable, for as the number of imperial troops in Paraguay grew, those of Argentina shrunk. The Montonero uprisings in the west had brought a new threat against the national government, and while the campaign against López might wait, that against Varela could not. In mid-November 1866 Mitre detached some one thousand Argentine troops from the main Allied army in Paraguay and sent them south to join with troops being raised by the Porteños and by the Santafecinos. The officer Mitre chose to command this new army was none other than General Wenceslao Paunero, hero of the Corrientes campaign. The general's raid on the Correntino capital dramatically enhanced his reputation because it upset the Marshal's timetable so convincingly that the Paraguayans never recovered momentum. Yet talented as Paunero might have been, he could not be in two places at once, and it was hardly surprising that as these new units mustered against the Montoneros, logistical problems prevented them from coalescing into an effective force. Varela and the Cuyano rebels kept advancing.

On 24 January 1867 the Argentine president announced that four more battalions of mounted artillerymen—eleven hundred men—would be added to Paunero's units for a major push against the western rebels. "If this proves insufficient," he wrote Vice President Paz, "then I will send from here double or triple the number, and if necessary I will go myself until the rebellion is suffocated." In this same message, Mitre emphasized that, as a constitutional leader, he had many duties to perform and that his actions in Paraguay counted for only some of these; traitors at home had complicated his efforts, and if the uprisings in the Argentine west continued to plague the quest for national unity, he would soon steam south to crush the "anarchy of the interior."[92]

On 31 January, after receiving further intelligence from Buenos Aires, Mitre announced his intention to retire together with thirty-six hundred of his fighters, all of whom would join Paunero's army. When Mitre communicated this news to Caxias, the marquis called it a dismal business. He claimed that he felt ill-prepared to command the entire Allied army in Paraguay, and could only accept Mitre's decision if the Argentine president first prepared a detailed plan for operations against Marshal López.[93]

As Mitre's steamer turned downriver on 9 February, there was no longer any doubt that ultimate command among the Allies had switched definitively into the hands of Caxias and the Brazilians.[94] What had been de facto became de jure, and, for the foreseeable future, the four thousand Argentine troops who remained in Paraguay under General Gelly y Obes had to follow the marquis's lead.

Cholera and Other Challenges

In conditions as terrible as those faced by soldiers on both sides of the Paraguayan War, it should come as no surprise that epidemic disease was added to the long list of calamities. Throughout 1865 and early 1866, the principal maladies were simple diarrhea, amoebic dysentery, and malaria.[95] Respiratory problems, fevers, trench foot, and the normal soldierly aches and pains filled out the remaining medical complaints. Now, with the dawn of another year, epidemic disease stood ready to hammer everyone at the front.

Measles, yellow fever, and smallpox had hit the Platine region before, with the last of these carrying away a substantial portion of the Paraguayan population in the mid-1840s.[96] Nearly twenty years later, the López government experimented with vaccination to contain any future threats. Instructional materials and smallpox vaccines were distributed to rural officials in 1862 and 1863, but it is not clear how far these programs extended or how effective they were.[97] They continued on an irregular basis at least through 1867, but again, it is difficult to determine how many people received treatment.[98] One thing is clear, however: while smallpox does occasionally appear on the roster of diseases found in Paraguayan military hospitals and in Asunción proper at the time, it never became a generalized epidemic in other parts of the country.[99]

This was not the case just behind the Brazilian lines in Mato Grosso. The province suffered dramatically because of the war, and even those areas far from the Paraguayan occupation experienced a wide range of troubles, not excluding measles, which appeared in a limited form in April and May 1866.[100] When smallpox also intruded the next year, there was no preparation and no real defense. Over half the population of Cuiabá died as a result.[101] It seems probable that the inhabitants of Mato Grosso suffered far more from smallpox than the Paraguayans.

The one epidemic disease to really run amok during the war was neither smallpox, nor measles, but Asiatic cholera, the worst form of infectious gastroenteritis. It had appeared in Russia in the early 1850s, leaving a million dead in its wake before moving on (via Crimea) to Western Europe, Africa, and eventually South America during the latter part of the decade. Medical authorities in the Platine states had largely contained the threat by the mid-1860s, but the war, with its filthy conditions and countless opportunities for physical contact among men, led to a horrible new incidence of the contagion. It turned up in Rio de Janeiro in February 1867, moved up the river from Buenos Aires, and finally gained the camps at Paso de la Patria by late March.[102] When it arrived in Paraguay, it acted like a maniac.

Cholera works its evil in a remarkably short time, progressing from the first liquid stool to shock in four to twelve hours, with death following a day or two later. Before antibiotics, an infected person required prompt oral rehydration if he hoped to survive, and the careful disposal of waste, clothing, and bedding was essential to keep the disease in check. As it was, it coursed through the Brazilian army in a scant three days. Peasants and farm boys, crowded with other men for the first time in their lives, proved especially susceptible. Four thousand of their number fell ill at Curuzú, and of these, twenty-four hundred, including eighty-seven officers, may have died.[103] The disease also left a terrible mark at Tuyutí.

By the end of April thirteen thousand Brazilians were incapacitated with the disease, straining all the hospital facilities on both sides of the Paraná. There was no universally accepted treatment; allied doctors had some good ideas of how to combat the contagion and how to prevent its spreading; they distributed soap and ordered the soldiers to burn any sheets or mattresses that sick patients had used. But they also had some bad ideas. They recommended, for example, that the afflicted seek help in alcohol, which caused a run on all the beer, wine, and hard liquor the sutlers had in stock.[104]

The medical authorities were overwhelmed with the sheer scale of the problem, and with the fact that once an individual became ill, he stood a better-than-even chance of dying—a fact that rendered the doctors as desperate as the men.[105] The Brazilian officer Dionísio Cerqueira repeated the tale of one overworked physician who served aboard a hospital ship. The doctor, whenever he entered the ward, automatically prescribed *vomitórios* for patients on the left side and *purgantes* for those on the right; upon his return the next day, the order of the prescription was reversed.[106]

Though it is easy enough to rebuke these physicians for incompetence, in fact the doctors and orderlies who had to contend with the disease did a better job than the common soldiers charged with keeping the camps clean. In far too many cases, the improper disposal of waste contaminated the water supply, which spread the disease down the line and into the Argentine and Uruguayan ranks.[107] No matter how often the doctors insisted on proper sanitation, the soldiers could not grasp that clean-looking water might nonetheless harbor deadly microbes. They insisted on sharing the metallic straw (*bombilla*) with which they drank their yerba mate. Everyone suffered accordingly. Teams of soldiers were dispatched to build sheds and barns at Potrero Pirís, and these filled with cholera patients overnight.[108] Each day seemed worse than the preceding one.

At the outset of the epidemic, the Allied commanders tried to disguise the extent of the problem and keep its worst manifestations concealed from both the civilian population and the enemy. Newspaper correspondents were forbidden entry into the frontline camps, and the use of the word "cholera" was ruthlessly excised from all official communiqués.

The presence of cholera among the troops in Paraguay should not have been surprising, for the scourge had already struck a number of communities downriver, including Buenos Aires, where some fifteen hundred inhabitants succumbed between 3 and 25 April 1867.[109] The denizens of Corrientes, who had caught more than a passing glimpse of the disease's effects, reacted with considerable alarm and threatened to burn down the Brazilian hospital rather than see such men in their midst. [110] In the absence of reliable information, the average civilian found it easy to imagine the worst. *La Nación Argentina* reported an unsubstantiated rumor that the epidemic had caused the remaining Argentine forces to relocate their main camp away from insalubrious Tuyutí.[111] Families feared for their sons, and even in France word of cholera in the Plata provided commentators with new reasons to oppose the war.[112]

As for Marshal López, he understood a good deal about the epidemic. Spies, who operated as laundresses and dayworkers in the Allied camp, had kept him well apprised of the increased activity in the field. These spies might have been tempted to gloat over the enemy's predicament as offering yet another proof that God was on their side. But they had little real time for such thoughts, for in short order they, too, felt the effects of the scourge. The medical troubles at Humaitá initially paralleled those of the Allies, but this was before the onset of serious malnutrition among the Paraguayans. Most epidemic diseases are opportunistic, and generally attack individuals already weak from other illnesses, with malnutrition supplying the serious catalyst. For the Paraguayans, food and medicines were becoming hard to find.[113]

The Marshal faced some difficult decisions. He ordered that any contact with the men in the opposite trenches cease at once, and his pickets pulled back accordingly. He had read all about cholera during his European tour in the previous decade, and may have seen its ravages during his travels.[114] López's own illness in the previous months may have made him doubly sensitive to the perception of disease, and he could not afford to discount the possibility that his entire army might be swept up in it.

The one man on the Allied side who kept his head during this difficult stage was Caxias. Aware of exactly what dangers cholera might encompass, the marquis took special care in his personal habits; he had his quarters scrubbed clean every day and limited himself to drinking bottled mineral water sent from Rio de Janeiro.[115] And he also lost no time in turning for organizational help to Doctor Francisco Pinheiro Guimarães, who had started his career as a naval surgeon and had already fought epidemics in Brazil.

The doctor worked quickly, isolating the known cholera cases and setting aside special wards within the hospitals to deal with the immediate threat. He strictly enforced standards for sanitation.[116] The town fathers at Corrientes began slowly to calm their nerves, convinced now that the threat had passed.[117] The same mood soon settled over the Allied camps closer to the front. Caxias, whose faith in Pinheiro Guimarães was well rewarded, called again on the doctor some weeks later, this time to go systematically through the Allied hospitals to search for malingerers, an effort that brought another twenty-five hundred men back into active duty.[118]

As the cholera epidemic subsided among the Allies in mid-May, it reached over the line at Paso Gómez and pounced upon the Paraguayans.[119] The effect was immediate. The epidemic proved worse for the Marshal's men than for those of Caxias, since the Allied soldiers at least had some access to food and modern drugs. Medical facilities on the Paraguayan side, already stretched, now had to cope with a far greater challenge. Some months earlier, engineers had erected a new hospital, located halfway between Humaitá and Paso Pucú, and its two thousand beds and hammocks filled with cholera patients virtually overnight.[120] Other aid stations went up in short order, as well as a dozen well-arranged huts reserved for senior officers at Paso Pucú.

The epidemic spread like an indiscriminate killer. Several of Paraguay's most noteworthy figures contracted the disease over the next weeks, but thanks to the attentions of William Stewart, the senior British doctor in the Paraguayan employ, all recovered. The afflicted included Generals Bruguez and Resquín, James Rhynd and Frederick Skinner (two of the other three British military doctors still in the Paraguayan service), and Benigno López, younger brother of the Marshal.[121] These men were the lucky ones, for many others perished.[122]

In the absence of modern medicines, the Paraguayan doctors fell back on herbs, donkey's milk, and other traditional remedies. Oddly enough, they had ice—which British engineers produced from ammonia—at their disposal.[123] This they used to provide cold compresses and to cool the medicinal beverages that often constituted the only relief.

Aware that the disease had spread through contaminated water, the doctors forbade their patients from drinking anything that had not been boiled. López gave orders to quarantine the afflicted men, and also to light fires to fumigate the camp with bay leaves and grass.[124] This left his headquarters clouded by near-constant smoke that irritated lungs and eyes yet failed to have any impact on the epidemic, which saw fifty deaths a day.[125]

The level-headed reaction that Caxias had displayed found some—but only *some*—resemblance in the comportment of the Marshal, who obsessively contradicted his medical personnel and interfered in many trifling ways. Following the lead of the Allied commander, he forbade the mention of the word "cholera." It was too late to avoid panic, however, and the soldiers responded to their leader's order by rechristening the disease *cha'í*, using the Guaraní word for "wrinkled" or "shrunken" (which is how a suffering man's body appeared after a day or two).[126]

López might be excused for his inconsistencies at this time. He was under considerable stress and was suffering himself from a weakened version of the disease, which came upon him not long after recovering from his previous illness. Cholera turned his habitual suspicions into something far more frightening. On one occasion, his fever induced an uncontrollable thirst that caused him to ignore his own rule against drinking unboiled water. With sweat pouring along his neck, he seized a pitcher and attempted to lift it to his lips. At the last moment, a medical orderly, Cirilo Solalinde, violently struck the vessel from his master's hands, sending it crashing onto the earthen floor. This act probably saved the Marshal's life, but his immediate response was predictably fierce. As he was on the verge of having the impertinent man arrested and shot, the bishop stepped forward and upbraided Solalinde as a cruel and stupid servant in not having permitted his master a single draft of water. This tongue-lashing satisfied López, who returned to bed without having taken a swallow and promptly forgot about the incident. Writing many years after the fact, Centurión lamented the orderly's quick thinking and courage: in putting himself between the Marshal and a possibly fatal danger, Solalinde may have acted honorably, but in saving López he condemned the Paraguayan people to three more years of butchery.[127]

The fever may have sapped the Marshal's reason and strength, but it did nothing to mitigate his stubbornness, and as he slipped in and out of consciousness, López began to perceive any number of enemies hovering near him. When he awakened, he would act on those impressions. He accused his doctors of slipping poison into his gruel, "in which charge he was seconded by the bishop."[128] López had never been patient, and on numerous occasions during the war, he evinced a palpable anger whenever the day's news went against him. His subordinates had long since learned to recoil at these shows of bad temper, which only Madame Lynch or his children seemed capable of alleviating.

López often gave in to an unbridled ferocity while in a bad temper—this much everyone recognized. In this case, however, the men around him had even more reason to tremble, for during his convalescence they witnessed a disturbing pattern that the Marshal's detractors preferred to call madness. This it almost certainly was not, but his growing exasperation surely brought reason to worry about the future. Paranoia, like old age, can steal upon an individual by slow degrees, which, even when obvious to others, are often unacknowledged by the afflicted individual. The cholera started to subside within the Paraguayan camps by early June, but the apprehension that López might slip more and more into a world of delusion never abated. It was subsumed within the broader tragedy of the war, and by the fact that cholera had spread to the civilian population in the winter of 1867. There it would rage with renewed vigor, killing, among others, the Marshal's one-year-old son.

6

INNOVATIONS
AND LIMITATIONS

The extended lull of 1866–1867 brought many challenges for both the Paraguayans and the Allies, all of which stemmed from a broad realization that the war could last indefinitely. The setback at Curupayty had weakened the unity of the Allied command, leaving generals as well as distant observers pointing fingers at each other and pondering what to do next. No one could say.

Mitre departed in February to deal with the Montonero threat, leaving Caxias to assume overall command. The marquis was in every sense a professional. He recognized that he needed time to stabilize the front, restore morale, reorganize supply and sanitation, and try to contain the cholera epidemic. He encouraged an important tactical innovation when he convinced Rio to import five thousand breech-loading rifles (Roberts) and two thousand repeaters (Spencers) from the United States. He hesitated, however, to make fundamental changes in strategy, in part because he thought Mitre would reassume command in short order. These limitations could only exasperate Caxias, who wanted to put a decisive face on his conduct. And yet, of all Allied commanders, he emerged as the most practiced in political matters—more so, even, than Mitre; if anyone could assure coordination between the politicians in Rio and the army at the front, surely it was Caxias. He need only wait for the reserves he required to take the offensive.

As for the Paraguayans, they weathered the early months of 1867 with a certain sangfroid. Curupayty had been their victory, and they had taken heart at Mitre's departure. They prayed that the "triple infamy" would come unraveled at these setbacks, at which point the various enemies of the republic would go home, and Caxias would come to realize that Paraguay could not be defeated on his terms. But, as it turned out, these were forlorn hopes. The lull may have been protracted, but the basic factors that guided Allied policy remained unchanged. Brazil and Argentina could still call on reserves of manpower and matériel, while Paraguay could never replace its losses. While it was true that Caxias controlled only nine square miles of Paraguayan territory ("a space hardly more than sufficient to contain, were they laid side by side, the bodies of those who had perished"), his forces were gaining strength while those of the Marshal were growing weaker every day.[1] López might still dream of survival—if not outright victory—but the odds against him were overwhelming.

The Paraguayan Homefront

Visitors to today's Paraguay are apt to wonder how the Guaraní republic could ever have hoped to resist the combined military might of Brazil, Argentina, and Uruguay. Of course, on one level, few contemporary Paraguayans ever expected it to. By 1866, the country was isolated save for an obscure overland route that connected it through occupied Mato Grosso to the communities of eastern Bolivia, which were themselves rather isolated.[2] Since the Paraguayans had little choice, they necessarily had to improvise a remarkable system in which all available resources, manpower, and the state bureaucracy were harnessed to the cause of military resistance. That this system worked at all was a major testimony to human ingenuity. Paraguay, it seems, had undergone a transformation. As was once said of Prussia, it was no longer a country that had an army, but rather an army that had a country.

History had prepared Paraguay to resist any number of outside pressures. For many generations, it had withstood Portuguese interlopers from the north and Guaicurú raiders from the west. These challenges bred a strong sense of self-reliance among the Paraguayans. They had their own essential institutions, including a conservative Catholic Church whose representatives insisted on the legitimacy of traditional hierarchies. The simple vision of good and evil that the clergymen offered the Paraguayans reinforced the popular mistrust of the "rational." It was natural to identify with the soil and the community, and with Guaraní as the language of both hearth and family. These inclinations set the province apart from those territories further south.

Today, it is easy to dismiss the tightly woven interpretations that López's government used to justify the war, but Paraguayans at the time accepted the basic premise of "us versus them." They made superhuman sacrifices because their leaders called upon them to do so. Distinct from the situation in Argentina, Brazil, and Uruguay—where criticism of the war received a daily and often strident airing—in Paraguay, the people could complain only in whispers. And they only had one version of events.

True enough, the government employed any number of "soft-footed" informers (*pyragües*) who made sure that any hint of defeatism was reported and ruthlessly stamped out. Yet any contemporary observer or later scholar who attributed Paraguayan steadfastness to the Marshal's use of coercion misread the national temper; men and women who fight for a dictator can do so for many reasons, not all of them pernicious.[3] Both the Paraguayan soldiers and their civilian counterparts fought hard, not because their inclinations were slavish or because they were forced to take up arms, but because their psychology—their sense of duty—left them no choice.[4] Nothing less than their survival as a people was at stake.

The careful manipulation of internal finances and a maximum mobilization of manpower and resources explain how the Marshal's government kept working so effectively.[5] The Paraguayan state put together a bureaucratic machine that harnessed every community to the war effort. It was backward in some ways, and it was certainly cold-blooded, but it was also resilient. Its many successes reflected the efforts of Domingo Francisco Sánchez, the elderly, rail-thin, clear-eyed vice president who organized the requisition of foodstuffs and other supplies and arranged for their transport to Humaitá.[6] This was a herculean task for an economy already seriously strained. Civilians had to eat, too, and food sent to the fortress could not be consumed at home.

At isolated ranches and farms, hoarding thus became widespread, and the government could do little to frustrate such practices. Some functionaries quietly held-back supplies for their own families, and the theft of food and other supplies by third parties was neither unusual nor frequently punished.[7] The villages had always witnessed intrigue, personal vendettas, and rank meanness, even in the best of times; there is no reason to suppose that a peasant's resentments toward his neighbor might subside just because the country was at war.

Asunción had its own requirements for food, and when these could not be met through normal channels clever traffickers sometimes gained access to military commissaries. They also had recourse to a limited but still active black market, which always managed to provide beef for the tiny foreign community.[8] As often happens in times of scarcity, the loudest patriots were the most eminent profiteers. They knew that in order to survive, dissimulation was not enough. To conceal, to bribe, to cajole—all this had its place in a time of near starvation—but shamming (*mbotavy*) was an essential part of the job. Independent minds that in other circumstances might have risen above the clamor of a public unanimity found it safer to join the crowd, mouth the familiar slogans, and take advantage where they could.

In all this, Vice President Sánchez still enjoyed some advantages. For one thing, the country already boasted a crude but effective command economy in which orders from the central government were rarely disobeyed.[9] Instructions from Asunción might involve the purchase of tobacco, maize, or beans for the consumption of troops in faraway garrisons, the donation of surplus cattle from state ranches for distribution among the poor, the payment of salaries for primary school teachers, or the conscription of laborers to clear trails through the forests. As we have seen, Sánchez had already managed similar duties with a marked competence for many years.[10]

In the first months of the conflict, the Paraguayan government had tried to raise outside loans for the army, but with the Allied blockade, any thought of foreign support vanished and the state had to fall back on internal financing. Properties confiscated from enemy nationals and forced "donations" added to the available reserves, and the government tried a variety of ways to coax citizens into relinquishing coins, silver cutlery—anything of value.

In Asunción and every village of the countryside Sánchez organized rallies that featured "patriotic acts." On these occasions, an air of pageantry prevailed. Municipal officers gathered around themselves the district's women, children, and toothless old men. With minimal prompting, these people proceeded first to murmur, then to bellow, hackneyed incantations of support for the Marshal. The assembled women were urged to step forward and donate their rings, bracelets, and other metallic baubles as proof of fealty to the nation.[11] Attendance at these rituals was compulsory, and the women did not disappoint. They joined in the ritual shouting that these meetings entailed, though a few believed—correctly, as it turned out—that their precious jewelry would end up in the hands of Madame Lynch.[12]

As luck would have it, these contributions from the "fair national sex" could not have made a difference to the war effort, for the Allied blockade prevented purchases of supplies from abroad.[13] The donations of silver and gold nonetheless postponed absolute depreciation of the Paraguayan peso until the last years of the conflict. Some silver coins were still being minted in Asunción in 1866, and between 1867 and 1868 new gold and silver specie appeared after another carefully orchestrated series of "donations." But these emissions were inconsequential; the state had long since opted to pay for its purchases with paper currency, and the more the government printing office issued, the less it was worth.[14]

That Paraguayan finances should decline was a foregone conclusion, and in Asunción prices for basic commodities had risen as much as 160 percent over the first nine months of the war.[15] Sánchez had to rely on more traditional sources of support. He could, for example, fall back on the production of state ranches, which in late 1864 could still boast 273,430 head of cattle, 70,971 horses, 24,122 sheep, and 587 mules. Many of these animals had already arrived at Humaitá by the waning months of 1866, after which Sánchez turned his attention to livestock held in private hands. This amounted to perhaps seven or eight times as many animals, most of which were purchased by the state under a quota arrangement.[16] The vice president also ordered rural functionaries to step up pressure against private ranchers to offer their livestock as patriotic contributions.[17]

In central Paraguay, the requisition and payment system that Sánchez had inaugurated was well administered and initially evenhanded. By 1868, however, the system had broken down, and owners could no longer expect to receive even depreciated currency in exchange for beeves taken, and outright seizure became the rule. In the far north, some of the more prosperous private ranches still held sizable herds late in the war, but these cases were exceptional, for everywhere else the state had taken all the available animals. As for horses, by mid-1867, the herds had grown so depleted that the government instructed ranchers in the far north to drive their remaining mounts the length of the country, from the Aquidabán River to Humaitá. Half of these animals died en route.

To be sure, Sánchez wanted more than livestock and a waving of the flag from civilian populations. Iron cooking pots, tin plates, old machetes, and nails were collected and sent to the arsenal or the foundry at Ybycuí to be cast into cannon balls and bullets. Bronze and copper were also collected.[18] The government instructed townspeople to donate their imported goods—paper, medicines, glassware, even buttons. The carpets from the National Club and railway station in Asunción were cut up into ponchos and *chiripás* for the soldiers, and textile operations were set up within the National Theater to weave cloth for uniforms.[19] Every village in the interior operated looms for the same purpose.

The peasants and smallholders had to provide tobacco, yerba, timber, manioc, firewood (for boilers), peanuts, citrus fruit, cornmeal, cloth, saltpeter (for gunpowder), leather goods, maize, greases, and especially salt, for which a dire need had developed among the soldiers.[20] These demands fell disproportionately on country women. Losses at the front had denuded the interior of its male inhabitants, save for children and very old men. Sánchez had already considered this fact when, in July 1866, he instructed the rural population to focus on farming: "every day, every season, even moonlit nights ... without distinction between the sexes ... in anticipation of the day in which the entire male population will have to abandon any pursuit that does not promote the expulsion of the perfidious enemy ... all must work, and it is necessary to utilize all forces to provide the necessities of life."[21]

Women had engaged in arduous farming since colonial times, when many young men worked in logging or in gathering yerba far from home. The absence of men at Humaitá presented a similar challenge. Sánchez periodically gave assistance to the poorest among these women, providing them exemptions on rents, or even diverting foodstuffs in their direction, but these were exceptional cases.[22] He had no doubt that women would make the appropriate sacrifices, and he chided them when they failed to do so.[23]

Paraguay has two annual growing seasons—a winter planting of April through September, and a summer planting of October through March. The vice president kept a meticulous record of the lands under cultivation in order to ascertain the quantity of foodstuffs an individual district could supply. In the winter of 1866, he began conducting a regular series of agricultural censuses in the interior communities and came up with some remarkable statistics. The republic had some 4,192,520 *liños* (rows) of food crops under cultivation, and it had planted some 135,757 fruit trees.[24]

The total area sown in these crops was some 50,000 liños below normal, but the government nonetheless chose to style this as a successful effort. The country had suffered a severe drought in the last months of the growing season, and little more could be expected of such dry soil. Sánchez did censure several villages for their lax attitude in meeting state objectives, and he promised swift punishment for any community that failed to adhere to his guidelines.[25] Sure enough, during the next season (the summer of 1866–1867), the total area of land under cultivation rose to 6,805,695 liños of food crops together with 215,189 fruit trees planted. And in the subsequent winter, Sánchez could report 7,532,991 liños of food crops and 212,997 fruit trees planted.[26]

On the surface, these figures seem impressive. Given the tremendous drain on manpower, the fact that officials recorded such high totals suggests an outstanding coordination between the vice president's agents and the women who performed the labor. Unfortunately, for all of their outward precision, the agricultural censuses can be trusted only so far. For one thing, the cultivation of fruit trees was an irrational assignment because they could not bear for some time after the first planting and therefore added nothing to the war effort. For another, the censuses recorded crops sown, not crops harvested, and in the tropical environment of Paraguay, with its insects and radical shifts in rainfall, it was—and remains—impossible to calculate the quantity of food crops produced during any given period.[27] No matter the specific numbers recorded by Sánchez, every reason existed for his officials to embellish the totals on the higher end, for, in the increasingly authoritarian environment of Lopista Paraguay, any community that fell behind on its established quota did so at great risk.

Not all of the agricultural work that supported the war effort involved heavy plowing. With tobacco and peanuts, supplies kept up fairly well with wartime demand. The same was true in the beginning for oranges, and for *guembé*, a common vine used for cordage. Both plants grew wild in many parts of the country. In these locales, women and children gathered vine and processed it into rope. They harvested oranges at the same time, and sent the whole fruit south when possible.[28] On other occasions, the fruit provided the basis for an alcoholic beverage consumed in the hospitals. It never gained much favor among the soldiers, who on all occasions preferred their native *caña* or *aguardiente*, but it helped ward off scurvy. The men also tended to dislike the tangy preserves fashioned from the fruit of the bitter orange (*apepú*) and mixed with sugar or molasses—another local confection.[29] Of course, hungry men will eat whatever is available, and the *dulces* shipped from Asunción did add variety to a limited diet.[30]

People in need will not only eat anything, they will also wear anything. Uniforms that had once seemed so brilliant and colorful had deteriorated into faded tatters. Luckily, Paraguayan cotton, coconuts, and *caraguatá* (a pineapple-like bromeliad) all supplied fibers in some abundance, and Vice President Sánchez insisted that women harvest the cotton, spin it into yarn, and weave it into serviceable, if rather rough, broadcloth for shirts, trousers, and *poiby* blankets.[31] The women grumbled about the impracticality of these orders; the process of spinning and weaving was laborious and slow, and it was not at all clear that demands could be met. The government responded, first with instructions to switch more and more to caraguatá, and then to the assignment of new quotas for raw cotton, awarding prizes for the increase in acreage devoted to its cultivation.[32]

Sánchez understood that his problems had less to do with production than with processing and transport. Manioc root offers a case in point. In normal circumstances, the tuber was cleaned, boiled, and then consumed whole as a starchy accompaniment to meat and vegetables. Now, military demands required that women toast the manioc, grind it into flour, bag it, and transport the product to the nearest railhead or navigable stream. Given the unreliability of river transport, and the common lack of oxen, these supplies might wait for weeks before they could reach the hungry troops at Humaitá, and the flour sometimes filled with weevils en route.

The country women cooked the flour into traditional breads, hardtack, or manioc loaves (*chipas*)—thus responding to yet another state demand—but the effort entailed yet more work for a population already pushed to the limit.[33] No matter that Sánchez managed to refine his organizational approach as the war dragged on; still the total production of foodstuffs and cloth tapered off precipitously, even in crops whose cultivation women had traditionally dominated. In 1867, the production of foodstuffs had fallen by one-third of its prewar level. With the gathering of yerba, the cutting of timber, and the handling of oxen, village women simply could not keep pace with the state's demand.[34]

Transport entailed a variety of problems as well. Paraguay's small flotilla of river steamers had survived the disastrous encounter with the Allies at Riachuelo in 1865; it was now used mainly to handle the supply run from Asunción northward to the garrisons in Mato Grosso and southward to Humaitá. The inadequacy of river transport meant that supplies could never keep up with demand. In general, ships operated from the protected Bay of Asunción, where they took on reinforcements, munitions, and special communications. Some miles downstream, they put in at Villeta or Villa Franca to receive cargos of foodstuffs, fuel, and other supplies before departing for Humaitá. As there were no permanent wharves at the latter site, the ships discharged their cargoes onto rafts or canoes just above the fortress. Special parties from individual battalions met the ships at the riverside and ferried their assigned rations straightaway to their units.

When the Allied blockade was first established during the springtime of 1865, the Marshal realized the inadequacy of this system of river transport, and gave orders for various villages to build 446 canoes to carry war-related cargo.[35] As some communities were located far from the river, the newly constructed canoes had to be carted a great distance over marshy territory before they could be deployed.

And this was only the beginning. The state requisitioned private craft under a system similar to that which Sánchez had used for seizing livestock. The shipyards in Asunción continued to work overtime building and repairing smaller ships and lighters, all of which ferried supplies to the army. López's British staff oversaw the evaluation of ships for damage, the organization of repairs, and the designing and casting of spare parts for steamers. Unfortunately, the number of workmen in the principal shipyard and the associated arsenal began to slip dramatically by the second year of the war. There had been 432 men working in those establishments in March 1864; by April 1866, the number had fallen to 290.[36]

The overland transport of foodstuffs and other supplies to port, or at least to a navigable stream, was inconceivable without oxcarts, and the army had already swept up so many of these that officials could no longer be sure of their availability. And they also had to consider the heavy winter rains, which flooded the usual landing places in the south, turning slow-moving streams into torrents, and interfering with the loading of vessels.

Transporting supplies by land was even more hazardous and problematic. Though the railway ran according to a set schedule, it went no further south than Sapucaí, and from that point, transport required oxcarts and mule teams.[37] The maps of the 1860s depicted several parallel roads running along the Paraguay River, but these were no better than rudimentary trails cut through the brush; since no one had ever perceived a need for overland routes in that direction, they were never designed as major arteries. Any heavy rain left the trails flooded and greatly hindered the passage of carts, and even livestock, especially during the winter months.[38] Single animals could get through with some trouble, but large herds could not be driven south with any certainty of success. With choices limited to either the makeshift trails or the even less practical passage through the Ñe'embucú swamps, the overland supply route to Humaitá could offer little aid to the soldiers facing the Allied armies.

The lack of imported medicines impaired the health of both civilians and soldiers. The use of locally manufactured gunpowder and the recourse to low-grade metals made the effective use of artillery difficult. The interruption of cheap cloth imports left the populace in rags, and caraguatá never became a serviceable substitute. Worst of all, despite the efforts of the women, the production of food crops declined in a very marked way, and those that were harvested often failed to reach Humaitá. While Sánchez displayed a great strength of mind and a knack for improvisation, these skills permitted him only a few fleeting successes, and these were never enough.[39]

Biding Time at Humaitá

Soldiers new to the front soon learned that the war was mostly a dull business. For every occasion that bred heroism or cowardice, there were a thousand that required only patience. All one could do was wait; when something did happen, it was rarely what one expected.

The Paraguayan soldiers in camp or in the trenches met many of the same challenges as the women at home. They understood that their prospects for military success were bleak. They were hungry, physically tired, and, as cholera worked its way through the ranks, discouraged in ways that precluded any easy recovery. But they were not beaten. The soldiers in the Marshal's army were still told to kill as many of the *macacos* as possible, or else face the terrible consequences the enemy would bring to their wives, their children, and their country. That the Paraguayans continued to think this way remained one of the most salient facts of the campaign, and was recognized as such by everyone from Marshal López and the Marquis of Caxias, to the various war correspondents and foreign observers, to the recently arrived recruits from the Brazilian interior who never imagined that they would ever set foot in Paraguay.

Humaitá has a certain beauty difficult to capture in words. On the one hand, there is a stark quality in the reddish promontory that juts west of the settlement and falls precipitously to the river. And yet, a certain softness also pervades the place, especially in the nearby forests and marshland, and in the tall grasses that adorn the riverbank. Humaitá was an active and substantial town, similar to the Allied camps some miles away at Paso de la Patria and Tuyutí. Before cholera hit, the camp boasted a population in excess of forty thousand people. About half of its inhabitants were active soldiers, but there were also medical personnel, engineers, clerics, civilian teamsters, telegraphers, carpenters, blacksmiths, camp followers, a few foreign observers and prisoners, and children whose fathers were stationed with the army. López had also transformed his headquarters at Paso Pucú into a large, if not exactly flourishing, subsidiary camp around which were bivvied three battalions of infantry, and four or five partial regiments of dismounted cavalry, altogether numbering perhaps twenty-five hundred men.[40]

Humaitá lacked the gaudier touches of the Allied camps. There were no sutlers or grocers, no restaurants, photographers' studios, gambling halls, or brothels, and what there was of the private life had to be snatched at odd moments when military duties or physical energy permitted.[41] On the other hand, women and children gave the fortress and adjacent camps some feeling of community, as if their debased existence could somehow provide a semblance of home life. Perhaps the secret of Paraguayan steadfastness lay in this unenviable situation, for suffering, when shared with relatives or friends, can perhaps be better endured over a long span of time.

The British pharmacist George Frederick Masterman had occasion to visit Humaitá in late 1865. He was not much impressed:

> I went down to Humaitá to inspect the hospital and field boticas [pharmacies], but I saw very little of the formidable batteries which have made it so famous. It is a dreary place, flat and marshy, the soil a retentive clay, so that a heavy rainfall makes a lake of it. On all sides stretch the dismal esteros, with narrow, bad roads wading through them. A little raised above the general surface would be a few neglected fields, a grove of ragged old orange trees, and a poor rancho; nothing else between the low parapet on the land side and the distant hills, a blue line on the horizon. Within the works there were long ranges of barracks, mere sheds built of adobès [sic] and thatched with reeds, a single-storied brick house, where the president resided, he at one end, the bishop at the other, and Mrs. Lynch between them, and a few squares of tiled rooms for the officers. ... The batteries were hidden by a belt of trees from the lines. They were principally earthworks, but there was one brick casement, called the London Battery. They mounted then about 200 guns, mostly thirty-twos. On the land side there was only a single parapet and ditch, with re-entering angles, commanded by field-pieces, mounted en barbette [atop a platform of earth and logs that permitted gunners to fire over the parapets], and bastions at long intervals, with four heavier guns in each.[42]

By 1867, the army had much expanded its defenses around the fortress, and far more men had moved into the trenches. On the landside, Humaitá was protected by three lines of earthworks, with eighty-seven guns dug in on the innermost line. The river batteries mounted forty-six guns—one 80-pounder, four 68-pounders, eight 32-pounders, and the rest a variety of calibers. The Curupayty battery, just opposite the Allied line, mounted thirty 32-pounders, and the center was defended by a hundred guns, including four 68-pounders and one Whitworth, supposedly a 40-pounder, recovered from the hulk of a Brazilian steamer after the battle of the Riachuelo. All told, there were nearly four hundred artillery pieces around Humaitá, nearly double what had been present earlier.[43]

In constructing the earthworks that guarded the southern approaches to the fortress, the Paraguayans took care to indent the line of rifle pits. They made sure that the positions were not subject to enfilade from any nearby ground. Where loose or wet soil was present, they set up revetments with branches or bamboo stakes, and they cut trees for abatis. The Allies might be able to lay siege to Humaitá, but a head-on attack in this quarter now seemed unthinkable. The Allies would never risk another Curupayty.

Life at Humaitá was monotonous. The irregular hours for meals, the want of green vegetables and salt, the sameness of the fare, all combined to wreck any pleasure that a man could take in eating. Fish from the river and lagoons, and game from the bush, occasionally offered a touch of variety to the soldiers' diet, but the nearby swamps were soon hunted out. Any venison or capybara meat now had to come from the Chaco. Soldiers soon learned to eat the whitish hearts from the palmettos that grew at the edge of the *carrizal*. At home they rarely ate these artichoke-like bites, but at Humaitá they chewed them raw or, less frequently, boiled. Together with maize, peanuts, and occasionally beans, the palm hearts made up the vegetable portion of what the soldiers generally ate. Beef remained the central item in their mess; boiled, barbecued, jerked, cooked in its own hide—it was always beef. And if portions became smaller with the passage of the months, no greater variety was forthcoming. Eventually the daily ration dropped from one-eighteenth of a steer per man to one-two hundredth.[44]

Paraguayan soldiers sometimes went looking for wild honey. Five or six species of bees and honey ants could be found in the country. Most were stingless, and all produced a sour honey, which in normal times was mixed with molasses to coax out its sweetness. This blend was mixed with five parts water (and sometimes the internal sap of the caranday palm) and left to ferment into a kind of beer (*kaguy*), which was the common beverage of the Chaco. It was not especially potent, though, and when possible, the men pilfered *caña* from the medical supplies, or waited for the occasional celebration when liquor was granted them as part of the festivities.

Sharpshooters had active service on the frontlines but only occasionally killed anyone. The frequent Allied bombardments, however, became the stuff of derision, for they were even less effective; one simply had to keep low in the dugouts.[45] The enemy almost never managed to hit the fortress itself, and those in the camp learned to think of the cannonades as no more threatening than rainstorms over the Chaco. Meanwhile, everything was dull. There was the sharpening of bayonets and lances to attend to, and the cleaning of muskets. Latrines had to be dug and messages ferried. As for other particulars, guard duty followed drill and drill followed guard duty until some senior officer would conceive a short raid or grant permission for soldiers to return to their quarters to sleep. Seemingly, every man in the army had at one point or the other cried the nighttime watchword: "¿Quién vive?," which would hopefully bring the standard countersign: "¡La república!"

There was rarely anything new to report, yet every man took pains to harass the enemy pickets whenever possible. As Thompson explained, the Paraguayans "used to play all sorts of pranks at night with the Brazilian guards, shooting at them with bows and arrows, and with '*bodoques*,' ball[s] of clay, baked in the sun, about an inch in diameter, [and] shot from a bow with two strings [held] with the right thumb and forefinger like an arrow."[46]

As to continued raiding, Paraguayan sappers sometimes penetrated the Allied lines in the dead of night. They put heel first when walking upon solid ground, and used the balls of their feet when walking through soft sand, so as to remain silent. The enemy troopers would awake in the morning to find their sentinels' throats had been cut. Such exploits were never all that frequent, but the few that did occur earned the Marshal's men a reputation for supernatural ferocity among the Allies, and on the other side helped to reinvigorate morale.

Discipline in the Paraguayan camp followed the old Spanish regulations, which on paper were meticulous and hierarchical. Major crimes or signs of defeatism received swift and heavy punishment, as in the case of Corporal Facundo Cabral of the 27th Regiment, who, in May 1867, was found guilty of having spoken in awe of the enemy fleet and earned five hundred lashes for such loose talk.[47] Lesser infractions brought lesser punishments, of course, but even these could be draconian. Theoretically, an accused man could be placed in leather "stocks" or strapped upon the wheel of an oxcart, where he might remain tied until an officer had decided that he had had enough. In practice, however, what tended to happen drew a good deal less from Spanish antecedents than from the rough justice and easy familiarity of the Paraguayan countryside. Fellowship in the trenches implied a certain intimacy, not the fictitious equality that served as one of the slogans of Mitre's Liberals, but a feeling rooted in common needs.

Such attitudes grew out of an established tradition of patriarchy. Soldiers called their superiors *tataí* (father) and were called *che raý* (my son) in response. A good officer took pride in his patient control of the men around him. He never beat them into insensibility, though beat them he did. A man laid raw by the leather thong of a horsewhip would be approached by his superior, who would ask him if he thought a father enjoyed beating his children. Before he could answer, the officer would touch him on the shoulder, offer reassurances, and tell him that good discipline was necessary in the Marshal's army.[48]

By 1867, the area allocated for barracks had grown to meet the needs of the newly arrived troops. Sometimes these were standard edifices fashioned from adobe, and similar to those that Masterman had noted above. But the soldiers also constructed simple huts from mud, straw, sticks, and cowhide. These could house two or perhaps three men, but were wet, uncomfortable, and infested with vermin. Even so, the huts were much sought-after, for the Paraguayans had few tents to speak of, nor any prospect of obtaining one. Soldiers were thus forced to sleep outside, their bodies hunched near their campfires, and their ponchos pulled over their heads. They had a difficult time finding protection from downpours or insects.

The main hospitals at Humaitá were situated directly behind the batteries. This represented poor planning, for medical facilities thus placed were apt to get hit with the shells the Allies meant to strike the gun placements. Casualties in the wards thus proved frequent, and on one occasion a single ball killed thirteen men as they lay in their beds and hammocks.[49] Those in hospital beds counted themselves lucky. The incidence of "walking wounded" was high among the Paraguayans at Humaitá, and sometimes whole units were composed of men with bad legs or arms. The British doctors managed to evacuate some of the sick and wounded to Asunción or Cerro León, but by 1867 the statistics on how many had received treatment were no longer maintained with any regularity. Masterman reported a terrible fate for most of those sent upstream to the capital:

> They came up, poor fellows, in the half-crippled steamers, from the front, after a journey of three or four days, and as a rule did not get a morsel of food on the way; by the[n], we must understand half or a third of those who were put on board [arrived], the rest had died and been thrown overboard. The condition in which they arrived was shocking beyond expression. ... Almost or quite naked, with their wounds untended, dirty and famished, and so emaciated that when dead they dried up without de-composition, they were carried up from the pier to the hospitals; and then had to lie, perhaps for a week, or till they died on the ground, but one never heard a word of complaint: they bore all with a silent heroism, which won them our heartiest sympathies.[50]

Women played a crucial role at Humaitá and the other military camps. They provided the men with cooked food, swept the camps clean, and with their companionship and sympathy, managed to take the edge off a difficult existence. They gathered firewood and fodder for the horses, and worked as laundresses. Upon every bush they placed sheets, trousers, starched blouses (*typoíes*), and the little scraps of cotton cloth that served as towels for the hospitals, all freshly washed and drying in the sun. They sometimes pressed jasmine flowers or the leaves of native patchouli into the recesses of the cloth to impart its perfume as a tiny concession to the sensual.

At first the women were not allowed to go to the soldiers' quarters after sunset, though the prohibition was eventually relaxed.[51] As nurses, herb doctors, and unofficial orderlies, their work was indispensable: they scrubbed the wards and brought cold well water for those who needed it; they lit candles and prayed; they dug jiggers from the feet of afflicted men and picked lice from their hair; and they held the hands of dying soldiers who could just barely murmur the words "acanundú, acanundú, che jhasy!" (Fever, fever, oh, how I hurt!)[52]

Every family was required to send one daughter or one sister to the hospitals to serve in the wards where their work was lauded as essential to the war effort.[53] Such women came under strict military discipline right away. They received a regular salary for their labor, but they were expected to work hard. The Paraguayan field commanders eventually organized these nurses, naming *sargentas* (female sergeants) to supervise their labor in the hospitals and in the camps generally.[54]

These same sargentas also organized dances, which became a regular feature of the limited social life in the military camps. They set up decorations, supplied table cloths and snacks, and saw to it that the assembled women looked their best. *Caña* flowed liberally at these events, which all the resident officers were obligated to attend in full-dress uniform. The military bands, which included harps, clarinets, trumpets, and violins, struck up well-known reels and other step tunes, including "La Palomita," the "Cielito," and the "London Karapé," and the participants danced with as much energy as they could manage.[55]

Such fetes provided opportunities, not only to snatch a moment of affection and tenderness from the depressing business of war making, but also to celebrate the national cause. No one could forget that the wooden dance rotunda that graced the central hall had once served as the deck of a Brazilian warship that the Paraguayans had forced aground at the Riachuelo. Favored occasions for dances included the Marshal's birthday, the anniversary of his election to the presidency, national independence, noted military victories, and sometimes even defeats in which Paraguayan forces had requited themselves with particular devotion.[56]

Musical events were not limited to dances, of course. The Paraguayan peasants had a long tradition of singing and guitar playing, and at Humaitá the soldiers arranged regular concerts. In the trenches, too, they happily gave in to this temptation, whiling away the hours by composing new ditties that pelted the enemy with a variety of amusing insults. Every folksong remembered from childhood received new lyrics. The Guaraní language has a wonderful repertoire of bawdy and piquant terms, and these received ample display in the forging and reforging of ballads and war chants.

The desire to escape boredom and relieve stress found many other outlets in the Paraguayan camp. Religious festivals, for instance, were celebrated on a regular basis and every effort was made to give them a certain luster. Attendance at mass ran high both at Humaitá and in the field. Members of every choir—and there were many—gathered on Sundays to sing hymns of praise to the Son of God (ñandejara Jesucristo), the sacred cause, and Marshal López.[57]

For all of his faults, the Marshal entertained many progressive notions about his country; one of them held that Paraguayans could improve their future prospects with education, and López never forgot this principle during the war. In mid-1866, just after his interview with Mitre at Yataity Corã, he ordered the then captain Juan Crisóstomo Centurión to set up an academy for soldiers at Humaitá. The effort proved successful, with officers and men who had witnessed every manner of horror lining up like excited schoolboys to take lessons in Spanish grammar, geography, French, and English. (The captain had spent considerable time in England, where he became a genuine aficionado of Shakespeare.)

Centurión, who understood how men under pressure can thirst for new knowledge, took to his new assignment with real enthusiasm. He told his students how the sciences could break the reign of ignorance in South America, and how every man could partake of the resulting prosperity if he would only eschew traditional xenophobia.[58] The academy continued to function for many months. One commentator observed that it was positively beautiful to see men "returning from an attack on enemy convoys in the swamps or from a charge with sword and bayonet, hanging up their arms and leather shakos, drying away their heroic sweat, and taking up the pencil to translate English or French."[59]

There was something surreal as well as poignant in these scenes. Though the horrors of combat could not be cancelled out by wishful thinking, even rank escapism had a place at the Paraguayan camp. Its strangest manifestation involved a magic lantern show that the Marshal had ordered from Paris and which arrived in Paraguay just before the blockade closed the river. Someone had mislaid the instructions for this "phantasmagoria," which was managed on a rather grand scale and included vividly colored cut-out figures of important European personages, landscapes, and recent events.

López ordered Thompson and Masterman to assemble the exhibition at Paso Pucú, and though the two were vexed at having been assigned this trifling duty, they ended up having some fun. When they inaugurated the show, the Marshal, the bishop, and "three or four generals" arrived en suite and made a detailed inspection to the sound of martial music. The two Britons then slipped effortlessly into the role of showmen. The various Paraguayan officials had little idea of what the images represented, but earnestly gestured at each and every one, offering comments and misconceived appraisals with the greatest show of seriousness. The Marshal, who could not know how silly he looked, stood on tiptoe to peer through the bull's-eyes at the "Bay of Naples by Moonlight," and a "Chasseur d'Afrique Engaging Ten Arabs at Once."

When the magic lantern show began, it presented still more opportunities to contemplate the bizarre. A wide passage connecting two courtyards was closed off with curtains placed at one end and the white screen at the other. Thompson set up the machine, adjusted the focus, and lit the requisite candles after chairs had been arranged in a semicircle for López and his entourage. The soldiers, for whom the amusement was supposedly intended, could find only standing room outside.[60] It was one of the more incongruous episodes in an incongruous war.

The Mato Grosso Campaign

During the entire course of the war, the Allies attempted only one major strategic initiative that offered at least a slim hope of changing the trajectory of the conflict. This was not the expected—and wholly rational—second front that should have developed through the Misiones and Encarnación, but rather a far riskier effort to dispatch the Brazilian army through the Mato Grosso bush to attack Paraguay from the north. On paper, the idea of such a campaign had much to recommend it; after his successful invasion of Mato Grosso in late 1864, the Marshal had done little to maintain the tiny outposts he had occupied in the province, which seemed to invite a diversionary attack in that quarter.

The problem, however, was that this idea ignored practical difficulties. Mato Grosso lay hundreds of miles from São Paulo, and the two were separated by some of the most difficult terrain in South America. Any Allied units that passed through the forests could never be adequately supplied, given the distances involved, and while the defense of López's garrisons in the north had been entrusted to small, second-rate units, they at least could expect support from contiguous areas in Paraguay proper. This should have prompted skepticism regarding any attack through Mato Grosso. But such a prudent stance held no appeal for the armchair generals in Rio de Janeiro, who wanted a cheap end to the war. The old proverb, "Deus é grande, mas o Mato é ainda maior" (God is great, but the Mato is greater still), went unheeded.

The objective conditions for a terrible disaster were already in place by April 1865, when a newly commissioned twenty-two-year-old military engineer, Alfredo d'Escragnolle Taunay, asked to join the proposed expedition to Mato Grosso. His participation would prove a major boon to Latin American letters, for his account of what happened, *A Retirada da Laguna*, became one of the classics of Brazilian literature.

Taunay fit the image of the enthusiastic aristocrat that dominated public imagination in the earliest stages of the war. He was eager and curious to visit the interior of Brazil, the land of the unending marshes, the hyacinth macaw, and the last of the "red Indians." Though he wrote in the "spirit" of the *bandeirantes*, in reality Taunay's inclinations were fundamentally romantic.[61] His epic account of the Mato Grosso campaign could be read as a bildungsroman, for not only did Taunay's experiences turn him into a hardened man; like many of his comrades-at-arms, they almost destroyed him.

On 10 April 1865, a column of 568 men left São Paulo for the interior. Command over the column was given to Colonel Manoel Pedro Drago, whom the emperor had named the new president of Mato Grosso. The colonel's instructions were to head for Uberaba in Minas Gerais, where he would receive reinforcements for the advance into Paraguay.

Despite his background as former head of police in Rio, Drago had few of the attributes of the war's other ex-police chief, the Paraguayan general José Eduvigis Díaz. While Díaz's drive and impetuosity had won him numerous accolades—and eventually got him killed—Drago proved a rather unmilitary sort of officer and a born procrastinator. Five days out from São Paulo, his column halted at Campinas, where it stayed for two months.

This mid-sized town was located at the hub of a major commercial artery, and as a result, was surprisingly rich and progressive.[62] The colonel took pleasure in the social life of the town, attending receptions, paying court to women, and smiling at musical recitals. Taunay, who had already cast himself in the role of Xenophon, enjoyed himself almost as much as his commander, later writing that the time spent at Campinas was "one of his happiest and most diverting [experiences], with its long succession of dinners, parties, picnics, fetes, and dances, one after another, without leaving us a moment of rest."[63]

Drago's delays at Campinas were not entirely of his own making. For one thing, having gilded the idea of the Mato Grosso expedition, the government ministers did little to support it. To move forward, Drago needed horses, carts, oxen, foodstuffs, medicines, and money to hire teamsters while en route. But the war minister gave him little more than promises. In addition, while at Campinas, Drago's column was hit by smallpox, which caused six deaths and 159 desertions.[64] The column departed Campinas in mid-June 1865, but not before Taunay recorded the passing of a huge shooting star, a veritable fireball that all the soldiers in his command saw as a harbinger of disaster.[65]

While Drago was frittering his time away, the tiny guards units in Mato Grosso had to defend the province with the minimal resources at hand. Apart from a few men trickling in from Goiás, they had seen no reinforcements or aid.[66] In fact, the hard-pressed defenders of Cuiabá remained ignorant of the expedition that had been raised on their behalf, and presumed that the empire had forgotten them one and all.[67] In their minds, there always existed a possibility that Bolivia might join with López and seize territories to the west, and that slaves in the province might rise in support of the invader.[68] Even if the Cuyabanos had been aware of the units coming to their aid, they lacked the supplies necessary to sustain even their own forces.[69]

On 18 July Drago reached Uberaba, where his column was reinforced by a brigade of 1,212 Mineiros (inhabitants of Minas Gerais) made up of police units and Voluntários led by Colonel Antonio da Fonseca Galvão.[70] Drago had already taken four months to travel less than three hundred miles, and all along the route troubles had plagued his column. Now, for another forty-seven days, the expeditionary force bivouacked outside Uberaba, a cattle town some 2,250 feet in elevation that earlier inhabitants had grandiloquently christened A Princeza do Sertão, though the little community could only boast an irregular grouping of one-story houses, the poorer ones covered with thatch.[71] Drago's column made itself at home and awaited the muster of still more troops.

As a matter of fact, desertions constituted a major problem at Uberaba. Ninety-six soldiers fled into the bush, 33 of whom died in the effort. Drago sent another 25 men into a makeshift prison as a warning to others, but the effort did little good; no one wanted to join the column, and those already a part of it doubted the wisdom of the whole enterprise. Eventually, another reinforcement of 1,209 men arrived, which brought Drago's troop strength to 1,575 soldiers. This was the total contingent, now styled the "Expeditionary Force in Operations in the South of Mato Grosso," that departed on 4 September 1865 with Cuiabá as its destination. The imperial government promised a force of 12,000 and delivered to Drago just over one-tenth that number. They boasted thirteen artillery pieces, all small cannon. And with this meager force they proposed to reconquer a piece of territory nearly as large as the Banda Oriental.

Just behind the columns followed a band of two hundred women, the lovers and wives of the soldiers, some of whom brought their children. No provisions had been allocated for these camp followers. The soldiers, the women, and the children alike suffered from diarrhea, malnutrition, and malaria, and the animals from equine beriberi.[72]

As the expeditionary force approached Mato Grosso from the east, the Paraguayans showed no obvious concern. Their occupation of the southern districts of the province had been, for the most part, unremarkable. After the initial rush of excitement in seizing Coimbra, Corumbá, and the small military posts along the Río Mbotety, they never bothered to advance further. The provincial capital Cuiabá thus remained in Brazilian hands throughout the war.

The Marshal's men conducted one major attack in April 1865 against Coxim, a small village that lay along the trails that ran past the edge of the Pantanal and connected Corumbá with communities further east. The initial results of this engagement were inconclusive.[73] The real significance of the Coxim gambit was strategic: if they could somehow isolate the provincial capital, the Brazilians would be unable to organize resistance anywhere in Mato Grosso. All depended on López's willingness to maintain a credible threat in the garrison he assigned to the village, but a sizable deployment was impossible. The Paraguayans at Coxim had to cope with minimal support. They spent the months growing maize and manioc, tending to the few cattle that fell into their hands, and generally avoiding contact with the enemy.[74]

At Uberaba, Colonel Drago received orders from Rio to deviate from the original plan by marching, not to Cuiabá, but to the southern districts, near the center of Paraguayan strength in the Mato Grosso. Brazilian ministers likely believed that the enemy garrisons were so depleted that Drago could easily reestablish imperial authority. Drago did receive further reinforcements from Goiás as his column passed through a small corner of that province, but the 2,080 men who entered into Mato Grosso proper hardly constituted a battle-worthy force.[75] The colonel himself never got the chance to test his men in combat, for on 18 October 1865, he received word from the imperial capital that he had been relieved. The stories of his exaggerated conviviality at Campinas had finally caught up with him, and he reluctantly passed command to Antonio da Fonseca Galvão.

No one knew if Galvão could do any better than his predecessor. The sickness and malnutrition that had dogged the men got worse, for this area of Mato Grosso proved especially insalubrious.[76] The Río Paraguay overflowed its banks throughout this latitude, and mosquitoes infested the soggy terrain everywhere; there were palometas, piranhas, caimans, and enormous serpents in the water; and there was hunger—always hunger.

Galvão could expect little help from the local Matogrossenses, and the provincial government had little to offer. Besides, the backwoodsmen (*sertanejos*) of these environs were apt to regard the newly arrived Brazilian troops with contempt. The sertanejos lived in water-logged clearings hewn from the forest, raised cattle, and showed little interest in the larger Brazilian community. True enough, they had little love for the Marshal and his men, either, but this animus was not easily joined to the emperor's cause. And more to the point, they had no discipline. If Galvão used such men on this occasion, he would take a great many chances.

The expeditionary force reached Coxim at the end of December 1865. The village had been abandoned. In the last stage of this advance, the column that had started at São Paulo covered some of the most difficult territory and were now badly in need of new supplies of food and horses. The men saw their situation deteriorate still further as the Pantanal rose, and isolated them from any support. This meant more sickness, more hunger, more desertions.

And reinforcements were not on the way. The provincial authorities at Cuiabá had mustered few new recruits during the final months of 1865, and those that did enter the rolls did so forcibly.[77] Neither could the officials at Cuiabá promise any cattle or foodstuffs, for there were none to spare.[78] No one knew what the Paraguayans might do next, and there were even rumors that the Indigenous people would take advantage of the disorder and launch incursions even more violent than those of the Marshal.[79]

Galvão's units remained at Coxim, surrounded by flooded terrain and stagnant water, until June 1866, when they set out for Miranda, still some three hundred miles to the southwest. It took three months to march this distance, for the intervening territory, near the Río Negro, was, if anything, worse than what the soldiers had already seen. It had taken Taunay and the men coming from Rio de Janeiro two full years to reach this site, and one-third of their number had died or deserted.[80]

The Paraguayans abandoned Miranda, just as they had Coxim. They destroyed the community's few buildings, which meant that the Brazilians could only use their own tents for shelter, and in such a wet environment, it was hardly surprising that still more men fell ill.[81]

Galvão himself took no satisfaction in the progress of his columns, for he had suddenly taken ill while crossing the swamps; he would die before he got out of them. The new commander of the expeditionary force—if it could still be called one—was Colonel Carlos de Morais Camisão, a short, black-eyed, bald-pated officer, forty-seven years of age, who had earned a field commission two decades earlier. He had had considerable experience in the province, and had taken part in the evacuation of Corumbá in 1865. Unfortunately, he had never risen above the aspersions cast against those who had supposedly failed to prevent that earlier defeat.[82] Taunay, though ever respectful, worried that the new commander would use this new opportunity to vindicate himself at the expense of his own exhausted men.[83]

The expeditionary force now comprised the 17th Voluntários of Minas Gerais, the 20th and 21st Infantry Battalions, an artillery detachment from Amazonas that operated four ox-drawn LaHitte rifled cannon, a small number of "Indian auxiliaries," and the ever-suffering camp followers. The units amounted to thirteen hundred men, but none were cavalry, which in these circumstances presented a serious drawback.[84]

To Camisão it made little difference. Sensibly enough, he regarded the campground at Miranda as undesirable, and on 11 January 1867, he ordered the entire force to advance toward Nioaque, which was dry and relatively high; the Marshal's men had also done a good job of maintaining it. But once again, they disappeared without a fight, leaving the Brazilians to occupy the site on 24 January. The Paraguayans, it turned out, had already moved the bulk of their forces to the opposite side of the Río Aquidabán several months earlier, and had destroyed the buildings they had abandoned, leaving only the niche of the little chapel intact.[85]

Camisão, who had no clear orders, evidently thought that his troops should cut a broad swath through northern Paraguay, occupy the town of Concepción, and in one fell swoop isolate the enemy garrisons upriver, where the Paraguayan force could be picked off at will. Looking at a map, this did not seem unreasonable; yet with all his previous experience of the Paraguayans and of the terrain in that part of the world, the colonel should have acted with greater caution. As it was, he told his exhausted men to advance out of Nioaque on 25 February, and about a week later, still without horses, still without provisions or munitions, they crossed the Río Apa into Paraguay.

They initially met little resistance, sighting only a few cavalrymen gallop-ing in the opposite direction. Up to this point, Taunay had believed that the Paraguayans could be won over with friendly arguments; his commander had even sent a message forward that referred to future amity among "civilized peo-ples."[86] But when the tiny outpost of Bella Vista fell into Camisão's hands, his soldiers encountered a cowhide nailed to a tree on which someone had carved an ominous message: "Advance, baldy! Fool of a general who comes in search of his sepulcher. The Brazilians think to be in Concepción before the holidays, but our men are waiting for them with bayonets and lead."[87]

For all of his audacity, Camisão saw that his situation was dire. The Paraguayans refused to offer battle, and time seemed to be on their side. The colonel was desperate for supplies: all his men were famished, while some had fallen sick with beriberi, and as there was no chance of obtaining support from the authorities in Cuiabá, they were on their own. A rumor had passed among the troops, however, that large cattle herds could be found at a nearby ranch, called "Laguna," supposedly the personal property of Marshal López. Camisão gave the order to march once again.

The vanguard reached the ranch on 1 May to find its buildings smoldering, with not a single head of cattle to be seen. Scouting parties later brought in some fifty animals, and this mollified the hungry men.[88] So did the unexpected ar-rival of a sutler coming from the north with three wagons of supplies.[89] Yet the Brazilian soldiers in Camisão's command had little time to enjoy their repast, for as they moved out in reconnaissance on 6 may, they met stiff resistance.

Those who initially planned the Mato Grosso gambit should have noted the Marshal's advantage in interior lines. He could call upon reinforcements, and indeed, troops under the command of Major Blas Montiel had just arrived from Humaitá. When joined with Major Martín Urbieta's depleted garrisons, the total amounted to around 780 men. These troops, who had not intended to go into action right away, had been instructed to wait for a clear opportunity to harass their foe. As always, however, a great deal of confusion attended the moment of contact between the two sides.

No one can say who fired the first shots. The Paraguayan soldiers had dug a small series of trenches at Bayendé, behind which they placed tents and wag-ons. In the early morning hours most men were still asleep. Though hardly well rested, they were in better shape than the men in the opposing columns. Colonel Camisão had intended to charge with bayonets, overwhelming the first Paraguayan units, and seizing their cannon, but with no cavalry, he could not scout enemy positions. Instead, his men had to approach the Paraguayans on foot, which was difficult to do surreptitiously.

At the beginning, the Brazilians enjoyed some success, for the better part of Urbieta's forces had yet to arrive on the scene: eighty Paraguayans were killed in the initial melee, compared to only one Brazilian.[90] Though Camisão failed to capture any of the six enemy cannon, his men did succeed in dismounting two.[91] An hour or so later, Paraguayan cavalry appeared from the forest and fell upon the Brazilian rear, which threatened to drive a wedge between Camisão's vanguard and the main column just to the north. Rather than allow that possibility, the colonel ordered a retreat.

Camisão meant this withdrawal to be temporary. On 8 May, however, a large Paraguayan force of perhaps two thousand men ambushed the retreating Brazilians near the Machorra Creek.[92] The Brazilians had tried to erect a line of reinforced trenches, but Urbieta sent two columns of mounted troops into them, killing some two hundred men, while losing only sixteen of his own.[93] Two days later, dragging themselves through the bush in as good an order as possible, the Brazilians recrossed the Apa into Mato Grosso.

Another ugly engagement occurred on 11 May near Nioaque, leaving perhaps another two hundred fifty corpses on the field. The Brazilians halted just long enough to bury their dead.[94] Even now, a month of skirmishing, starvation, and cholera still awaited the expeditionary force as it fled north; this retreat, which formed the focus of Taunay's classic work, was a veritable *via dolorosa* for everyone involved. Even though deep into Brazilian territory, and thus far from any support, Montiel and Urbieta kept up their daily harassment. They set brush fires that disrupted the enemy's path of retreat, attempted to steal the few head of cattle that the Brazilians still possessed, and cut down stragglers wherever they found them.[95]

It was a bitter march. Some of the Paraguayan wounded fell into the hands of the Brazilian's Guaicurú auxiliaries, who tortured them in gruesome fashion.[96] On another occasion, with many of his men struck down by disease, Camisão decided to abandon "more than 130 cholera patients," trusting without much hope in the mercy of the enemy. Every abandoned man was either killed by the Paraguayans or left by them to die (such was the fear of contagion).[97]

Colonel Camisão and his second-in-command both died of cholera over the next several weeks. So did the chief of engineers—Taunay's immediate superior—and a great many others. At an earlier stage of the campaign, the men could be urged forward with promises of home and family just beyond the horizon; now, simple survival was their clarion call. Food had almost completely disappeared, but the men kept moving thanks to the spongy palmetto hearts, the green oranges, and the wild manioc, whose roots they dug up and ate raw. Since many varieties of the latter plant were poisonous, the mortality in the retreating column actually increased as a result.[98]

The Paraguayans broke off their pursuit on 8 June. Perhaps Urbieta, Montiel, and the Marshal's other officers realized the senselessness of any further action, or perhaps their own fatigue got the better of them. Either way, the Brazilian column they had followed for weeks was broken, and the Paraguayans celebrated by playing cornets and bugles.[99] The larger portion of Montiel's force then returned to Humaitá, a distance of over three hundred miles.

Four days later, a tattered mass of skeletal Brazilian soldiers, a few Indigenous people, and even fewer women emerged through the brush from the south, and set up a bivouac at Porto Canuto on the Río Aquidauana. Those who could threw themselves into the water and clawed dust, mud, and parasites from their ulcerated bodies. Mindful of their weakness and hunger, they arranged themselves as best they could, rested, and enjoyed this newfound "land of beautiful waters." Food and other support arrived shortly thereafter from nearby villages.

Of the 1,680 men who had crossed into Paraguay with Camisão, only 700 remained alive.[100] The survivors had maintained their discipline from beginning to end, a fact that Taunay and others never ceased to applaud. The troops managed to drag back all four cannon with them, but the column as a whole was in shreds. And we can speculate that without his strong imagination, which had bolstered him under the twin spurs of depression and malnutrition, Taunay himself might not have survived.

The Brazilian expedition from São Paulo to Mato Grosso and northern Paraguay was not only disastrous—it was downright foolish. In this challenging environment, the Paraguayan defenders enjoyed all the advantages. Camisão's seniors had poorly prepared the expeditionary force, which was already weakened when it reached Mato Grosso, but his impulsiveness, his ambition, or perhaps his sense of mission never permitted him to admit the impossibility of his situation. The idea that such a column, lacking both provisions and horses, could succeed in taking Concepción, was nothing short of self-delusion; Camisão paid for this bravado with his life, as did many of his men. In retrospect, his best course of action would probably have been to move out of Paraguayan-occupied territory and reinforce his troops at Cuiabá. But for whatever reason, he failed to do this.

In the world of letters, of course, the retreat from Laguna made for an epic tale. Taunay repaired to Rio de Janeiro with word of the expedition's fate and was immediately acclaimed as the man of the hour. The government issued elaborate medals to all the participants, which began the process of transforming the military fiasco into a propaganda victory, replete with awesome tales of courage and sacrifice.

Taunay did his part in penning his classic account of the retreat, which, ironically for a distinctive work in the nationalist vein, first appeared in French in 1871. The author praised his comrades in elegiac terms, and whether he was describing Paulistas, Mineiros, or Matogrossenses, he attributed to them a constancy and heroism befitting the subjects of the emperor. And yet Taunay's account is a thick palimpsest, full of meanings not altogether clear—perhaps not even to the man himself. He reserved a vague admiration for the sertanejos of the interior provinces, men whose cunning, ruthlessness, and self-sacrifice he respected; with little evidence, he judged that they had saved the expeditionary force from annihilation time and again. He thought them uncouth, ignorant, and frighteningly violent, and yet, for all their rustic impulses, they acted, he claimed, as loyal Brazilians.[101]

Taunay could not have known that while his comrades were suffering their worst, the military situation in Mato Grosso had started to turn in Brazil's favor. In Cuiabá, the provincial president, José Vieira Couto de Magalhães, had pieced together a force to retake Corumbá. He reasoned that the Paraguayans had already abandoned Miranda and Nioaque along with the military colonies on the Mbotety, and that Corumbá could not be defended if he attacked right away. Camisão's regulars had already failed, but his Matogrossense guardsmen, who understood the land, just might succeed. On 10 June 1867 a mixed force of perhaps one thousand men left Cuiabá destined for Corumbá.

Corumbá had endured a two-year occupation at the hands of the Paraguayans, during which available resources diminished with each demand from the south. The Marshal's functionaries had tried to promote overland trade with Bolivia from this point, but the community shrunk anyway. Locals found the Paraguayan presence painful, especially since it had been preceded by a decade of commercial expansion. López, however, had removed a great many of the foreign merchants in the province to Paraguay in 1866, and ever since, food had been difficult to procure. At the same time, Lieutenant Colonel Hermógenes Cabral, the Marshal's field commander, remained under strict orders to reserve every scrap of available provisions for his garrison. This draconian policy made life difficult for anyone who stayed at Corumbá.[102]

At two thirty in the afternoon on 13 June the force from Cuiabá reached the occupied town and disembarked from five steamers as land units under Lieutenant Colonel Antonio Maria Coelho moved in from Dourados. Rumors of smallpox had caused Coelho to hasten his arrival at the site, and it appears that the Paraguayans were taken completely by surprise. The Brazilian troops penetrated the enemy's fortifications, and discovered that many of Cabral's 316 men were in hospital suffering from the epidemic. Those Paraguayans who could resist did so with the usual ferocity, but were overwhelmed nonetheless.[103] Cabral, his second-in-command, the Paraguayan chaplain, six other officers, and 160 men fought to their deaths.[104]

In the wake of this quick victory, Coelho and Couto de Magalhães hardly knew what to do. They had rescued five hundred individuals at Corumbá, including four hundred women, who, as a later commentator declared, "lived as slaves and [were constantly] subjected to the lascivious appetites of the Paraguayan soldiers."[105] Perhaps this accusation was accurate, perhaps not. In either case, what were these women's liberators supposed to do with them now—especially since so many had contracted smallpox? No extra provisions were available, nor any medicines; the threat of further contagion loomed over the community, and it was probably impossible for help from Cuiabá to arrive in time.

Though it does not appear to have been their first choice, Coelho, Couto de Magalhães, and the other Brazilian commanders opted to return to the provincial capital the next day.[106] They had thought the battle over, but did not count on Lieutenant Romualdo Núñez, the enemy naval commander, who had two steamers hidden in a bend of the river just to the north. Though the Paraguayan land forces had been driven from Corumbá, these two vessels still intended to exact a toll for the loss. They slipped past the Brazilian units at night and made south for Coimbra, where they picked up both munitions and men, and again steamed upriver.

The provincial president returned to Corumbá with a new contingent of regulars on 24 June. He had intended to evacuate those sick individuals who had been left behind, but little did he realize how much further the epidemic had spread among the civilian population. It took more than two weeks to get the sick embarked aboard lighters, which were escorted upriver toward Cuiabá by two tiny imperial steamers, the *Antonio João* and the *Jaurú*. The little flotilla had been headed north for several days when, on 11 July, the two ships dropped anchor near the mouth of the Río São Laurenço. At three in the afternoon, the Paraguayan warship *Salto de Guairá* steamed into view and fired her guns into the Brazilian vessels.

Núñez had returned, and with a vengeance. The Paraguayan lieutenant made at once for the *Jaurú*, which he badly damaged. The ship started to list at the shoreline right as a party of Paraguayan sailors boarded. The surprised Brazilians had just enough time to jump onto land and run into the sarandí. Meanwhile, the *Antonio João* managed at the last moment to maneuver into an advantageous position in the narrow river channel and got off several shots that hit the *Salto de Guairá*. The musket fire from the Brazilian troops on land proved even more lethal. Bullets filled the sky and Núñez and several of his crew fell wounded.

In one last lunge at the enemy before sunset, the Brazilians managed to recapture the hulk of the *Jaurú*, killing most of the Paraguayans on board. The *Salto de Guairá* broke off contact shortly thereafter and fled to Corumbá, which by this time had again fallen to the Marshal's troops. The wounded Núñez had the pleasure of forwarding to Paso Pucú a full account of the damage done the Brazilians on the São Laurenço.[107] Two days later, he received even happier news when his missing helmsman and two of his soldiers reappeared at Corumbá. They had escaped after the assault on the *Jaurú* and had made their way overland through the bracken to reach Paraguayan lines. They confirmed that the Brazilian vessel had been wrecked and that the enemy host had abandoned the site and fled to Cuiabá on foot.[108]

The two men could not have realized that still more tragic news awaited the Matogrossenses to the north. The smallpox that the infected individuals carried with them to Cuiabá, instead of finding its relief in the provincial capital, in fact spread rapidly once it arrived. Well over half the population of the city perished—between five and ten thousand people. So many died, in fact, that burial parties could not keep up with the labor, and bodies were simply thrown into the streets, where they were consumed by dogs.[109]

Government ministers in Rio de Janeiro chose to present the actions in Mato Grosso as heroic examples of Brazilian stoicism.[110] But there was no success, and the pride that adorned their reports and proclamations had a hollow ring. The Paraguayans continued to control Coimbra until April 1868, and might reasonably have claimed success for their force of arms in the province until that point.

Marshal López refused to accept such a simple verdict, however, and instead focused his ire at the temporary fall of Corumbá on 13 June. Unwilling to see that his men had been taken by surprise, he manufactured an account that referred to the supposed treachery of the Paraguayan commander: Cabral, he said, had sold the place to the Brazilians, and had, on the day they assaulted it, dispatched all the sound men into the woods and removed the guns from the trenches. López also claimed that when the sick men in hospital saw the Brazilians coming, they all stood to their arms, and though they were overpowered at first, the sick men ultimately drove the enemy away. He even said that "the Brazilians had chopped up Cabral and his priest into small pieces, and had eaten them, in payment for their treachery."[111] This fanciful version of events entered the official record in the pages of *El Semanario*, although few in Paraguay seemed to believe it.[112]

What neither the imperial government nor López cared to admit was that the entire Mato Grosso campaign of 1866–1867 was a sideshow—bloody and tragic, but with little influence over the larger course of the war. The Marshal's earlier efforts in the province had demonstrated that while the Brazilians could be defeated in local battles, the sheer vastness of the territory made it impossible for a lesser power to force an outright victory. In this case, however, the size of the empire worked against Brazilian interests; in the south, at Humaitá, both the fleet and the armies had been too big for the country, and their commanders found it difficult to maneuver no matter what. In Mato Grosso, by contrast, the country was too big for the armies.

Mitre Contemplates His Position

Casual observers might have supposed that Mitre's return to Buenos Aires was made necessary by the Montonero revolts in the west of Argentina; in fact, the political situation in the capital had deteriorated for many reasons, only some of them connected to the western uprisings. Vice President Marcos Paz had recently tried to quit his post over a trivial political dispute, and several cabinet ministers likewise tendered their resignations. The Autonomists had increased their influence at the expense of Mitre's Liberals, and there had been extensive complaints in Congress about the financial soundness of the loans that the national government had obtained from British banks (not all of which supported the war effort).[113] And there was the upcoming presidential election to consider.

Don Bartolo had full confidence that he could juggle these challenges. He called on Wenceslao Paunero to quash the western Montoneros and the general immediately set out from the Paraguayan front to put together a new army of five thousand men. Mitre then put the Argentine house in order. He rejected Paz's resignation, and through a combination of patient cajoling and measured threats managed to get the vice president back where he wanted him.[114] He made it clear that he would compromise with those Autonomists in Buenos Aires who wanted him to behave as a Porteño first and an Argentine second.[115] And he also asserted that if Entre Ríos joined the rebellion, he would arrange to dispatch Brazilian troops into the Litoral provinces to contain any challenge from Governor Urquiza.[116]

Perhaps most importantly, Mitre mobilized his support in the Argentine countryside, an area that both the Montoneros and Marshal López regarded as sympathetic to their interests.[117] Certain Liberal caudillos, such as the Taboada brothers in Santiago del Estero, harkened immediately to the president's call and organized an effective force. The Montoneros had gained territory and political influence with considerable aid from Chile in the form of armaments and at least two battalions of "volunteers."[118] But such help was too little, too late. On 1 April, a Liberal army hit the rebels in San Luis, sending the whole lot into precipitous flight. A week later, a second Liberal army under Antonino Taboada overwhelmed the Montonero general Felipe Varela in a seven-hour engagement just outside the town of La Rioja. Varela's gauchos had arrived at the scene of battle fatigued, thirsty, and ready for defeat at the hands of the veterans of the Paraguayan War. Several months later the Montoneros crossed the Bolivian frontier and the rebellion fizzled out.

The moment of danger had passed for Mitre. From this point onward, the Chileans kept a greater distance from Argentine political affairs, and the support that Urquiza had supposedly promised the Montonero uprising never materialized. When asked by Mitre to suppress certain provincial newspapers that voiced approval of the Cuyo insurgents, the Entrerriano governor did not hesitate to do as he was told.[119]

Having won in the field, Mitre took swift revenge on the Montoneros. While armed units of the national government occupied the western provinces, his recruitment officers conscripted every man suspected of harboring dissident opinions and sent them, under guard, to the Paraguayan front. In June 1867, the president announced to Congress that he was raising a new force of three thousand men "from the provinces that have contributed least to the war."[120] To the extent that Argentina would continue to sacrifice her sons to the war in Paraguay, they would now be sons that the fatherland could do without.

Mitre survived the military challenge of the Montoneros and restored some of his clout with the politicians in Buenos Aires. Yet he never succeeded in cauterizing the wound inflicted by the rebellions. His recruitment policies had alienated not only his *provinciano* enemies in the west, but many people elsewhere in the country. By transferring troops away from frontier garrisons in Buenos Aires province he shored up control in the west, but left the frontier open to raids by Indigenous people that damaged the interests of the ranchers whose good will he needed to govern successfully. To counter this, Mitre could have expended all his energies in support of his foreign minister, Rufino de Elizalde, who he hoped would succeed him in 1868.[121] Or, more importantly, he could win the war in Paraguay—better a tardy victor than an outright failure.

He ultimately chose the latter course, and Marcos Paz reassumed his administrative duties at Buenos Aires while once again Mitre set sail for Paraguay in July 1867. Technically, the Argentine president regained command over the Allied forces upon his return to the front. But in fact, Caxias continued to enjoy extensive authority and all the latitude needed to exercise it. In public, the marquis maintained a polite deference to the Allied commander, who was thirteen years his junior. But he must also have worried about the Argentine's every demonstration of power, which enhanced the material interests of Buenos Aires more than the Alliance.[122]

Indeed, Mitre and Caxias never liked each other. The marquis was acutely aware that, in Paraguay, he represented the majesty of dom Pedro, and that the elected president of a republic, no matter how excellent his personal qualities, could never rise above the status of partisan politician; the emperor, by contrast, while certainly a political figure, was also the living embodiment of all that distinguished Brazil. And if the nation itself had its share of backwardness, dom Pedro offered proof that the future was as stable as it was rosy. By contrast, the Argentine president could only promise a regular series of "revolutions" that, if they were not always violent, were certainly divisive. This was not the kind of politics that recommended itself to the marquis.

7

 THE ONGOING RESISTANCE

Caxias had spent the months of Mitre's absence strengthening his trench works from Tuyutí to Curuzú. He had his engineers reinforce the long line with packed earth and tree branches and build revetments at regular intervals; he improved the medical services and the commissary; he established guidelines for better hygiene in camp, and rewrote the field manuals to reflect the circumstances of the Paraguayan terrain; he obtained alfalfa and cornmeal for the horses (which previously had been left to forage for whatever they could find, sometimes developing mange or farcy as a result); and, in stark contrast to the prior custom among Brazilian commanders, who tended to reserve promotions for the well connected, he started to promote officers of proven ability and professionalism.[1]

No detail seemed too inconsequential for Caxias, and every man who showed slackness or who deviated from regulations found himself on charges.[2] The marquis managed to restore morale in the Allied army, as well as a renewed dedication to prosecuting the war. He even flattered certain government ministers and members of Parliament into thinking that all the resources expended had been worth it.[3]

By the beginning of July, the Allied desire for action against López was palpable all along the line. Some soldiers wanted to fight because their officers told them to, others because they perceived a score to settle. But the majority, it seemed, just wanted to get on with it because every battle placed them one step closer to home. Besides, their advantages had expanded. Under Caxias's care, the army now numbered around forty-five thousand effectives, of whom forty thousand were Brazilians, with just under five thousand Argentines. No more than six hundred troops, under General Castro, were Uruguayan.[4] To counter this enormous force, the Marshal could still depend on about twenty thousand malnourished and under-supplied men, of whom fifteen thousand were infantry, thirty-five hundred cavalry, and fifteen hundred artillery.[5]

Despite their obvious advantage in numbers, the Allies still had to cope with the challenges presented by the carrizal and by the poor intelligence about what lay north. They had experimented for a short time in 1867 with observation balloons, bringing in two North American "aeronauts" and a Polish military engineer to help map the areas south of Humaitá.[6] Yet the Paraguayans soon discovered that they could obscure the view by setting multiple fires and filling the air with smoke; this impeded any observation from balloons or mangrullos. The Pole, Major Roberto A. Chodasiewicz, stayed on with the Allies as a military cartographer, but in the absence of better information, even his prodigious talents counted for little.[7]

No one doubted that the Allies enjoyed numerical superiority, but many doubted that they had the will to use this power in pursuit of the obvious end. In fact, their commanders had a general plan of attack in place for nearly a year. Mitre had advocated a flanking maneuver that would take the bulk of the army beyond the southern face of the Paraguayan Cuadrilátero, and then across the Bellaco towards Tuyucué, where it would take up a position in front of the Cuadrilátero's eastern face; from there, the Allies could gradually extend to the right, cutting the road from Humaitá to the capital. They would move by a long circuit north of the marshes and, at Tayí, they would reach the Río Paraguay, thus completing the encirclement of the fortress on the eastern side of the river. The Allies could then strangle Humaitá. The plan was straightforward, and though flashy frontal assaults had rarely succeeded in this war, the simple maneuver that Mitre advocated could not fail to deliver the desired victory. While the Allies' earlier optimism now looked no better than wishful thinking, this plan, by contrast, could succeed.

Mitre had already outlined the specifics of the flanking maneuver in a letter to Caxias on 17 April 1867.[8] The marquis, who saw the rapid march to the northeast as a logical complement to the previous Brazilian advance on Curuzú, embraced the plan at first, but then begged off because of the outbreak of cholera. He surmised that time was on his side, however, and that the epidemic would weaken the Paraguayans more than his own troops.[9]

Caxias had already done the basic arithmetic and had concluded that, in the end, the weight of Allied manpower would prevail over Paraguayan courage. Though the Marshal's troops might sacrifice themselves on a colossal scale, they could only inflict death and destruction in proportion to their numbers. According to the marquis's ruthless but inescapable logic, the attrition had only to be continued long enough to obtain the desired result.

But Caxias still needed time. He had redeployed forty-five hundred of the six thousand men from Curuzú on 30 May and now had to integrate them into the main force at Tuyutí.[10] He also had to train the troops that arrived with General Osório in June. This column of recent recruits, some ten thousand strong, was thought by many observers to be destined for a new front through the Paraguayan Misiones from Encarnación.[11] But in the end the marquis decided to add the troops to the host gathering at Tuyutí. Osório, still the most audacious officer on the Brazilian side, had spent several months on medical leave and was now anxious to reenter the fray alongside Caxias.

The marquis gave the Riograndense general what he wanted: command over two divisions of Brazilian cavalry, two divisions and two brigades of Brazilian infantry, a regiment of "mounted," or horse, artillery, three companies of engineers, and the bulk of the Uruguayan forces. The latter units constituted the vanguard that spearheaded the movement around the Paraguayan left.[12] Altogether they counted around twenty-eight thousand men and sixty-nine artillery pieces.

General Porto Alegre (who did not get on with Osório) received instructions to remain at the main Allied camp with his 2nd Corps as a reserve of some ten thousand men.[13] Caxias kept this sizable force behind just in case Marshal López ordered his units along the Bellaco out of their rifle pits and into another frontal assault on Tuyutí. Argentine commentators may have castigated the marquis for his ponderous and tardy organization at this stage, but his preparations were commendable. And in fact, things went more or less according to his plan.

President Mitre had yet to put Paraguayan clay under his boots when Caxias launched the expected maneuver on 22 July. The Argentines might have been justified in questioning the timing of his attack as insufficiently considerate of their national interests, but the marquis could not have seen it that way. Instead, he realized that Mitre's return would occasion political difficulties that would likely vanish if the armies had already made good progress on the ground.[14] Caxias would present the Argentine president with a fait accompli.

Admiral Ignácio, whose fleet had pounded the Paraguayan positions since the end of the previous year, now coordinated the navy's deployment to help the land forces advance. The marquis had hoped that the fleet could tear apart the river defenses at Curupayty and Humaitá, or at least draw enemy fire while Osório marched parallel to the river.[15] To this end, Osório moved out of Tuyutí at six in the morning, accompanied by a general shelling of the Paraguayan lines. Behind him followed the main Allied army of thirty-five thousand men. Due to a misunderstanding among the field commanders, the Argentine troops under General Gelly y Obes marched around the right bank of the Bellaco instead of the left, thus finding themselves without appreciable cover from the Brazilians. Centurión later argued that if the Paraguayans had attacked the Argentines at this juncture, they would have sent the Allies flying.[16] But for want of manpower López failed to capitalize on the enemy's mistake; he already had some knowledge of the overall Allied plan through an indiscretion in the Argentine press, but he apparently felt that nothing could be done without risking his carefully prepared defenses against overwhelming numbers.[17] Osório thus continued to advance with minimal opposition. The ground was firmer on the other side of the Bellaco and the marshes soon yielded to open land, a fact that cheered the Allied troops after so many months in the mud.

Tightening the Noose

Tuyucué fell on 29 July. There had been a minor clash of cavalry units at the end of the advance, but otherwise little fighting took place. Although the seizure of Tuyucué assured the primary objective of Mitre's grand flanking maneuver, it did not solve the dilemma of how to properly invest Humaitá. Reduction of the place by famine was still out of the question because its northern approaches remained open; so long as the Marshal's men could drive cattle from that direction, or ferry supplies downriver from Asunción, the bastion could still hold.

Besides, though Humaitá was now almost in sight, the Paraguayans had already extended their line of trenches and traverses from Curuzú in such a way as to protect themselves on the east as well as the south.[18] Though, on a direct line, the distance between Tuyutí and Humaitá was less than ten miles, the intervening marshes and palmettos meant that the Allied army at Tuyucué could only be supplied by a long and circuitous route almost forty miles long, and Marshal López, whose contempt for the Brazilians was boundless, was ready to place a sharpshooter behind every bush along the way. Mobile forces could harass the Allied supply trains almost at will, and perhaps even secure some provisions for the Paraguayan units. Skirmishes would become daily events, and Allied success in these engagements was by no means assured. In some ways the Allied position had grown more precarious.

On 31 July Caxias ordered the main body of his army to Tuyucué, and on the same day Mitre reached the front and reassumed command. He brought with him a two-hundred-man escort of richly attired and seemingly professional artillerymen, but they were unable to restore an aura of invincibility to the Argentine president, who now headed an army composed mainly of Brazilians. The marquis expressed a willingness to receive Mitre's orders, but both men understood that political realities had changed. Even more than before, the war against Paraguay would henceforth become a Brazilian affair, run along Brazilian lines, and directed toward Brazilian ends.

The Paraguayans could not sustain their position as Caxias strengthened his grip around Humaitá. The Allied generals judged that a decisive battle was in the offing, and in faraway Buenos Aires, the editors of *The Standard* anticipated that the campaign was at last drawing to a close—possibly even "before the sailing of the English mail."[19] One might suppose that responsible observers would have avoided such optimistic predictions by now; the war had already swallowed many naive soothsayers—and would do so again—and while the Allies found themselves strong and well situated, the Paraguayans had yet to accept defeat.

Any army can be bludgeoned into submission. Many on the Allied side had long advocated hard and unremitting attacks, and now that the Marshal's forces seemed so deteriorated, taking the harshest approach seemed the logical. A drive towards all-out victory at this time, however, required political confidence and cohesion both within the high command and among the units of the Allied army. Caxias had yet to construct such solidarity. Mitre, as always, was full of elaborate ideas and strategies, but whether his notions could be cobbled into an early triumph at Humaitá was doubtful.

On 31 July 1867, the Allies took San Solano, a tiny ranch to the north of Tuyucué that had been converted into a temporary place of shelter for civilians displaced from the Misiones. Capturing this site (which bore the name of the Marshal's patron saint) afforded an opportunity to close off the fortress from the south and east. The full encirclement of Humaitá was now within reach. The Allies, no doubt pleased with their progress, observed considerable activity within the Paraguayan lines, with cattle being driven into the main camp, and the steady movement of men. In the late afternoon, the Marshal brought up two rocket tubes and four field pieces, which immediately fired upon the newly occupied Allied positions. The fire continued until after dusk.

The next day, Osório sent several units against these same enemy cannon, only to find that López had withdrawn the main pieces, leaving behind a single cavalry regiment. The Paraguayan horsemen proved no match for the Brazilian cavalry that followed into the fray. One hundred twenty Paraguayans were killed, another fifteen made prisoner, and small quantities of arms, munitions, and rocket tubes fell into Allied hands.[20]

This was the beginning of a much more active campaign of Allied harassment. Mitre had already arrived with a plan for the next stage of the Allied advance. It featured a general attack on the enemy lines of communication between the Cuadrilátero and Pilar, a sizable river town seven leagues to the north that had once served as the commercial hub for southern Paraguay.[21] Pilar had receded in importance since the construction of Humaitá in the 1850s, but it remained a significant community, one that might afford safe disembarkation for Allied troops.

The imperial government, with its aristocratic and mercantile inclinations, had long since committed itself to a policy that favored the navy over the army. While this preference made sense in light of Brazil's coastal geography, it could never be converted into an offensive strategy in Paraguay. Caxias understood this well enough. Unlike Mitre, who could never reconcile himself to any change of priorities, the marquis was determined to play to naval interests when he had to, and to override them gently when the strategy fit. Above all, he had no intention of breaking previous commitments to Ignácio.

Mitre agreed, though doing so vexed him. Once again he pressed the fleet for more action, and Caxias promised him support.[22] Despite his doubts, the marquis continued to behave with the deference due both his naval subordinate and his nominal superior on land. But his own strength as a military man had always rested on his lucid grasp of every situation. This was no exception. The press in Europe and the Allied countries had lately made much of a supposed falling out between the two commanders.[23] In fact, don Bartolo wanted simply to find an honorable way to cede more authority to the marquis, whose reputation at the front had waxed while Mitre's had waned. Both men realized that any deviation from established practice must hereafter originate with the Brazilians. Yet even with this understanding there was destined to be substantial jockeying when it came to Allied strategy.

On 3 August, Mitre dispatched the Uruguayan general Enrique Castro with a column of around three thousand cavalry to scout the trails leading north to Pilar. Just beyond San Solano, he encountered seven hundred Paraguayan horsemen, and, in a running fight, drove them back to a point two leagues below the town. He reported the enemy's losses as one hundred fifty killed and thirty-four prisoners, while his own command lost but a single man with eight wounded.[24] The Allies presumed that the Marshal had abandoned Pilar to concentrate on the defense of Humaitá—and yet Castro did not rush forward to take the place, since he could not yet hope to hold it. Instead, he cut the Paraguayan telegraph lines to Asunción at several points and returned to Tuyucué. Over the next weeks his cavalry conducted similar explorations and reconnaissance.[25]

The harassment did not just come from one side, however. The distance from Tuyutí to Tuyucué was more than twice the distance from the former site to Itapirú, and the trail north afforded the Paraguayans numerous opportunities to mount surprise attacks. Supplies for Tuyucué were dispatched through the palm forests from the main camp every two days, and the Marshal's spies kept him informed of these movements. He was determined to make the most of these opportunities.

On 11 August, a mounted force under Major Bernardino Caballero set up an ambush deep in the woods between Tuyutí and Tuyucué, where the Paraguayans swept down on an enemy escort, firing their muskets at close range; as the balls whistled past the opposing troops, the Allied teamsters panicked, jumped to the ground, and fled into the forests to the south. Caballero thus managed to secure a considerable number of supply wagons with minimal losses to his side—an achievement for which the Marshal rewarded him.[26]

This was only one of many such escapades. On another occasion, the Paraguayans made off with a herd of eight hundred cattle being driven to the Allied troops through the same wooded terrain.[27] On yet another occasion, the

Paraguayans captured a large quantity of writing paper, an article that had become scarce at Humaitá.[28] The most unusual sortie, however, came a short time later when a troop of the Marshal's men crept out at night, seized one of the enemy's mangrullos and moved the entire structure back across their own lines before the Allies could discover what had happened.[29]

Meanwhile, Mitre and the other Allied commanders dedicated themselves to fortification, constructing new batteries at Tuyucué to curb the regular enemy shelling of their position. The Prussian major von Versen, who observed the weakness of the Paraguayan defenses, later wrote that the Allies were wrong not to mount an attack, for instead of quickly "breaking the enemy position, they waited at a distance of a mile and a half, maintaining a vigorous bombardment over two days and setting up their own trench works." The Marquis of Caxias, he noted, tried to cut the Paraguayans off from Asunción by stationing ten thousand troops on the eastern flank at Solano while at the same time seeking to maintain contacts with Tuyutí. But this played into the Marshal's hands, for "the Paraguayans never ceased to appropriate various herds of cattle [while] López exhausted the forward posts of the enemy and disrupted their transport of all manner of supplies."[30]

The Allied commanders had decided to open a close siege of the Paraguayan position. It was reasonable to suppose that the superiority of their cavalry made it impractical for López to supply Humaitá for much longer. Yet, even now the Paraguayan position remained firm. López seems to have thought that the Allied flanking maneuver around San Solano had paved the way for a large-scale attack against his left. When this attack failed to materialize, he reevaluated his deployments and moved artillery pieces from Curupayty. Over the next weeks his men constructed a new road from Timbó, on the Chaco side of the river nine miles north of Humaitá, to Monte Lindo, a small landing place five miles above the Paraguay's confluence with the Tebicuary.[31] Eventually the Marshal ordered the remaining civilians out of Humaitá, northward along this road and away from possible Allied attack.

Meanwhile, the heavy harassment of the Paraguayan positions never let up, with the navy for once leading the way. Just before seven in the morning on 15 August, ten of Admiral Ignácio's ironclads succeeded in getting above the batteries at Curupayty. The Paraguayans fired at these steamers as they passed by, one after another, but took no fire in return.[32] The commander of the *Tamandaré* opened the window of his casement in an attempt to discharge a cannon, but was blown backwards by a Paraguayan shell before he could fire. He lost a leg in the process.[33]

All told, the Paraguayan gunners struck the Brazilian ships 246 times, though they failed to sink any, and the damage inflicted was soon repaired.[34] After a passage of two and a half hours, five vessels in the flotilla dropped anchor between Curupayty and Humaitá, while another five went upstream and moored behind a little island opposite the main fortress, beyond the range of its guns.[35]

The navy's passage of Curupayty lifted Allied morale, and soon thereafter the emperor rewarded Admiral Ignácio by ennobling him as Viscount of Inhaúma.[36] The admiral had shown—finally—that his naval units could move forward just like those on land.[37] Instead of taking satisfaction in this, however, he was less than reassured: in surveying the thirty-three Brazilians killed and wounded, as well as the many holes the Paraguayans had left in his ships (some of which were three inches deep), he could only conclude that getting past Humaitá in similar manner would prove costly.[38]

The navy's losses were thus far minimal compared with those on land, but this concerned Ignácio; also, as with the other Brazilian commanders (save for Osório), he still chafed under Mitre's command and wondered, sometimes aloud, if the Argentine president were conducting the conflict according to some hidden agenda aimed at weakening the empire.[39] As it was, all the effort expended in making the Argentine soldiers hate the Paraguayans only made them hate the war.

In strategic terms, though, Ignácio's achievement was significant. It rendered the Paraguayan hold on Curupayty untenable, leaving the Marshal with little choice but to order Colonel Paulino Alén to withdraw with most of his command from the site and proceed north to Humaitá, where he would take charge of the garrison (and begin to drink himself into serious trouble with the Marshal and his fellow officers). He left behind a token force under naval captain Pedro Victoriano Gill, nephew of General Barrios.

But for all of his supposed acumen, Ignácio had left his flotilla poorly situated at Curupayty, cut off from its supply bases at Corrientes and Paso de la Patria. Without the coal that these provided, his options for further progress along the river remained limited.[40] Provisions and other light supplies were ferried to him by canoe and along a bush-clogged trail that the Allies carved out along the Chaco side of the river. He needed these in far greater quantities, however, and this meant that he would have to wait for the land forces to advance.

The Allied navy spent many weeks in a spirited cannonade of the fortress. The Brazilian gunners' eyes smarted even worse than before as the upswell of smoke filled their ships' casements, and the din from their cannon shook houses as far away as Corrientes.[41] Still, the shelling did minimal damage, except to the brick chapel, the one structure at Humaitá visible from the ships' anchorage.

The five foremost ironclads had not yet gained sight of the lesser batteries mounted *en barbette*, nor of the heavier fortifications above the Batería Londres. In yet another failure of intelligence, the Allies had not learned that the Paraguayan garrison had shrunk to a mere two thousand troops, though these men could still contest *the* river approaches with pieces that Alén had brought from Curupayty. Most of the artillery had by now been sent eastward to counter Mitre and the Brazilians at Tuyucué, although it produced few positive results in that sector. A sufficient number of guns might be unavailable for use against the ironclads, but the passage remained hazardous, with torpedoes still bobbing in the water and the chain that the Marshal's troops had stretched across the river preventing any easy movement.

The poor placement of the Allied ships relative to Paso de la Patria occasioned renewed friction among the Allied commanders. Ignácio wrote to Caxias on 23 August to argue that he needed more provisions if he were to force the passage at Humaitá, and that if he failed to get help he could not maintain his situation above Curupayty. Even now, he noted, a retreat southward to Paso de la Patria might prove necessary.[42]

With his oxen and mules employed in ferrying provisions from Tuyutí to Tuyucué, the marquis could not increase the flow of supplies along the Chaco trails to Ignácio. Unable to agree to the admiral's request, and convinced that it made little difference to the offensive, Caxias ordered the ironclads downriver to resume their former anchorage. He reasoned that a temporary retreat involved little trouble because the Paraguayans had already removed their cannon from Curupayty and the enemy gunners could no longer menace the fleet's passage. Ignácio could renew operations against the Marshal's river batteries once he restocked his coal.

Time was not on the admiral's side, however. When the Marshal discovered that the ironclads were not steaming against Humaitá after all, he sent several cannons back to Curupayty. This had the salutary effect of boxing-in Ignácio's warships, and confirming Mitre's worries that time had been irretrievably lost.[43] Perhaps the Paraguayan position at Curupayty was not so untenable after all.

Caxias had discussed the fleet with the Argentine president on several occasions already, but giving the order for withdrawal without consulting his superior was a breach of military courtesy, and Mitre could not have felt pleased when he learned of it. On the night of 26 August, he met with the marquis to complain and was told that he ought to reflect on his current role within the Triple Alliance and recall that all matters concerning the navy remained the exclusive responsibility of the Brazilians. In fact, this was still an open question, and Mitre had every right to demand the appropriate subordination from his commanders—Caxias included.[44] At that moment, all the wounded pride of an aggrieved Argentine republican was ranged against the inbred hubris of a Brazilian aristocrat, and it was unclear who would flinch first.

Neither did. Instead, both men retired from the meeting to consider their words. The next day, the president sent the marquis yet another note to clarify his reasons for opposing even a temporary naval withdrawal: it had already taken so long to accomplish anything on the river; why, Mitre asked, should they contemplate even a momentary retreat? Caxias had anticipated just such a message, and well aware of Mitre's eloquence (and his own position of strength), he let him have the point. He responded that his order to Ignácio was no more than a suggested course of action, and had no imperative character. This, he declared, ought to satisfy His Excellency, for the fleet could stay where it was.[45]

Mitre was not happy. The marquis's note made no mention of any action against Humaitá and left issues of command unsettled. But rather than engage in a shouting match, Mitre agreed to submit his views in written form, which he did on 9 September. This extensive memorandum, which he published only in the early twentieth century, catalogued all the obstructionism that he had encountered from the navy since the time of Tamandaré. It further asserted that no real impediment had ever kept the fleet from getting past Humaitá—that indeed, the time was right to make an advance. The Paraguayans had yet to erect a credible defense either at the fortress or closer to Tuyucué. Mitre asserted that as commander in chief he had always supported full coherence between the armies and the fleet, and that he could thus claim authority over the Allied warships along with all the military units on dry land.[46]

To judge from a letter that Caxias directed to the minister on 11 September, the marquis was infuriated with Mitre, who seemingly took pleasure at the prospect of Brazilian vessels wrecked by the Marshal's gunners. Caxias argued that the empire had kept itself secure from the usurpations of neighboring republics because it maintained a formidable blue-water navy, and the tactic suggested by the Argentine president would cause many irreplaceable losses in the fleet. Brazil had to think of her own.[47]

This might have brought an open rupture between the two commanders, but neither was so impetuous as to allow this to happen, no matter what was stated in private correspondence. Caxias still held the high card, and both men knew it. Besides, there were more immediate matters to consider, such as credible rumors of a negotiated peace with the Paraguayans.

Prospects for Peace and the Question of the European Prisoners

In late July 1867, Gerald Francis Gould, the secretary of the British legation in Buenos Aires, received instructions from his government to steam northward to Paraguay to arrange for the evacuation of British subjects from the country. Unlike Washburn, whose efforts at mediation had received the approval of the US Congress, Gould lacked the credentials as well as the standing to engage in mediation. And yet, when the British warship *Doterel* reached Paraguayan waters and the secretary disembarked, he found it prudent to address the topic off the record.

The situation for foreign residents in Paraguay had grown precarious; not only had they suffered privations, but they had also become the objects of police surveillance. López, it seemed, had gone back and forth in his appreciation of these men and women. On the one hand, the engineers, skilled workers, and machinists among them had helped him build a formidable resistance, but on the other, their willingness to serve him indefinitely remained uncertain.[48] In the Marshal's erratic judgement, if such individuals were not loyal servants they might then be enemies, and that was enough to inspire concern.

The notion of the friendly neutral began to vanish in this atmosphere of mistrust. Americans, Italians, Portuguese—all were subjected to pressure, and even diplomatic personnel found it difficult to arrange an exit from Paraguay. The French consul, Laurent-Cochelet, had tried to negotiate the evacuation of his fellow citizens in April, but was told a month later that no passage could be arranged so long as the war lasted.[49]

Gould thus found himself in a quandary when he arrived for an interview on 18 August. He assumed that the Marshal would use those British subjects under his control as bargaining chips to force new discussions with the Allies, over whom Her Majesty's government might exercise some leverage. But Gould had limited authority and no experience of bluffing a head of state. López granted no immediate concessions, though he permitted Gould to converse with his countrymen at Paso Pucú (though never in private). The Briton failed, however, to contact those who lived elsewhere in Paraguay. Max von Versen visited him on several occasions and asked him to carry some open messages to Prussian agents in Buenos Aires, but Gould was reluctant to jeopardize his mission of evacuating British subjects by seeming to cooperate with this other man.[50]

The Marshal, in fact, had made up his mind that he still needed the British engineers. As Richard Burton observed a year later, "it was hardly reasonable to expect that the Marshal-President should dismiss a score of men—of whom sundry were in his confidence and knew every detail which it was most important to conceal from the enemy."[51] In the end, Gould managed to take just three or four widows and their children when he departed—and López rather regretted even that concession.[52]

Meanwhile, at the Marshal's instigation, Gould framed a series of negotiating points that the Allies might find acceptable. Perhaps he thought that he might thus rescue something from his frustrated mission, or perhaps the secretary was just playing for time. His hastily scribbled notes, when completed, amounted to a plan similar to that which Washburn had presented to Caxias some months earlier. The Allies, Gould insisted, would promise to respect Paraguay's territorial integrity, and leave all questions of frontiers to be decided later; both sides would release prisoners of war and forego reparations; Paraguay's military would withdraw from Brazil's Mato Grosso province and afterwards be reduced to a size appropriate for maintaining internal peace; and once hostilities had ended, the Marshal would leave the country for Europe, entrusting his government to Vice President Sánchez as provided for in the 1844 constitution.[53]

Amazingly enough, when shown these demands, López assented at once to the suggested terms. Thompson caught the essence of the Marshal's initial reaction to the proposal when he noted that "López was to leave with flying colours, making peace himself, and thus that great obstacle, his pride, was overcome, as it was scarcely interfered with."[54] The Marshal urged Gould to present Caxias with the outlined terms for peace.

Accordingly, on 11 September, the secretary carried the proposals under a flag of truce to the Allied camp, where the marquis received them with uncertain favor. Later that day, he conveyed the text to other Allied representatives, who hoped to find in it some germ of a future peace. In diplomatic interchanges, vagueness is seldom fatal since ambiguities can be clarified in later meetings and inconsistencies ironed out. Gould offered a spoonful of hope—there was nothing wrong in testing the proposals.

The positive Allied reaction produced a momentary rush of optimism on all sides. Mitre announced his conditional endorsement, and the chief of the imperial staff left at once in a special steamer for Rio de Janeiro, where the emperor was expected to signal his approbation.[55] From Buenos Aires, ex-foreign minister Elizalde also declared his approval, adding only an amendment by which Humaitá would be demolished as part of the price of peace.[56] Two days later, Gould returned to Paso Pucú in excellent spirits, hardly believing that he had managed to persuade so many people with so little effort.

Little did he know that he had failed to convince the one person who mattered most. When informed of the negotiations, López sent a reply through his secretary, Luis Caminos—who now denied that his master had ever agreed to leave the country—that "Paraguay [would] not stain her honor and glory by ever consenting that her President and defender, who has contributed to her so much military glory … should descend from his post, and suffer expatriation from the scene of his heroism and sacrifices, [that the] best guarantee for the country would be for Marshal López to follow the path that God has prepared for the Paraguayan nation."[57]

Never was a suicide note more ornately—or more absurdly—penned. Gould did not even bother to respond, and departed straightaway aboard the *Dotorel*, never to return. In measuring the Marshal's stubbornness on this matter, it is easy to cite the corruptive impulses of absolute power along with the isolated circumstances of the Paraguayan leader; indeed, he may have believed himself indispensable. Washburn, however, argued that news of further rebellions in Argentina had convinced him to hold out for better terms.[58] Besides, López "knew that there were scores of men whose families and friends he had treated so atrociously that only by keeping an army between him and them could he hope for a life lease of a single month."[59]

For his part, the ever-obsequious Luis Caminos claimed that it was unconstitutional for López to abandon his post in the way mandated by the proposed agreement. But this was a self-serving argument; after all, the Marshal had never let legal restrictions limit his actions before.[60] These terms were the best he was offered during the war, and he spurned them. Far too many Paraguayans were already in the cold clay for López to argue that he was saving them from a worse fate. It was easier to conclude that the Marshal was willing "to sacrifice the last man, woman, and child of a brave, devoted, and suffering people, simply to keep himself for a little while longer in power."[61]

Fighting In The Rain

The war between Paraguay and the Triple Alliance did not subside during the time of Gould's visit, but it did not move ahead either. Rain fell constantly at the beginning of September, paralyzing the movement of Allied troops. "On all sides," *The Standard* reported, "oxen, horses, or mules ... may be met with embedded in the mire, in many instances still alive, their heads and necks projecting above the quaggy [*sic*] mud, which is soon to become their deathbeds and graves."[62]

In spite of the rain, artillery exchanges were conducted at numerous places along the line, but no real progress was made against the Paraguayans. The muck along the trails prevented the adequate supply of Tuyucué, and so the Brazilian, Uruguayan, and Argentine forces simply held their ground and avoided contact with the enemy. They may have thought that the Marshal would launch an attack of his own, but it never came. Instead, troops on both sides contended with yet another wave of cholera. Though the effects of the disease proved less debilitating on this occasion than in April, the dread it inspired was just as palpable—particularly as the Brazilians also registered several cases of smallpox at Tuyutí. On 6 September, *The Standard* announced that one man in the Argentine hospital had already died of cholera, and that the disease might "soon be making havoc here [at Itapirú], where every loathsome species of filth abounds."[63]

Though sanitary conditions remained poor, Allied medical preparations had improved, and by the middle of the month, the number of patients at the Argentine hospital shrunk to a mere thirty-seven men, none of whom had cholera.[64] The disease still cropped up sporadically over the next two months, and instilled fear each time. On 11 October, the Allies announced that an Argentine general and a colonel had died from cholera and another three hundred men were sick with dysentery and other ailments.[65]

In the Paraguayan camp, the situation was worse, for malnutrition had set in at Humaitá. Epidemic diseases act opportunistically, of course, so that men who previously had been barely able to carry out their duties now fell ill. Those who succumbed numbered in the hundreds, and included officers, soldiers, civilians, and the ten-year-old recruits only recently arrived from Asunción.[66] The Marshal's latest *levée en masse* seemingly emptied the towns of the interior and the new recruits could not help but be exposed to the sickness, which added its own quotient of viciousness to the unfolding demographic disaster.[67]

Among those who died in the epidemic was Natalicio Talavera, the young reporter whose letters in *El Semanario* were so avidly consumed by readers on all sides of the conflict. On 28 September, he submitted his final missive, which betrayed a distress that, by now, appeared all too familiar.[68] The killing he had condemned continued throughout September and October with sharp, inconclusive engagements becoming the rule rather than the exception. For example, on 8 September, a force of 527 Paraguayan cavalrymen, members of the 21st Regiment, slammed into Allied positions near a cemetery one half-league from San Solano.

The attack, which the Paraguayans intended as a major surprise, was uncoordinated from the beginning and brought minimal losses to the defenders. Disabled horses covered the ground, while others, still on their feet, struggled in confusion and agony. Everywhere, dismounted riders were running in circles trying to get a bearing. A ball struck one man as he wandered disoriented in the direction of the enemy, severing his head from his body as cleanly as the blade of a guillotine.

He was not the only one to die. The Paraguayans left one hundred fifty dead before being driven back to their dugouts by Brazilian cavalrymen who had arrived from Tuyucué. In exchange for this loss of life, López's men gained one hundred head of cattle and a few horses.[69] That several men had deserted to the Brazilians and Correntinos during this engagement infuriated the Marshal, and he angrily dissolved the 21st Regiment, dividing its men among his infantry battalions, and executing or flogging the officers and sergeants who had failed to prevent the defections.

Despite all the talk of Paraguayan resolution, desertions had become an increasing problem at Humaitá. Cases of absence without leave occurred fairly regularly in the Paraguayan army even before the war, but those individual instances could not be ascribed to some general feeling of alienation on the part of the troops.[70] This was no longer true. The orders and instructions the soldiers had once willingly obeyed had of late become more dangerous, more unreasonable, and they were increasingly being based on irrational appraisals of the situation—all issued in an attempt to inspire a show of fealty to the Marshal. That some men recoiled from further sacrifice was understandable, but their hesitation made López and his officers even more ready to act arbitrarily. The desertions thus continued apace with the terrible punishments meted out to those caught trying to escape.[71]

A total collapse of discipline on the Paraguayan side, however, was improbable. After all, officers could still offer support and reassurance, as well as threats, and this sometimes cancelled out any nascent defeatism. The chaplains, though they were as hungry as the men, also did their best to inspire confidence, working their way through the trenches and rifle pits, suppressing their own fear, comforting those whom they could, and doing so without sleep.

For all of the bad news, the Paraguayans enjoyed a series of little victories that bolstered their faith in the struggle. On 20 September, the Brazilians took Pilar, but were soon driven off when a Paraguayan steamer landed reinforcements. The defenders of the port district made much of their defeat of the kambáes. They laughed raucously at the antics of a squad of Brazilians who, having upset a large container of molasses while despoiling a private residence, could not get the sticky substance from their hands and boots and retreated back towards San Solano looking like "circus clowns."[72] The Paraguayans should have reacted with less disdain, for the Allies took seventy-four prisoners during their brief occupation, along with two hundred head of cattle, sixty thousand cartridges and other arms and munitions, a quantity of charqui, and an intact chata, which they set on fire, along several canoes, before departing.[73]

On 24 September there was another engagement the Marshal's men could boast about. A three-thousand-man Allied column escorting a train of supply wagons spotted what appeared to be the tattered remnants of a Paraguayan detachment zigzagging toward the convoy from out of the marshes near the Paso del Ombú. The Brazilians permitted the oncoming troops to seize a wagon and several mules. Hoping to kill the foolish intruders, they attacked with five battalions of infantry and three regiments of cavalry.[74] This caused the Paraguayans to retreat back into the swamp. The Brazilians followed, only to realize too late that they had fallen into a trap. Colonel Valois Rivarola, a rich cattle rancher from the interior village of Acahay, had laid an intricate ambush, dispatching two battalions of infantry to punish the Brazilians, and blasting away at them with musketry and Congreve rockets from close range.

Caught in the muck, the Allied soldiers called for aid from the imperial cavalrymen, who were splendidly mounted with the finest roans and piebalds that Urquiza's ranches could supply. The horses soon found themselves up to their chests in water; according to Thompson, the Brazilians then charged the Paraguayan regiment, whose "miserable haggard horses could hardly move." The enemy came to "within 150 yards of the Paraguayans, when the latter made their horses canter to meet them, thus causing the Brazilians immediately to turn tail … and gallop away, [this being] the only movement made on either side, and at length the enemy retired, leaving about 200 dead on the field [with the Paraguayans losing] only about eighty killed and wounded."[75]

The engagement at Ombú was inconclusive, but because Allied losses exceeded the Marshal's, he treated the battle as a spectacular humiliation for the enemy. He praised Colonel Rivarola's audacity, and cheered the units involved, who responded with a grim exuberance that befitted the occasion.[76] But nothing had really changed.

Parecué

López had made a habit of sending out sizable cavalry units on daily forays. On a few occasions, these efforts resulted in significant skirmishes between forces numbering in the thousands. One such engagement occurred on 3 October 1867 at Parecué (Isla Tayí). At the break of day, Major Bernardino Caballero set out from Humaitá with one thousand cavalrymen bound for San Solano, where he hoped to disrupt the extreme right of the Allied position. He had little idea of what to expect. The enemy had detected his move and Caxias himself proceeded to the threatened point, setting in motion the various corps detailed to aid the defense.

Caballero was the Marshal's new favorite, an appropriate successor to Díaz. With his youthful exuberance, chiseled face, and piercing blue eyes, the major looked the part of a hero, and López enjoyed surrounding himself with such types.[77] Caballero never seemed to grasp operational strategy, however, and his successes were mostly limited to short, aggressive raids. Parecué, presented him with an opportunity to accomplish something better than the seizure of a convoy.

As Caballero neared the enemy position, he arranged his six mixed regiments in a broad column, the center of which deployed atop a small rise. Almost immediately, the Paraguayans drew carbine fire from a unit of Brazilian cavalry that sallied toward them from across the field. Caballero had no problem driving them back with saber and lance. He nonetheless lost some minutes in this skirmish, which allowed Caxias to bring up two field pieces to pound the Paraguayans. Sensing the danger and hoping to lure the Brazilians into his own enfilading fire, Caballero withdrew a portion of his troops into the wood and ordered his remaining forces back to the center to prepare an attack en masse once the marquis showed his hand.[78]

It was not clear if the Allies would be pulled into Paraguayan fire or the other way around. The Brazilians advanced upon the main enemy force with three regiments of cavalry and two battalions of infantry in the rear guard.[79] These units were then hit by an impetuous charge of Caballero's horsemen. The Brazilians lunged forward, moving faster and faster, the riders bending upon their horses' necks, but as they neared the Paraguayans, a din of musketry erupted and the vanguard broke under a storm of projectiles. Men and horses went down in heaps, and the piled bodies made an insurmountable barrier for those who followed. The Brazilians faltered, and Caballero counterattacked, slashing into the enemy.

Whether from fear that their cannon might fall into Paraguayan hands or because they realized how inaccurate their gunnery had been, the Brazilians pulled back their pieces and left the fighting to their cavalry, three more regiments of which swarmed over the field, waving their sabers; Caballero stopped these in turn, exhausting most of his ammunition. When the Allied cavalry failed to carry the day, Caxias sent in several battalions of infantry against the Paraguayans as they attempted to reassemble on a grass-covered island. He tried to maneuver his men out of the line of direct fire, but they fell back in disarray, fleeing in multiple directions.

Up to this point, the Brazilians seemed demoralized, with little sense of what to do next, but as the enemy hesitated and broke, Caxias's men took heart and charged with renewed determination. Most of the Paraguayan losses that day occurred over the next few minutes. Immediately thereafter, for reasons having as much to do with luck as with training and experience, the Marshal's troops regained their composure; this time, the Brazilians fled from the field. Although the Paraguayans made ready to resist yet another assault, it never came.[80]

Dead horses and dead men competed for space on the soggy ground, but neither Caballero nor the Allies had sufficient guarantee of security to stop and bury the slain. Only after the Brazilians fell back on San Solano later that day did the Paraguayans set about this grim task, and many of their men had bled to death in the interim.[81]

Some reports depicted Parecué as an Allied victory, for it did not allow the Paraguayans to recapture San Solano.[82] Caxias knew better, however, than to boast about what was actually a minor setback. But though he had no desire to repeat the mistakes of that day, the marquis could nonetheless take some comfort in the knowledge that he could afford the losses while the Marshal could not.

Tataiybá

On 21 October the marquis got a chance to avenge his fallen comrades. He prepared a trap, situating five thousand of his own cavalrymen behind palmettos in a flat expanse called Tataiybá, which sat in no-man's land about three miles north of Humaitá. As Caballero departed the fortress on one of his periodic raids, the Allied horsemen made ready for him. Though within rifle shot of the Paraguayan raiders, the Brazilians held their fire while Caxias dispatched a single regiment as bait. This force encountered Caballero watering his horses in a clearing, fired a few shots, and fled toward San Solano and the forests. The Paraguayans followed, falling upon the Brazilians and doubling them up. As the correspondent for *The Standard* observed, the "shrill war whoop [*sapukai*] of the pursuers echoed round the woods; and as the Paraguayans deemed the flying Brazilians to be merely an advanced guard for Osório, redoubled their efforts to catch them; but the delusion was momentary—the shrill trumpet call in the orange grove was the signal for the advance of the various Brazilian brigades."[83]

In terms of sheer savagery, what followed was one of the ugliest scrimmages of the entire war. Paraguayan survivors of the battle described the oncoming imperial regiments hitting them at midday from three sides—a veritable avalanche of soldiers.[84] The marshes made it difficult for anyone to maneuver, but rather than attempt a retreat, the Marshal's men charged headlong into the first enemy brigade, jabbing at the Brazilians with lance and saber. The Allied attackers boasted superior arms and a steady determination, but even a blind man among them would have recognized the courage of the Paraguayan soldiers that day.

The combat was unequal, with the Allies outnumbering their foes by five to one—and yet the fighting lasted more than an hour.[85] At one point, having already exhausted the majority of his effectives, Caballero plunged into the nearby estero as the fighting raged behind him. Almost all the Paraguayan horses were lost at this time, with some cut down in the field and others drowned in the swamp. Caballero's cavalrymen kept swinging their sabers in the hand-to-hand fight. Their resistance was horrible, but to judge from the evocations of later nationalist writers, it was beautiful in its fury.[86]

In earlier encounters Paraguayan steadfastness often caused the Allies to balk. Not this time: no matter how fierce the Paraguayans' resistance, the Brazilians came on and on, firing their rifles from a close distance. The Marshal's men retired slowly, halting to fire when they could, and crawling along the ground when they could not. For the whole three miles Caballero's force was surrounded, and yet he kept pushing the men headlong into the Brazilians. At length, they cut a breach in the enemy line and escaped through it. Caballero got back to Humaitá by the skin of his teeth, and with only a small fragment of his command intact.

Four hundred Paraguayans lay dead on the field; another 178 were taken prisoner, 40 of them wounded.[87] A few injured men—perhaps 50—arrived at Humaitá with Caballero, and another three hundred managed to survive by retreating in another direction, rendering a glancing blow against the line at Tuyucué, and fleeing north into the woods and safety. [88] The Brazilians lost some 150 killed and wounded, including 8 officers.

Tataiybá was a minor engagement, but the battle was noteworthy in one respect: it was planned and directed by the Marquis of Caxias, and thus presented a good opportunity to analyze his actions as field commander. Having formed a clear opinion of his opponents' strengths and weaknesses, and perceiving their inclination to engage in raids of a limited character, he judged that they would attempt something similar in short order—indeed he worked all the details of his ambush around this assumption. His victory was assured the minute that Caballero behaved as predicted. Military historians have tended to treat the marquis as a superior strategist, a dutiful officer, a martinet, and a politically talented general.[89] Tataiybá demonstrated his capabilities at the tactical level as well.

Potrero Ovella and Tayí

The movement of the Allied armies round the Paraguayan left had resulted in minimal opposition and brought worthwhile results: they took possession of a portion of the dry trail north to Asunción, and began to scout the outer edge of the Laguna Méndez that lay beyond it. This placed the Allies within reach of the village of Tayí, some fifteen miles upriver from Humaitá and a league south of Pilar. This was a critical point on the Paraguay River in late 1867, and its capture would close the gap around the fortress, leaving only the Chaco trail as a possible escape route.

Caxias left the next stage of the Allied advance to General João Manoel Mena Barreto, an elegant, forty-three-year-old Riograndense officer with a close-cropped beard and dark eyes. His father was Viscount of São Gabriel and he himself had been one of Caxias's closest protégés in the imperial army. João Manoel was also a born calculator, a commander who could measure and remeasure his advantages and limitations before his troops had struck their tents. His military talents had first been displayed in 1865 at the time of the Paraguayan invasion of his native Rio Grande do Sul. But he came into his own on 27 October 1867, when Caxias sent him out with five thousand men to take Tayí.

The operation was not easy; the intervening territory between Tayí and Humaitá contained nothing but thick forests, *carrizal*, and an endless expanse of thickets, across which the Marshal's men had just completed two intersecting roads. At the terminus, called Potrero Ovella, the Paraguayans had dug a new entrenchment that provided modest defilade. It was this position that João Manoel needed to carry; López had used the Potrero as a stock reserve for the troops at Humaitá, so its capture might rob him of cattle and drive yet another nail into the Paraguayan coffin.

At 7:00 a.m. on 29 October, the Brazilians began storming Ovella in the face of a fierce defense. João Manoel ordered three battalions into the enemy's center position and another three around its flank.[90] Three times his troops surged forward, and three times they were driven back by an overwhelming storm of cannon and musketry. This resistance convinced the Brazilian general of the strength of the enemy position, and he elected to pull back and shell the Paraguayans into submission.

In truth, Captain José González, a well-loved commander on the opposite side, had a mere three hundred men in his command, and by this time a third of them lay dead or wounded. When he grasped the odds against him, the captain opted to spike his cannons and retreat into the forests before the Brazilians could mount a barrage. For over an hour the Allied guns tore into the Potrero, downing a great many hardwood trees, but no further Paraguayans were killed, save, ironically, for González himself.[91]

João Manoel took forty-nine prisoners at Potrero Ovella—all wounded men who could not be evacuated. Eighty Paraguayans had died and as many as 85 Brazilians, including 9 officers, with another 310 wounded.[92] The Allies seized 1,500 head of cattle, which must have seemed a paltry number given the lives expended.[93] Caxias's plan had conformed to design, however, and Mena Barreto could now move on Tayí.[94] The next day the general dispatched a reconnaissance party to scout the paths leading north along the Paraguay. The cavalrymen went as far as the outskirts of Pilar, where they spotted two Paraguayan steamers bearing down hard upon them from the south. Concentrated cannon fire from these vessels—the *Olimpo* and the *25 de Mayo*—drove the Brazilian troops away from the riverbank and back towards João Manoel's main force.

For the Paraguayans, there was little time to lose. Within hours, the Marshal embarked four hundred of his troops at Humaitá aboard the same two steamers that had challenged the scouts. They returned upstream with orders to fortify Tayí in a last-ditch effort to keep the village out of Allied hands. The Marshal assigned Thompson the task of building the defenses at Tayí, but the Briton was not sure he could comply given the lack of time:

> We arrived there late in the afternoon, and after reconnoitering, found the enemy close by. ... Advanced guards were placed, and a redoubt traced out, with the river for its rear. Three steamers were placed to flank with their guns the front of the redoubt, and the work was begun at sunset on the 1st. Seeing an old guardhouse at Tayí, with a strong stockade all round it, I sent ... a dispatch advising López that the enemy was close by, and that the stockade could be made very defensible by the morning ... whereas the trench would, by the same time, be still very backward. He preferred, however, that the trench be [completed].[95]

This decision sealed the fate of Tayí. The next morning, João Manoel assailed the unprepared position with his full force, starting with a bayonet charge from his infantry.[96] The Paraguayans, as soon as they learned of his approach, got underneath the precipice that fell abruptly to the river and tried to fire over the bank at the oncoming Brazilians; escape for the defenders was well-nigh impossible, but at least they could stall the enemy advance while taking advantage of covering fire from the three steamers. But it was not enough. After an hour, João Manoel brought up his own artillery to the edge of the Río Paraguay and laid a heavy bombardment on both the land troops and the three vessels. Several

Paraguayans cast themselves into the river at this point and were lost in the current. All the rest died as they clung to the sides of the cliff.

The Brazilians, who had yet to finish the day's bloody work, now focused their remaining energies on the *25 de Mayo* and the *Olimpo*. They tore every inch off the vessels, killing most of the crewmembers in less than an hour; the heavy guns then finished the job, sending the ships to the bottom. Only the *Ygurey*, with Thompson aboard, managed to evade the full fire of Mena Barreto's gunners and escape downstream to Humaitá.[97] When the smoke cleared, the survivors counted some five hundred Paraguayan dead and sixty-eight wounded.

João Manoel had no intention of waiting for the Paraguayans to consider their poor position. Instead, he brought six thousand men forward to Tayí and erected extensive earthworks around the exposed spot—far more extensive than Thompson had envisioned. The Brazilian general also mounted fourteen artillery pieces on these new trenches and had his engineers stretch heavy chains across the Paraguay and onto a series of pontoon boats so as to prevent any supplies reaching Humaitá from the north.

At San Solano, meanwhile, Caxias readied ten thousand men to reinforce Tayí if López decided to attack. The marquis could take comfort in the Allied plan, which was now exclusively his own. If his field commanders could act with the same ruthlessness as Mena Barreto, they could bring the war to a speedy conclusion. The land forces had isolated the Marshal's men on the right bank of the Paraguay, and they had barred the way north. All that remained was for the Brazilian navy to force a passage above the fortress, which thereafter would fall to the Allies.

Second Tuyutí

The Marshal knew that time was running out for Humaitá. The Allied encirclement was essentially complete, and all that Mitre and Caxias needed to do was tighten the noose. Still, the enemy commanders had certain weaknesses in their tactical position that López wished to exploit. The supplies that the Argentines and Brazilians needed to invest the fortress had to be ferried overland from Tuyutí through some of the most inhospitable forests in southern Paraguay; Bernardino Caballero's raiders had hit these supply caravans on more than one occasion, disrupting the Allied timetable. These sorties stood no chance of crippling the enemy's offensive, however. For this, López needed something more convincing.

Paraguayan intelligence gathering still outshone that of the Allies, and the Marshal had long since learned how often supply caravans departed Tuyutí. He guessed that a caravan would leave the Allied camp in early November, accompanied by a sizable escort. Given that two battalions had just been dispatched to reinforce Tuyucué, this new deployment would leave the 2nd Corps undermanned, and vulnerable to a surprise attack. The sun had yet to peep over the horizon on 3 November 1867 when some nine thousand Paraguayan troopers burst from their hiding places near the edge of the Bellaco and pressed south across Yataity Corã. At that time of year, the air was balmy and filled with the grassy smells of moldering vegetation coming from the swamps. This tended to lull the Allied pickets into a false sense of security, and they failed to spot the oncoming troops, which swept unimpeded into the first line of trenches.

López had never intended to overwhelm the main Allied camp per se, as engaging in a pitched battle with superior forces was not possible at this stage of the campaign. Instead, he chose to launch a limited raid similar to those conducted the previous year against Itatí and Corrales. Now, he sought to take advantage of interior lines and strike through to the Potrero Pirís, hitting the enemy base of communication and supply, seizing all the artillery pieces that fell into his hands, and returning to his own trenches before his startled adversaries could regain their senses. A successful raid at this important site might force Mitre to redeploy troops from Tuyucué, upsetting Allied plans to encircle Humaitá.

The Marshal came close to achieving these goals, and was only frustrated when his emaciated men went beyond their orders. As it happened, the Paraguayan column advanced in loose file, and spread out in two divisions, with an infantry force of perhaps eight thousand men commanded by General Barrios falling on the enemy right.[98] The 2nd Division, consisting of Caballero's remaining cavalrymen, set up a series of harassing assaults against the Brazilian redoubt on the left.

The complacent Allied soldiers reacted with horrified surprise and fled precipitously as thousands of Paraguayan "savages" bore down upon them. Maddened horses bolted whether they had riders or not; also in flight were the soldiers of the Paraguayan Legion, including its commanders, Colonels Fernando Iturburu and Federico Guillermo Báez, who could have expected instant execution at the hands of their countrymen.[99] As it was, the Marshal's men raced against minimal opposition, punched several broad holes in the main line, and poured through. Only those Allied soldiers who found refuge in the innermost recesses survived.

The combat deepened around the Allied ramparts. By now, the Brazilians had started to stand their ground, fighting hand-to-hand to push the Marshal's soldiers back. In the end, however, they were themselves pushed back in the direction of Porto Alegre's headquarters, from where they could perceive the Paraguayan ensign waving over heaps of slain Allied soldiers at the first line of trenches. The camp at Tuyutí had been in Allied hands for a year and a half, and by now resembled a prosperous town, its many warehouses and sutlers' wagons well-stocked with goods and provisions. Though the 2nd Corps had stayed behind as a reserve force to protect the camp, the position was exposed.

If the Paraguayans had used a stronger force from the beginning, Tuyutí might have fallen.

The Paraguayans came close to penetrating the second line of Allied trenches within fifteen minutes. Four battalions of Brazilians, who were doing garrison duty there, dropped their weapons and fled posthaste towards Itapirú. When they reached the river, the terrified soldiers attempted to bribe the local ferrymen to take them across to Corrientes, and some intense bargaining ensued as the sounds of battle grew louder from behind.[100] The Allied resistance was perilously close to disintegrating.

Then an unexpected and frustrating thing happened. López had previously authorized the plundering of the Allied camp, an instruction that presupposed ongoing confusion among the enemy, but did not take into consideration the ravenous hunger of the malnourished Paraguayans.[101] Nor did it consider what should happen if Porto Alegre succeeded in checking the flight of his own troops—which is precisely what occurred. As Thompson relates it, the Brazilian general assembled troops to defend the citadel. This was easy, since the Paraguayans had all but disbanded—indeed, they had already begun looting—at which point the Brazilians fired into the enemy troopers, killing many. The wounded men immediately loaded themselves with plunder, and returned to the Paraguayan camp while the Brazilians charged. This left the Marshal's men to sack "the whole of the camp … drinking and eating handfuls of sugar, of which they were very fond [and at length] the Brazilians and Argentines came out of the citadel, butcher[ing] many of the Paraguayans, who were here, there, and everywhere—those who could do so making off with their booty." [102]

Porto Alegre himself acted with conspicuous gallantry throughout the engagement, his sword raised high, displaying all the valor and poise of an Osório. At one point, his horse was shot from under him; after mounting another, this animal too was shot down. Though badly hurt in the fall, the general mounted yet a third *pingo* and rode into the thick of the fight, wherein he drew a revolver and killed a Paraguayan major, firing three shots into him as he tried to plant his national colors atop the trench.[103]

The Marshal's troops, who had mocked the dour-faced corps commander as "Porto-Triste," now found reason to salute his courage, as did the Voluntários, who had already fled toward the Paraná.[104] Porto Alegre had turned his men about with sheer willpower. They raised a cheer at the example of their general and began to re-form their line, and at his signal, they charged back into the camp at the very moment that the Marshal's units had given themselves over to plundering.

The tide of battle abruptly shifted. Porto Alegre's counterattack included the Brazilian 36th, 41st, and 42nd Infantry Battalions along with the 3rd Artillery, all under the general's immediate command. These units were aided by Porteño and Correntino reinforcements that arrived fortuitously from Tuyucué along with imperial cavalry units commanded by João Manoel. The influx of these troops helped drive the Paraguayans from the camp, and then from the trenches, leaving the last among them with token spoils. General Barrios lost an opportunity to send in his reserve of one thousand men that had remained at Yataity Corã, and was roundly criticized as a result.[105]

Now it was the Paraguayan side that fell apart. In the pandemonium that followed, the Brazilians bounced back with tremendous vigor, and growing stronger with every foot taken. Their fire grew more accurate, and the Marshal's men started to drop by the wayside, filling the field with bodies. At this juncture, the Brazilian military band that had joined in the battle as foot soldiers captured some interesting booty of their own—thirty-five musical instruments belonging to the band members of López's 40th Battalion.[106] As the Brazilians chuckled at the change of fortune, their comrades cleared the enemy from the right flank. They then turned their gaze toward the left, anxious to make their victory complete.

Caballero, now a lieutenant colonel, had had a somewhat better time of it in his sector. Unnoticed, his cavalrymen had closed on the Allied trench works, jumped off their horses at the appointed time, and, with sabers drawn, mixed with the Brazilians. These men were just clearing the sleep from their eyes, and reacted with the same shock as their comrades on the right. One Allied officer instinctively lifted a white flag in token of surrender, and Caballero ordered his men to cease the attack; but when several of the Brazilians refused to throw down their arms, he told his troops to knife anyone who failed to submit.[107]

Caballero now controlled an extensive section of the enemy line, though with the Paraguayan infantry already in headlong retreat he could not hold onto it. He began to withdraw, taking 259 Brazilian prisoners, along with Major Ernesto Augusto da Cunha Mattos, one Argentine artillery officer, and six women. All were driven northward toward Paso Pucú and into a pitiless captivity.[108] Meanwhile, with bullets cracking all about his head, Caballero goaded his cavalrymen into one final, ill-considered assault. They carried two redoubts whose defending troops they killed to a man. This was the last advance of the day. Afterwards, with the sound of cannon and musket still ripping through the air, the remaining Paraguayan units raced back toward their own lines. It was 9:00 a.m. The battle had lasted over four hours.

While in temporary possession of Tuyutí, the Marshal's men inflicted considerable damage. They burned the Brazilian barracks, the Argentine hospital, the large depot owned by the arms merchant Anacarsis Lanús, and many of the sutlers' wagons.[109] They also torched a branch of the Commercial Bank that had been established in the camp, which led the correspondent for *The Standard* to call the event a "virtual godsend," since the thousands of destroyed bills would no longer have to be redeemed.[110] The Paraguayans would have wrought still more destruction had they delayed their looting for even a few minutes; instead, most of the enemy camp was left smoking.[111]

The spoil the Paraguayans took at Tuyutí consisted of every imaginable item, including rifles, battle standards, and items of food. Indeed, Colonel Thompson's eyes grew wide when the plunder was brought in:

> The only artichokes I ever saw in Paraguay were brought from the allied camp that day. A mail had just arrived from Buenos Aires, and was taken to López, who, on reading one of the letters, said "Poor Mitre! I am reading his wife's letter." ... A box was brought to López, which had just arrived for General Emilio Mitre, containing tea, cheese, coffee, and a pair of boots. New officers' uniforms were brought from a tailor's. Parasols, dresses, crinolines, shirts (Crimean shirts especially), cloth, were brought in large quantities, every man carrying as much as he could. A tripod telescope was brought from one of the watch-towers, and gold watches, sovereigns, and dollars were abundant.[112]

In terms of the guns seized by the Paraguayans, the take was more modest: a Brazilian Whitworth 32-pounder, an Argentine Krupp 12-pounder rifled breechloader, and eleven other pieces. Seizing the Whitworth proved difficult: as the Paraguayans dragged it back toward their lines, its wheels stuck fast in the mud. When López learned that the gun had been left behind in no-man's land within range of enemy sharpshooters, he sent the enthusiastic General Bruguez to fetch it.

The general took two battalions, twelve yoke of oxen, and extensive cordage with him, but before he departed camp, he complied with an order to execute two members of the Paraguayan Legion, men who had worked with the Argentine army and who had the misfortune to fall into the Marshal's hands. Bruguez shot both men in the back as worthy penalty for those who betrayed the nation. Finished with this duty, the general departed and, toward the end of the day, encountered the 32-pounder already being worked free by the Brazilians; a minor duel ensued, during which several men on both sides were killed before the Paraguayans secured their prize.[113] Some hours later, when López's artillerymen had the chance to examine the captured gun, they discovered that its copper vent-piece was twisted and burned inside so that the shell that remained therein could not be pricked.[114]

As always in the Paraguayan War, various calculations were submitted as to losses. In a letter to Vice President Paz, Mitre described "mountains" of Paraguayan cadavers on the field, the total number of which he estimated at around 2,000 (by noon on 4 November, 1,140 corpses had already been buried and the process was nowhere near complete). Mitre judged Allied losses at

400 killed and wounded.[115] The Brazilians estimated Paraguayan losses at 2,743 killed, at least 2,000 wounded, and 115 taken prisoner, while Allied losses were listed at 249 killed, 435 missing, and 1,198 wounded.[116] Thompson, who saw the results firsthand, set Paraguayan losses at 1,200 killed and a similar number of wounded, while the Allies, he estimated, lost about 1,700 men, killed, wounded, and prisoners.[117] *El Semanario*, never reticent to offer exaggerated statistics, reported 4,000 Paraguayan losses (killed and wounded), and between 8,000 and 9,000 for the enemy.[118]

Despite the stink of death and the unavoidable memories of First Tuyutí that it invoked, some chose to record the second battle as a magnificent victory. López issued promotions and medals to every officer and man of significance who had participated in the fight. True enough, the seizure of merchandise and military supplies humiliated the Allies, but they could repair their losses with relative ease. And though a successful raid could have driven the imperial government to sue for peace, the day had passed without long-term repercussions for the Allies.

Many historians—perhaps most—have judged Second Tuyutí a draw, but in fact it represented a serious setback for the Marshal.[119] On the one hand, though he could still conduct an innovative and risky maneuver, walking away with captured battle flags, wine, and sardines, he failed to take strategic advantage of the enemy's confusion.[120] Strictly speaking, this was not his fault: if his men had obeyed their orders, and returned to their lines with captured guns right away, they might have disrupted the intended Allied encirclement of Humaitá; and if the initial pursuit of Porto Alegre's units had not broken up when Barrios's men came in sight of the Allied stores, the Paraguayans might have even swept all the way to the Paraná, isolating Mitre's entire army in the process. But they never got the chance, for the starving soldiers could not control themselves in the midst of such quantities of food and drink; discipline gave way to temptation, order to disorder. Under these circumstances, even a limited raid stood no hope of success.

If Thompson was correct in his calculations, the Paraguayans lost a third of their attacking force at Second Tuyutí—losses the Marshal could never afford. If the Allies now faltered in the conquest of Humaitá, then it would be a reflection of their own incompetence, not the efficacy of Paraguayan resistance. As always, some in the Allied camp convinced themselves that victory was near. And yet the carnage continued. The optimistic predictions made a few months earlier now assumed a profound bleakness:

> Grim death may laugh with Satanic joy at the awful scenes now enacted in Paraguay. The scythe cannot sweep off at a stroke all the hapless victims on Paraguayan soil, and as if the horrors of

relentless war were insufficient, revengeful despotism is called to play on a poor harmless people, whose only crime is innocence, whose only offense fidelity. Who can read of the awful sufferings of this unfortunate people without a pang? ... Good God, has it come to this, that in the middle of the 19th century a whole people must be exterminated to dethrone one man? Is all our civilization but a hollow farce, that the last drop of Paraguayan blood must be shed before either party cries—"*hold*—enough."[121]

8

THE COST OF
ENDURANCE

By late 1867, the hopelessness of the Paraguayan position at Humaitá had become undeniable. João Manoel Mena Barreto had reinforced Tayí with artillery and placed chains across the main channel of the Río Paraguay to prevent any supplies from reaching the fortress by the usual route, and he cut the Paraguayan telegraph lines, thus making communication with the capital nearly impossible.[1] Meanwhile, Caxias and Osório strengthened the Allied lines at Tuyucué and San Solano so as to make them impervious to enemy assaults. Even Caballero's gutsy raids grew less and less frequent.

Just downriver lay Ignácio's fleet, whose warships continued to fire fitfully at Humaitá. The admiral's own supply problems came to an end when Brazilian engineers constructed a little railway line along the Chaco bank of the river. Up its tracks, the Allies shipped a daily allotment of 65 tons of munitions, fuel, and rations for the fifteen hundred men aboard Ignácio's warships.[2] Yet, the admiral refused to budge from his anchorage; he was down with fever, which made him physically listless, and he had yet to give the order to steam forward—though there was little doubt of his ability to do so whenever he chose.

This depressing reality was all too evident to the Paraguayans. A few months earlier, the men had hoped that an honorable peace might still be negotiated. Now, the soldiers resigned themselves to the fading prospect of release from the trap Caxias had set for them. The Paraguayans could not cook anything because their firewood was exhausted, along with the dried cow manure that had served as a substitute. Instead, they waited for orders and chewed ragged pieces of leather—old reins and lariats—when they could not get the charqui and fresh beef that had once been so plentiful. These, together with the dwindling quantities of Indian corn, manioc flour, and palm hearts, now made up the greater part of their diet.

Malnourished troops could never defend the Cuadrilátero, which accordingly softened into a barrier two shades more permeable than either the Marshal or the Allied commanders cared to admit. Troop reinforcements, even if they had been able to bypass Mena Barreto along the Chaco trails, were practically nonexistent. Still further north, the latest demands of conscription made it clear that Marshal López intended to consume Paraguay's seed corn in the form of boys barely able to lift a musket.[3]

We must ask ourselves two questions. First, given all their advantages, why did the Allies not attack and finish the Paraguayans? The troops were ready, anxious for the fight, and despite the humiliating raid at Tuyutí, they had more than enough matériel to make a good go of it. Of course, they could have used more horses and mules, but this was a perennial problem, one that should not have interfered with a final assault.

However, the tension that had characterized relations between the various commanders provided the main stumbling block yet again. Mitre wanted a victory to ensure the election of Elizalde and his fellow Liberals in the upcoming presidential election; Caxias, not surprisingly, was indifferent to Mitre's partisan concerns—he had no desire to risk his units at the hottest time of the year, especially when every day he got stronger while the Marshal got weaker.[4] Besides, the Allied army had evolved into *his* army, and he preferred to wait for the arrival of more troops and pack animals, the better to forge ahead to Asunción, and to vindicate the empire's policy towards Argentina.

The second question concerned the Marshal: why did he not surrender or flee? On various occasions, he had heard rumors of a "golden" bribe that other heads of state would have accepted as a perfectly honorable way out, but had refused to discuss any such offer. He had seen thousands of his fellow Paraguayans perish, and had even lost a child in the cholera epidemic. Yet he refused to step down.

The King Of Paso Pucú

In explaining the Paraguayans' protracted resistance after 1867, it is easy to emphasize Francisco Solano López's personal obduracy, but to delve more generally into his psyche is not so easy. The Marshal's thinking does not lend itself to precise analysis. His actions, moreover, have been so consistently lauded or vilified in the polemical literature that he often appears more as a personification of good or evil than as a human being with shortcomings and idiosyncrasies. Yet because the popular will in Paraguay and the active direction of the war were so intermingled with López's mandate, it is imperative for us to understand his mindset—more so than Mitre's or Caxias's. Above all, we need to ask what he still hoped to accomplish as the Allied army closed around Humaitá and the conflict entered its fourth year.

The time López spent at the front had amplified rather than erased his bad personal habits, and it inflated his arrogance into something approaching caricature. For example, though never regular in his diet, when he did eat, he consumed enormous quantities of beef, fish, and manioc. He made a great show of gobbling cakes and rich dainties that had been procured so as to gratify his pride rather than his stomach.[5] In matters of drink, he consumed more liquor than anyone in camp, and cared little, it seems, whether the beverage was the local *caña* or the finest Burgundy. The result of his drinking was easy to discern, for when in his cups, he leveled abuse at all those around him, screaming obscenities and insults and occasionally even sending men to be shot.

In taking the full measure of the man, however, we should admit to his points of sound thinking. He had once governed Paraguay with a mind to the future, promoting her exports and sponsoring such noteworthy innovations as a railroad, a telegraph system, and a national theater. He displayed a certain maturity in his administration that cannot be dismissed with jabs at his caprices or despotism. While many *políticos* in the region had prospered for a short time and then vanished, the Marshal remained an active force. Was this because he was lucky, or shrewd, or true to his ideals? Was his personal stance emblematic of a "gallant" nation, as *El Semanario* insisted, or was he simply an opportunist who did not know when to let go?

Perhaps the Marshal had grown too fond of his own propaganda. If so, he needed to defend these fantasies with all available resources, not the least of which was his dexterous understanding of the Paraguayan people. López regarded cunning as a virtue, not merely in politics and diplomacy, but in all human affairs. As a result, he larded his conversation with provocative statements, white lies, and monumental falsehoods. He seemed to take it for granted that his countrymen behaved in similar fashion, and even when he did not accuse them of shamming, he always thought them guilty of it. López surrounded himself with spies and toadies who offered material and rhetorical tributes to his greatness.[6] And yet, he tolerated this show of veneration only when it suited him; to do otherwise would be to invite predictability, which he would have regarded as unwise for a leader in his position.

In some ways, López behaved like Juan Manuel de Rosas, José Antonio Páez, or some other traditional caudillo who demanded absolute obedience from his semi-literate countrymen. But as a military commander with a modern, unmistakably Francophile orientation, he also despised the subservience of his fellow Paraguayans. He took pleasure in testing them, and no one could guess which mood might seize his fancy on any given day.[7]

The volatile tenor of López's administration gave rise to many tales of personal ferocity, including one that dated back to the Marshal's childhood, claiming—rather implausibly—that he took a visceral satisfaction from torturing small animals.[8] But López could show kindness, even at this exasperating stage of the war. He had real affection for children, and yet he was never shy about jostling with a favorite son over a preferred slice of beef. Toward those men who had received battle wounds he maintained an open and heartfelt tenderness, and from their pain derived every particle of vicarious glory. When in a good temper, or after a satisfying meal, he even burst out in spontaneous songs reminiscent of his earlier days in Europe.[9]

López remained an avid observer of the fighting during the months he spent at Paso Pucú. He made out the scenes of combat through his telescope, and he was always eager to hear daily reports from those who had fought the foe hand to hand.[10] In themselves, these accounts never satisfied him—not because he was losing the campaign, but because he longed to find in it something more substantial, more fulfilling. López, to put a fine point on it, wanted to be a hero. He regarded the spectacle of war as sublime, transcendental, and he thirsted for the laurels won by wielding his own sword.

Yet this aspiration, common enough in novice officers, was unattainable for the Marshal. He imagined that he could glimpse the divine spark in the bravery of his soldiers, but the more he reached out to it, the more it receded from his hands. To be sure, López might achieve some personal reaffirmation in the slaughter from seeing thousands of his men butchered, but he could never overcome his basic reservations about battle.

This dread or anxiety contrasted in general terms with the attitude shown by Allied leaders. Dom Pedro had yearned to get into the fight at Uruguaiana in 1865, but was prevented from doing so at the last moment by his ministers.[11] Both Mitre and Caxias exposed themselves to fire on more than one occasion during the war, and Flores positively reveled in battle. Only López recoiled from personal peril, and this was not a matter of him saving his life so as to save the cause—quite the contrary: whenever an Allied bombardment began, he raced for the safety of his thick-walled quarters, pushing his lieutenants to one side.[12]

From today's perspective, this trepidation makes the Marshal appear more human than those ferociously brave but somewhat wooden Paraguayan generals, such as Díaz and Elizardo Aquino. But López was a man of his own times, not of ours, and he had little interest in leaving an epitaph that underscored his humanity or emotional complexity: he preferred glory. Thus, since he had no patience for weakness in others, it followed that he felt conflicted when he discovered it in himself. Later critics portrayed the Marshal in an unambiguously negative light, as if his defects added up to something almost Satanic.[13] But these detractors have misunderstood him. What made López dangerous was not his wickedness, but his self-doubt and feelings of guilt. These inclinations made him ignore day-to-day challenges and think instead of destiny.

The rot had already set in by late 1867. Throughout this time, López had been thinking of his place in history. To the extent that Paraguay had entered the first rank of South American states it was thanks to his father's wise administration and the son's willingness to take on the executive responsibility after Carlos Antonio López died in 1862. To deprive the country of his leadership, as the Allies demanded, would be to choose personal comfort over the national welfare.

Such an undignified course held few attractions for the Marshal, who reasoned that neither dom Pedro nor any European monarch would ever contemplate such a disgrace.[14] The proof had come from Mexico, where, in June of 1867, Maximilian von Hapsburg stood his ground when given the opportunity to abdicate. Indeed, the Austrian archduke had never wavered in his loyalty to his adopted country, and he died together with his generals at Querétaro. All of Europe had gone into mourning. López had to be willing to make a similar sacrifice in order to rouse a similar sympathy.

Though laced with theatricality and narcissism, these rationalizations colored the Marshal's attitude on all occasions, and he refused to forsake them. A political opposition capable of convincing him to steer a different course did not exist in Paraguay. The exiles in Buenos Aires and the officers of the Paraguayan Legion had acted as open collaborators with the enemy and could hope for nothing but contempt from López.[15] That left the members of his family and entourage as the only individuals who could sway him in a direction that might still offer hope.

But courtiers failed to influence the Marshal. True enough, the bastions of privilege had grown rather porous in Paraguay, a country where parvenus drenched themselves in imported perfumes and dismissed the highborn with a gleeful contempt. And the Marshal encouraged their pride in ways that his father would never have done. For example, even before the war the government sponsored popular dances, band serenades, and formal balls, not just in the Club Nacional (the haunt of the old elite), but in every public plaza as well. At some locations, separate dance floors were maintained for the different classes, but all were prodded into attending by the police, who were under orders to assure good attendance at public amusements.[16] These dances did not diminish with all the military reverses, but in fact grew, for to cancel an engagement might suggest that there was something to fear rather than celebrate in the news from the front.[17]

Those who observed that wartime promiscuities in Paraguay were not that dissimilar from those in Buenos Aires should remember that, in Argentina, social niceties were constrained by tradition, not dictatorship. The Argentine equivalents of such men as Alén, Bruguez, or Resquín could never parade their "golden-combed" mistresses at public events and still hope to curry official favor.[18] In Paraguay, such comportment was not only possible, it was encouraged. This did not mean, of course, that every second lieutenant could gain the Marshal's ear—no one at Paso Pucú could afford to mistake his place. But since absolute rule provides its own definition for taste and good manners, in Paraguay the trend that counted was set by the presidential family, by Madame Lynch, and by López himself.

In understanding the Marshal's motivations and behavior, we might consider his overindulgent upbringing and lack of dispassionate counsel. Washburn put it best when he observed that, though López had many flatterers, he had no advisers. He had received command in his youth, and all those around him soon realized that the surest path to privilege was through adulation and flattery. Predictably, then, all heaped praise upon the Marshal until he came to regard any man who might express an opinion different from his own as an enemy. Whenever the conduct of the "war was discussed, [even] those … who had most of his confidence could never express a doubt as to what the issue might be without incurring his severest displeasure—their own safety required that they should tell him he was invincible."[19]

The members of the Marshal's family were not exempted from these rules of decorum, and they, too, had to observe a complicated etiquette. (Perhaps the old rumors suggesting his illegitimate birth had spoiled his relation with his brothers and sisters, for even if untrue, they must have been galling.)[20]

Once he was president, López brooked no familial opposition or presumption, not even from his mother. In previous years, Juana Pabla Carillo had dared to express a partiality for her youngest son Benigno, an excessively pomaded dandy who valued property over people. The resentment that this maternal predilection fostered proved long-lasting, for the adult Francisco Solano López demonstrated little warmth toward her.

López also started to regard his siblings, who had been his childhood playmates, with a marked wariness. In everyday matters, he favored the two sisters, Rafaela and Inocencia, both of whom shared his imperious humor, his cupidity, and his girth. But while they lived sumptuously and in close proximity to their mother all their lives, the sisters never got along, and enjoyed setting family members against each other. Each sister appeared to take greater pleasure in the other's flaws and misfortunes than in news of their brother's victories in the south. Certainly, they held no sway over him.[21]

Neither did the two brothers. On most occasions during the conflict the rather nondescript Venancio López exercised the post of war minister, and never once in the voluminous correspondence that passed between them did he address the president as anything other than "Excelentísimo Señor."[22] The obsequiousness did not stop there. In all formal interchanges, the members of the López family were obliged to treat Francisco Solano with fawning respect.[23]

Only one person, Eliza Lynch, seemed capable of scaling the cliff face of the Marshal's pride. Novelists have tended to treat her badly, placing her among the third-rate *horizontales de Paris*.[24] There is little fairness or accuracy in this: she was never a courtesan, though she was always controversial. She spent thirteen years with López and bore him seven children. On at least one occasion, Lynch publicly scratched his face after learning of a peccadillo, but she always pretended to forgive his inconstancy.[25] In return, he offered her trust as well as intimacy, and perhaps even loved her in a rough, unromantic way. Her support made it possible for López to enjoy something like a normal home life in the claustrophobic environment of Paso Pucú.

Whether she could ever convince him to make peace was another matter. If we are to judge by her many pregnancies, Lynch had always elicited the most powerful yearnings in the Marshal. Though he was attracted to numerous women, she was indisputably his favorite. No one else in Paraguay had her bearing, no one seemed so poised, and no one could speak French so sweetly. The grandes dames of Asunción, whose husbands lay dead at Tuyutí, had snubbed and maligned her.[26] But in her loyalty to the man whom she lovingly called "don Pancho," there was stolidity and clear thinking.

Although she enjoyed the perquisites of influence and standing, Lynch had to be a realist. In contrast to the Marshal, who displayed regal pretensions, she never fooled herself into thinking that she might one day assume a Paraguayan throne as empress.[27] Instead, she emphasized the practical side of her relationship with the president. Since the church had failed to legitimize her legal separation from her first husband—a French surgeon—she could not contract a new marriage with López; she thus needed to look after herself and their children in a manner unsanctioned by ecclesiastical law.

The easiest way to do this was through the acquisition of land. The Marshal had lavished all manner of gifts on her before the war began. Accordingly, she gained title to several homes and properties in Asunción and various parts of the nation. After the Allies had driven the Paraguayans from Curuzú, Lynch stepped up her purchase of available real estate. When she returned to South America after the war to assert claim over some of these lands, her lawyers contrived to portray her avarice as a sort of patriotism, but they made little headway with this interpretation.[28]

It is easy to see that Lynch's purchases amounted to an insurance policy in the event of catastrophe. At first, the properties she obtained were modest compared with what other members of the López family had assembled over the years.[29] At this penultimate stage of the campaign, however, she increased her holdings in a frenzied fashion, engaging in the profiteering that she pretended to disdain. Lynch came to own over three thousand square leagues in Paraguay and the occupied Mato Grosso.[30] Whether these transfers of land came through her own initiative or through the largesse of the Marshal, it remained the case that the best guarantee of her children's security lay in upholding the status quo.

In attempting to understand Madame Lynch—or "la Madama"—perhaps the most salient observation we can make is that she truly loved López, "with all her heart and soul," and worried incessantly about their future together.[31] In another time and place her devotion to him and to their children might have sustained them both; here it only helped preserve an air of unreality. Because Lynch loved the Marshal, she petted his most dangerous assumptions, just as a loyal consort in the mid-1800s was expected to do.

Lynch may have had an "abundance of that courage of which [López himself] was so greatly in want," but she never used that courage to challenge or moderate his excesses.[32] The Victorian milieu from which she came may have permitted her to thrive as the mistress of the most powerful man in Paraguay, but it also restricted the scope of her actions; she could neither gain the respectability she craved nor afford to act independently, and she never picked up a sword or mixed in the affairs of the Paraguayan state.[33] And she failed to push him toward that comfortable European exile that would one day be her lot. Though she continued to wheedle the Marshal for small favors and enjoy his more substantial concessions, she could never afford to forget that Paraguay was his country to command, even unto the end.

Paso Poí

The final days of 1867 held only false hope for Paraguay. The Marshal reviewed new offers of mediation from Washburn, which he found wanting in substance and impossible to pursue honorably.[34] He also continued to probe the new Allied lines at Tuyucué and San Solano, setting up limited nighttime ambushes. These efforts irritated Mitre and Caxias, but, safe in the knowledge that Allied attrition would wear down the Paraguayans, they knew they could afford a few pinpricks.

In mid-November, the Allied army in Paraguay consisted of 11,587 men at Tuyutí; 19,027 at Tuyucué; 6,777 at Tayí; and 1,098 in the Chaco, for a total of 38,489 men.[35] The Marshal had less than 20,000 emaciated soldiers to counter this force. G. F. Gould, who had seen these men two months earlier, noted that many

> were worn out with exposure, fatigue, and privations. They are actually dropping down from inanition. They have been reduced for the last six months to meat alone, and that of a very inferior quality. They may once in a while get a little Indian corn, but that mandioc [sic], and especially salt are so very scarce, they are, I fully believe, only served out to the sick. ... Many of the soldiers

are in a state bordering on nudity, having only a piece of tanned leather round their loins, a ragged shirt, and a poncho made of vegetable fiber."[36]

Given his usual trepidation, it may seem curious that López should choose to remain with these men at Humaitá after João Manoel had fortified Tayí and isolated the fortress. But on occasion his feelings of insecurity outweighed his sense of duty, and this may have been one of those times. His men could not eat his stubbornness, however, and common sense should have dictated their withdrawal northward to the Río Tebicuary while there was still time.

Two reasons explain the Marshal's unwavering hold on his established position. For one thing, Ignácio's well-supplied fleet had yet to steam past the key Paraguayan embrasures to link up with the Allied land forces at Tayí. Perhaps the admiral thought that Humaitá would fall without much of a naval effort. Caxias had made a similar calculation on land and that gambit had yet to play itself out. The fleet commander also complained, perhaps disingenuously, that he could not force the remaining river batteries without the three monitors being built at the time in Brazil.

Then there was the surprising success of the road constructed by the Paraguayans in the Chaco, between Timbó and Monte Lindo. This road had already done good service in facilitating a small traffic in supplies from above Tayí.[37] The Marshal then erected a battery of thirty guns at Timbó and stationed a strong garrison commanded by Colonel Caballero to cover the position. López also managed to reestablish telegraph contact with Asunción by stringing a wire across the Río Paraguay, then along the same Chaco line, and back across the river, where it reconnected to the old line.[38]

The supplies coming through the Chaco only prolonged the misery of the undernourished men at Humaitá; even those soldiers who had eaten something often fell sick with gastric ailments. The cattle driven to them through the Chaco were bony animals that could find no pasture at Humaitá and had to be butchered and consumed directly upon arrival.[39] It was hard to see how the army could last much longer.

Nonetheless, López attacked. Despite the hellish heat of the day, and the knots in their stomachs, the Paraguayan soldiers managed to summon up their old élan after one of the Marshal's adjutants rode in on 22 December and presented himself before the assembled troops at Humaitá. In an appropriately thunderous voice, the famished officer (whose name was not recorded) gave the standard salute: "How goes it, boys?" (*Mbaéteipa che lo mita?*). This was answered with a loud "Just fine" (*Iporãnte*), "awaiting orders to finish off the darkies!" The adjutant, in what by now looked like a well-rehearsed stage production, responded in the same theatrical fashion, booming out "Well and good, for that is why the Marshal has sent me!"[40] He conveyed his chief's instructions at once: the troops were to march out and destroy the Allied units at Paso Poí, a little redoubt equidistant between San Solano and Parecué.

Despite the men's enthusiasm, which under the circumstances was remarkable, the attack took two days to plan because few soldiers at Humaitá were fit for service. Once it got started, however, the raid went smoothly. One hundred sixty men moved with practiced stealth, wading through a series of waist-high lagoons after sunset, with sabers clenched between their teeth. The soldiers kept pushing ahead through the morass during the darkest hours of the night, and emerged from the water just before dawn on 25 December. They slid forward on their bellies like alligators, and just as the sun colored the eastern sky, they crawled atop the dry redoubt.

Then, in a flash, and like a horde of demons descending from the firmament, they fell upon the sleeping Voluntários. Crying "Long live Marshal López!" the Paraguayans swung hard with their sabers and cut up the four hundred men they encountered in the nearest dugouts. The Brazilians had no time to react. "Every blow was a sure mortality," Centurión wrote in his memoir, and within thirty minutes the Paraguayans had covered the position with torn and disfigured bodies. A temporary bridge previously built by Allied engineers was also covered with enemy corpses.[41] Awakened from their slumber by their comrades' startled cries, Allied infantrymen loosed a fusillade at the attackers from across the lagoon, but their bullets flew high and failed to hit a single man.

The Allied infantrymen raced away in sheer terror. A cavalry squadron whose commander attempted to gallop to the rescue met the Paraguayans in the shallow waters and received the same bowelless treatment meted out to the Voluntários. As the surviving horsemen disappeared into the distance, the Paraguayans took some forty or fifty minutes to retrieve the weapons and supplies the Brazilians had dropped in their confusion. To the Marshal's delight, they captured some regimental colors as well.

López never intended to hold Paso Poí with such a small force, and even before the Brazilians regained their composure, they had already begun to retreat through the muddy esteros to Paso Benítez. The long-faced Brazilian general José Joaquim de Andrade Neves (Baron of the Triumph) arrived on the scene at about this time, bringing with him several well-equipped units, both infantry and cavalry. The general had fought well at Potrero Ovella and in other engagements, but here the situation bewildered him. A quick scan of the field told Andrade Neves that the enemy raiders intended to regain Humaitá by the most direct overland route, so he ordered his horsemen to advance posthaste on a straight line toward the fortress, where they soon fell under cannon fire, and took still more casualties before retiring straightaway.

Caxias, who had rode in with his staff, was also thoroughly vexed by the chaos he encountered. A call to duty always gained a ringing endorsement from the marquis, but he found it exasperating to contend with the incompetence that Paso Poí suggested. He ordered an investigation, out of which came a court-martial for the lieutenant colonel whose Voluntário units the Paraguayans had come close to obliterating.[42]

Paraguayan sources claim that Allied losses at Paso Poí exceeded eight hundred men slain against a loss of just four of the Marshal's men.[43] This obviously exaggerated number was disputed by the Allies, with the Brazilians recognizing five men lost and seventeen wounded, compared to one man killed and five wounded for the Paraguayans.[44]

25 December did double duty as both Christmas and Paraguayan Independence Day, and news of the successful assault provided the Marshal's entourage at Paso Pucú with added reason for cheer. If Paraguayan soldiers could still win a victory, even now, they might yet accomplish all that López demanded of them. The military bands at Humaitá played patriotic marches the whole night long, and in Asunción, the festivities went on for days. The Paraguayan government even took the unusual step of releasing amputees from active service at Humaitá, sending them home with fairly ample pensions—one hundred pesos each for married men, and twenty-five for the unmarried.[45]

If Paso Poí taught López that he could not only survive against Mitre and Caxias, but even win, it reinforced a blatant recognition of the need for ruthlessness among the Allies. Many Allied soldiers—perhaps most—now believed that the Paraguayans would never quit, and would continue to fight until they were annihilated; the sooner they killed all the Paraguayans, the sooner they could go home. Gone was any romantic evocation of the enemy's virtues. Instead, savage feelings of murder filled the minds of the Brazilians and Argentines, and a violent impatience filled their hearts.[46]

Exit Mitre, Again

The Argentine president made no extensive comment on the Paraguayan raid at Paso Poí; instead, he found himself scanning reports from the lower provinces, where the news was anything but good. Cholera had also hit the capital, and Mitre now had to address the possibility of a widespread epidemic. With some irritation, moreover, he read that a new "revolution," probably of Urquicista inspiration, had just erupted in Santa Fe and was at that moment threatening the city of Rosario.[47] Provincial authorities had asked for national intervention, which raised fears of another round of internal revolts.

The Santafecino uprising turned out to be trivial, but that he had to deal with it at all suggested once again that Mitre, unlike Caxias, could not afford to devote himself exclusively to the Paraguayan campaign. Elizalde, the Taboada brothers, and Marcos Paz had acted as useful political allies, but they could never do without his guidance and support. Urquiza, as usual, was capricious, and the Europeans were less willing to deal with the Liberals on anything other than their own terms. If his army was overworked in Paraguay, the Argentine president proved even more fatigued in Buenos Aires.

Mitre had served as Allied commander for the better part of three years and, like General George McClellan in the United States, had provided the impetus in building the armed forces into something formidable and modern. He had handled the various diplomatic challenges of negotiating with the Brazilians and Uruguayans and he had succeeded in keeping the Alliance together—in itself no small feat. Although he had failed to gain his principal war objective, he had worked well with the Brazilians in formulating a strategy to bring López to his knees. The terrible setback of Curupayty, he could note, had at long last been forgotten, and the Allied army was once again on the move.

But Mitre had not yet vanquished the Marshal. Though the men at the front had heard many promises of victory as the New Year dawned, still they could perceive no sure sign of victory or peace. Humaitá had not fallen; the Paraguayan army remained active in the field (if in a less-decisive capacity); and don Bartolo's beard now had almost as much gray in it as the Marshal's. Worst of all, there was nothing to contemplate but more of the same.

On 2 January 1868, cholera took the life of Argentine vice president Marcos Paz. The fifty-four-year-old Tucumano had provided the political glue that had kept the national government together while Mitre was away at the front, and no one could replace him. Neither the Paraguayans nor the Brazilians could have wished for an event more compromising to Argentine—or at least Mitrista—interests. The president had no choice but to return south, this time for good. His wife and children were waiting for him, and he looked forward to a setting many times more comfortable than his billet at Tuyucué.

Many changes had occurred in his absence, however, and it was not clear what these new circumstances might require of him. With Paz's help, the national government had maintained a force of tens of thousands that had fought well against López, and the military had quashed opposition in the provinces, which made all the difference between a chaotic and a tranquil Argentina. Now, the generals wished to act as arbiters in a modern political order, something that Mitre hoped to forestall. There was no reason to suppose that the officers would throw their support to Elizalde, and without Paz on hand to check the Autonomist opposition, Mitre's Liberals had to look to their own.

The president could no longer waste time in pondering his historical legacy or in worrying about Humaitá, so he moved quickly, departing Paraguay on 14 January and leaving Caxias in overall command. From the Brazilian perspective, this was a key event, for the marquis could now prosecute the war according to his own dictates. For Mitre, by contrast, the departure from the front constituted a personal failure, yet another ambition thwarted by fate.

In the mid-1850s, Mitre had been the most versatile man in a generation of Argentine scholar-statesmen, and perhaps the most distinguished. Twelve years later, he looked much older, and he had also lost the patina of distinction that had set him on roughly the same level as Alberdi, and well above Urquiza. While he still could not claim the mantle of elder statesman, his political career no longer held the same promise as it had when he was younger. There was even talk about impeaching the president for having exceeded his war powers.[48]

As it turned out, Mitre spent several months trying to keep his political work from unraveling. He lost several of his most important allies in the government, and watched grudgingly while Elizalde fell by the wayside in the presidential election, defeated by Domingo Faustino Sarmiento, the Argentine minister to Washington. The latter figure, who, like Paz, had lost a son at Curupayty, was an unambiguous critic of the war.

To paraphrase Nicolas Shumway, it is difficult to separate Mitre's patriotism and hopes for Argentina from his more ignoble political ambitions since he possessed such a superb rhetorical command.[49] His eloquence, unmatched either by his Brazilian allies or his Paraguayan enemies, provided a lasting veneer to a life that comprised as much prevarication as it did high-minded philosophy. Mitre's modern detractors condemn his liberalism as the product of an elitist frame of mind; his political defects, they argue, originated in his faulty instinct for humanity.[50] When he should have reached out to the Argentine people and felt compassion for their poverty, he saw in their supposed backwardness something that needed to be overcome. In that sense, his Porteño-oriented patriotism served as a cover for a new kind of exploitation. The man himself was complex, sophisticated, and attractive, but the nationalism that he so carefully manufactured in his library, in his newspaper office, and in his billet at Tuyucué, was exclusive and incomplete.

Caxias "Todo-poderoso"?

Frankly, the death of Vice President Paz had no effect on the Marshal's perception of Allied strengths because he misunderstood what had happened; for weeks he believed that it was Mitre who had died, not Paz, and he insisted that all his underlings accept this mistaken opinion.[51] Only slowly did the truth come out. López's anger did not subside on learning the facts, however, for now he suspected the men who had previously confirmed his false assertions. "The phantoms which existed in the mind of the Roman emperor," Gibbon tells us, "had a real and pernicious effect on the government." And so it was for Paraguay.

Reality, of course, could not reassure the Marshal. Mitre's departure from Paraguay left the door open for Caxias, and what had for many months been de facto at Tuyucué in short order became de jure when, on 12 January 1868, the Brazilian general took over as Allied commander. Caxias granted that his Argentine predecessor was better read and in some ways more thoughtful, but that was no reason for the marquis to act as a willing subordinate to the younger man. His own experience in government was long and distinguished, and included two terms as president of the council (or prime minister). Even now, he was a lifetime member of the imperial senate.

Caxias knew from the beginning that the empire's status as senior partner in the Triple Alliance would provide all the power he needed. And he understood his strengths at that moment. The Argentine commander who stayed behind at Tuyucué, General Andrés Gelly y Obes, was a capable officer who could take orders. The Uruguayan contingent hardly counted. The Brazilian land forces would do their duty. And Admiral Ignácio, who owed Caxias for his show of support after the fleet went past Curupayty, could be trusted to fall in line as well.

Even now, it was not obvious that the time had arrived to crush Marshal López. Mitre's departure coincided with political crises in both Montevideo and Rio de Janeiro—the latter representing a potential threat to the Allied war effort. Radicals within the imperial government had adopted a skeptical pose toward the conflict, similar to that espoused by the Autonomists in Buenos Aires. Those members of Parliament who wished to displace Prime Minister Zacharias de Góes e Vasconcelos lent some support to this stance and censured the military for wasteful spending and poor planning.[52] These criticisms cut uncomfortably close for Caxias, threatening his command every bit as much as political shifts in Buenos Aires had hurt Mitre.

The marquis was a skilled politician who knew when to let rivals have their way and when to challenge them. He was, moreover, the leading Conservative stalwart, a statesman upon whose loyalty the emperor had always counted; not a single man of importance in the Brazilian political firmament believed that victory over the Paraguayans could be achieved without him. Now that Mitre had relinquished command, Caxias demanded unquestioned authority to get the job done.

Whatever they thought about Caxias's abilities as a general, Zacharias and his Liberal ministers had long opposed his political ambitions, and in February 1868, the marquis decided that he had had enough of their intrigues. He directed two letters to the war minister making his position transparent, and he requested leave to resign, citing reasons of health. The second missive, sent privately, enlarged on the marquis's displeasure with Liberal newspapers that had assassinated his character and undermined the success of Brazilian arms in Paraguay. If Caxias had lost the emperor's confidence—and he surely knew that he had not—then he was ready to set aside his command.

These two letters amounted to a bid for the emperor to replace Zacharías with a new Conservative ministry or else lose Caxias's services at the front. The prime minister had disliked the marquis ever since the Ferraz affair in 1866, but he could read between the lines and understand what he had to do next. On 19 February, Zacharias offered his cabinet's resignation, and, with the emperor's approval, referred the question to the Council of State, which would have to choose between the resignation of the general and that of the cabinet.[53] Pedro seemed to understand how nervous and conflicted this made the councilors feel, but he refused to entertain any false compromises or delay—they had to make the choice required of them. They ended up by dividing almost evenly, a clear sign that the emperor should now act as he saw fit.

Dom Pedro realized that the Conservatives were unwilling to take office at once, so he persuaded Zacharias to stay on as prime minister for a short time. At the emperor's prompting, the Conservatives then composed a letter to the Allied commander to express confidence in his generalship and to ask him to remain at his post. Zacharias swallowed his pride and did the same, writing an effusive letter to reaffirm the government's commitment to the war and to praise Caxias as the one man capable of assuring victory.

The partisan crisis within the Brazilian government was not averted, merely postponed. Zacharias continued to head the government until July, but the chamber as a whole showed scant enthusiasm about his deals with the Conservatives. Dom Pedro's actions in February were controversial. He might have believed that he was loading the Brazilian ship of state with necessary ballast, but in truth he was disturbing its equilibrium (though it may be overstating things to say that he thereby weakened the monarchical system, as some have claimed).[54] The 1824 constitution granted Pedro extensive authority under its "moderating power" provisions, but the emperor had always trod carefully so as to avoid any charge of tyranny. He was not always successful, but on this occasion, he got what he wanted: the war went on and Caxias continued in command. Yet no one in the imperial government could fail to notice that the emperor's hair had already lost its previous color and that he was looking "care-worn," much older than his forty-four years.[55]

The Running Of The Batteries

As far as the Allied campaign in Paraguay was concerned, the emperor's actions had the desired effect of reaffirming Caxias as commander. His conduct of the war would henceforth go unquestioned, and by mid-February 1868, the fighting had taken several positive turns. On 13 February, the three monitors built at Rio de Janeiro, which had only recently appeared on the scene, succeeded in getting past Curupayty in the dark of night. The Paraguayan batteries along the bank offered limited resistance and the newly arrived vessels linked up with Ignácio's ironclads further upriver. The monitors, having been adapted for fluvial operations, were a much-improved version of the design used four years earlier by the Union navy during the US Civil War. They boasted two separate boilers, a triple-thick hardwood hull clad with three or four inches of Muntz metal, a bronze ram, and an unusual turret.[56] Each ship came armed with a single Whitworth cannon, either a 70- or 120-pounder, and, as with the old chatas, the hulls were almost flush with the water line. This made the vessels difficult to hit—just the thing to test the Batería Londres.

Admiral Ignácio could no longer delay a naval assault on Humaitá. Mitre had departed, and with him the old excuse that the fleet needed to stay anchored to guard against any Argentine treachery; if Brazilian warships were wrecked in an attack on the fortress, the failure would rest on the marquis's shoulders. Caxias could promise Ignácio that a major land attack against Cierva would accompany the effort on the river. The admiral had always argued that land and naval units needed to act jointly in any advance on Humaitá, and he was therefore unable to oppose a mission that featured just such an attack. The marquis not only had López where he wanted him—he had trapped his own admiral as well.

On 19 February, the two commanders set the attack in motion by having the ironclad flotilla commence a heavy bombardment of the Paraguayan positions. By prearrangement, the wooden fleet off Curuzú did the same, as did two flat-bottomed vessels that the Allies had moved into the Laguna Pirís. Simultaneously, the Allied artillery at Tuyucué shelled Espinillo, and several battalions of infantry peppered the same position with musketry.

These barrages were all diversionary. The real action occurred along the main river channel, where the fleet forced a passage of the Humaitá and Timbó batteries. In Brazilian thinking, this was in many ways the great moment of the war, something that the Allied armies had anticipated for over two years, and from which the Paraguayans should never have been able to recover.

Two hours before dawn, three of the heaviest ironclads got steam up and eased forward into the main river channel. Each had a monitor lashed to her port side, away from the fortress. First came the *Barroso*, named for the victor of the Riachuelo, leading the monitor *Rio Grande*, followed by the *Bahia* with the *Alagoas* alongside, and finally, by the *Tamandaré* leading the *Pará*. The paired vessels approached the line of embrasures at Humaitá in single file, their guns blazing away.[57] Normally, it would still have been pitch black, but Paraguayan spies had revealed Allied intentions, and López had lit a series of huge bonfires along the river. These, together with the near-constant flashes of cannon fire and Congreve rockets, illuminated the sky with a terrible light.

The Marshal's artillery units threw huge quantities of shell and canister into the air as the enemy fleet neared. Perhaps one hundred fifty guns were firing simultaneously. The din was terrific, and it lasted for over forty minutes, during which the fleet made the transit above Humaitá. Allied fire had already wrecked the river booms across which the Paraguayans had stretched three obstacles in the form of intertwined chains, and López's troops had failed to repair them in time. High water covered what was left of the chains by ten or fifteen feet, so the vessels were not long detained in front of the main guns. Even so,

Ignácio's boilers could not give his ships the power to steam ahead at anything approaching breakneck speed.

The passage was difficult, though nowhere near as hazardous as Ignácio had envisioned. Under pressure from Caxias, he had dispatched his son-in-law, the talented Commodore Delphim Carlos de Carvalho, to oversee the operation from the deck of the *Bahia*. The commodore understood what he was up against. It was common knowledge that the channel was quite narrow just below the fort—a mere seven hundred yards across; it would thus have to be approached with care. The sharp bend in the river required any ships heading upstream to lower their speed so as to maneuver against the 4-knot current. Steering problems dogged the passage, and there were times when the ships presented their full length to the enemy gunners.

López's engineers had erected their most formidable batteries just above the bend, which permitted them to pour concentrated fire onto any vessel trying to pass. The number and heavy caliber of the Paraguayan guns (some of them 68-pounders) offered an intimidating prospect, as did the various obstacles and mines that the Marshal's men had dropped into the river during the preceding months. The fire from the Batería Londres and the fortress's other guns was tremendous; it "was well-sustained and true, but the balls flew into pieces on the plates of the ironclads [and, after] passing Humaitá, they went straight on, and ran past the battery of Timbó to Tayí" where Mena Barreto was waiting.[58] In some ways, Timbó, which was located on the Chaco side of the river, presented a more striking challenge than the fortress, for it was lower and thus better protected from Allied fire. At one point the *Bahia* lost its way and collided with the *Tamandaré* and the *Pará*, which followed behind. The latter vessel took on water but none of the others were seriously damaged, and they completed the passage in good time.

Perhaps the most terrifying part of the entire episode involved the little monitor *Alagoas*, which broke loose from the bow of the *Bahia* when shrapnel cut the forward cable. The prows of the two ships began at once to drift apart. Water resistance then caused the second cable to snap at the stern, setting the *Alagoas* downstream, her bow pointed at the enemy. In due course, she neared the Paraguayan embrasures without being able to get her engines adjusted. None of the other Brazilian ships turned about to help.[59]

The danger to the *Alagoas* was grave. Having drifted into the swiftest part of the current, the ship was carried some way from the fleet, coming within a hair's breadth of destruction in front of the Batería Londres. The ship's skipper, Lieutenant Joaquim Antônio Cordovil Maurity, stayed cool during ten minutes of sustained fire, finally getting his engines into working order at the last moment. The *Alagoas* then steamed as fast as possible away from the enemy guns. Later that day, when the damage was surveyed, it turned out that the "little tortoise" had been hit 187 times.

Colonel Caballero caught sight of Maurity's ship from the low banks of the Potrero Ovella and decided to intercept her with troops placed aboard twenty canoes. The chances of doing meaningful damage to the Allies would be quadrupled if he could capture such a ship. The Paraguayans therefore pressed

> furiously ahead, [and] succeeded in boarding the monitor, but were perplexed and confounded when they saw none of the [crew-members, who were] in the hold … and the hatchways were securely closed by heavy iron plates. Then the crew poured a withering fire from within the tower into the dense masses of Paraguayans surging over the deck, which was cleared in a brief time. Of those who managed to leap back into the boats some were killed by the fire from the tower and the others perished in the waves, when the monitor, in hot pursuit, crushed and sank the boats. The little steamer, turning now to the right and then to the left, ran down one after another of the wildly flying canoes. Only a few of them succeeded in reaching the sheltering canals where the monitor could not [or would not] pursue them.[60]

The *Alagoas* had just gotten her engines in proper working order, and, having struck the enemy canoes as they approached, proceeded to steam upriver to rejoin the other Brazilian ships at Tayí. Caballero seems to have bit into the hilt of his sword and spat as Maurity's monitor sped away to the north.

Not a single man aboard the Allied fleet was killed, and only ten were wounded in the action of 19 February. The ironclads all took hits, with the *Bahia* suffering 145 and the *Tamandaré* 170, but, as if to prove the efficacy of iron plating, none of the damage was serious. The flotilla encountered no mines, which had probably floated away in the recent rise of the river.

Under the circumstances, the many men in Allied uniform could wonder why the forcing of the batteries had seemed so easy, so predictable, and so expedient after so much time had been wasted. Perhaps Caxias and Ignácio thought the same, perhaps not.[61] Argentine critics seemed to believe that the tardy use of Brazilian naval power was part of a deliberate strategy to put the national government into the background. In any case, the old signatories to the Triple Alliance Treaty could not afford to feel very happy just yet. They were about to suffer another reverse.

The Alliance Mourns a Stalwart

A serious blow to the Alliance, if not to Allied military fortunes, came on the same day that the gunboats forced the passage of Humaitá. In circumstances that have never been fully explained, the empire's old ally, President Venancio

Flores, was murdered at midday as he emerged from his carriage in Montevideo. Unlike Mitre, Flores had seemed a man out of another age. For twenty years he had fought for a concept of Uruguayan patriotism that accentuated personal dignity and courage over national, "fusionist" ideals. As a p ̣nt of honor, Flores had insisted on paying a lavish political debt to Brazil, supplying not only men and matériel in Paraguay, but in Uruguay proper, where the presence of imperial troops had proven irksome to everyone.

The president's return to Montevideo after Curupayty witnessed a few successes. But for all of these achievements, Flores failed to plug the holes within his own Colorado Party, and he never managed to recapture the authority that he had seized in 1865. Pushed into a corner by renewed factionalism, the caudillo put on his most generous face in appealing for political support. This accomplished nothing, however, and he had few friends left when, in November 1867, he rigged congressional elections one too many times. His opponents—and even some of his friends—had no intention of sanctioning the fraud, and Flores made a fatal mistake when he turned to weak-handed cronies who defended him for pay, though with little conviction.

The Brazilians had always supported Flores as the best alternative among the Uruguayans.[62] But the imperial government was no more satisfied with him than were the dissident Colorados, who now coalesced into a new faction under Gregorio "Goyo" Suárez, the victor (and to some minds, the butcher) of Paysandú. Finally, although the government had suppressed the Blanco opposition, both in Montevideo and the countryside, there seemed little doubt that these perennial adversaries would reassert a place in the country's politics at any time.

Hoping to forestall such an eventuality, Flores's sons Fortunato and Eduardo attempted to stage a coup against their more conciliatory father, who fled the city in order to rally the part of his army that was not absent in Paraguay. This effort went nowhere, and on 15 February, Flores resigned the presidency. Don Venancio may have wanted to revive his dictatorship, or work out a new deal with the Brazilians, but before he could get going with this the Blancos launched their expected rebellion.

Ex-president Bernardo Berro, a hapless combatant in almost as many civil wars as Flores, was at the center of events. Together with twenty of his most trusted Blanco partisans, he chose the early hours of 19 February to challenge the Colorados by forcing his way into government house. Each insurgent brandished a weapon and, as they tried to break down the door, cried out "Down with Brazil! Long live Oriental independence! Long live Paraguay!"[63] The Colorado forces quickly rallied, however, and seized control of the streets. Shortly thereafter, Berro fell into their hands after failing to rendezvous with a river launch sent to ferry him to safety.

This unsuccessful action sealed his fate. Flores had heard of the attack right away, but may not have learned of Berro's detention when he set out across town for a hurried meeting with supporters. En route, he was accosted by unknown assailants who blocked his path with a carriage at the sunniest moment of the day. The police never identified Flores's murderers except as dark-clad men in ponchos who ran their daggers through his body with the ease of professional killers. They might have taken their orders from the Blancos, from Suárez, or from any one of the many embryonic factions seeking power in the Uruguayan capital.[64] Given the banquet of historical vendettas on offer in the city, it was even possible that the assassins were disgruntled veterans from Paraguay or individuals with purely personal motives.[65]

The murder opened a new round of chaos. Berro, who was held at the old government house, was killed within hours of Flores, shot down together with other political detainees after having been shown his rival's body. The Colorados interred Berro's corpse in a pauper's grave after having it carried through the streets in an oxcart driven by a Florista fanatic who wailed at the shuddered windows that such a fate awaited all *salvajes*.[66] Street fighting continued for the better part of a week.

In their concern for all this disorder and butchery, Uruguayans could easily forget that their country's destiny had once seemed so inextricably linked to the Marshal and his cause. The battles of Yataí, Tuyutí, and Boquerón, the death of Palleja, even the notion of a Platine balance of power—all seemed so trifling now, so far away. Flores was dead. Berro was dead. The violence in Paraguay went on.

The Raid on Asunción

At Tuyucué, the Marquis of Caxias showed little interest in delving into the mystery of Flores's death; he had a war to wage and took to that task with ease. His deliberate movements, his slow, honeyed smile, and the contemplative look in his heavy-lidded eyes did not accord with the usual image of a vigorous personality. But he was perhaps the most vigorous man at the front.

The navy's running of the batteries at Humaitá and Timbó had opened the river, at least conditionally. Caxias could now contemplate attacking Asunción itself. The Allied land forces—just under forty thousand men—still lagged behind in the vicinity of the fortress, building up their supplies and manpower before pushing on to the mouth of the Tebicuary, the seizure of which would open a navigable waterway into the Paraguayan interior, thus offering a new avenue of advance.[67] Caxias could not afford to leave any substantial Paraguayan units in his rear, however, and so persisted in shelling the fortress with unremitting determination.

This pressure had already manifested itself on the day the ironclads forced the Humaitá batteries. With a view to confusing his adversaries, López had established a redoubt at the spot traditionally called Establecimiento de la Cierva, some two miles north at the edge of the great marsh. His soldiers defended this position with nine minor guns and a garrison of five hundred. The redoubt had no value in itself, but as the Marshal had foreseen, the Allies mistook its basic function; they seemed to assume that it guarded a previously unidentified opening into the swamps (similar to the Potrero Ovella), or else secured communication with some other Paraguayan post further upstream.[68]

In fact, it did neither. Cierva was not located at a spot that facilitated communication between Timbó and Humaitá; it was not even situated on the Paraguay River proper, as the marquis had presumed. This lack of topographical information caused him to take substantial risk in following the false lead, and, on the 19 February, he sent seven thousand men to storm the Establecimiento. According to the plan developed with Ignácio, Caxias had tried to time this assault to coincide with the forcing of the batteries. As it turned out, the attack constituted an entirely separate engagement.

Thompson's description of the battle reveals the high price paid by the Allies for their lack of clear intelligence:

> At daylight, Caxias sent his first attack, headed by the famous needle-guns. These did not do much execution, as the Paraguayans were behind parapets, and poured into the Brazilian columns such a fire of grape and canister, at close quarters, that the needle-gun men ... were thrown back, and completely disbanded. Another column was immediately sent forward, [then] a third, and a fourth, [which] had no better luck than the first. While the fourth column was retreating, a Paraguayan in the re-doubt [called] out to his officer that the artillery ammunition was all finished, which encouraged the Brazilians to ... return to the attack. While they were doing this, [the Paraguayans retreated] on board the *Tacuarí* and *Ygurey*, which were close at hand, and had assisted with their fire. After exchanging shots, the two steamers [fled downriver] to Humaita."[69]

The three-hour engagement cost the Brazilians some twelve hundred killed and wounded, the Paraguayans one hundred fifty.[70] There had been many heroic displays that day. The Brazilian doctor Francisco Pinheiro Guimarães, who had done so much to contain the cholera threat the previous year, found himself again as an infantry officer at Cierva, and took pleasure in personally hauling down the Paraguayan tricolor at the climax of the engagement.[71] Even so, the Allies had captured a useless position and just nine cannon.

The Marshal took no time to savor his victory, and in fact seemed to think the battle a major reverse. The running of the Humaitá batteries had left the Paraguayan communities upriver open to any assault that the enemy navy cared to mount; besides, with Delphim in control of all the waters between Humaitá and Tayí, the telegraph connection with Asunción, only recently reestablished, would be broken once again.

Though the general trajectory of such engagements as Curuzú and Second Tuyutí might call into question the Marshal's grasp of strategy, his actions on this occasion were fluid and well considered. At the very moment the ironclads steamed past the fortress, he came alive. He declared martial law throughout Paraguay and telegraphed orders to Vice President Sánchez to evacuate the Paraguayan capital and intervening communities, and to relocate both the civilian population and the government to Luque, nine miles to the northeast.[72] The few military units left in Asunción were ordered to ready their guns at the riverfront and repulse any enemy ships approaching from downstream. Meanwhile, López made ready to retreat northward across the Chaco to a point above Tayí, where he could recross to the mouth of the Tebicuary.

Sánchez was an aged bureaucrat with inky fingers who a few years earlier had dreamed of retiring quietly to his country estates. On more than one occasion, however, the war had moved him to display an unexpected energy. In this case, he signaled his immediate compliance with instructions. He notified families to take what they could carry and abandon the capital without delay. From this time forward, any civilian who wished to return to Asunción could enter the city only under escort and with the clear understanding that any visit home would be brief. The authorities also instructed diplomatic and consular personnel to join the exodus. All complied, save for US Minister Washburn; since his legation constituted sovereign American territory, he insisted he could not evacuate it without explicit instructions from Washington.[73]

Washburn's decision, predicated as it was on a faulty grasp of international law and diplomatic procedure, was poorly considered. It caused him no end of trouble later, for in standing his ground in the face of the Marshal's direct instruction, he made himself the object of mistrust. To make matters worse, foreign residents in the capital—and not a few members of the terrified local elite—attempted to seek protection within the vacant rooms of the US legation. When Washburn declined to give them aid, they persuaded him instead to store their valuables—jewelry, coins, and the like.

To this request, the minister reluctantly and recklessly assented. Though he refused to take any formal responsibility for their property, the trunks and luggage belonging to various notables of the city nonetheless piled up in his personal quarters. Even Madame Lynch sent some wooden chests.[74] So many people solicited his help that he made another ill-considered move and hired two of his countrymen to help him arrange affairs at the legation. One was

Major James Manlove, a would-be privateer who had once been a major in the Confederate Army, and the other was an obscure note taker, Porter Cornelius Bliss.[75] The Paraguayan authorities had already marked both men as suspicious, and Washburn's newfound association with them registered deep disapproval. Every move that the minister made seemed calculated to place him in a disadvantageous light.

Meanwhile, the city plunged itself into the turmoil of forced evacuation, with masses of soldiers and noncombatants clogging the roads out of town. Some Asuncenos shut everything up, hoping against hope that some of their possessions might survive. But the majority, certain that their properties were bound for destruction, left their homes wide open, with doors and windows gaping and rooms stripped bare. There was much grieving and expression of fear from nervous children, who had never before seen their mothers weep. The printing presses for *El Semanario* and wagon-loads of archival documents followed in their wake, as did a train of cattle, oxen, sheep, and dogs. Grandparents too sick to walk were strapped atop cupboards, placed onto the wagons, and carted away like sticks of furniture.

The propertied classes, or what was left of them, became like all the war's refugees—homeless, impoverished, hungry. These city people, who had always turned their noses up at the poor peasants, soon found themselves depending on those same country people for all of their sustenance, for the state could offer no succor.

Benigno López, José Berges, the garrison commander, and other members of the military and Asunción city government had already met in a hastily convened meeting in which several men voiced profound worry. Paraguayan officers knew how to obey, but they found it difficult to make decisions independent of López. In this case, as city authorities had had no communication with the Marshal, they wondered frantically what they were expected to do.

A long debate followed. Benigno (who had acted as secretary to Sánchez but otherwise held no formal position in the government) claimed to speak for his brother Venancio, the war minister, who at that moment was supposedly bed-ridden with syphilis. There were many expressions of fear and frustration, but only one man, Father Francisco Solano Espinosa, spoke in favor of continued resistance. Benigno, acting as chairman, let every man have his say and then announced his intention to ride to Paraguarí to solicit help from militia officers in the interior.[76]

He convened another meeting there on 21 February in the railroad station. Military commanders and jefes políticos from Itá, Yaguarón, Ybycuí, Carapegua, Quiindy and Caacupe attended and listened carefully while Benigno outlined the gravity of the situation. He had had no word from his elder brother, who, for all he knew, had perished or fallen prisoner. He therefore insisted that the local officials make themselves ready to receive orders from the vice president—even if that meant making peace with the enemy. The assembled men agreed at once, less out of conviction than out of habit, and Benigno returned to the capital to report that the Paraguayan *provincianos* stood ready to obey the new orders.[77]

During his absence, several of the Asunción notables had met again and seem to have had a change of heart. Fearful of the Marshal's reaction should he learn of the unauthorized gatherings, the normally tight-lipped Sánchez cleared his throat to endorse Espinosa's words. The vice president reiterated his faith in the López family and stressed that all Paraguayans must fight the enemy in Asunción as well as Humaitá.[78] At this, the men nodded their assent in the same formulaic way that the functionaries at Paraguarí had done with Benigno. Of course, no one could have felt secure. They sank back into a posture of gloom. Outside, the rain fell in torrents.

As the US minister observed, the "long-threatened evil had now come."[79] The British engineers employed at the Asunción arsenal got word that Allied ironclads were fast approaching from the south. Their arrival was sure to unleash a furious bombardment of the city. Support for the Paraguayan cause appeared to be unraveling, and the foreign residents scurried to protect their families from whatever vengeance the Lopistas might exact at this late hour. Numerous Britons again approached Washburn, now as a group, and demanded that he place them under his protection. This time, he granted their request, insisting only that they obtain Paraguayan government approval before moving into the back rooms of the legation. Surprisingly, this was conceded, and Washburn found himself with forty-two persons under his roof.

He also inherited nine tame parrots, which he lodged on a long bamboo in the corridor and fed little slivers of manioc. One of these birds later gave rise to much apprehension in the legation, when, out of nowhere, she began to cry out, "Viva Pedro Segundo!" The minister, taken aback by this most unexpected and treasonous imprecation, glared at the parrot, who proudly turned her head to one side and again squawked "Viva Pedro Segundo!" as if she were celebrating a holiday on the Rua Ouvidor. "Wring that bird's neck directly," shouted Washburn to his secretary, "or we shall all get into trouble."[80]

Whether the minister or his avian houseguests expected Caxias's army to land in short order, many of the remaining inhabitants of Asunción believed that the hour had come. On 24 February, the ironclads *Bahia* and *Barroso* and the monitor *Rio Grande* steamed into view. The men aboard the ships glimpsed the volcanic cone of Lambaré, green and solitary, which still marks the southernmost edge of the Paraguayan capital. Just behind the hill, the river veered eastward, making a large bight that was partly sealed off by a half-sunken islet; this enclosure formed the "bay" of Asunción and within its watery limits was sufficient room for the entire imperial fleet.

Commodore Delphim remained at the opening of the bay, from which his ships began to shell the outskirts of the city. The Brazilians had already done much damage en route, having aided the Allied army in seizing the little Paraguayan post at Laureles and in raking enemy positions at Monte Lindo and Villa Franca. The civilians at the latter community had already buried many of their sons, but they had never before heard the loud reports of enemy cannon. Now, they had the chance to accustom themselves to the sound, for as they fled their homes, they could hear the concussions behind them.

The Brazilians encountered no real opposition on their voyage upriver, just empty canoes, all of which they destroyed. They slaughtered the small herds of cattle they spied grazing near the river.[81] And they also nearly captured one of the Marshal's last remaining gunboats, the *Pirabebé*, whose crew had been caught unawares while towing a damaged schooner. The Paraguayans had to burn the ship's bulwarks for want of fuel before managing to escape upriver. Though the Brazilians claimed to have sunk the accompanying schooner, the Paraguayans appear to have destroyed it themselves rather than see it fall into enemy hands.[82]

Ignácio and the other Allied naval officers later described the raid on Asunción as a reconnaissance, but to Washburn and the other foreign observers it seemed a prelude to invasion. The one fort that opposed the flotilla was located at San Gerónimo, near the Lambaré hill, located some 275 yards from the US legation. This placement afforded a clear view for Washburn and his colleagues, who positioned themselves on the roof.

The bombardment, however, inspired no confidence in any of these foreigners, many of whom were anticipating a Paraguayan defeat. The three Brazilian vessels fired continuously for four hours, but the "shots flew far wide of their mark, the greater number fell harmlessly into the river and a few into the city, the only damage being the destruction of a balcony on the presidential palace, a slice off the front of a house, and the demolition of a couple of dogs in the market-place."[83]

The fort at San Gerónimo boasted one heavy gun, the "Criollo," which the Paraguayans had cast at the arsenal a short time earlier. The inner workings of this "raging Beelzebub" were sound enough, but the engineers had done a poor job of mounting the cannon, and the Paraguayan gunners soon gave up, having fired three or four times without getting the enemy's range. The other field guns did no better (and their shot in any case would have been "as harmless as paper pellets against the heavy plates of the ironclads").[84]

Just one small cavalry unit stood in the way of Allied success, and Washburn, Masterman, and the other foreigners expected that more Brazilian vessels would join the flotilla and mount a landing in the city proper. Nothing of the kind happened, however. Instead, the little puffs of white smoke that marked the movements of the ironclads soon dissipated into the distance; the flotilla, having fled back to Tayí, hit the undefended Monte Lindo one more time as a consolation.

Commodore Delphim's official account referred to "having severely chastised the insolence of the Paraguayans in firing upon" the flotilla, but the damage at Asunción proved negligible.[85] If the raid on the Paraguayan capital had been conceived as a reconnaissance, the ironclads should have steamed into the bay to have gained a better knowledge of what the Allies faced at the city. Presuming that the Brazilians had sufficient supplies of coal, they could also have steamed further upriver to determine if the Marshal had any reserve forces available there. If, on the other hand, the attack at Asunción was meant as a more traditional raid, then the navy missed an opportunity to wreck the urban center and sow still more confusion. Delphim's command of the river was unquestioned, and he could have returned with at least some troops to occupy the port district (though probably not the whole of the city).

As it was, Washburn could not believe his eyes. His disgust at the navy's timidity and unwillingness even to attempt a landing knew no bounds: "being as yet ignorant of the perfection to which the Brazilians had attained in the art of carrying on war without exposing themselves to danger, we could not but believe … that at any moment we might hear the guns of the returning vessels."[86] Instead, they heard nothing.

Washburn was a diplomat with a rather narrow grasp of what was happening to the south and only an amateur's judgment on the overall military situation. There were still Paraguayan troops at Humaitá, at the mouth of the Tebicuary, and in the Chaco, and the Allied commanders had yet to ascertain the strength of these garrisons. Caxias could ill afford to leave sizable units of the enemy behind him while the navy launched an uncertain operation upriver; besides, Delphim had no way to know that Asunción was essentially defenseless. He had taken fire from San Gerónimo and there could have been sizable cavalry units ready to repulse any Brazilian landings in the port district. So Delphim chose the prudent course.

Perhaps that was enough. The marquis, for his part, could recognize the advantages of at least a minor naval foray against the Marshal's capital. Word of Delphim's achievement brought celebrations throughout Brazil.[87] If Caxias could provide the emperor with solid proof of further military success, all the doubts that the Liberals had voiced would disappear like cobwebs on a sunny morning.[88]

Delphim's decision to withdraw from Asunción seemed cowardly to Washburn. But it also produced a useful psychological impact—not just in Paraguay, but also in Rio de Janeiro, where the emperor ennobled the commodore as the Baron of the Passage on the same day the ironclads raided the enemy capital. The immediate military consequences of the raid may have been limited but no one could doubt its worthiness as a gambit. The marquis had good reason to suppose that hitting Asunción, even in a limited way, might inspire a panic similar to that caused by Paunero's raid on Paraguayan-held Corrientes in May 1865. That effort had upset the timetable for the Marshal's offensive in

Argentina and ultimately brought about his retreat. This time, the Allies hoped that the entire urban population would flee, causing the Marshal's army not just to pull back, but to disintegrate altogether.

In assuming a cautious stance at the time of the raid, the Allied commander likely missed another opportunity to shorten the war. Paraguay's civilian population had indeed panicked and could never again hope to supply Humaitá; so much confusion reigned at Luque and in the hill country behind Asunción that people could not obtain sufficient food for their own needs, much less provide real support to López's army. Had they known the state of affairs, the Allies might have taken advantage of the turmoil to bring their full force to bear on the enemy. It was another opportunity lost.

9

A CRUEL ATTRITION

Mitre, Caxias, and the majority of politicians in Buenos Aires and Rio had, at one time or another, predicted the weakening of the Marshal's resolve, only to witness the Paraguayan leader stand firm. This time, however, all indications suggested that something different was in the offing. The Allied fleet now operated on either side of Humaitá; João Manoel was well entrenched at Tayí; and Caxias's army was poised to strike from Tuyucué and San Solano. For a man so convinced of his own genius, López could occasionally face facts. And so, on 19 February—the same day that Delphim ran the Humaitá and Timbó batteries—he sent Madame Lynch and his children through the Chaco to Asunción.

Militarily, however, the situation was less certain than this picture suggests. Naval dispositions on the Paraguay River were erratic, with the wooden ships of the Allied fleet anchored below Curupayty, whose gunners remained active. Seven ironclads guarded the river between Curupayty and the fortress, but their commanding officers were unwilling to emulate the audacity of Commodore Delphim, who held the river at Tayí with the six vessels that had forced the batteries, three of which had just returned from raiding Asunción. This same flotilla had yet to establish regular communication with Admiral Ignácio, and, in any case, was isolated from the vessels downstream. As before, all the flotilla's supplies had to be brought overland through the esteros from Paso de la Patria. For the Paraguayan capital to be seized by way of the river, more warships, and a great many transports, would have to break through from the south.

Despite the tactical advantages the Allies boasted, they nonetheless forgot to plug an important hole. Had the naval commanders left even one ironclad between Timbó and the fortress, its guns could have prevented López from escaping through the Chaco brush.[1] The road north, which had thus far scarcely met the needs of the Humaitá garrison, might then have been barred to the Marshal's soldiers.

But failing to deploy an ironclad upriver was a glaring mistake, one from which López could immediately benefit. He had two steamers to transport the artillery across the river to Timbó; then came the sick and most of the remaining stores. The Marshal ordered the guns facing the interior lines brought into the fortress for transport to the Chaco side, leaving a few light guns at Curupayty, a single gun at the Paso Gómez, and twelve on the eastern face of the Cuadrilátero, directly opposing the main Allied force.

All was ready, it seemed, to ferry the remaining units to Timbó in preparation for a general redeployment to the Tebicuary, or some point further upstream. So far, the enemy had failed to detect the army's movements and there was every reason to suppose that the Paraguayans could reach the Chaco in safety. Before the troops could embark, however, the Marshal opted for one last throw of the dice. He understood that Ignácio had anchored his fleet in an erratic fashion all up and down the river; if he could wrest control of at least one ironclad, he could use it to destroy the remaining Brazilian ships, and the river would become Paraguayan once again.

Canoes Against Ironclads

The odds against victory seemed very long indeed. The operation depended on both Paraguayan courage, which was never in doubt, and surprise, which was. The Paraguayan naval commanders might well have had enough experience with the Brazilian ironclads to doubt the efficacy of the plan, but they also had enough sense not to insist on their opinion once López had declared his faith in the operation.[2] The Marshal always presumed that the Brazilians were spineless, and though this attitude had cost him in the past, he never abandoned it. He selected five hundred of his most dependable soldiers and out of them fashioned a corps of rowers (*bogabantes*), who received training in swimming, grappling, boarding, and gymnastics. They were given no muskets, however, and had to mount a complicated attack with sabers and hand grenades.[3]

The Río Paraguay reaches flood stage in mid-summer, and with the heavy flow of water comes *camalotes*—floating islets of brush, vines, and water hyacinths that combine into single entities with the clay that tumbles from the riverbanks. Camalotes provided an abode for ghosts in Guaraní mythology, and, in fact, are sometimes large enough to furnish involuntary refuge to capybaras. For an attacking force of canoes they could provide excellent camouflage, especially at night.

The ironclads *Cabral* and *Lima Barros* were moored below Humaitá at an anchorage that during daylight hours afforded an impressive view of the fortress and its batteries. Their position had kept them safe from the enemy guns, but as it always paid to take double precautions, Admiral Ignácio ordered guard boats to remain a hundred yards upstream to raise the alarm if need be.

The first attempt at seizing an ironclad came during the late evening of 1 March 1868, when a complement of Paraguayan canoes, in an attempt to scale the enemy ships, ran into each other in the darkness, causing a general pandemonium. The bogabantes apparently believed that the Brazilian guard boats were upon them and they tried to swim away. Meanwhile, several other canoes missed their target altogether and the current swept them toward Cerrito Island. At least one other canoe accidentally fell into a whirlpool, which forced its bogabantes to jump overboard and make for shore. Several men drowned in the effort.

The second attempt at capturing an ironclad brought a bloody encounter. On 2 March, at two in the morning, a Brazilian midshipman aboard one of the guard boats scratched the sleep from his eyes and noticed a large camalote drifting toward the anchored vessels. The darkness made it impossible to make out any details, but he soon noticed that it was not one but many camalotes bunched together—a phenomenon unusual enough to merit further attention. Then his jaw dropped, for coming from behind the vegetation was the movement of oars. Though he could still discern no sound above the rolling vibration of the river, he at once recognized the danger. Together with the crew of the guard boat, he rowed for dear life, and, as he approached the *Lima Barros*, shouted that the river had come alive with Paraguayans.

There were almost three hundred bogabantes, twelve men in each of the twenty-four canoes and a number of officers, all ready for the fight. Captain José Tomás Céspedes, a cavalryman from Pilar and perhaps the best swimmer in the Paraguayan army, had been assigned the position just behind the vanguard of the attacking force. According to plan, the canoes were tethered two by two with ropes sixty feet in length. In floating downstream from the fortress, he steered the paired boats so skillfully that the center of the connecting ropes struck the bows, first of the *Lima Barros*, and then of the *Cabral*.[4]

Up to this point, the Paraguayans enjoyed total surprise. The Brazilian midshipman had given his loud alarm, but the sailors aboard the *Lima Barros* only grasped what was happening when the enemy boarders swarmed on deck. It was still pitch black, and both officers and ratings had been sleeping topside to escape the heat of the interior quarters. The groggy sailors awoke only at the last moment; the Marshal's men killed the guards and hacked their way toward the tower, finally bringing fire from those officers who had drawn pistols.

The commander of the imperial squadron, Commodore Joaquím Rodrígues da Costa, rose half-dressed from his quarters amidst the turmoil, strapped on a sword, and rushed to join the sailors at the opposite side of the ship. He "fought furiously for his life but was overpowered and sank under the saber strokes of the enraged Paraguayans."[5] Captain Aurelio Garcindo Fernando da Sá, commander of the *Lima Barros* and a veteran of the battle of the Riachuelo, had better luck; a small man, he wiggled through a porthole into the ship's tower, but took a severe saber cut on his left shoulder even so.[6] Garcindo may have been the last man to get into the inner recesses of the ship before the mates fastened the hatchways against further intrusions. As for the officers and crew of the *Cabral*, they managed to reach safety within their own casement before the bogabantes commenced their murderous work topside.

The page then turned abruptly. On both ships, the Paraguayans rushed from one end of the deck to the other, vainly striking their sabers at the iron doors, setting off sparks but failing to break into the interior of either vessel. The Paraguayans dropped grenades down smokestacks, but only a few went off. The damage caused was minimal.

The Brazilians had recovered from their shock by now. They poured pistol and musket fire into the mobs of Paraguayans from behind the iron plating of the casements, resulting in much confusion among the bogabantes. Once the ships' captains in the imperial squadron saw what happened, they steamed forward, with the *Silvado* the first to intervene. In spite of the dimness and the danger of collision with his own ships, her skipper steered his ironclad between the *Cabral* and the *Lima Barros*, letting loose a withering volley of grape in both directions. The effects were horrible and immediate, with scores of lacerated Paraguayans dropping as if in clumps. A burnished moon had just started to peek above the eastern horizon, and its soft light illuminated the bloody panorama as Brazilian gunners reloaded and fired again.[7] Soon, several other Brazilian vessels steamed forward to add their fire to the *Silvado's*.

Mutilated corpses lay twisted upon the decks of the two ironclads. Céspedes was captured along with fifteen other Paraguayans, all severely wounded.[8] Those who sought to save themselves by swimming ashore were chased by the Brazilians and killed as they swam.[9] Though offered quarter, no more than a handful of the bogabantes accepted. The rest died gasping for air and spitting curses at the enemy. One captain lost an eye in the encounter, and was pulled from the river at the last moment by a burly sergeant of his own regiment. He woke in hospital, where medical orderlies counted sixty-one wounds on his body.[10]

Thirty-two Paraguayan bodies lay on the deck of the *Cabral* and another seventy-eight on the *Lima Barros*. A further fifty of the Marshal's men lost their lives in the water, and something like seventy imperial marines and sailors perished.[11] Downriver, in Buenos Aires, Mitre reflected on the slavish devotion of the Paraguayans and allowed himself a little contempt for his own people: "If we Argentines had done something so absurd, people would say that we [the government] had wasted the lives of our soldiers or that we were fools and our men were oxen being led to the slaughter; but … [our people] have no words to express their admiration for the heroism of the Paraguayans and the energy of López—look how our great people have fallen to this state of moral cowardice."[12]

A Retreat Through the Wilderness

Thus ended the Marshal's foolhardy attempt to change the military equation on the river. On 3 March 1868, he left the bulk of his army at Humaitá, and, with his guard units and staff, decamped to Timbó by way of the swollen Río Paraguay.[13] The presidential party began a rapid withdrawal through one narrow corner of the Chaco. The Marshal had an idea to turn several thousand previous evacuees into a new army further north, but first he had to reach the camp at Monte Lindo. From there, he could traverse the main river channel to the mouth of the Tebicuary, the logical place to anchor his line and check the Allied advance.

The Chaco is an intimidating place. To this day, travelers often comment on the inviting softness of the woods in eastern Paraguay, which seem to promise a tranquil respite from strenuous rambles. By contrast, the sun-besieged foliage of the Chaco offers a witch's brew of color and sound that continually assaults the senses. The proof of man's passing gets obscured in nature's excess, in which the struggle for existence seems to play itself out at a frenzied pace.

Here the vegetation appears sinister or callous. Vines strangle the boughs of hardwood trees, which grasp desperately for sunlight. Jaguars creep silently through the brush, and pounce in a flash upon their prey. Millions of termites and leaf-cutting ants lay waste to every inch of exposed ground, and the air swarms with flying insects, whose buzzing signals a lustful or violent intention. Even the white or blue-gray herons, who against the verdant background appear so stately, are in fact the ruthless killers of fish.

In such a setting, the soldiers could easily grow aware of their smallness, even those stationed in the tiny *puestos* that the Paraguayan government had maintained there since the time of the elder López. To make the passage to the Tebicuary, the Marshal had to depend on these men as guides along the trails northward. The main route, which the army had recently hacked out of the bush, led through swamps and irregular lowlands, the latter dotted with scrubby yataí palms and low-lying brush with thorns as long and sharp as penknives.

Oxcarts and contingents of men on horseback had moved up and down these paths over the preceding months—even Madame Lynch and the López children had already traversed this section of the Chaco. But it was one thing for a small party on horseback to ride across the wilderness, quite another to ferry heavy artillery pieces through the mud, as the Marshal now demanded. A brass 6-pounder weighs at least 5 hundredweight, and the prospect of pulling it to the riverside and onto a launch, then dragging it once again through the muck of the Chaco, was hardly attractive. Getting the guns to Monte Lindo required gut-wrenching labor from malnourished soldiers who had few mules and oxen to aid them.

The Allied ironclads kept their distance. This allowed the two Paraguayan steamers that had earlier escaped to Humaitá to finish transporting troops, field pieces, and the Marshal's private stores to Timbó. The Whitworth 32-pounder went first, then the Krupp 12-pounder. Eight 8-inch guns followed directly thereafter, leaving all the incapacitated and wounded soldiers for the final transit.

Thompson had gone ahead some days earlier to scout the best approaches to the Tebicuary and had reported the numerous streams and deep water that disrupted the line of march. He recommended that the army erect a battery at Monte Lindo to fend off the Allied ironclads, which otherwise would have free run of the river. If he could build batteries at the mouth of the Tebicuary, a far better defense would result—though this task, he emphasized, might take several days.[14]

The Marshal considered this suggestion. Unlike his men, who seemed hesitant about the adventure awaiting them in the Chaco, López radiated nervous energy. He could appreciate how vulnerable his overall position was, but this was not his main concern; he had grown visibly tired of the long siege at Humaitá—almost as tired as his opponents. He now contemplated a more mobile resistance.

The Marshal affected an affable, self-assured manner while on the march. He rode well in advance of his wagons, and, belying his usual timidity, almost dared the Chaco to make a stab at him. He had eaten well on fresh beef and was mounted on the best available steed. Putting on a good show before his bronze-helmeted Acá-Verá guards came naturally to him, and this time they responded with good humor as they finished the most difficult labors without complaint.[15]

While their buoyant display was essentially theater, the Marshal really was composed, even optimistic, in his conversations with his soldiers, and as frequently happened on such occasions, his Guaraní proved steady, colloquial, and reassuring. This was no mean feat, for not every commander can ingratiate himself with men for whom he feels contempt. Wellington could not do it in Spain and Lord Raglan could not do it in the Crimea. But Juan Manuel de Rosas could do it in 1840s Argentina, and for the same reason as López in Paraguay: both needed the obedience of the common soldiers if they hoped to continue fighting.

As the Marshal rode through the wilderness, his thoughts almost certainly fell back on those men who had supposedly challenged his instructions or otherwise sullied the national cause. He still raged at the kambáes, whose insults he intended to avenge. Yet he now nursed an even greater disgust for Sánchez and the other notables of Asunción, whose performance at the time of Delphim's raid had been pusillanimous, insubordinate, and, in the case of Benigno López, perhaps even treasonable. Had he not told Venancio to deal sternly with defeat-ists and traitors?[16] He would punish those laggards when the time was right, and neither Benigno nor Venancio would be exempt.

Meanwhile, the Marshal disregarded those who followed him in the train. The sick and wounded may have grown accustomed to rough or indifferent treatment, for they never uttered a sour comment.[17] Members of the staff, how-ever, expected at least some show of consideration, for Paraguay's continued existence depended on their skill and fortitude. And yet the Marshal ignored them. The wagon wheels broke, the horses grew feeble and stumbled, men be-came stomach-sick and dehydrated. The wind brought them a whiff of the stag-nant lagoons that guttered the land to the north. No one could avoid the mud, the snakes, the biting gnats, and every sort of nocturnal insect. Throughout it all, López kept his eyes peeled on the trail ahead, his jaw clenched.

On the first day out, the Marshal halted briefly at a site where the bulrushes and sarandí gave way to open space. Instead of the gala uniform he used at Paso Pucú, he now wore civilian dress—a gray poncho and straw hat.[18] At this desolate spot, with the forest all around him, he doffed the hat, dismounted and composed a message for the units still at Humaitá. Taking the opportunity both to reward and to inspire, he promoted a favorite aide-de-camp, Francisco Martínez, to full colonel and gave him joint command, together with Paulino Alén, over the beleaguered garrison of three thousand men, surely the most miserable soldiers at the front.[19]

Remigio Cabral and Pedro Gill, both naval captains, also received orders to remain behind as lieutenant colonels, third and fourth in command at the fortress.[20] How they were expected to defend a position that Caxias had caught in a pincer, no one could say. But López seemed to believe that his words would suffice to strengthen the mettle of his officers. He forbade them from negoti-ating with enemy officers, or receiving delegations under a flag of truce. They were to continue to launch river mines to harass the enemy and wait until all the remaining provisions were exhausted before slipping away to the Chaco in perhaps six months' time. The word "surrender" was never to be uttered.[21]

The Marshal himself needed to move along. He took the opportunity to send word to his engineers to begin constructing the Monte Lindo battery. Where there had been one Humaitá, there could still be another, and with this idea in mind, he dug his spurs into his animal, and rode into the Chaco with his guards and closest associates following behind.

The trek across the region, which a Jesuit missionary had once described as "a theater of misery for the Spaniards," was inescapably complicated for anyone with a soft body. In Thompson's telling, it required several days of heavy exer-tion during which the skills of the troopers were very much in evidence:

We had had to pass several deep lagoons, over some of which bridges were begun, but not yet finished. Some of these bridges were made by throwing quantities of brushwood upon beams laid in the water, and were intended, when sufficiently high, to be covered with sods. … We had then to cross the Bermejo, a torturous river with very red water, caused by the red clay through which it flows. … [The passage was accomplished] by means of canoes, swimming three horses on each side of a canoe, and then [riding] slowly up a hill through the woods, till we reached the general level of the Chaco. … We now had to ride through a league of wood, in mud three feet deep. … [The next day we] went through some leagues of bamboo forest, after which we crossed the Paso Ramírez in canoes, and had dinner there, feeding our horses with the leaves of the "pindó," a tall palm without thorns. … After dinner we went on to Monte Lindo, which we reached by dark. Here most of us found a roof to sleep under.[22]

The Marshal's guides led him through the Chaco without serious incident. Soon thereafter, he passed back over the Paraguay River and took up a position on the left bank just behind the Tebicuary, where he met many men—von Versen indicates twelve thousand—who had already withdrawn along the same route.[23] It turned out that instead of feeling crushed by the running of his key batteries and by the raid on Asunción, López had found a way to evacuate the greater part of his army. Let Caxias and Ignácio celebrate their achievements; he could now crow at their folly for underestimating him.

The Allies Follow

López guessed right when he assumed that Caxias would allow him time to complete the works. Thompson had initially thought otherwise, and for several days neither he nor the work parties under his command got any sleep; they journeyed several miles into the eastern forests to cut wood for gun platforms and ferry the heavy planking back to the river. They also erected a battery of four 8-inch guns raised en barbette three feet above the foxtail grass of an island near the Chaco bank. They optimistically christened this little spot "Fortín."[24]

A battalion of three hundred men and boys from Monte Lindo received orders to garrison the island to shield the gunners from any incursion. Three or four imperial warships did steam by some days later and fired on these positions, but the Paraguayans had already completed the main work, and the bombardment produced no result. Either Allied marksmanship remained poor, or the ironclads intended nothing more than normal harassment.

Meanwhile, using a design provided by Thompson, the Paraguayans constructed a series of minor works and dugouts on the eastern bank near the mouth of the Tebicuary. These they reinforced with additional batteries at two nearby positions. The British engineer and his men also erected a separate battery facing the Tebicuary proper, just in case the Allies should attempt a landing there. The Marshal understood that the Allies could not hope to outflank him on the east, as Caxias had done the previous July, for deep swamps more than a league wide enclosed the perimeter of the Tebicuary. Similar conditions prevailed on both banks of the river for thirty miles upstream. If the new defenses were properly arranged, therefore, they might yet keep the Allies back no matter what might happen at Humaitá.

As the batteries assumed their final form, the Marshal divided his time between Monte Lindo (which he soon vacated), a secondary camp at Seibo (also on the Chaco side), and his new headquarters at San Fernando. The latter site, which served as the army's main depot and nerve center for the next several months, was built on a dry outcropping just up the Tebicuary from its confluence with the main river. At first the troops had to set up their tents and wagons in the midst of the mud, but the ground was quickly drained, and soon San Fernando became a well-ordered community.[25] Like Paso Pucú, the new camp was comfortably distant from naval gunfire. It boasted a little octagonal chapel, a series of huts for the use of senior personnel, and unimpeded telegraphic communication with Asunción. Spacious quarters for López and Madame Lynch were built at the center of the camp, as well as barracks for common soldiers and a separate "district" for camp followers and female relatives.

Two steamers aided in supplying the needs of the newly established garrison of around eight thousand men.[26] The printing presses for *Cabichuí* were reestablished at the camp, and by mid-May, the Marshal's advocates were once again calling in print for further sacrifices, swathing the war's most bitter realities in the old bandages of delusion.[27] More important still, San Fernando also boasted a workshop for the repair of rifles and manufacture of cartridges, which, given the scarcity of paper, the Paraguayans now formed from the inner membrane of tanned hide.[28] The results proved less than encouraging, but the soldiers had made do before.

Caxias might well have thought the Paraguayans finished. The attrition that he had planned for Humaitá had already sapped their strength, and though he lacked information on how many had already escaped through the Chaco, he felt sure that the number was minimal; common sense suggested that he continue to apply pressure against the fortress and destroy the other enemy positions in due course. On 21 March, therefore, the Marquis launched a series of coordinated attacks against the southern perimeter of Humaitá, with General Argolo storming the trenches at Sauce, Osório emerging from Parecué and hitting the far left of the Paraguayan line at Espinillo, and Gelly y Obes making a minor feint on the right at "the Angle."

With so few Paraguayan troops guarding these positions, the Marshal could only manage a cursory resistance. The Brazilians had almost overwhelmed Espinillo, "sending shot, shell, and Congreve rockets with a right good will, taking in their turn a seemingly well-sustained cannonading and musketry."[29] Then, inexplicably, an Allied bugle sounded retreat. This brought a momentary respite for the overtaxed Paraguayans, but still they could not hold.

The chief complaint of the Argentines during the day's combat was that the marquis had failed to seize the opposite trenches, which would have been child's play. The irritation they showed at this lost opportunity was understandable. Though Caxias appreciated the Argentine soldiers well enough, he saw no need for their help in securing the Cuadrilátero.[30] By Thompson's reckoning, the Allies lost some two hundred sixty men that day, the Paraguayans an improbable twenty.[31]

On 22 March, the remaining Paraguayan units left behind the whole of their old works and, dragging their guns with them, withdrew into the fortress. When the Allies ventured into Curupayty a few hours later they were shocked to discover "a battery composed of forty sham guns made of the trunks of palm trees, covered with hides and mounted on old cart wheels" while "the troops in garrison consisted of some thirty to forty effigies, made of straw stuffed into hides, who were placed as sentinels in such positions as to be visible to the storming party."[32] The Paraguayans had departed Curupayty weeks earlier.

On 23 March, in an effort to correct a previous strategic weakness on the river, three of Ignácio's warships descended below the batteries at Timbó, and started to set up an anchorage between that site and Humaitá. Before they could drop anchor, however, Allied sailors spotted the *Ygureí* hidden behind an inlet and gave chase. The Paraguayan steamer, which had done good work in the evacuation of Tayí, had nowhere to go this time and started taking a great many hits. A 70-pound shot from the monitor *Rio Grande* struck the *Ygureí* below the water line soon thereafter, and in two or three hours she sank in deep water. Her crew survived by swimming to the Chaco bank.[33]

Meanwhile, the Brazilians had also caught sight of the *Tacuarí*, which they discovered while her crewmembers unloaded artillery pieces along a western tributary. On this occasion, the ironclad *Bahia* blocked the smaller channel, and, aided by the *Pará*, opened fire at the cornered enemy. The Marshal's sailors barely managed to get their last guns onto dry land as enemy shells riddled the vessel. Seeing no way out, the Paraguayans opened the main valves, and watched from the high grass of the Chaco bank as the *Tacuarí* sank. Her smokestack was still visible at low water three decades later.[34]

The crew of the onetime Paraguayan flagship fled into the Chaco and an uncertain future, leaving the Brazilians to savor their victory. The moment for satisfaction came a few hours later, when Admiral Ignácio's ships returned to the previously designated position between Timbó and the fortress. From this point, they could cut the communication, making it difficult—though even now not quite impossible—for the remaining members of the garrison to escape by the route that López had already taken.

The men at the fortress had to move fast. At eleven o'clock that same night, General Vicente Barrios ordered his men to drive the remaining horses at Humaitá across the river, and he himself followed with the members of his staff in canoes. It was a moonless night and the general chose to ride northward, parallel to the riverbank, approaching Timbó along a direct route. Centurión, who had returned to Humaitá from Paso Pucú a day or two earlier, explained that this route took the troop through the muddiest ground of the whole sector:

> We left at one in the morning and followed the riverside trail, [where the] mud was deep and sticky, and the horses had to make extraordinary efforts to get through, for their hooves stuck fast, and made that peculiar popping sound as they tried to pull them free. We spent the day in getting through the back-swamp along the riverbank right in front of an ironclad that anchored in the near distance. To make matters worse, the mule that carried the staff baggage fell into the mud, and as we tried to get her up, the ironclad grew aware of our presence and started to fire. Thankfully there were no [losses] save for an adjutant of Barrios, who was wounded. We arrived at Timbó at 5 in the afternoon, with our feet full of blisters and splinters. [This was due to the fact] that we had dismounted at Barrios's orders half-way through our journey in order to rest the animals, and had completed the trek on foot.[35]

At Timbó, Colonel Caballero assembled the last units that had gotten across the river before the final domino fell. During the previous months, ten to twelve thousand men had succeeded in retreating from Humaitá, a figure that had to embarrass the Allies. Most of the Paraguayans had gone on to Seibo and San Fernando, but some three thousand men had stayed behind with Caballero. Now, as the withdrawal came to an end, Generals Bruguéz and Resquín slipped through, arriving on 26 and 27 March, respectively.[36]

That any men got through at all brought scant credit to Caxias. As overall Allied commander, the marquis worked with unwavering dedication: he held conferences with subordinates; he rode all over the various camps making inspections and jotting down details for later consideration; and he did his best to increase discipline among both officers and men.[37] When he was wrong, however, his army paid the price. In this case, the Paraguayans got away clean, and had taken many of their heavy guns with them. Despite all their material advantages and good leadership, the Allies had gotten no further than Tayí. It proved that the Paraguayan fighting man could still count on a few resources—most notably, his perseverance.[38]

The Fist Begins to Close

The Allies first became aware of the Marshal's escape on 11 March, but they dismissed the news as unsubstantiated until two weeks had gone by.[39] It took them even longer to determine how many troops and artillery had fled northward along the same route.

It was not an easy position for the marquis, but though he lacked absolute knowledge of what lay ahead, he reacted firmly. Seeking to test what was left of Humaitá's defenses, he gave orders to bombard the fortress, and both naval guns and land-based artillery opened daily barrages throughout April.[40] More importantly, Caxias abandoned the old camps at San Solano and Tuyutí and advanced closer to the fortress. He moved the entire Brazilian 2nd Corps to Curupayty, and the 3rd Corps, part of the 1st Corps, and the remaining Uruguayan forces to Parecué opposite the Paraguayan left flank. The Argentines assumed the center position between these new points.

Meanwhile, Allied officers and various independent observers poured over López's former headquarters at Paso Pucú, and were puzzled when they saw what a ramshackle place it was. As the correspondent for *The Standard* sarcastically observed, there was much "wealth" in "the mock cannons of palms mounted on four sticks and covered with hides and the sentinels and guards of straw—what a rich store of relics … in the ranchos of López and his satellites, what a variety of utensils of 'cuero,' even vesture pantaloons cut after the true Parisian fashion of the hide of an ox."[41] Richard Burton, who visited the site five months later, was similarly unimpressed. In noting the evident leveling of the bomb-proof "bunker" that Thompson had prepared as a hideaway for the Marshal, he hinted that it had never existed.[42]

Such discoveries illustrated a disturbing tendency. Simply put, the Paraguayan camps had never been as strong as rumor held. Allied newspapers had never tired of depicting Humaitá as colossal and invulnerable, and they repeated this so often that the Brazilian and Argentine soldiers at the front tended to believe the tale. This would not be the first time that Allied planners had exaggerated the enemy's strength, but the true assets at Paso Pucú made them seem the dupes of their own hyperbole. Perhaps the "barbaric" Marshal López, with his false artillery pieces and nonexistent bunkers, had had the last laugh after all.

Caxias could bristle at the implication that the Paraguayans had fooled him and his officers, but he could also feel reassured that Allied strategy was still working according to his plan. The Marshal's withdrawal meant that Humaitá would soon fall, and though the Allies had made mistakes, they were inconsequential ones; the Paraguayan garrison remained encircled, and the new defenses that López had constructed to the north could never withstand the concerted force that the marquis intended to throw at them.[43]

As the Marshal set up his new batteries at the Tebicuary, he left the Humaitá garrison to its own devices. The scene was not reassuring. What could the two to three thousand men under Alén and Martínez do against the forty thousand soldiers arrayed against them? The Allies also had ironclads, fifty other warships, and hundreds of guns on both land and river. The Paraguayans had no hope of defending the fifteen thousand yards of trenches that surrounded the fortress. Fodder for the few remaining animals was almost nonexistent and powder and provisions could only be introduced at great risk by rafts coming from the Chaco under the full view of the enemy fleet.[44]

Even this slender reed soon withered. In mid-April, the marquis learned that though his land and naval forces had already closed the main supply routes to the fortress, the Paraguayans still retained a line of communication with it from the north.[45] This he attempted to terminate by dispatching the Uruguayan-born Ignacio Rivas, now an Argentine general, to find this trail at the beginning of May and interdict any supplies coming down from Timbó. Should any Paraguayan units choose to engage the Allied force in that isolated location, so much the better: Rivas could destroy them then and there.

The general, well attired in his *vicuña*-lined poncho and imported riding boots, arrived well south of Timbó on 2 May. The 2,000 men who accompanied him chopped their way through the brush over two days and two nights. In the midst of this labor, one battalion (composed of European recruits) was attacked and decimated before reinforcements could arrive.[46] Despite this setback, the Argentines pushed ahead and made contact with imperial units, also 2,000 strong, who had disembarked under fire some miles to the north. Men from several different Paraguayan battalions tried without success to drive this combined force back to the edge of the river. The Brazilians suffered 137 *hors de combat*, the Argentines 188, and the Paraguayans 105.[47] While Allied casualties were hardly insignificant, Caxias could always replace his losses—something the Paraguayans could not do.

Rivas sent out pickets to locate the trail that Caxias had sought. The muddy track over which Barrios had passed had indeed seen supplies transported to the fortress; this, it turned out, was the last link. The rutted "road" ran along a muddy ridge, three hundred yards wide, which bordered the Río Paraguay for four miles. On its western side, an extensive lagoon known as the Verá (or Ycuasy-y) faced the Chaco wilderness.

Rivas established himself atop the ridge at a spot called Andaí, located about halfway between Timbó and Humaitá. He destroyed the telegraph line he found there then fortified the position.[48] If the Paraguayans still hoped to save the fortress at this stage, Caballero needed to dislodge the Allied troops and re-open the trail. Recognizing the desperation of his countrymen to the south, the Paraguayan colonel decided to strike. Most senior officers in the Paraguayan army never received sufficient or clear operational orders, nor the freedom to act independently in unexpected circumstances, but Caballero enjoyed the Marshal's confidence.

Such freedom of action usually worked well for him—but not on this occasion. At dawn on 5 May, four battalions of infantry and two regiments of dismounted cavalry (around three thousand men) fell upon the Brazilians with saber and lance. The Paraguayans managed to penetrate the nearest abatis, but got no further before a devastating Allied fire started to take its toll. The Allies drove back the Marshal's men after about an hour and a half. A column of cavalry that Caballero had deployed as a reserve also came under fire and had to turn to retreat alongside the river, where it came under an unexpected and withering fire from the ironclads. Throughout the engagement, the fighting never varied in its intensity, and Rivas and the Brazilian officers soon had the situation well in hand. The Paraguayans lost at least three hundred men, the Brazilians fifty. The Argentines, who were somewhat distant on the left flank, suffered no losses.[49]

On the morning of 8 May, six battalions of Allied infantry made contact with the Paraguayan vanguard coming from Timbó. Though the Brazilians enjoyed cover fire from the fleet, the Paraguayans nevertheless put them to flight before retiring unscathed.[50] In truth, as with so many of the victories that the Marshal gloated about, this was an ephemeral business; no one present could question that Rivas's position had grown unassailable. Worse still for López, the Allies soon came upon a channel that linked the Verá with the Río Paraguay and by which the Argentine general could supply his division with artillery, ammunition, provisions, and above all, reinforcements. Caballero could do nothing to slow this process, and even the Paraguayan sharpshooters kept their distance.

When told of the day's events, the Marshal hastened from the safety of San Fernando to praise his loyal officers. He recommended that the wounded be evacuated as soon as practical and that his troops begin a series of ambushes to keep the enemy from consolidating his position. It was already too late for such harassment to have much effect, but over the next several weeks López sent multiple suggestions to Caballero. None of these stood any chance of successful execution.[51] The river and the lagoon prevented a flank movement and, for want of sufficient men, the colonel could not venture a frontal attack along the ridge.

Is there Hope?

The campaign had not gone as Caxias had envisioned. The quarrels over command that had plagued Allied cohesion before 1868 were no longer a factor, nor were there any shortages in manpower and supplies; the marquis's field officers enjoyed excellent dispositions on land; the fleet was positioned to provide more than adequate support. With all of these strengths, much was expected of him, and now that he enjoyed sole authority, he expected much of himself. And yet, the Paraguayans had frustrated every officer, and for all of his talent, Caxias had to deal with a great many aggravations and disappointments, some of them of his own making.

On 6 June, the marquis dispatched General João Manoel Mena Barreto from Tayí to reconnoiter and possibly destroy the Marshal's new batteries at the south of the Tebicuary.[52] The expeditionary force consisted of two brigades of National Guardsmen, four light cannons, and four hundred Argentines, for a total of fifteen hundred men on horseback, ready and able to do much more than conduct a reconnaissance in force.[53]

João Manoel still lacked adequate intelligence as to what lay ahead. He started off by keeping to the margin of the Ñe'embucu, bypassing Pilar, which the Paraguayans had by this time abandoned. Commodore Delphim's warships had already started to pound these positions at the Tebicuary, but given the seeming sophistication of the works that Thompson had prepared, the Brazilians could not guarantee the success of their gunnery. João Manoel, unlike Mitre at Curupayty, decided to postpone his advance for twenty-four hours just to make sure. The next day, thanks to the enfilading fire from the ironclads, he pushed ahead and cleared the riverfront of enemy pickets.[54] He advanced as far as the Yacaré creek, a tributary of the Tebicuary that bore the Guaraní name for caimans.

Pleased with his progress, the general dispatched several cavalry units across the river, whose opposite bank was thought to be undefended. Once they gained the far side, however, the Brazilian horsemen found themselves ambushed by a smaller—though more desperate—Paraguayan force of two hundred. Despite orders to penetrate further north, the surprised guardsmen whirled about in headlong retreat toward the Yacaré.[55]

Mena Barreto had some problem in recomposing his troop, but once this was accomplished, he withdrew to Tayí rather than face a force of uncertain size. The general had completed enough of his reconnaissance in any case.[56] His withdrawal left the Paraguayans laughing, after a fashion. *Cabichuí* offered its customary acclaim for the Marshal's leadership and sarcasm for the Brazilian antics; it dismissed the foray as yet another proof of *macaco* ineptitude in the service "of that gold and green slavocrat rag."[57]

Always inclined toward dramatic gestures whenever simple persistence seemed inadequate, the Marshal then chose to mount another canoe attack against the enemy ironclads. Having supposedly learned from the bitter experience of March, the survivors among the bogabantes expressed enthusiasm for the project, which López scheduled for July. This time the Paraguayans targeted the ships of the Tayí flotilla, the *Barroso* and the *Rio Grande*—two of the three vessels that had struck Asunción. If either or both of these vessels fell into their hands, it might still change the balance in river operations, or at least permit López to organize further evacuations from Humaitá.

This time, however, the Allies gained advance warning of the operation. A Paraguayan prisoner of war had revealed the essence of the plan, noting that the Marshal had been preparing a new unit of bogabantes to replace the men lost in March and that these rowers would soon be ready to assault the Allied warships at Tayí. The Brazilian commanders were determined not to be surprised like the sailors of the *Lima Barros*. Though the men of the flotilla might have assumed a complacent air while in their accustomed anchorage, in fact they were preparing for the new engagement.

The Paraguayans had planned their venture well. They had hidden twenty-four canoes, disguised as camalotes, in the backswamp at the mouth of the Bermejo. Each canoe carried ten bogabantes, one or two officers, and a number of engineers to operate any captured ships. As before, the men carried sabers and revolvers. And to assuage those who still felt uncertain, the engineers revealed a new type of hand grenade together with "metal tubes filled with a flammable, asphyxiant material" to wedge into the enemy casements if necessary.[58]

Sadly for the Marshal's bogabantes, their attack failed in exactly the same way as the earlier effort. The night chosen for the assault—9 July—was as dark as coal—a fact that seemed to portend good things for the rowers as they set out upon the Paraguay around 11:00 p.m., paddling south from the river's confluence with the Tebicuary. However, things went wrong immediately. The twelve canoes intended for the assault on the *Barroso* only approached the Brazilian ship, whose forewarned crewmembers let loose a blast or two of musketry as the bogabantes went past. That contingent of rowers at least escaped with their lives; the nighttime obscurity hid them from pursuit, and they spent the next day pulling their wounded comrades from the shallows at the Chaco bank of the river.

The bogabantes who struck at the *Rio Grande* had had a terrible go of it. At the outset, they boasted better luck than their fellows and succeeded in boarding the monitor largely unopposed. Then, their sabers drawn, the Paraguayans cut down both captain and crew as enemy sailors rushed on deck.[59] Those Brazilians who survived the initial attack shut themselves into the heavy casement, and just as had happened in March, the Paraguayans could find no way to pry open the hatch with sabers.

The *Barroso* then assumed the role of the *Silvado*, steaming alongside her sister ship and firing salvoes at the hapless Paraguayans on deck. The shouts of anger, irritation, and fear were drowned out by the thunderous report of the guns and the ricochet of shrapnel hitting metal. Almost all the bogabantes were killed or wounded within minutes. The luckiest among them succeeded in diving into the Paraguay, but few managed to reach the Chaco bank. Centurión, who was in Seibo or San Fernando at the time, provided the most succinct evaluation of the episode, which he condemned as a "sterile sacrifice of lives that would have been better saved for a more worthy enterprise."[60]

In spite of the Marshal's boasts, the death of his bogabantes represented just a minor part of a much wider Paraguayan defense, one focused on the broader objective of containing the Allied threat. This was increasingly difficult. At Humaitá, continued resistance had now become impossible, desertions were on the rise, and Paulino Alén had grown despondent. The end of the Humaitá campaign was not far off.[61]

A short man with thin eyebrows and a dark visage, Colonel Alén resembled the Marshal in appearance and bearing, but could never summon up his master's confidence. He could not hold as López had ordered, and yet his sense of duty prevented him from striking his colors. The Allies sent him numerous petitions begging him to capitulate for the sake of his family, but these were spurned. On one occasion, he responded to the marquis's offer of money and high rank by sarcastically lamenting his own inability to award gold; if the Allied commander would instead deliver up his own army, then Alén, with the Marshal's permission, was willing to promise Caxias the imperial crown of Brazil.[62] Such cheek might have felt reassuring, but it could not fill stomachs. The stores of food were nearly exhausted, and no hope of rescue existed from any direction. Worn-out, hungry, with the whole world against them, the men of Humaitá awaited the final challenge.

On 12 July, Alén, in a "fit of total despair," took a last cheroot from his mouth and reached across his table for a pair of revolvers. His orderlies came running at the sound of two discharges and found him on the hard-earth floor of his headquarters with blood gushing from his head and gut. Most of those present could sympathize with his attempted suicide, but the two wounds were not mortal; they left him incapacitated and subjected to intense agony.[63] Alén later had to endure still greater pain at an inquisition that the Marshal convened at San Fernando to judge the colonel's "treachery." Meanwhile, Colonel Francisco Martínez succeeded to full command at the fortress. But like Alén, he had no idea of what to do next.

In the Chaco, Caballero had been eyeing the Allied positions just to the south of Timbó. Though he dismissed any possibility of retaking the main camp at Andaí, he nonetheless refused to consider his situation hopeless. Above all, he needed to keep harassing Rivas, who even now might waver. The Paraguayan colonel might have been deluded, but he could feel happy that the bombardments from Humaitá against the Allied troops in the Chaco had continued.

The Allied army was growing stronger every day, and yet the Marshal's men continued with their show of impudence. One moving example came on the night of 14 July, when Martínez sent a messenger to swim the river with a note to remind López that while Caxias had surrounded the fortress, its garrison remained defiant, ready to carry out his orders.[64] Every man at Humaitá knew that a messenger stood no chance of getting through the Allied lines near Andaí, yet there was no dearth of volunteers for the assignment. What happened next was poignant in the extreme:

> After crossing the river, [the messenger] had to skirt along and partly ... cross a laguna ... at the upper end of which were stationed three Brazilian sentinels. ... It was two in the morning and, July being the middle of winter ... the position of these sentinels was not an enviable one. The shadow of a man was seen gliding by, but perfectly noiselessly. The usual [recognition sign] elicited no reply. All three simultaneously fired. Not a sound ensued; no cry, no groan; no splash in the water, or noise of anything falling. ... When morning dawned they saw at a distance of about twenty yards off, a dead Paraguayan, with his body half in the water and half on *tierra firme*. Going to examine it, they found the calf and thigh of one leg eaten off by a yacaré ... and that, although dead from a wound in his breast ... [the man still] held firmly clutched in his hand and pressed to his heart, the message of which he was the bearer. ... To the credit of the Brazilians, they buried him on the spot where he fell, and put a board over his grave with the simple inscription, "Here lies a brave man."[65]

Such displays filled the Allied soldiers with awe, and their officers with apprehension. They worried that, given the Paraguayans' unbending determination, only the most elaborate ruthlessness could beat them. Caxias hoped even now to buy López's submission, but he could not have felt too confident of success. All the Allied generals wished to punish the pathetic diehards at Humaitá and in the Chaco—and their fat master hiding away at San Fernando. It was his fault, after all, that the war went on, and he did not deserve the steadfast support of his men.

Generals eager to teach lessons frequently make mistakes. The Paraguayans speculated that Rivas might be coaxed into a blunder, and sought to tempt him with an easy target. Caballero had already established a line of tiny redoubts between Timbó and a site halfway down the ridge to Andaí. At this last position, which the Paraguayans called the Corã redoubt, the colonel deployed a single battalion of infantry that launched almost daily raids against the Allies.

As Caballero deduced, the apparent weakness of the Corã redoubt inflamed the ardor of the enemy commanders. By 18 July, Rivas had had enough of the constant provocations, and ordered the Rioja Battalion, forty or fifty skirmishers, and two Brazilian battalions to advance on the Paraguayans and drive back to Timbó. Caxias had already instructed Rivas to storm Corã. The Argentine general hesitated, however, thinking it preferable that his men not go beyond the temporary bridge that Caballero had recently erected at the redoubt.

Rivas was a gallant and reflective officer who had missed action since Curupayty, a battle in which he had been badly wounded.[66] On this occasion, he opted to stay behind with the main units at Andaí. He had not yet started out when he received word from the commander of the Riojanos, Colonel Miguel Martínez de Hoz, who had arrived at the point indicated and had already killed forty or fifty Paraguayans. The scion of one of the richest landowning families in Buenos Aires province, the colonel was an audacious and brave officer. Nonetheless, he probably should have waited for orders before moving; Rivas sent word that he was coming to his aid, but the colonel, it turned out, had advanced into a trap. When Rivas arrived, he discovered that saber-wielding Paraguayans had torn up the Argentine vanguard as soon as its men reached the abatis; the imperial units, who had fled, could not now cover a necessary retreat. The general sent word for the remaining troops to retire, but the message arrived too late.[67]

The Paraguayans pursued Rivas's units to the edge of Andaí, where the Argentine general obtained the support of two more battalions and succeeded in driving Caballero back, but only after a severe brawl. The color sergeant of the Argentine battalions received a fatal wound during the exchange of fire but saved his flags by throwing them into the river, where they were later retrieved by the Brazilian monitor *Pará*.[68]

Allied losses at this battle, called Acayuazá after the "tangled boughs" of the bush near Corã, amounted to at least four hundred Argentines killed and wounded.[69] Martínez de Hoz, whom the Bonaerenses had already lionized as "the most valiant of the valiant," had been deserted by his men and lay dead upon the field, his preferred Havana cigars still bulging from his pocket. His second-in-command, Lieutenant Colonel Gaspar Campos, was more fortunate in falling prisoner to Caballero's skirmishers, but afterwards suffered a terrible five months in chains, deprived of every human comfort, until he, too, succumbed.[70]

As for the Paraguayans, their losses were "hardly slight" according to *El Semanario*, and included at least nine junior officers and a large number of men.[71] The Marshal treated the limited tactical deception as a signal victory. The government issued—or at least planned to issue—a commemorative medal in the shape of a Maltese cross and emblazoned with the words "For Decisiveness and Bravery."[72] López promoted Caballero to general, and to the extent that the jefes políticos could still orchestrate them, festivities were observed all over unoccupied Paraguay. These celebrations proved bittersweet, for, as if to counterbalance any happy news coming from the Chaco, the news from Humaitá was very bad indeed.

The Fall Of Humaitá

Provisions at the fortress were almost exhausted and the garrison had no way to replenish them. Given this fact, Colonel Martínez understood that further resistance was useless—and yet he could not capitulate without orders. His previous instructions permitted the evacuation of only wounded and noncombatants, of whom some three hundred could still be found at Humaitá.[73] The Paraguayans held a tiny point of land on the Chaco bank opposite the fortress, and for several nights after 11 July, they ferried many people to it by canoe. The wounded Colonel Alén was among the first men evacuated. Whether any of them could get through Rivas's lines, Martínez had no way of knowing—but their movements on the river did not go unnoticed by the enemy ironclads, who reported to Caxias that the final evacuation had begun.

The marquis ordered an assault. The Humaitá garrison still counted two thousand men, and if they would not surrender, he would destroy them. At two in the afternoon on 15 July, Paraguayan pickets reported extensive troop movements along the line to San Solano, which pointed to the general attack that Martínez had long anticipated. Each company, battalion, and regiment hurried to its assigned place in the breastworks. With their thirty thousand men, the Allies could have carried the entire line, but the colonel expected them to limit the main attack to the northeast flank of his trenches. He ordered his remaining gunners to fire with round shot, saving the canister for the moment when the enemy forces penetrated his lines.

This guess—for such it was—proved correct. Rather than launch the assault with his entire army, Caxias assigned the honor of spearheading the attack to the Brazilian 3rd Corps alone. This placed the reluctant general Osório at the vanguard, together with his twelve thousand veterans, who, unlike their commander, were champing at the bit to be the first to violate the Marshal's sanctuary.[74]

The cavalry took the lead and encountered little opposition. The air at that moment had in it the perfume of Allied victory. As Albert Amerlan put it, with "bands playing and colors flying in the wind, the Brazilians advanced in magnificent style, as if on a parade ground, [growing] more confident of victory with every step—Humaitá was theirs; such were the thoughts which agitated the breasts of the attacking soldiers."[75]

Osório's troops had started to enter the second defensive line, when out of nowhere a hailstorm of Paraguayan canister and shrapnel hurled from the 68- and 32- pounders swept into their ranks. Martínez's gunners, who were not at all defeated, were firing point-blank into the enemy columns. The cannonade was so fierce, so unremitting, and so unexpected that Osório had no time to order a withdrawal.[76] He had two horses shot from underneath him, and as he struggled to mount a third, his men broke into a hasty flight. They left nearly two thousand comrades dead and wounded. The Marshal and his colonel alike must have taken satisfaction in this impressive repulsion of what had seemed an unstoppable advance.

Martínez could not afford to rest for very long, however, and he resolved to complete the evacuation quickly. On the night of 24 July, he began sending men across to the Chaco redoubt. He had thirty canoes available to ferry some twelve hundred men to the opposite bank within eight hours. Since this departure was expected by the Allies, and since three more Brazilian ironclads had by now forced the batteries at Humaitá, it was shocking, almost criminal, that no one took note of the many trips taken across the river.[77]

At sunrise the next day, Colonel Martínez fired a 21-gun salute to honor the Marshal's birthday—a clear indication that all was well within the fortress. In fact, he had ordered his military bands to occupy the forward trenches and play their martial music raucously as proof of the army's presence. While the music played, Martínez prepared the remaining members of the garrison to flee across the river. As had happened in previous years, the holiday was accompanied by dancing and revelries, and the Allies received no hint that it would be different this time. The music died down at midnight on 26 July, and there followed one last volley of muskets and loud cheers for López and the Paraguayan Republic. At five o'clock the next morning, after the guns had been spiked and rendered inoperable, the last man left Humaitá. [78]

Martínez and his entire force now occupied Isla Poí, a little spit of wooded land opposite the fortress. He still had to force a way through to Timbó, where Caballero was presumably waiting for him, but Rivas's units blocked his path and would be impervious in any case to a direct assault by such weakened troops. Martínez was determined to slip around the Allies by hauling up the canoes that he had left at the riverbank and using them to paddle to the northern limit of the Verá, which at that point was some two miles distant. Any movement across the lagoon would bring the canoe-borne troops under enemy fire, and after a few attempts to accomplish this transit during daylight brought only slaughter, Martínez concluded that any further attempts at flight should occur after sunset.

Rivas, however, was ready for this eventuality, too. He sent for reinforcements, and over several days Brazilian transports landed ten thousand men, some of whom took up positions on the west side of the lagoon where they could fire on the Paraguayans with relative ease. Meanwhile, some sixty Allied vessels sailed or steamed into the lagoon from the main river channel and added their firepower to that already arrayed against Martínez. Rivas now had eleven guns at Andaí and several thousand muskets that he could train on Isla Poí or at any spot on the Laguna Verá at any time of day or night.

Confounding the enemy ships on the lagoon, Paraguayan canoes continued their night passage from their "water-walled bulwark," and hand-to-hand combat took place on almost every occasion. Some of the canoes, outfitted as chata*s*, tried to return fire, leaving more than a few bodies floating in pink water.[79] Whenever the Paraguayan paddlers succeeded in shaking off the enemy and getting their men on dry ground, however, they gave off a yell of satisfaction, and set off once again through the murderous fire to retrieve more men.

Alén arrived safely at the other side of the Verá, together with a large number of the wounded. Caballero could not help any of them, however. The Paraguayans may have celebrated whenever one of their canoes got through, but such tiny successes could not go on indefinitely. Perhaps a thousand soldiers made the transit by the time the final Paraguayan canoe was sunk by gunfire in the last days of the month.[80] Seeing that the end was near, Rivas elected on 28 July to attack the remaining Paraguayan troops at Isla Poí. But Martínez had a few 3-pounders left, and when he exhausted his ammunition he had his men take the muskets of those who had been killed; they smashed the locks and fittings to use as shrapnel. Incredibly, these weary units drove the Allied attackers off.

The next night brought a frustrating sequel in the unexpected confusion of two imperial battalions returning from separate details and firing on each other in the dark. More than a hundred men were slain before anyone recognized the error.[81] On 2 August, Rivas followed up his heavy-handed efforts with an appeal to the enemy, but Martínez fired on the flag of truce that the Argentine general extended. Two days later, Rivas tried again, and received the same response. The Paraguayans had eaten the last of their horses and now managed on berries and a little gun oil, and still they resisted, perhaps hoping that some of their number might yet escape across the lagoon.[82]

Rivas felt bewildered. The Paraguayans were stubborn opponents—no question of that—but a normal definition of courage, he felt, ought to include yielding when further resistance was futile. Like many officers in the Allied army, Rivas had made a mystique of Paraguayan prowess, but now he found it difficult to understand their obstinacy. To crush the Paraguayans with sheer force at this point seemed little different from murder, and this idea, as much as anything, irked him. He felt ill at ease in the guise of an assassin.

Rivas decided on another tack. He summoned Ignacio Esmerats, a Catalan chaplain employed at the Brazilian hospital, and sent him into the Paraguayan lines to initiate negotiations.

> Esmerats took with him not only the flag of truce, but the cross, symbol of the faith common to him and them. Holding it before him, he penetrated to their camp in the jungle, and reminded them of the brave deeds they had already done for their country, of the hopelessness of longer resistance, of the courage and sufferings of their women, of the famine of their children. He showed them that the Allies had only to fire on them to turn their camp

into a slaughter ground, and he besought them by their common humanity and by the emblem of mercy which he carried to spare further suffering by surrender. Still they hesitated, fearing that they would be mowed down by the Brazilian guns when they left their cover. The priest then seized the cross, held it over his breast and declared that the sacred symbol was a protection which no shot or shell could pierce.[83]

In truth, Esmerats could not quite believe that the skeletal creatures he found lying prostrate upon the few dry spots of earth were human beings. He spoke softly to the two Paraguayan clerics present and distributed among the soldiers the little portion of bread and wine he had brought from the Allied camp. These pitiful men had no strength left.

The exhausted Colonel Martínez stepped forward. He had been with López from the beginning and had even served as his adjutant in arranging the 1866 Yataity Corã conference with Mitre. The colonel found it difficult even now to breach the topic of honorable surrender, but his officers had already endorsed the idea, mumbling as if with one voice that nothing else remained to do.[84]

The next day, 5 August 1868, Esmerats led Martínez to General Rivas, who was struck by his adversary's heart-rending appearance. The colonel's uniform was in rags, and as he had eaten nothing for four days, his face was gaunt and had taken on a saffron hue; he could barely speak as he saluted the general and his legs wobbled. Indeed, as Martínez contemplated his losses, he found it difficult to stand and he was only saved from embarrassment when two naval officers came forward to hold him erect.[85]

The former garrison of Humaitá now counted ninety-nine officers and twelve hundred men, one-third of them wounded, all of them horribly shrunken from want of food.[86] They now capitulated, relinquishing their flags and stacking their eight hundred remaining muskets with as much pride as the moment allowed. A few of the soldiers betrayed a sullen dignity but could not keep anger on their faces for very long. Rivas saluted their gallantry by embracing Martínez, wrapping him in his own luxurious poncho, and telling him that he had never fought a more valiant foe.[87]

The Paraguayan commander responded to this observation with a wan smile, but he could not ignore the high price his comrades had paid to obtain such praise. Their stomachs were empty and yet most of the men could hold their heads high even now. They had never once fraternized with the enemy; there had been no Christmas truces, no spontaneous shows of mutual admiration, no weakening of the call to duty; they had fought for the Marshal, for the Paraguayan nation, for their families, and for each other. That had always been enough.

Rivas permitted Martínez and his officers to retain their side arms. The general promised that none would be forced to serve in the Allied armies. With this matter settled, the Paraguayan soldiers passed quietly and in good order aboard the waiting Allied transports that took them back across the waterway and thence into detention.[88] They henceforth received ample food, new clothing, and an unbroken show of respect from their captors. The material comforts that they enjoyed after surrender would have been impossible to visualize back in the trenches. Most of the men captured at Isla Poí lived to see their families again. In this, however, the fate of the defenders of Humaitá was not always enviable, for in the months before the final peace much horror was visited upon their homeland. Every mother, father, and child would have new tales of dread to relate to returning veterans after the war.

10

THE NATION
CONSUMES ITS OWN

The Allies learned of Humaitá's evacuation ten hours after the last of Martinez's men departed. Caxias wasted no time in occupying the fortress—the object of his frustration for many months.[1] As had been true of Paso Pucú, many of his soldiers had spoken with tremendous awe for the place; everyone who put pen to paper had qualified it as vast, modern, and impregnable—a veritable Sebastopol at the edge of the South American wilderness. The primitive reality of the site must have come as a surprise, then. Indeed, Humaitá was inferior in its position and construction even to Curupayty.

The eight miles of earthworks that circled the fortress consisted of redans, curtains, and trenches sixteen feet wide and thirteen feet deep. Though part of the works dated from early in the conflict, the Marshal's engineers had never reinforced them with revetments. The parapets, sustained by trunks and interlaced palmettos, had not been maintained, either. The Paraguayans had dug the outermost line with salient angles to permit enfilade, but though the line could fit at least seventy-eight batteries, most of the guns had disappeared across the river—if they had ever been there at all.[2]

Of the eight batteries facing the main channel of the Paraguay, only the Batería Londres had any pretense to modernity. Casemated with brick and boasting embrasures for sixteen guns (rather than the rumored twenty-five), it had contested the passage of the Allied fleet for two years. And yet, when Richard Burton inspected it, in late August 1868, he dismissed it as a "Prince of Humbugs," eight of whose ports had been converted into workshops "because the artillerymen were in hourly dread of their caving in and crumbling down."[3]

The Allies captured one hundred eighty guns at Humaitá, but only half were serviceable.[4] Some had been dragged from the deep water, while others were so old that the military men could hardly believe that such museum pieces still existed.[5] The Marquis of Caxias doled out the captured guns among his units, with each Allied nation receiving a portion of the spoils. The "Cristiano," which had been the pride of the Marshal's artillery, ended up in Rio's Museu Histórico Nacional. The chains that had once stretched across the river and excited so much concern were dragged from the riverbank, cut in three pieces, and delivered to representatives of the three Allied powers. The soldiers also encountered ample furniture of a rudimentary design, and, amazingly, the remaining spoils from Second Tuyutí—bottles of wine and cooking oil and jars of fruit preserves.[6] They found no further souvenirs save for a few broken Spencer rifles and a seemingly endless number of cannon balls.[7]

The battered chapel at Humaitá still stood resolutely as the most visible symbol of Paraguayan determination. The Allies treated it with almost mystical trepidation, even after Brazilian gunners had blasted away its northern belfry. In its presence, visiting soldiers requited themselves with a hushed reverence—a mood all the more appropriate given the chapel's charred appearance and smell of burnt wood. In later years, veterans bragged of having stepped through the building, much as a Victorian tourist spoke of visiting Pompeii or the pyramids of Egypt.[8] Yet aside from the chapel, whose silhouette later decorated Paraguayan postage stamps, the most striking thing about the former enemy camp was its emptiness.[9]

The fallen fortress offered pause for reflection. When the Allies departed from Tuyutí, they left behind scores of emaciated dogs, some still tied to stakes and howling jackal-like with hunger. Had these animals been present at Humaitá, the Marshal's troops would have eaten them.

If such a dilapidated and forlorn site had functioned as the linchpin of Paraguayan resistance for two years, what did its collapse signify? Humaitá may have seemed powerful as a symbol, but its reality did not astonish; its defenses may have been barely adequate, but they hardly met an engineer's definition of beautiful. Something in the appearance of the ruined fortress was disappointing and all the more poignant as a result. Officials in Rio de Janeiro could only conclude that the Marshal was on his last legs, and this inspired renewed hopes for the future. From now on, the public speeches in Allied capitals promised a prompt end to the conflict and a just punishment for López.[10]

But what if these prognostications were mistaken? Humaitá's sad state could just as easily suggest that the Paraguayan resistance might go on no matter where the Marshal's weakened army established its next defenses. Burton, who likened the fall of Humaitá to that of Vicksburg five years earlier, believed that the Paraguayan position was hopeless. And yet, the Paraguayan prisoners he met insisted that the war had only begun, and that none but traitors would surrender.

One of them asked the medical officer of the HMS *Linnet* why the ship was there. "To see the end of the struggle," was the reply. "Then," rejoined the man, "Ustedes han de demorar muchos años" (You will have to wait many years.)[11]

A Time For Suspicion and Fear

Neither Caxias nor López had time for philosophical quandaries as they prepared for the next stage of the war. The marquis could see military advantages in the fallen fortress that neither his soldiers nor the numerous war correspondents who visited the site could appreciate. For one thing, the intact buildings offered billets, and his medical staff could adapt the hospital for their own wounded and sick. Besides, building up a strong Allied presence at Humaitá made Caballero's position at Timbó untenable, and with its elimination, Caxias's troops might take a leaf from the Marshal's book and bypass the batteries that Thompson had prepared further north.

The marquis's political position had also improved. The slow pace of the armies had seemed little better than a stalemate, and this lack of progress had not redounded to the credit of Prime Minister Zacharias. Indeed, among Brazilian politicians the slow rot of disenchantment had lately merged with a broader cynicism. The weakness of the prime minister's position in Rio, which had not improved since the parliamentary impasse of February, now provoked another crisis in which, surprisingly, Progressives and Liberals colluded. In a move that few could have predicted, they forced the emperor to name a Conservative ministry to head the government. Zacharias himself favored this ploy, as it assured his strong position in the opposition. Since the minority Conservatives could assume power only through Pedro's direct intervention, it followed that the other factions would subsequently reorganize themselves to reject the emperor's "despotism."[12]

This, in fact, is what happened when the Viscount of Itaboraí assumed office on 16 July 1868. The old Liberals lost little time in hypocritically calling foul and announcing that they would embrace a series of reforms that included a streamlining of the monarch's constitutional role. Much to his surprise, Zacharias failed to gain the support he craved either from the Liberals or from dom Pedro. In paving the way for a Conservative resurgence, moreover, he helped radicalize the political dialogue in the country, which in turn sapped the strength of the Bragança monarchy over the next two decades.

In Britain, Itaboraí had claimed that "peace with Paraguay was the only rational policy for Brazil," and he declared that he "would allow himself no rest till he had secured it."[13] At the same time, however, his ascendancy assured that Caxias's party would dominate imperial politics for some time.[14] Itaboraí was a more cautious and guarded politician than Zacharias. The new war minister, the Baron of Muritiba, proved expert at pulling political strings to favor the military, and he was hardly the kind of man to reject requests for aid from the marquis's headquarters in Paraguay.[15] This fact, coupled with the emperor's own intransigence, meant that the war would go on.

Marshal López could boast of no similar base of material support from Asunción, whose empty streets his troops patrolled in search of enemy infiltrators. The flow of supplies to the Paraguayan army had largely been stanched, and the government was now in more disarray than at any time since the López family took power. Much of the confusion derived from its precipitous flight from the capital and the faulty reestablishment of state authority at Luque. To make matters worse, cholera had returned, causing families to flee further inland or crowd into the few available homes in Luque in a hopeless scramble to escape.[16] Neither food nor drink was available in quantities sufficient for the displaced population, and no one who claimed to be in charge had any answers.

López still took it for granted, however, that all upright Paraguayans were ready to accept the war's challenges as a matter of duty. According to the Marshal, whenever public spirit showed any sign of flagging, this was merely reflected the egotism of bad Paraguayans. Fear he could comprehend, and occasionally even pardon. But disaffection posed a more serious challenge—it could spread, and the Marshal understood his responsibilities even if his underlings did not. Final victory required vigilance against traitors, and he made no exceptions for those whom his lieutenants had met with in Asunción in the wake of Delphim's raid. When out of touch with Humaitá, he reasoned, these men had stolen the first opportunity to try to subvert his authority and construct an alternative power base. Their deeds—or at least their inclinations—were more sordid than those of previous traitors, and deserved speedy punishment.

López was looking for a reason to fire a shot over the heads of his functionaries. As early as 10 March, he ordered the Asunción police chief, the interim war minister, the gravely ill José Berges, and his own brother Benigno south to Seibo on the first available vessel.[17] It was not clear that this order amounted to an arrest warrant, but the men soon realized that it did. They also discovered the truth of rumors concerning the arrest of the state treasurer, Saturnino Bedoya, who was the Marshal's brother-in-law. He had been held for a number of months in semi-detention, but now it emerged that he had suffered through several heavy-handed interrogations and had talked effusively.[18]

But what had he said? When he first appeared at the fortress, Bedoya had made the unpardonable mistake of wondering aloud (during confession no less) what might come to pass in Asunción now that enemy ironclads had run the Humaitá batteries.[19] Bishop Manuel Antonio Palacios, who showed no regard for the sanctity of the confessional, reported these remarks to López, who decided to extract further details from Bedoya by torture. The more the soldiers thrashed the treasurer, the more ornate his descriptions became. Afterwards no Paraguayan official could feel safe, least of all the López brothers, who now could grasp the cost of fraternal rivalry.

On 16 March, while still in the Chaco, the Marshal directed a telegram to Francisco Sánchez demanding an explanation for the latter's actions in Asunción. In the note, he cited Bedoya's claims that the vice president had made himself party to a conspiracy, that in acting as the "vile instrument" of Benigno's ambitions, he had betrayed the Paraguayan cause, and had given "to the enemy for the first time an advantage that [he, the Marshal] never would have expected."[20]

López held off ordering the old man's arrest, and over several days, Sánchez composed an appeal for clemency that was outwardly self-effacing if inwardly frantic. He quoted back his master's own words on patriotism, disassociated himself from the "anarchic propositions" of supposed renegades, and confessed much stupidity on his own part.

Earlier, the vice president had lacked the stomach for in-fighting with other members of the Marshal's cabinet. On this occasion, though, he attacked Bedoya by name, asking "how could anyone dare charge me with treasonous acts against my government without referring to a single act, or some expression on my part that would even hint at such a probability?"[21] The sincerity, or the abject submissiveness, of this appeal placated the Marshal; he took no further action against Sánchez, whose long, narrow body had started to bend like a candle. The ordeal left him stooped, but alive.[22]

The other members of the presidential entourage took his deliverance as a hopeful sign. By wrenching Sánchez into line, López had reestablished discipline in the government. Appropriate pressure could henceforth be applied at Luque and the interior villages by his police or his guardsmen in the Acá Carayá.[23] Their vigilance freed López to concentrate on those areas that were his proper preserve: military preparation, the conduct of battle, and diplomacy.

Yet the Marshal's anger had not vanished—in fact, it was only just beginning to show itself. In the last months before the fall of Humaitá, López had not discarded his qualms about his brothers or the members of his staff. His outbursts of pique grew so frequent and so strident during this time that his traditional critics could be forgiven for thinking him insane. But there was another possibility suggested by the British pharmacist George Masterman, who worked together with Porter Bliss in the US legation. He observed that López had resorted to the bottle, and when not actually inebriated, commonly spent "two or three hours a day kneeling or praying" in the chapel.[24] His newfound faith (or reaffirmation of his old faith) may very well have been genuine, but it seems to have added to his erratic behavior, providing a veneer for something more pernicious and ultimately more costly for himself and his people.

The fear that the Marshal inspired at the Paraguayan camps was palpable during late autumn and winter. A system of espionage had operated at every level of Paraguayan society since the colonial period, but now it flourished as never before.[25] López took the reports of spies in the morning, in the afternoon, and in the evening, and any contradiction that he detected in their testimony exacerbated his own anxiety. In contrast to the general run of men in camp, these agents provocateurs (or *pyragües*) never lost their tongues. In fact, they took every opportunity to make themselves indispensable to the Marshal, and the more he credited their words, the more powerful they became.

No one was safe. When Benigno arrived at Seibo in late March, he learned that his earlier display of independent thinking had been reported. In the presence of Colonel Caballero, the Marshal treated his brother with undisguised scorn. "And so," he is said to have asked, "what is it that you people were thinking of doing back at the capital?" Benigno explained his actions as if speaking to a high-ranking but misinformed patron: "Señor, since we had had no word from either you or the army since Humaitá came under siege, we believed that the time had come to save our persons and property." This statement may have had the ring of truth, but it elicited the gruffest response from the Marshal, who turned to Caballero and snarled: "See? These [blackguards] are darker than the kambáes."[26]

In spite of this insulting reprimand, Benigno was assigned a place that night at his brother's table next to Madame Lynch and the children, all of whom treated him affectionately as a much-loved uncle. Perhaps he thought that the worst was over. However, as soon as the army crossed the river to San Fernando, all familial warmth disappeared. Now Benigno was accused of plotting the Marshal's assassination. He was arrested and held incommunicado at a small hut where Venancio soon joined him as a prisoner. Some weeks later, Juana Pabla Carrillo came to camp to intercede for the two brothers, who by then were in irons, but her solicitude worsened rather than improved their lot.[27]

Meanwhile, on 14 May, Minister Washburn visited San Fernando to ask the Marshal's leave to communicate with American naval personnel aboard the steamer *Wasp*, which had dropped anchor just south of the Allied blockade. As had happened in 1866, the Allies refused to permit the ship's passage upriver. Washburn stressed that the US vessel had come upriver to evacuate members of the legation and their dependents, and that, while he personally preferred to stay on, he wanted his wife and staff removed to a place of safety.

López agreed to facilitate Mrs. Washburn's departure, but could not resist asking the minister about the men and women who had found refuge at the US legation. The Marshal had already been apprised of the North American's indiscretions, how he had insisted first on staying in Asunción, then on interceding on behalf of Porter Bliss and other foreigners, and, more recently, how he had secured the release of Major Manlove, the would-be privateer.[28] Manlove had used some sharp words in dealing with the Asunción police, and the minister had made no subsequent effort to apologize, except in a cursory way. Such effrontery could not go unnoticed, and now, without alluding to the incident itself, López intimated that he was annoyed.[29]

Washburn had anticipated the upbraiding. He had already received a series of reprimands from the foreign ministry, to which he responded with an evasive correspondence. He now wished to put the matter in correct perspective.[30] He quietly observed that the people in his care had lived for some time under terrible stress; given the circumstances, was not their lack of courtesy or foresight forgivable? These words seemed to soothe López. Mrs. Washburn and the other dependents at the legation had failed to escape at this time, it is true, but this was due less to any obstacles placed in her way by the Marshal than because of Caxias's attitude toward Captain William Kirkland, commander of the *Wasp*, who had wanted to steam north in the face of Brazilian refusal to cooperate.

Washburn had already observed that day-to-day life had grown more precarious at the front, such that those stationed at San Fernando had taken to greeting each other with foreboding in their voices. He noticed that his friends among the British engineers avoided his gaze. Even the gregarious Thompson let him know that he should not speak too openly about Paraguay's quest for an honorable peace. The minister returned to Asunción two days later rather more perplexed than reassured.[31] During his last night in camp, he had joined Thompson, Franz Wisner von Morgenstern, and Madame Lynch for a game of whist, but the camaraderie typical of these parties was missing. The players sent their greetings to Mrs. Washburn but otherwise kept their voices low and their eyes firmly fixed on their cards.

The "Tribunals of Blood"

Washburn wondered what all this awkwardness portended. He had long since grown accustomed to the authoritarian vagaries of Paraguay, but the hesitancy that he witnessed among his fellow card players betrayed a sense of anxiety far more pointed than what he expected to find among such privileged individuals. Things had in fact grown far worse than Washburn could have realized. Bedoya had evidently died of dysentery on 17 May, and therefore could no longer add—or invent—details to the tale of revolutionary plotting.[32] But its general parameters had nonetheless started to take shape in the Marshal's mind, and López placed the US minister at the center of this fantastic scheme.

In his memoirs, General Francisco Isidoro Resquín summarized the official version of what had happened. He claimed that Washburn had first connived with the Marquis of Caxias on one of his visits to the Allied camp in late 1866, and that the two men had been biding their time until they could enlist some powerful coconspirators. At length they were approached by Bedoya, who presented the minister with a quantity of gold pilfered from the Paraguayan treasury. To this bribe was supposedly added monies from Benigno, from the imperial coffers, and from the property stored within the US legation. As the enemy closed in on Humaitá, this cash became more central in the thinking of the plotters. Foreign Minister Berges, General Barrios, Monsignor Palacios, and the two López brothers eventually joined with Washburn, who, Resquín argued, sought to coordinate an uprising to coincide with Delphim's attack on Asunción.

When the commodore failed to occupy the capital, however, the rebellion was rescheduled for July, or whenever the Brazilians could overwhelm the Paraguayan batteries on the Tebicuary. Timing was crucial in the convoluted account, but the traitors supposedly felt optimistic. The Marshal's spies even purportedly intercepted a letter from Benigno to Caxias that outlined the details of the plan and presented incriminating evidence against more than eighty suspects.[33]

On the surface, this claim of conspiracy amounted to a pastiche of poorly digested information derived from unreliable informants, blended with the Marshal's preexisting fears, and presented as self-justification by the officer responsible for the mistreatment of the accused. The different elements in the account certainly compel our attention, but they hang together poorly. For one thing, though Washburn made little secret of his aversion to López, he had no more sympathy for Caxias, Benigno, and all the others who had purportedly lent their support to the plot.[34] The accused Paraguayans, moreover, lived in glass houses and knew from experience that their most innocent remarks were always reported to the police. They might very well share Washburn's distaste for the Marshal's politics, but they would have found it impossible to unite with the US minister in any revolutionary committee. Even the theory that Washburn provided indirect aid for their efforts (and eschewed a central role for himself) was ruled out by the fact that the man could never keep his mouth shut.

Both in his memoirs and in formal testimony before the US Congress in 1870, Washburn denied that he had ever conspired against the government to which he had been accredited.[35] He maintained then and for the rest of his life that his efforts at mediation between Paraguay and the Allies had been disinterested, and that his actions at the legation, as well as his later defense of resident foreigners, were fully consistent with proper diplomatic practice. It seems unlikely that European diplomatists in the Platine countries could have endorsed this interpretation, and even many of his own North American colleagues regarded the New Englander as a hothead.[36] Conspirators are rarely fashioned from among the indiscreet.

Nonetheless, many doubts hovered around the US minister, and, even today, some polemicists point a finger in his direction.[37] Two diametrically opposed views have developed in the historical literature to explain Washburn's conduct in Paraguay. Those who supported him in print during his lifetime had repeatedly fallen victim to the Marshal's excesses, and, though they thought the minister brash, they still owed their lives to his intercession.[38] Those who insisted on his complicity in a plot, by contrast, often had a great deal to conceal about their own comportment during the war.[39] If they could tie the country's downfall to foreign imperialists and local backstabbers, then perhaps they might secure their own reputation in years to come.

Amid this rat's nest of blame and counter blame, what we can clearly see is that the one man whose opinion mattered in May and June of 1868—Marshal Francisco Solano López—had yet to make up his mind about Washburn. López certainly harbored serious concerns about the US minister's capacity for intrigue, but he was similarly suspicious about the other foreign representatives. Benigno, Venancio, and the others he had already marked down as undependable, but he was unsure of what to do with them.

July saw another incident that helped corroborate the Marshal's worst fears. On 24 July—López's birthday—three imperial monitors struck at the batteries that Thompson had established at the mouth of the Tebicuary. It was not much of an engagement, and it interfered little with the celebrations on land. The Allied vessels managed to score several hits on positions south of San Fernando, but the Paraguayan gunners drove them off successfully.

In his account of the day's events, Thompson reported that, as the monitors steamed past, three individuals put their heads out of the turret of the *Bahia*, and one shouted at the Paraguayan soldiers who glared at them from the riverbank. As the British engineer noted, the moment they went by,

> I telegraphed to López the number which had passed, and proceeded to write another dispatch containing details, when I received a telegram from him saying, "what signal did the first ironclad make on passing the battery?" The telegraph clerk had already informed him. I then wrote and told him all about it, and that the men said it was the Paraguayan Recalde, who had formerly deserted from López. Hereupon he wrote me a terrible anathema against traitors, wondering that they had been allowed to pass in silence, and to open their polluted mouths to honest patriots. ... I wrote back that they had been well abused by all, which was a fact; he then wrote back that he was now "satisfied with my explanation." [But] he absolutely held me responsible for Recalde putting his head out of the turret of the ironclad.[40]

It seems that the Marshal had come to doubt the loyalty of his long-serving British subordinate. He also seemed to think it probable that turncoats in the pay of the marquis were communicating with men in his own army. This could only mean that the culmination of the treasonable plotting was at hand.

López moved swiftly. On 2 August, he issued a decree that invoked the Laws of the Indies in establishing a series of two-man tribunals to investigate accusations of treason.[41] *Jueces fiscales* (or judge-prosecutors) were chosen from among clerics and those officers the Marshal still considered reliable. He designated the bull-necked General Resquín as chief officer responsible for arraigning the defendants and carrying out whatever sentences the special courts determined. Scores, perhaps hundreds, of suspects were taken into custody, and the podgy Resquín, who was now drinking and eating almost as much as López, lost no time in arguing that they receive a severe grilling.

Arrests had already taken place further north. Former foreign minister Berges was detained at his country estate in Salinares, as was the Bolivian writer Tristan Roca, editor of *El Centinela*, in Areguá.[42] The two López sisters were also arrested, as was Gustave Bayon de Libertat, the assistant of French consul Paul Cuverville, and José María Leite Pereira, the honorary consul of Portugal.[43] Almost all the jueces de paz, jefes políticos, and militia commanders in the central zone from San Lorenzo to Villarrica—two hundred individuals in all—were detained and then concentrated in Luque. Most were eventually brought south to San Fernando by steamer.[44]

Prisoners of both sexes arrived in camp daily. The imprisoned women, nearly all of them members of the upper class, enjoyed the privilege of remaining unshackled. Each received a cured hide for a bed. Otherwise, they had to make do in the open air the same as the men and consume the same miserable fare of unsalted beef in portions smaller than those doled out to soldiers. Once a day the prisoners received a cow horn of water from the nearby lagoon. Given the reluctance of the guards to escort them from their place of confinement, the accused men and women often had to squat in their own filth. All prisoners were chained at night, where they sat "in rows, stretched on the damp, slimy ground."[45] Thus assembled, these "conspirators," already thin, declined rapidly.

The surrender of the Humaitá garrison came three days before the trials began. That event cast a noticeable pall over the proceedings at San Fernando and ushered in the Marshal's most egregious and controversial demonstration of ruthlessness. The gallant Colonel Martínez, whose long service and unshaken loyalty were soon forgotten, had joined his starving men in Allied captivity, and was now beyond López's reach. His round-faced young wife, Juliana Ynsfrán, had been evacuated to the Paraguayan interior, however, and her fate was different.

Doña Juliana was first cousin to the Marshal, one of the privileged members of the presidential family. She had resided at Madame Lynch's country house at Patiño Cue for several months. Then, one night in August, two soldiers appeared at her door, rapping melodramatically and demanding that she present herself for arrest. No sooner had she dressed when they seized her, taking her torn and disheveled to Asunción. At mid-morning, she met another party of soldiers at the arsenal, who loaded her with heavy fetters, and dragged her aboard a steamer bound for San Fernando, where she joined the growing ranks of the accused.[46]

The witch-hunt began in earnest. The two-man judicial teams received instructions to scour the entire country for possible traitors, and if we are inclined to doubt the efficacy of the Paraguayan government in delivering foodstuffs and in containing the threat from epidemic disease, we can be sure the state did an exemplary, if terrifying, job conducting the so-called tribunals of blood.[47] Unlike Mitre, who during the Montonero rebellions usually placed rebels before the firing squad without trial, the Marshal observed the legal conventions at San Fernando. So did his associates, who interpreted the letter of the law with unmistakable strictness.

The most remarkable of the *fiscales* to emerge from the tribunals of blood was Fidel Maíz, a tall, clear-eyed, forty-year-old priest from the tiny hamlet of Arroyos y Esteros. With a surname that evoked images of the countryside, Maíz had a good claim on being the most cultured Paraguayan of his generation. He earned lavish praise from his contemporaries for his scholarship, oratorical skills, and piety, and he occasionally dabbled in poetry, geography, and the sciences as well as theology.[48] Despite the isolation of Maíz's home parish, he strove to maintain close relations with the lettered portion of the Paraguayan elite, not excluding members of the presidential family.

Unfortunately for Father Maíz, there were those who envied his reputation and way with words. As a result, in 1862 he was arrested, fitted with irons and left to languish in military custody for nearly five years.[49] During that time he learned that he was little suited to the role of martyr. Nor did he relish being insulated from the tremendous challenges that his country had endured during his captivity. Eight of his ten brothers perished during the war. The Allied armies crossed the Paraná and pummeled his country at Tuyutí and Boquerón, and still he remained a prisoner, unable to come to her defense or improve his own condition.

The victory at Curupayty put Marshal López in a generous frame of mind and this, in turn, saved Maíz. Instead of facing the firing squad, he sought the intercession of the Marshal's patron saint and composed a petition for clemency. This fulsome and unctuous appeal, which appeared in *El Semanario*, was a model of blasphemous adulation, in which Maíz compared López to Jesus Christ—indeed, to the latter's disadvantage.[50] Any reader who lived outside Paraguay during the 1860s would have thought the petition a nauseating joke. Its publication, however, earned the cleric his freedom, and afterwards he worked on *Cabichuí* and served as chaplain to the men in López's guard.[51]

No one can doubt Father Maíz's brilliance as a writer and orator who spoke an incomparably fluent Guaraní. But for a man of the cloth to oversee the torture and execution of accused traitors requires explanation. On the one hand, his deeds at San Fernando were distinctly Faustian. Having for so long cringed in pain in the Marshal's jails, he now looked for every chance to redeem himself in López's eyes. At the same time, he could not fail to notice that the Paraguay of 1868 no longer reflected the static norms of the world into which he had been born. The Guaraní-speaking peasants of the interior—the land of his youth—had lately gained an ascendancy, even strength, in the service of Marshal López. Through them, Maíz perceived some residual hope for influence. He calculated that persecution of the established elite would reinforce the national sympathy that the Marshal sought to stir. In flogging the upper classes, the government might draw attention to the contrasting loyalty of the country people, over whom Maíz could claim some sway.[52]

Maíz's status as a cleric helps to explain this reasoning. He recognized a common thread between the social status of his peasant parishioners and the message of the Gospels that proclaimed the good news not just for the upper classes, but for all people. If his labors at San Fernando could suppress the ignoble ambitions of the elites—and separate them from their foreign baals—this would also promote the wider interests of Paraguayan Christianity.

We might speculate that whenever this religious imperative failed him, Maíz could also take refuge in the contradictions of politics. Having taken a "liberal" posture in the past, he could help foster the future welfare of Paraguay only by assuming an authoritarian stance in the present. This hope required a somersault in thinking, but it allowed him to qualify his actions as necessary, even commendable.[53] Whether he cloaked himself in an all-encompassing Catholic faith, or in an equally powerful nationalism, Maíz intended to do his conscientious duty as a *fiscal*.

There was much self-deception in all this, but Maíz was not alone in seeking to make the ends justify the means at San Fernando. There were many other willing collaborators. Juan Crisóstomo Centurión, the handsome staff officer who had overseen the "scientific" restructuring of Guaraní orthography and who left to posterity one of the most detailed memoirs of the war, himself barely missed being accused of plotting, and responded to this close call by joining the crusade against the internal enemy.[54] So did Colonel Silvestre Aveiro, the former private secretary of Carlos Antonio López; José Falcón, the sometime director of the National Archive; and Justo Román, another army chaplain with long experience at the altar.[55]

All five of these men were thoughtful, well-read individuals whose submission to the Marshal's caprices was troubling. But stronger men had already succumbed to the appeal of power during this war. The twenty to thirty fiscales named by López could recognize the absurdity of many accusations, yet they could never act on their doubts, not even *sotto voce*, for to question the process was tantamount to questioning the cause. And any show of defeatism might result in their own arrest.

In normal circumstances, people who turn their back on reality are soon set straight by the criticism and mockery of those around them. At San Fernando, however, no such correctives existed for functionaries who had already learned the price of dissension. Deception and self-deception was thus permitted to multiply as in a hall of distorting mirrors, so that even the grimmest of realities bore no resemblance to what accused men and women said they saw.

Angry Men Make Angry Justice

A stab-in-the-back interpretation of Paraguay's military decline had started to take root at San Fernando, and the fiscales saw no benefit in hindering it. Besides, acting as judges in these circumstances presupposed certain advantages. In a setting that had hitherto reserved absolute authority for one man alone, the fiscales saw their chance to exercise the power of life or death over many men, and they would not or could not resist the corruptive influences that such power entailed. One can depict them as bureaucrats doing an unpleasant but necessary service, as hard-bitten nationalist fanatics, or as hirelings who wished to guarantee their own survival by doing their master's bidding.

López himself had little to do with the judicial proceedings, and later expressed surprise that many loyal people had been detained.[56] Though he remained the judge of last resort (and evidently perused all the depositions), he rarely exercised his right of confirmation, commutation, or pardon.[57] Thompson even claimed that at San Fernando the Marshal "used to go out with his children to fish in a lagoon near his headquarters," so little did he care—or affect to care—about the trials.[58]

Instead, Maíz and the others enforced what the ancient law demanded, performing their tasks with a fervor that they found difficult to live down in later years.[59] The fiscales rejected simple evidence and looked instead for subtle motives to elucidate the purported actions of the accused, and they refused to concede that an individual's decisions could draw more from improvisation than conspiracy. By degrees, they convinced themselves and others that the revolutionary plots were real. These judges (or prosecutors, for martial law made no provision for defense attorneys) pressed hard to construct a consistent version of the truth, often resorting to the most grotesque measures to make the different accounts gel.[60]

The fiscales enjoyed the assistance of squads of regular soldiers delegated from the Marshal's guards. Like a procession of acolytes with heads kept low, these bare-backed adolescents went about their work in a silent, respectful manner, almost as if the trials had taken place in church. The scourge and the knotted rope were their chosen instruments, which they employed at a glance from the fiscales whenever a statement seemed sufficiently insolent to merit a reproach. Most of the time, however, the soldiers sat glumly in the background.

They may have taken a surreptitious pleasure in the trials, but they feigned in-difference, for they knew better than to spoil the ritual with a demonstration of emotion.[61]

Torture was common. The mildest form involved riveting three heavy irons to the legs, such that the accused was compelled to crawl rather than walk to the "courtroom." But this was the least onerous of the torments. Another approach involved "stretching" (*cuadro estacado*), in which the accused was pressed with his face to the ground and with his hands and feet bound to leather cords at-tached to stakes and pulled tight. This left the victim extended into the form of a Saint Andrew's cross and subject to the full rays of the scorching sun.[62] If a confession could not be compelled even under that burden, the soldiers first withheld water and then used their whips.

The most notorious method to elicit confessions was the *cepo uruguaiana*, a loathsome variation on bucking whereby the victim was forced face down onto the ground with hands lashed tightly behind him; his knees were then raised and bound to the neck with leather straps, after which the soldiers loaded heavy muskets one after the other upon the victim's back.[63] The procedure slowly dis-located the shoulders, tore the muscles along the ribcage and rendered one or both of the arms useless. The pain was always excruciating and invariably drew out every confession required.

Torture is inherently peculiar, for while its putative function is to extract truthful information, it in fact produces something quite different from the truth. The person undergoing physical coercion will say whatever his tormen-tors tell him to say. They know that he knows that they know how unreal his words appear—and it does not matter. The "truth" is preordained, and like the final product in the mind of a sculptor, it has a precise shape. In this case, those at San Fernando understood that reality was dispensable. All that was needed was for the accused men and women to fill out the contours of the conspiracy.

Yet some individuals did not understand how to confess. One of these was Juliana Ynsfrán, whose torture was prolonged and relentless. It is hard not to agree with Washburn when he ascribed her brutal treatment exclusively to the Marshal's vindictiveness:

> The fact that [her husband, Colonel] Martínez had surrendered rather than die of starvation was proof that he was one of the con-spirators, and his wife was ordered to confess that it was so, and give all particulars of the plan and the names of the parties to it. But the poor woman knew nothing and could not confess. ... She was then flogged with sticks, and the flesh literally cut from her shoulders and back. ... What could she tell? She knew nothing. Then the *cepo uruguaiana* was applied, which was never known to fail in bringing out any confession that was asked. ... The effect

of the *cepo* was such that persons subjected to it remained in a state of semi-consciousness for several days afterwards. Yet the wife of Martínez was kept alive long enough to undergo it at six different times, between whiles being flogged till her whole body was a livid mass.[64]

Doña Juliana was told that her husband had communicated with the commander of the Paraguayan Legion (he had—to scorn Allied demands for surrender), and that she had countenanced his treasonable missives.[65] In all her time under the lash, she never managed anything more than a bewildered cry of innocence. She escaped execution for several months, though not physical abuse, and when she was finally shot, in December 1868, it came as a blessing.[66]

Many others had preceded her, both at the scene of torture and before the firing squad. Several of the most outstanding figures of the prewar elite were reduced to groveling idiocy in the process. Such was the fate of José Berges. The longtime foreign minister possessed a vision rare among Paraguayan functionaries. He was shrewd and could appreciate the difference between what was desirable and what was possible—a trait that had served his country well, both in previous negotiations with representatives of the British, Argentine, and US governments, and also in his nimble administration of occupied Corrientes in 1865. In fostering amicable public relations there, Berges bought his country considerable goodwill while simultaneously demonstrating that the Paraguayan state favored diplomacy over force.

This was a flexible approach that the Marshal had not initially discouraged. After the retreat of 1866, however, Berges sank into irrelevance. The once voluminous correspondence he had carried on with Paraguayan agents in Europe shrunk dramatically, for now every letter or dispatch had to be carried over jungle trails through the Mato Grosso and Bolivia, and thence to the sea. Meanwhile, the official attitude towards his style of negotiation grew frostier, and the Marshal saw less and less use for a fat, pretentious civilian who failed to conceal his gifts behind the usual mask of servility.

At San Fernando, Berges nervously attempted to defend his record. He had always proven a gifted actor in the presence of outsiders, and he tried to apply his skills as a thespian to the proceedings.[67] His interrogators, however, could never have been swayed by facts; besides, they had a quota to fill.[68] The worldly Berges, who had been sick with various ailments for a year, may have consoled himself with the knowledge that the world was insane, but nothing could have saved him.[69]

The former foreign minister was only one of numerous highly placed Paraguayans accused and "processed" at San Fernando during August 1868 and at other spots over the next several months. These included Berges's successor, Gumercindo Benítez; the two López brothers, Benigno and Venancio; Dean

Eugenio Bogado; Bishop Manuel Antonio Palacios; eleven other clerics, and many lesser officials. Though he had lost an eye, the hapless Colonel Paulino Alén still managed to recover from his suicide attempt only to be accused of treason at San Fernando, where he was eventually dragged before the firing squad. The broad-bearded General Vicente Barrios attempted to emulate Alén's example by cutting his own throat on 12 August, but, as with the colonel, his life was saved by quick medical attention.[70] The Marshal's teenaged praetorians kept Barrios under close guard before finally shooting him in December.

Foreigners enjoyed no immunity from persecution. The European merchants and engineers who had come to the country in the late 1850s and early 1860s willingly left behind the gas-lit streets of London, Paris, or Bologna to look for their fortune in the New World. They tended to regard their sojourn as an adventure. But then they lost their enthusiasm in a wartime Paraguay that was less an earthly paradise than a dense thicket of trouble. Those European men who brought their wives and children with them fared best. Some of the others, however, made poor use of the power that López had permitted them vis-à-vis local subordinates. This arrogant attitude now worked against these foreigners, for strangers, colleagues, and acquaintances among the Paraguayans found it easy to condemn *forasteros* who behaved inappropriately or who had used their privileged position to assert an unwarranted superiority.[71]

When finally separated from Washburn in September, both George F. Masterman and Porter Bliss were promptly arrested and tortured. Bliss purchased a reprieve from the worst treatment by agreeing to write a florid—if wholly fictitious—account of Washburn's criminal intrigues. The Prussian major von Versen and several of the Marshal's British engineers eventually faced imprisonment (and sometimes the *cepo*) and survived the conflict thanks to the last-minute arrival of Brazilian troops.[72] Manlove was executed in mid-August, along with John Watts, a British machinist who had been decorated for his battle service on the *Tacuarí*. At least one other Briton was shot later, as well as an Italian riverboat captain, two Uruguayan diplomats, several of the Marshal's Correntino allies, and the Portuguese consul. Perhaps the most unusual foreigner to lose his life was an expatriate Swedish naturalist, Eberhard Munck, who was condemned in 1869 for "not having used his knowledge of witchcraft [!] to promote Paraguayan victory."[73]

While the tribunals of blood constituted an atrocious episode in an atrocious war, the affair still has its mysteries. Some witnesses claimed that the proceedings at San Fernando unfolded amidst an atmosphere of palpable gloom.[74] A surprising number of people, however, were unaware that anything out of the ordinary had happened—even in the camp itself. Richard Burton, who visited the site after the Paraguayan retreat, thought that witnesses had exaggerated the atrocities committed there. As proof, he noted that those Britons in the Paraguayan service, though reckoned among the Marshal's most ill-treated prisoners, in fact knew of these abuses only from hearsay. US naval officers, who appeared on the scene about the same time, were similarly disinclined to believe the most horrific tales.[75] To cite an even more revealing instance, Thompson, who was posted nearby, claimed an ignorance of the treason trials, and grew suspicious only when his friend Bruguez went missing.[76]

The question remains open as to whether a conspiracy ever existed, and if it did, whether it was it justified? As to the latter question, who could blame any Paraguayan for wanting to see the war come to an end in 1868? The country was practically destroyed, the people exhausted, and neither conspiracies nor executions could lift the diminished morale. Dismay at the Marshal's war policies had cropped up in every corner of Paraguay, along with the whispered griping that always accompanies a protracted struggle.

The preponderance of evidence argues against the existence of any revolutionary plot. That Benigno had had aspirations for power in 1862 was well known, but that he could have somehow contacted Brazilian agents operating through the US minister seems fanciful. Though Washburn was often pilloried as the ringleader of an anti-López scheme, he seemed a dubious choice for such a role. He was a prig—arrogant, oversensitive, and brash in the presence of people whom he thought beneath his station. He demanded absolute recognition of his country's dignity, yet was oblivious to her political interests. He always insisted that he was in the right and that everyone else was either wrong or badly informed.

That the US minister would have made a poor organizer for any conspiracy (and just as poor a follower) does not alter the fact that he knew more than he let on. Washburn was acquainted with Benigno, Minister Berges, and every other highly placed person in Asunción; he visited them regularly, often riding from the home of one friend to another, and rarely bothered to tailor his conversations to wartime conditions. He seemed to take pleasure in taunting the police in a most undiplomatic fashion.[77]

That Washburn refused to relocate the US legation to Luque when other foreigners acquiesced in the evacuation order appeared queer not just to López, but to everyone in Paraguay. So did his willingness first to house the property of a great many private persons (including Madame Lynch), then to arrange their money matters for them, and finally to take people in as if he were running a hotel for the rich.[78] Given all this, it is easy to understand why the police wanted to keep him under surveillance. But that does not mean that he was ever involved in a conspiracy.

Then there was the issue of his wife's curious statement. When she was evacuated from Paraguay in September 1868, a despondent and emotionally taxed Sallie Washburn blurted out to a US naval officer that a plan to transfer the presidency to Benigno had indeed been hatched with her husband's consent and foreknowledge.[79] During her stay in Paraguay, she had made much noise as the wife of the American minister, but it was never more than vulgar ostentation or pride in her friendship with members of the "better class." This time, however, her words came back to haunt her. And though she later claimed to have been misquoted, her testimony before Congress failed to improve much under examination.[80]

Washburn was neither the first nor the last US diplomat to intervene in some egregious way in a host country's politics. Both the French and Italian representatives in Luque reported his involvement in a plot to unseat the Marshal, though at what level or in what capacity they refused to speculate.[81] While in Paraguayan custody, Bliss produced an extensive report on the plot in which he accused his former protector of all sorts of sinister machinations. While both he and Masterman, who was compelled to offer similar testimony, disavowed their words once they were free, their confessions deserve attention from those in search of nuance in an already nebulous tale.[82] Several officers of the US Navy met both men later that year and concluded that they had lied about their mistreatment. Some of the San Fernando confessions, the officers remarked, "might be true."[83]

And well they might. It does seem probable that meaningful dissent in Paraguay was being composed into something resembling a conspiracy—or, to use Sallie Washburn's term, a "plan"—for a world without Marshal López. More likely, there were many "conspiracies," running the gamut from simple grumbling to an active evasion of orders, to stealing and hoarding, to thoughts of displacing the government, and even, perhaps, of assassination. The meetings that occurred in Asunción and Paraguarí at the time of Delphim's raid demonstrated that government officials could act without guidance from López. If Burton is correct, then their purpose was to "bell the cat."[84]

But the dissidents never got their chance. Over five hundred men and women were shot, lanced, or bayoneted as a result of the proceedings at San Fernando, and in subsequent months the names of even more individuals were appended to a long list of suspects.[85] Despite what many of his detractors subsequently argued, López's behavior at this time betrayed no hint of clinical paranoia, nor was it even neurotic when viewed in the context of Paraguay's sinking fortunes on the battlefield. The Marshal was at the end of his tether emotionally and politically, and he struck out at those around him for want of a more obnoxious foe. Seen in this light, his fear of betrayal was rational, whether or not a conspiracy actually took place.[86]

López could sometimes act entirely out of malice, as his persecution of Juliana Ynsfrán suggests. In general, however, he couched his brutality in terms of necessity. More was the pity for his country, for he clearly misjudged the impact of what he had set in motion. In attempting to smash a putative rebellion among his followers, the Marshal executed, or relieved from their posts, precisely those individuals who had served him best. In so doing, he made it even more difficult for his people to continue their legitimate struggle against the Allies. Those punished at San Fernando could not be replaced, and as Paraguay entered the darkest hour in its history, their absence would be sorely felt.

11

BLEEDING, DROP BY DROP

Historically, one of Paraguay's general misfortunes has been its leaders' obsession with imaginary enemies to the neglect of real ones. Perhaps the men and women executed at San Fernando had to die as an object lesson to others, but in suppressing the dubious plotters, the Marshal disregarded the fact that the Allies were massing to attack him. The treason trials may have provided an element of catharsis, at least for López, but they could not change the military equation. In fact, they probably made things worse. If the accusations had any truth to them, then the *patria* seethed with traitors, a situation that belied the Marshal's claim of universal support among the Paraguayan people. On the other hand, if the accusations of treason were false, then López had behaved with gross injustice to fellow citizens at a time of national crisis. Either way, Paraguayan society turned on itself at the very moment when the Allied army was poised to attack.

Regular logistical support for the Paraguayan army had declined dramatically after the evacuation of Asunción. There were areas in the north where livestock and supplies might still be requisitioned, but the organizational skill needed to make this happen was wanting.[1] In obliterating the alleged threat to the government of Paraguay, López had hobbled the state bureaucracy that his father had striven so meticulously to construct. Putting it back together again would be impossible.

The *jueces* of the countryside had previously managed to meet armed demands in a variety of ways. They had kept supply lines to Humaitá open despite profound difficulties. Now, having sung the song of national unity for ten seasons, they watched their own authority cheapened in the frantic search for traitors. In every village, *pyragües* sprung up in the form of children and old women, and it was unclear which of their incessant denunciations grew out of a genuine desire to protect the public weal from domestic enemies, and which issued from personal grievances.

Those functionaries operating in distant locales survived well enough. They remained at their posts, directing their thin and ever-shriller chorus of fellow citizens in official commemorations of Paraguayan victories or in public paeans to Marshal López. They still promoted a campaign to condemn not just the kambáes but Berges, Bedoya, and other traitors, both living and dead.[2] Doubts about the future could scarcely have been absent among them, however, and soon they would have to leave patriotism behind and look after their own.

To the Tebicuary and Beyond

The Allies enjoyed tremendous superiority in arms, supplies, and, for the time being, morale. The martial pride of their soldiers had been nourished by real advances in the field. Caxias had shown remarkable vitality when he first assumed command over the Allied armies, and he had kept up the momentum against Alén and Martínez for many months. His seizure of Humaitá had yet to deliver the long-sought victory, however, and he must have felt unsure about what to do next.

After several weeks, the marquis opted to advance as a response to the rumors, brought to him by Paraguayan deserters, of a revolution against López. At 7:00 a.m. on 26 August 1868, three brigades of cavalry under General Andrade Neves crossed the Yacaré. This time they encountered no surprises, and after a sharp fight, the Brazilians routed 300 Paraguayan cavalrymen, killing some 45 and seizing 126 horses.[3]

Two days later, the same imperial units stormed a redoubt on the south side of Tebicuary. Though of short duration, this engagement was hotly contested. The attacking troops initially got caught in the sharpened boughs of the enemy abatis, but laid such a heavy fire into the opposing force that the Brazilians were able to blast through the obstacle, driving on against minimal resistance. They then cut a much bigger gap in the line and poured the remaining units through it. Lacking ammunition, the Marshal's men held on with lances and sabers, but Andrade Neves mowed them down, killing 170 and taking 81 prisoners. On the Allied side, there were 21 killed and 132 wounded.[4]

The Brazilians may have captured three Paraguayan cannon, together with some stacked arms, horses, and oxen, but the key benefit they gained that day was strategic. Having dislodged the Paraguayans from the south bank of the Tebicuary, Caxias sent four of Ignácio's monitors up the waterway to impose an overwhelming advantage against any enemy works further inland. Then, on 1 September, the Allies discovered that the Marshal had abandoned the defenses that Thompson had previously established near the river; the troops boarded transports and occupied San Fernando unopposed. There they found a smoldering camp, signs of an abrupt departure, and the corpses of some three hundred fifty men, including that of the still-recognizable Bruguez.[5]

Dionísio Cerqueira, one of the first Brazilian officers to arrive on the scene, felt revulsion at the discovery of so many bodies and his horror at the prospect of finding further proof of slaughter as the Allies moved north:

> What a sight! Even today my mind recoils at the thought of it. … Close by we found an immense ditch piled high with corpses blackened with decay, all naked, some young, some old, all bearing horrible wounds from lances, bullets, and knives. They had slashed throats that swarmed with bluebottles, and chests torn open, with remnants of intestines that the buzzards had already worked through. All of the bodies were swollen with rot. Here and there I spied one with protruding eyes, but most were left with sockets pecked clean by the birds. … There were many such ditches near an orange grove, all left uncovered, and each one decorated with a pole driven through a throat or mouth, and bearing the warning "Traitors to the Fatherland." It was impossible to count the number of cadavers for everything was tossed about in disorder—but there were hundreds.[6]

In war, atrocities become fixed in the imagination. They take on a life of their own irrespective of their immediate military impact, and, in this case, the Allies reacted less with anger at the discovery of the executions than with apprehension about the future. These new proofs of the Marshal's stern hand did not portend a swift end to the fighting. The men and women whose bodies littered the grounds at San Fernando may have been Paraguayans, but so were their executioners—and they were still alive, somewhere up ahead, waiting to do battle. The marquis could delay his march, as he had done before on numerous occasions, or he could hasten to crush them before they could build yet another defensive line further upriver. Politics—and perhaps humanity—urged him to take the second course in an attempt to end the war before Christmas. Whether this made good military sense was another matter entirely.

The Marshal had maintained the defenses south of San Fernando for as long as he could. Ever since Martínez's surrender, Allied troops in the Chaco had been poised to make a frontal assault against Timbó. The fortifications that Caballero had constructed below that camp never presented the kind of obstruction that could stave off a concerted Allied attack, and the fleet had shelled the position on an almost daily basis. Once Rivas and the Brazilians succeeded in seizing the camp, they could outflank the Marshal's main units.

With this possibility already in mind, López considered abandoning Timbó as early as the end of June, but he decided to hold after Caballero showed unexpected resiliency in repulsing a Brazilian attack on 3 July.[7] Three weeks later, as setback after setback dimmed his chances along the eastern banks of the Paraguay, the Marshal changed his mind and ordered Caballero to evacuate the site before the Allies could flank it and secure the mouth of the Bermejo.[8]

At the same time, López ordered Thompson to reconnoiter the marshy areas north of the Tebicuary with a mind to establishing a new defensive position. The newly promoted colonel had already shown interest in the area around the Estero Poí, a narrow swamp similar to the Bellaco, and like its southern cousin, a natural extension of a vast inland lagoon. In this case, the Estero drained the Laguna Ypoá, Paraguay's largest lake, which was also the last natural obstacle of any size for a military force seeking to move northward toward Asunción.

Upriver of the Ypoá, the swamps gave way to lightly wooded hill country that until recently had been home to a sizable portion of Paraguay's rural population. It was also at the geographic center of the country's agrarian economy. The network of cart trails there could facilitate any Allied invasion of the Paraguayan heartland, wherein many farms and ranches beckoned as prizes. The Paraguayans desperately needed to hold on to these to prevent a general Allied offensive.

Thompson understood all of this. He located an attractive spot for a new defensive line at the mouth of the Pikysyry, a slow-flowing stream brimming with crayfish that emptied from the north end of the Ypoá into the main channel of the Paraguay. Near that confluence the *arroyo* was twenty yards across and relatively deep. This afforded an appropriate site for a fortified camp—so long as the colonel could find a sufficiently large span of dry land.

He soon discovered just what he was looking for at Angostura, along the north edge of the stream. When he reported his positive appraisal to the Marshal, Thompson received permission to erect a new series of batteries, throwing up earthworks and several gun emplacements en barbette using timber from nearby woods. In his estimation, Angostura held greater advantages for the defensive than the camps on the Tebicuary as the new site could not be flanked except on an impractically long semicircular trek through eastern Paraguay or on a similar trip through the Chaco.[9]

This fact appealed to the Marshal's sense of strategy. His mind had too often wandered from military matters in recent weeks, and it did him good to focus once again on killing Brazilians. He suggested that Thompson redeploy the guns held at Fortín, while he sent word to Asunción to have the Criollo brought down to Angostura. Guns were also brought from Timbó. Meanwhile, work began at a rapid pace at the new camp:

All means of conveyance were now put into requisition, both by land and water, and troops and guns were constantly arriving by steamers and by land. Quantities of ammunition were also brought. ... The riverside became crowded with stores of all kinds. The [adjoining] wood had to be cut down both for the river-batteries, and for opening a connection between them and the trenches, and for leaving an open space in front of them. It was very hard work to cut down this jungle, and make all so low that a rifleman could not hide himself behind any of the trees. However, it made a most excellent abatis.[10]

Thompson's men dug new trenches and dugouts and noted with evident pleasure that their position at Angostura placed them closer to their bases of supply. Oranges, manioc, and beef thus became available to them in quantities unseen for some time.[11] Health standards improved accordingly, and even though many areas of the Paraguayan interior were already seeing famine, at Angostura, the men ate.

A War of Movement

On 26 August, the same day that the Allies assaulted his forces on the Yacaré, Marshal López had abandoned San Fernando, leaving behind a number of observers and taking a slow overland route to Villeta, a rusty penny of a village located just above the Arroyo Pikysyry. The long train of retreating soldiers and camp followers that arrived at the town was noteworthy for its numbers, and for the rhythmical clanking of chained prisoners bringing up the rear.

Though the Allied fleet eventually succeeded in reaching the Tebicuary, for the moment Ignácio avoided the main channel of the big river, where his sailors still engaged in artillery duels with the battery on Fortín. On 28 August, however, the Paraguayan commander on the island received orders to retire. He pitched his three remaining guns into deep water and fled. The next morning, the crews of the imperial ironclads found themselves in virtual command of the river from the Pikysyry south.

As Colonel Thompson argued, Caxias should have taken the opportunity to instruct Ignácio to ascend the Paraguay and destroy any new batteries before the guns could be properly mounted. The marquis, however, was too busy celebrating the fall of Humaitá and the subsequent advance to the Tebicuary to see where his true advantage lay.[12] The marquis's circumspection was perhaps understandable—he was not a man of snap judgments—since it went against his idea of military planning to move precipitously when the intelligence on conditions further north remained hazy. He thus issued orders for the Allied army to halt, which gave the Paraguayans the time they needed to erect the defenses at Angostura. The batteries went up with little interference.

Perhaps Caxias could afford to bide his time. The Marshal needed a great many weeks if he wanted to mount any resistance. In April he had ordered his commander at Encarnación to redeploy his troops northward to the Tebicuary, and over several weeks some twelve hundred horsemen and another one hundred infantrymen made the trek from the Alto Paraná.[13] This left the southeastern corner of Paraguay undefended, save for small guerrilla bands that stayed behind to harass any enemy troops coming from the Misiones.[14]

López also ordered the evacuation of Mato Grosso in early March, first bringing his undermanned northern battalions to Asunción and integrating them into his main force. He left behind one small cavalry unit to act as observers on the Apa frontier. Amazingly enough, the Brazilians at Cuiabá were unaware of the fact that the Paraguayans had burned the port district at Corumbá before abandoning the province.[15] This omission may have reflected simple ignorance, or the willful policy of a Mato Grosso government tired of adventures; either way, the Brazilians failed to capitalize on it.

By the time Caxias realized what had happened in the north, the Paraguayan units that had bested Camisão in 1867 had long since joined the Marshal and moved on to Villeta; so, too, had the troops in Caballero's command—but only after 20 August, when the newly minted general abandoned Timbó.[16] In all, the army that the Marshal reestablished on the Pikysyry counted no more than twelve thousand men and few of these could be described as able. His adversaries had more than twice that number.

A number of Paraguayan deserters who had stumbled back to their old camp at Humaitá filled Caxias's ears with news that the Marshal intended to relinquish all of the territory on or near the Tebicuary. This made good sense militarily, but since it was still unclear where the enemy troops could go, the marquis elected to wait until the Paraguayans retired.[17] Besides, no less than nine hundred draft animals had been lost in the marshes on the trek from Humaitá to the Tebicuary, and Caxias had to consider that fact if he wished to establish secure bases of supply.[18]

As it turned out, the Allies acted with elaborate care in the weeks that followed. After taking Timbó, they razed the site and then redeployed some ten thousand men under General João Manoel out of Tayí and along the land route into Pilar, which the Marshal had emptied of its population over the previous season. Caxias had no idea where the town's defenders might have gone and so dispatched a strong unit inland through the Ñe'embucú marsh to search for stragglers.[19] The Brazilians often displayed reticence in thrusting deep into unknown territory, but on this occasion they took the risk and went through water up to their breasts. They caught sight of caimans, capybaras, and snakes, but found no Paraguayans and thus no threat to Allied lines of communication.

In fact, the Marshal's entire army had relocated to the north, and was busily constructing Thompson's new defenses. The weather was bad, and according to the colonel, the mud at the new battery went "so deep as nearly to hide an 8-inch gun."[20] And yet the Paraguayans achieved a great deal. The Allied leaders had insisted that the Marshal's troops were finished, but they continued to show signs of life.

The battery that Colonel Thompson's men built at Angostura was divided into two sections of nine guns each, some seven hundred yards apart, and so constructed that any Allied ironclad that ventured too close to the "port," which was located at the right battery, would come under fire from the left. The British engineer witnessed a test of this sort on 8 September, when three imperial vessels approached from the south. He concealed the guns of the left battery with boughs, and then, when the *Silvado* steamed into his line of fire, he hit her with a shell at the waterline. The smoke and noise surprised everyone on board and delighted the Paraguayan gunners. When she withdrew downriver a half hour later, the *Silvado* was struck with a 150-pounder on the other side, yet failed to sink.[21]

Among the many spectators at that day's gunnery was Marshal López, who sat safely at his new headquarters some four miles from the river atop a high hill called Loma Cumbarity. He had trimmed his beard, put on a clean uniform, and adjusted his telescope to observe the engagement with the ironclads. He looked refreshed and smiled knowingly as his artillerymen fired ball after ball at the "monkeys." It seemed like Paso Pucú all over again.

In declining battle at San Fernando, the Marshal bought himself some breathing space. Instead of pursuing the retreating Paraguayan army, the Allies settled into their new positions to begin preparations for a final offensive, as López had surmised. When the war was confined to Humaitá, it was a matter of an Allied hammer swinging over and over against a piece of Paraguayan masonry, which eventually broke into pieces under the blows. Now that the fortress had fallen, the conflict became a struggle not of armies, but of small units, dispersed over a vast area in which the Paraguayans no longer required a permanent base of operations. If the Marshal adopted an evasive strategy sooner rather than later, he could hold out in the hinterland, whether or not Caxias occupied Asunción. The marquis would have to destroy the enemy before this happened.

The Allied commander was clearly not thinking of Clausewitz's dictum, according to which the destruction of the enemy's ability to wage war constituted the foremost objective. The marquis's education, his upbringing, and his previous experience in Brazil's internal struggles all suggested that once the enemy capital fell, he could count the war over, and any guerrilla resistance that might come afterwards was hardly worth worrying about.

As always, the Allied commander lacked reliable intelligence. Maps were few, incomplete, and generally suspect. Chodasiewicz had done a fine job for the Allies in his 1867 balloon ascents, but his maps for the Humaitá area had no utility this far north. The Marshal successfully infiltrated spies into the enemy lines on most occasions. By contrast, Caxias had to depend on rumor or the word of untrustworthy Paraguayan deserters, and he could never be sure that he had gained an accurate picture. Though he questioned the viability of the Marshal's army, he was not the sort of commander to act decisively without verifiable information. He thus favored continual probes into Paraguayan territory, followed by more deliberate thrusts at the right time.

There was precious little of this in the early days of September 1868. Instead, the Allies built earthworks to fortify their own positions in the event of a López attack, which seemed unlikely but not impossible. Meanwhile, Ignácio's ships steamed up the Paraguay to learn whatever they could. The Brazilians spotted no torpedoes, no new chains, and relatively few Paraguayans, but the exact disposition of the Marshal's army remained hidden from them.

Exit Washburn

During this time, several unrelated factors asserted themselves in the minds of both López and his adversaries. For one thing, the commander of the *Wasp* had finally secured the marquis's permission to pass through the river blockade to retrieve Washburn. The US minister had spent the previous weeks shivering in the winter cold and eating manioc and beef consommé with his wife, all the while denying every accusation of complicity in a conspiracy. Then, in mid-August, Washburn wrote interim foreign minister Gumercindo Benítez to say that if the harassment of the representative of a friendly nation did not cease, he would retire from Paraguay. Before he could respond, however, the cultured and effete Benítez was swept up into the treason trials and an ugly fate. López replaced him with Luis Caminos, the sycophantic time-waster who had helped frustrate the Gould peace initiative in 1867, and on 2 September the US minister wrote to him to demand passports for himself, his family, and his retinue.[22]

With the *Wasp* now anchored off Villeta, no obvious reason for delay remained, save for the unanswered question of Bliss and Masterman, both of whom worked in the legation and who had been accused of complicity in the plot. Washburn insisted that the two men, both foreigners, enjoyed diplomatic immunity. Caminos, the police authorities, and presumably the Marshal himself challenged this interpretation, directing them to appear before a tribunal to explain their criminal comportment.

Washburn balked at the implied threat, though he did accede to a government request for an accounting of the properties still stored at the US legation. Over several days he received further demands for information.[23] Only then did he learn that specie from the treasury had supposedly been purloined by Bedoya and this money was what Caminos wished to find. The deficits may have resulted from poor bookkeeping, but Washburn evidently regarded the tale of lost silver as an excuse to steal any remaining coin that might turn up in private homes in Asunción. Hardly in good humor at these pointed suggestions, and frankly in fear for his life, the US minister informed Caminos that British subjects had previously removed their goods from the legation. As for the rest, the owners had requested that their properties be taken out of the country. No Paraguayan who had left property with Washburn dared to reclaim it, and with great reluctance, he left it all behind, later citing the possibility that López's agents might murder him had he delayed any longer.[24] More to the point, he had to consider his wife, who had reacted to the worsening situation with near-hysteria.

Captain Kirkland had no wish to involve his ship in any more diplomatic confrontations, and the Marshal refused to permit him to steam above Villeta. This left Washburn and his associates to fend for themselves. At midday on 10 September, the French and Italian consuls paid the US minister a final call, pressing their consular correspondence into his hands. Sallie Washburn and her little daughter walked the short distance to the Asunción quayside, the tiny Paraguayan steamer *Río Apa* having already arrived to carry the North American party to Villeta. Masterman stood at the door with Bliss, Washburn, and the consuls to watch as the minister's wife and her servants disappeared from view. In his memoir, the British pharmacist noted that the police then drew their swords, rushed forward, and roughly separated them from each other: "Good-bye, Mr. Washburn, don't forget us," Masterman implored, and the latter "half turned his face, which was deathly pale, made a deprecative gesture with his hand and hurried away."[25] The North American later claimed that he had instructed Bliss and Masterman to invent anything about him that could save them from torture.

Washburn tried to convince Kirkland to effect some kind of rescue, but the commander of the *Wasp* declined.[26] He pointedly omitted Washburn's strong words of protest when he met López for a final time on 11 September. The Marshal and Madame Lynch treated him with a flawless cordiality in this last interview, but when he returned to the *Wasp*, the commander discovered that the now ex-US minister to Asunción was not to be trifled with: Washburn, it emerged, had grown angry when presented with recently composed missives from Bliss and Masterman, who, from their place of confinement, demanded that the *Wasp* delay its departure and that their former chief relinquish any papers and "historical manuscripts." These letters were manifestly the product of duress, and could be safely dismissed, especially one sent to an imaginary Henry Bliss of New York, whose "son" informed him of Washburn's role as "the head of a revolution."[27]

His blood now boiling, Washburn composed a final missive to López; insultingly, it condemned the Marshal, like Nero, as the "common enemy of mankind." Kirkland saw to it that the letter went undelivered until his ship passed beneath the batteries at Angostura, thus saving his men from a shelling but also increasing Washburn's enmity for officers of the US Navy. As it was, the New Englander demanded to be taken to Caxias to provide the Allies with useful information. Not wanting to involve the United States in further difficulties in Paraguay, Kirkland quite appropriately denied the request.

During the entire voyage downriver, the ex-minister seethed with anger, and once he reached Buenos Aires, he gave interviews to the local press in which he commented in detail on Paraguayan military dispositions. This brought US neutrality into still greater uncertainty.[28] Washburn may have thought that his testimony would save lives and shorten the war, but his underlying rage, which was easy to discern, focused on settling scores against the US Navy, the Allied command, and, of course, López. The little whirlwind of complaints and demands for vindication thus set in motion resulted in a major congressional investigation in the United States less than a year later.[29]

Argentina Once Again

While Washburn's disclosures could have little impact at the front, they did succeed in diminishing Paraguay's standing as a David facing a monstrous Allied Goliath. The country's fame as a gallant underdog had sprung up with relative vigor in European capitals, and to a lesser extent, in the Allied countries themselves. This feeling was actuated in part by a nagging sense of guilt that the Paraguayans really had suffered too much as a result of the war, that, no matter how extensive the sins of the Marshal, his countrymen surely did not deserve such pain.[30] But Allied populations, having grown very tired of the war, also wanted it over as soon as possible, and were demanding some new political approach to bring this about. This attitude was increasingly present in Argentina.

That country was on the verge of inaugurating a new president, Domingo Faustino Sarmiento, and there was much change in the air. Elections had taken place in April and Mitre's chosen successor, Rufino Elizalde, had finished third behind the antiwar Sarmiento and the old federalist Urquiza. The Autonomists had split their presidential vote, but came together in the vice-presidential contest, which guaranteed the Bonaerenses a strong voice in the new government.[31]

Don Bartolo spent his "lame-duck" months brooding about his legacy and about the pro-Brazilian policies that he had designed and which now seemed so costly and ill-considered. The loans that his government had negotiated with provincial and British banks amounted to nearly six million pesos, and though the country's economic potential (and ability to repay) was substantial, this debt reminded the public of Mitre's failed approach to the war. The troops deployed in Paraguay had also gone without pay for twenty months, a fact that caused much bitterness in military circles.[32]

Mitre was still a comparatively young man, but his adherence to the alliance made him appear a gouty old uncle trying to find a chair in a drawing room full of more energetic *políticos*. Instead of actively campaigning in favor of Elizalde, he sat on the sidelines while military officers and heterodox Liberals pooled their energies in favor of Sarmiento, who was then serving as Argentine minister to Washington. Just a few years earlier, wags in Buenos Aires had dismissed Sarmiento as "don Yo," a provincial egomaniac who might fool foreigners with his grandiose schemes for the future but whom no one in the national capital could take seriously. At the same time, his basic competence, his commitment to economic development, European immigration, and public education were well known and approved. Mitre may have started Porteño elites thinking in terms of a country-wide modernization, but Sarmiento promised them that he could make the national transformation occur.

Part of this change required a new role for the military. Now that the Marshal's troops had been driven from the country, all citizens might benefit in avoiding a wider war. The Argentine people now had more to fear from Indigenous uprisings along the Patagonian frontier than from the Paraguayan military. A civil conflict in Corrientes, supposedly abetted by Urquicista agents, muddled the situation even more since it required a military response from the national government.[33]

The death of Sarmiento's son at Curupayty had snuffed out much of the new president's human warmth, so that in place of a once robust, forthright, and obdurate personality, there was left only frustration and peevishness.[34] Strangely enough, his personal loss failed to turn him into a fire-breathing extremist, and he did not seek revenge against the Marshal's people; in fact, his views on Paraguay remained ambiguous. As with many *provincianos* who found themselves in positions of responsibility in Buenos Aires, he retained a lingering sympathy for the Paraguayan soldiers. But at the same time he rejected everything in them that smacked, as he saw it, of native backwardness. He once noted, for example, that Paraguayan nationalism amounted to "the submission of the Indian, the slave, the barbarian, the ignorant man to his master" and that the "dog has the same obedience, the same courage, and the same fidelity to his owner."[35]

Sarmiento's view may have been racist, but he had no intention of letting it obscure his interpretation of Argentine interests. The country demanded not only victory over López, but also a broader geopolitical arrangement with the empire—something that would guarantee the cession of disputed territory while laying the groundwork for a lasting peace. Sarmiento felt that he had to adhere to the Triple Alliance Treaty but should also go beyond it in preparation for a new decade of Argentine prosperity.[36] Mitre had been a good ally to the Brazilians, but Sarmiento wished to be a smart politician.

Surubiy

The war had been cruel by every measure, but the Paraguayans had given up far more than the Allies. By the time that Humaitá fell, the Marshal had lost seventy thousand men along with eight steamships, thirteen floating batteries and chatas, fifty-one battle flags, seven Congreve rocket stands, and an enormous quantity of other munitions, powder, and supplies.[37] To this sad statistic must be added other tangible losses, like the damage done to the civilian economy and the system of internal trade, and the horrible impact on national morale. López could congratulate himself on the stubbornness of his soldiers, who were still willing to make the sacrifices he demanded. But the country was perilously close to collapse.

The Allies made more progress in September than in August. The navy conducted various reconnaissances along the river; on land, cavalry units under General Andrade Neves had taken the lead along the muddy or washed-out trails leading northward, and the main elements of Caxias's army were not far behind. It was rough going the whole way. The road was in a dreadful state, as described by the correspondent for *The Standard*:

> a succession of thick woods, thorns, and brushwood; during the three days' march the army was separated from the … river Paraguay, suffering dreadfully for want of water, because the water of the *pantanos* was undrinkable. … [The men] were however sustained by the idea that these were the last sacrifices imposed upon them for their country's sake, and … to prevent a tiger in human shape from continuing to oppress his own people.[38]

In the second week of the month, the Allies entered Villa Franca, another forgotten village that had previously loomed large in military matters because of its depots and small port. The Allies discovered supplies stockpiled there, including hundreds of dry uniforms, six hundred harnesses and tack, arms and powder, and sufficient rations to feed one thousand soldiers for a month.[39] Had his steamers worked as regularly as they once had, the Marshal could have gotten these provisions to the men who needed them.

When Caxias learned that the river had none of the predicted torpedoes, he decided on a more active use of the navy. The slow deliberation of his earlier deployments gave way—momentarily—to a flush of excitement as Allied troops crowded onto ships at Villa Franca and Humaitá, from whence they were steamed upriver to a point several leagues south of Angostura. There they were ordered to reassemble their ranks and advance directly against the enemy.

The time for action had finally come. At 5:30 a.m. on 23 September, the imperial cavalry launched an assault to gain possession of a drawbridge spanning a fast-moving stream, the Surubiy, located less than ten miles from the Pikysyry. The stream lacked an obvious ford for the horses, wagons, and oxcarts, and the adjacent ground was hilly and covered in brush. This gave the bridge its tactical value, and explains why the Marshal stationed skirmishers to guard the position, daring the enemy to attack.

The official account of the engagement that followed extolled Brazilian colonel João Niederauer Sobrinho as an intrepid and cold-blooded cavalry commander—a reputation he had earned in earlier battles.[40] On this occasion, however, his previous experience did not work for him. He suspected nothing while approaching the approximately two hundred Paraguayans guarding the north end of the bridge. These skirmishers displayed an odd composure as Niederauer's seven hundred horsemen advanced toward them. The colonel gave the signal to charge, and the Marshal's men poured a lively volley of musketry into the oncoming troops before retreating in mock surprise. Much to their regret, the Brazilians followed. Hidden in the nearby woods was a large unit of enemy cavalry, and as soon as Niederauer got across, these forces deployed from the woods, and there "ensued the real fight."[41] The Brazilians wheeled round and cut their way back to the bridge. Though they managed to reach the other side, the retreating horsemen became entangled with another unit of Brazilian cavalry moving up in support and were badly shot up. In their haste to flee the scene, the first unit had collided with the second and pushed it into a corner, where Paraguayan lancers rushed upon them with a fury.[42]

Since ancient times, generals have argued that armies should feign confusion and strike suddenly. This is what the Paraguayans accomplished at Surubiy. Given the Allied advantage in numbers, however, the Marshal's men could not hold out. General Andrade Neves sent eight battalions of infantry to aid the cavalrymen fighting in front of the bridge, and these were soon buttressed by a battalion of Voluntários. A Paraguayan force of some six hundred now faced thirty-five hundred of the enemy. Even this imbalance failed to bring on the expected retreat, for the men of the Acá Verá, who had hidden in the sarandí alongside the main trail, swooped down abruptly on the Brazilians, achieving total surprise. Confusion reigned until the bloodied Paraguayans withdrew northward, leaving behind a small rearguard to destroy the bridge.[43]

Angry that his troops had been deceived by the Marshal's soldiers, Caxias preferred a charge of cowardice against his own 5th Infantry Battalion, which he formally dissolved after a court-martial met on 28 September. While it was true that this battalion buckled under pressure, most of the other units were lost in the confusion as well, and it was excessive for the marquis to chastise this one detachment with a punishment "a thousand times crueler than death."[44] It was a display of impatience on his part. Politicians in Rio had demanded for months that Caxias stop wasting time, and move on to Asunción without further delay. He had answered their criticisms by insisting that the offensive be sure as well as swift. Surubiy suggested that he could expect neither, and that López still had many tricks at his disposal.

A Road Through the Chaco

General Gelly y Obes arrived at Villa Franca after Surubiy, and was soon poised to deploy his Argentine troops as the left wing of the Allied advance along the eastern bank of the Paraguay; Castro's Uruguayans were in the middle, and Caxias's main force of Brazilians on the far right. The latter troops had already moved up and secured the site formerly held by the Acá Verá, and Brazilian engineers soon rebuilt the bridge without any interference. The main defenses that Thompson had prepared at the Pikysyry still lay ahead, however, and recent experience suggested that the Allies could expect determined resistance. The Paraguayans had mounted just over a hundred guns at their new position, and had also dammed the water of the Pikysyry in three places so that the stream was over six feet deep on the high road.[45]

Caxias decided that the enemy defenses were too strong to be forced and resolved to turn the position from the rear. Having previously rejected an advance along the western bank of the Paraguay, he now resolved to get around the enemy batteries by constructing a road through the Chaco to a horseshoe bend in the river near Angostura; from there, he could recross the Paraguay at Villeta, move on the enemy's rear, and avoid the Marshal's batteries altogether. His engineers were far better placed to construct this road than López's men had been some months earlier. And now that Caballero's units had evacuated the Chaco, no Paraguayans could contest Allied progress through the wilderness.

The Marshal's units along the Pikysyry were weaker than their enthusiasm at Surubiy had implied. Access to provisions of beef, oranges, and manioc had improved the health and comportment of the troops, but not enough. The Paraguayans had left considerable arms and munitions behind in the rush from the south, and none of their artillery pieces could boast more than a hundred rounds.[46] Shipments of powder coming from the saltpeter deposits at Valenzuela had grown irregular.[47] As for manpower, it was likely that there were now no more than eighteen thousand men in the Paraguayan army, down two thousand from the previous month. There was little hope of reinforcement.

Though Caxias suspected that the Paraguayans had reached their final extremity, he still wanted positive proof. On 1 October, therefore, he directed Commodore Delphim to lead four ironclads and force the batteries at Angostura, testing whether the mouth of the Pikysyry was as well defended as rumored. The naval assault began before dawn and the ships succeeded in getting past the Paraguayan position. The four enemy vessels still took as many hits as they would have done by daylight, every shot of which struck an ironclad, giving out a flash of light. As Thompson related, the trees on the Chaco side threw a deep shade over half of the river, hiding the ironclads, which could only be seen by the moving reflection of their stacks on the water. After the sun rose "eight more ironclads came up to reconnoiter, and after them the *Belmonte*, a wooden gunboat with the admiral on board. ... [The Paraguayans] put a Whitworth 150-pounder shell into her at her water-line, upon which she immediately retreated."[48]

While Delphim's ships probed the Marshal's defenses from the river, Osório's troops moved forward from the south on land and conducted a reconnaissance at Villeta. This required that the Brazilians approach gingerly through hilly country above Angostura and strike at the Paraguayan left flank. With this in mind, Osório surged ahead at seven in the morning, encountering heavy resistance. He engaged the enemy at several spots, seized one redoubt, and drove the defenders from the trenches. Having determined the remaining number of enemy troops, he withdrew a short while later to his previous encampments. He lost 164 men, most of them wounded, while Paraguayan losses were negligible.[49]

For the next seven weeks, the Allies contented themselves with minor forays and regular naval duels with the Angostura batteries. The latter confrontations proved as inconclusive as those seen at Humaitá, and in his memoirs Thompson made much of the damage he inflicted on Ignácio's ironclads.[50] But the Brazilians developed considerable aptitude in repairing their vessels. The Paraguayans could observe from the opposite bank how the commodore's men emerged from the holds of their vessels to dump splinters, torn doors, glass, and other refuse into the water—Thompson's gunners had obviously perforated the interior of the steamers. The damage was nonetheless limited, and Ignácio's crews soon put the flotilla back into shape.

The Allies likewise proved competent in cutting a road through the Chaco. This required a herculean effort from the engineers. They had to establish a base on the Chaco side opposite Palmas, where the main Brazilian camp was situated, and slice through the foliage on a thirty-mile track around a series of lagoons until they could emerge again on the Paraguay just above Angostura. The road they constructed required felling thirty thousand caranday palms, which were laid transversally, side by side, on muddy ground liable to flood whenever the river ran high.

The elements worked against the thousand men delegated to aid the engineers. On any given day, they could be found waist-deep in water trying to fight off the snakes, insects, and their own exhaustion. Yet even in the driving rain they kept up their labors. They built five bridges across the deepest gullies and cut through heavy masses of tangled vines and palmettos, sometimes clearing over one thousand yards daily.[51] They also had to contend with a brief outbreak of cholera.[52]

The marquis, who came to visit on several occasions, wondered whether the effort to build a road through the Chaco might prove impractical.[53] His engineers knew better, and so did the Paraguayan pickets who operated nearby; they could not believe their eyes as the kambáes pushed relentlessly forward. Their own military had had no similar resources during the withdrawal some months earlier, and the officers had hoped, naively, that the jungle would delay the Allies indefinitely.

The pluck of the Paraguayans was all that the Marshal really had left in the Chaco. He had organized some two hundred soldiers into a roving strike force after Caballero retreated across the Paraguay in August. This small unit, commanded by a stern-faced young captain named Patricio Escobar, could be dispatched back into the Chaco at a moment's notice. Such a small number of men, however, could only offer passing harassment to an army of five thousand Brazilians. On the other hand, Escobar had lately fallen into disfavor and was anxious to strike at the enemy to prove his loyalty to the Marshal. On two different occasions, he assaulted the Allied vanguard, first on 16 October, and then again ten days later. Neither effort accomplished anything.[54] Escobar's courage added to the legend of Paraguayan ferocity, yet never slowed the Allied advance.[55]

About a mile below Villeta on the Chaco side lays a little stream called the Araguay, which empties into the Paraguay just out of sight of that community. Though the mouth of this arroyo was narrow, it provided enough room to admit one of the smaller Brazilian paddle steamers. The Paraguayans could do little to hamper Ignácio's transport of provisions through this opening and into safer anchorages. As the engineers completed the road from the south, Caxias dispatched supplies for the entire Allied army by means of the Araguay. Meanwhile, Argolo's troops constructed camps upstream from the confluence with the Paraguay. All were well situated to launch incursions against López's positions on the Pikysyry.

The Marshal could have directed Escobar or Caballero to slow Allied progress in the Chaco, but having beheld the soggy terrain at first hand, he gave little credence to the enemy's accomplishing much in that quarter.[56] He disregarded the reports of spies and treated the whole matter as a probable diversion from the real threat, which would come from a direct confrontation along the Pikysyry.[57]

Osório and the other Allied generals had already positioned their forces with just such an attack in mind. This left the Paraguayans with little choice but to prepare for an assault that might come from one direction or the other, or from both at the same time. That Caxias had placed the enemy into a vise was proof of his strategic acumen, for though he may have made slow progress initially, his efforts now appeared farsighted. The marquis's building of the Chaco road was a decisive achievement and the situation in November 1868 confirmed his view that the end was near.

The Marquis Crosses The River

Foreign military analysts have generally treated López as a third-class general and a fourth-class strategist. But he occasionally showed great skill in his use of the minimal resources available to him.[58] Once he realized that the marquis was more likely to move on Villeta, he responded energetically. He gave orders to construct a long line of trenches around the village, and he converted the greater part of his troops into a mobile reserve, leaving only enough men in the trenches to operate the artillery.[59] Five of the six Paraguayan battalions at Angostura were detached from Thompson's command to join this larger force, which the Marshal kept near his headquarters at Itá Ybaté, from whence he could deploy them at will.

A showdown of some kind was imminent, and it produced no end of worry. The news from San Fernando failed to reassure the foreigners, and the various European representatives expressed a common wish to prevent a general slaughter. As with Washburn, they feared for their fellow citizens still living in Paraguay and worried that López might kill them once the Brazilians succeeded in carrying the Pikysyry positions. But they also apparently believed, as the US minister had not, that the task of negotiating their release might prove more fruitful if conducted by naval personnel on the scene rather than by diplomats in Buenos Aires. Secretary Gould had traveled by steamer to Angostura at the end of September; he obtained nothing substantial before returning downriver rather than engage in a fruitless correspondence.

His Italian and French associates enjoyed better luck. During October and November, steamers from those two countries made almost daily transits between the chief Allied camp at Palmas and Thompson's batteries at Angostura.[60] Caxias had finally stopped interfering with the passage of neutral vessels, probably calculating the benefit to the Allies of preventing the murder of foreign noncombatants—or at least being able to hold López responsible for their deaths.

The Paraguayans received these delegations with a syrupy politeness, offering them many bottles of carefully hoarded wine. The negotiations to free the European residents were nonetheless protracted. Part of the problem involved the Brazilian warships, nine of which had run the Angostura batteries and were shelling the Paraguayans with such regularity that the Marshal postponed several meetings.[61] In the end, the Italian steamer *Ardita* took away some fifty-two individuals, mostly women and children, while the French *Decidée* rescued a smaller number.[62] Among the Frenchmen released was Gustave Bayon de Libertat, the chancellor of the consulate in Luque, whom the Paraguayans had held in irons since 31 August for having supposedly colluded in Benigno's "conspiracy."

French consul Paul Cuverville, who on at least one occasion had journeyed to Itá Ybaté along with his Italian colleague Lorenzo Chapperon, had been unable to shield Libertat with the diplomatic immunity that Washburn had used to protect Bliss and Masterman. A long and painful interrogation directed by Fathers Maíz and Román ensued, and it was only through the hard work of Cuverville and the officers of the *Decidée* that Libertat escaped with his life.[63] While under torture, he had already sworn that he had received forty thousand pesos from the conspirators and was sent down to Thompson to be delivered to the French captain as a criminal. The British engineer handed him over as instructed and noticed that the steamer "took away a number of heavy cases [that] … probably contained some of the ladies' jewelry, which had been collected in 1867, as well as a large number of doubloons."[64]

This passing reference to monies and jewelry transported on the French vessel explains another element in the Marshal's unexpectedly gracious reception of the naval officers: he wished to send his own funds through the Allied blockade and on to Europe, where it would provide a cushion for his family in the event of a forced exile. The intended recipient of these properties was the brother of Dr. William Stewart, who was expected to guard them until Lynch or López arrived in Edinburgh.[65] Though details on this whole affair remain nebulous, it does for once appear that the Marshal had adopted a practical attitude about his future.

Practicality was certainly called for. In early November 1868, Caxias inspected the Chaco road that his engineers had nearly completed. Having previously doubted their ability to make any headway, he now showed considerable confidence and announced a plan to promptly strike Villeta. This declaration was in fact a ruse, for he really wanted to cross the Paraguay at a place some distance north of the town, and hoped that the Marshal would waste time preparing for a nonexistent attack.

Over the next four weeks, his troops moved artillery pieces and munitions to forward areas along the Chaco road. Meanwhile, as his naval gunners peppered Angostura, his land forces conducted a series of short but sharp probes against the Pikysyry line.[66] The most serious of these occurred on 16 November, when Osório's horsemen attempted to capture several Paraguayan pickets in the hours before dawn. By one account, the Marshal's men slipped away before the cavalry could even approach them, and according to another, the Brazilians were driven from the field with heavy casualties.[67]

On 21 November, the main Allied infantry units crossed the river from Palmas and, unopposed, bivouacked at a new camp on the Chaco side called Santa Teresa. The next day, the same units made their way north along the road and linked up with Argolo's 2nd Corps, which was already well forward. Allied troop strength in the Chaco now amounted to some thirty-two thousand men, with ample artillery and cavalry accompanying the infantry.

A few days later, having established a new headquarters at one of the Chaco guard posts, Caxias learned of a rise in the river that threatened to turn the road into a morass. Rather than see his troops bogged down at this late date, he called a temporary halt. He had no desire to postpone his grand flanking maneuver, however, and decided to use the time to mount a major diversion.

On 28 November, Commodore Dephim and four ships of his flotilla surged north toward Asunción with orders to shell the city. This barrage, it was hoped, would draw the enemy away from the Pikysyry to help defend the former capital, drastically stretching his available resources. As it turned out, Caxias failed to trick the Paraguayans into thinking this bombardment would bring an incursion of the sort that Washburn had predicted. López telegraphed news of Allied naval movements, giving his own steamer, the *Piribebé*, just enough time to escape northward—but the Marshal kept his troops where they were.[68]

The bombardment of Asunción occurred the next day. Delphim targeted the government buildings nearest the bay, and this time scored hits against the arsenal, customs house, shipyard, and executive palace, which saw one of its four decorative pinnacles blown apart when a ball tore through a flagstaff bearing the national ensign. The symbolic value of the target was noteworthy, but the few Paraguayan defenders in Asunción took heart when the Brazilians failed to land troops.

Meanwhile, Caxias had taken up the march once again. The waters had receded from the high mark of the previous week, and the engineers repaired the damaged sections of the road. The full force of Brazilians and Argentines pushed steadily up the Chaco trail to a spot several miles above Villeta, where they crossed unopposed on 5 December in one of the best-executed maneuvers of the whole campaign. Only a tiny number of Paraguayan cavalrymen awaited them, and they withdrew at once to rejoin López on the Pikysyry. A larger column, composed of some two thousand cavalrymen under Luis Caminos, had been delegated to attack the invaders but inexplicably retreated east to Cerro León, having failed even to attempt to detain the enemy.[69]

By dusk, over fifteen thousand Allied troops landed on the eastern bank of the Paraguay River. Despite a steady rain, Caxias sent scouts to determine the strength of any enemy units in the vicinity.[70] Colonel Niederauer Sobrinho's cavalry crossed a little bridge that spanned the fast-flowing Ytororó, but as he met no enemy resistance he returned to the riverfront and declared the path to Angostura and the Pikysyry clear. This fact, he seemed to suggest, set the necessary conditions for the final assaults of the war.

Enter McMahon

On 3 December, the US warship *Wasp* reappeared off the Paraguayan position at Angostura, this time flying the colors of Rear Admiral Charles Davis, the commander of the US South Atlantic Squadron, and carrying Martin T. McMahon, the new American minister to Asunción. Like his counterpart in Rio, James Watson Webb, McMahon was a former army general. He had spent a month in Brazil and Argentina, interviewing key personages and reading the miscellaneous reports on Paraguay. The ministry to the inland republic was far removed from the normal diplomatic posting yet romantic enough to inspire some real interest in McMahon. The fact that Paraguay was at war only made the country more appealing. The new minister had already concluded that López needed to be treated with a firm hand and that Washburn's dabbling had obstructed the quest for peace, making the extraction of foreign nationals from the war zone that much more difficult.[71]

The visit of the HMS *Beacon* a few weeks earlier had secured the evacuation of a handful of British subjects, and with this precedent (and that the efforts of the French and Italian naval officers) in mind, the newly arrived minister decided to try his own luck with López.[72] He had brought Admiral Davis along to highlight the seriousness of US resolve, and to signal that where reason and charm failed, the Americans had recourse to the kind of force to which Captain Kirkland had alluded.

As it turned out, the Marshal was anxious to meet the new minister, whose arrival could redound to Paraguay's advantage. He put on a good show. In contrast to Ulysses S. Grant, who seems to have indulged in a single bout of hard drinking during four years of war (and was ever afterwards pilloried as a drunkard), the Marshal had lately evolved into a steady imbiber. He preferred brandy and imported clarets, but at length he moved on to the local caña, of which he grew inordinately fond, regarding it as a cure for his constant stomach distress and toothache. No one at Itá Ybaté, not even Madame Lynch, had dared to chide him for the habit.[73] Now, however, he needed to put on an attractive face and appear self-assured and sober. Captain Kirkland requested an interview directly after dropping anchor, and informed the Marshal that Admiral Davis wished to see him on a mission of mercy. Davis met with López that evening at Colonel Thompson's thatch-covered quarters in Angostura. Their conversation grew friendlier with every passing minute, it being obvious, among other things, that both men disliked the recently departed Washburn.

Davis observed that the detention of Bliss and Masterman had created an unnecessary rift in the good relation between Paraguay and the United States but this barrier could be surmounted if the Marshal now gave up the two men. López, having anticipated this request, responded affirmatively. Despite their obvious guilt, he had hoped for some time to arrange their evacuation but had been prevented from doing so by the tribunals, whose useful work had not yet concluded.[74] Davis had some arguments of his own "in the shape of 11-inch guns, which would have been applied in a more persuasive manner than the Brazilians did theirs."[75]

The admiral, however, saw no need to underscore his firepower since the Paraguayan leader proved perfectly happy to release the miscreants, provided that American authorities promise them an appropriate upbraiding and punishment. This meant that the former employees of the legation should foreswear all contact with Allied representatives, stop insisting on their innocence, and instead accept their true status as conspirators released through an act of clemency.

Whether or not the gray-whiskered Davis believed in their guilt, he agreed to these conditions. Masterman and Bliss, the latter bearing multiple copies of his notorious pamphlet, were released to US custody on 10 December. They spent the next several months in a comfortable semi-confinement on board a series of American warships before arriving at New York.[76] State Department functionaries escorted them to Washington to testify before Congress, where both exonerated Washburn, denounced their treatment by the US Navy, and castigated López as a sadistic criminal.[77]

Though these two men might have found it difficult to banish the Marshal from their thoughts, he had far more pressing things to do than concern himself with them. McMahon had disembarked on 12 December, but before he presented his credentials, the Marquis of Caxias launched the first incursion of the December campaign. At least fifteen thousand Brazilians had landed behind the Paraguayan lines. They were coming fast.

THE DECEMBER CAMPAIGN

The Marquis of Caxias was responsible for the efficient and largely bloodless way in which the Allied army attained its operational goals in the final months of 1868. This contrasted profoundly with the earlier sloppiness. Caxias had improved discipline throughout the Allied forces, promoting officers of proven ability and giving them command over vanguard units. He had maximized the use of his engineers and had kept up steady pressure against enemy defenses that were stronger in some ways than those at Humaitá. Now, in early December, the marquis offered an astonishing display, first, of a striking personal courage more often associated with Osório, and second, of an unforgivable clumsiness in letting the Marshal slip out of the trap once again.

General Argolo, who had crossed his entire 2nd Corps from the Chaco, dispatched mounted elements under Colonel Niederauer Sobrinho during the early evening hours of 6 December to reconnoiter the southeastern track towards Villeta. The colonel had minimal information about what lay ahead. He encountered many streams, which the troop found easy to cross, and then a more substantial creek, over which stretched an unguarded wooden bridge. Crossing it, Niederauer advanced a short distance to a forest, then pulled back rather than face sharpshooters in the nighttime. In returning to base he neglected to secure the bridge, whose centrality neither he, nor Argolo, nor anyone else, had properly recognized.[1]

On his side, the Marshal wasted no time dispatching General Caballero and his mobile reserve to occupy the bridge, which turned out to be the most defensible position in the whole sector. The rivulets that the Brazilians had discovered intermingled, intertwined, and ultimately joined together at this point into a single roiling torrent some fifteen feet across that sent up clouds of mist as it fell through a defile. The Ytororó, as the stream was called, was hemmed by masses of brambles and scrub. Only the bridge, and the clearing on the far side, offered passage for the troops, and Caballero had drawn up his thirty-five hundred men to protect it. They felt rushed and fatigued, having just arrived on the scene after a long night's march. But even so, they held the advantage, for the Brazilians could not outflank them.

Ytororó

Though by now Caxias understood how vital the bridge was, he saw no alternative but to storm the position with superior numbers. He ordered the attack for the early hours of the 7 December. Colonel Fernando Machado broke through the defile first, accompanied by four battalions of infantry. As they approached from the far side, they offered the enemy the narrowest of fronts, perfect for the enfiladed fire that Caballero poured upon them. The leading Brazilian battalions collapsed in disorder, then staggered back through other units still trying to advance. Bodies crumpled and flew into pieces as balls rent the air.

Realizing that the advance might disintegrate before it got started, Machado rode into the field of fire, beckoning his men to re-form their line and charge. Just as they came together, however, a shot blew the colonel from his horse. His men took little notice at first and they continued to advance without him, managing through sheer willpower to gain the far side of the bridge despite the withering fire. Then, after a bloody assault against the nearest artillery position, they seized two Paraguayan guns.

This would have given them cause for satisfaction had they had time to think; unfortunately, they discovered too late that the Marshal had prepared another ambush. Hidden among the foliage, just out of sight, were hundreds of Paraguayan infantrymen pressed low against the ground until their commanding officers, Colonels Valois Rivarola and Julián Godoy, gave the signal to attack. They then rose and plunged downward with their sabers and bayonets, flailing away at the stupefied enemy.[2]

For a time, the Paraguayan and Brazilian soldiers fought in such close quarters that they appeared to congeal into a single mass. Machado had already died trying to take the bridge, and his desperate subordinates barely rallied their men into defensive squares. The Brazilians could not hold against the furious charges coming at them from three directions, and in short order, they scattered back across the bridge, first the cavalry, then the infantry.[3]

Caxias witnessed the action through his spyglass: he could see the danger in failing to regain the momentum. Turning to Colonel Niederauer, he gave orders to charge the bridge with five regiments of Riograndense cavalry. The colonel, who had proven his bravery many times, raced towards the enemy. The horsemen succeeded in getting forward, but their progress was slowed by the many dazed survivors of the initial assault—and by the bodies that lay about them in clumps.

Cavalrymen of the mid-1800s generally believed that if they broke into a mass of infantry it would naturally fall to pieces, but such was not the case here. A single soldier with a machete could swing for a hamstring cut and both horse and rider would go down together. This happened many times over the next few minutes. Thrusting his saber to and fro, Niederauer somehow managed to seize four enemy cannon and, after a time, drove the Paraguayans into the bush. Rivarola and Godoy soon counterattacked, however, aided by fifteen hundred reinforcements who had made their way through the swamps and now joined their fire with that of the men already there.

The imperial cavalry and infantry units proceeded to disperse into three or four separate clusters, all of which began to break under the unremitting discharges. These soldiers had presumed that López had already been bested, and that his men could ill afford a show of determination on empty stomachs at this juncture. And yet, their unexpected strength could not be ignored. It served first to shock, then to terrify.

Although the Brazilians failed to see it, in truth, there was more than momentary indecision on the other side. Some of the newly arrived Paraguayans balked at the numbers they faced and started to edge away from the field, but just as one battalion started to break, one of the infantry commanders blustered in Guaraní that the soldiers were worse than old women.[4]

This did the trick. Those to whom the reproach was directed were teenaged boys who still smarted from an insult in a way that crusty veterans had long since learned to ignore.[5] The young soldiers gritted their teeth, turned around, and the other men followed. The Paraguayan ranks then closed, and with a superhuman effort, they succeeded in pushing the enemy back. The remaining Brazilians on the south side of the bridge broke ranks and crowded one upon another in an attempt to escape. Some fell into the torrent and drowned.

The marquis witnessed this reversal and immediately ordered General Hilario Gurjão to retake the bridge. The general hesitated not a moment, charging with all dispatch, leading the 1st Infantry Battalion, then the 36th Voluntários, and finally the 24th and the 51st. Still more battalions inched their way forward, and after much exertion, it appeared that Gurjão would clear the Paraguayans from the far side of the Ytororó. Suddenly, with the momentum still in his favor, the general barked out a final word of encouragement, but at that very moment a Minié ball tore into his left arm, cutting an artery and causing Gurjão to tumble, unconscious, from his mount. A sergeant who had served him as a personal retainer lifted the general over his back and, in spite of unremitting musket fire, managed to carry him to safety.[6] Meanwhile, the units Gurjão had led across the bridge fell back to where they had started.

The battle, which the Argentine general José Ignacio Garmendia likened to a bloody contest between red and black ants, had seesawed back and forth with some sixteen thousand men willing to do anything—or everything—to gain mastery over a single wooden bridge.[7] The Paraguayans still refused to cede the perimeter, so the marquis next directed General Argolo, commander of the 2nd Corps, to replace Gurjão, but he had no more success in moving his soldiers forward than those who had gone before, and, in fact, fell mortally wounded in the effort. Caxias next ordered twelve more battalions up from the 1st Corps, but the Paraguayans stopped them cold, too.

Brazilian casualties mounted rapidly and the marquis lost his patience. Glancing behind him to urge still more reinforcements forward, he unsheathed his sword and lifted it high over his head. The blade had stayed in its scabbard for so many seasons that when he drew it out, a cloud of rust supposedly followed.[8] Caxias had no intention of appearing romantic in this gesture, but, in spite of his sixty-four years, he still acted with the passion and determination of a young man. "All of you who are Brazilians, follow me!" he shouted, galloping at full speed toward the bridge with his remaining units behind him.[9] All who witnessed this spectacle admitted that it was the marquis's finest—or at least most melodramatic—hour. His action brought the envisioned result. Galvanized, the troops surged forward with cheers for Caxias. Niederauer's cavalry recovered from their previous awkwardness and closed rapidly. The fury that had been blunted now grew unstoppable.[10]

The Paraguayans, already tired from a battle that had lasted the whole day, needed no further persuasion to give way. They had already received word of the approach of General Osório's troops and now conceded the field. Caballero's cavalry offered just enough resistance to cover the infantry's withdrawal during the late afternoon, and then the horsemen disappeared from sight, hiding in the nearest woods. The Brazilians refused to follow, and at dawn the next day the Marshal's men retreated southward toward another creek, the Avay.

Ytororó was perhaps the hardest-fought engagement of the war. Limitations in both terrain and tactics made it the scene of terrible hand-to-hand combat.[11] Caxias's decision to attack frontally negated the numerical advantage he enjoyed and left his units open to enfilade. With his superiority in firepower he could have pummeled the enemy troops and forced their withdrawal, but the marquis dared not wait. The Paraguayans were so exhausted that they could offer no better than passing resistance anywhere above Angostura and they had not challenged his landing upriver. Perhaps the Allied commander had already drawn too many conclusions from that show of indecision. If that was the case, it was certainly costly.

Without censuring Caxias, whose eleventh-hour heroics quickly became legendary, we should give proper due on this occasion to Marshal López. Though not present at the bridge, he had seized the initiative before the battle began, spotted a dramatic weakness in the Allied line of advance, deployed his troops effectively, and, for once, allowed his field commanders sufficient freedom that they could exact a heavy toll for every inch of ground gained. To be sure, the Brazilians won at Ytororó, but at a heavy cost: three thousand killed, wounded, and missing against just twelve hundred for the Paraguayans. And among these casualties, the Allies counted several senior officers, including Generals Gurjão and Argolo.[12]

The marquis might perhaps be faulted for failing to enlist Osório's 3rd Corps in the action at Ytororó. The general had some five thousand men in his columns and they were advancing perpendicular to the main forces, some nine miles to the east. Though marching in the wrong direction, they could still have turned and offered support had anyone bothered to inform them. If the plan was for Argolo to attack in front and for Osório to attack in the rear of Caballero's forces, then Caxias must have misjudged either the lay of the land or the time required to turn the Paraguayan flank.[13] As he noted a few years later, the fault may have rested with a captured Paraguayan officer who had acted as a guide for Osório and, accidentally—or purposely, as the case may be—took the general around in circles so that he arrived thirty minutes too late to do any good.[14]

Caballero's men were now encamped five miles to the south. They had just relinquished many lives to the Brazilians, together with six guns, and they were keen to avoid any further clashes. But the Allied commander had no intention of letting them rest. Within hours of the Paraguayan retreat, he had his troops marching up from behind, ready for still more fighting. They camped outside the little village of Ypané, before pushing south again three days later.

The inconsistency of the climate favored neither side. The gritty *viento norte*, which blew sand in from the Chaco, battered the line of march toward the Avay so consistently that Brazilian soldiers found themselves choking and unable to see their way forward. The wind reminded every man present how hellish Paraguay can be in the summertime and how unimportant man can be in the scheme of things. As it was, the soldiers found themselves praying for rain, yet fearing what would happen if it fell upon them in the usual fashion, bringing mud and flooding.[15]

Caballero spent 9 and 10 December preparing his defenses at the Avay. He had consulted with the Marshal at Villeta and secured one extra battalion and twelve artillery pieces. This brought his total strength to fifty-five hundred men and eighteen guns, but it did little to improve his odds. López chose to retain some units along the line of the Pikysyry and at Angostura, and hoped that Caballero could make do. In contrast to the situation at the Ytororó, however, the general could not count on favorable terrain, which in this case afforded him no opportunity for enfilade.

López had shamed Caballero into setting up his defenses at a weak position. He had previously queried two of his corps commanders, Valois Rivarola and Germán Serrano, about the wisdom of establishing a defense at the Avay. His asking them at all was unusual, but so were their responses. The first stated bluntly that any such effort would fail, while the second expressed confidence, even pride, in the army's ability to hold back the enemy as the infantry had done at Ytororó. Ignoring the obvious fact that the Paraguayans lost the latter battle, the Marshal chose to credit Serrano's reassurances over Rivarola's doubts. When Caballero demurred and essentially seconded the latter's opinion, López overruled him, saying that if either man lacked the courage to fight the enemy, then he would find officers who could do the job.[16] This imputation of cowardice brought Caballero around. He now steeled himself for the slaughter to come.

Rivarola met with Serrano shortly thereafter atop a small hill at the south side of the Avay. The Marshal had just promoted Serrano to full colonel, a fact that did not sit so well with the other officer. Noticing the shiny stars that now decorated the younger man's epaulettes, Rivarola smirked: "Well, my friend, soon you will have an opportunity to parade your new stars. The enemy is closing in on us, and the kambáes are not coming with withered washcloths."[17] Serrano tried to smile but found no way to respond.

Avay

Caballero drew up his forces in a semicircle at the base of the hillock, locating ten guns at the center and four at either side. He dug trenches but realized that Caxias would never grant him enough time to do this properly. In the near distance, he spied a large open pasture from which the Allies could outflank his troops no matter how he deployed them. And, while the Ytororó could not be forded, the Avay was both shallow and slow moving, and the Allies could get across it at a dozen spots. It thus presented itself as a disaster in the making.

On 10 December, while the Marshal was negotiating with Admiral Davis, the Brazilians prepared the attack. General Osório had led the way from the Ytororó with his 3rd Corps, followed by the 1st and 2nd Corps, commanded by Generals Jacinto Machado de Bittencourt and Luiz Mena Barreto, respectively. Cavalry units under General Andrade Neves covered the right wing, and those under General Manoel Mena Barreto, who had replaced the dead Argolo, had charge of the left.[18] These troops had their problems, with many men displaying the symptoms of battle stress: jumpiness, cold sweats, an inability to make themselves understood, and a decided incidence of the "thousand yard stare." Even so, when taken together, the Allied host facing Caballero amounted to around twenty-two thousand men—four times what the Paraguayans had.

The marquis established his headquarters near the northern bank of the Avay, letting the Paraguayans contemplate his forces as they assembled for the attack. The temperature had fallen abruptly, and so many black clouds had gathered overhead that everyone present could have mistaken the morning hours of

11 December for nighttime. Despite the dimness, there was much bright color on display. As Chris Leuchars put it, the "awesome sight of tens of thousands of their enemies, led by bands playing, in uniforms of blue, white, and gray, together with their artillery and cavalry, must have been terrifying."[19] Indeed, Marshal López may have had second thoughts, for he sent a last-minute message urging Caballero to withdraw to safer ground.[20] Before the note arrived, however, the Allies began to shell the general's position at the Avay and the Paraguayans could not get themselves deep into their dugouts. Then, at 10:00 a.m. sharp, Caxias gave the order to attack at a moment that coincided with a colossal downpour.

Their powder wet, neither the Brazilians nor the Paraguayans could fire their guns properly, or even keep the water from their eyes. Muskets became drenched and could only serve as clubs; lances, sabers, and bayonets could not be efficiently wielded under the driving rain. But none of this lessened the viciousness of the fight, and on their side, the Paraguayans pressed on with grim desperation, inflamed by the idea that this might be their last chance.[21]

The Marshal's men repulsed the enemy once, and the Brazilians, deeming the odds against them sufficiently reduced, now lunged forward again, only to be driven back a second time with heavy losses. This happened over and over during the next four hours. At one juncture, General Caballero directed the bulk of his cavalry down the slope of the hill to attack the Brazilian center in a fanatical charge, forcing the Allies back. Not to be outdone, General Osório rushed to the scene, slashing his saber through the falling rain. His men, who had wavered in the face of the oncoming cavalry, now turned and poured a volley among their pursuers. At that moment, Osório paused for a split second to survey the ground. Almost on reflex, he lowered his saber, and as he did a Minié ball struck him and shattered his lower jaw.[22]

Osório was seriously wounded. Blood streamed through his beard and onto his saddle horn, and yet he remained at the head of his troops, gesturing toward the front with all his might, though he was now quite unable to speak. Somehow Osório stayed erect on his horse, hiding the damage done to his person. His men continued to advance until an aide, having caught sight of the general's twisted face, wrenched the reins from his hand and led him back through the lines. Soon shouts went from man to man that their general might die then and there. Despite his agony, however, Osório pulled himself straight and got free of his aides, taking one or two of his troopers by their shoulders and pinching them hard. He made them see that he wished to be driven up to the forward line. It was far better that his men see their commander grievously hurt than not see him at all.

The Riograndense general had survived a dozen battles, and unlike López, he knew that he needed to occasionally place himself under enemy fire. His seeming invulnerability on such occasions had served as a powerful talisman to his men since the onset of hostilities, and Caxias viewed Osório as an indispensable force of cohesion within the army. Any doubts created by his wound would surely bring trouble now that the final offensive had begun.

The marquis understood what he had to do. As at Ytororó, he unsheathed his sword and rode to the front line, the entire 2nd Corps following behind. The span of land between the original Brazilian position and that of the Paraguayans overflowed with cadavers—so many that in some spots a man could walk fifty yards stepping from one body to another. The marquis's enthusiasm was irresistible and the Brazilians surged forward once more. The rain was still pouring, and the guns and muskets functioned only in fits and starts, but, as the engagement entered its third hour, the violence astounded every observer. The carnage, though arranged on a smaller scale, had the same aspect as that seen at Tuyutí and Curupayty.[23]

In Rio de Janeiro's Museu Nacional de Belas Artes, visitors today can find an enormous commemorative tableau of the battle of Avay painted by Pedro Américo de Figueiredo e Melo between 1872 and 1877. The painting is wildly inaccurate. It misrepresents the terrain, the deployment of troops, the cut of the uniforms, the look of the sky, and the placement of the key figures involved.[24] In one aspect, however, it is strikingly true to the event, for it captures the terror, the sense of fear that the day epitomized for both sides. Caxias conducted himself well in the heat of the fight. He was remarkably clearheaded but he could never have denied the horror of the scene before him: a large stretch of ground glazed horribly with blood and rainwater, upon which torn bodies competed for space with shreds of uniforms, kepis, cartridge boxes, and broken sabers, all blending into a bouillabaisse of gore.

Caballero, who in later years tried to scrape from his brain every terrible memory of that day, could not help but recoil at the sight. The resistance he offered at the Avay had been hopeless from the start. Assaulted from the center by two well-armed corps, his little army fell to pieces, first in the front and then along the edges. At some point, the general ordered his men to form five defensive squares, but these, too, collapsed after Caxias sent Mena Barreto's corps to attack from the left.

The sky started to clear during the fourth hour of combat. Dry powder was then brought up, enough for the Brazilian cannons to let off repeated volleys and for a few Congreve rockets to explode overhead. The Paraguayan resistance began to wane in consequence. Cerqueira was close enough to witness every detail of the murderous process, every show of bravery and sacrifice, as the Marshal's men were finally overwhelmed by an avalanche of imperial troops.[25]

Darkness fell a few hours later, perhaps mercifully, for the visual expression of brutality at the Avay was now hidden by the night, though the cries of wounded men were still perceptible. The Southern Cross came out, the crickets sang, and exhausted men fell asleep. In the tents that served as field hospitals, the doctors sawed off arms and legs by the light of oil lamps—a depressingly familiar labor. One of the men they tried to save was Colonel Niederauer, the impetuous officer who took a hit in the last charge. They amputated his leg but he died of shock a few hours later.

The battle of the Avay seemed decisive. Of the five thousand soldiers under Caballero's command at the engagement, around three thousand were killed or wounded and another twelve hundred were captured.[26] One of those taken prisoner was Colonel Serrano, whose misreading of the situation had caused the day's debacle. Some of the Paraguayan prisoners, at least two hundred, succeeded in escaping over the next several days, but Serrano was not among them.[27] As for the Marshal, he could never make up his losses. Though Thompson cited a casualty figure of four thousand men for the Brazilians, the true number appears to have been less than half that.[28] Even granted the lower number, this amounted to a great many men put out of action. From the broader perspective of leadership and élan, the worst loss of the day for the Allies was General Osório, who later recovered from his wound, but who came perilously close to death at Avay.

Caballero managed to escape.[29] The general, it seemed, was less like José Díaz than either the Marshal or subsequent hagiographers might have cared to recognize. Caballero was an eager and ambitious man, but he always knew when to spur his horse and gallop away. In this case, a Brazilian trooper succeeded in knocking him to the ground and stripping his poncho from his back. He nonetheless wriggled free, grabbed the reins of another animal, and, leaping upon its back, rode off before anyone could draw a bead on him. Courage made little sense to Caballero if coupled with suicide. In this, he upheld a rational view of soldiering that contrasted with the all-or-nothing bravado favored by López—who, paradoxically, still admired the general.

As for Caxias, though he could not yet smile, he nonetheless had to take some satisfaction with the day's work. He had destroyed Caballero's forces and set the stage for further conquests. This he accomplished with superior manpower and doggedness, all of which suggested that his overall strategy had finally yielded decisive results. He had trapped López in a pocket to the south, and with columns bearing down on him from three directions, he could nearly taste victory.

Colonel Thompson, who was still at Angostura, thought that the Marshal had erred in ordering his army against Caxias in the open field at Avay, and should have maintained the units at the strong positions previously established along the Pikysyry.[30] Whether the Paraguayan defenses could hold the Allies back on the north as well as the south had never been clear, and, in any case, Caxias had already proven the basic vitality of his strategy of attrition. Had the Paraguayans stayed in their trenches at Angostura and the Pikysyry, it might have given the Marshal some breathing space. Inflicting casualties in the hope of buying time was, sadly, the only option left to the Paraguayans at that time, and it failed.

Now that the Allies had crushed Caballero at the Avay, the next target had to be Itá Ybaté, the center of Paraguayan defenses on the Pikysyry and the site of López's headquarters. The Marshal instructed Thompson to put together some last-minute preparations to deal with this threat. The colonel related what happened next:

> At my suggestion, a trench was begun from Angostura towards his headquarters, with its front towards Villeta, and flanked in the same manner by the right battery, as the old trench was by the left. It was, however, soon apparent that we had not sufficient men to execute a large work like this, and it was given up, and a star fort begun on a hill 2,000 yards on the way, intended to be one of a chain of forts; but the enemy did not give time for this either. López accordingly scraped together all the men he could, and collected about 3,000 at his headquarters, where he also had a number of guns sent, including the Whitworth 32-pounder. He had a ditch dug, two feet wide by two feet deep, and the earth thrown to the front, so that, by sitting down on the inner edge of the ditch, the men could be somewhat protected from rifle-bullets.[31]

López never had the time to get these ditches properly arranged. He directed his guardsmen into the trenches to prepare for the attack that would soon come. The long trench line at Pikysyry was garrisoned with around fifteen hundred men, who, in fact, were mostly boys and invalids. They had only forty guns of various calibers. Thompson turned these little batteries into individual redoubts by digging shallow trenches in a semicircle around each one, which provided just enough depth for the soldiers to avoid the canister. Caxias could not know that the northeastern end of the line had remained defenseless, there being too few troops to cover that position. This left open a limited number of narrow trails leading into the interior.[32]

The marquis directed his units to Villeta, which fell to him without a fight on the 11 December. There the troops rested and waited for supplies that could only come to them by way of the Chaco.[33] Just to the south, Argentine units under General Gelly y Obes were readying themselves for battle. The Marshal thus found his army almost encircled; any defenses that Thompson constructed could make little difference. The Paraguayans had no way to withdraw, save perhaps in small bands across marshy territory to the east. Any such movement could bring no meaningful threat to the Allies. The Paraguayans, it seemed, could not prevent the occupation of Asunción.

A Glimmer Of Hope, A Shadow of Resignation

López could count on a few days' respite. Luckily, this was the moment that the new US minister to Paraguay, General Martin T. McMahon, came upon the scene. The North American became a remarkable figure in the eyes of his Paraguayan hosts—friendly, supportive, sympathetic to a hard-pressed military, and willing to interpret his diplomatic responsibilities in a way that might yet save their country. Unlike Washburn, whom the Paraguayans considered neither a true Americanist nor a true republican, here was a man who might just be both.

Brevetted a major general of volunteers before he reached the age of thirty, McMahon had two brothers, both of whom died as a result of wounds sustained in battle while fighting for the Union. McMahon left the army after Lee's surrender at Appomattox, and spent two years as a corporate attorney for the city of New York before leaving for his diplomatic post in Paraguay. He had never heard of that nation before Washburn's misadventures gained public attention in the United States, but he read as much as he could about it while en route to South America. As he noted later in life, he already felt hostile to Brazil's planter elite (whom he equated with the worst of the Confederate slavocrats) and was convinced that Paraguay's fight for life paralleled the struggle for freedom in Ireland and Poland. As such, the little republic deserved the support of the United States, which had just finished four years of bloodletting in order to free its enslaved population.[34]

Whether McMahon held that opinion when he first set eyes on Marshal López and Madame Lynch is something we can never know. But López saw the hand of Providence in the arrival of this handsome diplomat, so full of industry, so anxious to do his best as the minister of a friendly power. Humaitá had fallen; so had Pilar, Villa Franca, and Villeta. But even now, as the "darkies" were poised to take the old capital, there remained a slim chance for Paraguay to escape the fate that Caxias had ordained. The last-minute intervention of this young North American might make the difference.

López received McMahon at Itá Ybaté on 14 December, and demonstrated his enthusiasm with a carefully worded letter of welcome. He announced in his first conversation with the new minister that because the Allies had isolated Luque, government functions had transferred to Piribebuy, a neglected village in the Cordillera of central Paraguay. It would be convenient, López suggested, for McMahon to stay on as his guest at headquarters while the government reestablished itself in the interior.

Either through naiveté or an honest enthusiasm for the underdog, McMahon developed a strong fondness for the Paraguayans. Both the Marshal and Madame Lynch appreciated finding someone so congenial, but today's scholars may find it odd that they forged a cozy relation with him in so short span of days. McMahon wanted to dispel the bad air left by Washburn. He made every attempt to cooperate, to prove that Washington still harbored good feelings towards Paraguay.

McMahon, it seemed, could always sympathize with men in the field, and especially with an army as threadbare as this one. He toured the Paraguayan camp, chatting with regular soldiers, tapping junior officers on the shoulder in an honest display of compassion and understanding. However, his admiration for these brave men whom the world had already written off was partly offset by a clear understanding of how much the war had already cost them, and how tragic their future might be.[35]

McMahon ate at the president's table over the next several days and found his host both cultured and thoughtful. Even though the minister spoke Spanish with difficulty, he believed that he and the Marshal shared in a "freemasonry of generals," an attitude of mutual respect among officers irrespective of national origin or circumstance.[36] It triggered conviviality between them, adding a buffer of sorts to the pressure-filled atmosphere of the war. So did the good food and charm that Madame Lynch had on full display.

What McMahon did not realize—or chose not to admit—was that the Marshal was still slaughtering his domestic opposition. This remained a priority for him, every bit as important as preparing military defenses. The tribunals that had opened at San Fernando had continued without interruption since the army's relocation to the Pikysyry. Bishop Palacios, who himself had "always recommended and approved the most sanguinary measures," was "processed" at the beginning of the month, with Fathers Román and Maíz presiding over the trial.[37] General Barrios, Colonel Alén, and Benigno López suffered the same fate, and all four were shot in the back as traitors before the dawning of the New Year.[38]

So was Juliana Ynsfrán, now totally broken in the cepo and still incredulous about her destiny.[39] The López sisters, whom the fiscales implicated in the same conspiracy as the other would-be Catalines, were rescued from the firing squad by the Marshal's commutation on 15 December. Both, however, witnessed the execution of their husbands, and they still ended up being scourged, as did their mother—whose early preference for Benigno now placed her in the worst light.[40] The other brother, Venancio, temporarily escaped with his life but was henceforth treated with undisguised contempt.

It seems odd that McMahon was unaware of these legal proceedings—or, for that matter, the tortures taking place a few hundred paces from where he slept. He may have already assumed an attitude so supportive of the Paraguayans that his eye could not discern what was obvious to others. More plausibly, he was too busy inspecting the military preparations at Itá Ybaté and getting his ministry organized to take notice. The Marshal had decided to move the capital to

Piribebuy, and McMahon had to consider whether he should follow, or depart Paraguay as the European representatives wished to do.

One foreigner who had voluntarily stayed behind with the Paraguayans, and whose behavior may throw light on McMahon's thinking, was Major Max von Versen. The Prussian adventurer had suffered terrible privations during his months spent in detention. His jailers had beaten him sporadically and he had never once eaten a full meal, yet he refused to abandon his plan to give the war a professional analysis. This project remained uppermost in his mind, and focusing on its details may even have kept him alive. He had spurned the opportunity to be evacuated aboard the *Beacon* in November, and had no intention now of ruining his standing through loose talk.

As with the US minister, von Versen had grown fascinated with the Marshal and his people, and he wanted to write about them.[41] There was much to comment upon over the next weeks. The Allies had sent out scouts almost every day, and these men reported on the progress of the fortifications that Thompson was preparing at Itá Ybaté. Not a one of the redoubts could hold back Caxias's army.

Itá Ybaté

On the night of 16 December, two ironclads got upstream of Angostura, with five more following three days later. This final run placed twelve ironclads above the Marshal's main river batteries and six just below. Ignácio could now bombard Angostura from two directions, and while the shelling had not yet proven effective, that could change at any moment. López had redeployed all but two thousand of his men away from the river, and crowding these troops into the trenches nearer his headquarters appeared to promise high casualties once the battle began.[42]

The imperial cavalry probed the Paraguayan lines on 19 December, decimating the Marshal's 45th Cavalry Regiment and returning with few losses.[43] Hoping that this augured a quick victory, Caxias sought to attack with his main forces right away. But a rainstorm intervened, and the principal attack instead came three hours before dawn on 21 December. The plan was for João Manoel Mena Barreto's cavalry to attack the Pikysyry line from the rear, while the marquis himself would assault the main position at Itá Ybaté and crush the remaining Paraguayans in the adjacent hill country, the Lomas Valentinas.

In their accounts of this penultimate stage of the war, Brazilian historians link the various engagements into a single operation they call the "Dezembrada," which suggests that the battles followed upon each other in logical sequence.[44] Paraguayan scholars have never warmed to this designation, arguing that the engagements are better understood as improvisations in poorly understood territory.[45] In this instance, the Brazilians probably have the better interpretation.

The Marquis of Caxias was no longer working in the dark and was willing to risk substantial losses in pursuit of a decisive engagement.

His combative spirit was much in evidence between 21 and 27 December. Despite his reconnaissance, Caxias still had not located the Paraguayan strong points on the Pikysyry line; he therefore opted to advance along two steep paths leading up the Loma Cumbarity to the Marshal's headquarters. Infantry units under General Bittencourt advanced on the left and more infantry under General Luiz Mena Barreto on the right. Cavalry units under General Andrade Neves provided support, with the idea of cutting the retreat of any enemy forces fleeing south or southeast.

The sky was still jet black when the Brazilians began their push on 21 December. López had predicted that an enemy attack would come within twenty-four hours, and expressed relief that after so much idleness the big battle was at last in the offing.[46] Everyone now tried to keep silent as the marquis's troops wound their way up the hill, but as the Brazilians could do no better than grope ahead in the dark, their presence was soon divined. Sharpshooters fired into them from a near distance. This caused the Brazilians to stumble among themselves before coming to a complete stop. At one point a shell from the Whitworth the Paraguayans had captured at Second Tuyutí came ripping through one battalion, beheading a corporal and killing a dozen others around him. Congreve rockets then lit up the heavens—but the Brazilians did not retreat.[47]

It was not until midday that they got going again, and this time the fighting was fierce and sustained. Dionísio Cerqueira, whose memoirs often alternated between a pretentious or excessively sincere tone, nonetheless provided a painfully realistic description of battle that few personal accounts of the campaign can equal:

> Our line was extensive. We ambled down the hill, reached the defile and started to climb up the slope, marching quick-step at the front, with rifles extended and shouting *vivas*. The enthusiasm was indescribable. But there the enemy was waiting for us in his trenches. The edge of the parapet flared up before us, and the cannonade began, tearing into us mercilessly. Like rain, the volleys of musketry fell down upon the brave men of the 16th Battalion, and quickly decimated the ranks. Still they advanced. I had to spur my horse to a gallop just to keep up. ... I don't know how long the shelling lasted. The bugler Domingos fell wounded but trumpeted the charge notwithstanding—it was his last. As we neared the opposite slope there were but a few of us left. The ground overflowed with soldiers of the 16th; but their gunners [kept falling] and our riflemen gave them no respite. Just a ditch and a parapet separated the combatants, and from their protected position the Paraguayans fired

hotly into us—and the greater part of them were in turn bayoneted to death. ... I had no idea where the commanding officer was, nor the major. Both had fallen. Suddenly, I felt on my left [cheek] a sharp and heavy blow, like a hammer. ... The horse reared up [and I] fell from the saddle, passing out. Afterwards, I know not how long, I found my tunic no longer white—it had reddened with the blood that spewed from my wounded face, blurring my vision. I felt no pain and got to my feet stunned. I glanced about and in fumbling for my cap all I could see were the dead and wounded.[48]

This was only the beginning of the engagement. The Brazilians attacked again and again. Mena Barreto, with three corps of cavalry, two brigades of infantry, and a few guns, slipped behind the Pikysyry trenches and assaulted the Paraguayans from the rear, before making his way to the same line of trenches that had stopped Cerqueira. The general killed seven hundred of the Marshal's soldiers, took two hundred prisoners, and then moved to the trenches to lick his wounds.[49] Bittencourt, meanwhile, forced his way up the trail as planned, dislodging the Paraguayans from the first line of trenches as Mena Barreto had done on the right.

The power of sheer numbers carried the day. A good many Paraguayans had already fled. Some took refuge in Angostura while others hurried to reinforce the Marshal's headquarters at Itá Ybaté. Caxias had anticipated gaining the summit of the hill with minimal resistance. Now that he had smashed the first defenses, he was surprised when the Paraguayans, fighting on open ground, pushed back his troops with an unexpected vigor. At one point, a cavalry unit under the seemingly impervious Valois Rivarola swept out of nowhere and scattered the imperial infantry. The marquis's troops staggered back to the same trench line that they had captured a few hours earlier yet got no further during the daylight hours.

Caxias called a halt around 6:00 p.m. His men had come within a hundred yards of penetrating the final line near López's headquarters, and they had captured ten Paraguayan guns, including the Whitworth—but still they could not claim a victory. Minister McMahon, a veteran of four years' fighting in Virginia, had little good to say about the Brazilian assault, noting, for example, that the marquis's troops had lost "more in their return than they would probably have lost had they swarmed over the intrenchments [sic] of the enemy, which their numbers should have certainly enabled them to do." Had the Brazilian cavalry deployed in lines instead of slow columns, the North American observed, they would have swept the "little handful of men resisting them, capturing the Paraguayan headquarters and probably López himself."[50]

The US minister was a model of indiscretion. He volunteered, for instance, to act as an escort for the López children, for whom he evinced an avuncular sympathy. He spent most of the battle with them, his own revolvers at the ready, staying by their side while Brazilian bullets flew through their tent from multiple directions.[51] No one was hurt and McMahon gained a reputation among the Paraguayans for his quixotic bravery, so unusual among diplomats. They also applauded his friendliness towards children, who, as he noted in his report to Secretary Seward, now comprised the greater portion of the Marshal's army.[52]

The successful defense of Itá Ybaté reveals much about the discipline of these young boys, who displayed a temperament that seemed to contrast strikingly with that of the Marshal. Thompson, who had dug in at Angostura, claimed that López had fled to the woods a mile distant from the fighting, but Centurión, who now engaged the enemy for the first time in the war, had him issuing orders within rifle shot of the enemy, while Aveiro had him on horseback at the head of his troops.[53] Whatever the truth, the cohesiveness of the Paraguayan command seemed questionable, a fact that made the steadfastness of the Marshal's boy-soldiers even more impressive. Whether out of habit or desperation or foolishness or simple bravery, they fought on.

The losses at Itá Ybaté proved high. The Brazilians took almost four thousand casualties that day, including the wounded General Andrade Neves, the Baron of the Triumph.[54] Paraguayan losses were likewise in the thousands—Resquín claims as many as eight.[55] Colonel Rivarola, who had fought with determination on every occasion, was grievously wounded along with many officers on the Paraguayan side. Colonel Felipe Toledo, the seventy-year-old commander of López's personal escort, was sent off to challenge the enemy and was soon killed along with the chief of artillery. Over the next night, the Brazilians never stopped firing their rifles.

Five Days of Fighting

In one sense, the battle at Itá Ybaté was a victory for Paraguay. The Brazilians should probably have won outright, but had to satisfy themselves with a line of trenches and the few guns captured in exchange for a heavy loss of men. The Paraguayans could not withstand another assault, however, and had to get help any way they could. The Marshal sent runners to Cerro León and the little interior village of Caapucú to bring back whatever men they could find, including those wounded who could still walk. López also tried to bring the remaining troops from Angostura and the south line of the Pikysyry. Little could come from either direction, however, for Thompson had no troops to spare and the Paraguayan forces to the south had troubles of their own.

When his forces facing Itá Ybaté stalled, Caxias sent word to General Gelly y Obes to launch another attack in that quarter. The Argentine general had nine thousand fresh troops at his disposal, along with the men of the Paraguayan Legion. The latter force had always seemed a comparatively weak asset, useful to some extent in propaganda, but militarily irrelevant. Now, however, with López nearly defeated, the legionnaires might prove far more important.

The relations between Gelly and the marquis had never been better than strictly correct. The former had repeatedly complained that Caxias wanted all the glory for himself.[56] At this moment, however, the Argentine commander praised his allies, signaling to the marquis that his brave Brazilians deserved repose, not more combat, and that the men of the Argentine army stood ready to do the dirty work.[57]

The assault of 22 December started off as a feint but it brought an unmistakable crumbling of the Paraguayan line. On the Marshal's side, there had been a wave of promotions since the fall of Humaitá, and many officers held commands well above their abilities. On the northern reaches of the Pikysyry, this had not mattered much, but on the south it was a key factor in assuring the collapse of the remaining Paraguayan force. The Allies split the Pikysyry line in two, and Angostura was left isolated to the south. The Marshal lost seven hundred men and thirty-one guns.[58]

The situation for Paraguay had gone from very bad to hopeless. McMahon and Centurión's accounts coincide in their depiction of the horrors seen in camp, with the North American offering more than a taste of the desperation that he witnessed:

> The condition of things within López's lines ... was deplorable. There were no means of caring for the wounded in such numbers, nor could men be spared to bring them off the field, or to bury the dead. Many children, almost unnoticed, were ... grievously wounded and silently waiting for death. ... Random bullets splintered the woodwork of the buildings from time to time, and an unearthly peacock, perched on the ridge-pole, made night hideous with his screams every time a shot came near enough to disturb his slumbers.[59]

On 22 and 23 December, minor reinforcements got through to López from Cerro León, Caapucú, and the small villages on the far side of the Ypoá. This brought up Paraguayan strength to around sixteen hundred infantry and cavalry, but few individuals in the reassembled force could be called able.[60] Given the dearth of weapons, these reinforcements could hardly make a difference, but the Marshal could still rely on his countrymen and their willingness to accept new sacrifices. As the new troops arrived, López dispatched a long train of women, children, and wounded down through the narrow trails to the east, and across the swollen Ypecuá, normally just a creek but now a large and swiftly flowing river, brimming perilously with poisonous snakes.[61] McMahon, accompanying the refugees together with the López children, was astounded at how well the refugees managed the difficult passage using dried hides as makeshift rafts. Far behind, they could still hear the peal of thunder, intermixed with the "dull reverberation of the heavy guns," as if man and nature had combined all their violence into a single phenomenon.[62]

Meanwhile, a curious episode unfolded on Christmas Eve that allowed López to reflect on what the war meant for his nation. Caxias, who believed that Paraguay was on the verge of collapse, issued an ultimatum. This demand for surrender, written in terse words, arraigned the Marshal "before his own people and the civilized world for all the evil consequences of the war." López spent some time in composing his answer, which Centurión, in a show of approbation, later called the "one classic note that the war produced."[63] Later generations might disagree, but an indissoluble sense of determination and tragedy permeated every sentence:

> Your Excellencies have informed me that you know my resources, and [intimate] that I know your preponderance in numbers and supplies, and your facilities for limitless reinforcement. I have no such knowledge; but I have learned from four years of fighting that the vast superiority [of which you speak] had never been sufficient to break the spirit of the Paraguayan soldier, who fights with the self-denial of a devoted citizen and Christian who prefers to see his country reduced to one vast tomb than permit her dishonor. [Neither have you any] right to charge me before the country that I have defended. I do defend her now and will defend her always. She has imposed this as a duty upon me, and I will perform it religiously to the end. For the rest, history will judge, and I owe no account save to God; and, if blood has yet to flow, He will not fail to affix the blame where it properly belongs. ... I am still even now disposed to treat for an honorable termination of the war, but I will not listen to the word "surrender!"[64]

The pride or arrogance that such a rejoinder exemplified commonly carries a heavy price, and in this case it proved very dear. Caxias hated being reminded that it was López who had sought reconciliation at Yataity Corã, and that Paraguay, moreover, deserved both to be praised for the bravery of her sons and to survive as an independent state. But the marquis refused to take the bait. He simply wanted to finish the war: the emperor demanded it and Brazil needed it.

On Christmas, the concentrated fire of forty-six Allied guns (and a great many rockets) battered the Paraguayan headquarters at Itá Ybaté.[65] Angostura was also heavily shelled. Simultaneously, rain poured down, sometimes in torrents, and though the bad weather slowed the barrage, it did not end it. At one point, the Marshal sent one of his last detachments of cavalry to scout a possible escape route to the north, but the Brazilians drove the Paraguayans back as the bombardment commenced again.

It was much the same the next day. All the hills in the Lomas Valentinas area were either ablaze from shellfire or pockmarked from previous barrages. The final attack, the one that Caxias had meant to be definitive, came only at daybreak two days later. The tactic that the marquis chose on this occasion was the same as he had used at Avay and which had cost so many lives.[66] This time, however, the Paraguayans were greatly weakened, and the Allied troops, most of them Argentines under the command of Ignacio Rivas, felt ready for the fight. A total of sixteen thousand soldiers (sixty-five hundred men attacking from the rear and ninety-five hundred from the front) swept over the first hill as a bugle sounded.

Unable to offer meaningful resistance, the Marshal's troops pulled back precipitously to the nearby woods, keeping up a sporadic fire as they withdrew. Irritated by the considerable number of hits they took, the Argentines edged forward against these thickets and were surprised, even shocked, when small units of cavalry and infantry emerged to strike at them. A melee ensued. Rivas's men stalled and pushed ahead again only when reinforcements moved up the hill in support. Shortly thereafter, the Argentines carried the Paraguayan redoubt. Some of its defenders were lucky enough to limp off towards the south, but more lay dead upon the ground. Their artillery pieces lacked shot and most of the guns were dismounted, so, as the Argentines closed with the line, not a single shell hindered their advance.[67]

Marshal López galloped away with his staff as the enemy neared. He was pursued by Allied infantrymen who could see him in the distance but failed to fire straight. Soon the Marshal crossed over the Potrero Mármol, the sole remaining route to safety in the east. The Allies had initially blocked this exit, but for some reason, amid the fog of battle, they had left the way open.[68] Unwilling to call this an accident, some in the Allied army repeated the rumor that Caxias had let López go.[69]

In truth, the Allies were busy elsewhere on the field. By now, the battle had moved on to the second hill, where Paraguayan resistance had coalesced around General Caballero. José Ignacio Garmendia, a young lieutenant colonel in the Argentine forces, witnessed this last stage of the battle, in which General Rivas swept behind the Paraguayan right flank with several Correntino units, bearing down hard upon Caballero's remaining men.[70] As they neared, the Paraguayan general passed a flask of caña among his stalwarts, asking if they had the strength to make one more charge. At this stage no one could tell the difference between enthusiasm and resignation, but when Ramona Martínez, a servant girl in the López household, stepped forward to seize a saber, everyone followed her example.[71]

Around four hundred Paraguayans lay dead or wounded around the Marshal's former headquarters, which fell to the Allies at midday. What was left of Caballero's force, just a handful of men, somehow managed to escape east, presumably taking the same route that López had used in his retreat across the Potrero Mármol and the Ypecuá. Madame Lynch accompanied him at that time rather than leave earlier with McMahon and the children.[72] All met up again later, first in Cerro León and then in Piribebuy. Behind them, on every knoll in the Lomas Valentinas and on the slopes and the flatland in between, all was smoke and devastation.

The ordeal had come to an end and Caxias could well afford his cup of satisfaction. He had smashed the Marshal and destroyed all his key emplacements. He had seized twenty-three battle flags and more than a hundred cannon. The war would surely conclude with this latest Paraguayan defeat, which seemed dramatic and comprehensive. Angostura still held out fitfully, and one could expect some minor guerrilla resistance in the rural environs where "ignorant peasants, fools to the last," might still choose loyalty to López. By every real calculation, however, the Paraguayan army no longer existed.

The proof for this came in the many cadavers visible around Itá Ybaté. The pain on seeing these horrors was something that Garmendia wrote about with eloquence and disgust. For it was not the thought of corpses that disturbed the sleep of the Allied conquerors on the night following the battle, but instead the cry of prepubescent boys, whose shrill voices emanated from the hospitals and aid stations.[73] There was no pride in this grisly victory, and no Allied soldier stepped forward to mutilate the dead.

Angostura

The destruction of the Marshal's forces around Lomas Valentinas left Colonel Thompson in a predicament. He had received orders to hold out, but unlike those men who prized self-sacrifice as the acme of devotion to López, the British engineer saw no grandeur in useless resistance. He intended to do his duty at Angostura but no more than that. After the war, Thompson sought to excuse his dedication to the Paraguayan cause as perfectly understandable for a man who had served so long in a position of trust. Whether we should accept this assertion as naïve or merely sad, we need to remember that it took shape only later, after considerable reflection. The challenges facing him at Angostura, by contrast, required immediate consideration.[74]

Before Itá Ybaté fell, the Marshal had told Thompson to obtain all necessary supplies from General Resquín. The colonel succeeded, however, in obtaining from him only three days' beef, and about twelve small sacks of Indian-corn. The garrison of the two batteries consisted of 3 chiefs (all field-officers), 50 officers, and 684 men, of whom 320 were artillerymen; and we had just ninety rounds of ammunition per gun. After the Pikysyry trenches were taken, on the 21st, we had an addition of 3 chiefs, 61 officers, and 685 soldiers, most of them having lost their arms, and the greater part being small boys. Besides these, we received 13 officers and 408 men, all badly wounded, whom we had to accommodate in the soldiers' quarters, and about 500 women; so that instead of 700 mouths to feed, I had to provide for 2,400, which for some days I managed by doling out very small rations. All these people were very much crowded, and suffered a good deal from the continual bombardment of the fleet.[75]

The want of rations for this substantial garrison necessitated some improvisation. On the night of 24 December, Thompson sent five hundred men on a raid into the Chaco, where they appropriated the personal belongings of the skipper of the ironclad *Brasil*, twenty-seven mules, and one hundred twenty boxes of claret with which the raiders got uproariously drunk. It emerged, however, that the majority of imperial troops had already departed, taking their provisions with them, and leaving the Paraguayans with nothing save for red wine.[76]

On 26 December, Thompson tried another tack. He mustered 550 troopers, from which 100 riflemen were selected and sent on a diversion along the old line of the Pikysyry trenches. The remaining troops made their way to a clearing about halfway to Villeta, where spies had reported a herd of livestock. Though the Allies fired on these Paraguayans, they failed to prevent their escaping with 248 head of cattle and 14 horses. As Thompson had exhausted his provisions the day before, the rations of meat the beeves provided made a great difference to his besieged soldiers.[77]

Before the last telegraphic link with Itá Ybaté was severed, the Marshal had assured Thompson that the Brazilians had suffered extensive casualties, so many that Caxias could neither move against the main Paraguayan positions nor advance on Angostura. This claim was delusional, and on 28 December, with López's former headquarters firmly in their hands, the Allies set up a general attack on the colonel's position.

It remained to be seen whether Angostura, which Thompson had fortified with skill, could still be defended with resolution. The colonel could not know that the Paraguayan battalions around Lomas Valentinas had collapsed. He tried to communicate with his superiors using signal flags, but although he could just glimpse the Marshal's camp in the distance, no one returned his signals. The camp had already fallen.[78]

Meanwhile, the Allied fleet kept up its bombardment of Angostura. The *Wasp* had anchored nearby and her officers had already expressed scorn for the way that Ignácio went about shelling the position. The Brazilian ironclads came into action in the morning and dropped down out of range at night. To those American officers who had suffered through the civil war at home the conduct of the Brazilian fleet in the Paraguayan campaign seemed nothing short of incompetent. Writing in the third person, their commander noted that "Admiral Davis had in his [own] squadron guns enough to have knocked this battery down in half an hour if American methods had [been] resorted to."[79] Fair or not, this evaluation reflected the general contempt that Anglo-Saxons had directed at the imperial navy since the time of Tamandaré.[80] Perhaps the fleet was improperly and pusillanimously deployed, perhaps not. Either way, time was on Ignácio's side.

On 28 December, as the Brazilian land forces readied their cannon, a monitor flying a flag of truce steamed up to Angostura but refused to halt when Paraguayan officers rowed out on a canoe to learn its intent. Thompson directed a protest to the Allied commanders the next day, noting that the ship's refusal to drop anchor at the proper moment constituted a serious abuse of the flag of truce.[81] The Allied generals could have responded to this letter using either harsh or conciliatory language. In the end, they did both, promising to address the matter in due course, while simultaneously offering evidence of Itá Ybaté's destruction, accompanied by a warning that Angostura would meet the same fate if Thompson continued to resist.

A commission of Paraguayan officers sent to the Allied camp returned with irrefutable proof of the Allied claim. Thompson still had around ninety rounds for each of his smaller guns. This perhaps would have served for two days' resistance but no more. He had only eight hundred able-bodied men as against twenty thousand on the Allied side, not counting the naval guns trained upon him from the river. There was no hope of any assistance from the Cordillera.

Thompson and his nominal superior, Colonel Lucás Carrillo, elected to do what no previous Paraguayan commanders had ever done: they solicited the opinion of every soldier in their command as to what course they should pursue. Save for one lieutenant, the officers and men opted for capitulation. Their decision suggests that, once free from the Marshal's pressure, the Paraguayans would choose surrender over suicide.[82] They were not the rigid fanatics that both Allied propagandists and certain nationalist writers of a later generation alleged.[83]

On the morning of 30 December, Thompson and Carrillo sent word of their intention to surrender, and the three Allied commanders—Caxias, Gelly y Obes, and Castro—announced approval of terms under which officers could keep their ranks and swords, and the Paraguayan units as a whole were accorded proper honors.[84] At noon, the band struck up a martial tune and the men filed out, stacking their arms in three separate piles for the Allies to parcel out among themselves. Lieutenant José María Fariña, who had distinguished himself during the "war of the chatas," could not tolerate the enemy taking his unit's flag, so he personally lowered it from its staff, wrapped it around a cannonball, and threw it into the river. Then, like the other soldiers, he passed into captivity—hungry, perhaps even starving, but alive.[85]

Later that day, Thompson received leave from Caxias to inspect Itá Ybaté, where he found seven hundred bloodied troopers crowded into the Marshal's former residence. There were corpses scattered all along the trail and little groups of wounded men stretched out underneath the many trees of the district. The marquis acceded to Thompson's request that several medical students who had accompanied him to Angostura be sent up to help those Paraguayans whose lives might still be saved. Gelly y Obes also sent some twenty-five of his own medical personnel to assist. Colonel Thompson, with his sword still strapped to his waist, remained near Angostura for another two days. He was then evacuated to Buenos Aires aboard the HMS *Cracker* after a brief visit to the now-deserted Asunción. He had been in Paraguay for just under eleven years.[86] It must have seemed like a century.

13

ANOTHER PAUSE

During the last days of December 1868, Allied commanders had three short-term goals in Paraguay, all of which lay within their grasp. Angostura had just fallen and the troops that had encircled it needed to be redeployed. Asunción beckoned only a few miles upriver, unprotected and ready, it seemed, to welcome the Allies as liberators. And the Marshal's army, now no better than a skeletal force in and around Cerro León, could not withstand even a minor blow from Caxias, who stood ready to strike at any time. The end of the war was in sight.

For the Paraguayans, meanwhile, home took the form of a devastated landscape, stripped of its human resources. Some towns in the interior, especially in the country's far north, had escaped the ravages, and could still boast a few head of cattle and quantities of manioc and cotton, though by now such things were luxuries. But these villages could not sustain a nation that every day grew more insubstantial. And yet the Paraguayan leadership had survived all manner of bitterness before. The fall of Angostura changed nothing, and nor did the idea of an occupied Asunción. Even now, Paraguay might fight again.

The Republic Moves Inland

The Allied successes of December 1868 badly shook López. Arms, munitions, his carriage, even his scarlet poncho with the embroidered Bragança device, fell into enemy hands. So, too, did a great many incriminating documents, including General Resquín's "diary," which listed individuals executed for treason over the previous months.[1] The loss of these materials was humiliating, but the real problem lay in putting the Paraguayan military back together. Command had disintegrated throughout the Lomas Valentinas, and soldiers had either abandoned their posts or wandered about waiting for orders that never came.

In the confusion, people held captive since before the fall of Humaitá unexpectedly recovered their freedom as their guards fled. Four Brazilian officers, three Argentines, and the redoubtable Major von Versen ultimately made it through the lines as the last defenses crumbled at Itá Ybaté. The former prisoners, ecstatic at their last-minute deliverance, were soon joined by Dr. William Stewart, Colonel Wisner, the British architect Alonzo Taylor, the German telegraphist Robert von Fischer-Treuenfeldt, and a substantial number of women and children left behind in the scramble.

Allied victory had been a foregone conclusion for some time, and the December engagements confirmed the wisdom of the marquis's military strategy. He had taken Angostura, thereby eliminating the Marshal's last positions on the Paraguay River. He had dispersed the enemy soldiers into the marshes and presumably thought that their army would never regain cohesion. Asunción was thus his for the taking.

Caxias needed to find some additional reserve of vitality and he could not find it in himself. Having spent December fighting stubbornly like Ulysses S. Grant, in the wake of victory he became more like George M. McClellan—cautious, slow, and overly dependent on precedent. He also failed to capture the Marshal, a fundamental error that, to his regret, Caxias only appreciated later. The war correspondent for *The Standard* summarized the consequences, observing that:

> Not if Paraguay was teeming with the diamonds of Golconda, or the mines of California, would it be worth the blood spilt at the Lomas Valentinas. Error, deep-lasting error, to have taxed humanity with such a sacrifice. Waterloo had an object; on it hung the fate of France, nay, of Europe. [Königgrätz] can be justified by the eternal feuds of the too bulky German family. But the Lomas Valentinas was a sterile victory since López was permitted to escape, and that terrible blunder will yet cost the Allies fresh torrents of blood and millions, aye millions, of treasure.[2]

These words were penned in early August 1869, long after López's army had regained sufficient strength to harass the Allies in a limited way. Eight months earlier, at the time of the Marshal's escape, the situation appeared less ominous, his getaway less relevant. The Allies had completely routed the Paraguayans—that was the paramount fact, and there was no obvious need to deal with stragglers.[3]

The reality of the battlefield losses seemed persuasive enough but the marquis's decision to press on to Asunción without bothering to chase the Marshal revealed his poor grasp of the country. Caxias had always considered his opponent a backwoods charlatan lacking in both integrity and courage, a man whose honor could be purchased and whose troops obeyed him out of fear. From this simplistic appraisal, it followed that once the Paraguayans were freed of their fetters, they would forsake the Marshal and welcome the Allied troops.

The opposite happened. The Allies assumed that Paraguayans thirsted for the kind of freedom that Brazil and Argentina offered them. In Paraguay, however, European-style freedom had a negligible value compared to community, and ultimately, to hope.[4] The marquis failed to grasp this fact. His clumsiness, or lack of foresight, ultimately tarnished his standing and provided fuel for political opponents who found it hard to believe that an intelligent general could have allowed López to escape. Some commentators—not all of them revisionists—looked for a more nefarious rationale to explain Caxias's failure to do the right thing.[5]

Their speculations—if that is the right word—assumed some odd and distorted shapes over the years. Thompson set off the cascade of accusations by suggesting that the marquis had acted either out of "imbecility," a desire to squeeze still more money out of the military budget, as an excuse for maintaining a Brazilian army in Paraguay, or perhaps merely "with the view of allowing López to reassemble the remainder of the Paraguayans, in order to exterminate them in 'civilized warfare.'"[6] Another equally implausible explanation (also hinted at by Thompson) held that Caxias had reached an agreement with López to facilitate the "escape" of Brazilian officers in Paraguayan custody in exchange for smoothing the flight of López and his entourage.[7] Perhaps the strangest rumor of all, however, depicted the Allied commander as a staunch Mason who was at pains not to humiliate a supposed fellow Mason and who therefore let the Marshal slip away as a sign of fraternal consideration.[8]

Such theses are overdetermined and a bit silly; Caxias and his officers were physically and mentally exhausted in late December 1868, and fatigued men rarely act with complete composure. Either through a misreading of their orders or through sloppy execution, the men of his command failed to seize the Marshal and terminate the war. Their mistake was necessarily the marquis's responsibility. He had repeatedly underestimated López and had never shaken off his contempt for the Paraguayan people, no matter how dedicated and resilient they had shown themselves to be.

This does not mean, however, that he or any other Allied officer facilitated the Marshal's escape. It was a crass mistake not to dispatch cavalry units to hunt him down, but though it was a blunder that other commanders may have made, Caxias has to take the blame. On the eve of his greatest achievement, he stumbled and could not get to his feet. As the Allied army moved northward to occupy Asunción, the ragged bands of old men and children drifted toward

López's refuge at the foot of the Cordilleras. They were, to belabor a now familiar point, not yet defeated.

Visitors to Cerro León are decidedly rare today, but all who come are struck by its funereal atmosphere, even in the brightness of day. The lowing of cattle provides the place with its principal soundtrack in the early twenty-first century, but at the end of 1868 it was bustling with noise and nervous activity. Its wounded and displaced men were in pain and had many questions.

López was inclined to see divine intervention in his escape. Cerro León might lie within range of Allied marauders, but Caxias was unlikely to divert his army away from the occupation of Asunción just to destroy this one small garrison. The Paraguayans would thus have time to assemble a resistance on their home ground, and with God's help, they would yet prevail. This was the tone that the Marshal struck in a proclamation of 28 December. Before he rested from the long ride from Lomas Valentinas, he addressed his long-suffering compatriots, reviewing the latest events and spurring them to still greater sacrifices in the name of the nation—and of the Almighty: "Our Lord intends to test our faith and constancy in order to give us a greater and more glorious fatherland," he intoned, "and all of you should feel hardened, as do I, with the blood spilt yesterday, drunk up by the soil of our birthplace; to avenge the loss and to save the nation, here I stand ... to purge the country of its enemies."[9]

Given the chaos of December, it was surprising that the country people could coordinate their efforts. In fact, when the news of the reverses at Lomas Valentinas first reached the interior villages, the result was panic. The Marshal's officials had had to face many challenges. The few crops hastily sown over the previous months had failed in the summer heat, which brought famine. Transit through the Paraguayan countryside had been exceptionally difficult due to the lack of mounts, and, save for shipments coming from communities located near the railhead, it had been impractical to get provisions to the front. And cholera had also returned to at least half a dozen towns in the interior.[10]

And yet, with all this, the Paraguayans kept faith with the Marshal. His ability to sway underlings had never been a matter of simple power or brutality. His Guaraní was impeccable, his use of supportive and endearing terms flawless. It was easy for men, even the elderly, to think of him as a father. Most important of all, for the average Paraguayan there existed no point of political or social reference that was not Lopista. To question the Marshal's genius was thus not merely unwise, it was unnatural, and when López arrived at Cerro León, those few army officers who had not participated in the latest engagements stepped forward. Long inured to the hardships of war, they had by now developed hearts of lead, and they intended to keep fighting. Over the next days and weeks, they were joined by other hardened men and boys who had somehow survived the worst challenges of December and had hid from the Allies ever since.[11]

Martin T. McMahon observed the change that came over the Paraguayan camp once the Marshal arrived. The US minister initially noted the gloom associated with the fall of Angostura, but this was now pushed aside by a new determination. In this respect, the fortitude of a single adolescent particularly impressed the North American, convincing him that, even now, the country could still count on men who, psychologically speaking, would never demobilize:

> There came a boy-sergeant of fourteen years, dripping from the swamps, through which, for nearly thirty hours, he had swum or waded; and he told the humiliating story of the surrender [at Angostura]—how gun-boats had been sent with flags of truce and plausible messages from the Allied chiefs; how Paraguayan deserters had misinformed the principal officers of the batteries, telling the old story, since periodically repeated, that López was trying to escape to Bolivia; how at last the whole garrison, more than two thousand, were marched out of their works and suddenly ordered to stack arms in the hated presence of the enemy; and how he, with many others, scorned the surrender, betook himself to the swamps, and rested not until he stood before his chief. All this he told with streaming tears and voice almost choked with sobs.[12]

After only a day, López established a new camp at Azcurra, two miles distant at the crest of the hills. He left behind six hundred men at Cerro León, and moved his remaining troops to the new site, which served as his military headquarters over the next months.[13] The view was panoramic, affording excellent scrutiny of the cultivated areas at the edge of Lake Ypacaraí, the adjacent villages of Areguá and Pirayú, the terminus of the train line that linked the countryside with Asunción and the many tents and lean-tos surrounding the hospital below. If Caxias were to approach, he would have to come this way. Meanwhile, from these sylvan heights, the Marshal could see everything.

As government functions shifted to Piribebuy, López reviewed his strategic options. He likely felt betrayed by incompetent underlings and turncoats like Thompson. On the other hand, Sánchez and the other functionaries might still rebuild the Paraguayan state according to changing needs. Though he was hardly optimistic, the Marshal had no intention of modifying his outlook on the war. The Paraguayans might still "win" simply by not losing, while the Allies could only win by destroying López's army.

The Sack of Asunción

The first Allied troops—some seventeen hundred Brazilian infantrymen—landed at Asunción on the afternoon of 1 January 1869. The damaged López palace, the customs house, legislature, railroad station, and cathedral soon came into sight but the Brazilians spied almost no people—and certainly no enemy batteries blazing at them. Instead, an eerie quiet predominated. It was the hottest time of year, and the riverfront shimmered with a haze, an effect that magnified the oddness of the place. Here was Asunción—the Mecca, the Timbuktu—towards which all Allied hopes had been directed for four years, the city that Bartolomé Mitre had once promised would fall in three months.

It was not impressive. The landing spot the Allies chose teemed with water rats, the air with insects. The nearby commercial establishments were of a sort familiar from Corrientes and the lower provinces—traditional affairs with adobe walls and high ceilings. But for all the rusticity, the former Paraguayan capital boasted some modern buildings constructed for the López regime. These edifices were large and ornate, designed to impress the poorest Paraguayans with the grandeur of the state. They gleamed with an ostentation that to many Allied soldiers seemed redolent of Europe. They hinted at a broader prosperity and a sure promise of spoils.[14]

The main Allied units arrived from Villeta on 5 January. Following Caxias's instructions, the parade of troops took the form of a triumphal procession, with bands striking up martial airs and every man donning dress uniforms with boots, buttons, and bayonets polished to a shiny luster. The marquis wished to present his conquest of the city as an occasion for spectacular rejoicing. The mission that the emperor had assigned him had finally been accomplished and Caxias evidently thought it appropriate to mark that victory as the culmination of his long military career.

The marquis issued a proclamation declaring an end to the war, which the fleet officers endorsed with a statement that boasted that "it was not impossible to achieve the impossible, we did it."[15] Caxias then prepared to relinquish command to his subordinates. He lacked permission to do this, but evidently was fed up with Paraguay, and longed to return to Rio for a much-deserved rest. The only concession he made to doubt lay in his decision to dispatch a mobile force north to Luque and up the rail line towards Areguá to defend against any unexpected trouble.

The marquis's men had more immediate objects in mind, and few of these redounded to their good name. Indeed, foreign observers unanimously condemned the behavior of the Allied troops who arrived at Asunción over the next weeks. Having fought for so long in the swamps and forests, these soldiers now had many demands to satisfy. The women and girls who wandered into the city at this time were therefore outraged in ways great and small. The Brazilians had already gained a bad reputation for their treatment of three hundred Paraguayan women who fell into their hands after Avay and were repeatedly raped.[16] The Asuncenas escaped most, though not all, of this bad treatment only because so few of them were present in the city.[17]

McMahon, who could not call himself a neutral observer, condemned the Brazilians as a "licentious and lawless horde who disgrace alike humanity and the name of soldier."[18] In coming to this estimation, however, he might well have addressed the vengeance motive that he had witnessed firsthand in Virginia. At least some of the soldiers who raped and abused women in Asunción reasoned that similar treatment had befallen their countrywomen in Corumbá during the Paraguayan occupation. This fact, of course, excused nothing.

A few Brazilian soldiers managed to turn a profit at this time by kidnapping children and holding them for ransom. This seems to have been an isolated phenomenon initially, but kidnapping for ransom grew into a wider problem after the Brazilians penetrated the hill country in July.[19] Though the Marshal's troops had also practiced kidnapping when they compelled a group of Correntino women to accompany them back to Paraguay in late 1865, their motivation was political and involved no demands for ransom.[20] The same cannot be said, however, for the "Italian Nicoles," whom the Paraguayans captured in Mato Grosso, and freed only after his friends paid a ransom of twenty-five million *milréis*.[21]

Rape and kidnapping were less prevalent than looting in the Asunción of 1869. Under the accepted rules of war senior officers could authorize the seizure of articles that might help sustain the enemy's army. The rules did not, however, permit trespass on private dwellings, nor did they envision looting as an object in itself. Yet, as the Paraguayans had shown in Corumbá and Uruguaiana, this is what happens in the absence of proper discipline.[22] The matter of scale may also be pertinent. Whereas the above-mentioned towns received merciless treatment from the Paraguayans, they were all tiny places. Asunción was a national capital, a city in which pillaging was symbolically more painful.

When Caxias celebrated a Te Deum in the Cathedral on 8 January, the nastiness was well underway. The soldiers started with the larger public buildings. The executive palace, not quite completed at the onset of hostilities, had suffered through Commodore Delphim's barrages. Now, as the Brazilian imperial standard was raised from its loftiest tower, the structure was systematically gutted. As a later observer noted, the palace's "shattered turrets, slivered cornices, and broken parapets announce only too faithfully the absolute devastation of the lone and dismantled interior, [from which] the Brazilian plunderers carried off whatever they could lay their hands on, even to the timbers of the floors and the steps of the staircases, besides hacking and defacing whatever, from its nature, could not be carried away."[23] And this was only the beginning. One German eyewitness reported that the empire's soldiers pillaged "the city thoroughly, leaving not a pane of glass, or mirror, or lock untouched, although the war was ostensibly waged against the tyrant López and not against the people of Paraguay."[24]

Allied officers had sanctioned liberal foraging, and the men proceeded to take whatever victuals and strong drink they could find. They fanned out into the urban neighborhoods, broke into foreign legations and ransacked churches, private homes, and warehouses in search of things to eat or sell.[25] They lit fires in buildings to illuminate their plundering during the evening hours, reducing more than a few to ashes. Even tombs they desecrated.[26]

At the outset, no one tried to curb these excesses. For one thing, the Brazilian soldiers were apt to feel themselves defrauded of an absolute right to pillage if their behavior were put under restraint, and the officers had had enough problems controlling them as it was. The worst offenders, moreover, could rationalize that they were only doing what the more rustic Paraguayans had done whether or not the Marshal had endorsed such behavior.[27] Even civilians rarely show mercy to other civilians in such circumstances.

The Argentine units, now commanded by General Emilio Mitre, were stationed a league outside the city at Trinidad, where they could conveniently deny having taken part in the abuses. The Argentines claim to have acted with greater circumspection than the Brazilians. Yet, their disdain was tinged with envy. Whenever they witnessed Brazilian troops loading chairs, tables, pianos, carpets, and pieces of art onto imperial warships, they mumbled *"ahijuna"* in wistful complaint that the furniture would never grace their own *ranchos*.[28] Yet the Argentine officers ultimately managed to secure a portion of the loot. And in April, when the new Allied commander passed through Buenos Aires, he caught sight of the Marshal's purloined chairs in the Argentine government house during a reception by Sarmiento.[29]

Furniture and assorted baubles were one thing, but the most valuable portion of the loot consisted of hides, tobacco, and yerba "requisitioned" from private and state warehouses. A surprising quantity of these export items had remained in Asunción and cargo holds of Allied merchant vessels soon bulged with the stuff, which made its way downstream on government account or on that of individual officers.[30] General Castro, the Uruguayan commander, was said to have commandeered a vessel filled with tannin-scented hides and stolen tobacco that he planned to sell on the Montevideo market.[31]

To be sure, some officers behaved badly, but pillaging also found its severest critics within the Allied command. Emilio Mitre, for instance, delivered strong reprimands to well-corned soldiers who had tolerated or engaged in thievery. The same revulsion was likewise expressed by members of the Paraguayan Legion, whose homes were among the buildings gutted. They had looked on helplessly, feeling an understandable contempt—and just a bit of fear—at the wanton behavior of their allies.[32]

There was a certain tragic irony in the plundering. When the Marshal's government ordered the city's evacuation eleven months earlier, a few Asuncenos concealed valuables in the masonry of their houses or buried them in family gardens.[33] They thus avoided the cupidity of López's soldiers only to have their property dug up and appropriated by the Allies. Worse still, the rumors of hidden treasure (*plata ybyguí*) inflamed the avarice of Paraguayans and foreigners alike. Everyone thought to wrest valuables from hiding places in the ground. Vandalism thus continued long after the fighting ended.[34]

The sacking of Asunción gave the lie to the professed desire among the Allied leaders to bring civilization to the downtrodden people of Paraguay. Yet some commentators defended theft as a natural consequence of war. *The Standard*, claiming that tales of wide-scale pilfering in Asunción had been exaggerated, noted that there was not much left to seize, and when the soldiers found the doors of the shops sealed by orders of López, "it was natural enough that … the butt end of a musket should be guided by curiosity in effecting an entrance." The principal pillage was directed "according to the articles of war towards Government property, such as piles of hides and yerba."[35] The Brazilian foreign minister made a similar observation. Meeting Paraguayan outrage with a bland expression of moral superiority, he asserted that the imperial soldiers had committed no great misconduct, and that the worst looting followed from the actions of foreign hucksters who had arrived in the wake of the army.[36]

There was a grain of truth in this claim. The flotsam of a dozen European countries came on the scene within days of the Allied landing, and it took sutlers no time to set up shops in the ruined buildings of the port district—one source noted one hundred twenty of these establishments by the third week of January.[37] These tight-fisted, sharp-elbowed men, mostly Italians (and a few Germans), were anxious to make a quick peso—the quicker the better. They lacked the romance and guileless fascination that had animated earlier visitors to Paraguay, and took pleasure in watching the parade of Allied soldiers—not because they fancied pageantry, but because more troops meant more profit. The looting that they envisioned was no different from that of the soldiers, just better organized.[38]

If these early commercial exchanges with Brazilian troopers amounted to bartering glassware, table linen, and silver drinking straws (*bombillas*) for liquor and foodstuffs, they nonetheless signaled a rebirth of Paraguayan commerce, which, for the first time since the 1810s, went unencumbered by state interference. The popularity of Paraguayan yerba in downriver ports had never abated and might now have served to stimulate the country's reintegration into the broader economy. That said, in 1869 the advantages of a more open trade were dubious and the Paraguayans had every right to denounce the Allies as robbers. The Bay of Asunción soon crowded with merchant vessels of every size and flag—over one hundred arriving in the first week alone (twice that figure by the end of the month). The sutlers and bagmen quickly filled the holds of their ships with captured booty and sent them on their way, leaving Paraguayans to seethe with a resentment that persists today as an element in nationalist discourse.

Exit Caxias

Sympathetic biographers have claimed that the Marquis of Caxias did everything in his power to curb the excesses of his soldiers. But Caxias was not merely fatigued in January 1869—he was sick. He had gone without sleep for nearly three days before his troops entered Asunción, and he literally fell into the bed that his servants had prepared for him in the elegant residence of the late General Barrios.[39] The temperature was now above one hundred degrees Fahrenheit, and the sixty-five-year-old marquis could hardly move for the heat.

He was not alone. In truth, many senior Allied officers had come down with fevers, which often aggravated previous illnesses. General Andrade Neves died on 6 January and the marquis's adjutant, Colonel Fernando Sebastião Dias de Motta, a short time later.[40] Both General Guilherme Xavier de Souza and Admiral Ignácio were so ill that they could not leave their respective sickbeds, and the latter had already asked to be relieved as commander of the fleet. Generals Osório and Argolo Ferrão had not yet recovered from their wounds and General Machado Bittencourt soon died of his.[41]

All this sickness among senior officers created a power vacuum in Asunción that placed even greater strain on Caxias. The victories in December involved a heavy loss of life and this fact weighed heavily on him. Even though he feigned indifference to public hectoring, the battering that the marquis had received in the Argentine and Brazilian press had likewise aggravated his sense of well-being. What had started as minor quibbles had surged into a campaign of whispered invective, and it evidently wounded his pride to think that he had lost the respect to which he was entitled.

The term "dignified" had so often fastened onto Caxias that he had long since ceased making excuses for any personal failings, and on this occasion it showed. He evidently felt unsure that he still enjoyed the confidence of the emperor, and, on 12 January, asked to be relieved or at least granted leave. Two days later, having received no word from Rio de Janeiro, he issued Order of the Day no. 272, which formally declared the war at an end.[42]

The marquis clearly understood that the struggle was not over, but he felt so fatigued and depressed that he desperately wanted to close the book. Then, while attending mass in the Asunción Cathedral on 17 January, Caxias fainted. His men carried him to his quarters, where he momentarily regained consciousness, then collapsed again. As reported in the English-language press, the reaction among doctors was unequivocal:

> His medical attendants did not deem it prudent for him to wait [for the war minister to confirm his successor] … and he embarked on Monday night on board the *Pedro Segundo*, and left early on Tuesday morning. On that day, as was to be expected,

López formed a subject for conversation, and his probable future movements, with the 8,000 men said to be under his command, were discussed. The Marquis put an end to the discussion amongst his officers by exclaiming: "What does it matter? Eight-thousand men can never finish these dregs [of Brazilian soldiers] that will stay behind [in Asunción]."[43]

Caxias's remark may have been spat out in haste and with aristocratic contempt for his own troops, but it conceded, at least, that the country was not yet pacified.

This fact could hardly have mollified the marquis's successor, General Guilherme Xavier de Souza, who was also sick (with liver disease) and anxious to go home. A former governor of Rio Grande do Sul, the new commander was a gifted political officer, and certainly no weakling, but he was decidedly out of his depth as head of Allied forces. He had none of Caxias's charisma, precious little of his now-vanished energy, and he was frankly perplexed by the turn of events that had placed him in command. Guilherme envisioned no changes to his predecessor's policies; he presumed that his command was temporary and that he ought to resist the temptation to mount new attacks against López.[44] He did act to impose more control in Asunción, to inventory the spoils then in the hands of sutlers, and, where possible, to return properties to their owners. These efforts could never have succeeded amid so much chaos, however. Indeed, the members of the commission that he named to supervise the return of stolen properties helped themselves to a portion of the loot (or took bribes to look the other way).[45]

When he complained to Guilherme and Emílio Mitre that Allied soldiers had wrecked his consulate at Luque, the Italian consul Chapperon was told to mind his manners and to remember that his right of diplomatic immunity could easily be revoked.[46] People were similarly jumpy in all of the nearby villages that had come under Allied control. A small number of Luque's inhabitants had remained hiding in their homes without daring to peep at the Brazilians. Many more, however, found it expedient to flee further inland, carrying their children and infirm parents upon their backs.

As for Caxias, he steamed homeward. His decision not to disembark at Buenos Aires inspired bitter comment from the Porteños, who could not help but think it an intentional snub or some expression of political chicanery. At Montevideo, the marquis did go ashore, not to consort with Uruguayan officials, but to convalesce in accommodations provided by the local Brazilian command.[47] The cumulative strain of overwork and depression had yet to run its course with him, though his fevers abated long enough to permit a brief meeting with Councilor José María da Silva Paranhos, who arrived in the Uruguayan capital at that time.

The imperial government had just named Paranhos special agent to Asunción. Although his duties were only vaguely defined, he had already amassed extensive power as foreign minister, and Paraguay's fate depended on how he chose to use it. Though a Conservative like Caxias, Paranhos had shown little patience with the manner of the marquis's departure from the seat of war, and like the emperor, he worried about what this action might portend. Final success had seemingly been snatched from Brazil's grasp, that old and broken man having thrown it away. In truth, victory had been delayed, not squandered, though at that particular moment this was not apparent.

The Porteño press ruminated that the marquis was dying, and so it appeared to people in Rio de Janeiro as well.[48] His arrival in the imperial capital proved the most consternating event of his life. As Caxias wearily made his way down the ramp from the warship and set foot in his native city, no official stepped up to greet him. He was treated as a private individual, deserving neither a formal reception nor a public expression of gratitude. This lack of appreciation, tantamount to a slap in the face, stung deeply, all the more so since it clearly emanated from the monarch.

Only on 21 February did Pedro condescend to receive Caxias at the São Cristóvão Palace. By now the emperor had opted to put aside his disappointment. It was true that the marquis had failed to capture López—an objective that Pedro deemed essential to preserving his imperial dignity—but the monarch recognized that Caxias had labored under tremendous pressure. He had won many battles, and had always proven a staunch defender of the dynasty. He had much to contribute even now, and it was best for all concerned that his achievements be duly honored.[49] Within a number of weeks, the emperor went one step further, according Caxias the noble title of duke. He was one of only three Brazilians ever to achieve this distinction.[50]

Pedro wished to send a message to the army, to members of the government, and to the public at large, but he failed to display a similar sympathy to Admiral Ignácio, who also returned "prematurely" to Rio de Janeiro at this time. Barely conscious and still wracked with fever, the ex-commander of the fleet was carried to the court in a litter, but the emperor refused to meet him. Distraught as well as ill, Ignácio retreated at once to his home on the Rua do Senado. His religion provided him with his only measure of solace in the three weeks remaining to him, and he succumbed destitute of any public homage save for the hasty praise of his sailors and a few journalists.[51]

Despite his poor treatment of Ignácio, Pedro's willingness to resolve his differences with Caxias was politically convenient, and it found easy support among Conservatives. It did not sit so well with Liberals, of course. They had not forgotten the emperor's use of his moderating power to help Caxias at their expense in February 1868.[52] Heated exchanges on the matter erupted in the newspapers, in the senate, and on the streets, and these brought neither resolution nor even much clarity. Members of Parliament spent more time evaluating the patriotism of their colleagues than in examining facts. Certain Liberals professed dismay at seeing Caxias ennobled as a duke when a heroic and equally deserving Liberal, General Osório, remained a mere marquis.

In July 1870, after the war was over, Caxias faced a senate inquiry into his decision-making during the final stages of the 1868 campaign. He was a member in good standing of that body, a fact that his colleagues recognized by assuming a scrupulously polite demeanor for the occasion. Caxias had recovered his health and much of his composure and was not interested in any lingering skepticism. He summarized what had occurred in Paraguay before he took command and what he accomplished in his twenty-seven months in the field, omitting no opportunity to eulogize his subordinate officers. He dismissed the question of his departure by disingenuously observing that since Montevideo was part of the military district "in operations in Paraguay," he had never really left his post. As for declaring the war at an end, he had simply stated an opinion, he said, nothing more.[53] The more significant matter of having let López escape was potentially explosive, but Caxias refused to be pulled into a long-winded debate.

The duke's testimony masked an exasperated contempt for the second-guessing of civilians. He was visibly upset at having to go through what seemed like an inquisition. He kept his comments brief, but nonetheless evoked what was known about the Paraguayan campaign at the beginning of 1869. Several things had been certain then. The Marshal's army had counted for little more than a shirtless rabble. They were militarily irrelevant, and unable to hinder the empire's plan to build a Paraguay without López; Brazilian commanders could liquidate the tiny bands of Lopista vagrants whenever they wished. Meanwhile, it was necessary to bring order to those parts of the country that the army had yet to occupy, and this mission could easily have been accomplished by a man in better health than Caxias.

These priorities recognized the military and political realities of the moment, and were in keeping with the emperor's magnanimity. In this assembly, no one could really afford to discount dom Pedro's will. This was as much a matter of self-interest as political procedure. The Senate was the natural domain for aristocratic grandees, the majority of whom wanted to clear Caxias of wrongdoing. Despite their earlier deprecations, every senator could agree that he merited the nation's esteem. He had won the victory by securing Asunción, and whether his military virtues proceeded from policy, personal pride, or the instinct of service, they still deserved to be lauded.

Caxias was honest enough to be disconcerted by a process that flayed him one moment and sanctified him the next. He had sought neither praise nor rehabilitation. But that did not stop him from reciprocating the senate's embrace and approving the soupy commendations ladled over the army that he had shaped into a modern force. With all these proofs of official acclaim already in the public consciousness, the senate hearings could not help but endorse what the emperor had already decided.

Foreign observers might reasonably have reacted with sarcasm. They could have wondered whether such flattery camouflaged a less-than-pristine record, as the events in Paraguay suggested. For the Brazilian elite, however, it was crucial that military success in no sense challenge their base of political power. It was bad enough that officers of humble birth, who held no titles and who owned no slaves, had played an effective role in the campaign against López. These men might still be co-opted over time. For now, Caxias stood out as the perfect symbol, not just among his own Conservative collaborators but also among Liberals, Progressives, and any others who defended the empire. He had to be a hero—nothing less was permissible.

Thus did Caxias undergo an apotheosis. Over the years that remained to him, he insensibly rose—or sank—into the role of an icon, the Duke of Iron, the symbol of military integrity for all subsequent generations of Brazilian officers. His place in the master narrative of the nation's history was guaranteed and his faults forgotten. Henceforth, his name was used to adorn barracks, railroad stations, and elementary schools.[54]

And the war in Paraguay continued without him.

Paranhos And The Allied Occupation

Perhaps Caxias showed so little concern about the country he had left behind because José María da Silva Paranhos had more or less taken his place. The councilor could be trusted to keep imperial interests in hand as he asserted civil authority in Paraguay and helped construct a new government out of many disparate factions. As a proponent (and practitioner) of realpolitik, Paranhos had always presumed that the Triple Alliance consisted of one dominant power—Brazil—and two subsidiary states—Argentina and Uruguay—both of which needed to comprehend their place in the changing world. 1869 was not 1865. Flores was dead, and the national government in Buenos Aires, though anxious to secure its promised territories in Misiones and the Chaco, could only have a titular interest in the alliance. The campaign in Paraguay had left the Brazilian army in a commanding position, and Paranhos saw no benefit to abandoning this supremacy through some misguided consideration of policy. It was natural that postwar Paraguay operated according to Brazilian rules, and Paranhos wanted this done economically, without giving offense to Argentina.

Like his spiritual descendants in today's Itamaraty Palace, the councilor preferred to achieve results through honest means. He had no desire to poison the atmosphere in Asunción any more than had already occurred, but he also recognized that the authority he appeared to hold could offer prizes for all concerned. It might be used to reconcile the feuding Paraguayan exiles (whose claim on power at that moment was illusory). It could also sideline any efforts by Buenos Aires to enhance the interests of Argentina's preferred candidates and frustrate their annexationist impulses. Above all, Paranhos could push every player—save López—into accepting the inevitable transition to a new and inoffensive Paraguay. A nation at peace. A gelding.

After consulting Caxias in Montevideo, Paranhos left in early February to visit Sarmiento in Buenos Aires. The councilor wished to avoid statements that might excite Argentine suspicions, and he kept the president mollified with his carefully crafted words. Sarmiento in turn promised continued support for Paranhos's mission to Paraguay, so long as it was cost-effective, reminding him only of the political and financial debts that linked the two governments.[55]

Paranhos made port in Asunción on 20 February, just as the hot weather started to break. Nothing could have prepared him, however, for the brash indiscipline of the occupying troops and the plethora of interested factions who claimed to speak for Paraguay. He had hoped to make the necessary changes without delay and get on with smashing López. Everyone, however, had been waiting on his arrival. They had done little to prepare any transition, and the challenges he faced were therefore considerable. As Sarmiento had already observed in a letter to General Emilio Mitre, the "indefinite protraction of the war leaves us with tied hands. Is there a country called Paraguay? Does it have inhabitants, does it have males? Can a Paraguayan government be organized? Where? When? With what men? To govern whom?"[56]

As a civilian navigating through a highly militarized environment, the councilor found himself at a disadvantage in trying to answer these questions. Yet he was widely seen as the only person capable of breaking through the logjam of ambition, incompetence, and avarice that passed for administration in occupied Asunción. Paranhos was indefatigable, and many in the city began to think of him as the de facto viceroy of Paraguay. He met with General Guilherme, with other Allied military commanders, with Paraguayan exile leaders recently returned from Buenos Aires and Europe, with foreign consular officials, and with representatives of the many traders in the city. He pinpointed Paraguayan exiles deserving of discreet cultivation. And he tried to deal with displaced people who, with the cooling weather, had lost their fear and who were now drifting back to the capital in increasing numbers.[57] Some refugees were honest victims of the Marshal's caprice. Others were spies. But most were scavengers in search of anything the looters had left behind.

The common Brazilian appraisal of Paraguayan liberals, anti-Lopistas, and supposedly ex-Lopistas mingled sincere appreciation with a pragmatic desire to find among them a faction willing to fall into line. Paranhos was more realistic than those Brazilians who thought it simple to enlist a coterie of collaborators. In dealing with Paraguayans, the other Brazilians had always favored the use of force even when they could gain their objectives through policy. The councilor wanted to find a better way.

The most efficient method to bring about stability in Paraguay was to create the right kind of government to succeed López. Various exile politicians and members of the Paraguayan Legion had asserted a claim to authority among their countrymen ever since early January. But these men failed even to curtail the looting, and they constantly quarreled among themselves. At one time, there were at least five men who announced an intention to assume the provisional presidency; not one was inclined toward political compromise.[58]

Every important exile family had a son in mind for the post. One group, led by Juan Francisco Decoud and his dashing son José Segundo, insisted that all political problems be put to rest through a prompt and open election.[59] This proposal was entirely impractical, but at least it admitted the right of Paraguayans to choose a future of their own design. Unfortunately, neither Paranhos, nor the Brazilian high command, nor the Argentines, nor the other Paraguayan liberals stood ready to consent to any change whose outcome could not be decided in advance.

The councilor discovered his most problematic candidates for power in Asunción not among the former exiles from Buenos Aires but from a small coterie of opportunists who had once served the Marshal. Chief among them was Cándido Bareiro, López's former agent in Paris, whom one scholar described as "a ruthless and cynical politician charged by his enemies with having no scruples whatever."[60] Bareiro arrived in Asunción in February, and, having set aside his previous commitment to López, now sought to create a government that would preserve much of the old Lopista spirit. He took the key role within the nucleus of a coalition favored by those legionnaires who could not stomach the Decoud family's arrogant claim to power. The Decoudistas—if such a term is permissible, given the constant shifting of alliances—remained stridently pro-Argentine, and thus misread the true disposition of power in Asunción, which always favored Paranhos.

In commenting on the befuddled politics of the day, Richard Burton observed that a president "without subjects enough to form a ministry … would be a palpable absurdity, and Paranhos could not lend himself to the farce of creating a nation out of war-prisoners."[61] But the councilor ended by doing something rather like that. He announced that a provisional government of anti-López Paraguayans could count on imperial patronage so long as political niceties were respected. By this, he meant that any anti-Brazilian sympathies that might arise within a new regime would have to be eradicated. Without addressing this stipulation, some three hundred thirty-five citizens signed a petition at the end of March that demanded a new government, and four emissaries were selected to carry the proposal to Buenos Aires.[62]

One of the emissaries begged off, but the remaining three soon departed downriver to the same city where the Triple Alliance Treaty had been signed four years earlier. They paid Paranhos a courtesy visit before they left. The interview tested the councilor's charm, and he offered the three men every sort of bonhomie that aristocrats reserve for inferiors who do not realize that they are inferiors: He flattered them one moment, berated them the next, all the while driving home a polite reminder that their success depended on his.

Paranhos had little trust for these men. Indeed, he slipped away from Asunción aboard an express packet that reached Buenos Aires hours before the three Paraguayans made port. He had started the process of rebuilding the nation and now intended to see it through without setting aside the empire's advantages or spoiling his notion of a lasting peace.

The Marshal Sets the Stage—Again

In all this muddled talk of nation-building, precious little was said about the obvious fact that López remained free. Though no one doubted that his forces had been seriously reduced in the interior departments, what he might choose to do with them was anyone's guess. The different factions in Asunción might argue all they wanted about the future—the Marshal intended to make war.

Except in scale, the struggle had not appreciably changed during the early months of 1869. López's army occupied a position in a well-watered and fertile district of the Cordillera, roughly twenty miles wide by forty long, and into which had concentrated around one hundred thousand people. Cerro León lay at the entrance of this district, near Pirayú and Sapucai. Directly to the east rose a chain of green hills, six hundred feet in elevation and home to a great many peasant farmers.

López, having left a rearguard force at Cerro León, moved the remainder of his army up the rocky slope to Azcurra, which he had engaged in fortifying ever since his flight from Itá Ybaté. He had twenty artillery pieces of various calibers at the new site and perhaps two thousand troops fit for service.[63] The few British engineers who remained received orders to begin casting cannon at a makeshift arsenal at nearby Caacupé. The foundry south of Ybycuí was also still operational. The main effort, however, focused on constructing earthworks at Azcurra.

Stories of Allied ill-treatment of the Asuncenos and Luqueños, which had spread all over unoccupied Paraguay, were much embellished in the telling; in truth, civilians had more to fear from the Marshal's press-gangs, which needed workers to assist in constructing the Azcurra defenses.[64] Luis Caminos had already drafted the women, children, and old men from the outlying towns and had driven the multitude forward over the previous weeks like so many cattle.[65]

They had lived in the open ever since, their few possessions piled atop bullock carts near their assigned places of labor.

Caapucú, Itá, Yaguarón, San Lorenzo, Villarrica, and Paraguarí lost substantial portions of their dwindling urban population, an estimated thirty to forty thousand persons having fled from the Allies into the hill country and an uncertain future. *The Standard's* war correspondent exaggerated little when he wrote in disgust of their ongoing tribulations:

> [Caminos had] ordered all the families to the mountains, the young, the old, the aged, and the infirm, were all swept before the ruthless guard; the first and best families in Paraguay are at present living … chiefly on mandioca and roasted corn. Clothes are unknown, even rags are scarce. The people are in the most deplorable state of misery, and without even a ray of hope; beef is allowed once a week to the unfortunates; women are alone; men there are none save those in the hospitals, or the few on duty.[66]

Hundreds of displaced families from all over Paraguay joined the residents of the Cordilleras in trying to survive with inadequate resources while keeping up the show of diehard resistance that Marshal López demanded.[67] Those Asuncenos who had rarely dirtied their hands in the soil found themselves begging the peasants for a measly portion of whatever roots or parched corn they had hoarded over the previous season.[68]

Outwardly, the majority of Paraguayans stood firm and cheered the Marshal's cause, their nationalism unperturbed. But in fact, most civilians, having already lived through some of the war's worst traumas, simply could not think of where else to go. So they stared at their wasted children—their protruding stomachs, their frail limbs knotty as dried wood, their hopeless eyes. And they did what the soldiers told them to do. Only a few took the road to Asunción. By now, every Paraguayan could see that the home front was the only front.

Aside from several limited scouting expeditions, the Allies had to continue gathering information through the usual less-than-satisfactory means. Since the Marshal's troops rarely moved out of Azcurra and Piribebuy, a large portion of eastern Paraguay, which had been well populated and prosperous before the war, effectively became a no-man's land. The Marshal had ordered the evacuation of the Misiones long before the fall of Humaitá, and no resettlement of any kind had occurred in the zone since. Other areas had largely been drained of male inhabitants by the government's ceaseless demands for recruits and workers to tend fields closer to the action.

Villarrica, the most important community in the department of Guairá, had suffered a severe decline when the Marshal ordered a new muster in the early months of 1868. The town's militia chief at that time listed 563 men on his roll: 283 boys aged 12 to 14; 7 more boys in a church band; 5 slaves; 8 former slaves (*libertos*); 29 wounded soldiers; 260 militiamen aged 50 and above; and a long list of "defectives," including 6 insane individuals, 4 men "completely blind," 3 "deaf and dumb," and one 90-year-old *anciano* who had "problems all over his body." Muster lists from Atyra, Caazapá, Yuty, and Concepción revealed a similar picture—and these statistics date from before the December campaign took its toll.[69]

It would be helpful to have complete and ongoing data to illustrate the demographic decline of Paraguay during the war, but in an environment where scriveners recorded extant manpower reserves on pieces of rawhide, fragmentary information was always the rule.[70] One of the clearest illustrations of the changing population can be garnered from one of the least numerous groups in the country: the freed blacks, whom the state listed in censuses from 1844 to 1868. Though an analysis of a small group reveals nothing about broader questions of mortality, all the same it presents a shocking picture for the final year that such records were kept. Only four districts (*partidos*), home at that time to the majority of Paraguay's blacks, received extensive attention:

		1850	1853	1856	1868
CAAPUCÚ:	born	20	11	19	8
	died	9	6	11	37
TABAPY:	born		24	35	4
	died		3	10	13
QUIINDY:	born	112	47		4
	died	34	15		36
QUYQUYÓ:	born	11	14	14	2
	died	4	2	5	8

Given the absence of men conscripted into the Nambí-í and other battalions of the army, fewer libertos were born in the communities surveyed in 1868 and a much smaller proportion of those born survived.[71] It is not hard to discern in these numbers a population on the verge of extinction.

Save for the liberto statistics, census data for the rural zones are entirely absent for the period 1868–1869. The unfolding disaster was nonetheless obvious to all observers. We can take at face value the statement of Lucás Carrillo, former Paraguayan commander at Angostura, who, when questioned by Allied officers in December, remarked that Paraguay's population had "been reduced to debris, with all property laid waste, every family left fatherless, and with a total population made up of women, children, invalids, and wounded."[72]

Except in a half-dozen communities on the northern periphery, food had grown very scarce, malnutrition had become chronic, and epidemic disease was raging. In earlier days, Paraguayan functionaries found ways to meet the army's needs while retaining sufficient supplies for local consumption. This was no longer possible. "War must nourish war," Cato once exclaimed in the Roman senate—an adage now ruthlessly adapted by the Marshal. To supply his army and keep the fight going, he now seized all of the much-diminished harvest of maize, manioc, and beans, and in so doing, left the civilians with nothing to eat. When he issued orders to concentrate displaced families closer to Azcurra, it simply compounded the pressure on remaining supplies, and spread cholera to areas hitherto unaffected by sickness.[73]

True to his convictions—or to his vanity—López admitted to no added burden in any of this. His people had made sacrifices before and they could do so again, and what they lacked in military stores they could more than balance with an unbending patriotism. Paraguay's continued independence was at stake, and while the kambáes wriggled to the right and left in search of turncoats to staff a puppet government, the Marshal's legitimate regime in Piribebuy continued to function. He organized those minimal sources of manpower, armaments, and provisions still left him with skill and forbearance.[74] At the same time, while his people struggled to stay alive, he displayed indifference not just to their pain but to the very circumstances that had brought that pain about.

Even more than usual, López seemed engrossed in his own personal drama. He had always carried an air of exclusivity about him, and now, amidst all this squalor, he more and more lost himself in it. The cult that had grown up around his name had taken ever more exaggerated forms during 1868, and he may have come to believe in his own propaganda. Certainly he ate more beef than ever before, drank more caña, prayed more fervently and in terms of greater familiarity to a deity that most Paraguayans would have thought unapproachable. He became an avid reader of religious texts, including Chateaubriand's *Genius of Christianity*, which gave him a casuistry to validate his actions.[75]

The Marshal occasionally tried to make out the balance sheet of his life. While chatting with Lieutenant Colonel Centurión at Azcurra, for instance, he spoke of the advantages that Paraguayans enjoyed in having chosen authority over legality:

> I could have been the most popular man, not only in Paraguay, but in all of South America. All I needed to do was to promulgate a constitution. But I did not wish to do so, for however easy it might have been, it would have brought disgrace on my nation. When I read the constitutions of the neighboring countries, they leave me enthusiastic in the contemplation of so much beauty, but

when I adjust my eyesight to see their practical effect, it fills me with horror.[76]

Thus did López attempt to cement the national destiny to his person and pass off his impulses as reflecting the public will.

The Marshal had always striven for glory, yet now there were also periods when his grip on reality seemed tenuous, and he appeared more and more to be looking for death. Perhaps a feeling of guilt had finally touched his soul. More likely, the darkness of his probable fate had so enveloped him that he sought release in delusion. Such inclinations might be judged pitiful in a harmless country gentleman like the knight of La Mancha, but as López retreated more and more into his dreams, he grew more frightening—and more arbitrary. No one could afford to ignore his whims or to forget that he still held the fortune of thousands of Paraguayans in the small of his hand.

On several occasions starting in late April, the Marshal dispatched cavalrymen on expeditions to Concepción, Horqueta, and other communities of the north. They had orders to root out and execute local traitors, with which the region supposedly abounded. López had long suspected the more prosperous families in the region of having preferred the candidacy of Benigno back in 1862. And now his spies had informed him that certain highly placed members of the old Concepceño elite had opened treasonable contact with the Brazilians.[77] With Marshal López, suspicion quickly became fact, and, since among his soldiers freedom from responsibility was more attractive than freedom from restraint, they now did their worst. Before his cavalrymen finished their grisly assignment, they had lanced nearly fifty "criminals," the great majority women and children.[78] Lopista agents were capable of even worse behavior, with one source noting 257 individuals executed in Pirayú and Azcurra over several months, both military men and civilians accused of defeatism and worse.[79] There were few natural brakes to contain this butchery.

Madame Lynch and the López children sometimes got through the Marshal's gloom, but they could also encourage his breaks with reality. In the National Archives in Asunción there is a torn and dusty letter of March 1869 from Panchito López to José Falcón. In it, the fourteen-year-old colonel asks the fifty-nine-year-old official to kindly arrange for the binding in fine leather of two volumes of music belonging to his mother, la Madama, with instructions to carefully tool her initials onto the cover of each book.[80] The almost surreal quality of this epistle, which presupposes affluent rather than normal circumstances, suggests how far the López family had slipped away from reality. So did the behavior of Madame Lynch, who spent her time at a makeshift treasury in Caacupé picking out jewelry from among the loot collected by state agents. She also continued to purchase private lands "for absurdly low prices; on occasion, she bought them in exchange for food."[81]

The strangeness of this little republic in the hill country was reflected not just in the comportment of the presidential family but also in the pages of *Estrella*. This was the final Lopista newspaper of the war, edited in Piribebuy and composed in Spanish by the Italian cleric Gerónimo Becchi and two Paraguayan assistants who filled it not just with the usual bloated patriotism and praise for the Marshal, but also with references to engagements that had never happened, victories that were never won. In earlier days, the various state newspapers tried to promote a strong nationalist sympathy among the undefeated Paraguayans. Though this same idea evidently guided *Estrella*, it was no longer a matter of casting the pearls of Lopista wisdom before the peasant swine, to somehow inflame their enthusiasm in this late hour. The pearls instead were being cast to the wind.[82]

The Count Takes Command

While the people of Paraguay did everything they could to survive their privations and the members of the López family basked in self-delusion, the Brazilians wondered what to do next. Citing the paucity of horses and fodder, General Guilherme did little to challenge the Paraguayans in the Cordillera during February and March.[83] López had wrecked the one locomotive left behind at Asunción, and while the Allies awaited the arrival of a new machine from Buenos Aires, their scouts followed the rail line on horseback past Areguá.[84] They noted a shattered bridge at the Arroyo Yuquyry that had to be rebuilt before any major advance up the line.

The scouts also confirmed the falseness of a rumor that the Marshal had placed warships on Lake Ypacaraí, a 56-square-mile body of tranquil water that obstructed the approach to the east. They then continued on towards Patiño Cue and Pirayú, noting little of interest, and returned to base along a more direct route. Other scouts, dispatched on a still longer ride, galloped past Paraguarí and edged Carapeguá in central Paraguay before they, too, returned empty-handed to Asunción.

Though the Allied armies avoided major confrontations, the navy did engage in smaller operations. A portion of the Allied fleet had already steamed upriver in mid-January in search of the López navy, whose ships, it emerged, had fled up the Manduvirá, an important tributary of the Paraguay just north of the capital.[85] The retreating Paraguayans left a half-sunken hulk at the mouth of the river before making their way further upstream and onto a swollen creek, the Yhagüy. Most Allied ships were too deep-drafted to follow without clearing the obstacle, and only Delphim's monitors succeeded in getting through. At length, however, they discovered that Paraguayan troops had dropped chains, stakes, and rock-filled oxcarts into the channel at various points, making what had been a difficult passage virtually impossible.

Meanwhile, other naval units proceeded up the Paraguay to inspect the Mato Grosso settlements that the Marshal had previously abandoned. The sailors were startled to learn that a new Brazilian fort had replaced the Paraguayan defenses at Corumbá. This new facility boasted a garrison of five hundred troops sent from the provincial capital. The new garrison met the imperial steamers with an initial volley of hot fire, thinking they were the Marshal's vessels coming to wreak havoc once again.[86]

López was not terribly concerned with remote events. He preferred to focus on building the works at Azcurra in the same way he had once prepared defenses at Humaitá. Yet he was still capable of tricks. On 10 March, a force of Brazilian engineers marched from Luque to the Arroyo Yuquyry to rebuild the railway bridge that had previously been destroyed. The Argentine locomotive had finally arrived in Asunción and the Allied command wanted to get it into operation as soon as possible.[87] The Paraguayans had been so quiet that no reason existed to suspect any opposition to the Brazilian effort. Then, as the troops lined up to receive their midday rations, a locomotive with six cars steamed up near the opposite bank. Two hundred Paraguayans jumped off all at once, and immediately let fire a volley of musketry.

The Marshal's gunners, having also mounted a small cannon on one of the six wagons, now used it to pour grape on the startled Brazilians, forty of whom fell dead over the next minutes. Allied cavalry eventually swept across the creek, but no one had the presence of mind to lay a log across the rails in the rear. This allowed the Paraguayans, with one man killed and three wounded, to get to their wagons and speed off towards Pirayú.[88] Thereafter the Brazilian generals carefully guarded the tracks between Areguá and the Yuquyry with upwards of fifteen hundred troops, but these did not impede periodic sabotage along the line.[89]

In truth, the Allies were busy elsewhere. Five days after the train attack, Allied warships conducted a reconnaissance of the Alto Paraná at the southeastern end of the country, nearly three hundred miles from the capital. They disembarked troops at Encarnación and found the town empty, stripped clean of everything useful. Brazilian cavalry units followed up this operation by mounting a brief foray deeper into the Misiones, destroying what they could of the meager Paraguayan stores found there.[90] These scouting operations brought negligible gains in matériel seized and intelligence gathered.

The main Allied units still made no move, however. The Argentines at Trinidad spent many weeks drilling in the mornings and giving formal balls at night, but their morale was poor and their rations even poorer. The beef, cooked in its own hide; the savory stews (*pucheros*); the plates of cornmeal crushed into a polenta that smelled of the home fire—in Paraguay, all these things were replaced by a humble fare of charqui and hardtack. It was no better for the

Brazilians. They drilled just like the Argentines, and spent their free time with amateur dramatics, gambling, and the inevitable singing songs of *saudade*.[91]

Military preparations for the final push went nowhere. Guilherme had been intermittently ill. Richard Burton, who met the Allied commander in mid-April, described him as a tall, thin man, peculiarly Brazilian in countenance, but with pallid, yellow skin that left him looking "almost corpse-like." Knowledge of his fainting spells had become common by now, and his officers dismissed him as little better than a *General da Corte*, joking that any second lieutenant could offer better leadership.[92] As Guilherme had supposed, moreover, the government in Rio showed no interest in assigning him the honor of obliterating López's army and instead was looking for some other candidate, preferably an aristocrat of the highest rank.

Most senior officers in the Brazilian army either lacked the necessary prestige, were politically unreliable, or had already fallen ill from fever in Paraguay. The most obvious remaining candidate was dom Pedro's son-in-law, Louis Philippe Marie Ferdinand Gaston d'Orléans, the Count d'Eu. The count had the requisite status and had already seen military service with Spanish forces in Morocco. But his nomination posed a challenge.[93] A generous impulse in 1864 had prompted Pedro to favor the suit of this minor Orleans prince who sought the hand of his daughter Isabel. Though the emperor had his reservations, the count found a sympathetic spirit in the imperial princess, and the newlyweds grew much attached to each other no matter what her father thought.[94]

Isabel enjoyed considerable esteem in Brazil and it was natural that the Count d'Eu should seek some public role through her. But Pedro always meddled, citing *raisons dynastiques* while in fact acting as a compulsive busybody. Whatever his faults, the count deserved better treatment. He dressed indifferently, spoke Portuguese poorly, and was presumptuously unconcerned with protocol. True, he was devoted to the Bragança monarchy, got along well with members of the court, and found friends in both the Conservative and Liberal camps. But the count's casual habits, which had gained him so many friends, grated on the emperor. So did the fact that Dona Isabel had thus far failed to conceive.

And there was another matter. In 1865 the Count d'Eu had accompanied the emperor to Rio Grande do Sul, where together they witnessed the Paraguayan surrender at Uruguaiana. Ever since, the younger man had thirsted for action. He sent five separate petitions to the Council of State asking for a field command and Pedro saw to it that all five petitions were quashed.[95] We can only guess the motivations behind the monarch's rebuffs. Possibly he wanted the count to focus on family matters. Also, so long as Mitre and Caxias held the overall command, His Royal Highness would have to take orders from social inferiors, and no matter how amenable and respectful the generals might be, such an inversion of rank on the part of Isabel's husband was unthinkable.

While these factors may have carried some weight, jealousy clearly framed the emperor's need to keep the count tethered to his home in Rio de Janeiro. Since the government had previously baulked at his own demand to serve as Brazil's first Voluntário, the monarch was unwilling to enlist the whiny Gaston, who understood the envy underlying the council's denial and hence resented it; he would find some way to demonstrate his patriotism whether the emperor liked it or not. Now, in February 1869, the situation had changed and so had Pedro's opinion. He directed a letter to the count, citing the urgent situation in Paraguay and assured him that as Allied commander he could leave diplomacy to Paranhos, choose his own officers, and concentrate on military affairs. "A steamship awaits your orders," the emperor wrote.[96]

The count had Pedro where he wanted him. In a three-hour interview, he enumerated the problems that stood in the way of his immediate assumption of the Allied command. For one thing, he had harshly criticized the manner of Caxias's departure from Asunción—something that the Conservatives would hold against him. In addition, the ministers responsible for the war had never included the count in their deliberations, and he would therefore be working in the dark about conditions at the front. And finally, he pointed out that Paranhos had strongly opposed his earlier requests for command, and could not now wholeheartedly support a promotion that made the count his virtual partner in Paraguay.[97]

The emperor had already reflected on these things, and he made every concession to settle the question of command. The count, now vindicated, nodded his assent, and then, as a final jab, he insisted that the Council of State confirm the nomination, and that Paranhos agree to the matter in writing. Tired of his son-in-law's chirpy voice—and of the many things that went unsaid between them—Pedro wearily assented. Both men got what they wanted in consequence: the embarrassed emperor had an aggressive commander in Paraguay who would hound López to the death, while the count had all the reassurances he needed so as not to be kept on a tight leash by anyone, least of all Pedro.[98]

If a blister had to be lanced in Paraguay, Gaston was the man to do it. He reached Asunción on 14 April 1869. Brazilian warships in the bay thundered a royal salute as he stepped onto dry land, lifted his kepi to the assembled soldiers, and accompanied the reception committee to the Cathedral for a Te Deum. Staff officers grimaced in noting more than a few errors in etiquette, but His Royal Highness "was never a very great stickler for such like, [and] seemed thoroughly to enjoy the consternation of some of his entourage at the various little 'contre-temps,' and the more serious they looked, the more he laughed."[99]

The count got busy the next morning. He was only twenty-seven years old and seemingly out of place in such a senior role, yet he showed a remarkable diligence that Brazilian historians have yet to properly acknowledge.[100] He visited Luque in the early hours, inspected the battalions guarding the approaches to Asunción, and re-formed the army into two corps. To Osório, who had yet to fully recover from his jaw wound, Gaston assigned command of the First Corps—perhaps the single most popular decision of the day.[101] With somewhat less enthusiasm, the soldiers greeted Polidoro as the count's chosen commander over the Second Corps. Gaston may have lacked the gravitas of Caxias, the introspection of Mitre, and the physical courage of Flores, but he had no intention of letting anyone doubt his perspicacity or the scope of his authority. He was determined to bring the inaction of recent months to an end.

Accompanying the Count d'Eu in this effort was Alfredo d'Escragnolle Taunay, the military engineer who had survived the torments of the Mato Grosso jungle and who now joined in the new deployment as the count's personal secretary. Among his duties was to write an evocative account of events to rival what he had already penned during the retreat from Laguna.[102] Once in Paraguay, Taunay offered effusive praise to his patron, noting the count's strength of mind, his careful and sympathetic interrogations of Paraguayan deserters, and his desire to put the army in order.[103]

Not all the soldiers in Asunción shared Taunay's enthusiasm for Gaston (and, in truth, the friendly relation between the two cooled after a time).[104] Building morale by assigning command to the count was a problematic business. Caxias's hackneyed argument that the war was fought by the entire Brazilian nation seemed contradicted by the emperor's choice of a foreign-born commander who was hard of hearing, spoke Portuguese like a French bourgeois, and who made the soldiers work too hard.[105]

Though many officers admired the man's zeal, the men never liked him. They took exception to anyone who might force them back into the fight, for they already knew much about the Paraguayans that the count presumably did not. He was a novice and the Allied soldiers stood every chance at suffering from his inexperience and, perhaps, his recklessness.

On one occasion, not long after his arrival at the front, Gaston boarded a hospital ship bearing sick and wounded to Buenos Aires. Calling the patients malingerers, he ordered four-fifths of them to return to their duties and prepare for combat.[106] Up to this point, many Brazilian soldiers had actually thought that they might survive the war and see their families again. Now no one knew for sure. A ditty sung at the time told the whole story:

> He who made it to Asunción
> [has already] finished with his mission.
> If López has stayed in the country,
> then it's because the Marquis wanted it that way.
> Whoever now marches to the Cordillera
> will have acted like a donkey.[107]

14

 RESISTANCE TO NO AVAIL

Military men of the nineteenth century frequently made the assumption that the patterns and tendencies they observed in the field could be sculpted into general principles of war.[1] The Paraguayan campaign, however, contradicted many of the most common suppositions about wartime behavior. Whether or not it was best for their country, and regardless of their tremendous losses, the Paraguayans kept rebuilding a fighting force long after other armies would have yielded to superior force. This happened so often that everyone on the Allied side grew exasperated with having their predictions of Paraguayan defeat so regularly frustrated.

López deserves credit—or blame—on precisely this point. Since his arrival at Azcurra in January, he had rebuilt the broken officer corps and the state bureaucracy that sustained the national cause. The army of 1869, now made up of invalids, old men, and children, could never replace that which Caxias had destroyed at Itá Ybaté. But while their stomachs ached for lack of food, the Marshal's soldiers could still nourish themselves on a diet of duty.

Despite the claims of state newspapers like *Cacique Lambaré*, the peasants and burden-bearers of the Paraguayan countryside had never identified with the state any more than they had to. In the context of the present conflict, however, it was crucial that the remaining masters identify more readily with the poor, granting them a measure of agency in the ongoing struggle. In such a campaign, survival counted almost as much as outright victory. If he could somehow hold on, the Marshal might still weaken the Allies through pinpricks, causing them to reconsider their conquest of his country. He could no longer hope for victory, but he could still buy time.

Postponing the final confrontation held few advantages, but no evidence has come to light to suggest that the Marshal ever considered raising the white flag. In this he was not alone. For every man who doubted the resiliency of the nation, there were others who doubted not a whit.[2] Colonel Patricio Escobar, who by now had battle scars thick as a jaguar's spots, succeeded in bringing troops from the Lomas Valentinas. A portion of the men who had surrendered at Angostura and had been released broke their parole and rejoined López, bringing up to strength those reserves that Luis Caminos had earlier led to Azcurra. And General Bernardino Caballero still had sufficient cavalrymen to cause mischief. If few of these soldiers at Azcurra ate well, still they ate something. And Madame Lynch, for one, made sure that they occasionally received cigars, *chipas*, and other foodstuffs.[3] It may not have been much, but it was sufficient for them to consider themselves ready for action.

The precise number of effectives available to the Marshal in early 1869 remains unclear, but he somehow found the able-bodied men he needed. Child recruits arrived from San Pedro, San Joaquín, Caaguazú, and other isolated hamlets. The two thousand men ready for service in January had doubled by March, and by mid-April had more than doubled again, with most sources citing a figure of between eight and thirteen thousand soldiers.[4]

Since General Guilherme avoided any harassing actions, the Paraguayans had time to prepare a passable defense. The artillery pieces that had graced the battery at San Gerónimo and those along the Pikysyry were dragged to the crest of the hills overlooking Cerro León. Blows from machetes cleared the way for new trench works and abatis at the site. In addition, a machine for rifling cannon that the Paraguayans had previously hidden arrived intact from the old arsenal and was transported to Caacupé, where the Marshal's British machinists continued their manufacture of arms. They had already cast thirteen new guns of a minor caliber to add to the batteries already in operation.[5]

What had looked in January like a transient camp for stragglers was by April almost formidable. Of course, the Paraguayans still had to contend with an army of twenty-eight thousand Brazilians, four thousand Argentines, and a hundred or so Uruguayans.[6] These Allied troops were well supplied with new provisions, blankets, tents, and extra munitions. They still lacked horses, however, and there were ongoing complaints about defective cartridges and the lack of certain comestibles. The Count d'Eu took a personal interest in pressuring Lanús and the other armorers to deliver the supplies that they had promised or else face cancellation of their contracts.[7] When they were slow to respond, he distributed his own canned sardines among the men, giving rise to a popular ditty that compared the trend in rations from the roast beef of Osório to the beans and jerky of Polidoro and Caxias to the "sardinhas de Nantes" of the Count d'Eu.[8]

The latter commander had already proven his worth as an organizer; now he proceeded to show his skill as a strategist. Unlike Caxias, who had focused his energies on taking Asunción, the count had in mind a Clausewitzian objective: to pursue and annihilate López's army. Though he lacked precise information on the enemy's strengths, he knew where the Paraguayans had concentrated their main units, and saw no reason to grant López another Curupayty. Instead, the count planned to flank Azcurra simultaneously from the north and south while leaving sufficient troops at Pirayú to suggest that he might come from the center. The planned pincer movement would cause the Marshal to abandon his fixed positions in an attempt to protect Piribebuy. The imperial troops could then charge in from both sides and sweep the adversary from the field.[9]

The strategy was simple but it required careful coordination among the Allied units. At the beginning of April, some two thousand Brazilian troops set off for the small interior town of Rosario. This effort, which Guilherme had designed as his final show of aggressiveness before Gaston arrived, succeeded in driving out a small Paraguayan force. This left the Allies well situated to march on Concepción, the site of many recent executions and the most substantial community in the Paraguayan north.[10] Set against the bloody panorama of the war's final months, the seizure of Rosario and the atrocities in Concepción seemed relatively insignificant. The next step in the Allied plan, however, was crucial to the count's broader success.

The Raid at Ybycuí

On 1 May, Gaston sent several exploratory columns to the south to prepare for a major deployment. The first column was a mounted unit of eighty men, nominally Uruguayan but in fact composed largely of Paraguayans serving with the Allies. Their commander was a Uruguayan major, Hipólito Coronado, who had received orders to destroy the Marshal's iron foundry near Ybycuí.

For more than ten years, the foundry of El Rosado had cast cannon balls, bullets, and other implements of war in considerable quantities, and the place gained a legendary status among the Paraguayans and Allies alike. What galled the latter was the knowledge that the Marshal's engineers had retooled spent Allied ordinance, forming them into new projectiles to use against those who had fired them.[11] And even in 1869 the ironworks permitted the Marshal to pretend that his army was something more than a rabble.

Coronado's objective at Ybycuí thus had a symbolic as well as a military aspect, and its capture or destruction might make—or salvage—the major's career in the Uruguayan army. As early as December 1868 General Castro had asked permission to depart from Paraguay together with his division but his request had been refused by the Allied command.[12] Like Flores before him, Castro had seen many disciplinary problems among his troops, and he wanted to withdraw before they got worse. Besides, he was wooing an Italian woman in Asunción and presumably was so busy in his romantic endeavors that he wanted no major complications in the field. With this in mind, he assigned Coronado command of the Ybycuí venture.[13]

The major had reason to worry about this assignment. Short in stature but long on stage presence, he had a reputation for impulsiveness. In April, he had deserted the Oriental Division to join one of the revolutionary factions in Corrientes, but Argentine troops apprehended him and turned him over to Castro for the prescribed execution. At the last minute, however, Castro agreed to pardon Coronado if he emerged victorious at Ybycuí—but he warned the major not to return alive if he failed.[14]

The foundry, located some sixty-five miles southeast of Pirayú, had also served throughout the war as a detention camp where Allied prisoners and displaced persons of every nationality toiled under heavy sun and rain with minimal rations available to them. The local commander, Captain Julián Ynsfrán, was related to the same Juliana Ynsfrán whom López had repeatedly tortured when her husband surrendered the Humaitá garrison. Captain Ynsfrán seems to have lived under a cloud since that time, and he drove his prisoners relentlessly as a result.

Four hundred Allied soldiers (and four officers) made up the principal labor force at Ybycuí, together with one hundred fifty foreign civilians, mostly Brazilians and Argentines.[15] The latter had fallen into the Marshal's hands in Corrientes and Mato Grosso, and very few could now be called fit. Though it was set in a beautiful green valley cut by a crystalline arroyo, the foundry was little better than Siberia as far as its prisoners were concerned.

The Uruguayan column moved steadily southward starting on 11 May. Coronado expected to find relatively few people at the site, but when he captured several Paraguayan scouts the second day out, they informed him that the defending force was larger than anticipated.[16] The major pushed ahead anyway. At half past seven on the morning of the 13 May, he found himself directly opposite the Ybycuí "mines" and immediately ordered fifty horsemen to advance at the gallop. His report on the subsequent engagement freely recognized the tenacity of Ynsfrán's men—as well as the joy that Allied prisoners displayed at the moment of their liberation:

> The skirmishers had nearly seized the place without firing a shot, as they reached it before the defenders rushed to their arms. ... [One] of the enemy's officers felt inclined to surrender, but Captain Ynsfrán ... ordered firing [to commence] at different points. I ordered the carbineers and lancers to dismount and charge the enemy, [whose position was] swept after an hour's fighting. ... We took prisoner Captain Ynsfrán and two officers, together with 53

men. 23 rank and file were killed and the rest fled. … How can I describe the shouts of joy that the Allied prisoners sent forth when they found themselves liberated after years of cruel suffering? They were almost all naked, worn, and with the mark of hunger upon their features. Some were limping about on makeshift crutches. All greeted us as their saviors, and told us of their many sufferings at the hands of López and his pitiless lackeys.[17]

After counting his three dead and ten wounded, Coronado set to work destroying the iron machinery. The former prisoners took delight in joining in the melee, wrecking these objects of so much anguish. They tore apart the water wheel and threw the various iron implements into the creek. The Uruguayan column then began the long march back, this time accompanied by hundreds of former inmates, one hundred thirty camp followers and children, and several score of peasant laborers who brought up the rear in oxcarts.

After the battle of Yataí in August 1865, the Uruguayans showed little mercy to their Paraguayan prisoners, cutting off the heads of more than a few.[18] On this occasion, Coronado was disinclined to do any different. Having rounded up the members of the former garrison, he separated out Captain Ynsfrán and four others and forced them to march ahead of the troop. At a convenient spot near an outcropping of trees the major called a halt, turned to Ynsfrán, and loudly accused him of abusing Allied prisoners.

"I obeyed my orders," murmured the captain, who now waited for a response. It came back as a shout: "You are not a soldier! You are nothing but a coward!" Gesturing to a sergeant and drawing two fingers across his own throat, Coronado ordered the five men beheaded in front of the entire company. No one moved at first. Then, as the sharp saber fell down on Ynsfrán, the major mockingly observed that perhaps he ought to lance all the remaining enemy prisoners.[19] He was dissuaded from this course when his own Paraguayan subordinates, visibly shaken, assumed a threatening posture.[20]

Though he later condemned Ynsfrán's killing, the Count d'Eu nonetheless benefited from Coronado's raid. It robbed López of a major source of cannon and undermined still further the Paraguayans' waning morale. In mid-June, after he had gathered more information, the count sent Brazilian engineers to demolish the foundry more completely than Coronado had.[21] All that could be destroyed was broken with axes, the buildings were burned, and the water sluices shut to flood the site. The old water wheel sunk into the creek, and within weeks was overgrown with vines. Meanwhile, Coronado returned to base, where he luxuriated in all manner of accolades from the Allied commanders. He was promoted in rank, and generally treated as a hero, except by the Paraguayans, who considered him a murderer.[22]

Exit McMahon

The Marshal could not have welcomed the foundry's destruction, but even more costly to the national cause was Washington's recall of Minister Martin T. McMahon—the one remaining foreigner whose support might have saved Paraguay. The former Union Army general had spent the intervening months in Piribuy, which he described as a rustic place, "consisting of four streets intersecting each other at right angles, and enclosing an open space or grass-covered plaza, about a quarter of a mile across." The population, normally three to four thousand, had "more than trebled by the women and children who had abandoned their homes outside the district of the Cordilleras; at night these unfortunates thronged the corridors and orange groves or slept by the roadside wherever night overtook them."[23]

They had no regular sources of sustenance, and had to eat carrion, a porridge made from manioc, or sometimes the marrow of cow bones. When women and children approached the soldiers to ask for food, they were driven away, for all of the Marshal's men were hungry. And if a new recruit complained about the lack of meat, the old veterans would dig the lice from their armpits and laughingly point to them as the only "cattle" left in Paraguay.

McMahon was billeted in a comfortable home near the residences of the vice president and other cabinet ministers. The food available to him sold in the marketplace for "enormous" prices—when it could be found. He had little work to do other than attend the dances sponsored by the government, so he busied himself in the flower gardens he encountered and strolled near the stream that ran along the foot of the nearby mountain. The suffering of average Paraguayans, especially the children, was visible on all sides and continued to dig at his temper.

McMahon still evinced a positive feeling for the Piribebuy government, only one step short of advocacy. Unlike Washburn, he committed few of his thoughts and calculations to paper.[24] López needed the US minister to effect some diplomatic solution, if that were still possible; if all were truly lost, however, then the general might at least provide some security for Lynch and the López children.

Already in late January McMahon had naively broached the subject of US mediation. He presented himself to López as a go-between in arranging a cease-fire, and offered to obtain North American asylum for the Marshal and his family. López received these suggestions kindly and assured the minister that he would willingly make any personal sacrifice and accept exile if by doing so he could ensure Paraguayan independence. But if "his people had to choose between subjugation and extermination he would remain with them and accept the latter."[25] McMahon then proposed the withdrawal of Allied troops as a condition of his leaving the country and the submission of all other questions to neutral arbitration.

The Marshal was doubtful, but he let McMahon put the plan in an official communication on 1 February. López waited an entire week before rejecting the offer, observing that Allied victories in December would disincline the enemy to serious negotiations.[26] If McMahon thought to restore peace on the basis of mutual concessions then it was already too late. The possibility of US mediation was discussed only one more time, with the Count d'Eu, who rejected the offer out of hand.[27]

McMahon proved helpful to the Marshal on at least two other occasions. In late February, the Argentines saw fit to award to the Paraguayan Legion the use of Paraguay's national colors, doubtless as a way to secure a broader recognition for its place within a new provisional government. López reacted with unconcealed fury when the Allied commanders followed through by formally presenting them with the flag in March. He demanded to know how a coterie of traitors could constitute themselves as the legitimate bearers of the national ensign—and who were the Argentines to authorize such a concession in the first place? McMahon, managing to soothe the Marshal's rage, helped him compose a sober diplomatic missive that recognized that the Allies might shed Paraguayan blood in legitimate warfare, but insisted that they had no right to discount the patriotism of those who continued to resist.

The US minister had had few communications with his superiors since that time because the Brazilians made a habit of firing on dispatch riders sent from Piribebuy. But on 12 May, two American naval officers arrived at the front with messages from Washington, and the count decided to let them through.[28] McMahon, it emerged, was being recalled. Secretary of State William Seward, who had held his post through the roughest years of the Civil War, had been replaced by Elihu B. Washburne, elder brother of the former minister to Asunción. The latter's tenure at the State Department proved brief—less than two weeks—but that was time enough to recall the man whose words and conduct had undermined his brother's many accusations against López.[29]

McMahon received the news of his recall with his usual placidity. He recommended that a new minister be sent at once to the beleaguered Paraguayans, then reluctantly informed López of Washburne's decision. He assured him that he would withhold official announcement of the recall for a day or so. This last constituted a personal favor to the Marshal, who took the opportunity to pen letters to the outside world and prepare seven cartloads of property to be transported through the lines with McMahon.[30] The foreigner, who had previously agreed to serve as guardian for the Marshal's sons and daughters, now agreed to carry out substantial quantities of coin intended for deposit in England for Madame Lynch.

For the US minister to carry Lynch's property was surely impolitic. She had amassed a considerable private fortune through legitimate means. In these matters, however, appearances are all-important, and many observers were ready to accuse McMahon of abetting her thievery. A great deal of speculation arose concerning the quantity of money and jewels involved. One anti-Lopista scholar, writing in the first decade of the twentieth century, asserted that nearly a million pesos changed hands, while others claimed less than a tenth of that figure.[31] McMahon himself later testified in an English court that he had carried eleven thousand pounds to England for Madame Lynch, another fifteen hundred to New York for the Marshal's son, Emiliano, and the remaining seven thousand he took out for several British subjects who stayed behind in Paraguay.[32]

As a matter of policy, diplomatic agents ought to avoid anything suggesting favoritism, but the Italian and French representatives had already made themselves available to Paraguayans in exactly this way. Even Charles Washburn had previously taken charge of foreign baggage (including some belonging to the López family), and, though he had never taken "responsibility" for this property, he had set a certain precedent.

At any rate, before departing on 21 June, McMahon collected eight or nine heavy trunks full of valuables.[33] He also carried eleven bales of yerba mate provided him for sale downriver as a means of defraying any costs in the transport of the trunks. The minister took the trunks with him on the long voyage first to Buenos Aires, then to England and the United States.[34] He never admitted to misusing his diplomatic privilege but he never lived down having rendered López this particular service either.[35]

Living in the rarefied isolation of Piribebuy, McMahon failed to grasp that people might treat his generosity with suspicion—but there were still things to do before he took his leave. Allied troops had displayed the Paraguayan tricolor during sorties against the main Paraguayan positions, and had refused to eschew this practice, which brought a strongly worded letter from the Marshal to the Count d'Eu. In this missive, López dropped the diplomatic niceties recommended by McMahon and observed sarcastically that he had expected more from a member of the illustrious house of Orléans. If the count failed to deliver up the ill-treated banner, he warned, he might be forced to deal harshly with Allied prisoners still in his custody.[36]

In his reply to this ultimatum, Gaston pointed out that political exiles had formed a fighting unit linked to the Triple Alliance and were then engaged in liberating their homeland; this unit alone used the Paraguayan flag and the whole Allied army ought not to be faulted for the disagreements of one faction of Paraguayans with another. The Allies had guaranteed the independence of Paraguay—that ought to be enough.[37]

McMahon could see where this was going. Seeking to save lives, he interjected himself into the exchange, and pointed out the absurdity of any claim that the republic had joined the Alliance against itself. Just because a few disgruntled officers had claimed a right to fight the Marshal was no reason to abandon the proper decorum of war.[38] Gaston pooh-poohed the minister's concerns, offering him a reply even more sarcastic in tone than those used in López's initial threat. McMahon had hoped for a minimal show of courtesy and got nowhere. He was on record as a man committed to peace. The count spurned his efforts, however, and there was nothing more to do.

The US minister bade farewell to López on the last day of June. As a tribute to Madame Lynch, he wrote a long elegiac poem in English to honor his host country and her long-suffering people.[39] He then rode past the Brazilian camps and down to Asunción where he was received frostily. While in the city, he inspected his country's former legation and found it plundered, with Washburn's meticulous records strewn all over the adjacent streets. Then, before leaving for Buenos Aires aboard the steamer *Everett*, he reflected that the Allies "are now enacting the farce of creating a new Paraguayan government ... [which though not yet established already has] accredited to it a Minister Plenipotentiary [in order] ... to prove that President López is a monster of cruelty and that the Allies are the humane regenerators of the land."[40]

He had hoped to save the lives of the people he left behind. Nothing stood between them and a final bloody reckoning—an appointment with Armageddon that could no longer be postponed. This troubling impression continued to occupy McMahon as he steamed downriver. Soldier that he was, he could not help but reflect on how terrible a thing war is. He wondered if he would ever again don his general's uniform. He did not find it convenient to return to the United States by way of Rio de Janeiro.

The Pincer Begins to Close

From late 1865 onward the disparity of resources was so great that Paraguay never stood a chance except against a disunited Alliance, and now that the empire no longer needed Argentine help or approval to crush their exhausted adversary—the only question remaining was one of time. Even now, López did not think the situation was irreversible: his defenses could withstand a frontal assault and there was little fear of any easy maneuvering on the part of the enemy; the passes and defiles leading up to Azcurra were intricate and afforded the Paraguayans numerous opportunities to ambush Allied troops; and besides, the adjacent trench works may have had a primitive aspect, but they provided good defilade from any forces moving up from the base of the hill.

This argued for an Allied envelopment of the Paraguayan positions from the flanks, an idea that had already occurred to the Count d'Eu. Invigorated with the cool airs of autumn, his troops cleared what was left of the Marshal's men from Luque and Areguá before advancing along the southern edge of the

Ypacaraí. They rebuilt the rails, then the Yuquyry bridge. As we have seen, they wrecked the Ybycuí foundry on the south side and seized territories on the north at Rosario, Concepción, and San Pedro.[41] Pirayú and Cerro León, in the center, fell on 25 May, and Paraguarí the day after.[42] On the last day of the month, Allied units met a force of twelve hundred Paraguayan infantry in the vicinity of San Pedro at Tupí-Pytá (or Tupí-Hu). Curiously, the Marshal's men had drawn up in line of battle in front of a shallow stream rather than behind it, with their right resting near a thick wood and their left at a stone fence. They had mounted four cannon on the opposite side of the creek and eight others along the center and left.

On the Brazilian side, the infantrymen were posted in columns, with skirmishers in front, eight cannon at the center, and two on the left. Four regiments of cavalry were deployed and a battalion of infantry and a regiment of cavalry remained in reserve. At 10:00 a.m., after pelting the Paraguayans with cannon fire, the Brazilian commander ordered a general charge and his troops swept the Paraguayans before them. The Brazilians killed at least five hundred troopers before withdrawing with three hundred fifty prisoners, sixteen small cannon (three dismounted), two standards, and nearly two thousand head of cattle that the Paraguayans had hoped to drive to Azcurra. Having no time to take the animals west, the Brazilians slaughtered them, leaving the carcasses for the vultures.[43]

The engagement at Tupí-Pytá constituted the Marshal's last effort to out-maneuver the Allies on the northern flank. The Count d'Eu had thus succeeded in cutting the last avenue of supply for the Marshal's army in the Cordillera.[44] Over the next week, a series of tremendous clouds gathered at the western horizon and soon covered everything with an unnatural darkness. This made way for a tempest, one of the most remarkable storms in living memory. Rain fell steadily day and night. The galloping wind tore through the treetops, and the thunder sounded like a symphony of kettledrums. Every man sought shelter. Every animal took fright. And every creek swelled into a river.

The bad weather stalled the main Allied columns. The smaller imperial units kept up reconnaissance in the south, with mounted troops under General João Manoel Mena Barreto dispatched towards Villarrica in early June. Had their forays occurred a year or two earlier, the horsemen would have ridden through well-tended fields, broken only occasionally by termite mounds. Now this same earth abounded with rain-drenched weeds; rows of maize remained unsown, and only a few straggling plants were seen, grown from fallen ears. The main pathways to the villages had become impassable, almost as if human beings had never stepped that way. The same desolation or neglect was apparent in every hamlet they passed. Instead of burning wood fires, little herds of goats, and the odors of cooked food, the villages smelled like rotting thatch. There were no dogs to be seen, no chickens, no turkeys. All had been eaten.

João Manoel saw few Paraguayans, either—perhaps an occasional child standing in the open spaces along the trails. Such displaced individuals had no further tears to shed, yet they always seemed more inquisitive than hateful. One story told of a group of peasant women who gaped at João Manoel's troops with an unwinking, jaw-hanging kind of look and then spoke rapidly in frank astonishment that monkeys in uniform really existed. "Holy Father!" one supposedly exclaimed: "Look! The monkeys have no tails!"[45]

On his sweep southward, João Manoel dispersed a Paraguayan force of sixty-five men near Sapucai, killing perhaps forty before marching on towards Ybytymí. When Marshal López became aware of his movements, he dispatched a column of three thousand soldiers under Caballero, supposedly to shield the families of Carapeguá, Acahay, and Quiindy.[46] More likely, since López had lost his supply route from the north, he hoped to frustrate a parallel development in the south.

Caballero arrived at Ybytymí under a torrential downpour on the night of 7 June. He had hoped to attack before morning's first light, but his drenched troops, fatigued from the previous day's march, lacked the energy for an early confrontation. At the same time, General João Manoel's scouts reported that the trail to Villarrica was extremely soggy, especially near the headwaters of the Tebicuary, and he opted to turn around.

As these units began their withdrawal in the late morning, Caballero stormed into them with some two hundred soldiers, blazing away with the few guns remaining to them. The Brazilians should have parried this attack with minimal trouble, but their units had become burdened when some four thousand women and children who unexpectedly attached themselves to the column outside Ybytymí.[47] Little bands of displaced civilians, it seems, had grown into a single large entity seeking safety behind the Allied lines. João Manoel did not know what to do with these people.

Then Caballero struck.[48] As his musketry went up, the Brazilian troops dashed for a nonexistent cover, and João Manoel had to abandon his rear guard as the Paraguayans trampled over several of the smaller enemy units. They killed over two hundred stragglers who could not keep pace with the main force of troopers, who now raced away precipitously. Caballero later boasted that the Brazilians fled with such a velocity that his own troops felt exhausted from chasing them. In truth, João Manoel might well have lost a greater portion of his units in the attack had the Paraguayans sufficient horses to pursue him. As it was, though the Brazilian general failed to re-form his troops until almost within sight of Paraguarí, the majority of the refugees nonetheless reached the Allied lines. Newspapermen wasted no time in commenting on their wretched appearance and on their joy at having escaped the Marshal's clutches.[49]

A great many fugitives, however, also followed Caballero when he went to rejoin the Marshal. They may have regarded Brazilian patronage with less sympathy than the other displaced people. In commenting on the matter, *Estrella* asserted that those women and boys who had begged for Allied protection had in fact been raped and carried off for additional abuse. The criminal lust of the kambáes, it was claimed, had gone unslaked since their sack of Ybytymí, so they turned against those Paraguayans least able to defend themselves.[50]

The Allied generals could not really take a captious view of João Manoel's inability to control his troops. The count was willing to pardon João Manoel and at one point rode out in person to rescue the general's rear guard.[51] With all this, however, His Royal Highness still betrayed a young man's impatience. He longed to see his boots caked with the mud of battle and it irked him to yield any spot to either man or nature. He had to plan carefully. He converted Pirayú into a major military encampment with a field hospital, canteen, and depot for provender and other supplies.[52] It was an excellent site, located near both water and grassland, and easy to patrol so as to frustrate infiltrators (or desertions by the count's own men).

The village offered many advantages, but Gaston could make little use of them given the sloppy logistics at Asunción and the mechanical inadequacies of the two Brazilian locomotives the army provided for transport.[53] These machines failed to move supplies as speedily as the staff officers had promised. And when an Argentine locomotive was fitted for the job, it proved more powerful but also more accident-prone. On two occasions, it ran off the tracks, stranding soldiers and dignitaries halfway between Asunción and the front, leaving Gaston to fall back on more traditional transport.

There were, however, some advantages in waiting. For one thing, the Allies had launched another incursion near Encarnación. Though the Paraguayan irregulars somehow managed to drive them back, no one thought that the Marshal's forces could continue to operate for much longer in that quarter.[54] The Allies might even open another line of supply from the south whenever Paraguayan resistance collapsed in that area.

Then there was the natural advantage guaranteed the stronger side in any war of attrition. The cruelest calculations that the count attended to during June and July involved the breakdown of Paraguayan supply and the effect this engendered among the defenders in the Cordillera. Allied raids had seriously impaired the flow of food, and the hungrier the Paraguayans became, the easier the Allies could advance whenever the time came for the final push. Sharing provisions with civilians would merely hasten the disintegration of the Marshal's units. The pox had also broken out again among the imperial troops; if the disease spread to the Paraguayans—a virtual certainty—it would complicate their situation, as cholera had already done.[55]

Contrary to the accusations of some twentieth-century commentators, the count was no sadist and he had no wish to treat the enemy with brutality.[56] But unlike Mitre and Caxias, he never evinced much respect for the Paraguayan fighting man. His time in Morocco and Paraguay taught him that whether savages wore burnooses or *chiripás*, they would never fight according to civilized rules. If they refused to surrender, then they needed to be bludgeoned into submission. The count recognized that the Paraguayans had shown an unwavering contempt for death, but he saw no valor in this, much less any patriotism. It was brutishness, and in a world where European civilization set the standard for progress and modernity, their backward inclinations deserved to be expunged.

If disease and starvation failed to sap Paraguayan resistance, then the count's soldiers stood ready to accomplish the task by every means available. Generals Sherman and Sheridan had perfected a system of hard fighting a few years earlier in Georgia and the Shenandoah Valley, campaigns that Gaston had known about from the press. The two American generals would have told him that a wise and responsible commander was necessarily ruthless, and that he should leave the supposed noncombatants in Paraguay "with nothing but their eyes to weep with over in the war."

López would have shown more approval for this kind of war-making were his own country not its obvious victim. At the end of May, he had relocated his private headquarters further east from Azcurra, halfway between Caacupé and Piribebuy.[57] This placed him in a comfortable, even bucolic, setting which his family enjoyed, living in a large thatched-roof dwelling near the summit of a hill. Unfortunately, the new headquarters afforded no clear view of the western approaches to the Cordillera, and as a result, he could not properly coordinate the troops he had spread out between the provisional capital and Azcurra.

The Allies failed to notice his departure until Argentine cavalry probed the Azcurra line on 4 July and found only a sprinkling of defenders at the slope. They came within a hundred yards of opposing sentinels during the darkest hour of the night and launched an assault against the main entrenchments at daybreak.[58] They killed two hundred drowsy Paraguayans, but the remaining troops slipped effortlessly into the trenches and returned fire. Pleased with their reconnaissance (and with their limited casualties), the Argentines withdrew toward Pirayú, carrying with them word that the Marshal's men were unprepared should the Allies attack in force.

This news should have pleased Gaston. Yet the Allied commander still could not measure what he was up against. Of the geographical features to the east, he knew only the names. Some informants told him that the territory beyond Azcurra was a tableland, perfect for the operation of cavalry—others, that it was only the beginning of a "mountain fastness." Scuttlebutt had the Marshal fleeing with a small band to Bolivia, retrenching his position at Piribebuy, or preparing for a long-term guerrilla struggle in the forested areas of the east.[59] As the correspondent for *The Standard* put it in mid-July, the intelligence that López had fallen back from Azcurra, and gained the almost inaccessible Caaguazú, had produced much anxiety in Asunción, as it is the settled conviction of even the most experienced Paraguayans that if he once takes to the mountains, and succeeds in removing his families thither, the war is interminable, and either the Allies must give up the chase, or make terms. The subject was much spoken of in Asunción, and the people escaping from Azcurra confirmed the rumor. Behind Caaguazú there is a fine open country, peopled by industrious Indians, and it is feared López will gain their support. [Meanwhile,] thousands on the slopes between Azcurra and Villarrica have died of sheer famine.[60]

The truth was only slightly less perturbing for Allied interests; there were no friendly Indigenous people to the east, and no way to reconstruct the Paraguayan army.

Continued sacrifices mattered little to López. On 24 July, in fact, he celebrated a birthday banquet at which he shared with his officers some of his last tinned delicacies and European wines. There was a quiet sense of urgency among these men, but the Marshal himself seemed unperturbed. He had participated beforehand in a solemn religious procession, carrying the statue of Saint Francis up the ridge at Azcurra and on towards Caacupé, and, along the way, his son Panchito thought that he saw the statue tilting its head and moving its eyes to signal the advent of a miracle.[61] López smiled at this good omen and ordered a salute fired at Pirayú. The cannons at Azcurra obeyed and the Allied soldiers listened apprehensively, wondering what fresh trouble this portended.

Piribebuy

The rain flooded vast areas of Paraguay during July, which permitted the Allied navy to steam up the Tebicuary, where the ships succeeded in reaching imperial cavalry units that had penetrated the district. The reinforcements brought by the navy allowed the Brazilians to drive the remaining Paraguayan troops toward Yuty and Caazapá and away from any chance of supporting Marshal López.[62] Central Paraguay thus lay open to any incursions that the Allies chose to launch.

In early August, Gaston's flanking maneuver began in earnest. The village of Sapucaí fell first, then Valenzuela, the site of the Marshal's gunpowder works.[63] It soon became clear that the Paraguayan defenders in the Cordillera had stretched themselves too thin. They had only five thousand able-bodied men left. Of these, less than half were present at Piribebuy, and such a modest garrison could not hope to resist an assault coming from any one direction— let alone several at once. This situation served Allied timetables. According to plan, the count delayed his advance from Valenzuela until the arrival of twelve hundred Argentines detached from Emilio Mitre's command.⁶⁴ The Argentines reached Pirayú on 10 August and then proceeded, together with some eighteen thousand Brazilians, towards Piribebuy. Total envelopment of the capital became a real possibility.

Dense thickets had shielded the Paraguayans in the Chaco and alongside the Estero Bellaco. Piribebuy, however, boasted little cover either for soldiers or for the thousands of women and children who had gathered there either in obedience to the Marshal's orders, or because they hoped that food might become available there. The troops that guarded—and abused—them found cover inside the several ditches that paralleled the roads leading up to the town. They had dragged several cannon from along the heights to Piribebuy, but had had no time to erect batteries. A garrison of fewer than three thousand men remained at Azcurra, which, with its revetments and gabions, could still offer a formidable defense, if only the Count d'Eu would mount a frontal attack against it.

His Royal Highness had no intention of doing so, though he did direct Mitre to advance on the village of Altos as part of a prearranged feint.⁶⁵ Meanwhile, the count brought artillery through Valenzuela, and flanked Piribebuy on the north, east, and south. Nominally in command at the town was Pedro Pablo Caballero, an obstinate colonel with a cow's face who ached to lead a final charge. But Paraguay had long since passed the noontide of any ability to resist. Caballero lacked reserves of men and ammunition, and saw no alternative to a spirited, if predictable, defense. He haughtily rejected the count's demand for surrender, noting that the women and children remained safe in his care, and that the Allied commander "could issue orders in Paraguayan territory only when there was no one left to resist them."⁶⁶

In the early morning hours of 12 August the Allies shelled the town with forty-seven of Emilio Mallet's guns. It was a foggy morning and the Brazilian gunners could only perceive the outlines of the enemy positions. This was still enough to do great damage. As for the Paraguayans, though they returned fire with their eighteen remaining cannon, they scored no hits.⁶⁷ Instead they tried to find shelter in hastily dug rifle pits. Many men clawed at the earth with their fingers, trying desperately to escape the shelling. The experience at Humaitá suggested that artillery had little effect on well-entrenched troops, but the Paraguayan soldiers at Piribebuy were inexperienced draftees, and their trenches were shallow. Worse still, in the confusion, women, children, and refugees of all kinds became intermixed with the troops. No one could prevent their panicking. Both soldiers and refugees screamed in terror as the balls flew among them. Town residents did the same, finding momentary shelter within their homes, but Allied shells overshot the trenches and hit the edifices, knocking down walls of stone and adobe. Even those children who hid in wells could hear the shouts, the rattling, the shrieking sounds of musketry, and the horrible thud that tells too well how each projectile found its mark.

The bombardment lasted four hours, and in the process Piribebuy was blown apart. Around eleven o'clock, now under a steady sun, a Brazilian bugle blew and General João Manoel's cavalry dashed en masse across the swollen creek at the edge of town. The current barely slowed their progress. Caballero had had no time to erect mangrullos and he could not respond effectively as the Brazilians approached. In short order, the count's men swept over the northern breastworks and the Paraguayans poured out to meet them.

Fury and fear blended and were everywhere on display. A Paraguayan military band struck up "El torito," a favorite tune of General Díaz.[68] This steeled the Paraguayans. Three times they beat back the Brazilians, who three times renewed their attack. At each go, the violence increased, and the din of arms, the shrieks of pain, and the groans of death commingled into a single sound. The Paraguayans kept firing but scored few hits, and, on one occasion, a group of their gunners was struck by the wheel of a cannon in its recoil, leaving several men with broken bones.

Years of braggadocio had furnished the Paraguayans with an impressive list of stock slogans in Spanish, and at this moment of supreme confusion, the youngest troopers fell back on these patriotic hosannas. In a language that few understood they screamed "Viva la república del Paraguay!" They cried with such vigor that the Allies could not help but flinch. It burst from their adolescent throats like the old *sapukaí*, the brazen war-cry of the Guaraní that signaled joy, pain, resolution, and the foreknowledge of death. In subsequent generations, writers shaped the sound of the sapukaí into a tale of boy-soldiers, who, like the medieval church's recruits to the Children's Crusade, maintained their faith no matter what.[69] To the participants at that moment, however, the cry was all too real, all too immediate.

For all its ferocity, the engagement was never in doubt. As João Manoel spurred his horse forward, his cavalry units followed, breeching the principal trench works while three columns of infantry converged on the main square. A unit of Argentine soldiers advanced together with the count's Brazilians on the right, who were commanded by a particularly ruthless Riograndense general named José Antonio Correia da Camara. The bandaged and still suffering General Osório attacked in the center and General Victorino pushed ahead on the left. A reserve force remained at some short distance to the north, but its participation was redundant (as was that of Argentine and Uruguayan units at Pirayú).[70]

Victorino and Camara ordered their stalwarts to move by the flank at the double-quick, while Osório's troops pushed ahead, taking casualties here and there, but never slowing their pace.[71] "Close up, men, close up! Close up there in the rear," Osório shouted. At length, the Brazilians broke through to the lesser Paraguayan trenches, and though the defenders fought with superhuman grit, they could not check the surge. Within minutes, the Paraguayans had nearly exhausted their ammunition, but in their desire to kill the foe, to rend his bones, the Paraguayans kept going, and hundreds of nearly naked boys jabbed at the Allied troops *en bastinado* and joined with old men to throw stones, adobe bricks, and dirt clods.

It was at that moment that the schoolmaster of Villarrica, a reserve major named Fermín López, directed his young charges to retreat in front of the church, placing the heavily timbered door to their rear. The Brazilians pursued them into the building and killed those who continued to raise cudgels in defiance. The gravely wounded Major López received no quarter, and, without further ado, was decapitated—an act witnessed by the boys whom he had taught to read and write.[72]

The confrontation involved every manner of sacrifice, both terrible and strange. In lauding the bravery of their own men, some officers on the Allied side later paid tribute to the undiminished devotion of the enemy. Dionísio Cerqueira, who had looked so foppish and out of place when the war began, had grown into a soldier's soldier, and could recognize martial courage when he saw it. At Piribebuy, he spotted an ancient Paraguayan peasant ignoring the rain of bullets to stand perfectly erect while shooting at the oncoming Brazilians, reloading and taking aim as if on a firing range. A bit later, Cerqueira discovered the body of a young mother, who had held her ground at the doorway to the church and had died together with her infant son, killed by the very same Minié ball beneath the Redeemer's tortured image.[73]

Soldiers treat killing as a necessary evil. They argue that a boy of tender years who wields a sharpened bamboo can offer just as much of a threat as a veteran with a carbine, and he deserves the same lethal response. Killing can nonetheless become exaggerated in the heat of battle and atrocious in its aftermath—and, in the eyes of most Paraguayans, this is what happened at Piribebuy.[74] The weight of nearly twenty thousand over two thousand men could never be denied. As the last pockets of resistance gave way, the Paraguayans dropped to the ground, fired their last salvoes, threw their last stones, and drew their bayonets. Then they were overwhelmed.

In the final moments of the engagement two Minié balls pierced General João Manoel in the midsection. Coughing blood, he passed out from the pain and never regained consciousness.[75] His death evidently triggered one of the worst Allied atrocities of the war. The Brazilian soldiers acted from great anger, for the gallant João Manoel enjoyed much support among his troops.[76] But the general had also become a particular favorite of the Count d'Eu, who was evidently incensed at the news of his friend's death and ordered—or did not order—a terrible retribution.[77]

They needed little encouragement. Although the count afterwards lauded the professional behavior of his men, what they did next deserved little praise. Already in full control of the field, the Brazilians vented their rage on those who lay prostrate upon the ground. They disemboweled men and boys who were still alive, and whose pallor and skeletal appearance might otherwise have moved the Brazilians to pity.[78] Cerqueira, who had already seen more than his share of killing that day, somehow managed to save one wounded boy:

> A bit later, a little Paraguayan who could not have been older than twelve, ran to my side. He was covered with blood and pursued from a close distance by one of our own soldiers, who was just about to seize him when [the poor wretch] reached out to me and implored my protection. … Just then, my comrade, Captain Pedra, rode past and shouted "kill him!" "No," I rejoined. "He's a prisoner, a poor child, and I aim to protect him." "What! Why argue over a Paraguayan?" "And why not? It's my duty, and you would do the same thing." And what I said was true, for Pedra was an honorable officer, incapable of murdering a prisoner. So, instead, he spurred his horse and galloped away. And I conveyed my little prisoner to the guard.[79]

Cerqueira might have saved this one individual but many more had their throats slashed. The Paraguayan garrison commander, Colonel Caballero, was decapitated after Allied soldiers had stretched him tight between two cannons and took turns flaying him in the presence of his wife.[80] Brazilians then turned to the local hospital, which was full of Paraguayan wounded. Though some of these unfortunates managed to escape, many more were dispatched as they tried to get to their feet. Rather than seize the building for later use by the Allied medical staff, the Brazilians set it ablaze, immolating six hundred men and women.[81] The Paraguayans never forgot this wanton act, the veracity of which went unquestioned save in Brazil, where many denied that the incident had taken place. In recounting the details of battle, it is common to depict victorious troops as feeling elated and the vanquished as feeling drained. At Piribebuy, however, every participant was exhausted and even greed fell momentarily to the side. When they took Asunción seven months earlier, the Brazilians grabbed whatever they could find, as if plundering were an involuntary function of the body. At Piribebuy, however, the Allies could only admit to a sense of numbness, and in some ways they were too shamefaced at all their killing to poke at the town's debris.

By the time their greed returned, the Allied soldiers had tallied their own losses at 53 killed and 446 wounded out of nearly 20,000 men in the attacking force.[82] The Paraguayans lost the greater part of their contingent at Piribebuy, some 700 killed and 300 wounded, with another 600 who fell prisoner or went missing. The number of surviving women and children who haunted the plaza amounted to thousands.

The Allied soldiers finally began to examine their spoils. Piribebuy was not Asunción, just a little village, and there was little to be had from its original population. Though the Marshal's functionaries had made a passable effort to convert the town into a national capital, it possessed little worth stealing, and most of that belonged to the López family. Taunay was one of the first to enter the residence where Madame Lynch had lived. His men found a small fortune in silver coins, while his attention was drawn to the piano that the Marshal's soldiers had so carefully transported to Piribebuy some months earlier. Despite the presence of a headless cadaver lying at the edge of the room, the future viscount could not resist the lure of such a fine instrument. He sat down to play while his fellow officers took a share of la Madama's porcelains and tea service. One man found a beautifully bound copy of the second volume of *Don Quixote* (wherein the mad knight regains his sanity). Taunay managed to secure the book for himself though he regretted not finding the first volume. The Brazilian officers also located a small but impressive wine cellar, from which they extracted bottle after bottle of champagne "of an indisputable and legitimate provenance."[83]

When the government relocated from Luque, state officials requisitioned several buildings to fill with documents, paper currency, furniture, inkwells, ledgers, and the other ephemera of bureaucracy. None of the Allied soldiers who now rifled these buildings bothered to examine these papers for useful intelligence. Instead, they made bonfires with them, and, in the tradition of victorious soldiers everywhere, took delight in using the enemy's currency to roll cigars. Orders eventually came to send fourteen cartloads of archival materials down to Asunción. Though some documents were eventually transferred to the Paraguay's provisional government, a great many more remained in Brazilian hands for over a century.[84]

Neither Resquín nor General Caballero had joined in the defense of Piribebuy, nor had Marshal López, who was with his army at Azcurra. Meanwhile, the Count d'Eu savored his victory. At one point, he beckoned to a pair of Paraguayan women, telling them to step forward, and he showed them a small printed portrait of the Marshal. "There is your God," he uttered sarcastically. "Yes, señor" one of the two responded, her commitment—or her resignation—still undiminished. "He is our God."[85] The count must have felt very old at that moment.

Ñú Guazú

A distant observer might be forgiven for thinking Piribebuy the last station of the Marshal's cross. But López did not think that way. When he first learned of the Allied investment of Piribebuy, he sent his troops on a forced march from Azcurra to intercept Gaston's army before it began the final assault. In this vain attempt to reach the provisional capital in time, the Marshal abandoned the earthworks and abatis he had so meticulously constructed. It was rather like Tuyutí, where he had chosen a risky offense over a carefully constructed defense. Before the troops from Azcrura got halfway down the trail, word came that things were going badly at Piribebuy and the Marshal countermanded his earlier order, one of the few times that he changed his mind about a military decision.[86] His troops turned about and reversed their steps, but before they regained their old position, López changed his mind again.

This time, rather than risk a head-on attack from the Allies, he conducted a measured withdrawal towards Caraguatay, a northern village even smaller and more isolated than Piribebuy. He divided his forces into two columns, the first of which consisted of some five thousand boy-soldiers under his immediate command and seconded by General Resquín. This column set out on the evening of 13 August and marched three long days until the troops, "almost dead from exhaustion, arrived at Caraguatay."[87]

The Marshal envisioned leaving behind a rear guard with most of the cannon and the only reasonably effective troops he had left. He assigned command over this column to Bernardino Caballero, who may have had experience in conducting raids but little in mounting a holding action of the sort that López envisioned. He hoped to buy time so that the remaining Paraguayan units could retreat unmolested to a point some miles north of Azcurra where they could regroup for some sort of Fabian resistance.

The evacuation of the Cordillera was not precipitous. The garrison spent twenty-four hours marching past Caacupé, the site of Paraguay's last remaining arsenal. The train of soldiers that went past the town was accompanied by three thousand women employed in carrying military supplies. Some of these women had come all the way from southern Paraguay, responding to appeals from Sánchez and the more palpable prodding of Caminos.[88]

The Allied armies reached Caacupé on 16 August. Everywhere en route they encountered starving people looking for food, clogging the trails and making it difficult for troops to move with the speed that the count had anticipated. The Brazilians found the machinery at the arsenal already smashed. Much to their surprise, however, they discovered intact the printing press that had accompanied the Marshal's army for so long and which still had its type set for a final edition of *Estrella*.

López had been thorough in other respects. He had scoured the remaining cattle from the district and had taken sixteen or seventeen of the sixty small cannon that his British machinists had cast at the site (the others not yet being ready for use). All these guns he transferred to Caballero, but he lacked the wagons to transport the projectiles, pikes, and lances from the arsenal, and these he left to the Allies.[89]

Also left behind were several thousand civilians in the town square and seven hundred wounded men in the local hospital. These people were in a state of total destitution. The count was nonetheless pleased to note among their number all but five or six of the Marshal's British employees.[90] These Europeans had toiled diligently for López, but had suffered grievously in recent months along with their wives and children. Sickness had thinned their ranks, and though Madame Lynch had occasionally sent medicines and food, the Britons had had a miserable existence. The arrival of the Allies turned their contemplation of a tragic future into a bad memory. As one of their number explained:

> we saw with unspeakable joy the Brazilian cavalry entering the village. We greeted them by waving hats and ran towards the soldiers, kissing their hands. They immediately understood our situation, asked us to return to our houses, assuring us that a guard would remain at Caacupé to protect us. At about 10 a.m. the Count d'Eu arrived with his staff and having had us called before him he spoke in English, asking for news of the whereabouts of López. Meanwhile, ten thousand Brazilians (infantry, cavalry, and artillery) occupied the village. One of the Prince's officers took down our names and ordered us to make the necessary preparations for leaving.[91]

The conditions these foreigners faced in Paraguay had stimulated much commentary in the European and North American press ever since the failure of Gould's mediation.[92] Few foreigners, however, showed a comparable concern for the fate of the Paraguayans.

The best way to conduct a holding action is to prepare sufficient cover, usually in the form of trench works bolstered by artillery, but with an escape route at the ready. López had ordered Caballero to construct such a defense. The general supposedly had threescore cannon, but few were battle-tested. He had limited shot and powder and only enough time to construct a few shallow dugouts, nothing more. His men had not eaten for three days. But López, who was moving towards Caraguatay, had no one else to turn to, and ordered Caballero to counter anything that the Allies could throw at him.

The battle of Ñú Guazú was the last major engagement of the war. The Guaraní expression "ñú guazú" denotes a large open field or pasture, and it was on just such an expanse, grass-covered and more than a league across, that Caballero made ready to meet the enemy. On 16 August, he signaled López to note the Allies approaching from the southeast. The Marshal acknowledged the message, then ordered twelve hundred of the soldiers under his immediate command to dig a trench across the road to Caraguatay. Meanwhile, Caballero's troops—perhaps three thousand in number—prepared to make their stand.

Though later accounts placed the site of this battle near the present-day town of Eusebio Ayala, in fact, no one today can be exactly sure where it took place, except to note that the Piribebuy and Yuquyry creeks ran close to each other through the pasture. Even the battle's proper appellation is debated; Brazilian accounts generally record its name as Campo Grande (a literal translation from the Guaraní) and many of the Paraguayan accounts as Rubio Ñú. The most common name encountered today—Acosta Ñú—was not adopted until after the war, drawing inspiration from a nearby ranch once owned by the Acosta Freyre family. The historian Efraím Cardozo, never one for imprecision, called it the Battle of the Children.

The Allies had always hoped to seduce the Paraguayans into a Cannae. They almost achieved this at Tuyutí, but after that, the Marshal had never given them another opportunity. This time, however, the best defense the Paraguayans could manage came from the youngest boys, who used false beards to make them appear mature veterans. Though they suffered from pangs of hunger, these boys still hoped to take down ten of the enemy for every man lost.[93] The Brazilians might think López's troops a pathetic rabble of youngsters only recently separated from their mothers, but Caballero would show the kambáes that they could fight like men.[94]

The battle commenced at about 7:00 a.m. and lasted into the mid-afternoon. The Paraguayans set up a long line, intending to retreat to two other lines if necessary. They initially loosed a weak fusillade, aided by their few artillery pieces, but the fire brought minimal damage to the foe and took too much time. Though they fought ferociously, the boy-soldiers failed to keep the imperial cavalry from sallying in and among them, retreating, and sallying forth again.

Not everything went against the Paraguayans, however. Even though they were covering the perfect terrain for cavalry, the Allies could not properly focus their charges, and it looked for a time like the Paraguayans would push the horsemen back. General Camara then changed his tactics, concentrating his fire on the Paraguayan left flank. The right and center continued to hold, however, and even the addition of Coronado's Uruguayan cavalry to the assaulting forces could not break the Paraguayans.[95]

The Allied regiments then assumed the form of an immense "V" and plunged into the forward Paraguayan position, knowing full well that Caballero had no time to improvise. They were therefore shocked to see the Paraguayans moving perpendicular to their previous lines, re-forming their units along the left bank of the Yuquyry. This bought some time. Around ten, the Allied infantry suddenly made their appearance. The flying columns of Emílio Mitre, in obedience to the count's order, had broken camp at Atyrã around midnight the night before and reached the scene of action at just the right moment. So did infantry units under General Victorino and the sixty-year-old General José Luiz Mena Barreto, yet another high-ranking officer of that surname, the older brother of João Manoel.[96] José Luiz had taken Osório's command one day earlier, leaving the crusty Baron of Herval to return to Asunción for a much-deserved convalescence.[97]

As José Luiz's infantry units came up they formed a line parallel to that of the opposing force, each unit extending to the right until the Allies could overlap the Paraguayan left. The fighting raged furiously and every spot along Caballero's line came under fire.[98] Pressured now on all sides, the Paraguayans exhausted their cannon shot, and hastily stuffed the gun barrels with stones and broken glass to fire at the enemy like a shotgun.[99] It wounded some but left others untouched.

As the improvised shot gave out, the boy-soldiers retreated to a new position alongside the other creek, the Piribebuy. At some point in this final interchange, the Count d'Eu galloped in with his saber raised high, urging his men to destroy what remained of the Marshal's troops. The Paraguayans fixed bayonets. And many died with their weapons still clutched in their hands.[100]

The Paraguayans resisted for more than five hours and lost nearly two thousand killed and wounded. The Allies lost less than five hundred.[101] In reflecting on this disproportionate toll, Taunay observed that the Paraguayans suffered from the obsolescent design of their guns. The weapons they left on the field included blunderbusses and ancient flintlocks that deserved a place "in some archaeological museum" as well as one Congreve rocket stand whose mechanism impressed all who saw it.[102]

More impressive still was the sheer number of Paraguayan slain visible in every direction. It seemed a "hallucinated" landscape of smoke, hundreds of wrecked wagons and carts, and the corpses of "bearded" children who were so thin as to look diaphanous. The Brazilians had good reason to doubt that starving boys could fight so hard for a lost cause, and when they did so, it brought a reaction of both contempt and futile horror. In fact, the Paraguayan losses would have been lower had not Allied troopers decided to lance every wounded boy they could find. This slaughter continued off and on for three days. No Allied officer bothered to squelch the excesses or punish those responsible.[103] Perhaps this reluctance to interfere manifested the disgust that Brazilian officers often expressed for men who, having given their parole, rejoined the fight. Or perhaps the Brazilians simply got caught in a frenzy of uncontrolled violence, their army converted into an engine of massacre.

After the killing had run its course, Allied interrogators asked an injured Paraguayan colonel how many men had fought under Caballero's command. His rejoinder spoke volumes: "I don't know, sir, but if you want an idea of the truth, go out to the battlefield and count the Paraguayan corpses, add the number of prisoners you have in custody, and you'll have the total."[104] The contempt suggested in the colonel's words was sadly irrelevant to the military realities at Ñú Guazú. All the Marshal's promises lay shattered alongside the wounded survivors who cried in pain for their mothers. The Paraguayans had been undone by the obvious fact that where well-fed and well-trained men had failed, children could never succeed.

The Allies, who knew this from the outset, now felt ashamed of their own ruthlessness. One of the more perverse myths that the Brazilians had propagated in explaining Paraguayan truculence and obstinacy was that they were a childlike race; at Ñú Guazú, the irony in this depiction became obvious. As Cerqueira observed, the field was left covered with enemy dead and wounded, "whose presence caused us great pain, due to the high number of *soldaditos* we saw, plastered with blood, with their little legs broken, having never reached the age of puberty." What "a terrible struggle between Christian piety and military duty," he continued. "Our soldiers all said that *there is no pleasure in fighting so many children*."[105]

Having finished with the day's work, the Allied soldiers piled the Paraguayan corpses into mounds just as they had at Boquerón and Tuyutí, and set the whole field aflame. The fire soon grew out of control, burning the wagons, the bodies, the cartridge boxes—everything. The threadbare tunics, once scarlet with dye and now reddened only with clay and blood, were consumed. A charge of gunpowder would periodically go off under the inferno as a final salute to the slain.[106] The boys who had wanted to die like men were now destined to be burned or buried in dung heaps. The next day, nothing but ashes marked the site.

But the war went on. The Count d'Eu counted his losses. Caballero managed to escape towards Caraguatay by barging past his wounded comrades with just a few companions—one source says five other men. He eventually made contact with the units the Marshal had left behind to construct a new defensive barrier. But the news of a rout, this time unvarnished with false hope, had preceded his arrival. The troops hastily hitched their wagons and the twelve artillery pieces with which they had sought to strengthen their half-constructed trenches and made ready to retreat again. Caballero rode on to Caraguatay. There he encountered López giving orders to the civilian population to make ready to accompany his truncated army into the wilderness.

15

THE NEW PARAGUAY
AND THE OLD

It is a maxim of military tactics to press relentlessly on the heels of a defeated foe, giving him no rest and destroying his forces before they can regroup.
Caxias had failed to do this after the December campaign, and the Count d'Eu
had no intention of repeating his predecessor's mistake. López was on the run
and it should be easy to catch him. In practice, however, the task proved far
more challenging than the count envisioned.

The balance of losses between June and August 1869 was heavily against
Paraguay. One eyewitness calculated that one hundred thousand men, women,
and children had died of disease and hunger during the Cordillera campaign.
This amounted to almost a quarter of the nation's entire population, and that
number had clearly grown since that time.[1] The Paraguayan army had suffered
more than six thousand casualties over the same period, but Allied losses were
only one-fifth that number, and the count had reserves available.[2]

The parameters of the war thus seemed set to everyone, save perhaps to
the Paraguayan boy-soldiers, who still maintained their dogged faith. For the
Allied leadership, final victory was within range. Though the generals and politicians had been fooled in the past, there now existed every reason to tend to
matters other than fighting. The average soldier may have looked for rest and
rations, but individuals in positions of authority understood that as the military
struggle faded, the political struggle was just beginning.

Nation-building and Allied Policy

As the Count d'Eu's army dislodged the Marshal's forces from Piribebuy and Ñú Guazú, much of consequence was happening in Asunción. For one thing, Councilor Paranhos had worked tirelessly to transform Paraguayan politics. In April he had steamed downriver to Buenos Aires to confer with Argentine foreign minister Mariano Varela and Uruguayan envoy Adolfo Rodríguez regarding the petition of Paraguayan exiles to form a sovereign regime.[3] The councilor needed to act quickly and with more than the usual decorum. He no longer feared any action on the part of Marshal López, but there was much that could still upset his plans. With bizarre rumors circulating that the United States might intervene to bring an end to the fighting, Paranhos initiated discussions about the country's future.[4]

While ostensibly inspired by the remote possibility of foreign interference in Platine affairs, these talks ended by highlighting tensions between the empire and Argentina. The councilor stressed that neither the inviolability of Paraguayan sovereignty nor the Allied claims on territory could be modified. The new government, whatever its composition, needed to accept those claims as a condition for peace, and though Rodríguez eventually fell into line on these interpretations, Varela demurred. While careful to reiterate his government's historical claims in Misiones and the Chaco, the Argentine foreign minister insisted that the 1 May 1865 treaty could not constitute the sole basis for peace. His government, he noted, had negotiated the treaty during the Marshal's invasion of Corrientes, when feelings still ran hot. At that juncture, each one of the Allied powers could pretend to the status of an offended party seeking redress in the common goal of ousting López from occupied territory. Now, with the Marshal on the run, and the Brazilians in charge at Asunción, the Argentines could only appear as late arrivals.

The Brazilians adamantly opposed any hint of a "Greater Argentina," but though Varela spoke of the historical links that tied Paraguay to the other Platine states, he lacked the power to do anything more than complain.[5] He assumed a posture that simultaneously expressed never-ending friendship for the Paraguayan people and a break on imperial ambitions. He did worry that putting together an interim regime in Asunción might constitute an unwelcome diversion as long as López was still at large. It was likewise far from clear that such a government, no matter how it was constituted, could negotiate the peace accord that Sarmiento defined as a priority.[6]

The Mitre government would never have risked confronting the councilor when Argentina could still profit commercially from the Alliance. Varela's assertiveness, however, revealed an obvious—and justifiable—fear about the empire's goals in the Plata, and suggested a reversion to the anti-Brazilian stance of the previous decade. Now, with Paraguay a shadow of its previous self, he had to prevent its becoming a Brazilian colony (as had already happened, to some extent, with Uruguay). The best way to do this was to work with the Paraguayans who had migrated to Buenos Aires during the 1840s and '50s. These were the same men who had formed the Sociedad Libertadora, the Asociación Paraguaya, and other exile organizations. A few subsequently officered the units of the Paraguayan Legion, and were generally seen as friendly to the Sarmiento government.

Whatever the orientation of the Paraguayan exiles, the task of putting together a new regime would not be easy. As the editors of *The Standard* put it, "the mission of Señor Paranhos, whatever its secret success may have been, has certainly not ... [led] to a hope that the war is near its close."[7] The councilor took Varela's points in good stride. He had his own criticisms of the Brazilian military's comportment in Asunción. He evidently saw the army as a poor custodian of the country, having too readily tolerated the graft that sutlers cultivated in the officer corps, and not knowing how to assist the civilians who flooded into the city. No infrastructure existed to cover the needs of these displaced people, who simply followed the Brazilian soldiers around in droves, begging without humility, their bony hands stretched out to take anything offered.

Paranhos could only act with cold realism. He had grown tired of the financial burden of Allied charity, which had cost the exchequer thousands of *milréis* in rations distributed out of army stores to the unfortunate refugees.[8] The councilor may have felt sympathy for their condition, but he also blamed them for having blindly followed the "despot" into penury and ruin. Now, with no obvious relief in sight, he preferred to pass responsibility for these wretches to some Paraguayan regime and attend to more pressing administrative tasks.[9]

No matter what Varela said, Brazilian preeminence over civilian and military affairs in occupied Paraguay could not be denied. The empire had earned the right to set the agenda, and its objectives were fourfold: signing peace treaties favorable to Brazil; fixing the amount of Paraguayan war reparations; establishing clear and unquestioned borders; and gaining recognition for long-term Paraguayan independence.[10]

The Argentine foreign minister had no way to alter Brazil's goals, and he eventually gave in to pressure not just from Paranhos, but also from the remaining Mitristas in the national government who wanted no confrontation with Brazil.[11] Besides, the Argentines coveted additional territories in the Paraguayan Chaco, an acquisition for which they had no legitimate claim; if they were to succeed on this matter, they could not afford to anger Paranhos. So, Varela, Rodríguez, and the councilor postponed consideration of the more controversial territorial questions for another day.[12] The Paraguayan delegates who witnessed their conversations were given no leave to object or to assert their own opinions.

The Cost of Factionalism

While seemingly anxious to grant the Paraguayans their proper share of freedom and the "generous sympathies of the Allied governments," Paranhos and
his associates insisted that any Paraguayan government "bind itself to proceed
in entire accord with the Allies until the termination of the war." They prohibited the new regime from any role in military matters and forbade unauthorized
contacts with the Marshal's agents.[13] The Paraguayan delegates agreed to the
Allied protocols on 11 June, but only after trading a great deal of insults among
each other. Resigned to the bickering that was sure to come, the delegates
steamed back to Paraguay with friendly messages from Paranhos and Varela.
Everyone hoped that the various parties in Asunción would simply support the
Allied commissioners.[14]

It was not easy. The exiles had already joined together with defectors from
the ancien régime to form several mutually antagonistic political clubs. These
associations asserted ideological goals, yet acted as though private grievances were paramount. The Asuncenos understood this and tended to qualify the
factions in personalist terms, as groupings of local grandees, their extended
families, and retainers. Despite the social ties that linked the groups together,
they all had constantly shifting memberships. It was not even clear that they
were uniformly anti-Lopista.[15]

Initially, the Brazilians favored Colonel Fernando Iturburu to head the
new government. He had commanded the Paraguayan Legion, and was a good
friend to both Mitre and the empire. The colonel's candidacy came naturally
to a man who enjoyed recognition among all the factions, and who boasted
prestige from earlier days. But Iturburu had an ambitious streak, and instead
of biding his time, he got involved in a scheme to place a presidential sash
around Juan Andrés Gelly y Obes. This notion of elevating an Argentine general to the Paraguayan presidency never stood much chance of success and when
Councilor Paranhos learned of it, he accused Colonel Iturburu of sidestepping
legitimate imperial concerns and perhaps even thinking of handing Paraguay
over to the Argentines.[16] Paranhos saw no reason to tolerate that.

As Iturburu's star set, the shape of the future government was left open. The
faction led by Colonel Juan Francisco Decoud and his twenty-one-year-old son,
José Segundo, had displayed considerable industry during Paranhos's absence
in Argentina. Though the elder Decoud could not always control this group of
men, his clientele remained the strongest force within it, and José Segundo was
clearly its brightest light. The faction-within-a-faction that he dominated was
sufficiently secure by late June 1869 that its members could announce its formal
organization as the Club del Pueblo, avowedly the most "liberal" of the various
inchoate Paraguayan political organizations.[17] Given their wide reading and
eloquent predictions of future prosperity, the Decoudistas might have seemed

innovative, but those Paraguayans who grew to manhood in Buenos Aires had heard liberal blather before. Rhetoric alone could never bring the Decouds any advantage over Paranhos. Nor could it guarantee them uncontested sway over the political actors vying for power in Paraguay.

The faction associated with Cándido Bareiro could claim a similar influence. It boasted a curious composition of former Lopista officials (who had sat out the war in Montevideo, Buenos Aires, and Europe), and the surprisingly large number of legionnaires and liberal exiles who could not stomach the Decouds. Organizers had met at Fernando Iturburu's residence at the end of March to establish the Club Unión Republicana, the "conservative" counterpart to the Decoudistas.[18] The 338 signatures affixed to the formal announcement of the founding of the organization suggested a wide following, much larger than the 50 or 60 men associated with their rivals.[19] But a good many names were evidently copied from tombstones at the Recoleta cemetery.[20] A more accurate account of membership numbers would probably reveal around 100 men, 74 of whom were legionnaires associated with Iturburu.[21]

Neither faction relished the role of procurer for Brazil or Argentina. Yet neither saw any option other than putting their members up to the highest bidder. As was true of their successor organizations in the 1880s—the Liberal and Colorado Parties—the ultimate character of the clubs was personalist no matter what the coloration of their flags. As Paranhos, Decoud, and all the other political contenders well understood, Paraguay was a small country that could ill afford to leave any talented man completely on the outside, so Bareiro had to be included and so had the Decouds.

The Allies had to tolerate divisions among their chosen friends; they knew what they wanted even though many Paraguayans did not. Paranhos directed that an emergency junta of three individuals shoulder the executive authority on a temporary basis until a constituent assembly could determine a permanent political structure for the republic. At its inception, Paraguay's provisional government thus took the form of a triumvirate more beholden to Paranhos than to the other Allied representatives. In exchange for their show of fealty, the triumvirs could demand Allied moral support and whatever material aid the Brazilians chose to throw their way. The provisional government maintained a facade as a purely Paraguayan body, but always responded to Allied interests. For example, one provision in the protocols of 11 June promised uncontrolled ingress and egress for foreign sutlers in Paraguay, which guaranteed that the smuggling that had gone on since January 1869 would continue indefinitely.[22]

The Club del Pueblo named Cirilo Antonio Rivarola as its candidate for president of the triumvirate. A lesser member of an important landholding family, Rivarola had studied law before the war but his injudicious talk constantly got him in trouble. He quarreled publicly with a *jefe político*, who jailed him for many months. In 1868, Rivarola was released (perhaps at the instigation of his uncle Valois) and then drafted into the army as a corporal. He fought at Lomas Valentinas, was captured by the Brazilians, escaped, and rejoined López, who promoted him to sergeant. But he remained free for only a short time before being rearrested later, this time for military ineptitude. He was rescued in May 1869 by the Brazilians, who thereafter treated him as a favorite. Grateful to his captors, Rivarola gave the Count d'Eu extensive information about Paraguayan dispositions in Azcurra and spoke freely of his hatred for López and hopes for the nation.

This was not the reaction that most Paraguayan soldiers displayed as prisoners; even those exiles who had fought in the Argentine ranks had their own agendas and scores to settle, and these had little link to the Allied cause. But Rivarola could be cut according to the empire's own standard. His Highness granted him automatic ingress among the Brazilians along with a safe-conduct pass to travel to and from Asunción.[23] There Rivarola made contact with different factions who bid for his attention, and accepted the support of José Segundo Decoud, who evidently thought to turn the man into a tool of the Club del Pueblo. In this curious manner Decoud nominated the improbable Sergeant Rivarola to head the provisional government.[24]

The Club Unión Republicana, not to be outdone by this odd selection of Rivarola, chose as its candidate Félix Egusquiza, a cousin of the Marshal who had acted as his commercial agent in Buenos Aires before the war. But despite this family relation, Egusquiza had lately cooperated with whichever group seemed most ready to take power.[25] The Argentine and Uruguayan commissioners had less faith in Rivarola, whom they usually dismissed as a pretentious mediocrity.

The Allied representatives must have felt annoyed at all the Paraguayans for their stubborn refusal to agree on a common candidate.[26] The leaders of the two clubs felt just as annoyed at the Allies for trying to define the character of Paraguayan patriotism, and still hoped to use Argentina against Brazil and vice versa. On 21 July, a grand assembly convened in the National Theater. It was composed of 129 notables but featured Paranhos as carefully pulling the strings from the side. The electoral procedures, which the Brazilian minister had already composed in private, were quickly accepted, leaving only an angry measure of ad hominem debate to follow.

The delegates' greed for power was inversely proportional to how little power there was to covet. Indeed, despite all the vituperation, the meeting had gone as Paranhos envisioned—and he was the one who mattered. When the electoral committee members met on 5 August, however, they omitted Rivarola's name from the three men chosen, and instead put forward the names of José Díaz de Bedoya, Carlos Loizaga, and Juan Francisco Decoud as potential stand-ins for José Segundo, the heir apparent.

This effort vexed Paranhos. All his subtlety had been wasted on these art-less rubes. So he set aside all pretense, raised his finger (but not his voice), and insisted that the committee drop the former colonel's name in favor of Rivarola or someone tied to the old Iturburu faction.[27] The Decoudistas then made ready to walk out en masse, and the meeting started to collapse into pandemonium. It fell to Paranhos to play the agglutinative role. From time to time during the proceedings he extracted a monogrammed handkerchief from his pocket, and passed it across his bald pate, mopping the sweat away in a deliberate motion. With this simple gesture he signaled that his patience had come to an end—he was willing to act as midwife but not as referee.

In due course, the participants assumed a more serious demeanor. Everything, they knew, could be gained from cooperating with this man, and much could be lost by seeming to oppose him. Though the councilor person-ally detested Juan Francisco Decoud, he approached the man directly and per-suaded him to withdraw his name; in exchange, the colonel accepted a series of appointments for his adherents to secondary positions in the new government. Rivarola warily concurred, and the meeting broke up.[28]

The triumvirate was formally installed in a public ceremony on 15 August, by custom, the day observed to honor Our Lady of the Ascension.[29] This was well chosen as a time for renewal, but things did not seem so well further in-land. Piribebuy had just fallen and only hours remained before the boy-soldiers at Ñú Guasú breathed their last. The war had not ended in the interior districts, where talk of the future seemed horribly out of place. It was as if there were two separate countries.

The installation of the provisional government provided the first opportuni-ty for celebration that Asuncenos had experienced in many months. Politicians read prepared speeches in the Plaza 14 de Mayo and bands played triumphal airs. Local inhabitants, sutlers, interested bystanders, and a few Lopista spies filed into the cathedral, where the Argentine military chaplain administered the oath of office to the triumvirs. This was followed by a deadpan declara-tion from Rivarola who promised cooperation with the Allies. There was much pomp, much fuss, much tricolored bunting to decorate the whole affair. And while the councilor hosted a luncheon for dignitaries at the Brazilian legation, the public was treated to a presentation of flamboyant street theater.[30]

The Provisional Government

For all of its false glitter, the symbolic passing of an era aroused more irony than jubilation. The time had not long gone when the Lopista regime had insisted on full public participation at national rituals during which all citizens were obliged to offer monetary contributions to the cause. People remembered how upper-class society women were forced to attend such festivities and dance with illiterate corporals until two in the morning. They remembered how "prostitutes" were elevated to positions of privilege. They had to ask themselves if this new regime would really be different.

The men who replaced the Marshal seemed more like morticians than honest patriots. The best among them acted at Paranhos's behest. A puppet regime could provide more than the oblivion that López offered, but no one expected the councilor to transmute Paraguayan factionalism into something sound. As chief of the new triumvirate, Rivarola was described by one prominent Decoudista as a "splenetic spirit, devoted to legal forms and with arbitrary and despotic instincts; a mixture of good and evil, of truth and falsehood ... a man without character."[31] Character he may have lacked, but he had sufficient liberal antecedents to make himself attractive. He could boast some knowledge of the law, which was a rare thing in Lopista Paraguay, and he also deserved recognition for having spoken in favor of peace with the Allies when such talk normally brought execution. The Count d'Eu had done everything he could to sculpt the barefooted Paraguayan sergeant into a figure of political substance. Even Councilor Paranhos recognized his potential and this was enough to earn Rivarola the senior position in the Triumvirate.

His fellow triumvirs, Carlos Loizaga and José Díaz de Bedoya, were distinctly less significant. Both were former members of the Asociación Paraguaya who had participated in the convoluted political haggling in Mitre's Buenos Aires and had switched in and out of various exile factions over the years. Neither had any experience of government administration.

Once an old fox and now merely old, the Decoudista Loizaga was a reader of poetry and adventure stories. Though he had suffered little compared to Rivarola, he appeared visibly fatigued and anxious to retire from public scrutiny.[32]

The stout, clean-shaven Díaz de Bedoya, who cut a figure vaguely reminiscent of José Berges, was the younger brother of Saturnino Bedoya, the onetime merchant who married the Marshal's sister and ultimately died before the firing squad as a "conspirator." Like his brother, Díaz de Bedoya was an opportunist, greedy and sparsely educated, but willing to conform to whatever policies Paranhos indicated. When sent to Buenos Aires shortly afterwards to obtain financial help for the provisional government, he disappeared into private life, absconding with silver taken from Paraguayan church altars that the new government wished to use as collateral.[33]

For those Asuncenos who had survived the fighting, Rivarola and his associates seemed little better than Brazilian lackeys. There were other men available for the job, but none stood any chance of success without Allied patronage. Those Paraguayans demanding a swift return to true sovereignty could only find disappointment. They could choose one anti-nationalist puppet over another, or resign themselves to the return of López or someone in his image. That said, a cup of water that is three-quarters empty can also be one-quarter-full.

Those Paraguayan exiles coming home from Buenos Aires professed a more optimistic attitude than those who had been in Asunción since the advent of Allied occupation. The newcomers regarded the earlier protocols as a reasonable starting base for the reconstruction of the country.

While some Paraguayans willingly gave the triumvirs a chance to build something out of very little, the foreign powers unanimously scoffed at the new government's legitimacy. The Marshal's friend, General McMahon, who was in Buenos Aires en route to London, observed with disgust that the Allies had sought

> to collect from all parts of the country such of the unhappy people of Paraguay whom famine and suffering compel to abandon the national cause, for the purpose of furnishing a constituency to this pretended government. These people … [are] paraded mercilessly through the streets for days naked and footsore to be exhibited to the army of traders, sutlers, and camp-followers who throng the city occupying the very homes of the poor unfortunates who are thus so publicly exhibited.[34]

McMahon still supported the Marshal, who at that moment was barely holding out. But even those diplomatic agents of foreign states with nothing positive to say of López could not be reassured by Allied designs for a new government. The British minister dismissed this state-in-the-making as "a shadow behind which the Allied governments will seek to elude some of their most serious and embarrassing responsibilities without dispossessing themselves of any material power." The Italians and the French voiced similar skepticism.[35]

Perhaps predictably, the same contempt for outside opinion that had animated the Marshal also found its place in the hearts of the men who succeeded him. The triumvirs knew that their long-term hopes for power rested on their short-term willingness to kowtow to the Allies. Meanwhile, to gain legitimacy, they had to supplant López in the minds of everyone concerned. The fathers had preferred exile to tyranny; the sons, power to anonymity.

They certainly wasted no time in making this priority known. On 17 August, the provisional government issued a decree that defined how the Marshal and his remaining supporters fit into the new politics:

> The first duty of every Paraguayan in this supreme moment is to endorse as far as possible the victory of the Republic and Allied governments, to whom our cordial thanks are due, by lending them assistance against the tyrant López, the scourge of the people. … Any citizen who continues to serve the tyrant, or who neglects to assist … the old men, women, and children forced to die

in awful misery in the forests, shall henceforth be considered a traitor. … [The provisional government likewise decrees] that the impious monster López … who has bathed the country in blood, [ignoring] every dictate of human and divine law, exceeding in cruelty every despot or barbarian mentioned in the page of history, be hereby declared an outlaw, to be ejected forever from the soil of Paraguay … as an enemy to the human race.[36]

The triumvirs had to find some way to differentiate themselves from the Marshal. They were builders, they insisted, not destroyers. They therefore issued a manifesto, printed on the Brazilian army's press, which alluded to the narrow "escape from martyrdom" that the Paraguayan people had made, and the need to break with traditions of "tyranny," with forced isolation, and with neighbor spying upon neighbor.[37]

As Paranhos had foreseen, the refugee problem had grown considerably by the time the provisional government came to office; *The Standard* left no room to underestimate the difficulties the triumvirs would face in this respect:

> The city is crowded in every part, and a house or a room cannot be obtained for love or money. There are about 10,000 natives, mostly women or children, and as the arrival of sufferers from the interior continues daily, the authorities are putting up tents for them in the outskirts. The Allies give out rations daily to those poor starving people. No words can describe the horrible condition of the refugees that each train from Pirayú brings in to the capital; they seem living skeletons, and some of them are boys of ten or twelve years old, for the most part shockingly mutilated with bullet and saber wounds. Strangers are quite astonished at the extraordinary endurance of these Paraguayans, who survive sufferings that must prove fatal to Europeans.[38]

The provisional government committed itself to a general reorganization. In a flurry of new legislation, the triumvirs named new jefes políticos in towns vacated by the Marshal's troops, eliminated tariffs, and authorized the sale of stamped paper. With an eye to raising revenues from rents, they declared as public property the National Theater and the slaughterhouse, and issued licenses for commercial establishments.[39] They convinced the Brazilian army to hand over stocks of yerba, tobacco, and hides stored in the city's warehouses and which could also be used to raise revenues.[40] In a move obviously inspired by the Count d'Eu, they formally abolished slavery in the country.[41]

Liberal ideology held that governments should derive their powers from the consent of the governed, but there was nothing liberal about the triumvirs;

they might dispense favors, but sharing power with the people was not part of their mental makeup. They told citizens that, from now on, the state would aid, rather than exploit them, and that they had to be satisfied with that.[42] The triumvirs set up work camps on abandoned farms outside Trinidad to provide food for those in the capital. They also established a commission to care for the needs of invalids and orphans. But they prohibited the siesta, which was "prejudicial to the [spirit] of activity the times call for," and proscribed the use of the Guaraní language in schools, because it had been used in *Cabichuí* and *Cacique Lambaré* to propagate *Lopismo*.[43]

Some of these decrees and prohibitions seemed absurd, others merely impractical. Now that the former exiles had a semblance of power they made promises that seemed just as hollow as the Marshal's evocations of national glory. Even the faction out of power used similarly turbulent rhetoric. The Club del Pueblo maintained great visibility thanks to *La Regeneración*, a newspaper funded by the Decoud family in October 1869. It claimed to champion the rights of those Paraguayans who had nothing, but its jeremiads against other factions make today's readers wince.[44] Eventually, the Bareiristas established their own newspaper, *La Voz del Pueblo*, which proved just as sulfurous in its rhetoric.[45]

To Paranhos, as virtual viceroy of Paraguay, political promises meant little. He was perfectly content to flatter the triumvirs despite a secret indifference to their troubles. To the masses still struggling for a piece of *chipa* or a scrap of dried meat, the slogans meant nothing at all, for the provisional government had little effect on those poor Paraguayans who most needed help.[46] The triumvirs boasted no more dedication to the lower classes than had the Marshal. And unlike López, the various liberal factions perceived no pressing need to mobilize the country people in order to survive. Brazilian patronage may have mattered, but Paraguayan public opinion did not. If the war continued into the new decade, it was not because the provisional government had any say-so in it—it was because the war had forged its own dynamic. And as the skeletal soldiers of the Paraguayan army fled into the forests with Marshal López, the final hand was ready to be played.

The Advance to Caraguatay

Any consideration of the provisional government provides evidence to prove that farce covers a greater expanse of human endeavor than philosophy. One could add that the arcane political posturing in Asunción had almost nothing to do with the ongoing war. Paraguay's continued existence as a nation was perhaps no longer in doubt, but the Paraguayans' survival as a people was quite another matter. While in the capital debate and political rancor provided color to an otherwise dreary tableau, the shenanigans were only minimally related to what mattered most in the interior districts: how to live to the next day.

Though the eastern half of Paraguay was and is the most settled section of the nation, in 1869 it still boasted vast stretches of unpopulated and heavily wooded territory. Aside from young men who had labored in the region's widely dispersed *yerbales*, few in the country had ever visited these areas, which on contemporary maps were marked simply as "forests." Yet it was precisely these districts that Marshal López had to traverse in his flight from enemy forces. And for the first time in the war, he knew as little about the terrain as did the Allies.

To the Marshal's rear, disaster was approaching. On the 17 August, the two enormous columns of the Allied army finally came together in the hill country between Caacupé and Ñú Guazú. These units, which included the Brazilian 1st and 2nd Corps and Emilio Mitre's Argentine units, had remained at some distance from each other for over a month as part of the count's plan to trap the enemy in a pincer movement. Though he had taken some casualties in the effort, Gaston's overall strategy had worked well. Thus far, the Brazilians and Argentines had won minor engagements along the southern edges of the Ypacaraí, at Tobatí, Pirayú, Cerro León, Valenzuela, and Ybytymí, along with two major victories at Piribebuy and Ñú Guazú. Unfortunately for the count, these victories failed to compel the Marshal's surrender and the final placement of the pincer left some units to the northeast, just outside the circle. Allied troops therefore had to move quickly on Caraguatay, a sleepy, fly-blown village, the last community of any significance for many miles. Perched on the brow of a semicircular range of hills, and hemmed in on one side by sarandí and the other by marshes, Caraguatay presented a good site for defense.[47]

Gaston had broken the Paraguayan army during the Battle of the Children, but he needed to finish it or else have López escape, leaving his men to disperse into bands of marauders that could maintain guerrilla warfare indefinitely. A Paraguayan army thus reduced was incapable of really threatening the Allied occupation, though it might still be strong enough to contemplate continued mischief in the interior districts.

Caraguatay beckoned, and the count needed to find a route through the nearby woods by which the Allied force could flank the Paraguayans and hopefully annihilate them. The mission obligated him to dispatch his available troops—nearly seventeen thousand strong—in three sizable columns toward the town.[48] Gaston accompanied them on the advance, all the time awaiting word of contact with the enemy. Scouts reported hundreds of starving refugees coming down the trails, but there was no sign of the Marshal.

While we know that the count felt tense and anxious to end the struggle once and for all, no comparable picture of López's attitude has come to light. He had sufficient presence of mind to order Caballero to prepare to a shallow trench line at Caraguatay, but the troops delegated to put together the resistance had no chance of slowing the enemy. When General Victorino assailed the prepared position on 18 August, he discovered some two thousand boy-soldiers under

Colonel Pedro Hermosa waiting. The Paraguayans were not deeply entrenched (there having been no time for such preparations), but they nevertheless tried to hold the line.

They got nowhere. Morale had plummeted among the Paraguayans in the twenty-four hours since Ñú Guazú and the fighting spirit that had once so impressed their enemies was just not in them that day. The engagement, sometimes dubbed the "battle" of Caaguy-yurú, may not deserve that appellation, for it was a simple scrimmage, quickly and decisively concluded. Hermosa stood no chance of countering the Allied attack through improvisation, and he enjoyed no luck. Though the field was covered with thick fog, the Brazilians discovered the enemy dispositions, while their adversaries knew neither the strength of the Allied units nor their direction of approach. Seven Brazilian battalions attacked the Paraguayans head-on at mid-morning. The fog obscured their advance, and they stormed the trenches just as Hermosa fired his twelve cannon, the shells going over the Brazilians' heads. A reserve battalion of Voluntários cut through the brush from the west and helped the infantry envelop the position.

Paraguayan losses were heavy. Brazilian fire disabled some of the enemy guns, but Taunay recorded that the Allies captured all 12 pieces intact. Colonel Hermosa lost 260 killed and another 400 of his men fell prisoner. Around 1,300 Paraguayans, including Hermosa, succeeded in escaping into the forest.[49] The Allies listed losses of 13 killed and 143 wounded, but the true figure probably exceeded twice that number.[50]

For all the obscurity of the encounter, the vengeance taken by the Brazilians at Caaguy-yurú was unmistakable. In the predawn hours, before the contending sides met in combat, two Brazilian teamsters leading pack mules accidentally stumbled across the Paraguayan position. The two men, who were carrying supplies of new uniforms for the Allied troops, had had trouble urging their animals through the woods, and had failed to notice the enemy sentinels who proceeded to shoot them down. The Marshal's soldiers found no provender among the various packs, and as they had no clothes of their own, they helped themselves to the uniforms, including those of the two dead men. When the main Brazilian units encountered the teamsters' naked corpses shortly thereafter, word went around that the Paraguayans had left them hanging from trees as if to kipper their bodies in the sun.[51]

Though Paraguayan defenders had had no time to commit the suspected atrocities, General Victorino beheaded eighteen Paraguayan officers anyway, one in the presence of his young son who had begged for his father's life.[52] This revenge sickened the Brazilian officers, who were eager to move on to Caraguatay and leave this place behind. They reached the town in the late afternoon. A once thriving community, it was now a forlorn place consisting of a dozen empty buildings, an absence of tilled fields, and nothing to pillage, not even chickens. A population of destitute women still lived at Caraguatay, however, and, in the evening, a group of girls, more curious than afraid, grew bold enough to approach the Allied soldiers to ask in ungrammatical Spanish if the Argentine military band would play them a number of dance tunes.[53]

López, to no one's surprise, had disappeared.

Destruction of the Fleet

As Allied troops explored their depressing prize, they presumed that the Marshal had fled to San Estanislao de Kostka, a village many miles to the north that the Paraguayans often call Santaní. In 1869 it was a profoundly isolated place that could only be reached after a long march over poorly known ground. While the generals pondered whether they should descend on the town or make some other move, word arrived concerning the missing Paraguayan fleet.

The previous January, it will be recalled, the Marshal had ordered its withdrawal into the interior of the country by way of the Río Manduvirá. The imperial fleet tried to follow in April, but the Brazilians only got so far as the river's confluence with the Yhagüy, where they discovered that the enemy had dumped carts, tree trunks, and other debris into the water to block the passage upstream.[54] Contenting himself with the knowledge that the Paraguayans could never use the ships they had taken into a cul-de-sac, Commodore Delphim steamed back to Asunción. He was confident that as far as the navy was concerned, the war had ended.[55]

Heavy rains had fallen during the intervening month, however, and this permitted the Paraguayan fleet to continue upriver into districts rarely reached by vessels with even the shallowest of drafts. Six ships—the *Apa*, *Anhambaí*, *Salto de Guairá*, *Ypora*, *Paraná*, and *Pirabebé*—pushed up a narrow channel, past forests of half-submerged, leafless trees wrapped with slimy lianas. The water receded a month later, leaving the ships stranded at a very remote spot later christened Vapor Cué (which in Guaraní denotes "where the steamships once were").

The little fleet remained secure over the next few months, but the crewmembers had to give up any thought of escape to the main channel of the Paraguay. Maneuver for the ships along the creek bed of the Yhagüy was likewise out of the question, so the sailors removed the ships' cannon and sent them south to Marshal López. This left them with only muskets to defend the site.

The war was coming their way and the crews had to scuttle the vessels upon which they had lived and fought for five years. Delphim (and, for that matter, Tamandaré) would have sympathized with their emotions, for it seemed like smothering a beloved but terminally ill family member. Certainly the sailors had no time to spare. Two days after Ñú Guazú, cavalry under General Câmara approached out of the woods that separated the site from Caraguatay. The sailors had heard the sounds of rifle fire coming from the village the previous afternoon, so what happened next came as no surprise. They hastily assembled at a forward position a half mile to the front of their ships. It was a foggy morning and they peppered the oncoming the Brazilian horseman as best they could with rifle shot. After only a few minutes' resistance, they fled into the eastern forests where they hoped to join Caballero in his retreat from Caraguatay.

Meanwhile, their comrades set charges in the ship engines, blasting them to pieces while fires spread upon the decks, rendering the vessels useless.[56] The ships settled into the shallow Yhagüy. Steam stacks, masts, and pieces of metallic hulls jutted out of the water in improbable configurations like headstones in a swampy cemetery. The hulks soon rusted and were covered by the verdigris of time, the once proud ships of the Marshal's navy eventually becoming indistinguishable from the muddy-green arroyo.

Hot Pursuit

While Brazilian engineers surveyed the wrecked fleet, the Count d'Eu had to wonder where the main Paraguayan columns had gone. It turned out that General Caballero, who now had charge of the Paraguayan rear guard, had succeeded in gaining the yerba districts some miles to the north. A few of the men in his units had served as *yerbateros* in these remote locales and could guide their fellows through the forests—an effort that involved more challenges than the Paraguayans had thus far experienced (with the possible exception of the Chaco).

Caballero never felt safe amidst so much foliage. He continued to press forward on a series of forced marches in which no one had anything to eat save for some charqui. He eventually arrived at the Arroyo Hondo, a short distance from a ranch that had belonged to the late Benigno López. The soldiers prepared a billet for the Marshal's family members but could not have tarried very long at the task, for Allied cavalry units were fast approaching. On 20 August, before he could reach Santaní, Caballero was overtaken by Allied horsemen who burst out of thick woods with the sun to their backs. As they waited for other units to arrive, an Argentine colonel sent across a surrender demand under a flag of truce. Hoping to buy time, the Paraguayans assembled a team of negotiators. The Marshal suggested a ruse by which Colonel Centurión, as head of the team, would brandish a pistol and take the enemy representatives prisoner at gunpoint. Luckily for the colonel, who was none too keen on the idea, López soon abandoned the notion as unworkable.[57]

The next day the Allies easily swept the position, subduing the Paraguayan troopers after a half hour's fight. Marshal López, as always, got away. So did Caballero.[58] Many of the soldiers who accompanied the two enjoyed no such luck. This left some four to five hundred Paraguayans dead or wounded on the field. Despite their threat to take no prisoners, the Allies did care for the injured, and afterwards sent many captives down the line towards Pirayú.[59] The Brazilians also captured five small cannon, a few remaining provisions, and an entire caravan of wagons and oxcarts that carried la Madama's personal baggage and that of former *fiscal* José Falcón.[60] The Allies lost fourteen men killed and seven wounded, one of whom was the same Argentine colonel who had tried to offer the Paraguayans an honorable way to surrender.[61]

On 23 August, the Marshal finally arrived at San Estanislao, where he expected to set up a long-term refuge just as he had at Itá Ybaté and Azcurra. It was a minuscule village, not much better than a clearing in the forest. The soldiers, no longer young despite their tender age, quietly set up camp within an orange orchard. Their morale was at an all-time low, and because of desertions and recent skirmishes, manpower had declined dramatically. To use a modern term, though, Marshal López was still living in denial. He gloried in moments of difficulty, for in his experience such challenges always preceded something better. At Humaitá and Lomas Valentinas, when things looked darkest for his people, his world actually seemed to improve. He could still point to his army and call it a cohesive force. The troops had accomplished the passage from Caraguatay, and now he expected the pursuing Allies to stumble as on so many previous occasions.

The Marshal's optimism (or wishful thinking) may have brought him some personal gratification but it was delusional. Sources of support for the Paraguayans had vanished and in the absence of fresh troops and supplies, any military operations were foredoomed to failure. López, however, still counted on the ineptitude of his enemies. He had never ceased to dismiss the kambáes as poor soldiers, and since the fall of Asunción, he had repeatedly mistaken serious Allied maneuvers for indecision or bewilderment. He underestimated both his opponents' resources and resolve and he kept trying to apply to this new state of affairs the lessons learned when his army was still young. He presumed, for instance, that the enemy units would run afoul of the terrain the deeper they penetrated into eastern Paraguay. He also misread the recent turn in politics, thinking that the Brazilians could no longer trust Emílio Mitre's Argentines or that coterie of traitors operating in Asunción.

The Marshal reasoned that he had time to gather supplies and he sent out parties to reconnoiter the territory west to Concepción, where he hoped to seize every head of cattle that might have eluded earlier round ups. These foraging details had twenty to thirty men led by an officer and followed by a wagon to collect all provisions acquired. This often involved not only taking manioc from storage sheds, but pulling it up by the root while still in the field. The officer would know which route the main Paraguayan column was following and would rejoin the force by the evening hours to send the supplies on to San Estanislao.

Marshal López now took the opportunity to promote half a dozen officers to senior rank. He likewise rewarded several of the chaplains, including Father

Maíz, with the National Order of Merit.[62] And he designated San Isidro de Curuguaty, a village even further north, the new provisional capital, sending Francisco Sánchez ahead to instruct local officials to prepare for the army's arrival.[63] The vice president brought orders for local laborers to sow community fields with maize and other food crops. Even here, however, state infrastructure was severely decayed and Sánchez and the other officials could not hope to comply. The Marshal remained adamant, nonetheless; he expected to make war again in short order, and neither his officers nor his civilian functionaries, nor even Madame Lynch, tried to convince him otherwise.

Back at Caraguatay, the Brazilians had settled in. Their commander, the Count d'Eu, may have looked like a boy but he acted like a seasoned commander. While still getting organized, he received a visit from José Díaz de Bedoya, one of the new triumvirs, who brought news of the establishment of the provisional government and the promise of future collaboration.[64] Gaston had less interest in new political questions than in finishing the old campaign, which he feared might degenerate into rural anarchy. In normal circumstances, once an army guts an enemy, the latter surrenders as a matter of course. Allied triumphs in the Cordillera had demonstrated the necessary supremacy, yet the Marshal still refused to yield. Would the count have to exterminate all the remaining Paraguayans? Or perhaps he might simply declare victory and go home (as Caxias had done), leaving the Marshal to be liquidated by the triumvirs as a common bandit.

The situation must have eaten at Gaston. The Marshal, he knew, could never mount another attack, nor even put together a limited holding action. Every day brought proofs of Paraguayan disintegration. The refugees who crowded along the trails to Asunción included not just women and children but starving deserters from the Paraguayan army. First they came as individuals, then in groups of ten or more, and now, seemingly, by the hundreds. This ought to have reassured the count. But he could not be comfortable in the role of a policeman chasing a gang of ill-kempt banditti. He had little patience for this ignominious sort of war-making, and was angry that Rio de Janeiro had provided so little material support. He dispatched numerous letters to the war minister asking to withdraw the bulk of his troops, who were terribly fatigued, and whose presence seemed superfluous.[65]

While waiting for some specific reply (a rejection that was predictably slow in coming), the count busied himself with the never-ending question of supply. On 22 August, his vanguard units lost track of Caballero's retreating forces. Since the number of near-lame animals in the Allied cavalry prevented any immediate pursuit into the forests, he reluctantly ordered the soldiers back to Caraguatay.[66] There they joined Argentine cavalry units, Brazilian infantry, and some five hundred Paraguayan prisoners who had defected over the previous two weeks.

These men drew on his available supplies in a way that the count could not have planned for.[67] The logistical demands of the Allied armies had always been greater than those of the enemy. The war had mostly been fought on Paraguayan soil, where the Marshal enjoyed interior lines. The invading Allied armies, by contrast, had to depend on complicated supply networks, river transport, and the dispatch of wagon trains into unfamiliar territory. Making this system work had taxed Caxias, who supposedly enjoyed support from the imperial war minister (and from Urquiza as purveyor of horses and livestock). For the Count d'Eu, who faced an imperial government anxious to declare the war at an end, it was nearly impossible.

Obtaining adequate numbers of horses remained the most pressing problem, just as it had been for Mitre and the marquis. Gaston had even heard rumors that the Argentines had solved some of their own supply problems by making nightly forays into the Brazilian corrals.[68] Whether or not this story was true, the absence of mounts clearly compounded the count's headaches, for just when his men seemed ready to pounce on López, their horses went lame.[69]

Then there was the problem of provisions. Bonaparte had always insisted that armies live off the land, thus permitting more freedom for maneuver through a lack of dependence on supply columns. The Count d'Eu could never afford such a tactic, for the enemy had already stripped the country clean. Gaston's troops saw their own rations cut in half, and, for the moment, could obtain nothing save palm hearts and charqui. The contracts with Lanús and other purveyors had lapsed and Gaston could think of no immediate solution, so he told his men to forage where he knew they would find nothing to eat.[70] He no longer had sardines to share with them.

The count was livid and evidently leaning closer to a nervous depression. He was pressed simultaneously by Paranhos and others who had no idea what the front looked like but who insisted on prompt, unambiguous victory.[71] Gaston could not show them his indignation, for he needed their support. But it was difficult for him to appear patient. Perhaps the Marshal intended something like a protracted guerrilla struggle, even though such a course was beyond his limited means. But the count could ill afford to be dismissive of the possibility.

If the troops on the Allied side were hungry, the privations experienced by their Paraguayan quarry can scarcely be imagined. There was little energy left in soldiers who generally got by on a diminishing ration of dried beef, maize, edible thistles, and bitter oranges (which at least staved off scurvy).[72] Yet, even in this extremity, López demanded loyalty and further sacrifices. The Allied leaders in Asunción remained convinced that he would ultimately turn west to Bolivia and leave his long-suffering soldiers to the vicissitudes of the forest—further proof that, even now, the Allies clearly did not know their enemy.[73] The Marshal had no intention of leaving Paraguay.

16

THE END OF IT

Councilor Paranhos spent the second half of 1869 trying to mold the various cliques of Paraguayan exiles into a provisional government beholden to Brazil. What he got in the triumvirate was hardly reassuring; the tense relation between the factions set the stage for political trouble in Paraguay well into the twentieth century. Paranhos had wanted stable lackeys and got squabbling, inconsistent courtiers instead.

Meanwhile, things in the interior were moving toward their expected end. López's stay at San Estanislao, though predictably brief, was long enough to uncover another "plot." Somewhere above Caraguatay a patrol chanced upon two Paraguayan men and a woman and placed them under arrest. They were very likely Allied spies. One of the men was shot down in an escape attempt, and the other two, when finally dragged before López at Santaní, openly cringed with fear. The Marshal had experienced increasingly fierce headaches during his retreat and had no patience for any dawdling.[1] The woman's face blanched and her voice grew atonal as she tried to speak. When she could not answer his questions, he lost his temper entirely, ordering Luis Caminos to beat every scrap of information from her. The flogging elicited a confession that the three individuals indeed worked for the Allies, and that they had made an agreement with an ensign of López's escort to rouse other members of that unit to murder the Marshal without further delay.

The ensign, who had been in very good odor with the Marshal, denied knowledge of any plot, but after suffering the cepo for a time, he started to denounce everyone in the escort. Eighty-six enlisted men were swiftly executed as traitors, along with sixteen officers. This included the commander of the escort, and his second, who died not because they had participated in the "plot," but because they had failed to uncover it. Each man was flogged to within inches of his life, and only then were they shot."[2]

If the count's army had not already sown sufficient dread among the Paraguayans, López's actions at San Estanislao certainly did. Soldiers in the Acá Verá and Acá Carayá escort regiments had always constituted a class apart—focused, inured to hardships, and utterly obedient to the Marshal. They had once looked so fine in their polished helmets, scarlet tunics, and high leather boots that they served López as gala reminders of Paris and his first days with Madame Lynch. These simple soldiers, whose devotion and loyalty had remained rock-solid during the worst of times, may not have been members of the perfidious elite that López hated so dramatically, but they had no way to insulate themselves as Paraguay unraveled. The Marshal personally attended all the executions that he had ordered—something that he had never done before. He watched as the bullets tore into the beardless peasant boys, and counted their corpses one by one. Now only thirty or forty remained alive.

Perhaps López's attendance at these events provided him with some sense of justice or relief, but it failed to check his anger. Any hint of dissension now sent the Marshal into a fury, causing him to rail against imaginary villains. He shouted that he had defended the *patria* through every campaign, and that in spite of all his sacrifices, there were Paraguayans that had turned on him. Those men who heard these outbursts prayed that he would somehow forget his anger. But it was not to be. On one occasion, his own bitterness left him humiliated and ashamed. Accused of defeatism, a certain lieutenant was lashed to death in the Marshal's presence, and before he fell unconscious, the man raised his voice plaintively. "Never forget, sir," he cried, "that there is a God whom we must all face on the Day of Judgment, and even Your Excellency may soon have to account for this act of injustice!"[3] López must have felt shaken at the lieutenant's reference to the Almighty, and he slunk away to the little chapel to pray.

At the end of August, Paraguayan scouts brought word that the count had dispatched a large force up the Paraguay to a spot near Concepción, where the troops composed themselves into two new columns, mainly cavalry. Even as the count had postponed his pursuit from the south, these forces could assault San Estanislao from the west.[4] López had no idea of how many troops were involved (there were at least six thousand in Concepción and another five in Rosario).[5] But the rumor that General Câmara headed one column and General Victorino the other could not have reassured him, since both were known to be hard-fighting commanders.

Once again, López ordered his troops to break camp and retreat, this time towards Curuguaty. He left a small force in the rear to make a final round up of cattle. Surprisingly, the Paraguayan soldiers located fifteen hundred animals, but the troops driving them were intercepted by the Allies before the herds reached Curuguaty and every head instead went south to supply Prince Gaston's army.[6]

The Marshal slipped across the Río Manduvirá in the second week of September. His was a demoralized and feeble force, no longer even plausibly military in appearance. At every step the soldiers retreated they had to look over their shoulders—not at their distant Brazilian pursuers, but rather at each other. Men who had known each other since Corumbá and Estero Bellaco bit their tongues and complained about nothing, even though their ulcerated feet made them ache with terrible pain.[7] They hurried through the shallower sections of the Aguaracaty, a semi-inundated plain some four hundred square leagues in extent, the best route through which to move surreptitiously to the northeast. At one point the column halted in the mud for six days, during which time the men who had fled from Caaguy-yurú and the site of the fleet's immolation caught up with them.

López slept little and drank much, which caused his suspicion to grow to extremes. He accused everyone, forgave no one. He reassembled the old tribunals under Maíz and the other fiscales, who evidently felt so afraid for their own lives that they behaved with even more elaborate zeal than they had shown at San Fernando. Just as an addict needs more and more opium, the Marshal needed ever more traitors executed.

The fiscales might have believed the terror of 1868 was justified as a means to restore discipline. But it is unclear how they could justify such methods now. Hundreds of men were questioned, and nearly as many endured the whip, their backs lacerated into something unrecognizable as human flesh. In the end, sixty more individuals fell to the executioner's lance.

Meanwhile, several minor encounters took place between Allied scouts and Paraguayan troops guarding the western approaches to Curuguaty.[8] On 20 September, Brazilian units from Concepción struck the Paraguayan rear guard, forcing the Marshal's men to abandon the field and all the civilian refugees they supposedly protected. This left open the way to San Joaquín, another tiny village that fell shortly afterwards.[9]

Via Crucis

López's remaining men—just over two thousand exhausted soldiers—had escorted a host of displaced civilians to a supposed refuge at Curuguaty. These people were the real victims of 1869: women, children, and old men staggering forward, uncared for, with little food and no hope, and yet essential to the Marshal's jejune claim that his cause was still synonymous with the Paraguayan nation. Malnutrition made it impossible for mothers to nurse their babies; despair and an intense experience of physical pain looked out from every face, and whenever a worn-out individual fell to the wayside, her companions lacked the energy to help. Religion had failed these people. Nationalism had failed them. The dreams of glory, counterfeit though they may have been in 1864, had once sustained them. Now, the same mindset brought emptiness. Old men did not hesitate to steal a sliver of manioc from a child's mouth. Soldiers violated the women in their charge with little fear of punishment, sometimes promising them a handful of parched corn as compensation, sometimes offering nothing.

The women in the train of refugees were divided into two groups: *residentas* and *destinadas*. The former included members of families who remained faithful to the Marshal after the Allies took Asunción, and whom Luis Caminos had evacuated into the hill country to serve as laborers. Though little recompensed for their farm work at Azcurra, they had, in fact, provided a considerable portion of the rations eaten by soldiers at Piribebuy. Now that the provisional capital had fallen, however, they once again took to the road.

The destinadas, by contrast, included the wives and relatives of men who had putatively turned against López. Some were foreigners, though the majority were members of the old elite, the crème de la crème of old Paraguayan society. In earlier days, the appearance of such well-bred women would have attracted the notice of the throng, but now not a single one of them betrayed even a trace of affluence. Unlike Juliana Ynsfrán, they survived their tortures only to be sent into internal exile at one of several isolated villages. That some of the women were the Marshal's former lovers was a telling irony.

Several destinadas left memoirs of their experiences, including one appropriately subtitled *Sufferings of a French Lady in Paraguay*. The author, Dorothée Duprat de Lasserre, was the wife of a French distiller who had contrived to sit out the war as an inoffensive neutral but was instead swept up into the maelstrom of accusations at the time of Benigno's supposed conspiracy. The undertow of these charges invariably pulled Monsieur Lasserre down, and off he went in chains to San Fernando. His wife received orders to take her family to Areguá and then Caacupé, after having already abandoned homes in Asunción and Luque. Everywhere she went, she lost money and property to state officials, who abused her unceasingly with petty excises.[10]

When officials ordered Doña Dorotéa east to Yhú in January 1869, all her horses save one were confiscated by a thuggish sergeant who "had the authority to take from anybody his things, his poncho, in fact anything he chose, so that [they] ought to be grateful for his forbearance."[11] Lasserre's mother rode the remaining animal and the other refugees, all of them ill with fever, made their way on foot.[12] When ordered north to Curuguaty in September, doña Dorotéa managed somehow to obtain a new oxcart, but her tribulations were just beginning:

> We left Yhú at midnight and held out as long as we could through mud and across arroyos with only fifteen pounds of starch, one

pound of black sugar, three pounds of grease, and a handful of salt …but, after traveling several days to the Ybycuí pass we encountered a woman who sold us a small piece of meat. … Towards eleven the next night several soldiers arrived, and ordered us to cross the arroyo, because if their officer found us, we should be lanced. … López himself [had given] strict orders to kill all the women who lagged behind from fatigue. … Thus we crossed the arroyo at one in the morning, [walking] along narrow paths through thick wood in total darkness. I kept falling into some very ugly holes … and over the next several days the arroyos [grew ever more] swollen, and in some the water was up to our waists.[13]

On 27 September Lasserre reached Curuguaty, where she learned of her husband's execution the previous year.[14] She also learned that the reign of terror had not yet spent itself, for even in Curuguaty charges were being made against senior functionaries. Hilario Marcó, the former police chief of Asunción, was flogged for supposedly seeking to orchestrate the escape of Venancio López and other members of the presidential family. Marcó was shot after six weeks as a warning to the López relatives, for whom the Marshal had another fate in mind.[15]

No one was safe. Lieutenant Colonel Centurión had spent nearly a month incapacitated with a high temperature and suppurating skin rashes, and had only heard about the new conspiracies from his orderly. One evening, when in particular pain, he received one of the Marshal's adjutants, who announced that López wished to see him. Filled with dread, Centurión struggled to present himself at the tent of his master, who beckoned him to take a seat beside Madame Lynch. Assuming the worst and shaking as much from fear as fever, he was handed the first of three cups of cognac. López then offered a friendly smile, and toasted the good health of "Colonel" Centurión, thereby announcing his promotion to full colonel. The man still could not stop shaking, but managed to mumble his gratitude for the honor bestowed. In the back of his mind, however, he worried that such favor carried with it a great many dangers.[16]

The destinadas understood the odd juxtaposition of brutality and festivity in Curuguaty. Madame Lasserre found the Paraguayan army intermingled with an unexpectedly large number of refugees, amounting to over three thousand individuals. As a complete surprise, government officers rode in and gave Lasserre and the others some meat from military stores. This food was welcome, and the residentas (and a few of the destinadas) made professions of thanks and loyalty to Marshal López. For their trouble, they received work assignments in fields just to the north near Ygatymí, which offered the prospect of regular food for the first time in months.[17]

Vague rumors that circulated throughout Paraguay held that the fighting would soon end. Councilor Paranhos and various Allied military officers had told their respective governments that the war had already concluded.[18] The Count d'Eu, however, saw no wish to endorse such an inaccurate view. He had already dispatched Brazilian units to occupy Villarrica. This meant that López had to contemplate moving the army and all the refugees once again. He had already designated Curuguaty as his new headquarters, sent out search patrols to round up cattle, and ordered the tilling of the local fields in anticipation of a long stay.

Curuguaty, however, was not Luque, nor Piribebuy, nor even Caraguatay—it was a tiny hamlet that could never sustain a flood of desperate newcomers. The local population consisted of rude farmers who occasionally supplemented their meager income by smuggling cattle across the border to Brazil. All had heard of Francisco Solano López, but none had ever seen him, and in the angry changeling who arrived among them they recognized something of what they expected of the nation's leader, as well as something they did not. They expressed readiness to obey him, as they would have done with his father, with Dr. Francia, or with some Bourbon representative. Mainly, however, they wanted him to leave.

The denizens of this remote district were mistrustful of all newcomers and habitually sided with the probable victor in whatever outside struggle impinged on their lives.[19] Such a stance at this stage could only inflame the Marshal's temper. Knowing this, some of the country people took to their heels, and those who remained behind assumed the most abject pose imaginable. Yet it was hardly enough. Vice President Sánchez could no more comply with orders to obtain provisions from them than he could promise to make the place an impregnable bastion. Like the refugees, he had no idea of what to do next.

Over the next weeks the Allies made some progress reconnoitering the territories outside San Joaquín. They encountered no troops, just more displaced people and headless corpses strewn along paths like so much crow bait.[20] The war, it seems, had turned even more brutal. Taunay, who saw the cadavers, could never harden his heart to such appalling sights.[21]

On 11 October, advanced Allied units occupied San Estanislao, which they found desolated.[22] Yhú fell two days later. And in southern Paraguay, the count's units destroyed the remaining Lopista bands one by one, obliterating the vestiges of the old government in those environs. López had by now given up all thought of a protracted guerrilla struggle against the Allies, their elimination of his forces in the south having effectively ended resistance everywhere save for the extreme northeast.

These successes had a positive impact. In Villarrica, the Paraguayans greeted the Brazilian conquerors with open arms. The Allies made a show of distributing foodstuffs, and then joined the local inhabitants in celebrating their liberation from López.[23] It was not obvious, however, whether the local Guaireños were welcoming the Allies as "liberators" (as some liberals argued), or merely as providers of food.

On 17 October the Paraguayans abandoned Curuguaty and made for Ygatymí. After Piribebuy, the Marshal had permitted some of his civilian supporters to withdraw to their homes. No longer. Now his soldiers drove forward all noncombatants like so many head of cattle. Any soldier who lacked a leather whip would tear a sapling from a nearby tree and bring it down with a will upon the back of anyone who tarried behind. Thus did the republic limp forward from one place of destitution to another.

For some of the boy-soldiers the indiscriminate brutality seemed like a game. As long as the cruelty of López focused on members of the Paraguayan elite, the guards viewed these peoples' discomfort with indifference, or perhaps with pleasure. But now the Marshal ordered that no Paraguayan be left behind alive, and to that end, he sent armed parties in all directions to search for stragglers. Some of the men in these parties themselves deserted, but most followed instructions. Whenever they encountered a group of civilians too numerous to drive back to the main column, they lanced them and moved on.

Thus, the helpless refugees were "forced to the severest kind of drudgery, while all of them were driven about through the wilderness, exposed by day to the scorching rays of the sun, with no shelter at night, and with only such food as the forest afforded."[24] At night, vampire bats left telltale signs of their forays, bloodying animals in the train. There were also botflies (*úra*), which during their nocturnal flights secreted their eggs on mosquitos, which in turn would thrust them into the sleeping Paraguayans. Victims later suffered painful, even debilitating, lesions as the fly larvae hatched out and dug their way to the surface of the skin.[25]

Dorotéa Lasserre and the other women could not avoid this round of torment. They had spent the previous fortnight in rural labor that had strained muscles but yielded nothing to eat. Hunger sent them foraging for green fruit, manioc, and honeycombs, while those few who still had jewelry to barter did so for miniscule quantities of food. The refugees numbered 2,014 when they started, and half perished before the war ended.[26] Now the destinadas and residentas took to the trail again, their line of march having grown indistinct, with constantly shifting destinations.

It was always the same thing: *monte* and wetland, wetland and *monte*, an unending struggle with tangled thickets. The "guides" who led the refugees tried to orient themselves by moving along streambeds from clearing to clearing, but this was risky, for no one could tell when a storm would turn gullies into raging torrents and carry away any child whose step was unsure.

Food, of course, was irregular. Madame Lasserre convinced her companions to consume the stillborn fetus of a donkey by telling them that people ate horseflesh in France. In the end, the ravenous women ate the animal's hide and hooves as well. More commonly, the refugees subsisted on bitter oranges, or on the gritty heart of the pindó palmetto, which, when ground into flour, made a barely digestible pancake (or *mbeyú*).[27]

The grim and pallid group rarely encountered signs of human habitation—a thatched hut occasionally, a patch of manioc, or an isolated orange grove at the end of a pasture, then nothing but forest. They saw no people. True enough, the Mbayá and Cainguá sometimes watched the procession pass. Their own knowledge of the conflict with the Triple Alliance was sketchy, not unlike that of most Europeans, who had heard of Paraguay, but could not place it on a map. For the Indigenous peoples, the war proved less tragic than mysterious, and they showed no sympathy for its victims, nor even much interest.[28]

Rumor held that a few tiny communities lay ahead, somewhere amid the Mbaracayú hills. The destinadas now entered an area of superabundant green, where hundreds of rivulets drained not into the Paraguay but into the Alto Paraná. They could only pray to find some dry place, and, in their imagination, they regarded the rumored villages with a kind of awe, much as those in hell must long for purgatory. The column that included Madame Lasserre reached one such spot, Espadín, about a week's march from Curuguaty. This hamlet lay east of the Mbaracayú hills in Brazilian territory. It offered temporary sanctuary but little food. Lasserre and the others spent more than a month at Espadín where they stayed alive by eating donkey meat and oranges, while their children "walked about like living skeletons, catching lizards."[29]

Eventually even these meager provisions gave out. This left Lasserre to doubt the chances of survival:

> No alternative seemed left to us save to die of starvation or to be lanced; we preferred giving ourselves to the Indians. We held a consultation and sent a deputation to the Indian tents to invite their chiefs to come and treat. It was a mad attempt—at nightfall more than two-hundred people left ... [but the guards eventually hunted all of them down]. ... As the entrance of the wood was so near I did not pay attention where we were going, and we kept going round and round, and lost ourselves among the weeds.[30]

Doña Dorotéa succeeded in finding her mother the next morning, and together with a few refugees, opted to fall back on Espadín, where word reached them that the Brazilians had penetrated the district. The whole band then set out across the arroyos and woods to meet them, worried every step of the way that López's troops would butcher them before they got far. They walked two leagues in moonlight on the night of 24 December and reached the count's encampment the next afternoon. In this dash to meet their deliverers, the "ground [seemed] like fire, and the pain to the feet intolerable, but the anxiety to save [themselves] was still stronger."[31]

The count's adjutant general gave the women a ration of meat, salt, and *farinha*, and they congregated about the encampment, watching as other refugees straggled in. Many had died along the nameless trails, lost and disoriented in their final days. Some four hundred reached Curuguaty by the end of the month.[32] This brought the total number of destinadas and residentas rescued by the Allies to around one thousand—the remnants of the old prewar elite, stripped of their rich apparel, and the poorest of peasant women all thankful to be alive.[33]

Last of the Boy-Soldiers

By late October 1869 the cohesion that had once characterized the Marshal's army had largely dissolved, but despite their lack of purpose—or perhaps because of it—the troops continued northward across the Río Jejuí. During this time, the Count d'Eu visited Asunción to coordinate the campaign with Paranhos and the provisional government. He left the pursuit of López to General Câmara, who pressed his units to advance despite the hot weather— over a hundred degrees Fahrenheit.[34] Câmara emerged as an exemplary soldier, especially bold when under the eyes of a superior or when a dirty job had to be finished with dispatch. He was not a talkative man or a strategist like Porto Alegre or Caxias, but he was always attentive to his duties, a trait that served him well in this final push against López.

The total number of Brazilian troops in Paraguay at this moment approached some 25,000 *praças*, with 2,300 men at San Joaquín; 1,500 with Victorino; 8,000 under Osório in the vicinity of Rosario and moving toward Santaní; 9,450 with Prince Gaston at Caraguatay; 2,000 at Asunción; and around half that number at Humaitá. This left around 2,300 men marching to the northeast directly under der Câmara's command. The Argentines still had 4,000 troops in Paraguay, but these had already been redeployed across the big river into the Chaco territory (which the national government in Buenos Aires coveted). One hundred nominally Uruguayan troops were also left. The Allies thus had far more troops than they needed to destroy López.

So long as Câmara kept on the move, the tattered remnants of the Paraguayan force could never rest. As the Marshal withdrew further into the woods, in Asunción the provisional government was testing the limits of its power. The triumvirs made modest attempts to raise revenues from the sutlers but these efforts were ineffective both in design and execution.

Foreign merchants found the hurly-burly of an uncontrolled market quite congenial, and they claimed every possible scrap of Allied patronage to keep things the way they were.[35] Unable to tax the only moneyed foreigners on the true value of their businesses, the triumvirs remained powerless to improve the country's condition. Aware of their impotence and wanting to make at least a symbolic show of sovereignty, they spent the final months of 1869 setting up a lending library, complaining, and trying to raise a foreign loan.[36] By feigning optimism in the face of so much misery, the triumvirs seemed to think that offering the public a thin reed of hope was healthier than offering nothing at all. Gaining legitimacy with both the councilor and the Paraguayan public could only happen when a constitutional convention oversaw the transition to a new government—and it might not happen even then.[37] More importantly, the Brazilians still had to destroy the Marshal's army.[38]

That the ancien régime still "functioned" in the distant forests had little direct impact on the provisional government, but its survival mattered a great deal to Paraguay. That the Marshal thought to take the offensive at this stage may seem hard to credit, but his creating a workshop at Ygatymi for repairing rifles suggested otherwise. He certainly had no intention of fleeing to Bolivia.[39] López had situated his shrinking column at Itanará-mí, a clearing equidistant between the two branches of the Río Jejuí, when word came that the Brazilians (and a few legionnaires) had attacked his rearguard force at Curuguaty. The children who composed the latter unit never stood a chance: several were shot down right away and the remainder wearily put up their hands.[40] When interrogated, they could only point to the northeast and declare that López was "*mombyry-ité*"—far, far away.

Indeed he was, still drinking European liqueurs, still eating fresh beef, still musing on victories that could not happen. Not only was the Marshal distant from the "front" in terms of miles, he had also distanced himself from the great political questions of the country. Instead, he fretted over desertions and the "plots" hatched against him. Novelists have tried to personalize the Paraguayan dilemma in 1869 by relating how López persecuted his own family.[41] His cruelty may have amounted to a final burst of vindictiveness or perhaps he still sought to instill discipline and political cohesion by showing that no one was above the cause, not even his relatives.

Either way, the first to fall victim was Venancio, the onetime war minister. The government had previously accused him of sedition, but he earned a reprieve in November 1868 through his brother's surprising show of leniency. Now Venancio was a sick man, sometimes delirious, whom informants had fingered for trying to escape to the Allied lines. Worse still, according to information supplied by spies, Venancio had hatched a plot to kill the Marshal with the help of sisters Rafaela and Inocencia and their mother, Juana Pabla Carrillo.[42]

It might seem odd that Marshal López had failed to shoot all four earlier, but he still seemed conflicted about how to deal with treacherous family members. He had to be careful; their role in Paraguay had once been nearly supreme and his treatment towards them now might send the wrong message. He wavered between ordering a firing squad and something less bloody though equally demonstrative. Washburn, now safe in the United States, related that López

> called together his principal officers and asked them if he ought not to bring his mother to trial. Resquín and all the others, with the exception of Aveiro, answered that it was better not to proceed formally to the trial of the old lady, at which López became furious, and called them sycophants and flunkies, praising Aveiro highly for having said that his mother should be tried like any other criminal. He said that among them all Aveiro was his only friend.[43]

The meaning of this statement was unmistakable, but the Marshal decided to forego the execution of his mother and siblings. He did make their lives miserable, however. He "processed" them, gave them nothing to eat, and berated them like common destinadas.[44] The three women, whose hands had never known calluses, survived by chewing cowhides.

Whenever the column halted for the evening, the Marshal had the women dragged from the old supply wagon that served as their conveyance. As he had done with Juliana Ynsfrán, he then had them whipped before his officers and men. López designated his "only friend" Aveiro to flog his unfortunate mother, who had defended Inocencia and Rafaela as she had once defended Benigno.[45] Juana Pabla seemed ready-made for caricature: stout and ponderous, habitually complaining, and extravagantly generous, she seemed a tragedy-queen straight out of Dickens. In moments of pressure, however, she demonstrated the same resilience and stamina as other Paraguayan women.[46]

Colonel Aveiro took pleasure in conducting cruel interrogations, and never explicitly denied his role in Juana Pabla's torture. This left him a marginally more honest figure than Centurión, Falcón, or Maíz.[47] As for Venancio, he tried to save himself by accusing others, but succumbed either to pneumonia or to the thrust of a lance sometime in December.[48] His sisters and mother all survived the war, but could never afterwards suppress their flinching whenever they saw a coachman whip a slow-moving horse.

One person who also fell at this time was Pancha Garmendia, whose name Paraguayans have always linked to romance and national tragedy. Her beauty, it was said, had enraptured López before he became president but she persistently rejected his advances, gaining a measure of acclaim for holding out even during the worst stages of the *via crucis*. For her part, Madame Lynch had always shown contempt for any woman "don Pancho" found attractive, even (and especially) anyone who refused his advances. Any denial of the Marshal's demands or passions could provoke bad comment and such gossip could prove lethal in Paraguay. For this reason, as much as any other, the Marshal had Pancha arrested.

Pancha followed the destinadas to Espadín, and later accompanied the Paraguayan army in its many peregrinations. Wrapped in a shawl that once had been red with white fringe but had now faded into a dirty rose, she always seemed "active and serene" in the role that fate reserved for her.[49] Cholera and deprivation slowly turned her into a specter with sunken eyes. But even now the Marshal continued to show curiosity towards her, and on at least one occasion he invited her to sup at his dinner table alongside Madame Lynch. As talk of the poison plot began in mid-1869, however, Pancha found herself unexpectedly complicit. At her execution in December, she was so feeble from hunger that she could barely stand, and the lances pierced her body as if going through parchment.[50]

Brutal and evocative though it was, the tale of Pancha Garmendia and the López women was no different in substance from that experienced by hundreds of anonymous men and women who have never found their poet. Hunger and disease had become their common attributes for many months. And yet the killing went on.

The Paraguayan army had successfully retreated since the fall of Piribebuy, and López had generally kept his units intact, but he could no longer do this with any confidence. It had been the Marshal's practice to deploy patrols at some distance from the main columns to provide rearguard functions and occasionally mount delaying actions.[51] Later, with troop strength reduced, the patrols limited themselves to reconnaissance, and they also tracked down and killed any civilians who failed to keep pace or who had dared flee toward Allied lines. Indeed, Lopista executioners seemed to compete with Brazilian scouts to see who could kill the most civilians.[52]

The command structure within these small patrols, as within the army as a whole, had always gone unquestioned. Now, however, with the Acá Carayá and Acá Verá shattered and loyal Lopistas dead or in chains, officers found it difficult to maintain control in units operating far from the main force. The soldiers that made up these units were as destitute and hungry as the civilians and, like them, apt to desert. On one occasion in mid-February, a party of Paraguayan medics fled to the Allied lines while on one of these patrols; among their number was Cirilo Solalinde, the medical orderly who had saved the Marshal from cholera.[53]

López sternly reminded his men that the Allies had given no quarter in earlier engagements, but this warning found less resonance than before.[54] He then reduced the number of patrols and attempted to reinforce discipline within the main column by flogging anyone for any reason at any moment. Such measures simply increased military burdens, causing his men to suspect each other and look for excuses to take revenge. Instead of bringing the army together, the measures did the reverse.

The march north had little coherence. The Paraguayans pushed through brush that was more than simply thick. On all sides, green foliage wrapped itself like bunting around dead logs, and creepers worked their way up every lapacho to provide awnings for scores of dark streams. This wooded environment seemed to grow stranger and stranger and even the birds supposedly refused to light on its tallest trees, which towered above the soldiers like so many obelisks.[55] The heat was oppressive, the air was filled with insects and the reek of vegetable fermentation.

Caraguatay and Curuguaty had been squalid sites but they were known villages. Now no one could say where the trail would lead. "The enemy is a mystery," recorded one Allied newspaper, and "his situation, his operations, and his numbers are all mysterious."[56] These things seemed equally puzzling to the Marshal's men, who, to use the words of Chris Leuchars, "staggered on, further and further into the interior, both figuratively and literally away from civilization."[57]

If any Allied leader could hasten military victory, and thereby terminate Paraguayan suffering, it was the Count d'Eu, but Gaston's position was hardly enviable. He received only intermittent aid from imperial officials in Rio. The count resented the government's insistence on running the war cheaply. A perfect military economy meant finding a balance in which the blows against López were devastating without stretching the Allied armies too far. As it was, Gaston faced a pervasive disenchantment with the Paraguayan imbroglio from within the war ministry, and no interest in greater expenditures. He had a surplus of manpower and a deficit of supplies. This frustrated his plans to end the campaign by Christmas.[58]

The Allied troops broke off active pursuit because the lack of horses permitted only sporadic reconnaissance. Enemy deserters gave the Count d'Eu some information but never enough to act with any decisiveness in hunting down López.[59] On the other hand, the Allied commander had no need for a full complement of troops to defeat such a weakened opponent. In late November, he withdrew units from Caraguatay to Rosario, leaving only three thousand men under General Câmara to probe around Ygatymí.[60]

Over the next two months the Marshal's troops closed with Allied detachments on several occasions, but the confrontations were ephemeral. López continued to retreat and at the brink of the New Year, he arrived at a large clearing in the forest euphemistically called "Panadero" (the baker). There he set up camp together with la Madama, Vice President Sánchez, Generals Resquín and Caballero, and the remaining members of his government and army. The total number amounted to just over one thousand men—a tiny fraction of the force that once carried the Paraguayan flag to Corrientes, Rio Grande do Sul, and Mato Grosso. Several hundred refugees and residentas had remained with the army, and each day, the soldiers pounced on those who could not keep up, shoving them roughly forward, even children whose faces were rounded with kwashiorkor.

In earlier days, López had accurate military intelligence, but spies no longer had a way to pass from the Allied camps to his headquarters. The barest whisper of an Allied incursion therefore sent the Marshal to his saddle to order a new retreat. Panadero might have offered his men a break in this respect but the paltry provisions available there gave out almost immediately.[61] Then López learned of Brazilian troops advancing from the south. Unaware of the far more substantial force moving up from the west, he decided that, as the sick and wounded were slowing his progress, he ought to leave them at Panadero together with most of the women and the few big cannon still in his possession.[62] The latter he hid in brambles, thinking to recover them later. Then he set off on 12 January 1870 with between six hundred and a thousand men, a few head of cattle, the smaller artillery pieces, and several bullock carts of money and plate. He moved northward across the Río Aguaray, then eastward towards the Alto Paraná.

The Paraguayans passed in close column over long expanses of spongy, water-logged terrain. In the distance rose the Mbaracayú hills, whose eastern slope the men skirted before veering into Brazilian territory for a week or two, following the Alto Paraná northward, and then recrossing back into Paraguay above the Río Ypané. The heat was like a stove—but this did not hinder the Marshal from imbibing a great deal of liquor.[63] His men drank water.

Despite some rumors that López might be heading for the Salto Guairá country of the Alto Paraná, it seemed more likely that his ultimate destination was Dourados, an abandoned Brazilian village more than a hundred miles north of Panadero.[64] This site was some two hundred fifty miles from Concepción, which General Câmara had recently taken. Charged by the Count d'Eu with bringing down the enemy, Câmara had perhaps three thousand troops ready, and in the last days of January, they set out along a diagonal course towards Dourados.[65] At the same time, another, somewhat smaller, force was deployed to come up the bush trail behind López. Câmara instructed this second force to avoid confrontations but keep close enough to harass the enemy as opportunity permitted. Whenever the Paraguayans gained Dourados, the two corps could come together to overwhelm the Marshal with sheer numbers.

Accordingly, General Câmara's columns advanced northward towards Bella Vista, a tiny outpost on the frontier previously occupied by a Brazilian brigade that guarded the northern bank of the Río Apa.[66] Câmara wanted to unite his army with those smaller units and move on to Dourados to intercept López. Before he reached Bella Vista, however, word came that the Paraguayans had veered away from Dourados and were moving westward along a path cut years earlier by *yerbateros*. Called the Picada de Chiriguelo, the trail led after some distance to an excellent campground set amid the Amambay highlands—Cerro Corá.

This site, whose apposite Guaraní name means "the corral of the hill country," had the shape of a natural bowl, Eden-like in its verdure and noteworthy for a large, stoneless pasture often described as a natural amphitheater.[67] It was surrounded by steep limestone hillocks more reminiscent of the *mogotes* in Cuba's Pinar del Río province than the rolling Cordilleras of Piribebuy. In military terms, the ground should have been easy to defend, but the Marshal no longer had the manpower.

Running along the northern edge of the Cerro Corã was the Aquidabán-niguí, a shallow, honey-colored tributary of its larger namesake. To the west, near the confluence with the main branch of the Aquidabán, lay another creek, the Tacuara, which was smaller still. Only two trails cut the expanse, one that followed the Picada de Chiriguelo along which the Paraguayans had come from the south, and the other running northeast toward Dourados. Like the picada, it was impenetrable at many points and would have to be cleared for the army to move carts along it.

Cerro Corã was a wild place, looking as if humanity had more or less passed it by, and even today, there are no towns or villages nearby to disturb its tranquility. It was not necessarily quiet, however, for the noises of howler monkeys provided unmistakable proof that nature regarded the Paraguayan soldiers as invaders just like the Brazilians.

The Marshal's unexpected arrival at this new encampment led General Câmara to reconfigure his attack.[68] He ordered the units at Bella Vista to make for Dourados, from where they would follow the track and shut off the northern outlet from Cerro Corã. The general himself hastened by forced marches to bottle up López from the opposite side, near the confluence with the Aquidabán. While still en route to this latter site, Câmara met with a Paraguayan deserter who told him that the Marshal knew nothing of the looming danger and still believed the Allies had yet to advance from Concepción. The Brazilian general smiled at this intelligence, and gave orders to redouble the pace of his march.

Cerro Corã

The Paraguayans needed a long repose. Nine hundred survivors had reached Cerro Corã, where they were essentially marooned by circumstances. They pitched their shabby tents in the usual uniform way at the main encampment, dug latrines, and kindled their cook fires to make the best of a fare of boiled cowhides and nettles. A few soldiers brought in game, which added protein to the mess but hardly enough to relieve the general want.

These Paraguayan soldiers may have been long on stoicism and short on words in earlier days, but life at Cerro Corã promised nothing more than continued fatigue and grumbling took energy that no one cared to expend. Officers and high-ranking civilian functionaries, better nourished than the rank and file, may have retained a bit of their previous bearing, but some worried that their actions at San Fernando, Concepción, and other places might soon bring a reckoning. Those who lacked López's death wish had to wonder if a future even existed.

The Marshal was powerless to prevent the disintegration of his army, but to keep going, to give the national struggle continued meaning, he clung to his religious faith and whatever historical precedents came to mind. He could never quite decide whether he was a Moses guiding his people through the wilderness, or an Alexander, who remained at the head of an ever-victorious army taking a long but necessary detour through the Syrian desert. In a conversation with Victor Silvero at about this time, López ruminated on the long-term historical impact of the Paraguayan campaign. Citing precedents from antiquity, he asserted that those who had fallen in battle were the real winners in war and that those who remained alive after the fighting deserved only pity. If the Paraguayan people had hitherto sacrificed themselves so selflessly in the struggle against the Triple Alliance, it was because they knew that he, as their commander, would face death alongside them. His people would achieve their apotheosis through him.[69]

By leaving behind the wounded along with most of the women and children at Panadero, López at least reduced his concerns to the military sphere. He found, however, that he could not manipulate the troops with the ease he once had and that he needed to do something different. On the night of 25 February, therefore, he assembled his officers and men for an important ceremony. Around five hundred soldiers and the few women remaining at the main camp came to attention in a large semicircle. It had been a brutally hot day and all were presumably thankful for the relative coolness of the evening. The Marshal spoke to the group softly, eschewing for a change the rhetoric of glory and imminent victory.

As in the past, the men listened attentively, though now their faces appeared empty in the dying light of the campfires. López started by praising their steadfastness. He repeated a few old jokes at the expense of the enemy, and damned the empire as an affront to civilization.[70] Then he got to the point, defining the contrast between vulgar militarism and national sacrifice:

> You who have followed me from the beginning know that I, your chief, am ready to die together with the last of you on the final field of battle. That moment is nigh. You must know that the victor is the man who dies for a beautiful cause, not the one who remains alive at the scene of combat. We will all be reproached by the generation that emerges from this disaster, the generation that will take defeat into its soul like a poison. … But generations to come will do us justice, acclaiming the grandeur of our immolation. I shall be mocked more than you. I will be the outcast of God and man, and buried beneath a mountain of ignominy. But … I will rise from the well of slander, to rise ever higher in the eyes of our

countrymen, and at length become that which our history had always meant me to be.[71]

The address, which featured prophecies more ironic than López could have guessed, at least recognized the certainty of defeat. His assertion that the costs had been worthwhile may have sounded hollow, but when he stated that all those present shared a common destiny, that they were comrades whom history would honor in good time, there was an element of truth in his words.

López then awarded a new decoration to all those who had survived the six-month retreat from Piribebuy. Distributing colored ribbons in lieu of the medals themselves, López described the award's design in loving detail and noted how deserving every soldier was of Paraguay's acclamation.[72] The presentation of this new medal provoked an instant reaction. The Marshal had loosened invisible chains and the crowd burst into sincere applause. "In all the history of the world," Cunninghame-Graham recorded, "no military order was instituted in stranger circumstances."[73] True enough, and if we are to believe Centurión, the news brought weary smiles to all present. López then waved to his fatigued and famished soldiers, dismissed the assembly, and retired for the night together with Madame Lynch and the children.

The men took in this *coup de theatre* and contemplated the fate that had brought them to this camp. They chatted only a little, then stared at the heavens before laying down to a nervous sleep. The Marshal had already dispatched patrols to search for cattle and other provisions. One such unit, composed of forty-three men and commanded by General Caballero, had gone into Mato Grosso on a foraging expedition and had not been heard from in several days.[74] As for the enemy, though the Brazilians were probably many days distant, the troops had already prepared some minor defenses. To the Paraguayan front lay the Aquidabán-niguí, with the Tacuara some three miles away on the extreme left. At the first waterway, the Marshal's men hid four small cannon to cover the ford leading to the main camp. At the second, two cannon and a sizable guard of infantry—several hundred strong—served as an outpost.[75] The Paraguayans had little ammunition, and given the exhaustion of the men, their efforts at building defenses were necessarily limited. Even so, the soldiers hoped to accomplish something over the next days.

General Câmara did not let them have their way. An hour or so before dawn on 1 March, a small party of his Brazilian cavalrymen succeeded in crossing the Tacuara without being detected.[76] At daybreak, they charged the little outpost and seized the cannon before the Marshal's men could open fire. The shocked Paraguayans immediately dispersed, but Câmara's troops chased them down. The Paraguayans then tried to set up an ambush between the two streams, but the Allied soldiers stormed the position before anyone could raise a general alarm. In the process, the Brazilians captured an officer who proved very talkative.[77] Several soldiers who had accompanied the man managed to slip away around six in the morning and rush to López's side. Up to that moment, he had no idea that the enemy had violated his sanctuary. "To arms!" he screamed, his voice breaking, and the men assembled into defensive positions as cavalry charged them.[78] Rifle rounds were exchanged in the usual frenzied way, but most Paraguayans held only sabers and lances.

On previous occasions, as Allied soldiers seized the momentum from the Paraguayans, their commanders would delay their assault until the Marshal had either withdrawn or assembled sufficient troops to control the field. General Câmara was not much more imaginative in his tactics than his predecessors, but, unlike them, he was determined to prevent López's escape. Câmara hastened to the fight, bringing up a force of around two thousand men. The Brazilian infantry, one battalion of which was commanded by Major Floriano Peixoto (future president of Brazil), deployed along the length of the Aquidabán-niguí, and fired at the few gunners on the other side. Bugles sounded, and cavalry and infantry bounded across the water. The Brazilians seized the light cannon, and routed a force that arrived too late to reinforce the defense. Then, with lancers at the front, the infantry advanced onto the open ground where the Paraguayans had set up their tents. Four hundred of the Marshal's troops, drawn up now in a single column, tried to meet the Allied force. At the last instant, however, Brazilian lancers swept round the column in a prearranged maneuver that blocked the trail leading away from the ground.

This effectively closed the trap. Brazilian riflemen assembled into a skirmishing line after emerging from the ford leading to the encampment. Wasting not a moment, their commander charged in to prevent the Marshal's escape. Although López's soldiers had by now recovered from their shock, they still faced a far superior force. The Brazilian riflemen swept forward relentlessly, firing their weapons in a manner both mechanical and furious, and eventually they enveloped the malnourished defenders. After fifteen minutes, the Paraguayan units broke and ran, leaving some two hundred of their number dead.[79]

Colonel Centurión tried to rouse the men to resistance but his horse took a hit and slipped, trapping the colonel underneath. As he struggled to get up, a Minié ball struck his cheek and splattered blood into his eyes so that he could barely see. He dragged himself to the far end of the camp as the bullets whizzed around. He felt groggy and uncertain of his footing. One of his final memories of the day was hearing López's familiar voice demanding to know who had abandoned the field, and being told by Panchito that it was the gravely wounded Centurión.[80]

At this moment of confusion, the Marshal's mother, who could presumably still feel the welts on her back from Aveiro's lashing, harkened to her son. "Save me, Pancho!" she shouted, but he answered only with a hurried retort—"Trust to your sex, madam!"—and was gone.[81] The heartlessness of this response hid many realities. The Marshal's view of his mother had always been complicated by jealousy and lack of warmth. She showed him more affection than he could find for her, and, just perhaps, at this moment of peril, his mind retreated to his youth and the whispered canards that he had been born a whoreson. Some claimed that López had already reserved a date for her with the firing squad, but instead now left the old woman to the clemency of the enemy as a greater humiliation.[82]

Certainly all was pandemonium and López could find no way out. He shoved Madame Lynch and the children into a carriage and the little party set off south along the picada, hoping to rejoin the Marshal after the confusion subsided. Meanwhile, bullets continued to fly as the Brazilian soldiers reached the Marshal's tent, which astounded them with its damask lining, provisions, and luxuries.

As his family vanished down the trail, López dug his spurs into the flanks of his horse and, together with his staff and half a dozen officers, galloped furiously toward the Aquidabán-niguí. His eyes were fixed on the opposite bank.[83] All the men had their swords unsheathed but before they could gain the arroyo and the wood beyond, Brazilian fire cut them down. Dead also was Caminos, the Marshal's flatterer and aide-de-camp. General Resquín, the only senior Paraguayan riding a mule that day, fell to the ground when his animal slipped. Covered in mud, he tried to get to his feet and reach for his sword but he failed to get his fingers properly wrapped around the hilt. As the Brazilians approached, he raised his hands, and fell prisoner.[84]

The Marshal had no intention of sharing his general's fate. He wheeled about for a moment and fled obliquely towards the arroyo as the sound of cavalry came up fast behind him. The ground suddenly grew soft under his horse's hooves, leading the animal to stumble. Sputtering with rage, López dropped from the saddle and sank knee-deep in the muck. He began to trudge across, but was thwarted in his course by the Brazilians, who called loudly for his surrender. They cursed him as a pig and a tyrant. Aveiro somehow caught up during this interchange and the Marshal screamed for him to "kill the monkeys." But it was too late.[85]

The threat of immediate violence can make cowards courageous or brave men waver, and the Marshal's cowardice, which had been so obvious on so many previous occasions, now made way for the one brave act of his career. He kept pushing ahead, trying to follow Aveiro's lead, all to no avail. Six enemy cavalrymen galloped up from the near distance, ordering him to cast down his sword, and in response, he cursed them as darkies, and damned them for profaning the soil of Paraguay. Although the testimony is contradictory, López might have then taken a shot to the chest or was perhaps cut by a saber.[86] In either case, however, he stood his ground.[87] General Câmara rode up during the melee and, recognizing the enemy commander, added his own strained voice to the clamor. He directed his men to hold fire and apprehend the Marshal, who continued to hurl insults at his pursuers as Colonel Aveiro got away.

The Brazilian government had offered a reward of 110 pounds sterling to whoever could bring the Marshal down. This enticement evidently proved too tempting for a fierce little Riograndense corporal named José Francisco Lacerda, who returned the profanity that López offered, then lunged forward on horseback. With all the skill of a picador—but none of the grace—he drove his lance into the Marshal's abdomen. The corporal, whom comrades had nicknamed "Frank the Devil," saw the pain he inflicted in the Marshal's face, and he took pleasure in the deed though it also caused him to wince just a bit.[88]

López's final moments, though iconic, remain obscure in their details. Some witnesses aver that he was shot in the chest but kept standing despite lance and bullet wounds. Others claim that he fell face first into the arroyo, rose in a final show of determination, and fell again. All agree that Câmara grew impatient and implored his tottering opponent to yield, but though the Paraguayan could not find the strength to rise, he did manage to summon a final measure of grit from deep inside his torn gut.[89] He pursed his lips, spat, and cried the words of his own eulogy: "¡Muero con mi patria!" (I die with my country!).[90]

López coughed, blood gushing from his side, and slipped into unconsciousness, his final gulp of air as hungry for life as a baby's first breath. His anger, his vanity, and his caprices ebbed away in seconds. He was the Marshal no more—just another corpse whose blood mixed with the mud and water of the Aquidabán.

Afterwards

Were the story of the Triple Alliance War a Homeric epic, it would have ended here, with Francisco Solano López stubbornly choosing honor in death over humiliation in life. In reality, he died amidst great confusion. Not everyone at Cerro Corã had realized that the war's chief antagonist had met his end. A few Paraguayans kept fighting along the nearby perimeter and a few more who were at some distance were not privy to the event. General Caballero, for instance, was off searching for provisions in the Mato Grosso.

For their part, the Brazilians indulged in a rampage against the Paraguayan survivors. The elderly Vice President Sánchez, so often the butt of López's mockery, stumbled from his tent with saber in hand. As the Brazilian lancers cut him down, the old man looked far more courageous than his master. Indeed Sánchez died fighting, as did three colonels, a lieutenant colonel, and five military chaplains.[91] A good many lesser officers and functionaries died as well, perhaps because the Allied commanders insisted that no member of the Marshal's government should escape alive.[92]

In a day full of poignant moments, perhaps the most poignant came when Brazilian cavalry caught up with Madame Lynch and her children. The Marshal and most of his men had died an hour or two earlier, leaving Allied troopers busily searching for stragglers. La Madama's carriage had made little or no progress down the Picada de Chiriguelo when Brazilian horsemen suddenly came galloping from behind. Their officer, a lieutenant colonel named Francisco Antonio Martins, rode at their head, and when he spotted the carriage, raised his voice to demand that the escort of boy-soldiers yield.[93]

Now a full colonel in his father's service, fifteen-year-old Panchito bristled, and when Martins turned his back momentarily, his young adversary drew his sword and struck him slightly on the forearm. "Give up, little boy!" Martins exclaimed with contempt, raising a saber to ward off further blows. Madame Lynch added her own appeal in the form of a shriek, pleading from the carriage window for her son to give up his charade of resistance. "A Paraguayan colonel never surrenders!" Panchito cried out with bravado, echoing the vacuous sentiment that had guided the Marshal since 1864.

Swinging his weapon in the air and growling at the Brazilians, Panchito's performance elicited more amusement than fear or pity. When his hand went for a revolver, however, they lost patience. A lancer jutted forward from his saddle and ran Panchito through.[94] His mother had just stepped down from her conveyance and was only three paces behind. "I'm an Englishwoman!" she cried, "Respect me!" Then she burst into tears, running forward to cradle the body of her firstborn. At this sight, her second son, the eleven-year-old José Félix, screamed uncontrollably. "Don't kill me! I'm a foreigner, the son of an Englishwoman!" Then he, too, was lanced—an utterly unnecessary and atrocious killing.[95] With a look of absolute dismay, Madame Lynch stood erect but could find no words to convey the depths of her misery. She now took the place of all the Paraguayan women before her and contemplated her dead children.

If the Brazilians had orders to take no prisoners, they certainly failed to comply, for many key figures in the Marshal's entourage made it out of Cerro Corã as captives. Colonel Centurión had received some grudging help from one of the residentas, who hid him in a grass hut from where he witnessed the Allies bayonet two boy-soldiers who had tried to surrender. The colonel later crawled to a stand of trees, where he spent many hours until he was finally noticed and brought in. He had had nothing to drink save his own urine. Amazingly, Colonel Patricio Escobar, whose heroism had facilitated the retreat at Ypecuá in December 1868, also survived the final confrontation.[96] So did Father Maíz, Generals Resquín and José María Delgado, Colonels Aveiro and Angel Moreno, an equal number of lieutenant colonels (including the faithful Correntino Victor Silvero), José Falcón, and other lesser members of government.

General Câmara ordered a litter constructed from saplings and had the Marshal's body ferried back to the main camp, where it lay on the ground for several hours. During that time, medical personnel completed an autopsy.[97] Sentries prevented the cadaver from being profaned, either by rowdy Brazilian troopers or by Paraguayan women who "had taken to sacking the carts [and when they saw the Marshal] routed, wanted now to dance on his corpse." It supposedly "cost no small trouble to prevent them."[98]

By now, the second Brazilian column had arrived from the Chiriguelo, which brought the full Allied contingent on the field to around six thousand men. Each soldier wanted to view the bodies of López and Panchito, who had been brought back to the main camp along with Madame Lynch. Doña Juana Pabla and the López sisters stepped up but refused to exchange words with the grieving woman. Only the Marshal's mother showed any emotion, weeping bitterly for her son and grandsons.

As for Madame Lynch, she now assumed the pose of a self-possessed, gallant widow, anxious to protect her remaining children but otherwise unwilling to betray any loss of dignity. General Câmara and Colonel Ernesto Cunha de Mattos were touched by this show and accorded her every consideration. Having fought so ruthlessly, Câmara wanted to appear magnanimous, while Cunha de Mattos remembered la Madama's personal kindnesses to him when he was a prisoner of the Paraguayans.

The Brazilians permitted Lynch to retain her properties and go about camp unmolested. "Although it was known that she had with her an immense value in brilliants and other jewelry, nothing was taken from her carriage; on the contrary, a Brazilian guard protected her from violence."[99] Cunha de Mattos acted as her escort on the return trip to Concepción. In placing himself at her orders, he hoped that fellow officers would endorse his scrupulous behavior, "for Brazilians were above [small-minded] suspicions."[100] Madame Lynch charmed these men just as she had charmed McMahon, Cuverville, and many foreigners at Asunción. Her "blend of arrogance and fine courtesy" worked its magic one final time.[101]

Still dressed in Parisian finery and carrying herself like a tragic heroine, Lynch begged permission to bury López and Panchito at the campsite. The Brazilian commander conceded this, assigning soldiers to help her dig the shallow graves. Former minister Washburn claimed—not very convincingly—that Câmara also provided her with extra guards to protect her from the residentas, who "would undoubtedly have dug her eyes out with bodkins ... and thrust her mutilated body into the Aquidabán to become food for the alligators."[102] The soldiers who helped Lynch must have felt vindicated, for the inhuman López was dead, and with him, all the aggression he had projected towards the empire. On the other hand, though they were hard men made harder by the war, they could not help but admire this handsome woman whose family they had just torn to shreds.[103] The interment was a rushed business: two holes dug into the soft earth, two bodies wrapped in white sheets, two simple wooden crosses, and no indication of who lay beneath. For more than a generation neither mound nor tablet marked the burial site.[104]

There were many other graves to dig at Cerro Corã and little time to waste. Câmara wished to return promptly to Concepción, where the Count d'Eu awaited details of the final engagement. The Riograndense general took with him some 244 Paraguayan prisoners, including those "precious trophies of the triumph," Madame Lynch and the López women.[105] The Allies had suffered a mere 7 men wounded on their side, while the Paraguayans lost over half their contingent of 500 defenders. Some were killed afterwards by the Brazilians, but many dashed into the bush and later joined the lines of refugees on the way to Asunción.

The Brazilians picked up many souvenirs of their victory, including López's sword, which Câmara sent on to Rio de Janeiro as a present for dom Pedro. Other men on the scene took various baubles—silver spurs, *bombillas*, etc. One man secured the Marshal's pocket watch. And Colonel José Vieira Couto de Magalhães, a bookish officer who later became Brazil's premier ethnographer, discovered in the Marshal's baggage a 1724 edition of Antonio Ruiz de Montoya's *Arte de la lengua guaraní*, which he kept as an object of study for many years.[106]

The train of prisoners that set off for the eleven-day journey to Concepción faced an unknown future. Most were glad that the war had ended, even though it meant a lengthy foreign occupation. Others worried about what kind of slavery the Brazilians had in mind for them—if it were to be hard labor alone, or if the emperor would parade them like caged animals before the public and shoot them when he tired of the game. The prisoners' notions of Paraguayan nationalism, which the Marshal had cultivated since the heady days of Curupayty, must have seemed unrecognizable by now. It was unclear that these people would ever see Asunción again.

As it turned out, neither Câmara nor the Count d'Eu had any intention of turning their high-ranking prisoners over to the summary justice of the triumvirs.[107] In fact, the Brazilians fraternized rather ostentatiously with their Lopista captives. Everyone took a fancy to Colonel Centurión, who quoted Shakespeare with ease and joked about his facial wound. The charming José Falcón was likewise admired and forgiven for having gotten involved with some shabby self-promoters.

And there were more tender links between victor and vanquished. Some claim that Inocencia López had a brief but passionate affair with General Câmara, who left her pregnant only days after his brother's death. Rafaela López definitely had a relation with Colonel Azevedo Pedra, for they married shortly thereafter and took up residence in Mato Grosso. For his part, Captain Teodoro Wanderley, a minor officer in the Brazilian command, became so enraptured with a daughter of Venancio that he stayed by her side not just to Concepción, but all the way to the Paraguayan capital.[108]

Once they arrived at the Brazilian base, the ranking Paraguayans received orders to sign a statement denouncing the Marshal; most signed, then repudiated the declaration later.[109] Resquín, Aveiro, Maíz, and a few others were then held incommunicado aboard a Brazilian warship. For his part, Aveiro had somehow managed to slip away from Cerro Corã, but having nowhere to go, he eventually turned himself in to Câmara, who asked him sharply why he had not killed López when he had the chance. Aveiro responded with impudence, asking why he, Câmara, had failed to kill the emperor, who was the real author of the war. The Brazilian general let this remark pass, then asked if it were true that Aveiro had flogged the Marshal's mother; when the colonel admitted to the deed, citing orders, Câmara cut him off, telling the Paraguayan that he was lucky to be alive, since doña Juana Pabla had explicitly demanded his execution. Aveiro found enough courage to risk still more effrontery, saying that Juana Pabla's murderous intent towards him was hardly surprising in a woman who had tried to assassinate her own son. At this, Câmara shook his head and terminated the interview.[110]

The count, who learned of Câmara's victory on 4 March while en route from Rosario, signaled the imperial government that though he held several important prisoners, the Marshal had preferred death. The war was over, Prince Gaston announced with final assurance, and his men deserved praise and rest.

The celebrations that followed in the Allied camp were boisterous, but probably not as loud as those in Rio de Janeiro.[111] The feeling of jubilation—if that is the correct term—was far more subdued in Buenos Aires, Montevideo, and the occupied Paraguayan capital. In the last of these three cities, little in the way of real celebration accompanied the war's end. The street poets of the capital, mostly Italians, were dancing on the great man's misfortune, but most Paraguayans simply felt relieved. Nearly every one of them had lost a son or a father.

La Regeneración, the newspaper of the Decoud faction, reflected the politics of both Paranhos and every Paraguayan liberal when it noted that the "1st of March will ever after mark the anniversary of freedom in Paraguay, sealed with the ignominious death of a monster who ruled bloodily and who exterminated her sons."[112] Whether most Paraguayans endorsed the politics behind this sentiment was irrelevant; they still wandered the countryside in small groups looking for food. Gradually, they learned that the Allies had won and that the nation had to come to terms with that fact. The Asuncenos had already learned this lesson. For their part, they were too preoccupied with immediate needs to waste pity on any refugees—or on the nation.

In April, General Caballero and his men finally emerged from the bush. They had located only a few head of cattle on the Mato Grosso frontier and learned of the Marshal's death some three weeks after leaving his side. They skirted the outlying districts of Dourados, where they heard that other strag-glers had died in clashes with Brazilian soldiers who had offered no quarter.[113] Whether this was true or not, Caballero had already decided to turn back to Concepción when his men spotted enemy horsemen in the distance. They later encountered other Allied cavalry as they neared the town. This time, when the enemy fired a few shots their way, Caballero threw up a white flag. His men were now almost completely naked, their tattered clothes having worn out during the final trek through the forests.

The balls that flew over their heads in this one-minute encounter were the last fired in the Triple Alliance War. The Allied cavalrymen disarmed the Paraguayan soldiers and gave them food and drink. As they had no clothing of their own to spare, the Brazilians gave their prisoners cowhides to cover them-selves. Dressed like troglodytes, the last Lopista soldiers marched into captivity.

Caballero ultimately joined the other high-ranking prisoners who had been sent on to Rio de Janeiro. The majority of his officers and men obtained their release upon arrival in Concepción, and were permitted to join the droves of refugees wandering toward the capital.[114] When they finally reached the city, few were thinking about war-making, self-sacrifice, Paraguayan nationalism, or loyalty to Marshal López. Heroism is not just about fighting and dying. Staying alive, too, requires bravery, and the Paraguayans needed every bit of courage to face the challenges of peace.

Epilogue

Though the protracted debacle had finally come to an end, no one could yet measure its long-term impact. Most participants had by now forgotten the war's causes, though its immediate effects were plain enough. The Allies emerged victorious, but they gained only a prostrate country whose independence they agreed to respect out of geopolitical self-interest. The Brazilians and Argentines had strained their national treasuries to crush López, and thousands of their soldiers lay dead. For a few officers and politicians, honor may have at long last been satisfied. But for the men in the field, the struggle had been without meaning for many months.

In military terms, the Paraguayan campaign offered few surprises. Any chance of the Marshal gaining a meaningful victory ended with the destruction of his fleet at the Riachuelo in mid-1865. From that point onward, the Paraguayans could never prevail, nor even rescue the Blanco regime in Montevideo. Their struggle instead took the form of a long attrition in which the Allies enjoyed all the material advantages and most of the political ones.

On occasion, the Brazilians and Argentines suffered reverses, including a spectacular defeat at Curupayty. The one major strategic innovation the Allies attempted—the Mato Grosso operation—also resulted in failure, after which they returned to their original idea of pounding Humaitá into collapse. This strategy brought the expected success only after a long effort. Caxias and the Count d'Eu certainly did most things right, of course. They adopted more up-to-date weaponry during the course of the fighting and dramatically improved both provisioning and medical support. And they assigned field command to officers who had already proven their worth in combat, thus demonstrating that military professionalism usually wins out over simple courage.

The other military lessons of the war were purely technical. Universal conscription provided a valuable source of dependable manpower, and the laying of telegraph lines proved essential to a good defense. Ironclad vessels, by contrast, were overrated as an offensive tool, for they failed to silence or even damage good earthen batteries. It was likewise problematic to place rifled cannon or muskets into the hands of troops whose commanders had had no training with such weapons. Despite the fact that they delivered less of a punch, lighter cannon proved superior to heavier guns because they were easier to transport. For a similar reason, Congreve rockets proved more successful than military planners had previously believed. Needle rifles had no positive impact on the conduct of close engagements and were rejected by all who used them. Cavalry forces had not generally succeeded as planners had predicted and war ministries would henceforth pay more attention to organizing and maintaining infantry units. Lighter-than-air balloons could provide good intelligence initially, but the enemy could hamper their effectiveness by setting fires whose smoke would obscure any observation. A well-organized supply system was vital in facing an opponent who enjoyed interior lines. And finally, though the loss of the *Rio de Janeiro* might suggest otherwise, river torpedoes really offered more of a threat in the minds of naval planners than they ever did in reality.

These conclusions were unlikely to shake the thinking of military men like von Versen, Manlove, and McMahon, who understood them already from wars in North America and the Crimea. What no one could have predicted, however, were the lengths to which the Paraguayans would go to defend their community and nation. It was ultimately not a question of why the Allies won the war but rather why it took the Paraguayans so long to lose. They tenaciously resisted the Allied onslaught after all chances for victory had ended and after every appeal for a negotiated peace was rejected as unacceptable. They resisted like the men and women of Masada, whose fate they shared, astonishing the world in the process.

The Paraguayan War brought many changes to the political milieu in each of the four nations involved, and it accelerated other changes that were already underway. The war cost Argentina some eighteen thousand combat deaths and at least as many from disease.[1] The national government had to absorb considerable financial costs, perhaps as much as fifty million dollars—money that could have been spent more productively on education and infrastructure.[2] Needless to say, some time passed before the loans were repaid to the various banks.[3]

Despite these costs, the war brought advantages to the merchants and cattlemen of Buenos Aires and the Litoral provinces. Justo José de Urquiza and Anacarsis Lanús were only two out of a great many men who grew rich as purveyors of livestock and supplies to the Allied armies. The profits earned by Bonaerense oligarchs helped bolster the national government, which took advantage of Brazil's obsession with Paraguay to consolidate power in the Argentine Interior and to strengthen the hand of the army. The *provincianos* witnessed a few final gasps in defense of their Federalist ideals and then gave way as their old quest for coequality with Buenos Aires faded.[4]

The tone of leadership—and the political direction in general—within the Argentine national government changed drastically as a result of the war. Bartolomé Mitre had acted as the booster of pro-Brazilian policies in the Plata.

He had supported the Triple Alliance as the best way forward for Argentina and after the Marshal's defeat, he sought to reinforce good relations with Brazil. To that end, he went to Rio de Janeiro as ambassador in the mid-1870s, and though he got on well with the emperor, he lost the support of imperial officials who argued that Argentina could no longer be trusted.[5]

Rejected as a suitor, Mitre searched for solace once again in Argentine national politics and was rejected there as well. More so than he had anticipated, his country was evolving. Mass immigration started to offer a bridge between the Creole regime of the past and the cosmopolitan nation of the future. Its promoters perceived European immigration as a eugenic solution for the nation's social ills, for, by replacing gauchos and "Indians" with "good European stock," the country could finally become the more "civilized" nation that Sarmiento had heralded. And indeed, by introducing barbed wire to the Pampas, sowing the grasslands with cereals for export, mechanizing the processing of beef, and building railroads, Argentina transformed itself into a terrible yet wonderful exemplar of "Progress" that José Hernández decried and that Mitre thought of as his life's work.[6]

Though the former head of state could take credit for many of these changes, he was increasingly out of step in the new environment. President Nicolás Avellaneda had the foresight to pardon Mitre after an ill-considered rebellion in the 1870s, but the old president could never forgive his successors for ignoring him. He focused on operating *La Nación*, still one of the country's great newspapers, and to some extent, he played the role of godfather to anyone who might listen to his counsel. But Mitre's life proved unfulfilling. His closest friends died before him, as did his wife, and several of his children (one of his sons a suicide). With each death, the bright spark that politics had once provided grew dimmer.

Mitre found solace in writing and in his magnificent home library. From the early 1880s onward, likely as not he could be found at any hour of the day wearing a stained frock coat and sitting, pen in hand, behind a rampart of books. They were his true friends, unwavering in their loyalty. As he aged, Mitre appeared less as the revered founder of a Liberal Argentina than as an eccentric collator of historical details, a *talmudiste manqué*. He wrote classic biographies of his heroes Belgrano and San Martín, received scientific delegations on occasion, and even dabbled in poetry.[7]

For a long time Mitre kept his opinions about the Paraguayan campaign to himself; he emerged from self-imposed silence only in 1903, when Brazilian veterans published a series of jeremiads questioning his effectiveness as Allied commander. He responded by releasing the *Memoria militar* that he had prepared for Caxias in September 1867, in which he defended his actions in his usual sharp-witted way. He then retired quietly to his library and died three years later, still haunted by memories of Paraguay and a thousand unrealized dreams.

Despite his frequent evocation of a happy future for Argentina, Domingo Faustino Sarmiento considered himself a personal failure after he left the presidency in 1872. He had to bear the responsibility for war-related debts that others had accumulated, and he grew bitter about this and much else. He wrote scathing articles about his political opponents, theorized about racial matters (while bemoaning the pluralistic society), and held his face in a perpetual grimace. Visions of Dominguito bleeding into the soil at Curupayty disturbed his nightly rest. Sarmiento ultimately died as a carbuncle-ridden exile in Asunción—of all places—sitting in a high-back chair suitable to a schoolmaster, alone and unmourned.

Like Argentina, the Empire of Brazil saw its political destinies change along with the character of its nationalism, even though these changes were endorsed with the greatest reluctance by traditional power brokers. Among the most influential (and most conservative) of these men was Caxias, the "Duke of Iron," who returned to political life in Rio in a state of public grace and private disdain. Six months after Cerro Corã, the Imperial Senate appointed him to the Council of State, and he retained that position while serving as senator. His refusal to pursue López after Lomas Valentinas was forgotten, and, in 1875, the emperor convinced the reluctant general to accept the prime ministry for a third time. Unlike Zacharias, Itaboraí, and Paranhos, he made few innovations, leaving the more ticklish affairs of government to younger colleagues. He stepped down in January 1878, leaving the reins of power to his Liberal adversaries, and died two years later, predeceasing the empire he had done so much to defend by less than a decade.

Though he spent the war years at some distance from actual combat, the duke's Imperial Master was also worn down by the Paraguayan War, which he had always seen as a matter of honor. As Liliana Moritz Schwarcz and John Gledson observed,

> At the beginning of the war, when he was forty, with his sturdy demeanor and uniform, Dom Pedro II presented the picture of a serene and confident ruler. ... At the time of the great battles, [he] was portrayed as a soldier in trying circumstances: after all, Brazil had spent 600,000 *contos* and worsened its financial dependence on Great Britain. Its leader, on horseback ... carrying a small spyglass with a battle scene behind him ... or surrounded by children, was a monarch symbolizing the nation at war. Yet the calm and tranquility with which the photos try to impress us cannot hide the real anxiety. Dom Pedro's famous beard ... was whitening in front of everyone's eyes, and the now well-known image of the old man, by which he is still recognized in Brazil ... was emerging. ...

> [The] official photographs hide the unease of a king who has gone
> to war ... and seen the less brilliant side of his Empire.[8]

Notwithstanding his physical decline, dom Pedro persevered, and for a long time few thrones appeared more secure. His reign might have lasted his entire lifetime if not for a certain lassitude that he took few pains to disguise. Inattentive to the temper of the new generation, the emperor failed to keep up with the times, and found himself constantly reacting to political challenges rather than initiating reforms. He grew tired of defending the monarchy with the same alacrity with which he pursued the campaign against López, and he failed to recognize that meaningful disenchantment had set in among military officers whose identities had been shaped by the war. These individuals (not all of whom were Positivists) refused to resume their status as nonentities and took umbrage when their sacrifices were discounted.

After Cerro Corã, most Brazilian soldiers returned home to a rousing welcome from the public.[9] From the imperial government, however, they perceived a certain worry—justified as it turned out—that men in uniform had gained an outsized prominence while in Paraguay. Now that the war was won, the parliamentarians sought to put the military genie back into the bottle through a series of demeaning gestures and budget cuts. It could be argued that the latter changes reflected normal adjustments to postwar conditions, but the military men nonetheless took offense at what seemed like calculated disrespect. One who expressed irritation was the Count d'Eu, who protested vociferously at any intimation that slighted the armed forces.[10] As an institution, the military swallowed its pride, but many officers in the middle ranks never forgot the rude treatment. Their thinking was henceforth defined more by their loyalty to the nation than to Pedro himself—and this was presumably true of their civilian supporters (including the thirty thousand soldiers who now returned to civilian life).[11] The military men believed, as presumably the monarch did not, that they would soon transform Brazil.

Before the war, the men of the armed forces recognized that though they already had a Brazil to defend, as yet they had no Brazilians. The war gave concrete meaning to Brazilian nationalism, however, and with total casualties amounting to sixty thousand dead and wounded, the state badly needed to justify their sacrifice.[12] Officers of humble origin had found considerable authority in Paraguay and discovered that they liked it. They had little interest in going back to the insignificant role of earlier days—and neither had their men. The Paulista, Carioca, Sertanejo, and Gaúcho soldiers developed a bond of unity in the trenches. The monarchy was only incidental to that cohesion. Now, in building a new military and ostensibly a new nation, they would need to be just as dedicated as the Paraguayans had been in defending their native soil.

The emperor had insisted on dictating the peace in Paraguay rather than negotiating it, but this preference had cost him dearly.[13] Paying off the various loans from foreign banks contributed to ongoing budgetary problems in the 1870s. As was true in Argentina, however, the Paraguayan War also stimulated the most modern economic sectors, and it helped spur the construction of Brazilian rail and port facilities. All of this strengthened the planter aristocracy at a time when coffee inspired a major export boom.

To keep pace with the growing economy, highly placed civilians proposed important political reforms. Unlike the junior officers, they contemplated these adjustments from within the confines of established procedure and with due deference to the emperor's opinions. This inclination was most obvious among the Liberals, who had suffered in Caxias's fait accompli of February 1868. In recovering from that blow, they sponsored decentralization, direct elections, the conversion of the Council of State into an exclusively administrative organ, the abolition of life tenure in the Senate, judicial autonomy, the extension of the franchise to non-Catholics, a new structure for public education, and the gradual emancipation of slaves.

This platform, though still avowedly monarchist, in fact weakened the established order, as can be seen in the subsequent career of Paranhos. After departing Paraguay in June 1870, the councilor was ennobled as the Viscount of Rio Branco and took office shortly thereafter as prime minister. Though his four-year administration generally received the same plaudits that he had earned in Asunción, he found that he could govern effectively only by ignoring his old associates, which, unfortunately, increased factionalism in the Conservative Party. In 1871, Paranhos oversaw the passage of the controversial Free Womb Law, which assured the ultimate elimination of Brazilian slavery.[14] Along with Caxias, he defended the emperor during his confrontation with the church in the 1870s, and worked hand in hand with the Liberals to keep the more radical politicians at bay during his time in office. He continued to enjoy public esteem after he stepped down in 1875, though parliamentarians of a younger generation sniggered at him behind his back.

The viscount had always enjoyed imported Havana cigars, and in retirement, his smoking habit led to cancer of the mouth. The painful affliction prevented his speaking with the customary lucidity and eloquence; it did not, however, stop him from quarreling with his son, whose public relation with a Belgian actress irked the elder Paranhos as much as López's antics had done in an earlier day. A statesman of the highest rank who aspired to a visionary role among Brazilians, he ended his days in petty bickering, trying with hand gestures to make himself understood.[15]

The changes that the Paraguayan War inspired and that Paranhos and the Liberals supported crept steadily into the body politic in Brazil. The process culminated in Princess Isabel's emancipation decree of 1888. Several of the system's staunchest defenders had already died or distanced themselves from governance, visibly spent by the unending political debates. The process of dissolution that in some ways commenced on the battlefields of Paraguay culminated in a military takeover in 1889, when Pedro was deposed and a nominal republic established. Broken, it seems, by the weight of events and the ingratitude of people whose loyalty he had taken for granted, the emperor sailed for Europe. He declined compensation for the properties that the new regime had seized and died in a Paris hotel in 1891.

Prince Gaston lived to see the various republican prohibitions against the imperial family lifted in the early twentieth century. He had spent thirty years in exile from his adopted fatherland, maintaining always his affection for Isabel and his fealty to the Bragança monarchy that she embodied. For her part, Isabel felt that the abolition of slavery had been worth the loss of a throne. Some Brazilians, their eyes clouded with nostalgia, increasingly saw her actions in that same patriotic light, and as for her foreign husband, he was not such a bad Frenchman after all.[16] In fact, well-wishers showered him with respect when, in January 1921, he disembarked at Rio de Janeiro, having escorted the bodies of dom Pedro and his empress on their long voyage home for final interment. Isabel, then virtually bedridden, could not accompany him, but she expressed satisfaction at the news of his enthusiastic reception. She died soon thereafter, having lived just long enough to celebrate the fifty-seventh anniversary of their marriage. The count survived her by less than a year. Invited back to the old imperial capital to attend the centennial celebration of Brazilian independence, he died at sea on 28 August 1922.[17] It seemed a fitting end for the man, caught so precariously between many allegiances to Old and New Worlds, and very distant indeed from the accusatory stares of Paraguayan phantoms.

For its part, Uruguay had entered the struggle against López as compensation for Brazilian aid to the Florista faction of the Colorado Party. The deaths of Colonel León de Palleja and a great many others assured payment on that debt, and the Uruguayans waited for some recompense now that the war had finally been won at Cerro Corã. This proved a vain hope, and in the end Uruguay had to be satisfied with a share of the battle flags in exchange for an expenditure of 6 million dollars and the lives of 3,119 men (out of a contingent of 5,583).[18] Unlike Brazil and Argentina, which witnessed the birth of nationalist sentiments as a result of the war, Uruguay experienced no comparable outburst of patriotism. The Uruguayans had to wait until the early 1880s for their measure of national affirmation, when dictator Lorenzo Latorre issued primers for schoolchildren that ascribed an improbable nationalist sympathy to José Gervasio Artigas.[19] This set the stage for the development of a full-blown Uruguayan national identity by the beginning of the 1900s—an identity that regretted the country's participation in the Triple Alliance War and refused to look upon it as a catalyst for anything healthy.

Neither the Argentines nor the Brazilians ever developed a dispassionate view of Paraguay, preferring to see the country as an historical aberration. The two wartime allies did find more ways to get along than either would have thought possible in 1869.[20] Yet when it came to negotiating a peace treaty with the defeated nation, the Brazilians preempted Buenos Aires and settled with the triumvirs not as a part of the Alliance, but as a separate government with separate interests. The Argentines feigned surprise at this decision but they had expected it all along.[21] A rapprochement of sorts occurred between the former Allies only in 1876, when the Brazilian occupation forces were withdrawn from Paraguay. But long-term trust was another matter.

In Paraguay itself, no one could ignore the war's effects. The nation was abused economically and politically, and the only thing that the triumvirs were really sure of was that they wanted no new López to ruin their lives once again. The provisional government made no comment when senior officials of the ancien régime were transported as prisoners to Rio de Janeiro, but protested loudly when Madame Lynch arrived at the Asunción quay in late March aboard the warship *Princesa*. Rivarola, who had already embargoed the López family's properties, upheld the petition of ninety Asuncenas that held that la Madama had stolen a quantity of jewels and that these must be returned to their rightful owners before she could be permitted to land.[22] The charge, which Lynch dismissed as slander, overstated how much property she had in her baggage and implicitly censured the Brazilians for their mock chivalry in protecting her. Paranhos dismissed the matter as trivial and Madame Lynch continued downriver. In May, the triumvirs toyed with the idea of bringing criminal charges against her, but by now she had reached Buenos Aires and would soon leave South America altogether. She returned only once, in 1875, but had no success in clearing her name or regaining any of her properties.[23]

Castigating Lynch was a popular move and cost the Paraguayan government nothing.[24] The fear of annihilation that López had so skillfully drummed into the heads of his countrymen had already dissipated. The appetite for brutality and indiscipline that the Brazilian troops had shown at Piribebuy was not repeated after 1870. To those Allied spokesmen who insisted that their soldiers had had clean hands, however, the Paraguayans could observe that there were few adult men left to murder. The great question now was simple survival. That much was obvious to every foreigner who passed through the country during the 1870s. Without exception, they felt jolted by the dire poverty and the mutilation of civil society. Like Richard Burton, these outsiders had not seen the earlier combat, but they reacted with horror and curiosity at the devastation they saw in its aftermath.[25]

One need not indulge in Paraguayan exceptionalism to point out the tremendous price the nation and its people paid during the war. The republic did not disintegrate over the next decade, as many citizens had feared, but its economy more or less collapsed. Ninety-nine percent of Paraguayan cattle were lost, and farming recovered only slowly.[26] In addition, Paraguay agreed to Allied claims on 55,000 square miles of disputed territory and was also assessed an impossibly huge indemnity.[27] The nation was gutted. It was one thing to see disabled veterans selling matches in the streets, just barely surviving "in a world that didn't care"; such sights were common in Rio, Montevideo, and Buenos Aires as well. It was quite another matter, however, to visit towns in the Paraguayan Cordillera that had no adult males, or to walk the streets of Luque, where women outnumbered men twenty to one.[28]

The demographic costs of the war were painful and obvious. Paraguay lost upwards of two hundred fifty thousand men, women, and children during the conflict, the great majority of whom died not as a result of combat but of disease and starvation.[29] In fact, the country enjoys the dubious distinction of having experienced the highest rate of civilian and military loss of life recorded in any modern war.[30] The fatalities were so high that the numbers horrified all foreign visitors and challenged the demographers of a later generation to provide convincing explanations for what happened.[31]

Rivarola and the other members of the provisional government clearly grasped the scale of the problem. The economic deterioration that accompanied the demographic collapse was the central fact of their time and the triumvirs recognized their inability to do much about it. The treasury was in de facto insolvency and the Allies' decision to demand a heavy indemnity promised no quick solution for Paraguay's economic woes. So the triumvirs pushed ahead with the political questions at hand. They had promised to hold a constituent assembly to determine the future structure of government, and in August 1870 they delivered on that promise.[32] The assembly, which met a total of eighty-three times, was inaugurated by Carlos Loizaga acting as representative of the triumvirs. In florid oratory, he denounced the dictatorships of the past—those monstrosities that had delivered the Paraguayan people to "the criminal passion of tyrants."[33] He promised in their place a nation founded in liberty. Whereas previous assemblies had subordinated themselves to the will of a despot, from now on, the government would reflect the public will.

It was not to be. Over the next four months, the assembled politicians produced a document that hid relevant issues behind a cloud of platitudes. The writing in the constitution drew largely from Argentine precedents. Yet never was a country so ill-prepared to learn from Alberdi's notions of nationhood as Paraguay in 1870. The assembly organized a bicameral structure of government when no need for a senate was convincingly demonstrated. The "Carta Magna," the politicians claimed, was guaranteed by popular support in the streets and legal checks within the halls of government—but no one understood what these checks might consist of. In the end, the political model they adopted guaranteed the celebration of the Argentine national holiday, 25 May, as Paraguay's own, and made it possible to dedicate the reborn nation to the modern age by prohibiting the use of Guaraní in public schools.

There was something surreal in this outcome. The assembly's deliberations had been accompanied by the worst pettifoggery. Belying their claim of devotion to proper procedure, the representatives plotted, made momentary alliances, and broke them as opportunity allowed. They treated each other with the same venom that the Marshal had reserved for the kambáes. At one point, the representatives even removed Cirilo Antonio Rivarola from the presidency of the triumvirate, only to bring him back again with the help of the Brazilian army.

The constitution of 1870 guaranteed no meaningful stability and the rest of the decade saw little improvement in the country's governance. Coups, counter-coups, and assassinations disgraced the Paraguayan scene right up to (and after) 1879, when the last Allied military force in the country—an Argentine garrison at Villa Occidental—finally withdrew. Throughout this time, the mass of Paraguayans never showed any meaningful resistance to the occupiers. But they were never empowered by their own government either, except as part of a confidence trick to purchase votes for a cup of caña.[34]

The Brazilians had released five hundred prisoners of war in November 1870, and these rough-and-ready boy-soldiers added their resentments to the political mix, sometimes siding with the "Liberals," sometimes with the "Traditionalists," and sometimes, it seemed, with both at the same time. The Brazilians also permitted the return to Paraguay of key Lopista officials like Caballero, Maíz, Escobar, Aveiro, and Centurión.[35] This coterie of veterans—a veritable who's who of Lopistas—ultimately supported the pretensions of Cándido Bareiro. They helped ease him into office as president in 1878, and when he died, they replaced him at the center of power.

By the end of the 1870s, the rural generals who had so assiduously supported López, and whose careers were formed by the struggle against the Triple Alliance, were firmly in power. Though Caballero, Escobar, and the others had benefited from the Marshal's patronage, they had no interest in a similar pursuit of national grandeur. Instead they devoted their energies to suppressing the Liberal heirs of their old opponents, and in profit-making in an "open" economy based on the export of yerba and *quebracho* wood. They also enriched themselves from the sale of thousands of hectares of state lands.

Looked at individually, the petty intrigues that made up their political work and the rackets they constructed merit little attention. Behind them, however, lay the more general goal of reconstructing the social barriers that had separated Paraguayans into classes during the colonial era. These had been weakened, first by the Marshal's explicit appeal to the peasantry to help him fight the war, and second, by the dramatic population shift in its aftermath. The new leaders felt no specific desire to turn the clock back. But under the guise of a nominal republicanism they asserted a claim to a traditional authority that might otherwise have shifted to poor Paraguayans demanding a greater right over their own lives. This, as much as anything, is why the Traditionalists—soon to be reconfigured within the ranks of the Colorado Party—chose some years later to turn Francisco Solano López into a national symbol.

It would be senseless to describe the Triple Alliance War without giving primacy to the Marshal and almost as difficult to categorize the subsequent period without alluding to his ghost. In life, López relished idolatry. In death, his name eventually subsumed his people's sacrifice, a development that occasioned many ironies and contradictions. The historical López, for instance, had always taken to his heels whenever danger threatened his personal safety. On such occasions, he never hesitated to abandon his men (or, for that matter, his family members) to face the wrath of the Brazilians.

In answer to any charge of cowardice, however, the Marshal could argue that his survival was indispensable, for without him, the Paraguayan nation would perish. This was not such a far-fetched idea. Chris Leuchars has pointed out that though Paraguay eventually lost a great swath of its territory to Argentina and Brazil, the amount was less land than the two countries had earlier demanded.[36] Had the Allies not formally agreed on 1 May 1865 to respect Paraguayan independence, they might have adopted an annexationist line, under which the country would have vanished like Poland in the eighteenth century. In this one narrow—and admittedly hypothetical sense—López stood out as a staunch defender of his country's interests.

It is one thing to stand firm in favor of one's nation and quite another to pass muster as a general. Though the Marshal's hagiographers have repeatedly stressed his military genius, they have never really made a convincing case.[37] López chose to invade Mato Grosso in 1864 and thereby spurned the opportunity to rescue the Uruguayan Blancos. He made Argentina an enemy when many in the Buenos Aires government were prepared to keep their country neutral. The Marshal's attack on Corrientes thus facilitated the signing of an unlikely military alliance that came perilously close to destroying Paraguay.

López then needlessly delayed his naval attack at Riachuelo until the Brazilians could counter it effectively, and he kept his land forces in Corrientes so far apart that they could never offer mutual support. He withdrew what remained of his army in Argentina before the units were effectively tested, and he later abandoned excellent defensive positions at Tuyutí to pursue a risky offensive strike. Perhaps worst of all, he never trusted his field commanders to do the right thing, even when circumstances favored their success. These were not the marks of a good commander, and where the Paraguayans succeeded militarily, they did so in spite of the Marshal's direction rather than because of it.

That said, much about López remains elusive. Even careful scholars can stumble while trying to separate the man from the marble that has been built around him. A good many historians have not even tried to find the human being in the history; they seem to prefer the rigid and artificial distinctions forged by Lopistas and anti-Lopistas to any careful consideration of the past.

The Marshal's Paraguayan detractors, mostly affiliated with the Liberal Party from the late 1800s onwards, regarded him as an unparalleled monster whose vanity required the extinction of his people. In their world of black and white, they painted him as darker than dark and his followers as little better than fools or barbarians.[38] On one occasion in 1898, for instance, a stationary store in the capital fomented a minor scandal when it marketed notebooks emblazoned with the Marshal's image. Their sale inspired a nasty confrontation when the Argentine director of the normal school refused to permit students to bring them to class. The police had to save the director when a mob of angry Lopistas threatened his life.[39]

An element of self-reproach has always suggested itself in the anti-Lopista interpretation, for how do such critics justify their opposition when the Paraguayan masses offered the Marshal so much during the worst of times? How do the Liberals, for that matter, explain their own recourse to authoritarian methods during the twentieth century?

There is no mystery in any of this for the nationalists, who depicted López as the personification of Paraguayan virtues—courage, constancy, and unquestioned defense of the fatherland. To Juan E. O'Leary and the others he was the *heroe máximo* and his war *la gran epopeya*, something beautiful and infinitely reaffirming.[40] The example of Francisco Solano López, they tell us, stirred the young men of 1932, who, when sent to fight the Bolivians in the thorn forests of the Chaco, showed the same grit as their grandfathers, and came back three years later singing Guaraní war songs and cheering the name of the Marshal. Their creation of a radical Febrerista Party, and then, under Natalício González, of a quasi-fascist wing of the Colorados, came about as a result of this inspiration. It was almost as if the Marshal's defeat and their own generation's victory gushed from the same spiritual fountain. They ultimately depicted authoritarianism in Paraguay as a benign and civilizing force, an assertion that brought them the patronage of dictators like Higínio Morínigo and Alfredo Stroessner.

People often show a great need for mythology, and whether they feel guided by nostalgia or the dictates of state interest, they take refuge in bygone days when the alternative is to wallow in the mundane and disappointing present. Stephen of Byzantium, writing in the sixth century, observed that mythology is "what never was but always is."[41] So it was with the various renderings of the Paraguayan War to appear during the 1900s. Today's Paraguayans are living through another reordering of these hero stories to fit the challenges posed by Brazilian economic dominance in the twenty-first century. In contemplating the earlier sacrifices, modern Paraguayans take no pleasure in the idea of a glorious precedent because they think it is true (or worthy of emulation): they think that it is true because they take pleasure in it.[42]

Such mythmaking and rank obfuscation is unfair to those who lived through the Triple Alliance War. Their concept of nationalism was not the product of López's heavy hand—indeed it only incidentally reflected his influence. From colonial times, the Paraguayans held deeply engrained notions about the need to protect the community from invaders. It mattered little whether those enemies were Brazilian soldiers, Porteño sutlers, or Guaicurú marauders.

The Paraguayans' zeal was genuine, their devotion to the fatherland—as they understood it—compelling. The Allies had always found it difficult to smirk at Paraguayan self-reliance, but to label it as the product of Lopista tyranny clearly misrepresented the facts. The majority of the people seemed ready to sacrifice themselves wholeheartedly, no matter what obstacles stood in the way. All of this suggests that we conclude this examination of the war with a requiem. It is painful to contemplate the trials of the Paraguayan people, for even those who survived were plagued with nightmares of gangrenous limbs, empty stomachs, and dead family members. For such individuals, the Paraguayan War never ended. They gave their lives, their property, and their hearts, and whether they couched the memories of their sacrifice in terms of courage or of fear, the war continued to consume them.

Notes

INTRODUCTION

1   Tulio Halperín Donghi, *The Aftermath of Revolution in Latin America* (New York, 1973).

2   Cecilio Báez, *La tiranía en el Paraguay* (Asunción, 1993); Cecilio Báez, *Ensayo sobre el doctor Francia y la dictadura en Sudamérica* (Asunción, 1996); Efraím Cardozo, *El sentido de nuestra historia* (Asunción, 1953).

3   Julio César Chaves, *El supremo dictador, Biografía de José Gaspar de Francia* (Madrid, 1964); Julio César Chaves, *El presidente López* (Buenos Aires, 1968).

4   Paraguayan historiography of the war has traditionally been divided into Lopista and Anti-Lopista camps. Though the dichotomy would seem to have grown stale long ago, it is still adhered to by many. Among the most significant Lopista works are Juan E. O'Leary, *El héroe del Paraguay* (Montevideo, 1930); *El mariscal Solano López* (Asunción, 1970); *El libro de los héroes* (Asunción, 1970); Arturo Bray, *Solano López. Soldado de la gloria y el infortunio* (Asunción and Buenos Aires, 1958); Carlos Pereyra, *Francisco Solano López y la guerra del Paraguay* (Buenos Aires, 1953); and Natalício González, *Solano López y otros ensayos* (Paris, 1926). The most noteworthy Anti-Lopista works include Héctor Decoud, *Sobre los escombros de la guerra: una década de vida nacional, 1869-1880* (Asunción, 1925); *La masacre de Concepción ordenada por el mariscal López* (Asunción, 1926); Cecilio Báez, *La tiranía*; and Jacinto V. Vicencio, *Dictadura del mariscal López* (Buenos Aires, 1874).

5   By the end of the 1840s, merchants in Buenos Aires, Montevideo, and Rio de Janeiro were all pressuring their respective governments to at least investigate better commercial and diplomatic relations with the "famed fairy-land of Paraguay, so long guarded by that wondrous ogre, Francia." See William Hadfield, *Brazil, the River Plate, and the Falkland Islands* (London, 1854), 305, and more generally, Thomas L. Whigham, *The Politics of River Trade. Tradition and Development in the Upper Plata, 1780-1870* (Albuquerque, 1991), 30-79.

6   Pablo Max Ynsfrán, *La expedición norteamericana contra el Paraguay*, 2 vols. (Mexico City and Buenos Aires, 1954-1958); Thomas Jefferson Page, *La Plata, the Argentine Confederation, and Paraguay* (New York, 1859), 271-287; Manuel Peña Villamil, *Historia de la diplomacia y las relaciones internacionales* (Asunción, 2000), 297- 304; Peter A. Schmitt, *Paraguay und Europa. Die diplomatischen Beziehungen unter Carlos Antonio López und Francisco Solano López* (Berlin, 1963), 89-237.

7   Thomas L. Whigham, *The Paraguayan War. Causes and Early Conduct* (Lincoln and London, 2002), 175–189.

8   Bray, *Solano López*, 132–136; Juan E. O'Leary, *El Paraguay en la unificación argentina* (Asunción, 1924).

9   Whigham, *Paraguayan War*, 139–144.

10   For revisionist historians like León Pomer, the supply of these arms was part of Mitre's broader plan to instigate a war on Paraguay. To summarize this curious interpretation: Mitre sent Flores into the Banda Oriental in 1863 with the idea that his presence would inspire a civil war between the Colorados and the Blanco government in Montevideo. The fighting would then aggravate the Riograndense ranchers, who would respond by calling on the empire to intervene in favor of the Colorados. Lacking outside support, the Blancos would have no option but to turn to Solano López for aid, whereupon Mitre's government—most regrettably—would join forces with Brazil in an ugly, but ultimately victorious, campaign against Paraguay. Argentina would emerge triumphant from this struggle, as would Mitre's capitalist friends in Great Britain. See León Pomer, *La guerra del Paraguay. ¡Gran negocio!* (Buenos Aires, 1968). If Mitre, in fact, had foreseen this sequence of events, he would not merely have been a political genius—he would have been a seer. What Pomer and other revisionists have never explained in all this bizarre assertion is why the national government in Buenos Aires would want to see the development of a conflict in which it would have so much to lose and so little to gain.

11   Foreign Minister José Berges to Cesar Vianna de Lima, Asunción, 30 August 1864, ANA-CRB I-30, 24, 26.

12   George Thompson, *The War in Paraguay* (London, 1869), 25.

13   Thompson, *The War in Paraguay*, 100.

14   The two men who had carried the smallpox into Paraguay were beaten until they confessed that they had been sent by Argentine president Mitre. Afterwards, they were flogged to death. See Thompson, *The War in Paraguay*, 115

15   In asking the question, "How Long Will the War Last?," the English-language *Standard* of Buenos Aires admitted to considerable frustration, implicitly blaming López and the Allied chiefs, and observing that the "war with Paraguay [was] a personal war, such as that which England waged against Napoleon, but we confess we look over the map of Paraguay with anxiety to discover the whereabouts of the future Waterloo." *The Standard*, 6 February 1866.

16   George F. Masterman, *Seven Eventful Years in Paraguay* (London, 1869), 110–11. In fact, summary executions for grumbling or utterances of defeatism became commonplace in the Paraguayan army in the months following the retreat from Corrientes. See, for example, Order for the Execution by Firing Squad of Captain José María Rodríguez, Paso de la Patria, 6 January 1866, ANA-SJC, vol. 1723.

17   The contempt that the Marshal felt for his people was palpable but hardly novel. In fact, he drew much of this negative sentiment from his father, and from José Gaspar Rodríguez de Francia, who ruled Paraguay as dictator between 1814 and 1840. Francia once notoriously remarked that the Paraguayans must lack the requisite number of bones in the neck, for none would lift their heads to look him in the face. See Johann Rudolph Rengger and Marcel Longchamps, *The Reign of Doctor Joseph Gaspard Roderick de Francia, in Paraguay; Being an Account of a Six Year's Residence in that Republic, from July 1819 to May 1825* (London, 1827), 202. This tale of a missing neck bone has made its way into the modern political folklore in the country, where pundits still allude to it as an explanation for the poor inroads that democracy has thus far made in Paraguay. See Helio Vera, *En busca del hueso perdido; tratado de paraguayología* (Asunción, 1990).

18 Charles Ames Washburn to William Seward, Corrientes, 8 February 1865, NARA, M-128, no. 1.

19 The Allies circulated a rumor that López had convinced his soldiers that whomsoever should die in combat for the fatherland would find himself reborn in Asunción. This ludicrous tale, which suggested that for the rural soldiers the capital city could substitute for the Elysian fields, spun misconceptions of Paraguayan society beyond all measure or patience. The rumor first appeared in print in *El Nacional* (Buenos Aires) in its issue of 6 February 1866, and was repeated (with an improbable attribution to the Bishop of Paraguay) in the *New York Times* on 13 July 1866.

20 A surprising number of the letters they wrote home still survive in the Archivo Nacional de Asunción. See, for instance, Francisco Cabrizas to Juan Y. Cabrizas, Paso de la Patria, 1 January 1866, ANA-NE 3273.

21 Every town and village in the country donated money and food for the hospitals, Humaitá, and the other military camps; only inadequate transport inhibited these supplies from getting to the troops right away. See, for example, "Actas de patriotismo y filanthropía," *Semanario de Avisos y Conocimientos Utiles* (Asunción), 13 January 1866. (Henceforth *El Semanario*.)

22 Richard Burton, *Letters from the Battle-fields of Paraguay* (London, 1870), 300.

23 Lista mayor… del ejército en el Sud. Paso de la Patria, 19 January 1866, MHM (A), Colección Gill Aguinaga, carpeta 63, no. 2.

24 Efraím Cardozo, *Hace cien años* (Asunción, 1970), 3: 11.

25 Most of the animals expired from exhaustion and inadequate pasturage right after gaining the Paraguayan bank of the river; a good many others died soon thereafter from eating a poisonous shrub that local cattle had long since learned to avoid. See Thompson, *War in Paraguay*, 97.

26 One unit within the Uruguayan contingent had so little food and equipment that by early December its commander was begging Mitre to incorporate the unit into the Argentine force. See Venancio Flores to Mitre, Ytacuaty, 8 December 1865, MHM, CZ, carpeta 150, no. 33.

27 Marcelino Reyes, *Bosquejo histórico de la provincia de La Rioja, 1543-1867* (Buenos Aires, 1913), 232.

28 André Rebouças, "Projeito para a Pronta Conclusão da Campanha contra o Paraguay," 9 September 1865, Arquivo Nacional (Rio de Janeiro), 9714983, lata 48 (Arquivo Particular do General Polidoro da Fonseca Quintanilha Jordão, Visconde de Santa Teresa).

29 In 1849, the Spanish minister in Montevideo noted the opinion of the famous French naturalist Aimé Bonpland, who thought that the Paraguayans could already field an army of twenty thousand soldiers "so brutally docile and disciplined that they [seemed] more like Russians or Prussians than soldiers hailing from a southern nation." See "Carlos Creus to Spanish government, Montevideo, 29 September 1849," in "Informes diplomáticos de los representantes de España en el Uruguay," *Revista Histórica* (Montevideo), nos. 139-41, 47 (1975), 854.

30 "Proclamation of Mitre, Buenos Aires, 16 April 1865," in *La Nación Argentina* (Buenos Aires), 17-18 April 1865.

31 For examples, see Hendrik Kraay, "Patriotic Mobilization in Brazil: the Zuavos and Other Black Companies in the Paraguayan War, 1865-70," in *I Die with My Country. Perspectives on the Paraguayan War*, Hendrik Kraay and Thomas L. Whigham, eds. (Lincoln and London, 2004), 61-80.

32 When shorn of its dubious Lamarckian inclinations, the classic work of Euclydes da Cunha, *Rebellion in the Backlands* (Chicago, 1957), 148, is still useful in understanding the earlier jagunço society of the Brazilian northeast.

33 Pomer, *La Guerra del Paraguay*, 340.

34 Juan Manuel Casal, "Uruguay and the Paraguayan War: the Military Dimension," in Kraay and Whigham, *I Die with My Country*, 119–139.

1 | THE ARMIES INVADE

1 Regarding life in the Allied camps, see Thomas Whigham, *La guerra de la Triple Alianza*, vol. 2, *El triunfo de la violencia, el fracaso de la paz* (Asunción, 2011), 271–287.

2 See, for example, Juan M. Serrano to Martín de Gainza, Ensenaditas, 7 January 1866, Museo Histórico Nacional (Buenos Aires), legajo 10613; Evangelista de Castro Dionísio Cerqueira, *Reminiscencias da Campanha do Paraguai, 1865–70* (Rio de Janeiro, 1948), 121.

3 Charles Ames Washburn to William H. Seward, Corrientes, 1 February 1866, WNL. (The Washburn-Norlands Library's collection of materials on Paraguay, while extensive, remains unorganized, a fact that will present problems to researchers seeking quick access to specific documents.) Other sources give a total number of Brazilian troops in the sector at between thirty and thirty-five thousand.

4 The Brazilian troops received some one hundred thousand sovereigns in salary by mid-January, so they had enough cash to spend on trifles. See *The Standard* (Buenos Aires), 10 January 1866. Even so, there were thieves among the men who stole more than an occasional head of cattle; on one occasion, the Hotel Dos Aliados was relieved of several hundred pesos, and quite a few Correntino homes were burglarized at the beginning of the Allied occupation. See Police Chief Juan J. Blanco to Provincial Minister Fernando Arias, Corrientes, 26 January 1866 (Concerning the arrest of a mixed gang of Argentine and Brazilian thieves), AGPC-CO 213, folio 39.

5 *Diário do Rio de Janeiro*, 21 March 1866.

6 Comments of John LeLong, *The Standard* (Buenos Aires), 10 January 1866.

7 "Sindbad," of *The Standard* (in the 8 March issue), noted that "street broils that invariably terminate in bloodshed are not noticed either by the police or the newspapers, so much have they become matters of course. Homicides and other crimes are perpetrated, which would call forth second editions and double-sheets in your papers, and not the slightest notice is taken thus much [*sic*] for progress and the march of intellect!" A month later things had not improved, if we are to judge by the words of one anonymous observer who noted that "the most open robbery is going on in Corrientes [with] Brazilian soldiers offering to sell officers swords for a Bolivian [peso], revolvers for two or three dollars, and even their very uniforms. No Argentine troops [are] in Corrientes, but crimes are committed every night." *The Standard* (Buenos Aires), 12 April 1866.

8 "Francisco M. Paz to Marcos Paz, Corrientes, 24 January 1866," in *Archivo del Coronel Dr. Marcos Paz* (La Plata, 1964), 5: 37; a half-dozen recalcitrant opponents of the war found themselves shut up in the *calabosos* of Corrientes, charged with being guilty of "incivism." *The Standard* (Buenos Aires), 17 January 1866.

9 *The Standard* (Buenos Aires), 17 January 1866.

10 The 1869 census revealed 415 individuals engaged in trade at the port, of whom 181 were foreigners, including three Swiss, one Austrian, and one Mexican (!). See AGN (BA) Censo 1869, legajos 210–212. To judge from notices placed in the Correntino newspapers, these merchants offered all sorts of goods to the Allied soldiers—even imported swords and dress uniforms were available for purchase. See commercial advertisements

in *El Nacionalista*, (Corrientes), 7 February 1866, and *El Eco de Corrientes*, 31 December 1867.

11 This figure includes the 157 men of the anti-López Paraguayan Legion, but not the Entrerriano artillery units that arrived in February and March. See Juan Beverina, *La guerra del Paraguay* (Buenos Aires, 1921), 3: 646-48, annex 52. A reorganization of the Argentine *Guardia Nacional* at the very end of January 1866 provided twenty-one battalions of infantry, four regiments of cavalry (and some Correntino irregulars), and two units of artillery. See Miguel Angel de Marco, "La guardia nacional argentina en la guerra del Paraguay," *Investigaciones y Ensayos* 3 (1967): 227–228.

12 *The Standard* reported with more optimism than fact that Mitre's "rough levies, who had never fired a musket previously, had arrived on the Paraná as an army of well-trained soldiers." See *The Standard* (Buenos Aires), 6 February 1866.

13 "Bartolomé Mitre to Marcos Paz, Paso de la Patria, 21 January 1866," in *Archivo del Coronel dr. Marcos Paz* (La Plata, 1966), 7: 132–134; Chris Leuchars, *To The Bitter End. Paraguay and the War of the Triple Alliance* (Westport, Connecticut, 2002), 91

14 Jorge Luis Borges captured exactly this sense of things in his 1969 poem "Los gauchos," which celebrates the career of the poet-soldier Hilario Ascasubi:

> They didn't die for this abstract thing, the fatherland, but rather for a
> casual patron, a whim, or at the invitation of danger.
> Their ashes are lost in remote regions of the continent,
> in republics whose history no one knows, in battlefields
> now famous.
> Hilario Ascasubi saw them singing and fighting.
> They lived their destiny like a dream without knowing who they were
> or what they were.
> Maybe the same is true of us.

See Borges, *Obras completas, 1923–1972* (Buenos Aires, 1974), 1001.

15 *The Standard* (Buenos Aires), 10 January 1866; the military history of Corrientes, which reflected the traditional gaucho culture of the Pampas more than it did the peasant-oriented life of Paraguay, has been the subject of considerable attention. See, for instance, Hernán Gómez, *Historia de la provincial de Corrientes. Desde la Revolución de Mayo al tratado del Cuadrilátero* (Corrientes, 1929), and Pablo Buchbinder, "Estado, caudillismo, y organización miliciana en la provincia de Corrientes en el siglo XIX: el caso de Nicanor Cáceres," *Revista de Historia de América* 136 (2005): 37–64.

16 One report from late January held that the "camps of Corrientes are covered with deserters, *peones* who were scarce, are now superabundant, but some cavalry picquets [*sic*] are scouring the country in search of deserters; just as the steamer was leaving, an officer and ten soldiers were brought in, in irons, and tied." *The Standard* (Buenos Aires), 1 February 1866.

17 Cardozo, *Hace cien años*, 3: 44.

18 León de Palleja, *Diário de la campaña de las fuerzas aliadas contra el Paraguay*, (Montevideo, 1960), 2: 10. The Paraguayan prisoners dispatched to Montevideo were all imprisoned in early March when it was rumored that they planned a rebellion together with Blanco partisans. Given the size of both Colorado and Brazilian garrisons in the Uruguayan capital, this rumor would seem to be absurd, but the Paraguayans often faced worse odds, so the story may be more than simple apocrypha, as events two years later seemed to suggest. See *The Standard* (Buenos Aires), 7 March 1866

19 On 25 January 1869, *El Nacional* (Buenos Aires) noted that "at the first sight of Paso de la Patria, they forget the slavery that they had endured, forget the floggings, the cruelties and the injuries of López and his followers, forget the nakedness, the hunger, and every

manner of misery; they likewise forget the commiseration we offered them, the treatment we gave them as comrades and brothers. All this they forget, and vanish [across the river], as if in a dream." See *El Nacional* (Buenos Aires), 25 January 1869. See also Eduardo Acevedo, *Anales históricos del Uruguay* (Montevideo, 1933), 2: 380-382.

20   *El Semanario* (Asunción), 16 December 1865; "Exercise de 5 avril 1866" (French Consul Emile Laurent-Cochelet), in Luc Capdevila, *Variations sur le pays des femmes. Echos d'une guerre américaine (Paraguay, 1864-1870/Temps present)* (Rennes, 2006), 373-374; Depositions of Cándido Franco and Pablo Guzmán, Paso de la Patria, 11 March 1866, ANA-SJC 1797.

21   The Marshal had a considerable fear of assassins, and surrounded himself from the beginning of his presidency with a double, and ultimately a triple, cordon of armed guards. See Thompson, *The War in Paraguay*, 114-115.

22   Memorias de teniente coronel Julian N. Godoy, edecán del mariscal López, Asunción, 13 April 1888, MHN (A), Colección Gill Aguinaga, carpeta 7, no. 3. (Henceforth "Memorias de Julián N. Godoy"). If we are to believe Charles Ames Washburn on this point, the Paraguayan raiders decapitated every Allied soldier who fell into their hands, thus proving to the world that little had changed since "the days of Alva and Torquemada." See Washburn to Seward, Corrientes, 1 February 1866, WNL.

23   *El Semanario* (Asunción), 9 December 1865.

24   This was one of the few times where Francisco Solano López publicly disavowed an atrocity. See "Memorias de Julián N. Godoy."

25   Mitre peevishly noted that the Paraguayans "have made themselves masters of the river with their flotilla of sixty canoes because the Brazilian squadron has no instructions even to advance to the mouth of the Paraguay." See "Mitre to Marcos Paz, Ensenadita, 1 February 1866," in *Archivo del Coronel Dr. Marcos Paz*, 7: 141; *El Pueblo* Buenos Aires, 25 January 1866.

26   *The Standard* (Buenos Aires), 27 February 1866. "Sindbad" was, in fact, John Hayes, an elderly American-born rancher "with much time in Corrientes." See Sallie C. Washburn Diary, 16 March 1866, WNL.

27   In his annotations to Louis Schneider's *A Guerra da Triplice Aliança* (São Paulo, 1945), 2: 43, José María da Silva Paranhos, the Baron of Rio Branco, claimed that López's purpose in launching so many raids was precisely to lure the Brazilians into shallow waters where they might run aground and be shelled by mobile artillery. The Argentine military historian Juan Beverina rightly dismisses this contention, noting that the "criminal inactivity" of the squadron had already become *de rigeur*, and that such an interpretation could not "withstand even the most superficial criticism." See Beverina, *La guerra del Paraguay*, 3: 391. Perhaps the simplest explanation for the inaction, however, is that any Brazilian naval commander who grounded his vessel would almost certainly face a court martial.

28   *La Tribuna* (Montevideo), 11 February 1866; *El Pueblo* (Buenos Aires), 14 February 1866; *The Standard* (Buenos Aires), 20 February 1866; María Haydeé Martin, "La juventud de Buenos Aires en la guerra con el Paraguay," *Trabajos y Comunicaciones* 19 (1969): 145-176.

29   See "Correspondencia de Buenos Ayres," *Jornal do Commercio* (Rio de Janeiro), 23 February 1866.

30   *The Standard* (Buenos Aires), 8 February 1866. For a more detailed account of this stage of the engagement, see Declaraciones del coronel Manuel Reyna, ayudante del general Nicanor Cáceres, aboard the riverboat *Cosmos*, 4 April 1888, MHM-CZ, carpeta 141, no. 27, and Pompeyo González (Juan E. O'Leary), "Recuerdos de gloria. Corrales. 31 de enero de 1866," *La Patria* (Asunción), 31 January 1903.

31 *El Pueblo* (Buenos Aires), 9 February 1866; Ignacio Fotheringham, *La vida de un soldado o reminiscencias de la frontera*, (Buenos Aires, n.d.), 1: 79–80.

32 Declaración del Sargento major Adriano Morales, sobre la expedition a Corrales, 31 January 1866, MHN (A) Colección Gill Aguinaga, carpeta 7, no. 3.

33 "Memorias de Julián N. Godoy."

34 The exact number of Argentine troops facing the two hundred fifty Paraguayans is much debated. *El Semanario* (Asunción), 10 February 1866, lists six thousand; Thompson, *The War in Paraguay*, 118, claims seventy-two hundred; José Ignacio Garmendia, *Guerra del Paraguay. Campaña de Corrientes y de Río Grande* (Buenos Aires, 1904), 517, notes 1,588 officers and men in the 2nd Division alone; and the Baron of Rio Branco noted that "if the listed troop strengths of the Argentine army were accurate, they had on that day close to 2,000 infantrymen and another 3,000 of cavalry." See Schneider, *A Guerra da Triplice Aliança*, 2: 4.

35 Juan Crisóstomo Centurión argues that Mitre should have taken some responsibility for what had happened at Corrales, but preferred to let Conesa carry the weight for its successes and failures. The colonel, for his part, composed an official account filled with self-serving exaggerations. He stressed, for instance, the diversity of arms and matériel captured ("new Minie rifles and ancient blunderbusses") and also noted, *inter alia*, the landing of five hundred enemy reinforcements on his right flank—something that never occurred. He likewise claimed a total Paraguayan loss of seven hundred men, that is, nearly three hundred more than actually faced him at any one time. To his credit, however, Conesa did offer elaborate praise to his subordinates, many of whom had suffered wounds like that of their colonel or worse. See Juan Crisóstomo Centurión, *Memorias o reminiscencias históricas sobre la guerra del Paraguay* (Asunción, 1987), 2: 31–32.

36 "Benjamín Canard to J. Antonio Ballesteros, Corrientes, 8 February 1866," in Canard, Joaquín Cascallar, and Miguel Gallegos, *Cartas sobre la guerra del Paraguay* (Buenos Aires, 1999), 73–75; see also Miguel Angel de Marco, *La guerra del Paraguay* (Buenos Aires, 2003), 157–94.

37 See anonymous report, Ensenaditas, 16 March 1866, in *The Standard* (Buenos Aires), 28 March 1866.

38 "Letter of Pastor S. Obligado, opposite Paso de la Patria, 3 Feb. 1866," in *La Tribuna* (Montevideo), 11 February 1866. See also *El Nacional* (Buenos Aires), 10 February 1866.

39 Cardozo, *Hace cien años*, 3: 112; Palleja, *Diário de la campaña*, 2: 64, argues that Paraguayan losses could not be "lower than one-thousand"; and Leuchars, *To the Bitter End*, 99, notes that Paraguayan losses were over five hundred, a figure that coincides with that mentioned by *The Standard* (Buenos Aires), 13 March 1866. It is difficult from the limited evidence to account for much more than two hundred.

40 Thompson, *The War in Paraguay*, 118, says that nine hundred Argentines were put out of action, while Mitre claimed a loss of only 295 killed and wounded (though he noted that reports of newly discovered casualties were still coming in). See Mitre to Marcos Paz, *Archivo del Coronel dr. Marcos Paz*, 7: 143–145. The true number of Allied casualties almost certainly lies between these two figures.

41 Several of the Porteño newspapers, including *The Standard* (Buenos Aires), 7 February 1866, portrayed the engagement as an Argentine success, though hardly "a bloodless one." The same article, however, recounted details of the battle that were odd or far-fetched, such as the notion that Conesa's retreat on the 30 January was a feint designed to pull the Paraguayans deeper into Corrientes, and that the Paraguayan withdrawal across the Paraná two days later was heavily contested by Allied sharpshooters.

42 The anxiety was understandable in that a majority of the Argentine troops involved in the engagement were of Porteño origin. See "Ford to the Earl of Clarendon, Buenos

Aires, 15 February 1866," in George Philip, ed., *British Documents on Foreign Affairs. Reports and Papers from the Foreign Office. Confidential Print. Part I: Series D, Latin America, 1845–1914*, vol. 1. *River Plate, 1849-1912* (London, 1991), 197.

43 *El Semanario* (Buenos Aires), 3 February 1866. Ironically enough, the correspondent of Rio's *Jornal do Commercio* also referred to the "painful lessons of the Peguajó," alluding to the lack of military preparation on the part of the Argentines. See *Jornal do Commercio*, 6 March 1866.

44 See Washburn, *History of Paraguay*, 2: 87–88, for the Marshal's reactions to the "treasonable" comportment of Colonel Estigarribia, who had surrendered the Paraguayan forces at Uruguaiana in October 1865.

45 This feeling of superiority over the Allies had a remarkably long life. Later in the war, when the Paraguayans had already been driven from their key defensive positions around Humaitá, the US minister to Asunción asked his Paraguayan hosts why the Allies had not followed up all "their advantages," and was offered the standard expression of contempt, "Son brasileros' ('They are Brazilians')." See Washburn, *History of Paraguay*, 2: 253–254.

46 Garmendia, *Campaña de Corrientes*, 557.

47 *La Tribuna* (Montevideo), 2 March 1866.

48 Thompson, *War in Paraguay*, 119; *The Standard* (Buenos Aires), 7 March 1866.

49 Report of José Díaz, Paso de la Patria, 21 February 1866, BNA-CJO; "Manuel N. Sánches to Nicanor Cáceres, Chilín-Cue, 20 February 1866," cited in María Haydée Martin, "La juventud de Buenos Aires," 167. A few days after retaking the village, the Allies conveyed the statue to what they hoped would be the safety of a private residence near the Paso de Enramada. Here a temporary sanctuary was established that received a regular flow of pilgrims until the statue could be returned to Itatí later in the war. See *The Standard* (Buenos Aires), 23 March 1866.

50 Cardozo, *Hace cien años*, 2: 141.

51 Cardozo, *Hace cien años*, 3: 139; Colonel Palleja reported that the commander of the Brazilian forces under Suárez had likewise received a letter from Osório telling him to retire his forces to prepare for a Paraguayan attack and not bother to aid the Uruguayans. See "Diary at Head-Quarters," *The Standard* (Buenos Aires), 8 March 1866.

52 Leuchars, *To the Bitter End*, 101, suggests that Tamandaré might have wished to deploy his squadron to the east to support such an invasion (and thereby reap the glory of a Brazilian—rather than an Allied—victory, over Núñez). If the admiral actually thought this way, then he was misinformed, for the shoals near the island of Apipé would have prevented the passage of all but the most shallow-drafted vessels. For his part, the Marshal had no worries about this front, so long as Núñez "obeyed his instructions." See Solano López to José Berges, Paso de la Patria, 17 March 1866, ANA CRB I-30, 13, 1.

53 See, for example, "La alianza y la escuadra," *La Tribuna* (Buenos Aires), 8 February 1866. The Spanish minister in Buenos Aires, Pedro Sorela y Maury, made extensive comment on the negative public reaction to Tamandaré's inaction ("even among the female population there is a marked aversion to the Brazilians"). See his 14 February 1866 report to his country's foreign ministry in Isidoro J. Ruiz Moreno, *Informes españoles sobre Argentina* (Buenos Aires, 1993), 1: 303–304. For his part, Tamandaré had little love for the Argentines, whose prisoner he had been for a time during the Cisplatine conflict of the late 1820s.

54 André Rebouças, then present in Corrientes as an army engineer, remarked that in the navy as well as the army there was a general contempt for Tamandaré's "irresolution, the timidity, the excess of precaution … that always looks ridiculous." See Rebouças, *Diário: a Guerra do Paraguai (1866)* (São Paulo, 1973), 29. Even the emperor was not averse to

expressing pique at the lack of harmony between the admiral and Osório. See Francisco Doratioto, *Maldita Guerra. Nova história da Guerra do Paraguai* (São Paulo, 2002), 201. One Argentine veteran of the war noted that this period was characterized not so much by inter-allied friction as by a simple lack of will on the part of naval commanders. See Carlos D. Sarmiento, *Estudio crítico sobre la guerra del Paraguay (1865-1869)* (Buenos Aires, 1890), 20-21.

55 See "Declaration of Paraguayan soldier Pedro Mendoza, Corrientes, 23 February 1866," *La Nación Argentina* (Buenos Aires), 7 March 1866.

56 Cardozo, *Hace cien años*, 3: 145-46; Barbara Potthast-Jutkeit, *"¿Paraíso de Mahoma" o "País de las mujeres"?* (Asunción, 1996), 247-53.

57 In a letter to his daughter, written on 20 March 1866, General Flores commented that all in camp were anxious to face the despot López. See Flores to Amada Agapa, Ensenada, 20 March 1866, AGN (M), Archivos Particulares, Caja 10, carpeta 13, no. 45; *The Standard* (Buenos Aires), 3 April 1866.

58 Thomas J. Hutchinson, *The Paraná, with Incidents of the Paraguayan War and South American Recollections from 1861 to 1868* (London, 1868), 260-261; see also "Correspondencia de Corrientes," *El Siglo* (Montevideo), 5 April 1866.

59 Centurión, *Memorias o reminiscencias históricas*, 2: 43. See also the image entitled "Explosión de una chata paraguaya en los combates con la bateria Itapirú del mes de marzo," *Correo del Domingo* (Buenos Aires), 8 April 1866.

60 *El Semanario* (Asunción), 31 March 1866. The most effective gunnery executed by the chatas came from a single man, Lieutenant José Fariña, who survived the engagements to become the most decorated officer in the Paraguayan navy. See Garmendia, *Campaña de Corrientes*, 576-581. See also "Importantes notícias de la escuadra imperial," *La Tribuna* (Montevideo), 4-5 April 1866; Carlos Careaga, *Teniente de Marina José María Fariña, heroe naval de la guerra contra la Triple Alianza* (Asunción, 1948); and most importantly, Juan E. O'Leary, *El libro de los heroes* (Asunción, 1922), 11-53, which contains Fariña's own story, as told in old age to the author.

61 "Francisco M. Paz to Marcos Paz, Ensenaditas, 29 March 1866," in *Archivo del coronel Dr. Marcos Paz*, 5: 84-87.

62 The commanding officer, Lieutenant Mariz e Barros, died after doctors amputated his shattered legs. The son of a former cabinet minister who was a personal friend of Tamandaré, the younger Mariz e Barros was badly hit in the groin and abdomen as well as the legs. One commentator suggests that he might have survived if he had taken a chloroform preparation offered by the medical staff, but saying that such potions were only for women, he endured the operation with a cigar clenched between his teeth, and succumbed to shock thereafter. See William van Vleck Lidgerwood to William Seward, Petropolis, 4 May 1866, NARA, M-121, no. 34; see also "Comments of Rebouças," *Jornal do Commercio* (Rio de Janeiro), 14 April 1866. In a letter to the countess of Barral, Dom Pedro expressed heartfelt sorrow at the loss of the brave lieutenant, saying that "the ironclads may have drawn too close to the enemy guns without remembering that nothing in the world is invulnerable." See "Pedro II to Condessa de Barral, Rio, 23 April 1866," in Alcindo Sodre, *Abrindo um Cofre* (Rio, 1956), 104.

63 *The Standard* (Buenos Aires), 4 April 1866; "Theatro da guerra," *Diário do Rio de Janeiro*, 21 April 1866.

64 An officer who served on the warship *Mearim* left considerable details on this stage of the fight against the chatas. See Miguel Calmon, *Memorias da Campanha do Paraguay* (Pará, 1888), 109-113. See also *The Standard* (Buenos Aires), 17 April 1866; and "Pedro Sorela y Maury Report, Buenos Aires, 12 April 1866," in Ruiz Moreno, *Informes españoles sobre Argentina*, 1: 308.

65   See "Marcos Paz to Mitre, Buenos Aires, 21 March 1866," in *Archivo del general Mitre*, 6: 58–59. Paz discussed at length the transport of hats, shoes, tunics, pants, and foodstuffs. And the Anacarsis Lanús company of Buenos Aires was promising much more (a daily ration of flour and rice and a pound and a half of charqui or two and a half of fresh meat, plus tobacco, yerba, soap, and salt). See "Contract celebrated with Lanús and Brothers, Buenos Aires, 28 Feb. 1866," in Beverina, *La guerra del Paraguay*, 3: 667-669, annex 54. Regarding the supply of Brazilian munitions and armaments see José Carlos de Carvalho, *Noções de Artilharia para Instrução dos Oficiais Inferiores da Arma no Exército fora do Império pelo Dr. … Chefe da Comissão de Engenheiros do Primeiro Corpo do Mesmo Exército* (Montevideo, 1866), 59. The Brazilian *carne do vento* was the charqui of the Argentines and the *biltong* of the Boers; it was made by cutting beef into long strips and exposing it to the sun for a number of days, then dipping it into orange juice, salt, and perhaps a little cinnamon to give it flavor.

66   Thompson, *War in Paraguay*, 122–125.

67   Thompson, *War in Paraguay*, 125, claimed that the island was of recent development, one of a myriad of tiny islets periodically thrown up by low water on the Paraná. Centurión, *Memorias o reminiscencias históricas*, 46, denied that this was the case, arguing that an island half a league long had always existed on the site. General Dionísio Cerqueira, however, finally put this minor question to rest in 1903, when, as a member of a border demarcation commission, he actually passed in a steamboat over the spot where Redención once lay. When asked what had become of the island, he was told that the Paraná had long since swallowed it. See Cerqueira, *Reminiscencias da campanha*, 137–139.

68   Rebouças, *Diário*, 65–79.

69   Charles Ames Washburn to Seward, Corrientes, 27 April 1866, WNL.

70   A. de Lyra Tavares, *Vilagran Cabrita e a Engenharia de Seu Tempo* (Rio de Janeiro, 1981), 119–131; Joaquím Antonio Pinto Junior, *Guerra do Paraguay. Defeza Heroica da Ilha de Redenção. 10 de Abril de 1866* (Rio de Janeiro, 1877), 4–5; *El Mercurio* (Valparaíso), 2 May 1866.

71   Rebouças, *Diário*, 9.

72   Thompson, *The War in Paraguay*, 125; *El Semanario* (Asunción), 21 April 1866.

73   A. de Sena Madureira, *Guerra do Paraguai. Reposta ao Sr. Jorge Thompson, autor da "Guerra del Paraguay" e aos Anotadores Argentinos D. Lewis e A. Estrada* (Brasília, 1982), 20.

74   For once, Brazilian and Paraguayan sources give similar numbers on casualties, although Rebouças, *Diário*, 85, implies that of the nine hundred to one thousand Paraguayans lost, the great majority were killed; while Centurión appears to think a higher proportion were wounded of the 960 total casualties he recorded. See also Calmon, *Memorias da Campanha*, 119; "Declaration of Captain [*sic*] Romero," *The Standard* (Buenos Aires), 19 April 1866; and "El capitán paraguayo Romero," *El Siglo* (Montevideo), 21 April 1866.

75   Theotonio Meirelles, *O Exercito Brazileiro na Guerra do Paraguay. Resumos Históricos* (Rio de Janeiro, 1877), 98. See also Dr. Moreira Azevedo, "O Combate da Ilha do Cabrita," *Revista Trimensal do Instituto Histórico, Geographico, e Etnographico do Brasil* 3 (1870): 5–20.

76   Thompson, *War in Paraguay*, 126, claimed a Brazilian loss of about one thousand killed—a very improbable figure. Pedro Werlang, an eyewitness, noted a loss of almost four hundred men. See "Diário de Campanha do Capitão Pedro Werlang," in Klaus Becker, *Alemães e Descendentes do Rio Grande do Sul na Guerra do Paraguay* (Canoas, 1968), 125.

77 *The Standard* (Buenos Aires), 20 April 1866; *Jornal do Commercio* (Rio de Janeiro), 3 May 1866.

78 A year and a half later, a war correspondent passed by the "sandbank where the ill-fated Cabrita perished like Wolfe, in the hour of his victory. A solitary crow marks his burial place." See "The War in the North," *The Standard* (Buenos Aires), 18 September 1867.

79 "Mitre to Paz, opposite Itapirú, 30 March 1866," in *Archivo del coronel Dr. Marcos Paz*, 7: 164–166.

80 "Mitre to Paz, opposite Paso de la Patria, 13 April 1866," in *Archivo del coronel Dr. Marcos Paz*, 7: 171–172.

81 Thirty years later, Mitre claimed exclusive credit for the invasion plan, which, he remarked, "was opposed by all Allied commanders save Tamandaré." The point of disembarkation, he carefully noted, was suggested by a Brazilian military engineer, whose name "could be found in my papers." See Bartolomé Mitre to Estanislao Zeballos, Buenos Aires, 6 April 1896, Museo Histórico de Luján (Papeles Estanislao Zeballos).

82 Guillermo Valotta, *La operación de las fuerzas navales con las terrestres durante la guerra del Paraguay* (Buenos Aires, 1915), 67–69.

83 Francisco Doratioto, *General Osorio. A Espada Liberal do Império* (São Paulo, 2008), 16–30.

84 Joaquim Luis Osório and Fernando Luis Osório, filho, *História do general Osório*, (Pelotas, 1915), 2; 182; Francisco Doratioto, *General Osório. A Espada Liberal do Império* (São Paulo, 2008).

85 The unit that came to Osório's rescue was commanded by Major Deodoro de Fonseca, who became first president of the Brazilian republic in 1889. See Cardozo, *Hace cien años*, 3: 232.

86 The same storm kept the Uruguayan contingent aboard the transport vessels. Flores found good reason to mistrust the weather in those parts, since only two weeks earlier one of his soldiers was killed by a lightning bolt and another five severely burned. See *La Tribuna* (Montevideo), 13 April 1866.

87 Cardozo, *Hace cien años*, 3: 234

88 Cited in *El Siglo* (Montevideo), 27 April 1866.

89 Both guns were discovered by the Allies and incorporated into their artillery. See Thompson, *The War in Paraguay*, 129.

90 The Argentines at this time suffered from a shortage of mounts, such that only the commanders of the division had reliable horses. It was little surprise, then, that the Argentine troops deployed on the Paraguayan side of the river were mostly infantry. See "Wenceslao Paunero to Marcos Paz, Paso de la Patria, 27 April 1866," in *Archivo del Coronel dr. Marcos Paz*, 5: 119–120.

91 *The Standard* (Buenos Aires), 26 April 1866.

92 Thompson, *The War in Paraguay*, 130.

93 Osório's engineers again did a splendid job in erecting piers, batteries, and pontoons, struggling not so much against the enemy as against the elements. See Jerónimo Rodrigues de Morães Jardim, *Os Engenheiros Militares na Guerra entre o Brazil e o Paraguay e a Passagem do Rio Paraná* (Rio de Janeiro, 1889); Luiz Vieira Ferreira, *Passagem do rio Paraná; Comissão de Engenheiros de Primero Corpo do Exercito em Operacões na Campanha do Paraguai* (Rio de Janeiro, 1890).

94 "Notícias da guerra," *Diário do Rio de Janeiro*, 17 May 1866. Not surprisingly, *El Semanario*'s account of these events omitted reference to the Marshal's absence, and emphasized that all at Itapirú went as planned. See *El Semanario* (Asunción), 5 May 1866.

95 Thompson, *The War in Paraguay*, 132; Testimony of Frederick Skinner, Asunción, 25 January 1871, Scottish Record Office, CS 244/543/19.

96 Tamandaré later raised the vessel and presented her clean and whole to the Argentine government, from which she had been taken a year before. See Calmón, *Memorias da Campanha*, 1: 137.

97 Thompson, *War in Paraguay*, 133. Ironically, the tactic that Thompson suggested was exactly that which was frequently adopted by the Paraguayans in the 1932–1935 Chaco War; over and over again (at the battle of Nanawa in January 1933), the numerically superior Bolivians wasted their troops in fruitless assaults against Paraguay's well-constructed, well-defended trenches. See José Félix Estigarribia, *Epic of the Chaco. Marshal Estigarribia's Memoirs of the Chaco War* (Austin, 1950).

2 | VAST FIELDS OF DEATH

1 *The Standard* (Buenos Aires), 27 April 1866.

2 Charles A. Washburn to William Seward, Corrientes, 4 May 1866, WNL.

3 One of these bridges was a floating affair one hundred thirty yards long and more than ten wide that the engineers had erected in less than twenty-four hours. See *La Nación Argentina* (Buenos Aires), 2 May 1866.

4 *The Standard* (Buenos Aires), 2 May 1866.

5 As a young man, Marshal López had had to obey orders of similar complexity in similar circumstances. In 1845, his father sent the eighteen-year-old Francisco Solano on a military incursion into Corrientes at the head of a force of nearly two thousand men, and on that occasion issued him a set of orders that went on for many pages and pretended to cover every imaginable contingency. It did not occur to the elder López that his son be given the freedom to act as circumstances dictated, and this same conviction (or feeling of doubt) guided many of the younger López's actions during the war against the Triple Alliance. See Instructions of Carlos Antonio López, Asunción, 9 December 1845, ANA-SH 272, no. 22, and, more generally, Manuel Florencio Mantilla, *Crónica histórica de la provincial de Corrientes* (Buenos Aires, 1929), 2: 140–144.

6 Revisionist historians have often castigated Britain as an omnipresent puppeteer, pulling strings to effect an imperialism that crushed the Latin American quest for an economic development independent of Albion's control. But these scholars and polemicists, who include José María Rosa, León Pomer, Julio José Chiavenato, and, more recently, Luis Agüero Wagner, have rarely permitted an inconvenient fact to play havoc with their conviction. They have never explained why the British should bother to reveal the complete wording of the Triple Alliance Treaty when its revelation would strengthen the Marshal's cause and the "anti-imperialist" sentiments of those Latin Americans who sympathized with it. The failure of the revisionists to address this question is more than a minor detail, for it disrupts their broader contentions about the workings of nineteenth-century imperialism in Latin America.

7 Cardozo, *Hace cien años*, 3: 157–158; Box, *Origins of the Paraguayan War*, 270–273. Strictly speaking, the text of the treaty contradicted long-standing Brazilian policy, which had generally sought to weaken Argentina at the expense of Paraguay and Uruguay, not the other way around. Ironically, the two major Allied powers outlined a common goal almost certain to set them at loggerheads once victory over López was assured. See Francisco Doratioto, "La politique paraguayenne de l'Empire du Brésil (1864–1872)." Paper presented at the Colloque International "Le Paraguay a l'Ombre de ses Guerres," Maison de l'Amerique Latine, Paris, 17 November 2005.

8   *La América* (Buenos Aires), 5–6 and 13 May 1866; Cardozo, *Hace cien años*, 3: 270–271, and José Fabián Ledesma to Juan Bautista Alberdi, Buenos Aires, 10 May 1866, Archivo Alberdi (Luján), 4529, no. 5114. Allied officials tried with minimal success to counter the resulting criticism in Europe and the United States with a pro-Allied press campaign; in one pamphlet, issued with the help of the Brazilian legation in Washington, the unnamed author states that the "Allies, far from designing to usurp territories that do not rightfully belong to them, are only defending their own rights [to those territories]." This claim, which might have seemed reasonable had it not been cloaked in a stated need for secrecy, met with near-universal scorn. See *The Paraguayan Question. The Alliance between Brazil, the Argentine Confederation and Uruguay versus the the Dictator of Paraguay. Claims of the Republics of Peru and Bolivia in Regard to this Alliance* (New York, 1866), 12.

9   An anonymous *El Semanario* article of 31 March 1866 entitled "Los reclutas" expressed the concern for national survival in almost nihilistic terms: "Save the Fatherland or die for her!!! [*sic*] is the solemn pledge that all Paraguayan citizens make ... [such that we] profess our love for the Fatherland and [offer] our maximum confidence in our brilliant Marshal López's [campaign] to defeat the barbarous enemy."

10   Thompson, *The War in Paraguay*, 138.

11   Palleja, *Diário de la campaña*, 2: 218; "Más detalles sobre el combate del 2," *El Siglo* (Montevideo), 12 May 1866; "2 de mayo de 1866," *La Patria* (Asunción), 2 May 1894.

12   José Ignacio Garmendia, *Campaña de Humaytá* (Buenos Aires, 1901), 88; Paulo de Queiroz Duarte, *Os Voluntários da Patria na Guerra do Paraguai* (Rio de Janeiro, 1985), 2, bk. 4: 175–181.

13   The officer delegated to transport these guns back to the Paraguayan lines was a young cavalry lieutenant, Bernardino Caballero, who would play an exemplary role in the later engagements of the war and eventually became president of Paraguay (1880–1886). See Gregorio Benítes, *Primeras batallas contra la Triple Alianza* (Asunción, 1919), 154.

14   Centurión, *Memorias o reminiscencias históricas*, 2: 71–72.

15   Silvestre Aveiro, *Memorias militares, 1864–1870* (Asunción, 1989), 38.

16   Correspondent to D. M. Rodríguez, aboard *Proveedor* at Paso de la Patria, 10 April 1866, in *El Siglo* (Montevideo), 17 April 1866.

17   Julio César Chaves, *El general Díaz. Biografía del vencedor de Curupaity* (Buenos Aires and Asunción, 1957), 64–65. See also "Batalla de 2 de mayo. Estero Bellaco," *El Independiente* (Asunción), 2 May 1888.

18   Colonel Conesa, whose conduct at Corrales had caught the appreciative eye of Brazilian officers, now returned the compliment by assigning to Osório "the greatest glory of the day and the appreciation of the entire [Argentine] army." See Conesa to Martín de Gainza, Yataity, 20 May 1866, cited in Doratioto, *Maldita Guerra*, 213.

19   Never one to whitewash the failures of his fellow officers, Centurión noted that few tacticians among Paraguayan commanders could have arranged a maneuver in time to assure a meaningful victory at the Estero Bellaco. Centurión, *Memorias o reminiscencias*, 2: 72. See also José María Sandoval to his brother Bernardino Sandoval, Yataity, 1 May 1866, ANA-CRB I-30, 20, 47.

20   Decree of López [condemning Robles to death together with two assistants], Paso de la Patria, 6 January 1866, ANA-CRB I-30, 28, 2, no. 11; "Destitución de Robles," *La Nación Argentina* (Buenos Aires), 9–10 August 1866.

21   Colonel Silvestre Aveiro, one of the Marshal's most ardent defenders in later years, implicitly criticized this particular failure in his 1874 reminiscences, noting that if López "had [correctly] calculated the effect of his surprise [attack] perhaps he would have launched his entire army [into the fray; as it was, however, Díaz hesitated] to ask

for support [until it was too late] … for it to arrive." See Aveiro, *Memorias militares*, 38. See also Manuel Avila, "Rectificaciones históricas. Estero Bellaco," *Revista del Instituto Paraguayo*, 2, no. 22 (Nov–Dec. 1899): 143–151, who argues that Díaz had little room for meaningful maneuver and could not exceed orders to reconnoiter the ground and return.

22   Colonel Thompson put Allied losses at the Estero Bellaco at an improbable twenty-five hundred (see *The War in Paraguay*, 136), while in Sena Madureira's "response," the Brazilian countered with an equally unlikely one thousand men lost (see his *Guerra do Paraguai*, 22); Mitre's own report to Vice President Paz put Allied casualties at 656 ("the majority wounded") with Paraguayan losses "more than 1,200 dead, three artillery pieces, two flags, around 800 rifles, and a great number of prisoners, for the most part wounded." See "Mitre to Marcos Paz, Estero Bellaco, 3 May 1866," in Jorge Thompson, *La guerra del Paraguay* (Buenos Aires, 1869), xxxii–iii; the *Correio Mercantil* (Rio de Janeiro), 16 July 1866, provided eleven columns on the first two pages with the names of the Brazilians killed and wounded, for a total of 425 killed, 2,192 wounded, and 127 lightly wounded (*contusos*); the most exaggerated recounting of losses, however, came from a junior officer in Osório's command, whose diary noted only four hundred total Allied casualties as against three thousand for the Paraguayans. See "Diário do Alferes João José da Fonseca. Natural da Cidade de Castro na Guerra do Paraguai (17/Dezembro de 1865 até 19/Novembro de 1867)," *Boletim do Instituto Histórico, Geográfico e Etnográfico Paranaense*, 34 (1978): 137.

23   Flores to Querida Agapa, Paso de la Patria, 11 May 1866, AGN (M), Archivos Particulares, Caja 10, carpeta 13, no. 48.

24   Pecegueiro later issued an extended defense of his actions, which included an angry denunciation of several fellow officers. See Lopes Pecegueiro, *Combate de 2 de maio de 1866* (Rio de Janeiro, 1870).

25   *El Semanario* (Asunción), 5 May 1866. The Allied press liked to pretend that the distresses caused by the war were having a palpable effect in Asunción, where war widows could express their "desperation and sadness only in the bosom of their homes." See "Teatro de guerra," *El Siglo* (Montevideo), 18 May 1866. At this stage of the conflict, in fact, there was little proof that many Paraguayan women were thinking this way.

26   The *Jornal do Commercio* (Rio de Janeiro) reported on 20 May 1866 that López had directed the Paraguayan attack from the front lines at the Estero Bellaco, but this was clearly not the case at any time during the battle. See James Schofield Saeger, *Francisco Solano López and the Ruination of Paraguay. Honor and Egocentrism* (Lanham and Boulder, 2007), 148.

27   Dionísio Cerqueira, *Reminiscencias da Campanha do Paraguai* (Rio de Janeiro, 1948), 167. See also Doratioto, *Maldita Guerra*, 213.

28   In 1862 the Brazilian army had imported several "carros ambulâncias" from France. These stagecoach-like vehicles, with spring suspension, gave a much smoother ride than was possible with cacolets and were much used later in the war; see also Report of Brigadier Polidoro to Colonel Director of the Arsenal. Rio de Janeiro, 18 June 1862, which describes the initial allocation of the ambulances. Arquivo Nacional, Coleção Polidoro da Fonseca Quintinilha Jordão.

29   Although the Brazilian medical services were much criticized, in fact, certain impressive innovations had already occurred over the preceding decade, one example being the deployment of specialized orderlies for combat conditions. Previously, musicians from the military band were sent to retrieve the wounded from the battlefield (and this continued as the practice for all armies during the Paraguayan conflict). The Brazilians nonetheless established a field nursing company. General Osório, with more than a touch of racist disdain for his own Black troops, delegated this particularly onerous duty to the

Zuavos Battalion from Bahia. See Kraay, "Patriotic Mobilization in Brazil. The Zuavos and Other Black Companies," in *I Die with My Country. Perspectives on the Paraguayan War*, Hendrik Kraay and Thomas L. Whigham, eds. (Lincoln and London, 2004), 76–78. Concerning the Argentine medical services, which usually earned greater praise from observers than those of the Brazilians, see Miguel Angel de Marco, *La guerra del Paraguay* (Buenos Aires, 2003), 157–194.

30   For general details on the role of Argentine military chaplains, see de Marco, *La guerra del Paraguay*, 223–240. On the Paraguayan side, see the extensive treatment in Silvio Gaona, *El clero en la guerra del 70* (Asunción, 1961), and Rafael Eladio Velásquez, "El clero en la guerra del 70," *La Tribuna* (Asunción), 6 January 1963.

31   The correspondent of the Buenos Aires *Standard* described the hospital complex at Saladero (a league south of Corrientes) as an infinity of tents and eight separate wooden buildings, one of which was 200 yards long by 10 yards wide, the remaining seven edifices each being 60 by 10. The establishment was therefore capable of handling several thousand wounded men. See *The Standard* (Buenos Aires), 8 June 1866, and Hutchinson, *The Paraná*, 281–282.

32   J. Arthur Montenegro, "Hospital Fluctuante," in *Fragmentos Históricos. Homems e Factos da Guerra do Paraguay* (Rio Grande, 1900), 102–104.

33   Efraím Cardozo noted that the many Paraguayan wounded were taken by skiffs and schooners up to Asunción, where the military hospital was quickly filled. Private homes were then opened, including that of War Minister Venancio López. See *Hace cien años*, 3: 273.

34   "They seemed to remember so little, and would never think for themselves, never try to go through any process of reasoning. And their prejudices, the old wretched nonsense they had learnt from their grandmothers, always stood in the way. If they once got a wrong idea into their heads, nothing could remove it. They are like the Indians of Central America, who, having confounded *envierno* (winter) with *infierno* (hell) could never be persuaded by the Jesuits that the latter was hot." George Frederick Masterman, *Seven Eventful Years in Paraguay*, 117.

35   Masterman, *Seven Eventful Years in Paraguay*, 117–118. An intriguing document from mid-1866, which goes on for thirty-six densely annotated pages, lists 24,551 pesos worth of drugs and medical supplies that the state had recently purchased from Asunción pharmacists. This document also indicates that private drugstores still possessed supplies of foreign-produced medicines in impressive quantities this late in the war, and that the state was still willing to pay for such materials, rather than simply confiscate them. See Nota de los efectos de Botica entregados con venta al Estado, 6 June 1866, ANA-NE 1711. As for locally produced *remedios*, the commandant of the Villa de Salvador reported at the end of 1867 that he was sending the hospitals several demijohns of fever medicine, which "had always given good results with head-aches." See Rafael Ruiz Díaz to War Minister, Divino Salvador, 15 December 1867, ANA-NE 820.

36   Anselmo Aquino Report, Encarnación, 11 November 1865, ANA-NE 2375. Measles seems to have made a circuitous journey among the Paraguayan troops; by April 1866, we find the commandant of the tiny, isolated fort of Olimpo (in the northern Chaco) reporting fourteen of his soldiers down with the disease (two in danger of dying). See Pedro Ferreira to War Minister, Olimpo, 9 April 1866, ANA-NE 1733.

37   Lucilio del Castillo, "Enfermidades reinantes en la campaña del Paraguay," *Album de la guerra del Paraguay*, 1(1893): 341–343, 357–359, 2 (1894): 25–30, 43–47, 63–64.

38   Masterman, *Seven Eventful Years in Paraguay*, 139.

39   Thomas Whigham "Building the Nation While Destroying the Land: Paraguayan Journalism during the Triple Alliance War, 1864 –1870," *Jahrbuch für Lateinamerikanische*

Geschichte 49 (2012): 157–180; María Lucrecia Johansson, *Soldados de papel. La propaganda en la prensa paraguaya durante la guerra de la Triple Alianza (1864-1870)* (Cádiz, 2014).

40   "Francisco M. Paz to Marcos Paz, Bellaco, 9 May 1866," in *Archivo del coronel Dr. Marcos Paz* (La Plata, 1964), 5: 134–137.

41   *La Tribuna* (Buenos Aires), 15 May 1866.

42   The ancient Greeks called this latter phenomenon *ignis fatuus* (the fire of fools), a red or greenish light produced by the spontaneous combustion of methane coming from decaying marsh plants. Individuals lost at night would make for these lights in "foolish" fashion, thinking them the lanterns of friends, and would find themselves hopelessly mired in the swamp as a result. See Robert Southey, *Common-place Book* (London, 1849), 730, for a particularly evocative example of the phenomenon. As for fireflies, Masterman reported two different varieties in southern Paraguay—a smaller insect, which emitted an intermittent yellow light and was never seen except over wet ground, and a larger variety, which emitted a steady green light; he also reported "another light-bearer of even greater beauty, the larva of a beetle, a grey ungainly worm by day, but at night a bracelet for Titania herself, a double chain of living emeralds, with a clasp of a single ruby." See *Seven Eventful Years in Paraguay*, 124–125.

43   Joaquim Silverio de Azevedo Pimentel, *Guerra do Paraguai. Episodios Militares* (Rio de Janeiro, 1978), 14–15. As used here, the word *negro* or *negrinho* in Portuguese or *kambá* in Guaraní, probably comes closer in its contempt to the English term "nigger," which, however, is so laden with nuances today as to be of doubtful utility in this older Paraguayan context; the substitute term "darkie" perhaps provides the least anachronistic epithet for that time and place. The Paraguayans, whose disdain for the Brazilian blacks was ubiquitous, also called them *kaí*, the Guaraní equivalent for *macaco*, or "monkey," the one forest animal that laughs uncontrollably at his own antics and who never takes a serious step. The common Paraguayan slur for Argentines, *kurepí* ("pig bellies"), evidently comes from a later period; it derives from the white color of the underside of hogs, which, to Paraguayan thinking, resembled that of Argentine faces. One frequently hears the latter term even today, and it is just as unflattering now as when it was first coined. *Kaí* and *kambá*, on the other hand, have dropped out of usage as derogatory terms for Brazilians.

44   Decree of Vice President Sánchez concerning the evacuation of all civilians from the southern districts, Asunción, 23 November 1865, ANA-SH 334, no. 1.

45   Some anti-López Paraguayans had been organized into a minor military force called the Paraguayan Legion, which had served under Argentine command since mid-1865. Juan Bautista Gill Aguinaga's, *La asociación paraguaya en la guerra de la Triple Alianza* (Buenos Aires,1959).

46   Washington Lockhart, *Venancio Flores, un caudillo trágico* (Montevideo, 1976).

47   Cited in the *New York Times*, 29 June 1866.

48   Thompson, *The War in Paraguay*, 141.

49   Manuel Martínez to Colonel José Luis Gómez, President of the Centro de Guerreros del Paraguay, Montevideo, 26 March 1916, MHN-M Colección Guerreros del Paraguay; Floriano Müller, "O Batahão 'Vilagran Cabrita' na Guerra do Paraguai," *Revista Militar Brasileira*, 62: nos. 1–2 (1955): 78.

50   Thompson, *The War in Paraguay*, 142.

51   Centurión, who was awarded with the Knight's Star of the National Order of Merit for his work in the execution of the attack, did not hesitate to call it capricious and point the finger directly at the Marshal. See *Memorias o reminiscencias*, 2: 84–85.

52   On 23 May, the Paraguayans captured a Brazilian spy who revealed the plans for an Allied attack in two days' time. From today's perspective, it seems obvious that the man invented a story to tell his tormentors what they wanted to hear and thus end the flogging the Paraguayans meted out. See Adolfo I. Báez, *Tuyuty* (Buenos Aires, 1929), 55–56.

53   Cited in Albert Amerlan, *Nights on the Río Paraguay. Scenes of War and Character Sketches* (Buenos Aires, 1902), 40–41.

54   It was an unfortunate habit of López to communicate to each chief only that which concerned him, so that none of them should presume to take the overall command himself. Thus his field officers frequently failed to understand the Marshal's general aim and could not work to affect it as a whole. See Amerlan, *Nights on the Río Paraguay*, 42.

55   Thompson cites a figure of twenty-three thousand men in the attacking Paraguayan force, but bizarrely omits mention of Marcó's column. See *The War in Paraguay*, 143. Cardozo, in *Hace cien años*, 3: 301, mentions an attacking force of eighteen thousand Paraguayans with another seven thousand (and eight artillery pieces) in reserve. Battalions with full complements were always a rarity.

56   Cardozo, *Hace cien años*, 3: 298–299; Wisner, a consummate survivor and eccentric who had come to Paraguay during the early Carlos Antonio López period, managed to live through the Triple Alliance conflict in relative comfort with his many children, and served the postwar governments with as much dedication as he had that of the Marshal. See Gunther Kahle, "Franz Wisner von Morgenstern. Ein Ungar im Paraguay des 19. Jahrhundert," *Mitteilungen des* Österreichischen *Staatsarchivs*, 37 (1984): 198–246.

57   *Le Courrier de la Plata* (Buenos Aires), 29 May 1866, attributed this story to Paraguayan prisoners who later fell into Allied hands, and Colonel Palleja repeated the tale in his diary, though he seems to have doubted its veracity. See *Diário de la campaña*, 2: 266; Centurión, *Memorias o reminiscencias*, 2: 104, chides Palleja for giving a voice to this falsehood: "I do not understand why officers so brave and enlightened should stoop to denigrate [the natural courage] of our countrymen who fought [so hard] to defend their soil."

58   Cerqueira, *Reminiscencias da Campanha do Paraguai*, 183.

59   Báez , *Tuyuty*, 51.

60   Thompson, *The War in Paraguay*, 144.

61   John Hoyt Williams, "'A Swamp of Blood.' The Battle of Tuyutí," *Military History* 17, no. 1 (April 2000): 60. General Sampaio was from Ceará, one of the very few senior officers in the Brazilian army to hail from the northeastern provinces.

62   See eulogies in *Diário do Rio de Janeiro*, 21 July 1866; "Sampaio. 200 Anos," *Revista do Exército Brasileiro*, 147, special edition (2010); and Paulo de Queiroz Duarte, *Sampaio* (Rio de Janeiro, 1988), 288–315.

63   Garmendia, *Campaña de Humaitá*, 204. This tale might possibly be accurate, though Garmendia did tend to praise the efforts of his own Argentine comrades while underestimating those of his Brazilian allies.

64   Azevedo Pimentel, *Episódios Militares*, 88–89.

65   "Seeber to 'Querido amigo,' Tuyutí, 30 May 1866," in Seeber, *Cartas sobre la guerra del Paraguay* (Buenos Aires, 1907), 93. This same Seeber later had a successful career as a businessman and served for a year as mayor of Buenos Aires (1889–1890). Jakob Dick, a German-born gunner with the Brazilian forces, noted with pride that the best Allied artillerymen were likewise Germans (veterans of the earlier campaign against Rosas), who, on this day, "saved the cause." See "Diário do Forriel Jakob Dick," in Klaus Becker, *Alemães e Descendentes do Rio Grande do Sul na Guerra do Paraguai* (Canoas, 1968), 160.

66   "Relato dos Acontecimentos de 24 de Maio. Batalha de Tuiuti. Manuscrito de Autor Não-mencionado," IHGB Arquivo, lata 335, pasta 26 (1866?).

67   Juan E. O'Leary, *24 de mayo. Tuyuty. Estero Bellaco* (Asunción, 1904), 61.

68   Gilbert Phelps, *The Tragedy of Paraguay*, 151. Mallet's guns were LaHittes 4 (with a bore dimension of 88 mm), which fired a 3.7 kg shell (the shrapnel grenades weighed 4.45 kgs). The Brazilians were fond of the LaHitte cannon and used its French design when constructing their own cannon at the Naval Arsenal. Reginaldo J. da Silva Bacchi, personal communication, São Paulo, 23 October 2005.

69   Thompson, *The War in Paraguay*, 144.

70   "Friendly fire" casualties were common throughout the Paraguayan War; this case was unusual, however, in that Colonel Palleja admitted that the guns of his Florida Battalion were at fault in killing many of his Argentine allies. See Palleja, *Diário de la campaña*, 2: 268. General Paunero, another victim of this same bombardment, lost part of his right ear. See *La Tribuna* (Montevideo), 31 May 1866.

71   The Argentine painter Cándido López recorded that these Paraguayan troops carried no weapons save "heavy machetes, so new that they still bore the green [paper] label that identified their English manufacture." See López's notes for 24 May 1866, in Franco María Ricci, *Cándido López. Imagenes de la Guerra del Paraguay* (Milan, 1984), 142.

72   See *La Nación Argentina* (Buenos Aires), 12 June 1866; General Osório's adjutant later sent what was left of this flag as a trophy to Admiral Tamandaré, who responded by offering an eloquent tribute to the Paraguayan soldier's devotion to his country. See *El Siglo* (Montevideo), 24 June 1866.

73   The Paraguayans kept playing their music over the next several days to hide the disarray of their situation. Cerqueira took this to mean that they had received reinforcements and were so enthused and ready to fight once again that some of their solders were already popping out "of their entrenchments to take pot-shots at our advance [units]." See Cerqueira, *Reminiscencias da Guerra*, 163.

74   Báez, *Tuyuty*, 99.

75   "Bartolomé Mitre to Marco Paz, Tuyutí, 24 May 1866," in *Archivo del coronel Dr. Marcos Paz*, 7: 198.

76   Colonel Thompson could not resist a touch of derision as he tallied the losses:

> Major Yegros (who had been imprisoned and in irons ever since
> López II was elected President [in 1862]), Major Rojas, and Captain
> Corvalán—all of them ex-aides-de-camp of López, and in whom
> he formerly had great confidence—were taken out of their irons (no
> one knew why they had been put in them) and sent to fight, degraded
> to the rank of sergeant; they were all killed in the battle or mortally
> wounded. José Martínez, ... [one of the Marshal's favorites, had
> been made] a captain after the "2nd May," when he was wounded [at
> the battle of the Estero Bellaco] ... and was now made a major
> just before he died. ... Many of the merchants of Asunción, who
> had just been recruited for the army, were also among the killed.

See *The War in Paraguay*, 145–146.

77   Palleja, *Diário de la campaña*, 2: 266–267; see also "Jacobo Varela to his brothers, Tuyutí, 24 May 1866, 10 pm," *La Tribuna* (Montevideo), 2 June 1866.

78   Allied accounts of Paraguayan sacrifice at Tuyutí and other battles were always heart-wrenching. They invariably stressed the courage, not the foolishness, of the enemy. See, for example, "Official Report of Field Marshal Osório, Tuyutí, 27 May 1866," *Jornal*

do Commercio (Rio de Janeiro), 20 June 1866, and the various "partes oficiales" in *El Siglo* (Montevideo), 31 May 1866.

79 Washburn to Seward, Corrientes, 8 June 1866, NARA, M-128, no. 2.

80 Thompson recorded eight thousand casualties on the Allied side—an improbably high figure. See *The War in Paraguay*, 146; Leuchars, reflecting the early testimony of Mitre and the more refined analyses of Garmendia, puts the figure of total Allied killed and wounded at just under four thousand. See *To the Bitter End*, 124.

81 See Seeber, *Cartas sobre la guerra del Paraguay*, 86–87.

82 Masterman, *Seven Eventful Years in Paraguay*, 137; "Más sobre el combate del 24 de mayo," *El Pueblo. Organo del Partido Liberal* (Asunción), 4–5 June 1895.

83 "Dr. Manoel Feliciano Pereira de Carvalho to the Baron of Herval, 27 May 1866," *Jornal do Commercio* (Rio de Janeiro), 15 July 1866.

84 An absorbing account of an Argentine field hospital on the 24 and 25 May can be garnered from José Juan Biedma, "Por un pan de jabón," *Album de la guerra del Paraguay*, 1 (1893–1894), 69–72.

85 *The Standard* (Buenos Aires), 8 June 1866; in the same report we find a curious story of three camp followers taken aboard the *Presidente* at the same time:

> Two of the trio were wounded, one not so severely as to prevent her from using her wicked tongue. She was a Correntina 'china.' The other associate, a Cordevesa, a white woman, was desperately hurt. Her right hand had been pierced through with a lance, her left arm broken at the elbow by a ball, five other grievous wounds upon her head and body made up the score. … The surgeon at once pronounced her to be a hopeless case. She still possessed consciousness, imploring the Mother of Mercies to "look down in pity" upon her sufferings. As this was passing, the Correntina, in a no unmistakable tone, began to mimic the last accents of one who probably had been a rival:
>
> Oh! Woman
>
> When to ill thy mind is bent,
>
> All hell contains no fouler fiend.
>
> The nymph received a caution "to shut up," at the same time a threat that another breath would be the signal to be thrown overboard. It need not be added after this there was no further mimicry.

86 Manuel Biedma, the Argentine officer who directed the disposal of the cadavers, noted with amazement how the fire failed to engulf them and how instead they dried into the form of Egyptian mummies: "The Paraguayans never surrender, not even to the flames!" Cited in Cardozo, *Hace cien años*, 3: 312. The Bate Company photographers of Montevideo immortalized the scene with shots of corpses piled one on top of the other; these images soon went on sale in downriver ports and still offend the eyes today. See Miguel Angel Cuarterolo, "Images of War: Photographers and Sketch Artists of the Triple Alliance conflict," in *I Die with My Country. Perspectives on the Paraguayan War, 1864–1870*, Hendrik Kraay and Thomas L. Whigham, eds. (Lincoln and London, 2004), 154–178.

87 Captain Seeber considered the Marshal's unwillingness to focus his attack on the Argentines the key Paraguayan error of the day. See *Cartas sobre la guerra del Paraguay*, 86–87.

88 Aveiro, *Memorias militares*, 42. I have adjusted the colonel's Guaraní to conform with modern orthography, but he seems to have left a word or two out of the original: "Aipebú ndeve los kambá, xe Karaí, pero ndambogüi."

89 Centurión, *Memorias o reminiscencias*, 2: 94.

90 Sometime later, López told Resquín that he had deserved to be shot for his poor conduct at Tuyutí but was saved by the fact that the Marshal might then have had to shoot his

brother-in-law Barrios, who had shown a similar ineptitude. See Garmendia, *Campaña de Humayta*, 227; in his memoirs, perhaps not surprisingly, Resquín omits reference to this upbraiding. See Francisco I. Resquín, *La guerra del Paraguay contra la Triple Alianza* (Asunción, 1996), 46.

91   Centurión, *Memorias o reminiscencias*, 2: 95.

92   See *El Semanario* (Asunción), 26 May 1866.

93   Centurión, *Memorias o reminiscencias*, 2: 98; French consul Emile Laurent-Cochelet, then in Asunción, noted that in the Paraguayan capital the government represented the disaster at Tuyutí as a brilliant victory, though his own testimony suggests that few really believed this interpretation. See his "Exercise de 5 juillet 1866" (Asunción), in Capdevila, *Variations sur le pays des femmes*, 380.

3 | A MARCH THROUGH THE SWAMPS

1   Thompson, *The War in Paraguay*, 153–154.

2   See, for example, Mitre to Marcos Paz, Estero Bellaco, 10 May 1866, and Evaristo López to Mitre, Corrientes, 14 June 1866 (regarding the expropriation of horses in Corrientes), both in the *Archivo del coronel Dr. Marcos Paz, 7*: 184–185 and 192–194, respectively; Mitre to Foreign Minister Rufino de Elizalde, Tuyutí, 5 July 1866, in *Correspondencia Mitre-Elizalde* (Buenos Aires, 1960), 284–285; an article entitled "The Horse Panic" appeared in *The Standard* later that month that described the many subterfuges horse owners in Buenos Aires used to keep their animals from being seized for war service. See *The Standard* (Buenos Aires) 17 July 1866. In Uruguay, similar appeals were made to citizens to contribute their horses to the army (and with similar negative results). See "Caballos para el ejército," *El Siglo* (Montevideo), 11 July 1866.

3   Cardozo, *Hace cien años*, 4: 32.

4   Circular of Francisco Sánchez, Asunción, 1 June 1866, cited in Cardozo, *Hace cien años*, 4: 9; the specific exemption of slaves in this recruitment gives the lie to Garmendia's assertion that López built his new army out of a force of "six-thousand slaves and other contingents." See *Recuerdos de la guerra del Paraguay. Primera parte (Batalla de Sauce—Combate de Yataytí Corá—Curupaytí)* (Buenos Aires, 1890), 43.

5   One report noted the passage of 863 new recruits and thirty-two convalescents southward aboard the steamer *Ygurey*. See Captain Francisco Bareiro to Francisco Solano López, Asunción, 14 June 1866, ANA-NE 3280.

6   Centurión, *Memorias o reminiscencias*, 2: 133; Garmendia, *Recuerdos de la guerra del Paraguay*, 43, puts the figure at thirty thousand.

7   Palleja, *Diário de la campaña*, 2: 353.

8   *The Standard* (Buenos Aires), 7 June 1866. The situation had still not improved a week and a half later when the same newspaper reported that "the state of the hospitals, the gross neglect and want of doctors, and the number of unfortunates found dead each morning in their catres [cots] is really unfit for publication. It is a crying sin that doctors are not sent up … by the score." See *The Standard* (Buenos Aires), 20 June 1866.

9   Francisco Seeber, *Cartas sobre la guerra del Paraguay*, 110–112.

10   On various occasions the high command sought to curb the activities of these sutlers, who caused much jealousy and disorder among the rank and file. See de Marco, *La guerra del Paraguay*, 146–147.

11   *The Standard* (Buenos Aires), 10 June 1866. *La Nación Argentina* had already reported as astounding the sight of the "floating bakeries, whose curious brick ovens [were

constructed] atop every deck as if built on solid ground." See *La Nación Argentina* (Buenos Aires), 9 February 1866.

12 Lucio Mansilla, *Una excursion a los indios ranqueles* (Caracas, 1984), 34–37.

13 Paraguayan intelligence likely had a good notion of Flores's movements at this time. See Leuchars, *To the Bitter End*, 129–131.

14 *El Semanario* (Asunción) issued a special number on 15 June 1866 that claimed an enemy loss of a "minimum of six battalions of infantry," but there was no reason to doubt the more measured statistic recorded by Palleja in his *Diário de la campaña*, 2: 306–307.

15 *Boletín de campaña*, no. 7 (15 June 1866); "Correspondencia de Wenceslao Fernández," unidentified clipping, Palmar de Estero Bellaco, 14 June 1866, BNA, CJO. See also *La Tribuna* (Montevideo), 22 June 1866.

16 Palleja, *Diário de la campaña*, 2: 340.

17 *El Nacional* (Buenos Aires), 22 June 1866.

18 Alberdi had criticized the Triple Alliance from the beginning. His opponents subsequently branded him a traitor, though various commentators, many of them Paraguayans, stepped forward to defend his actions as essentially patriotic. See David Peña, *Alberdi, los mitristas, y la guerra de la Triple Alianza* (Buenos Aires, 1965), and Liliana Brezzo, "Tan sincero y leal amigo, tan ilustre benefactor, tan noble y desinteresado escritor: los mecanismos de exaltación de Juan Bautista Alberdi en Paraguay, 1889–1910." Paper presented at the XXVII Encuentro de Geohistoria Regional, Asunción, 17 August 2007.

19 In its issue of 8 August 1866, *El Siglo* (Montevideo) presented the official Allied line on the suppression of *La América*, noting that, while freedom of the press was a "wonderful thing," it had to be coupled with responsible use, and this was where de Vedia's comportment deserved more than simple censure.

20 The way had been prepared for the arrest with a sharp critique in the 19 July 1866 issue of *La Nación Argentina* (Buenos Aires), in which *La América* was impugned as a throwback to the despotic age of Rosas. The newspaper had its defenders, including Carlos Guido y Spano, who had previously supplied it with articles, and the poet Olegario V. Andrade, who denounced Mitre's actions against free speech in "La suspensión de 'La América,' " *El Porvenir* (Gualeguaychú), 1 August 1866. The *Jornal do Commercio* usually kept silent on internal dissension in Buenos Aires, but on this occasion it lashed out at *La América*, noting that "every day it [revealed itself as] a more pronounced organ of Paraguay." See *Jornal do Commercio* (Rio de Janeiro), 21 July 1866.

21 *El Nacional* (Buenos Aires), 22 June 1866.

22 Guido y Spano, "El gobierno y la alianza," *La Trubuna* (Buenos Aires), 20–25 March 1866; see also Patricia Barrio, "Carlos Guido y Spano y una visión de la guerra del Paraguay," *Todo es Historia* 216 (April 1985): 38–44.

23 The poet Olegario V. Andrade, with his usual flair for the elegiac, referred to the national government's having "sold for foreign gold the fatherland's ancient virtues and glories in pursuit of a stupid ambition." See *El Porvenir* (Gualeguaychú), 12 August 1866. See also Guido y Spano, *Rafagas* (Buenos Aires, 1879), 388–91.

24 The normally pro-government *Standard* admitted with more than normal candor that the war had enriched the country, as would any similar conflict in future, so long as Argentina could "find as rich an ally as Brazil, and so many hungry soldiers to feed with our beef at 7 petacones for each cow." See *The Standard* (Buenos Aires), 20 June 1866.

25 Beatríz Bosch, "Los desbandes de Basualdo y Toledo," *Revista de la Universidad de Buenos Aires*, 4, no.1 (1959): 213–45.

26   Taken from an anonymous flysheet entitled "El nube y el arco iris" (probably written by former Finance Minister Luis Domínguez) and cited in *The Standard* (Buenos Aires), 17 July 1866.

27   Erasmo, *Ao Povo. Cartas políticas* (Rio de Janeiro, 1866), 12–24 and 70–72; *Ao Emperador. Novas cartas políticas* (Rio de Janeiro, 1867?). Alencar was one of the first significant writers in Brazil to set out consciously to create a national literature; his "Indian" novels, especially *O Guarany* (1857), and *Iracema* (1865), introduced a constellation of specifically "Indian" virtues to complement those that the Portuguese had brought from Europe. He hoped to convince the public that such virtues provided a positive gloss to the new Brazilian society; his readers must have recognized, however, that the "American" elements he praised were indistinguishable from the "unspoiled" and "natural" patriotism that other authors had extolled in the Paraguayans. See Manuel Cavalcanti Proença, *José de Alencar na Literatura Brasileira* (Rio de Janeiro, 1966).

28   See Marcos Paz to Mitre, Buenos Aires, 11 July 1866, in *Archivo del general Mitre*, 4: 193, and Juan Manuel Casal, "Uruguay and the Paraguayan War," in *I Die with My Country. Perspectives on the Paraguayan War, 1864–1870* , Hendrik Kraay and Thomas L. Whigham, eds., 132–133.

29   "Mediaciones inaceptables," *El Siglo* (Montevideo), 24 June 1866; "Noticias do Rio da Prata," *Diário do Rio de Janeiro*, 26 June 1866.

30   Cardozo, *Hace cien años* 4: 15–16; in its issues of 23 and 24 June 1866, *La Nación Argentina* (Buenos Aires) referred to mediation offers by France and Chile, and noted that such propositions were wholly inopportune, given that the war "would soon end through the definitive victory of Allied arms." Over the next months, the governments of Peru, Chile, Ecuador, and Bolivia developed a common position on the war that featured a pro-Paraguayan neutrality. For an early example of this argument, see Foreign Minister Toríbio Pacheco to Benigno G. Vigil, Lima, 9 July 1866, ANA-SH 343, no. 16. This letter and related correspondence first appeared in *El Peruano* (Lima), 11 July 1866, and were later reprinted in the Secretaría de Relaciones Exteriores, *Correspondencia diplomática relativa a la cuestión del Paraguay* (Lima, 1867). See also "De la protesta de los Estados Americanos (9 July 1866)," in José Falcón, "Memoria documentada de los territories que pertenecen a la República del Paraguay," MG 64, and Report of Spanish Minister Pedro Sorela y Maury, Buenos Aires, August 1866, in Ruiz Moreno, *Informes españoles sobre Argentina*, 1: 320–322.

31   The man shot for defeatism had been one of the Marshal's mulatto slaves (the son of the woman who had suckled López as a baby). One evening the man was overheard expressing an innocent admiration for the music of the Allied bugler, who, in the distance, had played the *diana* so sweetly. This casual remark cost him his life. Not surprisingly, the Allies depicted his execution as capricious and cruel, whereas the Paraguayans saw it as the product of a necessary firmness. *La Nación Argentina* (Buenos Aires), 20 June 1866.

32   *El Semanario* (Asunción), 7 July 1866.

33   The exasperated Washburn once observed that "the people in Corrientes could not understand why the minister of a great and powerful nation should be hanging on in the rear of the Allied army like a camp follower, and I heard of numerous discussions [about] whether or not I was an accredited minister or an impostor." See Washburn, *The History of Paraguay with Notes of Personal Observations and Reminiscences of Diplomacy under Difficulties* (Boston and New York, 1871), 2: 120; for two examinations of Washburn's conflicted relations with his family members (who included in their number two governors, a senator, an admiral, and a sometime secretary of state), see Theodore A. Webb, *Seven Sons. Millionaires & Vagabonds* (Victoria, 1999), 192–196; and Kerck Kelsey, *Remarkable Americans. The Washburn Family* (Gardiner, Maine, 2008), 182–205.

34 Porto Alegre, it should be noted, could not use Tamandaré's fleet to smash the little Par-
    aguayan flotilla off Encarnación because the shoals near the island of Apipé prevented
    the passage of anything but shallow-draft vessels up the Alto Paraná (except when the
    river was in flood). Porto Alegre to War Minister, 8 May 1866, in Augusto Tasso Fragoso,
    História da Guerra entre a Tríplice Aliança e o Paraguai (São Paulo, 1959), 3: 61–62.

35 *The Standard* (Buenos Aires), 20 June 1866. The 25 July 1866 issue of the same periodical
    explained Porto Alegre's slow pace as resulting from difficult terrain. But Edward Thorn-
    ton, the British minister in Rio de Janeiro, observed that if Porto Alegre had "crossed the
    Upper Paraná at Itapúa, he might have marched to the rear of President López's army,
    and cut him off from his supplies and from the most populous part of the country, the
    inhabitants of which would probably have declared against him … it is this apparent
    absence of proper discretion which makes one doubt as to the future success of the allied
    forces." See Thornton to the Earl of Clarendon, Rio de Janeiro, 7 July 1866, in George
    Philip, *British Documents on Foreign Affairs: Reports and Papers from the Foreign Office
    Confidential Print. Part I: Series D, Latin America, 1845–1914* (London, 1991), 1: 202–203.

36 Colonel Palleja, in one of his final dispatches to the Montevideo and Buenos Aires news-
    papers, noted the superiority of the Marshal's rockets to anything the Allies possessed:
    "if only the Paraguayans knew how to properly direct their [fire] … they would have a
    terrible effect." See *Diário de la campaña*, 2: 363–364; *La Tribuna* (Buenos Aires), 18 July
    1866.

37 Garmendia, *Recuerdos de la guerra del Paraguay*, 124–125, argues that the Paraguayan
    withdrawal was part of a planned maneuver, but offers no proof to illustrate the point.
    See also "Triunfo sobre los paraguayos," unidentified clipping, Tuyutí, 12 July 1866,
    BNA-CJO; the Italian-born General Daniel Cerri, who witnessed the battle as a young
    officer, later emphasized that despite all the smoke and uncertainty, the Argentine forces
    never withdrew from their initial defensive line, no matter that certain Paraguayan
    sources (in particular, Juan Silvano Godoi's *Monografías históricas*) claimed otherwise.
    See "El combate de Yataitic," *La Nación* (Buenos Aires), 28 April 1893.

38 Cardozo, *Hace cien años*, 4: 91; Flores to "Mi querida Agapa," Tuyutí, 12 July 1866, AGN
    (M) Archivos Particulares. Caja 10, carpeta 13, no. 51.

39 *El Semanario* (Asunción), 14 July 1866. See also Pompeyo González [Juan E. O'Leary],
    "Recuerdos de gloria. 16 de julio de 1866. Yataity Corã," *La Patria* (Asunción), 11 July
    1902.

40 Thompson, *The War in Paraguay*, 159.

41 See "Correspondencia del Río Paraguay… julio 15 [1866]," unidentified clipping,
    BNA-CJO.

42 Thompson's success as a military engineer was all the more surprising given his lack
    of training. He was completely self-taught, and relied principally on ragged copies of
    Macaulay's *Field Fortifications* and the *Professional Papers of the Royal Engineers*. See
    Leuchars, *To the Bitter End*, 133. As for Thompson's reputation among the Paraguayans,
    his fellow British engineers noted that he "was beloved by all classes of the natives." See
    Michael G. Mulhall, *The English in South America* (Buenos Aires, 1878), 365.

43 Thompson, *The War in Paraguay*, 160–161; "Segundo viaje al teatro de la guerra," MHM-
    CZ, carpeta 144, no. 1. For a graphic representation of this trench work, and of the
    adjacent terrain, see "Acción de Boquerón. Croquis," *El Pueblo Argentino* (Buenos Aires),
    4 August 1866, and "Reconocimiento de las posiciones ocupadas por nuestras fuerzas
    el 16 y 18 de julio de 1866. Croquis leventado por el ingeniero [Roberto] Chodasiewicz,
    Tuyutí, 23 de julio de 1866," Museo Mitre. Sección Mapas.

44 Osório's gout troubled him immensely, so much so that he had to go barefoot at Tuyutí,
    and, in a letter to his son written from Pelotas on 13 August 1866, he noted that his leg

was "swollen to the groin," and that he was glad to have delivered command to Polidoro, a "well-placed and talented man" destined later to be ennobled as the Viscount of Santa Thereza. See Joaquim Luis Osório and Fernando Luis Osório, *História do General Osório* (Pelotas, 1915), 2: 271; the general's affliction added to his legendary status, and many years later, when an equestrian statue of the hero was unveiled in Rio de Janeiro, the sculptor was roundly criticized for depicting him with a boot upon his swollen foot.

45   Mitre commented some days later that Polidoro "had more of the qualities of a general than Osório, but he had [neither the] experience, [nor the charisma] of his predecessor. … In any case, Osório's command was greater than his capacities; he himself knew it, and this made him morally [sic] as well as physically ill." See Mitre to Vice President Marcos Paz, Yataity, 25 July 1866, in *Archivo del coronel Dr. Marcos Paz*, 7: 232–233.

46   See "Partes relatives ao ataque do 16 de julho ultimo," *Jornal do Commercio* (Rio de Janeiro), 29 December 1866.

47   Leuchars, *To the Bitter End*, 134.

48   Of this plethora of high-ranking Allied officers, Centurión snidely commented: "what a luxury of generals, and see how much [consequent] honor for our modest colonels and captains, the commanders of battalions!" See *Memorias y reminiscencias*, 2: 158–159.

49   Ordem do dia no. 3 (General Polidoro da Fonseca Quintinilha Jordão, Tuyutí, 20 July 1866), cited in Theotonio Meirelles, O Exército Brasileiro na Campanha do Paraguay (Rio de Janeiro, 1877), 163.

50   Palleja, *Diário de la campaña*, 2: 361.

51   Palleja, *Diário de la campaña*, 2: 382–383.

52   Garmendia, *Recuerdos de la guerra del Paraguay*, 73. See also "Parte official del coronel Cesáreo Domínguez," Tuyutí, 20 July 1866, in *La Nación Argentina* (Buenos Aires), 31 July 1866.

53   Iwanovski was born Heinrich Reich in the Prussian city of Posen in 1827. He first came to South America as a recruit to the Brazilian army in 1851 and served in the Caseros campaign. Finding himself destitute in Montevideo, he appeared before the Marques de Castiglione, who was in the Uruguayan capital recruiting troops for Buenos Aires in its struggle against the confederation. Initially, the Marques had no room for Reich, but when a Polish recruit named Iwanovski failed to appear for the muster, the Prussian stepped forward and took his name and place. He served throughout the war with Paraguay and was wounded several times. A general by 1874, Iwanovski was caught by a rebellion in the province of San Luis and died with a revolver in his hand, shouting in his bad Spanish, "I no surrender, I no surrender!" See De Marco, *La guerra del Paraguay*, 75. Ignacio Fotheringham, another immigrant who knew the man well, insisted that his real name was Karl Reichert. See *Vida de un soldado o reminiscencias de las fronteras*, 1: 332. Juvêncio Saldanha Lemos mentions a João Reicher as having served in the 27th of Caçadores during the 1850s, but it is not clear that this is the same man. See *Os Mercenários do Imperador* (Rio de Janeiro, 1996), 571.

54   Domingo Fidel Sarmiento to Editor of *El Pueblo*, Tuyutí, 18 July 1866, BNA-CJO; Giuffra died of his wounds two weeks later in a Correntino hospital. See *La Tribuna* (Buenos Aires), 8 August 1866.

55   Emilio Mitre to Martín de Gainza, Yataity, 19 July 1866, Museo Histórico Nacional (Buenos Aires), 3843.

56   Cuarterolo, "Images of War," 163. The newly arrived troops, though basically unprepared for the fight, were quickly incorporated into Flores's depleted units; for details, see Orden General, Tuyutí, 8 July 1866, in Archivo del Centro de Guerreros del Paraguay, Museo Histórico Nacional (Montevideo), tomo 77.

57 See, for example, "Un episodio del valor oriental. El capitán Pareja [sic]," in Pane, *Episodios militares*, 115–118. The Uruguayan government declared a day of mourning, and the newspapers vied with each other in covering the most lugubrious details of his passing. See *El Siglo* (Montevideo), 1–2 August 1866.

58 Palleja was born José Pons y Ojeda in Seville in 1817, and by the age of twenty had already affiliated with the rebels of Don Carlos. With the latter's defeat in 1839, Pons immigrated to Uruguay, changed his name to Palleja, and joined his new country's army. Like Iwanovski, he served with distinction at Caseros, and had already retired when called back into active service for the Paraguayan campaign, a conflict he regarded as a "stupid error." Palleja wrote sixty-four letters from the front that were published in Montevideo's *El Pueblo* and *El Siglo*, and occasionally republished in Rio's *Jornal do Commercio*, Buenos Aires's *La Tribuna*, and, in English translation, in *The Standard*. See Alberto del Pino Menck, "Armas y letras: León de Palleja y su contribución a la historiografía nacional," senior thesis, Universidad Católica del Uruguay (Montevideo, 1998), revised version presented at Segunda Jornadas Internacionales de Historia del Paraguay, Universdidad de Montevideo, 15 June 2010.

59 "Parte del Mariscal Polidoro, general-en-jefe del primer cuerpo del ejército brasilero," Tuyutí, 23 July 1866, in *Archivo del general Mitre*, 4: 125.

60 Garmendia, *Recuerdos de la guerra del Paraguay*, 79.

61 Centurión, *Memorias o reminiscencias*, 2: 165.

62 Leuchars, *To the Bitter End*,138; *The Standard* (Buenos Aires), 1 August 1866.

63 Garmendia, *Recuerdos de la guerra del Paraguay*, 109; "Teatro de guerra. Combates del 16 y 18," *El Siglo* (Montevideo), 1 August 1866.

64 Doratioto, *Maldita Guerra*, 234.

65 Centurión, *Memorias o reminiscencias*, 2: 166–167.

66 Cuarterolo, "Images of War," 164.

67 Garmendia absolved Flores of all blame for the setback, claiming that the praise accorded the Uruguayan president was unanimous on the Allied side. On the surface, this seems an odd observation, but the gist of Garmendia's dubious interpretation seems to be that Flores's actions saved the Argentines from a worse fate. See *Recuerdos de la guerra del Paraguay*, 101.

68 General Tasso Fragoso notes very different interpretations of the first stages of the battle in the reports filed by Flores, Brigadier Vitorino, and Colonel Domínguez. See *História da Guerra entre a Tríplice Aliança e o Paraguai*, 3: 33–35. See also *Diário do Rio de Janeiro*, 12 August and 1 September 1866.

69 Centurión, *Memorias o reminiscencias*, 2: 168.

4 | RISKS AND SETBACKS

1 See Vicente Barrios to Marshal López, Asunción, 20, 24, and 26 June 1865, ANA-NE 2824.

2 See *La Nación Argentina* (Buenos Aires), 27 June 1866; *Diário do Rio de Janeiro*, 5 July 1866; "Diário da Esquadra," *Jornal do Commercio* (Rio de Janeiro), 21 July 1866.

3 Since the 1850s, the Blyth Brothers of Limehouse, London, had supplied the Paraguayan government with construction materials, engines, iron goods, and the services of foreign machinists and engineers for various state development projects, many, though not all, of them associated with the military. See John Hoyt Williams, "Foreign Técnicos and

the Modernization of Paraguay, 1840–1870," *Journal of Interamerican Studies and World Affairs*, 19, no. 2 (1977): 233–257.

4   Thompson, *The War in Paraguay*, 152, gives the date for this event as 20 June, and also notes that two mines broke loose from their moorings with one striking the *Bahia* and the other the *Belmonte*. The other sources, which claim that a single mine was purposely launched against the *Bahia*, make no reference to the other Brazilian warship, and it appears that Thompson erred in his details.

5   Darryl E. Brock, "Naval Technology from Dixie," *Américas* 46 (1994): 6–15. See also Julio Alberto Sarmiento, "Empleo de minas submarinas en la guerra del Paraguay (1865–1870) y esquema de la evolución del arma hasta fines del siglo XIX," *Boletín del Centro Naval*, 79, no. 648 (1961): 413–427.

6   Though imported chemicals were impossible to find in Paraguay by this point, the Asunción arsenal still possessed good quantities of saltpeter, sulfur, and charcoal for fabricating gunpowder. In fact, each week during this period, shipments of explosives were sent downriver to Humaitá and thence to the front. See, for example, Francisco Bareiro to Solano López, Asunción, 27 July 1866, ANA-SH 350, no. 2, which mentions the transport of sixteen hundred *arrobas* (forty thousand pounds) of powder.

7   Centurión, *Memorias o reminiscencias*, 2: 175; Manuel Avila, "La Controversia Caxias-Mitre,' *Revista del Instituto Paraguayo*, 5, no. 46 (1903): 291–293, argues that it might seem incredible that empty demijohns alone could have kept a powerful squadron in check, but even the Brazilian admiral believed the mines made for a "terribly dangerous [situation], useless to attempt a passage upriver."

8   "Visconde de Tamandaré sobre operações da guerra (1866)," IHGB, lata 314, pasta 4; Lieutenant Francisco de Borja Marques Lisboa added an appendix on Paraguayan mines to his translation of C.W. Sleeman's *Os Torpedos e seu Emprego* (Rio de Janeiro, 1881), 297, in which he noted that they carried between six hundred and fifteen hundred pounds of powder.

9   In a letter to Secretary of State Seward, Charles Washburn emphasized the suspicions of "men better informed of the politics of this country than I am" to the effect that the empire intended to annex not only Uruguay but the Argentine provinces of Corrientes and Entre Ríos as "compensation for the expenses it has incurred." See Washburn to Seward, Buenos Aires, 14 August 1866, WNL.

10   See miscellaneous correspondence of Tamandaré in the Arquivo do Serviço de Documentação Gerald a Marinha (Rio de Janeiro) and in José Francisco de Lima, *Marqués de Tamandaré. Patrono da Marinha* (Rio de Janeiro, 1982), 509–553.

11   Tasso Fragoso, *História da Guerra entre a Triplice Aliança e o Paraguai*, 3: 76–79; Doratioto, *Maldita Guerra*, 234–235.

12   Thompson, *The War in Paraguay*, 167.

13   Pompeyo González (Juan E. O'Leary), "Recuerdos de gloria. 3 de septiembre de 1866. Curuzú," *La Patria* (Asunción), 4 September 1902.

14   Ouro Preto, *A Marinha d'Outrora*, 145.

15   The only officer to survive the sinking of the *Rio de Janeiro* was Lieutenant Custodio José de Melo, who, as an admiral twenty-seven years later, led a major naval mutiny against the new republican government. On the sinking itself, see Cardozo, *Hace cien años*, 4: 196–197; report from war correspondent "Falstaff" (Hector Varela), Vapor *Guaraní*, Corrientes, 7 September 1866, *La Tribuna* (Buenos Aires), 11 September 1866; and "As Experiencias do Capitão James H. Tomb na Marinha Brasileira, 1865–1870," *Revista Marítima Brasileira* (January–March 1964): 45.

16   Thompson, *The War in Paraguay*, 170.

17   See Leuchars, *To the Bitter End*, 143.

18   See "Parte do commandante do Segundo Corpo de Exercito a respeito da tomada de Curuzú, (September 1866)," in *Jornal do Commercio* (Rio de Janeiro), 6 October 1866; Amerlan, *Nights on the Rio Paraguay*, 53.

19   *La Nación Argentina* (Buenos Aires), 12 September 1866, reported a Paraguayan prisoner's claim that the Curuzú garrison numbered 12,700 men, but this number was never believable except to readers far from the front.

20   "Parte do Coronel Manoel Lucas de Lima, Commando da Terceira Divisão, Acampamento nas ruinas do Forte do Curuzú," 3 September 1866, Arquivo Nacional (Rio de Janeiro), 547 vol. 9.

21   "Notas sobre Forças Militares, 1867 [*sic*]," Biblioteca Nacional (Rio de Janeiro), Coleção A.C. Tavares Bastos, 17, 1, 25, no. 15.

22   Amerlan, *Nights on the Rio Paraguay*, 54.

23   Report of Lieutenant Colonel Luis Inácio Leopoldo de Albuquerque Maranhão, Curuzú, 3 September 1866, in Paulo de Queiroz Duarte, *Os Voluntários da Pátria na Guerra do Paraguai* (Rio de Janeiro, 1986), 2, bk. 5: 104–105.

24   His claim of extensive military service notwithstanding, the man was ultimately imprisoned in his home province while officials investigated his status. See "Perguntas feitas ao crioulo Felippe [José Luiz de Souza Reis]," Salvador, 10 June 1870, Arquivo Público do Estado da Bahia, Seção de Arquivo Colonial e Provincial, maço 6464 (as extracted by Hendrik Kraay).

25   Captain Henrique Oscar Wiederspahn, "Tomada de Curuzú," *Revista do Instituto Histórico e Geográfico do Rio Grande do Sul* (1948): 155–164. Report of war correspondent "Falstaff" (Héctor Varela), *La Tribuna* (Buenos Aires), 11 September 1866.

26   *La Nación Argentina* (Buenos Aires), 12 September 1866.

27   Centurión, *Memorias o reminiscencias*, 2: 188.

28   The number of Brazilian losses at Curuzú was, as usual, much disputed, with an improbably high figure of two thousand dead suggested by Colonel Thompson, *The War in Paraguay*, 170, while the baron's own report listed a more believable 772 men (including fifty-three officers) killed, wounded, and missing. See "Parte do Commandante do Segundo Corpo," Curuzú, 14 September 1866, *Jornal do Commercio* (Rio de Janeiro), 6 October 1866. Wiederspahn, "Tomada de Curuzú," 162, offers a total casualty figure of 933, which included the losses suffered by the Brazilian naval forces.

29   See "Officios e correspondencias dos generales Polidoro e Porto Alegre," Rio de Janeiro, 7 October 1866, IHGB lata 312, pasta 14.

30   "Parte do Commandante do Segundo Corpo," *Jornal do Commercio* (Rio), 6 October 1866; Tasso Fragoso, *História da Guerra entre a Triplice Aliança e o Paraguai*, 3: 92.

31   Centurión, *Memorias o reminiscencias*, 2: 189–190.

32   Centurión, *Memorias o reminiscencias*, 2: 191, note b.

33   O'Leary, *Nuestra epopeya (Primera parte)*, 171 (I have slightly altered O'Leary's Guaraní text so as to eliminate any obvious errors of syntax).

34   Confidential Reports of Councilor Octaviano, Tuyutí, 6 September 1866, and General Polidoro, 15 September 1866, both in Tasso Fragoso, *História da guerra entre a Triplice Aliança e o Paraguai*, 2: 95–98. See also Francisco Xavier da Cunha, *Propaganda contra o Imperio. Reminiscencias na Imprensa e na Diplomacia, 1870 a 1910* (Rio de Janeiro, 1914), 26–29, and "Curupayty," *El Pueblo. Organo del Partido Liberal* (Asunción), 12 March 1895.

35   Centurión, *Memorias o reminiscencias*, 2: 197.

36   Adolfo J. Báez, *Yatayty Cora. Una conferencia histórica (Recuerdo de la guerra del Paraguay)* (Buenos Aires, 1929), 22–23.

37   *El Semanario* (Asunción), 15 September 1867; see also Julio César Chaves, *La conferencia de Yataity Corã*, (Buenos Aires, 1958), 18.

38   "La conferencia de Yataitícorá," *La Nación Argentina* (Buenos Aires), 19 October 1866; "Conferencias de paz," and "La entrevista de los generales Mitre y López," *El Siglo* (Montevideo), 23 September 1866; Báez, *Yatayty Cora*, 27–28.

39   Centurión believed that López had had no other motive than to buy time, but the colonel's own annotator, Major Antonio E. González, found this interpretation unconvincing. Instead, he argued that the Marshal could have achieved the same goal by simulating his acquiescence in the treaty of 1 May 1865, and then demanding time to study its provisions more closely. Mitre would certainly have granted this request and López could thus have gained at least several days of cease-fire. Just because such a ploy was open to the Marshal is no reason to suppose that he thought of it. See *Memorias o reminiscencias*, 2: 196, note 27; see also Pedro Calmon, "La entrevista de Iataiti-Cora," *La Nación* (Buenos Aires), 8 August 1937.

40   Centurión felt surprised that López retained this imperial device, wondering how an individual with such strongly anti-Brazilian predilections could wear such an emblem. See *Memorias o reminiscencias* 2: 200.

41   Thompson, *The War in Paraguay*, 175; Juansilvano Godoi, *Monografías históricas* (Buenos Aires, 1898), 138–139; Emanuele Bozzo, *Notizie Storiche sulla Repubblica del Paraguay e la Guerra Attuale* (Genoa, 1869), 54.

42   "Theatro da Guerra," *Diário do Rio de Janeiro*, 4 October 1866.

43   Cited in *Jornal de Commercio* (Rio de Janeiro), 4 October 1866.

44   *The Standard* (Buenos Aires), 19 September 1866.

45   Mitre was fatigued when he wrote this message—it being two in the morning—and begged that a fuller account wait until he had a less-occupied moment. He nonetheless stressed the friendly tone of the meeting and noted that López "sustained his cause in a dignified and orderly manner, in language that was sometimes eloquent." See Mitre to Marcos Paz, Curuzú, 13 September 1866, in *Archivo del coronel Dr. Marcos Paz*, 7: 247–248.

46   Juansilvano Godoi, *Monografías históricas*, 141–142; "Proposiciones de paz," *La Nación Argentina* (Buenos Aires), 19 September 1866.

47   Cardozo, *Hace cien años*, 4: 223; "Relación hecha por el general Mitre el día 5 de septiembre de 1891, comiendo en casa de Mauricio Peirano con el teniente general Roca, doctor E.S. Zeballos y doctor don Ramón Muñíz y el consul de Italia cav. Quicco," in *Historia Paraguaya* 39 (1999): 444–445.

48   Many years later Mitre received a visit from the Marshal's son, Enrique Venancio López, who happened to be in Buenos Aires. As a memento of their pleasant conversation, the aged ex-president presented the younger man with this same riding crop, which today is on display at the Museo del Ministerio de Defensa in Asunción. See Valentín Alberto Espinosa, "Las fustas de Yatayty Cora," *Mayo. Revista del Museo de la Casa de Gobierno*, 3, no. 6–7 (1971): 234.

49   Memorandum of the Interview of Yataity Corã, in "Documentos oficiales" (printed matter), BNA-CJO; *La Tribuna* (Buenos Aires), 20 October 1866.

50   *The Standard* (Buenos Aires), 20 October 1866.

51   Carlos M. Urien, *Curupayty. Homenaje a la memoria del teniente general Bartolomé Mitre en el primer centenario de su nacimiento* (Buenos Aires, 1921), 53–54; see also

Lieutenant Colonel Enrique Jáuregui, "Curupaity," *La Nación* (Buenos Aires) 23 September 1916.

52 Centurión, *Memorias o reminiscencias*, 2: 214–215.

53 Azevedo Pimentel, *Episodios Militares*, 99.

54 "Plan detallado de las operaciones que se efectuarán para atacar Curupaity, las que serán iniciadas por la Escuadra y completadas por las fuerzas de tierra … Curuzú, 16 September 1866," in *Archivo del coronel Dr. Marcos Paz*, 7: 249–251; see also "Ofício confidencial do Almirante Tamandaré (?) ao Marqués de Paranaguá," aboard steamer *Apa*, off Curuzú, 28 October 1866, IHGB, lata 314, pasta 19 and Juan Beverina, *La guerra del Paraguay (1865-1870). Resumen histórico* (Buenos Aires, 1973), 236–238.

55 *The Standard* (Buenos Aires), 27 September 1866.

56 Antonio da Rocha Almeida, *Vultos da Pátria* (Rio de Janeiro, 1961), 1: 150; the Brazilian minister in London forwarded one hundred pounds sterling to the crewmembers of the *Affonso* as reward for their courage in the incident but the sailors insisted that the money be given to the survivors of the *Ocean Monarch*, many of whom had been left penniless in the disaster. Queen Victoria later rewarded Tamandaré with a gold- and jewel-encrusted chronometer inscribed with testimony of the admiration of her government for "the gallantry and humanity displayed by him in rescuing many British subjects from the burning wreck." See J. Arthur Montenego, *Fragmentos Históricos. Homens e Factos da Guerra do Paraguay* (Rio Grande, 1900), 85–87.

57 Fotheringham, *La vida de un soldado*, 2: 119–120.

58 Thompson, *The War in Paraguay*, 178, and First Lieutenant Antonio E. González, "Curupayty," unpublished manuscript, BNA-CJO.

59 Mitre to Rufino Elizalde, 13 September 1866, in Doratioto, *Maldita Guerra*, 229.

60 Seeber, *Cartas sobre la guerra del Paraguay*, 157–158. Garmendia later wrote a heartfelt and poignant eulogy for Roseti that appeared in *La cartera del soldado (Bocetos sobre la marcha)* (Buenos Aires, 2002), 69–74.

61 *The Standard* (Buenos Aires), 11 October 1866.

62 Centurión, *Memorias o reminiscencias*, 2: 217. See also E. A. M. Laing, "Naval Operations in the War of the Triple Alliance, 1864-70," *Mariner's Mirror* 54 (1968).

63 See "Partes dos Commandantes de Divisão de Navíos," (23 September 1866), *Diário do Rio de Janeiro*, 7 Oct. 1866; "Sobre el combate de 22 de septiembre," *El Pueblo* (Buenos Aires), 13 October 1866; and Theotonio Meirelles, *A Marinha da Guerra Brasileira em Paysandu e durante a Guerra do Paraguay. Resumos Históricos* (Rio de Janeiro, 1876), 150–152.

64 Report of Admiral Tamandaré, on board the steamer *Apa*, off Curuzú, 24 September 1866, in *Diário do Rio de Janeiro*, 6 October 1867, and *El Siglo* (Montevideo), 17 October 1866.

65 O'Leary, *Nuestra epopeya (Primera parte)*, 183.

66 See Tamandaré to Naval Minister, Río Paraguay, 22 September 1866, in Arquivo Tamandaré. Serviço Documental Geral da Marinha (Rio de Janeiro).

67 Many scholars and commentators, including Centurión, Godoi, Leuchars, Kolinski, and Carlos Urien, alluded to bugles and drums initiating the Allied assault, but eyewitness Cándido López commented that "scarcely a bugle was heard among the open formations, and … even the march from the encampment was muted and without music." See notes by López in Ricci, *Cándido López. Imagenes de la guerra del Paraguay*, 154.

68 The *sapukai* is almost certainly related to the war whoop of the early Tupi-speakers, whose shrill and ecstatic character was commented upon in the mid-1500s. See Philipp

Camerarius, *Operae horarum sucisivarum sive meditations historicae auctiores quam ante edita* (Frankfurt, 1650).

69 Leuchars, *To the Bitter End*, 150.

70 Thompson, *The War in Paraguay*, 179.

71 See Daniel Cerri, *Campaña del Paraguay* (Buenos Aires, 1892), 29.

72 *La Tribuna* (Buenos Aires), 2 October 1866.

73 Garmendia, *La cartera de un soldado*, 29–38; Belén Gache, "Cándido López y la batalla de Curupaytí: relaciones entre narratividad, iconicidad, y verdad histórica." Paper presented at the II Simposio Internacional de Narratología, Buenos Aires, June 2001; a ninety-five-minute documentary film on the artist's life and accomplishments, entitled *Cándido López y los campos de batalla*, was produced by Argentine cineaste José Luis García in 2004.

74 See José María Avalos to Estanislao Zeballos, Rosario (?), October 1889, MHM-CZ, carpeta 149, no. 15; Calixto Lassaga, *Curupaytí (el abanderado Grandoli)* (Rosario, 1939); and the miscellaneous materials stored in the Archivo del Museo Histórico Provincial de Rosario, legajo "Grandoli."

75 Garmendia, *Recuerdos de la guerra del Paraguay*, 184–190.

76 Miguel Angel de Marco, "La Guardia Nacional Argentina en la guerra del Paraguay," *Investigaciones y Ensayos* 3 (1967): 238.

77 *The Standard* (Buenos Aires), 11 October 1866.

78 Before the engagement began, the Brazilian officers had not shared the same doubts as Roseti and the other Argentines, though they later added their voices to the critical clamor. Even Luiz de Orléans-Bragança, grandson of Pedro II, reluctantly admitted that the defeat had been inevitable. See his *Sob o Cruzeiro do Sul* (Montreaux, 1913), 397.

79 The Viscount of Ouro Preto claimed that the company succeeded in seizing four Paraguayan cannon before being overwhelmed, but this does not appear to have been true. See *A Marinha d'Outrora*, 151.

80 "Parte do Tenente Coronel Alexandre Freire Maia Bittencourt," Curuzú, 23 September 1866, Arquivo Nacional (Rio de Janeiro), Coleção Quintinilha Jordão, vol. 547, no. 1.

81 Mitre's initial notes on the engagement, though extensive, are not especially lucid on this phase of the battle. See Mitre to Acting War Minister Julián Martínez, Curuzú, 24 September 1866, in Urien, *Curupayty*, 215–216.

82 Commentary of the Viscount of Maracajú ("Grande Combate de Curupaity"), Rio de Janeiro, December 1892, IHGB, lata 223, doc. 19 (6–8).

83 Leuchars, *To the Bitter End*, 152.

84 Lucio Mansilla's Private Gómez was one of the men who survived by pretending to be dead. See *Una excursion a los indios ranqueles*, 28.

85 Writing in the early 1890s, Colonel Centurión noted that the unfortunate man—a former draftee in the Argentine forces—was still at that moment in the insane asylum. See *Memorias o reminiscencias*, 2: 220, note a.

86 Centurión, *Memorias o reminiscencias*, 2: 220, note 31.

87 "Detalles sobre el ataque de Curupaiti," *El Siglo* (Montevideo), 3 October 1866, and *El Nacional* (Buenos Aires), 29 September 1866.

88 When moved from the scene of battle, the semi-comatose captain suddenly came to. Mistaking the medical orderlies for Paraguayans on the verge of picking his pocket, he drew a revolver and made ready to shoot, but died before he could pull the trigger. See *La Tribuna* (Buenos Aires), 2 October 1866; see also Andrés M. Carretaro, *Correspondencia*

de Dominguito en la guerra del Paraguay (Buenos Aires, 1975), 9–15; and Juan Antonio Solari, "Dominguito," *La Prensa* (Buenos Aires) 26 June 1966.

89   See the various "Partes Officiaes" issued by the Brazilian corps commanders after the battle, which enumerate the losses in nauseating detail, *Jornal do Commercio* (Rio de Janeiro), 7 December 1866.

90   Report of Joaquim Aniceto Vaz, Major in Command of the 46th Battalion of Voluntários of Bahia, Curuzú, n.d., in Queiroz Duarte, *Os Voluntarios da Pátria*, 2: V, 93; and Tasso Fragoso, *História da Guerra entre a Triplice Aliança e o Paraguay*, 3: 140, 719, 721.

91   How María Curupayti managed to encounter a Paraguayan cavalryman or any enemy soldier during a battle in which the Allies failed to penetrate the enemy line has never been explained. In any case, she recovered from her wound and stayed close to the army for the remainder of the campaign, even serving again in battle with the 42nd Voluntários. She later returned to Rio de Janeiro and was still living there in poverty some thirty years later. See Azevedo, *Episodios Militares*, 149–150. María Curupayti's story was hardly unique among the Brazilians, who were much attracted to romantic interpretations of the war. Another female Voluntária, Jovita Alves Feitosa, was hailed as a sort of Jeanne d'Arc in the earliest stages of the Paraguayan campaign and became even more famous after having committed suicide after her British lover abandoned her in Rio de Janeiro. See *Diário do Rio de Janeiro*, 11 October 1867, and *O Correio Mercantil* (Rio de Janeiro), 11 October 1867.

92   As we have seen, the precise number of casualties at every engagement tended to be disputed in the scholarly literature. Curupayty presents an exception, for although some debate exists as to Allied losses (with Thompson reporting an impossibly high figure of nine thousand Argentines and Brazilians slain), no one seems to question that Paraguayan losses were ridiculously low, certainly no more than two hundred fifty killed and wounded. The figure of fifty-four deaths on the Paraguayan side comes from Colonel Thompson, who may very well have counted them personally. See *The War in Paraguay*, 180.

93   Thompson notes that at Corrientes alone 104 Argentine officers and one thousand men were interned at the hospitals. Brazilian wounded from Curupayty were probably only slightly fewer. See *The War in Paraguay*, 180.

94   Thompson, *The War in Paraguay*, 181; see also report of Juan José Decoud, Curuzú, 23 September 1866, in *La Nación Argentina* (Buenos Aires), 8 October 1866.

95   Thompson, *The War in Paraguay*, 181.

5 | THE ALLIES STUMBLE

1   In a letter to his wife, the Brazilian officer Benjamín Constant noted that the "armed peace" between the Allies and the Paraguayans was designed to starve the Paraguayans, to empty them of all resources, before recommencing the advance. See Constant to his wife, Corrientes (?), 1 November 1866, in Renato Lemos, *Cartas da guerra. Benjamín Constant na Campanha do Paraguai* (Rio de Janeiro, 1999), 56.

2   Thompson, *The War in Paraguay*, 184.

3   Various Colorado leaders had been calling for his return to settle outstanding difficulties among them; in a 5 September 1866 article entitled "El regreso del general Flores," *El Siglo* (Montevideo) insisted that party men were willing to trust in his disinterested attitude and patriotism, but one gets the impression that supporters wanted him back in the Uruguayan capital as soon as possible.

4   Some months earlier Flores remarked in a letter to his wife how ill at ease he felt with modern war: "They do everything by mathematical calculations [and] drawing lines … they postpone all important actions." See Flores to María García de Flores, Campamento de San Francisco, 3 May 1866, in Antonio Conte, *Gobierno provisorio del brigadier general Venancio Flores* (Montevideo, 1897–1900), 1: 412–413.

5   Proclamation of Flores, 25 September (?) 1866, in *La Tribuna* (Buenos Aires), 2 October 1866.

6   "El arribo del general Flores," *El Siglo* (Montevideo), 30 September 1866.

7   Flores to Polidoro, Montevideo, 20 October 1866, cited in Doratioto, *Maldita Guerra*, 249.

8   *New York Times*, 1 December 1866; Flores to Castro, Montevideo, 2 Oct. 1866, AGN (M). Archivos Particulares. Caja 69, carpeta 4.

9   Cardozo, *Hace cien años*, 5: 16.

10   Doratioto, *Maldita Guerra*, 248; government critics in Pernambuco expressed an angry vindication at the news of Curupayty and recast the defeat as anti-monarchist propaganda:

And they speak of Russia! The [imperial] authority
has managed to establish a passive obedience, such
that the only words heard from the mouths of its agents
are *I obey orders*. And through such subservience, the
Brazilians are being conducted to a beheading … without
permitting them the least reflection. … The war with
Paraguay has cost us more than three-hundred *contos*, and
more than 40,000 men, and we still do not know why,
because His Majesty, as they say, does not want peace.

See *O Tribuno* (Recife), 25 October 1866. See also Viscount of Camaragibe to Military Commander, Recife, 6 November 1866, Biblioteca Nacional (Rio de Janeiro), I-3, 8, 10.

11   Rosendo Moniz, "A Victoria de Curuzú," *Jornal do Commercio* (Rio de Janeiro), 6 October 1866. At the beginning of the conflict, the Cariocas had flocked to see dramatic presentations at the São Pedro de Alcantara theater that popularized service in the war—but such presentations were by now long forgotten. See Thomaz de Aquino Borges, *O soldado Voluntário, scena dramática* (Rio de Janeiro, 1865).

12   Recruitment had been exceedingly poor, and a brisk business was now conducted with substitutes for the sons of prosperous families drafted into the National Guard (at a cost of between one hundred and one hundred fifty pounds sterling for each substitute). See, for example, the various advertisements for substitutes in the *Jornal do Commercio* (Rio de Janeiro), 5 January 1867. In addition, as the *Brazil and River Plate Mail* (Rio de Janeiro), in its issue of 22 December 1866, observed: "the Government called out the National Guard, a preliminary step to making drafts from the same for the army, [but] citizens composing the guard have refused to assemble. The war is not popular, but the Government wants men and says it will have them; the people are disinclined to leave their homes for honor and glory." See also "O recrutamento na provincia das Alagoas," *Jornal do Commercio* (Rio de Janeiro), 15 January 1867; *Relatório apresentado á Assembléa Legislativa Provincial [Espírito Santo] no dia da abertura da sessão ordinaria de 1866, pelo presidente, dr. Allexandre Rodrigues da Silva Chaves* (Vitória, 1866), 4–5; "Soldados de Minas Gerais na Guerra do Paraguai," *Revista de História e Arte* 3–4 (April–September 1963): 94–96; Tomás José de Campos a João Lustosa da Cunha Paranaguá, Rio Grande, 1 December 1866, IHGB, lata 312, pasta 23; and Hendrik Kraay, "Reconsidering Recruitment in Imperial Brazil," *The Americas* 55, no. 1 (July 1998): 1–33. As for São Paulo,

previously one of the provinces most abounding in volunteers for war service, between November 1866 and May 1867, of the 1,331 of its men sent to the Paraguayan front, only eighty-seven were volunteers. See Doratioto, *Maldita Guerra*, 265–267. The Paulista experience with recruitment offered considerable material for satirists throughout the war. For examples, see *O Cabrião* (São Paulo), 18 November 1866, 26 May 1867, and 15 September 1867; and *O Mosquito* (São Paulo) 24 October 1869.

13   Speech of Evaristo Ferreira da Veiga, 24 June 1866, in *Annães do Parlamento Brazileiro. Câmara dos Senhores Deputados* (Rio de Janeiro, 1866), 3: 238.

14   Wilma Peres Costa, *A Espada do Dâmocles* (São Paulo, 1996), 222–225.

15   Letter of 8 October 1866, cited in Barman, *Citizen Emperor*, 211 (emphasis in the original).

16   In a subsequent letter to former war minister Ferraz, Polidoro outlined the various failures of command at Curupayty—carefully exempting himself from any criticism –and noted how tired he had grown of all the assorted "accusations." See Polidoro to Àngelo Muniz da Silva Ferraz, Tuyutí, 29 October 1866 and 31 October 1866, IHGB, lata 312, pastas 18 and 12, respectively; see also Firmino José Dória to Marquis of Paranaguá, Estero Bellaco, 4 October 1866, IHGB, lata 18, pasta 22.

17   Adriana Barreto de Souza, *Duque de Caxias. O Homem por Trás do Monumento* (Rio de Janeiro, 2008).

18   Even today, among military officers and the general public in Brazil, the term "caxias" is reserved in common parlance for someone obsessively concerned with discipline and correct bearing. See http://dictionary.reverso.net/portuguese-english/caxias.

19   Cited in Barman, *Citizen Emperor*, 170.

20   *New York Times*, 1 December 1866.

21   Laurindo Lapuente, who spent most of his time dreaming up piquant denunciations of the president, looked back in 1868 to Curupayty and averred that Mitre "had never seized a flag and led his men forward, never had been the first in the attack, never the last in the retreat. [And at Curupayty] … don Bartolo's clock, instead of marking the hour of victory, marked the hour of defeat; once again the prophet Mitre had brought on a fiasco." See *Las profecias de Mitre* (Buenos Aires, 1868), 26–31.

22   The maudlin character of many of the eulogies for the honored dead of Curupayty was quite striking in 1866 and assumed greater proportions in later years. Domingo Faustino Sarmiento's feeling of loss over the death of his son drips from nearly every paragraph of *Vida de Dominguito* (Buenos Aires, 1886), while Vice President Marcos Paz adopted a wholly funereal tone in his equally lugubrious *Una lágrima sobre la tumba de tres soldados* (published posthumously in Buenos Aires in 1873), which describes the martyrdom of his son Francisco, and two other Argentine officers, Julián Portela and Timoteo Caliba. See also B. Moreno, "Domingo Fidel Sarmiento," *La Nación Argentina* (Buenos Aires), 22 September 1867

23   The writer José Marmol was a case in point; in a letter to his friend, the Uruguayan Colonel Emilio Vidal, he asked a series of pointed questions about the conduct of the war, and observing that no progress had taken place since April, concluded by asking whether the time had come to actually make peace. See Marmol to Vidal, Buenos Aires, 15 October 1866, AGN (M). Archivos Particulares. Caja 10, carpeta 18, no. 18.

24   Elizalde to Mitre, Buenos Aires, 3 October 1866, Museo Mitre. Archivo, doc. 1033; see also "El general Mitre y el Brasil," *La Nación Argentina* (Buenos Aires), 3 October 1866.

25   As early as 5 October 1866, the "Americanist" newspaper *El Pueblo* was demanding that General Paunero or some high ranking Argentine officer replace Mitre as commander of Allied forces—better this than any Brazilian general, all of whom had shown their true colors at Curupayty by "fleeing treacherously from the danger." One can see from this

estimation that the attractions of a much-reduced Argentine commitment did not express themselves as a pro-Brazilian sentiment. And *El Pueblo* was far from alone in this attitude: *La Tribuna* (Buenos Aires), 21 October 1866, and *El Nacional* (Buenos Aires), 23 October 1866, made similar observations.

26   *The Standard* (Buenos Aires), 24 October 1866. Eleven months later, a part-time correspondent of the same newspaper caught the basic sense of contemporary Argentine feelings toward their Paraguayan foes when he observed that it was "amusing to hear in the streets the constant use of the word 'Paraguayo' applied to an obstinate mule, a kicking horse, a drunken man, and by women to frighten children. In history we read that the Saracens used to frighten their little ones by threatening to show them Richard Coeur de Leon." See "Another Voice from the War," *The Standard* (Buenos Aires), 18 September 1867.

27   Cited in *The Times* (London), 21 November 1866.

28   A boom in wool exports created by the US Civil War subsided in 1866 due to the imposition of new tariffs by Washington, and Argentine suppliers worried that this might engender a general downturn in the local economy, but the negative effects were generally counterbalanced by the sale of supplies, horses, and cattle to the Brazilians. See McLynn, "Argentina under Mitre: Porteño Liberalism in the 1860s," *The Americas* 56, no. 1 (July 1999): 58–59. The Mitristas, it should be noted, were so associated with sales to the Brazilian army that contemporary critics in Buenos Aires commonly styled the Liberals the "partido de los proveedores" (the party of the suppliers),

29   Though it is tempting to think of the Argentine Congress of those times as an Augean stable of confidence men and plunderers, the representatives that met in Buenos Aires, unlike their Brazilian counterparts, at least held no slaves, and they never forgot that fact when comparing themselves to their nominal allies. The resulting anti-Brazilian sympathies, which were clear and unmistakable, never lost their resonance in the streets of the Argentine capital, even when the Alliance was winning. See Hélio Lobo, *O Pan-Americanismo e o Brasil* (São Paulo, 1939), 44.

30   The white-whiskered Santafecino governor, Nicasio Oroño, was a thoughtful exception to the general run of opportunists among the provincial Mitristas. Initially a pro-war activist, he continued to dispatch troops and matériel to the north in spite of Curupayty, and he did so irrespective of the poor reaction that he knew this measure would bring in the countryside. See Oroño to Marcos Paz, Rosario, 19 October 1866, and José M. de la Fuente to Marcos Paz, Rosario, 20 October 1866, in *Archivo del Coronel dr. Marcos Paz*, 5: 231–233. Later, after Mitre had left office and the success of Allied arms was no longer in doubt, Oroño became senator from his home province and a strong proponent of a phased withdrawal from Paraguay, eloquently arguing that Argentine honor had been satisfied and that further effusion of blood was pointless. See "Cuestión moral. Un decreto injusto y su refutación," in Oroño, *Escritos y discursos* (Buenos Aires, 1920), 469–470, and Miguel Angel de Marco, *Apuntaciones sobre la posición de Nicasio Oroño ante la guerra con el Paraguay* (Santa Fe, 1972), 13–17. In Córdoba, the dominant political factions aligned themselves with Governor Urquiza of Entre Ríos, and as long as he stayed loyal to the national government, so did they; compared to other provinces this fealty cost them little and in any case, the Cordobeses badly needed the goodwill of Buenos Aires given that Indigenous rebels had already taken advantage of domestic confusion to launch attacks against isolated communities. See F.J. McLynn, "Political Instablity in Córdoba Province during the Eighteen-Sixties," *Ibero-Amerikanische Archiv* 3 (1980): 251–269, and León Pomer, *Cinco años de guerra civil en la Argentina. 1865-1870* (Buenos Aires, 1986), 47–52. Corrientes, for its part, wavered back and forth between an unconditional support for Mitre and the war, and a position more conditionally associated with that of Urquiza. See *El Eco de Corrientes* (Corrientes), 27 November 1866. As for Santiago del Estero, that province remained strongly pro-Liberal thanks to the efforts of

the Taboada brothers, whose friendly links with Mitre dated from the 1850s. See Gaspar Taboada, *"Los Taboada." Luchas de la organización nacional* (Buenos Aires, 1929), and David Rock, "The Collapse of the Federalists: Rural Revolt in Argentina, 1863–1876," *Estudios Interdisciplinarios de América Latina y del Caribe* 9, no. 2 (July–Dec. 1998): 6–9. In Tucumán politicians engaged in a lively debate on the province's ambiguous stance during the war. See María José Navajas, "Polémicas y conflictos en torno a la guerra del Paraguay: los discursos de la prensa en Tucumán, Argentina (1864–1869)." Paper presented at the V Encuentro Annual del CEL, Buenos Aires, 5 November 2008.

31   Marcos Paz to Mitre, Buenos Aires, 27 October 1866, in *Archivo del general Mitre*, 6: 152–154, and Fernando Cajías, "Bolivia y la guerra de la Triple Alianza." Paper presented at the V Encuentro Annual del CEL, Buenos Aires, 5 November 2008.

32   *La Epoca* (La Paz), 11 July 1866; newspapermen in Montevideo also signaled out for contempt much of the Peruvian press, especially *El Nacional* (Lima), which had spared no effort in convincing its readers of the righteousness of the Paraguayan cause. See "El Paraguay y la prensa peruana," *El Siglo* (Montevideo), 19 December 1866, and Cristóbal Aljovín, "Observaciones peruanas en torno a la guerra de la Triple Alianza." Paper presented at the V Encuentro Annual del CEL, Buenos Aires, 5 November 2008.

33   Cardozo, *Hace cien años*, 5: 24–25.

34   Burton, *Letters from the Battle-fields of Paraguay*, 202–203. As a standard racist epithet for Brazilians, the term "macaco" has a long history among Platine peoples. It likely derives from folkloric antecedents in Paraguay, with this important difference: while Urquiza's attitude was plainly racist in the "modern" sense of the term, the Paraguayans tended to see Brazilian blacks as inferior because of their slavish status, their race being relatively unimportant. As we have seen, the supposed similarity of "darkies" to howler monkeys (*kaí* or sometimes *karajá*) explicitly reflects their status as buffoons or ill-tempered pests, which is how they are depicted in traditional folklore and in the propaganda directed against Brazil by the López government.

35   José M. Lafuente to Mitre, 10 October 1866, cited in F.J. McLynn, "General Urquiza and the Politics of Argentina, 1861–1870" (PhD diss., University of London, 1976), 242–243. More generally, see David Rock and Fernando López-Alves, "State-Building and Political System in Nineteenth-Century Argentina and Uruguay," *Past and Present* 167, no. 1 (2000): 178–190.

36   Revisionist historians have been particularly active in developing the analysis of the various Montonero rebellions against Buenos Aires (and the many links with the Paraguayan War). In this quite ample literature, which vainly seeks to link Mitre with British imperialism, several works stand out, most particularly Ramón Rosa Olmos, *Historia de Catamarca* (Buenos Aires, 1957), José María Rosa, *La guerra del Paraguay y las montoneras argentinas* (Buenos Aires, 1964), Fermín Chávez, *El revisionismo y las montoneras. La "Unión Americana," Felipe Varela, Juan Saá, y López Jordán* (Buenos Aires, 1966), and Norberto Galasso, *Felipe Varela. Un caudillo latinoamericano* (Buenos Aires, 1975).

37   *El Nacional* (Buenos Aires), 4 January 1867.

38   Ariel de la Fuente, "Federalism and Opposition to the Paraguayan War in the Argentine Interior, La Rioja, 1865–67," in *I Die with My Country*, Hendrik Kraay and Thomas L. Whigham, eds (Lincoln and London, 2004), 146–149; F.J. McLynn, "The Ideological Basis of the Montonero Risings in Argentina during the 1860s," *The Historian*, 46: (Feb. 1984): 235–251. For a contemporary source (prepared in Chile before the rebellion actually began), see Felipe Varela in *Manifesto del jeneral Felipe Varela a los pueblos americanos sobre los acontecimientos políticos de la república Arjentina en los años 1866 y 1867*, Rodolfo Ortega Peña and Eduardo Luis Duhalde, eds. (Buenos Aires, 1968), 80–82, 87.

39　Mitre was not the only man at the front who now regarded the war as endless. One war correspondent begged his readers to face facts about the situation:

> I am not a military man, but as an eyewitness I have seen how the Paraguayans fight from a close quarter. I have seen them fall amid the slaughter crying "Viva López!" Those that I have seen in our hospitals, treated with all affection and care, refuse to condemn the tyrant of their Fatherland. I have seen Paraguayans that have resided years among us refuse to recognize their closest relatives only because they have joined our forces. In recognizing with total impartiality all these things, I think I am not mistaken in assuring you that the war has only just started, and that much blood will yet be shed before the Allied flags will wave [in] Asunción.

See "Tenacidad paraguaya," *El Siglo* (Montevideo), 1 December 1866. Only five days later, the same newspaper repeated the rumor of an anti-López uprising in the Paraguayan camp—yet another case of grasping at straws. See "La sublevación de los paraguayos," *El Siglo* (Montevideo), 6 December 1866.

40　Thompson, *The War in Paraguay*, 186–187.

41　Cardozo, *Hace cien años*, 5: 88; "Correspondencia de Falstaff," *La Tribuna* (Buenos Aires), 14 December 1866 (which gives the number of troops available to Osório at ten thousand).

42　Elizalde to Mitre, Buenos Aires, 6 November 1866, Museo Mitre. Archivo. Doc. 1039.

43　*Ordem do Dia no. 1*, Quartel General, Tuyutí, 18 November 1866; Thompson, *The War in Paraguay*, 187.

44　Thompson claimed that whole battalions of Paraguayan soldiers were henceforth outfitted in Allied uniforms. See *The War in Paraguay*, 181–182.

45　At the Cerro León camp, four officers and 2,110 soldiers were down with wounds and various illnesses at the beginning of December (forty-six had died the previous week). And this was only one of nearly a dozen hospitals filled with the incapacitated. See Francisco Bareiro to War Minister, Asunción, 2 December 1866, ANA-NE 1733.

46　The Paraguayan authorities dealt harshly with any show of defeatism or inclination toward desertion. In early November 1866, the commandant at Humaitá reported the case of a camp follower who had evidently fallen in love with a deserter and who was planning to abscond with him to San Juan Bautista when their liaison was discovered. The woman was arrested and ruthlessly interrogated. The deserter himself escaped into the swamps, and though his pursuers found several campsites he had left behind, the man himself had yet to be captured. See Commandant of Humaitá to War Minister, Humaitá, 3 November 1866, ANA-NE 2408. Individuals found guilty of desertion were commonly sentenced to run a gauntlet of one hundred men four times, and if they survived, they received four years in the public works wearing ball and chain. For examples, see *Proceso* of Simón Aquino, Pilar, 30 January 1865, ANA-SJC 1843, no. 1; *Proceso* of Florencio Godoi, Villa Franca, 9 April 1866, ANA-SJC 1796, no. 10; and *Proceso* of Ildefonso Guyraverá, 15 November 1866, ANA-SJC 1796, no. 9.

47　For details on the establishment and operation of the Paraguayan telegraph, see Robert von Fischer Treuenfeldt to Francsico Solano López, Asunción, 26 May 1864, ANA-CRB I-30, 5, 12, no. 2; von Fischer Truenfeldt to Venancio López, Asunción, 25 August 1864, ANA-CRB I-30, 19, 170; von Fischer Truenfeldt to War Minister, Asunción, 1 December 1864, ANA-CRB I-30, 21, 167–178, no. 11; *El Semanario* (Asunción), 25 June and 9 July 1864; Eliseo Alfaro Huerta, "Documentos oficiales relativos a la construcción dek telégrafo en el Paraguay," *Revista de las Fuerzas Armadas de la Nación* 3 (Oct. 1943): 2381–2390; and, more generally, Benigno Riquelme García, "El primer telégrafo nacional, 1864–1869," *La Tribuna* (Asunción), 13 June 1965.

48　Hutchinson, *The Paraná, with Incidents of the Paraguayan War*, 306.

49   Amerlan, *Nights on the Rio Paraguay*, 89–90.

50   The term "Cuadrilátero" evidently derived from the line of fortress cities that had guarded the Hapsburgs' Italian provinces in the 1850s. See Burton, *Letters from the Battle-fields of Paraguay*, 351–362.

51   Leuchars, *To the Bitter End*, 155–156.

52   Thompson noted that these improvised guns never quite worked right, their range being only fifteen hundred yards. See *The War in Paraguay*, 191.

53   Thompson, *The War in Paraguay*, 191–192; regarding the production of cannon and shell at the foundry at this time, see Francisco Bareiro to War Minister, Asunción, 2 July 1866, ANA-SH 350, no. 2, and 5 August 1866, ANA-NE 761. See also Whigham, "The Iron Works of Ybycui: Paraguayan Industrial Development in the Mid-Nineteenth Century," *The Americas* 35, no. 2 (1978): 213–217

54   The existence of deposits of saltpeter had been recognized in Paraguay since colonial times, but received more attention with the onset of the war. Regarding gunpowder manufacture and the dangers of periodic and unplanned explosions, see Francisco Bareiro to War Minister, Asunción, 12 August 1866, ANA-NE 1731; Bareiro to Commandant of Concepción, Asunción, 24 January 1867, ANA-NE 3221; Twite to War Minister, Valenzuela, 3 July 1867, ANA-NE 2465; and Zenón Ramírez to Juansilvano Godoi, Asunción, 10 March 1918, UCR Godoi Collection, Box 5, no. 91.

55   Thompson, *The War in Paraguay*, 205; one woodcut published in the satirical newspaper *Cabichuí* shows the Marshal's gunners catching the shells fired at them by the Allies for reuse with their own artillery ("thus do the Paraguayans know how to make use of everything, [not excluding] the shells given them as gifts)." See *Cabichuí* (Paso Pucú), 5 December 1867.

56   Centurión, *Memorias o reminiscencias*, 2: 235.

57   Even before Allied troops arrived on Paraguayan soil, rumors circulated that France and the United States would intervene to force a cessation of hostilities. Though this was clearly wishful thinking at the time, in the aftermath of Curupayty, the idea no longer seemed so improbable. See Francisco Bareiro to War Minister, Asunción, 6 March 1866, ANA-NE 681; "La guerra del Paraguay," *El Siglo* (Montevideo), 16 October 1866; and Gregorio Benítes to Alberdi, Paris, 15 November 1866, Archivo Alberdi, no. 1079.

58   Washburn to José Berges, Asunción, 12 November 1864, WNL.

59   Washburn frequently committed his ruffled feelings to paper, producing a seemingly unending correspondence, full of complaints to friends, family, and US officials in Washington. These letters, many of which can be found today in the Washburn-Norlands Library in Livermore Falls, Maine, reveal much about Asunción society in the mid-1860s; but they also reveal a profoundly irritable man, ill-suited to his occupation, who found himself with rather more time on his hands than is healthy in a diplomat. He had an affair with a Paraguayan woman during his early stay, from which issued a child that he never formally recognized but never denied either. The descendants of this child are still living in Asunción today. See Letter of former US minister to Paraguay Martin McMahon in *New York Evening Post*, 13 January 1871.

60   The *Shamokin* was not the only ship whose passage upriver had been impeded by Allied fiat. Only six weeks before, Tamandaré had prevented the transit of the French warship *Decidee*, even though her captain insisted that he carried important diplomatic correspondence for the French consul in Asunción. See Sallie C. Washburn Diary, entry of 30 September 1866, WNL. See also Thomas Whigham and Juan Manuel Casal, eds., *Charles A. Washburn, Escritos escogidos. La diplomácia estadounidense en el Paraguay durante la Guerra de la Triple Alianza* (Asunción, 2008), 197.

61   Sallie C. Washburn Diary, entry of 5 November 1866, WNL.

62 Cardozo, *Hace cien años*, 5: 84–90. Washburn later ventured that this sickness was political, a result of the Marshal's disappointment that Tamandaré had not forced an incident with the Americans. See Washburn, *History of Paraguay*, 2: 137.

63 Washburn, *History of Paraguay*, 2: 138–155.

64 Cardozo, *Hace cien años*, 5: 125–126.

65 Berges to Washburn, Asunción, 30 November1866, ANA-CRB I-22, 11, 2, no. 1. See also "Presencia del señor Washburn en la república," *El Semanario* (Asunción), 10 November 1866.

66 Frank O. Mora and Jerry W. Cooney, *Paraguay and the United States. Distant Allies* (Athens, Georgia, and London, 2007), 43–53, 64–65, 69–72, 82–87, 122–123, 179–181, 251–252.

67 There was even talk after Appomattox of Grant leading an army of Union veterans who would immigrate to Mexico and help Juárez there. See Robert Ryal Miller, "Matías Romero: Mexican Minister to the United States during the Juárez-Maximilian Era," *Hispanic American Historical Review*, 45, no. 2 (1965): 242–245, and more generally, Thomas David Schoonover, *Dollars over Dominion: The Triumph of Liberalism in Mexican-United States Relations, 1861-1967* (Baton Rouge, 1978).

68 Watson Webb to William H. Seward, Rio de Janeiro, 7 August 1866, Department of State, *Papers Relating to Foreign Affairs* (Washington, 1866), 2: 320.

69 Cong. Globe, 39th Cong., 2nd Sess. 37 (1866–1867), bk. 1: 152.

70 Peterson, "Efforts of the United States to Mediate in the Paraguayan War," 6; a caricature in the Argentine satirical magazine *El Mosquito* (13 January 1867) portrays Uncle Sam as a cowboy, holding revolvers against both Mitre and López and proclaiming, "Ugh. You two have been fighting for so long that I have come to make the peace, and I have brought with me two little pieces of hardware to make you see reason." It is doubtful that the Argentine satirist was aware of Washburn's previous experience as a duelist in California, but in this one sense, the caricature was more apposite than anyone might have known.

71 S.D. to "Querido Amigo," in unidentified newspaper clipping, 22 December 1866, in BNA-CJO.

72 Artur Silveira da Mota, *Reminiscencias da Guerra do Paraguai* (Rio de Janeiro, 1982), 102–108.

73 Antonio da Rocha Almeida, *Vultos da Pátria* (Rio de Janeiro, 1965), 3: 129.

74 Viscount of Ouro Preto, *A Marinha d'Outrora*, 155.

75 Thompson, *The War in Paraguay*, 186.

76 Washburn, *History of Paraguay*, 2: 158–159.

77 Washburn, *History of Paraguay*, 2: 159.

78 Berges to Washburn, Asunción, 29 December 1866, ANA-CRB, I-22, 11, 2, no. 4. López had at first declined to release those Americans who had been in the Argentine naval service and had been captured aboard their ships when Paraguay occupied Corrientes in 1865; Washburn argued that the men ought not be held responsible for any hostile intent towards Paraguay, as a state of war with Argentina did not yet exist when they were captured. The Marshal, who understood that his government's acceptance of such an argument would put the irregularity of his attack on Corrientes into question, initially refused to budge on the matter and only relented as an explicit gesture of friendship to the United States.

79 Washburn, *History of Paraguay*, 2: 150–161.

80 Washburn, *History of Paraguay*, 2: 164.

81 Foreign Residents to Editor, Asunción, 28 December 1866, in *El Semanario* (Asunción), 29 December 1866.

82 Cardozo, *Hace cien años*, 5: 192.

83 Gelly y Obes to Estanislada Alvarez de Gelly y Obes (Talala), Itapirú (?), 1 January 1867, in Gelly y Obes, "Guerra de la Triple Alianza contra el Paraguay," *Revista de la Biblioteca Nacional*, 21, no. 51 (1949): 149–150.

84 "Correspondencia del ejército," *El Semanario* (Asunción), 12 January 1867.

85 "Rasgos biográficos, honores fúnebres y discursos pronunciados sobre la tumba del ciudadano José Díaz," *La Democrácia* (Asunción), 10 July–1 August 1892. See also Letter of Cleto Romero to Ignacio Ibarra, (July 1892), MHN (A), Colección Gill Aguinaga, Carpeta 154, no. 2.

86 Testimony of Captain Pedro V. Gill, Asunción (24 April 1888), MHM (A)-CZ, carpeta 137, no. 10.

87 The sword, the wreath, and the book of valedictories were paid for with public subscriptions. At a time when the Paraguayan population was starting to go hungry, an extensive outlay of money was wasted on these baubles, and yet any person who failed to contribute risked consequences more fearful than an empty stomach. See "Adhesión de las damas de San Pedro al proyecto del obsequio de una guirnalda de oro y brillantes al Presidente," (San Pedro, 1867), ANA-SH 352, no. 10; "El mariscal López frente a los enemigos de la patria," *Cabichuí* (Paso Pucú), 24 July 1867; and "Al gran mariscal López, vencedor de la triple alianza," *El Centinela* (Asunción), 7 November 1867. Perhaps the most obsequious examples of this public reverence came, however, from the interior villages, where justices of the peace and private parties were constantly wasting precious paper in composing letters of praise to be read before their respective citizens. See, for example, Letter of Juana B. Valdovinos de Benítez, Itauguá, 1867(?), ANA-NE 684.

88 The expression "más paraguaya que la mandioca" is modern, but perfectly encapsulates a particular Paraguayan type, of which Díaz was a good example. On Paraguayan national identity, "ideal types," and the universality of the Guaraní language, see Helio Vera, *En busca del hueso perdido (tratado de paraguayología)* (Asunción, 1995).

89 Juansilvano Godoi, *"El jeneral Díaz,"* in Monografías históricas (Buenos Aires, 1893), 12–14; Pablo Duarte, *Jeneral Díaz.Conferencia dada en el pueblo de Pirayú con motivo de la colocación de la primera piedra fundamental del monumento a la memoria del héroe de Curupaiti, en Setiembre 24 de 1911* (Asunción, 1913), 7–8.

90 Chaves, *El general Díaz*, 118–119; and, more generally, Silvano Mosqueira, *General José Eduvigis Díaz* (Buenos Aires, 1900).

91 Every town in the country went into official mourning, and Díaz's name was henceforth used when still more patriotic sacrifices were demanded of the people. Regarding memorial services in Villarrica, see Ramón Marecos to War Minister, 21 March 1867, ANA-NE 758. More generally, see eulogies in *El Semanario* (Asunción), 9 February and 16 February 1867.

92 Mitre to Paz, Yataity, 24 January 1867, in *Archivo del coronel Dr. Marcos Paz*, 7: 282–285.

93 This particular story, which has the ring of overstatement, first appeared in the annotations of Diego Lewis and Angel Estrada, Argentine translators of the first Spanish edition of the Thompson memoirs. See Thompson, *La guerra del Paraguay*, 2nd edition (Buenos Aires, 1910), 1: 193; though the interchange does not appear in the original English version, Mitre did subsequently send Caxias extensive comments on strategic questions, though this did not happen before mid-April 1867. See Thompson, *La guerra del Paraguay*, 2nd edition (Buenos Aires, 1910), 2: 5–6.

94 Caxias to Lustosa da Cunha Paranaguá, Tuyutí, 10 February 1867, IHGB lata 313, pasta 5.

95   Diarrhea could be fatal for men so undernourished. At the end of May 1866, the officer in charge of the Asunción military hospital reported that two officers and eighty-six men had died over the previous week, with one officer and thirty-two men dying from wounds, the rest from diarrhea. See Francisco Bareiro to War Minister, 27 May 1866, ANA-NE 681; 652 deaths were recorded at the Cerro León hospital between 23 June and 29 September 1866, the great majority from diarrhea, and most of the rest from "fevers." See "Lista de los individuos muertos en el hospital," Campamento Cerro León 23 June through 6 October 1866 (seven separate reports), ANA-NE 2438.

96   To judge from the reports of small-town officials, the Paraguayan countryside was particularly affected during this earlier epidemic. See Francisco Pereyra to Carlos Antonio López, Pilar. 29 February 1844 in ANA-SH 395; Julián Bogado to López, Santa Rosa, 27 May 1844 (which records seventy-three Indigenous people dead from smallpox since 16 April), ANA-NE 1376; Juan Pablo Benítez to López, Villarrica, 25 June 1844 (which records seventy deaths since 2 April), ANA-NE 1376; Agustín Ramírez to López, Itauguá, 6 November 1844 (which records 556 deaths over the previous season), ANA-NE 1376; and especially "Cuaderno que contiene … listas de los fallecidos de la peste de viruelas, correspondiente al año de 1845," ANA-NE 805.

97   See Francisco Sánchez to Gefe de Urbanos of Atýra, Asunción, 23 December 1862, ANA-SH 331, no. 22; "Legajos de participantes de los juices de campaña sobre la inoculación de viruelas [1863–65], ANA-SH 417, nos. 1 and 7; and "Instrucción para la vacunación e inoculación de la viruela" (Asunción, nd), ANA-SH 340 no. 8. On the Brazilian side, army regulations insisted that all recruits be vaccinated against smallpox, but given the number of men hospitalized for the disease not just in Mato Grosso but at Tuyutí, we can presume that the effort was only partially effective. Out of 10,506 patients listed in hospital at the latter encampment in May 1867, 390 had smallpox. See Manoel Adriano da Sá Pontes ao Ajudante General Francisco Gomes de Freitas, Tuyutí, 10 May 1867, Arquivo Nacional (as extracted by Adler Homero Fonseca de Castro). More generally, see Whigham, *La guerra de la Triple Alianza*, 2: 288–297

98   See Ramón Marecos to War Minister, Villarrica, 30 April 1866, ANA-NE 758 (which notes that 295 children had been inoculated against smallpox); and "Instrucción para los empleados de campaña sobre el regimen a observarse en la epidemia de la viruela según algunos casos, particularmente en la actualidad en que se carece de la vacuna" (Asunción, 22 October. 1866), ANA-NE 3221.

99   In a report to his superiors in Paris, the French minister to Asunción claimed that more than a tenth of the Asunceno population had succumbed to smallpox between March and May 1867, but it is difficult to know what to make of this statistic as the other sources made no similar references. The minister was strongly in favor of introducing modern methods of inoculation and perhaps this emphasis led him to exaggerate the prevalence of the disease in the Paraguayan capital. See Report of Emile Laurent-Cochelet, no. 61, Asunción, 31 May 1867, in Capdevila, *Une Guerre Totale*, 420–421.

100   See Francisco Bareiro to War Minister, Asunción, 16 April 1866, ANA-NE 681; Martín Urbieta to Solano López, Mbotety en Nioac, 18 April 1866, ANA-CRB I-30, 11, 56; and Bareiro to Teniente Núñez, Asunción, 16 May 1866, ANA-NE 767.

101   *Relatório com que o Exm. Snr. Dr. João José Pedrosa, Presidente da Provincia de Matto-Grosso abrió a Primeira Sessão da 22a Legislatura da Respectiva Assembléa no Dia Primeiro de Novembro* (Cuyabá, 1878), 32; Luiz de Castro Souza, *A Medicina na Guerra do Paraguai* (Rio de Janeiro, 1971), 107–115.

102   Alexandre José Soeiro de Faria Guaraní, "Esboço Histórico das Epidemias de Cólera-Morbos, que Reinaram no Brasil desde 1855 até 1867," in *Anais da Academia de Medicina do Rio de Janeiro*, tomo 55 (1889–1890); Enrique Herrero Ducloux, "Juan J. J. Kyle," *Anales de la Sociedad Quimica Argentina*, 7, no. 31 (1919): 9–10; and

"Correspondencia, (Tuyutí, 14 March 1867)," in *Jornal do Commercio* (Rio de Janeiro), 13 April 1867. One rather obscure Buenos Aires newspaper, *El Inválido Argentino*, suggested on 5 March 1867 that the epidemic had actually begun not in the south, but in the war zone itself, where, it was claimed, both the Paraguayans and the Brazilians often disposed of their cadavers in the river, and thus contaminated all the waters downstream. This ludicrous argument was easily refuted by individuals with medical experience. See Miguel Angel de Marco, "La sanidad argentina en la guerra con el Paraguay (1865–1870)," *Revista Histórica* 4, no. 9 (1981): 75–76.

103 Thompson, *War in Paraguay*, 189; an "unsubstantiated Buenos Aires telegram" claimed that twenty-seven hundred of the six thousand men stationed at Curuzú had died of cholera in only four days. See *The Times* (London), 3 June 1867.

104 Cardozo, *Hace cien años*, 6: 83. A more extensive analysis of the disease, with similar suggestions as to its treatment, can be found in Lucilo del Castillo, *Enfermedades reinantes en la campaña del Paraguay*. Tesis (Buenos Aires, 1870).

105 José María Penna, writing thirty years later of the virulence of the disease during the war, noted, somewhat improbably, that the rate of mortality among Allied soldiers sick with cholera ranged from 61 percent among the Brazilians to 77 percent among the Argentines. See Penna, *El cólera en la república argentina* (Buenos Aires, 1897).

106 Cerqueira, *Reminiscencias da Campanha do Paraguai*, 279–280.

107 The commander of the Uruguayan units remaining in Paraguay after Flores's departure reported that cholera went through the Brazilian and Argentine ranks first and only reached the Uruguayans at the end of May 1867; thirteen cases had been registered within those same units in the first week of exposure, of which nine died. See Enrique Castro to Venancio Flores, Tuyutí, 6 June 1867, AGN (M). Archivos Particulares. Caja 10, carpeta 10, no. 48.

108 Leuchars, *To the Bitter End*, 158.

109 *Anglo-Brazilian Times* (Rio de Janeiro), 8 May 1866.

110 Caxias sent troops to protect the hospitals against this eventuality. See Miscellaneous Correspondence and Reports on Correntino Hospitals (1867), MHM (A), Colección Gill Aguinaga, carpetas 3, nos. 1–17, and 91, nos. 1–25; "Correspondencia de Corrientes," (5 May 1867), in *La Nación Argentina* (Buenos Aires), 9 May 1867; and Cardozo, *Hace cien años*, 6: 90.

111 "La enfermedad reinante," *La Nación Argentina* (Buenos Aires), 18 April 1867; "Ejército del Paraguay," *Nación Argentina* (Buenos Aires), 27 April 1867. (The Argentines did, in fact, move a large portion of their troops to a new camp some months later).

112 In a short note written just before the onset of epidemic conditions at the front, General Gelly y Obes begged his old associate Colonel Alvaro Alsogaray to reassure their mutual friends in Buenos Aires that the tales of a new cholera crisis were "complete nonsense." See Gelly y Obes to Alsogaray, 7 April 1867, MHM (A)-CZ, carpeta 149, no. 33. The general's comment reflected a misplaced hope, and by the time news of the epidemic reached Europe, it had already grown outlandishly in the public mind and was frequently cited by Juan Bautista Alberdi as yet another monstrous byproduct of the alliance with Brazil. See Alberdi to Gregorio Benítes, Saint André, 17 November 1867, MHN (BA), doc. 2303.

113 The circumstance of malnutrition and lack of medicines provides the context for a curious article in one of the state newspapers on the utility of the coca plant, not a part of the native Paraguayan flora, but very useful in the Bolivian Altiplano in providing energy and in staving off the effects of hunger. See "La coca," *El Centinela* (Asunción), 26 September 1867.

114 López to José Berges, Paso Pucú, 18 April 1867, ANA-CRB I-30, 13, 2, no. 5.

115 Cerqueira, *Reminiscencias da Campanha do Paraguai*, 215.

116 See "Medidas que de prompto se devem tomar nos acampamentos dos exercitos alliados para prevenir-se o apparecimento de qualquer enfermidade epidemica," (Tuyutí, 31 Mar 1867), in "Exterior," *Jornal do Commercio* (Rio de Janeiro), 18 May 1867.

117 Miguel Arcanjo Galvão to João Lustosa da Cunha Paranaguá, Montevideo, 28 May 1867, IHGB lata 312, pasta 55 (Coleção Marqués de Paranaguá).

118 Francisco Pinheiro Guimarães, *Um Voluntário da Patria* (Rio de Janeiro, 1958), 222. Only a few months earlier Caxias had complained with good reason that many men in hospital were shamming and that the instances of illness in camp were exaggerated; but the epidemic character of the disease on this occasion could not be doubted. See Caxias to Marquis de Paranaguá, Tuyutí, 30 January 1867, IHGB lata 313, pasta 4.

119 "Correspondencia," (Corrientes, 24 May 1867) in *Jornal do Commercio* (Rio de Janeiro), 3 June 1867.

120 Thompson, *The War in Paraguay*, 201.

121 Regarding Dr. Rhynd, whose services to the Paraguayan cause had earned him the National Order of Merit the previous year, see Juan Gómez to Fausto Coronel, Asunción, 8 June 1867, ANA-NE 2459. In a telling aside, Colonel Thompson attributed Benigno López's sickness to "fright," but given the virulence of the cholera epidemic at the time, there is no reason to suppose that such a senior figure could not also fall ill. See Thompson, *The War in Paraguay*, 202.

122 Victor I. Franco, *La sanidad en la guerra contra la Triple Alianza* (Asunción, 1976), 80; Dionísio M. González Torres, "Centenario del cólera en el Paraguay," *Historia Paraguaya* 2 (1966): 31–47.

123 See, for instance, Receipt of 15 pesos to pay salaries for six peones working to produce ice for the national government (27 January 1867), ANA-NE 1765.

124 Ships coming from Humaitá were also subjected to a quarantine of ten days once they reached the Paraguayan capital. See French minister Laurent-Cochelet to the Marquis de Moustier, Asunción, 31 May 1867, cited in Milda Rivarola, *La polemica francesa sobre la Guerra Grande* (Asunción, 1988), 161.

125 Centurión, *Memorias o reminiscencias*, 2: 257.

126 Dionísio M. González Torres, *Aspectos sanitarios de la guerra contra la Triple Alianza* (Asunción, 1966), 63.

127 Centurión, *Memorias o reminiscencias*, 2: 256–257.

128 Thompson, *The War in Paraguay*, 202.

6 | INNOVATIONS AND LIMITATIONS

1 G. F. Gould to George Buckley Matthew, Buenos Aires, 26 April 1867, cited in Rock, "Argentina under Mitre," 49.

2 *El Semanario* (Asunción), 1 December 1866 and 23 February 1867.

3 Charles Ames Washburn, who never missed an opportunity to castigate the Marshal, nonetheless expressed praise for the valor of the common soldier while denouncing the barbarism of López: "they do not surrender even though inevitable death be the consequence of refusal, [replying always that] their orders are to fight and not to surrender—and they literally obey this command; their enemies say that this blind desperation results from a superstitious fear … of López [who would put them] to inconceivable torture, [and who uses] a system of vicarious punishment [by which] he visits the most terrible cruelties on the families of all who by surrendering escape from his [clutches]; but whatever the cause they admit that the Paraguayans fight with wonderful courage and endurance." In this, the US minister could just as easily have been describing the

temperament of Paraguayan civilians. See Washburn to Seward, Corrientes, 8 February 1866, WNL.

4   In his *Francisco Solano López and the Ruination of Paraguay*, James Saeger emphasizes the role of force in explaining the collusion of the Paraguayan people in the worst of the Marshal's excesses. He thereby contradicts the greater part of eyewitness testimony and misses an important opportunity to delve into the more frightening side of group psychology. The appeal to duty, which is lauded in both literature and recruitment drives, can command a powerful influence in many countries, and was recognized as crucial by the Paraguayans before and after the war. In an article in *La Unión. Organo del Partido Nacional Republicano* (Asunción), 5 August 1894, a representative of the veteran's association ridiculed the idea that force had had anything to do with his comrades' comportment during the war: "our opponents do not say—because they cannot—that we were cowards, so they affirm with an incredible audacity that [we fought] out of fear of López's punishments, as if in the field of battle we did not face certain death." Loyalty, even to a bad leader, thus explains far more than force why the Paraguayan people behaved the way they did.

5   Jerry W. Cooney, "Economy and Manpower. Paraguay at War, 1864-1869," in *I Die with My Country. Perspectives on the Paraguayan War*, Hendrik Kraay and Thomas L. Whigham, eds. (Lincoln and London, 2004), 23–43.

6   Olinda Massare de Kostianovsky, *El vice-presidente Domingo Francisco Sánchez* (Asunción, 1972); Juan F. Pérez Acosta, "El vice-presidente Sánchez: Curiosos detalles de su administración," in *El Orden* (Asunción), 17, 18, 19, 22, 23, 24, 29, and 30 December 1924. US minister Washburn described the vice president in typically derisive terms, calling him "a decrepit old man of about eighty-two ... [with] a good share of Jesuitical craft, and an easy style not wanting in dignity ... [who] was without ambition ... and never had anything to suggest of his own volition, and hence never provoked the jealousy of either of the despots he served." See *History of Paraguay*, 2: 228–229.

7   Insecurity drove the average person to invest what silver they had in a small and easily concealed bulk. Thus the idea of hidden treasure—so much a part of the Solano López legend—in fact has some basis in traditional practices. As for outright theft, see miscellaneous legal records concerning robberies of food, wine, money, cloth, etc. (for 1866-1867) in ANA-NE 1720, and for a specific instance concerning the theft of a poncho at Humaitá, see Vicente Osuna to War Minister, Humaitá, ANA-NE 2408.

8   The smuggling of foodstuffs was more of a problem than the government cared to admit. See Sallie Cleveland Washburn Diary, entry for 27 August 1867 and 30 November 1867, in Whigham and Casal, *La diplomacia estadounidense*, 232, 243.

9   Cooney, "Economy and Manpower," 23–24.

10   Sánchez had always been an exceptionally capable state official, but the presidential family nonetheless treated him with a public contempt. Masterman tells the story of a British diplomat who visited Asunción in the late 1850s and made the mistake of addressing correspondence to then Foreign Minister Sánchez as "His Excellency," an honorific perilously close to that reserved for President Carlos Antonio López; the matter filled Sánchez with fear and the president with vexation, after which the latter gruffly observed, "Call him what you please, he will remain but a blockhead still." See *Seven Eventful Years in Paraguay*, 37–38.

11   The quantities of jewelry contributed were extensive, as was the paperwork generated in praise of the contributors. See, for example, Blas Espínola to President of Commission, Pirayú, 1 September 1867, ANA-NE 2454; "Donaciones de alhajas y joyas," (1867), MHM (A), Colección Gill Aguinaga, carpeta 24, nos.1–72; and, more generally, the carefully annotated list of contributions in six enormous tomes, that today can be consulted (in an unorganized section) of the Archivo Nacional de Asunción. Using these contributions to

purchase arms and munitions from outside sources would have been nearly impossible given the blockade, though later in the war certain neutral ships did reach Asunción and may have ferried some of the silver out at that time. US minister Washburn and his successor, Martin McMahon, were both accused of having illegally exported what jewels remained, though it is more likely that Allied soldiers did the deed. Even so, the fate of the jewelry remains the stuff of legend in Paraguay and over the years has fueled any number of treasure hunts, scholarly examinations, and novelistic speculations. See "Joyas de familias paraguayas," *El Liberal* (Asunción), 11 and 13 June 1925; Héctor Francisco Decoud, "Las celebres alhajas de la guerrra," *La Tribuna* (Asunción), 5–7 and 11 February 1926.

12 Leuchars, *To the Bitter End*, 195. In a letter written after the war, the British physician William Stewart observed that Madame Lynch's collection of jewelry even then was still "worth more than 60,000 pounds sterling ... most of it the spoils of the poor Paraguayans." See Stewart to Charles Washburn, Newburgh, Scotland, 20 October 1871, WNL.

13 Encarnación Bedoya, a young woman from a prominent family, recounted that when "the tyrant López wanted the rich families to give up their jewelry for the maintenance of the war, the gold that was gathered was for him alone and Doña Fulana [Madame Lynch] ... [and, thus,] when asked for the jewelry, nobody gave anything except rings from wire and old earrings ... [since we knew who had demanded] the jewelry and nobody gave anything save those pieces that they could spare anyway." See Potthast, "Paraguayan Women in the 'Great War,' " 48–52, and Thompson, *The War in Paraguay*, 200–201.

14 Cooney, "Economy and Manpower," 24–25; Vera Blinn Reber, in "A Case of Total War: Paraguay, 1864–1870," *Journal of Iberian and Latin American Studies* 5, no. 1 (1999): 27, makes the odd observation that "With decreased revenues, the government printed currency to finance military expenditures, and it paid no attention to the relationship of paper currency to gold or silver." In fact, as the article itself demonstrates, the Paraguayan state paid careful and detailed attention to that relationship.

15 Laurent-Cochelet to Drouyn de L'Huys, Asunción, 6 February 1865, in Rivarola, *La polémica francesa sobre la Guerra Grande*, 154.

16 See, for example, "Lista de contribuyentes de ganado," Paraguarí, 31 May 1866, ANA-NE 2831; John Hoyt Williams, "Paraguay's Nineteenth-Century *Estancias de la República*," *Agricultural History* 47, no. 3 (1973): 215.

17 "Circular sobre la remisión de ganados al campamento de Humaitá," (1867), ANA-SH 352, no. 23; "Lista nominal de los individuos de este partido que han contribuido Ganado para gastos del Ejército," San José de los Arroyos, 27 May 1866, ANA-NE 2831; Mariano González to Comandante de Villarrica, 22 June 1866, ANA-NE 3258; "Lista nominal de ... individuos que han contribuido Ganado bacuno para consumo de los Ejércitos," Quyquyó, 1 December 1867, ANA-NE 2445; and "Lista nominal de las personas contribuyentes de reses," Yuty, 17 December 1867, ANA-NE 1731.

18 See "Circular de Saturnino Bedoya sobre cobre y bronce" (Asunción), 1 January 1867, ANA-SH 352, no. 21, and "Lista nominal de los individuos entregantes de cobre y bronce," Paraguarí, 17 January 1867 (which lists 92 contributors), and Villa Concepción, 28 January 1867 (which lists 133 contributors), both in ANA-NE 760.

19 Thompson, *The War in Paraguay*, 208.

20 As was true of livestock obtained from private parties, farmers were paid for their crops with increasingly worthless currency. See, for example, Justo González and Francisco Gómez to State Treasurer. Caacupé, 27 January 1867 (regarding state purchase of maize), ANA-NE 1765; and Félix Candia and Juan Manuel Benítez to Vice President Sánchez, Itauguá, 1 May 1867 (regarding state purchases of maize, beans, cotton, and caña), ANA-NE 912.

21   "Circular sobre trabajos de agricultura," Sánchez to Militia Commanders and Justices of the Peace, Asunción, 18 July 1866, ANA-SH 351, no. 1. The cultivation of food crops remained an exasperating, though not impossible, task that Paraguayan women alone handled during the war years, a fact that Washburn and other foreign observers depicted as utterly exploitative: "The country is thoroughly exhausted. All the manual labor is done by women. The women must plant what of corn or cane or *mandioca* there is planted or nothing can be raised. Women yoke the oxen and serve as teamsters. Women are the butchers who slaughter the cattle, take them to market, and sell the beef in the stalls. They do all the rough labor that elsewhere is done by men for there are no men to do it." See Washburn to Seward, Paso Pucú, 25 December 1866, NARA M-128, no. 2. It may be, as Washburn suggests, that the War of the Triple Alliance enhanced certain opportunities for women, but the heavy burden that peasant women routinely carried in Paraguay well before the war would argue against any major transformation of their role during the conflict. One could just as easily argue that the very fact of the fighting tended to legitimize conventional masculinity in the country.

22   Potthast relates the story of Patricia Acosta, a poor woman of Ybytymí who wrote to Sánchez in the winter of 1867 to ask for farm implements and two cows. She noted that her six sons had gone into the army, and four had already died, leaving her with a sick, half-blind mother and no sustenance. The vice president sent the requested help, but the archival documentation offers no proof that he made a habit of charity—usually it was quite the opposite. See Potthast, "Protagonists, Victims, and Heroes," 46–47, and Sánchez to Jefe de Milicias de Ybytymí, Asunción, 3 July 1867, ANA-SH 352, no. 1.

23   In a letter to one village official, Sánchez noted that the "primitive Cainguá Indians" successfully cultivated all sorts of crops without the use of oxen, horses, or metal plows, intimating with little subtlety that the women of the official's community should be able to do so as well; see Sánchez to Justice of the Peace at Itá, Asunción, 18 July 1866, ANA-NE 2396.

24   "La agricultura," *El Semanario* (Asunción), 11 May 1867.

25   Census information for various districts in the interior is scattered throughout many legajos of the Archivo Nacional de Asunción; see, for example, "Participaciones mensuales sobre sembrados" (1866), ANA-SH 419, nos. 2–3; "Informes de agricultura de todo el país," (1866), ANA-NE 2405, 2406, and 2410; "Informes de agricultura de todo el país," (1867), ANA-SH 355, no. 1; "Informe mensual del estado de la agricultura de todo el país," (1868), ANA-SH 356, nos. 1–2. Even communities in occupied Mato Grosso occasionally supplied data for these censuses; see Martín Urbieta to War Minister, Fortín de Bella Vista, 25 August 1866, ANA-NE 1733.

26   *El Semanario* (Asunción), 19 October 1867; see also Rafael Ruiz Díaz to War Minister, Divino Salvador, 31 July 1867, ANA-NE 2472.

27   This unfortunate fact invalidates much of what Vera Blinn Reber has claimed about the limited impact of demographic decline in Paraguay during the war: how can the population be falling so precipitously, she quite reasonably asks, if food crops are being produced at such high levels? Leaving aside the question of exactly what constituted a liño, we must observe that while the censuses tell us something about cultivation, alas, they tell us nothing about production or distribution and cannot be used therefore to bolster any argument about demographic stability or decline. See Reber, "The Demographics of Paraguay: A Reinterpretation of the Great War, 1864–1870," *Hispanic American Historical Review* 68, no. 2 (1988): 289–319; Thomas L. Whigham and Barbara Potthast, "Some Strong Reservations: A Critique of Vera Blinn Reber's 'The Demographics of Paraguay: a Reinterpretation of the Great War,'" *Hispanic American Historical Review* 70, no. 4 (1990): 667–676.

28 Regarding the shipment of oranges to Humaitá, see Francisco Bareiro to War Minister, Asunción, 9 August 1866, ANA-NE 1731.

29 See *El Semanario* (Asunción), 26 January and 12 October 1867.

30 See Receipt for 2,097 pesos 2 reales paid out to twenty-seven women in payment for *dulces*, Asunción, 14 February 1867, ANA-NE 872.

31 "Circular sobre el tejido de poivy para uso del Ejército" (1867), ANA-SH 352, no. 25; Thomas Whigham, "Paraguay and the World Cotton Market. The 'Crisis' of the 1860s," *Agricultural History* 68, no. 3 (1994): 1–15. The use of coconut fibers in weaving cloth never got far beyond the earliest stages during the war; see Justo Godoy to Sánchez, San José de los Arroyos, 14 March 1866, ANA-NE 2402. As for caraguatá, it was also used extensively as a substitute for paper, which in turn was used in the manufacture of currency. See "¿Nos vencerán por asedio?," *El Centinela* (Asunción), 16 May 1867.

32 See López Decree, Paso Pucú, in *El Semanario* (Asunción), 16 February 1867, and Cooney, "Economy and Manpower," 28–29. The government, seeking to promote the use of caraguatá in the production of paper, also recommended that resins and tree saps be collected to use as adhesives in the same manufacture. See "Circular de Saturnino Bedoya," Asunción, 14 June 1867, ANA-NE 2496.

33 Chipas appear more commonly in the documents in the period before Curupayty. See Receipt for 225 pesos worth of chipas purchased by the state for consumption at the Campamento Cerro León, Itauguá, 19 April 1866, ANA-NE 1714. One exception to the general rule could be found in the Indigenous *pueblos*, where, for example, the village of Guarambaré produced just under forty-eight *arrobas* (twelve hundred pounds) of chipas for the army in March 1867. See Lorenzo Pasagua and José Luis Lugo to Tesorero General, Guarambaré, 20 March 1867, ANA-NE 2869.

34 Only villages in the extreme north continued to supply yerba to the army after 1866. See, for instance, "Razón de la yerba recibida de la villa de Ygatymí," Asunción, 9 January 1867, ANA-NE 1763, and "Razón de la yerba traída de la Villa de Concepción," Asunción, 16 August 1867, ANA-NE 2867.

35 López to Commander and Justice of the Peace at Villarrica, Asunción, 12 October 1865, ANA-SH 345, no. 2.

36 Josefina Pla, *The British in Paraguay, 1850–1870* (Richmond, Surrey, 1976), 152. The Asunción shipyards were still actively engaged in the construction and repair of warships throughout 1866, but a year later their efforts had grown sporadic and the officials in charge no longer issued regular reports. See "Razón de las obras trabajadas" (Asunción, 18 March 1866), ANA-NE 1011; "Razón del estado en que se hallan las obras de la maestranza de ribera" (Asunción, 9 August 1866), ANA-NE 728; and "Razón de las obras trabajadas" (Asunción, 14 October 1866), ANA-NE 1089.

37 The Marshal commissioned Thompson to design a rail line from Curupayty past Paso Pucú, and then on to Sauce, but the line was never constructed. See Thompson, *The War in Paraguay*, 203. See also Harris G. Warren, "The Paraguay Central Railway, 1856–1889," *Inter-American Economic Affairs* 20, no. 4 (1967): 3–22.

38 Saturnino Bedoya to Military Commanders and Justices of the Peace, Asunción, 12 June 1867 (circular), ANA-SH 352.

39 James Saeger has argued that "from September 1866 until August 1867, López oversaw a partial recovery of his nation and army," but this observation is accurate only in a limited sense. The Marshal did succeed in ruthlessly shoring up support for the war, but no economic recovery of any kind occurred. As with so much else in Lopista Paraguay, "recovery" was a matter of self-delusion. See Saeger, *Francisco Solano López and the Ruination of Paraguay*, 159.

40 Masterman, *Seven Eventful Years in Paraguay*, 203.

41   Life for the common soldier in the Allied camps during the long lull of 1866–1867 is detailed in Whigham, *La guerra de la Triple Alianza*, 2: 277–288.

42   Masterman, *Seven Eventful Years in Paraguay*, 122–123.

43   Masterman, *Seven Eventful Years in Paraguay*, 123.

44   Leuchars, *To the Bitter End*, 160.

45   Washburn reported "that the average of killed and wounded is less than one per day, and that it costs the Brazilians at least six-hundred shot or shell, and all from cannon of a large caliber, to kill or wound one Paraguayan." See Washburn to Seward, Paso Pucú, 11 March 1867, NARA, M-128, no. 2.

46   In peacetime, the weapon was used by Paraguayan boys to shoot parrots. See Thompson, *The War in Paraguay*, 243.

47   Summary Accusations against Cabral (May 1867), ANA SH 347, no. 12.

48   A corporal could freely administer three blows with a cane to any soldier at any time. A sergeant could administer twelve, and an officer almost as many as he liked. See Thompson, *The War in Paraguay*, 56–57. The flogging of miscreants in the ranks dated from colonial times and was not abolished even with the establishment of a supposedly modern regime in 1870; in fact, as late as 1895, opposition politicians were still calling the practice criminal and demanding its elimination. See "Los azotes en el cuartel deben suprimirse," *El Pueblo. Organo del Partido Liberal* (Asunción), 7 June 1895.

49   Masterman, *Seven Eventful Years in Paraguay*, 123–124.

50   Masterman, *Seven Eventful Years in Paraguay*, 128–129.

51   Thompson, *The War in Paraguay*, 206.

52   The Guaraní term "acá," when it stands alone, means "head," as in the head of a man; the syllable "nundú," when repeated several times, is said to represent the throbbing ache that a sick man feels in his head when in a fever. Female nurses were common on both sides of the conflict from the beginning, of course, and acted in exactly the same capacity, but it suited Allied propagandists to depict Brazilian women as inspirational volunteers, as "encouraging the wounded" and "laughing in the face of bullets and cannon blasts," whereas those women who served López were no better than "lambs to the slaughter." See *A Semana Illustrada* (Rio de Janeiro), 3 September 1865.

53   See Vicente Osuna to War Minister , Humaita, 11 August 1866, ANA-NE 2408 (which mentions 233 women serving in the hospital). Full lists of women serving as nurses at hospitals in Asunción, Cerro León, Caacupé, Encarnación, Villeta, and in the smaller *bóticas* has been assembled by Juan B. Gill Aguinaga in "La mujer de la epopeya nacional," *La Tribuna* (Asunción), 30 May 1971.

54   Virtually all observers made positive comments on these nurses, whose discipline, hard work, and dedication mirrored that of the soldiers. See Masterman, *Seven Eventful Years in Paraguay*, 224; Thompson, *The War in Paraguay*, 207–208; and Max von Versen, *Reisen in Amerika und der Südamerikanische Krieg* (Breslau, 1872), 153–154. See also Potthast, "Protagonists, Victims and Heroes," 47–48; an anonymous article concerning Ña Severa, a sergeant of the great war, in *El Orden* (Asunción), 5 March 1927; and "Paraguayan Woman Dies at 107; Fought in War Sixty Years Ago," *New York Times*, 6 February 1931, which recounts the story of Señora Aranda, who had served as a sergeant of nurses during the war.

55   Masterman, *Seven Eventful Years in Paraguay*, 78–79, provides some detailed illustrations of a similar dance event in the countryside at about this same time.

56   Cardozo, *Hace cien años*, 3: 222.

57 The most detailed account of the mass held at the Humaitá church dates from a few years before the war. See Blas Garay, "La bendición de la iglesia de Humaitá," *La Prensa* (Asunción), 14 March 1899.

58 Centurión, *Memorias o reminiscencias*, 2: 208–210.

59 Antonio E. González annotation, cited in Centurión, *Memorias o reminiscencias*, 2: 210.

60 Masterman, *Seven Eventful Years in Paraguay*, 125–127.

61 Carlos de Koseritz, *Alfredo d'Escragnolle Taunay, Esboço Caracteristico* (Rio de Janeiro, 1886), 12–16.

62 Alfredo d'Escragnolle Taunay, "Relatório Geral da Commissão de Engenheiros junto as forças em Expedição para a Provincia de Matto Grosso, 1865–1866," *Revista do Instituto Histórico e Geographico Brasileiro* 37, no. 2 (1874): 93.

63 Taunay, *Memórias do Visconde de Taunay* (São Paulo, 1948), 119.

64 Doratioto, *Maldita Guerra*, 121.

65 Kolinski, *Independence or Death!*, 111.

66 Alexandre Manoel Albino de Carvalho, *Relatório apresentado ao Ilmo. E Exm. Snr. Chefe de Esquadra Augusto Leverger, Vice-Presidente da Provincia de Matto-Grosso ... em Agosto de 1865* (Rio de Janeiro, 1866), 12–13; Augusto Ferreira França, *Falla apresentada a Assemblea Legislativa Provincial de Goyaz, em o Primeiro de Agosto de 1866* (Goiás, 1867), 11–12.

67 President Alexandre Albino de Carvalho to War Minister, Cuiabá, 8 June 1865, in *Relatório do Presidente da Província do Mato Grosso, 1865* (Cuiabá, 1865), 44–45. In July of the same year, the provincial president released 107 men from military duty so that they could plant food crops for their families. See Augusto Leverger to José Ildefonso de Figueiredo, Cuiabá, 29 July 1865, APEMT, fol. 25, and Leverger to Ilmo. Senhor, Cuiabá, 23 August 1865, APEMT, liv. 220, no. 65.

68 Luiza Rios Ricci Volpato. *Cativos do Sertão. Vida Cotidiana e Escravidão em Cuiabá em 1850/1888* (São Paulo, 1993), 61; though a few slaves escaped to the Paraguayan-held areas, no general uprising occurred. See Police Chief Firmo José de Matos to Albino de Carvalho, Cuiabá, 11 March 1865, APEMT, Caixa 1865 G (which speaks of detaining a certain "Manoel Perreira da Silva for 'seducing' slaves in the parish of Santo Antonio, [telling] them to abandon their labors and head at once for Corumbá, where they will almost certainly be liberated").

69 The local newspaper at Cuiabá described the predicament in plain language, noting that "We can defend the capital and perhaps [a few other] spots, [but] our fields are deserted, our axes silenced, our scythes without movement ... our industries paralyzed, our trade lifeless, our coffers without money." See *A Imprensa de Cuyabá* (Cuiabá), 24 February and 5 March 1865. Given the severe shortages, the province could hardly support the needs of the expeditionary force that would soon arrive on the scene. A short but rather prophetic letter of 1 May 1865 (that purported to come from an individual familiar with Mato Grosso) declared that the Paraguayans had taken thousands of head of cattle to the south, and the livestock that remained to the province (some 251,000 head) would not be enough to feed an eight- to ten-thousand-man army together with the inhabitants that remained north of the line. See "Mato-Grosso," *Jornal do Commercio* (Rio de Janeiro), 2 May 1865.

70 "O ex-Comandante do corpo policial mineiro com destino a Mato-Grosso," *Jornal do Commercio* (Rio de Janeiro), 9 September 1865.

71 Uberaba had twenty-five hundred inhabitants at the time. See Taunay, "Relatório Geral da Commissão," 134–136; Matthew M. Barton, "The Military's Bread and Butter: Food

Production in Minas Gerais, Brazil during the Paraguayan War." Paper presented at the Latin American Labor History Conference, Duke University, 1 April 2011.

72   Taunay, *Em Matto Grosso Invadido (1866–1867)* (São Paulo, 1929?), 60–61.

73   Coxim switched hands back and forth between the Paraguayan raiders and the local Brazilian forces over the next months, though generally the Marshal's men held the territory. See "Mato-Grosso," *Jornal do Commercio* (Rio de Janeiro), 28 September 1865; Carvalho, *Relatório ... em Agosto 1865*, 38; and Albino de Carvalho to Commander of Goiano Battalion, Cuiabá, 3 October 1865, APEMT, liv. 209, no. 22.

74   The reports sent to Asunción from Paraguayan commanders throughout the Mato Grosso catalogued an unending series of complaints about the lack of provisions, the frequency of desertions, and the scourge of diseases. See Martín Urbieta to War Minister, Nioac, 10 January 1866, ANA-NE 761; Urbieta to War Minister, Nioac, 31 January 1866, ANA-SH 347, no. 8; Juan F. Rivarola to ?, Corumbá, 14 February 1866, ANA-NE 3273; Urbieta to War Minister, Nioac, 23 May 1866, ANA-NE 2436; Hermógenes Cabral to ?, Corumbá, 9 June 1866, ANA-CRB I-29, 16, no. 6; Urbieta to War Minister, Bellavista, 3 November 1866, ANA-NE 2831; Urbieta to War Minister, Bellavista, 29 December 1866, ANA-NE 2831; Patricio Galiano to War Minister, Estrella del Apa, 30 November 1867, ANA-CRB I-30, 15, 196; Hermógenes Cabral to Marshal López, Corumbá, 18 March 1866 through 1 August 1866, IHGB lata 321, doc. 6; and Romualdo Núñez to War Minister, Corumbá, 12 October 1865 through 15 January 1868, ANA-CRB I-30, 17, 55, nos. 1–17.

75   "Goyaz" (21 September 1865), in *Jornal do Commercio* (Rio de Janeiro), 2 November 1865; "Provincia de Matto Grosso," *Diário do Rio de Janeiro*, 8 December 1865.

76   Luiz de Castro Souza, "A Medicina na Guerra do Paraguai (Mato-Grosso)," *Revista de História* 40, no. 81 (1970): 113–136.

77   Augusto Leverger to Commander of Guards Troops, Cuiabá, 29 September 1865, APEMT liv. 220, no. 89; Leverger to Commander of Guards Troops, 2 October 1866, APEMT liv. 220, no. 91; Leverger to Commander, Cuiabá, 18 October 1865, APEMT liv. 220, no. 104; Vice President to Acting Commander of Guards Troops, Cuiabá, 14 November 1865, APEMT. Registro, ofícios expedidos pela presidencia, 1865–1866, fol. 44v.

78   Baron de Melgaço to José Antonio Fonseca de Galvão, Cuiabá, 16 January 1866, APEMT liv. 209, no. 29, and José Antonio Fonseca de Galvão to Councilor Nabuco de Araújo, Distrito do Taquarí, 20 February 1866, IHGB, lata 363, pasta 49. In April, provincial authorities did report the dispatch of a supply of rice, beans, arrowroot, and salt to the troops encamped at Coxim, but the quantities mentioned—three cartloads—were hardly inspiring. See "Carta particular de Minas Gerais, Uberaba, 21 April 1866," in *Jornal do Commercio* (Rio de Janeiro), 11 May 1866.

79   Baron de Melgaço to Galvão, Cuiabá, 22 March 1866, APEMT liv. 209, no. 32. Rumors of impending troubles with local Indigenous people had been rife since the onset of the war. See, for example, "Os Indios Coroados," *Imprensa de Cuyabá* (Cuiabá), 11 December 1865.

80   Taunay, *Memorias*, 171–172.

81   An unsigned letter (probably written by Taunay), from Miranda and dated 6 December 1866, recorded various men in hospital due to stomach ailments (brought on by bad water) and also wondered about the frightening possibility of an alliance between the Paraguayans and the Indigenous people. See "Mato Grosso," *Jornal do Commercio* (Rio de Janeiro), 23 February 1867.

82   After the fall of Corumbá, a highly critical pamphlet had circulated among Brazil's senior officers that unfairly accused Camisão and others of cowardice. See Fernando dos Anjos Souza, "A Liderança dos Chefes Militares durante a Retirada da Laguna na Guerra

do Paraguai," *Monografia da Escola de Comando e Estado-Maior do Exército* (Rio de Janeiro, 1994), 24–25.

83 Taunay, *A Retirada da Laguna* (São Paulo, 1957), 38.

84 Doratioto, *Maldita Guerra*, 124 (Kolinski, *Independence or Death!*, 112, gives the figure as sixteen hundred men). The "Indian auxiliaries" were armed with Minié rifles. See "Expedition to Matto-Grosso," *The Standard* (Buenos Aires), 6 November 1866.

85 In his account of the subsequent actions, Taunay gave extensive attention to José Francisco Lopes, guide (or *baqueano*) to the expeditionary force. A middle-aged rancher of Mineiro origins and local habits, Lopes seemed to the budding author a model of the uncivilized man—honorable, brave, and pure of heart, almost a force of nature. Taunay compared him explicitly to Fenimore Cooper's Nattie Bumpo, and in truth, Lopes did seem a prototype of the Matogrossense *sertanejo*, the modest denizen of the frontier who was surprised by the war, but accepted its consequences with grim resignation. In a conflict in which decisions were made by generals, presidents, and emperors, the sacrifices and experiences of men such as Lopes were frequently forgotten. And yet, such men could be found on all sides and at all times. See Taunay, *A Retirada da Laguna*, 39-40, 47; Taunay, *Cartas da Campanha. A Cordilheira. Agonía de Lopez (1869–1870)*, 104; and Rocha Almeida, *Vultos da Patria*, 3: 144–149.

86 This message, written in Spanish, Portuguese, and French, was curious in many ways, but, above all, showed a remarkable ignorance of national sensibilities in that it presumed that the Paraguayans could be coaxed away from the Marshal's cause with mere words. See Centurión, *Memorias o reminiscencias*, 2: 260–263.

87 Taunay, *A Retirada da Laguna*, 62.

88 Taunay, *Memorias*, 236, and more generally, Fano, *Il Rombo del Cannone Liberale*, 2: 268–274.

89 Doratioto, *Maldita Guerra*, 127.

90 Cardozo, *Hace cien años*, 6: 160. J. Arthur Montenegro gives a figure of over two hundred Paraguayans killed in this engagement, as against twelve killed and eighteen wounded for the Brazilians. See "Campaña de Matto-Grosso (inedito). Toma del atrincheramiento de Bayende (6 de mayo de 1867)," in *Album de la Guerra del Paraguay*, 2 (1894): 281–283.

91 Cardozo, *Hace cien años*, 6: 158–160; it is hard to accept the judgment of Montenegro, who, indulging in more than a little hyperbole, called the battle of Bayende a "decisive victory" for the Brazilians, who "once again proved the superiority of their soldiers." See "Campaña de Matto-Grosso," 283.

92 "Los laurels de la campaña del norte," *El Centinela* (Asunción), 18 July 1867, and "La espedición brasileira del Norte," *Cabichuí* (Paso Pucú), 22 July 1867.

93 This recounting of *hors de combat* seems to have been exaggerated in favor of the Paraguayans, who almost certainly lost more than the figure suggested. See "La invasión del norte," *El Semanario* (Asunción), 13 July 1867.

94 Taunay, *A Retirada da Laguna*, 86.

95 Lobo Vianna, *A epopeia da Laguna. Conferencia pronunciada no Club Militar* (Rio de Janeiro, 1938); João Lustoza da Cunha Paranaguá, *Relatório Apresentado a Assembléa Geral na Segunda Sessão da Deceima Terceira Legislatura* (Rio de Janeiro, 1868), 83–88.

96 Camisão threatened his Indigenous allies with execution if they continued such wanton activities, but it was not clear that his warnings did any good. See Cardozo, *Hace cien años*, 6: 165.

97 Taunay, *A Retirada da Laguna*, 114–115. The Brazilians later claimed that the men left behind were decapitated by the Paraguayans (and something like that was supposedly reported by a survivor). See "Falla dirgida a Assembleia Legislativa da Provincia de S.

Pedro do Rio Grande do Sul pelo Presidente Dr. Francisco Ignácio Maicondes Homen de Mello (Porto Alegre, 1867)," MHM (A), Colección Gill Aguinaga, carpeta 135, no 3. Walter Spalding, *A Invasão Paraguaia no Brasil* (São Paulo, 1940), 614–619; and Genserico de Vasconcellos, *A Guerra do Paraguay no Theatro de Matto-Grosso* (São Paulo, 1921?), 57–58. The Brazilians themselves were accused of beheading a much larger number of Paraguayans who fell into their hands after Corumbá was momentarily retaken in June 1867.

98   Antonio Fernandes de Souza, *A Invasão Paraguaia em Matto-Grosso* (Cuiabá, 1919), 47.

99   Cardozo, *Hace cien años*, 6: 233–234.

100 Taunay, *A Retirada da Laguna*, 137.

101 Regarding the figure of the *sertanejo*, which in Brazilian letters tends to play the role reserved for the gaucho in Argentine literature, see Peter Beattie, "National Identity and the Brazilian Folk: The *Sertanejo* in Taunay's *A retirada da Laguna*," *Review of Latin American Studies*, 4, no.1 (1991): 7–43.

102 Emmanuelle Cavassa, an Italian merchant several years resident in Corumbá when the Paraguayans came in 1865, left a short but edifying memoir on what happened to him and his family (who were removed to Paraguay in August 1866) and what happened to those who stayed behind in Mato Grosso. See Valmir Batista Corréa and Lúcia Salsa Corréa, *Memorandum de Manoel Cavassa* (Campo Grande, 1997), 19–42. For other details on the Paraguayan occupation of the province, see "Guerre du Paraguay. Faits Authentiques de l'occupation d'une Province Brésilienne par les Paraguayens," Archivo de Itamaraty. Lata 281, maço 1, p. 15.

103 Romualdo Núñez survived the war only to be accused of desertion in General Resquín's memoirs (see *La guerra del Paraguay contra la Triple Alianza*, 144). Partly to defend his actions and partly to leave a record of his war experiences for his children, Núñez composed a short memoir that included descriptions of his time in Mato Grosso; this was eventually published as "Rectificación histórica. La reconquista de Corumbá por los brasileños," *La Opinión* (Asunción), 22 July 1895. See also Valério D'Almeida, *Primer Centenario da Retomada da Vila de Corumbá: 1867–1967* (Corumbá, 1967).

104 Again, there are many different opinions as to the number of men supposedly involved in this engagement. Mario Monteiro de Almeida, in *Episódios Históricos da Formação Geográfica do Brasil* (Rio de Janeiro, 1951), 430, claims that the attacking force comprised only 430 men while the Paraguayan defenders could count a garrison of 313; by contrast, Cardozo, in *Hace cien años*, 6: 241, sets the number of defenders at 316 and the number of attackers at over three thousand. (It is hard to credit this latter figure in a province where manpower shortages had been chronic since 1865). Doratioto, in *Maldita Guerra*, 129, gives a figure of one thousand for the attacking force—a figure probably closer to the fact.

105 Vasconcellos, *A Guerra do Paraguay no Theatro do Matto-Grosso*, 66. One wishes to be judicious on this point, but today's scholars should perhaps remember that hungry people will do almost anything in order to eat, and that the sexual "appetite" of desperate men might be uncontrollable or might be constrained by the same hunger that forced women to prostitute themselves for a piece of manioc. Centurión claimed that an aged naval officer had told him that Cabral, the Paraguayan commander at Corumbá, had "sold his affections to a Brazilian girl" in the town, but whether this bit of gossip could indicate a general picture of life in the occupied community is another matter. Simply put, no one knows for certain what happened. See *Memorias y reminiscencias*, 2: 263–264.

106 "Recuperación de Corumbá," *La Nación Argentina* (Buenos Aires), 1 September 1867.

107   See Núñez Correspondence (June–August 1867), ANA-CRB I-30, 14, 137–139. The official Brazilian account of the engagement can be found in "Partes officiaes e Ordens do Dia Relativa ao Combate do Alegre," in Fernandes de Souza, *A Invasão Paraguaya em Matto-Grosso*, 77–97.

108   Núñez, "Rectificación histórica;" Monteiro de Almeida, *Episódios históricos*, 387.

109   Doratioto, *Maldita Guerra*, 129, and *Relatório com que o Exm. Snr. Dr. João José Pedrosa, Presidente da Província de Matto-Grosso abrió a Primeira Sessão da 22a Legislatura da Respectiva Assembléa no Dia Primeiro de Novembro*, 32; "La guerra, el hambre, y la peste," *La Nación Argentina* (Buenos Aires), 30 November 1867.

110   Few Brazilian politicians were willing to criticize the expeditionary force after so many lives were lost; one exception was Teófilo Ottoni, who, in the parliamentary session of 7 August 1867, remarked about how unwise it had been to launch an attack across the Apa without horses. See Camara de Diputados, *Perfis Parlementares 12. Teófilo Ottoni* (Brasília, 1979), 999–1009.

111   Thompson, *The War in Paraguay*, 204.

112   "Una traición y una victoria," *El Semanario* (Asunción), 20 July 1867.

113   These discussions had already come to a head in early September 1866, when Autonomist senators complained bitterly that new loans would be required to cover repayments and assure new credit in London. See Congreso de la Nación Argentina. *Diario de sesiones de la Camara de Senadores (1866)* (Buenos Aires, 1893), 401–402 (session of 1 September 1866).

114   Mitre to Paz, Buenos Aires, 12 June 1867, and Paz to Mitre, Buenos Aires, 12 June 1867 in *Archivo del general Mitre*, 6: 212–213.

115   Miguel Angel de Marco, *Bartolomé Mitre* (Buenos Aires, 2004), 343.

116   Rock, "Argentina Under Mitre," 54; the ongoing fear regarding Urquiza's intentions was entirely groundless, for the Entrerriano strongman had long since traded the role of revolutionary leader for that of livestock purveyor to the Allied armies. See F.J. McLynn, "Urquiza and the Montoneros: An Ambiguous Chapter in Argentine History," *Ibero-Amerikanische Archiv* 8 (1982): 283–295. Even Caxias was a touch worried about Urquiza's commitment, and wondered in a letter to the war minister if the Entrerrianos might join the western rebels. See Caxias to Marquis de Paranaguá, Tuyutí, 7 April 1867, IHGB, lata 313, pasta 6.

117   In his previous campaign in Corrientes, López had presumed that provincial sympathies would favor his incursion, and that even Urquiza would eventually join his side. Very little of this support ever developed, but the Marshal continued to hope that "friends" in the Litoral provinces would eventually rally to him. See Whigham, *The Paraguayan War*, 274–276.

118   Trinidad Delia Chianelli, *El gobierno del puerto* (Buenos Aires, 1975), 250.

119   Marcos Paz to Mitre, Buenos Aires, 6 February 1867, in *Archivo del general Mitre*, 6: 201–203; *La Nación Argentina* (Buenos Aires), 5 February 1867.

120   Cited in *El Nacional* (Buenos Aires), 11 June 1867. As David Rock has noted, over the next few months, most of the Argentines to die at the Paraguayan front came from battalions raised in La Rioja. See "Argentina under Mitre," 55.

121   For a variety of reasons, Elizalde was also favored by the Brazilians, not least because he had recently married the daughter of the Brazilian minister to Buenos Aires. See José Luis Busaniche, *Historia argentina* (Buenos Aires, 1976), 773.

122   Busaniche, *Historia argentina*, 769; Sena Madureira, for his part, ascribed an indifferent rather than anti-Brazilian attitude to Mitre, arguing that instead of organizing the Paraguayan campaign in proper fashion, the Allied commander wasted his time in his

"chalet," writing works of literary merit and playing chess, "of which he was exceedingly fond." See *Guerra do Paraguai*, 52.

7 | THE ONGOING RESISTANCE

1   The Brazilians initially had no sure system of promotion based on merit during war—and in peacetime promotions occurred strictly on the basis of seniority. Caxias started the process of granting field commissions during the 1866–1869 campaign, but the practice greatly expanded under his successor, the Count d'Eu. See Pinto de Campos, *Vida da Grande Cidadão Luis Alves de Lima e Silva*, 372–373.

2   The officer in charge of a battalion in which a sentry was found without the regulation boots was placed under arrest, as was a lieutenant who had absented himself when fodder was distributed to the animals. See Leuchars, *To the Bitter End*, 168.

3   The 4 June 1867 issue of the London *Times* reported that "in the month of April 1867, the Allies were in possession of but 30 square miles of Paraguayan soil, for which the Empire of Brazil was said to be paying at the rate of … 200,000 sterling [a day]."

4   "Diários do Exército em Operações sob o Commando em Chefe do Exmo. Sr. Marechal de Exército Marquez de Caxias (Acampamento em Tuiuti, Marcha para Tuiu-Cué," *Revista do Instituto Histórico e Geographico Brasileiro* 91–145 (1922): 43 (entry of 26 July 1867).

5   Kolinski, *Independence or Death!*, 149.

6   Walter Spalding, "Karai-ambaé. A Aerostação na Guerra contra Solano Lopez. Bartolomeu de Gusmão. Julio César. Santos Dumont," *Jornal do Dia. Suplemento Internacional* (Porto Alegre), 21 January 1953; Doyen to Caxias, Tuyutí, 26 December 1866, Arquivo Nacional. Documentos da Guerra do Paraguai. Vol. 10 (1866), folhas 217–218. Nelson Freire Lavenére-Wanderley, "Os Balões de Observação da Guerra do Paraguai," *Revista do Instituto Histórico e Geográfico Brasileiro* 299 (1973): 205–206; F. Stansbury Haydon, "Documents Relating to the First Military Balloon Corps Organized in South America: The Aeronautic Corps of the Brazilian Army, 1867–1868," *Hispanic American Historical Review* 19, no.4 (1939): 504–517; and Thomas L. Whigham, "El cuerpo de globos brasileño en la Guerra del Setenta, o la historia de un éxito efímero," in *Paraguay: Investigaciones de historia social y política*, Whigham and Casal, eds., 119–128.

7   Though the Polish Major remained optimistic about the uses of military balloons, the Marshal's men felt nothing but scorn for this odd innovation. The 8 August 1867 issue of *El Centinela* (Asunción) included a woodcut image of Paraguayan soldiers confidently guarding their Humaitá battery while bearing their naked backsides to Caxias, who appears as a hapless aeronaut in an outsized balloon. Sir Richard Burton offered a short sketch of Chodasiewicz in his *Letters from the Battle-fields of Paraguay* (London, 1870), 381–383, but the best overall account of the engineer's life, which details how bitter he became after the war, is the article by Harris Gaylord Warren, "Roberto Adolfo Chodasiewicz: A Polish Soldier of Fortune in the Paraguayan War," *The Americas* 41, no. 3 (1985): 1–19.

8   Mitre to Caxias, Buenos Aires, 17 April 1867, in *Archivo del General Mitre*, 3: 124–131

9   Caxias to Mitre, 30 April 1867, cited in Cardozo, *Hace cien años*, 6: 145–146.

10 Talavera, "Correspondencia del egército," *El Semanario* (Asunción), 31 May 1867. The Brazilian satirical newspaper, *Ba-Ta-Clan* (Rio de Janeiro), 27 July 1867, made extensive and caustic comment on the navy's failure to provide adequate cover fire on this occasion ("Cet imbecile d'Ignacio! Moi qui comptais sur lui pour avoir encore un prétexte à alléguer!").

11   The Paraguayan Misiones experienced an unending series of raids and counter-raids during the war, making it perhaps the most unstable territory along the entire front, and a breeding ground for subsequent banditry. See Francisco Bareiro toWar Minister, Asunción, 13 June 1866, ANA-NE 767; "Alto Uruguay," *La Nación Argentina* (Buenos Aires), 17 February 1867; Francisco Fernández to War Minister, Asunción, 13 June 1867, and Venancio López to Marshal López, Asunción(?), 22 January 1868, ANA-CRB I-30, 28, 16, no. 1.

12   Cardozo, *Hace cien años*, 6: 340; Osório to Wife, Paso de la Patria, 17 July 1867, in Osório, *História do General Osório*, 364.

13   Centurión put the land forces at a slightly higher total, with 38,500 in the vanguard, and thirteen thousand in the reserve. See *Memorias o reminiscencias*, 3: 6. The friction between Porto Alegre and Osório was political rather than military, and dated to a time when the two men affiliated with different factions of the Liberal Party in Rio Grande do Sul.

14   A minor controversy erupted in 1903 when Brazilian journalists published a series of articles celebrating the centenary of Caxias's birth. These articles, which evinced a highly critical view of Mitre's leadership during the war, attributed the plan to flank the Paraguayans at Tuyucué to the genius of the marquis. Mitre was still alive at this time, however, and he promptly responded by releasing confidential correspondence and other documents that unimpeachably showed the plan as his own. The Brazilian press bullheadedly refused to yield on the issue, and was in turn challenged by Argentine newspapers that condemned Caxias as "a dead weight the whole time." Caustic missives in favor of one champion or the other continued for some time, with one Paraguayan author, Manuel Avila, reminding all concerned that the maneuver failed to overwhelm Humaitá in any case. See Luiz Jordão, "O General Mitre e a Guerra do Paraguay," *Jornal do Brasil* (Rio de Janeiro), 5 October 1903; Jacques Ourique, "Caxias e Mitre," *Jornal do Commercio* (Rio de Janeiro), 11 October 1903; Carlos Balthazar da Silveira, "Campanha do Paraguay," *Jornal do Commercio* (Rio de Janeiro), 13 October 1903; Pedro de Barros, "Guerra do Paraguay," *Jornal do Commercio* (Rio de Janeiro), 27 October 1903; Affonso Gonçalves, *Guerra do Paraguay. Memoria. Caxias e Mitre* (Rio de Janeiro, 1906); clipping collection of Argentine reactions (taken from various newspapers in Buenos Aires, San Pedro, Quilmes, Carmen de Flores, San Nicolás, Rosario, Belcarce, etc.), BNA-CJO; and Avila, "La controversia Caxias-Mitre. Notas ligeras," *Revista del Instituto Paraguayo* 5, no. 46 (1903): 286–293.

15   The US minister in Buenos Aires reported that the Brazilian fleet had already "received orders to ascend the rivers and pass Humaitá in spite of all the obstacles, and even if half its ships were to be lost in the attempt." See A. Asboth to Seward, Buenos Aires, 11 July 1867, NARA, FM-69, no. 17; and Guilherme de Andrea Frota, ed., *Diário Pessoal do Almirante Visconde de Inhaúma durante a Guerra da Triplice Aliança (Dezembro 1866 a Janeiro de 1869)* (Rio de Janeiro, 2008), 105 (entries for 21, 22, 23, and 24 July 1867).

16   Centurión, *Memorias o reminiscencias*, 3: 6–7.

17   Cardozo, *Hace cien años*, 6: 252–254.

18   "Correspondencia," *Jornal do Commercio* (Rio de Janeiro), 3 September 1867; the Brazilian military historian Tasso Fragoso noted that "the situation did not correspond at all to what Mitre and Caxias had expected as the trail had already been hermetically sealed with defensive works in which the [Paraguayans] appeared as confident as they did [further south]." See *História da Guerra entre a Triplice Aliança e o Paraguai*, 3: 254.

19   *The Standard* (Buenos Aires), 11 August 1867.

20   *Anglo-Brazilian Times* (Rio de Janeiro), 23 August 1867.

21 Mitre to Paz, Tuyucué, 3 August 1867, in *Archivo del coronel Dr. Marcos Paz*, 7: 301–302, and, in more detailed form, Mitre to Caxias, Tuyucué, 5 August 1867, IHGB, lata 312, pasta 33.

22 Cardozo, *Hace cien años*, 7: 31–33.

23 See, for example, "Noticias do Rio da Prata," *Diário do Rio de Janeiro*, 4 September 1867, which claimed that "General Mitre has been the only cause of the prolongation of the war and of the misuse of so many Brazilian sacrifices." *La Tribuna* (Buenos Aires) offered an emphatic, if not quite measured, response to such attacks on the "warrior spirit" of the Argentine president in its 8 September 1867 edition. *El Pueblo* (Buenos Aires) went one step further in its 14 September 1867 edition, noting that Mitre "might be a general *de salon*, but [Caxias] has yet to get beyond the antechamber."

24 "South America," *The Times* (London), 21 September 1867

25 See, for example, José Luiz Mena Barreto to Mitre, San Solano, 10 August 1867, in *Archivo del coronel Dr. Marcos Paz*, 6: 230–231, and "Teatro de la guerra," *La Tribuna* (Buenos Aires), 27 August 1867.

26 In "Nupã ha'e chúra cacuaa," *Cacique Lambaré* (Asunción) predictably made much of this seizure, noting with some truth that the Paraguayans had captured substantial quantities of "flour, sugar, yerba, *galleta*, beer, wine, *aguardiente*, cognac and gin," and also, with tremendous exaggeration, that the nation happily celebrated "the 500 monkey cadavers left behind [to provide] a banquet for the buzzards." See issue of 22 August 1867.

27 "Teatro de la guerra," *La Tribuna* (Buenos Aires), 9 August 1867. This achievement was celebrated in one of *Cabichuí's* more elaborate woodcuts wherein Paraguayan soldiers accompanied by wasps are depicted as driving the animals to the Marshal's camp. See *Cabichuí's* (Paso Pucú), 16 January 1868).

28 Centurión, *Memorias o reminiscencias*, 3: 21.

29 Thompson, *The War in Paraguay*, 224.

30 von Versen, *Reisen in Amerika*, 129–130.

31 Thompson, *The War in Paraguay*, 212.

32 Natalício Talavera argued that the Brazilian vessels refused to return fire out of cowardice, and that, "despite the fact that they were ironclads, they still worried about defeat; and thus they resolved on a foolhardy action—they closed their eyes and started off into the abyss." See "Correspondencia del ejército," *El Semanario* (Asunción), 17 August 1867. In point of fact, the Brazilians acted prudently, for there was no sense in detaining their progress in front of the Paraguayan batteries where the enemy's strength was manifest. This was common sense, not fear.

33 "A Passagem de Curupaity," *Jornal do Brasil* (Rio de Janeiro), 15 August 1895; Ouro Preto, *A Marinha d'Outrora*, 161–163; and Barros, *Guerra do Paraguay. O Almirante Visconde de Inhaúma*, 220–235.

34 "Facts from Brazil," *New Orleans Daily Picayune*, 24 October 1867; Washburn to Seward, Asunción, 31 August 1867, NARA, M-128, no. 2; and "Breves Apontamentos sobre a Campanha do Paraguai. A Passagem do Humaitá, 1866 [*sic*]," IHGB, lata 335, pasta 9.

35 *Anglo-Brazilian Times* (Rio de Janeiro), 7 September 1867; the French anarchist writer Elisée Reclus wrote an article at the end of 1867 in which he claimed that the Brazilian passage of Curupayty was only the first stage of a more ambitious plan of attack and that, in failing to move past Humaitá that same day, Admiral Ignácio had essentially assured a "disaster" for the Allies. See Reclus, "La guerra del Paraguay," *La Revue des Deux Mondes* (Paris), 15 December 1867, 934–965. A.J. Victorino de Barros (a highly regarded Masonic historian who made the study of the Catholic admiral part of his life's work)

treated this argument as a vapid apologia for the Paraguayans, noting quite correctly that there had never been any plan to move on Humaitá at that time. See *Guerra do Paraguay. O Almirante Visconde de Inhaúma*, 227–231.

36   "Chronique," *Ba-Ta-Clan* (Rio de Janeiro), 21 March 1868.

37   Diary entries of 14–18 August 1867, in Guilherme de Andrea Frota, *Diário Pessoal do Almirante Visconde de Inhaúma durante a Guerra da Triplice Aliança* (Rio de Janeiro, 2008), 110–112.

38   In a typical show of contempt, Washburn belittled Ignácio's achievement, arguing that "had the squadron passed immediately on after getting above Curupaity, in one hour it would have been above Humaitá and this war could soon have ended, but the [Brazilians,] instead of pushing on, have given López three weeks' time to ... bring up his guns and [strengthen his defenses once again. And the Allies] think that by this course they may tire out and exhaust Paraguay! Perhaps they may, but it is more likely that they will exhaust and ruin themselves." See Washburn to Watson Webb, Asunción, 5 September 1867, WNL. Washburn was not the only American to find fault with the imperial navy's progress at this stage of the war. In a letter to Secretary of State Seward, the US minister to Buenos Aires, General Asboth, repeated the observations of the *La Tribuna's* war correspondent, to the effect that either the Brazilian ironclads were of an inferior class, or the effectiveness of Paraguayan gunnery was greater than could be supposed from comparable American experience during the Civil War. See Asboth to Seward, Buenos Aires, 12 September 1867, NARA, FM-69, no. 17.

39   In a letter of 3 August 1867, Ignácio wondered if the recent Argentine reinforcement of the island of Martín García might signal a plan to annihilate the Brazilian fleet; and in a similar missive of 11 September, he worried that risking the greater number of his vessels in Paraguayan waters might inspire other enemies of the empire with a desire to settle Platine affairs in a manner not to Brazil's advantage. Cited in Nabuco, *Um Estadista do Império*, 2: 73–76.

40   Théodore Fix, *Conférence sur la Guerre du Paraguay* (Paris, 1870), 57–58; Asboth to Seward, Buenos Aires, 26 August 1867, NARA, FM-69, no. 17; "Teatro de la guerra," *La Tribuna* (Buenos Aires), 20 August 1867; and Cardozo, *Hace cien años*, 7: 177–178 (which describes the Brazilian sailors forced to cut firewood in the Chaco for want of coal).

41   "The War in the North," *The Standard* (Buenos Aires), 25 August 1867.

42   Ignácio to Caxias, off Curupayty, 23 August 1867, in Cardozo, *Hace cien años*, 7: 64–65. See also Mitre to Arturo Silveira de Mota, Buenos Aires, October 1869, in *La Nación Argentina* (Buenos Aires), 11 November 1869 (in which the former Argentine president recapitulates his frustrations with Ignácio and Caxias for the slow progress of the fleet).

43   Antonio Sousa Junior, "Guerra do Paraguai," in *História Geral da Civilização Brasileira*, Sergio Buarque de Holanda, ed. (São Paulo, 1985), 4, bk.2: 307.

44   Caxias to Mitre, Tuyucué, 26 August 1867, in *Archivo del general Mitre*, 4: 281–282.

45   *Archivo del general Mitre*, 4: 286–289; Tasso Fragoso notes that Caxias composed a more elaborated response to the Argentine president on 24 December 1867, in which the marquis cited many cases in the recently concluded US Civil War that contradicted Mitre's understanding of naval tactics; when he sent a copy of this missive to functionaries in Rio de Janeiro, Caxias set aside his usual decorum and asserted that many of Mitre's "theories were not in accordance with the practice of war, and others had been entirely disproven." See *História da Guerra entre a Triplice Aliança e o Paraguay*, 3: 385–389.

46   Mitre to Caxias, Tuyucué, 9 September 1867, in *Archivo del general Mitre*, 4: 289–292.

47   Cardozo, *Hace cien años*, 7: 116–117.

48   In Asunción, the government kept a particularly close eye on the city's three resident foreigners, of whom eighty-four were Italians, sixty-one Argentines, forty-six Spaniards,

forty-six Brazilians, thirty-two Frenchmen, six Germans, and twenty-five of other nationalities. The great majority of Gould's countrymen, who worked as engineers and machinists, appear to have been listed separately, for in an August 1867 reckoning the number of Britons listed for the capital city amounted to an impossibly low five men. See List of Resident Foreigners, 6, 8, and 19 August 1867, ANA-NE 1738.

49 Report of Laurent-Cochelet, no. 60, Asunción, 8 March 1867, and a follow-up letter of 5 September 1867, in Capdevila, *Une Guerre Totale*, 417–420, 424–425. There were also a total of nearly three hundred Italian subjects in Paraguay, but little diplomatic effort was ever made to help them. See Lorenzo Chapperon to Italian Foreign Minister, Asunción, 18 March 1868, Archivio Storico Ministero degli Esteri (Rome) [as extracted by Marco Fano].

50 Von Versen, *Reisen in Amerika*, 139.

51 Burton, *Letters from the Battle-fields of Paraguay*, 329.

52 *The Standard* (Buenos Aires) characterized Gould's quest in biblical terms, noting that the secretary was "working hard like Moses in Egypt, to move the heart of López to 'let my people go,' whilst their promised land, the *Doterel*, remains here until wanted" (see issue of 27 August 1867). As it turned out, the British women were mistakenly permitted to disembark at Montevideo, where they told all they knew to the local press; this greatly irked the Marshal, who never forgot that Gould had seemingly gone back on his word. See Burton, *Letters from the Battle-fields of Paraguay*, 330.

53 Thompson, *The War in Paraguay*, 218–219 and *El Semanario* (Asunción), 14 December 1867; Sallie Cleaveland, the indiscreet wife of Charles Washburn, habitually noted in her diary the many bits of gossip that reached the foreign legations in Asunción, and in her entry of 30 August, she related how Madame Lynch had spoken of the Paraguayan president's fierce reaction to Gould's having failed to pass along diplomatic correspondence to the US minister. If López was indeed angry with the British secretary, he gave no signs of it at Paso Pucú, but Cleaveland's observation remains relevant nonetheless, since it shows how all potential negotiations were affected by the Marshal's fragile temper. See Washburn diary, 30 August 1867, WNL.

54 Thompson, *The War in Paraguay*, 219; see also G.F. Gould to George Mathew, Paso Pucú, 11 September 1867, in Philip, *British Documents on Foreign Affairs, Latin America, 1845–1914*, 1, pt. 1, Series D: 228–230.

55 In fact, he did nothing of the kind. We can easily reprimand the Marshal's unfortunate stubbornness throughout the war, though on this occasion, when Dom Pedro learned of the Gould proposals, his own reaction betrayed a similar inflexibility. In a letter to the Countess of Barral, the emperor noted that

the Secretary of the British legation at Buenos Aires, entirely *motu proprio*, went to Humaitá to protect British subjects and returned from there with peace proposals. Brazilian agents only listened to him. They were inadmissible; even López through his own declarations ruined the efforts of the secretary whose failure may counsel greater circumspection in the future in the matter of intervention into alien affairs.

See Pedro to Countess of Barral, Rio, 8 October 1867, in Sodré, *Abrindo um cofre*, 136; Kolinski, *Independencia o Muerte!*, 136–137; and "Chronique," *Ba-Ta-Clan* (Rio de Janeiro), 5 October 1867.

56 Chris Leuchars suggests that Elizalde probably had in mind asserting future Argentine sovereignty over the riverbank opposite the fortress, a very likely explanation of the temporarily unemployed foreign minister's thinking. See *To the Bitter End*, 167; in a subsequent letter, Vice President Paz reiterated the standard position that the Argentine national government had taken according to the Treaty of Alliance with Brazil, that

under no circumstances could López retain an official capacity in Paraguay. See Paz to Mitre, Buenos Aires, 25 September 1867, in *Archivo del general Mitre*, 6: 260–62.

57   "Las proposiciones de paz," *El Centinela* (Asunción), 19 December 1867.

58   The rumors about renewed Montonero violence in western Argentina were not wholly without foundation, and as late as November 1867, the Marshal's ministers were still trying to communicate with General Saa and other Federalist leaders whose forces had not been entirely contained by the national government. See José Berges to Antonio de las Carreras, Asunción, 24 November 1867, ANA-CRB I-22, 12, 2, no. 91.

59   Washburn, *History of Paraguay*, 2: 204–205. In an unintentionally ironic observation written in 1874, Colonel Silvestre Aveiro averred that López had consulted the "notable personages" of Asunción on the advisability of accepting Gould's conditions and was told that the country could never do without its head of state, and that the Marshal subsequently rejected the Briton's suggestion on the basis of their opinion. In authoritarian Paraguay, such a consultation—had it even occurred—could have elicited only one possible response, for any other words would have brought a violent punishment (these "notable personages" being precisely the people who would have preferred to see López hanged). See Aveiro, *Memoria militares*, 48.

60   Luis Caminos to G. Gould, Paso Pucú, 14 September 1867, in *La diplomacia estadounidense*, Whigham and Casal, eds., 365–368.

61   Thompson, *The War in Paraguay*, 220.

62   "War in the North," *The Standard* (Buenos Aires), 11 September 1867.

63   "War in the North," *The Standard* (Buenos Aires), 11 September 1867.

64   "War in the North," *The Standard* (Buenos Aires), 18 September 1867. See also Mitre to Paz, Tuyucué, 17 October 1867, in *Archivo del coronel Dr. Marcos Paz*, 8: 336.

65   M.A. de Mattos to Querido Amigo, Tuyucué, 11 October 1867, in *La Nación Argentina* (Buenos Aires), 16 October 1867.

66   *The Anglo-Brazilian Times* (Rio de Janeiro) reported that cholera "in a milder form than before was threatening the Allied forces, and deserters from Humaitá represent it as being very destructive in the Paraguayan encampments." (See issue of 23 October 1867). The *Jornal do Commercio* (Rio de Janeiro) went much further, claiming that the "Paraguayans are on the verge of dying either from cholera or hunger. In these circumstances, the Paraguayan War will end within a month." (See issue of 19 Oct. 1867).

67   In 2001, a minor (and rather artificial) controversy arose in the Carioca press when scholars associated with the Universidade Federal do Rio de Janeiro resuscitated an old canard concerning the existence of an 18 September 1867 letter of Caxias in which he admitted to having thrown the cadavers of cholera victims into the Paraná so as "to carry the contagion to the riverine populations of Corrientes, Entrerios [*sic*] and Santa Fe, cities still under the domination of the enemy Solano López." See Alexandre Werneck, "Bactéria foi arma de Caxias," *O Jornal do Brasil* (Rio de Janeiro), 21 October 2001; this charge of having conducted bacteriological warfare bears all the hallmarks of fabrication, historical blindness, and willful ignorance, and it cannot be sustained by the facts, for even had the Allies "launched" contaminated bodies into the Paraná (a very dubious idea), there were no Paraguayans in any province *downriver* from Itapirú in 1867. Nor can cholera be spread over hundreds of miles in the way this "correspondence" suggests. If writers committed to a conspiracy theory wish to smear the reputation of the Marquis of Caxias, they will have to do better than this. See General Luiz Cesário da Silveira Filho, "A verdade sobre Caxias," *Jornal do Brasil* (Rio de Janeiro), 11 November 2001, with a 25 November rejoinder in the same newspaper from Alberto Magno ("A guerra bacteriológica do Brasil"), who makes the irrelevant but rather telling observation that history itself is an "invention."

68 *El Semanario* (Asunción), 28 September 1867.

69 Caxias to Mitre, Tuyucué, 7 September 1867, in *La Noticia* (Buenos Aires), 19 September 1867.

70 The archival record is replete with cases of desertion throughout the 1860s. See, for example, Miguel González to López, Tranquera de Loreto, 13 March 1863, ANA-CRB I-30, 16, 7, no. 1; Court-martial of Sixto Mendes [1865], ANA-SJC 1512, no. 7; Interrogation of deserter Juan Bautista Espinosa, Headquarters of 47th Battalion, 15 February 1866, ANA-NE 780; Juan Gómez to War Minister, Headquarters of 47th Battalion, 7 June 1866, ANA-NE 755; Francisco Bareiro to López, Asunción, 16 August 1866 [regarding desertions from the foundry at Ybycuí], ANA-SH 350, no. 2; Court-martial of Anastasio Báez, Paso Pucú, 22 July 1867, ANA-SJC 1798, no. 1; and Miscellaneous documentation on "treason" trials at Paso Pucú (1867), ANA-SH 352, no. 9.

71 That desertions expanded in 1867 is illustrated by an incomplete record from June, July, and August of that year that lists fifty-one separate cases of deserters detained, flogged, or executed during the course of those months. See unidentified document of 1867, ANA-NE 768. Toward the end of the year, General Enrique Castro reported that Paraguayan deserters were coming over to the Allied side every day, and that only the previous evening a corporal had come across with promises of "bringing many others" if only a signal rocket could be arranged. See Castro to Flores, Tuyucué, 24 December 1867, AGN (M). Archivos Particulares. Caja 69, carpeta 21.

72 Cardozo, *Hace cien años*, 7: 142–144; *El Semanario* (Asunción), 28 September 1867.

73 Caxias to Mitre, Tuyucué, 23 September 1867, in *Archivo del coronel Dr. Marcos Paz*, 6: 343–344.

74 Dispatch of General Porto Alegre to Caxias, Tuyutí, 24 September 1867, in *Archivo del coronel Dr. Marcos Paz*, 6: 344–345.

75 Thompson, *The War in Paraguay*, 223–224; Centurión, *Memorias o reminiscencias*, 3: 21–23; Queiroz Duarte, *Os Voluntários da Pátria*, 3, bk. 1:132–134 and bk. 2: 173–175.

76 In its issue of 3 October 1867, *El Centinela* (Asunción) published an article that celebrated the "splendid triumph" at Ombú. It was accompanied by an elaborate woodcut illustration of the combat that improbably noted "600 dead Blacks, [other] prisoners taken, many wounded, and an entire battalion armed with the weapons seized in this engagement."

77 Ill-intentioned gossip had it that it was Madame Lynch, rather than López, who felt drawn to the handsome Caballero, who could trace his unprecedented promotions to an intimate relation with her. A parallel story, perhaps invented by the same busybodies, held that Caballero's sister, María de la Cruz Caballero, had had an ongoing affair with the Marshal and it was due to her influence, rather than that of the Madame, that her brother rose so quickly. See Frota, *Diário Pessoal do Almirante Visconde de Inhaúma*, 344, no. 487. It is certainly true that Caballero was better known as a ladies' man than as a soldier. After he became president of Paraguay in 1880, he entirely neglected his status as military hero, never wore his medals, and did not even own a uniform (see "Informes del general don Bernardino Caballero, ex-presidente de la república (Asunción, 1888), MHM (A)-CZ carpeta 131); he seems, however, to have fathered at least thirty-two children by almost as many women. According to a well-known family tradition, these children met at the official residence at the end of each month to receive a regular subvention from their father (Guido Rodríguez Alcalá, personal communication, Asunción, 8 June 2009). Probably the best-known work on Caballero, entirely hagiographic in its orientation, is Juan E. O'Leary, *El centauro de Ybycuí. Vida heróica del general Bernardino Caballero en la guerra del Paraguay* (Paris, 1929).

78   "Correspondencia del ejército," *El Semanario* (Asunción), 9 October 1867. See also Cardozo, *Hace cien años*, 7: 183–188.

79   There is a great disparity in the sources—more so than usual—as to the number of units involved in the engagement, with Thompson and Centurión claiming four Brazilian regiments (*The War in Paraguay*, 224; *Memorias o reminiscencias*, 3: 24), and Resquín a full division (*La guerra del Paraguay contra la Triple Alianza*, 66). It does seem that Caxias had far more units in reserve than he chose to deploy that day.

80   "Battle of Isla Taiy. Paraguayan Version," *The Standard* (Buenos Aires), 9 November 1867.

81   Altogether the Brazilians lost about five hundred men and the Paraguayans three hundred (killed and wounded); see Thompson, *The War in Paraguay*, 224; and Enrique Castro to Juan Bautista Castro, Tuyucué, 10 October 1867, AGN (M). Archivos Particulares. Caja 69, carpeta 23.

82   See, for example, "Splendid Victory by the Allies," *The Standard* (Buenos Aires), 9 October 1867.

83   "Great Brazilian Victory. The Battle of the Groves," *The Standard* (Buenos Aires), 31 October 1867.

84   Pompeyo González (Juan E. O'Leary) "Recuerdos de Gloria. Tatayibá, 21 de octubre de 1867," *La Patria* (Asunción), 21 October 1902, and Mitre to Paz, Cuartel general (Tuyucué), 24 October 1867, in *Archivo del coronel Dr. Marcos Paz*, 7: 340–341.

85   "Revista del mes de octubre," *El Semanario* (Asunción), 2 November 1867; "Teatro de la guerra," *La Nación Argentina* (Buenos Aires), 30 October 1867; marechal Visconde de Maracajú, *Campanha do Paraguay (1867 e 1868)* (Rio de Janeiro, 1922), 39–44.

86   González, "Recuerdos de Gloria. Tatayibá;" Ramón Cesar Bejarano, *El Pila. Señor del Chaco* (Asunción, 1985), 277–278.

87   Mitre to Paz, Cuartel general (Tuyucué), 24 October 1867, in Thompson, *La guerra del Paraguay*, xciv–xcv. See also Osório to "Chiquinha," Tuyucué, 27 October 1867, in Osório and Osório, *História do general Osório*, 2: 397.

88   "Great Brazilian Victory. The Battle of the Groves," *The Standard* (Buenos Aires), 31 October 1867.

89   For general treatments on this theme see Joaquim Pinto de Campos, *Vida do Grande Cidadão Brazileiro Luiz Alves de Lima e Silva, Barão, Conde, Marquez, Duque de Caxias* (Lisbon, 1878); Raymundo Pinto Seidl, *O Duque de Caxias. Esboço de Sua Gloriosa Vida* (Rio de Janeiro, 1903); and Tasso Fragoso, *História da Guerra entre a Triplice Aliança e o Paraguai*.

90   Tasso Fragoso, *História da Guerra entre a Tríplice Aliança e o Paraguai*, 3: 354–356; "Papéis e Notas Incompletos de Rufino Enés Galvão sobre o Ataque do Potreiro Ovelha, (1867)," IHGB, lata 223, doc. 19; Cunha Paranaguá, *Relatório Apresentada a Assembléa Geral*, 66–69.

91   "Crónica del ejército," *El Semanario* (Asunción), 4 December 1867.

92   Cardozo, *Hace cien años*, 7: 259–260.

93   "Otra carta del ejército," *La Nación Argentina* (Buenos Aires), 9 November 1867.

94   Caxias to Mitre, Tuyucué, 29 October 1867, in *La Nación Argentina* (Buenos Aires), 7 November 1867; da Cunha, *Propaganda contra o Imperio*, 34–35.

95   Thompson, *The War in Paraguay*, 226–227.

96   "Correspondencia do Jornal do Commercio (Buenos Aires, 14 November 1867)," *Jornal do Commercio* (Rio de Janeiro), 20 November 1867.

97   Washburn to Seward, Asunción, 13 December 1867, NARA, M-128, no. 2; Queiroz Duarte, *Os Voluntários da Pátria*, 3, bk. 1: 34–38 and bk. 2: 85–91.

98 Francisco Manoel da Cunha Junior, *Guerra do Paraguay. Tujuty. Ataque de 3 de Novembro de 1867* (Rio de Janeiro, 1888), 17; see also Queiroz Duarte, *Os Voluntários da Pátria*, 3, bk. 1: 134–137, bk. 2: 5–54, 112–116, 175–180, 206–212, and bk. 3: 82–87, 117–123, 227–228.

99 The Legion, which on paper consisted of just over seven hundred troops, had been constituted as a unit in the Argentine army since 1865. Not surprisingly, the Marshal's government treated as traitors the soldiers that composed its ranks, and yet, the number of uniformed legionnaires was never so great as that of the small-time Paraguayan opportunists, men and women, who sought to turn the war to their own advantage in the Allied camp. Honest collaborators among the Paraguayans were rare, turncoats even more so. At Tuyutí, the legionnaires had their bivouac alongside one of the main Argentine mangrullos and that is where Barrios's men found them. See "The Tuyutí Surprise," *The Standard* (Buenos Aires), 15 November 1867; Cunha Junior, *Guerra do Paraguay. Tujuty*, 15–16; Juan E. O'Leary, *Los legionarios* (Asunción, 1930).

100 Thompson noted a painfully exaggerated rise in the fares that the boatmen charged for such transport. See *The War in Paraguay*, 231.

101 Malnutrition can have insidious effects. In its early stages, before total listlessness sets in, it can inspire a crazed need for protein that is hard to ignore even among the most disciplined men. This appears to have happened with the Paraguayan soldiers at Second Tuyutí (although a less charitable view holds that the greedy Paraguayans made straight for the liquor). One deserter who came across the lines from Curupayty affirmed that meat rations in the Paraguayan trenches had by now almost completely stopped, and that the civilians could no longer trade for manioc root and maize, for such provisions could not be found. See Declaration of Corporal José Benítez of the 45th Battalion, Tuyucué, 19 November 1867, in *Archivo del coronel Dr. Marcos Paz*, 6: 432–433.

102 Thompson, *The War in Paraguay*, 231–232; "A Guerra," *O Tribuno* (Recife), 5 December 1867. In a telling passage, Centurión described the "shameful" scene of his countrymen being shot down while they crammed their mouths from sacks of sugar: "But who was responsible for this shame? Let the reader answer for us"—an obvious intimation that López had caused the starvation that brought out such behavior in his men. See *Memorias y reminiscencias*, 3: 40–41. The uncontrolled hunger of troops too long in the line has often upset calculations among commanders and campaign planners, as, for instance, during the German offensive of 1918, when General Ludendorff had to abandon his timetables because captured Allied stores proved too tempting to his hungry men.

103 "Batalla de Tuyu-Tí," *La Nación Argentina* (Buenos Aires), 9 November 1867.

104 Thompson spoke for many when he observed that "Porto Alegre *himself* behaved bravely, but his army did not." See *The War in Paraguay*, 231. See also "Correspondencia," (Curuzú, 30 Jan. 1868), in *Jornal do Commercio* (Rio de Janeiro), 13 February 1868.

105 Both General Resquín and Colonel Centurión later adopted a sharply critical view of Barrios's comportment on this occasion, an opinion broadly shared by many other Paraguayans. Resquín, *La guerra del Paraguay contra la Triple Alianza*, 72, and Centurión, *Memorias y reminiscencias*, 3: 41–42.

106 Pimentel, *Guerra do Paraguay. Episódios Militares*, 65–68.

107 Centurión, *Memorias o reminiscencias*, 3: 42.

108 In its issue of 28 November 1867, *El Centinela* (Asunción) offers a woodcut image of these downtrodden prisoners, depicted without exception as Brazilian blacks, being led off to Paso Pucú by a company of well-clothed and stalwart-looking Paraguayans.

109 A slave to money-making, Lanús had acted as armorer for the Paraguayan military before the war and since 1865 had worked for the Argentine national government in a similar capacity. See Whigham, *Paraguayan War. Causes and Early Conduct*, 239, 313, 354.

Brazilian sources claimed that Lanús's losses were inconsequential as they were limited to "rations for 20,000 men." See "A Batalha de Tuyuty," *O Tribuno* (Recife), 10 February 1868.

110   "The War in the North," *The Standard* (Buenos Aires), 16 November 1867.

111   As Sindbad of *The Standard* rather peevishly put it: "if the Paraguayan soldiers had obeyed their officers and abstained from drinking, Itapirú and all appertaining to it would have been a prey to the flames." See issue of 16 November 1867. One Uruguayan eyewitness to the Paraguayan pillaging (and the subsequent beating they took) tended to agree with this observation, as did Julián Godoy, the Marshal's adjutant. See Manuel Martínez to Colonel José Luis Gómez, President of the Centro de Guerreros del Paraguay, Montevideo, 26 March 1916, MHN-M Colección Guerreros del Paraguay, and "Memorias de teniente coronel Julián Godoy."

112   Thompson, *The War in Paraguay*, 235.

113   Cunha Junior, *Guerra do Paraguay. Tujuty*, 34–37.

114   Despite the extensive damage to the cannon's mechanism, the Marshal's engineers worked all night to repair it, and by the next day had transported it to Curupayty where it was placed at the right of the battery within full view of Ignácio's ships (which kept carefully out of its range). See Centurión, *Memorias o reminiscencias*, 3: 44, 49.

115   Mitre to Paz, Tuyucué, 4 November 1867, in *Archivo del coronel Dr. Marcos Paz*, 7: 349–350.

116   Tasso Fragoso, *História da Guerra entre a Triplice Aliança e o Paraguai*, 3: 375–376 (which summarized the official statistics reported by Caxias and others).

117   Thompson, *The War in Paraguay*, 234.

118   Cited in Cardozo, *Hace cien años*, 7: 278.

119   Phelps, *Tragedy of Paraguay*, 195–197; Bejarano, *El Pila*, 280–281; Kollinski, *Independence or Death!*, 154.

120   It was entirely predictable that the Marshal's pluck was the principal factor that the government gazette emphasized in its official account of the battle (though Barrios and Caballero also earned plaudits). See "Movimientos del enemigo," *El Semanario* (Asunción), 16 November 1867. At the end of the war, while still in Brazilian detention, General Resquín supposedly argued that the Marshal had had much more than a raid intended when he attacked the Allied camp at Tuyutí—that López really believed the Paraguayans could retain control at that point, which in turn would force the Allies to abandon their strong positions at San Solano. See "Declaración del general Francisco Isidoro Resquín, jefe del estado mayor paraguayo, prestada en el cuartel general del commando del Ejército Brasilero en Humaitá, en 20 de marzo de 1870," in *Papeles de López. El tirano pintado por si mismo* (Buenos Aires, 1871), 151–152.

121   "The War in the North," *The Standard* (Buenos Aires), 6 November 1867.

8 | THE COST OF ENDURANCE

1   Miscellaneous Correspondence of Mena Barreto (?) to Caxias, Tayí, January–March, 1868, IHGB, lata 447, doc. 82.

2   Jaime Gomes Argolo Ferrão, "Relatório sobre a Estrada de Ferro do Chaco," in Levy Scavarda, "Centenário da Passagem de Humaitá," *Revista Marítima Brasileira* 8, nos. 1–3 (1968): 35–40. There is an extant letter of Caxias requesting that the Baron of São Borja arrange that firewood cut for the ironclads be sent northward along this line. See Caxias to São Borja, 15 February 1868, IHGB, lata 447, doc. 84; in fact, the engineers who designed the rail line made a crucial mistake in locating it too close to the edge of

the Paraguay, for when the river waters rose precipitously in January, they flooded the rails and made it impossible for a time for supplies to reach the fleet. See "The War in the North," *The Standard* (Buenos Aires), 8 January and 11 February 1868.

3   The pressure to send to the front every man, young or old, sick or healthy, had never abated during this time. In a muster roll from the beginning of 1868, the parish priest of one interior village listed 487 "recruits," mostly very old men or children (the few men of intermediate age were all ill, wounded, infirm, insane, or functionally blind). See Report of Domingo Tomás Candía, Ybycuí, 18 January 1868, ANA-NE 982. The *jefe de milícias* of another interior town confirmed this general picture in his report of the same period, which listed 498 officers, soldiers, and "recruits" present in his district, 104 of whom were over sixty-five years of age. One man, Ysidro Escobar, was 101(!) and there were several other men in their nineties. See Report of Juan B. Campos, San José de los Arroyos, 20 January 1868, ANA-NE 982.

4   In a letter of 29 November 1867, the war correspondent of *The Standard* (Buenos Aires) reported that temperatures at the front were hovering between ninety-six and one hundred five degrees Fahrenheit (issue of 1 December 1867). Two weeks later, the same correspondent noted that "Ordinary thermometers [were] of no use, not being manufactured for such a rapid and extensive expansion of the fluid metal ... judging from one's sensations, [the temperature] may be called terrific ... the hot atmosphere ... brings roundly before the imagination Dante's infernal regions, at least a moderate foretaste of Purgatory" (issue of 18 December 1867).

5   In endorsing this general picture of a man jealous of his status and indifferent to the quality—though not the quantity—of his food, Washburn remarked that the Marshal was a "gourmand but not an epicure," with a decided preference for the "greasier dishes." See *History of Paraguay*, 2: 48.

6   See miscellaneous paeans to Marshal López in the 29 July 1865 issue of *El Semanario* (Asunción). As we have seen, at a time when malnutrition had begun to hit both Asunción and the interior towns, public subscriptions were held all over the country to pay for a jewel-encrusted sword the likes of a Tizona, a golden wreath, and a book of valedictories for presentation to the Marshal in tribute to his "many sacrifices" for the fatherland. For examples, see "Adhesión de las damas de San Pedro al proyecto del obsequio de una guirnalda de oro y brillantes al Presidente" (San Pedro, 1867), ANA-SH 352, no. 10, and "Adhesión de los pueblos al obsequio de guirnalda de oro y gorro triunfal" (1867), ANA-SH 353, no. 1.

7   Orión [Héctor F. Varela], *Elisa Lynch* (Buenos Aires, 1934), 217–218. Masterman observed that "it was one of the peculiarities of López that he distrusted everybody who tried to serve him, and treated those worst to whom he was the most indebted." See *Seven Eventful Years in Paraguay*, 223.

8   Robert Bontine Cunninghame Graham attributed to General Resquín this story of López's torturing animals in his childhood. See *Portrait of a Dictator* (London, 1935), 93. To be fair, Cunninghame Graham appears to be the only one arguing this as an explicit fact, for neither in the declaration he made while in Brazilian custody in 1870, nor in the memoir he published some years afterwards, does Resquín claim anything of the kind. Furthermore, though the Marshal was often cruel and always ruthless, there is little to suggest that he was clinically sociopathic. See "Importante documento para la historia de la guerra del Paraguay. Declaración del General Francisco Isidoro Resquín, Humaitá, 20 Marzo de 1870," BNA, Colección Enrique Solano López, no. 1094.

9   R.C. Kirk (?) to Hamilton Fish, Buenos Aires, 31 August 1869, NARA, FM-69, no. 18.

10   Thompson, *The War in Paraguay*, 241.

11   In 1865, Pedro had threatened to abdicate if kept from participating in the war at the head of his troops; to this his ministers reluctantly assented, but they slowed down his

progress toward the Riograndense front so as to coincide with the Paraguayan surrender at Uruguaiana, and afterwards convinced the emperor that his proper place was at Rio de Janeiro and that he should leave field command to Mitre and later Caxias. His willingness to fight, and perhaps to sacrifice himself, no one seemed to question. See Barman, *Citizen Emperor*, 202–203; Whigham, *The Paraguayan War*, 380–384.

12   Charles Ames Washburn perhaps showed the most florid contempt for the cowardice of the "great tyrant," but he has not been the only individual to qualify López in these terms. See Washburn, *History of Paraguay*, 2: 568–570; Thompson, *The War in Paraguay*, 328; Saeger, *Francisco Solano López and the Ruination of Paraguay*, 9–10, 180–182, 201, 208.

13   Cecilio Báez, *La tiranía en el Paraguay, sus causas, caracteres y resultados* (Asunción, 1903); Héctor Francisco Decoud, *La masacre de Concepción ordenada por el mariscal López* (Asunción, 1926); and more recently, James Schofield Saeger, *Francisco Solano López and the Ruination of Paraguay*.

14   As a matter of fact, dom Pedro did step down twenty years later when he saw that the monarchist cause was lost in Brazil. Whether the younger emperor would have displayed such grace in an untenable position is impossible to know, of course, but the truculence and obstinacy he showed in pursuing the war against Paraguay was manifestly absent during the military takeover of 1889, and it ultimately proved easy for him to accept the inevitable (particularly as his family shielded him from some of its uglier effects). Besides, we are concerned here with the Marshal's estimation of dom Pedro as a leader, not the estimation of Pedro himself. See Barman, *Citizen Emperor*, 353–366.

15   These exiles had been operating against the López regime for many years, in some cases, dating back to the time of the Marshal's father. See, for example, *Carta primera de don Luciano Recalde al Presidente López del Paraguay* (Buenos Aires, 1857), and, as a rebuttal, *Ojeada histórica sobre el Paraguay, seguida del vapuleo de un traidor, dividida en varias azotainas, administradas el extraviado autor de las producciones contra el Paraguay, conocido vulgarmente por el nombre de Luciano el Zonzo, escrita en verso y prosa por el ciudadano paraguayo Juan J. Brizuela* (Buenos Aires, 1857).

16   Washburn tells the anecdote of two sisters from Limpio, Anita and Conchita Casal, who happened to be in Asunción when one of these dances was held. Curious at the event, they approached the plaza during the late hours, and, when spotted by a policeman, were forced to join in the festivities or "go to the calaboose." Trembling with fear, they danced in the company of the roughest soldiers and common prostitutes until they found an opportunity to slip away unnoticed, running "away like frightened deer." See Washburn, *History of Paraguay*, 2: 100–101. In a letter to the British representative at Buenos Aires, G.F. Gould expressed the opinion that women had been flogged to death for refusing to attend the dances. See Gould to Mathew, Paso Pucú, 10 September 1867, in Philip, *British Documents on Foreign Affairs*, 1, pt. 1, series D: 224.

17   Even in classical times, commentators noted that as the power of a state declines, the pageantry increases—and this was always the case in Paraguay. The author, who was present in Asunción during the late 1980s, noticed a sharp, almost exponential expansion in the number of beauty competitions being shown on local television. This happened at a time of dotage for dictator Alfredo Stroessner, whose failure to name a successor had exacerbated the divisions within the ruling Colorado Party. The reason for televising the beauty competitions appeared obvious even then, and mirrored the rationale for the dance craze of the 1860s: in both cases, an authoritarian government sought to distract the public with meaningless amusements while, beneath the surface, political decay had already done considerable damage.

18   According to Thompson, the "golden combs" was "a name given to a class invented at the beginning of the dancing mania, and consisting of all the third-class girls who had any pretension to good looks, and were tolerably loose in their morals. They all wore

immense golden combs in their back-hair. They were brought forward by the Government to spite the ladies, most of whom refused to dance at these places, though under danger of their lives." See Thompson, *The War in Paraguay*, 44.

19   Washburn, *History of Paraguay*, 2: 95–96.

20   Though of uncertain origin, the tale of López's illegitimate birth is oft-repeated, with the usual version holding that Carlos Antonio López (himself the son of a tailor) had married the pregnant Juana Pabla Carrillo as part of a business deal with her father. This story was endlessly alluded to by both the Marshal's enemies and some of his associates. When Estanislao Zeballos visited Asunción in 1888, he discovered that all who had known Francisco Solano López believed that his true father was "one Señor Rojas," whom he physically resembled. See "Segundo Viaje al teatro de guerra, 1888. Varias noticias recogidas en la Asunción," MHM (A)-CZ, carpeta 127. This "Rojas" was Lázaro de Rojas Aranda, one of the richest men in Paraguay, who left his fortune to his godson, the future Marshal, "because he had no sons of his own." See Pastor Urbieta Rojas, "La infancia de Solano López," Ñandé 5, no. 109 (15 October 1963).

21   On occasion, a rather questionable treatment can summon up an accurate image. Such would appear to be the case with Anne Enright's supposedly stylish but in fact ostentatious novel, *The Pleasure of Eliza Lynch* (New York, 2002), which describes the two López sisters as "ghastly … equally fat, equally swaddled; their moustachios bristling, their bosoms heaving, and their armpits stained with sweat" (49). Most witnesses confirmed this unflattering physical portrayal, but it is also true that the two women suffered extensively at the hands of gossip mongers who thought them venal, ignorant, and spiritually empty. Unlike their brother, they have yet to find a champion among later scholars or polemicists (Alfredo Boccia, personal communication, Asunción, 3 November 2009). Regarding Rafaela's subsequent life with a Brazilian attorney, see Alfredo Boccia Romañach, "El caso de Rafaela López y el Bachiller Pedra," *Revista de la Sociedad Científica del Paraguay* 7, nos. 12–13 (2002): 89–96.

22   Dante, we should recall, reserved a filth-laden spot in the eighth circle of Hell for abject flatterers, among whom Venancio would surely have felt at home. Washburn described him as a man with many faults. For one thing, he was a lecher, "the terror of those families that, not belonging to the upper class, had yet some regard for decency and the reputation of their daughters." At the same time, the war minister was uncertain of his own place, "in a chronic fright," and that made him a most unusual figure, for

> all his countrymen were as afraid to visit him as he was to talk to them. Nevertheless, he nominally held a high official position, being commandant of arms, and having duties to perform that required him to visit the arsenal, barracks, and fort at Asunción every day. … What had he done that he appeared even more frightened and depressed than others who were afterwards accused of being his fellow-conspirators? Probably nothing; but he knew better than they did the terrible character of his brother, who, he was even then aware, had ceased to respect his mother's gray hairs, and regarded all ties of consanguinity as matters of indifference.

See Washburn, *History of Paraguay*, 1: 391–392 and 2: 212–213. Venancio may or may not have had the *peste française*, but the idea that he had been incapacitated (or "ruined") by the disease seems improbable given both his very active work schedule and the regularity of his correspondence. See Siân Rees, *The Shadows of Elisa Lynch* (London, 2003), 227.

23   In an otherwise banal report on troop movements written to the Marshal on the last day of the year, his brother began with the following salutation, versions of which had become more or less de rigueur by this time: "Most Excellent Sir, Marshal President of the Republic, [I feel] honored to have received Your Excellency's dispatches nos. 5 through 29, and [feeling] highly gratified at the news of Your Excellency's good health … I lift my vote to heaven so [that God may] conserve Your Excellency's much-desired happiness."

See Venancio López to López, 31 December 1867, ANA-CRB I-30, 26, 1, no. 13. Such observances and honorifics were so jealously upheld by the Marshal that officials had to be punctilious in their usage. We can point to an earlier letter to a minor official at Concepción, in which the treasury minister warns him never again to allude to the minister's "important life," that such a designation did not correspond to someone of such petty rank. One can easily imagine the Marshal's spies—who read every scrap of correspondence that came to and from Asunción—emphatically nodding their approval of this admonition. See Mariano González to Justice of Peace of Concepción, 19 January 1866, ANA-SH 348, no.1.

24   Alyn Brodsky, *Madame Lynch & Friend: A True Account of an Irish Adventuress and the Dictator of Paraguay, who Destroyed that American Nation* (New York, 1975); Anne Enright, *The Pleasure of Eliza Lynch*; and, to a lesser extent, Lily Tuck, *The News from Paraguay. A Novel* (New York, 2004).

25   One British witness claimed that the Marshal had eight mistresses, and that the "chiefs and judges of the districts were in the habit of selecting the most handsome of the girls to gratify [his] lusts." See "Testimony of Dr. Skinner (Asunción, 25 January 1871)," in Scottish Record Office, CS 244/543/19. The names of several of these women are known to us, and one of them, Pancha Garmendia, has over the years become a posthumous anti-Lopista heroine for her refusal to yield to his intentions. See "Pancha Garmendia," *El Orden* (Asunción) 22 July 1926; Victor Morínigo, "Los amores del Mariscal. Pancha Garmendia, Juanita Pesoa y Elisa Lynch," *Revista de las FF.AA. de la Nación* 3, no. 31 (1943): 1870–1834; and J.P. Canet, *Pancha Garmendia. El libro que no debe faltar en ningún hogar paraguayo y cristiano* (Asunción, 1957).

26   The malice that typified Lynch's reception by the society ladies of Asunción (and also by Madame Cochelet, wife of the French minister) has generated considerable material for novelists, who seem to have drawn principally from Varela and local gossips. Despite these problematic sources, the outline of her negative experiences in society appears believable. See, for instance, Hector Pedro Blomberg, *La dama del Paraguay. Biografía de Madama Lynch* (Buenos Aires, 1942), 42–46; William E. Barrett, *Woman on Horseback. The Story of Francisco López and Elisa Lynch* (New York, 1952), 84–86; and most recently, Lily Tuck, *The News from Paraguay*. In their well-documented and thoughtful biography, Michael Lillis and Ronan Fanning note that Lynch showed little ill feeling in the face of all the abuse she received; indeed, she never returned the contempt of the elite women of Paraguay, which, under the circumstances, was a decidedly enlightened response. See Lillis and Fanning, *The Lives of Eliza Lynch. Scandal and Courage* (Dublin, 2009), 89–90, 199–200.

27   The rumor that López aspired to convert the Paraguayan government into a monarchy and himself into an emperor was extensively commented-upon in diplomatic circles. In a letter of 3 November 1863 to the US secretary of state, Washburn alluded to a conversation with the future Marshal in which the latter claimed that the idea of creating a Paraguayan empire had been raised by the Brazilians, but that he had not yet "entertained any such idea himself." Commenting on this with his usual acidity, Washburn observed that "little [meaningful] change would be required, for the government is already more despotic, more completely under the absolute control of one man than any empire in the world." See Washburn to Seward, Asunción, NARA, M-128, no. 1; and, for parallel observations from French representatives, see M. Maillefer to Foreign Minister Drouyn de Lhuys, Montevideo, 14 October 1863, in "Informes diplomáticos de los representantes de Francia en el Uruguay (1859–1863)," *Revista Histórica* 19, nos. 55–57 (1953): 472. An analogous story held that the young Francisco Solano López had once initiated negotiations with dom Pedro for the hand of one of the imperial princesses, thinking thereby to marry into the monarchical institution and protect his country in the process. These negotiations, if they ever took place, supposedly foundered on the emperor's opposition

to any marriage with a commoner (both women married European princes in 1864). The whole episode offers ample room for speculation but never really rises above apocrypha. Even so, in the Museo Histórico Nacional in Buenos Aires there is a curious model for a crown that López supposedly ordered from Paris for a future coronation. See Alcindo Sodré, "Solano López, Imperador," *Revista do Instituto Histórico e Geográfico Brasileiro* 182 (1944): 105–115; R. Magalhães Junior, *O Império em Chinelos* (Rio de Janeiro and São Paulo, 1957), 103–110; Lillis and Fanning, *The Lives of Eliza Lynch*, 93–94; and, most curious of all, a "Contrato entre o representante da comissão de senhoras paraguayas e o Sr. [Paul] de Cuverville, gerente do consul frances, encarejado de mandar confeccionar em Paris uma corôa de ouro e brilhantes para ser ofrecido ao Marechal Presidente," (1868), IHGB doc. 5, lata 321.

28   *Exposición. Protesta que hace Elisa A. Lynch* (Buenos Aires, 1875), 56–57. See also Washburn to Seward, Asunción, 14 October 1867, NARA, M-128, no. 2, which makes specific reference to properties purchased within the capital by the López family and the consequent unlikelihood of an early evacuation.

29   The scale of land holdings sold in private arrangements to various members of the López family could only be described as colossal. The López mother, Juana Pabla Carillo, had been particularly active in this respect, as had Venancio and Benigno. See, for example, Contract of Juana Carillo with Pedro B. Moreno, Asunción, 13 January 1864, ANA-NE 3266; Miscellaneous land transfers (1850s–1860s), ANA-CRB I-30, 24, 38; I-30, 6, 98; I-29, 30, 46; "Cuenta formada de los alquileres de … las casas de la señora Juana Carrillo de López" (1 July 1865–30 April 1866), ANA-NE 3277; and more generally, Thompson, *The War in Paraguay*, 8–12.

30   Lynch's yearning to accumulate an immense treasure may be excused by the apprehension of her lover's death or eviction, which would have left her children destitute. See Junta Patriotica, *El mariscal Francisco Solano López* (Asunción, 1926), 17; Andrés Moscarda, *Las tierras de Madama Lynch. Un caso de prescripción contra el fisco* (Asunción, 1920?); and Carlos Pastore, *La lucha por la tierra en el Paraguay* (Montevideo, 1972), 148–157. The López sisters evidently detested Lynch, whom they thought responsible for their husbands' deaths; they also accused her of making off with considerable sums of their money and other properties (though their own avarice was well established). See "Testimony of Inocencia López de Barrios, (Asunción, 17 January 1871), in Scottish Record Office, CS 244/543/19 (90–93).

31   She contrasted the depth of her love with the shallower feelings she encountered among Latins, for "when an Englishwoman loves, she loves truly." See Orión, *Elisa Lynch*, 236; and if la Madama loved López, he loved her in turn and he particularly loved his children. In a rare letter from Panchito López to his mother at the beginning of 1868, see ample references to the Marshal's tenderness and his desire that his family members not expose themselves to unnecessary peril. See Juan F. López to Mi Querida Mamita, Humaitá (?), 3 January 1868, UCR-Godoi Collection, box 8, no. 92.

32   Washburn, *The History of Paraguay*, 2: 397; in her statement of 1875, Lynch explicitly denied responsibility for the domestic policies and deeds of her paramour: "I was far from being involved in the government … nor did I involve myself during the war in anything more than attending to the wounded and to the families of the [soldiers], and trying to reduce the general suffering I found." See *Exposición*, 208.

33   The tall tales that seemed to adhere like mucilage to Madame Lynch's life in Paraguay were constantly repeated in the nineteenth century and afterwards. Some argued that she headed an Amazon corps in the Paraguayan army; others that every piece of jewelry collected by her lover's government ended up in her possession; and still others that she had previously been mistress to the Correntino governor and had urged López to attack Argentina as revenge for that failed dalliance or because a newspaper editor in

that community had ridiculed her in a satirical article. Burton even heard it said that she directed military operations at Humaitá from a leather-covered *mangrullo*, "an unusual precaution intended to conceal petticoated ankles." See *Letters from the Battle-fields of Paraguay*, 357. What these many canards have in common is their utility as propaganda, for the Marshal's enemies drew great succor from the false image of a Lady MacBeth, who "flattered the vain, credulous, and greedy savage into the belief that he was destined to raise Paraguay from obscurity, and make it the dominant power in South America." See Masterman, *Seven Eventful Years in Paraguay*, 59. As should be obvious by now, López needed no extra encouragement to think himself a man of destiny. As for Eliza Lynch, it is hard not to concur with the judgment of her daughter-in-law, Maud Lloyd, who remarked that Lynch "was not the lurid, intriguing adventuress they make her out to be. Like most women living 'without benefit of clergy' [she] was the victim of circumstances. ... She was a warm hearted, sentimental, early Victorian Irishwoman with a ready sympathy for anyone in trouble ... [But] her influence with López was very limited." Cited in Michael Lillis and Ronan Fanning, *The Lives of Eliza Lynch, Scandal and Courage* (Dublin, 2009), 199–200.

34   Cardozo, *Hace cien años*, 7: 303–305; unbeknownst to Washburn, the US government had again tendered its good offices to the Allies in trying to arrange a negotiated peace, but the offer, sent from Washington on 25 December 1867, went unanswered by the Brazilians, who insisted on consulting with the Argentine government. The death in mid-January of General Asboth, the US minister to Buenos Aires, prevented the offer from reaching Argentine authorities before February, but afterwards they rejected it, as did the Brazilians, finally and definitively, in April 1868. See "Transactions in the Region of the La Plata," US Senate, 40th Congress, 3rd Session, ex. Doc, no. 5, 33–35, 44–45.

35   Mitre to Paz, Tuyucué, 14 November 1867, in *Archivo del coronel Dr. Marcos Paz*, 7: 360.

36   Gould to George B. Mathew, Paso Pucú, 10 September 1867, in Philip, *British Documents on Foreign Affairs, Latin America, 1845–1914*, 1, pt. 1, Series D: 225–226.

37   The war minister reported in late December that a party of military scouts had traversed nineteen river passes and creeks in the Chaco wilderness and had successfully arrived at the Pilcomayo River after only twelve days. This suggests that the Paraguayans had plans to go to still further lengths in establishing a supply route for the besieged troops at Humaitá. See Venancio López to López, Asunción, 27 December 1867, ANA-CRB I-30, 26, 1, no. 10.

38   Cardozo, *Hace cien años*, 7: 364–365.

39   Von Versen, *Reisen in Amerika*, 145–146, and Statement of Paraguayan deserter Gaspar Cabrera, aboard steamship *Princesa de Joinville*, 21 December 1867, in *Archivo del coronel Dr. Marcos Paz*, 6: 440.

40   Centurión, *Memorias o reminiscencias*, 3: 69–70.

41   Centurión, *Memorias o reminiscencias*, 3: 73; Pompeyo González [Juan E. O'Leary], "Recuerdos de gloria. Paso Poí. 24 de diciembre de 1867," *La Patria* (Asunción), 24 December 1902; Queiroz Duarte, *Os Voluntários da Pátria*, 3, bk. 1: 186–187.

42   Cardozo, *Hace cien años*, 7: 416; *El Semanario* (Asunción), 28 December 1867.

43   "Apéndice de los festejos del aniversario de nuestra independencia nacional," *Cabichuí* (Paso Pucú), 28 December 1867 (special edition).

44   General Tasso Fragoso dedicated a mere paragraph to the Paso Poí raid, which seems rather ungenerous given the importance that the Paraguayans attached to the engagement. See *História da Guerra entre a Triplice Aliança e o Paraguay*, 3: 384.

45   Leuchars calls these pensions generous, and so they would have been had they involved payment in coin. As it was, the monies were paid out largely in scrip valid only for use in state commissaries, just a few of which remained in operation in Paraguay after 1867

(Asunción being a prominent exception). In speculating that the Marshal wished to repopulate the country with these handicapped veterans, Leuchars would appear to indulge in an overly charitable interpretation. It seems more likely that López wanted to save himself the cost of feeding men who could add little or nothing to the war effort. See *To the Bitter End*, 177, and Telegram of López to Venancio López, Humaitá (?), 26 December 1867, ANA-CRB I-30, 28, 18.

46   This remorseless attitude, which had rarely been admitted to publicly and which specifically dehumanized the Paraguayans, now regularly disgraced the Allied press. The *Jornal do Commercio* (Rio de Janeiro) averred at the beginning of the new year that the "Paraguayans never were human beings; the Jesuits succeeded in reducing them to a perfect animated machine ... it is not the form of the government [that counts among them], but the character of the governed." See "Correspondencia, (Curuzú, 15 January 1868)" in issue of 31 January 1868.

47   Cardozo, *Hace cien años*, 7: 405, and Nicasio Oroño to Marcos Paz, Santa Fe, 22 December 1867, in *Archivo del coronel Dr. Marcos Paz*, 6: 443.

48   "The Impeachment of the President," *The Standard* (Buenos Aires), 18 April 1868.

49   Nicolas Shumway, *The Invention of Argentina* (Berkeley, 1991), 212–213.

50   Fermín Chavez, *Alberdi y el Mitrismo* (Buenos Aires, 1961); Atilio García Mellid, *Proceso al liberalismo argentino* (Buenos Aires, 1957).

51   "La muerte de Mitre," *Cabichuí* (Paso Pucú), 12 January 1868; "Testimony of Dr. William Stewart, late of Paraguay," (London, 9 December 1869), WNL; not surprisingly, the Argentine press lampooned the Paraguayan claims as yet another ridiculous expression of the Marshal's depravity. See "Los panfletos de López," *La Nación Argentina* (Buenos Aires), 28 January 1868.

52   Forced recruitment had become common practice in many areas of the empire, provoking a general disgust for the government's violent comportment. See, for example, *O Diário do Povo* (Rio de Janeiro), 21–22 October 1867; Comments of President José Costa Machado de Souza, in *Relatório que a Assembléa Legislativa Provincial de Minas Gerais apresentou na Sessão Ordinaria de 1868* (Outo Preto, 1868), 9–12; Comments of Baron of Villa Bella, in *Relatório apresentado a Assembléa Legislativa Provincial de Pernambuco pelo Presidente ... na Sessão do Primeiro de Março de 1868* (Recife, 1868). Desperate for recruits, Parliament had previously approved the purchase of slaves who were given conditional letters of emancipation, freed convicts from prison, and conducted forcible impressments against men normally exempted from regular military service. And yet there were always new demands coming from Caxias. Recruitment for the war ended up "indiscriminately mixing strata of the free poor at the front," while exacerbating an already problematic political scene at home. See Peter M. Beattie, "Inclusion, Marginalization, and Integration in Brazilian Institutions: the Army as Inventor and Guardian of Traditions." Paper presented at the Brazil Strategic Culture Workshop, Florida International University, Miami, November 2009.

53   The text of Zacharias's letter to the emperor can be found in Joaquím Nabuco, *Um Estadista do Império. Nabuco de Araújo, Sua Vida, Suas Opiniões, Sua Epoca* (Rio de Janeiro, 1897), 3: 100–101.

54   Wanderley Pinho, grandson of the Baron of Cotegipe, downplayed the February 1868 crisis as a factor in the decline of support for the emperor. See "O Incidente Caxias e a Quéda de Zacharías em 1868," in *Política e Políticos no Império: Contribuições Documentães* (Rio de Janeiro, 1930), 65–93, and Barman, *Citizen Emperor*, 217–219.

55   Louis and Elizabeth Agassiz, *A Journey in Brazil* (Boston, 1868), 58.

56   Adler Homero de Fonseca and Ruth Beatríz S.C. de O. Andrada, *O Pátio Epitácio Pessoa: seu Histórico e Acervo* (Rio de Janeiro, 1995), 84–86.

57   "Relatório da Passagem de Humaitá pelo seu Comandante Capitão-de-Mar-e-Guerra Delfim Carlos de Carvalho (aboard the *Bahia*, 20 February 1868)," in Scavarda, "Centenário da Passagem de Humaitá," 28–32.

58   Thompson, *The War in Paraguay*, 247; *El Semanario* (Asunción), 9 March 1868; eight months later, the *London Illustrated Times* published a relatively accurate illustration of the running of the batteries, then mistakenly captioned it "The Advanced Division of the Brazilian Fleet Forcing the Paraguayan Batteries at Tebicuary." (See issue of 3 October 1868).

59   The ships were lashed together by rope cables running from bollards in the deck, in the bow and stern of both ships. Since the cables were set perpendicular to the river bank, they offered a minimum target for the enemy batteries, but nonetheless a very lucky Paraguayan shot managed to cut the bow cable as described. In his analysis of the events, Admiral Carlos Balthazar da Silveira rhetorically asks why the other vessels in the fleet did nothing to help, and in supplying his own answer, argued that to risk further ships in an uncertain rescue was unwarranted. See *Guerra do Paraguay. A Marinha Brazileira* (Rio de Janeiro, 1900), 53–54.

60   Amerlan, *Nights on the Río Paraguay*, 108; Ouro Preto, *A Marinha D'outrora*, 185–186; Ricardo Bonalume Neto, "River Passage Sought," *Military History* (December 1993): 66–73, 95–98; Arthur Jaceguay and Vidal de Oliveira, *Quatro Séculos de Actividade Marítima, Portugal e Brasil* (Rio de Janeiro, 1900), 2: 469–471, 485–486 (which hints that the cable linking the *Alagoas* to the Bahia was cut not by shot or shrapnel but by a saboteur's axe).

61   Certain of Caxias's detractors in Argentina expressed no surprise at the tardy passage of the Humaitá batteries, claiming, perhaps with some justice, that the marquis had delayed the operation until he could get Mitre out of the way. See Rottjer, *Mitre militar*, 200–207. Another reason frequently cited for the delay was that most ships in the Brazilian fleet had wooden hulls and these could not possibly survive a pelting from the Paraguayan gunners; as it turned out, the wooden fleet got past the batteries at Curupayty in early March without any losses. See Ouro Preto, *A Marinha D'outrora*, 189–192. The future Baron of Jaceguay rather disingenuously claimed a year and a half later that the wooden vessels could never have gotten past the Curupayty batteries until after the Paraguayan guns had been removed—but how could he have known that since the fleet had never tried to run the position? See Silveira de Mota to Mitre (?), Montevideo, 13 November 1868, in *The Standard* (Buenos Aires), 17 November 1869.

62   The Viscount of Maracajú admired Flores, whom he described as a "brave general who was also our dedicated ally … [a man who invariably] gave proofs of his great valor." See *Campanha do Paraguay*, 76. Sena Madureira felt the same way, characterizing the dead man as "the most sincere and loyal friend the empire had in the Río de la Plata." See *Guerra do Paraguai*, 52. Some of the most effusive praise on the Brazilian side, however, came from men who had never met Flores personally. In faraway Pernambuco, for instance, the members of the town council of Recife offered *solemnes exequias* to the murdered president and ally of the emperor. See *Jornal do Recife*, 28 March 1868.

63   Juan E. Pivel Devoto, *Historia de los partidos politicos en el Uruguay* (Montevideo, 1942–1943), 2: 23.

64   Eduardo Acevedo noted that Flores had narrowly escaped assassination once before, in 1867, when a German engineer in the pay of conservative Colorados had planted a bomb under government house. It failed to detonate and clear responsibility for the attempted murder was never established. See *Anales históricos del Uruguay*, 3: 406–407. The same was true for the successful assassination of 1868; indeed, there are almost as many interpretations of Flores's death as there are Uruguayan scholars and polemicists who have examined the theme. See "Correspondencia de Montevideo, 21 February 1868," *Jornal do Commercio* (Rio de Janeiro), 27 February 1868; "La muerte del general Venancio Flores.

Un estudio del doctor José Luciano Martínez. Páginas de un libro próximo a aparecer," *La Razón* (Montevideo), 19 February 1912; "El asesinato del general Flores. Datos interesantes e desconocidos," *La Razón* (Montevideo), 3 July 1912; and Lockhart, *Venancio Flores*, 88–96.

65 In a letter of condolence to Flores's widow, General Enrique Castro noted with his usual embellishment that the president's assassination had had a bad effect at the front. See Castro to María G. de Flores, Tuyucué, 13 March 1868, AGN (M) Archivos Particulares. Caja 69, carpeta 21. The widow, whom the French minister dismissed as a "plebeian Agrippina," believed that Suárez and the military had joined with the Blancos in the conspiracy to kill her husband. Considering the visceral hatred that the Blancos felt for General "Goyo," the suggestion that they could have made common cause with him was inescapably absurd. See M. Maillefer to Marquis of Moustier, Montevideo, 14 March 1868, in "Informes diplomáticos de los representantes de Francia en el Uruguay," 311–315.

66 Pivel Devoto, *Historia de los partidos políticos*, 2: 22–23.

67 Rodolfo Corselli, *La Guerra Americana della Triplice Alleanza contro il Paraguay* (Modena, 1938), 459.

68 Caxias to Baron of São Borja, Tuyucué (?), 4 February 1868, IHGB, lata 447, doc. 83; Queiroz Duarte, *Os Voluntários da Pátria*, 3, bk. 1: 40–42; bk. 2: 14–20, 153–158.

69 Thompson, *The War in Paraguay*, 250–251; Von Versen, *Reisen in Amerika*, 147–148; for extensive Brazilian accounts of the engagement, see Cerqueira, *Reminiscencias da Campanha*, 255–264, and Ordem do Dia no. 4 (Tuyucué, 21 February 1868) in *Ordens do Dia*, 3: 159–176.

70 Centurión, *Memorias o reminiscencias*, 3: 92; Brazilian sources cite a variety of statistics on this engagement. For instance, the BNRJ's copy of the *Boletím do Exército* (Tuyucué, 20 February 1868) recorded a rather improbable loss of 529 killed and wounded. Perhaps making use of the same source, Tasso Fragoso noted 608 Brazilians killed and wounded. See *História da Guerra entre a Tríplice Aliança e o Paraguay*, 3: 423. Sena Madureira, for his part, recorded Allied losses at 120 men killed, 253 wounded, and a Paraguayan loss "of more than a thousand." See *Guerra do Paraguai*, 54.

71 Kolinski, *Independence or Death!*, 155; in its final issue printed at Paso Pucú, the Marshal's war newspaper recorded this engagement as yet another major victory for Paraguay, even offering the readership a paean in Guarani that alluded to a comprehensive smashing of the "stinking darkies." See "Cierva," *Cabichuí* (Paso Pucú), 24 February 1868. A somewhat more thoughtful article, which compared the battle to Thermopylae, appeared as "Paralelo," in *El Semanario* (Luque), 7 March 1868.

72 Declaration of Vice President Sánchez, 22 February 1868, ANA-SH 355, no. 2; "¡Arriba todos!" *El Semanario* (Luque), 29 February 1868.

73 The moustachioed Italian consul, Lorenzo Chapperon, who had only arrived in Paraguay at the end of 1867, wrote a short but telling description of the capital's evacuation. The consul thought Washburn's obstinacy ill-advised considering that not only Asunción, but the intervening towns of Oliva, Mercedes, Pilar, Villeta, Villa Franca, and Lambaré had been declared war zones. See Chapperon to Foreign Minister, Luque, 31 March 1868, Archivio Storico Ministero degli Esteri (Rome) (as extracted by Marco Fano).

74 Washburn agreed to store some of Lynch's property, but his contempt for her was undiminished even in these trying circumstances:

> The ambitious plans that had induced her to invest such large sums of money in furniture and adornments … seem to have miscarried. Two-hundred thousand dollars [pesos], the price of the toil and the sweat and blood of thousands of half-fed, overworked Paraguayans seemed about to fall into the hands of the hated

Brazilians … she only thought of saving her life and the lives of her children, and escaping with her ill-gotten gains to Europe.

See Washburn, *History of Paraguay*, 2: 239.

75 Bliss was born in upstate New York in 1839, the son of missionaries who had worked among the Indigenous people of the Adirondack Mountains. He attended Hamilton College and then Yale in the late 1850s, and though he did well at neither institution, his skill as a researcher was noticed by members of the Massachusetts Historical Society who secured him employment for a time. In 1861 he journeyed to Brazil where he served as tutor to the children of US Minister Webb, and then moved on to Buenos Aires in late 1862. There the national government asked him to conduct a survey of Indigenous languages along the Bermejo River (which abutted Paraguayan territory). Caught by the war in Asunción, Bliss took on a variety of jobs, including the writing of a Paraguayan national history for Marshal López; this latter work, which was never published, served as the key source for volume one of Washburn's *History of Paraguay*. See *New York Times*, 5 January 1885.

76 Liliana M. Brezzo, "Testimonios sobre la guerra del Paraguay (IV)," *Historia Paraguaya* 45 (2005): 421–435; a slightly different recounting of these two meetings is offered by Centurión, whose *Memorias o reminiscencias*, 3: 96–98, make it clear that confusion rather than concord marked the proceedings. One man who seems to have thought otherwise was Juan Esteban Molinas, nephew of the jefe político of Paraguarí, who subsequently learned of the meeting from his father, and who testified in a letter written forty-nine years later that the meeting constituted the beginnings of a concerted plot against the Marshal. See Molinas to Father Fidel Maíz, Paraguarí, 17 May 1917, in Maíz, *Etapas de mi vida* (Asunción, 1986), 170–171, and Statement of José I. Acosta, Itá, September 1918, BNA-CJO.

77 Manuel Avila, "Apuntes sobre la conspiración de 1868. Pequeña contribución a la historia de la guerra con la Triple Alianza y de la tiranía de López," *Revista del Instituto Paraguayo* 2, no. 17 (1899): 216–222.

78 Cardozo, *Hace cien años*, 8: 139–142.

79 Washburn, *History of Paraguay*, 2: 224.

80 Masterman, *Seven Eventful Years in Paraguay*, 228–229.

81 Tasso Fragoso, *História da Guerra entre a Tríplice Aliança e o Paraguay*, 3: 424–425.

82 Thompson, *The War in Paraguay*, 249–250.

83 Masterman, *Seven Eventful Years in Paraguay*, 226–227; Washburn, *History of Paraguay*, 2: 241–242.

84 Washburn, *History of Paraguay*, 2: 242; Venancio López to López, Asunción, 15 February 1868, ANA-NE 989.

85 Masterman, *Seven Eventful Years in Paraguay*, 227. Doratioto notes that Delphim had originally sought to bludgeon the capital into surrender, but changed his mind when faced with the "Criollo," and mistakenly concluded that resistance was more substantial than it actually was. See *Maldita Guerra*, 323.

86 Washburn, *History of Paraguay*, 2: 243.

87 News of the running of the batteries made excellent copy in Brazil, and the resulting festivities in the imperial capital lasted three days. The various paeans to Delphim that followed were predictably turgid; one typical example compared the Commodore's feat to actions at Troy and Trafalgar. See Antonio da Crus Cordeiro, *Episódio da Esquadra Brasileira em Operação nas Aguas do Paraguay, a 19 de Fevereiro de 1868* (Paraíba, 1868). São Paulo also witnessed several days of festivities, including a Te Deum held in the cathedral to thank God for the successful passage of the Humaitá batteries. See *Atas da Câmara da Cidade de São Paulo (1865–1870)* (São Paulo, 1946), 54: 42–43. In Bahia,

whose inhabitants enjoyed the opportunity for a celebration, an "extraordinary number of citizens of all classes, divided into three groups and forming a battalion, preceded by bands and flags … passed through the principal streets of the city," loudly cheering the emperor and the armed forces. See *Diário da Bahia* (Salvador), 3 March 1868. The reaction in Montevideo and Buenos Aires was understandably more muted, which led Mitre's *Nacion Argentina* (Buenos Aires; issue of 12 March 1868) to denounce those Argentine and Uruguayan writers who had scoffed at the Brazilian achievement. One Argentine writer who had not scoffed at Delphim was the poet José Hernández, who used the occasion to jab, not at the Brazilians, but at his old enemy Mitre:

> Humaitá got screwed,
> And López carried off to the Devil,
> What Mitre had not accomplished in two years,
> Caxias got done in a month's time.

See Hernández to Martínez Fontes, Corrientes, 19 February 1868, in Tulio Halperín Donghi, *José Hernández y sus mundos* (Buenos Aires, 1985), 41.

88   General James Watson Webb, the US minister to Brazil, put his finger on the irony of the situation when he observed that the navy's triumph at Humaitá occasioned "great rejoicings … throughout Brazil [though] such was the state of public sentiment that the most prudent and loyal people of all classes freely admitted that if the army did not achieve a victory within a month, the government must consent to a peace in order to avoid a revolution." See Webb to Seward, 9 March 1868, NARA M-121, no. 35.

9 | A CRUEL ATTRITION

1   The Correntino pilot Enrique Roibón, who knew the waters off Humaitá better than most Paraguayans, rather unexpectedly defended the Brazilian decision not to place warships between Timbó and the fortress, noting that supplies of coal were insufficient and the danger very great. See E. R. Cristiano [Roibón], "En honor a la verdad histórica," *La Libertad* (Corrientes), 3 April 1908.

2   Captain Pedro V. Gill, who witnessed these discussions (and who designed the main plan of attack), noted the obstinacy with which other naval officers expressed their opposition to the plan, and the insulting response the Marshal gave in return, threatening each man with four bullets for "cowardice" or dumb insolence. See "Testimony of Pedro V. Gill, (Asunción, 24 April 1888), MHM-CZ, carpeta 137, no. 10. In fact, the Paraguayan naval officers all survived López's wrath on this occasion.

3   The specific details of the plan were revealed to Allied commanders by a Paraguayan sergeant who deserted across the lines on 3 March. See "Importantes notícias de la escuadra," *La Nación Argentina* (Buenos Aires), 10 March 1868.

4   In his rather abbreviated account of the engagement, Thompson confuses the *Lima Barros* with the *Herval*, which was located slightly downriver that night. See *The War in Paraguay*, 253–254; several other Paraguayan sources make this same mistake, but the official account offered by the Brazilians clearly identifies the ship as the *Lima Barros*. See "Parte official del asalto de los paraguayos a los encorazados brasileros (Tuyucué, 14 March 1868)," in *La Nación Argentina* (Buenos Aires), 22 March 1868.

5   Amerlan, *Nights on the Río Paraguay*, 111. As we have seen, in his diary entry on the forcing of the Humaitá batteries, Admiral Ignácio claimed that the men aboard the enemy canoes that assaulted the *Alagoas* were Payaguá people; in this case, his diary entry notes the supposed presence among the bogabantes of "Brazilians!!! Englishmen, Italians, and Frenchmen!!!" In neither case does the claim seem credible. See Frota, *Diário Pessoal do Almirante Visconde de Inhaúma*, 173–174 (entry of 1-2 March 1868).

6   Silveira, *Campanha do Paraguay. A Marinha Brazileira*, 56–59.

7   Sena Madureira, *Guerra do Paraguai*, 56.

8   Cardozo, *Hace cien años*, 8: 175; Vittone, *Calendário histórico*, 27–28.

9   Several of the Brazilian sources claim that Céspedes was taken prisoner together with two other officers and twelve bogabantes. See Bonalume Neto, "River Passage Sought," 96.

10 Thomas Joseph Hutchinson, "A Short Account of Some Incidents of the Paraguayan War," *Proceedings of the Literary and Philosophical Society of Liverpool* 60, no. 25 (1871): 27–28; another man, whose surname was Izquierdo, managed to reach the Chaco bank. The Scottish writer Cunninghame-Graham, who made his acquaintance in the early 1880s, censured him at that time as a "roguish" sort of country lawyer, but nonetheless lauded his commitment to duty, his courage under fire, and the loathing he subsequently expressed for the dictator who had sent him out on the river in the first place. The man's recounting of the night's action and his ensuing struggle for life brought chills to grown men who had been children during the war:

> Armed only with long knives and swords, [he and his comrades] for a few minutes … were masters of the ship. Then, mowed down by volleys from a *mitrailleuse*, they were all killed but three, who dived into the stream and emerged safely, all wounded, on the Chaco side. The river where the adventure happened is a mile in breadth. … Wounded and almost naked, exposed to the attacks of every kind of flying insect, their state was desperate. Food, naturally, they had none, or means of killing any game. For two long days they sustained life on what wild fruits they found, whilst their untended wounds festered and made their lives a misery. Then, seeing they must either starve or their wounds mortify, they took the desperate resolution … to try to swim across [to the eastern bank of the Paraguay]. The current runs at least four miles an hour. … Of the three, Izquierdo only reached the other side, and lay exhausted, with his leg swollen to an enormous size, upon the sand. Discovered by some women washing clothes, and taken to their huts, he at length recovered, although lame for life.

See Cunninghame-Graham, *Portrait of a Dictator*, 77–78. (The author would appear to be mistaken about the breadth of the river, which even at flood stage is only half the figure cited at the point).

11 "Campanha do Paraguai. Diário do Exercito em Operações sob o Commando em Chefe do Exmo. Sr. Marechal de Exercito Marquez de Caxias," in *Revista do Instituto Histórico e Geographico Brasileiro* 91, no. 145 (1922): 298–302 (entry of 2 March 1868).

12 Mitre to Gelly y Obes, Buenos Aires, 15 July 1868, in *Archivo del general Mitre*, 3: 259; "Paraguay," *El Siglo* (Montevideo), 22 February 1868.

13 The Allies gained proof positive of the Marshal's flight only at the end of the month when a soldier in a Paraguayan artillery unit deserted to the Allied lines with the news that López and Madame Lynch had departed in the way described in the other sources. See "Declaración del soldado paraguayo de artillería de Humaitá, (Tuyucué, 22 March 1868)," in *La Nación Argentina* (Buenos Aires), 1 April 1868, and "Correspondencia," *Jornal do Commercio* (Rio de Janeiro), 1 April 1868.

14 Thompson, *The War in Paraguay*, 251–252.

15 The men worked all night in the water of one deep stream, constructing a bridge over which they wrenched the Marshal's carriage the next morning. See Thompson, *The War in Paraguay*, 258.

16 "Instrucciones para el Coronel López, comandante general de armas," Paso Pucú, 30 December 1867, ANA-CRB I-30, 28, 17, no. 34.

17 The onetime British consul at Rosario witnessed the agonies of a sick Paraguayan prisoner on the HMS *Dotorel* while sailing downriver in 1865 and gave this account, which he

clearly meant as being typical of behavior among the Marshal's men (which was just as true in the Chaco as it had been after the battle of the Riachuelo):

> I saw the Paraguayan sergeant, who had command over them, approach the bedside of the man suffering from inflammation in the bowels, now groaning with much pain. One word uttered by the sergeant stopped the complaints. Then the same official pronounced a harangue in Guaraní, and which the pilot on board translated for me as follows: "Dog of a bad Paraguayan! Are you not ashamed to let the enemies of your country hear you complain, and give them reason to laugh at you? The glory of having been wounded fighting for your country does not appear sufficient without crying for sympathy in your sufferings! Do not let me hear another groan from you, or I shall report you to the highest power"—meaning, of course, Field-Marshal López. From that moment the poor sufferer never uttered a moan, although he died four hours afterwards, evidently in dreadful torture. Some Argentines who were on board—no doubt those described as "enemies of his country" called this "Paraguayan stolidity or stupidity," but to me it seemed the perfection of discipline, joined to the highest class of moral and physical bravery.

See Thomas J. Hutchinson, *The Paraná. With Incidents of the Paraguayan War from 1861 to 1868* (London, 1868), 308. It seems rather doubtful that soldiers in modern armies today would describe this attitude as the "perfection of discipline."

18 Manuel Trujillo, *Gestas guerreras (de mis memorias)* (1911; Asunción, 1923), 28.

19 A Paraguayan deserter reported that the Humaitá garrison, save for a single battalion, consisted entirely of adolescent boys, and, there being no other rations, each individual among them was eating only a tiny piece of meat per day. See Gelly y Obes to Mitre (?) (Tuyucué, 18 March 1868), in *La Nación Argentina* (Buenos Aires), 24 March 1868.

20 Godoi, *El comandante José Dolores Molas*, 18.

21 Testimony of Captain Pedro V. Gill (Asunción, 24 April 1888), MHM (A)-CZ, carpeta 137, no. 10.

22 Thompson, *The War in Paraguay*, 256–258.

23 Von Versen, *Reisen in Amerika*, 145; Doratioto, *General Osório*, 176, notes a figure of ten thousand Paraguayans evacuated.

24 Thompson, *The War in Paraguay*, 259–261.

25 A surprising amount of personal correspondence from San Fernando has survived, but most of it concerns mundane matters (reports of illnesses and fatalities, requests for information on missing relatives). See Riveros (?) to Pablo Antonio González, San Fernando, 28 March 1868, ANA-NE 2491; Germán Serrano to Ramón Marecos, San Fernando, 4 April 1868, ANA-NE 2497; Domingo Riveros to Marcelino Gómez, San Fernando, 13 April 1868, ANA-NE 2490; José Gaspar Zavala to Josefa Zavala de Rojas, San Fernando, 2 May 1868, ANA-NE 2500; and Angel Cabrizas to Juan Isidoro Cabrizas, San Fernando, 15 June 1868, ANA-NE 2893.

26 In its "Chronique" of 15 June 1868, *Ba-Ta-Clan* (Rio de Janeiro) claimed that the Paraguayans might have as many as fifteen thousand men under arms at the San Fernando front and wondered if it might still be possible for López to reassemble a total force of over thirty thousand in the field. It was not.

27 "El Mariscal López," *Cabichuí* (San Fernando), 13 May 1868.

28 Leuchars, *To the Bitter End*, 184.

29 "The War in the North (Tuyucué, 24 March 1868)," *The Standard* (Buenos Aires), 1 April 1868. See also the BNRJ's copy of the 22 March 1868 *Boletim do Exército*, and Argolo to Caxias, Tuyutí, 22 March 1868, in "Campanha do Paraguai. Diário do Exercito em Operações sob o Commando do Marquez de Caxias," 321–326.

30 Gelly y Obes to Wenceslao Paunero, Tuyucú, 23 March 1868, in Thompson, *Guerra del Paraguay*, cv–cvi; see also Maracajú, *Campanha do Paraguay*, 83–89.

31 Thompson, *The War in Paraguay*, 254. Julián Godoy affirmed that Paraguayan losses were light, there "having been nothing in the way of hand-to-hand combat." See "Memorias de teniente coronel Julián Godoy." General Daniel Cerri offered a more believable recounting, citing Paraguayan losses at three hundred. See *Campaña del Paraguay*, 46.

32 Phelps, *Tragedy of Paraguay*, 204.

33 "Nuevos triunfos," *La Nación Argentina* (Buenos Aires), 29 March 1868.

34 Centurión, *Memorias o reminiscencias*, 3: 107–108.

35 Centurión, *Memorias o reminiscencias*, 3: 108–109.

36 Resquín, *La guerra del Paraguay contra la Triple Alianza*, 85.

37 The orders of the day issued by Caxias as Allied commander are replete with cases of courts-martial with punishments meted out to drunkards, to those taking French leave, brawling, and otherwise disrupting the good discipline. See, for example, Ordem do Dia no. 200 (Tuyucué, 18 March 1868); no. 202 (Tuyucué, 26 March 1868); no. 206 (Parecué, 19 April 1868); and no. 221 (Tuyucué, 17 June 1868), respectively in *Ordens do Dia*, 3: 229–231, 244–247, 325–327, and 448–453. A substantial number of the men accused of infractions were released for want of proof, the threat of punishment alone having been sufficient to maintain the proper discipline. Those men caught in the act of desertion, however, were invariably shot according to article 14 of the Military Code.

38 The Argentine colonel Agustín Angel Olmedo, writing after Humaitá fell, commented on the blame that went around after it was discovered that so many Paraguayans had escaped undetected: "The Argentines say that it happened because the *macacos* were all asleep … and the Brazilians say it was all the fault of the Argentines, *filhos da … gringo* thieves … that the Paraguayans got away. It's now clear that both were at fault." See *Guerra del Paraguay. Cuadernos de campaña. (1867–1869)* (Buenos Aires, 2008), 257 (entry of 31 July 1868).

39 Cardozo, *Hace cien años*, 8: 196; G.F. Gould to Lord Stanley, Buenos Aires, 10 April 1868, in Philip, *British Documents on Foreign Affairs, Latin America, 1845–1914*, 1, pt. 1, Series D: 238; Elizalde to Juan N. Torrent, Buenos Aires, 11 April 1868, Museo Andrés Barbero, Colección Carlos Pusineri Scala (Asunción).

40 See, for example, Caxias to General Vitorino José Carneiro Monteiro, Tuyucué, 31 March 1868, IHGB, lata 447, doc. 94 (which contains orders to establish batteries at the Potrero Ovella in order to shell the fortress). The Argentine commander, General Gelly y Obes, evidently thought this display of firepower less than superfluous, as it accomplished nothing but cover the grounds at Humaitá with cannon balls. See Gelly y Obes to Mitre, Tuyucué, 18 April 1868, in Cardozo, *Hace cien años*, 8: 298–299.

41 "The War in the North (Tuyucué, 24 March 1868)," *The Standard* (Buenos Aires), 1 April 1868. Bitter surprises of this sort are common in every war; for instance, when the supposed COSVN headquarters of the Communist forces was discovered in the Cambodian "Fish-hook" toward the end of the struggle in Vietnam, it turned out to be little more than a hole in the ground, and this irritating fact engendered the same sarcasm and disbelief among US generals that the Allies had expressed when they first inspected Paso Pucú.

42 Burton, *Letters from the Battle-fields of Paraguay*, 357. Despite the relatively short time he spent in Paraguay, Burton managed to produce a memoir of considerable depth and sophistication. Though he did not act the role of trailblazer or grand explorer, as he did when visiting Mecca in the guise of an Afghan *fakir*, he did read extensively on the war, omitted no references, and when possible, visited sites and interviewed eyewitnesses. Above all, he brought to the topic an unmatched worldliness, honed by many years spent

in the most exotic settings imaginable. Curiously, however, he made few efforts to get to know the Paraguayans, whose courage under extreme pressure might have appealed to his romanticism, much as Bedouins, Pathans, and Abyssinians had inspired his pen on earlier occasions.

43 "Teatro de la guerra (Tuyucué, 26 March 1868)," *La Nación Argentina* (Buenos Aires), 31 March 1868.

44 More than one hundred thousand head of cattle were still available in Paraguay that could have fed the Humaitá garrison if a way could have been found to drive the animals to the fortress. See Cardozo, *Hace cien años*, 8: 316–317 (which mentions mid-April donations from a score of interior villages including Arroyos y Esteros, 38,168 head; Rosario, 1,381 head; Yuty, 22,859 head; Quiindy, 17,755 head; San Joaquín, 6,097 head; and Mbuyapey, 14,248 head).

45 Amazingly, the isolated men at Humaitá were still receiving their salaries, as attested to in a receipt for 19,118 pesos sent through to the fortress by way of the Chaco in late April. See Alén to Luis Caminos, Humaitá, 29 April 1868, ANA-CRB I-30, 23, 103.

46 G.F. Gould to Lord Stanley, Buenos Aires, 12 May 1868, in Philip, *British Documents on Foreign Affairs*, 1, pt. 1, Series D: 239–240; Cerri, *Campaña del Paraguay*, 51–54.

47 Cardozo, *Hace cien años*, 8: 339; "Correspondencia," (Curupayty, 14 May 1868), *Jornal do Commercio* (Rio de Janeiro), 4 June 1868; "Secondo notizie de fonte paraguaiana," *La Stampa* (Turin), 7 June 1868.

48 Rivas to Caxias, Campamento-en-marcha frente a la isla Arasá, 3 May 1868, in *La Nación Argentina* (Buenos Aires), 12 May 1868.

49 Centurión, *Memorias o reminiscencias*, 3: 118–119; "The War on the Paraná [*sic*]," *New York Times*, 21 July 1868.

50 Resquín, *La guerra del Paraguay contra la Triple Alianza*, 90; Olmedo, *Guerra del Paraguay. Cuadernos de campaña (1867–1869)*, 166-169 (entries of 7–8 May 1868).

51 Cardozo, *Hace cien años*, 8: 372–375, 409; 9: 15, 63–64, 104–105.

52 Leuchars seems to have conflated this reconnaissance with a similar effort made a few days earlier at the mouth of the Ñe'embucú by General Andrade Neves, the Baron of the Triumph. See *To the Bitter End*, 186.

53 Tasso Fragoso, *História da Guerra entre a Triplice Aliança e o Paraguai*, 3: 476–477.

54 "Campanha do Paraguai. Diário do Exercito em Operações sob o Commando do Marquez de Caxias," 396–401 (entries of 9–10 June 1868), and Ordem do Dia no. 222 (Parecué, 18 June 1868) in *Ordens do Dia*, 4: 455–461.

55 Thompson, *The War in Paraguay*, 267.

56 Caxias to War Minister, Parecué, 19 June 1868, IHGB, lata 313, pasta 21.

57 "Nuevas zurribandas," *Cabichuí* (San Fernando), 8 June 1868.

58 Cardozo, *Hace cien años*, 9: 98; "Nuevo asalto a los encorazados," *La Nación Argentina* (Buenos Aires), 15 July 1868.

59 "Campanha do Paraguai. Diário do Exercito em Operações sob o Commando do Marquez de Caxias," 426–431 (entries of 10 July 1868).

60 Centurión, *Memorias o reminiscencias*, 3: 120–121. In *La guerra del Paraguay contra la Triple Alianza* (91), General Resquín used almost exactly the same words to describe the fiasco. See also Pereira de Sousa, "História da Guerra do Paraguai," *Revista do Instituto Histórico e Geographico Brasileiro* 102, no. 156 (1927): 316.

61 A very odd rumor, current among the Allied soldiers, held that deserters from both sides had set up a joint camp in the far reaches of the Chaco, and like the Brazilian slaves who had escaped into the forests, these men intended to live indefinitely beyond the law's

reach. Almost certainly this Chaco camp (or *quilombo*) never existed. See Burton, *Letters from the Battle-Fields of Paraguay*, p. 430.

62   Centurión, *Memorias o reminiscencias*, 3: 119–120; Cardozo, *Hace cien años*, 9: 113. Despite the slight difference in the spelling of his surname, Alén was in fact a distant relative of Leandro Além, one of the founders of the Unión Cívica Radical, which came to dominate Argentine national politics in the second decade of the twentieth century.

63   Pedro Gill had witnessed Alén's degeneration into a state of near-insanity, noting that the day before his suicide attempt he left the safety of his gun battery to wander down to the river. In full uniform and with his sword dangling, he attempted, Christ-like, to walk upon the water and was only saved from drowning when an officer pulled him from the current. See "Testimony of Pedro V. Gill, (Asunción, 24 April 1888)," MHM-CZ, carpeta 137, no. 10.

64   Several sources claim that the messenger had been dispatched by Colonel Alén, but this makes no sense, as he had shot himself two days earlier and had already been succeeded by Martínez. See Cardozo, *Hace cien años*, 9: 127, 135–136; and Centurión, *Memorias o reminiscencias*, 3: 126–127.

65   Hutchinson, "A Short Account of Some Incidents of the Paraguayan War," 28–30. Centurión relates the same story, offering the messenger's name as Francisco Ortega, and noting that the account of his fortitude (which Hutchinson styles a "martyrdom") had been related to the British diplomat by Miguel Lisboa, son of the Brazilian minister to Lisbon. See *Memorias o reminiscencias*, 3: 127.

66   Burton, *Letters from the Battle-fields of Paraguay*, 336.

67   Rivas to Caxias, Chaco, 18 July 1868, in Thompson, *La guerra del Paraguay*, cvii–cix; Resquín, *La guerra del Paraguay contra la Triple Alianza*, 91–92; "Terrible News from Paraguay," *The Standard* (Buenos Aires), 26 July 1868.

68   Thompson, *The War in Paraguay*, 273; Burton noted that in insisting on getting a receipt for the flags, the skipper of the *Pará* decidedly embarrassed his Argentine allies, a slight that no one, least of all General Gelly y Obes, was willing to overlook. See *Letters from the Battle-fields of Paraguay*, 333.

69   Cardozo, *Hace cien años*, 9: 147–149. The "Diário do Exército" mentions sixty Brazilians killed, 224 wounded, and ninety-two Argentines killed and twenty-nine wounded—yet another example of divergent reporting of losses. See "Diário do Exército," 447 (entry of 18 July 1868), and "Acayuazá," *El Semanario* (Luque), 19 July 1868.

70   The general Argentine view has always held that Campos was brutalized while in captivity and perished in late 1868 as a result of physical mistreatment; but Major Antonio E. González, the annotator of the Centurión memoirs, claims that the he died of natural causes in camp at a time when many Paraguayans were also seriously ill. See *Memorias y reminiscencias*, 3: 125na; Héctor F. Decoud completely contradicts this assertion, noting that those imprisoned in the Paraguayan camp had never seen a man so brutally abused over such a length of time as Campos. See *La masacre de Concepción*, 177–178; and also Garmendia, *La cartera de un soldado*, 87–97, which, in a section entitled "Los mártires de Acayuazá," argues much the same thing about the unfortunate Campos.

71   Cardozo, *Hace cien años*, 9: 149.

72   Fano, *Il Rombo del Cannone Liberale*, 330.

73   Resquín claimed that at this late stage there were still nine hundred women at Humaitá, but he is the only observer who offered such a high estimate of the number of noncombatants then at the fortress. See *La guerra del Paraguay contra la Triple Alianza*, 93.

74   Osório had expressed reservations about the plan of attack. General Vitorino Carneiro Monteiro, by contrast, offered even stronger opposition, noting with good reason that Humaitá had ceased to have much military value and that the Allies should concentrate

on pursuing López's army rather than waste lives in capturing a position of such limited importance. See Cardozo, *Hace cien años*, 8: 390.

75 Amerlan, *Night on the Río Paraguay*, 115–116; see also "Ocorrencias do Combate Proveniente do Reconhecimento feito nas Trincheiras Paraguaias no forte de Humaitá em 16 [*sic*] de Julho de 1868," IHGB, lata 335, documento 23; and "The Battle of Humaitá," *The Standard* (Buenos Aires), 23 July 1868.

76 "Parte Oficial do General Osório," Parecué, 20 July 1868, and Osório to Estimada Mãe, Parecué, 17 July 1868, in Osório and Osório, *História do General Osório*, 441–445, 447–451; *El Semanario* (Luque), 19 July 1868. Count Joannini, the Italian minister to Buenos Aires, noted that in the wake of this engagement, the reputation of Caxias declined while Osório's vastly expanded, and that "everyone wishes that [the latter] be assigned supreme command." See Joannini to Foreign Minister, Buenos Aires, 27 July 1868, Archivio Ministero degli Esteri (as extracted by Marco Fano).

77 *The Standard* (Buenos Aires), in its issue of 1 August 1868, compared the evacuation of the fortress with that of Sebastopol the previous decade, noting that the latter was deemed a "masterly" accomplishment of the Crimean conflict; but "what was it in comparison to the tactics of the shoeless commander of Humaitá, who drew off his whole force under the very nose of the besiegers, crossed the rapid torrents of the Paraguay river, and gained the opposite shore before even Gelly—the sleepless Gelly—heard a word about it."

78 *Anglo-Brazilian Times* (Rio de Janeiro), 22 August 1868; Leuchars notes that sixty of the one hundred eighty guns left behind were still sufficiently operable to be used later against their former owners. See *To the Bitter End*, 187.

79 Centurión, *Memorias o reminiscencias*, 3: 132–133; "Relación de un viejo Sargento," *El Paraguayo Ilustrado* (Asunción), 2 August 1896. (The old sergeant was, in fact, a young Emilio Aceval, who served as president of Paraguay from 1898 to 1902.)

80 "Notícias del ejército. Ataque a Timbó. 400 Prisoneros," *La Nación Argentina* (Buenos Aires), 2 August 1868; "Testimony of Pedro V. Gill, (Asunción, 24 April 1888)," MHM-CZ, carpeta 137, no. 10.

81 Thompson, *The War in Paraguay*, 275.

82 Rivas to Caxias, Chaco, 4 August 1868, in Thompson, *Guerra del Paraguay*, cix–cxi; Centurión, *Memorias o reminiscencias*, 3: 134. Resquín, in implying that Martínez had given up sooner than was strictly necessary, claimed that three hundred Paraguayans at Isla Poí actually succeeded in reaching Caballero's troops by swimming the distance to Timbó on the very day of the surrender. See *La guerra del Paraguay contra la Triple Alianza*, 93.

83 "An Episode of the War," *New York Times*, 24 September 1868; an intriguing—and not altogether fanciful—image of the surrender negotiations appeared first as "Le Réverend Pere Esmerata," in *L'Illustration* (Paris), 26 September 1868, and as "The War in Paraguay: Pere Esmerata Persuades Paraguayans to Surrender," in the *London Illustrated Times*, 3 October 1868. The image, it seems, was provided to the press by the Baron de Rio Branco, who was then visiting the European capitals in his role as an imperial diplomat. See Roberto Assumpção, "Rio-Branco e 'L'Illustration,'" *Revista do Instituto Histórico e Geográfico Brasileiro* 188 (1946): 10–13.

84 The Paraguayan prisoners were divided among the Allied armies and allowed to choose their place of captivity. Most chose Buenos Aires. See "La visita de nuestro corresponsal a Humaitá," *La Nación Argentina* (Buenos Aires), 30 August 1868, and Rivas to Caxias, Cuartel general, 5 August 1868, in Thompson, *La guerra del Paraguay*, cxiv–cxvi.

85 Martínez was questioned by his captors but refused to cooperate, relenting only in October, when he addressed a letter to the Argentine president demanding better treatment for his men. See Martínez et al to Sarmiento, Buenos Aires, 19 October 1868, in *The*

Standard (Buenos Aires), 31 October 1868. When this appeal was granted in January 1869, he finally supplied a short account of his activities at Humaitá. He censured the severe discipline and cruelty of Marshal López, who by now had vented his rage against the colonel's family. See "Exposición del coronel paraguayo Francisco Martínez," *Album de la guerra del Paraguay* 2 (1894): 205–207; Captain Gill's reminiscences of the last stand at Isla Poí were assembled by his descendant Juan B. Gill Aguinaga in *Un marino en la guerra de la Triple Alianza* (Asunción, 1959), 16–18.

86   Carlos Pereyra, *Francisco Solano López y la guerra del Paraguay* (Buenos Aires, 1953), 123. The correspondent for Mitre's newpaper claimed a figure of fourteen hundred Paraguayan prisoners. See "Teatro de la guerra," *La Nación Argentina* (Buenos Aires), 11 August 1868. Colonel Agustín Angel Olmedo, who witnessed the surrender, later spoke of the sad scene. When he tried to converse with the Paraguayans, "they could only stare straight ahead and murmur 'I want to eat.'" See *Guerra del Paraguay. Cuadernos de campaña*, 264 (entry of 5 August 1868).

87   Centurión, *Memorias o reminiscencias*, 3: 135, and "Rendição da guarnição de Humaitá e sucesos posteriores," (Humaitá, 6 August 1868), ANA-CRB I-30, 29, 24, no. 2.

88   Rivas to Mitre, Curupayty, 8 August 1868, in *La Nación Argentina* (Buenos Aires), 12 August 1868. A good many of these prisoners ended up as laborers in Buenos Aires. Contracts between police commissioners and private parties in the Argentine capital show several hundred men employed in this capacity (listing names, salaries, and termination of contract); see AGN X 32-5-6 (for 1866 through 1871).

10 | THE NATION CONSUMES ITS OWN

1   As it happened, the first two men to scout the abandoned fortress were an itinerant Italian sutler and a French baker, who slipped a few minor baubles to the Allied pickets to secure the honor—or the opportunity—of being the first to enter the Paraguayan camp. "To their ecstatic joy, they found the place completely deserted," but they were unable to loot the site before the main Allied units put in an appearance an hour or two later and did the job themselves. See "The Fall of Humaitá," *The Standard* (Buenos Aires), 6 August 1868.

2   Burton, *Letters from the Battle-fields of Paraguay*, 314–322; Olmedo, *Guerra del Paraguay. Cuadernos de campaña*, 250–254 (entries for 26–28 July 1868).

3   Burton scoffed at his Brazilian hosts when he ridiculed the Batería Londres as "an exposed mass of masonry which ought to have shared the fate of the forts from Sumpter [sic] to Pulaski; and when granite fails, brick cannot hope to succeed." See *Letters from the Battle-fields of Paraguay*, 319–320.

4   Thirty-six of these guns were bronze, the rest iron. At Isla Poí, six bronze field pieces and two iron guns were captured, for a total of 188 cannon (and six Congreve rocket stands). See Silva Paranhos notes to Louis Schneider, *A guerra da Triplice Aliança contra o governo da República do Paraguai*, 3: CDXXXVIII–CDLII.

5   Two cannons bearing the Spanish arms were spotted in the workings, one bearing the date 1671 and the other 1685. See "La visita de nuestro corresponsal especial a Humaitá," *La Nación Argentina* (Buenos Aires), 30 August 1868.

6   *Anglo-Brazilian Times* (Rio de Janeiro), 22 August 1868.

7   "Humaitá," *The Standard* (Buenos Aires), 15 August 1868; "Inventário de Humaitá, (Campamento de Paso Pucú, 5 August 1868)," in *La Tribuna* (Buenos Aires), 12 August 1868.

8   The Paraguayans were not exempt from the awe that the demolished chapel invariably excites in visitors. See C.S., "Las ruinas de Humaitá," *El Pueblo. Organo del Partido Liberal* (Asunción), 22 January 1895.

9   Images of the ruined interior of the Humaitá chapel were widely distributed in the Allied countries and in Europe, where they appeared in *L'Ilustration* (Paris), 26 September 1868. Of the two blue-and-white towers that graced the chapel before the war, the southernmost structure largely survived the Allied shelling, only to be torn down in subsequent years by local landowners who used the bricks to construct their outside ovens (*tatacuás*) and storage sheds. Today, tourists in Asunción who show an interest in purchasing chess sets carved from local hardwoods and featuring motifs of the Paraguayan War, will notice that the white rooks, when placed together, assume a form reminiscent of the Humaitá chapel.

10   *O Diário do Rio de Janeiro*, 4–5 August 1868. See also [O'Leary?] manuscript "Humaitá," BNA-CJO.

11   Burton, *Letters from the Battle-fields of Paraguay*, 340.

12   Needell, *The Party of Order*, 244–248. It will be remembered that the "moderating power" principle of the 1824 gave Pedro an extensive authority over Parliament but he generally sought to avoid the use of this authority lest he be accused of despotism. By contrast, though the Paraguayan constitution of 1844 gave López considerable authority as president, he never showed any restraint in going beyond its provisions to achieve a political end. In this sense, his opponents were correct in dubbing his government despotic.

13   *The Times* (London), 17 August 1868.

14   According to General Webb, the US minister in Rio, Itaboraí refused to enter office unless dom Pedro promised to consider peace proposals whenever Humaitá should fall. When the fortress did fall, however, the prime minister discovered that the Council of State had again endorsed the emperor's unbending position that "the war [needed to be continued] until the objects originally aimed at were attained." All the new ministers supposedly "complained of how they had [been deceived]" in this, but they did not proceed to deprive Caxias of the material and political support that he needed. In truth, lest Caxias be tainted as a warmonger, it should be noted that in August he himself proposed the cancellation of that proviso of the Triple Alliance Treaty that required López to step down before peace negotiations could commence—but dom Pedro vetoed the marquis's suggestion, even threatening to abdicate the throne if the matter were pursued against his wishes. See Webb to Seward, Rio de Janeiro, 25 August 1868, NARA, M-121, no. 35; Cardozo, *Hace cien años*, 8: 277–278; and Doratioto, *Maldita Guerra*, 337–339.

15   "Chronique," *Ba-Ta-Clan* (Rio de Janeiro), 18 July 1868.

16   Cholera had struck regularly at Luque and other villages of the Paraguayan interior since at least mid-March, and no medicines or facilities were available to help stave off an epidemic. See Telegram of Francisco Sánchez to Asunción garrison commander, Luque, 18 March 1868, ANA-CRB I-30, 16, 12, no. 23. The disease does not seem to have had a comparable effect on military men; of the 793 soldiers in hospital at Cerro León in July, 236 were listed as wounded, while 167 were down with foot sores caused by jiggers and lesions caused by botflies. Cholera does not even appear as one of the debilitating factors among the patients (though some of the miscellaneous respiratory ailments and fevers listed might possibly refer to the malady). See "Razón de infermos y heridos," Cerro Léon, 27 July 1868, ANA-CRB I-30, 28, 13.

17   As Benigno was absent at one of his northern ranches, he could not respond immediately to his brother's order, but left for Seibo only on 15 March. See Centurión, *Memorias or reminiscencias*, 3: 97–98, and Cardozo, *Hace cien años*, 8: 207.

18   The treasurer had visited Humaitá in late December 1867 to present López with a jewel-encrusted sword that had been prepared for him as a "voluntary" gift of the citizens. Bedoya's arrest came as something of a mystery, with the most convincing explanation being offered by Washburn:

Bedoya was arrested for no cause that I could ever learn, except that the French consul, Cuberville, had told Benigno that, in case the president should abdicate, [Bedoya] would be the proper man for the succession. There may have been other reasons, but anyone knowing López would regard that as sufficient... A whispered possibility that there might be a change was high treason in López's eyes, and though it was the consul who made it, yet it was enough to awaken the suspicion that the brother and brother-in-law were already providing for the succession. With this, I believe, commenced the first idea of a conspiracy in López's mind.

See Washburn, *History of Paraguay*, 2: 263.

19   Centurión, *Memorias o reminiscencias*, 3: 95–96.

20   Testimony of Sánchez, Luque, 27 March 1868, cited in Liliana M.Brezzo, "La Argentina y la organización del Gobierno Provisorio en el Paraguay. La mission de José Roque Pérez," *Historia Paraguaya* 39 (1999): 283, and Cardozo, *Hace cien años*, 8: 210–212. Benigno had studied at the Imperial Naval Academy in Rio de Janeiro, a fact that was remembered to his discredit during the worst excesses of 1868.

21   Sánchez to López, Luque, 27 March 1868, MHM (A), Colección Gill Aguinaga, carpeta 135, no. 1; and Centurión, *Memorias o reminiscencias*, 3: 253–258.

22   In subsequent months, Sánchez sought to redeem himself in the Marshal's eyes by using his own heavy hand against perceived dissidents and malingerers in Luque and elsewhere, sending several to the firing squad. See Manuel Avila, "El vice-presidente Sánchez fusilando. Espíritu de imitación por miedo," *Revista del Instituto Paraguayo* 6, no. 52 (1905): 32–38.

23   According to Italian consul Chapperon, police functions in Luque during 1868 were partly covered by women. See Fano, "Fiesta en la guerra," *ABC Color* (Asunción), 4 October 2011.

24   See Masterman, *Seven Eventful Years in Paraguay*, 208–209. Amerlan repeats the story, noting with emphasis that López used to enter "the chapel and returned crawling on his knees, beating his breast with his fist, he prostrated himself before the altar, tore his hair and demeaned himself like the most wicked and contrite of sinners." See *Nights on the Rio Paraguay*, 120.

25   William Oliver, a British subject who had come to Paraguay in 1863 to work as a farmer in partnership with Dr. William Stewart, explained the omnipresence of spies in the country:

To express a doubt of López's success in the war, was sufficient to cause any person's imprisonment; and later on in the war many were lanced for charges of less importance than that. Every time I went into Asunción after war commenced, a league before arriving I was met by a policeman in disguise, who followed me to near the town, where there was another man to relieve the first, and to follow me to the house where I stopped. I knew that all respectable persons, men and women, were spied [upon] incessantly by the police. I have seen the police take away under arrest many inoffensive persons, who I do not believe were capable of speaking a word against the Government. ... The want of confidence amongst natives was well-founded. In Ibicuy [sic], a young man who had returned to his house from the army was betrayed by his sister, and was taken away again in irons. Deserters were always shot.

See "Testimony of William Oliver (Asunción, 12 January 1871)," in Scottish Record Office, CS 244/543/19 (25–26).

26   This comment had the usual racist connotation and might be better translated as "more Brazilian than the Brazilians." See Centurión, *Memorias o reminiscencias*, 3: 145–146.

27   Thompson, *The War in Paraguay*, 267; Washburn(?), "Chronological Synopsis of the Administration of Marshal Francisco Solano López, second President of Paraguay," WNL.

28 Major James Manlove was one of those enigmatic, nonconformist figures who rarely recommend themselves to the official world. At the time of the evacuation of the capital, many local residents had hastily sold their ducks, chickens, pigs, and even cattle to those inmates at the US legation who intended to stay on at Asunción. With the prospect of foodstuffs getting scarcer by the day, Manlove took it upon himself to care for the cattle. One day in late February, while returning from this duty, he galloped across one of the city plazas, though this had been forbidden by the police, who detained him because of the infraction. While in custody, he acted in a most surly fashion. He failed to salute an army captain, saying in his poor Spanish, that, as a major, he was the one to whom a salute was due. Things went downhill from there, and Washburn extricated him from the predicament only with much difficulty. Within weeks, the Marylander was arrested once again, this time for supposedly breaking into the house of a French friend of the US minister. See Cardozo, *Hace cien años*, 8: 175–176, 186; Washburn to Francisco Fernández, Asunción, 5 March 1868; Manlove to Washburn, Asunción, 5 March 1868 (wherein the major notes, that as a former Confederate, he was not sure that he was entitled to the "protection of the flag of your [the latter word crossed through and replaced with 'our'] country"); Washburn to Gumercindo Benítez, Asunción, 24 March 1868; Gumercindo Benítez to Washburn, Luque, 29 March 1868; Washburn to Gumercindo Benítez, Asunción, 4 April 1868, all in WNL; *Correspondencia diplomática entre el Gobierno del Paraguay y la Legación de los Estados Unidos de América y el consul de S.M. el Emperador de los Franceses* (Luque, 1868?); *Correspondencia cambiada entre el Ministerio de relaciones exteriores de la república y el señor Charles A. Washburn, ministro residente de los Estados Unidos de América, sobre la conspiración fraguada contra la patria y el Gobierno en combinación con el enemigo; y el atento de asesinato a la persona del Exmo. Señor Mariscal López por los nacionales y estrangeros* (Luque, 1868); and "Sallie C. Washburn Diary," entries for 2 and 24 March 1868 (wherein Manlove is upbraided for "always making a fool of himself"), also in WNL.

29 Masterman, *Seven Eventful Years in Paraguay*, 235.

30 See Gumercindo Benítez-Washburn Correspondence, 20 March through 6 August 1868, ANA-CRB I-22, 11, 2, nos. 35–64, and NARA M-128, no. 2.

31 Washburn, "Memorandum of a Visit to the Paraguayan Camp in San Fernando, May 1868," WNL.

32 Aveiro claims that Bedoya died not in May, but in the winter months, and not of dysentery, but of a gangrenous leg. See *Memorias militares*, 63. Other sources speak of the former treasurer having been executed still later in the year. See "Testimony of Frederick Skinner, (Asunción, 25 January 1871)," Scottish Record Office, CS 244/543/19 (138); and Washburn, *History of Paraguay*, 1: 320.

33 Resquín, *La guerra del Paraguay contra la Triple Alianza*, 94–95.

34 Washburn seems to have despised all the Brazilian leaders. He once referred in print to Admiral Tamandaré (who had obstructed his passage to Asunción earlier in the war) as a "genius of imbecility." See *History of Paraguay*, 1: 553.

35 For his part, Caxias dismissed all talk of his involvement in a conspiracy with Washburn as so much tosh, affirming that had a plot even existed, he would never have participated in it either directly or indirectly. See "A Conspiração do Paraguay," *Jornal do Commercio* (Rio de Janeiro), 14 November 1868, and Caxias's "declaration" in John LeLong, *Les Républiques de la Plata et la Guerre du Paraguay. Le Brésil* (Paris, 1869), 43–44.

36 Burton, who was British consul at the Brazilian port of Santos, used rather skeptical language to sum up the general opinion of his colleagues on Washburn's refusal to move the US legation: "I hardly think that such a proceeding would have been adopted by Europeans. ... Asunción might have been attacked at any moment by a squadron of ironclads, and the Marshal-President of the Republic was to a certain extent answerable for

the lives of foreign agents accredited to him." See Burton, *Letters from the Battle-Fields of Paraguay*, 409.

37   Leonardo Castagnino, *Guerra del Paraguay. La triple alianza contra los países del Plata* (Buenos Aires, 2011); Javier Yubi, "Al gran Mariscal," *ABC Color* (Asunción), 24 July 2011.

38   Bliss and Masterman had every reason to be grateful to Washburn, but the latter none-theless observed that the US minister "did talk most imprudently. Amongst ourselves it was all very well to say what we thought of the war and the character of López; but he used, in his blundering Spanish, to tell things to natives … which, perfectly right in themselves as mere personal opinions, became treason and conspiracy if the point of view were shifted a little." See Masterman, *Seven Eventful Years in Paraguay*, 245.

39   Maíz, Resquín, Aveiro, and (somewhat more parenthetically) Centurión should probably be included in this group. See, for instance, Centurión, *Memorias o reminiscencias*, 3: 263–286.

40   Thompson, *The War in Paraguay*, 263–264. If anyone on board the ironclads had really wished to signal friends along the river, they would probably have used flags or hand motions rather than rely on shouted instructions.

41   Strictly speaking, the government had suppressed the Laws of the Indies in Paraguay during the early 1840s, but it seems that the regulations concerning treason, as defined first in the Siete Partidas and then in the Military Ordinances of Charles III, were still in force as part of the reigning code of military justice (Jerry W. Cooney, personal commu-nication, Longview, Washington, 9 April 2010).

42   Regarding Roca's experiences in Paraguay, see Zacarías Rivero to Basilio de Cuellar, San-ta Cruz, 17 January 1870, in Antonio Díaz, *Historia política y militar de las repúblicas del Plata* (Montevideo, 1878), 11: 171–176.

43   Inocencia López de Barrios is commonly depicted in unflattering terms as a Renoir woman with a Guaraní accent, who went about barefooted, and who betrayed just a touch of the slattern in her leer. But she was also an honest victim of her brother's wrath. She remained in custody in camp from August until December 1868, and during all that time was under constant threat of torture. Her sentence of death was commuted, it is said, on the same day that the authorities shot her husband, General Barrios. See "Tes-timony of Inocencia López de Barrios (Asunción, 17 January 1871)," in Scottish Record Office, CS 244/543/19 (83–84, 90). The two López sisters, both of whom survived the war, were ordered into detention at Yhú, an isolated village in the southeast of the country, but were rescued by their mother while en route to that destination, and were hidden away in the hill country of central Paraguay. Regarding Bayon de Libertat, see Fano, *Il Rombo del Cannone Liberale*, 2: 336; Maíz, *Etapas de mi vida*, 64-66; and Cuverville Correspondence (1868) in Kansas University Library, Natalício González Collection, ms. E222. As for the Portuguese consul, he stood accused of having secretly aided Brazil-ian prisoners of war; this brought the revocation of his exequatur in July and his arrest shortly thereafter. See Decree of López, San Fernando, 20 July 1868, ANA-CRB I-30, 28, 26, no. 9.

44   José del R. Medina to Francisco Fernández, Luque, 30 July 1868, ANA-CRB I-30, 25, 26, no. 15; see "List of Accused Prisoners aboard Steamer *Añambay*, (7 August 1868)," in Cardozo, *Hace cien años*, 9: 215–216.

45   Amerlan, *Nights on the Rio Paraguay*, 124.

46   Washburn, *History of Paraguay*, 2: 269–270.

47   The term "tribunals of blood" may appear to suggest a connection to the Black Legend, for that was the name English Protestants used in denouncing the Duke of Alba's six-teenth-century Council of the Troubles in the Netherlands. In point of fact, in describing the events at San Fernando, it was the Paraguayans themselves who first used the term,

and it has by now entered the broader political and cultural discourse in the country. Alcibiades González Delvalle's play "San Fernando," published in Asunción in 2011 but written twenty years earlier, could not be presented in Paraguay at that time because contemporary comparisons with the "bloodletting" of López's day seemed a bit too obvious for the defenders of the Stroessner dictatorship.

48   Among Maíz's many published works, one can mention the various editions of his memoirs, *Etapas de mi vida*, as well as *La Virgen de los Milagros* (Asunción, 1883); *Pequeña geografía* (Asunción, 1886); *25 de noviembre en Arroyos y Esteros* (Asunción, 1889); and *Discurso del Pbro. Fidel Maíz. Pronunciado hace 21 años en Piribebuy* (Asunción, 1922). His collected works can be found in Carlos Heyn Schupp, ed., *Escritos del Padre Fidel Maíz, I. Autobiografía y cartas* (Asunción, 2010).

49   One anonymous writer, possibly Washburn, observed that it "was whispered that, as Rector of the Theological Seminary, [Maíz] was inculcating the most horrible, dangerous and revolutionary doctrines to his unsuspecting pupils. … [He was ultimately] convicted and removed from [his] post by a decree, which recited in the vaguest possible language [his] horrid crimes and misdemeanors, concerning which nothing tangible was ever published." These "revolutionary doctrines" were almost certainly the standard European liberalism of the mid-1800s. See "Chronological Synopsis of the Administration of Marshal López," WNL.

50   *El Semanario* (Asunción), 1 December 1866.

51   Maíz also managed to perform a task that was very dear to the Marshal's heart. At the suggestion of Natalicio Talavera, he was ordered to compose a refutation of the Pope's Bull of 1866, which assigned ecclesiastical authority over the Paraguayan dioceses to the Bishop of Buenos Aires. Maíz's argument, which was reminiscent of the regalist doctrines of an earlier age, would have had the effect of strengthening state control over the church in Paraguay if it had been upheld in peacetime; as it was, during the war, the state held all the power anyway. See Maíz Rebuttal in *El Semanario* (Asunción), 2 February 1867 and Maíz Papers in UCR Juansilvano Godoi Collection, Box 1, no. 26.

52   Questions of race and class were historically intertwined in Paraguay, and one could just as easily paint the wartime estrangement that the Guaraní-speaking peasantry felt for the urban elite in ethnic as well as class terms. Von Versen probably put it best when he remarked that the "Guaraníes [*sic*] assisted [in this persecution of the elite] with a disguised but natural glee, hoping [thereby] to witness the complete elimination of those Spaniards who had enslaved them." See *Reisen in Amerika*, 173.

53   In a somewhat convoluted speech offered when in his dotage to an audience of admirers, Maíz stressed the desirability of a truly civil society, noting that it was all good and well to disagree when "under the breezes of a beautiful democratic freedom, but sometimes a tempest brings about a [broader] agitation from which surge forth new and impassioned disunions, and drive the ancient and hateful rivalries [like a dagger] into the breast of the Paraguayan family." See Maíz, *Desagravio* (Asunción, 1916), 76–77.

54   While never able to admit to remorse, Centurión was clearly vexed about his role at San Fernando, where he had taken notes at some of the most brutal interrogations. Frederick Skinner, one of the British doctors employed by the Paraguayan state, later claimed that the colonel had been a sadistic participant in the worst abuses:

> I cannot find language strong enough to express my opinion of him, which is that which all the people in the country have of him. He was one of López's *fiscales*, and his executioner-in-chief. I have repeatedly seen him gloating over tortures and cruelties. They say that he has buried women alive in ant hills, but I cannot vouch for this. He is a great liar, and neither his word nor his oath deserves credit. He is a greater scoundrel than López himself.

See "Declaration of Frederick Skinner, Asunción, 28 January 1871," in Scottish Record Office, CS 244/543/19 (141). After the war, Centurión evidently wanted to escape both from his country and from his nightmares, and ended up for a number of years in England, where he married a wealthy Cuban pianist, Concepción de Zayas y Hechevarría. He seems to have developed a natural flair for literature during this time, and composed a novel of mystical inclination, the *Viaje nocturno de Gualberto o reflexiones de un ausente*, the text of which seemed to beg sympathy and pardon from those who had never found it necessary to compromise their values under the pressure of orders. Centurión thought it convenient, perhaps even appropriate, to publish the work pseudonymously in a foreign city—New York, in 1877. Few Paraguayans ever read it. One year later, the colonel returned to Paraguay, where he found many among his countrymen still unwilling to shake his hand. He devoted himself thereafter to legal and diplomatic work, contributed to the *Revista del Ateneo Paraguayo*, and he eventually wrote the memoirs for which he is principally remembered today. In 1890, when an aspirant for a Paraguayan consular appointment at Montevideo publicly claimed that the colonel had attended the torture and execution of Uruguayan suspects at San Fernando, Centurión reacted swiftly, soliciting letters of support from a long list of veterans who swore that he had been nowhere near the events described. See *Memorias y reminiscencias*, 3: 258–262. Colonel Centurión died in 1902.

55   Aveiro was a complex figure, well-educated and loyal, but also cunning, spiteful, and perhaps a bit cruel. He left a brief but useful account of his experiences during the war in which he admits, among other things, that he personally flogged the Marshal's mother, for "such had been the orders." See *Memorias militares*, 108. In his own memoirs, which went missing for several generations and which were only recently rediscovered, Falcón took a far more circumspect—if hypocritical—view of the events at San Fernando, casting every ounce of blame on López:

> Hundreds of distinguished men, priests, and women were taken from the capital to that spot and there sacrificed to the whim or dream that [López had] conceived of a conspiracy against his life; there occurred the most horrendous torments against innocent persons who did not even know the cause of their torture. They died as martyrs crying out their innocence and they heard nothing but the noise of fetters, chains, lashings, screams, and cries for mercy.

See Falcón, *Escritos históricos*, 95. One would presume that Falcón was an unwilling spectator at these terrible events, and that, in accusing the Marshal, he was at least partly absolving himself for having done so little to prevent the torture. In fact, he acted as one of the *fiscales* appointed to conduct the interrogation of, among others, Masterman, and that, together with Maíz, he directly oversaw the Englishman's torture (though Maíz denied any knowledge of Masterman in his 1889 letter to Zeballos). See Masterman, *Seven Eventful Years in Paraguay*, 256–258, and "The Atrocities of López," *The Standard* (Buenos Aires), 15 May 1869.

56   In late December, with the tribunals of San Fernando now a thing of the past, the British architect Alonzo Taylor happened to meet Madame Lynch and the Marshal when the latter rode past the *Guardia* at Lomas Valentinas. Taylor had been a prisoner since July and had frequently been tortured, as had many foreigners who had worked for the Paraguayan government:

> We were ordered to stand in a row, and he came up to us and asked, "are you all prisoners?" We replied, "Yes," and then Mr. Treuenfeld [the telegraphist] appealed to His Excellency, who asked him why he was there. Mr. Treuenfeld said he did not know, and the President told him he was at liberty, and might retire. I then approached, and said I should be grateful for the same mercy. López asked me who I was, and affected great surprise when he heard my name, and said, "What do you

do here? You are at liberty." Then the other prisoners, ten in number, came up and received the same answer.

See "Taylor Narrative," in Masterman, *Seven Eventful Years in Paraguay*, 330.

57 Save perhaps for a truncated excerpt, the written transcripts of the San Fernando trials appear not to have survived. Scholars, however, can consult some of the earlier reports assembled at Luque to get an idea of the evidence to which the *fiscales* had access. See Miscellaneous testimonies, Luque, 8 May–2 June 1868, ANA-CRB I-30, 24, 46; "Plano y organización de la conspiración tramada en el Paraguay, 1866 [*sic*]," BNA-CJO, Manuel Avila, "Apuntes sobre la conspiración de 1868. Pequeña contribución a la historia de la guerra con la Triple Alianza y de la tiranía de López," *Revista del Instituto Paraguayo* 2, no. 17 (1899): 215–231, and 3, no. 23 (1900): 3–30; and more generally, Godoi, *Documentos históricos*, 131–145. Dr. William Stewart maintained that Marshal López was well informed about the proceedings at San Fernando, and also of all the tortures. "At table he told us that Mr. So-and-So begged to be shot, but that Father Maíz would reply 'have no fear for that, when we have done with you, we will shoot you.' " See "Testimony of Stewart," WNL. Stewart himself was an interesting witness to all these events. A favorite among the foreigners who frequented Madame Lynch's "salon," he always exhibited an air of tranquil superiority, except when the Marshal's name was mentioned; on such occasions, he posed as a model of obsequiousness, and yet always managed to seem manly (unlike Wisner, whose effeminacy was noted by all).

58 Thompson, *The War in Paraguay*, 328.

59 Father Maíz represents a case in point. After visiting Rome in the 1870s to help rectify Paraguay's relations with the Vatican, he returned to Arroyos y Esteros and quietly administered the parish school. He felt some guilt for his past brush with power, and in several of his final letters about the war, he laid aside the topic of his own conduct to focus on the sacrifices made by all the Paraguayan chaplains. See, for example, Maíz to O'Leary, Arroyos y Esteros, 24 February 1915, BNA-CO. Maíz died in 1920, a few days short of his ninety-second birthday.

60 Toward the end of his life, Maíz justified his behavior with words similar to those uttered by the various petty tyrants tried at Nuremburg in the late 1940s. "In truth," he remarked, "I obeyed the undeniable orders of the first magistrate of the Republic … keeping strictly to the law and all the legal precedents [knowing that if] the law was rigid, cruel, and perhaps barbarous, I could not depart from its letter and spirit. … I have nothing to repent." See Maíz, *Desagravio*, 23–24.

61 Masterman evinced considerable sympathy for the soldiers delegated to guard him, brutal though they were, for they were also mere children caught in terrible circumstances:

> Lying awake at night, I have heard the younger ones, perhaps ten or twelve years of age, crying bitterly, from terror at being left alone in the dark, gloomy vault, or from cold or hunger. Once I saw a chubby flaxen-haired boy, holding his musket like a pole before him, his tears running down his cheeks, trying to weep silently, but a big sob shook him at intervals. I asked him in a whisper what was the matter. "I want to go home to my mother," he whimpered most unheroically, "and I am afraid of the dark." Poor little fellow, I thought, you are even more miserable than I.

See *Seven Eventful Years in Paraguay*, 168.

62 Amerlan, *Nights on the Rio Paraguay*, 127.

63 Washburn, *History of Paraguay*, 1: 510. The *cepo uruguaiana* was supposedly used by soldiers of the Uruguayan army against Paraguayan prisoners during the 1865 siege of Uruguaiana. For reasons unclear, the same torture was sometimes referred to in the documentation as the *cepo colombiano*.

64   Washburn, *History of Paraguay*, 2: 269–271; Alonzo Taylor saw doña Juliana on many occasions over the months of her captivity, and conceived a great pity for her after learning that she had been through the cepo on six separate occasions: "She was very anxious to know if a large black mark she had over one of her eyes would disappear or if it would disfigure her for life … [and] when I saw her led out to execution on the 16th or 17th of December, the mark was still there." See "Taylor Narrative" in Masterman, *Seven Eventful Years in Paraguay*, 327.

65   "Correspondencia (Buenos Aires, 28 May 1868)," in *Jornal do Commercio* (Rio de Janeiro), 5 June 1868.

66   Matías Goiburú, another one of the Marshal's fiscales at San Fernando, left a short account of the sufferings of Juliana Ynsfrán. He blamed López for all her misfortune. See Cardozo, *Hace cien años*, 9: 241.

67   There is a tendency in the anti-Lopista literature to lump together all of the Marshal's victims, as if their common fate somehow reduced their individuality to useless detail; in truth, they were very different from each other and had different talents, different ambitions, and different weaknesses. Berges was perhaps the only one of the Marshal's ministers who could think "outside the box". The minister's administration of the port of Corrientes in 1865 offered an appropriate example, since it wedded a carefully constructed notion of Correntino "autonomy" to the gloved use of Paraguayan force in a way that actually gained the Asunción government some friends. See Olinda Massare de Kostianovsky, *José Berges. Malogrado estadista y diplomático* (Asunción, nd), 12–17. The former foreign minister's "defense" at San Fernando, such as it is, can be consulted in ANA-CRB I-30, 27, 96 [August (?) 1868].

68   In one of his many (and oft-times contradictory) letters on the subject of the tribunals, Father Maíz claimed that López generally penciled an "x" against the names of those who were to be found guilty and executed. See Maíz to Zeballos, Arroyos y Esteros, 7 July 1889, AHM (A)-CZ, carpeta 122. Though this does not seem out of keeping with the Marshal's temper, it nonetheless appears overstated, since he usually kept his distance from the inquisitions. The fiscales, of course, could not rely on his absenting himself if they wished to remain safe. Amerlan tells the story of one judge who earned himself four bullets to the brain when the Marshal learned that he had given Benigno a glass of water. See *Nights on the Rio Paraguay*, 128–129.

69   Aveiro maintained that the ex-foreign minister's distempers were largely a sham. See *Memorias militares*, 64. Berges faced the cepo uruguaiana various times before his execution. See Cardozo, *Hace cien años*, 10: 81.

70   Barrios was a stiff, rather limited officer who had acted as his future brother-in-law's procurer during the 1850s and later commanded the invasion forces in Mato Grosso in 1864. See "Sumario instruido contra el Ministro de Guerra y Marina, General de división ciudadano Vicente Barrios, sobre el suicidio que ha intentado de perpetrar degollándose con una navaja de barba el día 12 de agosto [de 1868]," ANA-SH 355, no. 9; Aveiro, *Memorias militares*, 68–69; and "Informes del general don Bernardino Caballero, ex-presidente de la república (Asunción, 1888)," MHM (A)-CZ carpeta 131.

71   In Paraguay, the foreign engineers had displayed the dull and self-conscious integrity of company men. Seeing their Paraguayan underlings invariably as "wogs," the engineers treated them accordingly and were little respected for it, however much they were obeyed. On the other hand, local masters, if anything, acted with even greater contempt for their subordinates. See Masterman, *Seven Eventful Years in Paraguay*, 54–55, and Pla, *The British in Paraguay*.

72   Though still detained as a suspected enemy agent, von Versen had enjoyed the freedom of the Paraguayan camp in San Fernando until mid-July when Resquín's men came to formally arraign him on conspiracy charges. He was kept in a sort of cage for a time but

was not subjected to the cepo. Later, once the Paraguayan camp had moved to Pikysyry, he was bound day and night together with various Allied prisoners of war. He was later released and then rearrested once again. See Cardozo, *Hace cien años*, 9: 151–152, 246, 352–353; 10: 25–26; and von Versen, *Reisen in Amerika*, 187–196.

73   Magnus Mörner, *Algunas cartas del naturalista sueco Eberhard Munck af Rosenchöld escritas durante su estadía en el Paraguay, 1843–1868* (Stockholm, 1956), 5; Visconde de Taunay, *Cartas da Campanha. A Cordilheira. Agonia de Lopez (1869–1870)* (São Paulo, 1921), 42.

74   Centurión referred to the proceedings as a "hellish vortex" that brought horror to everyone involved. See *Memorias o reminiscencias*, 3: 155–156.

75   Burton, *Letters from the Battle-Fields of Paraguay*, xi, 128. Regarding the skepticism of the foreign naval officers, see *The Times* (London), 11 December 1868.

76   The general, who had done such fine work as a gunner at Redención Island and elsewhere, managed to run afoul of the Marshal in a manner not entirely clear. Perhaps he was accused as an accomplice in the conspiracy; in any case, he disappeared one day and was later bayoneted to death. See Thompson, *The War in Paraguay*, 266. Bruguez, it seems, had been an intimate friend of Benigno López and therein lies, almost certainly, the explanation of his fate. In addition to his skills as a gunner, the general was known as a loving foster father to his many nephews and nieces whose own parents had died earlier in the war. See Decoud, *La masacre de Concepción*, 174–175.

77   In his memoirs, Washburn evidently felt no regret for his various displays of disrespect towards López, seemingly thinking that, as representative of a free country, he should be free to act any way he wished: "It may not have been diplomatic, and certainly was not courtier-like, but I took a sort of malicious pleasure, when everyone else in the room was standing, to sit in a conspicuous place, indifferent to whether the President were standing or not," an offense that was "laid up against me, to be brought up years afterwards." See *History of Paraguay*, 2: 104.

78   Many well-to-do people, mostly foreigners, had taken advantage of his generosity—or self-absorption—to turn their cash over to him in 1868, and there are many divergent tales of what finally happened to all the money and jewels. See, for example, "Los misterios del Paraguay," *La Nación Argentina* (Buenos Aires), 23–24 December 1868. One curious document at the Washburn-Norlands Library in Maine is a promissory note James Manlove, dated 13 August 1868, to pay Washburn the sum of two hundred fifty dollars in gold, with interest. This was only days before the major was shot.

79   Sallie Washburn emerges from the documentation as a smug, rather bigoted figure, boastful of her material advantages and the social position she enjoyed through her husband's status as US minister. The diplomatic personnel who made her acquaintance tolerated rather than liked her. She appears to have had a nervous breakdown en route to Buenos Aires, and it is hard to know what to make of her controversial assertion given her state of mind. See "Testimony of Commander W.A. Kirkland (New York, 28 October 1869)" in the *Paraguayan Investigation*, 215; In a letter to General Webb later cited in a note to Washburn's successor as US minister to Asunción, her husband amplified on her mental state, observing that

> while the danger lasted and we did not know but I should be arrested, tortured to death or shot, and she sent on foot to the Cordilleras, she kept up bravely. But the danger passed and she has completely broken down. Visions of imprisonment fettered and stripes for your humble servant disturb and haunt her; and her doctor tells me today she must keep entirely quiet and not go out for weeks. ... What she most needs is quiet together with sleep undisturbed by horrid visions of López and torture.

See Webb to Martin F. McMahon, Rio de Janeiro (?), 6 October 1868, and Washburn to Israel Washburn, Buenos Aires, 12 October 1868, both in WNL.

80 Sallie Washburn may have let slip a dangerous secret, or, more likely, she was deluding herself in thinking she knew more than she did. Months later, she denied that she had said any such thing, testifying before Congress that "I could not have said that there was a plan or a conspiracy because I did not then believe it; but I may have said that at one time we may have supposed there was, because of the arrest of people. ... I do not remember definitely what occurred on the voyage, as I was very nervous and suffered a great deal." See "Testimony of Mrs. Washburn (New York, 29 October 1869)," in the *Paraguayan Investigation*, 217. Given the rancor that developed between her husband and the US naval officers on the South American station, it is possible that her naval interlocutor, Captain William A. Kirkland, heard her comment the way he wanted to and interpreted it in such a way as to embarrass the Washburn family. For his part, the former minister denied that his wife could have disclosed a conspiracy, for no one who "had escaped from the hands of López believes there had been one." See Washburn letter, New York, 16 November 1869, in *New York Daily Tribune*, 17 November 1869.

81 Distinct from his predecessor Emile Laurent-Cochelet, French consul Paul Cuverville had never warmed to the New Englander and had little problem believing the worst of him. See Cuverville to French Foreign Minister, Luque, 23 October 1868, in Capdevila, *Une Guerre Totale*, 456–457. The Frenchman's suspicions, which in every detail reflected the official attitude of the Marshal's government, were widely credited in a Metropolitan France still resentful of the US's role in the Mexican fiasco. One result, perhaps, was the reception accorded the subsidized publication of a pamphlet entitled *M. Washburn et la Conspiration Paraguayenne. Une question du droit des gens* (Paris, 1868). This work contrived to implicate many Paraguayans and resident foreigners in the 1868 conspiracy. See Gregorio Benítes to Benjamín Poucel, Paris, 18 December 1868, BNA-CO Benítes Papers, which discusses monies paid out for this project.

82 Originally published as a series in *El Semanario*, this report was later published in multiple copies as *Historia secreta de la misión del ciudadano norte-americano Charles A. Washburn cerca del gobierno de la República del Paraguay* (Luque?, 1868). Even those who believe in a conspiracy can recognize the unmistakable hand of coercion in this work. Bliss spent three months composing it, calculating that the longer he stayed at the task, the greater the possibility of his rescue by the Allied army. He was daily bullied throughout this time by Father Maíz, who, though he never tortured the North American, warned that things might go badly for him if he failed to write in the prescribed way. In the end, the "pamphlet" reached 323 pages, and included a fictitious biography of Washburn and as many poems and "ridiculous old jokes" as Bliss could recall ("believing that this publication would inevitably fall into the hands of the Allies and be interpreted by them correctly, I resolved to make it the medium of informing them and all the world in regard to the atrocities committed by President López").

83 "Testimony of Rear-Admiral C.H. Davis (New York, 27 October 1869)," and "Testimony of Commander W.A. Kirkland (New York, 28 October 1869)" in *Paraguayan Investigation*, 186–209. Thomas Q. Leckron, a captain's clerk aboard the *Wasp* at the time of Bliss's release, chanced to talk with the reluctant author of the *Historia secreta* and quoted him as saying that he had never been mistreated, save that "he could not go any distance from his quarters without being accompanied by a Paraguayan soldier." See Leckron to W.A. Kirkland, Montevideo, 18 May 1869, in *Paraguayan Investigation*, 200–201. The ship's doctor aboard the same vessel testified that neither Masterman nor Bliss showed any sign of torture. See "Testimony of Marius Duvall (New York, 25 October 1869)," in *Paraguayan Investigation*, 166–173. With this kind of testimony and counter-testimony, we can only reiterate the observation of Harris G. Warren that someone "certainly was lying." But who? See Warren, *Paraguay. An Informal History*, 257.

84 Burton, *Letters from the Battle-fields of Paraguay*, 407.

85 As usual, there is considerable debate as to how many people were executed as a result of these various proceedings. General Resquín's diary, retrieved by the Allies after the Lomas Valentinas campaign, included summary dispositions on the various cases. These aptly titled "Tablas de Sangre" reported 432 individuals shot (*pasados por las armas*), five bayoneted, one lanced; 167 died in captivity; 216 taken out to work in the trenches; two (Bliss and Masterman) expelled from Paraguayan territory; one sent to the capital; and ten released. Of those shot, 289 were Paraguayans, 117 foreigners, and twenty-six listed without designation of national identity (the dispositions included several Correntinos, one Mexican, one Swiss, and one Russian). See *La Tribuna* (Buenos Aires), 20 February 1869; *Anglo-Brazilian Times* (Rio de Janeiro), 23 February 1869; and A. Rebaudi, *Guerra del Paraguay. Un episodio. "¡Vencer o morir!"* (Tucumán, 1920), 97–104.

86 In his unpublished (and unedited) *Historia del Paraguay*, now housed in the Nettie Lee Benson Library at the University of Texis, Austin, Dr. William Stewart offered an explanation of the Marshal's psychology that roughly coincided with the opinion expressed by Washburn:

> López became a victim of a limitless *amour-propre* that prevented him from giving proper weight to the happy perspectives that his position afforded him. Suspicious and taciturn, his life was surrounded by a dense shadow [and] to escape from society, the official sphere became the one thing that absorbed his attention. ... We took every occasion to awake in him noble aspirations of political greatness [that could be manifested in] the moral and material progress [of his country], but all was in vain. The efforts of the physician were arrested by opposing influences that developed into neurosis, which was the central element in my diagnosis.

11 | BLEEDING, DROP BY DROP

1 Despite the disorder, certain communities in the interior still managed to send herds of cattle to the army even into September. We see, for example, in the first week of the month, the following figures for cattle received at the camps at Pikysyry: 217 head from Altos; 122 from Salvador; 400 from Rosario; 928 from San Pedro; 370 from Villarrica; 70 from Curuguaty; and 130 from Paraguarí. Another one thousand head of cattle (and a few horses) arrived later in the month from Caazapá, Quiindy, San Estanislao, and once again from Rosario. See Cardozo, *Hace cien años*, 9: 300, 342.

2 Rural communities used their dwindling supplies of paper to copy effusive statements of loyalty. These letters, which attested to a common willingness to sacrifice "the last drop of blood" for the national cause, were apparently signed by every adult resident that the *jefe político* could find—and affirmed by many more who could not write. Invariably, the treason of Berges and others received a florid censure as utterly unbecoming of loyal Paraguayans. See Statement of Loyalty of Citizens of Itauguá, 27 July 1868, ANA-CRB I-30, 28, 3, no. 8; of Limpio, 5 August 1868, UCR-JSG box 15, no. 13; and of San José de los Arroyos, 9 August 1868, ANA-CRB I-30, 28, 13, no. 1.

3 "Parte oficial, Humaitá, 30 August 1868," in *Jornal do Commercio* (Rio de Janeiro), 16 September 1868; Gelly y Obes to Mitre, Humaitá, 30 August 1868," in *The Standard* (Buenos Aires), 2 September 1868; and Tasso Fragoso, *História de Guerra entre a Triplice Aliança e o Paraguay*, 4: 5–14.

4 *American Annual Cyclopedia of and Register of Important Events of the Year 1868* (New York, 1871), 8: 613 (which apparently used the *Anglo-Brazilian Times* as its primary source); and, more generally, Tasso Fragoso, *História da Guerra entre a Triplice Aliança e o Paraguay*, 4: 14–18.

5   Bruguez had been executed on 26 August, the Marshal's last full day at San Fernando. The general died together with eighteen other individuals, the majority of them soldiers or clerics. See Cardozo, *Hace cien años*, 9: 271–272.

6   Cerqueira probably exaggerated the number of victims, but there remains little doubt that there were many. See *Reminiscencias da Campanha do Paraguai*, 308–309. So suddenly had the Paraguayans departed from San Fernando that the officer in charge of one of the outlying posts came into camp to report as usual, only to find the Allies in possession of the site. See Leuchars, *To the Bitter End*, 188.

7   Cardozo, *Hace cien años*, 9: 101–103.

8   Cardozo, *Hace cien años*, 9: 173.

9   Thompson, *The War in Paraguay*, 279.

10 Thompson, *The War in Paraguay*, 280; Garmendia, *Recuerdo de la guerra del Paraguay. Segunda parte. Campaña de Pikyciri* (Buenos Aires, 1890), 243–245

11 Concerning supplies of cattle and foodstuffs available to the army at this time, see Juan Pedrueza to Colector General, Concepción, 8 October 1868, ANA-NE 2494; Pascual Melgarejo to Colector General, Barrero Grande, 27 October 1868, ANA-NE 2893; and especially List of Livestock Holdings, Estancia Gazory, 29 October 1868, ANA-CRB I-30. 14, 77, no.1 (which lists 15,088 head of cattle, mostly confiscated from ranches in Concepción and San Pedro).

12 Thompson, *The War in Paraguay*, 281.

13 Bengoechea Rolón, *Humaitá*, 194.

14 The desultory Paraguayan resistance in the Misiones represents one of the many untold chapters of the Triple Alliance War. Allied units had penetrated the area both from Corrientes and from the east relatively early in the conflict but never in sufficient numbers to entirely dislodge the Paraguayans even from the south bank of the Alto Paraná. The Marshal had not bothered to reinforce the little garrisons he maintained in this quarter and this left the Misiones "front" a minor business—except to the men who fought and died there. Francisco Bareiro to War Minister, Asunción, 15 December 1866, ANA-NE 1737; Bareiro to War Minister, Asunción, 11 April 1867, ANA-NE 785; See Francisco Fernández to War Minister, Asunción, 13 June 1867, ANA-SH 352, no. 1; Venancio López to López, Asunción, 22 January 1868, ANA-CRB I-30, 28, 16, no. 1; Gabriel Sosa to War Minister, Campichuelo, 6 July 1867, ANA-NE 763; Romualdo Prieto to Garrison Commander, Encarnación, 26 August 1868, ANA-CRB I-30, 14, 129; Reports of Romualdo Prieto to War Minister, Encarnación, 24 October 1868, ANA-CRB I-30, 14, 48, no. 1; Juan José Venegas to Garrison Commander at Encarnación, Santa Rosa, 15 November 1868, ANA-CRB I-30, 28, 4, no. 4; and Ciriaco Gauto to Garrison Commander at Josemi de la Villa Encarnación, Posta en Atingues, 16 November 1868, ANA-CRB I-30, 28, 4, no. 5.

15 Exploratory parties went as far downriver as Albuquerque in late September 1868 and found no Paraguayans. See "Important from Brazil," *The Standard* (Buenos Aires), 10 October 1868.

16 Regarding the siege at Timbó, see "Chronique," *Ba-Ta-Clan* (Rio de Janeiro), 15 August 1868; "La toma de Timbó," *El Nacional* (Buenos Aires), 25 August 1868; "The War in the North," *The Standard* (Buenos Aires), 26 August 1868; and "Important [News] from the Seat of War," *The Standard* (Buenos Aires), 1 September 1868.

17 "Teatro de guerra," *La Patria* (Buenos Aires), 28 August 1868.

18 *American Annual Cyclopedia 1868*, 8: 613. Since a team of six horses daily ate as much as twenty men, the care and feeding of the animals had to be a major concern for Caxias or any other commander. He could not afford to give any less attention to this matter than to the care and supply of his troops.

19 "The War in the North," *The Standard* (Buenos Aires), 26 August 1868.

20 Thompson, *The War in Paraguay*, 281–282.

21 Cardozo, *Hace cien años*, 9: 311–312.

22 Washburn to Caminos, Asunción, 2 September 1868, NARA, M-126, no. 2.

23 Caminos to Washburn, Luque, 4 September 1868, ANA-CRB I-30, 27, 58, and another missive written on the same day, again from Caminos to Washburn, ANA-CRB I-22, 11, 2, no. 27. The WNL boasts an incomplete list of the silver held in Washburn's legation for various British engineers. The quantities involved were substantial, with Thompson's hoard, for instance, amounting to over a thousand pesos in several bags.

24 Washburn, *History of Paraguay*, 2: 416–417.

25 Masterman, *Seven Eventful Years in Paraguay*, 250.

26 Washburn's account of the interview between López and Kirkland has the latter threatening the Marshal with dire consequences if he did anything to harm the US minister: "I advise you not to touch that man, for if you do, the United States will hunt you through Europe [and] will have your head sure." See *History of Paraguay*, 2: 438. This particular braggadocio, which does not seem atypical for North American naval men at the time, was later enlarged upon by Captain Kirkland in a letter to his superior that was read into the Congressional record. See W.A. Kirkland to Admiral C.H. Davis, Montevideo, 28 September 1868, in *Paraguayan Investigation*, 195.

27 This letter was clearly meant to convey the fact that no missive composed in the Paraguayan camp could be treated as containing truthful information. Porter Bliss to Henry Bliss, Esq., Paraguay, 11 September 1868, WNL. Bliss's brother Asher, in a letter to the *Fredonia Censor* in early December, noted the existence of this absurd letter, correctly giving it the interpretation intended by his imprisoned brother. See *New York Times*, 4 December 1868.

28 On page 411 of *Letters from the Battle-fields of Paraguay*, Burton remarked that the material that Washburn put before the public eye in Buenos Aires would have filled 240 pages. *The Standard* (Buenos Aires) received access to this collection of reports and correspondence, and proceeded to publish the whole compilation in a supplementary edition of 26 September 1868. The ex-minister also finished a valedictory dispatch for Secretary Seward (Buenos Aires, 24 September 1868), found in NARA, M-128, no. 2 (with portions repeated in the 17 November 1868 issue of the *New York Tribune*). But perhaps the most interesting, or at least the most touching, of the letters he composed at this time was a short note to his eldest brother that expressed relief at finally being out of the Marshal's clutches, noting that Sallie had by now completely broken down ("For a long time she could not sleep without horrid visions of prisons and fetters"). See Washburn to Israel Washburn, Buenos Aires, 12 October 1868, WNL.

29 The Congressional hearings, which Charles Ames Washburn had insisted on as a way to clear his name, produced no clear-cut findings or recommendations. The political influence of Washburn's brother may have prevented the former minister from being officially reprimanded. See "Interview between Secretary Fish and General McMahon," *New York Herald*, 29 October 1869.

30 The weaker that Paraguay became, the more European newspapers depicted it as a "gallant little nation." Though the struggle with the Triple Alliance never really made the headlines on the continent, the coverage that did appear tended to be more sympathetic to the Paraguayan people in 1867–1868 (though not especially sympathetic to López). See Juan Carlos Herken Krauer and María Isabel Giménez de Herken, *Gran Bretaña y la guerra de la Triple Alianza* (Asunción, 1982). The attention the European press gave to the war was in any case limited; in a political setting defined by growing tensions between Bonapartist France and Hohenzollern Prussia, the affairs of the faraway South

American states seemed of minimal significance at the time. See Gregorio Benítes to "Amigo Lacalle," Paris, 28 September 1868, BNA-CJO, Benítes Papers, Copiador de cartas. For his part, the Argentine jurist Juan Bautista Alberdi, an opponent of the war living in a self-imposed French exile, welcomed the rumors of a domestic insurrection in Paraguay, evidently hoping that this would at last bring peace to that benighted country. See Alberdi to Benítes, Caen, 1 September 1868, Museo Histórico Nacional (Buenos Aires), doc. 3935.

31   Elizalde was married to a Brazilian, and the longer the war lasted, the more often this fact was thrown in his face. See Fano, *Il Rombo del Cannone Liberale*, 2: 366–371, and F.J. McLynn, "The Argentine Presidential Election of 1868," *Journal of Latin American Studies* 11, no. 2 (1979): 303–323.

32   de Marco, *Bartolomé Mitre. Biografía*, 355–357; Roberto Cortés-Conde, *Dinero, deúda y crisis. Evolución fiscal y monetaria en la Argentina, 1862–1890* (Buenos Aires, 1989), 17–77; and Olmedo, *Guerra del Paraguay. Cuadernos de campaña*, whose diary entry for 16 November1868 goes into great detail on the irregularity of pay and the rancor this engendered (see 329–330). An editorial cartoon in *El Mosquito* (Buenos Aires), 4 June 1868, depicts Mitre in a nightcap being ejected from the bed of a symbolic Argentina: "You have replaced me with another, señora, and now you expect me to keep quiet?" "What do you care?" she retorts, and, pointing down to a baby marked "the war in Paraguay," she continues: "Isn't it enough that you have left me with this ugly and ravenous child?"

33   F.J. McLynn, "The Corrientes Crisis of 1868," *North Dakota Quarterly* 47, no. 3 (1979): 45–58, and Dardo Ramírez Braschi, *Evaristo López. Un gobernador federal* (Corrientes, 1997).

34   Though born in the province of San Juan, Sarmiento was always at pains to convince others to disregard his provincial roots. See Leopoldo Lugones, *Historia de Sarmiento* (Buenos Aires, 1931); Natalio Botana, *Los nombres del poder. Domingo Faustino Sarmiento. Una aventura republicana* (Buenos Aires, 1996); and Tulio Halperín Donghi et al, *Sarmiento. Author of a Nation* (Berkeley, 1994).

35   Sarmiento to Editors, Boston, 3 June 1868, in *Boston Daily Advertiser*, 6 June 1868.

36   Sarmiento's willingness to stand by Brazil, at least for the purposes of finishing with López, drew much criticism from his supporters, but, in truth, he had little choice. See "La gran traición del sr. Sarmiento a su partido," *La Nación Argentina* (Buenos Aires), 31 October 1868.

37   Garmendia, *Recuerdo de la guerra del Paraguay. Segunda parte. Campaña de Pikyciri* (Buenos Aires, 1890), 229.

38   "The War in the North," *The Standard* (Buenos Aires), 24 September 1868. See also Percy Burrell and Henry Valpy to Interim War Minister, Surubiy, 7 August 1868, ANA-CRB I-30, 22, 76 no. 2.

39   Even some Paraguayan musical instruments fell into Allied hands. See *Boletim do Exercito* (Villa Franca, 13 September 1868), in *Jornal do Commercio* (Rio de Janeiro), 27 September 1868; "The War in the North," *The Standard* (Buenos Aires), 24 September 1868; Cardozo, *Hace cien años*, 9: 332.

40   *Boletim do Exército* (Estancia do Surubi-hy, 26 September 1868), BNRJ.

41   "The War in the North." *The Standard* (Buenos Aires), 7 October 1868; "Correspondencia de Palmas (28 September 1868)," *Jornal do Commercio* (Rio de Janeiro) 14 October 1868; Corselli, *La Guerra Americana*, 475.

42   "Correspondencia da Esquadra, 28 September 1868," *Jornal do Commercio* (Rio de Janeiro), 15 October 1868.

43   The Paraguayans lost five officers and 125 men killed at Surubiy, together with one battle standard, several dozen horses, and a few muskets and sabers. A small number of Paraguayans fell prisoner. The Brazilians lost twelve officers killed and twenty-six wounded,

along with seventy-eight soldiers killed and 178 wounded, for a total of 292 men lost, not counting those few who went missing. See Garmendia, *Campaña de Pikyciri*, 269–270.

44   Garmendia, *Campaña de Pikyciri*, 270. Cerqueira noted that many soldiers in the field shared the contempt that Caxias had expressed for the 5th Infantry, and had rechristened the unit with a contemptuous nickname, "the runner." See *Reminiscencias da Campanha*, 262.

45   Thompson, *The War in Paraguay*, 283.

46   Thompson, *The War in Paraguay*, 283–284. Provisions continued to be stockpiled within the Paraguayan lines for a time, and even as late as early December, small herds of cattle were brought to the camp from the interior villages. See, for instance, Pedro Pablo Melgarejo to War Minister, Quyquyo, 5 December 1868, ANA-CRB I-30, 11, 67.

47   Carlos Twite to Eusebio González, San Juan Nepomuceno, 27 September 1867, ANA-NE 2483; Twite to War Minister, Minas de Azufre (Valenzuela), 18 January 1868, ANA-NE 2488; Gelly y Obes to Colonel Alvaro J. Alsogaray, January 1868, MHM (A), Colección Zeballos, carpeta 149, no. 29; Twite to War Minister, Valenzuela, 27 September 1868, ANA-NE 2495; The real problem at Valenzuela was transport, not production. The same was generally true for the foundry at Ybycuí, which even at this late date continued to produce cannonballs, bullets, hammers, lances, leg-irons, grenades, and replacement parts for the remaining Paraguayan steamers. See Cardozo, *Hace cien años*, 10: 60–61.

48   Thompson, *The War in Paraguay*, 285-286; Visconde de Maracajú, *Campanha do Paraguay (1867 e 1868)*, 133–134; Frota, *Diário Pessoal do Almirante Visconde de Inhaúma*, 240–241 (entries for 30 September and 1–3 October 1868).

49   Cardozo, *Hace cien años*, 10: 9–12.

50   Thompson, *The War in Paraguay*, 286–287.

51   Tasso Fragoso, *História da Guerra entre a Triplice Aliança e o Paraguai*, 4: 52–57; Corselli, *La Guerra Americana*, 467–468.

52   Cardozo, *Hace cien años*, 10: 72–74; the *Jornal do Commercio* (Rio de Janeiro), 20 October 1868, speaks of the incidence of cholera, previously limited to a dozen cases monthly, having lately expanded to three times that number, and it appeared that the disease had spread from the front to Montevideo aboard one of the merchant ships returning from upriver. See also "Chronique," *Ba-Ta-Clan* (Rio de Janeiro), 17 October 1868.

53   Report of Caxias, Asunción, 14 January 1869, in *Jornal do Commercio* (Rio de Janeiro), 27 January 1869.

54   Cerqueira, *Reminiscencias da Campanha*, 282–284.

55   Centurión, *Memorias o reminiscencias*, 3: 189–191.

56   Garmendia, *Campaña de Pikyciri*, 273.

57   Cardozo, *Hace cien años*, 10: 107–108.

58   Loren Scott Patterson, "The War of the Triple Alliance: Paraguayan Offensive Phase—A Military History" (Ph.D dissertation, Georgetown University, 1975); Juan Beverina, *La guerra del Paraguay (1865–1870): Resúmen histórico* (Buenos Aires, 1973).

59   The extension of these works eventually amounted to nearly ten thousand yards, not counting the trench line prepared around the batteries at Angostura. See Garmendia, *Campaña de Pikyciri*, 288. Concerning the mobile reserve, see *Boletím do Exército*, (Surubi-hy, 27 October 1868), BNRJ.

60   The Italian naval officers made no secret of the favor they showed the Paraguayan cause, a partiality that was sometimes shared, though in more ambiguous terms, by their French, British, and North American counterparts. See Manfredi to Count Joannini, Montevideo, 28 November 1868, Archivio Storico Ministerio della Marina (Rome) [as extracted by Marco Fano].

61   On at least one occasion, the Brazilian ironclads fired at the Angostura batteries over the bows of the Italian steamer, a serious breach in the understanding with the neutral powers. As Colonel Thompson noted, the "English gunboat was the only one they respected." See *The War in Paraguay*, 291. See also Luis Caminos to Gregorio Benítes, Pikysyry, 9 November 1868, ANA CRB I-30, 22, 58, no. 1. Thanks to this perceived influence, the HMS *Beacon* did manage to take away seventeen British subjects at this time, Dr. Fox and sixteen women and children. See John T. Comerford, "Journal of her Majesty's ship Beacon (1868–1871)," Coleção Privada Michel Haguenauer (Rio de Janeiro).

62   In addition to the women and children mentioned (as well as a baker, a butcher, a bricklayer, and several unemployed sailors) the Italian officers also secured the liberty of three individuals captured at the beginning of the war while serving aboard the Argentine warship *25 de Mayo*. See Cardozo, *Hace cien años*, 10: 65, 165, and "La quistione delle prigioniere," *La Nazione Italiana* (Buenos Aires), 22 December 1868. A partial list of monies sent out of the country with the Italians can be found in Circular del Gobierno, Luque, 2 December 1868, ANA-CRB I-30, 28, 14, no. 6.

63   The Libertat conspiracy trial is one of the few for which ample documentation exists. See Cardozo, *Hace cien años*, 10: 64–65, 67–68, 71, 74–75, 77–78, 80, 84–85, 88, 90–91, 94, 100–101, 103–104, 109, 112, 115–116; Cuverville Correspondence (1868), Kansas University Library, Natalício González Collection, ms. E222; and French Consular Documentation (November-December 1868), ANA CRB I-30, 11, 29, nos. 67–79.

64   Thompson, *The War in Paraguay*, 290.

65   Washburn put a value on these monies of between five and six thousand dollars (and this figure did not count the silver of other persons left in the US charge). See Washburn to Martin McMahon, Buenos Aires (?), 11 November 1868, WNL. After the war, Madame Lynch embarked on a complex and ultimately fruitless lawsuit to regain the fortune she deposited with the Stewarts. See Cecilio Báez, "Los grandes despojos," *El Orden* (Asunción), 22 December 1923. The legal documentation on the Lynch lawsuit—a voluminous mass—can be found in the Scottish Record Office, CS244/543/8–9; 12; 19; 25; 26; 28; and 247/3230–3231.

66   "Chronique," *Ba-Ta-Clan* (Rio de Janeiro), 12 December 1868.

67   Tasso Fragoso, *História de la Guerra entre a Triplice Aliança e o Paraguai*, 4: 59–60.

68   Official Paraguayan sources remain nearly mute on this second bombardment of Asunción, and scholars have mostly depended on Brazilian reports. See Cardozo, *Hace cien años*, 10: 193–194.

69   Many of the Marshal's subordinates had been shot for less, but the obsequious Caminos survived once again. This was no small feat; as Burton snidely observes, Caminos played the same disastrous role for Paraguay that General Emmanuel de Grouchy did for France at Waterloo. See *Letters from the Battle-fields of Paraguay*, 428.

70   "The War in the North," *The Standard* (Buenos Aires), 8 December 1868.

71   The US minister to Rio de Janeiro strongly advised McMahon not to bother assuming his duties in Paraguay before receiving the Marshal's assurances about Bliss and Masterman. McMahon ignored this advice. See J. Watson Webb to General Martin T. McMahon, Boa Viagem, 23 October 1868, WNL; Mora and Cooney, *Paraguay and the United States*, 30-31.

72   Cardozo, *Hace cien años*, 10: 126–127; "Testimony of Dr. William Stewart," WNL.

73   Even in his public statements Marshal López's tone had of late taken on a more religious character, as, for example, in a proclamation of mid-October in which he noted that the Lord "never despises the humble prayer to assist our arms." See Proclamation of López, Pikysyry, 16 October 1868, in *The Standard* (Buenos Aires), 15 November 1868.

74   This assertion was palpably untrue, for the Marshal had only to lift his finger to cancel a meeting of the tribunal. Bliss and Masterman seem to have undergone some fearful handling during the three months of their confinement (though not all testimony endorses their claim of mistreatment). Masterman asserted that the Paraguayans had routinely tortured him in the cepo and singled out for particular condemnation those clerical fiscales (Maíz he thought merely "terrible," while Román presented "an admirable study for Torquemada.") See *Seven Eventful Years in Paraguay*, 250–309.

75   Thompson, *The War in Paraguay*, 291.

76   Dr. Stewart claimed that the confinement that Bliss and Masterman were subjected to aboard the US vessels was not so comfortable, a fact that gave much amusement to López when he subsequently heard the tale from General McMahon. See "Testimony of Dr. Stewart," WNL.

77   See *Paraguayan Investigation*, 306–307; Burton, *Letters from the Battle-fields of Paraguay*, 128–129.

12 | THE DECEMBER CAMPAIGN

1   In *Maldita Guerra*, 361–362, Doratioto stresses that the marquis ultimately took responsibility for this battle (and all of its setbacks) rather than see any slander directed at his subordinate Argolo, who died in the engagement. The dignified behavior certainly would be in keeping with the marquis's standards for personal comportment among officers, but the truth is that we do not really know. See also "Breve Resumo das Operações Militares dirigidas pelo metódico general Marqués de Caxias na Campanha do Paraguai," *O Diário do Rio de Janeiro* (23 February 1870).

2   Godoy later explained to Estanislao Zeballos that his troopers were under orders to economize with their cartridges, which by this time were down to sixty rounds a man; besides "the success of our arms had always [come] through bayonet charges [which] the Brazilians do not resist." See "Memorias de Julián N. Godoy."

3   Tasso Fragoso suggests that Machado's infantry was ordered back by General Argolo to support the advance of cavalry units under Niederauer that were at that moment heading across the bridge, but this interpretation suggests a deliberation or coolness in the Brazilian troop movements that was largely or entirely absent on the field. See *História da Guerra entre a Tríplice Aliança e o Paraguai*, 4: 79; see also Testimony of Teófilo Ottoni, Chamber of Deputies, Rio de Janeiro, 25 September 1869, in *Camara dos Diputados. Perfis Parlementares* (Brasília, 1979), 12: 1074–1085.

4   Garmendia, *Campaña de Pikyciri*, 318.

5   See Manuel Avila manuscript, "Itá Ybaté," in BNA-CJO.

6   Gurjão was evacuated by steamer to the Allied military hospital at Humaitá, but died of shock shortly thereafter. See Centurión, *Memorias o reminiscencias*, 3: 204.

7   Garmendia, *Campaña de Pikyciri*, 320; Hector F. Decoud, "6 de diciembre de 1868. Sangrienta batalla de Ytororó," *La República* (Asunción), 5 December 1891; "Itororo," *La Opinión* (Asunción), 9 April 1895.

8   Taunay, *Memórias do Visconde*, 434.

9   Tasso Fragoso, *História da Guerra entre a Tríplice Aliança e o Paraguai*, 4: 81–82; William Warner, *Paraguayan Thermopylae—the Battle of Itororó* (Norfolk, 2007), 8–10.

10   Cerqueira, *Reminiscencias da Campanha do Paraguai*, 324; "Correspondencia, Ruinas de Humaitá, 15 December 1868," in *Jornal do Commercio* (Rio de Janeiro), 28 December 1868.

11   Although neither the Paraguayan nor the official Allied sources mention it, the battle
      may not have been necessary. Leuchars cites the experience of Dionísio Cerqueira, who

> had had the good fortune to spend the battle with the reserve in a
> small clearing to the left of the allied line. When the firing stopped,
> he walked a short distance to his left and noticed that in that place
> the stream was shallow enough to be crossed and could have served
> as a useful, and less costly, place from which to outflank the enemy.
> Perhaps wisely, he chose to keep his thoughts to himself.

      See *To the Bitter End*, 199. Leuchars may very well have exaggerated this last point, which
      Cerqueira mentions only briefly and without irony. In any case, once the frontal assault
      had been decided upon, the battle took a predictably bloody course. See also Caxias to
      War Minister, Villeta, 13 December 1868, in *Jornal do Commercio* (Rio de Janeiro), 26–
      27 December 1868, and "Boletín del Ejército," in *La Nación Argentina* (Buenos Aires), 22
      December 1868.

12   "Esquadra Encouraçada, Villeta, 12 Dez. 1868," *Semana Illustrada* (Rio de Janeiro), 14
      December 1868 (3366); Cerqueira, *Reminiscencias da Campanha do Paraguai*, 326; the
      Brazilian losses were so high that Caxias dissolved six battalions and distributed the
      survivors among the other corps. See Arturo Rebaudi, *Lomas Valentinas* (Buenos Aires,
      1924), 6. There were some of the usual inconsistencies in the reporting of casualties,
      though the figures cited here are the most commonly encountered; Sena Madureira
      writes that the Brazilian losses were less than half those claimed by Thompson. See
      Guerra do Paraguai, 67; General Resquín qualified the Paraguayan losses as 13 officers
      and 317 soldiers killed, and 29 officers and 757 soldiers wounded. See *La guerra del Para-
      guay contra la Triple Alianza*, 99.

13   Doratioto asserts that Caxias was physically and psychologically exhausted, and had he
      been properly rested, he would have sent Osório's troops in hot pursuit of Caballero. See
      Maldita Guerra, 363. The scholarly treatment of Brazilian conduct at Ytororó has grown
      annoyingly partisan over the years. The hagiographic accounts of Caxias cast blame for
      the miscalculations on Osório rather than on the marquis, whereas those seeking to cele-
      brate the Riograndense general have asserted precisely the reverse. Without once taking
      the "fog of war" into consideration, Paraguayan writers have taken both commanders to
      task for the sloppy execution of poorly considered tactics and have generally portrayed
      Caballero as a brilliant field commander. In responding to this interpretation, the Italian
      marshal Badoglio, who knew something about losing battles, expressed more than a
      touch of impatience. He roundly condemned O'Leary's attempt to portray Osório as
      incompetent or even disloyal on this occasion, noting that the habit of always depicting
      Allied officers as fools did little to make Caballero look heroic, for where is the glory in
      defeating a bungler? See Brezzo, "¿Qué revisionismo histórico? El intercambio entre Juan
      E. O'Leary y el mariscal Pietro Badoglio en torno a *El Centauro de Ybicuí*."

14   Cited in Doratioto, *Maldita Guerra*, 361. This Paraguayan officer was the same Céspedes
      who had helped the Brazilians with their balloon ascents earlier in the war.

15   This was not an idle preoccupation. The rains fell so hard for several days in late No-
      vember that the Allied hospital on the island of Cerrito was flooded, and six patients
      drowned. See "The War in the North," *The Standard* (Buenos Aires), 25 November 1868,
      and "Chronique," *Ba-Ta-Clan* (Rio de Janeiro), 5 December 1868.

16   Centurión, *Memorias o reminiscencias*, 3: 208.

17   The Guaraní expression ("Eio pygüe nderebicuá gallon pyajhú tuyá"), taken in this case
      from testimony related long afterward by Caballero, loses something in translation but
      roughly meant that the Brazilians would certainly fight hard and never offer a lukewarm
      offense. See Centurión, *Memorias o reminiscencias*, 2: 209.

18   The Mena Barreto family of Rio Grande do Sul produced many army officers of national importance in Brazil over more than two hundred years. Six members of the family, all senior officers, were present in the December 1868 campaign in Paraguay. See João de Deus Noronha Menna Barreto, *Os Menna Barreto. Seis Gerações de Soldados* (Rio de Janeiro), 159–322. Both primary and secondary sources tend to confuse these officers and it is not always obvious which man is being described. The case of the Mena Barretos (and, for that matter, of the Lima e Silva family) demonstrates that the imperial army was rife with nepotism.

19   Leuchars, *To the Bitter End*, 200; Héctor F. Decoud, "11 de diciembre de 1868. Batalla de Avay," *La República* (Asunción), 11 December 1891; "Los triunfos del 6 y 11 del corriente," *El Nacional* (Buenos Aires), 20 December 1868; and "Combate de Itororo y los movimientos precursors," anonymous manuscript, Kansas University Library, Natalício González Collection, Ms. E202.

20   The Marshal had set up an ancillary telegraphic line with his commander at Avay (or perhaps Villeta) and was thus in regular contact with his frontline troops—or could at least claim to be. See "Memorias de Julián N. Godoy."

21   *The Standard* likened the Paraguayan defenders at Avay to "a living wave [of soldiers], cheering wildly, [that] literally sprang upon the Brazilian line." See "The Seat of War, Corrientes, 17 Dec. 1868," in issue of 25 December 1868. The official Paraguayan account, which was not published until nearly three months later, qualified the Marshal's resistance in similar terms (for "such was the resolution of the army and the entire Paraguayan people that under the leadership of the illustrious Marshal, shout 'Long live the holy cause that we are defending!' " See "¡¡Batalla de Abay!!" *Estrella* (Piribebuy), 6 March 1869; and Corselli, *La Guerra Americana*, 478–481.

22   "The War in the North," *The Standard* (Buenos Aires), 23 December 1868.

23   The Brazilian army's *Boletim do Exército* (Villeta, 13 December 1868) was careful to distinguish between the engagement at Ytororó, which the command deemed a "combat," and that at Avay, which was termed a "battle." See also "The War in the North," *The Standard* (Buenos Aires), 23 December 1868.

24   It says much about the aging Caxias that, when the Avay painting was unveiled, he snarled at its inaccuracies and coldly asked the artist when "he had ever seen him [Caxias] with an unbuttoned frock." The marquis (by then, in fact, a duke), had become personally emblematic of military rectitude and proper etiquette and resented the suggestion that he could ever have gone into battle improperly attired. Indeed, the angry journalist Melo Morais Filho considered the depiction "an aggression of the artist against the dignity of [both] the general and the army." See *Gazeta de Noticias* (Rio de Janeiro), 16 April 1879.

25   Cerqueira, *Reminiscencias da Campanha do Paraguai*, 332.

26   Noting the high proportion of Paraguayans killed as opposed to wounded, Garmendia remarked that the Marshal's many atrocities had so hardened Allied hearts by now that engagements were "no longer battles but a horrible slaughter." See *Campaña de Pikyciri*, 345; "Batalla de Abay," anonymous manuscript, Kansas University, Natalício González Collection, Ms. E202.

27   Colonel Serrano proved quite voluble with his captors, and while a prisoner aboard the *Princesa*, offered them considerable information, carefully omitting all references to his service as executioner and military aide to the fiscales at San Fernando. See "Declaration of the Paraguayan Prisoners," *The Standard* (Buenos Aires), 27 December 1868, and "Esquadra Encouraçada, 26 Dez. 1868," *Semana Illustrada* (Rio de Janeiro), 28 December 1868 (3382).

28 Thompson, *The War in Paraguay*, 296. Sena Madureira notes a loss of just over one thousand men for the Brazilians, a figure reduced to eight hundred by Leuchars. See *Guerra do Paraguai*, 68, and *To the Bitter End*, 203. In his note to the secretary of state, General McMahon claimed that the Brazilians had lost six thousand men "according to the Paraguayan account ... [it being] quite certain that the battle was very disastrous to the Allies." See McMahon to Seward, off Angostura, 11 December 1868, in NARA M-128, no. 3. It was, in fact, far from certain that the Allies had been dealt the blow that this account described.

29 The Brazilians thought that they had killed the Paraguayan general and reported him as dead in the 13 December 1868 *Boletim do Exército*. See also "Correspondencia, Buenos Aires, 16 Dec. 1868," in *Jornal do Commercio* (Rio de Janeiro), 28 December 1868.

30 In this respect, Avay seems to have illustrated the same senseless lack of foresight that López had shown at Tuyutí in 1866. See Thompson, *The War in Paraguay*, 296–297.

31 Thompson, *The War in Paraguay*, 297.

32 Thompson, *The War in Paraguay*, 297; "Correspondencia, 15 Dec. 1868," *Jornal do Commercio* (Rio de Janeiro), 28 December 1968.

33 *Anglo-Brazilian Times* (Rio de Janeiro), 7 January 1869.

34 Here we have another example of outsiders drawing broad comparisons between the Paraguayan situation and circumstances encountered in other parts of the world. The Argentine Montoneros saw Tsarist Russia in Brazil, and McMahon saw Ireland in Paraguay. Lest outsiders take all the blame for this unfortunate or simplistic interpretation, one should recall that Marshal López had earlier equated the circumstance of the Platine Republics specifically with that of the Danubian countries, an analogy that, in part, had paved the way for war. See Lillis and Fanning, *The Lives of Eliza Lynch*, 134. Arthur Davis, *Martin T. McMahon, Diplomático en el estridor de las armas* (Asunción, 1985); Lawrence Robert Hughes, "General Martin T. McMahon and the Conduct of Diplomatic Relations between the United States and Paraguay," MA thesis (Boulder, University of Colorado, 1962); Michael Kenneth Huner, "Saving Republics: General Martin T. McMahon, the Paraguayan War and the Fate of the Americas (1864–1870), *Irish Migration Studies in Latin America* 7, no. 3 (March 2010), http://www.irlandeses.org/1003huner.htm.

35 "The Paraguayans are a very peculiar people," he later observed. "They have always been accustomed to an arbitrary sort of government ... but when the question of independence [from] a foreign nation comes up, there never has been a people who have a stronger love of [it] than the Paraguayans, from the lowest to the highest, who would more readily die to preserve it." See "Testimony of Martin T. McMahon, Washington, 15 Nov. 1869," in *Paraguayan Investigation*, 280.

36 Mora and Cooney, *Paraguay and the United States*, 31; though he was not present for any of the interviews between McMahon and López, Washburn concluded that the newcomer was willfully predisposed in favor of the Marshal's caprices. He also implied that McMahon held a reactionary Papist viewpoint that the civilized, (i.e. Protestant) world had left behind but which the Marshal would find both congenial and convenient. See *History of Paraguay*, 2: 556–558. Such characterizations tell us more about Washburn than they do about McMahon.

37 Meliá, "El fusilamiento del Obispo Palacios," 36–39; "Declaración de don Manuel Solalinde (10 Jan. 1870)," in Junta Patriotica, *El mariscal Francisco Solano López* (Asunción, 1926), 249–251; Juan Silvano Godoi, *El fusilamiento del Obispo Palacios y los tribunals de sangre de San Fernando. Documentos históricos* (Asunción, 1996); and *Causa celebre: don Manuel A. Palacios, Obispo del Paraguay procesado y declarado reo de muerte por los presbiteros Fidel Maíz y Justo Román, y fusilado en Pikisyry el 21 de diciembre de 1868* (Corrientes, 1875).

38   The Marshal's sister, Juana Inocencia López de Barrios, later testified *in extenso* about these executions, which she blamed on the malevolent influences of Madame Lynch, "the enemy of all respectable women." See, in Scottish Record Office, CS 244/543/19: Testimony of López de Barrios, Asunción, 17 January 1871.

39   Gelly y Obes to Mitre, Lomas de Pikysyry, 24 Dec. 1858 [*sic*], in *La Nación Argentina* (Buenos Aires), 31 December 1868. Colonel Alén, still in pain from his attempted suicide, managed to stand erect before the tribunal and in the final moment before judgment, intoned a clear denial of culpability: "I have *never* been a traitor to my country." He was shot together with the other condemned men, one by one, on 21 December. See Cardozo, *Hace cien años*, 10: 258, 269–270.

40   The Marshal had commuted Vanancio's death sentence on 4 November 1868, the younger brother having cooperated with the fiscales in providing details about the conspiracy that implicated a wide circle of people, including Benigno, the López sisters, and even Juana Pabla Carrillo. See Cardozo, *Hace cien años*, 10: 116–117; Federico García, "La prisión y vejámenes de doña Juana Carrillo de López. Antes del ultraje de una madre. Breve itinerario," *El Liberal* (Asunción), 1 March 1920, and Aveiro, *Memorias militares*, 67–72.

41   Von Versen, *Reisen in Amerika*, 202.

42   Thompson, *The War in Paraguay*, 298; *Boletim do Exército* (Villeta, 19 December 1868) in BNRJ.

43   The Paraguayans lost one hundred forty as against only three wounded for the Brazilians. See Leuchars, *To the Bitter End*, 204.

44   Doratioto, *Maldita Guerra*, 360–374; Ministério da Defesa. Exército Brásileiro. Estado-Maior, *Manuel de Campanha. Emprego da Cavalaria* (Brasília, 1999), 2–13; and "Dezembrada" in http://www.historiabrasileira.com/guerra-do-paraguai/dezembrada/. The term is by now ubiquitous and appears in the Online Portuguese Dictionary at http://www.dicio.com.br/dezembrada/.

45   Bejarano, *El Pila*, 306–322; Efraím Cardozo, *Paraguay independiente* (Asunción, 1987), 242–245; O'Leary, *Nuestro epopeya*, 311–378.

46   Cardozo, *Hace cien años*, 10: 263; "Batalla de 21 de diciembre en Itaybaté," *Estrella* (Piribebuy), 10 March 1869; Pampeyo González [Juan E. O'Leary] "Recuerdos de Gloria. 21 a 27 de diciembre de 1868. Itá Ybaté," *La Patria* (Asunción), 22 December 1902.

47   Cerqueira, who witnessed this scene first-hand, remembered the horror of the moment many years later, describing it as the worst thing he had ever seen. See *Reminiscencias da Campanha*, 337; Martin T. McMahon, "The War in Paraguay," *Harper's New Monthly Magazine* 239: 40 (April 1870), 637.

48   Cerqueira joined the mass of bloodied and torn men at the field hospital later that day, but even he did not know how long he had wandered amid the scene of destruction. See *Reminiscencias da Campanha*, 338–340.

49   Gustavo Barroso, *A Guerra do López* (Rio de Janeiro, 1939), 185–189.

50   McMahon, "The War in Paraguay," 637–638.

51   The minister witnessed several intriguing acts of bravery on the part of the López children. On one occasion, an Allied barrage began while the family dined with McMahon, and a bullet ricocheted onto the plate of one of the López boys, who smilingly picked up the object and waved it at the Marshal, exclaiming "Look what Caxias has given me as a gift!" See "Correspondencia [of Taunay] (Pirayú, 7 July 1869)," *Jornal do Commercio* (Rio de Janeiro), 24 July 1869.

52   The tragedy he witnessed affected him deeply:

> I regret to say that more than one-half of the Paraguayan army
> is composed of children from ten to fourteen years of age. This

circumstance rendered the battle of the 21st and the ensuing days peculiarly dreadful and heart rending. These little ones in most cases absolutely naked, came crawling back in great numbers, mangled in every conceivable way. … They wandered helplessly toward the headquarters without tear or groan. I can conceive of nothing more horrible than this slaughter of innocents by grown men in the garb of soldiers … and I mention it here precisely as I saw it because I believe it would justify the immediate intervention of civilized nations for the purpose of putting a stop to the war.

See McMahon to Seward, Piribebuy, 31 January 1869, cited in Hughes, "General Martin T. McMahon and the Conduct of Diplomatic Relations," 54.

53   Thompson, *The War in Paraguay*, 304; Centurión, *Memorias o reminiscencias*, 3: 222–223; Aveiro, *Memorias militares*, 73. Von Versen, who was also close at hand, claims that the Marshal hid so low within a bower that he could see nothing, and every time a bullet hit nearby, he treated the occurrence with awe and fled. See *Reise in Amerika*, 207.

54   Andrade Neves was a cavalryman who had frequently deployed his forces in the Allied vanguard. At Itá Ybaté, however, he was fighting on foot when he received his mortal wound. Taken by fever (or pneumonia) while in a field hospital, he lived just long enough to see Asunción occupied, and he died in the Brazilian hospital there on 6 January 1869. His last words were, reportedly, "One more charge, my fellows!" See José de Lima Figueiredo, *Grandes Soldados do Brasil* (Rio de Janeiro, 1944), 77.

55   Resquín, *La guerra del Paraguay contra la Triple Alianza*, 102. McMahon left an indelible portrait of the wounded and dying Paraguayans in the aftermath of the battle. See McMahon, "The War in Paraguay," 639–646.

56   Gelly y Obes to "Talala," Tuyucué, 18 March 1868; Gelly to "Talala," Paso Pucú, 15 April 1868; and Gelly to "Talala," 16 December 1868, in Biblioteca Nacional (Buenos Aires), Sección Manuscritos, documentos 15.683, 15.694, and 15.708, respectively.

57   Garmendia, *Campaña de Pikyciri*, 384; "War in the North," *The Standard* (Buenos Aires), 29 December 1968; Olmedo, *Guerra del Paraguay. Cuadernos de campaña*, 356–368 (entries of 22–27 December 1868).

58   Leuchars, *To the Bitter End*, 208; "The War in the North," *The Standard* (Buenos Aires), 30 December 1868.

59   McMahon, "The War in Paraguay," 638; Centurión, *Memorias o reminiscencias*, 3: 226–228; Lillis and Fanning, *The Lives of Eliza Lynch*, 153; and "Testament de López," *Le Courrier du Plata* (Buenos Aires), 31 December 1868.

60   In his comments to Estanislao Zeballos, Colonel Godoy claimed credit for organizing new units out of these men, who had come through the swamps "in groups of three or more." See "Memorias de Julián N. Godoy."

61   The army's transit of the Ypecuá, one of the lesser-known episodes of the war, received its due attention from Juan O'Leary, who, under his pseudonym Pompeyo González, published a short account entitled "Recuerdos de Gloria. Ypecuá, 27 de diciembre de 1868," in *La Patria* (Asunción), 27 December 1902; one survivor of the passage, José Guillermo González, also published a brief memoir of his experience as a sixteen-year-old battalion commander, who, badly hurt with three suppurating wounds, nonetheless managed to make the crossing. See *Reminiscencias históricas de la guerra del Paraguay. Pasaje de Ypecuá* (Asunción, 1914). Gaspar Centurión, another wounded officer, made the same crossing and escaped unscathed to Carapeguá. See his *Recuerdos de la guerra del Paraguay* (Asunción, 1931), 20–22.

62 McMahon, "The War in Paraguay," 640–641; Caxias to War Minister, Lomas Valentinas, 26 December 1868, in *Jornal do Commercio* (Rio de Janeiro), 8 January 1869.

63 McMahon, "The War in Paraguay," 638–639; Centurión, *Memorias o reminiscencias*, 3: 233; Hector F. Decoud, "24 de diciembre de 1868. Intimación de rendición al Mariscal López," *La República* (Asunción), 24 December 1891. Critics of such brave rhetoric can legitimately observe that talk is cheap, and that López could have saved his country at any time by agreeing to leave.

64 There are multiple English translations of this note, some better than others. See McMahon, "The War in Paraguay," 639; Thompson, *The War in Paraguay*, 301–303; Kolinski, *Independence or Death!*, 222–223; "President López's Reply," *The Standard* (Buenos Aires), 1 January 1869; *New York Times*, 22 February 1869; and William Van Vleck Lidgerwood to Seward, Petropolis, 25 January 1869, in NARA M-121, no. 36.

65 Avila manuscript, "Itá Ybaté."

66 Leuchars, *To the Bitter End*, 210.

67 "Gran triunfo," *El Liberal* (Corrientes), 30 December 1868; *Boletim do Exército* (28 December 1868), in BNRJ.

68 According to the war correspondent at *The Standard*, a "large column of cavalry under General Rivas and the Baron del Triunfo were immediately dispatched in pursuit of the fugitives," but, if this were the case, then someone fumbled in its execution, for the Marshal got away cleanly. See "The War in the North," *The Standard* (Buenos Aires), 10 January 1869. Juan Asencio, a young soldier wounded in covering the retreat of the Marshal, found no great mystery in the latter's abrupt departure, the "son-of-a-bitch was a coward (*Ypia miri co añá raý*)," he claimed, and fled at the first moment the Allied bullets fell nearby. See Asencio letter in *El Liberal* (Asunción), 14 November 1919.

69 Doratioto, *Maldita Guerra*, 374–382.

70 Garmendia, *Campaña de Pikyciri*, 422–465.

71 Juan E. O'Leary, *Lomas Valentinas. Conferencia dada en Villeta el 25 de diciembre de 1915* (Asunción, 1916), 37–38

72 Pedro Werlang, the German-born Riograndense captain, claimed to have witnessed Lynch, the Marshal, his generals, and senior staff escaping in a bunch toward the east, encountering no obstructions in their path, "which would have been easy enough to [erect had] Caxias thought it convenient to detain them." See Klaus Becker, *Alemães e Descendentes*, 143.

73 Garmendia, *Campaña de Pikyciri*, 475–477.

74 In a personal communication of 27 August 2009, the Italian scholar Marco Fano suggested that Thompson's memoirs were likely edited by persons unknown to make them appear like an anti-López diatribe—even though the colonel had previously shown no such sentiments. In this altered form the reminiscences arrived in Buenos Aires and Rio de Janeiro and were thus translated in the months before the war concluded. There may be something to this idea, for, as Fano observes, the placement of anti-López commentary in certain points in the text does seem a tad forced, ill-considered, and artificial. I am persuaded, however, that this phantom editor was none other than Thompson himself trying to come to terms with his earlier loyalties and hoping to ingratiate himself with those Paraguayans who had chosen the winning side. One wonders in this context what words the colonel might have used in describing his former commander in chief had he lived to see the man championed by O'Leary and others some thirty or forty years later. Much the same might be asked of Cunninghame Graham, who noted at the beginning of the twentieth century that he had never met anyone in Paraguay "who had a good word to say of López, but all condemned him, [speaking of] his cruelty, his love of bloodshed." Having made this unequivocal statement, the Scottish author promptly

contradicted himself, noting that there were those in the country who wished to "set up a legendary national hero as a rallying point for Paraguayan patriotism." See *Portrait of a Dictator*, 79–81.

75 Thompson, *The War in Paraguay*, 309; Garmendia, *Campaña de Pikyciri*, 485.

76 Thompson, *The War in Paraguay*, 309–310; McMahon seems to have been misinformed about the state of readiness within the Angostura line, noting that they had sufficient provisions to hold out a month. See "The War in Paraguay," 647.

77 Thompson, *The War in Paraguay*, 310–311.

78 Angostura was distant from the Marshal's former headquarters by a mere 800 yards. See "War in the North," *The Standard* (Buenos Aires), 27 December 1868; "Teatro de guerra, Palmas, 29 Dec. 1868," *El Liberal* (Corrientes), 1 January 1869.

79 Davis, *Life of Charles Henry Davis*, 321–325.

80 To suggest that American tactics would have easily won the day was doubly offensive in its arrogance. The Allied fleet off Angostura counted more than fifty vessels armed with hundreds of guns while the total number of US ships on the Paraná and Paraguay amounted to only five, and these had a mere thirty-eight guns. To think that the latter force could outperform the Brazilian navy under such circumstances seems unlikely, even granting the Americans some points for marksmanship. See Davis, *Life of Charles Henry Davis*, 324.

81 Thompson and Lucas Carrillo to Allied Commanders, Angostura, 29 December 1868, in Garmendia, *Campaña de Pikyciri*, 487–488 (this letter was reproduced in the pages of *La Estrella* on 17 March 1869 while Piribebuy was still in the Marshal's hands); the Allied rejoinder can be found in Gelly y Obes to Mitre (?), Cumbarity, 29 December 1868, in *La Nación Argentina* (Buenos Aires), 5 January 1869.

82 Manuel Trujillo, who attended the discussions among the Paraguayan soldiers, suggested that Thompson and Carrillo were no more inclined than previous officers to share the military facts with the men, but had lost so much authority with them the previous week that they saw no other option if they wished to avoid a mutiny. Trujillo claimed that almost no one wanted to capitulate initially and that the men changed their minds only after much urging from the officers. See *Gestas guerreras*, 37. For his part, Colonel Centurión criticized the two commanders not for the surrender, which was inevitable, but for their unwillingness to save honor by enduring at least one Allied assault, observing that "the surrender at Angostura was even more shameful than that at Uruguaiana, which resulted from starvation." See *Memorias o reminiscencias*, 3: 248. Both Brazilian analyses and that of Rodolfo Corselli supports this observation, with the Italian general chiding the Paraguayan units at Angostura for not having attempted a least a diversionary attack in favor the Marshal. See *La Guerra Americana*, 492–494.

83 "Revista das tropas paraguaias," *Vida Flumenense* (Rio de Janeiro), 30 May 1868 (figure 5), provides a sarcastic image of the much-reduced Paraguayan army of that period, still ready to fight. Among the later Paraguayan nationalist writers who attempted to explain the sources of their countrymen's obstinacy in the face of sure defeat, see, for example, Manuel Domínguez, *El alma de la raza* (Asunción, 1918); Justo Pastor Benítez, *El solar guaraní* (Buenos Aires, 1947), 89–94; and J. Natalício González, *Proceso y formación de la cultura paraguaya* (Asunción, 1988).

84 Thompson and Carrillo to Allied Commanders, Angostura, 30 December 1868, and Caxias, Gelly y Obes, and Castro to Thompson and Carrillo, Headquarters opposite Angostura, 30 December 1868, in "Fall of Angostura," *The Standard* (Buenos Aires), 10 January 1869; "Correspondencia, (Humaitá, 29 Dec. 1868)," *Jornal do Commercio* (Rio de Janeiro), 11 January 1869; "Ultima hora," *El Liberal* (Corrientes), 1 January 1869.

85 Now at a safe distance from Paraguay, former minister Washburn made a shrewd obser-
    vation in comparing the situation that had faced Thompson at Angostura with that of
    Martinez at Humaitá, that, "fortunately for Thompson, he had no wife in the country, on
    whom López and Lynch could exercise their ingenuity in torture." See *History of Para-
    guay*, 2: 571.

86 Thompson had one final opportunity to assert his authority as a Paraguayan officer,
    when, just before leaving for Britain, he learned that Caxias's successors in the field had
    enrolled Paraguayan prisoners into the Allied army, this latter action being contrary
    to the surrender agreement reached with the marquis in December. Thompson sent a
    spirited message to Caxias to complain about this practice, which "doubtless happened
    through the absence of the Marquez de Caxias from the seat of war." See Thompson to
    Caxias, Rio de Janeiro, 12 March 1869, in *The War in Paraguay*, 346. In later times, the
    British engineer was censured on all sides. He was condemned by the Lópista faction of
    the early twentieth century for his having "treacherously" denounced the Marshal after
    having served him so faithfully, and by the Liberals, who claimed that he was an op-
    portunist who acted with willful ignorance of the atrocities that López had committed.
    Relatively little of this criticism was directed at him during his lifetime, however, and
    like many of the foreigners who had once worked for the Paraguayan government, he
    came back to live in the country after the war. He married, had a family, and worked as
    an official in the Paraguay Central Railroad before dying at age thirty-seven in 1879. His
    wartime reminiscences have proven of enduring value, and even such critics as Antonio
    de Sena Madureira, Diego Lewis, and Angel Estrada were mostly reduced to carping
    about details. Thompson's condemnation of the Marshal does indeed seem tardy, of
    course, though no more so than similar testimony offered by Dr. Stewart, Colonel Cen-
    turión, Father Maíz, and Colonel Wisner.

13 | ANOTHER PAUSE

1 Richard Burton later examined these documents, which threw "a fierce light upon the
   shades of Paraguayan civilization." They included information on slavery (which had
   yet to be abolished in Paraguay), the disposition of monies collected through forced
   contributions, courts martial records, descriptions of punishments meted out for various
   offenses in the army, and some of the Marshal's private correspondence. See *Letters from
   the Battle-fields of Paraguay*, 472–481.

2 "Special Mission to Paraguay. Lomas Valentinas," *The Standard* (Buenos Aires), 1 August
   1869. President Sarmiento reacted to the Marshal's escape with considerable frustration,
   demanding of General Emilio Mitre how it could have happened, and reminding him
   that chasing López might cost an additional "four or six millions pesos that we do not
   have." See Sarmiento to E. Mitre, Buenos Aires (?), 21 January 1869, in *Obras de Domingo
   Faustino Sarmiento* (Buenos Aires, 1902), 50: 126–128.

3 The naval correspondent of *A Semana Illustrada* (who may have been Admiral Ignácio
   himself), wrote insultingly of the Marshal's decision to flee, calling him a recreant for
   not having killed himself like the brave Negus Theodore [Tewodros] of Ethiopia, who
   had chosen suicide rather than yield to the British the preceding April. See "Esquadra
   Encouraçada, 26 Dez. 1868," *A Semana Illustrada* (Rio de Janeiro), 28 December 1868
   (3382). Comparisons with Ethiopia came naturally to Britons at this time, for Englishmen were then being held hostage by supposedly insane jailers both in Paraguay and in
   the benighted empire in East Africa. See "The Fate of Paraguay," *Fraser's Magazine*, 81
   (1870): 181–183.

4 The pattern of favoring community values and interests over those of the individual
   was established early in the colonial period in Paraguay. See Efraím Cardozo, *Apuntes*

de historia cultural del Paraguay, I: Epoca colonial (Asunción, n.d.), 167–181, and, more genrally, Juan Bautista Rivarola Paoli, *La colonización del Paraguay, 1537–1680* (Asunción, 2010).

5   Cecilio Báez, *Politica americana* (Asunción, 1925), 41; Julio José Chiavenatto, *Os Voluntários da Pátria* (São Paulo, 1983), 107; and more generally, Doratioto, *Maldita Guerra*, 374–382.

6   Thompson, *The War in Paraguay*, 308; the violent implications of the colonel's latter speculation were seconded by the longtime Lopista official José Falcón, who wrote in the 1870s that the Brazilian leadership had wanted all Paraguayans dead. See *Escritos históricos*, 100. With the exception of this one man, the imputation of a genocidal policy among the Allies received less than a ringing endorsement during the nineteenth century, but it has excited a passionate reaction from among the more eccentric and exasperating revisionist writers a hundred years later. The most obvious example of this trend was journalist Júlio José Chiavenato, who chose letters dripping with blood to sensationalize the cover illustration of his *Genocídio Americano. La guerra del Paraguay* (Asunción, 1989). The term "genocide," which Chiavenato uses with considerable imprecision, was coined in 1943 by Raphael Lemkin, a lawyer of Polish birth who wished to attract international attention to "crimes of barbarity," alluding, first, to the organized slaughter of Armenians by the Ottoman Turks earlier in the century, and second, to the Nazi butchery of the Jews. The General Assembly of the United Nations passed a convention on the topic in 1948 that incorporated much of Lemkin's language, defining genocide as "acts committed with intent to destroy, in whole or in part, a national, ethnical, racial, or religious group." Since the historical record makes no reference to any premeditated plan on the part of the Allies akin to a "Final Solution" for the Paraguayan "problem," to uncover a genocidal intent in their words and actions seems wildly and unforgivably exaggerated. It did sometimes happen that Paraguayan prisoners were killed out of hand (as in the aftermath of the 1865 battle of Yataí), but Allied prisoners were slain in similar circumstances by López from time to time. To use the word "genocide" to describe every atrocity panders to emotional reactions. It is bad enough that Chiavenato's text provides only the thinnest catalog of facts to serve as a basis for critical judgment, but in accusing the Allies of genocide, he stokes the baser attitudes of xenophobes in today's Paraguay who hate Brazilians just because they are Brazilians.

7   Thompson, *The War in Paraguay*, 308; McMahon's own testimony has nothing whatsoever in it to corroborate this story, and only affirms that, in his retreat, the Marshal "narrowly escaped capture by galloping almost unattended through the *monte*" and "was pressed at first by the enemy's infantry, who fired excitedly and too high." See McMahon to Seward, Piribebuy, 31 Jan. 1869 in NARA, M-128, no. 3, and "The War in Paraguay," 639.

8   Carlos Pusineri, the longtime director of the Casa de la Independencia in Asunción made this argument explicitly when interviewed for the 1987 Sylvio Back film "Guerra do Brasil." He should have known better, for despite the claims of certain conspiracy theorists, Masonic organizations played no role in Lopista Paraguay. Nor could they have, for their secretive bonds and esoteric rituals would surely have attracted the attention of the police. The idea that the Marshal was himself a Freemason, moreover, strains credulity for two obvious reasons. First, his Catholicism, which he learned from his uncle (the Bishop of Asunción), was expressly reactionary in its estimation of the Masons. Second, if there had been any lodges in the country their presence would presuppose a brotherhood of equals or near-equals and the Marshal never admitted his coequality with anyone, not with Mitre, Flores, or Caxias (all of whom were Masons), and certainly not with his own brothers Venancio and Benigno. Hence, any explanation for his escape that hinges on Masonic connections or a fraternal sympathy for his plight seems farfetched. While it is true that individual Masons were present in the foreign community of

Asunción before the war, they kept their heads low and formed no official associations. The British architect Alonzo Taylor does tell the curious story of Ernesto Tuvo, an Italian confidence man who attempted to extort money from foreigners resident in Paraguay as the price of their enrollment in an entirely fictitious lodge. Taylor's brief contact with this "mountebank" provided the excuse for the Briton's detention at the time of the San Fernando tribunals. The obscurity of the whole affair speaks for itself. See Taylor's testimony in Masterman, *Seven Eventful Years in Paraguay*, 319–320. Freemasonry did enjoy a vogue among the officers of the Paraguayan Legion, who established lodges in Asunción during the 1870s and whose "irritating sarcasm" was predictably condemned by Catholic clerics in Paraguay throughout the twentieth century. See Fidel Maíz to Juan Sinforiano Bogarín, Arroyos y Esteros, 29 April 1900, in *Autobiografía y cartas*, 265–268.

9   Proclamation of López, Cerro León, 28 Dec. 1868, in ANA-CRB I-30, 24, 43, reprinted in *La Estrella* (Piribebuy), 24 February 1869.

10   Washburn reported at the beginning of 1868 that cholera was "raging in the capitol [sic] and vicinity." See Washburn to Elihu Washburne, Asunción, 15 Jan. 1868, in WNL. His fears about the spread of an epidemic were confirmed three weeks later by the jefes políticos of Concepción, who noted that the disease had spread to his district and beyond. See Gaspar Benítez to War Minister, 3 February 1868, in ANA-CRB I-30, 15, 156.

11   Colonel Aveiro argues convincingly that, while "no one could justify the despotic acts of López, in truth he was much admired in life both by civilians and the men of the army, [and] despite his severity, he knew how to treat each of them well." See *Memorias militares*, 79. This was not so much charisma, which López also clearly possessed, as it was a natural affinity for commanding those beneath him (*saber mandar*). To the extent that this ability could be reduced to a traditional paternalism, the Marshal could depend on a Paraguayan society that regarded a father figure as absolutely necessary, particularly in times of crisis.

12   McMahon, "The War in Paraguay," 647.

13   To the Allied soldiers, Azcurra was a kingdom tantalizingly close to their forward lines that was nonetheless cunningly arranged along the heights of the hill, access to which could only be gained by a single pass whose limits and dangers they could not easily discern. See Resquín, *La guerra del Paraguay contra la Triple Alianza*, 110.

14   Alfredo d'Escragnolle Taunay, who arrived on the scene in April, immediately noted the transparent irony of a nominally republican president occupying such a gaudy palace, while his own imperial master lived in a relatively modest home in Rio de Janeiro. See Taunay, *Cartas da Campanha*, 8 (entry of 20 April 1869).

15   Proclamation of Fleet Commander, Asunción, 6 January 1869 (?), in BNRJ documents collection.

16   Centurión, *Memorias o reminiscencias*, 3: 213; Without allowing for the possibility that Argentine and Uruguayan soldiers were likewise capable of bad comportment vis-à-vis the women that fell into their hands, a disgusted General Garmendia denounced the Brazilians responsible for the mass rape after Avay, stating that they had "opened the valves to their savage lasciviousness, and those unhappy women who had seen their husbands, sons, and lovers perish, now suffered the outrage of the [enemy's] lust in that darkest of dark nights." See Garmendia, *Campaña de Pikyciri*, 346. The facts of this brutal incident are not disputed, but the tone of Garmendia's observation, which appears to single out Brazilian blacks, clearly owes much to the racism that all too often typified scholarly writing in the early twentieth century.

17   Though there were few local women in town at that moment, the streets soon "filled up with the most filthy Indian women [from the Chaco], who go about the city, their long hair down to the heels, and in the most perfect state of nudity; yet these women find a hearty welcome [from the soldiers]." "Important from Asunción," *The Standard* (Buenos

Aires), 20 January 1869. According to *La Tribuna* (Buenos Aires), one reason that there were so few Paraguayan women in sight was that the Brazilians were sending captured women north to the settlements in Mato Grosso, there to serve like "the Sabine women of ancient Rome" in founding a new society. Cited in Cardozo, *Hace cien años*, 11: 58–59. The story is ridiculous stated this way; but it was nonetheless true that some (but not all) Paraguayan women found Brazil more amenable than home. Whenever possible, they went north, presumably because their wrecked country offered them no future. In the mid-1870s, their presence evidently became a real problem and the Mato Grossense authorities started complaining about "gangs" of displaced *paraguayas* who, hungry and overbearing, were taxing civic virtue in their communities. It is unclear whether they arrived in the province during the war or immediately thereafter. Either way, the Brazilian officials thought them harpies ready to devour every portion of comestibles they could find and pounce on any unmarried man they could find. The officials were anxious to rid themselves of the displaced women "of the lowest possible class who bring with them the most repugnant vices, and ... and [who run] from washing clothes and every other aspect of proper women's work." See statement of João Lopes Carneiro da Fonseca, Corumbá (?), 17 February 1876, in Potthast-Jutkeit, *"¿Paraíso de Mahoma" o "País de las mujeres"?*, 328.

18   McMahon to Hamilton Fish, Buenos Aires, 19 July 1869, cited in Warren, *Paraguay and the Triple Alliance*, 19; Huner, "Saving Republics;" and Correspondence of Manuel A. de Mattos, Asunción, 27 February 1869, in *The Standard* (Buenos Aires), 5 March 1869 (which discusses the murder in broad daylight of a Paraguayan woman by a Brazilian corporal who acted from jealousy). The subject of rape as a byproduct of war has lately received much attention because of its widespread incidence in Africa and the Balkans since the 1990s. See Jonathan Gottschall, "Explaining Wartime Rape," *Journal of Sex Research* 41, no. 2 (2004): 129–136. Anthony Beevor's *The Fall of Berlin 1945* (New York, 2002), 409–415, cites a figure of 2 million German women and girls raped by Soviet soldiers "as a part of the extended celebrations" that marked the end of the war. The Russians clearly felt justified in avenging themselves for previous Nazi brutality on the Eastern Front. But it is doubtful that the revenge motive for wartime rape could have played a tremendous role in the fall of Asunción, for the Brazilians had never suffered any abuses at the hands of the Paraguayans that remotely approximated what the Nazis did in Russia. Nor had Allied officers ever issued orders or instructions for their men to follow the advice of Nestor of Pylos, who told his Greek hosts in the second book of *The Iliad* that they should "suffer no man to hurry homeward until he had first lain alongside the wife of some Trojan." To the extent that vengeance did play a role in events in early 1869, it harkened back to the Paraguayan occupation of towns in Mato Grosso and Rio Grande do Sul, and appropriately focused on looting rather than on rape. If vengeance deserves much attention as a motive in 1869, it was so intermingled with personal greed that it was hard to distinguish as a separate motivation. See Héctor Francisco Decoud, *Sobre los escombros de la Guerra. Una década de vida nacional* (Asunción, 1925), 1: 19–20, which records Brazilian soldiers sacking a private home and leaving behind upon its barren wall a scrawl or graffito that (quite falsely) alleged that the "Paraguayans were worse in Uruguaiana and Corrientes."

19   Doratioto, *Maldita Guerra*, 386; Juan B. Gill Aguinaga, "Excesos cometidos hace cien años," *Historia Paraguaya* 12 (1967–1968): 17–25. Manuel Domecq García, the child kidnapped in Asunción, was ransomed from the Brazilians for eight pounds sterling, and as an adolescent joined the Argentine navy, where he eventually rose to the rank of admiral. He served as minister of marine in the cabinet of Marcelo T. de Alvear (1922–1928). See also Bartolomé Yegros to Juan E. O'Leary, Recoleta, 8 January 1919, in O'Leary, *El libro de los heroes*, 471, who confirms (from his personal experience as a boy of nine years) that the kidnapping of children became commonplace in 1869.

20 The Paraguayans had imprisoned the wives of several Correntino officers who had resisted the Marshal's occupation of their province in 1865; five such women were removed at the end of the year to the interior of Paraguay, where they remained in captivity until 1869. See Testimony of María Bar de Ceballos, in *El Liberal* (Corrientes), 12 September 1869; "A Romance of the War" (regarding the misadventures of another Correntino captive, Carmen Ferré de Alsina, whose name is incorrectly given as Carmen M. de Pavón), *The Standard* (Buenos Aires), 25 September 1869; Delfor R. Scandizzo, "Entonces la mujer. La larga odisea de las cautivas correntinas," *Todo es Historia* 383 (June 1999): 44–46; Hernán Félix Gómez, *Ñaembé. Crónica de la guerra de López Jordán y de la epidemia de 1871* (Corrientes, 1997), 13; and Ramírez Braschi, *La guerra de la Triple Alianza a través de los periódicos correntinos (1865-1870)*, 198–201.

21 Adler Homero Fonseca de Castro, personal communication, Rio de Janeiro, 7 April 2011.

22 The Paraguayans had plundered freely on many occasions. But it should also be noted that friends as well as enemies can loot. In liberating Corrientes from Paraguayan occupation in 1865, Allied soldiers tore into many private residences and took what they wished from helpless residents. This opened a decades-long series of lawsuits conducted against the national government that demanded indemnities for losses sustained. See *Documentos que justifican la legitimidad de las deudas contra el gobierno de la Nación por suministros hechos al ejército de vanguardia nacional en Corrientes en armas contra el del Paraguay* (Buenos Aires, 1870), and Dardo Ramírez Braschi, *Consecuencias de la guerra contra el Paraguay en la provincia de Corrientes. Una aproximación al estudio de los daños, perjuicios, e indemnizaciones* (unpublished manuscript).

23 "From Montevideo to Paraguay," *Littel's Living Age* (5th ser.), 51 (July–September 1885): 98–99, and William Eleroy Curtis, *The Capitals of Spanish America* (New York, 1888), 638–640. See also Francisco Ignácio Marcondes Homem de Mello, "Viagem ao Paraguay em Fevereiro e Março de 1869," *Revista Trimensal do Instituto Histórico, Geographico e Etnographico Brasileiro*, (3rd Trim.) (1873): 22–25, which describes most of the other major public buildings after a month of Brazilian occupation.

24 Amerlan, *Nights on the Rio Paraguay*, 144; *La Tribuna* (Buenos Aires), 16 January 1869; Juan E. O'Leary, "El saqueo de Asunción," *La Patria* (Asunción), 1 January 1919; and Carlos Zubizarreta, "Asunción saqueada por las fuerzas aliadas," *La Tribuna* (Asunción), 19 December 1965.

25 The Brazilian soldiers emptied out the US Legation, seizing the furniture and archived papers, the official character of which Marshal López and his police had always respected, even during the confrontations with Washburn. See H. G. Worthington to Seward, Buenos Aires, 11 March 1869, in NARA, FM-69, roll 17. The consulates of Italy, Portugal, and France were also ransacked. Cited in Cardozo, *Hace cien años*, 11: 17.

26 Allied troops supposedly tore into family crypts at the Recoleta cemetery, stripping cadavers of their finery, but for some reason they spared the tomb of General Díaz, who even in death enjoyed a charmed existence. See Cardozo, *Hace cien años*, 11: 25–26.

27 As early as 1865, in fact, López authorized his officials in the countryside to execute burglars as a war measure. See Disposition of López, Asunción, 16 May 1865, in ANA-SH 343, no. 5.

28 Some of the Argentine soldiers got their wish in this respect, for the plunderers were sometimes willing to trade their spoils for comestibles. As the correspondent of *The Standard* (Buenos Aires) noted in the issue of 20 January 1869, "we hear of a brass bedstead being exchanged for a piece of beef and a few biscuits; a pound of potatoes is worth more than the best arm chair in Government House."

29 See "Editor's Table," *The Standard* (Buenos Aires), 31 March 1869; "Notícias locales. El conde d'Eu," *La República* (Buenos Aires), 3 April 1869; *La Capital* (Rosario), 27 January 1869; Decoud, *Sobre los escombros de la guerra*, 1: 37.

30 "Important from Asunción," *The Standard* (Buenos Aires), 20 January 1869; Martín de Gainza to Emilio Mitre, Buenos Aires, 23 Janury 1869, in Museo Histórico Nacional (Buenos Aires), Lc. 11811/11; "Más sobre el saqueo," *El Nacional* (Buenos Aires), 24 January 1869.

31 Warren, *Paraguay and the Triple Alliance*, 17–18. According to *The Standard* (Buenos Aires), 27 January 1869, General Mitre embargoed a large shipment of dried hides bound on Uruguayan account for the port of Montevideo, stopping the vessel as it entered Argentine waters.

32 The Legion had doubled in size since the fall of Humaitá—to eight hundred men in two units, one cavalry and one infantry. Argentine commentators were unwilling to exclude its members from charges of looting Asunción, placing them fourth in the list of perpetrators after the Brazilians, the camp followers, and the sutlers. See *La Capital* (Rosario), 13 and 24 February 1869, and *El Nacional* (Buenos Aires), 24 January 1869; Liliana M. Brezzo, "Civíles y militares durante la ocupación de Asunción: agents del espacio urbano, 1869," *Res Gesta* 37 (1998–1999): 32–34.

33 The Paraguayan vice president had issued a directive at the beginning of December that authorized the inhabitants of Asunción to return to the city by rail to remove furniture or other properties in advance of expected Allied depredations. From subsequent testimony, it does not appear that many people took advantage of this opportunity, which was in force for six days. The Allies later liked to claim that the sacking of the Paraguayan capital began before their troops came on the scene and point to this decree as proof that the Marshal's soldiers were free to do what they wished with any properties they found in the city. This was not an argument well calculated to justify the rampant looting engaged in by Brazilian and Uruguayan troops. See Decree of Sánchez, Luque, 1 Dec. 1868, in *La Nación Argentina* (Buenos Aires), 23 January 1869. Though he arrived in Asunción only in April, after the looting had mostly run its course, the Viscount of Taunay made much of the story that López's agents had looted the city during the previous December. Some of this had happened, in fact, but Taunay engaged in a bit of willful exaggeration when he claimed that the Marshal's "agents had fashioned skeleton keys or wrenched locks away" so as to sack houses at the Marshal's will. There was, to put a fine point on it, much left in the city for the Allies to plunder. See Visconde de Taunay, *Recordações da Guerra e de Viagem* (São Paulo, 1924), 98.

34 Although an occasional coin has turned up along the paths of retreat that the Marshal had taken, no large cache of *plata ybyguí* has ever been reported. The folkloric ramifications of hidden treasure are discussed in León Cadogan, "Plata Yviguy. Tesosoros escondidos," in Colección Félix. *Antología ibérica y americana del folklore* (Buenos Aires, 1953), 243–245.

35 "Latest from Asunción," *The Standard* (Buenos Aires), 23 January 1869; and "Sobre el saqueo de Asunción," *El Nacional* (Buenos Aires), 21 February 1869. Richard Burton was likewise willing to forgive the plundering, reminding those who would castigate the Brazilians "to remember certain glass houses at Hyderabad, Sind, and the Summer Palace, China." See *Letters from the Battle-fields of Paraguay*, 443.

36 Manoel Francisco Correia, "Saque de Assumpção e Luque atribuido ao Exército Brasileiro na Guerra do Paraguay: Refutação," *Revista do Instituto Histórico e Geographico Brasileiro* 59 (1896): 376–391 (originally composed in May 1871 as a reply to French claims for damages); *El Nacional* (Buenos Aires), 14 and 21 February 1869. See also Letter of Candido Carlos Prytz, Vice-Consul of Brazil, Corrientes, 13 January 1869, in *El Liberal* (Corrientes), 15 January 1869.

37 "Important from Asunción," *The Standard* (Buenos Aires), 20 January 1869.

38 The reason that so few of these foreign merchants left memoirs of their time in Paraguay was simply that there was no profit in it. Instead, they assembled an ongoing bazaar

adjacent to the Brazilian camps, near where the Allied soldiers operated a "furniture depot," where they traded loot for liquor, comestibles, and various consumer goods. In an intriguing twist on commodity fetishism, these soldiers grew uncommonly fond of the floral perfumes that the sutlers had in their stock; the men in uniform would empty whole bottles upon their persons and thereby enjoyed a concession to luxury. The less imaginative among them drank the stuff as a tonic. All their simple bartering, reminiscent of rural markets everywhere, made many sutlers momentarily wealthy (especially compared to their predecessors at Paso de la Patria). While it is true that a good number of these merchants eventually lost their fortunes, there were some who succeeded in turning their Asunción shops into major establishments during the 1870s. A new and highly influential elite of foreign-born businessmen (mostly Italians) developed in the Paraguayan capital from this early beginning, and eventually spread into the interior during a heyday of land-grabbing in the 1880s. In analyzing their impact during the final decades of the nineteenth century, see Juan Carlos Herken Krauer, "Economic Indicators for the Paraguayan Economy: Isolation and Integration (1869–1932)" (PhD dissertation, University of London, 1986).

39 Cardozo, *Hace cien años*, 11: 49. Senior officers appropriated all of the best residences in Asunción, with Emilio Mitre, for instance, setting up his personal quarters in Venancio López's former house.

40 "Correspondencia, Buenos Aires, 20 Jan. 1869," *Jornal do Commercio* (Rio de Janeiro), 29 January 1869; Homem de Mello, *O General José Joaquim de Andrade Neves*, 43–44; Canabarro Reichardt, "Centenário da Morte do Brigadeiro José Joaquim de Andrade Neves, Barão de Triunfo, 1869–1969," *Revista do Instituto Histórico e Geográfico Brasileiro* 285 (1969): 21–34.

41 João Carlos de Souza Ferreira to "meu Conselheiro [Paranhos?]," Rio de Janeiro, 8 February 1869, in IHGB DL 983.15, no. 2. Wounded in the liver during the Lomas Valentinas engagements, Machado Bittencourt died in Asunción on 4 April 1869.

42 "Ordem do Dia, no. 272, Asunción, 14 Jan. 1869," in Tasso Fragoso, *História de Guerra entre a Triplice Aliança e o Paraguai*, 4: 181–185.

43 "Important from Paraguay," *The Standard* (Buenos Aires), 31 January 1869 (the Caxias quote is in Portuguese in the original). Caxias never wavered in his class-based disdain for the plebeian soldiers under his command. In a note to the war minister of 2 September 1868, the marquis remarked that the majority of these men were the sort that "society repudiates for their vile qualities." See Arquivo Nacional. Codice 924, V. 4.

44 It was said that Guilherme's inaction smacked of an unwillingness to operate without clear instructions, seeing in this a degree of incompetence or even cowardice, with *The Standard* (Buenos Aires), 6 March 1869, going so far as to call the man a "poltrinaire" [*sic*]. This interpretation (or calumny) seems manifestly unfair to the general, who, besides being very sick, could not be expected to operate effectively in the absence of clear instructions from Rio de Janeiro. See [Quentino Souza de Bocaiuva], *Guerra do Paraguay. A Nova Phase.(Carta a um Amigo)* (Montevideo, 1869), 15–17. Bocaiuva later became a key leader of the anti-Positivist faction of the Republican movement.

45 Warren, *Paraguay and the Triple Alliance*, 19; Olmedo, *Guerra del Paraguay. Cuadernos de campaña*, 397–399 (February 1869); the functions of this commission evidently devolved in March into the hands of a commercial tribunal made up of three Brazilians, two Argentines, and two Uruguayans. The new body had no more success in imposing its decisions than that which preceded it. See "Teatro de la guerra," *La República* (Buenos Aires), 17 March 1869.

46 Chapperon to General Guillermo de Souza, Asunción, 6 February 1869, and Declaration of General Xavier de Souza, Asunción, 14 February 1869, in Fano, *El Consúl, la guerra, y la*

muerte, 132–138; Rufino de Elizalde to Bartolomé Mitre, Asunción, 17 March and 22 March 1869, in *Archivo del general Mitre*, 5: 220–222, and Brezzo, "Civiles y militares," 37–44.

47   The Uruguayan leaders received Caxias perfunctorily and with the same coldness that the Porteños had shown. See M. Maillefer to the Marquis de La Valette, Montevideo, 20 February 1869, in "Informes diplomáticos de los representantes de Francia en el Uruguay (1866–1869)," *Revista Histórica* 26, nos. 76–78 (1956): 357.

48   "Important from Rio. Caxias Dying," *The Standard* (Buenos Aires), 7 March 1869; Xavier Raymond, "Don Lopez et la Guerre du Paraguay," *Revue de Deux Mondes* 85 (1870): 1019.

49   "Pedro II e Cotegipe," *Revista do Instituto Histórico e Geographico Brasileiro* 98, no. 152 (1925): 280–281.

50   *Exército em Operações na Republica do Paraguay sob o commando em chefe interino de S. Ex. O Sr. Marechal de Campo Guilherme Xavier de Souza, Ordens do Dia, 1-13 (1869)* (Rio de Janeiro, 1877), 69, 145–146; Rocha Almeida, *Vultos da Pátria*, 143–147.

51   In its issue of 15 March 1869 the Carioca newspaper *Ba-Ta-Clan* upbraided the Conservative Party for having failed to contribute money to Ignácio's family during the time of his illness. Caxias was too ill to attend the admiral's funeral.

52   The institution of the monarchy had not fared well since February 1868, for politicians in Rio de Janeiro, as elsewhere, had long memories and had not forgotten the emperor's earlier support for Caxias. Ten months later, an anonymous poet, almost certainly a Liberal or a Republican, slipped an innocuous adulatory poem into the pages of *O Jornal do Commercio* (Rio de Janeiro), 2 December 1868. This turned out to be anything but innocuous or adulatory. The newspaper staff evidently failed to notice that the poem was an acrostic, with the first letters of each stanza spelled out "O bobo do rei faz annos" (the fool of a king is having a birthday), an unbelievably impudent allusion to dom Pedro that the opposition *Opinião Liberal* (Rio de Janeiro), gleefully pointed out—or celebrated—in its issue of 3 December. The justice minister reportedly called for the prosecution of the *Jornal's* owners, but eventually let the matter drop, possibly at the insistence of Pedro. The author of the poem was never identified, but his effrontery suggested that the Bragança monarchy needed a boost in 1869—and the Senate was clearly happy to oblige by once again proffering its support to Caxias. Hendrik Kraay, personal communication, Calgary, Alberta, 10 December 2010. A more conventional poem that celebrated the monarch and his generals can be found in A. J. Santos Neves, *Homenagem aos Herois Brasileiros na Guerra contra o Governo do Paraguay* (Rio de Janeiro, 1870).

53   *Discurso que o Marechal d'Exército José Joaquim de Lima e Silva, Duque de Caxias, pronunciou no Senado na Sessão de 15 de Julho de 1870* (Bahia, 1870), 21, 23–26, 30, 32–33; and Corselli, *La Guerra Americana*, 499–501.

54   Caxias's posthumous reputation might seem exaggerated to non-Brazilians, but for those who grew up in the light of his iconic image, it seemed a natural progression from hero to demigod. See, for example, Joaquim Pinto de Campos, *Vida do Grande Cidadão Brasileiro Luiz Alves de Lima e Silva* (Lisbon, 1878); Raymundo Pinto Seidl, *O Duque de Caxias. Esboço de Sua Gloriosa Vida* (Rio de Janeiro, 1903); Eugenio Vilhena de Moraes, *O Duque de Ferro* (Rio de Janeiro, 1933); and Manuel César Góes Monteiro, "Caxias, a Expressão do Soldado Brasileiro," *Correio da Manhã* (Rio de Janeiro), 12 July 1936.

55   Mariano Varela to José María da Silva Paranhos, Buenos Aires, 12 January 1869, in ANA-CRB I-30, 29, 29; Decree of Sarmiento, Buenos Aires, 10 February 1869, in *The Standard* (Buenos Aires), 12 February 1869.

56   Sarmiento to Emilio Mitre, Buenos Aires (?), 21 January 1869, in Sarmiento, *Obras*, 50: 126–128.

57   The 7 March 1869 issue of *The Standard* (Buenos Aires) reported, "López's men in many parts have abandoned his cause, and are daily flocking to the capital; and from the poor

people who now and then escape from the mountains it is known that the general feeling of the sorrowing population of that ruined land is to get rid of López and return to their homes." There was less to this observation than met the eye, for many refugees coming from the back country were fleeing not from the Marshal but from starvation, and would probably have rejoined López in the same way that refugees from Uruguaiana had risked everything to escape and serve the Marshal once again.

58   "Important from Paraguay," *The Standard* (Buenos Aires), 4 March 1869; Thomas Whigham, *La guerra de la Triple Alianza. Volumen III: Danza de muerte y destrucción* (Asunción, 2012), 319–324.

59   [José Segundo (?)] Decoud, "Después de la guerra," *El Liberal* (Corrientes), 24 January 1869; Warren, *Paraguay and the Triple Alliance*, 50–52; Juansilvano Godoi, *El baron de Rio Branco. La muerte del Mariscal López. El concepto de la patria* (Asunción, 1912), 229; "Informes del Dr. José Segundo Decoud (Asunción, 20 Apr. 1888)," in MHM (A)-CZ carpeta 125.

60   Warren, *Paraguay and the Triple Alliance*, 52.

61   Burton, *Letters from the Battle-fields of Paraguay*, 446.

62   A perusal of the 335 appended names—and the affirmative references within this document to the "valiant corps of volunteers"—attests to its strong *Legionario* orientation. The subsidizing of the Paraguayan Legion had been managed by the Argentines in a routine way, and most of the Paraguayans involved retained an affinity for their sponsors in Buenos Aires and shared their mistrust of the empire. Whether this mistrust could serve Argentine interests over the long run only time would tell. See Petition of Paraguayan Citizens to the Governments of the Alliance, Asunción, 20 February 1869, in Hector Francisco Decoud, *Los emigrados paraguayos en la guerra de la Triple Alianza*, 39–49; Eduardo Amarilla Fretes, *La liquidación de la guerra de la Triple Alianza contra el Paraguay (negociaciones diplomáticas)* (Asunción, 1941), 32–35.

63   Olmedo, *Guerra del Paraguay. Cuadernos de campaña*, 384 (entry of 11 January 1869).

64   Agricultural Censuses (1868–1869), in ANA-CRB I-30, 26, 78, nos. 1–33; "Notícias del 7 de marzo de 1869," in MHM (A), Colección Gill Aguinaga, carpeta 1, no. 21.

65   A labor draft for women had existed informally since at least 1866, when the vice president issued a circular ordering every family to labor in the fields "even on moonlit nights." See Circular of Sánchez, Asunción, 18 July 1866, in ANA-SH 351, no. 1. In subsequent years what had once been de facto along these lines became de jure. See, for example, Decree of Sánchez, Piribebuy, 9 January 1869, in ANA-CRB I-30, 28,3, no. 1; Circular of Sánchez, Piribebuy, 14 February 1869, in ANA-SH 356, no. 9; and the Resquín Order of 18 December 1868, which the Argentine compiler saw fit to denominate "Round-up of Women," in *Papeles de López. El tirano pintado por si mismo*, 81–82. In the end, there may have been upwards of one hundred fifty thousand women cultivating fields in the Cordillera during 1869, the great majority of whom refugees from other parts of Paraguay.

66   "The Paraguayan War," *The Standard* (Buenos Aires), 24 and 27 January 1869.

67   The juez político of Tobatí reported that three hundred displaced families had entered his *partido* in the hill country by mid-February, and that, while he was doing all in his power to support them with rations of corn that support could not last forever. See Cardozo, *Hace cien años*, 11: 109.

68   As late as 1868, the Paraguayan state provided periodic assistance to needy families displaced by the war, but this support (and the private support that the government also encouraged) generally came to an end once Asunción fell to the Allies. See List of Funds Provided for Deserving Families [1865], in ANA-SH 418, no. 1; Contributions to the Rural Poor, Recoleta, 4 March 1865, in ANA-SH 346, no. 4; Jueces de Paz to Marshal López,

5 Feb. 1868, in ANA-NE 1010; Decree of López, Paso Pucú, 25 February 1868, in ANA-SH 355, no. 5; Francisco Sánchez to Militia Chief at Valenzuela, Luque, 5 April 1868, in ANA-CRB I-30, 28, 3; and Gumersindo Benítez to Consul Cuverville, Luque(?), 18 April 1868, in ANA-CRB I-22, 11, 2, no. 39.

69   Fuerza efectiva records for Villarrica and other partidos (1868), in ANA-NE 1012.

70   For an example of a muster roll written on rawhide, see List of Able-bodied Troopers, 2nd Company, 4th Squadron, 32nd Regiment, Azcurra(?), 2 May 1868, in MG 2003.

71   John Hoyt Williams, *Rise and Fall of the Paraguayan Republic*, 221.

72   Statement of Lucás Carrillo (February 1869) in Cardozo, *Hace cien años*, 11: 136.

73   In a brief note, the *jefe político* at Villarrica informed the authorities of the many women and children passing through his district as refugees on the way to the Cordillera, hinting broadly that the threat of epidemic disease was driving them forward as much as any government dicta. See José Antonio Basaral to Luis Caminos, Villarrica, 4 February 1869, in ANA-CRB I-30, 27, 62, no. 5.

74   Several of the interior communities were still able to send supplies to the Marshal's army between February and May 1869. Cattle came from Caazapá, Valenzuela, Ajos, San Estanislao, Yuty, and Mbocayaty; maize from Caazapá, Tobatí, Caraguatay, and the very distant Ygatymí; cloth and clothing from Tacuatí, Itacurubí de la Cordillera, San Estanislao, and San Joaquín; molasses from Mbocayaty and Itapé; onions from Carapeguá and Mbocayaty; and yerba mate—the standard beverage—from the single distant community of Unión. See Seferino Colmán to War Minister (?), San Estanislao, 28 February 1869, in ANA-NE 2508; Pantaleon Insaurralde to Luis Caminos, San Joaquín, 13 May 1869, in ANA-CRB I-30, 27, 66, no. 1; and Cardozo, *Hace cien años*, 11: 109, 119–120, 122–124, 159, 183–184, 192, 228–229, 233, 236, 239, 254, 258, 262, and 311.

75   Centurión thought the Marshal's interest in Chateaubriand constituted a "distraction for his spirit, as a way to ease his conscience from [the weight] of so many deeds that were difficult or impossible to justify." See *Memorias o reminiscencias*, 4: 28–29.

76   Cited in Héctor Francisco Decoud, *La convención nacional constituyente y la carta magna de la república* (Buenos Aires, 1934), 40.

77   Pedro A. Alvarenga Caballero, "Villa Real de Concepción en los días de la ocupación brasileña," *Historia Paraguaya* 39 (1999): 59–68; historically the central government found good reasons to suspect the elaboration of strong dissident factions in Concepción, San Pedro, and the other northern towns. So it was with Dr. Francia in 1813–1816, with Higínio Morínigo in 1946–1947, and with the Colorado traditionalists in 2007–2008.

78   Héctor F. Decoud described the slaughter as the cruelest and most unjustifiable act of the entire war. The atrocity does not improve on closer examination. See Decoud, *La massacre de Concepción ordenada por el Mcal. López* (Asunción, 1926); Nidia R. Areces, "Terror y violencia durante la guerra del Paraguay: 'La massacre de 1869' y las familias de Concepción," *European Review of Latin American and Caribbean Studies* 81 (October 2006): 43–63; Cardozo, *Hace cien años*, 11: 319, and 12: 86–88; and Resquín, *La guerra del Paraguay*, 113–114. The chief culprit in the Concepción atrocity, an antediluvian figure best known by his evocative nickname, "Bull-Strong," (Toro Pichaí), was a cavalry major who after the war worked as a foreman on the Decoud estate outside Emboscada.

79   This figure amounted to about half the individuals executed at San Fernando and along the Pikysyry during the period of the tribunals of blood. See "Victimas de la tiranía," *El Orden* (Asunción), 21 December 1923.

80   Juan F. López to José Falcón, Azcurra, 15 March 1869, in ANA CRB I-30, 27, 93.

81   "Testimony of Dr. Skinner (Asunción, 25 Jan. 1871)," in Scottish Record Office, CS 244/543/19.

82 In the inaugural issue of *Estrella* (Piribebuy), 24 February 1869, the editor defined his mission as promoting "the duties of man to the Patria and its Government; to stimulate and fulfill those duties; to attack vice wherever it is found; to combat indolence and excite in all a holy enthusiasm for the national cause." These stated objectives, while appropriate coming from a priest, shed little light on who the editor considered his readership to be. It may have been distributed in limited numbers at Azcurra, but the men who saw it were monolingual speakers of Guaraní and unlikely to understand the nuances the writers placed in their articles. The limited number of Spanish speakers in the Cordillera could not justify the expenditure of paper and ink needed to print each edition. It seems reasonable, therefore, to suppose that the readership for this last Lopista newspaper was mostly limited to the López entourage and to the Marshal himself—a supposition that provides still more proof for the oddity of the political atmosphere in unoccupied Paraguay. See Victor Simón Bovier, "El ultimo combatiente: Estrella," *La Tribuna* (Asunción), 26 April 1970.

83 Elizalde to Mitre, Asunción, 22 March 1869, in *Correspondencia Mitre-Elizalde*, 460–461; "Teatro de la guerra," *La República* (Buenos Aires), 18 March 1869. Regarding fodder, though scrub-grass was hardly lacking in Paraguay, the horses had shown little taste for it, and while starving or malnourished men can sometimes fight well, horses tend to be useless without adequate feed.

84 Olmedo, *Guerra del Paraguay. Cuadernos de campaña*, 388–389, 400–401 (March 1869).

85 Cardozo, *Hace cien años*, 11: 18–20, 323; E.A.M. Laing, "Naval Operations in the War of the Triple Alliance, 1864–70," *Mariner's Mirror* 54 (1968): 278; Ouro Preto, *A Marinha d'Outrora*, 210–212.

86 Cardozo, *Hace cien años*, 11: 93; "Latest from Paraguay," *The Standard* (Buenos Aires), 5 March 1869.

87 The locomotive did not become operational until the last days of April. See "Fetes and Fights," *The Standard* (Buenos Aires), 5 May 1869; "Correspondencia, Luque 14 May 1869," *Jornal do Commercio* (Rio de Janeiro), 31 May 1869.

88 On the first leg of their journey from Pirayú, the Paraguayan raiders were accompanied by Madame Lynch, General Caballero, the war minister, and Minister McMahon, but it seems that all of these high-placed individuals got off before the train reached the Yuquyry. "Sucesos del ejército," *La Estrella* (Piribebuy), 24 March 1869. The Brazilians reported a mere five men wounded, but Burton, who arrived in Asunción a bit later, thought the figure closer to forty. He also reported that the train was armored as a "railway battery." See *Letters from the Battle-fields of Paraguay*, 449.

89 "Chronique," *Ba-Ta-Clan* (Rio de Janeiro), 5 April 1869; "Correspondencia, Asunción, 14 Apr. 1869," *Jornal do Commercio* (Rio de Janeiro), 29 April 1869; Elizalde to Mitre, Asunción, 11 March 1869, in *Correspondencia Mitre-Elizalde*, 453.

90 *Jornal do Commercio* (Rio de Janeiro), 7 April 1869.

91 Olmedo, *Guerra del Paraguay. Cuadernos de campaña*, 400–401 (entry of 15–31 March 1869); "Latest from Paraguay," *The Standard* (Buenos Aires), 5 March 1869; Cardozo, *Hace cien años*, 11: 285–286.

92 Burton, *Letters from the Battle-fields of Paraguay*, 465–467.

93 Eldest son of the Duke of Nemours, Gaston was six years old when he witnessed the catastrophe that drove the whole family of his grandfather, Louis Philippe, King of the French, into exile. His family had never regained its previous luster in Europe, but in associating himself with the House of Bragança, he left behind a quiet life of leisurely indulgence and embarked on one of action. See Heitor Moniz, *A Corte de D. Pedro II* (Rio de Janeiro, 1931), 73–80; Helio Vianna, *Estudos de História Imperial* (São Paulo, 1950), 239–255.

94 William Scully, *Brazil. Its Provinces and Chief Cities* (London, 1866), 3; Roderick J. Barman, *Princess Isabel of Brazil. Gender and Power in the Nineteenth Century* (Wilmington, 2002), 61–119; Pedro Calmon, *A Princesa Isabel "a Redentora"* (São Paulo, 1941); Lourenço L. Lacombe, *Isabel a Princesa Redentora (biografia baseada em documentos inéditos)* (Petrópolis, 1989).

95 See Gaston d'Orléans to War Minister, Petropolis, 28 January 1868, in IHGB, lata 314, pasta 10, no. 14.

96 Alberto Rangel, *Gastão de Orleans (o ultimo Conde d'Eu)* (São Paulo, 1935), 209; Barman, *Citizen Emperor*, 226–228.

97 In a letter to the Argentine president, General Wenceslao Paunero observed that Gaston felt it dishonorable to assume leadership over an army that had won the war already and did everything in his power to decline the offer of command. See Paunero to Sarmiento, Rio de Janeiro, 28 March 1869, in Doratioto, *Maldita Guerra*, 398–399.

98 Barman, *Citizen Emperor*, 211–212, 216–217, 227–228. One of the few who voiced disapproval of the count's taking command in Paraguay was Dona Isabel, who clearly wanted her husband to stay at home. She did not mince words with her father, to whom she wrote, "I remember, Daddy, that by the Tijuca waterfall three years ago, you told me that passion is blind. I hope that your passion for the war has not blinded you! It seems that you want to kill my Gaston. … [Our physician] strongly advises him against too much exposure to the sun, and no rain and damp; how can he avoid these things if he is in the midst of a war?" Cited in Schwarcz, *The Emperor's Beard*, 243.

99 "The Seat of War," *The Standard* (Buenos Aires), 28 April 1869.

100 In his *História da Guerra entre a Triplice Aliança e o Paraguai*, 5: 5–47, General Tasso Fragoso gives the count some credit as a field commander but generally ignores his work as an organizer of the troops. Francisco Doratioto does much the same in *Maldita Guerra*, 396–402, stressing instead that Prince Gaston really did not wish to be in Paraguay in the first place.

101 Osório's courage was one of the great staples of the imperial army, like feijão or hardtack, and everyone wished to partake of it once again. Osório could not effectively use his lower jaw, however, and was still suppurating from the earlier wound. He accepted command of the 1st Corps only on condition that doctors always accompany him to the field. This stipulation was granted, for the Baron of Muritiba understood that the Riograndense's natural aggressiveness would lift moral among the Brazilian troops. See Doratioto, *Maldita Guerra*, 400.

102 Taunay, *Recordações de Guerra e de Viagem* (São Paulo, 1924), 10–11, 18–22; *Memórias do Visconde de Taunay* (n.p., 1960), 320–323.

103 Taunay thought that the count's efficiency and professionalism exceeded that of all the previous Allied commanders. See *Recordações de Guerra e de Viagem*, 31.

104 Taunay who owed political debts to the Conservatives, and did not take kindly to the count's order that he tender his services as war correspondent to the Liberal newspaper *A Reforma*. This might seem like a trivial matter, but the two men were equally unyielding, and refused for a time to converse with each other except while on duty. See Taunay, *Memórias*, 320–325.

105 With friends like the Swiss zoologist Louis Agassiz and his wife, the Count d'Eu always seemed "gay, easy, cordial, and with the self-possession and unconsciousness of perfect good breeding." See Elizabeth Cary Agassiz to Mrs. Thomas G. Cary, Rio de Janeiro, 25 January 1872, in Lucy Ellen Paton, *Elizabeth Cary Agassiz: A Biography* (Boston, 1919), 124. Others held the opposite opinion. Brazilian critics of a later generation portrayed the count as the problem child of the Paraguayan conflict, but getting a proper sense of the new Allied commander was already difficult in 1869. His contemporaries revered or reviled him, and always compared unfavorably him to Caxias. Gaston was by turns attractive and repugnant,

honest and deceitful, fanatically patriotic, and too obviously a foreigner for the taste of most Brazilians. In the 1860s and '70s his efforts were misunderstood, though his sincerity went unquestioned, and in later years it was the other way around. See Rocha Almeida, *Vultos da Pátria*, 2: 98–104; Barman, *Princess Isabel*, 104–110.

106   Leuchars, *To the Bitter End*, 218; morale among the Brazilian troops had been seriously tested by Caxias's departure and by the political calculations of Carioca Liberals, who saw to it that their newspapers, brimming with antiwar sentiments, circulated among the men stationed in Asunción. See Doratioto, *Maldita Guerra*, 395.

107   An English translation does poor service to the rhythm scheme of this tune, which was sung by soldiers on the way from Asunción to the battlefront in the hill country. The Portuguese runs:

> Quem chegou até a Assumpção
> Acabou a sua missão.
> Si o Lopes ficou no paiz
> Foi porque o Marquez o quiz!
> Quem marcher p'ra Cordilheira
> Faz uma grande asneira!

O Alabama (Salvador da Bahia), 5 June 1869.

14 | RESISTANCE TO NO AVAIL

1   The search for "laws" or "principles of war" goes back to at least as far as Caesar's *Commentaries on the Gallic Wars*. In the nineteenth century the Baron de Jomini was particularly known for his elaboration on this quest, but the American Henry Wagner Halleck and the Germans Colmar Freiherr von der Goltz and Hans Delbrück also provided impressive examples of this trend in military scholarship. The experience of the First World War and the general decline of positivism in the military academies and staff colleges witnessed a broad rejection of this approach in later generations. See J. D. Hittle, *Jomini and His Summary of the Art of War* (Harrisburg, 1959); Halleck, *Elements of Military Arts and Science* (New York, 1862); von der Goltz, *Das Volk in Waffen, ein Buch über Heerwesen und Kriegführung unsere Zeit* (Berlin, 1883); Delbrück, *History of the Art of War* (Lincoln and London, 1990); and, more generally, Peter Paret et al., eds., *Makers of Modern Strategy from Machiavelli to the Nuclear Age* (Oxford, 1986).

2   Writing in late April, US minister Martin T. McMahon noted with egregious imprecision that the Paraguayan army had "greatly improved in numbers and in enthusiasm and looks forward with extraordinary confidence to the next encounter with the enemy, which there is good reason to believe will be the decisive battle of the war." See McMahon to Secretary of State, Piribebuy, 21 April 1869, in NARA, M-128, no. 3.

3   Cirilo Solalinde, who had saved the Marshal's life earlier in the war, saw no generosity in Madame Lynch's distribution of food to the soldiers. Indeed, while

> the army was in Cordilleras, she ordered the local authorities to bring to her all the provisions. The order was fulfilled, and she appropriated for her own use a great quantity of those provisions; so that, up to the close of the war, she had a superabundance of everything, while thousands of soldiers and women and children were dying of hunger. In 1869 salt was very scarce and dear. The soldiers did not get a grain, and for that want many died, whilst all the time Madame Lynch had four hundred arrobas (10,000 lbs.) in store; but she would not part with an ounce of it, except now and then in the purchase of some jewelry still remaining in the possession of its owner. The result was that the greater part of the salt, which would have done much good, was lost; for in January 1870 it was thrown away, to prevent

its falling into the hands of the enemy. The only portion which was rendered useful was what soldiers of the guard could carry away with them.

See "Testimony of Dr. Solalinde (Asunción, 14 Jan. 1871)," in Scottish Record Office, CS 244/543/19. Despite the above criticism (and that of Stewart, Skinner, and other witnesses), there were individuals who continued to praise Madame Lynch's personal generosity and affection long after the war ended.

4   The war correspondent of the *Jornal do Commercio* (Rio de Janeiro) stated in the issue of 12 March that the Marshal's garrison had grown to some five thousand men. A month and a half later this number had expanded by two thousand, though this calculation included boys of ten years old scoured from the most remote communities still under Paraguayan control. See Falcón, *Escritos históricos*, 99–100.

5   *The Standard* (Buenos Aires) reported in its issue of 25 April 1869, that the Caacupé arsenal "is almost the last vestige of civilization [in Paraguay]; here the greatest activity still reigns, the few foreign engineers that yet remain are compelled under pain of death to turn out so many guns, drums, and swords each day." The European machinists were still receiving pay for their work in the Caacupé arsenal as late as June 1869. See pay receipts for 1 April, 1 May, and 1 June 1869, in ANA-NE 780, and request for salary for Jakob Wladislaw, Piribebuy, 4 June 1869, in ANA-NE 2509. Eventually, the arsenal produced eighteen cannon, two of iron and sixteen of bronze. See Resquín, "Declaración," in *Papeles de López. El tirano pintado por si mismo*, 156.

6   Leuchars, *To the Bitter End*, 216.

7   Taunay, *Memórias*, 367–368, 372–374; Dispatch of the Count d'Eu, Pirayú, 28 June 1869, in NARA, M-121, no. 37.

8   In Portuguese, the verse went:

> Osório dava churrasco
> E Polidoro farinha.
> O Marqués deu-nos jabá,
> E sua Alteza sardinha!

See Cerqueira, *Reminiscencias da Campanha*, 160.

9   "The Seat of War," *The Standard* (Buenos Aires), 14 May 1869, and Cardozo, *Hace cien años*, 11: 273–274.

10 Cerqueira, *Reminiscencias da Campanha do Paraguai*, 348–350; Cardozo, *Hace cien años*, 11: 294–296; Hélio Vianna, *Estudos de História Imperial* (São Paulo, 1950), 235–237. One man who wished to participate in the Allied advance, but whose services were rejected, was Antonio de la Cruz Estigarribia, the Marshal's former commander at Uruguaiana, who had spent four years living in comfortable circumstances as a prisoner of war in Rio de Janeiro, and who evidently wished to thank his hosts by offering to act as a guide for Prince Gaston's troops. His somewhat pathetic petition to that effect never received an answer from the emperor, and the Paraguayan colonel dropped out of sight once again. He died of plague in Asunción in December 1870, having returned to his country only a few days earlier. See Walter Spalding, *A Invasão Paraguaia no Brasil* (São Paulo, 1940), 282–283; "Recortes de jornais trazendo notícias da guerra," in ANA-CRB I-30, 30, 24; and Pedro Zipitria to Darío Brito de Pino, Fortaleza de San Juan (Rio de Janeiro), 6 December 1865, in AGN (M). Archivos Particulares, caja 10, carpeta 22, no 17 (in which an imprisoned Blanco officer laments his own misery at the hands of the Brazilians while "that rapist, incendiary, and plunderer" Estigarribia lives "luxuriously in a hotel with 300 *petacones* a month given him to satisfy his various whims").

11 Just before First Tuyutí, the foundry's commandant listed eighty-six cannonballs produced over the preceeding two weeks along with pieces for the waterwheels of the Paraguayan steamers. See Julián Ynsfrán, 17 May 1866, in ANA-NE 2436. Monthly reports

from 1868 attest to a continued production of cannonballs, sabers, bayonets, and the like, though quantities had fallen appreciably. See Ynsfrán to War Minister, Foundry of Ybycuí, 31 January 1868, in ANA-CRB I-30, 14, 154, nos. 1–3; Ynsfrán to War Minister, Foundry of Ybycuí, 31 March 1868, in ANA-CRB I-30, 14, 158, no. 1; Ynsfrán to Treasurer, Foundry of Ybycuí, 18 August 1868, in ANA-NE 2495; Ynsfrán to War Minister, Foundry of Ybycuí, 30 September 1868, in ANA-CRB I-30, 14, 162, nos. 1–3; Ynsfrán to War Minister, Foundry of Ybycuí, 16 October 1868, in ANA-CRB I-30, 14, 166; and Benigno Riquelme García, "La fundición de Ybycuí, 1849–1869," *La Tribuna* (Asunción), 20 May 1965.

12   The Count d'Eu may have viewed his (ostensibly) Uruguayan allies rather like a bag of ferrets around his neck, but he had no intention of seeing them slip away from their commitments. See Casal, "Uruguay and the Paraguayan War," 136.

13   Castro married the woman, Teresa Meraldi, in mid-June. See Marriage certificate, Asunción, 14 June 1869, in AGN (M). Archivos Particulares, caja 70, carpeta 1.

14   Casal, "Uruguay and the Paraguayan War," 135.

15   Gustavo Barroso, *A Guerra do Lopez* (Rio de Janeiro, 1939), 219. Some twenty European engineers were also present at the ironworks until early 1868, but it appears that they had been withdrawn to Caacupé before the December campaign. See Pla, *The British in Paraguay*, 147. See also José Antonio Seifert, *Os Sofrimentos dum Prisioneiro ou o Martir da Pátria* (Fortaleza, 1871).

16   "The Seat of War," *The Standard* (Buenos Aires), 29 May 1869.

17   Hipólito Coronado to Enrique Castro, near Franco Islas, 15 May 1869, in Tasso Fragoso, *História da Guerra entre a Tríplice Aliança e o Paraguai*, 4: 217–219; "Correspondencia, Luque, 20 May 1869," *Jornal do Commercio* (Rio de Janeiro), 12 June 1869.

18   Whigham, *The Paraguayan War*, 370–371.

19   Barroso, *A Guerra do Lopez*, 223–224; Several sources, most notably José Bernardino Bormann, claim that the initial decision was to shoot the Paraguayan captain, but Coronado ordered the decapitation when he discovered that the Allied prisoners had received similar treatment. See *História da Guerra do Paraguay*, 1: 22. Coronado later attempted to justify the killing by claiming that Captain Ynsfrán had brought on needless bloodshed in defending the foundry and had sought to execute his prisoners at the time of the Allied approach; though his soldiers had disobeyed this order, any man capable of issuing it, the major reasoned, deserved a swift execution. The obvious injustice of Coronado's thinking and his own brutality were widely condemned, even by General Castro and the Count d'Eu. The latter, who noted that executions were neither habitual among the Allies nor permitted by the rules of war, nonetheless observed that Ynsfrán's death was loudly applauded by those prisoners who had suffered at his hands. See Campanha do Paraguay. Comando em Chefe de S.A. o Sr. Marechal do Exército Conde d'Eu. *Diário do Exército* (Rio de Janeiro, 1870), 30.

20   Edgar L.Ynsfrán, "Fin de la 'Fabrica de fierro' de Ybycuí (13 de mayo de 1869)," *La Tribuna* (Asunción), 11 June 1972.

21   Juan F. Pérez Acosta, *Carlos Antonio López. Obrero máximo. Labor administrativa y constructiva* (Asunción, 1948), 194–196; "Chronique," *Ba-Ta-Clan* (Rio de Janeiro), 3 July 1869.

22   Coronado's exploit won the Oriental Division a general promotion from the Montevideo government for all those ranked sergeant and above. See Martínez, *Vida militar de los generales Enrique y Gregorio Castro*, 269–270; Olmedo, *Guerra del Paraguay. Cuadernos de campaña*, 411 (31 May 1869); Casal, "Uruguay and the Paraguayan War," 135.

23   McMahon, "The War in Paraguay," 644–645; Potthast-Jutkeit, *"¿Paraíso de Mahoma" o "País de las mujeres"?*, 269–279; Juan Martín Anaya to Sánchez, Valenzuela, 25 July 1869,

in ANA-NE 2509; and, more generally, Cardozo, *Hace cien años*, 11: 124, 130–131, 139, 144, 181, 275, 284.

24   From the time he landed in Paraguay to his return to the Argentine capital in July 1869, McMahon sent only nine dispatches to the State Department. These missives dealt exclusively with the official conduct of his mission and reveal little concerning the more controversial side of his activities. McMahon's relations with López have offered considerable room for speculation, but their diplomatic intercourse was largely confined to verbal communication after the minister took up his duties in Piribebuy. See Hughes, "General Martin T. McMahon and the Conduct of Diplomatic Relations," 47–48.

25   McMahon to Seward, Piribebuy, 31 January 1869, in NARA, Records Group 59. *The Times* (London) reported a false rumor in its 25 June 1869 issue to the effect that López had at last agreed to leave the country, thanks to the efforts of the US minister.

26   Cardozo, *Hace cien años*, 11: 116–117.

27   Cardozo, *Hace cien años*, 11: 88–89; Taunay, *Cartas de Campanha*, 62–65.

28   "Correspondencia, Asunción, 20 May 1869," in *Jornal do Commercio* (Rio de Janeiro), 15 June 1869.

29   McMahon to Luis Caminos, Piribebuy, 20 June 1869, in ANA-CRB I-30, 11, 17, nos. 1–2. For reasons best known to him, Elihu appended an *e* to the end of his surname, a choice that all of his descendants have had to live with.

30   Along with official messages for his agents in Europe, the Marshal also sent a letter with McMahon addressed to his estranged son Emiliano Victor, who was then living in Paris. He advised the young to move to the United States to take up the legal profession and help Paraguay accordingly. See López to Emiliano López, Azcurra, 28 June 1869, in *Proclamas y cartas del mariscal López* (Asunción), 192–199; Cardozo, *Hace cien años*, 12: 173–174; Saeger, *Francisco Solano López and the Ruination of Paraguay*, 183–185.

31   See Cecilio Báez, *La tiranía en el Paraguay, sus causas, caracteres y resultados* (Asunción, 1903), 179, which claims that the "counting of coin went on for several days and nights in an office situated to the back of the police station in Piribebuy, [and that] large boxes were taken away one morning beneath the gaze of the entire population." In a letter from Dr. Stewart's brother to Washburn, it was noted that among the papers found on Madame Lynch after she fell prisoner in March 1870 was a copy of a letter written to McMahon, which entrusted "to him some money to be deposited with the Bank of England, amounting to several thousand pounds." See C. Stewart to Washburn, Galashiels, 27 November 1870, in WNL. For other estimations on the quantity of coin and other valuables the minister carried out of Paraguay, see Cardozo, *Hace cien años*, 12: 180–181; Warren, *Paraguay and the Triple Alliance*, 20; and Hughes, "General Martin T. McMahon and the Conduct of Diplomatic Relations," 69–70.

32   Harris G. Warren, "Litigations in English Courts and Claims against Paraguay Resulting from the War of the Triple Alliance," *Inter-American Economic Affairs* 22, no. 4 (1969): 31–46.

33   The Allied press speculated endlessly about these trunks. Some gossips reported having seen as many as thirty boxes, each one weighing so much that it required eight men to lift it. See "Los catorce cajones del General MacMahon," *La Nación Argentina* (Buenos Aires), 9 July 1869. The then Argentine minister to the United States noted in a missive to the wife of Horace Mann that McMahon's baggage "must have included jewels and other valuables sent out by López … while the naked Paraguayans are dying from hunger." See Manuel R. García to Mary Mann, Berkeley Springs, 24 August 1869, in Mary Mann Papers. US Library of Congress. Ms. 2882. Mary Mann, it will be recalled, was Sarmiento's English translator, providing him, most notably, with the standard English version of his classic essay, "Facundo."

34   A. Rebaudi, *El Lopizmo*, 45–48. The perambulations of unopened trunks of Lopista loot presented a major focus for many would-be treasure seekers in later years. McMahon appears to have carried all the coin entrusted to him to London and New York and turned it over to designated parties in those cities. With Washburn, however, the uncertain circumstances in Asunción resulted in many properties formally under his care being lost or left in the care of others. The US government did eventually deliver to Paraguayan authorities one box of minor baubles left behind at the American Legation at Petrópolis. By then, however, sixty years had passed and inventories had been lost or thrown away. See Victor C. Dahl, "The Paraguayan 'Jewel Box,'" *The Americas* 21, no. 3 (1965): 223–242. Madame Lynch, we should remember, had on several occasions sent monies out on neutral ships (Italian and French as well as American).

35   McMahon's detractors made him into a receiver of stolen property. One congressional representative from Kentucky speculated openly that the former minister received money for the help he gave the Marshal and Madame Lynch: "He ingratiated himself with [the two, and guarded their interests] faithfully. … I hold in my hand an inventory of a part of what was thus entrusted to General McMahon's charge as executor; and it is worthy of remark that five percent commission would give him in that capacity three times the salary of any American Minister." See "Statement of Representative Beck of Kentucky," Cong. Globe, 41st Congress, 3rd Sess. 1 (1866–1867), bk. 1: 339. In making much the same accusation against McMahon, General José Bernardino Bormann noted that "for many men, the dollar has a magical power." See *História da Guerra do Paraguay*, 1: 36.

36   Aveiro, *Memorias militares*, 82–85; *La República* (Buenos Aires), 17 March 1869.

37   López to Allied Commander in Chief, Headquarters, 29 May 1869, in *The Standard* (Buenos Aires), 10 June 1869; Count d'Eu to López, Pirayú, 29 May 1869, in *The Standard* (Buenos Aires), 11 June 1869; ANA-SH 356, no 5, and ANA-CRB I-30, 21, 69.

38   McMahon Letters (15–18 June 1869), in ANA-CRB I-30, 11, 16, nos. 1–4. The Paraguayan government expended most of its precious supplies of paper in publishing multiple copies of this correspondence in *Documentos oficiales relativos al abuso de la bandera nacional paraguaya por los gefes aliados* (Piribebuy, 1869), 1.

39   The poem was placed in an album owned by Madame Lynch, and rested unexamined for many years in a private historical collection in Rio de Janeiro. It was afterwards translated into Spanish by Pablo Max Ynsfrán and published as "Resurgirás Paraguay!" *Historia Paraguaya* 1 (1956): 66–68. The original English-language version is included as an appendix in Hughes, "General Martin T. McMahon and the Conduct of Diplomatic Relations," 99–101.

40   McMahon to Fish, Buenos Aires, 19 July 1869, in NARA, Records Group 59.

41   Cerqueira, *Reminiscencias da Campanha*, 348–360.

42   "Sucesos del ejército," *Estrella* (Piribebuy), 3 June 1869; Taunay, *Cartas da Campanha*, 36–37.

43   Cardozo, *Hace cien años*, 12: 86–88; *Campanha do Paraguay. Diário do Exército*, 75 [entry of 2 June 1869]; Doratioto, *Maldita guerra*, 403–404; Resquín, *La guerra del Paraguay contra la Triple Alianza*, 114–115; Lidgerwood to Seward, Rio de Janeiro (?), 24 July 1869, in NARA, M-121, no. 37.

44   General Resquín claimed that after the battle the Brazilians despoiled all the poor families of the district, stealing everything they could find, raping women and boys, and sowing the seeds of real hatred for the Allies throughout the region. See *Guerra del Paraguay*, 114–115. Dionísio Cerqueira mentioned the women who fell into Brazilian hands at some length, but made no admission of his countrymen having raped anyone. See *Reminiscencias da Campanha*, 362–366. Cecilio Báez mentions the thefts but not the

rape. See Báez to Juan B. Dávalos, Asunción, 1924, in "La guerra del Paraguay. Matanza de familias, oficiales, y soldados," *El Orden* (Asunción). 28 August 1924.

45 See Kolinski, *Independence or Death!*, 182.

46 Centurión, *Memorias o reminiscencias*, 4: 57–59; "Correspondencia (Buenos Aires, 9 June 1869)," *Jornal do Commercio* (Rio de Janeiro) 16 June 1869.

47 The war correspondent for *The Standard* (Buenos Aires), 17 June 1869, reported that the "families rescued by General Mena Barreto exceeded 12,000 in number" but this figure must surely be an error. Perhaps he meant 12,000 individuals, but even that number, given what Centurión and other eyewitnesses claimed, would seem exaggerated. The *Jornal do Commercio* (Rio de Janeiro), 21 June 1869, mentions 4,000 families saved.

48 Taunay, *Diário do Exército, 1869-1870*, 69–70; Paraguayan sources hint that these people were forced to accompany the Brazilians on their retreat towards Pirayú, but there was no precedent for any coercion in such matters, and there seems little reason to doubt that they came of their own free will "to get out of their misery." See Centurión, *Memorias y reminiscencias*, 4: 58–59; Resquín, *La guerra del Paraguay contra la Triple Alianza*, 115–116.

49 See "Brazil. Letters of López and the Count d'Eu. Progress of the Allies. Their Recent Successes," *New York Times*, 20 July 1869; "The Seat of War," *The Standard* (Buenos Aires), 2 July 1869. The Viscount of Taunay remembered them as "walking cadavers." See *Recordações de Guerra e de Viagem*, 42, and *Cartas da Campanha*, 50–51.

50 "Asombrosas hazañas del Conde-arlequin," *Estrella* (Piribebuy), 16 June 1869.

51 Most of João Manoel's rear guard saved themselves by abandoning their horses and by taking to the woods. See *American Annual Cyclopedia of and Register of Important Events of the Year 1869*, 9: 556.

52 Taunay, *Cartas da Campanha*, 79–80; *Diário do Exército*, 109 (entry of 27 July 1869).

53 Azevedo Pimentel, *Episódios Militares*, 11–13.

54 On 24 June, a small Paraguayan unit attacked a Brazilian force of some twelve hundred men near the Paso Jara. In the skirmish, the Brazilians lost ten men killed and forty wounded, but the Paraguayans lost more than a hundred before falling back towards Yuty. See *The Standard* (Buenos Aires), 6 August 1869; Centurión, *Memorias o reminiscencias*, 4: 60–62. Allied naval units managed to reinforce the Brazilian land forces in this area shortly thereafter, effectively ending Paraguayan resistance.

55 "The Seat of War," *The Standard* (Buenos Aires), 2 July 1869.

56 Juan E. O'Leary, *El mariscal Solano López* (Asunción, 1970), 275–277; Hugo Mendoza, *La guerra contra la Triple Alianza, 1864-1870, 2nda parte* (Asunción, 2010), 77–78; Chiavenato, *Genocído Americano*, 159–161.

57 Centurión, *Memorias o reminiscencias*, 4: 33–34.

58 Tasso Fragoso, *História da Guerra entre a Tríplice Aliança e o Paraguay*, 4: 273; "Chronique," *Ba-Ta-Clan* (Rio de Janeiro), 31 July 1869.

59 *La Stampa* (Turin), 31 March 1869, held that López was attempting to escape, not to Bolivia, but to the United States.

60 "Important from Paraguay," *The Standard* (Buenos Aires), 22 July 1869.

61 Centurión observed of this occasion that the "comic and the ridiculous always combine even in the most serious acts and most solemn moments of life." See *Memorias o reminiscencias*, 4: 67–68.

62 "Correspondencia (Asunción, 31 July 1869)," *Jornal do Commercio* (Rio de Janeiro), 15 August 1869.

63 Taunay, *Recordações de Guerra e de Viagem*, 42–44, and *Memórias*, 343; at Sapucai, the Brazilians encountered a self-appointed *tenienta* of infantry, who resisted bravely, her sword tied jauntily to a belt made of rope. Her striking demeanor suggested that, while "there were no Charlotte Cordays to be found among the Paraguayan women, there were still many Joans d'Arc." See "Correspondencia (Asunción, 31 Aug. 1869)," in *Jornal do Commercio* (Rio de Janeiro), 16 September 1869.

64 Roque Pérez to Foreign Minister, Rosario, 10 August 1869, in *The Standard* (Buenos Aires), 11 August 1869; "Interrogatório de Felix Paraó," Piribebuy (?), 13 August 1869, in ANA-CRB I-30, 28, 14, no. 5.

65 The Altos feint successfully distracted the Marshal's garrison at Azcurra while Gaston's main forces approached Piribebuy. Mitre not only conquered the little town, he brought back to the main camp at Pirayú another two thousand refugees, most of them women and malnourished children. A small number were Brazilians who had fallen prisoner in Mato Grosso. See Doratioto, *Maldita Guerra*, 407, and Tasso Fragoso, *História da Guerra entre a Triplice Aliança e o Paraguai*, 4: 347–350.

66 Centurión, *Memorias o reminiscencias*, 4: 70–71.

67 "Correspondencia (copia) entre o Conde d'Eu e o General Osório," in IHGB, lata 276, doc. 27. Tasso Fragoso, *História da Guerra entre a Triplice Aliança e o Paraguai*, 4: 310–322.

68 Pompeyo González [Juan E. O'Leary] "Recuerdos de Gloria. Piribebuy. 12 de agosto de 1869," *La Patria* (Asunción), 12 August 1902.

69 Andrés Aguirre, *Acosta Ñú. Epopeya de los siglos* (Asunción, 1979); Mendoza, *La guerra contra la Triple Alianza*, 82.

70 Campanha do Paraguay. *Diário do Exército*, 169 (entry of 12 August 1869); O'Leary has the order of battle arranged differently, with Osório on the left, Victorino in the center, and the count on the right. See "Recuerdos de gloria. Piribebuy."

71 Tasso Fragoso, *História da Guerra entre a Triplice Aliança e o Paraguai*, 4: 312–313; "Correspondencia (Asunción, 16 Aug. 1869)," *Jornal do Commercio* (Rio de Janeiro), 30 August 1869.

72 Cardozo, *Hace cien años*, 12: 307. See Taunay, *Diário do Exército*, 131 (entry of 12 August 1869).

73 Cerqueira, *Reminiscencias da Campanha do Paraguai*, 375–377.

74 Allied comportment at Piribebuy has been widely censured in Paraguayan historiography up to the present day, with both liberal and revisionist scholars making the same arguments regarding the scale of Brazilian atrocities. See Juan Bautista Gill Aguinaga, "Excesos cometidos hace cien años," *Historia Paraguaya* 12 (1967–1968): 22–23; Efraím Cardozo, *Paraguay independiente*, 250; Hugo Mendoza, *La guerra contra la Triple Alianza*, 77–79.

75 There are two alternative views of the general's death, one having him shot at close range by a Paraguayan sharpshooter and the other having him felled by a randomly fired ball in a final cannonade. See "The Paraguay-Brazilian War," *Herald and Star* (Panama City), 14 October 1869, and Doratioto, *Maldita Guerra*, 408, 548.

76 João Manoel Mena Barreto always led from the front, and was generally recognized as one of the bravest officers in that famous military family. When the Paraguayans first invaded his home province in 1865, the then-colonel made a great show of parading in full uniform within rifle shot of the enemy. This was a ruse, designed to facilitate the escape of a full battalion of Voluntários, but it took extraordinary valor. See Francisco Pereira da Silva Barbosa, "Diário da Campanha do Paraguay," http:webarchive.org/web/2002106050712/http://www.geocities.com/cvidalb2000/.

77 Centurión, *Memorias o reminiscencias*, 4: 72–73, notes both Gaston's horrified reaction to Mena Barreto's death and the violent response that he ordered in consequence. The Welsh travel writer John Gimlette, who never offers a simple explanation when a sensational one is at hand, claims that Gaston and the Riograndense general "conducted an uncomfortably public and torrid affair," and that when João Manoel was slain, the "Prince of Orleans's grief was genocidal." See *At the Tomb of the Inflatable Pig. Travels Through Paraguay* (New York, 2003), 205, 212. There is, in fact, no proof whatsoever of an intimate relation between the two men. Had there been one, it could never have escaped notice and condemnation in the Allied camp, and López would surely have learned of the story and used it as propaganda. But no such talk circulated at the time, which leaves us to ask where Gimlette got his evidence. João Manoel had lost his wife to illness while he was at the front earlier in the war, and by 1869 he had taken a mistress (or *china*) who accompanied him into combat and in whose arms he was found at the time of his death. Most of the Brazilian senior officers kept mistresses in the field (Osório, who was an unrepentant womanizer, had several). But a homosexual encounter of the sort alleged by Gimlette would have aroused considerable commentary, and none of this occurred in 1869. Hence, it is not difficult to read the accusation as an intentional canard of fairly recent vintage. See Taunay, *Memórias*, 346, 350, 353.

78 Contrary to the speculations of certain twentieth-century writers, there was nothing genocidal in this spilling of blood, no plan, no "final solution" for the Paraguayan "problem." The count may have seen some advantages in a prompt and proportionate vengeance, but needless slaughter was beyond his ken. Piribebuy was not Auschwitz or Srebrenica; it instead was a site where angry soldiers abandoned their discipline, and their officers did nothing to stop them. The Paraguayans engaged in some of this same butchery at Curupayty and had developed a reputation for not taking prisoners. One of the Brazilians who admitted to having participated in the Piribebuy atrocities was the German immigrant Pedro Werlang, who made no excuses for having acted badly in the heat of the moment. See Werlang Diary in Becker, *Alemães e Descendentes*, 146–171, and more generally, Ary G. Prado, *O Capitão Werlang e seu Diário de Campanha Escrito Durante e Após a Guerra do Paraguai* (Canoas, 1969). Despite Werlang's contention that beheading prisoners was "normal after a battle," some Brazilian officers managed to show restraint. One was General Emílio Mallet, the gunner whose skill won the day for the Allies at Tuyutí. At Piribebuy, Mallet intervened at several junctures to save the lives of wounded Paraguayans, including Manuel Solalinde, the acting justice of the peace in the town, who was also an army captain and second-in-command after Caballero. See Cardozo, *Hace cien años*, 12: 307 and Doratioto, *General Osório*, 197. For a polemical example of the "Allies as butchers" interpretation, see Nebro Ariel Cardozo, *De Paysandu a Cerro Cora o el genocidio de los "civilizadores"* (Montevideo, 1970).

79 Cerqueira, *Reminiscencias da Campanha do Paraguai*, 376. Taunay confirmed the general outlines of Cerqueira's account, noting that Paraguayans were commonly killed in cold blood after battles and that he, too, had saved a *soldadito* from being decapitated and that afterwards the boy refused to leave him, even sleeping near his feet. See *Recordações da Guerra e da Viagem*, 48.

80 Gill Aguinaga, "Excesos cometidos hace cien años," 67, records this loss as typical. José Guillermo González, who was present with the Paraguayan artillery during the battle and fell prisoner to the Brazilians afterwards, evidently witnessed the torture and execution of Colonel Caballero. See "Reminiscencias históricas," *La Democracia* (Asunción), 27 December 1897.

81 Paraguayan historians have made much of these atrocities, taking their lead generally from the synoptic accounts of Colonels Centurión and Aveiro and from Father Maíz. The latter minced no words in denouncing the Brazilians for having "committed the most execrable cruelties; savagely cutting the throat of the brave and stoic Caballero, and

other prisoners, including children in their mothers' arms; the burning of the hospital with all the sick and wounded … horribly burned to death." See *Etapas de mi vida*, 70–71, and Maíz to Juan O'Leary, Arroyos y Esteros, 15 October 1907, in *Escritos del Padre Fidel Maíz, I. Autobiografía y cartas*, 311–313. Aveiro, *Memorias militares*, 87; Letter of "Mefistófeles," *La Tribuna* (Buenos Aires), 24 August 1869; and O'Leary, "Recuerdos de Gloria. Piribebuy," which claims that long after the event the flesh of wounded men trying to escape the burning building was still visible as greasy smudges upon the scorched walls. In his *Episódios Militares* (96–99), General Azevedo Pimentel claims that spontaneous combustion was a common occurrence in the grasslands of central Paraguay and perhaps had that fact in mind as a possible excuse for what happened in Piribebuy, though he does not make this argument explicitly.

82 This figure included fifteen Argentines killed and ninety-six wounded. See Tasso Fragoso, *História da Guerra entre a Triplice Aliança e o Paraguai*, 4: 320, and Emilio Mitre to Martín de Gainza, Altos, 13 August 1869, in MHN (BA), doc. 6690.

83 In going over these treasures, which seemed so out of place amid such devastation, Taunay observed how "vast and pernicious an influence this imperious and intelligent woman had had over the spirit of Solano López." See *Memórias*, 349–350. The presence of a volume of *Don Quixote* among the Marshal's possessions was ironic, for, as more than one observer noted, the Paraguayans had been tilting at windmills since 1864.

84 In retaining a large portion of this material for his personal collection, Councilor Paranhos unfavorably affected relations with the Paraguayans for over a century. In fact, the absence of the documents was later cited as one reason the Asunción government failed to justify its many claims against Brazil during the postwar period. See Acevedo, *Anales históricos del Uruguay*, 3: 371 (which notes an angry letter from the mid-1870s in which diplomat Jaime Sosa Escalada tells President Salvador Jovellanos that he finds it difficult to advise on foreign policy without the documents in hand). The "Piribebuy archive" remained with Paranhos until his death, and was afterwards donated by his family to the Biblioteca Nacional in Rio. The Carioca librarians took exceptionally good care of the Paraguayan materials in the Coleção Rio Branco, eventually microfilming them and organizing a highly useful catalog for the collection. Their organizing principle proved so efficient that it was retained by the Archivo Nacional de Asunción when the Brazilians finally returned the documents to Paraguay in the 1970s. See Hipólito Sánchez Quell, *Los 50.000 documentos paraguayos llevados al Brasil* (Asunción, 1976).

85 Letter of Julio Alvarez to O'Leary, Asunción, 3 November 1922, in "Los crimenes del Conde d'Eu. Informe de una victima sobreviviente," in BNA-CJO (this letter purports to record the experience of Alvarez's aunt, Juana Mora de Román, who had been cut terribly in the face at Piribebuy and given up for dead, but succeeded nonetheless in observing the count's conversation with the two women).

86 Aveiro, *Memorias militares*, 88; "Nouvelles du Paraguay," *Le Courrier de la Plata* (Buenos Aires), 22 August 1869.

87 Washburn, *History of Paraguay*, 2: 582–583.

88 Testimony of William King, Asunción, 18 October 1869, in Museo Andrés Barbero, Colección Carlos Pusineri Scala.

89 Cardozo, *Hace cien años*, 12: 319; Corselli, *La Guerra Americana*, 521–522.

90 Though their access to rations was constricted, the engineers had continued to draw their salaries during their time in the Cordillera. See Salary Receipts for 13 Foreign machinists (and three Paraguayans), Piribebuy, 4 June 1869, in ANA-NE 2509 (with partial copies in the BNA-CJO, and in the ANA-CRB I-30, 25, 27, no. 6). Several Britons continued to follow López after the retreat from Caacupé and still enjoyed his favor, but only one, Dr. Frederick Skinner, went with him the entire distance to the northeast.

91 "Testimony of William Eden," in Rebaudi, *Vencer o Morir*, 91–95; and "Arrival of the British Sufferers," *The Standard* (Buenos Aires), 26 August 1869.

92 A. Jourdier Communications in *L'Etendard* (Paris), 19 and 22 March 1868; W. R. Richardson Letter, in *The Times* (London), 3 April 1868; "The British in Paraguay," *The Times* (London), 7 August 1868; "Review for Europe" and "Foreigners in Paraguay," *The Standard* (Buenos Aires), 25 September 1868; "Mr. Washburn; Foreigners in Paraguay," *The Times* (London), 4 November 1868; "The War in the North. The English in Paraguay," *The Standard* (Buenos Aires), 19 November 1868; "Mr. Washburn and the British in Paraguay," *The Times* (London), 8 and 11 December 1868; "List of British in Paraguay," *The Times* (London), 2 January 1869; "Letter of a British Resident in Paraguay," *The Times* (London), 12 January 1869; "Mr. Washburn. List of the British in Paraguay," *The Times* (London), 25 March 1869; "The British in Paraguay," *The Times* (London), 4 October 1869; Documents Regarding British Prisoners in ANA-CRB I-30, 28, 10, nos. 1–7; and Cardozo, *Hace cien años*, 12: 18–19.

93 "Un heroe de 13 años," and "La mujer de Rbio [*sic*] Ñú," in Justo A. Pane, *Episódios militares* (Asunción, 1908), 12–22, and 41–49; Victor I. Franco, "Las heroínas mujeres del Acosta Ñú," *La Tribuna* (Asunción), 9 March 1969; and Doratioto, *Maldita Guerra*, 409.

94 The Paraguayans have set aside 16 August as Children's Day, and a very curious secular festival it is. In other countries, similar holidays celebrate the youthful innocence and sweet exuberance that childhood supposedly encompasses. In Paraguay, Children's Day pays tribute to the prepubescent soldiers of Ñú Guazú who willingly took on the most adult responsibility imaginable and fought to the death in futile combat. It should be remembered, of course, that while the Paraguayan boy-soldiers displayed implacable courage at Ñú Guazú, they had only recently shown an execrable brutality toward their own people. The sniggering executioners at San Fernando were nearly all teenagers. See Barbara Potthast, "¿Niños heroes o víctimas? Niños soldados en la guerra de la Triple Alianza," *II Jornadas Internacionales de la Historia del Paraguay* (Universidad de Montevideo), 15 June 2010; and Cooney, "Economy and Manpower," 41–43.

95 Manoel Luis da Rocha Osório to General Osório, Caraguatay, 20 August 1869, in *História do General Osório*, 2: 617–618; Altair Franco Ferreira, "Batalha de Campo Grande, 16 de Agosto de 1869," *A Defesa Nacional*, 5: 626 (July–August 1969), 65–121; and Corselli, *La Guerra Americana*, 523–524.

96 Taunay, *Recordações da Campanha e da Viagem*, 57–58; J. Estanislao Leguizamón, *Apuntes biográficos históricos* (Asunción, 1898).

97 The baron was not allowed leave until December. See Doratioto, *General Osório*, 197–200.

98 "The War," *The Anglo-Brazilian Times* (Rio de Janeiro), 7 September 1869. A somewhat fictionalized account of the engagement, replete with blood and loss of innocence, can be found in two of Adriano M. Aguiar's short stories, "Los dos clarínes," and "Yaguar-í paso," in *Yatebó y otros relatos. Episódios de la guerra contra la Triple Alianza* (Asunción, 1983), 145–158, 198–203.

99 "Chronique," *Ba-Ta-Clan* (Rio de Janeiro), 4 September 1869. The Paraguayans had used stones and broken shards as standard grapeshot since the beginning of the war (though now there was more stone than iron available). The grape, which was encased in leather boxes, caused many wounds but also ruined the bores of the cannon. See José Carlos de Carvalho, *Noções de Artilharia para Instrução do Oficiais Inferiores da Arma no Exército em Operações fora do Imperio* (Montevideo, 1866), 60.

100 Pompeyo González [Juan E. O'Leary] "Recuerdos de Gloria. Rubio Ñú. 16 de agosto de 1869," *La Patria* (Asunción), 16 August 1902; Andrés Aguirre, *Acosta Ñú*, 71–77; Antonio Díaz Acuña, *Homenaje al centenario de Acosta Ñú* (Asunción, 1969).

101   Tasso Fragoso, *História da Guerra da Triplice Aliança e o Paraguai*, 4: 342. Doratioto, *Maldita Guerra*, 417, records a more modest loss for the Allies—26 killed and 259
wounded—but this figure seems to represent the casualties recorded in the *Diário do
Exército* (184) for the 1st Corps alone; other Brazilian units took hits on the field that day
and the *Diário* does acknowledge those losses (though it excludes those sustained by
the Argentine and Uruguayans). Like Doratioto, Altair Franco Ferreira argues for a low
casualty total for the Allies, but he stresses that the high number of KIA among the Paraguayans could only derive from their fanaticism, the backwardness of their supporting
arms, and the technical sloppiness or lack of training in their lower ranks. See Ferreira,
"Batalha do Campo Grande," 105.

102   Taunay, *Memórias*, 527.

103   Doratioto, *Maldita Guerra*, 418. If one compares the figures of men lost at Piribebuy and
Ñú Guazú with the casualties suffered at Tuyutí, it is possible to see at once how trivial in
the military sense these engagements were; but the Paraguayans suffered mightily from
this "bloodbath" and they never forgot.

104   Centurión, *Memorias o reminiscencias*, 4: 90; Victor I. Franco, *Coronel Florentín Oviedo*
(Asunción, 1971). The Allies took from one thousand to twelve hundred prisoners at
Ñú Guazú, most of whom had initially dispersed into the forests but who delivered
themselves into Allied hands over the next two days. One of their number was a young
sergeant, Emilio Aceval, who served as Paraguayan president between 1898 and 1902.

105   Cerqueira, *Reminiscencias da Campanha do Paraguai*, 390–391 (emphasis in the
original).

106   O'Leary, "Recuerdos de Gloria. Rubio Ñú. 16 de agosto de 1869." Taunay saw with his
own eyes a wounded Paraguayan boy-soldier upon the ground, twisted into the fetal position and simpering with pain and coughing with the irritation of the smoke. Between
coughs he called out to a comrade to dispatch him before the fire could consume his person; the other soldier, with a look of resignation, responded by firing a single shot into
the heart of the prostrate boy. See Taunay, *Recordações da Guerra e da Viagem*, 68–69.

15 | THE NEW PARAGUAY AND THE OLD

1   This calculation is attributed to one of the Englishmen liberated at Caacupé in mid-August, a man who was clearly not exaggerating when he made the point that he expected the figure to grow over the next months. See "Correspondencia, Asunción, 18 Aug.
1869," in *Jornal do Commercio* (Rio de Janeiro), 1 September 1869.

2   "Correspondencia (Caraguatay, 28 Aug. 1869)," in *Jornal do Commercio* (Rio de Janeiro),
15 September 1869.

3   The Paraguayan exiles still hoped to win major concessions because the Allied powers
seemed even more riven by dispute than themselves. See Misc. Correspondence of Paraguayan exiles in UCR-JSG, Box 14, nos. 11–13, 15; Declaration of Paraguayan Citizens,
Asunción, 31 March 1869, and José Díaz de Bedoya, J. Egusquiza, and Bernardo Valiente
to Mariano Varela, Buenos Aires, 29 April 1868 [*sic* 1869], in Díaz, *Historia política y
militar de las repúblicas del Plata*, 11: 199–203.

4   The rumor of a possible American intervention was likely started by McMahon, who
wished to buy López some time. See Washburn, *History of Paraguay*, 2: 578–580. Paranhos knew enough of US policy considerations to doubt the validity of this tale, but he
could not afford to ignore the reactions of Conservative members of Parliament who
might happen to believe it. See Francisco Doratioto, "La política del Imperio del Brasil en
relación al Paraguay, 1864–1872," in Richard et al., *Les Guerres du Paraguay*, 39.

5   Ex-president Mitre strongly opposed the drift suggested by Varela, which he thought
tantamount to throwing away his country's territorial claims in Misiones and the Chaco

in exchange for nebulous political considerations. See Doratioto, "La ocupación política y militar brasileña del Paraguay (1869–1876), *Historia Paraguaya* 45 (2005): 256.

6   The Argentine Congress resisted the idea of sending a diplomatic mission to Asunción, arguing that the signing of a comprehensive peace treaty needed to come first. See *Congreso Nacional. Camara de Senadores. Diario de sesiones* (Buenos Aires, 1869), 238–239 (Session of 26 June 1869).

7   "The War in the North," *The Standard* (Buenos Aires), 17 March 1869.

8   The number of displaced persons flowing into Asunción continued to increase over the next months. According to one source, the cost of supplying rations to these refugees had grown by September to 100,000 milréis a day, a huge sum for which the Brazilians had made no allowance. See "Enormous expenses," in unidentified clipping attached to Lidgerwood to Seward, Petrópolis, 24 September 1869, in NARA M-121, no. 37.

9   Though imperial officials preferred to leave formal charity work to others, the generosity and compassion of individual Brazilian troops (and their officers) should not be doubted. Particularly striking was the work of Ana Néri, the Florence Nightingale of Brazil, who had effectively administered military hospitals in Corrientes and Asunción, and sometimes managed to get food to displaced Paraguayan children in the capital. Before returning to Bahia at the end of the war, she adopted four Paraguayan orphans she had helped in this way. See Cybelle de Ipanema, "No Centenário de D. Ana Justina Ferreira Néri," *Revista do Instituto Histórico e Geográfico Brasileiro* 334 (1982): 145–154, and João Francisco de Lima, *Ana Néri. Heroina da Caridade* (São Paulo, 1977). Just as striking were the efforts of Argentine Freemasons, who, in mid-July 1869, established an asylum in Asunción to house the poor. Located near the cathedral in a former clerical school, the asylum featured clean, whitewashed dormitories and some access to food and medical care. A little chapel was also provided for the inmates. Unfortunately, there was only room for one hundred fifty of the latter—hardly sufficient to deal with the problem. See "Paraguayan Asylum," *The Standard* (Buenos Aires), 22 July 1869.

10   The Brazilians were anxious to resurrect Paraguay as a viable entity, so that it could serve as a buffer state and effectively cancel out any Argentine pretensions to northern territories abutting the Mato Grosso. The Argentines had already displayed some interest in the Chaco districts opposite Asunción, and it was a matter of long-term Brazilian interest that Buenos Aires not get those lands. Hence, the empire looked with approval on any policies that strengthened the hand of a post-Lopista Paraguay. See Doratioto, *Maldita Guerra*, 463–470.

11   José S. Campobassi, *Mitre y su época* (Buenos Aires, 1980), 2: 213.

12   For many months, the members of the Alliance had seemed no better than the Graiae, the three primordial witches who shared a single eye among them and could see no further than what that one eye permitted. Now, however, the Allies had rediscovered some of their mutual animosity and were confronting each other (at least rhetorically) almost as much as they confronted the Marshal's army. See Cardozo, *Paraguay independiente* (Asunción, 1987), 248.

13   "Provisional Government of Paraguay. Agreement of the Allies," 2 June 1869, in Díaz, *Historia política y militar de las repúblicas del Plata*, 11: 206–210, and unidentified clipping in Asboth to Hamilton Fish, Buenos Aires, 21 July 1869, in NARA, FM-69, no. 18.

14   Some of the jibes were directed at the Paraguayan delegates who had met with Varela and Paranhos, others at men who had been in Asunción for some time and who now wished to assume the status of courtiers. See "De lo que han sido capaces," *La Verdad* (Buenos Aires), 19 June 1869, and Juansilvano Godoi, *El baron de Rio Branco. La muerte del mariscal López. El concepto de la patria* (Asunción, 1912), 232–233.

15   "Importantes notícias del Paraguay," *La Nación Argentina* (Buenos Aires), 8 April 1869.

16 Decoud, *Sobre los escombros de la guerra*, 87–90; Gill Aguinaga, *La Asociación Paraguaya en la guerra de la Triple Alianza*, 24.

17 The liberal opponents of the López regime often spoke among themselves in French and used Guaraní only when they wished to express contempt. Ironically, they were not far removed in this habit from the Marshal, though for López French was the language of intimacy, not of intellectual discourse. With regards to the latter, it might be submitted that, in spite of well-read intellectuals like the Decoud brothers, the Argentine model for liberalism that the Paraguayans adopted was somewhat passé—at least insofar as it reflected European impulses, which by the late 1860s had moved away from the ideals of Mazzini and the Frankfurt liberals. See Nicolas Shumway, *The Invention of Argentina* (Berkeley, 1991); Tulio Halperín Donghi, *Contemporary History of Latin America* (Durham and London, 1993), 105–121, 135–139.

18 Cardozo, *Hace cien años*, 11: 269–271.

19 Act of Foundation of the Club Unión, Asunción, 31 March 1869, in MHM, Colección Gill Aguinaga (uncataloged section).

20 Héctor Francisco Decoud, *Sobre los escombros de la guerra*, 105.

21 F. Arturo Bordón, *Historia política del Paraguay* (Asunción, 1976), 43.

22 This provision, the inclusion of which demonstrates just how far sutler power extended, read that "All individuals, ships, provisions, forage, and other material of whatever species, belonging to the Allied armies or to its contractors shall have ingress into and egress from the Republic, free of all and every onus or search, the same as granted to the generals and diplomatic representatives of the Allied Governments." See Tasso Fragoso, *A Paz com o Paraguai depois da guerra da Triplice Aliança* (Rio de Janeiro, 1941), 47–48; Warren, *Paraguay and the Triple Alliance*, 54.

23 Decoud, *Sobre los escombros de la guerra*, 145–146.

24 Lopista officials never quite trusted don Cirilo's independent streak, which doubtlessly explains why he never attained an officer's rank. They remembered that his father had also quarreled publicly, first with Dr. Francia's sub-*delegados*, and then with Carlos Antonio López, whose accession to power the elder Rivarola had opposed in 1844. Nor had the Marshal forgotten that the younger Rivarola had uttered "defeatist" remarks on several occasions. Such accusations were commonly directed at anyone with a recognizable surname during the final years of the war, but it was not always the case that Marshal López believed the rumor. In this case, he evidently took pleasure at the man's escape from Caxias, and promoted him as a reward. Unfortunately, the Marshal's satisfaction with Rivarola did not last. When two wounded troopers in his charge drowned during a torrential downpour at Cerro León, the sergeant was brought up on charges, given forty strokes, and kept tied to a tree just outside the encampment. The court-martial had intended him to post him to a vanguard unit to be killed in action, but when the count's troops stormed the camp in May, they liberated him without further ado. He proved grateful to his captors, who hoped to make of him a useful instrument. See Decoud, *Sobre los escombros de la guerra*, 145–147.

25 Paranhos had sought the inclusion of Egusquiza in the provisional government as proof of the empire's willingness to enlist old Lopistas. This was a typical concession to the politics of the moment, in which the councilor appeared so mild and judicious to the Brazilians, and so infamous to Paraguayans of every political stripe. See Doratioto, "La rivalidad argentine-brasileña y la reorganización institucional del Paraguay," *Historia Paraguaya* 37 (1997): 231.

26 Ernesto Quesada, *Historia diplomática nacional: la política argentina-paraguaya* (Buenos Aires, 1902), 33; Warren, *Paraguay and the Triple Alliance*, 55.

27   "He's quite a devil this Decoud," said a perturbed Paranhos at one point. See *Sobre los escombros de la guerra*, 134–136. Another of the Decoud sons, Juan José, had for some time used the pages of a Correntino newspaper to spit bile on Paranhos and the count's military regime. The Brazilian foreign minister, who took the insults personally, saw no reason to cater to any one of that surname after that, and so put his foot down when the matter of candidates for the triumvirate arose. See Godoi, *El baron de Rio Branco*, 236–237; and Whigham, *La guerra de la Triple Alianza*, 3: 402–411.

28   The old Lopista system had always taken the form of a rigid court hierarchy consisting of rival paladins seeking the Marshal's blessing; the provisional government was similar in that each faction sought the patronage of Paranhos. Colonel Decoud, head of the Club del Pueblo, was made chief of the Asunción police. His son Juan José was named attorney general, and José Segundo first became Rivarola's private secretary, and later minister of education. Even Ferreira earned a post in the new government as port commander at Asunción. Though the Decoudistas were kept out of the most senior positions in the new government, their presence in the second tier was very prominent—all the result of political payoffs from Paranhos and Rivarola rather than from serious compromises. See Bordón, *Historia política*, 49–52; Godoi, *El barón de Rio Branco*, 250–251; Carlos Centurión, *Los hombres de la convención*, 10–11, 19–20.

29   Act of Installation of the Provisional Government (Asunción, 15 August 1869), in *Registro Oficial de la República del Paraguay correspondiente a los años 1869 a 1875* (Asunción, 1887), 3–4.

30   Tasso Fragoso, *História da Guerra entre a Tríplice Aliança e o Paraguai*, 5: 267; Cardozo, *Hace cien años*, 12: 316–317; according to *The Standard's* description, this street theater "partook of some grotesque features." See "Installation of the Paraguayan Triumvirate," in the 25 August 1869 issue.

31   Wilfredo Valdez [Jaime Sosa Escalada], "La guerra futura. La guerra de Chile y Brasil con la República. La Alianza—la caura común. Estudio de los hombres del Paraguay—el Triumvirato," *Revista del Paraguay* 2, no. 3–9 (1892): 257–260.

32   Valdez, "La guerra future," 196; "Correspondencia" (Asunción, 7 August 1869), *Jornal do Commercio* (Rio de Janeiro), 21 August 1869.

33   Though Juansilvano Godoi almost certainly overstates the silver pilfered by Díaz de Bedoya as "300 or more arrobas [7,500 pounds]," the quantity taken was surely large. See *El barón de Rio Branco*, 242–243, 278–279.

34   McMahon to Hamilton Fish, Buenos Aires, 19 July 1869, cited in Warren, *Paraguay and the Triple Alliance*, 54.

35   Cited in Warren, *Paraguay and the Triple Alliance*, 54.

36   Decree of the Provisional Government, Asunción, 17 August 1869, in Lidgerwood to Seward, Petropolis, 11 September 1869, in NARA, M-121, no. 37; Decoud, *Sobre los escombros*, 168–169.

37   *La república del Paraguay. Manifiesto del Gobierno provisorio* (Asunción, 1869). The Paraguayan people might have been able to claim a certain moral authority by virtue of their terrible suffering, but such cannot be said for the members of the provisional government, who were capable of displaying an ostentatious, almost oriental, disregard for their countrymen's plight. It was therefore indecorous for the triumvirs to presume to teach them their duties. See Alberto Moby Ribeiro da Silva, "Bailes e Festas Públicas em Asunción no pós-guerra da Tríplice Aliança: Mulher e Resistencia Popular no Paraguai," *Estudos Ibero-Americanos* 25, no. 1 (1999): 43–52, and more generally, *La noche de las Kygua Vera. La mujer y la reconstrucción de la identidad nacional en la posguerra de la Triple Alianza (1867-1904)* (Asunción, 2010).

38   See "Important from Paraguay," *The Standard* (Buenos Aires), 21 September 1869. See also *El Nacional* (Buenos Aires), 17 September 1869, which speculates that cholera was again about to fall upon these poor people; and Brezzo, "Civiles y militares," 45–51.

39   See Decrees of 1–10, 11, 13, 15, 17, 18, 21, 23, 24, 25, 27, 28, and 29 September 1869 in *Registro Oficial de la República del Paraguay*, 11–27. *El Nacional* (Buenos Aires), 15 October 1869, reported that sutlers were organizing to oppose the government licensing of their activities.

40   Doratioto, *Maldita Guerra*, 432–433; "Chronique," *Ba-Ta-Clan* (Rio de Janeiro), 23 and 29 October 1869. These efforts to raise revenues were inconclusive. As *The Times* (London) noted, the new government was anxious to "restore the country to order, but destitute as it is of resources, without a trade save the army supply, without a solitary staple wherewith to feed the people, and without even the vestige of a treasury, it is impotent and every way unequal to the task." See issue of 6 December 1869.

41   See Decree of 2 October 1869, in *Registro Oficial de la República del Paraguay*, 29–30; Cardozo, *Hace cien años*, 12: 400–401, 13: 12–13; "O Conde d'Eu e a Escravidao no Paraguay," in Nabuco, *Um Estadista do Imperio*, 162–165; and Ana Maria Arguello, *El rol de los esclavos negros en el Paraguay* (Asunción, nd), 92.

42   It cannot be said that the Allied commissioners and directors of the military government were unaware of the scale of the problem. In a personal note to Foreign Minister Mariano Varela, the Argentine commissioner remarked that "what was most horrible and degrading in the liberated zones was the unfortunate state of the families. Hunger, misery, suffering, and nudity abound, and even in the streets [one can see] a mass of cadavers. This, my friend, no one can imagine, it is necessary to see." He might have shown great sympathy in noting this terrible business, but he could do nothing—or would do nothing—to help bring it to an end. Concern in words, indifference in actions would seem to have been the rule at that time. See *El Nacional* (Buenos Aires), 29 August 1869.

43   Williams, *Rise and Fall of the Paraguayan Republic*, 225; in addition to these decrees passed to supposedly favor the poor, the displaced women and children huddled into the plazas of the city were expelled to their home districts "as a hygienic measure." See Godoi, *El barón de Rio Branco*, 262–263.

44   Mitre and the financial backers of *La Nación Argentina* had evidently planned to establish a liberal newspaper in occupied Asunción tentatively called *El Sol de Lambaré*, but, for a variety of reasons, the project never came off. This left the field open for *La Regeneración*, which was edited by Decoud and radiated his political viewpoints as if the type were inked with pitchblende. Juansilvano Godoi regarded the paper, which appeared three times a week, as progressive in spirit, as favoring a broad concept of social welfare and public education for women. See *El barón de Rio Branco*, 267–270. Other readers might argue that there was less in *La Regeneración* than met the eye. See "Important from Paraguay," *The Standard* (Buenos Aires), 4 March 1869; Harris Gaylord Warren, "Journalism in Asunción under the Allies and the Colorados, 1869–1904," *The Americas* 39, no. 4 (1983): 483–498.

45   Incongruously, *La Voz del Pueblo*, which did not issue its first number until 24 March 1870, was founded by Miguel Gallegos, the surgeon who had served as head of the Argentine medical corps during the Humaitá campaign, and who thus played the role that fate assigned the Correntino Victor Silvero in his editorial work for *Cabichuí*. See Carlos Centurión, *Historia de la cultura paraguaya* (Asunción, 1961), 1: 317. Both *La Voz del Pueblo* and *La Regeneración* ceased publication in September 1870 when their respective offices were wrecked in the night by parties unknown (though it is not difficult to point the finger at government agents). See Warren, "Journalism in Asunción," 485.

46 While we might censure the triumvirs for concentrating on partisan politics when so many people faced starvation, in truth, the scale of the challenge would have confounded any responsible authorities. Conditions were so bad that, on 1 December 1869, Rivarola admitted to "the difficulty of transporting cadavers to the public cemeteries for lack of men to convey them, the task [having been relegated] to women already sunken from hunger and fatigue [brought on by living] under the yoke of Solano López, who had [sought] to exterminate the Paraguayan nationality." He ordered his little militia to aid in the interment of the dead wherever they were found, not bothering to carry them "to more distant burial grounds. See Circular of Rivarola, 1 December 1869, in *Registro Oficial*, 38–39.

47 "A March in Paraguay," *The Standard* (Buenos Aires), 25 November 1869.

48 Taunay, *Diário do Exército*, 163 (entry of 21 August 1869).

49 Councilor Paranhos initially reported that Hermosa had died during the attack, but he evidently survived by hiding in the scrub brush and later turned himself in as a prisoner of war. See Paranhos to Sr. Carvalho Borges, Rosario, 25 August 1869, in *La Nación Argentina* (Buenos Aires), 26 August 1869; and Centurión, *Memorias o reminiscencias*, 9: 91.

50 Taunay, *Diário do Exército*, 160–161 (entry of 19 August 1869); Tasso Fragoso, *História da Guerra entre a Triplice Aliança e o Paraguai*, 4: 355–357; *Anglo-Brazilian Times* (Rio de Janeiro), 7 September 1869; Alexandre Barros de Albuquerque to Francisco Vieira de Faria, Caraguatay, 21 August 1869, in IHGB, lata 449, doc. 54.

51 The Paraguayan side of this incident is presented in Victor Franco, "Crueldades imperiales en el combate de Caaguy-yurú," *La Tribuna* (Asunción), 9 April 1972, while the Brazilian side is presented in "Correspondencia (Caraguatay, 28 Aug. 1869)," *Jornal do Commercio* (Rio de Janeiro), 15 September 1869, and, more evocatively, in Cerqueira, *Reminiscencias da Campanha do Paraguai*, 392 (the latter does not claim to have seen the bodies of the dead men himself, but he leaves no doubt that Victorino's units took their revenge).

52 Centurión speculated that Victorino's bloodthirstiness, and the inflexibility of his order, suggested that it had originated from higher authority (possibly the count). See *Memorias o reminiscencias*, 4: 91–92.

53 It might seem odd that undernourished girls would beg for music rather than food, but such odd and coquettish happenings were far from uncommon. See Olmedo, *Guerra del Paraguay. Cuadernos de campaña*, 466 (entry of 18 August 1869). Robert Bontine Cunninghame Graham was far from the only one to notice how Paraguayan women in those sad moments often looked at men the way "a cannibal might stare at a young, well-fed missionary out in La Nouvelle or the New Hebrides." See "La Alcaldesa," in *Charity* (London, 1912), 40–41.

54 J. B. Otaño, *Orígen, desarrollo, y fin de la marina desaparecida en la guerra de 1864–70* (Asunción, 1942), 16–17.

55 Carlos Balthazar Silveira, *Campanha do Paraguay. A Marinha Brazileira* (Rio de Janeiro, 1900), 69–70.

56 Taunay notes that the force of the explosion of one ship's magazine sent shards of metal into the air, killing a Brazilian sergeant and wounding another man. See *Diário do Exército*, 162 (entry of 19 August 1869); Levy Scarvada, "A Marinha no Final de uma Campanha Gloriosa," *Navigator* 2 (1970): 36; and Olmedo, *Guerra del Paraguay. Cuadernos de campaña*, 473 (entry of 24 August 1869).

57 Centurión, *Memorias o reminiscencias*, 4: 95–96.

58 "Correspondencia, Asunción, 20 Aug. 1869," *Jornal do Commercio* (Rio de Janeiro), 2 September 1869.

59   Amerlan, *Nights on the Rio Paraguay*, 147; Rocha Osório to General Osório, Caraguatay, 27 August 1869, in Osório y Osório, *História do General Osório*, 622–623; "Don Lopez et la Guerre du Paraguay," *Revue des Deux Mondes* 85 (1870): 1024–1025; *La América* (Buenos Aires), 26 August 1869.

60   One of the Marshal's remaining British stalwarts, whom the pseudonymous author of a letter in *The Standard* (Buenos Aires) identified as Captain [Charles?] Thompson, had taken charge of this baggage (which included fruit preserves, bonbons, fine wines, dinnerware and the Marshal's gold-embossed boots). The Briton managed to flee into the woods when his troops were cut up at this engagement, and fell prisoner a day or two later. See "H. F." to Cranford, Asunción, 27 August 1869, in issue of 3 September 1869. See also "Correspondencia (Caraguatay, 28 Aug. 1869)," *Jornal do Commercio* (Rio de Janeiro), 15 September 1869.

61   Taunay, *Diário do Exército*, 165–166 (entry of 22 August 1869), "The Seat of War," *The Standard* (Buenos Aires), 1 September 1869.

62   Maíz, *Etapas de mi vida*, 71.

63   In such remote sites, López's civilian functionaries still went through the motions of governing in his name. They dispatched reports to a central government that no longer had a fixed seat of power, and they recorded minimal acreage sown with maize, peanuts, and cotton to supply a largely nonexistent army. In truth, however, the well-oiled state apparatus that had provided a bulwark for the Marshal's regime was increasingly replaced by direct military fiat. See Centurión, *Memorias o reminiscencias*, 4: 102–103.

64   Cardozo, *Hace cien años*, 12: 331–332; Díaz de Bedoya's behavior on this occasion proved that it was easier to begin collaboration than to stop, but his example was not much copied. The *jefe político* of San José de los Arroyos arrived on the scene at about this time, and immediately put himself under Allied orders. "This was the first defection from López's side," observed one Argentine officer, "and we will see how many will [soon] follow him." There were very few. See ? to Pedro José Agüero, Campamento, 22 August 1869, in *La Nación Argentina* (Buenos Aires), 2 September 1869.

65   A few months later, he threatened to resign his command and leave Paraguay if something were not done to help his soldiers. Doratioto, *Maldita Guerra*, 446–448.

66   Cardozo, *Hace cien años*, 12: 338.

67   Emilio Mitre remarked in a letter from Caraguatay on 25 August that he had just returned to the village after eight days searching for López's army and that he hoped to obtain victuals and new mounts from the Brazilians. He apparently believed that Gaston's stores to allow him to join the chase again fairly promptly. It turned out, however, that his Allies were just as destitute of supplies as he was. See *La Nación Argentina* (Buenos Aires), 2 September 1869, and Mitre to Martín de Gainza, Caraguatay, 30 August 1869, in MHN (BA), doc. 6693.

68   The horses the Argentines stole likely ended up in pucheros, for Emilio Mitre's troops were even hungrier than the Brazilians. See Kolinski, *Independence or Death!*, 183; a related tale has the Argentines at Cerro León turning the stolen animals into sausages, "horses and mules all alike." See "Startling from Paraguay," *The Standard* (Buenos Aires), 7 November 1869. General Mitre himself had long cited the inadequacy of the horses remaining to him as a factor in his army's inability to pursue López, but no one thought that his men would ultimately eat them. See Mitre to Martín de Gainza, Caraguatay, 25 August 1869, in MHN (BA), doc. 4294.

69   The dearth of horses continued to hamper Allied operations well into October. See Polidoro to Victorino, Asunción, 27 September 1869; Victorino to Polidoro, Caraguatay (?), 28 September 1869; Polidoro to Victorino, Asunción, 29 September 1869; Victorino

to Polidoro, Caraguatay (?), 30 September 1869; and Carlos Resin to Victorino, San Joaquín, 8 October 1869, in IHGB lata 447, nos. 107, 116, 108, 117, and 20, respectively.

70   Provisioning problems vexed Allied operational effectiveness for many months. See Cardozo, *Hace cien años*, 13: 57–58, 70, 72, and 121. On one occasion, a small Brazilian unit managed to capture a number of milk cows—a great rarity—and these were sent on to His Highness as a token of esteem (13: 64).

71   Taunay, *Memórias*, 367–369.

72   The Brazilians were also very hungry. General Azevedo Pimentel tells the story of a large macaw that his men had shot from a tree to provide something for the otherwise inconsequential mess; the soldiers had fired simultaneously, hitting the poor bird with eight bullets, and thus rendering their meal into pieces too small to eat. See *Episódios Militares*, 35–39.

73   "Correspondencia, Asunción, 31 Aug. 1869," *Jornal do Commercio* (Rio de Janeiro), 15 September 1869; Cerqueira, *Reminiscencias da Campanha do Paraguai*, 398; the *New York Tribune* reported in its 9 October 1869 issue that López had safely arrived in Bolivia, "to which country he had retreated from the mountains, attended by a few of his personal adherents." It had not happened.

16 | THE END OF IT

1   A double, or triple, espionage could transform an informer into the accused, and toward the end of the campaign, López found it difficult to trust anyone. On this occasion, he executed the sergeant who let the supposed spy escape. See Washburn, *History of Paraguay*, 2: 583.

2   "Declaración del general Resquín (Humaitá, 20 May 1870)," in *Papeles de López. El tirano pintado por si mismo*, 158–159. Centurión confirms the story, supplying details on the conversation between López and Aquino that bought the latter a few days, but which condemned many other members of the Acá Verá. See *Memorias y reminscencias*, 4: 103–107; "Declaración de Coronel Manuel Palacios," in Rebaudi, *Guerra del Paraguay. Un episódio*, 72–73; Tasso Fragoso, *História da Guerra entre a Tríplice Aliança e o Paraguai*, 5: 26–27; "Importante declaración de don Manuel Palacios (aboard Brazilian warship *Iguatemy*, Asunción, 20 May 1870)," in Masterman, *Siete años de aventuras en el Paraguay* (Buenos Aires, 1911), 2: 370–371. See also "Declarations of 2 Paraguayan Women," *The Times* (London), 19 November 1869.

3   Centurión, *Memorias o reminiscencias*, 4: 106. According to Dr. Skinner, the lieutenant enjoyed a natural talent for mimicry and had frequently provided amusement for López's family, as if he were a jester. See "Testimony of Dr. Frederick Skinner," in Scottish Record Office, CS 244/543/14, 1010.

4   Luis María Campos to Martín Gainza, Caraguatay, 4 September 1869, in MHN(BA), doc. 6602.

5   Cardozo, *Hace cien años*, 12: 339, records the total manpower of the Allied army at this juncture as 30,000 men, with 10,042 operating in Villa de Rosario and Concepción; 8,160 in the "central" districts; 2,140 in Villarrica; 1,000 in Asunción; 500 in Pirayú; 3,000 with the Count d'Eu in Caraguatay and San José; and 2,229 in various convoys. See also "Correspondencia (Asunción), 17 Sept. 1869," *Jornal do Commercio* (Rio de Janeiro), 2 October 1869; and Centurión, *Memorias y reminiscencias*, 4: 107.

6   The Brazilians also managed to take two small cannon from the Paraguayans on this occasion. They must have been among the few artillery pieces left in the Marshal's army. See Centurión, *Memorias y reminiscencias*, 4: 109–110.

7   Ulrich Lopacher had been present when Argentine troops reached Caraguatay, and had noted on that occasion that the northeast abounded with the so-called "Santa Fe grass, sharp as a knife, whose blades stabbed upward, and bloodied both feet and lower leg." It was the same further east. See *Un suizo en la guerra del Paraguay*, 38.

8   Centurión, *Memorias y reminiscencias*, 4: 109–110.

9   Several hundred Paraguayan soldiers were killed or deserted to the Allies the day before. See Leuchars, *To the Bitter End*, 225.

10 Dorotéa Lasserre, *The Paraguayan War. Sufferings of a French Lady in Paraguay* (Buenos Aires, 1870), 14–17. Other destinadas included Elizabeth Cutler, whose account of her time on the road can be seen in *The Standard* (Buenos Aires), 29 August 1869; Casiana Irigoyen de Miltos, who described her experiences in a single letter written from Asunción on 8 October 1871 to her brother Manuel V. Irigoyen, and which can be found in the private collection of Cristobal Duarte (Washington, D. C.); Concepción Domecq de Decoud, the mother of José Segundo Decoud, whose 1888 testimony can be found in MHM(A), Colección Zeballos, carpeta 128; María Ana Dolores Pereyra, mother of the late Bishop Palacios, whose declaration of 3 January 1870 can be found in *The Standard* (Buenos Aires), 2 February 1870, and *La Regeneración* (Asunción), 19 January 1870; Susana Céspedes de Céspedes, whose short declaration can be found in *La Regeneración* (Asunción), 15 December 1869; Encarnación Mónica Bedoya, whose memoir was reproduced in Guido Rodríguez Alcalá, *Residentas, destinadas y traidores* (Asunción, 1991), 91–97; and Silvia Cordal de Gill, whose abbreviated notes can be seen in Manuel Peña Villamil and Roberto Quevedo, *Silvia* (Asunción, 1987). Manuel Solalinde, a Paraguayan captain who surrendered to the Brazilians in September 1869, recorded six camps set aside for the destinadas. See Solalinde Testimony, Asunción, 16 September 1869, in Museo Andrés Barbero, Colección Carlos Pusineri Scala.

11 Lasserre, *The Paraguayan War*, 17; Potthast-Jutkeit, *"¿Paraíso de Mahoma" o "País de las mujeres"?*, 279–288.

12 En route to Yhú, they occasionally received kind treatment and food from local farmers, but it never amounted to much more than a handful of maize, for at least fifty displaced families had preceded them. Héctor Francisco Decoud recorded 2,021 displaced individuals in Yhú, mostly women and children. See *Sobre los escombros de la guerra*, 209–215.

13 Lasserre, *The Paraguayan War*, 23–25.

14 Testimony of Auguste Carmin, Asunción, 24 September 1869, in Museo Andrés Barbero, Colección Carlos Pusineri Scala.

15 Cardozo, *Hace cien años*, 12: 433–444; Centurión, *Memorias y reminiscencias*, 4: 111–113. Dr. Skinner attributed the mistreatment of Colonel Marcó to Madame Lynch, who was supposedly jealous of the attentions that the Marshal paid the colonel's wife. See "Skinner Testimony," in Scottish Record Office, CS 244/543/19, 1018.

16 Centurión, *Memorias o reminiscencias*, 4: 114–115.

17 They had to "sow maize and mandioca, making holes in the ground with their hands or with the jaw-bone of a cow." See "Declaration of the Bishop's Mother," *The Standard* (Buenos Aires), 2 February 1870.

18 Cardozo, *Hace cien años*, 12: 365, quotes a letter to this effect written by Councilor Paranhos to the Baron of Cotegipe at the end of August; two weeks later, General Castro announced his own intention to return to Montevideo because the fighting had ended. See Castro to José Luis Benalasreto, Cerro León, 9 September 1869, in AGN (M), Archivos Particulares, caja 69, carpeta 21; as for Emilio Mitre, he had already recognized that the struggle "had concluded, and now nothing yet remained but to pursue that maniac to finish even with the last shadow of the war." See Emilio Mitre to Mitre (?), Caraguatay, 2 September 1869, in *La Nación Argentina* (Buenos Aires), 10 September 1869.

19   Jerry Cooney has pointed out how long-lived the tendency toward independent poses was in this region of the Curuguaty and Ygatymí frontier, and how flexible it could become under outside pressure. See Cooney, "Lealtad dudosa: la lucha paraguaya por la frontera del Paraná, 1767–1777," in Whigham and Cooney, *Campo y frontera. El Paraguay al fin de la era colonial* (Asunción, 2006), 12–34.

20   Frederick Skinner saw an "infant on the road trying to eat human blood," only one of many hundreds destined to die in similar squalor. See "Skinner Testimony," in Scottish Record Office, CS 244/543/14, 1014. Comments of Brazilian general Carlos de Oliveira Nery, in Acevedo, *Anales históricos del Uruguay*, 3: 549–550; Testimony of Hipólito Pérez, Asunción, 6 September 1869, in Museo Andrés Barbero, Colección Carlos Pusineri Scala.

21   *Cartas de Campanha*, 100–101 (entry of 24 December 1869).

22   Tasso Fragoso, *História da Guerra entre a Tríplice Aliança e o Paraguai*, 5: 34–37; *Anglo-Brazilian Times* (Rio de Janeiro), 4 November 1869; Victorino to Polidoro, 10 October 1869, in IHGB, lata 447, doc. 112.

23   Cardozo, *Hace cien años*, 13: 21. One of those happiest to see the Brazilians was William Oliver, a British engineer who had worked at Ybycuí, and whose want of money prevented his buying food for his adopted children. See Oliver Testimony, Asunción, 15 September 1869, in Museo Andrés Barbero, Colección Carlos Pusineri Scala.

24   Washburn, *History of Paraguay*, 2: 575.

25   Cerqueira offers a rather gruesome account of how vampire bats assaulted his favorite horse. See *Reminiscencias da Campanha do Paraguai*, 397. As for the *úra*, the Spanish editor Ildefonso Antonio Bermejo offered an exaggerated observation a decade earlier, which repeated the myth that the troublesome insect was in fact a colossal moth whose "urine" could bring on death. Many denizens of the Paraguayan countryside repeat this story about moths today—all entomological proofs to the contrary. See *Vida paraguaya en tiempos del viejo López* (Asunción, 2011), 81–83.

26   Lasserre, *The Paraguayan War*, 27.

27   These pancakes had such a gritty taste that the women would "almost have preferred to eat pure dirt." See Decoud, *Sobre los escombros*, 230.

28   The destinadas encountered neither Brazilians nor Paraguayans in these districts, and the few Guayakí or Mbayá people who showed themselves offered no help. Some *caciques* were greater poseurs than the sutlers in Asunción. They were ready, they indicated, to make an alliance with any of the belligerents, and provide the women with foodstuffs, but only in exchange for goods that the women did not have. See Testimony of Francisco Benítez, 19 November 1869, in IHGB, lata 449, doc. 74; Cardozo, *Hace cien años*, 13: 273–274. One intriguing, almost certainly fabricated, account of late October has some crafty Cainguá offering to furnish López's with a hundred squadrons of ninety warriors each (with another similar group of warriors being offered by the "Mbaracayú") for any Paraguayan women the warriors might to wish to take for wives. See "López with the Caiguay Indians," *The Standard* (Buenos Aires), 11 December 1869. It is hard to credit a story whose veracity depends on the agency of nonexistent Indigenous groups and dubious traditions. That said, the Indigenous people were always on the lookout for advantages they might gain from any confrontations between the Brazilians and Paraguayans, and were willing to tell a good many lies to forward their interests generally.

29   Lasserre, *The Paraguayan War*, 28; Bormann, *História da Guerra do Paraguay*, 1: 407–409; the bishop's mother noted that the refugees were eventually reduced to eating "frogs and serpents." See "Declaration of the Bishop's Mother;" one rumor held that the Cainguá sold the women at Espadín a measure of "bush-meat," that turned out to be human

flesh cut from cadavers. See Cardozo, *Hace cien años*, 13: 100, 154, and Decoud, *Sobre los escombros*, 234–235.

30   Lasserre, *The Paraguayan War*, 29–30; *La Regeneración* (Asunción), 5 January 1870.

31   Lasserre, *The Paraguayan War*, 31.

32   This train of refugees included the bishop's mother, Decoud's wife, the sister of General Barrios, various representatives of the Gil, Aramburu, Aquino, Dávalos, and Haedo families, and Madame Lasserre. See Taunay, *Cartas da Campanha*, 114–115 (entry of 28 January 1870); Taunay, *Campanha das Cordilleiras*, 323–326; *Jornal do Commercio* (Rio de Janeiro), 28 January 1870.

33   *Diário do Exército*, 316 (entry of 28 December 1869); Cardozo, *Hace cien años*, 13: 254; Tasso Fragoso, *História da Guerra entre a Tríplice Aliança e o Paraguai*, 5: 104–109.

34   "Startling from Paraguay," *The Standard* (Buenos Aires), 7 November 1869. Whoever went about without a broad-brimmed hat in this weather risked heatstroke. General Joaquim S. de Azevedo Pimentel tells of a long-range patrol deployed from Rosario that experienced heat so intense that the men almost died of thirst and were saved by their horses, who smelled water in the distance. See *Episódios Militares*, 28–30.

35   The lawless commercial environment in Asunción had finally begun to stabilize, with lawyers, photographers, physicians, and retail merchants setting up local businesses. Even the Polish engineer Robert Chodasiewicz, who had recently separated from the Brazilian army, offered his services to the Asunción public as architect and engineer. See Cardozo, *Hace cien años*, 13: 68–69. In November, the triumvirs tried to license billiard parlors, hotels, and consignment houses, announcing that any establishment that failed to display the appropriate license would be fined double the price of the license; it is not clear that the government had any better luck with this measure than with those that preceded it. See *Registro official, 1869–1875*, 33.

36   *La República* (Buenos Aires), 15 and 18 January and 9 February 1870; *The Standard* (Buenos Aires), 19 January 1870.

37   *La Regeneracion* (Asunción) had already offered an outline for constitutional changes in its 10 October 1869 issue, but this "barometer of progress" bore the mark of the Decoudistas, and was denounced as such both in Asunción and Buenos Aires. Mitre's *La Nación Argentina* (Buenos Aires), 7 December 1869, continued to argue—not implausibly—that the provisional government did not "represent the opinion of the ... population in Asunción, nor of any broader view [in the country, and the men of the triumvirate now] bite the hand of those who yesterday they had joined so as to get to Asunción."

38   With only slight exaggerations, the US minister to Rio observed in this respect that the provisional government was "extremely feeble, and all the interest both on the part of those at the head of it, and the Allies who sustain it, is concentrated in the constant anxiety regarding General López; if his person could be secured it would be a solution of all their difficulties, but as long as he remains alive and free on the soil of Paraguay the pledges of the Allies will be a most serious embarrassment." See Henry T. Blow to Hamilton Fish, Petropolis, 23 November 1869, in NARA, M-121, no. 37.

39   Plausible accounts of the Marshal's movements cropped up in the oddest places. In the 17 January 1870 issue of the *Hartford* [Massachusetts] *Daily Courant*, a Bolivian exile was definitely ruled out, for when "last heard from, [the Marshal was] wandering with a few followers about the deserts [sic] of the Brazilian provinces."

40   Centurión, *Memorias o reminiscencias*, 4: 117–118.

41   See, for example, William E. Barrett, *Woman on Horseback* (New York, 1952); Lily Tuck, *The News from Paraguay*, 180–182; Katharina von Dombrowski, *Land of Women. The Tale of a Lost Nation* (London, 1935), 381–449; and Enright, *The Pleasure of Eliza Lynch*.

42   Aveiro, *Memorias militares*, 92–93. Scholars have generally depicted Venancio López as the innocent victim of his brother's ambition, without recollecting that he himself had once coveted power, just like Benigno, and had he gained the top position, he was just as capable as the Marshal of consummating a policy of revenge and murder. See Cardozo, *Hace cien años*, 13: 29, 48.

43   Washburn, *History of Paraguay*, 2: 585; Federico García, "La prisión y vejamenes de doña Juana Carrillo de López ante el ultraje de una madre," in Junta Patriotica, *El mariscal Francisco Solano López*, 73–98.

44   Centurión offered extensive information on their "trial," making comparisons with Julius Caesar and other classic figures who had to prosecute their relatives. See *Memorias y reminiscencias*, 4: 118–124; by contrast, Father Maíz, who headed the investigation, offered relatively little information on exactly what happened. See Maíz letters, in MHM (A)-CZ, carpeta 122, nos. 4–5.

45   Washburn ascribed this brutality to rank sadism on the part of López, who "was careful not to have them punished beyond the power of endurance. For this object he kept his mother, his sisters, and his brother alive for a considerable time, and they were flogged most unmercifully as often as could be done without danger of hastening their death." See *History of Paraguay*, 2: 586. It is difficult to know how often this occurred in fact, but the hatred that his sisters reserved for the Marshal after the war never abated. In her testimony during the Stewart case, Inocencia offered detailed comments on the brutal treatment meted out to her and her siblings, the cruel boasting of the fiscales, and the culpability of Marshal López for all that took place. See "Testimony of Señora Juana Inocencia López de Barrios, (Asunción, 17 Jan. 1871)," in Scottish Record Office, CS 244/543/19, 84.

46   Dr. Frederick Skinner evidently felt less scandalized by the Marshal's mistreatment of his relatives than by the indifference he showed to his countrymen as a whole. "Who else," he asked Washburn, has "exterminated a whole people by starvation, while he, his mistress and bastards, passed a life of comfort, feasting, nay, drinking choice wine *ad libitum*, surrounded by every convenience attainable in a retreat from a retreating army?" See Skinner to Washburn, Buenos Aires, 20 June 1870, in Washburn, *History of Paraguay*, 2: 586.

47   Aveiro, who flogged the Marshal's mother until the sinews showed, had not started out as a brutal enforcer. In fact, he had shown considerable diligence in seeking personal advancement since his time as Carlos Antonio López's secretary, but in other ways he was entirely ordinary, just possibly the embodiment of what Hannah Arendt termed the "banality of evil" in *Eichmann in Jerusalem* (New York, 1963). Much like his predecessors at San Fernando, Aveiro regarded obedience of orders as his supreme responsibility. So, to his discredit, did Centurión. See *Memorias o reminiscencias*, 4: 148–150.

48   Colonel Patricio Escobar was one of the officers delegated to monitor the ex-war minister, and one morning discovered him dead of "hunger and misery." Escobar immediately penned a note to the Marshal to inform him that don Venancio had died, but before he could send the message, his arm was caught by General Caballero, who advised him to scratch the honorific "don" from the paper or risk throwing suspicion upon himself. Escobar complied and Marshal López neither answered the note nor afterwards showed any concern over his brother. See "Informes del General Escobar, coronel en Cerro Corá, presidente de la república ahora (Asunción, 1888)," in MHM (A)-CZ, carpeta 129. An anonymous letter written by an eyewitness confirms Escobar's account of Venancio's death; see ? to Colonel Juan Crisóstomo Centurión, Asunción, 18 July 1891, in Museo Andrés Barbero, Colección Carlos Pusineri Scala. For his part, Father Maíz denied any role in Venancio's death, remarking in a letter to Escobar that he had been away with the general staff at the time, and found out about his demise only later. See Maíz to Escobar,

Arroyos y Esteros, 4 July 1893, in Museo Andrés Barbero, Colección Carlos Pusineri Scala. In the 1 February 1870 issue of *The Standard* (Buenos Aires), the editors mistakenly reported Venancio still alive, that the López family was "blessed with a naturally 'strong constitution,' " for Venancio had received "enough lashes to kill twenty ordinary men, and more probably than have been given to the 'mauvais sujets' of the British army within the last quarter of a century."

49 Testimony of Concepción Domecq de Decoud (Asunción, 1888) in MHM(A), Colección Zeballos, carpeta 128.

50 Leuchars, *To the Bitter End*, 226; Cecilio Báez, "Pancha Garmendia," *El Combate* (Formosa), 14 May 1892; "Pancha Garmendia," *El Orden* (Asunción), 22 July 1926; Jacinto Chilavert, "La Leyenda de Pancha Garmendia," *Revista de las FF.AA. de la Nación*, año 3 (July 1943); Aveiro to Centurión, Asunción, April 1890, in Centurión, *Memorias y reminiscencias*, 4: 208–212; and Cardozo, *Hace cien años*, 13: 101–102, 104, 121–122, 203–204.

51 Actions in October and November 1869 cost the Paraguayans another two hundred men killed and wounded—a tiny loss compared to Tuyutí or Boquerón, but a very heavy one at this juncture. See Corselli, *La Guerra Americana*, 535–536; Gaspar Centurión, *Recuerdos de la guerra del Paraguay*, 25–28; and Cardozo, *Hace cien años*, 13: 77–79, 83–86, 169–172. Comments from the Brazilian side of these short engagements can be found in "Correspondencia," *Jornal do Commercio* (Rio de Janeiro), 10 November 1869; "Correspondencia de Asunción 31 Oct. 1869," *Jornal do Commercio* (Rio de Janeiro), 17 November 1869; "Correspondencia de Asunción 9 Nov. 1869," *Jornal do Commercio* (Rio de Janeiro), 7 December 1869; and "Diário de Francisco Pereira da Silva Barbosa," which offers extensive details not just on the wasted condition of the Paraguayan troops, but on the dearth of provisions among the Allies.

52 Falcón, *Escritos históricos*, 103–104.

53 Resquín, *La guerra del Paraguay contra la Triple Alianza*, 149–150. Solalinde later opened a hospital at his Asunción house, where he treated many veterans, including the naval officer Romualdo Núñez, who afterwards never failed to express gratitude to the "deserter." See Riquelme García, *El ejército de la epopeya*, 2: 392. Later still, Solalinde sold his rural properties in San Pedro department to Friedrich Nietzsche's sister and her anti-Semitic husband for the establishment of a "pure" German colony at the site. Today only about eighty households are found in this isolated community, which was grandiloquently christened Nueva Germania in 1888. See Ben MacIntyre, *Forgotten Fatherland. The Search for Elisabeth Nietzsche* (New York, 1992), 119–124.

54 Allied patrols were avid to find the Paraguayan troops who had escaped their clutches at Tupí-pytá and executed those survivors who fell into their hands—a fact that López noted on many occasions during the subsequent retreat. See Centurión, *Memorias o reminiscencias*, 4: 140–142.

55 José Falcón reported that, in its lack of birds, the area seemed like a huge wasteland, notable only for the miserable people who passed through it and the mounds of "six, eight, and even ten persons dead of hunger lying alongside the trail." See *Escritos históricos*, 104–105. If the Allies had paid better attention, they could have tracked the Paraguayan retreat by following the line of corpses.

56 *La Prensa* (Buenos Aires), 3 November 1869.

57 Leuchars, *To the Bitter End*, 227.

58 Some cattle were sent by steamer from Asunción to Rosario, but the supplies were never enough and the official records of the Allied armies alluded constantly to serious hunger among the troops throughout this time. See Cardozo, *Hace cien años*, 13: 70, 82, 87, and Olmedo, *Guerra del Paraguay. Cuadernos de campaña*, 499–501, 510–511 (entries of 28 and 30 September and 15–16 October 1869). *The Standard* (Buenos Aires), 14 November

1869, reported that the Brazilian 1st Corps had "had to subsist for three days on the pith of the palm trees, and in consequence there have been several deserters, amongst them twelve officers; the same thing occurred in the 2nd Corps commanded by General Victorino." Argentine merchants had already responded in writing to the Allied demand for supplies but as of late October, provisions had yet to arrive in Paraguay. See Juan J. Lanusse to Paranhos, Asunción, 20 and 29 October 1869, in ANA-CRB I-30, 29, 35, and Campanha do Paraguay, *Diário*, 281 and 287 (entries of 14 and 19 November 1869). Regarding horses, see Antonio da Silva Paranhos to Victorino, Concepción, 31 December 1869, in IHGB lata 448, doc. 62. On cattle, see "Nota detallada de las cabezas de ganado conducidas al Rosario desde el 17 de octubre al 3 de noviembre," Asunción, 9 November 1869, in ANA-CRB I-30, 23, 178.

59 Interrogation of Paraguayan Captain Ramón Bernal, Concepción, 10 November 1869, in IHGB, lata 449, doc. 79; Interrogation of Italian Abraham Sartorius, resident in Paraguay since 1862 (and in service to the López government), Rosario, 22 December 1869, in IHGB, lata 449, doc. 75 [and *Jornal do Commercio* (Rio de Janeiro), 16 January 1870]; and Interrogation of Paraguayan Sergeant Antonio Benítez, 4 January 1870, in IHGB lata 449, doc. 78. See also Colonel Antonio da Silva Paranhos to General Victorino, Concepción, 12 November 1869, in IHGB, lata 448, doc. 60.

60 See "Teatro de la guerra, (Patiño Cué, 20 Nov. 1869)," *La Prensa* (Buenos Aires), 27 November 1869, and Tasso Fragoso, *História da Guerra entre a Triplice Aliança e o Paraguai*, 5: 111–115.

61 Centurión relates how soldiers came back from the bush with *aracitú* fruit (wild chirimoya), which in normal times would have provided a wonderfully sweet dessert, but which caused the men to get sick, so little accustomed were they to eating anything remotely rich. See *Memorias o reminiscencias*, 4: 154–155.

62 *Jornal do Commercio* (Rio de Janeiro), 14–15 February 1870; it is unclear how many of the men recovered from their wounds and illnesses, though the dearth of foodstuffs suggests that most of the seven hundred or so perished. See Centurión, *Memorias o reminiscencias*, 4: 150. As for the women and children, a good number evidently escaped Panadero and joined the numerous trains of refugees wandering through the Cordilleras. The luckier ones encountered Allied troops who shared rations with them. The luckiest of all eventually reached Luque and Asunción. See Count d'Eu to Osório, Rosario, 22 February 1870, in IHGB, lata 276, doc. 27.

63 *La Nación Argentina* (Buenos Aires) reported that as of early February "López has taken to drink and is perpetually tight." See issue of 5 February 1870. Other witnesses were saying similar things.

64 "Latest from Paraguay," *The Standard* (Buenos Aires), 16 February 1870. The "seven cataracts" of the Salto Guairá was once a strikingly beautiful spot where iridescent rainbows coexisted in permanent embrace with tropical foliage. It served as an Ultima Thule for explorers coming upstream along the Paraná since Jesuit times, and had only been mapped with any degree of precision in the early 1860s as part of a geographical and hydrographical survey organized by Carlos Antonio López just before his death and completed by order of his son. See *Diario de un viage por el Paraná desde el puerto de Encarnación hasta el Salto de Guairá por el teniente Domingo Patiño* (Asunción, 1881). One hundred years later the "Sete Quedas" were flooded by the waters of an artificial lake created during the construction of the Itaipú hydroelectric complex.

65 *The Standard* (Buenos Aires), 16 February 1870; Tasso Fragoso, *História da Guerra entre a Tríplice Aliança e o Paraguai*, 5: 159–172; Cardozo, *Hace cien años*, 13: 271–273, 313–314; "Aquidabán," *Jornal do Commercio* (Rio de Janeiro), 5 March 1904.

66 "Correspondencia da Vila do Rosario (14 Feb. 1870)," *Jornal do Commercio* (Rio de Janeiro), 28 February 1870; Antonio da Silva Paranhos to Victorino, Concepción, 12–13

February 1870, in IHGB lata 448, doc. 67; *Jornal do Commercio* (Rio de Janeiro), 31 March 1870.

67   Centurión, *Memorias o reminiscencias*, 4: 161–164.

68   See Marco Antonio Laconich, "La campaña de Amambay," *Historia Paraguaya* 13 (1969–1970): 17–18. Several sources claim that the precise movements of the Marshal's forces into Cerro Corã were revealed to the Brazilians by Cirilo Solalinde, the doctor who had escaped to Allied lines a few days earlier. See Amerlan, *Nights on the Río Paraguay*, 151–153.

69   This conversation, remembered by Silvero in old age, was related to Juansilvano Godoi in Buenos Aires at the end of the 1800s. See *El baron de Rio Branco. La muerte del Marsiscal López* (Asunción, 1912), 119–122. The Correntino journalist and former member of the province's Junta Gubernativa, Silvero supposedly penned a memoir of his experiences but it was never published and evidently disappeared soon after his death in 1902.

70   The Marshal could still impress his soldiers with shows of camaraderie and bravado common in many commanders. On one occasion at Cerro Corã, the men were amused to see López strip off all clothes, jump into a fast-flowing stream, and defeat the current with ease, thereby illustrating how victories could be obtained through audacity. See Centurión, *Memorias o reminiscencias*, 4: 156–157.

71   Cardozo, *Hace cien años*, 13: 423.

72   Decree of Francisco Solano López, Campamento General Aquidabaniguí, 25 February1870, in ANA-SH 356, no. 17; Centurión, *Memorias o reminiscencias*, 4: 168–170.

73   Napoleon held that it was by "such baubles" that men were led (an opinion that Marshal López doubtlessly shared). See Cunninghame Graham, *Portrait of a Dictator*, 262. Panchito López was among those who earned this decoration. See Luis Caminos to Juan F. López, Aquidabaniguí, 26 February 1870, in Ramón Cesar Bejarano, *Panchito López* (Asunción, 1970), 59.

74   "Primero de marzo de 1870. Cerro-Corã," *Revista del Instituto Paraguayo* 6 (1897): 374; Cardozo, *Hace cien años*, 13: 380–383; Resquín gives twenty-three as the number of men accompanying Caballero. See Resquín Testimony in Masterman, *Siete años de aventutas*, 2: 419.

75   Tasso Fragoso, *História da Guerra entre a Triplice Aliança e o Paraguai*, 5: 144–146. Centurión claims that nine hundred men were present at the Tacuara outpost, but this number seems wildly out of synch with other accounts; the total number of Paraguayan effectives, after all, had fallen significantly since the army abandoned Panadero, and those that remained had dispersed in several directions. See *Memorias o reminiscencias*, 4: 164. Cardozo records for all the Cerro Corã encampments a total of only 351 men "ready for combat." See *Hace cien años*, 13: 402. Amerlan notes 400 men and 500 women present. See *Nights on the Río Paraguay*, 149.

76   Most of the men were mounted on mules rather than horses, the former animals having a better record withstanding the fatigues associated with such protracted labor. See Da Cunha, *Propaganda contra o Imperio. Reminiscencias*, 60–61; Tasso Fragoso, *História da Guerra entre a Tríplice Aliança e o Paraguai*, 5: 172–176.

77   One anonymous commentator in the next generation (possibly a young Juan E. O'Leary) held that "two traitors had guided the Brazilian forces in their surprise against the small garrison [at the Tacuara Pass]." See "Cerro Corã," *La Opinión* (Asunción), 8 April 1895, and more generally, "Noticias del Paraguay," *Jornal do Commercio* (Rio de Janeiro), 31 March 1870; Mozart Monteiro, "Como foi morto Solano López," *Diário de Notícias* (Rio de Janeiro), 11 September 1949; Aguiar, *Yatebó*, 50–54.

78   "La fuga del mariscal," in Junta patriotica, *El mariscal Francisco Solano López*, 158–162.

79   Maíz to O'Leary, Arroyos y Esteros, 16 May 1911, in Maíz, *Autobiografía y cartas*, 333–334; Cardozo, *Hace cien años*, 13: 434–435.

80   Centurión, *Memorias o reminiscencias*, 4: 172–173; Olinda Masarre de Kostianovsky, "Cuatro protagonistas de Cerro Corã," *Anuario del Instituto Femenino de Investigaciones Históricas* 1 (1970–1971): 48–49.

81   See Junta patriotica, *El mariscal Francisco Solano López*, 155–169.

82   Aviero, *Memorias militares*, 102; Cerqueira, *Reminiscencias da Campanha*, 400.

83   *A Gazeta de Noticias* (Rio de Janeiro), 20 March 1880; Ignacio Ibarra, "1 de marzo de 1870. Cerro-Cora," *La Democrácia* (Asunción), 1 March 1885.

84   Not surprisingly, Resquín told the story differently, claiming that López had delegated him to escort Madame Lynch out of the line of fire. See Resquín, *La guerra del Paraguay contra la Triple Alianza*, 152–154; "Another Account of the Death of López [testimony of Colonel José Simão de Oliveira, Brazilian engineers]," *The Standard* (Buenos Aires), 6 April 1870; and Amerlan, *Nights on the Río Paraguay*, 154.

85   Aviero, *Memorias militares*, 103–104.

86   An obscure second lieutenant named Franklin M. Machado claimed to have fired the shot that wounded López, but the preponderance of evidence argues in favor of the Marshal's being wounded by a saber, and only later being shot—in the back. See *A Reforma* (Rio de Janeiro), 27 September 1870, Walter Spalding, "Aquidabã," *Revista do Instituto Histórico e Geográfico do Rio Grande do Sul* 23, no. 90 (1943): 205–211; James Schofield Saeger seems to think it significant—or at least indicative of cowardice—that the Marshal was shot in the back, but a survey of every modern war finds no end of heroes who died with bullets in their backs. True enough, López had never displayed much courage, but at Cerro Corã, he refused to yield in the face of certain death. See *Francisco Solano López and the Ruination of Paraguay*, 187.

87   Francisco Xavier da Cunha asserted that the Marshal succumbed to a rifle shot rather than a lance thrust. See *Propaganda contra o Imperio. Reminiscencias*, 62. Rodolfo Aluralde, an Argentine sutler who accompanied Câmara's troops to Cerro Corã claimed that the Brazilian general himself gave orders to shoot López. Cited in Godoi, *El baron de Rio Branco*, 126. In his *Francisco Solano López y la guerra del Paraguay* (Buenos Aires, 1945), 134–155, the Mexican historian Carlos Pereira asserts that in the flurry of the attack, the Marshal also received a saber slash across his head, which failed to kill him. Following the lead of General Câmara and a great many other Brazilian sources, Gustavo Barroso claims that it was a shot to the back that killed López. See *A Guerra do López* (Rio de Janeiro, 1939), 238, as well as Da Cunha, *Propaganda contra o Imperio*, 62, and Arnaldo Amado Ferreira, "Um Fato Histórico Esclarecido, Marechal Francisco Solano López," *Revista do Instituto Histórico e Geográfico de São Paulo* 70 (1973): 365–376.

88   Lacerda was a killer and he looked the part: jet-black hair outlining a fierce face; cruel, sensuous lips; and a square jaw suggestive of passion. As was their wont, the Brazilian soldiery included this unlikely man in their list of popular heroes, even rewarding him with a clever ditty to mark his achievement: "O cabo Chico diabo do diabo chico deu cabo" (Corporal Frank the Devil has finished off the devil Francisco). The imperial government provided Lacerda with a more tangible token of the emperor's appreciation, and he went home to Rio Grande do Sul one hundred pounds richer. See Francisco Pinheiro Guimarães, *Um Voluntário da Pátria*, 156; Azevedo Pimentel, *Episódios Militares*, 169–170; Núñez de Silva, "O Chico Diabo," *El Día* (Buenos Aires), 25 January 1895; and Luis da Camara Cascudo, *López do Paraguay* (Natal, 1927), 19–68.

89   Héctor F. Decoud has the Marshal asking General Câmara at this moment whether he would guarantee his life and property, and when the Brazilian agreed to the first but not to the second, López chose death. See "1 de marzo de 1870. Muerte del mariscal López,"

La República (Asunción), 2 February 1892. Ildefonso Bermejo notes having received a letter from one of the Marshal's agents in Europe that claimed that López was lanced while still on horseback, fell, and when called upon to surrender, growled that death was better than submission to the emperor. It was then that the Brazilians shot him in the head. See *Vida paraguaya en tiempos del viejo López*, 170.

90 The Marshal's last words are variously recounted. Some writers have appended "and with a sword in my hand!" to the familiar "I die with my country!" Others (including Centurión, for example), recorded the words as "I die *for* my country!" The difference between the two expressions is held by many Paraguayans to be essential in understanding López's role in their national history, and has engendered more than a few bitter polemics. The Marshal's twentieth-century idolaters eventually turned his words into something canonical, designed, so we are led to believe, with posterity in mind. But the tongue-tied often find eloquence in their last moments, and it is perfectly obvious that López spoke extemporaneously. Juan E. O'Leary gilded the Marshal's words with glory, but it would be more accurate to see them as precipitous, human, perhaps even trite. See *Nuestra epopeya*, 569, and *El heroe del Paraguay* (Montevideo, 1930), 59–75; Henrique Oscar Wiederspahn, "O Drama de Cerro Corá," *A Gazeta* (São Paulo), 14 November 1950; J. B. Godoy, "A Enigmática Morte de Solano Lopes," *Diario Trabalhista* (Rio de Janeiro), 3, 4, 6, 7, 8, 9, 10, 16, 17, 20, 23, and 24 January 1953.

91 Cardozo, *Hace cien años*, 13: 448–449; Sánchez and Caminos—the Rosencrantz and Guildenstern of political conformity in Lopista Paraguay—played their prescribed roles to the very end, laying down their lives for the Marshal when both probably could have survived the war unscathed.

92 If such orders did exist, it is difficult to explain how a good many highly ranked Paraguayans managed to survive. See Leuchars, *To the Bitter End*, 230, and Fano, *Il Rombo del Cannone Liberale*, 456; writing from a great distance in terms of space if not of time, a reporter for the *New York Herald* (12 May 1870) had no hesitation in labeling the Brazilian actions at Cerro Corã a "horrible massacre"; in his official report on this final engagement, General Câmara admitted no wrongdoing on the part of his men, though there is no more reason to believe his word on this matter than the words of the *New York Herald*. See Official Report (Concepción, 13 March 1870), in *Revista del Instituto Paraguayo* 12 (1892): 414–421.

93 "Noticias do Paraguay," *Jornal do Commercio* (Rio de Janeiro), 4 April 1870 (includes correspondence from Martins and other officers).

94 Opinion is divided as to whether Panchito López met his death by lance or by bullet, with the former position being argued, among others, by Washburn, *History of Paraguay*, 2: 593; Phelps, *Tragedy of Paraguay*, 259; Blomberg, *La dama del Paraguay*, 118; Amerlan, *Nights on the Río Paraguay*, 155; and Agustín Pérez Pardella, *Cerro Corá* (Buenos Aires, 1977), 150–151; and the latter position by Leuchars, *To the Bitter End*, 230; Centurión, *Memorias o reminiscencias*, 4: 183; and General Louis Schneider, "Guerra de la Triple Alianza," in *Revista del Instituto Paraguayo* 12 (1892): 462.

95 Cardozo, *Hace cien años*, 13: 446–447; *La Regeneración* (Asunción) 11 March 1870.

96 Escobar's capture occurred while he was bringing up one of the last Paraguayan cannons. Brazilian horsemen surrounded him and shouted the news that López was *hors de combat*. Escobar laid down his sword, and immediately sent word to General Francisco Roa to tell him of the Marshal's death. But Roa thought the message an Allied ruse, and continued to fight until seriously wounded. The Brazilians beheaded the prostrate Roa once the fighting subsided, an atrocity for which Escobar held himself responsible. See "Testimony of Patricio Escobar," in MHM (A)-CZ, carpeta 129; Juan Sinforiano Bogarín, "Anecdota histórica de Cerro Corã," Asunción, September 1936, in Museo Andrés Barbero, Colección Carlos Pusineri Scala; Maíz to O'Leary, Arroyos y Esteros, 5 April

1904, in Maíz, *Autobiografía y cartas*, 276–279; and Benigno Riquelme García, "General Francsico Roa. Un artillero inmolado en Cerro Corã," *La Tribuna* (Asunción), 25 August 1968. The late Washington Ashwell published an Escobar "memoir" found in an old chest of drawers at the Paraguayan Academy of History. This work asserts that it was a Paraguayan rather than a Brazilian bullet that killed the Marshal. Unfortunately, this "memoir" is manifestly a modern forgery using anachronistic language to make a series of absurd claims (including the idea that Escobar, then a virtually unknown twenty-seven-year-old colonel, was in active contact with Pedro II while en route to the Aquidabán, and that he also maintained correspondence with officials at Brazil's Itamaraty Palace, an edifice not constructed until the 1890s). Of course, as any reader of Sir John Mandeville or Marco Polo knows, a false document can occasionally contain accurate materials, and it is only improbable, not impossible, that the Marshal died at the hands of his own men "to save him from being mocked by the Brazilians." See Ashwell, *General Patricio Escobar. Guerrero, diplomático, y estadista* (Asunción, 2011). Public response in Paraguay to this weird "memoir" was predictably contentious and largely divided along factional lines. See *Ultima Hora* (Asunción), 8, 10 November 2011, and *ABC Color* (Asunción), 9, 10, 11, 13, 20 November and 16 December 2011.

97   The doctors issued a report only after returning to Concepción. They found a three-inch cut to the front (probably from a saber), two major wounds from thrusts driven downward into the abdomen, one of which penetrated to the intestines, and the other, through the peritoneum into the bladder. They also found a bullet wound in the back from which they extracted the Minié ball. See "Certification of the Wounds Causing the Death of Marshal Francisco Solano López by Brazilian Army Surgeons Manoel Cardoso da Costa Lobo and Militão Barbosa Lisboa," Concepción, 25 March 1870, in ANA-SH 356, no. 18.

98   See *The Standard* (Buenos Aires), 6 April 1870; Amerlan, *Nights on the Río Paraguay*, 155.

99   *The Standard* (Buenos Aires), 6 April 1870.

100   See Cunha Mattos testimony in von Versen, *História da Guerra do Paraguai* (Rio de Janeiro, 1913), 263–267.

101   Schneider, "Guerra de la Triple Alianza," 463. Major Floriano noted that Lynch "caused a great sensation" among the Allied officers. See Floriano Peixoto to Tiburcio Ferreira, Arroyo Guazú, 4 March 1870, in Roberto Macedo, *Floriano na Guerra do Paraguai* (Rio de Janeiro, 1938), 43–44.

102   *History of Paraguay*, 2: 593. Washburn echoed the common Brazilian rationale for Lynch's guard, but, as Barbara Potthast-Jutkeit points out, those women who had followed the Marshal to Cerro Corã had other reasons for doing so than to murder his lover. See *"¿Paraíso de Mahoma,"* 296, no. 169.

103   The story repeated by O'Leary (and alluded to in novelistic form by Manuel de Gálvez), which has a Brazilian trooper responsible for cutting the left ear from the Marshal's cadaver to settle a wager, stretches credulity given the presence of senior officers who wanted to take López prisoner and who would have interfered to prevent such an act. Just as unlikely is the assertion that one man danced upon the Marshal's bloodied belly before being driven away by Major Floriano Peixoto. See Cardozo, *Hace cien años*, 13: 446, 450. Doratioto refers parenthetically to the ear mutilation, and to another story involving soldiers who knocked out several of López's teeth and tore out a tuft of his hair, but he does not appear to believe either tale. See *Maldita Guerra*, 453. Slightly more credible is the account offered by Father Maíz, who condemns the Brazilians ("those human hyenas") for having forced Paraguayan prisoners to march over the Marshal's grave as they departed the next day. See *Etapas de mi vida*, 75.

104   In 1936, the Febrerista government exhumed the Marshal's bones and those of Panchito for reburial in the Panteón Nacional, but almost immediately questions arose about their authenticity. Evidence for the specific location of the earlier graves depended entirely on

the testimony of one ancient veteran, who revisited Cerro Corã ten years after the last engagement and found that the crosses that marked the two López graves had fallen—or had been thrown—to one side. He replaced the crosses where he thought they belonged and cut a notch into a nearby tree to further mark the spot. He returned again in 1897 and could find only the machete cut in the tree, the crosses having vanished in the interim. The team that visited the site in the 1930s had only his testimony to work with, and he was by that time a very rheumy old man. Modern DNA research might be able to determine whether the remains in the Panteón really belong to López, but no one as yet seems interested in reopening what could prove a politically charged case. See *La Hora. Organo de la Asociación Nacional de ex-Combatientes* (Asunción), 5 September and 14 October 1936; Juan Stefanich commentary, *La Nación* (Asunción), 23 September 1936; and Efraím Cardozo, "¿Donde estan los restos del mariscal López?" *La Tribuna* (Asunción), 29 March 1970. The scene of battle at Cerro Corã passed during the 1880s into the hands of La Industrial Paraguaya, the country's foremost yerba concern. The Morínigo dictatorship then expropriated the land for a national park in 1945.

105   Official Report of General Câmara (Concepción, 13 March 1870), in *Revista del Instituto Paraguayo* 12 (1892): 421.

106   Couto de Magalhães (1837–1898) rose to the rank of general after the war and earned acclaim as a scholar long before his retirement. His 1876 study, *O Selvagem*, stimulated folkloric studies in Brazil. In 1907 his nephew presented this rare Jesuit text taken from the Marshal's belongings to the diplomat Manoel de Oliveira Lima, who included it in the famous collection of books and documents he donated to the Catholic University in Washington, D. C., where it remains today.

107   General Resquín paid tribute on this count to Paranhos, whose refusal to hand the Paraguayan officers over to the triumvirs for almost certain execution marked him and his countrymen as civilized men, quite distinct from "perfidious traitors" like Rivarola and Loizaga. See *La guerra del Paraguay contra la Triple Alianza*, 158–160.

108   Pinheiro Guimarães, *Um voluntário da Pátria*, 44; General Câmara never recognized his paternity in the case of Adelina López, the daughter born to Inocencia after her return to Asunción. Wanderley, by contrast, married Venancio's daughter.

109   Centurión purposely signed this statement "Centauro" as his way of invalidating the document. See *Memorias o reminiscencias*, 4: 200.

110   Aveiro, *Memorias militares*, 107–108.

111   There was dancing in the streets of the imperial capital when word arrived of the Marshal's death, and then again in May, when the first units returning from Cerro Corã paraded before the jubilant Cariocas. Dom Pedro appeared as excited as all the others when he first received the news but his temper soon cooled when he learned how López was slain. In a letter of 4 April 1870, the war minister wrote to Paranhos about this concern, noting that the emperor "had no wish to consent to the conferring of honors on Corporal Chico [Lacerda] until all was cleared up," and that perhaps it would be "convenient to satisfy him with money." See Pinheiro Guimarães, *Um Voluntário*, 156–158; Kolinski, "The Death of Francisco Solano López," *The Historian* 26, no. 1 (November 1963): 90; *Anglo-Brazilian Times* (Rio de Janeiro), 25 March 1870.

112   *La Regeneración* (Asunción), 9 March 1870; *La Prensa* (Buenos Aires), 17 March 1870.

113   Two days after the engagement at Cerro Corã, the same unit that had killed General Roa caught up with a small unit of Paraguayans under Colonel Juan Bautista Delvalle, who had fled with several wagons of silver plate and other valuables. Though Delvalle and the others raised their hands in surrender, the Brazilians killed every man among them save one, then divided the loot. Resquín claimed that the number of Paraguayan victims in this encounter exceeded two hundred men (although that figure is almost certainly too high). See Centurión, *Memorias o reminiscencias*, 4: 192–195; Bejarano, *El Pila*, 390–391;

and Leuchars, *To the Bitter End*, 231. That the Brazilians gave no quarter on this occasion certainly argued against Caballero's prompt surrender, but Delvalle's killing may have had less to do with refusing quarter than with simple indiscipline.

114   Telegram of Paranhos, 10 March 1870, in *Jornal do Commercio* (Rio de Janeiro), 25 March 1870; Centurión, *Memorias o reminiscencias*, 4: 189–190.The prisoners from Cerro Corã, some three hundred officers and men (excluding the highest ranks), reached Asunción by the end of the month, and were promptly released. See *Jornal do Commercio* (Rio de Janeiro), 14 April 1870.

EPILOGUE

1   One source notes a loss of twelve thousand men from disease, but this either represents a typographical error for a far greater loss or is simple understatement. See "End of the Paraguayan War," *The Standard* (Buenos Aires), 23 November 1869.

2   The US minister to Buenos Aires offered this estimate of costs, adding in his dispatch to Washington that Argentina suffered less than the empire, which had incurred nearly six times as much in war expenditures. Indeed, he expected the resulting budgetary shortfalls to cripple Brazil's economy for some time. See R. C. Kirk to Hamilton Fish, Buenos Aires, 11 September 1869, in NARA FM-69, no. 18. For more details, see *La Prensa* (Buenos Aires), 18 October 1869 and *La Nación Argentina* (Buenos Aires), 27 October 1869.

3   Both the Banco de la Provincia de Buenos Aires and the Bank of London benefited from Argentina's conflict with Paraguay. The latter institution had provided a substantial loan to the national government at a rate of 18 percent, and saw its reserves rise tenfold during the war years, despite having paid 87.5 percent of capital invested in salaries and dividends. See H. S. Ferns, *Britain and Argentina in the Nineteenth Century* (London, 1960), 359.

4   Ironically, Urquiza did not long survive Marshal López, and died a victim of one of the last Federalist uprisings in the Litoral provinces. Urquiza's final trajectory mirrored the fate of Venancio Flores. Both men had started off as minor rural chieftains; both maneuvered their way into power with the connivance of local politicians who underestimated their abilities; both sought Brazilian patronage that seemed valuable initially but which in due time became a liability; and both were murdered by men whose notions of statecraft were even more antiquated than their own. See María Amalia Duarte, *Urquiza y López Jordán* (Buenos Aires, 1974), and Beatríz Bosch, *Urquiza y su tiempo* (Buenos Aires, 1980), 705–714.

5   Armando Alonso Piñeiro, *La mission diplomática de Mitre en Rio de Janeiro, 1872* (Buenos Aires, 1972).

6   The unrestrained money-grabbing, ostentation, and self-delusion of the era eventually converted the gauchos (who had constituted the bulk of the Argentine troops in Paraguay) from "worthless vagabonds" into quaint rustics, the objects of curiosity. José Hernández was only one of many figures who noticed the contradictions in this process. Whether Mitre ever evinced a similar nostalgia is doubtful, but it is nonetheless obvious that he felt uncomfortable in the world he had helped create. Regarding the economic changes that Argentina experienced during these years, see James R. Scobie, *Revolution on the Pampas. A Social History of Argentine Wheat, 1860–1910* (Austin, 1977). Regarding the political changes, see Natalio Botana, *De la república possible a la república verdadera, 1880–1910* (Buenos Aires, 1997), and Botana, *El orden conservador* (Buenos Aires, 1998).

7   Mitre was Argentina's premier historian during the nineteenth century, though in some ways he acted less as a scholar than a promoter of civic values. In an attempt to anchor

his version of Argentine nationalism to the aspirations of an earlier generation, Mitre promoted the figure of Manuel Belgrano, in life a rather ambiguous actor on the Platine stage (who once argued for an Incaic "restoration," but who looked every inch a hero and visionary). Mitre later transferred the same characteristics to San Martín, another curious choice, for the southern liberator's monarchism shrank in Mitre's hands until it nearly disappeared. Don Bartolo may have taken a leaf from the book of Thomas Carlyle in his choice of Romantic heroes, and in asserting that the Argentine nation followed from a teleology or providential plan that only required human will to actuate. True enough, Mitre upheld a modern standard in insisting on documentary evidence to illustrate historical accounts, but his prose style had a built-in gravity, in which every word was accorded weight. As a result, he often turned the trivial into the magnificent and succeeded only in boring the middle-class readers who made up his intended audience. See Eduardo Segovia Guerrero, "La historiografía argentina del romanticismo," (PhD diss., Universidad Complutense, Madrid, 1980); Guillermo Furlong Cardiff, "Bartolomé Mitre: El hombre, el soldado, el historiador, el politico," *Investigaciones y Ensayos* 2 (1971): 325–522; and Tulio Halperín Donghi, *El enigma Belgrano* (Buenos Aires, 2014).

8 Liliana Moritz Schwarcz and John Gledson, *The Emperor's Beard*, 248.

9 Brazilian military engineer André Rebouças recorded that when the count first arrived at Rio de Janeiro it "wasn't enthusiasm; it was delirium. You had to struggle to keep your feet on the ground … you cannot have an idea of the excitement that unfolded throughout the entire city of Rio. During four consecutive evenings there was not a single house that was not illuminated." Cited in Barman, *Citizen Emperor*, 230. See also Kraay, *Days of National Festivity in Rio de Janeiro, Brazil, 1823–1889* (Stanford, 2013), 259–260.

10 Manuel de Oliveira Lima, *O Império Brasileiro, 1822–1889* (São Paulo, 1927), 146. Though he was not properly recognized for it, the count remained an indefatigable defender of veterans' interests for the rest of his life. See Hélio Viana, "O Conde d'Eu: Advogado dos que serviram na Guerra. Dez cartas inéditas do Príncipe Gastão de Orléans," *Cultura Política* 31 (August 1943): 321–327. The count's diaries and personal papers on these (and many other questions concerning the war) can be found in the Archives Nationales (Paris), Archives de la Maison de France (branche d'Orléans), Papiers personnels de Gaston, comte d'Eu (1842–1922), dosier 300 AP IV 278.

11 These men were mostly *caboclos*, or poor whites, who settled into *bairros* on the peripheries of São Paulo and other cities, took advantage of land grants and monetary rewards offered to veterans, and saw their children converted into a lower-middle class that definitely sided with political change and against the status quo. See Pedro Calmon, *História da Civilização Brasileira* (São Paulo, 1940), 226–229, and Kolinski, *Independence or Death!*, 195.

12 The total fatalities suffered by the Brazilian armed forces during the war are difficult to determine, though the most complete statistics seem to suggest that at least 29,000 Brazilians died in combat, with another 30,000 dead from other causes (and missing). See Robert L. Scheina, *Latin America's Wars* (Washington, 2003), 331. Citing materials gleaned from the *Ordens do Dia*, General Tasso Fragoso provides a list of 23,917 men lost up to August 1869, but this statistic seems low even before we correct for the seven missing months (and to be fair to the general, he admits that he had no time to confirm the figures, having concluded that an analysis of military "operations was more useful and interesting than any numerical index"). See *História da Guerra entre a Triplice Aliança e o Paraguai*, 5: 278. Cerqueira, *Reminiscencias da Campanha do Paraguai*, 401, argued for a loss of 100–150,000 Brazilians, inclusive of those who died from disease. *Ba-Ta-Clan* (Rio de Janeiro), 9 October 1869, made the same claim.

13 As with all other statistical information concerning the war, the monetary expenditures of the empire are much debated. See Doratioto, *Maldita Guerra*, 461–462; "The Cost

of the War to Brazil," *The Standard* (Buenos Aires), 26 November 1869; João Nogueira Jaguaribe, "Quanto custou a guerra contra o Paraguay?" in *O Conde de Bagnuoli* (São Paulo, 1918), 89–100; and the *Anglo-Brazilian Times* (Rio de Janeiro), 23 July 1870. Carlos Pereira notes that to obtain 91 million from British banks, the imperial government in Rio had had to recognize a debt of 125 million and this took much effort to repay. The government compounded its problem by covering wartime domestic expenses through the issuance of bonds and paper currency, both of which held little value afterwards. See *Solano López y su drama*, 81. Thus, though commerce increased in Brazil during the 1860s, the financial health of the nation remained doubtful.

14   In an earlier day, Paranhos had expressed ambivalence about the place of the peculiar institution in Brazilian society. With time, however, he came to regard slavery as a major obstacle not just to social progress, but to good relations with the rest of the world. It stung him that foreign abolitionists were singling out his country for contempt. See Robert Edgar Conrad, *The Destruction of Brazilian Slavery, 1850–1888* (Berkeley, 1972), 106–117, and Jeffrey D. Needell, *The Party of Order. The Conservatives, the State, and Slavery in the Brazilian Monarchy, 1831–1871* (Stanford, 2006), 254–256.

15   Paranhos's tenure as prime minister was the longest of the imperial era. See José Murilo de Carvalho, *D. Pedro II* (São Paulo, 2007), 58–59; Lidia Besouchet, *José Maria Paranhos. Vizconde do Rio Branco* (Buenos Aires, 1944), 251–262.

16   Barman, *Princess Isabel*, 232–249. To judge by the results of the 1993 constitutional referendum, the Bragança cause evidently still has its adherents in Brazil; the electorate on that occasion returned an estimated 22 percent in favor of a restoration of the monarchy. See http://en.wikipedia.org/wiki/Brazilian_constitutional_referendum,_1993.

17   Hermes Vieira, *A Princesa Isabel no Cendrio Abolicionista do Brasil* (São Paulo, 1941); Barman, *Princess Isabel*, 232–234, 249.

18   Garmendia, *Recuerdos de la campaña del Paraguay y de Rio Grande* (Buenos Aires, 1904), 493; Doratioto, *Maldita Guerra*, 462; Warren, *Paraguay and the Triple Alliance. The Postwar Years*, 31.

19   The choice of José Gervasio Artigas as a "national" hero for Uruguay was odd, for the Protector de los Pueblos Libres (1764–1850) had never envisioned or contemplated a separate Uruguayan state, and in fact spent the last thirty years of his life in Paraguayan exile. See Guillermo Vázquez Franco, *La historia y los mitos* (Montevideo, 1994) and *Francisco Berra: la historia prohibida* (Montevideo, 2001).

20   The mutual admiration commonly expressed in the Brazilian and Argentine press was unexpectedly prevalent before the Misiones land dispute of the 1890s. See Ori Preuss, *Bridging the Island. Brazilians' Views of Spanish America and Themselves, 1865–1912* (Madrid, Orlando, and Frankfurt, 2011).

21   After the signing of an initial peace protocol in June 1870, considerable debate erupted among the Brazilian councilors of state as to whether the empire should negotiate separately with the provisional government on land questions or whether such negotiations should take place within the bounds of the Triple Alliance. Not surprisingly, imperial interests won out. See Senado Federal, *Atas do Conselho de Estado* (Brasília, 1978), 8: 117–133 (ata de 26 April 1870). See also Treaty of Peace, Asunción, 9 January 1872; Treaty of Limits, Asunción, 9 January 1872; Treaty of Extradition, Asunción, 16 January 1872; Treaty of Friendship, Trade, and Navigation, Asunción, 18 January 1872, in Justo Pastor Benítez, *República del Paraguay. Colección de Tratados* (Asunción, 1934), 380–423; Doratioto, "La ocupación política y militar brasileña del Paraguay (1869–1876)," 274–283; Tasso Fragoso, *A Paz com o Paraguai depois da Guerra da Tríplice Aliança* (Rio de Janeiro, 1941), 55–80; and Antonio Salum Flecha, *Derecho diplomático del Paraguay de 1869 a 1994* (Asunción, 1994), 29–51.

22   Decree of 19 March 1870, in *Registro official, 1869–1875*, 63–64; though the charges against her were wildly exaggerated, it did not stop the Asunción elites from treating her with contempt that even the conservative *Voz del Pueblo* saw fit to endorse: "All of Paraguayan society knows how that evil woman stole their jewels, took their valuables and even fine clothing, sometimes violently, sometimes with serious injury. Every family has a claim against her and every citizen has knowledge of the violence she committed … she will now enjoy the wealth of many unfortunates who today have not a piece of bread for their children." Cited in *La Nacion Argentina* (Buenos Aires), 31 March 1870.

23   Lynch remained a sedulous caretaker of her consort's memory, and a staunch, if somewhat unsuccessful, defender of her family's finances. She returned to Paraguay in September 1875, but within three hours the government put her back aboard the steamer that had brought her from Buenos Aires. Then, after making a trip to the Holy Land, she eventually settled into a quiet life in Paris. She had the satisfaction of seeing her children raised to positions of relative prosperity. One son, the unfailingly charming Enrique Solano López, became superintendent of public instruction in Paraguay a few years after *la Madama's* death and a senator for the Colorado Party sometime after that. See Eliza A. Lynch, *Exposición y protesta que hace Eliza A. Lynch* (Buenos Aires, 1875); *La Tribuna* (Buenos Aires), 26 September 1875; *Artículos públicados en "El Paraguayo" referents a la reclamación Coredero* (Asunción, 1888); and Victor Simón, *Enrique Solano López. El periodista* (Asunción, 1972).

24   Though her critics cast her as a would-be Marie Antoinette, Madame Lynch acted with charity toward prisoners and the poor during the war years, but she tended to concentrate on her own affairs and those of her children. This she continued to do in the conventional fashion one would expect of a mid-Victorian widow—a genteel respectability accompanied by a stiff upper lip and a rustling of crinoline. A lock of her blond hair made its way to Asunción together with the announcement of her passing, and was eventually incorporated into the Juan E. O'Leary Collection at the Biblioteca Nacional. The Alfredo Stroessner government transferred her remains from Paris in the early 1960s, but as she had never married the Marshal, the church objected to her being interred next to him in the Panteón Nacional. She now rests across town at La Recoleta. See Lillis and Fanning, *Lives of Eliza Lynch*, 196–207.

25   K. Johnson, "Recent Journeys in Paraguay," *Geographical Magazine* 2 (1875): 267–269; and, more generally, Herken Krauer, *El Paraguay rural entre 1869 y 1913*, 76–80.

26   Irene S. Arad, *La ganadería en el Paraguay, 1870–1900* (Asunción, 1973), 8.

27   Imposing an indemnity on the defeated Paraguayans seemed a petty, or at least stupid, act, one that made them pay in money what they had already expended in blood. In any case, the new government in Asunción could not pay. The former Allied countries eventually forgave the debt and returned many, though not all, of their war trophies. See Cesar López Moreira, "La deuda de la guerra del Paraguay de 1865/70, reconocida a los países de la Triple Alianza," *Revista del Centro Estudiantes de Ciencias Económicas* 35 (1942): 161–166; *Deuda argentine-paraguaya. Petición presentada al Honorable Congreso Nacional al abrir sus sesiones en 1901* (Buenos Aires, 1901); and Arturo Brugada, *La deuda de guerra paraguaya. Su condenación por el Uruguay en 1883. Antecedentes históricos* (Asunción, 1926). Some of the trophies taken by Argentina were not returned to Paraguay until the time of General Perón. See "No serán devueltos los trofeos," *La Opinión* (Asunción), 22 August 1928; José Angio, *A propósito de la devolución de los trofeos de la guerra del Paraguay* (Paraná, 1954); and Liliana M. Brezzo, "Juan Domingo Perón y la devolución de los troféos de la guerra de la Triple Alianza al Paraguay: entre la fiesta y lo efímero," *Historia Paraguaya* 42 (2002): 267–292. Brazil has taken even longer to return its portion of the trophies.

28 M. L. Forgues, "Le Paraguay. Fragments de journal et de correspondences, 1872–1873," *Le Tour du Monde* 27 (1874): 369–416.

29 The population decline seemed unprecedented, and more than a century later, its analysis unleashed a major debate between "low-counters" and "high-counters." The former asserted a total loss in Paraguay between 1864 and 1870 of less than 20 percent of the population, while the latter upheld the more traditional depiction of Taunay, Centurión, and others, who stated that over 50 percent of Paraguayans died from disease, starvation, and combat. See Vera Blinn Reber, "Demographics of Paraguay: A Reinterpretation of the Great War, 1864–1870," *Hispanic American Historical Review* 68, no. 2 (1988): 289–319; Thomas L. Whigham and Barbara Potthast, "Some Strong Reservations: A Critique of Vera Blinn Reber's 'The Demographics of Paraguay: A Reinterpretation of the Great War,' " *Hispanic American Historical Review* 70, no. 4 (1990): 667–676. *La Regeneración* (Asunción), 31 December 1869, alludes to staggering losses recorded in a preliminary census, findings also asserted shortly thereafter by Paraguayan doctor Cirilo Solalinde, who saw the disaster at firsthand during the final months of the conflict. He held that the Paraguayan population had fallen to less than one hundred thousand individuals, a shocking figure that, given its provenance, must carry considerable weight. See Solalinde Testimony (Asunción, 14 January 1871), in Scottish Record Office, CS 244/543/19.

30 Today's Lopista revisionists, who might be called "ultra-high-counters," seem to have purposely exaggerated the findings of "high-counters" to bolster a xenophobic depiction of Brazilians as genocidal maniacs. The modern Lopistas (and their foreign admirers) who make these claims do a disservice to the men and women of the past in thinking that the louder they shout their claims, the more convincing they become. See, for example, Daniel Pelúas and Enrique Piqué, *Crónicas. Guerra de la Triple Alianza y el genocídio paraguayo* (Montevideo, 2007), 197, who posit a total loss of between 750,000 to 800,000 Paraguayans, "all of whom died in battle." This is rather like saying twice as many people perished in the war as actually lived in the country. Moreover, following the Pelúas and Piqué logic, if 99 percent of the men did die between 1864 and 1870, then the only possible way for the population to have righted itself subsequently would be for the great-great-grandfathers of today's Paraguayans to have been Brazilian soldiers—a politically unthinkable reality for the Lopistas.

31 In the late 1990s, a previously undiscovered national census for 1870–1871 came to light in the archive of the Paraguayan defense ministry, and the high losses it recorded provided a new impetus to the demographic debate. The census had a few structural shortcomings that historians and geographers were quick to point out, but even after taking these weaknesses into consideration, the picture revealed was still unimaginably bleak. See Censo general de la república del Paraguay según el decreto circular del Gobierno Provisorio de 29 de septiembre de 1870," in Archivo del Ministerio de Defensa Nacional (Asunción); Whigham and Potthast, "The Paraguayan Rosetta Stone: New Insights into the Demographics of the Paraguayan War, 1864–1870," *Latin American Research Review* 34, no. 1 (1999): 174–186; Reber,"Comment on the Paraguayan Rosetta Stone," *Latin American Research Review* 37, no. 3 (2002): 129–136; Jan M. G. Kleinpenning, "Strong Reservations about 'New Insights into the Demographics of the Paraguayan War,' " *Latin American Research Review* 37, no. 3 (2002): 137–142; Whigham and Potthast, "Refining the Numbers: A Response to Reber and Kleinpenning," *Latin American Research Review* 37, no. 3 (2002): 143–148. *La Reforma* (Asunción), 6 August 1876, references yet another census, in this case, for April 1872, that records a total population in Paraguay of 231,194 individuals, with adult men only 28,777 in number. The Dutch geographer Jan Kleinpenning, whose own analyses placed him at the lower end of the "high-counters," sadly observed that, though Paraguay's total fatalities were "somewhat less dramatic than [those] calculated by Whigham and Potthast, [they are] still of a pitiful magnitude." See Kleinpenning, *Paraguay, 1515–1870* (Frankfurt, 2003), 1581.

32 Héctor Francisco Decoud, *La convención nacional constituyente y la Carta Magna de la República* (Buenos Aires, 1934); Carlos R. Centurión, *Los hombres de la convención del 70* (Asunción, 1938); Juan Carlos Mendonça, *Las constituciones paraguayas y los proyectos de constitución de los partidos políticos* (Asunción, 1967).

33 Warren, *Paraguay and the Triple Alliance. The Postwar Decade*, 80. More than half of the delegates who attended the constituent assembly felt so threatened or disgusted with the proceedings that they abandoned politics thereafter. One man who did not was José Segundo Decoud, who broke with his liberal allies during the next decade and helped establish the Associación Nacional Republicana (Partido Colorado). This fact vexes today's Colorado ideologues, who hope to find a one-to-one correspondence between former legionnaires and the founders of the rival Liberal Party and instead have to accept Decoud as one of their own.

34 Votes had little value in Paraguay. Men had votes in Italy in the time of the Gracchi, and the exercise of the franchise had saved no one in those days. In Paraguay, only factional allegiances counted, and the sanctity of the ballot box seemed a foreign innovation that both Colorados and Liberals found inconvenient. See Warren, *Rebirth of the Paraguayan Republic*, 39–133; Gómes Freire Esteves, *El Paraguay constitucional, 1870–1920* (Buenos Aires, 1921); Florentino del Valle, *Cartilla cívica: proceso politico del Paraguay, 1870–1950. El Partido Liberal y la Asociación Nacional Republicana (Partido Republicana) en la balanza de la verdad histórica* (Buenos Aires, 1951); and Manuel Pesoa, *Orígenes del Partido Liberal Paraguayo, 1870–1887* (Asunción, 1987).

35 Most prominent individuals in the Marshal's government served only minimal time in Allied detention. For instance, Colonel Wisner de Morgenstern, who had worked for the Paraguayan state since the early 1840s, continued to do so during the 1870s. Allowed by the Brazilians to take up residence in Asunción after the December campaign, he irritated his liberal sponsors by speaking positively of the Lopista cause and turning his nose up at the Allied soldiers who guarded the streets of the capital. A year after Cerro Corã, President Rivarola directed the Hungarian to inventory the Marshal's remaining property so that any hidden monies or valuables could be taken by the state rather than by thieves in Brazilian uniforms. He also aided Colonel George Thompson in the administration of the railroad and ran the government's immigration office. See Warren, *Paraguay and the Triple Alliance. The Postwar Decade*, 133, 144, 206. The majority of the Marshal's officials held prisoner in Rio de Janeiro returned after an unpleasant sojourn, and took up where they had left off. One such man was Falcón, who kept a revealing diary of his captivity in the Brazilian capital (where he and the others were treated as objects of curiosity much in the manner of exhibits in a zoo). Like Centurión, Caballero, and Aveiro, he survived his humiliations and assumed important posts in the new Paraguayan government. He served as senator and foreign minister before passing away at a ripe old age in 1881. See Falcón, "Diario de los prisioneros de guerra," in *Escritos históricos*, 109–156; Centurión, *Memorias o reminiscencias*, 4: 200–202; and Resquín, *La guerra del Paraguay contra la Triple Alianza*, 158–160.

36 Leuchars, *To the Bitter End*, 235.

37 See, for example, Luis Vittone, *Con motivo de la muerte heroica del Mariscal Francisco Solano López en Cerro Cora* (Asunción, 1970). James Saeger, *Francisco Solano López*, 208–221, appropriately condemns these claims as part of a "Big Lie" promoted by O'Leary and other right-wing Lopistas. That the claims also find some support on the populist left is illustrated by the recent decision of the Cristina Kirchner government to rename the 2nd Armed Artillery Group of the Argentine army for Marshal López. See *La Nación* (Buenos Aires), 6 December 2007.

38 Cecilio Báez, the bookish proponent of anti-Lopismo in Paraguay, once sneered in a public forum at the "cretinism" of the Paraguayan people for having followed such a man. See *La tiranía en el Paraguay, sus causas, caracteres y resultados* (Asunción, 1903).

39   The liberal newspapers *La Opinión* and *El Pueblo* severely criticized the young Colorado historian Blas Garay for having instigated the near riot. See Warren, *Rebirth of the Paraguayan Republic*, 111–114, and Francisco Tapia, *El tirano Francisco Solano López arrojado de las escuelas* (Asunción, 1898). The effort of Garay and O'Leary to dismiss Báez and other Liberal writers as antiquated hacks was not totally without effect, for the anti-Lopista position seemed largely in retreat for many decades. Intriguingly, James Schofield Saeger's *Francisco Solano López and the Ruination of Paraguay*, though written by a foreigner, seems to wholly resurrect the polemical style of nineteenth-century anti-Lopista writers (and bears comparison, in this respect, to the denunciations of Washburn).

40   The term "Lost Cause," which foreigners sometimes applied to the Paraguayan War, was borrowed from Sir Walter Scott's romantic depiction of the failed struggle for Scottish independence in 1746, retooled to describe the defeat of the secessionists in the United States 119 years later, and finally resurrected to describe Paraguay's fate in the Triple Alliance War. Twentieth-century Lopistas argue that the war represented the apex of Paraguay's history, when the country stood firmly in defense of her own freedom. O'Leary is most commonly associated with this opinion, but there have been a great many others, some of whom blame British imperialists and bankers more than the kambáes. Others see a natural (though, in fact, improbable) link between Francisco Solano López, Dr. Francia, Juan Manuel de Rosas, and sometimes even Juan Domingo Perón and Fidel Castro. See O'Leary, *Los legionarios* (Asunción, 1930), 192–216, and *El mariscal Francisco Solano López* (Asunción, 1970); Victor N. Vasconcellos, *Juan E. O'Leary: el reivindicador* (Asunción, 1972); Alfredo Stroessner, *En Cerro Corã no se rindió la dignidad nacional* (Asunción, 1970); León Pomer, *La guerra del Paraguay.¡Gran negocio!* (Buenos Aires, 1971); José María Rosa, *La guerra del Paraguay y las Montoneras argentines* (Buenos Aires, 1986); and Eduardo H. Galeano, *Open Veins of Latin America. Five Centuries of Pillage of a Continent* (New York, 1997).

41   This same sentiment is revealed for modern Paraguay by Helio Vera, whose *En busca del hueso perdido*, 131, suggests that the "Paraguayan past does not exist as history, only as legend, and because of this, we have no historians, only troubadours, emotive singers of epics."

42   Prosperous citizens in today's Asunción can speak of current events while enjoying ice cream at the Marshal López Shopping Center. In such a pleasantly air-conditioned (and ironically named) setting, they can ignore the painful chapters in Paraguay's history or remake them to suit modern tastes. They can complain, for example, about Brazilian agribusiness, the latest fees for internet service, and the lack of parking spaces for their Chinese-made cars. In their parents' time, the Lopista interpretation of Paraguay's past received formal support from General Stroessner (as a glance at *Patria* or *Cuadernos Republicanos* will show). This "official account" came to dominate the popular conception of the war, and stays alive today not so much because of state mandate as by the workings of the media. YouTube, which in effect privatized the old nationalism, has become a far greater purveyor of Lopista hyperbole than O'Leary's pamphlets could ever aspire to. Whether the general public in Paraguay will ever give scholarship a place of importance amid the many nationalist or *marxisant* fantasies repeated on the internet remains a matter of intense debate, and it is noteworthy that even the leftist guerrilla organization the Ejército Paraguayo del Pueblo bears on its flag an image of Marshal López on horseback. See Luc Capdevila, "Patrimoine de la défaite et identités collectives paraguayennes au XXe siècle," in *Patrimoine. Sources et paradoxes de l'identité*, Jean-Yves Andrieux, ed. (Rennes, 2011), 205–218; Peter Lambert, "Ideology and Opportunism in the Regime of Alfredo Stroessner, 1954–89," in *Ideologues and Ideologies in Latin America*, Will Fowler, ed. (Westport, 1997), 125–138; and Jennifer L. French, "'El peso de tanta pena': La guerra de la Triple Alianza como trauma intergeneracional," in *Paraguay en la historia, la literature, y la memoria. Actas de las II Jornadas Internacionales de Historia del Paraguay en la Universidad de Montevideo*, Juan Manuel Casal and Thomas L. Whigham, eds. (Asunción, 2011), 321–342.

Glossary

Abati: a defensive obstacle formed by felled trees with sharpened branches.

Acá Carayá: "monkey heads," one of Marshal López's two escort battalions, so called from the tails of howler monkeys used to decorate individual helmets.

Acá Verá: "shiny heads," another of Lopez's escort battalions, so called from the highly polished metallic plates used to decorate individual helmets.

Aguardiente: generic term for distilled spirits, often flavored with fruit or sweetened herbs.

Ahijuna: an interjection of gaucho origin indicating surprise or frustration.

Apepú: bitter orange, the juice of which is sometimes used to flavor alcoholic beverages, and the leaves for making petitgrain oil.

Arroyo: stream or creek.

Banda paí: Paraguayan term for military band.

Bandeirantes: Brazilian backwoods pathfinders or slave catchers.

Barbette: an earthen platform or raised mound fashioned at the edges of forts or reinforced positions to facilitate defensive fire over the parapet.

Batería Londres: the most lethal of the twenty odd batteries facing the Paraguay River at Humaitá.

Bersagliere: a member of a Piedmontese infantry corps organized around 1850 as sharpshooters or riflemen.

Bodoque: marble-sized balls of fire-hardened mud used by Paraguayans as shot for a sling.

Bogobantes: rowers, as with canoes.

Bombilla: a metallic straw, usually of silver, through which yerba mate is sucked.

Bonaerense: an inhabitant of the province of Buenos Aires

Cabichuí: stinging wasp.

Cacolet: one of a pair of chairs or litters mounted on a horse or mule.

Camalote: floating island of aquatic vegetation.

Caña: sugarcane liquor.

Caraguatá: species of agave plant useful in the making of rope and substitutes for paper.

Caranday: a palm tree of Paraguay and the Gran Chaco known for an internal reservoir containing water that is sometimes used in the preparation of a fermented beverage, *copernicia alba.*

Carioca: an inhabitant of the city of Rio de Janeiro.

Carrizal: marsh, slough, or shallow swamp.

Caudillo: military or political chieftain.

Cepo uruguaiana: a painful form of torture employed by the Paraguayans whereby legs and hands were tied together and heavy muskets place upon the back and under the knees to insure that the musculature would slowly be pulled from the bones.

Charqui: dried, salted beef in strips, often used as a ration in both Allied and Paraguayan armies.

Chata: a flat-bottomed raft equipped with a single cannon and towed into position for river operations.

Che ray: "my son" (Guaraní).

Chipa: bread made from manioc flour, eggs, and cheese.

Chiripá: leather undergarment worn at the waist by vaqueros and gauchos in lieu of trousers.

Chucho: malaria.

Congreve rocket: an iron-tipped, British-designed rocket used in the Mysore Wars and the War of 1812; largely obsolete as an offensive weapon by the mid-nineteenth century, but still encountered in some armies around the world.

Correntino: native of the Argentine province of Corrientes.

Cuadro estacado: a form of torture practiced by both sides in the Paraguayan campaign whereby the victim is stretched upon the ground with leather cords attached to his wrists and ankles and pulled tight, leaving him to the full rays of the sun in the form of a Saint Andrew's cross.

Cuero: cowhide.

Destinada: the wife or other female relative of a man who turned against Marshal López in the later months of the war, and held as prisoners as the Paraguayan army retreated inland.

Dulces: sugar sweets often made in Paraguay from guava paste or coconut.

Entrerriano: native of the Argentine province of Entre Ríos.

Estancieros: ranchers or estate owners.

Estero: swamp.

Farinha: manioc flour; arrowroot.

Feijão: black beans, issued as a ration in the Brazilian army.

Forastero: outsider; foreigner.

Galleta: hardtack or heavy cracker, often tasteless, issued as a common ration in the Allied armies.

Galopa: a lively dance tune of gaucho origin, named after the fastest running gait of a horse.

Generale di Divisione: Italian military rank corresponding to lieutenant general.

General da Corte: armchair general or staff officer attached exclusively to the imperial court.

Guaireño: inhabitant of the Paraguayan town and district of Villarrica.

Guembé: fibrous reed used as a rope substitute.

Horizontale: low-class courtesan or prostitute.

Hors de combat: military losses; killed in action and wounded in action.

Jefe de milícia: commander of local militia.

Jefe político: political boss, usually in the rural districts.

Juez fiscal: judge-prosecutor.

Juez de paz: justice of the peace; lower-level town official.

Kaguy: liquor or firewater; literally "drunk-water" (Guaraní).

Kambá: a pejorative term of Guaraní origin, referring to African blacks or to Brazilians more generally; "darkie."

Karaí: father figure or senior individual, sometimes used as a synonym for "señor."

Lapacho: a hardwood of Paraguay and the Argentine Northeast (*Tabebuia*)

Liño: a row of plants.

Litoral: the Argentine provinces edged by the Río de la Plata and its tributaries: Entre Ríos, Corrientes, Santa Fe, and the territories of the Misiones and the Chaco.

Macaco: racist epithet referring to Brazilians, and meaning "monkey" ("Kaí" or "Karajá" in Guarani.

Malambo: a rhythmic dance tune of gaucho origin.

Mangrullo: a primitive observation platform or lookout tower, constructed of tree limbs.

Maquinas infernales: river mines.

Mate: a gourd used as a vessel in the drinking of yerba mate.

Mbaragui: stinging gnats native to Paraguay and the Argentine Northeast.

Mbareté: Guaraní term for both strength and intransigence in political matters

Mbotavy: shamming; lying in order to deceive or evade responsibility.

Mineiro: inhabitant of the Brazilian province of Minas Gerais.

Minié ball: a muzzle-loading spin-stabilized rifle bullet in use in many armies during the nineteenth century, from the time of the Crimean War onward.

Mon dá: theft (Guaraní).

Monte: brush or woodlands.

Montoneros: lower-class rebels, usually referring to gaucho insurgents in the western provinces of Argentina.

Nambí-í: "Little Ears" (Guaraní), a celebrated unit in the Paraguayan army composed exclusively of Afro-Paraguayan soldiers.

Ñandejara Jesucristo: our lord, Jesus Christ, a common Guaraní interjection.

Needle gun: a firearm, usually a rifle, that has a needle-like firing pin, which passes through the paper cartridge case to strike a percussion cap at the bullet base. Associated with the Dreyse design of the 1830s, the weapon was standard for a short time in the Prussian service before being abandoned as inefficient.

Ñú: Guarani term for meadow or opening within a grassy field.

Oriental: Uruguayan.

Palometa: razor fish or piranha.

Pantano: swamp.

Patria: fatherland.

Peón: peasant retainer on a rural estate.

Picada: a trail cut by hand through scrub forest.

Pindó: a hardy feather palm tree native to Paraguay, Argentina, and Uruguay (*Butia capitata*).

Pingo: affectionate gaucho name for pony or small horse.

Plata ybyguí: hidden treasure.

Poihy: cotton blanket of Paraguayan design.

Político: politician, or political hack.

Porteño: an inhabitant of the city of Buenos Aires.

Potrero: field or pasture.

Praça: enlisted man in Brazil's imperial army.

Provinciano: a term commonly used among the Argentines to refer to inhabitants of the countryside (as opposed to citizens of the city of Buenos Aires).

Puchero: a meat-based stew common in the Platine countries.

Pueblito: village.

Puesto: medical aid station.

Purgantes: laxatives.

Pyragüe: Guaraní term meaning "soft-" or "hairy-footed;" a spy or informer.

Quai d'Orsay: French Foreign Ministry.

Residenta: a female member of families who stayed loyal to Marshal López in the later years of the war but who were nonetheless used as forced laborers during the army's retreat inland.

Salvaje: "savage," often used pejoratively to refer to citified political opponents or liberals, and more generally, to any political opponent.

Sapukai: a cry or war-whoop associated with feelings of great anger or exaltation (Guaraní).

Sarandí: tall grass usually found alongside creeks and rivers in the Argentine Northeast and Paraguay.

Sargenta: informal title for women who served as head nurses or medical aides at Humaitá and elsewhere in Paraguay.

Saudade: loneliness and sometimes homesickness or nostalgia, a longing for things distant in time and space (Portuguese).

Sertanejo: backcountry cowboy of the Brazilian interior, usually (though not always) denoting an inhabitant of the Northeastern provinces.

Telégrafo ambulante: mobile telegraph system.

Tereré: a cold or room-temperature infusion of yerba mate.

Toldería: Indigenous encampment or collection of huts.

Torpedo: river mine.

Turútutú: cow-horn cornet, used by the Paraguayans to mock the poor gunnery of the allies.

Úra: botflies.

Viento norte: a hot, gritty wind that blows seasonally out of the Gran Chaco and into Paraguay and is often blamed for lapses in temperament and occasional shows of violent anger.

Viento sur: a cold wind that blows northward out of Argentina and cools tempers in Paraguay as the viento norte heats them up.

Vomitorios: emetic.

Yacaré: caiman.

Yataí: a palm tree of Paraguay, Northeastern Argentina, and the Gran Chaco known for its edible inner stalk (*Areca olerácea*).

Yerba mate: a green herb (*ilex paraguaiensis*) used in South America as a highly caffeinated tea.

Yerbal: wild stand of yerba mate, also called *minerales de la yerba*.

Bibliography

Archives, Libraries, Museums

Archivio Storico Ministero degli Esteri, Rome
Archivo General de la Nación, Buenos Aires
Archivo General de la Nación, Montevideo
Archivo Nacional de Asunción
Arquivo do Instituto Histórico e Geográfico Brasileiro, Rio de Janeiro
Arquivo do Serviço de Documentação Geral da Marinha, Rio de Janeiro
Arquivo Histórico do Itamaraty, Rio de Janeiro
Arquivo Nacional, Rio de Janeiro
Arquivo Publico do Estado do Mato Grosso do Sul, Campo Grande
Biblioteca Nacional de Asunción
Juansilvano Godoi Collection, University of California, Riverside
Museo de Arte Hispanoamericano Isaac Fernández Blanco, Buenos Aires
Museo Histórico de Luján
Museo Histórico Militar, Asunción
Museo Histórico Nacional, Montevideo
Museo Mitre, Buenos Aires
Museu Histórico Nacional en Rio de Janeiro
National Archives and Records Administration, Washington, DC
Washburn-Norlands Library, Livermore Falls, Maine

Newspapers

A Gazeta (São Paulo)
A Imprensa de Cuyabá (Cuiabá)
A Opinião Liberal (Rio de Janeiro)
A Reforma (Rio de Janeiro).
A Regeneração (Rio de Janeiro)
A Revista Ilustrada (Rio de Janeiro)
A Semana Ilustrada (Rio de Janeiro)
A Vida Fluminense (Rio de Janeiro)
ABC Color (Asunción)

Anais da Academia de Medicina do Rio de Janeiro
Anales de la Sociedad Química Argentina (Buenos Aires)
Anglo-Brazilian Times (Rio de Janeiro)
Ba-Ta-Clan (Rio de Janeiro)
Baltimore American and Commercial Advisor
Boston Daily Advertiser
Cabichuí (Paso Pucú)
Cabrião (São Paulo)
Cacique Lambaré (Asunción)
Caras (Lima)
Congressional Globe (Washington, DC)
Correio da Manhã (Rio de Janeiro)
Correo del Domingo (Buenos Aires)
Daily Picayune (New Orleans)
Diário da Bahia (Salvador)
Diário do Rio de Janeiro
El Araucano (Santiago de Chile)
El Centinela (Asunción)
El Combate (Formosa)
El Constitucional (Mendoza)
El Correo del Domingo (Buenos Aires)
El Eco de Corrientes
El Independiente (Asunción)
El Inválido Argentino (Buenos Aires)
El Liberal (Asunción)
El Mercurio (Valparaíso)
El Mosquito (Buenos Aires)
El Nacional (Buenos Aires)
El Nacional (Lima)
El Orden (Asunción)
El Peruano (Lima)
El Porvenir (Gualeguaychú)
El Pueblo (Buenos Aires)
El Pueblo Argentino (Buenos Aires)
El Pueblo. Organo del Partido Liberal (Asunción)
El Río de la Plata (Buenos Aires)
El Semanario (Semanario de Avisos y Conocimientos Utiles) (Asunción)
El Siglo (Montevideo)
Estrella (Piribebuy)
Gazeta de Noticias (Rio de Janeiro)
Herald and Star (Panama City)
Hoy (Asunción)

Jornal do Brasil (Rio de Janeiro)
Jornal do Commercio (Rio de Janeiro)
Jornal do Dia (Porto Alegre)
Jornal do Recife
L'Etendard (Paris)
L'Illustration (Paris)
La América (Buenos Aires)
La Aurora (Asunción)
La Democracia (Asunción)
La Epoca (La Paz)
La Esperanza (Asunción)
La Esperanza (Corrientes)
La Mañana (Montevideo)
La Nación (Asunción)
La Nación Argentina (Buenos Aires)
La Nazione Italiana (Buenos Aires)
La Noticia (Buenos Aires)
La Opinión (Asunción)
La Palabra de Mayo (Buenos Aires)
La Palabra de Mayo (Buenos Aires)
La Patria (Asunción)
La Patria (Buenos Aires)
La Prensa (Asunción)
La Prensa (Buenos Aires)
La Razón (Montevideo)
La República (Asunción)
La Tribuna (Asunción)
La Tribuna (Buenos Aires)
La Tribuna (Montevideo)
La Unión, Órgano del Partido Nacional Republicano (Asunción)
La Voz del Pueblo (Buenos Aires)
Le Courrier de la Plata (Buenos Aires)
Liberdade (Rio de Janeiro)
London Illustrated Times
New York Daily Tribune
New York Evening Post
New York Herald
New York Times
New York Tribune
Ñandé (Asunción)
O Alabama (Salvador da Bahia)
O Constitucional (Ouro Preto)

O *Correio Mercantil* (Rio de Janeiro)
O *Diário de São Paulo*
O *Diário do Povo* (Rio de Janeiro)
O *Tribuno* (Recife)
Opinião Liberal (Rio de Janeiro)
Paraguai Ilustrado (Rio de Janeiro)
Revista de História e Arte (Belo Horizonte)
Revista de la Escuela Militar (Asunción)
The Standard (Buenos Aires)
The Times (London)
Última Hora (Asunción)

Secondary Works

Abente, Diego. "Foreign Capital, Economic Elites, and the State in Paraguay during the Liberal Republic (1870–1936)." *Journal of Latin American Studies* 21, no. 1 (1989): 61–88.

Acevedo, Eduardo. *Anales históricos del Uruguay.* 3 vols. Montevideo: Barreiro y Ramos, 1933–1936.

Agassiz, Louis and Elizabeth. *A Journey in Brazil.* Boston: Ticknor and Fields, 1868.

Aguiar, Adriano. *Yatebó. Episodio de la guerra del Paraguay.* Montevideo: Imprenta y Librería Vázquez Cores y Montes, 1899.

Alfaro Huerta, Eliseo. "Documentos oficiales relativos a la construcción del telégrafo en el Paraguay." *Revista de las Fuerzas Armadas de la Nación* 3 (1943): 2381–2390.

Aljovín, Cristóbal. "Observaciones peruanas en torno a la guerra de la Triple Alianza." Paper presented at V Encuentro Anual del CEL, Buenos Aires, 5 November 2008.

Almonacid, Vicente A. *Felipe Varela y sus hordas en la provincia de La Rioja.* Córdoba: Imprenta del Eco de Córdoba, 1869.

Alonso Piñeiro, Armando. *La misión diplomática de Mitre en Rio de Janeiro, 1872.* Buenos Aires: Institución Mitre, 1977.

Amaral, Antonio José do. *Indicador da Legislação Militar em Vigor no Exército do Imperio do Brasil.* Rio de Janeiro: Tipografia Nacional, 1871.

Amaral, Raúl. *Escritos paraguayos. Introducción a la cultura nacional.* Asunción: Ediciones Paraguayas, 2003.

———. *Escritos paraguayos. Primera parte.* Asunción: Mediterráneo, 1984.

Amerlan, Albert. *Nights on the Río Paraguay. Scenes of War and Character Sketches.* Buenos Aires: H. Tjarks, 1902.

Andrade, Oswald de. *Poesias reunidas.* São Paulo: Difusão Européia Do Livro, 1966.

Angió, José *A propósito de la devolución de los trofeos de la guerra del Paraguay.* Paraná: La Acción, 1954.

Aponte B., Leandro. *Hombres … Armas … y batallas de la epopeya de los siglos.* Asunción: Imprenta Comuneros, 1971.

Arad, Irene S. "La ganadería en el Paraguay, 1870–1900." *Revista Paraguaya de Sociología* 10, no. 28 (1973): 183–223.

Areces, Nidia R. "Terror y violencia durante la guerra del Paraguay: 'La masacre de 1869' y las familias de Concepción." *European Review of Latin American and Caribbean Studies* 81 (2006): 43–63.

Arendt, Hannah. *Eichmann in Jerusalem. A Report on the Banality of Evil.* New York: Viking Press, 1963.

Argüello, Ana María. *El rol de los esclavos negros en el Paraguay.* Asunción: Centro Editorial Paraguayo, 1999.

Ashwell, Washington. *General Patricio Escobar. Guerrero, diplomático y estadista.* Asunción: Medusa, 2011.

Assumpção, Roberto. "Rio-Branco e 'L'Illustration.' " *Revista do Instituto Histórico e Geográfico Brasileiro* 188 (1946): 101–103.

Aveiro, Silvestre. *Memorias militares, 1864–1870.* Asunción: Ediciones Comuneros, 1989.

Ávila, Manuel. "Apuntes sobre la conspiración de 1869. Pequeña contribución a la historia de la guerra con la Triple Alianza y de la tiranía de López." *Revista del Instituto Paraguayo* 2, no. 3 (1899): 215–228, and 3, no. 1 (1900): 300–301.

———. "La controversia Caxias-Mitre. Notas ligeras." *Revista del Instituto Paraguayo* 5, no. 46 (1903): 286–293.

———. "Rectificaciones históricas. Estero Bellaco." *Revista del Instituto Paraguayo* 2, no. 22 (1899): 143–151.

———. "El vice-presidente Sánchez fusilando. Espíritu de imitación por miedo." *Revista del Instituto Paraguayo* 6, no. 52 (1905): 32–38.

Ayrosa, Plínio. *Apontamentos para a Bibliografía da Lingua Tupí-Guaraní.* São Paulo: USP, 1943.

Azevedo Pimentel, Joaquim Silveiro de. *Episodios Militares.* Rio de Janeiro: Biblioteca do Exército, 1978.

Báez, Adolfo I. *Tuyuty.* Buenos Aires. Talleres Gráficos Ferrari Hnos., 1929.

———. *Yatayty Cora. Una conferencia histórica (Recuerdo de la guerra del Paraguay).* Buenos Aires: Imprenta y Papelería Juan Perrotti, 1929.

Báez, Cecilio. *La tiranía en el Paraguay, sus causas, caracteres y resultados.* Asunción: El País, 1903.

Baillie, Alexander F. *A Paraguayan Treasure. The Search and the Discovery.* London: Simpkin, Marshall & Co.: 1887.

Baratta, Victoria. "La guerra de la Triple Alianza y las representaciones de la nación argentina: un análisis del periódico *La América* (1866)." Paper presented at the Segundo Encuentro Internacional de Historia sobre las Operaciones Bélicas durante la Guerra de la Triple Alianza, Asunción-Ñeembucú, October 2010.

Barman, Roderick. *Citizen Emperor: Pedro II and the Making of Brazil, 1825-1891.* Stanford: Stanford University Press, 1999.

———. *Princess Isabel of Brazil. Gender and Power in the Nineteenth Century.* Wilmington: Scholarly Resources, 2002.

Barreto de Souza, Adriana. *Duque de Caxias. O Homen por Tras do Monumento.* Rio de Janeiro: Civilização Brasileira, 2008.

Barrett, William E. *Woman on Horseback. The Story of Francisco López and Elisa Lynch.* New York: Doubleday & Company, 1952.

Barrio, Patricia. "Carlos Guido y Spano y una visión de la guerra del Paraguay." *Todo es Historia* 216 (1985): 38-44.

Barros, A. J. Victorino de. *Guerra do Paraguay. O Almirante Visconde de Inhaúma.* Rio de Janeiro: Typ. do Imperial Instituto Artístico, 1870.

Barroso, Gustavo. *A Guerra do López.* Rio de Janeiro: Getúlio M. Costa, 1939.

Barton, Matthew M. "The Military's Bread and Butter: Food Production in Minas Gerais, Brazil, During the Paraguayan War." Paper presented at the Latin American Labor History Conference, Duke University, 1 April 2011.

———. *Sons of the Forest: Perceptions of the Brazilian Indians during the Paraguayan War.* Master's thesis, University of Chicago, 2006.

Beattie, Peter M. "Inclusion, Marginalization, and Integration in Brazilian Institutions: the Army as Inventor and Guardian of Traditions." Paper presented at the Brazil Strategic Culture Workshop, Florida International University, November 2009.

———. "National Identity and the Brazilian Folk: The *Sertanejo* in Taunay's *A retirada da Laguna.*" *Review of Latin American Studies* 4, no. 1 (1991): 7-43.

———. *The Tribute of Blood. Army, Honor, Race, and Nation in Brazil, 1864-1945.* Durham and London: Duke University Press, 2001.

Becker, Klaus. *Alemães e Descendentes do Rio Grande do Sul na Guerra do Paraguay.* Canoas: Editorial Hilgert, 1968.

Bejarano, Ramón César. *Panchito López.* Asunción: Editorial Toledo, 1970.

———. *"El Pila," señor del Chaco.* Asunción: Editorial Toledo, 1985.

Bengoechea Rolón, Felipe E. *Humaitá. Estampas de epopeya.* Asunción: Editorial Don Bosco, 2008.

Benítes, Gregorio. *Anales diplomáticos y militares de la guerra del Paraguay.* 2 vols. Asunción: Muñoz Hnos., 1906.

———. *Primeras batallas contra la Triple Alianza.* Asunción: Talleres Gráficos del Estado, 1919.

Bermejo, Ildefonso. *Vida paraguaya en tiempos del viejo López.* Buenos Aires: EUDEBA, 1973.

Besouchet, Lidia. *José Maria Paranhos. Vizconde do Rio Branco.* Buenos Aires: Viau, 1944.

Beverina, Juan. *La guerra del Paraguay: las operaciones de la Guerra en territorio argentino y brasileño.* 7 vols. Buenos Aires: Ferrari Hnos., 1921.

———. *La guerra del Paraguay (1865–1870). Resumen histórico.* Buenos Aires: Círculo Militar, 1973.

Bezerra Neto, José Maia. "Nos bastidores da guerra: fugas escravas e fugitivos na época da Guerra do Paraguai (Grão Pará: 1864–1870)." *História & Perspectivas* 20–21 (January–December 1999): 85–115.

Blomberg, Héctor Pedro. *La dama del Paraguay. Biografía de Madama Lynch.* Buenos Aires: Editora Inter-Americana, 1942.

Bocaiúva, Quintino Souza de. *Guerra do Paraguay. A Nova Phase (Carta a um Amigo).* Montevideo: Typographia Sul-Americana, 1869.

Boccia Romañach, Alfredo. "El caso de Rafaela López y el Bachiller Pedra." *Revista de la Sociedad Científica del Paraguay* 7, no.12–13 (2002): 89–96.

Bogado Bordón, Catalo. *Natalicio de María Talavera. Primer poeta y escritor paraguayo.* Asunción: Casa de la Poesía, 2003.

Bonalume Neto, Ricardo. "River Passage Sought." *Military History* 10, no. 5 (1993): 66–75, 95–98.

Bordón, F. Arturo. *Historia política del Paraguay.* Asunción: Orbis, 1976.

Borges Fortes, Heitor. "Atuação do Corpo de Artilharia do Amazonas na Força Expedicionária a Mato Grosso e Retirada da Laguna." *Revista Militar Brasileira* 53, no. 4/86 (1967): 32–35.

Borges, Jorge Luis. *Obras Completas, 1923–1972.* Buenos Aires: Emecé, 1974.

Bormann, José. *História da Guerra do Paraguay.* 3 vols. Curitiba: Impressora Paranaense, 1897.

Bosch, Beatriz. "Los desbandes de Basualdo y Toledo." *Revista de la Universidad de Buenos Aires* 4, no. 1 (1959): 213–245.

———. *Urquiza y su tiempo.* Buenos Aires: EUDEBA, 1980.

Botana, Natalio. *El orden conservador.* Buenos Aires: Sudamericana, 1998.

Box, Pelham Horton. *The Origins of the Paraguayan War.* New York: Russell and Russell, 1930.

Bozzo, Emanuele. *Notizie Storiche sulla Repubblica del Paraguay e la Guerra Attuale.* Genoa: Tip. del Commercio, 1869.

Bray, Arturo. *Hombres y épocas del Paraguay (Parte Segunda).* Buenos Aires: Ediciones Nizza, 1957.

———. *Solano López, soldado de la gloria y del infortunio.* Buenos Aires: Guillermo Kraft, 1945.

Brezzo, Liliana M. "Armas norteamericanas en la guerra del Paraguay." *Todo es Historia* 325 (1994): 28–31.

———. "Civiles y militares durante la ocupación de Asunción: agentes del espacio urbano, 1869." *Res Gesta* 37 (1998–1999): 23–53.

———. "¿Qué revisionismo histórico? El intercambio entre Juan E. O'Leary y el mariscal Pietro Badoglio en torno a *El Centauro de Ybicuí*." Paper presented at the Segundas Jornadas Internacionales de Historia del Paraguay, Montevideo, 16 June 2010.

——. "Tan sincero y leal amigo, tan ilustre benefactor, tan noble y desinteresado escritor: los mecanismos de exaltación de Juan Bautista Alberdi en Paraguay, 1889–1910." Paper presented at the XXVII Encuentro de Geohistoria Regional, Asunción, 17 August 2007.

Brock, Darryl E. "Naval Technology from Dixie." *Americas* 46 (1994): 6–15.

Browning, Christopher R. *Ordinary Men: Reserve Police Battalion 101 and the Final Solution in Poland.* New York: Harper Collins, 1993.

Buchbinder, Pablo. "Estado, caudillismo y organización miliciana en la provincia de Corrientes en el siglo XIX: el caso de Nicanor Cáceres." *Revista de Historia de América* 136 (2005): 37–64.

Bulfinch, S. G. "Paraguay and the Present War." *North American Review* 109, no. 225 (1869): 510–544.

Burton, Isabel and W. Y. Wilkins. *The Romance of Isabel, Lady Burton. The Story of Her Life.* New York: Dodd Mead & Company, 1899.

Burton, Richard. *Letters from the Battle-fields of Paraguay.* London: Tinsley Brothers, 1870.

Caballero Aquino, Ricardo. *La 2ª República paraguaya. Política, economía, sociedad.* Asunción: Edipar, 1986.

Caballero Campos, Hérib and Cayetano Ferreira Segovia. "El periodismo de guerra en el Paraguay." *Nuevo Mundo. Mundos Nuevos* (Coloquios), 2006. http://nuevomundo. revues.org/index1384.html.

Cadogan, León. "Plata Yviguy. Tesoros escondidos." In *Antología ibérica y americana del folklore,* edited by Félix Coluccio, 243–245. Buenos Aires: Kraft, 1953.

Cadogan, León and A. López Austin. *La literatura de los guaraníes.* Mexico City: Mortiz, 1970.

Cajías, Fernando. "Bolivia y la guerra de la Triple Alianza." Paper presented at the V Encuentro Anual del CEL, Buenos Aires, 5 November 2008.

Calmon do Pin Lisboa, Miguel. *Memorias da Campanha do Paraguay.* Pará: Typ. de A. F. da Costa, 1868.

Calmon, Pedro. *A Princesa Isabel "a Redentora."* São Paulo: Companhia Editora Nacional, 1941.

Campobassi, José S. *Mitre y su época.* Buenos Aires: EUDEBA, 1980.

Campos Arrundão, Bias. *Ending the War of the Triple Alliance. Obstacles and Impetus.* PhD diss., University of Texas at Austin, 1981.

Canard, Benjamín, Joaquín Cascallar, and Miguel Gallegos. *Cartas sobre la guerra del Paraguay.* Buenos Aires: Academia Nacional de la Historia, 1999.

Canton, Eliseo. *Historia de la medicina del Río de la Plata.* Madrid: Impr. G. Hernández y Galo Sáez, 1928.

Capdevilla, Luc. "O gênero da nação nas gravuras. *Cabichuí* e *El Centinela,* 1867–1868." *ArtCultura* 9, no. 14 (2007): 55–69.

——. *Une guerre totale, Paraguay 1864–1870. Essai d'histoire du temps présent.* Rennes: Presses Universitaires, 2007.

————. *Variations sur le pays des femmes. Echos d'une guerre américaine (Paraguay 1864–1870/Temps présent)*. Rennes: Presses Universitaires, 2006.

Cardozo, Efraím. *Hace cien años: crónicas de la guerra de 1864–1870 publicadas en La Tribuna*. 13 vols. Asunción: Ediciones EMASA, 1968–1982.

————. *Paraguay independiente*. Asunción: Carlos Schauman Editor, 1987.

Careaga, Carlos. *Teniente de Marina José María Fariña, héroe naval de la guerra contra la Triple Alianza*. Asunción: 1948.

Carretaro, Andrés M. *Correspondencia de Dominguito en la guerra del Paraguay*. Buenos Aires: Ediciones Librería El Lorrain, 1975.

Carvalho, Alexandre Manoel Albino de. *Relatório apresentado ao Ilmo. e Exm. Snr. Chefe de Esquadra Augusto Leverger, Vice-Presidente da Provincia de Matto-Grosso, em Agosto de 1865*. Rio de Janeiro, 1866.

Carvalho, José Carlos de. *Noções de Artilharia para Instrução dos Oficiais Inferiores da Arma no Exército fora do Império pelo Dr. [...] Chefe da Comissão de Engenheiros do Primero Corpo do Mesmo Exército*. Montevideo, 1866.

Casal, Juan Manuel. "Uruguay and the Paraguayan War: the Military Dimension." In *I Die with My Country. Perspectives on the Paraguayan War, 1864–1870*, edited by Hendrik Kraay and Thomas L. Whigham, 119–139. Lincoln and London: University of Nebraska Press, 2004.

Casal, Juan Manuel and Thomas L. Whigham, eds. *Paraguay en la historia, la literatura, y la memoria. Actas de las II Jornadas Internacionales de Historia del Paraguay en la Universidad de Montevideo*. Asunción: Tiempo de Historia, 2011.

————, eds. *Paraguay: Investigaciones de historia social y política. III Jornadas Internacionales de Historia del Paraguay en la Universidad de Montevideo*. Asunción: Tiempo de Historia, 2013.

Castro, Celso. "Entre Caxias e Osório: a criação do culto ao patron do exército brasileiro." *Estudos Históricos* 14, no. 25 (2000): 103–118.

Cavalcanti Proença, Manuel. *José de Alencar na Literatura Brasileira*. Rio de Janeiro: Civilização Brasileira, 1966.

Centeno, Miguel A. *Blood and Debt: War and the Nation-State in Latin America*. University Park: Pennsylvania State University Press, 2002.

Centurión, Carlos R. *Historia de la cultura paraguaya*. Asunción: Biblioteca Ortiz Guerrero, 1961.

————. *Los hombres de la convención del 70*. Asunción: El Arte, 1938.

Centurión, Gaspar. *Recuerdos de la guerra del Paraguay*. Asunción: Ariel, 1931.

Centurión, Juan Crisóstomo. *Memorias o reminiscencias históricas sobre la guerra del Paraguay*. 4 vols. Asunción: El Lector, 1987.

Cerqueira, Dionísio Evangelista de Castro. *Reminiscências da Campanha do Paraguai, 1864–1870*. Rio de Janeiro: Gráfica Laemmert, 1948.

Cerri, Daniel. *Campaña del Paraguay*. Buenos Aires: Tipografía Del Pueblo, 1892.

Chasteen, John Charles. *Heroes on Horseback. A Life and Times of the Last Gaucho Caudillos.* Albuquerque: University of New Mexico Press, 1995.

Chaves, Julio César. *La conferencia de Yataity Corã.* Buenos Aires: Biblioteca Histórica Paraguaya de Cultura Popular, 1958.

———. *El general Díaz. Biografía del Vencedor de Curupaity.* Asunción: Ediciones Nizza, 1957.

Chávez, Fermín. *El revisionismo y las montoneras: la "Unión Americana," Felipe Varela, Juan Saá y López Jordán.* Buenos Aires: Ediciones Theoria, 1966.

———. *Vida y muerte de López Jordán.* Buenos Aires: Ediciones Theoria, 1957.

Chesterton, Bridget María. *The Grandchildren of Solano López. Frontier and Nation in Paraguay, 1904-1936.* Albuquerque: University of New Mexico Press, 2013.

Chevalier, François. "'Caudillos' et 'caciques' en Amérique: contribution á l'étude des liens personnels." In *Melanges offerts a Marcel Bataillon par les Hispanistes Français.* Special Edition, *Bulletin Hispaniques* 64 (1962): 30-47.

Chianelli, Trinidad Delia. *El gobierno del puerto.* Buenos Aires: Ediciones La Bastilla, 1975.

Chiavenato, Júlio José. *Genocídio Americano. La guerra del Paraguay.* Asunción: Carlos Schauman, 1989.

Clausewitz, Carl von. *On War.* Princeton: Princeton University Press, 1984.

Coelho Neto, Henrique Maximiano. *Bazar.* Oporto: Chardron, de Lello & Irmã, 1928.

Comando en Jefe del Ejército. *Historia de las comunicaciones en el ejército argentino.* Buenos Aires, 1970.

Congreso Brasileiro. *Camara dos Diputados. Perfis Parlementares.* Brasilia: Congreso Brasileiro, 1979.

Congreso de la Nación Argentina. *Diario de sesiones de la Cámara de Senadores (1866).* Buenos Aires: Congreso de la Nación Argentina, 1893.

Congress (US). *Report of the Committee on Foreign Affairs on the Memorial of Porter C. Bliss and George F. Masterman on Relation to their Imprisonment in Paraguay. House of Representatives, May 5, 1870 (The Paraguayan Investigation).* Washington, DC: GPO, 1870.

Conrad, Robert Edgar. *The Destruction of Brazilian Slavery, 1850-1888.* Berkeley: University of California Press, 1972.

Conte, Antonio. *Gobierno provisorio del brigadier general Venancio Flores.* Montevideo: Imprenta Latina, 1897.

Cooney, Jerry W. "Economy and Manpower. Paraguay at War, 1864-1869." In *I Die with My Country. Perspectives on the Paraguayan War, 1864-1870,* edited by Hendrik Kraay and Thomas L. Whigham, 23-43. Lincoln and London: University of Nebraska Press, 2003.

———. "Lealtad dudosa: la lucha paraguaya por la frontera del Paraná, 1767-1777." In *Campo y frontera. El Paraguay al fin de la era colonial,* edited by Thomas L. Whigham and Jerry W. Cooney, 13-34. Asunción: Servilibro, 2006.

Cornejo, Escipión. *La verdad histórica. Invasión y montonera de Felipe Varela.* Salta, 1907.

Corréa, Valmir Batista and Lúcia Salsa Corréa. *Memorandum de Manoel Cavassa*. Campo Grande: UFMS, 1997.

Correia, Manoel Francisco. "Saque de Assumpção e Luque atribuido ao Exército Brasileiro na Guerra do Paraguay: Refutação." *Revista do Instituto Histórico e Geográfico Brasileiro* 59 (1896): 369–393.

Corselli, Rodolfo. *La Guerra Americana della Triplice Alleanza contro il Paraguay*. Modena: Tipografia delle Reale Accademia di Fanteria e Cavalleria, 1938.

Cortés-Conde, Roberto. *Dinero, deuda y crisis. Evolución fiscal y monetaria en la Argentina, 1862–1890*. Buenos Aires: Sudamericana, 1989.

Costa, Dora L. and Matthew E. Kahn. *Heroes and Cowards: The Social Face of War*. Princeton: Princeton University Press, 2008.

Costa Sobrinho, José L. da. "Guerra do Paraguay. Pela Verdade Histórica." *Revista Americana* 9 (1919).

Cotrim, Alvaro. *Pedro Américo e a Caricatura*. Rio de Janeiro: Pinakotheke, 1983.

Creydt, Oscar. *Formación histórica de la nación paraguaya*. n.p., 1963.

Cruz Cordeiro, Antonio da. *Episódio da Esquadra Brasileira em Operação nas Aguas do Paraguay, a 19 de Fevereiro de 1868*. Paraíba: Tipografia J. R. da Costa, 1868.

Cuarterolo, Miguel Ángel. "Images of War. Photographers and Sketch Artists of the Triple Alliance Conflict." In *I Die with My Country. Perspectives on the Paraguayan War, 1864–1870*, edited by Hendrik Kraay and Thomas L. Whigham, 154–178. Lincoln and London: University of Nebraska Press, 2004.

Cunninghame Graham, Robert B. *Portrait of a Dictator, Francisco Solano Lopez (Paraguay, 1865–1870)*. London: W. Heinemann Ltd., 1933.

———. *Progress*. London: Duckworth and Co., 1905.

Curtis, William Elroy. *The Capitals of Spanish America*. New York: Harper & Bros., 1888.

D'Almeida, Valério. *Primer Centenario de la Retomada da Vila de Corumbá: 1867–1967*. Corumbá, 1967.

Da Camara Cascudo, Luis. *López do Paraguay*. Natal: Tipografia d'A República, 1927.

Da Cunha Paranaguá, João Lustoza. *Relatório Apresentado a Assembléa Geral na Segunda Sessão da Deceima Terceira Legislatura*. Rio de Janeiro: Perservança, 1868.

Da Cunha, Francisco Xavier. *Propaganda contra do Imperio. Reminiscencias na Imprensa e na Diplomacia, 1870 a 1910*. Rio de Janeiro: Imprensa Nacional, 1914.

Dahl, Victor C. "The Paraguayan 'Jewel Box.'" *The Americas* 21, no. 3 (1965): 223–242.

Da Mota, Artur Silveira. *Reminiscencias da Guerra do Paraguai*. Rio de Janeiro: Serviço de Documentação Geral da Marinha, 1982.

Davis, Arthur. *Martin T. McMahon, Diplomático en el estridor de las armas*. Asunción: Imp. Militar, 1985.

Davis, Charles H. *Life of Charles H. Davis. Rear Admiral, 1807–1877*. Boston and New York: Houghton Mifflin, 1899.

Davis, William Columbus. *The Last Conquistadors. The Spanish Intervention in Peru and Chile, 1863–1866*. Athens: University of Georgia Press, 1950.

De Castro Souza, Luiz. "A Medicina na Guerra do Paraguai (Mato-Grosso) (III)." *Revista de História* 40, no. 81 (1970): 113–136.

De la Fuente, Ariel. *Children of Facundo. Caudillo and Gaucho Insurgency during the Argentine State-Formation Process (La Rioja, 1853–1870).* Durham and London: Duke University Press, 2000.

———. "Federalism and Opposition to the Paraguayan War in the Argentine Interior, La Rioja, 1865–67." In *I Die with My Country. Perspectives on the Paraguayan War, 1864–1870,* edited by Hendrik Kraay and Thomas L. Whigham, 140–154. Lincoln and London: University of Nebraska Press, 2004.

De Lima, José Francisco. *Marqués de Tamandaré. Patrono da Marinha.* Rio de Janeiro: Francisco Alves, 1982.

De Marco, Miguel Ángel. *Apuntaciones sobre la posición de Nicasio Oroño ante la guerra con el Paraguay.* Santa Fe, 1972.

———. *Bartolomé Mitre.* Buenos Aires: Emecé, 2004.

———. "La Guardia Nacional Argentina en la guerra del Paraguay." *Investigaciones y Ensayos* 3 (1967): 215–241.

———. *La guerra del Paraguay.* Buenos Aires: Planeta, 2003.

———. "La sanidad argentina en la guerra con el Paraguay (1865–1870)." *Revista Histórica* 4, no. 9 (1981).

De Martini, Siro and Oscar Rodríguez. "Los globos aerostáticos en la guerra de la Triple Alianza." *Boletín del Centro Naval* 109, no. 760 (1990): 121–154.

Dealy, Glen. *The Public Man. An Interpretation of Latin American and Other Catholic Countries.* Amherst: University of Massachusetts Press, 1977.

Decoud, Héctor Francisco. *La convención nacional constituyente y la carta magna de la república.* Buenos Aires: Talleres gráficos argentinos L. J. Rosso, 1934.

———. *Los emigrados paraguayos en la guerra de la Triple Alianza.* Buenos Aires: Talleres gráficos argentinos L. J. Rosso, 1930.

———. *La masacre de Concepción ordenada por el Mcal. López.* Asunción: Imprenta Serantes, 1926.

———. *Sobre los escombros de la guerra: una década de vida nacional, 1869–1880.* Asunción: Talleres Nacionales de H. Kraus, 1925.

Del Castillo, Lucilo. *Enfermedades reinantes en la campaña del Paraguay.* Buenos Aires, 1870.

Del Pino Menck, Alberto. "Armas y letras: León de Palleja y su contribución a la historiografía nacional." Paper presented at the Segundas Jornadas Internacionales de Historia del Paraguay, Universidad de Montevideo, 15 June 2010.

Del Valle, Florentino. *Cartilla cívica: proceso político del Paraguay, 1870–1950. El Partido Liberal y la Asociación Nacional Republicana (Partido Colorado) en la balanza de la verdad histórica.* Buenos Aires: Talleres Gráficos Lucania, 1951.

Díaz, Bárbara. *La diplomacia española en Uruguay en el siglo XIX. Génesis del tratado de paz de 1870.* Montevideo: Universidad de la República, 2008.

Díaz, Antonio. *Historia política y militar de las repúblicas del Plata*. 13 vols. Montevideo: Imprenta Comercial, 1878.

Dobrizhoffer, Martin. *An Account of the Abipones. An Equestrian People of Paraguay.* London: J. Murray, 1822.

Doratioto, Francisco. *General Osório. A Espada Liberal do Império*. São Paulo: Companhia das Letras, 2008.

———. *Maldita Guerra. Nova história da Guerra do Paraguai*. São Paulo: Companhia das Letras, 2002.

———. "La política del Imperio del Brasil en relación al Paraguay, 1864–72." In *Les guerres du Paraguay aux XIXe et XXe Siècles*, edited by Nicolas Richard, Luc Capdevila, and Capucine Boidin, 33–48. Paris: CoLibris, 2007.

Duarte, Pablo. *Jeneral Díaz. Conferencia dada en el pueblo de Pirayú con motivo de la colocación de la primera piedra fundamental del monumento en memoria del héroe de Curupaiti, en Setiembre 24 de 1911*. Asunción, 1913.

Duarte Miltos, Cristóbal G. *Las penurias de la iglesia paraguaya bajo los gobiernos a lo largo del primer centenario de la república y algunos sucesos históricos, 1813–1920*. Asunción: Servilibro, 2011.

Duprat de Lasserre, Dorothée. *The Paraguayan War. Sufferings of a French Lady in Paraguay*. Buenos Aires: Standard Office, 1870.

Earle, Rebecca. *The Return of the Native. Indians and Myth-Making in Spanish America, 1810–1930*. Durham and London: Duke University Press, 2007.

Enright, Anne. *The Pleasure of Eliza Lynch*. New York: Atlantic Monthly Press, 2002.

Ensinck, Oscar Luis. "Las epidemias de cólera en Rosario." *Revista de Historia de Rosario* 1 (1964): 6–7.

Escobar, Ticio. "L'art de la guerre. Les dessins de presse pendent la Guerra Guasú." In *Les guerres du Paraguay aux XIXe et XXe Siècles*, edited by Nicolas Richard, Luc Capdevila, and Capucine Boidin, 509–524. Paris: CoLibris, 2007.

Expilly, Charles. *Le Brésil, Buenos-Aires, Montevideo et le Paraguay devant la Civilization*. Paris: H. Willems, 1866.

Falcón, José. *Escritos históricos*. Asunción: Servilibro, 2006.

Fano, Marco. *El Cónsul, la guerra y la muerte*. Rome: Privately printed, 2011.

———. *Il Rombo del Cannone Liberale. Guerra del Paraguay, 1864/70*. Rome: Privately printed, 2008.

Fernandes de Souza, Antônio. *A Invasão Paraguaia em Matto-Grosso*. Cuiabá: J. Pereira Leite, 1919.

Fernández, Juan José. *La república de Chile y el imperio del Brasil. Historia de sus relaciones diplomáticas*. Santiago: Editorial Andrés Bello, 1959.

Ferns, H. S. *Britain and Argentina in the Nineteenth Century*. Oxford: Clarendon Press, 1960.

Ferreira França, Augusto. *Falla apresentada a Assembléa Legislativa Provincial de Goyaz, em o Primero de Agosto de 1866*. Goiás, 1867.

Ferreira Moutinho, Joaquim. *Notícias sobre a Provincia de Matto Grosso.* São Paulo: Typographia de Henrique Schroeder, 1869.

Fix, Théodore. *Conférence sur la Guerre du Paraguay.* Paris: Tanera, 1870.

Fois Maresma, Gladis. *El periodismo paraguayo y su actitud frente a la guerra de la Triple Alianza y Francisco Solano López.* Master's thesis, University of New Mexico, Albuquerque, 1970.

Fonseca de Castro, Adler Homero. *Muralhas de Pedra, Canhões de Bronce, Homens de Ferro. Fortificações do Brasil de 1504 a 2006.* Rio de Janeiro: Fundação Cultural Exército Brasileiro, 2009.

———. "Uniformes da Guerra do Paraguai." Biblioteca Nacional, Rede de Memória Virtual Brasileira, 2006. http://catalogos.bn.br/guerradoparaguai/artigos/Adler%20 Uniformes%20Guerra%20do%20Paraguai.pdf.

Fonseca de Castro, Adler Homero, and Ruth Beatriz S. C. de O Andrada. *O Pátio Epitácio Pessoa: seu Histórico e Acervo.* Rio de Janeiro: Museu Histórico Nacional, 1995.

Foreign Office. *Correspondence Respecting Hostilities in the River Plate.* London: British Foreign Office, 1866.

Fotheringham, Ignacio H. *Vida de un soldado o reminiscencias de las fronteras.* 2 vols. Buenos Aires: Ediciones Ciudad Argentina, 1998.

Franco, Víctor I. *Coronel Florentín Oviedo.* Asunción: Academia Paraguaya de la Historia, 1971.

———. *La sanidad en la guerra contra la Triple Alianza.* Asunción: Círculo Paraguayo de Médicos, 1976.

Franco Vera, Optaciano. *General José Elizardo Aquino (héroe de Boquerón del Sauce e hijo dilecto de Luque).* Asunción, 1981.

Freire Esteves, Gomes. *El Paraguay constitucional, 1870–1920.* Buenos Aires: Empresa Gráfica del Paraguay, 1921.

French, Jennifer. "La Guerre du Paraguay Dans l'oeuvre de Lucio V. Mansilla." Paper presented at International Conference on Paraguay a l'Ombre des ses Guerres, Paris, 18 November 2005.

Freyre, Gilberto. *Order and Progress.* New York: Alfred A. Knopf, 1970.

Frota, Guilherme de Andréa, ed. *Diário Pessoal do Almirante Visconde de Inhaúma durante a Guerra da Tríplice Aliança (Dezembro 1866 a Janeiro de 1869).* Rio de Janeiro: IHGB, 2008.

Gache, Belén. "Cándido López y la batalla de Curupaytí: relaciones entre narratividad, iconicidad, y verdad histórica." Paper presented at II Simposio Internacional de Narratología, Buenos Aires, June 2001.

Galasso, Norberto. *Felipe Varela. Un caudillo latinoamericano.* Buenos Aires: Ediciones Tiempo Latinoamericano, 1975.

Gálvez, Manuel. *Humaitá, escenas de la guerra del Paraguay.* Buenos Aires: Editorial Tor, n.d.

———. *Jornadas de Agonía.* Buenos Aires: Losada, 1948.

Ganson, Barbara. "Following Their Children into Battle: Women at War in Paraguay, 1864–1870." *The Americas* 46, no. 3 (1990): 335–371.

Gaona, Silvio. *El clero en la guerra del 70*. Asunción: El Arte, 1961.

Garavaglia, Juan Carlos , and Raúl Fradkin, *A 150 años de la Guerra de la Triple Alianza contra el Paraguay*. Buenos Aires: Promoteo, 2016.

Garmendia, José Ignacio. *Campaña de Corrientes y de Río Grande*. Buenos Aires: Peuser, 1904.

———. *Campaña de Humaytá*. Buenos Aires: Peuser: 1901.

———. *La cartera de un soldado (Bocetos sobre la marcha)*. Buenos Aires: Círculo Militar, 2002.

———. *Recuerdos de la guerra del Paraguay. Primera parte (Batalla de Sauce—Combate de Yataytí Corá – Curupaytí)*. Buenos Aires: Peuser, 1890.

———. *Recuerdos de la guerra del Paraguay. Segunda parte. Campaña de Pikyciri*. Buenos Aires: Peuser, 1890.

Gaston, James McFadden. *Hunting a Home in Brazil. The Agricultural Resources and other Characteristics of the Country. Also, the Manners and Customs of the Inhabitants*. Philadelphia: King and Baird Printers, 1867.

Gelly y Obes, Juan Andrés. "Guerra de la Triple Alianza contra el Paraguay." *Revista de la Biblioteca Nacional* 21, no. 51 (1949): 149–150.

Gill Aguinaga, Juan Bautista. *La asociación paraguaya en la guerra de la triple alianza*. Buenos Aires: privately printed, 1959.

———. *El capitán de navío Pedro V. Gill*. Asunción: Talleres Gráf, 1957.

———. "Excesos cometidos hace cien años." *Historia Paraguaya* 12 (1967–1968): 17–26.

———. *Un marino en la guerra de la Triple Alianza*. Asunción: Imprenta Paraguay, 1959.

Gimlette, John. *At the Tomb of the Inflatable Pig. Travels Through Paraguay*. New York: Alfred A. Knopf, 2003.

Godoi, Juansilvano. *El Baron de Rio Branco. La muerte del mariscal López. El concepto de la patria*. Asunción: Talleres Nacionales, 1912.

———. *El comandante José Dolores Molas*. Asunción: Talleres Nacionales, 1919.

———. *Documentos históricos. El fusilamiento del Obispo Palacios y los Tribunales de Sangre de San Fernando*. Asunción: El Liberal, 1916.

———. *Monografías históricas*. Buenos Aires: Félix Lajouane Editor, 1893.

———. *Ultimas operaciones de guerra del jeneral Díaz*. Buenos Aires: Félix Lajouane, 1897.

Góes e Vasconcelos, Zacharias de. *Da natureza e limites do poder moderador*. Brasilia: Senado Federal, 1978.

Gómez, Hernán Félix. *Historia de la provincia de Corrientes. Desde la Revolución de Mayo hasta el tratado del Cuadrilátero*. Corrientes: Imprenta del Estado, 1929.

———. *Ñaembé. Crónica de la guerra de López Jordán y de la epidemia de 1871*. Corrientes: Amerindia Ediciones Correntinas, 1998.

Gómez Florentín. Carlos *El Paraguay de la post-guerra, 1870–1900*. Asunción: El Lector, 2010.

Gonçalves, Affonso. *Guerra do Paraguay. Memoria. Caxias e Mitre.* Rio de Janeiro: Typ. Do Brazil, 1906.

Gondra, César. *El general Patricio Escobar.* Buenos Aires: Librería e Impr. Europea M. A. Rosas & Cía., 1912.

González Alsina, Ezequiel. *A cien años de Cerro Corá.* Asunción: Editorial del Centenario, 1970.

González Arrili, Bernardo. *Vida de Rufino Elizalde. Un constructor de la República.* Buenos Aires: Francisco A. Colombo, 1948.

González, José Guillermo. *Reminiscencias históricas de la guerra del Paraguay. Pasaje de Ypecuá.* Asunción: La Democracia, 1914.

González, Natalicio. *El Paraguay eterno.* Asunción: Guarania, 1935.

———. *Solano López y otros ensayos.* Paris: Editorial de Indias, 1926.

González Torres, Dionisio M. *Aspectos sanitarios de la guerra contra la Triple Alianza.* Asunción: Universidad Nacional de Asunción, 1996.

———. "Centenario del cólera en el Paraguay." *Historia Paraguaya* 36 (1996): 31–47.

Graham, Richard. *Patronage and Politics in Nineteenth-Century Brazil.* Stanford: Stanford University Press, 1990.

Gratz, George A. "The Brazilian Imperial Navy Ironclads, 1865–1874." *Warship* (1999–2000): 140–162.

Gray, J. Glenn. *The Warriors. Reflections on Men in Battle.* New York: Harcourt Brace, 1959.

Guevara, Ernesto. *Guerrilla Warfare.* Lincoln and London: University of Nebraska Press, 1998.

Guido y Spano, Carlos. *Ráfagas.* Buenos Aires: Igón hermanos, 1879.

Guthke, Karl S. *Last Words. Variations on the Theme in Cultural History.* Princeton: Princeton University Press, 1992.

Halperín Donghi, Tulio. "Argentines Ponder the Burden of the Past." In *Colonial Legacies. The Problem of Persistence in Latin American History,* edited by Jeremy Adelman, 151–174. New York and London: Routledge, 1999.

———. *Contemporary History of Latin America.* Durham and London: Duke University Press, 1993.

———. *José Hernández y sus mundos.* Buenos Aires: Editorial Sudamericana, 1985.

Halperín Donghi, Tulio, Ivan Jaksic, Gwen Kirkpatrick, and Francine Maciello, eds. *Sarmiento. Author of a Nation.* Berkeley: University of California Press, 1994.

Haydon, F. Stansbury. "Documents Relating to the First Military Balloon Corps Organized in South America: The Aeronautic Corps of the Brazilian Army, 1867–1868." *Hispanic American Historical Review* 19, no. 4 (1939): 504–517.

Henríquez Ureña, Pedro. *A Concise History of Latin American Culture.* New York: Praeger, 1967.

Herken Krauer, Juan Carlos. *Economic Indicators for the Paraguayan Economy: Isolation and Integration (1869–1932).* PhD diss., University of London, 1986.

———. *El Paraguay rural entre 1869 y 1913: Contribución a la historia económica regional del Plata*. Asunción: Centro Paraguayo de Estudios Sociológicos, 1984.

Hersch, Robert Conrad. *American Interest in the War of the Triple Alliance, 1865–1870*. PhD diss., New York University, 1974.

Heyn Schupp, Carlos, ed. *Escritos del Padre Fidel Maíz, I. Autobiografía y cartas*. Asunción: Union Académique Internationale y Academia Paraguaya de la Historia, 2010.

Homem de Mello, Francisco Ignácio Marcondes. *O General José Joaquim de Andrade Neves. Barão do Triumpho. Biografia*. Rio de Janeiro, 1869.

———. "Viagem ao Paraguay em Fevereiro e Março de 1869." *Revista Trimensal do Instituto Histórico, Geographico e Etnographico do Brazil* 36, no. 2 (1873): 5–54.

Hughes, Laurence Robert. "General Martin T. McMahon and the Conduct of Diplomatic Relations between the United States and Paraguay". Master's thesis, University of Colorado, Boulder, 1962.

Huner, Michael Kenneth. "Cantando la república: la movilización escrita del lenguaje popular en las trincheras del Paraguay, 1867–1868." *Páginas de Guarda* 4 (2007): 115–134.

Hutchinson, Thomas J. *The Paraná, with Incidents of the Paraguayan War and South American Recollections, from 1861–1868*. London: Edward Stanford, 1868.

———. *A Short Account of Some Incidents of the Paraguayan War. Paper Read before the Liverpool Literary and Philosophical Society*. Liverpool, 1871.

Izecksohn, Vitor. *Slavery and War in the Americas. Race, Citizenship, and State-Building in the United States and Brazil, 1861–1870*. Charlottesville and London: University of Virginia Press, 2014.

Izecksohn, Vitor and Peter M. Beattie. "The Brazilian Home Front during the War of the Triple Alliance, 1864–1870." In *Daily Lives of Civilians in Wartime Latin America. From the Wars of Independence to the Central American Civili Wars*, edited by Pedro Santoni, 123–146. Westport: Greenwood Press, 2008.

Jaceguay, Barão de and Carlos Vidal Oliveira de Freitas. *Quatro Séculos de Atividade Marítima: Portugal e Brasil*. Rio de Janeiro, 1900.

Jaksic, Iván, ed. *The Political Power of the Word: Press and Oratory in Nineteenth-Century Latin America*. London: University of London, 2002.

Johansson, María Lucrecia. *Soldados de papel. La propaganda en la prensa paraguaya durante la guerra de la Triple Alianza*. Cádiz: Ayuntamiento de Cádiz, 2014.

Johnson, Keith. "Recent Journeys in Paraguay." *Geographical Magazine* 2 (1875): 200–203, 264–273, 308–313, 342–345.

Jomini, Antoine-Henri. *The Art of War*. Philadelphia: J. B. Lippincott, 1862.

Jover Peralta, Anselmo. *El Paraguay revolucionario. Significación histórica de la revolución de febrero*. Asunción: Editorial Tupã, 1946.

Junta Patriótica. *El mariscal Francisco Solano López*. Asunción, 1926.

Kahle, Gunther. "Franz Wisner von Morgenstern. Ein Ungar im Paraguay des 19. Jahrhundert." *Mitteilungen des Österreichischen Staatsarchivs* 37 (1984): 198–246.

Kleinpenning, Jan M. G. *Paraguay 1515–1870. A Thematic Geography of its Development.* Frankfurt: Iberoamericana, 2003.

———. "Strong Reservations about 'New Insights into the Demographics of the Paraguayan War.' " *Latin American Research Review* 37, no. 3 (2002): 137–142.

Kelsey, Kerck. *Remarkable Americans. The Washburn Family.* Gardiner, Maine: Tilbury House, 2008.

Kolinski, Charles. "The Death of Francisco Solano López." *The Historian* 26, no. 1 (1963): 75–91.

———. *Independence or Death! The Story of the Paraguayan War.* Gainesville: University of Florida Press, 1965.

Koseritz, Carlos de. *Alfredo d'Escragnolle Taunay, Esboço Caracteristico.* Rio de Janeiro: Leuzinger & Filhos, 1886.

Kraay, Hendrik. "O Abrigo da farda: o exército e os escravos fugidos, 1800–1888." *Afro-Asia* 17 (1996): 29–56.

———. "Patriotic Mobilization in Brazil: the Zuavos and Other Black Companies in the Paraguayan War, 1865–70." In *I Die with My Country. Perspectives on the Paraguayan War,* edited by Hendrik Kraay and Thomas L. Whigham, 61–80. Lincoln and London: University of Nebraska Press, 2004.

———. "Reconsidering Recruitment in Imperial Brazil." *The Americas* 55, no. 1 (1998): 1–33.

Kraay, Hendrik, and Thomas L. Whigham, eds. *I Die with My Country. Perspectives on the Paraguayan War.* Lincoln and London: University of Nebraska Press, 2004.

Lacombe, Lourenço L. *Isabel a Princesa Redentora (biografia baseada em documentos inéditos).* Petrópolis: Instituto Histórico de Petrópolis, 1989.

Laconich, Marco Antonio. "La campaña de Amambay." *Historia Paraguaya* 13 (1969–1970): 15–22.

Lacoste, Pablo. "Las guerras hispanoamericana y de la Triple Alianza. La revolución de los colorados y su impactos en las relaciones entre Argentina y Chile." *Historia* 29 (1995–1996): 125–158.

Laing, E. A. M. "Naval Operations in the War of the Triple Alliance, 1864–70." *Mariner's Mirror* 54 (1968): 253–280.

Lapuente, Laurindo. *Las profecías de Mitre.* Buenos Aires: Imprenta Buenos Aires, 1868.

Lassaga, Calixto. *Curupaytí (el abanderado Grandoli).* Rosario: Tipografía La Cervantina, 1939.

Lavenère-Wanderley, Nelson Freire. "Os Balões de Observação da Guerra do Paraguai." *Revista do Instituto Histórico e Geográfico Brasileiro* 299 (1973): 202–240.

Leguizamón, J. Estanislao. *Apuntes biográficos históricos.* Asunción, 1898.

LeLong, John. *Les Républiques de la Plata et la Guerre du Paraguay. Le Brésil.* Paris: E. Dentu, 1869.

Lemos, Renato, ed. *Cartas da guerra: Benjamín Constant na Campanha do Paraguai.* Rio de Janeiro: IPHAN, 1999.

Leuchars, Chris. *To the Bitter End: Paraguay and the War of the Triple Alliance*. Westport: Greenwood Press, 2002.

Lillis, Michael and Ronan Fanning. *The Lives of Eliza Lynch. Scandal and Courage*. Dublin: Gill & Macmillan, 2009.

Lima Figuereido, José de. *Grandes Soldados do Brasil*. Rio de Janeiro: Livraria José Olympio Editora, 1944.

Lima, Francisco de. *Ana Néri. Heroina da Caridade*. São Paulo: Nova Época Editorial, 1977.

Lima, Herman. *Histórica da Caricatura no Brasil*. Rio de Janeiro: José Olympio Editora, 1963.

Lobo, Hélio. *O Pan-Americanismo e o Brasil*. São Paulo: Cía. Editora Nacional, 1939.

Lockhart, Washington. *Venancio Flores, un caudillo trágico*. Montevideo: Ed. de la Banda Oriental, 1976.

Lopacher, Ulrich and Alfred Tobler. *Un suizo en la guerra del Paraguay*. Asunción: Editorial del Centenario, 1969.

Lopes Pecegueiro, Manuel. *Combate de 2 de maio de 1866*. Rio de Janeiro: Typ. Lobo Vianna, 1870.

López de Decoud, Adelina. *Biografía de don Héctor Francisco Decoud*. Buenos Aires: Librería Cervantes, 1937.

López, Francisco Solano. *Proclamas y cartas del Mariscal López*. Buenos Aires: Editorial Asunción, 1957.

Lugones, Leopoldo. *Historia de Sarmiento*. Buenos Aires: Babel, 1931.

Lustig, Wolf. "Die Auferstehung des Cacique Lambare. Zu Konstruktion der guarani-paraguayischen Identität während der Guerra de la Triple Alianza." Paper presented at "Selbstvergewisserung am Anderen order Der fremde Blick auf der Eigene," Mainz, 18 September 1999.

———. "¿El guaraní lengua de guerreros? La 'raza guaraní' y el avañe'e en el discurso bélico-nacionalista del Paraguay." In *Les guerres du Paraguay aux XIXe et XXe Siècles*, edited by Nicolas Richard, Luc Capdevila, and Capucine Boidin. 525–530. Paris: CoLibris, 2007.

Lynch, Elisa. *Exposición y protesta que hace Elisa A. Lynch*. Buenos Aires, 1875.

Lynch, John. *Massacre in the Pampas, 1872*. Norman: University of Oklahoma Press, 1998.

Lyra Tavares, Aurelio de. *Vilagran Cabrita e a Engenharia de Seu Tempo*. Rio de Janeiro: Bibliex, 1981.

Macchi, Manuel. "Guerra de montoneros. Pozo de Vargas." *Trabajos y Comunicaciones* 11 (1963): 127–147.

Macedo, Roberto. *Floriano na Guerra do Paraguai*. Rio de Janeiro: Bedeschi, 1938.

Magalhães Junior, R. *O Imperio em Chinelos*. Rio de Janeiro and São Paulo: Civilização Brasileira, 1957.

Maíz, Fidel. *La cuestión religiosa en el Paraguay*. Asunción, 1877.

———. *Desagravio*. Asunción: La Mundial, 1916.

———. *Discurso del Pbro. Fidel Maíz. Pronunciado hace 21 años en Piribebuy*. Asunción, 1922.

———. *Etapas de mi vida*. Asunción: El Lector, 1986.

———. *Pequeña geografía para los niños de Arroyos y Esteros*. Asunción: Biblioteca Nacional, 1886.

———. *Vía crucis. Importancia de esta preciosa devoción. Solemne creación del camino de la Cruz en la Iglesia de la Encarnación*. Asunción, 1886.

———. *La Virgen de los Milagros de Caacupé: su origen, su santuario y su pueblo*. Asunción: Kraus, 1898.

Mansilla, Lucio. *Una excursión a los indios ranqueles*. Caracas: Ayacucho, 1984.

Maracajú, Marechal Visconde de [José Ubaldino Motta do Amaral]. *Campanha do Paraguay (1867 e 1868)*. Rio de Janeiro: Imprenta Militar, 1922.

Martin, María Haydée. "La juventud de Buenos Aires en la guerra con el Paraguay." *Trabajos y Comunicaciones* 19 (1969): 145–176.

Martínez, Pedro Santos. "La rebelión jordanista y el Brasil, 1870." *Investigaciones y Ensayos* 46 (1996): 73–88.

Massare de Kostianovsy, Olinda. *José Berges. Malogrado estadista y diplomático*. Asunción: Tall. Gráf. de la Penitenciaría Nacional, 1969.

———. "La mujer en la historia del Paraguay. Su contribución a la epopeya de 1864/70." *Historia Paraguaya* 12 (1967–1968): 215–218.

———. *El vice-presidente Domingo Francisco Sánchez*. Asunción: Escuela Técnica Salesiana, 1972.

Masterman, George Frederick. *Seven Eventful Years in Paraguay*. London: S. Low, Son and Marston, 1869.

———. *Siete años de aventuras en el Paraguay*. Buenos Aires: Imprenta Americana, 1870.

———. *Siete años de aventuras en el Paraguay*. Buenos Aires: Juan Palumbo Editor, 1911.

Matveeva, N. R. *Paragvai i paragvaiskaia voina 1864–1870 godov I politika inostrannykh derzhav na La Plate*. PhD diss., State University of Moscow, 1951.

McLynn, F. J. "The Argentine Presidential Election of 1868." *Journal of Latin American Studies* 11, no. 2 (1979): 303–323.

———. "The Corrientes Crisis of 1868." *North Dakota Quarterly* 47, no. 3 (1979): 45–58.

———. *General Urquiza and the Politics of Argentina, 1861–1870*. PhD diss., University of London, 1976.

———. "The Ideological Basis of the Montonero Risings in Argentina during the 1860s." *The Historian* 46 (1984): 235–251.

———. "Political Instability in Córdoba Province during the Eighteen-Sixties." *Ibero-Amerikanische Archiv* 3 (1980): 251–269.

———. "Urquiza and the Montoneros: An Ambiguous Chapter in Argentine History." *Ibero-Amerikanische Archiv* 8 (1982): 283–295.

McMahon, Martin T. "Resurgirás Paraguay!" *Historia Paraguaya* 1 (1956): 66–68.

———. "The War in Paraguay." *Harper's New Monthly Magazine* 40, no. 239 (1870): 633–647.

Meirelles, Theotonio. *O Exército Brasileiro na Guerra do Paraguay. Resumos históricos.* Rio de Janeiro: Typ. do Globo, 1877.

———. *A Marinha de Guerra Brasileira em Paysandú e durante a Campanha do Paraguay: Resumos Históricos.* Rio de Janeiro: Typ. Theatral e Commercial, 1876.

Mendonça, Juan Carlos. *Las constituciones paraguayas y los proyectos de constitución de los partidos políticos.* Asunción: EMASA, 1967.

Mendoza, Hugo and Rafael Mariotti. "La fundición de hierro de Ybycuí y la guerra del 70." In *Memoria del Segundo Encuentro Internacional de Historia sobre las operaciones bélicas durante la guerra de la Triple Alianza.* 203–216. Asunción: Tiempo de Historia, 2010.

Menna Barreto, João de Deus Noronha. *Os Menna Barreto. Seis Gerações de Soldados.* Rio de Janeiro: Gráfica Laemmert, 1950.

Mitre, Bartolomé. *Archivo del General Mitre.* 28 vols. Buenos Aires: La Nación, 1910–1914.

———. *Correspondencia Mitre-Elizalde.* Buenos Aires: Instituto de Historia Argentina "doctor Emilio Ravignani," 1960.

Moby Ribeiro da Silva, Alberto. "Bailes e Festas Públicas em Asunción no pós-guerra da Tríplice Aliança: Mulher e Resistencia Popular no Paraguai." *Estudos Ibero-Americanos* 25, no.1 (1999): 43–52.

———. *La noche de las Kygua Vera. La mujer y la reconstrucción de la identidad nacional en la posguerra de la Triple Alianza (1867–1904).* Asunción: Intercontinental, 2010.

Mörner, Magnus. *Algunas cartas del naturalista sueco Eberhard Munck af Rosenchöld escritas durante su estadía en el Paraguay, 1843–1868.* Stockholm, 1956.

Moniz, Heitor. *A Corte de D. Pedro II.* Rio de Janeiro: Livraria Freitas Bastos, 1931.

Monteiro de Almeida, Mario. *Episódios Históricos da Formação Geográfica do Brasil.* Rio de Janeiro: Pongetti, 1951.

Montenegro, J. Arthur. "Campaña de Matto-Grosso. Toma del atrincheramiento de Bayende (6 de mayo de 1867)." In *Album de la Guerra del Paraguay,* edited by José C. Soto. 281–283. Buenos Aires: Peuser, 1894.

———. *Fragmentos Históricos. Homens e Factos da Guerra do Paraguay.* Rio Grande: Typographia da Livraria Rio-Grandense, 1900.

———. *Guerra do Paraguay. Memorias de Mme. Dorothéa Duprat de Lasserre.* Rio Grande: Livraria Americana, 1893.

Mora, Frank O. and Jerry W. Cooney. *Paraguay and the United States. Distant Allies.* Athens and London: University of Georgia Press, 2007.

Moreira de Azevedo, M. D. "O Combate da Ilha do Cabrita." *Revista Trimestral do Instituto Geographico, e Etnographico do Brasil* 3 (1870): 5–20.

Morgan, Zachary R. "Legislating the Lash: Race and the Conflicting Modernities of Enlistment and Corporal Punishment in the Military of the Brazilian Empire." *Journal of Colonialism and Colonial History* 5, no. 2 (2004).

Moritz Schwarcz, Lilia and John Gledson. *The Emperor's Beard: Dom Pedro II and his Tropical Monarchy in Brazil.* New York: Hill and Wang, 2004.

Mosqueira, Silvano. *General José Eduvigis Díaz*. Buenos Aires: Talleres S. Oswald & Cía., 1900.

Murilo de Carvalho, José. *Elite and State-Building in Imperial Brazil*. PhD diss., Stanford University, 1975.

———. *D. Pedro II*. São Paulo: Companhia das Letras, 2007.

Nabuco, Joaquim. *Um Estadista do Imperio: Nabuco de Araujo, Sua Vida, Suas opinhões, Sua época*. 2 vols. Rio de Janeiro and Paris: Garnier, 1897.

Navajas, María José. "Polémicas y conflictos en torno a la guerra del Paraguay: los discursos de la prensa en Tucumán, Argentina (1864–1869)." Paper presented at V Encuentro Anual del CEL, Buenos Aires, 5 November 2008.

Needell, Jeffrey D. *The Party of Order. The Conservatives, the State, and Slavery in the Brazilian Monarchy, 1831–1871*. Palo Alto: Stanford University Press, 2006.

Nogueira Jaguaribe, João. *O Conde de Bagnuoli*. São Paulo: O Pensamento, 1918.

O'Leary, Juan E. *El Centauro de Ybycuí. Vida heróica del general Bernardino Caballero en la guerra del Paraguay*. Paris: Livre Libre, 1929.

———. *El héroe del Paraguay*. Montevideo: Talleres gráficos Prometeo, 1930.

———. *El libro de los héroes*. Asunción: Ministerio de Hacienda, 1970.

———. *Lomas Valentinas. Conferencia dada en Villeta el 25 de diciembre de 1915*. Asunción, 1916.

———. *Los legionarios*. Asunción: Editorial de Indias, 1930.

———. *El mariscal Francisco Solano López*. Asunción: Editorial Paraguaya, 1970.

———. *Nuestra epopeya (primera parte)*. Asunción: Mediterráneo, 1985.

———. *Recuerdos de Gloria. Artículos Históricos sobre la Guerra contra la Triple Alianza*. Asunción: Servilibro, 2008.

Oliveira Lima, Manuel de. *O Império Brasileiro, 1822–1889*. São Paulo: Melhoramentos, 1927.

Olmedo, Agustín Ángel. *Guerra del Paraguay. Cuadernos de campaña (1867–1869)*. Buenos Aires: Academia Nacional de la Historia, 2008.

Oneto y Viana, Carlos. *La diplomacia del Brasil en el Río de la Plata*. Montevideo: Imp. El Siglo Ilustrado, 1903.

Orléans Bragança, Luiz de. *Sob o Cruzeiro do Sul*. Montreaux, 1913.

Oroño, Nicasio. *Escritos y discursos*. Buenos Aires: La Facultad, 1920.

———. *La verdadera organización del país o la realización de la máxima "gobernar es poblar."* Buenos Aires, 1869.

Orué Pozzo, Aníbal. *Periodismo en Paraguay. Estudios e interpretaciones*. Asunción: Arandurã Editorial, 2007.

Osório, Joaquim Luis and Fernando Luis Osório. *História do general Osório*. 2 vols. Pelotas: Diário Popular, 1915.

Otaño, J. B. *Origen, desarrollo y fin de la marina desaparecida en la guerra de 1864–70*. Asunción: La Colmena, 1942.

Palleja, León de. *Diario de la campaña de las fuerzas aliadas contra el Paraguay.* 2 vols. Montevideo: Talleres Gráficos Bareiro y Ramos, 1960.

Pane, Ignacio A. *El Paraguai [sic] intelectual. Conferencia pronunciada en el Ateneo de Santiago de Chile el 26 de noviembre.* Santiago, 1902.

Pane, Justo A. *Episodios militares.* Asunción: R. Monte Domecq & Cía., 1908.

Papeles de López. El tirano pintado por sí mismo. Sus publicaciones. Buenos Aires: Imprenta América, 1871.

Paz, Marcos. *Archivo del Coronel Doctor Marcos Paz.* 7 vols. La Plata: Universidad Nacional de La Plata, 1964.

———. *Una lágrima sobre la tumba de tres soldados.* Buenos Aires: Imprenta de Mayo, 1873.

Peltzer, Federico. *Aquel Sagrado Suelo.* Buenos Aires: Emecé, 2000.

Pelúas, Daniel and Enrique Piqué. *Crónicas. Guerra de la Triple Alianza y el genocidio paraguayo.* Montevideo: Arca Editorial, 2007.

Penna, José María. *El cólera en la república argentina.* Buenos Aires: Peuser, 1897.

Penna Botto, Carlos. *Campanhas Navais Sul-americanas.* Rio de Janeiro: Imprensa Naval, 1940.

Peña Villamil, Manuel. "Los corsarios sudistas en la guerra de la Triple Alianza." *Historia Paraguaya* 11 (1966): 147–156.

Peña Villamil, Manuel and Roberto Quevedo. *Silvia.* Asunción: Criterio, 1987.

Peña, David. *Alberdi, los mitristas, y la guerra de la Triple Alianza.* Buenos Aires: Peña y Lillo Editor, 1965.

Pereira de Sousa, Octaviano. "História da Guerra do Paraguai." *Revista do Instituto Histórico e Geográfico Brasileiro* 156, no. 102 (1927): 7–497.

Peres Costa, Wilma. *A Espada do Dâmocles.* São Paulo: HUCITEC, 1996.

Peres Fernandes, Lia Silvia. "Guerra contra a Memória: a Devolução de Peças do Acervo do Museu Histórico Nacional ao Paraguai." *Anais. Museu Histórico Nacional* 42 (2010): 77–96.

Pereyra, Carlos. *Francisco Solano López y la guerra del Paraguay.* Buenos Aires Talleres Gráficos Buschi, 1953.

———. *Solano López y su drama.* Buenos Aires: Ediciones de la Patria Grande, 1962.

Pérez Acosta, Juan F. *Carlos Antonio López. Obrero máximo. Labor administrativa y constructiva.* Asunción: Guarania, 1948.

Pérez Maricevich, Francisco. *Revistas literarias paraguayas. I: "La Aurora." Contenido y significado.* Asunción: Cuadernos Republicanos, 1975.

Pérez Pardella, Agustín. *Cerro Corá.* Buenos Aires: Editorial Plus Ultra, 1977.

Perú, Secretaría de Relaciones Exteriores. *Correspondencia diplomática relativa a la cuestión del Paraguay.* Lima: El Progreso, 1867.

Pesoa, Manuel. *General doctor Benigno Ferreira. Su biografía.* Asunción: Intercontinental, 1995.

———. *Orígenes del Partido Liberal Paraguay, 1870–1887.* Asunción: Criterio-Ediciones, 1987.

Peterson, Harold F. *Argentina and the United States, 1810–1960.* New York: State University of New York, 1964.

———. "Efforts of the United States to Mediate in the Paraguayan War." *Hispanic American Historical Review* 12, no. 1 (1932): 2–17.

Phelps, Gilbert. *The Tragedy of Paraguay.* London and Tonbridge: Charles Knight, 1975.

Philbin, Stephanie. "Saddam: the Middle East's Francisco Solano López." *Times of the Americas* (Miami), 23 January 1991.

Philip, George, ed. *British Documents on Foreign Affairs. Reports and Papers from the Foreign Office. Confidential Print.* Bethesda, MD: University Publications of America, 1991.

Pinheiro Guimarães, Francisco. *Um Voluntário da Patria.* Rio de Janeiro: J. Olympio, 1958.

Pinho, Wanderley. *Política e Políticos no Império: Contribuições Documentães.* Rio de Janeiro: Imprensa Nacional, 1930.

Pinto de Campos, Joaquim. *Vida do Grande Cidadão Brazileiro Luiz Alves de Lima e Silva, Barão, Conde, Marquez, Duque de Caxias.* Lisbon: Imprensa Nacional, 1878.

Pinto Junior, Joaquim Antonio. *Guerra do Paraguay, Defesa Heroica da Ilha de Redenção, 10 de Abril de 1866.* Rio de Janeiro: Typ. Domingo Luiz dos Santos, 1877.

Pinto Seidl, Raymundo. *O Duque de Caxias. Esboço de Sua Gloriosa Vida.* Rio de Janeiro: Typ. Luiz Macedo, 1903.

Pivel Devoto, Juan E. *Historia de los partidos políticos en el Uruguay.* Montevideo: Atlantida, 1942–1943.

Plá, Josefina. *The British in Paraguay, 1850–1870.* Richmond, Surrey: Richmond Publishing, 1976.

Poggi, Rinaldo Alberto. *Alvaro Barros en la frontera sur. Contribución al estudio de un argentino olvidado.* Buenos Aires: Fundación Nuestra Historia, 1997.

Poma, Cesare. *Di un Giornale in Guaraní e dello Studio del Tupí nel Brasile.* Turin: Tip. Eredi Botta di L. Clemente Crosa, 1897.

Pomer, León. *Cinco años de guerra civil en la Argentina, 1865–1870.* Buenos Aires: Amorrortu Editores, 1986.

———. *La Guerra del Paraguay ¡Gran negocio!* Buenos Aires: Ediciones Caldén, 1968.

Potthast-Jutkeit, Barbara. *"¿Paraíso de Mahoma" o "País de las mujeres"?* Asunción: Instituto Cultural Paraguayo Alemán, 1996.

Potthast, Barbara. "Protagonists, Victims, and Heroes: Paraguayan Women in the 'Great War.'" In *I Die with My Country. Perspectives on the Paraguayan War, 1864–1870,* edited by Hendrik Kraay and Thomas L. Whigham, 44–60. Lincoln and London: University of Nebraska Press, 2004.

———. "Residentas, Destinadas, y otras heroínas: el nacionalismo paraguayo y el rol de las mujeres en la Guerra de la Triple Alianza." In *Las mujeres y las naciones: Problemas de inclusión y exclusión,* edited by Barbara Potthast and Eugenia Scarzanela, 77–92. Frankfurt and Madrid: Iberoamericana/Vervuert, 2001.

Prado, Ari G. *O Capitão Werlang e seu Diário de Campanha Escrito Durante e Após a Guerra do Paraguai*. Canoas: Ed. Hilgert e Filhos, 1969.

Preuss, Ori. *Bridging the Island. Brazilians' Views of Spanish America and Themselves, 1865-1912*. Madrid, Orlando, and Frankfurt: Vervuert, 2011.

Puiggrós, Rodolfo. *Pueblo y oligarquía*. Buenos Aires: Jorge Álvarez Editor, 1965.

Queiroz Duarte, Paulo de. *Sampaio*. Rio de Janeiro: Biblioteca do Exercito Editora, 1988.

———. *Os voluntários da patria na guerra do Paraguai*. 3 vols. Rio de Janeiro: Biblioteca do Exército, 1982.

Quesada, Ernesto. *Historia diplomática nacional: la política argentina-paraguaya*. Buenos Aires: Bredahl, 1902.

Quiroga, Horacio. *La gallina degollada y otros cuentos*. Buenos Aires: Centro Editor de América Latina, 1967.

Ramírez Braschi, Dardo. "Análisis de expediente judicial por traición a la patria a Víctor Silvero, miembro de la junta gubernativa correntina en 1865." Paper presented at the XX Congreso Nacional y Regional de Historia Argentina, Academia Nacional de la Historia, La Plata, 21–23 August 2003.

———. *Evaristo López. Un gobernador federal: Corrientes en tiempos de la Triple Alianza*. Corrientes: Camara Argentina del Libro, 1997.

———. *La guerra de la Triple Alianza a través de los periódicos correntinos*. Corrientes: Camara Argentina del Libro, 2000.

Ramírez Russo, Manfredo. *El coronel Centurión: Historiador y diplomático*. Asunción: Partido Colorado, 1972.

Rangel, Alberto. *Gastão de Orleans (o ultimo Conde d'Eu)*. São Paulo: Companhia Editora Nacional, 1935.

Raymond, Jean François de. *Arthur de Gobineau et le Brésil*. Grenoble: Presses Universitaires de Grenoble, 1990.

Raymond, Xavier. "Don Lopez et la Guerre du Paraguay." *Revue de Deux Mondes* 85 (1870), 988–1027.

Rebaudi, Arturo. *Guerra del Paraguay. Un episodio. "¡Vencer o morir!"* Tucumán: Imp. Constancia, 1920.

———. *Lomas Valentinas*. Buenos Aires: Serantes, 1924.

Rebello de Carvalho, Francisco. *A Terminação da Guerra*. Rio de Janeiro, 1870.

Reber, Vera Blinn. "A Case of Total War: Paraguay, 1864–1870." *Journal of Iberian and Latin American Studies* 5, no. 1 (1999): 15–40.

———. "Comment on the Paraguayan Rosetta Stone." *Latin American Research Review* 37, no. 3 (2002): 129–136.

———. "The Demographics of Paraguay: A Reinterpretation of the Great War, 1864–1870." *Hispanic American Historical Review* 68, no. 2 (1988): 189–219.

Rebouças, André. *Diario: a Guerra do Paraguai (1866)*. São Paulo: Universidade de São Paulo, 1973.

Reclus, Elisée. "L'election présidentielle de la Plata et la Guerre du Paraguay." *La Revue des Deux Mondes*, 15 August 1868.

———. "La guerra del Paraguay." *La Revue des Deux Mondes*, 15 December 1867.

Rees, Siân. *The Shadows of Elisa Lynch. How a Nineteenth-Century Irish Courtesan Became the Most Powerful Woman in Paraguay.* London: Review, 2003.

Reichardt, Canavarro. "Centenário da Morte do Brigadeiro José Joaquim de Andrade Neves, Barão deo Triunfo, 1869–1969." *Revista do Instituto Histórico e Geográfico Brasileiro* 285 (1969): 21–34.

Rengger, Johan Rudolph and Marcel Longchamps. *The Reign of Doctor Joseph Gaspard Roderick de Francia, in Paraguay, being an Account of a Six Year's Residence in that Republic, from July 1819 to May 1825.* London: Thomas Hurst Edward Chance, 1827.

Resquín, Francisco I. *La guerra del Paraguay contra la Triple Alianza.* Asunción: El Lector, 1996.

Reyes, Marcelino. *Bosquejo histórico de la provincia de La Rioja, 1543–1867.* Buenos Aires: Tall. Gráf. de H. Cattáneo, 1913.

Ricci, Franco María. *Cándido López. Imágenes de la guerra del Paraguay.* Milan: Ricci, 1984.

Richard, Nicolas, Luc Capdevila, and Capucine Boidin, eds. *Les guerres du Paraguay aux XIXe et XXe Siècles.* Paris: CoLibris, 2007.

Rios Ricci Volpato, Luiza. *Cativos do Sertão. Vida Cotidiana e Escravidão em Cuiabá em 1850/1888.* São Paulo: Editora Marco Zero, 1993.

Riquelme García, Benigno. *El ejército de la epopeya.* Asunción: Ediciones Cuadernos Republicanos, 1977.

Rivarola Matto, Juan Bautista. *Diagonal de Sangre.* Asunción: Ediciones NAPA, 1986.

Rivarola, Milda. *La polémica francesa sobre la Guerra Grande.* Asunción: Editorial Histórica, 1988.

Roa Bastos, Augusto. *El trueno entre las hojas.* Buenos Aires: Losada, 1953.

Rocha Almeida, Antonio da. *Vúltos da pátria. Os brasileiros mais ilustres de seu tempo.* Rio de Janeiro: Globo, 1961.

Rock, David. "Argentina under Mitre: Porteño Liberalism in the 1860s." *The Americas* 56, no. 1 (1999): 31–63.

———. "The Collapse of the Federalists: Rural Revolt in Argentina, 1863–1876." *Estudios Interdisciplinarios de América Latina y el Caribe* 9, no.2 (1998).

Rock, David and Fernando López-Alves. "State-Building and Political System in Nineteenth-Century Argentina and Uruguay." *Past and Present* 167, no.1 (2000): 178–190.

Rodriguez de Morães Jardim, Jerónimo. *Os Engenheiros Militares na Guerra entre o Brazil e o Paraguay e a Passagem do Rio Paraná.* Rio de Janeiro: Neves Pinto, 1889.

Romero, Roberto A. *Protagonismo histórico del idioma guaraní.* Asunción: Rotterdam Editora, 1992.

Rosa, José María. *La guerra del Paraguay y las montoneras argentinas.* Buenos Aires: Peña y Lillo, 1964.

Rottjer, Enrique. *Mitre militar*. Buenos Aires: Círculo Militar, 1937.

Ruiz Moreno, Isidoro J. *Informes españoles sobre la Argentina*. Buenos Aires: Museo Social Argentino, 1993.

Sábato, Hilda. *The Many and the Few: Political Participation in Republican Buenos Aires*. Stanford: Stanford University Press, 2002.

Sábato, Hilda and Alberto Lettieri, eds. *La vida política en la Argentina del siglo XIX: Armas, votos, y voces*. Buenos Aires: FCE, 2003.

Saeger, James Schofield. *Francisco Solano López and the Ruination of Paraguay. Honor and Egocentrism*. Lanham and Boulder: Rowman & Littlefield, 2007.

Saldanha Lemos, Juvêncio. *Os Mercenários do Imperador*. Rio de Janeiro: Biblioteca do Exército, 1996.

Salles, Ricardo. *Guerra do Paraguai: escravidão e cidadania na formação do exército*. Rio de Janeiro: Paz e Terra, 1990.

———. *Guerra do Paraguai. Memórias e Imagens*. Rio de Janeiro: Biblioteca Nacional, 2003.

Salum Flecha, Antonio. *Derecho diplomático del Paraguay de 1869 a 1994*. Asunción: Ediciones Comuneros, 1994.

Sánchez Quell, Hipólito. *Los 50.000 documentos paraguayos llevados al Brasil*. Asunción: Ediciones Comuneros, 1976.

Santos Neves, A. J. *Homenagem aos Herois Brasileiros na Guerra contra o Governo do Paraguay*. Rio de Janeiro: Laemmert, 1870.

Sarmiento, Carlos D. *Estudio crítico sobre la guerra del Paraguay (1865-1869)*. Buenos Aires: Talleres de La Impresora, 1890.

Sarmiento, Domingo Faustino. *Obras*. 9 vols. Buenos Aires: Organización Estado de Buenos Aires, 1902.

———. *Vida de Dominguito*. Buenos Aires: Félix Lajouane Editor, 1886.

Sarmiento, Julio Alberto. "Empleo de minas submarinas en la guerra del Paraguay (1865-1870) y esquema de la evolución del arma hasta fines del siglo XIX." *Boletín del Centro Naval* 79, no. 648 (1961): 413-427.

Scantimburgo, João de. *História do Liberalismo no Brasil*. São Paulo: Editora LTr, 1996.

Scavarda, Levy. "Centenário da Pasagem de Humaitá." *Revista Marítima Brasileira* 8, no. 1-3 (1968): 35-40.

Scheina, Robert. *Latin America: A Naval History 1810-1987*. Annapolis: Naval Institute Press, 1987.

Schneider, Louis. *A Guerra da Tríplice Aliança contra o governo da República do Paraguai*, 2 vols. São Paulo: Edições Cultura, 1945.

Schulz, John Henry. *The Brazilian Army and Politics, 1850-1894*. PhD diss., Princeton University, 1973.

Scobie, James R. *Revolution on the Pampas. A Social History of Argentine Wheat, 1860-1910*. Austin: University of Texas Press, 1977.

Scully, William. *Brazil. Its Provinces and Chief Cities*. London: Murray & Co., 1866.

Seeber, Francisco. *Cartas sobre la guerra del Paraguay 1865-1866*. Buenos Aires: Talleres Gráficos de L. J. Rosso, 1907.

Segovia Guerrero, Eduardo. *La historiografía argentina del romanticismo*. PhD diss., Universidad Complutense, Madrid, 1980.

Seifert, Antonio. *Os Sofrimentos dum Prisioneiro ou o Martir da Pátria*. Fortaleza: Tipografia Constitucional, 1871.

Sena Madureira, Antônio de. *Guerra do Paraguai. Resposta ao Sr. Jorge Thompson, autor da "Guerra del Paraguay" e aos Anotadores Argentinos D. Lewis e A. Estrada*. Brasilia: Ed UNB, 1982.

Shumway, Nicolas. *The Invention of Argentina*. Berkeley: University of California Press, 1991.

Sienra Carranza, José. "Respecto del Paraguay. Notas sobre el decenio 1870–1880." *Cuadernos Republicanos* 10 (1975).

Silva Paranhos, José María da, Baron of Rio Branco. *A guerra da Tríplice Aliança contra o gobernó da República do Paraguay*. São Paulo: Edições Cultura, 1945.

Silvado, Americo Brazilio. *A Nova Marinha. Reposta a Marinha d'Outrora*. Rio de Janeiro: Carlos Schmidt, 1897.

Silveira, Carlos Balthazar da. *Campanha do Paraguai. A Marinha Brasileira*. Rio de Janeiro: Tipografia do Jornal do Commercio, 1900.

Silveira, Mauro César. *A Batalha de Papel. A Guerra do Paraguai através da Caricatura*. Porto Alegre: L&PM Editora, 1996.

Soares, Pedro Paulo. *A Guerra da Imagem: Iconografia da Guerra do Paraguai na Imprensa Ilustrada Fluminense*. Master's thesis, Universidade Federal do Rio de Janeiro, 2003.

Sodré, Alcindo. *Abrindo un Cofre*. Rio de Janeiro: Editora Livros de Portugal S. A., 1956.

Soto, José C., ed. *Album de la guerra del Paraguay*. 2 vols. Buenos Aires: Peuser, 1893–1894.

Souza, Fernando dos Anjos. "A Liderança dos Chefes Militares durante a Retirada da Laguna na Guerra do Paraguai." *Monografia da Escola de Comando e Estado-Maior do Exército*. Rio de Janeiro, 1994.

Souza, Maria Regina Santos de. *Impactos da Guerra do Paraguai na Provincia do Ceará (1865–1870)*. PhD diss., Universidade Federal do Ceará, 2007.

Spalding, Walter. "Aquidabã." *Revista do Instituto Histórico e Geográfico do Rio Grande do Sul* 23 (1943).

———. *A Invasão Paraguaia no Brasil*. São Paulo: Companhia Editora Nacional, 1940.

Squinelo, Ana Paula. *150 Anos Após—A Guerra do Paraguai: Entreolhares do Brasil, Paraguai, e Uruguai*. 2 vols. Campo Grande: Editora UFMS, 2016.

———. "A Guerra do Paraguai e suas interfaces: memoria e identidade em Mato Grosso do Sul (Brasil)," Paper presented at the V Encuentro Anual del CEL, Buenos Aires, 4 November 2008.

Stefanich, Juan. *La restauración histórica del Paraguay*. Buenos Aires: Editorial El Mundo Nuevo, 1945.

Stroessner, Alfredo. *En Cerro Corá no se rindió la dignidad nacional.* Asunción: Cuadernos Republicanos, 1970.

Taboada, Gaspar. *"Los Taboada." Luchas de la organización nacional.* Buenos Aires: Imprenta López, 1929.

Talavera, Natalicio. *La guerra del Paraguay. Correspondencias publicadas en El Semanario.* Asunción: Ediciones Nizza, 1958.

Tasso Fragoso, Augusto. *História da Guerra entre a Tríplice Aliança e o Paraguay.* 5 vols. Rio de Janeiro: Biblioteca do Exército, 1957.

———. *A Paz como o Paraguai depois da guerra de Tríplice Aliança.* Rio de Janeiro: Imprensa Nacional, 1941.

Taunay, Alfredo d'Escragnolle. *Cartas da Campanha. A Cordilheira. Agonía de Lopez (1869–1870).* São Paulo: Melhoramentos, 1921.

———. *Diário do Exército, 1869–1870. De Campo Grande a Aquidabã. A Campanha da Cordilheira.* São Paulo: Melhoramentos, 1958.

———. *Em Matto Grosso Invadido (1866–1867).* São Paulo: Melhoramentos de S. Paulo (Weiszflog Irmãos), [1929?].

———. *Memórias do Visconde de Taunay.* São Paulo: Instituto Progresso Editorial, 1948.

———. *Recordações da Guerra e de Viagem.* São Paulo: Melhoramentos, 1924.

———. "Relatório Geral da Commissão de Engenheiros junto as forces em Expediçao para a Provincia de Matto Grosso, 1865–1866." *Revista do Instituto Histórico e Geographico Brasileiro* 37, no. 2 (1874): 79–177, 250–334, 337–340.

———. *A Retirada da Laguna.* São Paulo: Melhoramentos, 1957.

Thompson, George. *The War in Paraguay with a Historical Sketch of the Country and Its People and Notes upon the Military Engineering of the War.* London: Longmans, Green, and Co., 1869.

Thompson, Jorge. *La guerra del Paraguay.* Buenos Aires: Imprenta Americana, 1869.

Toral, André. *Adéus Chamigo Brasileiro. Uma História da Guerra do Paraguai.* São Paulo: Companhia das Letras, 1999.

———. "Entre Retratos e Cadáveres: a Fotografía na Guerra do Paraguai." *Revista Brasileira de História* 19, no. 38 (1999): 283–310.

———. *Imagens em Desordem. A Iconografia da Guerra do Paraguai (1864–1870).* São Paulo: Humanitas/FFLCH/USP, 2001.

Tovar, Enrique D. and Alfonso B. Campos. *Homenaje al Paraguay. Homenaje al Perú.* Caras, Perú: Prensa de Huailas, 1919.

Trujillo, Manuel. *Gestas guerreras (de mis memorias).* Asunción, 1923.

Tuck, Lily. *The News from Paraguay. A Novel.* New York: Harper Collins, 2004.

Tuohy, John H. *Biographical Sketches from the Paraguayan War, 1864–1870.* Charleston: Createspace, 2011.

Urien, Carlos M. *Curupayty. Homenaje a la memoria del teniente general Bartolomé Mitre en el primer centenario de su nacimiento.* Buenos Aires, 1921.

Valdez, Wilfredo [Jaime Sosa Escalada]. "La guerra futura. La guerra de Chile y Brasil con la República. La Alianza—la causa común. Estudio de los hombres del Paraguay—el Triunvirato." *Revista del Paraguay* 2, no. 3–9 (1892): 137–144, 197–200, 256–269, 289–306, 353–366, 398–409.

Valotta, Guillermo. *La operación de las fuerzas navales con las terrestres durante la guerra del Paraguay.* Buenos Aires: Ministerio de Marina, 1915.

Varela, Felipe. *Manifiesto del jeneral Felipe Varela a los pueblos americanos sobre los acontecimientos políticos de la república Arjentina en los años 1866 y 1867.* Buenos Aires: Rodolfo Ortega Peña and Eduardo Luis Duhalde, 1968.

Varela, Héctor F. [Orión]. *Elisa Lynch.* Buenos Aires: La Cultura Popular, 1934.

Vasconcellos, Genserico de. *A Guerra do Paraguay no Theatro de Matto-Grosso.* Rio de Janeiro: Confiança, [1921?].

Vasconcellos, Víctor N. *Juan E. O'Leary: el reivindicador.* Asunción. 1972.

Vázquez Franco, Guillermo. *Francisco Berra: la historia prohibida.* Montevideo: Mandinga, 2001.

———. *La historia y los mitos.* Montevideo: Cal y Canto, 1994.

Vera, Helio. *En busca del hueso perdido (tratado de paraguayología).* Asunción: RP Ediciones, 1995.

Viana, Hélio. *Estudos de História Imperial.* São Paulo: Companhia Editora Nacional, 1950.

Vianna, Lobo. *A Epopeia da Laguna. Conferencia pronunciada no Club Militar.* Rio de Janeiro, 1938.

Vianna Filho, Arlindo. "Tamandaré e a Logística Naval na Guerra do Paraguai." *A Defesa Nacional* 69, no. 708 (1983): 117–128.

Vieira Ferreira, Luiz. *Passagem do rio Paraná; Comissão de Engenheiros de Primero Corpo do Exército em Operaçoes na Campanha do Paraguai.* Rio de Janeiro, 1890.

Villagra-Batoux, Delicia. *El guaraní paraguayo. De la oralidad a la lingua literaria.* Asunción: Expolibro, 2002.

Vilhena de Moraes, Eugenio. *O Duque de Ferro.* Rio de Janeiro: Calvino Filho, 1933.

Viotti da Costa, Emilia. *The Brazilian Empire. Myths and Histories.* Chicago and London: University of Chicago Press, 1985.

Visconde de Ouro Preto [Afonso Celso de Assis Figueiredo]. *A Marinha d'Outrora.* Rio de Janeiro: SDGM, 1981

Vittone, Luis. *Calendario Histórico de la guerra de la Triple Alianza contra el Paraguay.* Asunción: Ediciones Comuneros, 1970.

Versen, Max von. *História da Guerra do Paraguai.* Rio de Janeiro: Imprensa Nacional, 1913.

———. *Reisen in Amerika und der Südamerikanische Krieg.* Breslau: Malzer, 1872.

Walzer, Michael. *Just and Unjust Wars: A Moral Argument with Historical Illustrations.* New York: Basic Books, 2006.

Warner, William. *Paraguayan Thermopylae—the Battle of Itororó.* Norfolk: Privately printed, 2007.

Warren, Harris Gaylord. "Brazil and the Cavalcanti Coup of 1894 in Paraguay." *Luso-Brazilian Review* 19, no. 2 (1982): 221–236.

———. "Dr. William Stewart in Paraguay, 1857–1869." *The Americas* 25, no. 3 (1969): 247–264.

———. "Journalism in Asunción under the Allies and the Colorados, 1869–1904." *The Americas* 39, no. 4 (1983): 483–498.

———. "Litigations in English Courts and Claims against Paraguay Resulting from the War of the Triple Alliance." *Inter-American Economic Affairs* 22, no. 4 (1969): 31–46.

———. "The Paraguayan Image of the War of the Triple Alliance." *The Americas* 13, no. 1 (1962): 3–20.

———. *Paraguay and the Triple Alliance. The Postwar Decade, 1869–1878.* Austin: University of Texas Press, 1978.

———. "The Paraguay Central Railway, 1856–1889." *Inter-American Economic Affairs* 20, no. 4 (1967): 3–22.

———. *Rebirth of the Paraguayan Republic. The First Colorado Era, 1878–1904.* Pittsburgh: University of Pittsburgh Press, 1985.

———. *Revoluciones y finanzas.* Asunción: Servilibro, 2008.

———. "Roberto Adolfo Chodasiewicz: A Polish Soldier of Fortune in the Paraguayan War." *The Americas* 41, no. 3 (1985): 1–19.

Washburn, Charles A. *The History of Paraguay with Notes of Personal Observations and Reminiscences of Diplomacy under Difficulties.* 2 vols. Boston and New York: Lea and Shepard, 1871.

Webb, Theodore A. *Seven Sons, Millionaires & Vagabonds.* Victoria: Trafford, 1999.

Whigham, Thomas L. "Building the Nation While Destroying the Land: Paraguayan Journalism during the Triple Alliance War, 1864–1870." *Jahrbuch für Geschichte Lateinamerikas* 49 (2012): 157–180.

———. *La Guerra de la Triple Alianza.* 3 vols. Asunción: Taurus, 2010–2012.

———. "La guerre détruit, la guerre construit: Esssai sur le development du nationalism en Amérique du Sud." In *Les guerres du Paraguay aux XIXe et XXe Siècles*, edited by Nicolas Richard, Luc Capdevila, and Capucine Boidin. 23–32. Paris: CoLibris, 2007.

———. "The Iron Works of Ybycui: Paraguayan Industrial Development in the Mid-Nineteenth Century." *The Americas* 35, no. 2 (1978): 201–218.

———. "Paraguay and the World Cotton Market. The 'Crisis' of the 1860s." *Agricultural History* 68, no. 3 (1994): 1–15.

———. *The Paraguayan War. Causes and Early Conduct.* Lincoln and London: University of Nebraska Press, 2002.

———. *The Politics of River Trade: Tradition and Development in the Upper Plata, 1780–1870.* Albuquerque: University of New Mexico Press, 1991.

———. *Lo que el río se llevó. Estado y comercio en Paraguay y Corrientes, 1776–1870.* Asunción: CEADUC, 2009.

Whigham, Thomas L. and Barbara Potthast. "Some Strong Reservations: A Critique of Vera Blinn Rebert's 'The Demographics of Paraguay: A Reinterpretation of the Great War.' " *Hispanic American Historical Review* 70, no. 4 (1990): 667–676.

Whigham, Thomas L. and Juan Manuel Casal, eds. *Charles A. Washburn. Escritos escogidos. La diplomacia estadounidense en el Paraguay durante la Guerra de la Triple Alianza.* Asunción: Servilibro, 2008.

Wiederspahn, Henrique Oscar. "Tomada de Curuzú." *Revista do Instituto Histórico e Geográfico do Rio Grande do Sul* 26, no.105–108 (1948): 155–164.

Williams, John Hoyt. "Paraguay's Nineteenth-Century Estancias de la República." *Agricultural History* 47, no. 3 (1973): 206–216.

———. *The Rise and Fall of the Paraguayan Republic, 1800–1870.* Austin: University of Texas Press, 1979.

———. "A Swamp of Blood. The Battle of Tuyutí." *Military History* 17, no. 1 (2000): 58–64.

Zavalía Matienzo, Roberto. *Felipe Varela a través de la documentación del Archivo Histórico de Tucumán.* Tucumán: Archivo Histórico, 1967.

INDEX

Davis, Charles, 295–97, 320
De Matos, Joaquim Fabricio de, 117
De Souza, Guilherme Xavier, 83–84, 332–33, 344, 346, 350, 541n44
Decidée, 293
Decoud, José Segundo, 338, 376, 378
Decoud, Juan Francisco, 338, 376, 378–79
defenses, construction of, 10–11, 30, 35, 131
Delgado, Jose Maria, 411
Delphim, Carlos de Carvalho, 221, 228, 230, 238, 247, 260, 264, 290–91, 295, 345, 386
demographics, 475n27, 580n29–31
desertion, 17–18, 284, 466n46
destinadas, 394–95, 397–99, 401–2, 565n10
Dezembrada, 311
Dias de Motta, Fernando Sebastião, 332
Díaz, Alejandro, 117
Díaz, José Eduvígis, 19, 26–27, 33, 48–51, 59, 61–62, 67, 80–82, 87–88, 100–101, 109–10, 113, 115, 118, 139–42, 165, 208, 364
Díaz de Bedoya, José, 378, 380
Dom Affonso, 110
Domínguez, Cesáreo, 86–87
"donations," 152, 433n21
Dourados, 404–5, 415
Drago, Manoel Pedro, 165–66
dysentery, 7, 29

E

Egusquiza, Félix, 378
El Centinela, 266
El Cristiano, 131
El Nacional, 75–76
El Semanario, 34, 51, 78, 81, 119, 142, 174, 190, 202, 207, 227, 267
Elizalde, Rufino de, 124, 188, 215–17, 286
Encarnación, 28, 41
Ensenaditas, 17, 29
Entre Ríos, 11, 77, 91, 126, 175
Escobar, Patricio, 350, 411, 426, 568n48, 573n96
Esmerats, Ignacio, 254–55
Espadín, 398, 402
espina de corona, 57

Espinillo, 220
Espinosa, Francisco Solano, 227
esprit de corps, 17
Establecimiento de la Cierva, 225
Estero Bellaco, 40, 46–47, 49, 53–54, 62, 95, 100, 110
Estigarribia, Antonio de la Cruz, 9, 548n10
Estrella, 344, 368, 545n82
Eu, Count de (Louis Philippe Marie Ferdinand Gaston d'Orleans), 346–48, 350–51, 353, 356–57, 360–63, 365–66, 369, 371–74, 378, 380, 382, 384, 387, 389–90, 396, 399, 403, 413, 417, 421, 423, 554n77
Eusebio Ayala, 369
Everett, 357
expropriations, 152–53

F

Falcón, José, 268, 388, 411, 516n55
Farrapo Rebellion, 83
feijão, 81
Fidelis, 35
Figueiredo e Melo, Pedro Américo de, 306
floating bakeries, 74
Flores, Venancio, 3, 13, 18, 28, 39, 43, 45–46, 48–50, 55–56, 70, 72, 74, 77, 80–82, 85–86, 90, 101, 103, 106, 117, 120, 222–24, 351–52
Florida Battalion, 47, 50, 60, 85, 87
Fort Henry, 12
Fortín, 240, 280
Fôsso de Mallet, 56, 62, 67
Fraga, Manuel, 114, 117
France, 4, 132, 146, 324
Francia, José Gaspar Rodríguez de, 2–3
Freemasonry, 325, 536n8
Fuentes, Ruperto, 111

G

galopas, 75
Galvão, Antônio da Fonseca, 165, 167
garbanzos, 10
Garmendia, José I., 111, 317–18
Garmendia, Pancha, 401–2

Kruger, William, 92–93
Krupp, 201, 238

L

La América, 46, 76
La Nación Argentina, 8, 146
La Regeneración, 414
La Rioja, 127
Lacerda, José Francisco ("Chico Diabo"),
 410, 572n88
Lafuente, José M., 126
Laguna Brava, 15
Laguna Méndez, 96, 109, 169
Laguna Pirís, 44, 46, 220
LaHitte cannons, 33, 83, 448n68
Lake Ypacaraí, 327, 344, 384
Lambaré, 228–29
Lanús, Anacarsis, 418
Lasserre, Dorothée Duprat de, 394–95,
 397–98
Latorre, Lorenzo, 423
Laurent-Cochelet, Emile 139, 187
leadership, 50–51, 70, 418, 484n14
Legión Paraguaya, 338, 375, 491n99
Leguizamón Pass, 80
Leite Pereira, José Maria, 266
Lettsom, William Garrow, 45
Leuchars, Chris, 305, 403
Liberal Party, Argentina, 76, 111, 175, 216
Liberal Party, Brazil, 122, 259, 334, 336, 346,
 422
Liberal Party, Paraguay, 428
Libertad Battalion, 61
libertos, 341
Lima Barros, 97, 112, 234, 236, 248
Lincoln, Abraham, 133
liquor, 16, 74
Litoral provinces, 6, 11, 75, 126–27, 174, 418
Liverpool, 110
Loizaga, Carlos, 378, 425
Lomas Valentinas, 311, 317–20, 324, 326, 350,
 388, 420
London battery, 158, 220–21, 257
looting, 327–31
Lopes Pecegueiro, Manoel, 50

López, Benigno, 210, 227, 239, 260, 262–65,
 271, 273, 310, 343
López, Cándido, 114
López, Carlos Antonio, 2–3, 209, 268
López, Emiliano, 356
López, Fermín, 365
López, Francisco Solano, 2–4, 6–7, 9, 24, 26,
 38–41, 44, 50, 58, 64, 66–67, 69, 72, 78,
 92, 100–101, 103–5, 108, 111, 116, 125,
 128, 132, 137–38, 148, 157, 162–63, 174,
 180–81, 187, 189, 197, 207–12, 215, 217,
 233, 238, 241, 260–61, 264–67, 273,
 277, 281–82, 285, 293–95, 302, 309, 316,
 329, 330–31, 333–34, 337, 339, 342–43,
 345, 349, 354–57, 359, 367, 372–73,
 380, 383–84, 390–92, 395–97, 399, 401,
 403–10, 412, 414, 421, 427–29, 573n90,
 574n104
López, Inocencia, 210, 400–401, 413, 514n43
López, Panchito, 343, 411–12
López, Rafaela, 210, 400–401, 413, 495n21
López, Venancio, 210, 239, 265, 271, 395,
 400–401, 495n22
López Jordán, Ricardo, 126
Lopismo, 431n4
Luque, 226, 260–61, 274, 293, 328, 333, 357,
 394
Lynch, Eliza, 19, 72, 105, 110, 210–11, 226,
 237, 241, 263, 273, 296, 309, 318, 343,
 355, 357, 388, 392, 395, 401–2, 411–13,
 424, 474n13, 497n30, 547n3, 579n23–24

M

Machado, Fernando, 300
Machorra Creek, 170
Magalhães, José Vieira Couto de, 172, 413
Magé, 96
magic lantern, 163
Maíz, Fidel, 268–69, 294, 310, 389, 411, 414,
 426
maize, 10
malambos, 75
malaria, 57, 73
Mallet, Emílio Luiz, 56, 62, 363
malnutrition, 71, 191, 397–98, 491n101

Osório, Manoel, 15, 27, 29, 33, 36–37, 39, 41, 43, 48–49, 56, 60–62, 64, 70, 82–83, 94, 113, 129, 140, 179, 181, 241, 252, 291, 299, 302–5, 307, 332, 335, 364, 370

P

Páez, José Antonio, 207
Palacios, Manuel Antonio, 260, 264, 272, 310
Palleja, León de, 18, 38, 41, 47, 50, 63–64, 85, 88, 120, 423, 455n58
Palmar Island, 96
Palmas, 291–93
palmhearts, 159
Panadero, 403–4, 406
Pará, 220–21, 251
Paraguarí, 274, 340, 358–59
Paraguay River, 15, 19, 36, 324
Paraná, 386
Paraná River, 6, 19, 29
Paranaguá, João Lustosa da Cunha, 124
Paranhos, José María da Silva, 333–34, 336–37, 339, 374–76, 379–80, 383, 391, 395, 414, 420, 422, 555n84
Parecué, 192–93, 241
Parnahyba, 112
Paso Carreta, 48–49
Paso de la Patria, 10, 19, 28–30, 33, 36–37, 39–41, 44, 56, 74, 233
Paso del Ombú, 191
Paso Fernández, 57, 70
Paso Gómez, 57, 70, 89, 128, 132, 234
Paso Lenguas, 38
Paso Poí, 212, 215
Paso Pucú, 55, 58, 104, 110, 130, 134, 139, 208, 211, 215, 241, 257
Passage of Curupayty, 183–84
Passage of Humaitá, 219–22
Patiño Cué, 344
patriarchy, 160
"patriotic acts," 152
patriotism, Paraguayan, 9, 13, 342
Paunero, Wenceslao, 24, 36, 80, 114, 143, 175, 230
Pavón, 3, 72, 124
Paysandú, 5, 6, 25

Paz, Francisco, 117
Paz, Marcos, 17, 28, 35–36, 107, 124, 143, 175, 201, 215–16
peanuts, 10
peasantry, Brazilian, 77
peasantry, Paraguayan, 19
Pedra, Azevedo, 413
Pedro II, 3, 7, 8, 35, 45, 77–78, 103, 122, 141, 176, 208, 219, 334, 420, 423
Peguajó creek, 21–22
Peixoto, Floriano, 408
Pereira de Carvalho, Manoel Feliciano, 65
pests, 16
photography, 89, 157, 449n86
picada, 85
Picada de Chiriguelo, 404–5, 411
Pikysyry stream, 280–81, 290, 292, 295, 303, 307–8, 310–13
Pilar, 181, 309
Pimentel, Joaquim Silverio de Azevedo, 55
Pirabebé, 229, 295, 386
piranhas, 167
Pirayú, 327, 339, 344–45, 351, 384
Piribebuy, 309, 327, 340–44, 351, 356, 362–66, 371, 384, 397, 405, 407
plata ybygui, 331, 473n7
Polidoro, Fonseca Quintinilha Jordão da, 83, 94, 101–3, 107, 117, 123
pornography, 16
Porteños, 6
Porto Alegre, Baron of, 28, 41, 72, 79, 81, 94–102, 113, 118–19, 123, 179, 198–99, 202
Porto Canuto, 171
Positivism, 421
Potrero Marmol, 317
Potrero Ovella, 195–96, 214
Potrero Pirís, 56–57, 59–60, 66, 81, 145, 198
Potrero Sauce, 57, 63, 70, 81
Praia Vermelha, Escola Militar da, 35
Presidente, 65
Prieto, Celestino, 21, 23
Princesa, 424
Progressive League, 122, 259, 336
Provisional Government, 377, 379, 381
punishments, 160, 190

CPSIA information can be obtained
at www.ICGtesting.com
Printed in the USA
LVHW02s0457080318
569072LV00005B/5/P

9 781552 388099